JOSE
MACIAS

$5.00

University Casebook Series

May, 1984

ACCOUNTING AND THE LAW, Fourth Edition (1978), with Problems Pamphlet (Successor to Dohr, Phillips, Thompson & Warren)

> George C. Thompson, Professor, Columbia University Graduate School of Business.
> Robert Whitman, Professor of Law, University of Connecticut.
> Ellis L. Phillips, Jr., Member of the New York Bar.
> William C. Warren, Professor of Law Emeritus, Columbia University.

ACCOUNTING FOR LAWYERS, MATERIALS ON (1980)

> David R. Herwitz, Professor of Law, Harvard University.

ADMINISTRATIVE LAW, Seventh Edition (1979), with 1983 Problems Supplement (Supplement edited in association with Paul R. Verkuil, Dean and Professor of Law, Tulane University)

> Walter Gellhorn, University Professor Emeritus, Columbia University.
> Clark Byse, Professor of Law, Harvard University.
> Peter L. Strauss, Professor of Law, Columbia University.

ADMIRALTY, Second Edition (1978), with Statute and Rule Supplement

> Jo Desha Lucas, Professor of Law, University of Chicago.

ADVOCACY, see also Lawyering Process

AGENCY, see also Enterprise Organization

AGENCY—PARTNERSHIPS, Third Edition (1982)

> Abridgement from Conard, Knauss & Siegel's Enterprise Organization, Third Edition.

ANTITRUST: FREE ENTERPRISE AND ECONOMIC ORGANIZATION, Sixth Edition (1983), with Problems in Antitrust Supplement

> Louis B. Schwartz, Professor of Law, University of Pennsylvania.
> John J. Flynn, Professor of Law, University of Utah.
> Harry First, Professor of Law, New York University.

ANTITRUST SUPPLEMENT—SELECTED STATUTES AND RELATED MATERIALS (1977)

> John J. Flynn, Professor of Law, University of Utah.

BUSINESS ORGANIZATION, see also Enterprise Organization

BUSINESS PLANNING (1966), with 1983 Supplement

> David R. Herwitz, Professor of Law, Harvard University.

BUSINESS TORTS (1972)

> Milton Handler, Professor of Law Emeritus, Columbia University.

UNIVERSITY CASEBOOK SERIES—Continued

CHILDREN IN THE LEGAL SYSTEM (1983)

Walter Wadlington, Professor of Law, University of Virginia.
Charles H. Whitebread, Professor of Law, University of Southern California.
Samuel Davis, Professor of Law, University of Georgia.

CIVIL PROCEDURE, see Procedure

CLINIC, see also Lawyering Process

COMMERCIAL LAW (1983)

Robert L. Jordan, Professor of Law, University of California, Los Angeles.
William D. Warren, Professor of Law, University of California, Los Angeles.

COMMERCIAL LAW, CASES & MATERIALS ON, Third Edition (1976), with 1982 Bankruptcy Supplement

E. Allan Farnsworth, Professor of Law, Columbia University.
John Honnold, Professor of Law, University of Pennsylvania.

COMMERCIAL PAPER, Third Edition (1984)

E. Allan Farnsworth, Professor of Law, Columbia University.

COMMERCIAL PAPER (1983) (Reprinted from COMMERCIAL LAW)

Robert L. Jordan, Professor of Law, University of California, Los Angeles.
William D. Warren, Professor of Law, University of California, Los Angeles.

COMMERCIAL PAPER AND BANK DEPOSITS AND COLLECTIONS (1967), with Statutory Supplement

William D. Hawkland, Professor of Law, University of Illinois.

COMMERCIAL TRANSACTIONS—Principles and Policies (1982)

Alan Schwartz, Professor of Law, University of Southern California.
Robert E. Scott, Professor of Law, University of Virginia.

COMPARATIVE LAW, Fourth Edition (1980)

Rudolf B. Schlesinger, Professor of Law, Hastings College of the Law.

COMPETITIVE PROCESS, LEGAL REGULATION OF THE, Second Edition (1979), with Statutory Supplement and 1982 Case Supplement

Edmund W. Kitch, Professor of Law, University of Chicago.
Harvey S. Perlman, Professor of Law, University of Virginia.

CONFLICT OF LAWS, Eighth Edition (1984)

Willis L. M. Reese, Professor of Law, Columbia University,
Maurice Rosenberg, Professor of Law, Columbia University.

CONSTITUTIONAL LAW, Sixth Edition (1981), with 1983 Supplement

Edward L. Barrett, Jr., Professor of Law, University of California, Davis.
William Cohen, Professor of Law, Stanford University.

CONSTITUTIONAL LAW: THE STRUCTURE OF GOVERNMENT (Reprinted from CONSTITUTIONAL LAW, Sixth Edition), with 1983 Supplement

Edward L. Barrett, Jr., Professor of Law, University of California, Davis.
William Cohen, Professor of Law, Stanford University.

CONSTITUTIONAL LAW, CIVIL LIBERTY AND INDIVIDUAL RIGHTS, Second Edition (1982), with 1983 Supplement

William Cohen, Professor of Law, Stanford University.
John Kaplan, Professor of Law, Stanford University.

UNIVERSITY CASEBOOK SERIES—Continued

CONSTITUTIONAL LAW, Tenth Edition (1980), with 1983 Supplement (Supplement edited in association with Frederick F. Schauer, Professor of Law, College of William and Mary)

Gerald Gunther, Professor of Law, Stanford University.

CONSTITUTIONAL LAW, INDIVIDUAL RIGHTS IN, Third Edition (1981) (Reprinted from CONSTITUTIONAL LAW, Tenth Edition), with 1983 Supplement (Supplement edited in association with Frederick F. Schauer, Professor of Law, College of William and Mary)

Gerald Gunther, Professor of Law, Stanford University.

CONSUMER TRANSACTIONS (1983), with Selected Statutes and Regulations Supplement

Michael M. Greenfield, Professor of Law, Washington University.

CONTRACT LAW AND ITS APPLICATION, Third Edition (1983)

The late Addison Mueller, Professor of Law, University of California, Los Angeles.
Arthur I. Rosett, Professor of Law, University of California, Los Angeles.
Gerald P. Lopez, Professor of Law, University of California, Los Angeles.

CONTRACT LAW, STUDIES IN, Third Edition (1984)

Edward J. Murphy, Professor of Law, University of Notre Dame.
Richard E. Speidel, Professor of Law, Northwestern University.

CONTRACTS, Fourth Edition (1982)

John P. Dawson, Professor of Law Emeritus, Harvard University.
William Burnett Harvey, Professor of Law and Political Science, Boston University.
Stanley D. Henderson, Professor of Law, University of Virginia.

CONTRACTS, Third Edition (1980), with Statutory Supplement

E. Allan Farnsworth, Professor of Law, Columbia University.
William F. Young, Professor of Law, Columbia University.

CONTRACTS, Second Edition (1978), with Statutory and Administrative Law Supplement (1978)

Ian R. Macneil, Professor of Law, Cornell University.

COPYRIGHT, PATENTS AND TRADEMARKS, see also Competitive Process

COPYRIGHT, PATENT, TRADEMARK AND RELATED STATE DOCTRINES, Second Edition (1981), with Problem Supplement and Statutory Supplement

Paul Goldstein, Professor of Law, Stanford University.

COPYRIGHT, Unfair Competition, and Other Topics Bearing on the Protection of Literary, Musical, and Artistic Works, Third Edition (1978)

Benjamin Kaplan, Professor of Law Emeritus, Harvard University,
Ralph S. Brown, Jr., Professor of Law, Yale University.

CORPORATE FINANCE, Second Edition (1979), with 1982 New Developments Supplement

Victor Brudney, Professor of Law, Harvard University.
Marvin A. Chirelstein, Professor of Law, Yale University.

CORPORATE READJUSTMENTS AND REORGANIZATIONS (1976)

Walter J. Blum, Professor of Law, University of Chicago.
Stanley A. Kaplan, Professor of Law, University of Chicago.

UNIVERSITY CASEBOOK SERIES—Continued

CORPORATION LAW, BASIC, Second Edition (1979), with 1983 Case and Documentary Supplement

Detlev F. Vagts, Professor of Law, Harvard University.

CORPORATIONS, see also Enterprise Organization

CORPORATIONS, Fifth Edition—Unabridged (1980), with 1983 Supplement

The late William L. Cary, Professor of Law, Columbia University.
Melvin Aron Eisenberg, Professor of Law, University of California, Berkeley.

CORPORATIONS, Fifth Edition—Abridged (1980), with 1983 Supplement

The late William L. Cary, Professor of Law, Columbia University.
Melvin Aron Eisenberg, Professor of Law, University of California, Berkeley.

CORPORATIONS, Second Edition (1982), with 1982 Corporation and Partnership Statutes, Rules and Forms

Alfred F. Conard, Professor of Law, University of Michigan.
Robert N. Knauss, Dean of the Law School, University of Houston.
Stanley Siegel, Professor of Law, University of California, Los Angeles.

CORPORATIONS, THE LAW OF: WHAT CORPORATE LAWYERS DO (1976)

Jan G. Deutsch, Professor of Law, Yale University.
Joseph J. Bianco, Professor of Law, Yeshiva University.

CORPORATIONS COURSE GAME PLAN (1975)

David R. Herwitz, Professor of Law, Harvard University.

CORRECTIONS, SEE SENTENCING

CREDIT TRANSACTIONS AND CONSUMER PROTECTION (1976)

John Honnold, Professor of Law, University of Pennsylvania.

CREDITORS' RIGHTS, see also Debtor-Creditor Law

CRIMINAL JUSTICE, THE ADMINISTRATION OF, Second Edition (1969)

Francis C. Sullivan, Professor of Law, Louisiana State University.
Paul Hardin III, Professor of Law, Duke University.
John Huston, Professor of Law, University of Washington.
Frank R. Lacy, Professor of Law, University of Oregon.
Daniel E. Murray, Professor of Law, University of Miami.
George W. Pugh, Professor of Law, Louisiana State University.

CRIMINAL JUSTICE ADMINISTRATION, Second Edition (1982), with 1983 Supplement

Frank W. Miller, Professor of Law, Washington University.
Robert O. Dawson, Professor of Law, University of Texas.
George E. Dix, Professor of Law, University of Texas.
Raymond I. Parnas, Professor of Law, University of California, Davis.

CRIMINAL LAW, Third Edition (1983)

Fred E. Inbau, Professor of Law Emeritus, Northwestern University.
James R. Thompson, Professor of Law Emeritus, Northwestern University.
Andre A. Moenssens, Professor of Law, University of Richmond.

CRIMINAL LAW (1982), with 1983 Supplement

Peter W. Low, Professor of Law, University of Virginia.
John C. Jeffries, Jr., Professor of Law, University of Virginia.
Richard C. Bonnie, Professor of Law, University of Virginia.

UNIVERSITY CASEBOOK SERIES—Continued

CRIMINAL LAW, Third Edition (1980)

    Lloyd L. Weinreb, Professor of Law, Harvard University.

CRIMINAL LAW AND PROCEDURE, Sixth Edition (1984)

    Rollin M. Perkins, Professor of Law Emeritus, University of California, Hastings College of the Law.
    Ronald N. Boyce, Professor of Law, University of Utah.

CRIMINAL PROCEDURE, Second Edition (1980), with 1983 Supplement

    Fred E. Inbau, Professor of Law Emeritus, Northwestern University.
    James R. Thompson, Professor of Law Emeritus, Northwestern University.
    James B. Haddad, Professor of Law, Northwestern University.
    James B. Zagel, Chief, Criminal Justice Division, Office of Attorney General of Illinois.
    Gary L. Starkman, Assistant U. S. Attorney, Northern District of Illinois.

CRIMINAL PROCEDURE, CONSTITUTIONAL (1977), with 1980 Supplement

    James E. Scarboro, Professor of Law, University of Colorado.
    James B. White, Professor of Law, University of Chicago.

CRIMINAL PROCESS, Third Edition (1978), with 1983 Supplement

    Lloyd L. Weinreb, Professor of Law, Harvard University.

DAMAGES, Second Edition (1952)

    Charles T. McCormick, late Professor of Law, University of Texas.
    William F. Fritz, late Professor of Law, University of Texas.

DEBTOR–CREDITOR LAW (1984)

    Theodore Eisenberg, Professor of Law, Cornell University.

DEBTOR–CREDITOR LAW, Second Edition (1981), with Statutory Supplement

    William D. Warren, Dean of the School of Law, University of California, Los Angeles.
    William E. Hogan, Professor of Law, New York University.

DECEDENTS' ESTATES (1971)

    Max Rheinstein, late Professor of Law Emeritus, University of Chicago.
    Mary Ann Glendon, Professor of Law, Boston College.

DECEDENTS' ESTATES AND TRUSTS, Sixth Edition (1982)

    John Ritchie, Emeritus Dean and Wigmore Professor of Law, Northwestern University.
    Neill H. Alford, Jr., Professor of Law, University of Virginia.
    Richard W. Effland, Professor of Law, Arizona State University.

DECEDENTS' ESTATES AND TRUSTS (1968)

    Howard R. Williams, Professor of Law, Stanford University.

DOMESTIC RELATIONS, see also Family Law

DOMESTIC RELATIONS, Successor Edition (1984)

    Walter Wadlington, Professor of Law, University of Virginia.

ELECTRONIC MASS MEDIA, Second Edition (1979)

    William K. Jones, Professor of Law, Columbia University.

UNIVERSITY CASEBOOK SERIES—Continued

EMPLOYMENT DISCRIMINATION (1983)

Joel W. Friedman, Professor of Law, Tulane University.
George M. Strickler, Professor of Law, Tulane University.

ENERGY LAW (1983)

Donald N. Zillman, Professor of Law, University of Utah.
Laurence Lattman, Dean of Mines and Engineering, University of Utah.

ENTERPRISE ORGANIZATION, Third Edition (1982), with 1982 Corporation and Partnership Statutes, Rules and Forms Supplement

Alfred F. Conard, Professor of Law, University of Michigan.
Robert L. Knauss, Dean of the Law School, University of Houston.
Stanley Siegel, Professor of Law, University of California, Los Angeles.

ENVIRONMENTAL POLICY LAW (1982)

Thomas J. Schoenbaum, Professor of Law, Tulane University.

EQUITY, see also Remedies

EQUITY, RESTITUTION AND DAMAGES, Second Edition (1974)

Robert Childres, late Professor of Law, Northwestern University.
William F. Johnson, Jr., Professor of Law, New York University.

ESTATE PLANNING, Second Edition (1982), with Documentary Supplement

David Westfall, Professor of Law, Harvard University.

ETHICS, see Legal Profession, and Professional Responsibility

ETHICS AND PROFESSIONAL RESPONSIBILITY (1981) (Reprinted from THE LAWYERING PROCESS)

Gary Bellow, Professor of Law, Harvard University.
Bea Moulton, Legal Services Corporation.

EVIDENCE, Fifth Edition (1984)

John Kaplan, Professor of Law, Stanford University.
Jon R. Waltz, Professor of Law, Northwestern University.

EVIDENCE (1968)

Francis C. Sullivan, Professor of Law, Louisiana State University.
Paul Hardin, III, Professor of Law, Duke University.

EVIDENCE, Seventh Edition (1983), with Rules and Statute Supplement (1984)

Jack B. Weinstein, Chief Judge, United States District Court.
John H. Mansfield, Professor of Law, Harvard University.
Norman Abrams, Professor of Law, University of California, Los Angeles.
Margaret Berger, Professor of Law, Brooklyn Law School.

FAMILY LAW, see also Domestic Relations

FAMILY LAW (1978), with 1983 Supplement

Judith C. Areen, Professor of Law, Georgetown University.

FAMILY LAW AND CHILDREN IN THE LEGAL SYSTEM, STATUTORY MATERIALS (1981)

Walter Wadlington, Professor of Law, University of Virginia.

UNIVERSITY CASEBOOK SERIES—Continued

FEDERAL COURTS, Seventh Edition (1982), with 1983 Supplement

Charles T. McCormick, late Professor of Law, University of Texas.
James H. Chadbourn, late Professor of Law, Harvard University.
Charles Alan Wright, Professor of Law, University of Texas.

FEDERAL COURTS AND THE FEDERAL SYSTEM, Hart and Wechsler's Second Edition (1973), with 1981 Supplement

Paul M. Bator, Professor of Law, Harvard University.
Paul J. Mishkin, Professor of Law, University of California, Berkeley.
David L. Shapiro, Professor of Law, Harvard University.
Herbert Wechsler, Professor of Law, Columbia University.

FEDERAL PUBLIC LAND AND RESOURCES LAW (1981), with 1983 Supplement

George C. Coggins, Professor of Law, University of Kansas.
Charles F. Wilkinson, Professor of Law, University of Oregon.

FEDERAL RULES OF CIVIL PROCEDURE, 1984 Edition

FEDERAL TAXATION, see Taxation

FOOD AND DRUG LAW (1980), with Statutory Supplement

Richard A. Merrill, Dean of the School of Law, University of Virginia.
Peter Barton Hutt, Esq.

FUTURE INTERESTS (1958)

Philip Mechem, late Professor of Law Emeritus, University of Pennsylvania.

FUTURE INTERESTS (1970)

Howard R. Williams, Professor of Law, Stanford University.

FUTURE INTERESTS AND ESTATE PLANNING (1961), with 1962 Supplement

W. Barton Leach, late Professor of Law, Harvard University.
James K. Logan, formerly Dean of the Law School, University of Kansas.

GOVERNMENT CONTRACTS, FEDERAL (1975), with 1980 Supplement

John W. Whelan, Professor of Law, Hastings College of the Law.
Robert S. Pasley, Professor of Law Emeritus, Cornell University.

INJUNCTIONS, Second Edition (1984)

Owen M. Fiss, Professor of Law, Yale University.
Doug Rendleman, Professor of Law, College of William and Mary.

INSTITUTIONAL INVESTORS, 1978

David L. Ratner, Professor of Law, Cornell University.

INSURANCE (1971)

William F. Young, Professor of Law, Columbia University.

INTERNATIONAL LAW, see also Transnational Legal Problems and United Nations Law

INTERNATIONAL LAW IN CONTEMPORARY PERSPECTIVE (1981), with Essay Supplement

Myres S. McDougal, Professor of Law, Yale University.
W. Michael Reisman, Professor of Law, Yale University.

UNIVERSITY CASEBOOK SERIES—Continued

INTERNATIONAL LEGAL SYSTEM, Second Edition (1981), with Documentary Supplement

Joseph Modeste Sweeney, Professor of Law, Tulane University.
Covey T. Oliver, Professor of Law, University of Pennsylvania.
Noyes E. Leech, Professor of Law, University of Pennsylvania.

INTRODUCTION TO LAW, see also Legal Method, On Law in Courts, and Dynamics of American Law

INTRODUCTION TO THE STUDY OF LAW (1970)

E. Wayne Thode, late Professor of Law, University of Utah.
Leon Lebowitz, Professor of Law, University of Texas.
Lester J. Mazor, Professor of Law, University of Utah.

JUDICIAL CODE and Rules of Procedure in the Federal Courts with Excerpts from the Criminal Code, 1984 Edition

Henry M. Hart, Jr., late Professor of Law, Harvard University.
Herbert Wechsler, Professor of Law, Columbia University.

JURISPRUDENCE (Temporary Edition Hardbound) (1949)

Lon L. Fuller, Professor of Law Emeritus, Harvard University.

JUVENILE, see also Children

JUVENILE JUSTICE PROCESS, Second Edition (1976), with 1980 Supplement

Frank W. Miller, Professor of Law, Washington University.
Robert O. Dawson, Professor of Law, University of Texas.
George E. Dix, Professor of Law, University of Texas.
Raymond I. Parnas, Professor of Law, University of California, Davis.

LABOR LAW, Ninth Edition (1981), with 1983 Case Supplement and 1977 Statutory Supplement

Archibald Cox, Professor of Law, Harvard University.
Derek C. Bok, President, Harvard University.
Robert A. Gorman, Professor of Law, University of Pennsylvania.

LABOR LAW, Second Edition (1982), with Statutory Supplement

Clyde W. Summers, Professor of Law, University of Pennsylvania.
Harry H. Wellington, Dean of the Law School, Yale University.
Alan Hyde, Professor of Law, Rutgers University.

LAND FINANCING, Second Edition (1977)

The late Norman Penney, Professor of Law, Cornell University.
Richard F. Broude, Member of the California Bar.

LAW AND MEDICINE (1980)

Walter Wadlington, Professor of Law and Professor of Legal Medicine, University of Virginia.
Jon R. Waltz, Professor of Law, Northwestern University.
Roger B. Dworkin, Professor of Law, Indiana University, and Professor of Biomedical History, University of Washington.

LAW, LANGUAGE AND ETHICS (1972)

William R. Bishin, Professor of Law, University of Southern California.
Christopher D. Stone, Professor of Law, University of Southern California.

UNIVERSITY CASEBOOK SERIES—Continued

NEW YORK PRACTICE, Fourth Edition (1978)
Herbert Peterfreund, Professor of Law, New York University.
Joseph M. McLaughlin, Dean of the Law School, Fordham University.

OIL AND GAS, Fourth Edition (1979)
Howard R. Williams, Professor of Law, Stanford University.
Richard C. Maxwell, Professor of Law, University of California, Los Angeles.
Charles J. Meyers, Dean of the Law School, Stanford University.

ON LAW IN COURTS (1965)
Paul J. Mishkin, Professor of Law, University of California, Berkeley.
Clarence Morris, Professor of Law Emeritus, University of Pennsylvania.

PATENTS AND ANTITRUST (Pamphlet) (1983)
Milton Handler, Professor of Law Emeritus, Columbia University.
Harlan M. Blake, Professor of Law, Columbia University.
Robert Pitofsky, Professor of Law, Georgetown University.
Harvey J. Goldschmid, Professor of Law, Columbia University.

PERSPECTIVES ON THE LAWYER AS PLANNER (Reprint of Chapters One through Five of Planning by Lawyers) (1978)
Louis M. Brown, Professor of Law, University of Southern California.
Edward A. Dauer, Professor of Law, Yale University.

PLANNING BY LAWYERS, MATERIALS ON A NONADVERSARIAL LEGAL PROCESS (1978)
Louis M. Brown, Professor of Law, University of Southern California.
Edward A. Dauer, Professor of Law, Yale University.

PLEADING AND PROCEDURE, see Procedure, Civil

POLICE FUNCTION, Third Edition (1982), with 1983 Supplement
Reprint of Chapters 1–10 of Miller, Dawson, Dix and Parnas's CRIMINAL JUSTICE ADMINISTRATION, Second Edition.

PREPARING AND PRESENTING THE CASE (1981) (Reprinted from THE LAWYERING PROCESS)
Gary Bellow, Professor of Law, Harvard Law School.
Bea Moulton, Legal Services Corporation.

PREVENTIVE LAW, see also Planning by Lawyers

PROCEDURE—CIVIL PROCEDURE, Second Edition (1974), with 1979 Supplement
The late James H. Chadbourn, Professor of Law, Harvard University.
A. Leo Levin, Professor of Law, University of Pennsylvania.
Philip Shuchman, Professor of Law, Cornell University.

PROCEDURE—CIVIL PROCEDURE, Fifth Edition (1984)
Richard H. Field, late Professor of Law, Harvard University.
Benjamin Kaplan, Professor of Law Emeritus, Harvard University.
Kevin M. Clermont, Professor of Law, Cornell University.

PROCEDURE—CIVIL PROCEDURE, Third Edition (1976), with 1982 Supplement
Maurice Rosenberg, Professor of Law, Columbia University.
Jack B. Weinstein, Professor of Law, Columbia University.
Hans Smit, Professor of Law, Columbia University.
Harold L. Korn, Professor of Law, Columbia University.

UNIVERSITY CASEBOOK SERIES—Continued

LAW, SCIENCE AND MEDICINE (1984)
Judith C. Areen, Professor of Law, Georgetown University.
Patricia A. King, Professor of Law, Georgetown University.
Steven P. Goldberg, Professor of Law, Georgetown University.
Alexander M. Capron, Professor of Law, Georgetown University.

LAWYERING PROCESS (1978), with Civil Problem Supplement and Criminal Problem Supplement
Gary Bellow, Professor of Law, Harvard University.
Bea Moulton, Professor of Law, Arizona State University.

LEGAL METHOD (1980)
Harry W. Jones, Professor of Law Emeritus, Columbia University.
John M. Kernochan, Professor of Law, Columbia University.
Arthur W. Murphy, Professor of Law, Columbia University.

LEGAL METHODS (1969)
Robert N. Covington, Professor of Law, Vanderbilt University.
E. Blythe Stason, late Professor of Law, Vanderbilt University.
John W. Wade, Professor of Law, Vanderbilt University.
Elliott E. Cheatham, late Professor of Law, Vanderbilt University.
Theodore A. Smedley, Professor of Law, Vanderbilt University.

LEGAL PROFESSION (1970)
Samuel D. Thurman, Dean of the College of Law, University of Utah.
Ellis L. Phillips, Jr., Professor of Law, Columbia University.
Elliott E. Cheatham, late Professor of Law, Vanderbilt University.

LEGISLATION, Fourth Edition (1982) (by Fordham)
Horace E. Read, late Vice President, Dalhousie University.
John W. MacDonald, Professor of Law Emeritus, Cornell Law School.
Jefferson B. Fordham, Professor of Law, University of Utah.
William J. Pierce, Professor of Law, University of Michigan.

LEGISLATIVE AND ADMINISTRATIVE PROCESSES, Second Edition (1981
Hans A. Linde, Judge, Supreme Court of Oregon.
George Bunn, Professor of Law, University of Wisconsin.
Fredericka Paff, Professor of Law, University of Wisconsin.
W. Lawrence Church, Professor of Law, University of Wisconsin.

LOCAL GOVERNMENT LAW, Revised Edition (1975)
Jefferson B. Fordham, Professor of Law, University of Utah.

MASS MEDIA LAW, Second Edition (1982)
Marc A. Franklin, Professor of Law, Stanford University.

MENTAL HEALTH PROCESS, Second Edition (1976), with 1981 Su
Frank W. Miller, Professor of Law, Washington University.
Robert O. Dawson, Professor of Law, University of Texas.
George E. Dix, Professor of Law, University of Texas.
Raymond I. Parnas, Professor of Law, University of California, D

MUNICIPAL CORPORATIONS, see Local Government Law

NEGOTIABLE INSTRUMENTS, see Commercial Paper

NEGOTIATION (1981) (Reprinted from THE LAWYERING PR
Gary Bellow, Professor of Law, Harvard Law School.
Bea Moulton, Legal Services Corporation.

UNIVERSITY CASEBOOK SERIES—Continued

PROCEDURE—PLEADING AND PROCEDURE: State and Federal, Fifth Edition (1983)

David W. Louisell, late Professor of Law, University of California, Berkeley.
Geoffrey C. Hazard, Jr., Professor of Law, Yale University.
Colin C. Tait, Professor of Law, University of Connecticut.

PROCEDURE—FEDERAL RULES OF CIVIL PROCEDURE, 1983 Edition

PRODUCTS LIABILITY (1980)

Marshall S. Shapo, Professor of Law, Northwestern University.

PRODUCTS LIABILITY AND SAFETY (1980), with 1983 Case and Documentary Supplement

W. Page Keeton, Professor of Law, University of Texas.
David G. Owen, Professor of Law, University of South Carolina.
John E. Montgomery, Professor of Law, University of South Carolina.

PROFESSIONAL RESPONSIBILITY, Third Edition (1984), with 1984 Selected National Standards Supplement

Thomas D. Morgan, Dean of the Law School, Emory University.
Ronald D. Rotunda, Professor of Law, University of Illinois.

PROPERTY, Fifth Edition (1984)

John E. Cribbet, Dean of the Law School, University of Illinois.
Corwin W. Johnson, Professor of Law, University of Texas.

PROPERTY—PERSONAL (1953)

S. Kenneth Skolfield, late Professor of Law Emeritus, Boston University.

PROPERTY—PERSONAL, Third Edition (1954)

Everett Fraser, late Dean of the Law School Emeritus, University of Minnesota.
Third Edition by Charles W. Taintor, late Professor of Law, University of Pittsburgh.

PROPERTY—INTRODUCTION, TO REAL PROPERTY, Third Edition (1954)

Everett Fraser, late Dean of the Law School Emeritus, University of Minnesota.

PROPERTY—REAL AND PERSONAL, Combined Edition (1954)

Everett Fraser, late Dean of the Law School Emeritus, University of Minnesota.
Third Edition of Personal Property by Charles W. Taintor, late Professor of Law, University of Pittsburgh.

PROPERTY—FUNDAMENTALS OF MODERN REAL PROPERTY, Second Edition (1982)

Edward H. Rabin, Professor of Law, University of California, Davis.

PROPERTY—PROBLEMS IN REAL PROPERTY (Pamphlet) (1969)

Edward H. Rabin, Professor of Law, University of California, Davis.

PROPERTY, REAL (1984)

Paul Goldstein, Professor of Law, Stanford University.

PROSECUTION AND ADJUDICATION, Second Edition (1982), with 1983 Supplement

Reprint of Chapters 11–26 of Miller, Dawson, Dix and Parnas's CRIMINAL JUSTICE ADMINISTRATION, Second Edition.

UNIVERSITY CASEBOOK SERIES—Continued

PUBLIC REGULATION OF DANGEROUS PRODUCTS (paperback) (1980)

Marshall S. Shapo, Professor of Law, Northwestern University.

PUBLIC UTILITY LAW, see Free Enterprise, also Regulated Industries

REAL ESTATE PLANNING (1980), with 1980 Problems, Statutes and New Materials Supplement

Norton L. Steuben, Professor of Law, University of Colorado.

REAL ESTATE TRANSACTIONS (1980), with Statute, Form and Problem Supplement

Paul Goldstein, Professor of Law, Stanford University.

RECEIVERSHIP AND CORPORATE REORGANIZATION, see Creditors' Rights

REGULATED INDUSTRIES, Second Edition, 1976

William K. Jones, Professor of Law, Columbia University.

REMEDIES (1982)

Edward D. Re, Chief Judge, U. S. Court of International Trade.

RESTITUTION, Second Edition (1966)

John W. Wade, Professor of Law, Vanderbilt University.

SALES (1980)

Marion W. Benfield, Jr., Professor of Law, University of Illinois.
William D. Hawkland, Chancellor, Louisiana State University Law Center.

SALES AND SALES FINANCING, Fourth Edition (1976), with 1982 Bankruptcy Supplement

John Honnold, Professor of Law, University of Pennsylvania.

SALES LAW AND THE CONTRACTING PROCESS (1982)

Reprint of Chapters 1–10 of Schwartz and Scott's Commercial Transactions.

SECURED INTERESTS IN PERSONAL PROPERTY (1984)

Douglas G. Baird, Professor of Law, University of Chicago.
Thomas H. Jackson, Professor of Law, Stanford University.

SECURED TRANSACTIONS IN PERSONAL PROPERTY (1983) (Reprinted from COMMERCIAL LAW)

Robert L. Jordan, Professor of Law, University of California, Los Angeles.
William D. Warren, Professor of Law, University of California, Los Angeles.

SECURITIES REGULATION, Fifth Edition (1982), with 1983 Cases and Releases Supplement and 1983 Selected Statutes, Rules and Forms Supplement

Richard W. Jennings, Professor of Law, University of California, Berkeley.
Harold Marsh, Jr., Member of the California Bar.

SECURITIES REGULATION (1982), with 1983 Supplement

Larry D. Soderquist, Professor of Law, Vanderbilt University.

SENTENCING AND THE CORRECTIONAL PROCESS, Second Edition (1976)

Frank W. Miller, Professor of Law, Washington University.
Robert O. Dawson, Professor of Law, University of Texas.
George E. Dix, Professor of Law, University of Texas.
Raymond I. Parnas, Professor of Law, University of California, Davis.

UNIVERSITY CASEBOOK SERIES—Continued

SOCIAL WELFARE AND THE INDIVIDUAL (1971)
Robert J. Levy, Professor of Law, University of Minnesota.
Thomas P. Lewis, Dean of the College of Law, University of Kentucky.
Peter W. Martin, Professor of Law, Cornell University.

TAX, POLICY ANALYSIS OF THE FEDERAL INCOME (1976)
William A. Klein, Professor of Law, University of California, Los Angeles.

TAXATION, FEDERAL INCOME (1976), with 1983 Supplement
Erwin N. Griswold, Dean Emeritus, Harvard Law School.
Michael J. Graetz, Professor of Law, University of Virginia.

TAXATION, FEDERAL INCOME, Fourth Edition (1982)
James J. Freeland, Professor of Law, University of Florida.
Stephen A. Lind, Professor of Law, University of Florida.
Richard B. Stephens, Professor of Law Emeritus, University of Florida.

TAXATION, FEDERAL INCOME, Volume I, Personal Income Taxation (1972), with 1983 Case Supplement; Volume II, Taxation of Partnerships and Corporations, Second Edition (1980), with 1983 Legislative Supplement
Stanley S. Surrey, Professor of Law, Harvard University.
William C. Warren, Professor of Law Emeritus, Columbia University.
Paul R. McDaniel, Professor of Law, Boston College Law School.
Hugh J. Ault, Professor of Law, Boston College Law School.

TAXATION, FEDERAL WEALTH TRANSFER, Second Edition (1982)
Stanley S. Surrey, Professor of Law, Harvard University.
William C. Warren, Professor of Law Emeritus, Columbia University.
Paul R. McDaniel, Professor of Law, Boston College Law School.
Harry L. Gutman, Instructor, Harvard Law School and Boston College Law School.

TAXATION OF INDIVIDUALS, PARTNERSHIPS AND CORPORATIONS, PROBLEMS in the (1978)
Norton L. Steuben, Professor of Law, University of Colorado.
William J. Turnier, Professor of Law, University of North Carolina.

TAXES AND FINANCE—STATE AND LOCAL (1974)
Oliver Oldman, Professor of Law, Harvard University.
Ferdinand P. Schoettle, Professor of Law, University of Minnesota.

TORT LAW AND ALTERNATIVES, Third Edition (1983)
Marc A. Franklin, Professor of Law, Stanford University.
Robert L. Rabin, Professor of Law, Stanford University.

TORTS, Seventh Edition (1982)
William L. Prosser, late Professor of Law, University of California, Hastings College.
John W. Wade, Professor of Law, Vanderbilt University.
Victor E. Schwartz, Professor of Law, American University.

TORTS, Third Edition (1976)
Harry Shulman, late Dean of the Law School, Yale University.
Fleming James, Jr., Professor of Law Emeritus, Yale University.
Oscar S. Gray, Professor of Law, University of Maryland.

UNIVERSITY CASEBOOK SERIES—Continued

TRADE REGULATION, Second Edition (1983)

Milton Handler, Professor of Law Emeritus, Columbia University.
Harlan M. Blake, Professor of Law, Columbia University.
Robert Pitofsky, Professor of Law, Georgetown University.
Harvey J. Goldschmid, Professor of Law, Columbia University.

TRADE REGULATION, see Antitrust

TRANSNATIONAL LEGAL PROBLEMS, Second Edition (1976) with 1982 Case and Documentary Supplement

Henry J. Steiner, Professor of Law, Harvard University.
Detlev F. Vagts, Professor of Law, Harvard University.

TRIAL, see also Evidence, Making the Record, Lawyering Process and Preparing and Presenting the Case

TRIAL ADVOCACY (1968)

A. Leo Levin, Professor of Law, University of Pennsylvania.
Harold Cramer, of the Pennsylvania Bar.
Maurice Rosenberg, Professor of Law, Columbia University, Consultant.

TRUSTS, Fifth Edition (1978)

George G. Bogert, late Professor of Law Emeritus, University of Chicago.
Dallin H. Oaks, President, Brigham Young University.

TRUSTS AND SUCCESSION (Palmer's), Fourth Edition (1983)

Richard V. Wellman, Professor of Law, University of Georgia.
Lawrence W. Waggoner, Professor of Law, University of Michigan.
Olin L. Browder, Jr., Professor of Law, University of Michigan.

UNFAIR COMPETITION, see Competitive Process and Business Torts

UNITED NATIONS LAW, Second Edition (1967), with Documentary Supplement (1968)

Louis B. Sohn, Professor of Law, Harvard University.

WATER RESOURCE MANAGEMENT, Second Edition (1980), with 1983 Supplement

Charles J. Meyers, Dean of the Law School, Stanford University.
A. Dan Tarlock, Professor of Law, Indiana Unversity.

WILLS AND ADMINISTRATION, Fifth Edition (1961)

Philip Mechem, late Professor of Law, University of Pennsylvania.
Thomas E. Atkinson, late Professor of Law, New York University.

WORLD LAW, see United Nations Law

*

University Casebook Series

EDITORIAL BOARD

DAVID L. SHAPIRO
DIRECTING EDITOR
Professor of Law, Harvard University

EDWARD L. BARRETT, Jr.
Professor of Law, University of California, Davis

ROBERT C. CLARK
Professor of Law, Harvard University

OWEN M. FISS
Professor of Law, Yale Law School

JEFFERSON B. FORDHAM
Professor of Law, University of Utah

GERALD GUNTHER
Professor of Law, Stanford University

HARRY W. JONES
Professor of Law, Columbia University

HERMA HILL KAY
Professor of Law, University of California at Berkeley

PAGE KEETON
Professor of Law, University of Texas

JOHN RITCHIE
Emeritus Dean and Wigmore Professor of Law, Northwestern University

SAMUEL D. THURMAN
Professor of Law, University of Utah

REAL PROPERTY

By

PAUL GOLDSTEIN

Professor of Law
Stanford University

Mineola, New York
THE FOUNDATION PRESS, INC.
1984

COPYRIGHT © 1984 By THE FOUNDATION PRESS, INC.
All rights reserved
Printed in the United States of America

Library of Congress Cataloging in Publication Data

Goldstein, Paul, 1943–
  Real property.

  (University casebook series)
  Includes index.
  1. Real property—United States—Cases. I. Title.
II. Series.
KF569.G6 1984   346.7304'3   84–5919
ISBN 0–88277–170–1 347.30643

Goldstein-Real Property UCB

TO JAN AND ELIZABETH

PREFACE

Real property law represents society's effort to order the ownership and use of land. It is real property law that requires B to obtain A's permission if he wishes to use her land. It is also real property law that prescribes the rights and liabilities of owner A and user B as between themselves, and as against the rest of the world.

Real property law has two unifying purposes. One purpose is to assure that land is put to its most productive use. The second purpose is to assure that land is put to its most humane use. Interests in productivity and humanity, in efficiency and equity, will often be jointly served by the same real property rule. Sometimes, however, they will not, and the resulting conflicts have galvanized some of the most spirited debates in real property law. Should landlords be forced to provide impoverished tenants with habitable premises? Should landlords be constrained in the amount of rent they can charge these tenants? What effect will such controls have on landowners' incentives to build new rental housing for the poor? In reading this book, you will find many such hard questions and hard choices.

The purpose of this casebook is to introduce you to the fundamentals of real property law. All of the topics traditionally covered in the first-year property course are included here and all of the basic rules are explored. Many of the notes and materials in the book aim to expose both the theoretical and historical foundations of the real property system as well as the more worldly, day-to-day practice of lawyers engaged in structuring real property transactions for their clients. My experience in academe convinces me that theory and principle should play a substantial role in guiding the evolution of real property law. My experience in practice convinces me that policymakers should attend closely to the practicalities of real property arrangements before proposing changes in real property law.

Many, many people have helped to bring this casebook from its earliest stages to its present form. Stanford law students have provided inestimable help in preparing research memoranda, checking citations, proofreading manuscript and attending to countless other important details. I am deeply grateful to John Barlow, Sarah Diehl, Catherine Glaze, Robert Sternbach, Peter Stone, Diana Van Etten and Janice Weiner. Their work was supported by the Stanford Legal Research Fund, made possible by a bequest from the Estate of Ira S. Lillick and by gifts from other friends of the Stanford Law School.

I am also very grateful to colleagues who have reviewed or taught from earlier versions of all or part of this book: Wayne G. Barnett, Lillian R. BeVier, Robert C. Ellickson, Mark G. Kelman, Robert Kreiss,

PREFACE

George P. Smith II and Howard R. Williams. I am indebted to Marvin R. Baum and Ronald Willig, of the New York Bar, for providing me with the forms reproduced in the section on land transfer and finance, and to Gregg Davis, of the Texas Bar, for gathering the materials for the section on the zoning system at work.

Stanford Law School has, as usual, provided a wonderfully congenial setting for research and writing. My former real property colleague and dean, Charles J. Meyers, encouraged me to take on this effort and helped in its formative stages. Deans John Hart Ely, J. Keith Mann and Thomas F. McBride have also been generous with their support. Staff members of the Robert Crown Law Library, under the expert guidance of Public Service Librarian Iris J. Wildman, were unfailingly conscientious and cheerful in their help; I am grateful to them for assisting so many times in so many ways. Finally, I am deeply indebted to my secretaries, Emily Chatfield and Bernice Zamora, for preparing the manuscript through its several drafts—performing, graciously and well, a task that must, at times, have seemed an endless burden.

A Note on Style. Most of the cases and other materials appearing in these pages have been edited. The deletion of sentences and pargaraphs is indicated by ellipses; the deletion of citations is not indicated. Most footnotes have been excised. The remaining footnotes retain their original numbering. Author's footnotes are lettered.

P. G.

Stanford, California
April, 1984

SUMMARY OF CONTENTS

	Page
PREFACE	xxi
TABLE OF CASES	xxxi

PART ONE. THE REAL PROPERTY SYSTEM

		Page
I.	Why Property?	1
	A. Trespass: The Right to Exclude	8
	B. Balancing the Rights of Neighbors	86
II.	Land Transfer and Finance	152
	A. A Typical Land Sale	152
	B. Title Assurance	310
	C. Land Finance	407
	D. Federal Income Taxation	446

PART TWO. PRIVATE ARRANGEMENTS FOR POSSESSION AND USE

		Page
I.	Possessory Interests: Present, Future, Concurrent	467
	A. The Estates System	467
	B. Promoting Alienability and Marketability	567
	C. Shared Ownership	606
II.	Nonpossessory Interests: Easements, Covenants, Servitudes	670
	A. Easements	673
	B. Covenants and Servitudes	719
	C. Interpreting Easements, Covenants and Servitudes	787
	D. Terminating Easements, Covenants and Servitudes	799
III.	Landlord and Tenant	816
	A. The Leasehold Estate	816
	B. Residential Leases: The Problem of Substandard Housing	908
	C. Commercial Leases: The Shopping Center	1010
IV.	Building on the Basics: The Condominium	1044
	A. Management and Control	1047
	B. Restraints on Alienation	1053
	C. Restrictions on Occupancy and Use	1059

PART THREE. PUBLIC CONTROL OF OWNERSHIP AND USE

		Page
I.	The Sources and Limits of State Power	1077
	A. "Health, Safety, Welfare and Morals"	1077
	B. "Takings"	1094
	C. Aesthetics	1116
	D. Exclusionary Effects	1128

SUMMARY OF CONTENTS

		Page
II.	Planning Law and Administration	1147
	A. The Comprehensive Plan	1152
	B. The Zoning System	1165
	C. Subdivision Regulation	1272
III.	Eminent Domain	1287
	A. "Public Use" and "Public Purpose"	1287
	B. "Just Compensation"	1301
IV.	Reprise: Why Property?	1329
	ACKNOWLEDGEMENTS	1343
	INDEX	1349

TABLE OF CONTENTS

	Page
PREFACE	xxi
TABLE OF CASES	xxxi

PART ONE. THE REAL PROPERTY SYSTEM

				Page
I.	Why Property?			1
	A.	Trespass: The Right to Exclude		8
		1.	Theory of Protection	8
		2.	Adverse Possession	24
			a. Theory of Protection	24
			b. Required Elements	37
			i. "Actual," "Open," "Visible," "Notorious" and "Exclusive"	37
			ii. "Hostile" (and "Under Claim of Right"?)	43
			iii. "Continuous"	50
		3.	The Improving Trespasser	60
		4.	Limits on the Right to Exclude	70
	B.	Balancing the Rights of Neighbors		86
		1.	Nuisance	90
			a. The Calculus of Rights	90
			b. Remedies	105
		2.	Lateral and Subjacent Support	126
II.	Land Transfer and Finance			152
	A.	A Typical Land Sale		152
		1.	Arranging the Sale	156
			a. The Lawyer's Role	156
			b. The Broker's Role	171
		2.	The Contract of Sale	186
			a. The Statute of Frauds	189
			b. Conditions	196
			i. Marketable Title	196
			ii. Financing	200
			c. Remedies	212
			d. Risk of Loss	226
		3.	Closing the Contract: The Deed	237
			a. Deed Construction	239
			b. Description of the Land Conveyed	244
			c. Delivery	260
		4.	Liabilities That Survive the Deed	279
			a. Fitness of the Premises	281
			b. Title	295

TABLE OF CONTENTS

	Page
II. Land Transfer and Finance—Continued	
B. Title Assurance	310
1. The Record System	310
a. Types of Recording Acts	317
b. Statutory Conditions of Protection	321
i. Purchaser Without Notice	321
ii. Purchaser for Value	337
2. The System at Work: The Title Search	343
a. The Indices	343
b. Extent of Search	356
3. Abstracts, Opinions and Title Insurance	363
a. Abstracts and Lawyers' Opinions	366
b. Title Insurance	373
4. Reforming the Title Assurance System	388
a. Marketable Title Acts, Statutes of Limitations, Curative Acts	388
b. Title Registration	397
C. Land Finance	407
1. The Forms of Land Finance	411
2. Obligations of Debtor	422
3. Default	430
D. Federal Income Taxation	446
1. Property Used as a Personal Residence	446
2. Property Held for Investment, Income or Business Purposes	448

PART TWO. PRIVATE ARRANGEMENTS FOR POSSESSION AND USE

	Page
I. Possessory Interests: Present, Future, Concurrent	467
A. The Estates System	467
1. Classification of Estates in Land	476
a. The Fee Simple	476
i. Fee Simple Absolute	479
ii. Defeasible Fees	485
b. The Fee Tail	501
c. The Life Estate	512
2. Future Interests	521
a. Classification	528
b. Rights of Future Interest Holders: Waste	549
B. Promoting Alienability and Marketability	567
1. Rule Against Perpetuities	567
2. Rule Against Restraints on Alienation	587
3. Statutory Limitations	599

TABLE OF CONTENTS

			Page
I.	Possessory Interests: Present, Future, Concurrent—Continued		
	C. Shared Ownership		606
	1. Concurrent Estates		606
	a. Joint Tenancy or Tenancy in Common?		607
	i. Classification		607
	ii. Severance		616
	b. Rights and Liabilities of Cotenants		624
	c. Partition		640
	2. Property Rights of Husband and Wife		646
	a. The Common Law System		647
	b. The Community Property System		656
	c. Administering Marital Property Systems		663
II.	Nonpossessory Interests: Easements, Covenants, Servitudes		670
	A. Easements		673
	1. Creation		673
	a. By Instrument		673
	b. By Implication and Necessity		684
	c. By Prescription		698
	2. Enforcement By and Against Successors in Interest		707
	a. Who Is Bound? Does the Burden Run?		707
	b. Who Is Benefited? Does the Benefit Run?		709
	B. Covenants and Servitudes		719
	1. Creation		719
	a. By Instrument		719
	b. By Implication		730
	2. Enforcement By and Against Successors in Interest		744
	a. Who Is Bound? Does the Burden Run?		744
	i. Intent and Notice		745
	ii. Privity		746
	(A) "Horizontal" Privity		746
	(B) "Vertical" Privity		750
	iii. Touch or Concern		755
	b. Who Gets the Benefit? Does the Benefit Run?		765
	c. Enforcement at Equity: Equitable Servitudes		780
	C. Interpreting Easements, Covenants and Servitudes		787
	D. Terminating Easements, Covenants and Servitudes		799
III.	Landlord and Tenant		816
	A. The Leasehold Estate		816
	1. Classification		823
	a. Types of Tenancies		823
	i. Term of Years		823
	ii. Periodic Tenancy		824
	iii. Tenancy at Will		824
	iv. Tenancy at Sufferance		825
	b. The Holdover Tenant		825

TABLE OF CONTENTS

III. Landlord and Tenant—Continued
- A. The Leasehold Estate—Continued **Page**
  - 2. Tenant Rights and Remedies 834
    - a. The Right to Possession 834
    - b. The Right to Quiet Enjoyment 843
    - c. The Right to Safe Premises 858
    - d. The Right to Assign and Sublet 868
  - 3. Landlord Rights and Remedies 877
    - a. Tenant Breaches and Refuses to Leave 878
    - b. Tenant Breaches and Leaves 892
- B. Residential Leases: The Problem of Substandard Housing 908
  - 1. The Market for Substandard Housing 917
  - 2. Efforts to Regulate Quality 927
    - a. Administrative Enforcement 927
    - b. Common Law Doctrine 936
      - i. Contract 937
        - (A) Illegality 937
        - (B) Implied Warranty of Habitability 941
      - ii. Remedial Strategies 959
  - 3. Regulation of Price and Access 973
  - 4. Alternatives to Regulation 990
- C. Commercial Leases: The Shopping Center 1010
  - 1. The Retail Lease 1011
  - 2. Tenant's Duties 1016
  - 3. Landlord's Duties 1032

IV. Building on the Basics: The Condominium 1044
- A. Management and Control 1047
- B. Restraints on Alienation 1053
- C. Restrictions on Occupancy and Use 1059

PART THREE. PUBLIC CONTROL OF OWNERSHIP AND USE

I. The Sources and Limits of State Power 1077
- A. "Health, Safety, Welfare and Morals" 1077
- B. "Takings" 1094
- C. Aesthetics 1116
- D. Exclusionary Effects 1128

II. Planning Law and Administration 1147
- A. The Comprehensive Plan 1152
- B. The Zoning System 1165
  - 1. The Zoning Ordinance 1165
  - 2. Flexibility in Zoning 1168
    - a. The Constitutional Setting 1168
      - i. Nonconforming Structures and Uses 1168
      - ii. Vested Rights 1173

TABLE OF CONTENTS

II. Planning Law and Administration—Continued
   B. The Zoning System—Continued
      2. Flexibility in Zoning—Continued   **Page**
         b. Administrative Decisions: Variances and Special Exceptions _____ 1179
         c. Legislative Decisions _____ 1186
            i. Rezoning _____ 1186
            ii. Floating Zones and PUDs _____ 1196
         d. Community Decisions _____ 1204
      3. The Zoning System at Work: The 2030 Vallejo Case 1213
         a. Factual and Legal Background _____ 1213
         b. The Administrative Process_____ 1220
         c. Judicial Review of the Administrative Process __ 1251
         d. Postscript _____ 1264
   C. Subdivision Regulation _____ 1272

III. Eminent Domain _____ 1287
   A. "Public Use" and "Public Purpose" _____ 1287
   B. "Just Compensation" _____ 1301
      1. Partial Takings _____ 1312
      2. Divided Interests _____ 1321

IV. Reprise: Why Property? _____ 1329

ACKNOWLEDGEMENTS _____ 1343

INDEX _____ 1349

*

TABLE OF CASES

The principal cases are in italic type. Cases cited or discussed are in Roman type. References are to pages.

Abel v. Zoning Board of Appeals, 1183
Abo Petroleum Corp. v. Amstutz, 544, 547
Acadia California, Ltd. v. Herbert, 125
Addison v. Addison, 664
Adrian v. Rabinowitz, 838
Agins v. City of Tiburon, 1114
Alsup v. Montoya, 596, 597
Ambler Realty Co. v. Village of Euclid, 1092
American Book Co. v. Yeshiva University Development Foundation, Inc., 875
American National Bank & Trust Co. v. City of Chicago, 1178
Amezquita v. Hernandez-Colon, 35
Anderson v. Grasberg, 623
Andrews v. Lake Serene Property Owners Association, Inc., 721
Appeal of (see name of party)
Arlington Heights, Village of v. Metropolitan Housing Corp., 1146
Armory v. Delamirie, 23
Arthur v. Lake Tansi Village, Inc., 730, 739, 740
Associated Home Builders of Greater East Bay, Inc. v. City of Walnut Creek, 1284
Aurora, City of v. Burns, 1091
Avner v. Longridge Estates, 292
Aztec Ltd., Inc. v. Creekside Investment Co., 705

Backhausen v. Mayer, 708
Baker v. Weedon, 563
Baker, State v., 1093
Baliles v. Cities Service Co., 189, 194
Banberry Development Corp. v. South Jordan City, 1283
Barash v. Pennsylvania Terminal Real Estate Corp., 845, 855, 858
Barclay v. DeVeau, 1047
Barela v. Superior Court, 970
Barnes v. North Carolina State Highway Commission, 1320
Barrier v. Randolph, 239
Barrows v. Jackson, 501
Baseball Publishing Co. v. Bruton, 674, 680, 683

Batten v. United States, 1113
Baumann v. Ross, 1286
Baylis v. City of Baltimore, 1194
Belle Terre, Village of v. Boraas, 1088, 1091, 1092, 1093, 1115, 1124, 1145, 1175
Belleville v. Parrillo's, Inc., 1168, 1175, 1176
Bennion, Van Camp, Hagen & Ruhl v. Kassler Escrow, Inc., 279
Berenson v. Town of New Castle, 1142
Berg v. Wiley, 878, 888, 889, 890
Bergesen v. Clauss, 48
Berkeley, State ex rel. Stoyanoff v., 1117
Berlier v. George, 235
Berman v. Parker, 1300
Berman & Sons, Inc. v. Jefferson, 954
Berry v. Union National Bank, 585
Beverley's Case, 526
Blackett v. Olanoff, 857, 858, 877, 952
Blagg v. Fred Hunt Co., 287, 292, 293
Block v. Hirsh, 976
Board of Education of Central School District No. 1 v. Miles, 603
Board of Education of School Dist. No. 68 v. Surety Developers, Inc., 1274, 1281
Board of Public Instruction v. Town of Bay Harbor Islands, 1327
Board of Supervisors of Fairfax County v. DeGroff Enterprises, Inc., 1284
Board of Supervisors of Fairfax County v. Medical Structures, Inc., 1173, 1176, 1178
Boomer v. Atlantic Cement Co., 105, 121, 122, 123, 124, 125
Boston Housing Authority v. Hemingway, 953
Bourgoin v. Fortier, 180
Bove v. Donner-Hanna Coke Corp., 104
Brattle Square Church v. Grant, 582
Breen v. Morehead, 363
Breene v. Plaza Tower Association, 1053, 1059
Brice v. Griffin, 427, 428
Broadway, Laguna, Vallejo Association v. Board of Permit Appeals, 1256, 1263, 1264

TABLE OF CASES

Brokaw v. Fairchild, 560, 561
Brooks v. Reynolds, 762
Brown v. Lober, 297, 302
Brown v. McAnally, 1298
Brown v. Safeway Stores, Inc., 1029
Brown, State v., 887
Brown v. Southall Realty Co., 937, 940, 969
Brown v. Wrightman, 604
Browning v. Sacrison, 540
Bryan v. City of Chester, 1116, 1121
Buchanan v. Warley, 500
Buffalo, City of v. J. W. Clement Co., 1311
Bump v. Dahl, 335
Burt, Inc., Charles E. v. Seven Grand Corp., 856
Bushmiller v. Schiller, 200, 206, 211
Butler v. Acme Markets, Inc., 1042

Campbell v. Race, 86
Capitol Federal Savings & Loan Association v. Smith, 494, 501
Carlson v. Libby, 752
Carpenter v. Coles, 49
Cashion v. Ahmadi, 183, 184
Cast v. National Bank of Commerce, Trust & Savings Association of Lincoln, 597
Causby, United States v., 1112, 1113
Cazares v. Ortiz, 954, 955
Centex Homes Corp. v. Boag, 222
Central Financial Services, Inc. v. Spears, 439
Charlotte v. Charlotte Park & Recreation Comm'n, *1321,* 1325
Charlotte Park & Recreation Commission v. Barringer, 501, 1326
Cheek v. Wainwright, 37, 39, 40
Cheney v. Mueller, 684, 694, 696, 697
Cheney v. Village 2 at New Hope, Inc., 1196
Church v. Town of Islip, 1193
City of (see name of city)
Clayton v. Jensen, 703
Cogan v. Kidder, Matthews & Segner, Inc., 181
Colman v. Butkovich, 257, 258
Commissioner of Internal Revenue v. Tufts, 453
Conger v. Conger, 561
Conklin v. Davi, 196, 207
Connor v. Great Western Savings & Loan Association, 294, 295
Consolidated Edison Co. of New York v. Hoffman, 1184

Cooke v. Chilcott, 786
Cornelison v. Kornbluth, 430, 444
Corrigan v. Buckley, 501
Costello v. Johnson, 224
County of (see name of county)
County Council for Montgomery County v. District Land Corp., 1178
Cramer v. Jenkins, 703
Crane v. Commissioner, 452
Crimmins v. Gould, 813, 814
Crowder v. Vandendeale, 293
Crum v. McCoy, 181, 183

D'Arundel's Case, 471, 478, 501
Daugharthy v. Monritt Associates, 422, 427
Davis v. Bruk, 797
Davis v. Huey, 746
Davis, Inc., William J. v. Slade, 940
Dennen v. Searle, 477, 478
Dennison v. State, 1318
Diamond Housing Corp. v. Robinson, 940
Dickhut v. Norton, 969
Dickson v. Alexandria Hospital, Inc., 512, 520
DiDonato v. Reliance Standard Life Insurance Co., 209
Dieffenbach v. McIntyre, 834, 842
Dobbs, Inc., Ellsworth v. Johnson, 182, 184
Doctor v. Hughes, 526, 527
Donnellan v. Rocks, 184
Donnelly Advertising Corp. v. Flaccomio, 825
Dorsey v. Speelman, 549, 559
Dover Pool & Racquet Club, Inc. v. Brooking, 209
Duke of Norfolk's Case, 586
Dumpor's Case, 874
Dunlap v. Bullard, 750, 754
Dunn Bros., Inc. v. Lesnewsky, 709, 714
Dupree v. Worthen Bank & Trust Co., 857
Durant v. Hamrick, 624
Dussin Investment Co. v. Bloxham, 856
Dutton v. Thompson, 50
Dyett v. Pendleton, 843, 854, 855, 952
Dzuris v. Kucharik, 43

Eagle Enterprises, Inc. v. Gross, 762
East Haven Associates, Inc. v. Gurian, 850, 855, 952
Eastlake v. Forest City Enterprises, Inc., 1204, 1212, 1213
Echols v. Olsen, 400
Edwards v. Habib, 969

TABLE OF CASES

Eldridge v. City of Palo Alto, 1114
Erickson v. Erickson, 613, 614
Estate of (see name of party)
Euclid, Village of v. Ambler Realty Co., 1077, 1091, 1092, 1093, 1115, 1175

Fairlawn Plaza Development, Inc. v. Fleming Co., 1022, 1032
Fanti v. Welsh, 335
Farr v. Newman, 336
Fasano v. Board of County Commissioners, 1192, 1193
Ferguson v. Caspar, 268, 278
Fidelity Federal Savings & Loan Association v. De La Cuesta, 429
Finn v. Williams, 692, 694, 695, 696, 697, 698
First Universalist Society of North Adams v. Boland, 582
First Wisconsin Trust Co. v. L. Wiemann Co., 856, 907
Fitts v. Hanks, 856
564.54 Acres of Land, United States v., 1309
Flagg Brothers, Inc. v. Brooks, 891
Fletcher v. Hurdle, 520
Flora Logging Co. v. Boeing, 1298
Florida Power & Light Co. v. Rader, 336
Florida Publishing Co. v. Fletcher, 86
Flureau v. Thornhill, 224
Foisy v. Wyman, 957
Fontainebleau Hotel Corp. v. 4225 Inc., 102
Forbis v. Honeycutt, 173, 181
Fowler v. Bott, 816, 820
Fox, State ex rel. Haman v., 704, 705
Frank v. Jansen, 214
Frankland v. City of Lake Oswego, 1203
Franklin, Estate of v. Commissioner of Internal Revenue, 462
Friendswood Development Co. v. Smith-Southwest Industries, Inc., 130
Fuentes v. Shevin, 891
Funk v. Funk, 868, 874, 875, 876

Gagner v. Kittery Water District, 324, 336
Gardner v. Keteltas, 854
Gibbens v. Weisshaupt, 705
Girsh, Appeal of, 1144
Gleason v. Title Guarantee Co., 372
Gnash v. Saari, 209
Goldberg v. Zoning Commission of Town of Simsbury, 1285
Goldblatt v. Town of Hempstead, 1109

Golden v. Planning Board of Town of Ramapo, 1145, 1164
Gordon v. Village of Wayne, 1282
Grace v. Croninger, 1042
Graham, In re Marriage of, 664
Grant v. Leith, 148
Great Atlantic & Pacific Tea Co. v. Bailey, 1041
Green v. Superior Court, 955, 958, 959
Greene v. Lindsey, 891
Greenfield & Co., Albert M. v. Kolea, 816, 820
Gruman v. Investors Diversified Services Inc., 904

Hadacheck v. Sebastian, 1091
Hagemann v. National Bank & Trust Co., 567, 581
Hall v. Garson, 891
Halleck v. Halleck, 614
Haman, State ex rel. v. Fox, 704
Hankins v. Mathews, 587, 596
Hannah v. Peel, 24
Hannan v. Dusch, 839
Hanson v. Cheney, 694
Hanson v. Zoller, 346
Harbison v. City of Buffalo, 1177
Hargrove v. Taylor, 623
Hatcher v. Chesner, 803, 812
Haywood v. Brunswick Building Society, 786
Hecht v. Meller, 181
Helmsley v. Borough of Fort Lee, 977
Hewitt v. Hewitt, 664
Hidden Harbour Estates, Inc. v. Basso, 1068
Highbaugh Enterprises, Inc. v. Deatrick & James Construction Co., 796
Hillis Homes, Inc. v. Snohomish County, 1282
Hoffmann v. Kinealy, 1176
Holden v. Lynn, 8, 21, 32
Holiday Homes of St. Johns, Inc. v. Lockhart, 180
Home Builders League, Inc. v. Township of Berlin, 1144
Hood v. Hood, 278
Hopkins v. Hill, 703
Horn v. Lawyers Title Insurance Corp., 387
Hornsby v. Smith, 707
Houston Gas & Fuel Co. v. Harlow, 100
Howard v. Kunto, 50, 55
Hudson View Properties v. Weiss, 980, 986, 989

TABLE OF CASES

Humphreys County Board of Education v. Baker, 548
Hurd v. Curtis, 752

In re (see name of party)
Industrial Development & Land Co. v. Goldschmidt, 1042
Inganamort v. Borough of Fort Lee, 974
Interstate Restaurants, Inc. v. Halsa Corp., 1041
Isen v. Giant Food, Inc., 586
Isham v. Cudlip, 58

Javins v. First National Realty Corp., 941, 951, 952, 953, 954, 956, 957, 969, 971, 1041
Jee v. Audley, 582
Jeminson v. Montgomery Real Estate & Co., 295
Johnson v. Carman, 225
Johnson v. Myers, 754
Johnston v. Michigan Consolidated Gas Co., 716, 729
Joiner v. Janssen, 43, 48
Jolliff v. Hardin Cable Television Co., 791, 796, 797
Jones v. Alfred H. Mayer Co., 501, 989
Jones v. Grow Investment & Mortgage Co., 302
Jordan v. Talbot, 890
Josefowicz v. Porter, 209

Kakalik v. Bernardo, 210
Karesh v. City Council of City of Charleston, 1297
Kelly v. Schmelz, 787, 795
Kemp v. Lake Serene Property Owners Association, Inc., 335, 728
Keppel v. Bailey, 785
Kinley v. Atlantic Cement Co., 125
Klauder, Klotz & Venitt v. Rose's Stores, Inc., 1031
Kline v. Burns, 866
Kline v. 1500 Massachusetts Avenue Apartment Corp., 858, 867, 952, 969
Knapp v. Cirillo, 148
Knight v. City of Billings, 1113
Knight v. Thayer, 363
Koenig v. Van Reken, 416, 418
Kovarik v. Vesely, 210
Kozesnik v. Township of Montgomery, 1162
Krause v. Crossley, 622
Krencicki v. Petersen, 702
Krieger v. Helmsley-Spear, Inc., 875

Kriegler v. Eichler Homes, Inc., 292
Kroger Co. v. Chemical Securities Co., 1016, 1029, 1031

Lafferty v. Payson City, 1283
Lake Meredith Development Co. v. City of Fritch, 335
Lanza, In re, 165, 169, 170, 336
Leonard v. City of Bothell, 1212
Letts v. Kessler, 707
Levine v. Stein, 444
Lien v. Pitts, 206
Limpus v. Armstrong, 210
Lindsey v. Normet, 971, 972, 1145
Lionshead Lake, Inc. v. Wayne Township, 1144
Loda v. H. K. Sargeant & Associates, Inc., 211
Lohmeyer v. Bower, 209
Long v. Long, 503, 504
Long v. Short, 518, 520
Loretto v. Teleprompter Manhattan CATV Corp., 1108, 1111, 1112
Los Angeles, City of v. Gage, 1176
Los Angeles, City of v. Wolfe, 1319
Louisville, City of v. Kavanaugh, 1164
Lovering v. Worthington, 581
Lown v. Nichols Plumbing and Heating, Inc., 337, 343
Lucas, In re Marriage of, 657, 664
Lux v. Haggin, 814

McCarty v. Natural Carbonic Gas Co., 90, 100, 102, 103, 124
McDaniel v. Lawyers' Title Guaranty Fund, 336
McDonnold v. Weinacht, 25, 32, 33
McIntosh v. Vail, 752
McKnight v. Basilides, 624, 636, 637, 638
Maguire v. Yanke, 13, 21
Maioriello v. Arlotta, 696
Marcus Brown Holding Co. v. Feldman, 976
Marengo Cave Co. v. Ross, 41
Marini v. Ireland, 956
Marmont v. Axe, 904
Marshall v. Hollywood, Inc., 393
MAR–SON, Inc. v. Terwaho Enterprises, Inc., 903
Martin v. Martin, 126
Martin v. Port of Seattle, 1113
Martin v. Reynolds Metals Co., 103
Martin v. Seigel, 194
Martin v. Union Pacific Railroad Co., 103
Martinez v. Martinez, 679
Marvin v. Marvin, 664

## TABLE OF CASES

Mastbaum v. Mastbaum, 638
Maxwell v. Redd, 302
Melms v. Pabst Brewing Co., 552, 560
Merrill Trust Co. v. State, 1312, 1317, 1320
Metromedia, Inc. v. City of San Diego, 1123, 1124
Metropolitan Housing Development Corp. v. Village of Arlington Heights, 1146
Meyer v. Law, 41
Meyers v. Ridley, 501
Michael's Estate, In re, 607, 613, 614
Midkiff v. Tom, 1299
Mid-State Equipment Co. v. Bell, 741
Miller v. Green, 328, 336
Miller v. Weston, 583
Mister Donut of America, Inc. v. Kemp, 321
Mitchell v. W. T. Grant Co., 891
Moore v. City of East Cleveland, 1093
Morley v. J. Pagel Realty & Insurance, 185
Morris v. Austraw, 884, 887
Morris v. Nease, 806, 812
Morse v. Aldrich, 752
Morse v. Curtis, 356, 362, 363

National Land & Investment Co. v. Kohn, 1143, 1144
Nebbia v. New York, 976
Nectow v. City of Cambridge, 1085, 1115, 1183
Nedry v. Morgan, 639
Nelson v. American Telephone & Telegraph Co., 682, 683
Neponsit Property Owners' Association, Inc. v. Emigrant Industrial Savings Bank, 755, 760, 761, 764, 765, 778, 811
Neuberger v. City of Portland, 1192
New Orleans, City of v. Impastato, 1124
New York, City of v. United States, 560
Nicholson v. 300 Broadway Realty Corp., 761
Norcross v. James, 762, 763
Norsco Enterprises v. City of Fremont, 1285
North Georgia Finishing, Inc. v. DiChem, Inc., 891
North Shore Steak House, Inc. v. Board of Appeals of Incorporated Village of Thomaston, 1179, 1183, 1185
Northern Terminals, Inc. v. Smith Grocery & Variety, Inc., 1040
Northern Transportation Co. v. City of Chicago, 1108

Oakland, City of v. Oakland Raiders, 1300, 1308
Oakwood at Madison, Inc. v. Township of Madison, 1141
O'Connor v. Village Green Owners Association, 1059
O'Keeffe v. Snyder, 58, 59
Oldfield v. Stoeco Homes, Inc., 485, 497, 498, 499, 500, 548
Oliver v. Ernul, 680
Oliver v. Thomas, 42, 43
Orchard Homes Ditch Co. v. Snavely, 763
Osborn v. City of Cedar Rapids, 1311
Owen v. Neely, 372
Owensboro, City of v. McCormick, 1297

Pace v. Carter, 698, 701, 703
Pace v. Culpepper, 575, 586
Pacesetter Homes, Inc. v. Village of Olympia Fields, 1124
Packer v. Welsted, 695
Paine v. Meller, 234, 235
Pakenham's Case, 729, 779
Park West Management Corp. v. Mitchell, 954
Pascack Association, Ltd. v. Mayor & Council of Township of Washington, 1141
Penfield v. Jarvis, 640, 646
Penn Central Transportation Co. v. New York City, 1100, 1107, 1108, 1115, 1124, 1125, 1175
Pennsylvania Coal Co. v. Mahon, 1094, 1107, 1108, 1109, 1110, 1115
Peters v. Juneau-Douglas Girl Scout Council, 39
Petersen v. Beekmere, Inc., 786
Petition of (see name of party)
Petrosky v. Zoning Hearing Board of Upper Chichester Township, 1179
Pettitt v. City of Fresno, 1178
Pharr, City of v. Tippitt, 1186, 1191
Phillips v. Johnson, 222
Pickens v. Daughterty, 548
Pierson v. Post, 149
Poletown Neighborhood Council v. City of Detroit, 1287, 1295, 1296, 1297
Pollock v. Morelli, 1032, 1040, 1041
Prah v. Maretti, 101
Pressman v. City of Baltimore, 1194
Professional Realty Corp. v. Bender, 184
Pruneyard Shopping Center v. Robins, 70, 84, 85, 1043, 1111, 1298
Pumpelly v. Green Bay Co., 1108

TABLE OF CASES

Puritan Holding Co. v. Holloschitz, 100, 101
Pyrke v. Waddington, 207

Ramsey, County of v. Miller, *1301*, 1307, 1308
Rangeley v. Midland Railway Co., 718
Rayner v. Preston, 235
Redarowicz v. Ohlendorf, 293
Regan v. Lanze, 207
Reid v. Architectural Board of Review, 1124
Remilong v. Crolla, 729
Reno, City of v. Matley, 779
Rich v. Emerson-Dumont Distributing Corp., 184
Ridge Park Homeowners v. Pena, 811
Riley v. Bear Creek Planning Committee, 742, 743
Robinson v. Diamond Housing Corp., 959, 969, 970, 971
Robinson v. 12 Lofts Realty, Inc., 1058
Robinson Township v. Knoll, 1145
Rothman Realty Corp. v. Bereck, 184
Rozny v. Marnul, 259
Rushing v. Hooper-McDonald, Inc., 22
Ryczkowski v. Chelsea Title & Guaranty Co., 386

Sabo v. Horvath, 358, 362, 363
Sagamore Corp. v. Willcutt, 892, 901, 902
St. Louis, Iron Mountain & Southern Railway v. O'Baugh, 779
St. Louis Gunning Advertising Co. v. City of St. Louis, 1121
San Antonio School District v. Rodriguez, 1145
San Diego Gas & Electric Co. v. City of San Diego, 1114
Sanborn v. McLean, 743
Sansom Street, In re, 1286
Santa Barbara, City of v. Adamson, 1094
Sargent v. Ross, 866
Sawada v. Endo, 650, 664
Schad v. Borough of Mt. Ephraim, 1123, 1124
Schimenz, State ex rel. Zupancic v., 1194
Scoville v. Fisher, 703
Seattle, Petition of City of, 1297
Sebastian v. Floyd, 413, 418
Shack, State v., 85, 86
Shelley v. Kraemer, 500, 501
Shorter v. Shelton, 889
Shotwell v. Transamerica Title Insurance Co., 379

Shroyer v. Shroyer, 260, 278
Sikora v. Sikora, 623
Simon v. Solomon, 952
Simonsen v. Todd, 703
Skelly Oil Co. v. Ashmore, 226, 235
Smirlock Realty Corp., L. v. Title Guarantee Co., 386
Smith v. McEnany, 856
Smith v. Warr, 212, 224
Sniadach v. Family Finance Corp., 891
Snow v. Van Dam, 773, 778
Solly v. Toledo, 1108
Soltis v. Miller, 798
Somerville v. Jacobs, 60, 66, 67, 68, 122, 795
Sommer v. Kridel, 894, 903, 904
South of Sunnyside Neighborhood League v. Board of Commissioners of Clackamas County, 1162
Southern Burlington County N.A.A.C.P. v. Township of (Mt. Laurel I), 1124, *1128*, 1141, 1142, 1143, 1175, 1282
Southern Burlington County N.A.A.C.P. v. Township of Mt. Laurel (Mt. Laurel II), 1141, 1142, 1143
Spann v. City of Dallas, 1091
Speight v. Anderson, 702
Spencer's Case, 760
Spur Feeding Co. v. Superior Court of Maricopa County, 124, 148
Spur Industries, Inc. v. Del E. Webb Development Co., 113, 122, 123, 124, 125
Stachnik v. Winkel, 194
Stark v. Stanhope, 49
State v. ——— (see opposing party)
State Bar of Arizona v. Arizona Title & Trust Co., 185, 365
State Bar of New Mexico v. Guardian Abstract & Title Co., 365
State by Rochester Association v. City of Rochester, 1193
State Department of Ecology v. Pacesetter Construction Co., 1110
State Dept. of Highways v. Schumacher, 1327
State ex rel. ——— (see opposing party)
State Theatre Co. v. Smith, 1211, 1213
Stewart v. Lawson, 856
Stockdale v. Yerden, 711, 714, 715, 716, 718
Stoner v. Zucker, 676, 680, 682, 683, 702
Stout's Estate, In re, 560
Stover, People v., 1122
Stoyanoff, State ex rel. v. Berkeley, 1117, 1121, 1124

xxxvi

TABLE OF CASES

Strain v. Green, 69, 70
Suchan v. Rutherford, 223
Suffield v. Brown, 696
*Sun Oil Co. v. Trent Auto Wash, Inc.,
780*, 785, 786
Surrick v. Zoning Hearing Board of the
Township of Upper Providence, 1142
Symms v. Nelson Sand & Gravel, 1319

Taltarum's Case, 503
Teaff v. Hewitt, 69
Tefft v. Munson, 363
Tenhet v. Boswell, 616, 620, 622
Teodori v. Werner, 1036, 1041
Thompson v. Baxter, 825
Thompson v. Watkins, 560
Thornton's Estate, In re, 664
Threatt v. Rushing, 632
Thurlow v. Crossman, 86
Topanga Association for a Scenic Community v. County of Los Angeles, 1264
Tresemer v. Albuquerque Public School District, 36
Triangle, Inc. v. State, 1320
Tristram's Landing, Inc. v. Wait, 176, 181, 182, 184
Trustees of Schools of Township No. 1 v. Batdorf, 599, 603
Tulk v. Moxhay, 785, 786
Turner v. Blackburn, 444
Turners Crossroad Development Co., Matter of, 766, 778, 779
219 Broadway Corp. v. Alexander's Inc., 822

Udell v. Haas, 1152, 1162, 1163
United States v. _____ (see opposing party)
United States National Bank of Oregon v. Homeland, Inc., 902, 904

Van Sant v. Rose, 778
Varjabedian v. City of Madera, 1318
Vawter v. McKissick, 903
Village of (see name of village)
Villar, In re, 584

Waggener v. Leggett, 22
Waggoner, Estate of v. Gleghorn, 697
Walker v. Community Bank, 445
Walters v. Tucker, 252, 259
Walton v. Dana, 697
Warfel v. Vondersmith, 126, 147
Warth v. Seldin, 1146
Wawak v. Stewart, 281, 291, 293
Weisner v. 791 Park Avenue Corp., 1058
Wellenkamp v. Bank of America, 428, 597
Werner v. Graham, 742
Wetherbee v. Green, 68
Wheeler v. Schad, 746, 753, 754, 779
Whitcomb v. Brant, 902
White v. Brown, 479, 520
Whitinsville Plaza, Inc. v. Kotseas, 762
Wierzbicki v. Alaska Mutual Savings Bank, 295
Williams v. Polgar, 366, 371, 387
Wilson v. Parent, 103
Wilson v. Schneiter's Riverside Golf Course, 312, 316, 317
Wilson v. Wilson, 649
Witt v. Reavis, 799, 811
Wolek v. Di Feo, 335
Wolfe v. Henry Shelley, 526
Wong v. Di Grazia, 586
Woodard v. Marshall, 21
Woods v. Garnett, 362
Woodward v. Blanchard, 48
Wright v. Conner, 561
Wright's Estate, In re, 583

Young v. American Mini Theatres, Inc., 1122, 1123, 1124

Zirinsky v. Sheehan, 224
Zomisky v. Zamiska, 611, 614
Zupancic, State ex rel. v. Schimenz, 1194
Zylka v. City of Crystal, 1185

REAL PROPERTY

*

Part One

THE REAL PROPERTY SYSTEM

I. WHY PROPERTY?

GREY, THE DISINTEGRATION OF PROPERTY
XXII NOMOS 69-74, 76-77 (1980).

In the English-speaking countries today, the conception of property held by the specialist (the lawyer or economist) is quite different from that held by the ordinary person. Most people, including most specialists in their unprofessional moments, conceive of property as *things* that are *owned* by *persons*. To own property is to have exclusive control of something—to be able to use it as one wishes, to sell it, give it away, leave it idle, or destroy it. Legal restraints on the free use of one's property are conceived as departures from an ideal conception of full ownership.

By contrast, the theory of property rights held by the modern specialist tends both to dissolve the notion of ownership and to eliminate any necessary connection between property rights and things. Consider ownership first. The specialist fragments the robust unitary conception of ownership into a more shadowy "bundle of rights." Thus, a thing can be owned by more than one person, in which case it becomes necessary to focus on the particular limited rights each of the co-owners has with respect to the thing. Further, the notion that full ownership includes rights to do as you wish with what you own suggests that you might sell off *particular aspects* of your control—rights to certain uses, to profits from the thing, and so on. Finally, rights of use, profit, and the like can be parceled out along a temporal dimension as well—you might sell your control over your property for tomorrow to one person, for the next day to another, and so on.

Not only can ownership rights be subdivided, they can even be made to disappear as if by magic, if we postulate full freedom of disposition in the owner. Consider the convenient legal institution of the trust. Yesterday A owned Blackacre; among his rights of ownership was the legal power to leave the land idle, even though developing it would bring a good income. Today A puts Blackacre in trust, conveying it to B (the trustee) for the benefit of C (the beneficiary). Now no one any longer has the legal power to use the land uneconomically or to leave it idle—that part of the rights of ownership is neither in A nor B nor C, but has disappeared. As between B and C, who owns Blackacre? Lawyers say B has the legal and C the equitable ownership, but upon reflection the question seems meaningless: what is important is that we be able to specify what B and C can legally do with respect to the land.

The same point can be made with respect to fragmentation of ownership generally. When a full owner of a thing begins to sell off various of his rights over it—the right to use it for this purpose tomorrow, for that purpose next year, and so on—at what point does he cease to be the owner, and who then owns the thing? You can say that each one of many right holders owns it to the extent of the right, or you can say that no one owns it. Or you can say, as we still tend to do, in vestigial deference to the lay conception of property, that some conventionally designated rights constitute "ownership." The issue is seen as one of terminology; nothing significant turns on it.

What, then, of the idea that property rights must be rights in things? Perhaps we no longer need a notion of ownership, but surely property rights are a distinct category from other legal rights, in that they pertain to things. But this suggestion cannot withstand analysis either; most property in a modern capitalist economy is intangible. Consider the common forms of wealth: shares of stock in corporations, bonds, various kinds of commercial paper, bank accounts, insurance policies—not to mention more arcane intangibles such as trademarks, patents, copyrights, franchises, and business goodwill.

In our everyday language, we tend to speak of these rights as if they attached to things. Thus we "deposit our money in the bank", as if we were putting a thing in a place; but really we are creating a complex set of abstract claims against an abstract legal institution. We are told that as insurance policy holders we "own a piece of the rock"; but we really have other abstract claims against another abstract institution. We think of our share of stock in Megabucks Corporation as part ownership in the Megabucks factory outside town; but really the Megabucks board of directors could sell the factory and go into another line of business and we would still have the same claims on the same abstract corporation.

Property rights cannot any longer be characterized as "rights of ownership" or as "rights in things" by specialists in property. What, then, *is* their special characteristic? How do property rights differ from rights generally—from human rights or personal rights or rights to life or liberty, say? Our specialists and theoreticians have no answer; or rather, they have a multiplicity of widely differing answers, related only in that they bear some association or analogy, more or less remote, to the common notion of property as ownership of things.

Let me briefly list a number of present usages of the term property in law, legal theory, and economics.

1. The law of property for law teachers and law students typically is the whole body of law concerned with the use of land: the doc-

trines of estates in land, title registration and transfer, the financing of real estate transactions, the law of landlord and tenant, public regulation of land use (including zoning and environmental regulation), and public subsidy and provision of low-income housing. The only thing these doctrines have in common with each other is that they concern real estate as distinguished from other aspects of the economy.

2. Lawyers (and some economists) identify property rights with rights *in rem* (rights good against the world), as distinguished from rights *in personam* (rights good against determinate persons). This distinction does not fit closely with popular notions of property; for example, the rights to life, bodily security, and personal liberty protected by criminal laws against murder, assault, and kidnapping are on this account "property rights." Neither the application of the distinction nor its purpose is very clear; for example, *in personam* contract rights shade into property rights as they become freely assignable, and assumable, and as "interference with contractual relations" is recognized as a tort.

3. Some economists seem to adopt, implicitly, a purposive account of property, including among property rights all and only those entitlements whose purpose (in some sense) is to advance allocative efficiency by allowing individuals to reap the benefits and requiring them to bear the costs generated by their activities. Again, on this account rights to life, liberty, and personal security are included within the field of property. On the other hand, legal entitlements to transfer payments, such as are conferred by welfare and social security laws, are presumably excluded.

4. By contrast, some modern legal theorists have stressed that a traditional purpose of private property has been to protect security and independence, and that public law entitlements to social minima serve this purpose in the modern economy, and hence should be considered a "new property." This view has been embodied in the construction the courts have given to the constitutional requirement that persons not be "deprived of . . . property without due process of law." Protections offered to property have been extended to entitlements conferred by, for example, welfare and public education law.

5. Another contrasting view of property is suggested by the prevailing interpretation of another constitutional provision, the prohibition against "taking" private property except for a public purpose and upon the payment of just compensation. Here, the kind of property that can be taken is confined to those conglomerations of rights that, in the popular mind, have been reified into "things" or "pieces of property." Thus, the Supreme Court recently held that designation of Grand Central Station as a historic monument, and the consequent prohibition of construction of a skyscraper over the station, did not "take" any property of the landowners—the right to use the airspace over the building, an economically valuable entitlement, was

not sufficiently thing-like to be subject to the just compensation requirement. (This body of "takings" law, which most nearly corresponds to popular conceptions of property as thing ownership, is difficult to rationalize in the terms of modern legal and economic theory.)

6. Another specialized usage distinguishes between "property" and "liability" rules according to the nature of the sanctions imposed upon their violation. Property rules are enforceable by injunction or criminal sanctions or both—sanctions designed to prevent violation even when it would be cost justified in terms of market valuation. Liability rules are enforced only by the award of money damages, measured by the market valuation of the resources lost to the victim. This conception departs widely from popular usage; thus, a person's ownership of his car, for example, is protected by both liability rules (tort doctrines of conversion and liability for negligent damage to property) and property rules (criminal laws against theft).

The conclusion of all this is that discourse about property has fragmented into a set of discontinuous usages. The more fruitful and useful of these usages are those stipulated by theorists; but these depart drastically from each other and from common speech. Conversely, meanings of "property" in law that cling to their origin in the thing-ownership conception are integrated least successfully into the general doctrinal framework of law, legal theory, and economics. It seems fair to conclude from a glance at the range of current usages that the specialists who design and manipulate the legal structures of the advanced capitalist economies could easily do without using the term "property" at all.

II

It was not always so. At the high point of classical liberal thought, around the end of the eighteenth century, the idea of private property stood at the center of the conceptual scheme of lawyers and political theorists. Thus, Blackstone wrote: "There is nothing which so generally strikes the imagination, and engages the affections of mankind, as the right of property."[11] And the French Civil Code had as its "grand and principal object" (in the words of one of its authors) "to regulate the principles and the rights of property."[12] Kant began his discussion of law in the *Metaphysics of Morals* with an analysis and justification of property rights.[13] The earliest American state constitutions proclaimed property as one of the natural rights of man.

The conception of property held by the legal and political theorists of classical liberalism coincided precisely with the present popular idea, the notion of thing-ownership. Thus, Blackstone described

11. Sir William Blackstone, *Commentaries on the Laws of England* 11th ed. (London, 1791), vol. II, p. 2.

12. Quoted by Richard Schlatter, *Private Property: The History of an Idea* (New Brunswick, N.J., 1951), p. 232, from J.G. Locre, *La Legislation Civil de la France* (Paris, 1827), vol. 31, p. 169.

13. Kant, *Philosophy of Law*, trans. W. Hastie (Edinburgh, 1887), pp. 81–84.

property as "that sole and despotic dominion which one man claims and exercises over the external things of the world, in total exclusion of the right of any other individual in the universe." [15] And, in perfect concord, the French Civil Code defined property as "the right of enjoying and disposing of things in the most absolute manner."[16]

It is not difficult to see how the idea of simple ownership came to dominate classical liberal legal and political thought. First, this conception of property mirrored economic reality to a much greater extent than it did before or has since. Much of the wealth of the preindustrial capitalist economy consisted of the houses and lots of freeholders, the land of peasant proprietors or small farmers, and the shops and tools of artisans.

Second, the concept of property as thing-ownership served important ideological functions. Liberalism was the ideology of the attack on feudalism. A central feature of feudalism was its complex and hierarchical system of land tenure. To the rising bourgeoisie, property conceived as a web of relations among persons meant the system of lord, vassal, and serf from which they were struggling to free themselves. On the other hand, property conceived as the control of a piece of the material world by a single individual meant freedom and equality of status. Thus Blackstone denounced the archaisms of feudal tenure. The French Civil Code marked the culmination of a revolution that abolished feudal property. Hegel wrote that the abolition of feudal property in favor of individual ownership was as great a triumph of freedom as the abolition of slavery. Jefferson contrasted the free allodial system of land titles in America with the servile English system of feudal tenure.

Third, ownership of things by individuals fitted the principal justifications for treating property as a natural right. In England and America, the dominant theory was Locke's; rightful property resulted from the mixing of an individual's labor with nature. The main rival to Locke's theory within liberal thought was the German Idealist conception of Kant and Hegel, who saw original property resulting from the subjective act of appropriation, the exercise of the individual will over a piece of unclaimed nature. On this view, property was an extension of personality. Ownership expanded the natural sphere of freedom for the individual beyond his body to part of the material world.

. . . The dissolution of the traditional conception of property erodes the moral basis of capitalism. Capitalism has commonly been conceived, by friends and enemies alike, as a system based on the existence and protection of private property rights. Given this conception, the view that property rights have intrinsic worth must strengthen the case for capitalism—at least so long as "property

15. Blackstone, op. cit., p. 2.

16. Code Civil, Art. 544, quoted in Schlatter, op. cit., p. 232.

rights" are viewed as a single coherent category. But the phenomenon of the "death of property" breaks the connection between simple thing-ownership and the legal entitlements that make up the framework of the capitalist organization of the economy. And it is simple thing-ownership that has been justified in classical liberal theory, and I think in popular consciousness, as having intrinsic worth.

The theories that support an intrinsic moral right to property can be roughly divided into the labor and personality justifications for private ownership. The labor theory expresses the intuition that the individual owns as a matter of natural right the valued objects he has made or wrested from nature. Thus, the farmer naturally owns the land he has cleared and the crops he has grown; the artisan owns the tools he has fashioned, the raw materials he has gathered, and the products he has made. The idealist "personality" theory rests on the different but no less powerful idea that human beings naturally come to regard some objects as extensions of themselves in some important sense. This idea gains its intuitive force from the way most people regard their homes, their immediate personal effects, and other material things that play a double role as part of their most immediate environment in daily life and at the same time as expressions of their personalities.

NOTES

1. *The Right to Exclude.* Consider the plight of Professor Grey's farmer in a state of nature, before property or law. To clear land and grow crops would involve considerable peril, for without property law the farmer has nothing but constant vigilance and the threat of force to keep his neighbor or roving marauders from appropriating the fruits of his labor. Because the venture is so perilous, and defense so costly, the farmer will soon drop agriculture for hunting and foraging. Property law, however, erects invisible, largely invincible, walls around land, thus enabling the farmer to reap the returns on his investment and thus attracting investment to farming—a more productive use of land than hunting or defense.

Property law can also control the overuse of land. The farmer whose land borders an open, unclaimed pasture is free to let his cattle graze on this commons—as are his neighbors. Because the pasture is free, the farmer will increase the number of cattle he lets graze there—as will his neighbors. Although these increases mean that the pasture will at some point become overgrazed, the farmer will increase his stock still more, for the market pays him fully for each additional steer he raises, while his neighbors share the costs of overgrazing. But it has been observed that each neighbor sharing the commons will reach this conclusion. "Therein is the tragedy. Each man is locked into a system that compels him to increase his herd without limit—in a world that is limited." Hardin, The Tragedy of the Commons, 162 Science 1243, 1244 (1968). By contrast, property law can bound the commons, empowering its owner to exclude everyone and thus to ration the right to enter—by price or other mechanism—so that only the correct level of grazing occurs.

2. *Transferability.* Property attracts investment to the productive use of land by conferring a right to exclude. But only if this right is transferable can it begin to attract investment to the *most* productive use of land. If, for example, the value of the farmer's parcel is $10,000 put to agricultural uses, but $110,000 put to use as a shopping center, the land will probably be put to its more valuable use only if the farmer can sell it to a shopping center developer. An owner can often put land to still more productive uses by parcelling out individual interests in her "bundle of rights." For example, the shopping center developer can transfer interests in the parcel to various tenants and secured lenders for sums that, in the aggregate, may far exceed the $110,000 she paid for the parcel.

3. No real property system offers rights that are completely exclusive, for circumstances always exist in which courts or legislatures will excuse private and public intrusions on land. Indeed, exclusivity is necessarily unattainable. One owner's exclusive use of her land—playing the clarinet at 3:00 A.M., or painting her house neon pink—will inevitably interfere with a neighbor's exclusive use of *his* land—sleeping through the night or viewing the landscape without the need for dark glasses. Nor are property rights completely transferable. Courts and legislatures sometimes limit transferability in order to promote more general interests in the free alienability of land.

As you read each case in this book, consider the extent to which it dilutes exclusivity or curtails transferability, and how likely the dilution or curtailment is to discourage investment in land.

4. *The Roles of Property Law.* Property induces investment and property law channels it. A handful of classificatory schemes circumscribe the landowner's choices in dividing up interests in Blackacre. These doctrinal limitations on forms of transfer pose what is perhaps the greatest challenge for the real estate lawyer: to manipulate longstanding, highly formalized doctrinal categories into investment vehicles that will serve the speculative, financing and tax objectives of today's investor.

Why should property law, presumably aimed at increasing investment and investment opportunities, impose these limits on the freedom with which an owner can divide interests in Blackacre? Are transaction costs significantly lowered when the private parties making these divisions—and the courts called on to enforce them—are limited to a small number of well-known forms of transfer? Is certainty of outcome substantially increased by the use of accepted forms?

5. What are the effects of uncertainty on real estate investment? An investor seeking a parcel on which to erect an apartment building will presumably pay less for the parcel in a city that will limit her

rents through rent control than in one that will put no cap on her returns (say she will pay $2 million without rent control as compared to $1.5 million with rent control). How much will this investor pay for a parcel in a city in which the question of rent control, though under discussion in the city council, has not yet been resolved? Say that she offers to pay $1.7 million for a parcel in this city, the discount from $2 million reflecting her estimate of the likelihood that rent control will be passed. The seller rejects this offer, accepting instead another investor's bid of $1.8 million, the parcel's value as the site of a warehouse. Can you comfortably say that, developed as a warehouse, the parcel is being put to its highest and best use?

How effectively are legislatures constrained from passing laws that upset the expectations on which investments have been made? Say that a city enacts a rent control ordinance. Will a real estate developer who paid $2 million for her development site, under the reasonable expectation that the city would not enact a rent control ordinance, succeed in her claim that the city's action unconstitutionally takes her property without just compensation? Say that, spurred by this first city's enactment, other cities begin to discuss the possibility of rent control. Would landowners in these other cities succeed in their claim that, by increasing the probability of rent control in their own cities, and thus reducing the value of their properties, the first city unconstitutionally took their property without just compensation?

How effectively are courts constrained from rendering decisions that upset the expectations upon which investments have been made? Real property law is often said to be more conservative and steadfast in its adherence to precedent than other bodies of common law. Is inflexibility in the face of change a more or less dangerous attribute in real property law than in other areas?

A. TRESPASS: THE RIGHT TO EXCLUDE

1. THEORY OF PROTECTION

HOLDEN v. LYNN

Supreme Court of Oklahoma, 1911.
30 Okl. 663, 120 P. 246.

AMES, C. The plaintiff sued the defendant in a justice court of Osage county for $100, the alleged value of certain corn and fodder destroyed by defendant's cattle. Judgment was rendered for the plaintiff, and an appeal was taken to the county court, where, on a retrial, judgment was again rendered for the plaintiff, in the sum of $65, and the defendant brings error.

Three questions are involved: (1) Did the bill of particulars state a cause of action? (2) Did the court err in excluding evidence tending to show that the land on which the corn was grown belonged to an Osage Indian, and was not under lease approved by the Secretary of the Interior? (3) Can the suit be maintained against the defendant alone, when the cattle belonged to a partnership?

1. The objection urged against the bill of particulars is that the plaintiff does not allege therein that he was the owner of the crops destroyed; and it does require the application of exceedingly liberal rules of construction to ascertain from the bill of particulars who owned the cattle, but, in view of the fact that this is a justice of the peace case, that a justice court is not a court of record, that the evidence did establish that the defendant owned the cattle, and that no substantial right of the defendant can be affected, we are not disposed to reverse the case. . . .

2. On the trial it appeared that the corn involved was grown on the "Old Lady Corndropper place"; that it had been cut and shocked; that the plaintiff bought it from the man who raised it; that it was surrounded by a wire fence; and that the defendant's cattle broke down this fence and ate the corn. The defendant offered to prove that this was Osage Indian land, that the man who raised the corn did not have a lease approved by the Secretary of the Interior, and the court refused to permit this evidence. This ruling is assigned as error. The defendant's contention is that under the act of June 28, 1906, c. 3572, § 7, 34 Stat. 539, providing "that all leases given on said lands [Osage] for the benefit of the individual members of the tribe entitled thereto, or for their heirs, shall be subject only to the approval of the Secretary of the Interior," this lease was void; and that therefore the plaintiff could not recover for trespass to his corn bought from the lessee. In support of this contention, he cites Light v. Conover, 10 Okl. 732, 63 Pac. 966; Megreedy v. Macklin, 12 Okl. 666, 73 Pac. 293; and Williams v. Steinmetz, 16 Okl. 104, 82 Pac. 986. Light v. Conover and Megreedy v. Macklin hold that, when an Indian lease does not carry the approval of the Secretary of the Interior, it is absolutely void, and that no rent can be recovered under the lease.

These cases rest upon the well-established rule that the courts will not enforce an invalid contract, whether malum in se or malum prohibitum; and that therefore the plaintiff cannot recover in any action where it is necessary for him to prove the illegal contract, in order to make out his case. In the case at bar, as it was not necessary for the plaintiff to prove title to the land, or to prove the existence of any lease at all, the principle on which these cases were decided does not apply.

Williams v. Steinmetz, supra, however, presents a different question. In that case certain land in Caddo county had been allotted to Robert L. Williams, a son of W.G. Williams (a white man, who had been adopted into the Caddo tribe) and of a Caddo Indian woman.

Steinmetz and Painter leased this land from Robert L. Williams, took possession of it, and planted it to corn and cotton. The lease was not approved by the Secretary of the Interior. The cultivated land was inclosed by a good fence. The cattle of W.G. Williams and Robert L. Williams broke down the fence and destroyed the corn. Suit was brought by the lessees against the owners of the cattle, and judgment was rendered in their favor by the trial court. On appeal, the Supreme Court of the territory, in an opinion delivered by Justice Burwell, after holding that the lease was void, held that by reason of that fact the plaintiffs could not recover damages for the trespass. The principal discussion in the opinion is as to the validity of the lease, and it seems to have been taken for granted by the court that if the lease was invalid the plaintiffs could not recover. At page 109 of 16 Okl., at page 988 of 82 Pac., the court says:

"These provisions are an exception to the general rule, and authorize the leasing of the lands of those Indians who cannot, by reason of age or other disability, personally and with benefit to themselves occupy or improve their allotments, or any part thereof, under such terms, regulations, and conditions as shall be prescribed by the Secretary of the Interior. Robert L. Williams does not come within this exception. He was not prevented by reason of his age or other disability from farming the land profitably. The purpose of the government in allotting lands to Indians in severalty is to encourage them in the cultivating of such lands, and to induce them, if possible, to establish fixed places of abode and acquire habits of industry. The allottee is supposed to live on the land and cultivate it himself. It may be leased only if he, by reason of age or disability, cannot properly cultivate and care for it himself. The lease in question was made in violation of a positive statute of the United States; and therefore the courts will not aid the parties in enforcing it. Nor will they grant relief when its terms have been violated. The lessees had no right on the allotted land of Robert L. Williams, and they planted and cultivated the crops at their own peril. For their destruction, they cannot recover damages. Light v. Conover [10 Okl. 732] 63 Pac. 966; Mayes v. Cherokee Strip Live Stock Ass'n et al. [58 Kan. 712] 51 Pac. 215."

It will be noted from the quotation that the two cases cited by the court in support of the conclusion reached are Light v. Conover and Mayes v. Cherokee Strip Live Stock Ass'n. We have called attention to the fact that Light v. Conover was an action to recover rent; and this is likewise true of Mayes v. Cherokee Strip Live Stock Ass'n. In both of those cases, recovery was denied, on the ground that the plaintiff would have to prove an illegal contract, and that, as the law will not aid the parties in enforcing an illegal contract, recovery could not be had. That principle, however, did not apply in Williams v. Steinmetz, nor does it apply in the case at bar.

It will be noticed that the exact question involved here is whether the *defendant* could offer evidence concerning this leasehold interest. If it devolved upon the defendant to prove this state of facts, then it is clear that it was not necessary for the plaintiff to do so, and if the plaintiff did not have to prove the illegal contract, he, of course, did not rely upon it, and the court, by giving the relief sought, would not be enforcing or lending its aid to the enforcement of an illegal agreement. If a man who raises a crop of corn on Indian land, without a lease executed in the manner required by law, acquires no rights whatever to the corn after it is grown and harvested, even as against a willful trespasser, and if a man who purchases this corn from such a lessee acquires no rights whatever, even as against a willful trespasser, then the plaintiff in this case should not have recovered. But if such an owner has a property interest, good against a bare trespasser, the ruling of the trial court was correct. A few questions ought to demonstrate the rule. If a thief enters the corncrib of such a lessee, should he go free, because the lease had not been approved by the Secretary of the Interior? And should a passer-by have the right to enter the barnyard of such a lessee and take his hogs, which had been raised upon the land, merely because the lease had not been approved by the Secretary of the Interior? If a trespasser should enter upon the premises of such a lessee and commence harvesting his wheat crop, would the lessee be remediless in the courts? Does a man who takes possession of land under a void lease become thereby outlawed?

So far as our attention has been called to the authorities, and so far as our own examination has taken us, Williams v. Steinmetz stands alone in the history of English and American jurisprudence. . . .

In Reed v. Price, 30 Mo. 442, 446, it is said: "The possession of the plaintiff being conceded, and the defendant claiming no title to the premises or license from the owner to enter, the question is whether evidence of want of title in the plaintiff was admissible. The law has been too long and too well settled to render it necessary to cite authorities in support of the position that possession is sufficient to maintain an action of trespass. In this action the defendant may dispute the plaintiff's possessory right by showing that the title and possessory right are vested in himself or another, under whom he claims, or whose authority he has. But if the plaintiff prove possession merely that will suffice, if the defendant cannot show a superior right in himself or another, under whom he can justify. It is true the plaintiff must prove such a lawful possession as the defendant had no right to disturb, but any possession is a legal possession as against a wrongdoer. Graham v. Peak, 1 East, 246; Lambert v. Strakin, Willes, 219; Cottoirs v. Cowper, 4 Taunt. 546; [Inhabitants of Barnstable v. Thacher] 3 Metc. [Mass.] 242; First Parish in Shrewsberry v. Smith, 14 Pick. [Mass.] 303. In the case last cited, the general principle and reasons upon which the doctrine rests is well stated by Chief

Justice Shaw, in delivering the opinion of the court. He says: 'There are many cases where acts have been done intended to constitute a good and valid title, where grants have been made and titles transferred, but where, through negligence, ignorance, or mistake, especially where corporations, public bodies, and official agents are concerned, such titles cannot be legally proved. Upon a close investigation, a flaw in the title would be discovered. If a lawful owner, in whom the legal title remains, chooses to interfere and set up his legal claims, the law, in consistency with its own rules in regard to the transmission of title, may be compelled to admit his claim. But if such owner, upon considerations of propriety, equity, and conscience, chooses to acquiesce and permit the party in possession to retain that possession, notwithstanding any defect of title, by what rule of law, of equity, or of sound policy can a mere stranger be allowed to interfere, and by his own act violate the actual and peaceable possession of another, and thereby compel him to disclose a title, in the validity or invalidity of which such stranger has no interest?'"

In Duncan v. Potts, 5 Stew. & P. (Ala.) 82, 24 Am.Dec. 766, 767, it is said: "But it is not only here, but elsewhere, that many may be found in the occupancy of lands to which they can show no legal title; and wherever this is the case, if prior peaceable possession did not give a preference in the right of enjoyment, the same consequences would arise. This is the reason of the common law that any possession is sufficient to sustain trespass against a wrongdoer, or a person who cannot make out a title prima facie entitling him to possession. It is held that 'a tenant for years, a lessee at will, and a tenant at sufferance, may support this action against a stranger, or even against his landlord, unless a right of entry be expressly or impliedly reserved.' 1 Chit.Pl. 178, and authorities. Also it is said: 'The action of trespass vi et armis is termed a possessory action, to distinguish it from those actions in which the plaintiff must show a title. Being founded on an injury to the possession, it is essential that the plaintiff should be in possession of the close at the time when the injury is committed; but, as against a stranger or wrongdoer, it is immaterial whether such possession be founded on a good title or not. Even a tortious possession will support trespass against a wrongdoer.' 2 Wheat. Selw. 1018. Various other authorities to the same effect might be cited, but the principle is considered too clear to require it."
. . .

In view of the uniform holdings in other states, as well as in the Supreme Court of the United States, and that we believe every consideration of justice protects one in possession against the acts of mere trespassers, we cannot follow the decision of the Supreme Court of the territory, and Williams v. Steinmetz, 16 Okl. 104, 82 Pac. 986, is overruled on this point. . . .

PER CURIAM. Adopted in whole.

MAGUIRE v. YANKE

Supreme Court of Idaho, 1978.
99 Idaho 829, 590 P.2d 85.

DONALDSON, Justice.

In 1975, Claude Porter leased a tract of property located in Blaine County from McCulloch Properties, Inc. The McCulloch property is situated approximately one and three-quarter miles west of Hailey, Idaho. The property is intersected by the Croy Creek Road which runs in an east-west direction across the property. On June 6, 1975, Porter subleased to the plaintiff-respondent Maguire, some 82 acres located on the south side of Croy Creek Road. The 82 acres were described as hay and alfalfa land, and Maguire used the property for raising hay. The hayland was surrounded by a fence but the fence was in a state of disrepair. Sometime in June 1975, Porter subleased to the defendant-appellant Yanke the property on the north side of Croy Creek Road. This property was pasture land and was also fenced. The lease agreement between Yanke and Porter provided that Yanke would pasture cattle on the land, and Yanke would maintain the fence around the pasture to ensure confinement of his livestock. In June 1975, Yanke moved 130 cows, 130 calves, and 8 bulls into the pasture. The Yanke and Maguire properties were not located in a herd district. Testimony was received that the area had been historically one of enclosed lands.

On numerous occasions between mid-July 1975 and August 2, 1975, several of Yanke's cattle broke through the pasture fence and strayed onto Maguire's alfalfa land south of the road. On August 2, 1975, a major breakout of Yanke's cattle occurred, and approximately 137 head of cows and calves entered Maguire's hayfield. At the time, Maguire had baled hay in the field which was substantially damaged by the cattle. Substantial damage was also done to the growing second crop of hay. When Maguire learned of the breakout, Yanke was called and the cattle were promptly removed.

Maguire thereafter filed this action against Yanke for damages. Maguire sought $3,818 actual damages and $10,000 punitive damages. The district court awarded Maguire a judgment of $3,818 to compensate him for his actual damages. The district court refused to allow any punitive damages, finding that Yanke had not acted wilfully. In finding that Yanke was liable for the damages done by the cattle to Maguire's hay and land, the district court stated in its conclusions of law:

I

It was the lawful duty of Yanke to maintain his fences so that his cattle would not escape through the same. This duty arose through the agreement with Porter as well as the fact that it was illegal for Yanke's cattle to trespass upon the county road.

II

In addition to Conclusion No. 1, it was the duty of Yanke to keep his cattle fenced in because this was not an open range area, and was an area of enclosed lands.

I

The trial court reasoned that Maguire had no duty to fence Yanke's cattle off his property, since it bordered on a county road which cattle could not legally trespass upon; and in addition that it was Yanke's duty to keep his cattle fenced in because the land was situated in what was historically an area of enclosed lands and not in open range.

Yanke contends the trial court erred in allowing Maguire recovery for damage to his crops caused by Yanke's cattle when Maguire's land is not located in a herd district or enclosed by a legal fence. Yanke argues that, with the exception of herd districts and liability to motorists for livestock that stray on highways, it is a long-standing rule in Idaho that livestock are permitted to roam and graze upon unenclosed lands without any liability accruing to the owner of the livestock for damage caused by them.

A review of the law relating to the liability of an owner of livestock for damage caused by his stock straying on another's land is necessary to the resolution of the issues presented in this case. At common law it was the duty of the owner of livestock to fence them in, and no duty was placed upon the adjoining landowner to fence them out. 4 Am.Jur.2d Animals § 49 (1962); Restatement (Second) of Torts § 504(1) (1976). The owners of livestock were liable for the damage caused by their stock straying upon another's land whether the land was enclosed or not. An early English case stated the rule as follows: "[W]here my beasts of their own wrong without my will and knowledge break another's close I shall be punished, for I am the trespasser with my beasts . . . for I am held by the law to keep my beasts without their doing wrong to anyone." W. Prosser, Handbook of Law of Torts 496 (4th ed. 1971), *quoting* 12 Hen. VII, Keilwey 3b, 72 Eng.Rep. 156.

Western cattle states generally rejected the common law, holding that livestock roaming at large committed no trespass when they strayed on unenclosed private land. Idaho, concurring with the approach of its neighboring states, also rejected the common law rule. Kelly v. Easton, 35 Idaho 340, 207 P. 129 (1922); Johnson v. Oregon Short Line Ry. Co., 7 Idaho 355, 63 P. 112 (1900). The Idaho rule was stated as follows: "The common-law rule that every man must confine his own cattle to his own land does not obtain in this state, and in

Strong v. Brown, 26 Idaho 1, 140 P. 773, 52 L.R.A.,N.S., 140, Ann. Cas.1916E, 482, it is held that under our statute (C.S., c. 82), if a landowner fails to fence out cattle lawfully at large, he may not recover for loss caused by such livestock straying upon his unenclosed land." Kelly v. Easton, 35 Idaho at 344, 207 P. at 130. However, one who willfully and deliberately drives his stock upon the lands of another, whether enclosed of unenclosed and grazes them upon such land without the permission of the owner, is liable in damages for the trespass.

In an effort to provide a remedy for landowners whose property was damaged by roaming cattle, most western states including Idaho passed fence laws. Idaho Code §§ 35–101 and 35–102 define what constitutes a legal fence, prescribing standards relating to height, length, number of rails and materials. Idaho Code § 25–2202 provides that a landowner who encloses his property with a legal fence has a cause of action against the owner of animals that break the enclosure.[2] The United States Supreme Court, commenting on a Texas fence law, in Lazarus v. Phelps, 152 U.S. at 85, 14 S.Ct. at 478, states the object of such fence statutes:

> As there are, or were, in the state of Texas, as well as in the newer states of the west generally, vast areas of land, over which, so long as the government owned them, cattle had been permitted to roam at will for pasturage, it was not thought proper, as the land was gradually taken up by individual proprietors, to change the custom of the country in that particular, and oblige cattle owners to incur the heavy expense of fencing their land, or be held as trespassers by reason of their cattle accidentally straying upon the land of others.

The legal fence laws of the State of Idaho provide a remedy to the landowner whose property, although enclosed by a legal fence, is nonetheless damaged by roaming cattle. Contrary to the finding of the trial court in the instant case, the legal fence laws of the State of Idaho are "fencing out" statutes. These legal fence statutes recognized the rancher's right to allow cattle to roam.

Although the "fence out" rule prevails in this state, there are some important legislative exceptions to the rule. Idaho and other western states provide for the creation of herd districts as an alternative to landowners who wish to protect their land from damage caused by roaming stock, but do not wish or cannot afford to fence their land. Idaho Code § 25–2401 et seq. permits districts within a county to petition for the creation of a herd district. If a majority of the landowners owning more than fifty percent of the land in the dis-

---

2. "25–2202. Animal breaking inclosure—Recovery of damages.—If any animal before mentioned breaks into any inclosure or through any fence conforming to the requirements of chapter 1 of title 35, the owner of such animal must, for such trespass, pay to the party injured the full amount of damages he has sustained by reason of such trespass, to be recovered with costs in any court having jurisdiction."

trict vote to create a herd district, livestock are prohibited from running at large within the district, and a landowner may recover for damages caused by animals straying upon his property, regardless of whether it is enclosed by a legal fence.³ In essence the creation of a herd district in Idaho reinstates the English common law within that district, placing a duty on the livestock owner to fence in his stock and holding him liable for damages caused if his stock escapes onto another's land, regardless of whether that land is fenced or not.

In 1963, the Idaho Legislature amended the herd district law, I.C. § 25–2402, to not allow inclusion of open range in a herd district.⁴ Open range was defined as follows: "all uninclosed lands outside cities and villages upon which by custom, license or otherwise, livestock, excepting swine, are grazed or permitted to roam." The legislature also added to the section a provision that excepts from the application of herd district laws any livestock roaming or straying into the district from open range, unless the district is enclosed by a legal fence.

In 1961, the Idaho Legislature passed a statute, I.C. § 25–2118,⁵ relieving owners of livestock roaming on open range of the duty to keep such stock off the highway and absolving them of liability for damages caused by a collision between a vehicle and the livestock. Open range was defined as "all uninclosed lands outside of cities, villages and herd districts, upon which cattle by custom, license, lease or permit, are grazed or permitted to roam." Idaho Code § 25–2118 impliedly makes it the duty of the person owning, or controlling the possession of livestock, to keep them off any highway not located in open range; and does not absolve such a person of liability for damages caused by a collision between a vehicle and the animal, unless the highway is in open range.

3. I.C. § 25–2402 reads in part:
"Petition for district.—A majority of the landowners in any area or district described by metes and bounds not including open range and who are also resident in, and qualified electors of, the state of Idaho may petition the board of county commissioners in writing to create such area a herd district. Such petition shall describe the boundaries of the said proposed herd district, and shall designate what animals of the species of horses, mules, asses, cattle, swine, sheep and goats it is desired to prohibit from running at large, also prohibiting said animals from being herded upon the public highways in such district; and shall designate that the herd district shall not apply to nor cover livestock, excepting swine, which shall roam, drift or stray from open range into the district unless the district shall be inclosed by lawful fences and cattle guards in roads penetrating the district so as to prevent livestock, excepting swine, from roaming, drifting or straying from open range into the district. . . .

Open range means all uninclosed lands outside cities and villages upon which by custom, license or otherwise, livestock, excepting swine, are grazed or permitted to roam."

4. 1963 Idaho Sess.Laws, ch. 264, p. 674.

5. "25–2118. Animals on open range—No duty to keep from highway.— No person owning, or controlling the possession of, any domestic animal running on open range, shall have the duty to keep such animal off any highway on such range, and shall not be liable for damage to any vehicle or for injury to any person riding therein, caused by a collision between the vehicle and the animal. 'Open range' means all uninclosed lands outside of cities, villages and herd districts, upon which cattle by custom, license, lease, or permit, are grazed or permitted to roam."

II

The prior review of Idaho law reveals that there are two geographical areas other than cities and villages recognized in this state in relation to the liability of livestock owners for damage done by their stock to another's land. First, herd districts created pursuant to I.C. § 25–2401 *et seq.* where within the district the English common law rule of prohibiting livestock from running at large is reinstated. Since 1963 herd districts could not contain "open range," which was defined as "all uninclosed land outside cities and villages which by custom, license or otherwise, livestock, excepting swine, are grazed or permitted to roam." 1963 Idaho Sess.Laws, ch. 264, p. 674. The second area contains "open range" as defined by I.C. § 25–2402 and all other areas of the state not within cities, villages, or already created herd districts. Herd districts may be created in this area by the landowners for protection against roaming livestock so long as the land in question is other than "open range" as defined by I.C. § 25–2402. It is in this area where the rule that livestock owners are not required to fence their stock in and are not liable for damages caused by their stock to another's land unless the landowner's property is enclosed by a legal fence obtains.

The trial court held that it was the duty of Yanke to keep his cattle fenced in because the area was an area of enclosed lands and not located in open range. Testimony was received at trial that the area in question had been one of enclosed land where cattle were not permitted to roam for more years than any witness could remember to the contrary. It appears that the trial court relied on this testimony and the definitions of "open range" contained in I.C. § 25–2402 in determining the area was not in open range and thus placing a duty on Yanke to fence his livestock in. Maguire concurs with the trial court that the right of livestock to roam freely is restricted to "open range" and that the controlling definition of "open range" is contained in I.C. § 25–2402 and § 25–2118, which includes only land where historically livestock were grazed or permitted to roam.

This analysis, in essence, creates a third area relating to liability for damage caused by roaming livestock. This area would encompass all land which livestock by custom, license, lease, or permit are not permitted to roam at large or graze. In this region, a livestock owner would have a duty to fence his cattle in, and there would be no duty on a landowner to fence cattle out in order to recover damages caused by roaming livestock.

Yanke contends that the trial court erred in using the analysis above in determining he had a duty to fence his cattle in. Yanke argues that this Court's rejection of the English common law duty to keep one's livestock enclosed in Johnson v. Oregon Short Line Ry. Co., *supra*, and the adoption of the rule of no duty to fence in livestock in later cases, plus the enactment of fence laws by the Idaho

Legislature, firmly establish that within this state there is no duty for a livestock owner to fence his cattle in. Yanke asserts that notwithstanding the fact that the area in question was not one where by custom livestock were grazed or permitted to roam, no liability attaches to a livestock owner for damage done by his stock straying onto another's land, unless the damaged landowner's property is enclosed with a legal fence. Yanke argues that the only method by which a landowner may relieve himself of his duty to fence livestock out and place upon the livestock owner the duty to fence his stock in is the creation of a herd district. We agree.

The abrogation of the English common law duty of a livestock owner to fence his stock in and the passage of fence laws which placed the duty on the landowner to fence livestock out is a phenomenon of the western cattle states. Since the western states adopted such rules in response to a common problem during the early settlement of this region in the late 1800's and early 1900's, as did Idaho, a review of these states' approach to the question of a livestock owner's liability for damage caused by their trespassing stock would be helpful in determining the meaning of our own legislation. "Countless avenues and forms of communication and interaction among the jurisdictions lead to so much parallelism among the laws of different states as the result of emulation, adaptation and outright copying that common patterns and standard modes of dealing with common problems become evident." Sutherland, Statutory Construction § 52.03 (4th ed. Sands rev.1973).

We have extensively reviewed the statutory and case law of Washington, Oregon, Montana, Wyoming, Nevada, Colorado, Arizona and New Mexico and we find no support for the appellant Maguire's position that a livestock owner has a duty to fence his stock in areas where livestock have not historically been grazed or permitted to roam. On the contrary, these states have adopted the general rule that livestock owners may range their stock in all areas of the state with no obligation to prevent them entering upon the unenclosed premises of another. These states require that a landowner cannot recover for damage to his lands caused by trespassing livestock unless their land was enclosed by a legal fence.

In Washington, Oregon, Montana, Wyoming, New Mexico and Arizona the respective state legislatures adopted legislation, the equivalent of our herd district law, which permit certain counties or parts of the states by a vote of the people within such subdivision to determine whether livestock should continue to be allowed to run at large and landowners be compelled to rely on a legal fence for protection, or whether livestock owners should be required to fence their stock in and landowners allowed to recover for damage caused by trespassing stock, regardless of whether their land is enclosed by a legal fence. The case law and legislation from these jurisdictions clearly shows that in all other areas in the state not designated as herd districts livestock are permitted to run at large and it is the duty of the landowner to fence the stock out.

The trial court erred in restricting the right of livestock owners to roam stock to only those areas where by custom, license, or permit livestock are grazed or permitted to roam. The adoption of such a rule creates de facto herd districts in areas where by custom livestock have not been permitted to roam and thereby renders I.C. § 25–2401 *et seq.* unnecessary. The trial court, in effect, applied herd district rules relating to liability for roaming livestock to these areas without requiring the creation of a herd district. It is a general rule of statutory construction that courts should not nullify a statute or deprive a law of potency or force unless such course is absolutely necessary. It appears the intent of the legislature in enacting I.C. § 25–2401 *et seq.* was that for areas where the historical use has been one of enclosed lands, the landowners in that area must petition and vote to designate that area a herd district in order to change the Idaho law regarding liability for damage by roaming livestock.

The statutory definitions of "open range" as set forth in I.C. §§ 25–2402 and 25–2118 are inconsistent with the case law concept of "open range" as unfenced, unenclosed, public range, domain or common. It is a matter of common understanding that definitional provisions do not purport to prescribe what meanings shall attach to the defined terms for all purposes and in all contexts but generally only establish what they mean where they appear in that same act.

Prior to 1963, I.C. § 25–2402 contained no definition of "open range." Herd districts were allowed to be created in any part of this state. This permitted persons within a geographical area to reinstate in that area the English common law duty of a livestock owner to confine his stock that was abolished in Idaho by the holding in Johnson v. Short Line Ry., *supra,* and to avoid the necessity of constructing a legal fence as required by I.C. § 25–2202 in order to recover damages caused by trespassing stock. In 1963, as was previously discussed, the legislature inserted a definition of "open range" in I.C. § 25–2402 and stated that herd districts could not be created in such area. It is respondent Maguire's contention that this definition of "open range" should be applied to our entire body of case law and thus limit the rights of livestock owners to roam their stock at large to "open range" as defined by the statute. This interpretation is inconsistent with not only our case and statutory law, rules of statutory construction, but also the common pattern of dealing with this problem in the West as evinced by the laws of eight of our sister states. Prior to 1963, herd districts could be created in any part of Idaho. It is clear the amendment of I.C. § 25–2402 by the inserting of a definition of "open range" was designed to protect the rights of livestock owners by prohibiting herd districts in areas where they historically grazed stock, rather than limiting the area where livestock owners were free to let their stock roam at large. Under our decision, herd districts may still be created in any area not within "open range" as defined in I.C. § 25–2402. The passage of I.C. §§ 25–2402 and 25–2118, with their accompanying definition of "open range" in terms of historical use, was not intended to and does not change the law of this state that with the exception of cities, villages, and herd districts, livestock may run at large and graze upon unenclosed lands in this state.

III

The trial court also appeared to base its finding that Yanke had a duty to fence his cattle in on the fact that the pasture where the cattle were grazed was bounded on one side by a highway. Yanke did have a duty to keep his stock off the highway since his land was not located in open range under the definition of I.C. § 25–2118. Idaho Code § 25–2118 was passed to protect the livestock owner running stock on open range from liability caused by collisions of vehicles with livestock; and, impliedly, to place a duty on the livestock owner not running on open range to keep the stock off the highway. The statute would seem, however, to have reference to the relationship existing between livestock owners and motorists and is inapplicable to the relationship between livestock owners and adjoining landowners. In construing a statute, not only should the terms of the statute be examined, but legislative intent is also to be collected from the context, occasion and necessity of the law, from the mischief felt, and from the remedy in view. It is obvious that the statute addresses itself to the problem of the increasing spread of highways and the flow of high-speed traffic through areas of open range grazing of livestock and where liability should be placed when a collision between livestock and auto occurs. It does not address itself to the question of liability of a livestock owner for damage caused by his stock straying across a highway and on to adjoining landowner's property. Yanke had a duty to keep his cattle off the highway, but this duty was owed to motorists on that road, not to Maguire.

The trial court erred in holding that Yanke had a duty to fence his cattle in and that Maguire had no duty to fence the cattle out in order to recover for the damages occasioned by the cattle straying upon his land. The rule simply stated is that in all areas in this state, with the exception of herd districts, villages, and cities, there is no duty for a livestock owner to confine his cattle to his own land and that no liability attaches to that livestock owner for damage occasioned by his stock straying onto another's property, unless the damaged landowner's property is enclosed by a legal fence.

Judgment reversed.

McFADDEN and BISTLINE, JJ., concur. [The opinion of BAKES, J., concurring in the reversal, but dissenting in the disposition, is omitted.]

NOTES

1. What is the holding of Holden v. Lynn? Is it that a possessor of land has an action for trespass notwithstanding his lack of title to the land? Or is it that a possessor of crops has an action for their misappropriation notwithstanding his lack of title to the crops? Or is it that the possessor of crops has an action for their misappropriation notwithstanding his grantor's lack of title to the land on which the crops were grown? Does the second proposition necessarily follow from the first? Does the third necessarily follow from the first or the second? See R. Brown, Law of Personal Property § 17.4 (W. Raushenbush 3rd ed. 1975).

One rationale for giving possessors of land an action against all but the rightful owner is that the possessor will frequently have obtained possession from the rightful owner through a transaction that, but for some unwitting failure to comply with a conveyancing formality, would have given the possessor good title. The grantor will typically be as ignorant of the error as the grantee. Should the rule favoring possessors be limited by this curative rationale and not extended to possessors without color of title? Should the trespass action be given to possessors under illegal leases?

Some courts distinguish between injuries to the possessory interest and injuries to the ownership interest, and hold that possessors without title can recover for injuries to the first, but not the second. For example, in Woodard v. Marshall, 14 N.C.App. 67, 187 S.E.2d 430 (1972), the court ruled that "where the plaintiff claims damages for unlawful cutting of timber, he is claiming permanent damages to the freehold, or damages to the ownership interest, and his right to recover depends on his establishing his *title* to the described lands. The *possession* of real property is not a sufficient interest upon which to base a recovery for permanent damages to the freehold—the ownership interest." 14 N.C.App. 68–69, 187 S.E.2d 431.

2. Does the common law fencing-in rule reveal any preference as between farming and ranching activities? Does the Idaho fencing-out rule reveal any preference between the two activities? What preference underlies the statutory authorization of herd districts? The 1963 Idaho amendment excluding open range from herd districts? The rules respecting liability for animals straying onto highways in and out of open range? The court's decision in Maguire v. Yanke? What is the probable behavior of farmers and ranchers under each set of rules? Is this behavior likely to lead to the most desirable allocation of costs and benefits in each setting?

3. Trespass law erects barriers that are higher and deeper than any stone wall or wooden fence. A possessor's rights extend not only to the surface of the land but also to the entire column of space below—*usque ad inferos*—and above—*usque ad coelum*. The only limit to the possessor's subsurface rights is that the ancient rule of

capture holds that anyone is free to withdraw underlying oil, gas and water. See pages 130 to 151 below. More recently, with the growth of air travel, the possessor's above-surface rights have been limited in favor of free use by aircraft; the reason commonly given is that the invaded air space lies outside the surface occupant's sphere of actual or potential use. See 6A American Law of Property § 28.4 (A.J. Casner ed. 1952). Is this reasoning circular? If surface occupants were given exclusive rights to the column of air space above their land, is it not likely that they would use the resource by licensing others—such as airlines—to fly through it? Should anything of consequence turn on whether a resource is used by its immediate owner or by some licensee or grantee of the owner who, presumably, can put it to a more productive use? Is there some other, better economic rationale for excusing invasions by aircraft?

4. There are several remedies for trespass. One is damages. The basic measure of damages is the difference between the land's value before and after the trespass. In some states, damages will be measured by the cost of repair—if the injury is reparable and if the cost of repair is less than the diminution in the property's value. See e.g., Waggener v. Leggett, 246 Miss. 505, 150 So.2d 529 (1963). The victim is also entitled to compensation for all injuries that naturally and proximately result from the trespass—including personal injuries (physical, mental or reputational) and injuries to personal property. If the trespass is willful, wanton or malicious, punitive damages may also be given. See e.g., Rushing v. Hooper-McDonald, Inc., 293 Ala. 56, 300 So.2d 94, 98 (1974) ("A jury is warranted in awarding punitive damages in the case of trespass if the trespass is attended by rudeness, wantonness, recklessness or an insulting manner or is accompanied by circumstances of fraud and malice, oppression, aggravation, or gross negligence").

The victim can recover the land from the trespasser through a common law ejectment proceeding or through the far quicker statutory vehicle of unlawful detainer. A decree of ejectment may be accompanied by an award of mesne profits, measured by the rental value of the property during the period of the trespass. The victim can obtain an injunction against the trespass if she can demonstrate that her legal remedy is inadequate—typically because damages will not make her whole or will require a multiplicity of lawsuits.

5. Trespass to real property is often made a crime. Some states, focusing on the unauthorized entry on land, treat criminal trespass as an offense related to burglary. See e.g., New York—McKinney's Penal Law §§ 140.05; 140.10; 140.17. Criminal trespass in New York can range from a class D felony (trespass in building with deadly weapon or explosives; punishable by a maximum sentence of 7 years and a minimum sentence of 1 year) to a class B misdemeanor (trespass on fenced or otherwise enclosed premises; $500 fine, three-month sentence) to a mere violation (trespass on premises; $250 fine,

15-day sentence). Other states include various trespassory acts among "crimes against property." See e.g., Miss. Code 1972, §§ 97-17-89; 97-17-93 (1981 Supp.) (trespass and destruction or carrying away vegetation not amounting to larceny—fine not exceeding $500.00 or six-month imprisonment or both; trespass on enclosed lands after posted notice—fine not exceeding $250.00).

6. *Personal Property: The Law of Finders.* Personal property law governs rights in *chattels*—movable things such as corn, cows, and cars. It also governs many aspects of *choses in action*—legal claims against third parties, such as promissory notes and bank accounts. Should personal property law and real property law follow parallel paths? To what extent does the fact that chattels are movable, while land is immovable, require that the two paths diverge?

One issue on which personal property law and real property law follow closely parallel paths is, what rights accrue from possession? Under personal property law, one who finds and takes possession of a chattel is given ownership rights in it as against the entire world, except the true owner. For example, in the much-cited Armory v. Delamirie, 1 Strange 505, 93 Eng.Rep. 664 (K.B.1722), plaintiff, "a chimney sweeper's boy," brought a jewel that he had found to the shop of defendant, a goldsmith, to determine its value. The goldsmith's apprentice, "under pretence of weighing it, took out the stones, and calling to the master to let him know it came to three halfpence, the master offered the boy the money, who refused to take it, and insisted to have the thing again; whereupon the apprentice delivered him back the socket without the stones." The court ruled for plaintiff: "the finder of a jewel, though he does not by such finding acquire an absolute property or ownership, yet he has such a property as will enable him to keep it against all but the rightful owner." As to damages, "several of the trade were examined to prove what a jewel of the finest water that would fit the socket would be worth; and the Chief Justice directed the jury, that unless the defendant did produce the jewel, and shew it not to be of the finest water, they should presume the strongest against him, and make the value of the best jewels the measure of their damages: which they accordingly did."

Why give possessors of chattels rights against all but the true owner? Since personal property transfers have few of the formalities required for real property transfers, real property law's curative rationale, discussed in Note 1, above, would seem not to apply. Would a rule that favored a subsequent finder over the first finder be likely to encourage people to "find" things that had perhaps not been lost?

Why not give possessors of chattels rights against the true owner as well as against the rest of the world? Such a rule might appear more conducive to the productive use of resources since a finder will be more willing to improve a chattel through processing or manufacturing if he knows that there is no risk that it will later be reclaimed by the true owner. Is it just a coincidence that virtually all finders cases involve chattels that have already been fully processed, manufactured or otherwise brought to their most valuable form?

Finders are not necessarily keepers, nor losers weepers, and someone lucky enough to "find" a valuable jewel or sack of cash may in fact occupy a treacherous position. The finder is subject not only to the true owner's claim, but is also subject to criminal prosecution for theft if it can be proved that he retained the chattel knowing, or with reasonable means for discovering, the whereabouts of the true owner. See, for example, West's Ann.Cal.Penal Code § 485 ("One who finds lost property under circumstances which give him knowledge of or means of inquiry as to the true owner, and who appropriates such property to his own use, or to the use of another person not entitled thereto, without first making reasonable and just efforts to find the owner and to restore the property to him, is guilty of theft").

Consider how you would advise your client, an army sergeant who, while quartered in a private home that had been requisitioned by the army from its owner, discovered a brooch lodged behind a window frame; when the sergeant cleaned off the cobwebs and dirt, the brooch revealed the inscription, "From *R.B.* to *E.B.B.*" As between your client and the landowner, who would have paramount rights in the brooch? *Cf.* Hannah v. Peel, [1945] 1 K.B. 509. Would your answer differ if, instead of being legally quartered on the premises, your client had been a trespasser? See R. Brown, The Law of Personal Property § 3.2 (W. Raushenbush 3d ed. 1975). As between your client and her employer, the United States Army, who would have paramount rights? As between your client and the true owner of the brooch?

What steps, if any, should your client take to track down the mysterious *E.B.B.*, or, for that matter, *R.B.*? You would do well to determine at the outset whether your jurisdiction has a statute prescribing the steps to be followed with respect to lost property. See, for example, N.Y.—McKinney's Personal Prop.Law Art. 7–b.

2. ADVERSE POSSESSION

a. Theory of Protection

OLIVER WENDELL HOLMES, JR., LETTER TO WILLIAM JAMES, APRIL 1, 1907, IN 2 R. PERRY, THE THOUGHT AND CHARACTER OF WILLIAM

JAMES 461–462 (1935): . . . I am reminded by some things you say of an observation of mine to which I attach some value in the legal aspect. I say that truth, friendship, and the statute of limitations have a common root in time. The true explanation of title by prescription seems to me to be that man, like a tree in the cleft of a rock, gradually shapes his roots to his surroundings, and when the roots have grown to a certain size, can't be displaced without cutting at his life. The law used to look with disfavor on the statute of limitations, but I have been in the habit of saying it is one of the most sacred and indubitable principles that we have; which used to lead my predecessor Field to say that Holmes didn't value any title that was not based on fraud or force . . .

McDONNOLD v. WEINACHT

Supreme Court of Texas, 1971.

465 S.W.2d 136.

WALKER, Justice.

M. McDonnold, Jr. et al. brought this trespass to try title suit against L.A. Weinacht et al to recover title to and possession of the NW/4 of Section 39, Block 13, H. & G.N. Ry. Co. Survey in Reeves County. Plaintiffs are the record owners, and defendants claim title under the ten-year statute of limitations. Art. 5510, Vernon's Ann. Civ.Stat. The trial court rendered judgment on the verdict in defendants' favor, and the Court of Civil Appeals affirmed. In our opinion there is no evidence to support the finding of the jury that defendants held adverse possession of the land for ten years.

If defendants have title by adverse possession, it must be through use of the land by L.A. Weinacht, hereinafter referred to as Weinacht. His two sons, to whom Weinacht conveyed the disputed tract in 1963, will be referred to by their given names, Charles and Don. The present suit was filed on January 9, 1964. In the summer of 1954, there were changes in the fences so that the land in controversy became part of a different enclosure. Since this occurred less than ten years prior to the institution of this suit, we will confine our statement of the facts to the situation as it existed from 1940 to 1954. Our treatment of the case in this manner is not to be taken as indicating approval of the holding by the Court of Civil Appeals that defendants were in adverse possession of the disputed tract after the fences were changed in 1954. We simply do not reach that question.

The tract in controversy contains 160 acres. Its eastern and southern boundaries are indicated by broken lines on the following plat:

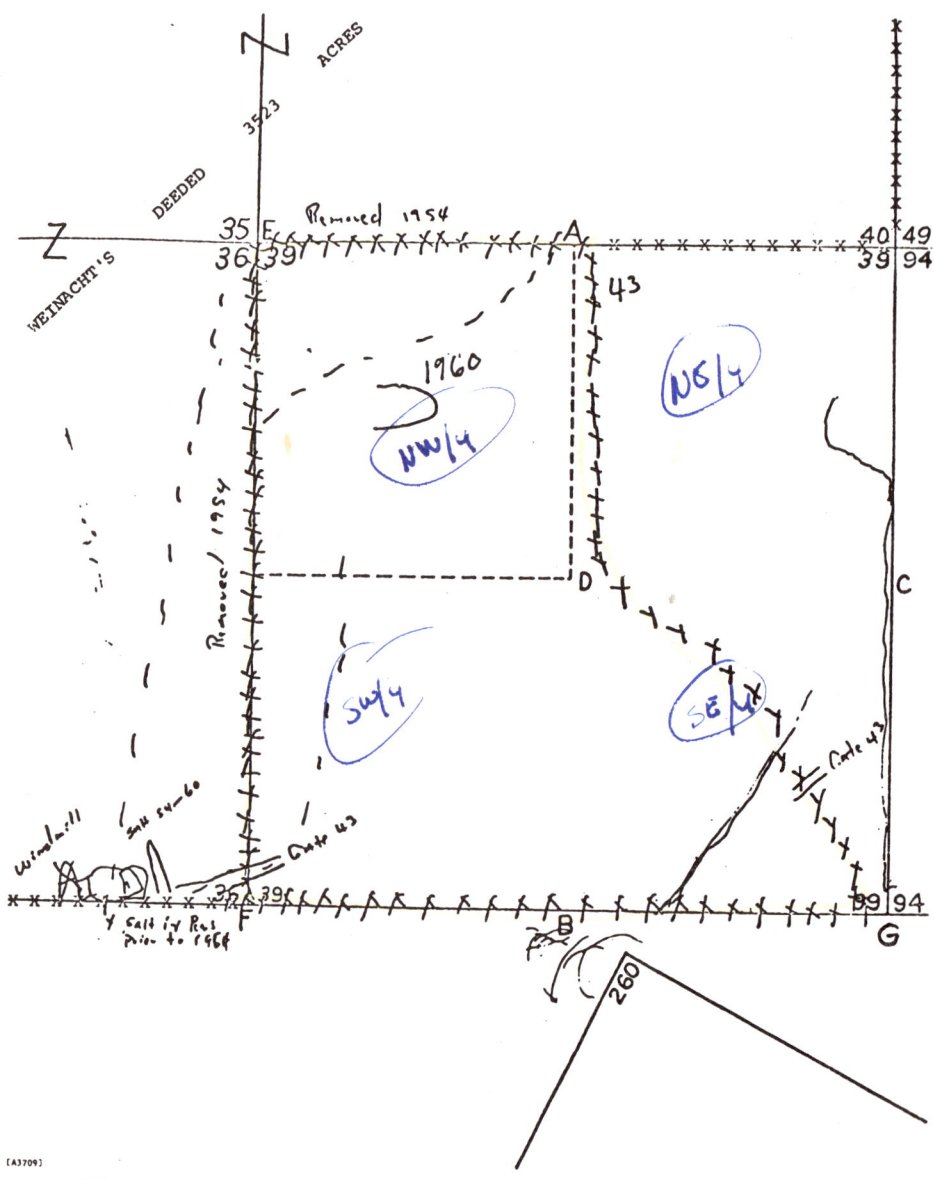

The foregoing plat is a reproduction of Plaintiffs' Exhibit 41 with the following changes made by us: (1) addition of a legible letter "G" at the southeast corner of Section 39; (2) addition of words and symbols indicating the location of adjacent deeded land owned by Weinacht in Sections 35, 36 and 40; (3) elimination of markings indicating a fence from D to B that was built by Weinacht in 1954, less than ten years prior to institution of this suit; and (4) addition of X's made with a typewriter and indicating Weinacht's boundary fences on the south line of Section 36, the east line of Section 40, and from A to the southeast corner of Section 40. The location of all other fences was marked by Don with pen and ink on Plaintiffs' Exhibit 41 during the trial, and defendants adopted the exhibit as a correct portrayal of the ground situation.

Weinacht acquired the Meier Ranch from Mrs. Mary J. Gould et al. by deeds dated November 15, 1940. This ranch consists of five and one-half sections, including Sections 35, 36 and 40, and contains about 3523 acres. It was completely surrounded by fences. No part of Section 39 was included in the deeds to Weinacht. The fences in and around Section 39 at that time, and as they continued to exist until 1954, are depicted by X's marked by Don on the above plat. The land in controversy was thus in an enclosure of about 400 acres, hereinafter referred to as the trap, that included the NW/4, the SW/4 about half of the SE/4, and apparently a strip off the west side of the NE/4, of Section 39. The record is silent as to when, by whom or for what purpose any of the fences were originally built.

Weinacht knew that the land in controversy was not included in his deed. Mrs. Gould advised him that she had the SW/4 of Section 39 under lease, however, and she told him to go ahead and use it. He paid pasture rent on the SW/4 to Mrs. Gould every year from 1943 to 1949, and he continued to hold the same under Mr. Gould after her death. From 1958 until the time of trial, he held the SW/4 under lease from and paid pasture rent to Delbert Loos et al. who were then the record owners.

Shortly after acquiring the Meier Ranch in 1940, Weinacht repaired all of the fences around his deeded land. These included the fence on the east line of his Section 36 and the south line of his Section 40, which incidentally were the fences bounding the trap on the west and north. He also repaired the fences bounding the trap on the south and east. All of the evidence concerning repairs made at that time comes from Weinacht, whose testimony is inconsistent in several respects and far from clear on a number of points. According to Weinacht's testimony, he found that the fences around his deeded land and around the trap "were all up pretty good" except those on the west and south lines of Section 39. The two last mentioned fences were "practically down in places." Posts that were broken off or rotted in the west fence were replaced, and all of the wire in this fence was restretched. As for the south fence, "it was up in pretty good shape—nothing excellent. We repaired it all." Later he stated that he "rebuilt that [from F to B] as a real fence right after I got the thing." "We also rebuilt that fence" from E to A, but the nature and extent of the work done on the north and south fences is not disclosed by the evidence. The east fence extending from A to D to G "wasn't too good a fence." He "repaired it"; "we didn't build too good a fence on that part right there, but it would turn horses and cattle." It seems fairly clear then that Weinacht made substantial repairs to at least part of the fences surrounding the trap, but there is no evidence that he changed their location or character or built any new fences. After doing his initial work, Weinacht continued to maintain the fences in repair from 1941 to 1954.

There was a lane leading from the SW/4 of Section 39 at its southwest corner to a large watering lot in the southeast portion of Weinacht's deeded Section 36. Cattle grazing on the large pasture on the deeded ranch also had access to the watering lot, but the fences were so arranged that cattle in the main pasture could not enter the trap. There were watering troughs and a windmill in the lot, and salt for livestock in the trap was placed there. Weinacht kept horses and brood mares in the trap, and used it to hold wormy cattle and calves, continuously from 1941 to 1954. Once or twice each year during that period, the trap was used for gathering and holding cattle that were to be sold. Each year Weinacht and his employees chopped the cockleburs and inkweed growing on the 400 acres. This was done because the burs "are bad on horses and cows—get in their tails and manes." The inkweed is very poisonous—"it just takes a few hands full to kill a cow."

Weinacht did not ever claim the SW/4 or the portion of the SE/4 that was in the trap. According to his testimony, he did claim the NW/4 of Section 39 continuously from 1941 until it was conveyed to his two sons in 1963. However, he guarded his claim carefully. Until about three years before the institution of this suit, he never gave written or verbal expression to the claim except to members of his immediate family. The only testimony that he claimed the disputed tract came from Weinacht and his two sons. They testified that he claimed the land but not that he ever told anyone of his claim. His neighbor and kinsman who held a lease on the NE/4 of Section 39 never heard Weinacht or any of his family make claim to any part of the NW/4. This was also true of the County Surveyor who had been surveying land in the area for 20 years and who, in 1963, surveyed the right of way for Interstate Highway 10 across the Weinacht Ranch.

The claim was also kept secret from the taxing authorities until 1961. Weinacht's state and county rendition sheet for 1960 was offered in evidence, and he admitted that he signed and swore to the rendition. The oath he took was in the usual form that "this inventory rendered by me contains a full, true and complete list of all taxable property owned or held by me . . . in this county." The NW/4 of Section 39 was not listed, although the rendition did include one acre owned by Weinacht in the northeast corner of the same section. It was stipulated that, in so far as material to this suit, all of his state and county rendition sheets for prior years were similar to the 1960 rendition. No taxes were paid by Weinacht on the NW$^1/_4$ of Section 39 for those years.

On August 5, 1952, Weinacht wrote a letter to two individuals at Quincy, Illinois. In this letter he stated that his map indicated that the addressees "own the NW/4 of Section 39, Block 13, in Reeves

County." The letter further stated that he "would like to get a grazing or grass lease on this 160 acres" and would "give ten cents per acre for a one or three year grass lease." Weinacht admitted writing this letter which, if received by the true owner, was calculated to induce the belief that the writer was not claiming to own the land himself.

If plaintiffs had suspected an adverse claim and made inquiry of Weinacht, it is not at all certain that he would have told them that he was claiming the land. His own testimony shows that he was somewhat less than open and frank with plaintiff McDonnold, who first became interested in the disputed tract when he obtained oil and gas leases from the record owners in 1963. Later that year he visited Weinacht for the purpose of attempting to buy mineral royalty interests in the latter's ranch. In the course of the conversation, McDonnold showed Weinacht a map on which the land in dispute had been colored in purple. Weinacht inquired why the tract was colored, and McDonnold replied that he had obtained an oil and gas lease from the record owners and was on his way to pay the delinquent taxes. Weinacht did not then advise either that he was claiming the land or that he had been paying the taxes since 1961. Upon paying the delinquent taxes, McDonnold learned that Weinacht had paid the taxes for several years. He again visited Weinacht and offered to refund the taxes paid by the latter. According to McDonnold's testimony, Weinacht stated, "that won't be necessary; I have had some use of the land." Weinacht admitted that he said nothing to McDonnold about claiming to own the land, and his only explanation of this continued secrecy was that "I don't never tell all of my business to everybody."[1]

There is good reason then for the rule that to constitute adverse possession under the ten-year statute, the appropriation of the land must be of such character as to indicate unmistakably an assertion of a claim of exclusive ownership in the occupant. Defendants here re-

---

1. Weinacht testified on cross-examination as follows:

Q Did you tell him you didn't claim it or didn't own it?

A I didn't tell him yes or no.

. . .

Q You never did tell any of these land owners or Mr. McDonnold or anybody else that you claimed that land up until the time you filed that deed to your boys, did you?

A I don't never tell all of my business to everybody.

. . .

Q In other words, you were going to wait until he drilled a well or something before you told Mr. McDonnold?

A I would have waited until he started, yes, sir.

Q And let him go ahead and spend any amount of money he could spend on it and then tell him, is that what you intended to do?

A That would have been his business.

Q And you then deliberately did not tell him because you just wanted to wait and see what he would do with that land, is that right?

A Why, absolutely.

. . .

Q Why did you not tell him at that time that you claimed this land? Wasn't that the most natural thing in the world to do?

A I don't see why.

ly, as they must, upon the grazing of livestock, chopping weeds, and repair of existing fences. The tract in controversy was never separately enclosed, and no one has ever resided upon or cultivated the land in the trap. During the 1940–1954 period, there was no improvement of any kind on the 400 acres, not even a watering trough or salt box or improved road. The closest semblance to a road on the NW/4 was a trail made by driving vehicles and extending from the gate at the southwest corner of the 400 acres to a point just across the south line of the land in controversy. "It didn't go anywhere. It just went out in the pasture."

Our courts have never recognized the common law rule of England that requires every man to restrain his cattle either by tethering or by enclosure. Unenclosed land has always been regarded as commons for grazing livestock in Texas, and it is well settled that the use of unenclosed land for grazing livestock does not, of itself, constitute adverse possession. A claimant who builds and maintains fences for the purpose of enclosing the land and grazes the same continuously may be in adverse possession, but not every enclosure capable of turning livestock will suffice.

Part of the unenclosed commons might become enclosed as a result of being fenced out by surrounding owners. The grazing of an enclosure thus "casually" or "incidentally" created has never been regarded as an actual and visible appropriation of the land within the meaning of Article 5515, Vernon's Ann.Civ.Stat. In the absence of special stock laws, an owner who does not properly fence his property has no cause of action for damage done by cattle of ordinary disposition that enter the land. If the owner of land enclosed with that of another wishes to prevent the latter's livestock from grazing on his property, his remedy is to construct a suitable fence for that purpose. It would be rather strange then to hold that a person might acquire limitation title by simply doing that which he is legally entitled to do, i.e. permit his livestock to wander and graze upon land that he happened to find enclosed with his own deeded or leased land.

It is accordingly well settled that the mere grazing of land incidentally enclosed as a result of the construction of fences built for another purpose does not constitute possession that will ripen into title by limitation. The adverse claimant who relies upon grazing only as evidence of his adverse use and enjoyment must show as part of his case that the land in dispute was designedly enclosed.

. . . Here there is no proof that the fences were originally built for the purpose of enclosing the NW/4 of Section 39, and neither the enclosure itself nor the work done by Weinacht on the fences warrants the conclusion that plaintiffs' land was designedly enclosed. His repair or rebuilding of the fences along the east line of his deeded Section 36 and along the south line of his deeded Section 40 is clearly referable to his deed. They were designed to and did form part of the enclosure of his deeded land, and the fact that they also bounded the trap on the north and west was purely incidental. In these circumstances and in view of Weinacht's lease of the SW/4 from the Goulds, his repair of the fences bounding the trap on the south and east does not evidence an intention to enclose the disputed tract. It was simply the easiest and most economical way of maintaining an enclosure that would permit grazing on the SW/4.

We accept Weinacht's statement that cattle and horses were kept in the trap "all of the time," but he did not attempt to say how many animals were generally kept there. According to Don's undisputed testimony, the average number kept on the entire ranch over the years was ten or twelve brood mares and horses and about 80 to 100 head of cattle. It seems fair to assume, therefore, that relatively few animals regularly grazed in the trap. Be that as it may, the only salt and water provided for them were in the water lot on Weinacht's deeded land. Since plaintiffs' land was never separately enclosed, the animals would naturally move at times from the water lot across the unclaimed land enclosed therewith to the tract in controversy. It was always necessary, however, for them to return to the water lot to obtain water and salt. Weinacht was under no legal obligation to fence off the NW/4 and in the absence of a violation of some statute would have incurred no liability to the record owner simply because his cattle did not stop their grazing when they reached its unfenced south line. We thus have a classic case of incidental enclosure and incidental grazing, and these are insufficient as a matter of law to constitute a visible appropriation of the land.

Defendants argue that the cutting of burs and poisonous weeds in the 400-acre trap adds something to their case. There is testimony that the weeds were cut "every year," but no one undertook to say whether this was done more than once a year or how long each operation lasted. Weinacht evidently had the right to cut weeds on the SW/4 he held under the Goulds, and his keeping the trap free of weeds could hardly be considered an appropriation of the remainder of the land in the enclosure. It is settled, moreover, that the cutting of weeds is "not such use of the property as to meet the requirements of Article 5510 V.A.C.S. for establishing title by adverse possession." City of Dallas v. Etheridge, 152 Tex. 9, 253 S.W.2d 640. This is in accordance with the general majority rule that cutting and gathering a natural crop does not constitute adverse possession. Here the cutting of weeds was no less incidental than the grazing of the tract or its inclusion in the enclosure maintained by Weinacht.

. . .

The judgments of the courts below are reversed, and the cause is remanded to the district court with instructions to render judgment for plaintiffs.

[The concurring opinion of POPE, J., and the dissenting opinion of REAVLEY, J., omitted here, are summarized in Note 3, below.]

NOTES

1. Under the rules discussed in Holden v. Lynn, a possessor without title can exclude all but the land's true owner. Under the statute of limitations governing actions to recover the possession of real property, the possessor without title can, once the limitations period has elapsed, exclude the true owner as well. The running of the statute does more than bar the true owner's claim. It also divests him of title and vests title in the adverse possessor. To justify this dramatic result, and to assure that the true owner has notice of his claim while the limitations period is running against him, states generally require that the adverse possession be actual, visible, hostile and continuous, and that the true owner be competent to bring suit, throughout the limitations period.

Should the impact of these requirements differ depending on the context in which the adverse possession arises? For example, if the true owner and adverse possessor were originally grantor and grantee under a conveyance that, but for some formal defect unknown to both, would have effectively transferred title from one to the other, will the putative grantee's actual, visible, hostile and continuous possession for the limitations period likely give the grantor notice of his claim? Compare the situation in which the true owner is not in the position of grantor but rather, as in *Weinacht*, is the adverse possessor's neighbor. Consider whether it should matter that the adverse possessor is occupying the true owner's land: under color of title (the deed by which the adverse possessor took title to his parcel erroneously describes his parcel to include part of the true owner's parcel); without color of title, but in good faith (the adverse possessor's deed correctly describes his parcel but, relying on a faulty survey, the adverse possessor builds an improvement encroaching on the true owner's land); without color of title and in bad faith (the adverse possessor knowingly trespasses on the true owner's land, hoping to gain title by adverse possession).

What surveillance burdens do the requirements for adverse possession place on true owners in each of these four contexts? In the first case, in which the adverse possessor is occupying under a formally defective conveyance, is there anything that the true owner could—or should—be able to do to guard against title passing to the adverse possessor? What steps must a neighboring owner take, and how often, to guard against losing part or all of his parcel by adverse possession? Will the neighbor's burden differ depending on whether the adverse possessor is claiming under color of title; without color of title, but in good faith; in bad faith? Would it be better in any of these cases to shift the risk of loss to the adverse possessor?

2. Are there any connections between the substantive law of trespass and the governing statute of limitations? As a substantive matter, for the true owner to prevail in a trespass action, she need

only show some intentional interference with her possession, and need not show that she has suffered any injury. The rationale commonly given for allowing the action without proof of injury is that the true owner might otherwise lose title by adverse possession through acts that cause her no harm. See 6–A American Law of Prop. § 28.12 (A.J. Casner ed. 1952).

Is this reasoning circular? If injury *were* an element of the cause of action for trespass, the statute of limitations for the recovery of real property would not begin to run until injury occurred, with the result that the true owner would never lose her title to an adverse possessor whose possession was harmless. Consider whether the real function of the rule excusing the true owner from proof of injury is to save her from the consequences of a mistaken judgment as to whether the trespass caused injury or not.

3. Would *Weinacht* have gone the other way if, more than ten years before filing suit, McDonnold had attempted to convey the NW/4 of Section 39 to Weinacht through a deed that, unknown to both parties, was formally defective? If Weinacht had built a house on the parcel? If Texas followed the English common law rule that "requires every man to restrain his cattle either by tethering or enclosure"?

Under the Texas rule, which treats unenclosed land as a commons, can continuous grazing ever produce title by adverse possession? In the view of Justice Pope, concurring, " 'mere' grazing or 'occasional' grazing, or 'casual' grazing will not provide the necessary notice of the claim. However, active and total use to the limits of the pasture's capacity and to the exclusion of all others, with a claimant's livestock continuously present and visible, will give that notice and support a claim of adverse possession. This is particularly true in the case of land which is suitable for no other purpose." 465 S.W.2d at 144. What cause of action would McDonnold have had against this grazing, and when would the statute of limitations for that cause of action have begun to run?

Were Weinacht's annual efforts to clear the disputed parcel of inkweed and cockleburs inconsistent with the parcel's status as a commons? Would it have been preferable for the Texas Supreme Court to view these efforts in connection with Weinacht's other activities on the parcel, rather than to analyze them separately? Justice Reavley, dissenting, thought that this would have been the preferable approach, and was also disturbed by the court's cavalier treatment of the trial court's fact finding. "The jury found, in answer to the customary inquiry, that Weinacht 'had and held peaceable and adverse possession' of the land, 'cultivating, using or enjoying the same' for a period of ten consecutive years or more prior to January 9, 1964 when this suit was instituted. Using the statutory language, the court instructed the jury that 'peaceable possession' means continuous possession and that 'adverse possession' means 'an actual and visible appropriation of the land, commenced and continued under a claim of right inconsistent with and hostile to the claim of another.'" 465 S.W.2d at 145.

4. *Squatting.* Title by adverse possession is usually acquired in good faith—through possession under a formally defective instrument or under a mistaken deed description or survey. Yet, title is sometimes acquired through an act of sheer, unmistaken will by squatters—adverse possessors who have no belief that the lands they occupy belong to them. It is usually the poor and the displaced who, in their quest for shelter, take possession of land without claim of right.

Although squatting patterns differ, their object—a roof over one's head—is always the same. Squatting in the lesser-developed countries is typically an urban phenomenon, the last step in a flight from the impoverished countryside. According to one slightly dated but conservative estimate, forty-five percent of the population of Ankara, Turkey consisted of squatters; twenty percent of Manila, Philippines; thirty-five percent of Caracas, Venezuela; and twenty-five percent of Santiago, Chile. C. Abrams, Man's Struggle for Shelter in an Urbanizing World 13 (1964). In England in the 1970's, masses of urban poor moved into dwellings that had been vacated for urban renewal; by summer, 1975, London alone had thirty thousand squatters. Trimborn, Outcast Squatters Stir Homeowners' Fears, Los Angeles Times, 3 August 1975, section 1 at column 1. In the United States, a tradition of squatting began virtually with the first colonial settlers and continued, primarily on government lands, as the American pioneers moved west. In New York City in the 1960's, squatting became as much a political as an economic phenomenon, with groups of five or more families, organized by community activists, moving into abandoned but still livable buildings. See, generally, Allen, A Frontier Challenge to the Urban Landowner: Squatters in New York, 49 J. Urban L. 323 (1971); Manaster, Squatters and the Law: The Relevance of the United States Experience to Current Problems in the Developing Countries, 43 Tul.L.Rev. 94 (1968).

Common law principle, and sympathy for the plight of the homeless poor, have sometimes combined to give squatters substantial protection against even the true owner. Although squatters have no legal right to exclude the true owner before the statute of limitations has run against their trespass, they can at least put the true owner to the considerable expense and delay of an action to evict. And, if the exasperated owner seeks to remove squatters through self-help, the squatters may be able to invoke the criminal sanction, and also obtain damages, under the applicable forcible entry and detainer statute. (Forcible entry and detainer statutes in this country trace more or less to England's original Forcible Entry Act, 5 Richard II, ch. 7 (1381), making forcible entry onto another's quiet possession of land a crime, even if the entrant held good title to the land as against the occupant.) See Comment, Defects in the Current Forcible Entry and Detainer Laws of the United States and England, 25 UCLA L.Rev. 1067 (1978).

5. What rights do squatters have as against the state? In Amezquita v. Hernandez-Colon, 518 F.2d 8 (1st Cir. 1975), members of the Villa Pangola, a squatter group occupying part of a farm owned by the Land Authority of the Commonwealth of Puerto Rico, brought an action against the Authority and the Commonwealth, claiming that the Authority's forcible removal of their structures violated their civil rights. The district court held for the squatters and ordered "the defendants and their agents to refrain from violating the civil rights of herein plaintiffs by destroying plaintiffs' property and invading plaintiffs' privacy without previously obtaining a judicial order to that effect."

The Court of Appeals for the First Circuit reversed. In its view, the lower court "apparently thought that the due process clause of the fourteenth amendment barred eviction without prior judicial authorization. Under this theory if a homeless family moved into a vacant apartment in a state housing project, the state would be constitutionally barred from evicting by self-help." Rejecting this theory, the court concluded that a "similar answer is required to the question whether there is a protected 'property' interest. We turn to Commonwealth law to determine whether such a protected interest exists. Germane to this issue are two Puerto Rico statutes:

'He who builds, plants, or sows in bad faith on another's land, loses what he has built, planted or sown, without having any right to indemnity.' 31 L.P.R.A. § 1165.

'The owner of the land on which any one has built, planted or sown in bad faith, may exact the demolition of the work or the removal of the planting or sowing and the replacing of everything in its former condition, at the expense of the person who built, planted or sowed.' Id. § 1166.

These statutes preclude us from recognizing in the plaintiffs a 'property' interest in the land which could not be disturbed without procedural preliminaries." 518 F.2d at 10, 13.

Would the squatters in *Amezquita* have had any greater rights if the government had been acting not as landowner but rather in its more traditional policing capacity, seeking to restore title to its lawful source? Apart from constitutional considerations, can you think of any good reason for the state to confirm title in squatters as opposed to the true owner? Under the 1841 Preemption Law, the United States, as landowner, gave squatters the right of first refusal to buy the land they occupied at established minimum prices. See A. Bertrand & F. Corty, Rural Land Tenure in the United States, 52 (1962).

6. *Transfers by Parol Agreement, Estoppel and Acquiescence.* As a general rule, the Statute of Frauds allows interests in land to be transferred only through properly executed written instruments. Adverse possession is one of four major exceptions to the Statute's requirement of written land transfers. A second theory, *parol agreement*, enables courts in appropriate circumstances to enforce neighbors' oral agreements settling their boundaries. Under a third theory, *estoppel* (or *estoppel in pais*), one who develops or otherwise invests in land relying on his neighbor's representation as to the true boundary between their parcels will gain title to all land up to the represented boundary. Fourth, many states allow boundary lines to be fixed by *acquiescence.* The requirements for acquiescence are that "(1) adjoining landowners (2) who occupy their respective tracts up to a clear and certain line (such as a fence), (3) which they mutually recognize and accept as the dividing line between their properties (4) for a long period of time, cannot thereafter claim that the boundary thus recognized is not the true boundary." Tresemer v. Albuquerque Public School District, 95 N.M. 143, 144, 619 P.2d 819, 820 (1980).

Adverse possession, parol agreement and acquiescence overlap at several points. For example, a substantial number of states measure acquiescence's required "long period" by the statute of limitations applicable to adverse possession. And some states require that, for adverse possession to be proved, the owner must have acquiesced in the adverse claimant's possession. See pages 698–702, below. Some states will enforce a parol boundary agreement only if the neighbors have acquiesced in the boundary for a long time, and many courts that purport to rely on acquiescence alone nevertheless treat acquiescence as evidence of an agreement between the parties. Browder, The Practical Location of Boundaries, 56 Mich.L.Rev. 487, 505–506 (1958).

Courts differ widely, often within the same jurisdiction, in their willingness to employ any of the four theories and, if willing, in the manner in which they will apply it. Indeed, it is hard to find an area of real property law in which the rules are more open-ended, tentative and confused. Is this confusion, and the resulting uncertainty, likely to discourage productive investment in land? To produce wasteful behavior in the surveillance of boundaries? If so, why has there not been greater pressure for clarification of the law?

b. REQUIRED ELEMENTS

i. "Actual," "Open," "Visible," "Notorious" and "Exclusive"

CHEEK v. WAINWRIGHT

Supreme Court of Georgia, 1980.
246 Ga. 171, 269 S.E.2d 443.

CLARKE, Justice.

This controversy involves ownership of a parcel of land located in Land Lot 85 of the 14th Land District, Taylor County, Georgia. Appellants, plaintiffs below, contended that the disputed parcel, upon which appellee proposed to cut timber and conduct other activities, belonged to them. They filed suit in the Superior Court of Taylor County alleging that appellees were trespassing and should be enjoined from continuing to do so. Appellees denied that appellants owned the property in question, and the case came on for jury trial on January 24, 1979, resulting in a verdict and judgment in favor of appellees on the basis of adverse possession and prescriptive title.

The disputed land, a rectangular strip of approximately 62 acres, was located in the southern portion of Land Lot 85. Appellee Wainwright in 1945 purchased some 202.5 acres, the deed for which described the land as being in Land Lot 86. The land is coterminus with the southern boundary of Land Lot 85. In October, 1966, appellants purchased a piece of property from the estate of J.F. Posey which purportedly included the "Mosley Place" and the "Shoupe Place." According to the deed, the Shoupe Place embraced some ten acres in Land Lot 85. Appellees contend that ten acres in Land Lot 85 were included in the "Sanders Place," which they had purchased in 1945. Appellants obtained a deed of correction, executed in December, 1970, which described the Mosley Place as containing all of Land Lot 85. The case went to the jury on the question of appellees' contention that they had acquired prescriptive title to the disputed 62 acres in Land Lot 85 by adverse possession for twenty years. . . .

Wainwright testified that after purchase of the Sanders Place in 1945, he worked the property up to a hedgerow which he thought was the line between the Sanders Place and the Mosley Place. He planted peppers and cotton in the area which now is the subject of this lawsuit in 1946 and 1947. In 1947, he began tree farming on the disputed land and since that time has planted pine trees in rows, has thinned pine trees, and has furnished lumber for the Sanders house. There was testimony that the planted trees were visible from a county road. This evidence was supported by similar testimony of three other witnesses.

Adverse possession is defined in Code Ann. § 85–402 as follows: "Possession to be the foundation of a prescription must be in the right of the possessor, and not of another; must not have originated in fraud; must be public, continuous, exclusive, uninterrupted, and peaceable, and be accompanied by a claim of right. Permissive possession cannot be the foundation of a prescription, until an adverse claim and actual notice to the other party." Code Ann. § 85–403 provides that actual possession of lands is evidenced by "inclosure, cultivation, or any use and occupation thereof which is so notorious as to attract the attention of every adverse claimant, and so exclusive as to prevent actual occupation by another."

Cultivation, tillage of the soil, planting and harvesting a crop are superior indicia of possession. Therefore, the evidence of cultivating the land by growing cotton and peppers in 1946 and 1947 is sufficient to establish actual possession for those years. The question remaining is whether the testimony as to acts of tree farming support the finding of continuous possession. Timber cutting as evidence of possession has been held to be of little value and standing alone has been held totally insufficient. In this case, trees were planted in rows on land which had been open and cultivated land previously and the planting of the trees was on an area visible from a public road. We must decide whether this coupled with periodic harvesting authorized the jury to find a continuation of the possession which began with crop cultivation.

The essence of actual possession is use of the land to such an extent and in such a manner as to put the world on notice. This notice is achieved when the use is so notorious as to attract the attention of every adverse claimant. In this case, Wainwright went into possession by carrying out acts which have been universally recognized as acts of actual possession. Two years later, he continued his possession by changing the very nature and appearance of the land through the planting of trees on previously open land. Trees planted in rows along a public road give a clear and lasting notice that someone is exercising possession by even changing the nature of the real estate.

In Memory v. Walker, 209 Ga. 916, 76 S.E.2d 698 (1953), a highly restrictive rule was set down as to actual possession of timberlands. Even boxing pines, plowing fire breaks, planting pines, marking corners, keeping fire and trespassers off of the land and returning the land for taxation was held not to be evidence of actual possession. This case has been criticized as ignoring the realities of turpentine and forestry farming. We must also join in the disapproval of this holding. The development of tree farming as a major segment of agriculture has caused this enterprise to move outside of the realm of occasional removal of trees from wild lands and into the mainstream of modern economy and technology. There is a state and public interest in the law providing for prescription by adverse possession. This interest is mainly served by removing doubts as to land titles.

It is not reasonable to hold that a major portion of the real estate in Georgia cannot be affected by the law dealing with prescription. Although this case is not intended to place a stamp of approval upon mere cutting of trees as evidence of actual possession, we do hold that tree farming when carried out in such a manner as to attract the attention of every adverse claimant can be evidence of actual possession.

[margin note: holding]

This case arose from an action to enjoin a trespasser on land. The question in such a case is whether the plaintiff has title in fact. If the evidence is conflicting, it is for the jury to decide, and a verdict based on any competent evidence which has the approval of the trial judge will not be disturbed on appeal. We find that under the circumstances of this case, there was competent evidence upon which the jury could have based its verdict in favor of defendants. . . .

Judgment affirmed.

All the Justices concur, except JORDAN, P.J., and NICHOLS, J., who concur in the judgment only.

NOTES

1. Statutes and common law variously require that, for adverse possession to ripen into title, it must be "actual," "open," "visible," "notorious," "exclusive" or some combination of these elements. *Cheek*, for example, required Wainwright's possession to have been "public," "exclusive," "actual," and "notorious." There is considerable overlap between these terms and little constancy in their use from state to state or even within a single state. Is it possible that the terms do not express several discrete requirements but rather represent several ways of expressing a single requirement? If so, what is that single requirement? Is it that the claimant's use be sufficiently visible to put the true owner on notice of the adverse claim so that she can file suit before the statute of limitations runs? Or is it the less modest requirement suggested in *Cheek*—"use of the land to such an extent and in such a manner as to put the world on notice"?

Consider the observation of the Alaska Supreme Court in Peters v. Juneau-Douglas Girl Scout Council, 519 P.2d 826, 830–831 (1974): "[T]he main purpose of nearly all the requirements is essentially the same, that is, to put the record owner on notice of the existence of an adverse claimant. That purpose should, therefore, be kept in mind when deciding whether any given set of circumstances satisfies the exclusive use requirement. An owner would have no reason to believe that a person was making a claim of ownership inconsistent with his own if that person's possession was not exclusive, but in participation with the owner . . . . [T]he adverse claimant's acts must 'evince a purpose to exercise exclusive dominion over the property.' . . . a claimant's 'possession need not be absolutely exclusive; it need only be a type of possession which would characterize an owner's use.'"

2. *"Actual, Open and Notorious."* As a practical matter, how will landowner *A* discover that neighbor *B* is encroaching on his land? The requirement that the encroachment be actual, open, notorious and exclusive only goes part of the way toward communicating the fact of trespass, for although *A* may know that *B* is in possession of a piece of land, *A* will usually not know that title to that land is in him rather than in *B*. The true legal boundary between *A's* and *B's* parcels will typically not appear on the land at all, but only in the legal description appearing in the deed to each of their parcels, a description that will usually be phrased in terms of abstract and technical surveying references. (Indeed, it is *A's* and *B's* natural expectation that observable phenomena such as a stream or fence, rather than the technical, legal line, constitute their boundary that so often leads to loss of title by adverse possession.) To discover his parcel's true boundaries, *A* must employ a surveyor who will convert the abstract references in the deed to physical markings on the ground with stakes or pins. These survey markers will then become reliable physical evidence of the boundaries—so long as they are not moved by natural or unnatural forces.

Does this fact—that boundaries, unlike possession, are characteristically not actual, open and notorious, and are discoverable only through a survey or close examination of the ground for recently placed survey markers—suggest that adverse possession's visibility standard is unnecessarily high? If *A* or his surveyor traces *A's* boundaries once every limitations period, will not the scrutiny needed to establish the boundary line be sufficiently close to detect encroachments that fall short of the actual, open and notorious standard?

Is the common law's insistence on actual, highly visible possession really aimed at serving some policy other than quiet titles? Does *Cheek's* reference to "cultivation, tillage of the soil, planting and harvesting a crop" as "superior indicia of possession" indicate that the actual, open and notorious requirement is concerned not so much with giving the true owner notice as with rewarding those who are making what is perceived to be the more productive use of land, and that courts will leave title in the true owner only if the adverse possessor is not making a productive use? This emphasis on proof of productive activity might appear to connect with adverse possession's notice rationale at one point: for the true owner to have notice of the trespass, the adverse possessor must act as if he were the true owner of the land, and one thing a true owner does is to invest in his land's development and exploit its resources. But do true owners invariably behave this way? What of the investor who determines that it is best to postpone the land's development for five, ten, or twenty years? Is this any less—or more—a productive use of the land than its immediate exploitation?

Consider whether the following judicial approach properly deals with the productivity question: "The concept of adverse possession is an ancient and, perhaps, somewhat outdated one. It stems from a time when an ever-increasing use of land was to be, and was, encouraged. Today, however, faced, as we are, with problems of unchecked over-development, depletion of precious natural resources, and pollution of our environment, the policy reasons that once supported the idea of adverse possession may well be succumbing to new priorities. A man who owns some virgin land, who refrains from despoiling that land, even to the extent of erecting a fence to mark its boundaries, and who makes no greater use of that land than an occasional rejuvenating walk in the woods, can hardly be faulted in today's increasingly 'modern' world. Public policy and stability of our society, therefore, require strict compliance with the appropriate statutes by those seeking ownership through adverse possession." Meyer v. Law, 287 So.2d 37, 41 (1973).

3. Can a subterranean use ever be "actual, open and notorious"? In Marengo Cave Co. v. Ross, 212 Ind. 624, 10 N.E.2d 917 (1937), the adverse possessor had developed a cavern under his land and opened it to the paying public; the cavern extended under lands of the true owner, 700 feet from the cave opening. Asserting exclusive possession of the cave for twenty-one years after the true owner's purchase, the adverse possessor claimed fee title to all of the cave that lay under the true owner's land. The true owner instituted an action to quiet title.

The Indiana Supreme Court affirmed the lower court's judgment for the true owner on the ground that the adverse possession was not sufficiently open to put the true owner on notice. To begin with, "the possession of the appellant was not visible. No one could see below the earth's surface and determine that appellant was trespassing upon appellee's lands. This fact could not be determined by going into the cave. Only by a survey could this fact be made known." Further, "appellant's possession was not notorious. Not even appellant itself nor any of its remote grantors knew that any part of the 'Marengo Cave' extended beyond its own boundaries, and they at no time even down to the time appellee instituted this action made any claim to appellee's lands." 212 Ind. at 635–636, 10 N.E.2d at 922.

Was *Marengo* correctly decided? Was the presence of the cave entrance, 700 feet from the boundary, sufficient to put the true owner on notice that there might be an underground encroachment? Would it have been much more burdensome to conduct an underground survey than a surface survey? As between true owner and adverse possessor, which was making the more productive use of the underlying space? If the adverse possessor had been extracting coal from under the true owner's surface, would—and should—the court have been more willing to confer title by adverse possession?

4. Say that A purchases Blackacre under a deed that erroneously locates Blackacre's western boundary twenty feet into B's neighboring parcel, Whiteacre. Relying on the erroneous description, A builds a house that encroaches fifteen feet onto Whiteacre. If all the requirements for adverse possession have been met, to what part of Whiteacre will A gain title—the entire twenty-foot strip, or just the part on which the house is physically situated? Strictly applied, the actual, open and notorious requirement would appear to limit A's title to that part of Whiteacre on which the house physically rests since this is the only part that A has actually occupied. Does this result properly balance A's expectations against B's need for notice?

As a general rule, "where entry is made under an invalid deed or other written instrument which purports to transfer title to the possessor, actual possession of a small portion of the parcel described in the record of such instrument gives constructive possession of the rest of the parcel included within the description described in the deed without proof of such acts of user of the unoccupied part and without proof of fences or other visible boundaries. Actual physical possession of a part by the usual open and notorious acts of ownership under such an instrument establishes intent to control and claim the entire tract, and the bounds described in the instrument take the place of the fences and other visible boundaries which are necessary in the absence of such instrument. This is called constructive possession under 'color of title' of such part not actually occupied." 3 American Law of Property § 15.11 (A.J. Casner ed. 1952).

Is the rule a good one? As a practical matter, and from the perspective of true owner B, is it realistic to say that "the bounds described in the instrument take the place of the fences and other visible boundaries which are necessary in the absence of such instrument"? B, making a survey, would presumably discover the encroaching house; but neither a survey nor an inspection of the land would disclose the extent, beyond the house, of the boundary on which A relied. Is it five feet or fifty? Only an examination of A's deed will provide the answer. Is it appropriate to place this burden of inspection on B? Could A have avoided the problem by inspecting B's deed? Is it appropriate to place this burden of inspection on A?

Say that the description in A's deed was correct but that, relying on a faulty survey locating Blackacre's boundary twenty feet within Whiteacre, A builds a house encroaching fifteen feet onto Whiteacre. Does A constructively possess the remaining five feet?

5. *Exclusivity.* How "exclusive" must the adverse possession be? In Oliver v. Thomas, 173 Neb. 36, 112 N.W.2d 525 (1961), plaintiff had used the disputed parcel as pasture for his cattle, horses and mules "to the exclusion of all others for that purpose," while defendant concurrently used the parcel to hunt game. The court rejected plaintiff's claim of adverse possession on the ground that "title may not be granted or quieted on the theory of adverse possession in the

absence of proof of exclusive possession for a purpose to which the land is adapted for the statutory period of ten years;" while plaintiff had established "actual, open, exclusive, and continuous possession for use over the area as pasturage for more than ten years, he did not however establish exclusive possession against the other purpose for which it was adapted, that is hunting." 112 N.W.2d at 529.

What result would *Oliver* require if the only interruption of the adverse claimant's exclusive possession had been the true owner's flooding of the claimed land once or twice a year over an eighteen-year period? See Dzuris v. Kucharik, 164 Colo. 278, 434 P.2d 414 (1967) (claimant's possession not exclusive; title not gained by adverse possession).

ii. "Hostile" (and "Under Claim of Right"?)

JOINER v. JANSSEN

Supreme Court of Illinois, 1981.
85 Ill.2d 74, 51 Ill.Dec. 662, 421 N.E.2d 170.

UNDERWOOD, Justice:

Plaintiffs, Hobart and Catherine Joiner, brought suit to quiet title to a strip of land 14 feet wide adjacent to the east line of their residential lot in the village of Tiskilwa, claiming title by adverse possession under the 20-year statute of limitations (Ill.Rev.Stat.1977, ch. 83, par. 1). The rough diagram appearing below will assist in an understanding of the facts.

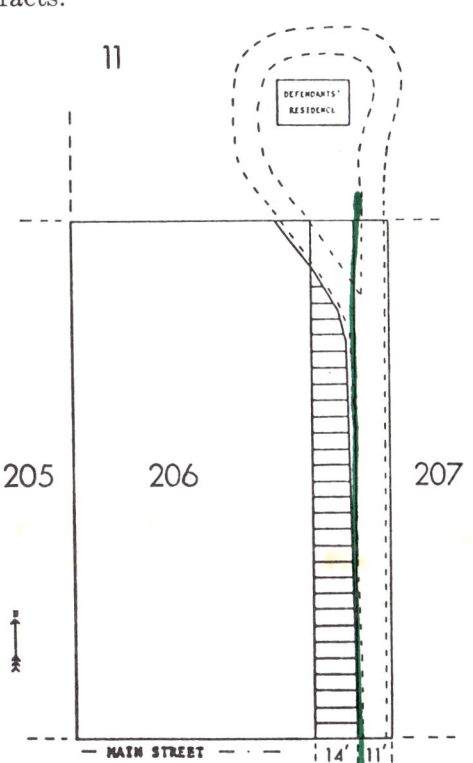

The portion of the east 14 feet of lot 206 claimed by the plaintiffs is marked with horizontal lines. The driveway which circles the defendants' house on lot 11 is marked with dotted lines.

The defendants, Alfred and Blanche Janssen, who live on lot 11 adjoining plaintiffs on the north, claimed title to the 14-foot strip under a warranty deed. The north and south driveway serving defendants' property is located principally on an 11-foot strip of land adjoining the 14-foot strip on the east. The driveway does, however, gradually veer over on the 14-foot strip as it nears the north lot line, and the west fork of the driveway actually crosses the northeastern corner of plaintiffs' lot. The disputed property is that which lies in the 14-foot strip and west of a line of trees and bushes forming both the western boundary of the driveway and the eastern boundary of that portion of the 14-foot strip claimed by plaintiffs. Following a bench trial in the circuit court of Bureau County the plaintiffs were found to have established title by adverse possession. The judgment divided the 14-foot strip between the plaintiffs and defendants according to a survey which approximated plaintiffs' claimed boundary line. The Appellate Court for the Third District reversed, one judge dissenting (84 Ill.App.3d 462, 39 Ill.Dec. 856, 405 N.E.2d 835), the majority stating that it was bound by a decision of the Second District, with the logic of which it expressed some "uneasiness" (84 Ill.App.3d 462, 465, 39 Ill.Dec. 856, 405 N.E.2d 835). The essence of that majority holding is that, because the strip of land in question was excluded in the legal description in plaintiffs' purchase contract and deed, plaintiffs were on notice that they did not have title to the land. Consequently, according to that holding, plaintiffs' possession could not be hostile in the sense necessary to establish adverse possession. We granted plaintiffs' petition for leave to appeal, and we now reverse.

The trial judge indicated that he found the plaintiffs and the witnesses on their behalf more credible, and our review of the record indicates his findings of fact are not against the manifest weight of the evidence. As our diagram indicates, three adjoining lots, 205, 206 and 207, are bordered by Main Street on the south. Lot 11 adjoins lots 206 and 207 on the north. Defendants obtained title to lot 11 and the east 14 feet of lot 206 in 1945 and have since resided in their home on lot 11. The west 11 feet of lot 207 over which defendants' driveway actually passes was never conveyed by the common grantor of all the lots in question. Quitclaim deeds to that 11-foot strip were obtained by defendants from surviving heirs of the common grantor, who died in the 1930's, and defendants now hold title to that 11-foot strip. The driveway from lot 11 was supposed to have been on the 14-foot strip of lot 206 rather than the 11-foot strip of lot 207, and thus all parties mistakenly considered the tree and bush line on the 14-foot strip as the boundary.

Plaintiffs purchased on contract in 1951 the east part of lot 205 and all of lot 206 except the east 14 feet and have since resided thereon. Plaintiffs' house is on lots 205 and 206 west of the 14-foot strip in question. In 1958 they paid the balance of the contract and obtained a deed to the property. At the time of their purchase plaintiffs were taken by the seller on to the lot, and it was then indicated to them that the east boundary was the tree and bush line adjoining the driveway. Plaintiffs believed this line to be the actual boundary, and went into possession of the property to that line. They did not erect a fence, but the evidence indicates that this tree and bush line formed a definitely ascertainable boundary. Plaintiffs mowed the grass on the 14-foot strip in question, raked leaves, planted and removed trees, bushes and flowers, gave away trees, bushes and flowers from the land as gifts, buried their pet dog on the strip when it died, shoveled snow from the walk in front of the strip, and generally maintained the property, thus indicating to neighbors and members of the community that they were in possession of and claiming ownership to the ground west of the line of trees and bushes.

Defendants seem to have acquiesced in this line as the boundary until 1977, when a survey made at their request revealed the mistake. Defendants thereafter claimed the land pursuant to their deed and attempted to go into possession by removing rocks and bushes from the tree and bush line. Plaintiffs then filed this action and obtained an injunction restraining defendants from entering the property west of the tree and bush line.

Although the trial court was satisfied that plaintiffs had established an adverse possessory title, the appellate court reversed because it regarded as dispositive and binding upon it the Second District Appellate Court panel's opinion in Hansen v. National Bank (1978), 59 Ill.App.3d 877, 17 Ill.Dec. 366, 376 N.E.2d 365. The *Hansen* court indicated that where the disputed land is specially excluded from the legal description the possessor is put on notice that he does not own the excluded land and therefore his subsequent possession of it cannot be adverse to the true owner, stating, "When an adverse claimant comes into possession of land thinking that he is not the record title holder, such possession lacks the requisite hostility for obtaining title by adverse possession." (59 Ill.App.3d 877, 879, 17 Ill. Dec. 366, 376 N.E.2d 365.) The quoted statement which the appellate panel in this case deemed binding and dispositive is simply not an accurate statement of the law, as is evident from the opinions of this court hereinafter cited.

The essence of the doctrine of adverse possession is the holding of the land adversely to the true titleholder. "A party, claiming title by adverse possession, always claims in derogation of the right of the real owner. He admits that the legal title is in another. He rests his claim not upon a title in himself, as the true owner, but upon holding adversely to the true owner for the period prescribed by the Statute of Limitations." (Mercer v. Wayman (1956), 9 Ill.2d 441, 445–46, 137 N.E.2d 815). To hold that because the possessor knows or should know that record title is in another precludes any possibility of the possessor's title being adverse is the antithesis of the doctrine of adverse possession as it has existed in this State. The possessor's good faith in claiming title is, of course, required by the statutory provisions relating to possession for seven years under color of title (Ill. Rev.Stat.1977, ch. 83, pars. 6, 7); it is not relevant under the 20-year doctrine (Ill.Rev.Stat.1977, ch. 83, par. 1).

What is essential in order to establish title under the 20-year adverse-possession doctrine incorporated in section 1 of the Limitations Act (Ill.Rev.Stat.1977, ch. 83, par. 1) is that there must be 20 years' concurrent existence of the five elements: (1) continuous, (2) hostile or adverse, (3) actual, (4) open, notorious, and exclusive possession of the premises, (5) under claim of title inconsistent with that of the true owner. Presumptions are in favor of the title owner, and the burden of proof upon the adverse possessor requires that each element be proved by clear and unequivocal evidence. The incidents of that possession determine its character. The "hostile" nature of the possession does not imply actual ill will, but only the assertion of ownership incompatible with that of the true owner and all others. "Where there has been an actual, visible and exclusive possession for twenty years it is not essential to the bar of the Statute of Limitations that there should have been any muniment of title or any oral declaration of claim of title, but it is sufficient if the proof shows that the party in possession has acted so as to clearly indicate that he did claim title. 'No mere words could more satisfactorily assert that the defendant claimed title than its continued exercise of acts of ownership over the property for a period of twenty years does. Using and controlling property as owner is the ordinary mode of asserting claim of title, and, indeed, is the only proof of which a claim of title to a very large proportion of property is susceptible.' [Citations.] . . . Such improvements or acts of dominion over the land as will indicate to persons residing in the immediate neighborhood who has the exclusive management and control of the land are sufficient to constitute possession. [Citations.]" Augustus v. Lydig (1933), 353 Ill. 215, 221–22, 187 N.E. 278.

Since the claim to ownership need not be spoken or supported by title documents, and one's actions can adequately convey the intent to claim title adversely to all the world including the titleholder, it is apparent that what the property description in a deed held by the adverse possessor excludes or includes is irrelevant to the adverse-possession issues.

As we earlier noted, the possession forming the claimed ownership in the present case was based upon the mistaken belief of the parties that the boundary was the tree and bush line. In these circumstances some jurisdictions have applied a subjective test, holding that the intention of the possessor is the controlling factor in determining whether possession to a mistaken boundary is hostile. Thus, if a landowner through mistake or ignorance takes possession to a boundary beyond the true line intending only to claim to the true line and not intending to claim the additional land if it should be ascertained that the boundary is not as he thought it, then such possession is not adverse or hostile. Elsewhere, including Illinois, occupancy to a visible and ascertained boundary for the statutory period is deemed the controlling feature in determining hostility in mistaken-boundary cases. The difficulty with the subjective test is that it affords no protection to the landowner who innocently and mistakenly occupies and improves land beyond his boundaries. He can never acquire title thereto. Conversely, he who deliberately sets out to steal adjacent land may succeed. Consequently, "[i]n a growing number of jurisdictions occupancy to a visible and ascertained boundary for the statutory period is deemed the controlling feature in determining hostility in mistaken boundary-line cases. Thus, it is held with increasing frequency that an open, notorious, and hostile possession of property for the statutory limitation period is sufficient for the acquisition of title by adverse possession, and the fact that the possession was taken under mistake or ignorance as to boundary lines is immaterial." 3 Am.Jur.2d Adverse Possession sec. 39, at 125–26 (1962).

In a case where an adverse possessor is claiming to a mistaken or disputed boundary he bears the burden of establishing by clear and convincing proof the location of the boundary. "The proof must be such as to establish with reasonable certainty the location of the boundaries of the tract to which the five elements of adverse possession are applied and all of the elements must extend to the tract so claimed. While it is not necessary that the land should be enclosed by a fence, the boundaries must be susceptible of specific and definite location." (Schwartz v. Piper (1954), 4 Ill.2d 488, 493, 122 N.E.2d 535.) Plaintiffs here have proved the existence of their claimed boundary line, supporting the survey by testimony and documentary evidence. Defendants argue that plaintiffs have not met the 20-year test since plaintiffs' deed to their property was not recorded until 1958 and they brought suit in 1977. As we have noted, however, possession is the important feature in adverse possession, not the date of a deed or other muniment of title. It is clear that the plaintiffs went into possession of their property, including the strip west of the tree and bush line, in 1951, when they acquired equitable title under the contract of purchase.

For the reasons stated, the judgment of the appellate court is reversed and the judgment of the circuit court affirmed.

Appellate court reversed; circuit court affirmed.

NOTES

1. Why do you suppose Illinois varies the limitations period depending on the basis of the adverse possessor's claim—seven years if the claim is under color of title, twenty years if the claim is not?

Would the Janssens have received notice of the Joiners' claim any earlier or more clearly if the Joiners had possessed the fourteen-foot strip under color of title? Would the Joiners have behaved any differently? Should the seven-year color of title statute be applied across the board to cases involving boundary disputes in which one neighbor has relied on an erroneous deed description, and to title disputes between grantor and grantee under a formally defective deed?

Among the reasons given for Illinois' seven-year statute is that it "provided for the exigencies of settlers, in quieting possession and protecting titles, either from patentees, or under tax or execution sales." Unable to meet the technical requirements of the existing statute, a settler "was left exposed for twenty years to litigation and the loss, not only of his possession and title, but for all his labor and improvements. This state of things greatly retarded the settlement, improvement and development of the agricultural interests of the State, and more particularly, in the district for military bounty lands. Viewing thus the provisions of the existing laws, and the evil, we may more readily comprehend the true spirit of the proposed remedy in the act of 1839." Woodward v. Blanchard, 16 Ill. 424, 428 (1855).

Does the "true spirit" of the seven-year statute require that forged deeds be treated as color of title? In Bergesen v. Clauss, 15 Ill.2d 337, 343–344, 155 N.E.2d 20, 23 (1958), the Illinois Supreme Court faced the question for the first time, and answered in the affirmative: "[A] forged deed cannot itself ever be anything but a forged deed. It cannot ever convey title. It can, however, as a color of title, constitute one step needed as a condition precedent for the acquisition of title by reason of the operation of § 6 of the Limitations Act—a result that cannot be reached by a forged deed alone." The *Bergesen* court added that, for a forged deed to constitute color of title, it must have been taken in good faith, in the belief that it was genuine. Would Joiner v. Janssen let an adverse possessor, who holds under a deed that she knows to have been forged, acquire title under the twenty-year statute?

2. *"Hostile."* Almost all states require that for possession to ripen into title it must be hostile, and virtually all take hostility to mean that possession must be adverse, rather than subordinate, to the true owner's title; it must be without, rather than with, the true owner's permission. Hostility does not require that possession be taken in the spirit of conquest, nor does it require animus on the part of the adverse possessor.

Kansas departs from this general pattern by focusing on the claimant's mental state. Kan.Stat.Ann. 60–503 (1976) requires possession "either under a claim knowingly adverse or under a belief of ownership." According to a commentator on the statute, "In the language of the statute 'belief of ownership' has been substituted for the common law element of 'hostile' holding. It may be assumed the change will make it more difficult to challenge the character of the holding, belief being a state of mind whereas hostile holding involves a state of intent, normally evidenced by overt acts or statements in respect to such holding. . . . Belief of ownership as a substitute for 'hostile' holding is not without limitation. In cases where there has been an admission or recognition of doubt or uncertainty as to the true boundary line the requisite 'belief of ownership' does not exist under the statute. Further, it must be recognized that in cases where possession has been 'under a claim knowingly adverse' hostility remains an essential element. . . ." Commentary, Kan.Civ. Proc.Code Ann. § 60–503 (1981). See generally Stark v. Stanhope, 206 Kan. 428, 480 P.2d 72 (1971).

Is the Kansas rule preferable to the general rule in any respect?

3. *"Claim of Right."* Some courts and legislatures require that possession not only be hostile, but also that it be accompanied by a "claim of right," "claim of title," or "color of title." The requirement, which enjoyed its greatest popularity in the first quarter of the nineteenth century, has been widely discarded or diluted today. Most states that employ the term today mean by it "nothing more than the intention of the disseisor to appropriate and use the land as his own to the exclusion of all others. To make a disseisin it is not necessary that the disseisor should enter under color of title, or should either believe or assert that he had a right to enter. It is only necessary that he enter and take possession of the lands as if they were his own, and with the intention of holding for himself to the exclusion of all others." Carpenter v. Coles, 75 Minn. 9, 77 N.W. 424 (1898). On the origins of the requirement, see Bordwell, Disseisin and Adverse Possession, 33 Yale L.J. 141 (1923).

What justification is there for a claim of right requirement, however loosely formulated? Can a squatter who occupies without claim, color or even mistake of title ever acquire title by adverse possession in a state that requires possession under claim of right? Does the claim of right requirement encourage or discourage the productive use of land? See generally, Helmholz, Adverse Possession and Subjective Intent, 61 Wash.U.L.Q. 331 (1983).

4. *Taxpaying as a Requirement of Adverse Possession.* Several states, primarily in the West, Southwest and Midwest, require that for the adverse possessor to gain title she must have paid taxes on the occupied parcel throughout the limitations period. A few states, like California, make taxpaying a categorical requirement. West's Ann.Cal.Civ.Proc.Code § 325. Others require tax payments only in special circumstances—if the parcel is claimed under an abbreviated limitations period, Ariz.Rev.Stat. §§ 12–524, 12–525 (1982), or is claimed other than in a boundary dispute, Minn.Stat.Ann. § 541.02 (1982 Supp.).

What rationale or rationales underlie the taxpaying requirement? An early Texas decision offers three: "It is not very clear why the legislature made the payment of taxes necessary in order to sustain the defense of limitation based on five years' adverse possession under a recorded deed. It may have been, to this extent, to require evidence of good faith on the part of the occupant, to secure to the state and its municipal subdivisions the payment of taxes due on the land, or to give further notice of the adverse claim and of the time it would mature into title, if possession be not interrupted, than afforded even by adverse possession under a recorded deed." Dutton v. Thompson, 85 Tex. 115, 119, 19 S.W. 1026, 1028 (1892).

It was, apparently, the nineteenth-century lobbying efforts of large landowners—of whom the railroads were the largest—that led to enactment of the taxpaying requirement. The railroads were primarily concerned that the vast, undeveloped and unoccupied tracts given to them by the federal government would over time be lost by adverse possession to the ever present and perennially troublesome squatters. Although "color of title" and "claim of right" requirements went far to protect these landowners from squatters' claims, a taxpaying requirement was even more effective in flushing out adverse claimants who were paying taxes, and in excluding squatters who were not. See generally, L. Friedman, A History of American Law 360–361 (1973). What impact does the taxpaying requirement have on claims in the three other recurrent adverse possession contexts: possession under a defective deed, possession under a faulty deed description and possession under a faulty survey?

iii. "Continuous"

HOWARD v. KUNTO

Court of Appeals of Washington, 1970.
3 Wn.App. 393, 477 P.2d 210.

PEARSON, Judge.

Land surveying is an ancient art but not one free of the errors that often creep into the affairs of men. In this case, we are presented with the question of what happens when the descriptions in deeds do not fit the land the deed holders are occupying. Defendants appeal from a decree quieting title in the plaintiffs of a tract of land on the shore of Hood Canal in Mason County.

At least as long ago as 1932 the record tells us that one McCall resided in the house now occupied by the appellant-defendants, Kunto. McCall had a deed that described a 50-foot-wide parcel on the shore of Hood Canal. The error that brings this case before us is that the 50 feet described in the deed is not the same 50 feet upon which McCall's house stood. Rather, the described land is an adjacent 50-foot lot directly west of that upon which the house stood. In other words, McCall's house stood on one lot and his deed described the adjacent lot. Several property owners to the west of defendants, not parties to this action, are similarly situated.

Over the years since 1946, several conveyances occurred, using the same legal description and accompanied by a transfer of possession to the succeeding occupants. The Kuntos' immediate predecessors in interest, Millers, desired to build a dock. To this end, they had a survey performed which indicated that the deed description and the physical occupation were in conformity. Several boundary stakes were placed as a result of this survey and the dock was constructed, as well as other improvements. The house as well as the others in the area continued to be used as summer recreational retreats.

The Kuntos then took possession of the disputed property under a deed from the Millers in 1959. In 1960 the respondent-plaintiffs, Howard, who held land east of that of the Kuntos, determined to convey an undivided one-half interest in their land to the Yearlys. To this end, they undertook to have a survey of the entire area made. After expending considerable effort, the surveyor retained by the Howards discovered that according to the government survey, the deed descriptions and the land occupancy of the parties did not coincide. Between the Howards and the Kuntos lay the Moyers' property. When the Howards' survey was completed, they discovered that they were the record owners of the land occupied by the Moyers and that the Moyers held record title to the land occupied by the Kuntos. Howard approached Moyer and in return for a conveyance of the land upon which the Moyers' house stood, Moyer conveyed to the Howards record title to the land upon which the Kunto house stood. Until plaintiffs Howard obtained the conveyance from Moyer in April, 1960, neither Moyer nor any of his predecessors ever asserted any right to ownership of the property actually being possessed by Kunto and his predecessors. This action was then instituted to quiet title in the Howards and Yearlys. The Kuntos appeal from a trial court decision granting this remedy.

At the time this action was commenced on August 19, 1960, defendants had been in occupancy of the disputed property less than a year. The trial court's reason for denying their claim of adverse possession is succinctly stated in its memorandum opinion: "In this instance, defendants have failed to prove, by a preponderance of the evidence, a continuity of possession or estate to permit tacking of the adverse possession of defendants to the possession of their predecessors."

Finding of fact 6, which is challenged by defendants, incorporates the above concept and additionally finds defendant's possession not to have been "continuous" because it involved only "summer occupancy."

Two issues are presented by this appeal:

(1) Is a claim of adverse possession defeated because the physical use of the premises is restricted to summer occupancy?

(2) May a person who receives record title to tract A under the mistaken belief that he has title to tract B (immediately contiguous to

tract A) and who subsequently occupies tract B, for the purpose of establishing title to tract B by adverse possession, use the periods of possession of tract B by his immediate predecessors who also had record title to tract A?

In approaching both of these questions, we point out that the evidence, largely undisputed in any material sense, established that defendant or his immediate predecessors did occupy the premises, which we have called tract B, as though it was their own for far more than the 10 years as prescribed in RCW 4.16.020.[5]

We also point out that finding of fact 6 is not challenged for its factual determinations but for the conclusions contained therein to the effect that the continuity of possession may not be established by summer occupancy, and that a predecessor's possession may not be tacked because a legal "claim of right" did not exist under the circumstances.

We start with the oft-quoted rule that:

[T]o constitute adverse possession, there must be actual possession which is *uninterrupted*, open and notorious, hostile and exclusive, and under a *claim of right* made in good faith for the statutory period.

(Italics ours.)

We reject the conclusion that summer occupancy only of a summer beach home destroys the continuity of possession required by the statute. It has become firmly established that the requisite possession requires such possession and dominion "as ordinarily marks the conduct of owners in general in holding, managing, and caring for property of like nature and condition." Whalen v. Smith, 183 Iowa 949, 953, 167 N.W. 646, 647 (1918).

We hold that occupancy of tract B during the summer months for more than the 10-year period by defendant and his predecessors, together with the continued existence of the improvements on the land and beach area, constituted "uninterrupted" possession within this rule. To hold otherwise is to completely ignore the nature and condition of the property.

We find such rule fully consonant with the legal writers on the subject. In F. Clark, Law of Surveying and Boundaries, § 561 (3d ed. 1959) at 565: "Continuity of possession may be established although

---

5. This statute provides:

"4.16.020 Actions to be commenced within ten years. The period prescribed in RCW 4.16.010 for the commencement of actions shall be as follows:

"Within ten years;

"Actions for the recovery of real property, or for the recovery of the possession thereof; and no action shall be maintained for such recovery unless it appears that the plaintiff, his ancestor, predecessor or grantor was seized or possessed of the premises in question within ten years before the commencement of the action."

the land is used regularly for only a certain period each year." Further, at 566:

> This rule [which permits tacking] is one of substance and not of absolute mathematical continuity, provided there is no break so as to sever two possessions. It is not necessary that the occupant should be actually upon the premises continually. If the land is occupied during the period of time during the year it is capable of use, there is sufficient continuity.

We now reach the question of tacking. The precise issue before us is novel in that none of the property occupied by defendant or his predecessors coincided with the property described in their deeds, but was contiguous.

In the typical case, which has been subject to much litigation, the party seeking to establish title by adverse possession claims *more* land than that described in the deed. In such cases it is clear that tacking is permitted.

In Buchanan v. Cassell, 53 Wash.2d 611, 614, 335 P.2d 600, 602 (1959) the Supreme Court stated:

> This state follows the rule that a purchaser may tack the adverse use of its predecessor in interest to that of his own where the land was intended to be included in the deed between them, but was mistakenly omitted from the description.

The general statement which appears in many of the cases is that tacking of adverse possession is permitted if the successive occupants are in "privity." The deed running between the parties purporting to transfer the land possessed traditionally furnishes the privity of estate which connects the possession of the successive occupants. Plaintiff contends, and the trial court ruled, that where the deed does not describe *any* of the land which was occupied, the actual transfer of possession is insufficient to establish privity.

To assess the cogency of this argument and ruling, we must turn to the historical reasons for requiring privity as a necessary prerequisite to tacking the possession of several occupants. Very few, if any, of the reasons appear in the cases, nor do the cases analyze the relationships that must exist between successive possessors for tacking to be allowed.

The requirement of privity had its roots in the notion that a succession of trespasses, even though there was no appreciable interval between them, should not, in equity, be allowed to defeat the record title. The "claim of right," "color of title" requirement of the statutes and cases was probably derived from the early American belief that the squatter should not be able to profit by his trespass.

However, it appears to this court that there is a substantial difference between the squatter or trespasser and the property purchaser, who along with several of his neighbors, as a result of an inaccurate survey or subdivision, occupies and improves property exactly 50 feet to the east of that which a survey some 30 years later demonstrates that they in fact own. It seems to us that there is also a strong public policy favoring early certainty as to the location of land ownership which enters into a proper interpretation of privity.

On the irregular perimeters of Puget Sound exact determination of land locations and boundaries is difficult and expensive. This difficulty is convincingly demonstrated in this case by the problems plaintiff's engineer encountered in attempting to locate the corners. It cannot be expected that every purchaser will or should engage a surveyor to ascertain that the beach home he is purchasing lies within the boundaries described in his deed. Such a practice is neither reasonable nor customary. Of course, 50-foot errors in descriptions are devastating where a group of adjacent owners each hold 50 feet of waterfront property.

The technical requirement of "privity" should not, we think, be used to upset the long periods of occupancy of those who in good faith received an erroneous deed description. Their "claim of right" is no less persuasive than the purchaser who believes he is purchasing *more* land than his deed described.

In the final analysis, however, we believe the requirement of "privity" is no more than judicial recognition of the need for some reasonable connection between successive occupants of real property so as to raise their claim of right above the status of the wrongdoer or the trespasser. We think such reasonable connection exists in this case.

Where, as here, several successive purchasers received record title to tract A under the mistaken belief that they were acquiring tract B, immediately contiguous thereto, and where possession of tract B is transferred and occupied in a continuous manner for more than 10 years by successive occupants, we hold there is sufficient privity of estate to permit tacking and thus establish adverse possession as a matter of law.

We see no reason in law or in equity for differentiating this case from Faubion v. Elder, 49 Wash.2d 300, 301 P.2d 153 (1956) where the appellants were claiming *more* land than their deed described and where successive periods of occupation were allowed to be united to each other to make up the time of adverse holding. This application of the privity requirement should particularly pertain where the holder of record title to tract B acquired the same with knowledge of the discrepancy.

Judgment is reversed with directions to dismiss plaintiffs' action and to enter a decree quieting defendants' title to the disputed tract of land in accordance with the prayer of their cross-complaint.

ARMSTRONG, P.J., and PETRIE, J., concur.

NOTES

1. What purposes are served by the requirement that the claimant's possession be continuous? One obvious purpose is practical: if the adverse possession is not continuous throughout the limitations period, the true owner who inspects his boundaries only once every limitations period may not be aware of the adverse claim. Another purpose is technical: since the adverse claimant's rights subsist only so long as he is in possession, abandonment will terminate his rights and revest constructive possession in the true owner, thus ending the true owner's cause of action. Should it make a difference for practical purposes, technical purposes, or both, whether the discontinuity in the claimant's possession was caused by the true owner's interference, by interference from an unrelated third party, or by the claimant's own voluntary act?

Did Howard v. Kunto apply the continuity requirement correctly? For practical purposes? For technical purposes? Would, or should, the result in the case have differed if, during the winter months, a trespasser had lived in the house that the adverse possessor occupied during the summer months? Should the answer turn on whether the adverse possessor would have had the right to exclude the trespasser?

2. *Tacking.* Tacking recognizes that land will rarely be held by the same person for the entire limitations period and provides that successors can add the original adverse possessor's holding period to their own for purposes of the statute of limitations. If the succeeding claimant did not take possession consensually, but rather ousted the former claimant or simply took possession after the former claimant's departure, she will not be allowed to tack her predecessor's holding period to her own, and the limitations period will start anew. By allowing tacking between successors under written instruments, but not between occupants under successive dispossessions, courts seek to honor occupants' reasonable expectations without disserving true owners' interests in having notice of their claims.

What if the succeeding claimant, like her predecessor, claims and possesses more land than is described in her deed? As stated in *Kunto*, most courts today allow tacking in this context, under an expectations rationale. Was *Kunto* correct to expand the rule still further to allow tacking when *none* of the land occupied by the adverse possessor coincided with the parcel described in her deed? Does the dilution, and in some places disappearance, of the "claim of right" requirement suggest that tacking's privity requirement should also be diluted or dropped entirely? Should the answer depend on whether adverse possession is viewed as a device for protecting the expectations of possessors or as a device for encouraging surveillance by true owners?

3. The limitations period for adverse possession varies significantly from state to state, with periods generally longer in the East and shorter in the West. Limitations periods can generally be grouped in multiples of five and seven. A substantial number of eastern states prescribe a twenty-year period, and a substantial number of midwestern and southern states split between fifteen- and ten-year periods. See 7 R. Powell, Real Property ¶ 1014[1] (1983). Ohio has a twenty-one year statute, Ohio Rev.Code § 2305.05 (1981), and Arkansas a seven-year statute, Ark.Stats. § 37–101 (1962). Some states prescribe different periods depending on whether the adverse possessor has color of title or has paid taxes throughout the limitations period.

4. *Adverse Possession Against the Government.* Some statutes do not allow title to pass by adverse possession against governmental owners on the theory that "time does not run against the King." See, for example, 48 U.S.C.A. § 1489 (1952) ("No prescription or statute of limitations shall run, or continue to run, against the title of the United States to lands in any territory or possession or place or territory under the jurisdiction or control of the United States; and no title to any such lands of the United States or any right therein shall be acquired by adverse possession or prescription, or otherwise than by conveyance from the United States"). Other statutes allow time to run against the sovereign, but more slowly than as against private landowners, some states doubling the private limitations period, others lengthening it in multiples of fives and sevens. See, for example, N.C.Gen.Stat. § 1–35 (1969) (standard seven- and twenty-year periods for adverse possession with and without color of title extended to twenty-one and thirty years, respectively.)

What reason underlies this greater solicitude for governmental landowners? Is government any less able to watch over its boundaries than private landowners? Approximately 40% of all land in the United States is government-owned—33% by the federal government, 7% by state and local governments—and 95% of all land in the United States is essentially undeveloped, devoted to agricultural, forest, recreational, wildlife, national defense and wasteland uses. See Chantfort, Land for All Reasons, 3 Farmline 4 (1982). Will government's ability to identify and proceed against trespassers differ depending on the context of the trespass—whether, for example, the trespasser is occupying under a formally defective deed or is squatting without color of title?

In 1970 the Public Land Law Review Commission published its recommendation that "the doctrine of adverse possession be made applicable against the United States where land has been occupied in good faith." U.S. Public Land Law Review Commission, One Third of the Nation's Land 261 (U.S. Govt. Print. Off. 1970). Recognizing that the "principle that the United States cannot lose title to its lands by adverse possession by a private party is treated as axiomatic by the courts," the Commission observed that "private citizens do occupy public lands in technical trespass, but in good faith believe that the land is theirs. Often valuable improvements are placed upon such lands in ignorance of the Federal claim. Partly because of the protection the Government enjoys, including inapplicability of the doctrine of adverse possession, such occupancies, although known to the Government's agents, are sometimes permitted to exist until there is a Federal use for the lands. At other times they simply remain undiscovered until there is a Federal requirement for the lands." *Id.* at 262. For a sharp criticism of the Commission's recommendation, see Million, Adverse Possession Against the United States—A Treasure for Trespassers, 26 Ark.L.Rev. 467 (1973).

5. *Disabilities.* Should the true owner be protected from loss of title if, at some point during the adverse claimant's possession, the true owner was under a disability that may have prevented him from learning that he had a cause of action for trespass? An English statute, 21 Jac. 1, c. 16 (1623), provided that if the true owner was an infant, a married woman ("femme covert"), insane, imprisoned or "beyond the seas," at the time the cause of action first accrued, the limitations period would be extended to compensate for the disability. American legislation generally follows the pattern of the English statute but varies the definition of disability. Although infancy and insanity continue to be disabilities in America, the disability of coverture has been lifted as married women have become entitled to sue. Some, but not all, American statutes make imprisonment and absence from the country a disability. Other statutes use the general term, "legal disability," and leave it to the courts to determine what facts should constitute disability in any particular case.

States differ on other points as well. Some provide that the statute of limitations will not begin to run until the disability ends. See, for example, Ariz.Rev.Stat. § 12–528 (1982). Others toll the statute but prescribe a shortened limitations period within which the action must be brought once the disability is removed. See, for example, Iowa Code Ann. § 614.8 (1981). Others prescribe a maximum period beyond which the statute's period will not be extended even if the disability continues. See, for example, West's Fla.Stat.Ann. § 95.051 (1982). And while some states provide that, for the statute to be suspended, the disability must exist at the time the cause of action first accrued, others provide that intervening disabilities will correspondingly extend the limitations period.

What is the purpose of these disability provisions? Do they properly balance the true owner's interest in obtaining effective notice against the reasonable expectations of the adverse possessor? What effect do these rules have on certainty respecting titles and, consequently, upon the costs of land transfer?

6. *Personal Property: Transfer of Title Through Adverse Possession and Abandonment.* Time heals defects in title to personal

property as well as to real property. One who possesses a chattel unlawfully may acquire title to it through adverse possession once the limitations period has run against the true owner's action to recover the chattel. The doctrine of abandonment, though conceptually separate from adverse possession, also relies on elapsed time to transfer title to a chattel from true owner to possessor: the longer the true owner is out of possession, the more likely it is that a court will hold her to have abandoned the chattel, vesting title in the new possessor.

Adverse Possession. At least nominally, the requirements for acquiring personal property by adverse possession are identical to those for real property: "By analogy to adverse possession of real estate . . . possession of goods or chattels to be adverse possession for the applicable limitations period must be hostile, actual, visible, notorious, exclusive, continuous and under claim of ownership . . . if there is adverse possession for the required time, title to the property becomes thereby vested in and acquired by the possessor. . . ." Isham v. Cudlip, 33 Ill.App.2d 254, 268, 179 N.E.2d 25, 32 (1962).

Do the different characteristics of real and personal property dictate that the requirements for adverse possession be applied differentially? The New Jersey Supreme Court addressed that question in O'Keeffe v. Snyder, 83 N.J. 478, 416 A.2d 862 (1980). Plaintiff, the prominent artist, Georgia O'Keeffe, brought an action to recover possession of three paintings that had allegedly been stolen thirty years earlier and, through a series of transfers, had come into defendant's hands. Defendant responded that O'Keeffe's action was barred by New Jersey's six-year limitations period governing actions to recover personal property and that, consequently, he had gained title by adverse possession. The trial court gave summary judgment to defendant. The intermediate appellate court reversed and entered judgment for O'Keeffe on the ground that all the elements required for adverse possession had not been met. The New Jersey Supreme Court reversed and remanded for a complete hearing.

The principal disagreement between the supreme court and the two lower courts turned on whether the case should be controlled by the traditional requirement that the adverse possession be "visible, open and notorious," or whether a rule should be adopted "that is more responsive to the needs of the art world than the doctrine of adverse possession." 83 N.J. at 497, 416 A.2d at 872. The supreme court concluded that a new requirement was needed, and found it in the so-called "discovery rule": "in an appropriate case, a cause of action will not accrue until the injured party discovers, or by exercise of reasonable diligence and intelligence should have discovered, facts which form the basis of a cause of action." 83 N.J. at 491, 416 A.2d at 869. The advantage of the discovery rule over adverse possession's traditional elements seemed manifest: "if jewelry is stolen from a municipality in one county in New Jersey, it is unlikely that the owner would learn that someone is openly wearing that jewelry in another county or even in the same municipality. Open and visible possession of personal property, such as jewelry, may not be sufficient to put the original owner on actual or constructive notice of the identity of the possessor." 83 N.J. at 496, 416 A.2d at 871.

The court's prescription for owners of personal property was clear: "By diligently pursuing their goods, owners may prevent the statute of limitations from running. The meaning of due diligence will vary with the facts of each case, including the nature and value of the personal property. For example, with respect to jewelry of moderate value, it may be sufficient if the owner reports the theft to the police. With respect to art work of greater value, it may be reasonable to expect an owner to do more. In practice, our ruling should contribute to more careful practices concerning the purchase of art. The considerations are different with real estate, and there is no reason to disturb the application of the doctrine of adverse possession to real estate. Real estate is fixed and cannot be moved or concealed. The owner of real property knows or should know where his property is located and reasonably can be expected to be aware of open, notorious, visible, hostile, continuous acts of possession on it." 83 N.J. at 499, 416 A.2d at 873.

Could the *O'Keeffe* court have reached the same result by a modest expansion of orthodox adverse possession rules? Many, if not most, states have shaped the traditional requirement of "open, visible and notorious" possession to meet the special circumstances of personal property: "The cause of action accrues only when the possession becomes clearly hostile to the rights of the owner, as when demand for return of the property is made and refused. Again, not only must the holding be adverse but it must also be open and notorious. While an innocent removal of the chattel from the locality or even from the state does not alone prevent the statute operating, simple morality requires that one who intentionally, by removal, concealment, or otherwise prevents the owner from ascertaining his property's whereabouts should not by such means defeat the latter's cause of action and acquire title to the withheld goods. While it is possible that a thief, or a purchaser from a thief, with knowledge may hold so openly and notoriously as to acquire title, secret rather than open holding will be presumed." R. Brown, The Law of Personal Property § 4.2. (W. Raushenbush 3d ed. 1975).

Abandonment. One who finds and takes possession of abandoned property will become its owner, with exclusive rights against both its former true owner and the rest of the world. What constitutes abandonment by the former owner? Abandonment is traditionally said to turn strictly on the former owner's intent: "Abandonment occurs when there is a 'giving up, a total desertion, and absolute relinquishment' of private goods by the former owner. It may arise when the owner with the specific intent of desertion and relinquishment casts away or leaves behind his property; or when after a casual and unintentional loss all purpose further to seek and reclaim the lost property is given up." R. Brown, The Law of Personal Property § 1.6 (W. Raushenbush 3d ed. 1975). Yet intent, particularly intent respecting conduct long since past, is virtually impossible to prove directly. As a consequence, courts accept longstanding nonuse by the former owner as almost irrebuttable evidence of intent to abandon.

How can someone coming upon an unclaimed chattel determine whether the chattel was "lost"—and thus subject to the paramount claim of the true owner—or "abandoned"—and thus hers to keep and do with as she wishes? One clue will doubtless be value. A valuable diamond ring can be presumed lost, while a stripped and rusting automobile might properly be assumed abandoned. Does the difference in value explain the difference in rules? Since the diamond ring continues to have value to its former owner (although not sufficient value for her to have effectively guarded against its loss), the finder should be entitled only to temporary possession, awaiting its reclamation by the former owner. By contrast, where the chattel has little or no value to its former owner, the finder who is willing to invest in its restoration should be encouraged to do so through such inducements as exclusive title.

3. THE IMPROVING TRESPASSER

SOMERVILLE v. JACOBS

Supreme Court of West Virginia, 1969.
153 W.Va. 613, 170 S.E.2d 805.

HAYMOND, President:

The plaintiffs, W.J. Somerville and Hazel M. Somerville, herein sometimes referred to as the plaintiffs, the owners of Lots 44, 45 and 46 in the Homeland Addition to the city of Parkersburg, in Wood County, believing that they were erecting a warehouse building on Lot 46 which they owned, mistakenly constructed the building on Lot 47 owned by the defendants, William L. Jacobs and Marjorie S. Jacobs, herein sometimes referred to as the defendants. Construction of the building was completed in January 1967 and by deed dated January 14, 1967 the Somervilles conveyed Lots 44, 45 and 46 to the plaintiffs Fred C. Engle and Jimmy C. Pappas who subsequently leased the building to the Parkersburg Coca-Cola Bottling Company, a corporation. Soon after the building was completed but not until then, the defendants learned that the building was on their property and claimed ownership of the building and its fixtures on the theory of annexation. The plaintiffs then instituted this proceeding for equitable relief in the Circuit Court of Wood County and in their complaint prayed, among other things, for judgment in favor of the

Somervilles for $20,500.00 as the value of the improvements made on Lot 47, or, in the alternative, that the defendants be ordered to convey their interest in Lot 47 to the Somervilles for a fair consideration. The Farmers Building and Loan Association, a corporation, the holder of a deed of trust lien upon the land of the defendants, was on motion permitted to intervene and be made a defendant in this proceeding. . . .

By final judgment rendered June 11, 1968, the circuit court required the defendants within 60 days to elect whether they would (1) retain the building and pay W.J. Somerville $17,500.00 or suffer judgment against themselves in his favor in that amount, or (2) convey title to Lot 47 of Homeland Addition to W.J. Somerville for the sum of $2,000.00 cash. From that judgment this Court granted an appeal and supersedeas upon application of the defendants on October 17, 1968. . . .

As previously indicated the material facts, which are not disputed, were stipulated and set forth in the agreed statement of the attorneys representing the parties, and the questions presented for decision are questions of law.

The stipulation concerning the facts is in this form:

"1. The plaintiffs, W.J. Somerville and Hazel M. Somerville, in mistaken reliance upon a surveyor's report and plat, constructed the building described in the Complaint upon Lot No. 47 of Homeland Addition to the City of Parkersburg, in Wood County, West Virginia, believing that they were constructing the building upon Lot No. 46 of said addition.

"2. Lot No. 47 was and still is owned by the defendants as joint tenants with the right of survivorship, title to said Lot No. 47 having been acquired by William L. Jacobs and Marjorie S. Jacobs by Deed dated February 21, 1966, and duly admitted to record in the Office of the County Clerk of Wood County, West Virginia, on March 14, 1966, as appears of record in Deed Book 513, at Page 317.

"3. The defendants were not aware of the fact that said building had been constructed on their property until after the completion of said building by the plaintiff, W.J. Somerville, its purchase by the plaintiffs, Fred C. Engle and Jimmy C. Pappas, and its occupancy as a tenant by the plaintiff corporation, Parkersburg Coca-Cola Bottling Company.

"4. The fair market value of said Lot No. 47 immediately prior to the erection of said building was $2,000.00.

"5. The fair market value of said Lot No. 47 immediately subsequent to and by reason of the erection of said building was $19,500.00.

"6. By deed dated January 14, 1967, the plaintiffs, W.J. Somerville and Hazel M. Somerville, who are husband and wife, conveyed to the plaintiffs, Fred C. Engle and Jimmy C. Pappas, Lots 44, 45 and 46 of said Homeland Addition under the mistaken belief that the warehouse building described in the complaint was situate on Lot 46, for a total purchase price of $19,500.00, and the plaintiffs Engle and Pappas paid the plaintiffs, W.J. Somerville and Hazel M. Somerville the said sum of $19,500.00 under the mistaken belief that said warehouse was situate on said Lot 46.

"7. The plaintiffs, Fred C. Engle and Jimmy C. Pappas, leased the said warehouse building to the plaintiff, Parkersburg Coca-Cola Bottling Company beginning as of January 1, 1967, and continuing up until the time of the filing of this action for a monthly rental of $250.00, that being the fair rental value of said warehouse building.

"8. Since the filing of the above styled action, the plaintiff, W.J. Somerville, has constructed on said Lot 46 a warehouse building identical with the one previously constructed by him on said Lot 47 and the plaintiff, Parkersburg Coca-Cola Bottling Company is now occupying said building as a tenant and paying to the plaintiffs, Fred C. Engle and Jimmy C. Pappas the sum of $250.00 as a monthly rental on said premises pursuant to the terms of the lease to which reference is hereinabove made."

The controlling question for decision is whether a court of equity can award compensation to an improver for improvements which he has placed upon land not owned by him, which, because of mistake, he had reason to believe he owned, which improvements were not known to the owner until after their completion and were not induced or permitted by such owner, who is not guilty of any fraud or inequitable conduct, and require the owner to pay the fair value of such improvements or, in the alternative, to convey the land so improved to the improver upon his payment to the owner of the fair value of the land less the value of the improvements.

Though there are numerous decisions by this Court relating to improvements to land, the precise question here involved is one of first impression in this jurisdiction. The statute dealing with allowance for improvements to real estate, Article 5, Chapter 55, Code, 1931, provides for allowance for improvements only to a defendant against whom a decree or judgment shall be rendered for land where no assessment of damages has been made and permits such defendant, at any time before the execution of a decree or judgment, to present a petition to the court rendering such decree or judgment praying that he may be allowed the fair and reasonable value of such improvements. That statute has no application to the facts of this case, and this case, for that reason, is not within the statute.

Though the precise question here involved has not been considered and determined in any prior decision of this Court, the question has been considered by appellate courts in other jurisdictions and though the cases are conflicting the decisions in some jurisdictions, upon particular facts, recognize and sustain the jurisdiction of a court of equity to award compensation to the improver to prevent unjust enrichment to the owner and in the alternative to require the owner to convey the land to the improver upon his payment to the owner of the fair value of the land less the improvements. . . .

In Section 625, Chapter 11, Volume 2, Tiffany Real Property, Third Edition, the text contains this language:

"Since the rule that erections or additions made by one who has no rights to land are fixtures, and therefore not removable by him, even though he made them in the belief that he was the owner of the land, is calculated to cause hardship to an innocent occupant of another's land, by giving the benefit of his labor and expenditures to the landowner, the courts of this country, without either imputing fraud or requiring proof of it, hold it inequitable to allow one to be enriched under such circumstances by the labor and expenditures of another who acted in good faith and in ignorance of any adverse claim or title. Applying this doctrine of 'unjust enrichment,' a court of equity will, on the principle that he who seeks equity must do equity, refuse its assistance to the rightful owner of land as against an occupant thereof unless he makes compensation for permanent and beneficial improvements, made by the latter without notice of the defect in his title.

"According to one line of decisions, the innocent occupant will be allowed compensation for such improvements upon a bill filed by him against the true owner for the purpose.

"Under other decisions relief of this character is accorded only in a proceeding instituted by the true owner, as an incident to the relief given him."

From the foregoing authorities it is manifest that equity has jurisdiction to, and will, grant relief to one who, through a reasonable mistake of fact and in good faith, places permanent improvements upon land of another, with reason to believe that the land so improved is that of the one who makes the improvements, and that the plaintiffs are entitled to the relief which they seek in this proceeding.

The undisputed facts, set forth in the agreed statement of counsel representing all parties, is that the plaintiff W.J. Somerville in placing the warehouse building upon Lot 47 entertained a reasonable belief based on the report of the surveyor that it was Lot 46, which he owned, and that the building was constructed by him because of a reasonable mistake of fact and in the good faith belief that he was constructing a building on his own property and he did not discover his mistake until after the building was completed. It is equally clear that the defendants who spent little if any time in the neighborhood were unaware of the construction of the building until after it was completed and were not at any time or in any way guilty of any fraud or inequitable conduct or of any act that would constitute an estoppel. In short, the narrow issue here is between two innocent parties and the solution of the question requires the application of principles of equity and fair dealing between them.

It is clear that the defendants claim the ownership of the building. Under the common law doctrine of annexation, the improvements passed to them as part of the land. This is conceded by the plaintiffs but they assert that the defendants can not keep and retain it without compensating them for the value of the improvements, and it is clear from the testimony of the defendant William L. Jacobs in his deposition that the defendants intend to keep and retain the improvements and refuse to compensate the plaintiffs for their value. The record does not disclose any express request by the plaintiffs for permission to remove the building from the premises if that could be done without its destruction, which is extremely doubtful as the building was constructed of solid concrete blocks on a concrete slab, and it is reasonably clear, from the claim of the defendants of their ownership of the building and their insistence that certain fixtures which have been removed from the building be replaced, that the defendants will not consent to the removal of the building even if that could be done.

In that situation if the defendants retain the building and refuse to pay any sum as compensation to the plaintiff W.J. Somerville they will be unjustly enriched in the amount of $17,500.00, the agreed value of the building, which is more than eight and one-half times the agreed $2,000.00 value of the lot of the defendants on which it is located, and by the retention of the building by the defendants the plaintiff W.J. Somerville will suffer a total loss of the amount of the value of the building. If, however, the defendants are unable or unwilling to pay for the building which they intend to keep but, in the alternative, would convey the lot upon which the building is constructed to the plaintiff W.J. Somerville upon payment of the sum of $2,000.00, the agreed value of the lot without the improvements, the plaintiffs would not lose the building and the defendants would suffer no financial loss because they would obtain payment for the agreed full value of the lot and the only hardship imposed upon the defendants, if this were required, would be to order them to do something which they are unwilling to do voluntarily. To compel the performance of such an act by litigants is not uncommon in litigation in which the rights of the parties are involved and are subject to determination by equitable principles. And the right to require the defendants to convey the lot to the plaintiff W.J. Somerville is recognized and sustained by numerous cases cited earlier in this opinion. Under the facts and circumstances of this case, if the defendants refuse and are not required to exercise their option either to pay W.J. Somerville the value of the improvements or to convey to him the lot on which they are located upon his payment of the agreed value, the defendants will be unduly and unjustly enriched at the expense of the plaintiff W.J. Somerville who will suffer the complete loss of the warehouse building which by bona fide mistake of fact he constructed upon the land of the defendants. Here, in that situation, to use the language of the Supreme Court of Michigan in Hardy v. Burroughs, 251 Mich. 578, 232 N.W. 200, "It is not equitable . . .

that defendants profit by plaintiffs' innocent mistake, that defendants take all and plaintiffs nothing."

To prevent such unjust enrichment of the defendants, and to do equity between the parties, this Court holds that an improver of land owned by another, who through a reasonable mistake of fact and in good faith erects a building entirely upon the land of the owner, with reasonable belief that such land was owned by the improver, is entitled to recover the value of the improvements from the landowner and to a lien upon such property which may be sold to enforce the payment of such lien, or, in the alternative, to purchase the land so improved upon payment to the landowner of the value of the land less the improvements and such landowner, even though free from any inequitable conduct in connection with the construction of the building upon his land, who, however, retains but refuses to pay for the improvements, must, within a reasonable time, either pay the improver the amount by which the value of his land has been improved or convey such land to the improver upon the payment by the improver to the landowner of the value of the land without the improvements. . . .

The judgment of the Circuit Court of Wood County is affirmed.

Affirmed.

CAPLAN, Judge, dissenting:

Respectfully, but firmly, I dissent from the decision of the majority in this case. Although the majority expresses a view which it says would result in equitable treatment for both parties, I am of the opinion that such view is clearly contrary to law and to the principles of equity and that such holding, if carried into effect, will establish a dangerous precedent. . . .

I am aware of the apparent alarmist posture of my statements asserting that the adoption of the majority view will establish a dangerous precedent. Nonetheless, I believe just that and feel that my apprehension is justified. On the basis of unjust enrichment and equity, the majority has decided that the errant party who, without improper design, has encroached upon an innocent owner's property is entitled to equitable treatment. That is, that he should be made whole. How is this accomplished? It is accomplished by requiring the owner of the property to buy the building erroneously constructed on his property or by forcing (by court edict) such owner to sell his property for an amount to be determined by the court.

What of the property owner's right? The solution offered by the majority is designed to favor the plaintiff, the only party who had a duty to determine which lot was the proper one and who made a mistake. The defendants in this case, the owners of the property, had no duty to perform and were not parties to the mistake. Does equity protect only the errant and ignore the faultless? Certainly not.

It is not unusual for a property owner to have long range plans for his property. He should be permitted to feel secure in the ownership of such property by virtue of placing his deed therefor on record. He should be permitted to feel secure in his future plans for such property. However, if the decision expressed in the majority opinion is effectuated then security of ownership in property becomes a fleeting thing. It is very likely that a property owner in the circumstances of the instant case either cannot readily afford the building mistakenly built on his land or that such building does not suit his purpose. Having been entirely without fault, he should not be forced to purchase the building.

In my opinion for the court to permit the plaintiff to force the defendants to sell their property contrary to their wishes is unthinkable and unpardonable. This is nothing less than condemnation of private property by private parties for private use. Condemnation of property (eminent domain) is reserved for government or such entities as may be designated by the legislature. Under no theory of law or equity should an individual be permitted to acquire property by condemnation. The majority would allow just that.

I am aware of the doctrine that equity frowns on unjust enrichment. However, contrary to the view expressed by the majority, I am of the opinion that the circumstances of this case do not warrant the application of such doctrine. It clearly is the accepted law that as between two parties in the circumstances of this case he who made the mistake must suffer the hardship rather than he who was without fault.

I would reverse the judgment of the Circuit Court of Wood County and remand the case to that court with directions that the trial court give the defendant, Jacobs, the party without fault, the election of purchasing the building, of selling the property, *or* of requiring the plaintiff to remove the building from defendant's property.

I am authorized to say that Judge BERRY concurs in the views expressed in this dissenting opinion.

NOTES

1. Is the rule of Somerville v. Jacobs fair? Efficient? As between improving trespasser and true owner, who is better placed to insure against or avoid the kind of error that occurred there? If it was the surveyor's error that caused the Somervilles' mistake, and if the surveyor had failed to exercise reasonable care in preparing his report and plat, the Somervilles could have proceeded against him on a negligence theory. And, regardless of negligence, the Somervilles could have purchased a guaranteed survey under which they would have been held harmless by proceeding against the surveyor on his guarantee. Does *Somerville* encourage lackadaisical reliance on low-cost and sloppy surveys? What, if anything, could the Jacobs have done to protect themselves? Does *Somerville* heighten the landown-

er's duty, implicit in adverse possession rules, to inspect his boundaries once during every limitations period?

Should the *Somerville* rule be applied in favor of trespassers who occupy and improve land under color of title, such as a forged deed? Although no amount of care can eliminate the risk of a forged deed, it is customary for title insurance policies to insure against this risk and to compensate the insured at least for the amount he paid for the land. Is one effect of *Somerville* to discourage land developers from purchasing extra title insurance coverage to protect themselves against the loss of their improvements?

Do you agree with Judge Caplan's observation in dissent that, "for the court to permit the plaintiff to force the defendants to sell their property contrary to their wishes . . . is nothing less than condemnation of private property by private parties for private use"? Would a finding that there was no trespass in the circumstances have deprived defendants of their property *without* compensation? Would the remedy proposed by Caplan—giving Jacobs "the election of purchasing the building, of selling the property, *or* of requiring the plaintiff to remove the building from defendant's property—" stack the deck too heavily in Jacobs' favor? What do you expect the Somerville-Jacobs negotiations following such an order would look like?

2. "As stated by the American authorities the common law rule is that the improvements, whether made in good or bad faith, belong to the owner of the land. If the owner sues for rents and profits the value of the improvements can be set off against them. In equity the good faith improver will be protected if the owner stood by and allowed him to improve knowing of his mistake. There is some authority to the effect that restitution will be allowed the good faith improver by way of defense in an equitable action brought by the owner, as where he brings an action to quiet title, on the principle that he who seeks equity must do equity. And there are, finally, a few cases giving the improver an independent equitable action of his own for restitution. However, the majority of the cases recognize no such equitable action or defense." Merryman, Improving the Lot of the Trespassing Improver, 11 Stan.L.Rev. 456, 465–66 (1959).

Professor Merryman traces the common law rule to the "complex, subtle and somewhat fluid" Roman law on the subject: "A bad faith trespasser loses everything, but a good faith improver may recover his materials if they are ever severed. If the owner of the land brings an action for possession the good faith improver can recover the cost of materials and labor or retain possession if the owner refuses to pay." Although the common law rules are "directly traceable to the Roman law," the "story is one of degeneration rather than development. . . . The numerous refinements of the *Digest* and the commentators have vanished. We are left with a rule whose source is not the law of England, which it purports to represent, but the law of Rome, which it disfigures." 11 Stan.L.Rev. 458–461.

3. Statutes in an overwhelming majority of states have significantly modified the common law and equitable rules. Most of these statutes follow the approach taken in *Somerville,* entitling the true owner of the land to elect between paying for the improvement and selling the land to the trespasser. Most also require that the trespasser enter under color of title and act in good faith. See, e.g., Utah Code Ann.1953, 57-6-1—57-6-3.

4. *Personal Property: Accession.* Say that the Somervilles had found a stack of oak logs on lot 47; believing that the logs belonged to them—although in fact they belonged to the Jacobs—the Somervilles cut and fashioned the logs into wine casks. Who owns the casks—the Jacobs, who unwittingly contributed the raw material, or the Somervilles, who innocently contributed the labor? The common law of accession generally makes the answer turn on the degree to which the innocent converter has transformed the raw materials and increased their value: the greater the degree, the more likely it is that the converter will be given title. For example, in Wetherbee v. Green, 22 Mich. 311 (1871), an innocent converter who increased the value of another's timber from $25 to nearly $700 by making it into barrel hoops, was held to have title in the hoops. Note, however, that this rule applies only to innocent converters. If the converter knows the raw materials are not hers, she must return them, as improved, to their owner. Is this latter rule fair? Efficient? The leading commentator has observed that whether the rule "would be followed in a case where the value of the resulting product is out of all proportion to the value of the original materials may be doubted, but no cases have been found which confirm the doubt." R. Brown, The Law of Personal Property § 6.2 (W. Raushenbush 3d ed. 1975).

Say that the converter contributes not only her labor, but also her own raw materials, to another's chattels; for example, the Somervilles take possession of the Jacobs' pick-up truck, paint it and replace its seat covers. The law of accession will give title to the owner of the "principal goods"—presumably, in this case, the Jacobs as owners of the truck. The most striking feature of this rule is that it is indifferent to the converter's state of mind. Thus, if the Somervilles knowingly stole paint and fabric from the Jacobs' garage in order to restore the Somerville family car, the Somervilles would retain title to the car *and* the paint and fabric.

Can these two sets of accession rules, respecting added labor and added materials, be reconciled with each other? With the majority opinion in Somerville v. Jacobs? With Judge Caplan's minority opinion in *Somerville?* Consider whether reconciliation is aided by accession rules respecting damages. When the converter is given title, the original owner can recover damages measured by the value of her contributed materials. However, when the original owner is awarded title, the converter will not, as a general rule, be given damages for either the labor or materials she added, regardless of her good faith.

5. *Personal Property: Fixtures.* A fixture is a chattel that, though originally personal property, and though retaining its original separate identity, is considered to have become real property by reason of its annexation to land. The determination whether a chattel has become a fixture is important in several contexts. When A contracts to sell "all my real property, known as Blackacre" to B, B will be entitled to receive not only the land but also every chattel—the furnace, perhaps, and possibly the chandeliers, mirrors and drapes— that, as a fixture, also constitutes part of A's "real property." When A, as tenant, annexes his chattels to the rented premises in such a way that they become fixtures, his landlord, B, will become entitled to them, together with the rest of the real property, at the end of A's term, unless the lease specifically provides otherwise. When the county condemns Blackacre to build a parking garage, it must compensate A for all the real property taken—land *and* fixtures.

What rules govern the determination whether a chattel has become a fixture? Courts frequently cite a test formulated in a nineteenth-century case, Teaff v. Hewitt, 1 Ohio St. 511, 530 (1853): "the united application of the following requisites will be found the safest criterion of a fixture:

1. Actual annexation to the realty, or something appurtenant thereto.

2. Appropriation to the use or purpose of that part of the realty with which it is connected.

3. The intention of the party making the annexation, to make the article a permanent accession to the freehold—this intention being inferred from the *nature* of the article affixed, the *relation* and *situation* of *the party* making the annexation, the structure and mode of annexation, and the purpose or use for which the annexation has been made."

Despite *Teaff's* claims of objectivity and predictability, its test has proved to be essentially circumstantial. For example, does "annexation" require that the chattel be embedded in the land, or will attachment with nuts and bolts, or even by sheer weight, suffice? What is the "purpose" of the connected realty, and what constitutes "appropriation" to that purpose? Although courts have lately inclined to merge these first two criteria into the third—the annexor's intention—this criterion, too, is highly malleable.

As indicated in *Teaff,* courts inquiring into intent will focus on the position of the annexor and the nature of the chattel. Strain v. Green, 25 Wn.2d 692, 172 P.2d 216 (1946), typifies the inquiry. Defendants, upon selling their house, removed the hot water tank and electric heater, venetian blinds, several lights, including a "beautiful crystal chandelier," and three mirrors, two of which could not be removed without damaging the plaster. Plaintiff buyer sued for the return of these articles. The trial court held that the venetian blinds—which had been specially designed for the house—and the hot water tank were fixtures, and ordered defendants to return them and pay for the re-installation. The court found, however, that the lights and mirrors were personal property. On appeal, the Washington Supreme Court held that the lights and two mirrors were fixtures. Rejecting defendants' contention, based on an 1899 case, that lights are not fixtures, the court noted that the law of fixtures changes with the times and "the luxuries of a given generation become the necessities of the next." The court discounted the defendants' testimony that they had never intended the items to become fixtures and, indeed, had previously removed and transported these articles from each of their prior homes. In the court's view, the fact that the sellers had owned the land at the time they annexed the chattels was sufficient evidence of an intent to make them permanent additions to rebut any claim to the contrary.

The court in Strain v. Green followed the usual approach to fixture cases. It attempted to divine the annexor's intent respecting the status of his chattels from the nature of his estate in the underlying land. Courts generally assume that an annexor who owns the land outright intends to "enrich the freehold" and thus the addition becomes a fixture. Conversely, an annexor who is only a tenant on the land presumably intends that the addition remain his personal property. Would it have been better for the court to focus on the intent of the Strains and the Greens at the time they made their contract? Clearly buyer and seller could at that time have expressly agreed on the disposition of all the disputed items and adjusted the contract price accordingly. What kind of fixture rule will most effectively induce buyers and sellers to express their expectations respecting ownership of annexed chattels in the contract of sale?

4. LIMITS ON THE RIGHT TO EXCLUDE

PRUNEYARD SHOPPING CENTER v. ROBINS

Supreme Court of the United States, 1980.
447 U.S. 74, 100 S.Ct. 2035, 64 L.Ed.2d 741.

Mr. Justice REHNQUIST delivered the opinion of the Court.

We postponed jurisdiction of this appeal from the Supreme Court of California to decide the important federal constitutional questions it presented. Those are whether state constitutional provisions, which permit individuals to exercise free speech and petition rights on the property of a privately owned shopping center to which the public is invited, violate the shopping center owner's property rights under the Fifth and Fourteenth Amendments or his free speech rights under the First and Fourteenth Amendments.

I

Appellant PruneYard is a privately owned shopping center in the city of Campbell, Cal. It covers approximately 21 acres—5 devoted to parking and 16 occupied by walkways, plazas, sidewalks, and buildings that contain more than 65 specialty shops, 10 restaurants, and a movie theater. The PruneYard is open to the public for the purpose of encouraging the patronizing of its commercial establishments. It has a policy not to permit any visitor or tenant to engage in any publicly expressive activity, including the circulation of petitions, that is not directly related to its commercial purposes. This policy has been strictly enforced in a nondiscriminatory fashion. The PruneYard is owned by appellant Fred Sahadi.

Appellees are high school students who sought to solicit support for their opposition to a United Nations resolution against "Zionism." On a Saturday afternoon they set up a card table in a corner of PruneYard's central courtyard. They distributed pamphlets and asked passersby to sign petitions, which were to be sent to the President and Members of Congress. Their activity was peaceful and orderly and so far as the record indicates was not objected to by PruneYard's patrons.

Soon after appellees had begun soliciting signatures, a security guard informed them that they would have to leave because their activity violated PruneYard regulations. The guard suggested that they move to the public sidewalk at the PruneYard's perimeter. Appellees immediately left the premises and later filed this lawsuit in the California Superior Court of Santa Clara County. They sought to enjoin appellants from denying them access to the PruneYard for the purpose of circulating their petitions.

The Superior Court held that appellees were not entitled under either the Federal or California Constitution to exercise their asserted rights on the shopping center property. It concluded that there were "adequate, effective channels of communication for [appellees] other than soliciting on the private property of the [PruneYard]." The California Court of Appeal affirmed.

The California Supreme Court reversed, holding that the California Constitution protects "speech and petitioning, reasonably exercised, in shopping centers even when the centers are privately owned." 23 Cal.3d 899, 910, 153 Cal.Rptr. 854, 860, 592 P.2d 341, 347 (1979). It concluded that appellees were entitled to conduct their activity on PruneYard property. In rejecting appellants' contention that such a result infringed property rights protected by the Federal Constitution, the California Supreme Court observed:

" 'It bears repeated emphasis that we do not have under consideration the property or privacy rights of an individual homeowner or the proprietor of a modest retail establishment. As a result of advertising and the lure of a congenial environment, 25,000 persons are induced to congregate daily to take advantage of the numerous amenities offered by the [shopping center there]. A handful of additional orderly persons soliciting signatures and distributing handbills in connection therewith, under reasonable regulations adopted by defendant to assure that these activities do not interfere with normal business operations would not markedly dilute defendant's property rights.'" *Id.*, at 910–911, 153 Cal. Rptr., at 860–861, 592 P.2d, at 347–348.

The California Supreme Court thus expressly overruled its earlier decision in Diamond v. Bland, 11 Cal.3d 331, 113 Cal.Rptr. 468, 521 P.2d 460 (*Diamond II*), cert. denied, 419 U.S. 885, 95 S.Ct. 152, 42 L.Ed.2d 125 (1974), which had reached an opposite conclusion. 23 Cal.3d, at 910, 153 Cal.Rptr., at 860, 592 P.2d, at 347. Before this Court, appellants contend that their constitutionally established rights under the Fourteenth Amendment to exclude appellees from adverse use of appellants' private property cannot be denied by invocation of a state constitutional provision or by judicial reconstruction of a State's laws of private property. We postponed consideration of the question of jurisdiction until the hearing of the case on the merits. We now affirm.

II

We initially conclude that this case is properly before us as an appeal under 28 U.S.C. § 1257(2). It has long been established that a state constitutional provision is a "statute" within the meaning of § 1257(2). Here the California Supreme Court decided that Art. 1, §§ 2 and 3, of the California Constitution gave appellees the right to solicit signatures on appellants' property in exercising their state rights of free expression and petition.[2] In so doing, the California Supreme Court rejected appellants' claim that recognition of such a right violated appellants' "right to exclude others," which is a fundamental component of their federally protected property rights. Appeal is thus the proper method of review.

III

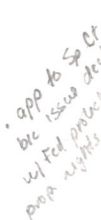

Appellants first contend that Lloyd Corp. v. Tanner, 407 U.S. 551, 92 S.Ct. 2219, 33 L.Ed.2d 131 (1972), prevents the State from requiring a private shopping center owner to provide access to persons exercising their state constitutional rights of free speech and petition when adequate alternative avenues of communication are available.

---

2. Article 1, § 2, of the California Constitution provides:

"Every person may freely speak, write and publish his or her sentiments on all subjects, being responsible for the abuse of this right. A law may not restrain or abridge liberty of speech or press."

Article 1, § 3, of the California Constitution provides:

"[P]eople have the right to . . . petition government for redress of grievances."

Lloyd dealt with the question whether under the Federal Constitution a privately owned shopping center may prohibit the distribution of handbills on its property when the handbilling is unrelated to the shopping center's operations. The shopping center had adopted a strict policy against the distribution of handbills within the building complex and its malls, and it made no exceptions to this rule. Respondents in *Lloyd* argued that because the shopping center was open to the public, the First Amendment prevents the private owner from enforcing the handbilling restriction on shopping center premises. In rejecting this claim we substantially repudiated the rationale of Food Employees v. Logan Valley Plaza, 391 U.S. 308, 88 S.Ct. 1601, 20 L.Ed.2d 603 (1968), which was later overruled in Hudgens v. NLRB, 424 U.S. 507, 96 S.Ct. 1029, 47 L.Ed.2d 196 (1976). We stated that property does not "lose its private character merely because the public is generally invited to use it for designated purposes," and that "[t]he essentially private character of a store and its privately owned abutting property does not change by virtue of being large or clustered with other stores in a modern shopping center." 407 U.S., at 569.

Our reasoning in *Lloyd*, however, does not *ex proprio vigore* limit the authority of the State to exercise its police power or its sovereign right to adopt in its own Constitution individual liberties more expansive than those conferred by the Federal Constitution. In *Lloyd*, *supra*, there was no state constitutional or statutory provision that had been construed to create rights to the use of private property by strangers, comparable to those found to exist by the California Supreme Court here. It is, of course, well established that a State in the exercise of its police power may adopt reasonable restrictions on private property so long as the restrictions do not amount to a taking without just compensation or contravene any other federal constitutional provision. *Lloyd* held that when a shopping center owner opens his private property to the public for the purpose of shopping, the First Amendment to the United States Constitution does not thereby create individual rights in expression beyond those already existing under applicable law.

IV

Appellants next contend that a right to exclude others underlies the Fifth Amendment guarantee against the taking of property without just compensation and the Fourteenth Amendment guarantee against the deprivation of property without due process of law.

It is true that one of the essential sticks in the bundle of property rights is the right to exclude others. Kaiser Aetna v. United States, 444 U.S. 164, 179–180, 100 S.Ct. 383, 392–393, 62 L.Ed.2d 332 (1979). And here there has literally been a "taking" of that right to the extent that the California Supreme Court has interpreted the State Constitution to entitle its citizens to exercise free expression and petition rights on shopping center property.⁶ But it is well established that "not every destruction or injury to property by governmental action has been held to be a 'taking' in the constitutional sense." Armstrong v. United States, 364 U.S. 40, 48, 80 S.Ct. 1563, 1568, 4 L.Ed.2d 1554 (1960). Rather, the determination whether a state law unlawfully infringes a landowner's property in violation of the Taking Clause requires an examination of whether the restriction on private property "forc[es] some people alone to bear public burdens which, in all fairness and justice, should be borne by the public as a whole." This examination entails inquiry into such factors as the character of the governmental action, its economic impact, and its interference with reasonable investment-backed expectations. When "regulation goes too far it will be recognised as a taking." Pennsylvania Coal Co. v. Mahon, 260 U.S. 393, 415, 43 S.Ct. 158, 160, 67 L.Ed. 322 (1922).

Here the requirement that appellants permit appellees to exercise state-protected rights of free expression and petition on shopping center property clearly does not amount to an unconstitutional infringement of appellants' property rights under the Taking Clause. There is nothing to suggest that preventing appellants from prohibiting this sort of activity will unreasonably impair the value or use of their property as a shopping center. The PruneYard is a large commercial complex that covers several city blocks, contains numerous separate business establishments, and is open to the public at large. The decision of the California Supreme Court makes it clear that the PruneYard may restrict expressive activity by adopting time, place, and manner regulations that will minimize any interference with its commercial functions. Appellees were orderly, and they limited their activity to the common areas of the shopping center. In these circumstances, the fact that they may have "physically invaded" appellants' property cannot be viewed as determinative.

This case is quite different from Kaiser Aetna v. United States, *supra*. *Kaiser Aetna* was a case in which the owners of a private pond had invested substantial amounts of money in dredging the pond, developing it into an exclusive marina, and building a surrounding marina community. The marina was open only to fee-paying members, and the fees were paid in part to "maintain the privacy and security of the pond." *Id.*, at 168, 100 S.Ct., at 386. The Federal Government sought to compel free public use of the private marina on the ground that the marina became subject to the federal navigational servitude because the owners had dredged a channel connecting it to "navigable water."

---

6. The term "property" as used in the Taking Clause includes the entire "group of rights inhering in the citizen's [ownership]." United States v. General Motors Corp., 323 U.S. 373, 65 S.Ct. 357, 89 L.Ed. 311 (1945). It is not used in the "vulgar and untechnical sense of the physical thing with respect to which the citizen exercises rights recognized by law. [Instead, it] denote[s] the group of rights inhering in the citizen's relation to the physical thing, as the right to possess, use and dispose of it. . . . The constitutional provision is addressed to every sort of interest the citizen may possess." *Id.*, at 377–378, 65 S.Ct., at 359.

The Government's attempt to create a public right of access to the improved pond interfered with Kaiser Aetna's "reasonable investment backed expectations." We held that it went "so far beyond ordinary regulation or improvement for navigation as to amount to a taking. . . ." *Id.*, at 178, 100 S.Ct., at 392. Nor as a general proposition is the United States, as opposed to the several States, possessed of residual authority that enables it to define "property" in the first instance. A State is, of course, bound by the Just Compensation Clause of the Fifth Amendment, but here appellants have failed to demonstrate that the "right to exclude others" is so essential to the use or economic value of their property that the state-authorized limitation of it amounted to a "taking."

There is also little merit to appellants' argument that they have been denied their property without due process of law. In Nebbia v. New York, 291 U.S. 502, 54 S.Ct. 505, 78 L.Ed. 940 (1934), this Court stated:

> "[N]either property rights nor contract rights are absolute . . . . Equally fundamental with the private right is that of the public to regulate it in the common interest. . . .
>
> . . .
>
> ". . . [T]he guaranty of due process, as has often been held, demands only that the law shall not be unreasonable, arbitrary or capricious, and that the means selected shall have a real and substantial relation to the objective sought to be attained." *Id.*, at 523, 525, 54 S.Ct., at 510–511.

Appellants have failed to provide sufficient justification for concluding that this test is not satisfied by the State's asserted interest in promoting more expansive rights of free speech and petition than conferred by the Federal Constitution.

V

Appellants finally contend that a private property owner has a First Amendment right not to be forced by the State to use his property as a forum for the speech of others. They state that in Wooley v. Maynard, 430 U.S. 705, 97 S.Ct. 1428, 51 L.Ed.2d 752 (1977), this Court concluded that a State may not constitutionally require an individual to participate in the dissemination of an ideological message by displaying it on his private property in a manner and for the express purpose that it be observed and read by the public. This rationale applies here, they argue, because the message of *Wooley* is that the State may not force an individual to display any message at all.

Wooley, however, was a case in which the government itself prescribed the message, required it to be displayed openly on appellee's personal property that was used "as part of his daily life," and refused to permit him to take any measures to cover up the motto even though the Court found that the display of the motto served no important state interest. Here, by contrast, there are a number of distinguishing factors. Most important, the shopping center by choice of its owner is not limited to the personal use of appellants. It is instead a business establishment that is open to the public to come and go as they please. The views expressed by members of the public in passing out pamphlets or seeking signatures for a petition thus will not likely be identified with those of the owner. Second, no specific message is dictated by the State to be displayed on appellants' property. There consequently is no danger of governmental discrimination for or against a particular message. Finally, as far as appears here appellants can expressly disavow any connection with the message by simply posting signs in the area where the speakers or handbillers stand. Such signs, for example, could disclaim any sponsorship of the message and could explain that the persons are communicating their own messages by virtue of state law.

Appellants also argue that their First Amendment rights have been infringed in light of West Virginia State Board of Education v. Barnette, 319 U.S. 624, 63 S.Ct. 1178, 87 L.Ed. 1628 (1943), and Miami Herald Publishing Co. v. Tornillo, 418 U.S. 241, 94 S.Ct. 2831, 41 L.Ed.2d 730 (1974). *Barnette* is inapposite because it involved the compelled recitation of a message containing an affirmation of belief. This Court held such compulsion unconstitutional because it "require[d] the individual to communicate by word and sign his acceptance" of government-dictated political ideas, whether or not he subscribed to them. 319 U.S., at 633, 63 S.Ct., at 1183. Appellants are not similarly being compelled to affirm their belief in any governmentally prescribed position or view, and they are free to publicly dissociate themselves from the views of the speakers or handbillers.

Tornillo struck down a Florida statute requiring a newspaper to publish a political candidate's reply to criticism previously published in that newspaper. It rests on the principle that the State cannot tell a newspaper what it must print. The Florida statute contravened this principle in that it "exact[ed] a penalty on the basis of the content of a newspaper." 418 U.S., at 256, 94 S.Ct., at 2839. There also was a danger in *Tornillo* that the statute would "dampe[n] the vigor and limi[t] the variety of public debate" by deterring editors from publishing controversial political statements that might trigger the application of the statute. *Id.,* at 257, 94 S.Ct., at 2839. Thus, the statute was found to be an "intrusion into the function of editors." *Id.,* at 258, 94 S.Ct., at 2839. These concerns obviously are not present here.

We conclude that neither appellants' federally recognized property rights nor their First Amendment rights have been infringed by the California Supreme Court's decision recognizing a right of appellees to exercise state-protected rights of expression and petition on appellants' property. The judgment of the Supreme Court of California is therefore

Affirmed.

Mr. Justice BLACKMUN joins the opinion of the Court except that sentence thereof, which reads: "Nor as a general proposition is the United States, as opposed to the several States, possessed of residual authority that enables it to define 'property' in the first instance."

Mr. Justice MARSHALL, concurring.

I join the opinion of the Court, but write separately to make a few additional points.

I

In Food Employees v. Logan Valley Plaza, 391 U.S. 308, 88 S.Ct. 1601, 20 L.Ed.2d 603 (1968), this Court held that the First and Fourteenth Amendments prevented a state court from relying on its law of trespass to enjoin the peaceful picketing of a business enterprise located within a shopping center. The Court concluded that because the shopping center "serves as the community business block" and is open to the general public, "the State may not delegate the power, through the use of its trespass laws, wholly to exclude those members of the public wishing to exercise their First Amendment rights on the premises." *Id.*, at 319, 88 S.Ct., at 1609. The Court rejected the suggestion that such an abrogation of the state law of trespass would intrude on the constitutionally protected property rights of shopping center owners. And it emphasized that the shopping center was open to the public and that reasonable restrictions on the exercise of communicative activity would be permitted. "[N]o meaningful claim to protection of a right of privacy can be advanced by respondents here. Nor on the facts of the case can any significant claim to protection of the normal business operation of the property be raised. Naked title is essentially all that is at issue." *Id.*, at 324, 88 S.Ct., at 1611.

The Court in *Logan Valley* emphasized that if the property rights of shopping center owners were permitted to overcome the First Amendment rights of prospective petitioners, a significant intrusion on communicative activity would result. Because "[t]he large-scale movement of this country's population from the cities to the suburbs has been accompanied by the advent of the suburban shopping center," a contrary decision would have "substantial consequences for workers seeking to challenge substandard working conditions, consumers protesting shoddy or overpriced merchandise, and minority groups seeking nondiscriminatory hiring policies." *Ibid.* In light of these realities, we concluded that the First and Fourteenth Amendments prohibited the State from using its trespass laws to prevent the exercise of expressive activities on privately owned shopping centers, at least when those activities were related to the operations of the store at which they were directed.

In Lloyd Corp. v. Tanner, 407 U.S. 551, 92 S.Ct. 2219, 33 L.Ed.2d 131 (1972), the Court confined *Logan Valley* to its facts, holding that the First and Fourteenth Amendments were not violated when a State prohibited petitioning that was not designed to convey information with respect to the operation of the store that was being picketed. The Court indicated that a contrary result would constitute "an unwarranted infringement of property rights." 407 U.S., at 567, 92 S.Ct., at 2228. And in Hudgens v. NLRB, 424 U.S. 507, 96 S.Ct. 1029, 47 L.Ed.2d 196 (1976), the Court concluded that *Lloyd* had in fact overruled *Logan Valley*.

I continue to believe that *Logan Valley* was rightly decided, and that both *Lloyd* and *Hudgens* were incorrect interpretations of the First and Fourteenth Amendments. State action was present in all three cases. In all of them the shopping center owners had opened their centers to the public at large, effectively replacing the State with respect to such traditional First Amendment forums as streets, sidewalks, and parks. The State had in turn made its laws of trespass available to shopping center owners, enabling them to exclude those who wished to engage in expressive activity on their premises. Rights of free expression become illusory when a State has operated in such a way as to shut off effective channels of communication. I continue to believe, then, that "the Court's rejection of any role for the First Amendment in the privately owned shopping center complex stems . . . from an overly formalistic view of the relationship between the institution of private ownership of property and the First Amendment's guarantee of freedom of speech." Hudgens v. NLRB, *supra*, at 542, 96 S.Ct., at 1047 (dissenting opinion).

II

In the litigation now before the Court, the Supreme Court of California construed the California Constitution to protect precisely those rights of communication and expression that were at stake in *Logan Valley, Lloyd,* and *Hudgens*. The California court concluded that its State "Constitution broadly proclaims speech and petition rights. Shopping centers to which the public is invited can provide an essential and invaluable forum for exercising those rights." 23 Cal.3d 899, 910, 153 Cal.Rptr. 854, 860, 592 P.2d 341, 347 (1979). Like the Court in *Logan Valley*, the California court found that access to shopping centers was crucial to the exercise of rights of free expression. And like the Court in *Logan Valley*, the California court rejected the suggestion that the Fourteenth Amendment barred the intrusion on the property rights of the shopping center owners. I applaud the court's decision, which is a part of a very healthy trend of affording state constitutional provisions a more expansive interpretation than this Court has given to the Federal Constitution.

Appellants, of course, take a different view. They contend that the decision below amounts to a constitutional "taking" or a deprivation of their property without due process of law. *Lloyd*, they claim, did not merely overrule *Logan Valley's* First Amendment holding; it overruled its due process ruling as well, recognizing a federally protected right on the part of shopping center owners to enforce the preexisting state law of trespass by excluding those who engage in communicative activity on their property. In my view, the issue appellants present is largely a restatement of the question of whether and to what extent a State may abrogate or modify common-law rights. Although the cases in this Court do not definitively resolve the question, they demonstrate that appellants' claim has no merit.

Earlier this Term, in Martinez v. California, 444 U.S. 277, 100 S.Ct. 553, 62 L.Ed.2d 481 (1980), the Court was also confronted with a claim that the abolition of a cause of action previously conferred by state law was an impermissible taking of "property." We responded that even if a pre-existing state-law remedy "is a species of 'property' protected by the Due Process Clause . . ., it would remain true that the State's interest in fashioning its own rules of tort law is paramount to any discernible federal interest, except perhaps an interest in protecting the individual citizen from state action that is wholly arbitrary or irrational." *Id.*, at 281–282, 100 S.Ct., at 557. Similarly, in the context of a claim that a guest statute impermissibly abrogated common-law rights of tort, the Court observed that the Due Process Clause does not forbid the "creation of new rights, or the abolition of old ones recognized by the common law, to attain a permissible legislative object." Silver v. Silver, 280 U.S. 117, 122, 50 S.Ct. 57, 58, 74 L.Ed. 221 (1929). And in Munn v. Illinois, 94 U.S. 113, 24 L.Ed. 77 (1877), the Court upheld a statute limiting the permissible rate for the warehousing of grain. "A person has no property, no vested interest, in any rule of the common law. . . . Rights of property which have been created by the common law cannot be taken away without due process; but the law itself, as a rule of conduct, may be changed at the will . . . of the legislature, unless prevented by constitutional limitations. Indeed, the great office of statutes is to remedy defects in the common law as they are developed, and to adapt it to the changes of time and circumstances." *Id.*, at 134.

Appellants' claim in this case amounts to no less than a suggestion that the common law of trespass is not subject to revision by the State, notwithstanding the California Supreme Court's finding that state-created rights of expressive activity would be severely hindered if shopping centers were closed to expressive activities by members of the public. If accepted, that claim would represent a return to the era of Lochner v. New York, 198 U.S. 45, 25 S.Ct. 539, 49 L.Ed. 937 (1905), when common-law rights were also found immune from revision by State or Federal Government. Such an approach would freeze the common law as it has been constructed by the courts, perhaps at its 19th-century state of development. It would allow no room for change in response to changes in circumstance. The Due Process Clause does not require such a result.

On the other hand, I do not understand the Court to suggest that rights of property are to be defined solely by state law, or that there is no federal constitutional barrier to the abrogation of common-law rights by Congress or a state government. The constitutional terms "life, liberty, and property" do not derive their meaning solely from the provisions of positive law. They have a normative dimension as well, establishing a sphere of private autonomy which government is bound to respect. Quite serious constitutional questions might be raised if a legislature attempted to abolish certain categories of common-law rights in some general way. Indeed, our cases demonstrate that there are limits on governmental authority to abolish "core" common-law rights, including rights against trespass, at least without a compelling showing of necessity or a provision for a reasonable alternative remedy.

That "core" has not been approached in this case. The California Supreme Court's decision is limited to shopping centers, which are already open to the general public. The owners are permitted to impose reasonable restrictions on expressive activity. There has been no showing of interference with appellants' normal business operations. The California court has not permitted an invasion of any personal sanctuary. No rights of privacy are implicated. In these circumstances there is no basis for strictly scrutinizing the intrusion authorized by the California Supreme Court.

I join the opinion of the Court.

Mr. Justice WHITE, concurring in part and concurring in the judgment.

I join Mr. Justice Powell's concurring opinion but with these additional remarks.

The question here is whether the Federal Constitution forbids a State to implement its own free-speech guarantee by requiring owners of shopping centers to permit entry on their property for the purpose of communicating with the public about subjects having no connection with the shopping centers' business. The Supreme Court of California held that in the circumstances of this case the federally protected property rights of appellants were not infringed. The state court recognized, however, that reasonable time and place limitations could be imposed and that it was dealing with the public or common areas in a large shopping center and not with an individual retail establishment within or without the shopping center or with the property or privacy rights of a homeowner. On the facts before it, "[a] handful of additional orderly persons soliciting signatures and distributing handbills . . . would not markedly dilute defendant's property rights." 23 Cal.3d 899, 911, 153 Cal.Rptr. 854, 860–861, 592 P.2d 341, 347–348 (1979).

I agree that on the record before us there was not an unconstitutional infringement of appellants' property rights. But it bears pointing out that the Federal Constitution does not require that a shopping center permit distributions or solicitations on its property. Indeed, Hudgens v. NLRB, 424 U.S. 507, 96 S.Ct. 1029, 47 L.Ed.2d 196 (1976), and Lloyd Corp. v. Tanner, 407 U.S. 551, 92 S.Ct. 2219, 33 L.Ed.2d 131 (1972), hold that the First and Fourteenth Amendments do not prevent the property owner from excluding those who would demonstrate or communicate on his property. Insofar as the Federal Constitution is concerned, therefore, a State may decline to construe its own constitution so as to limit the property rights of the shopping center owner.

The Court also affirms the California Supreme Court's implicit holding that appellants' own free-speech rights under the First and Fourteenth Amendments were not infringed by requiring them to provide a forum for appellees to communicate with the public on shopping center property. I concur in this judgment, but I agree with Mr. Justice Powell that there are other circumstances that would present a far different First Amendment issue. May a State require the owner of a shopping center to subsidize any and all political, religious, or social-action groups by furnishing a convenient place for them to urge their views on the public and to solicit funds from likely prospects? Surely there are some limits on state authority to impose such requirements; and in this respect, I am not in entire accord with Part V of the Court's opinion.

Mr. Justice POWELL, with whom Mr. Justice WHITE joins, concurring in part and in the judgment.

Although I join the judgment, I do not agree with all of the reasoning in Part V of the Court's opinion. I join Parts I–IV on the understanding that our decision is limited to the type of shopping center involved in this case. Significantly different questions would be presented if a State authorized strangers to picket or distribute leaflets in privately owned, freestanding stores and commercial premises. Nor does our decision today apply to all "shopping centers." This generic term may include retail establishments that vary widely in size, location, and other relevant characteristics. Even large establishments may be able to show that the number or type of persons wishing to speak on their premises would create a substantial annoyance to customers that could be eliminated only by elaborate, expensive, and possibly unenforceable time, place, and manner restrictions. As the Court observes, state power to regulate private property is limited to the adoption of reasonable restrictions that "do not amount to a taking without just compensation or contravene any other federal constitutional provision."

I

Restrictions on property use, like other state laws, are invalid if they infringe the freedom of expression and belief protected by the First and Fourteenth Amendments. In Part V of today's opinion, the Court rejects appellants' contention that "a private property owner has a First Amendment right not to be forced by the State to use his property as a forum for the speech of others." I agree that the owner of this shopping center has failed to establish a cognizable First Amendment claim in this case. But some of the language in the Court's opinion is unnecessarily and perhaps confusingly broad. In my view, state action that transforms privately owned property into a forum for the expression of the public's views could raise serious First Amendment questions.

The State may not compel a person to affirm a belief he does not hold. See Wooley v. Maynard, 430 U.S. 705, 97 S.Ct. 1428, 51 L.Ed.2d 752 (1977); West Virginia State Board of Education v. Barnette, 319 U.S. 624, 63 S.Ct. 1178, 87 L.Ed. 1628 (1943). Whatever the full sweep of this principle, I do not believe that the result in Wooley v. Maynard, *supra*, would have changed had the State of New Hampshire directed its citizens to place the slogan "Live Free or Die" in their shop windows rather than on their automobiles. In that case, we said that "[a] system which secures the right to proselytize religious, political, and ideological causes must also guarantee the concomitant right to decline to foster such concepts." 430 U.S., at 714, 97 S.Ct., at 1435. This principle on its face protects a person who refuses to allow use of his property as a marketplace for the ideas of others. And I can find no reason to exclude the owner whose property is "not limited to [his] personal use. . . ." A person who has merely invited the public onto his property for commercial purposes cannot fairly be said to have relinquished his right to decline "to be an instrument for fostering public adherence to an ideological point of view he finds unacceptable." Wooley v. Maynard, *supra*, 430 U.S., at 715, 97 S.Ct., at 1435.

As the Court observes, this case involves only a state-created right of limited access to a specialized type of property. But even when no particular message is mandated by the State, First Amendment interests are affected by state action that forces a property owner to admit third-party speakers. In many situations, a right of access is no less intrusive than speech compelled by the State itself. For example, a law requiring that a newspaper permit others to use its columns imposes an unacceptable burden upon the newspaper's First Amendment right to select material for publication. Miami Herald Publishing Co. v. Tornillo, 418 U.S. 241, 94 S.Ct. 2831, 41 L.Ed.2d 730 (1974). Such a right of access burdens the newspaper's "fundamental right to decide what to print or omit." Wooley v. Maynard, *supra*, 430 U.S., at 714, 97 S.Ct., at 1435; see Miami Herald

Publishing Co. v. Tornillo, *supra*, 418 U.S., at 257, 94 S.Ct., at 2839. As such, it is tantamount to compelled affirmation and, thus, presumptively unconstitutional.

The selection of material for publication is not generally a concern of shopping centers. But similar speech interests are affected when listeners are likely to identify opinions expressed by members of the public on commercial property as the views of the owner. If a state law mandated public access to the bulletin board of a freestanding store, hotel, office, or small shopping center, customers might well conclude that the messages reflect the view of the proprietor. The same would be true if the public were allowed to solicit or distribute pamphlets in the entrance area of a store or in the lobby of a private building. The property owner or proprietor would be faced with a choice: he either could permit his customers to receive a mistaken impression or he could disavow the messages. Should he take the first course, he effectively has been compelled to affirm someone else's belief. Should he choose the second, he has been forced to speak when he would prefer to remain silent. In short, he has lost control over his freedom to speak or not to speak on certain issues. The mere fact that he is free to dissociate himself from the views expressed on his property, cannot restore his "right to refrain from speaking at all." Wooley v. Maynard, *supra*, 430 U.S., at 714, 97 S.Ct., at 1435.

A property owner also may be faced with speakers who wish to use his premises as a platform for views that he finds morally repugnant. Numerous examples come to mind. A minority-owned business confronted with distributers from the American Nazi Party or the Ku Klux Klan, a church-operated enterprise asked to host demonstrations in favor of abortion, or a union compelled to supply a forum to right-to-work advocates could be placed in an intolerable position if state law requires it to make its private property available to anyone who wishes to speak. The strong emotions evoked by speech in such situations may virtually compel the proprietor to respond.

The pressure to respond is particularly apparent when the owner has taken a position opposed to the view being expressed on his property. But an owner who strongly objects to some of the causes to which the state-imposed right of access would extend may oppose ideological activities "of *any* sort" that are not related to the purposes for which he has invited the public onto his property. To require the owner to specify the particular ideas he finds objectionable enough to compel a response would force him to relinquish his "freedom to maintain his own beliefs without public disclosure." *Ibid.*[3] Thus, the right to control one's own speech may be burdened impermissibly

---

3. The problem is compounded where, as in shopping centers or in the lobby areas of hotels and office buildings, stores are leased to different proprietors with divergent views.

even when listeners will not assume that the messages expressed on private property are those of the owner.

II

One easily can identify other circumstances in which a right of access to commercial property would burden the owner's First and Fourteenth Amendment right to refrain from speaking. But appellants have identified no such circumstance. Nor did appellants introduce evidence that would support a holding in their favor under either of the legal theories outlined above.

On the record before us, I cannot say that customers of this vast center would be likely to assume that appellees' limited speech activity expressed the views of the PruneYard or of its owner. The shopping center occupies several city blocks. It contains more than 65 shops, 10 restaurants, and a theater. Interspersed among these establishments are common walkways and plazas designed to attract the public. Appellees are high school students who set up their card table in one corner of a central courtyard known as the "Grand Plaza." They showed passersby several petitions and solicited signatures. Persons solicited could not reasonably have believed that the petitions embodied the views of the shopping center merely because it owned the ground on which they stood.

Appellants have not alleged that they object to the ideas contained in the appellees' petitions. Nor do they assert that some groups who reasonably might be expected to speak at the PruneYard will express views that are so objectionable as to require a response even when listeners will not mistake their source. The record contains no evidence concerning the numbers or types of interest groups that may seek access to this shopping center, and no testimony showing that the appellants strongly disagree with any of them.

Because appellants have not shown that the limited right of access held to be afforded by the California Constitution burdened their First and Fourteenth Amendment rights in the circumstances presented, I join the judgment of the Court. I do not interpret our decision today as a blanket approval for state efforts to transform privately owned commercial property into public forums. Any such state action would raise substantial federal constitutional questions not present in this case.

NOTES

1. Was Justice Rehnquist, who wrote for the *PruneYard* majority, saying that PruneYard was not unconstitutionally deprived of its property because its bundle of rights did not contain the right to exclude pamphleteers, or because, although its bundle did contain such a right, the right was only "regulated," not "taken"? Could the California Supreme Court have avoided the taking issue entirely by rest-

ing its decision on a common law, rather than a constitutional, ground? For example, could the California court have ruled that trespass occurs only when the gravity of harm to the victim exceeds the utility of the intruder's conduct, and that under this balance the injury to the shopping center did not exceed the value of the pamphleteers' conduct? Would the United States Supreme Court be barred from second-guessing the state court's interpretation of California law on the ground that "as a general proposition . . . the United States, as opposed to the several States," is not "possessed of residual authority that enables it to define 'property' in the first instance"?

Was Justice Rehnquist saying that state courts are free to define property rights as they wish but, once having defined these rights, they cannot upset them without violating the constitutional prohibition against takings of property? If state courts are free to set these rules, why not state legislatures? Does it matter whether the rules are given retrospective as well as prospective force?

Was Justice Marshall addressing only retroactive application when he observed that "quite serious constitutional questions might be raised if a legislature attempted to abolish certain categories of common law rights in some general way"? Did Marshall have both retrospective and prospective laws in mind when he announced the sweeping principle that "there are limits on governmental authority to abolish 'core' common law rights, including rights against trespass, at least without a compelling showing of necessity or a provision for a reasonable alternative remedy"? Is it relevant that the cases Marshall cited in support of this proposition generally involved state limitations on civil liberties, and not on property rights? Is there any reason not to give property rights equal standing with civil rights?

What is your answer to Justice White's question, "May a state require the owner of a shopping center to subsidize any and all political, religious, or social-action groups by furnishing a convenient place for them to urge their views on the public and to solicit funds from likely prospects?" What if a California statute required that, for every twenty stores rented in a shopping center, the center must set aside one storefront for use by political groups? Would it matter that the statute was limited to shopping centers built after its effective date?

2. *PruneYard* was the unusual case in which trespass law becomes the object of competing constitutional claims. The right to exclude is more commonly shaped in the crucible of common law decision. In State v. Shack, 58 N.J. 297, 277 A.2d 369 (1971), the New Jersey Supreme Court reversed the criminal trespass convictions of a health services worker and a Legal Services lawyer who had sought to give medical and legal aid to migrant workers housed on a farmer's land, and had refused to depart on the farmer's demand. Avoiding the proffered constitutional grounds, the New Jersey court rested

its decision on a nonconstitutional ground instead: "The reason is that we are satisfied that under our State law the ownership of real property does not include the right to bar access to governmental services available to migrant workers and hence there was no trespass within the meaning of the penal statute." 58 N.J. at 302, 277 A.2d at 371–372.

In the court's view, "property rights serve human values. They are recognized to that end, and are limited by it. Title to real property cannot include dominion over the destiny of persons the owner permits to come upon the premises." 58 N.J. at 303, 277 A.2d at 372. Thus, the "quest is for a fair adjustment of the competing needs of the parties, in the light of the realities of the relationship between the migrant worker and the operator of the housing facility. Thus approaching the case, we find it unthinkable that the farmer-employer can assert a right to isolate the migrant worker in any respect significant for the worker's well-being. The farmer, of course, is entitled to pursue his farming activities without interference, and this defendants readily concede. But we see no legitimate need for a right in the farmer to deny the worker the opportunity for aid available from federal, State or local services, or from recognized charitable groups seeking to assist him. Hence representatives of these agencies and organizations may enter upon the premises to seek out the worker at his living quarters. So, too, the migrant worker must be allowed to receive visitors there of his own choice, so long as there is no behavior hurtful to others, and members of the press may not be denied reasonable access to workers who do not object to seeing them." 58 N.J. at 307, 277 A.2d at 374.

Applying the *Shack* analysis, consider whether you would characterize any of the following intrusions as nontrespassory and, if so, how you would rationalize the result in nonconstitutional terms:

> A traveller on an obstructed highway drives over neighboring private land to avoid the obstruction. Campbell v. Race, 7 Cush. 408 (Mass.1851) (no trespass).

> A news photographer enters a fire-damaged residence for the purpose of photographing the disaster scene. Florida Publishing Co. v. Fletcher, 340 So.2d 914 (Fla.Sup.Ct.1976) (no trespass).

> A coastal warden parks his car on private lands while investigating illegal clam-digging activities nearby. Thurlow v. Crossman, 336 Mass. 248, 143 N.E.2d 812 (1957) (no trespass).

B. BALANCING THE RIGHTS OF NEIGHBORS

Real property law encourages the development of land through the grant of exclusive rights. Yet, to award an exclusive right to one owner often implies withholding it from another. If a carbonic acid factory has the exclusive right to use its land as it pleases, it will be free to belch thick black soot and smoke, even if this means fouling the air above a neighboring homeowner's parcel. If the homeowner has the exclusive right to use her land as she pleases, she will be entitled to have the factory's pollution enjoined. One function of trespass law—and of nuisance law—is to resolve this sort of conflict.

How should the law allocate rights between factory and homeowner? Should the factory be given the right to pollute so that the neighbor, to enjoy her home free of soot and smoke, must buy off the factory? Or should the homeowner be given the right to clean air so that the factory, to continue operating as before, must buy her off? One answer, frequently offered by environmentalists, is that the factory should be made liable for its emissions because smoke damage represents a cost—specifically a "social cost"— of producing carbonic acid that is properly borne not by the homeowner, but by the producer; imposing liability on the factory will force it to account for the full cost of its production and, as a result, the factory will properly pollute less than if it bore no liability for its emissions.

The argument that the factory rather than the homeowner should bear the cost of pollution rests on the premise that it is the factory that causes the harm. In fact, it is equally plausible to say that the homeowner causes the harm, for if the house were not there—if the lot were vacant or occupied by another factory—there would be no injury to residential use. The damage that attends the factory's and the homeowner's use of the ambient atmosphere can thus be viewed either as a cost of producing carbonic acid in a factory adjoining a residence or as a cost of living in a residence adjacent to a factory. Or, perhaps, more accurately, the damage can be viewed as a joint cost of the two activities.

Looking at factory and homeowner in this light suggests that, *a priori*, there is no reason to prefer the activities of one to the other. On what basis, then, are rights to be assigned? Some numbers may help explain the effects of alternative assignments. Say that the homeowner suffers $800 damage from the factory's emissions and that the factory values the right to emit smoke and soot at $1,200 (because it allows the factory to use soft coal which costs $1,200 less than the cleaner hard coal). If the applicable legal rule imposes liability on the factory, giving the homeowner the right to be free of emissions, the factory should be willing to pay the homeowner some amount less than $1,200, and the homeowner should be willing to accept some amount greater than $800, in exchange for the homeowner's release of her legal right. Both would profit by the exchange. If, by contrast, the applicable legal rule imposed no liability on the factory, the exchange would not occur. The factory would not accept any payment less than $1,200 (the amount of its benefit under the rule of no liability) and the homeowner would pay no more than $800 (the amount of her cost under the rule of no liability). The most striking fact is that the uses made of the two parcels will be identical under either assignment of rights: the factory will continue emitting pollutants. What would the result be if the numbers were reversed—with the factory valuing its right to emit smoke and soot without liability at $800 and the homeowner's harm being $1,200?

Do these results mean that nothing turns on whether the factory owner is made liable? Certainly it matters to the parties. The homeowner will be wealthier, and the factory poorer, under a rule that makes the factory liable than under a rule that leaves it free to pollute. Thus, if it is property law's province to judge whether one class, such as homeowners, is more entitled to wealth than some other class, such as factory owners, and if courts and legislatures are capable of making such generalized judgments, this could justify the choice of one liability rule over another.

There is another reason why liability rules matter. Transaction costs—the costs of negotiating the transfer of rights between factory and homeowner—sometimes make a deal so costly to execute that the deal will not be struck, with the result that the law's initial allocation of rights will not be altered by private bargain. In the example just given, where the factory placed a $1,200 value on the right to emit particulates and the homeowner placed an $800 value on the right to be free of them, the factory will be unwilling to negotiate with the homeowner, even if the law imposes liability on the factory, if it expects that legal fees and other expenses of the transaction will exceed $400. Also, transaction costs multiply as more parties become involved. Apart from the cost of identifying all 98 affected homeowners, how does the factory deal with the one who holds out for a price higher than that sought by the other 97? How does it deal with a neighboring factory that, though contributing to the pollution, refuses to chip into the fund out of which homeowners are to be paid? In each of these situations, although the factory *should* have acquired the right to pollute, transaction costs will prevent it from doing so.

Does the problem of transaction costs suggest that, in allocating liability, courts and legislatures should attempt to assign rights to the party that would have negotiated for and obtained the rights in the absence of transaction costs? What about imposing the burden on the party that faces the lowest transaction costs? Remember that the governmental intervention and fact-finding necessary for these judgments are themselves not costless.

Property rights are rarely absolute. If the factory is given the right to pollute, it will probably not be without limit. If the homeowner is given a right, it will likely be to air that is clean, but not absolutely so. In the presence of transaction costs, which is better—a rule of absolute liability or a rule that makes liability turn on the degree of harm? Does the largely absolutist law of trespass adequately respond to the problem of transaction costs?

NOTES

1. The view that, absent transaction costs, resources will be efficiently allocated regardless of how liability is assigned was first systematically advanced by Ronald Coase in his celebrated essay, The Problem of Social Cost, 3 J. Law & Econ. 1 (1960). The Coase theorem has attracted expositors, critics and defenders. See, for example, R. Posner, Economic Analysis of Law 27–64 (2d ed. 1977); Demsetz, When Does the Rule of Liability Matter?, 1 J. Legal Studies 13 (1972); Calabresi, Transaction Costs, Resource Allocation and Liability Rules—A Comment, 11 J. Law & Econ. 67 (1968); Nutter, The Coase Theorem on Social Cost: A Footnote, 11 J. Law & Econ. 503 (1968); Coase Theorem Symposium, Part I, 13 Nat. Resources J. 557 (1973); Part II, 14 Nat. Resources J. 1 (1974); Kelman, Consumption Theory, Production Theory, and Ideology in the Coase Theorem, 52 S.Cal.L.Rev. 669 (1979); Kennedy, Cost-Benefit Analysis of Entitlement Problems: A Critique, 33 Stan.L.Rev. 387 (1981); Cooter, The Cost of Coase, 11 J. Legal Studies 1 (1982).

2. Legal rules that favor the most highly valued of two or more competing uses can be justified on the ground that, even in the presence of transaction costs, they assure the dedication of land to its most productive use. One important implication of this approach is that the law's assignment of rights will change as the values of competing uses change. What effect does this prospect of constant change in legal rules have on long term incentives to invest in the productive use of land? How will the factory owner, who knows today that he need not pay the homeowner for the right to pollute, behave if he also knows that when the factory's social value declines and other more valuable uses enter the neighborhood, he will lose the right to pollute? In calculating an offering price, should land buyers be expected to account for such contingencies—that land uses will change, that transaction costs will prevent exchanges, and that the law will value one use higher than another?

Would interests in productivity over the long and short term be better advanced by a clear rule that, without balancing or exception, gave the first user the right to be free of any interference? Although the homeowner could not be certain that a factory would not locate next door, she would at least know that the factory would have to pay her for the right to be there. Does such a rule make sense in the presence of possibly disabling transaction costs? Transaction costs aside, what would be the effect of such a rule on the timing and location of land development? Would such a rule entitle one homeowner to exact payments from a second homeowner who builds next door?

1. NUISANCE

a. The Calculus of Rights

McCARTY v. NATURAL CARBONIC GAS CO.

Court of Appeals of New York, 1907.
189 N.Y. 40, 81 N.E. 549.

VANN, J. This action was brought to restrain the defendant from so operating its manufactory as to cause smoke, soot and dust emitted from it chimneys to gather and settle about the dwelling house of the plaintiff to his annoyance and injury.

The trial court found the following facts in substance: For four years prior to the 13th of July, 1904, when this action was commenced, the plaintiff owned certain premises on South Broadway in the village of Saratoga Springs, consisting of a lot of land with a frame dwelling house thereon, known as the "Anna Therese." Said house is situated in a country district suitable for country homes, "although not as yet so appropriated by others than the plaintiff." The defendant is a foreign corporation engaged in the manufacture of carbonic acid gas in a semi-fluid form convenient for shipment to market by compressing the natural gas found on its premises, and for this purpose it maintains a plant containing machinery operated by steam, which is generated from two boilers with a capacity of 100 horse power. It has two smokestacks, each 90 feet high, situated 840 feet from the residence of the plaintiff. From two and one-half to four tons of soft coal are used daily by the defendant and its chimneys continuously pour forth "a thick black smoke, large in volume and larger, denser and thicker when the fires are freshened twice" every hour during the twenty-four that the plant is in operation, Sundays excepted.

When the wind is right the smoke blows down upon the plaintiff's house and comes upon and around it. When the atmosphere is dense "clouds of smoke proceeding from the defendant's chimneys gather and settle about the plaintiff's house, enveloping it and sometimes obscuring it from view." Said smoke "has caused the exterior of the house of the plaintiff to become discolored with soot and has caused plaintiff and his family much discomfort and annoyance and some financial injury." The defendant causes this damage and injury by the use of soft coal, yet by the use of anthracite coal it would obtain the same result in manufacturing although at a greater expense, and if the use of soft coal were abandoned the discomfort experienced by the plaintiff would be entirely avoided. "The present use of soft coal is not a necessary use for the practical management and running of its plant" and "under all the circumstances of the case the present discomfort of the plaintiff is not occasioned by any reasonable use by the defendant of its own property." The plaintiff had owned his property for several years before the defendant erected its factory. Another factory like the defendant's was located in the neighborhood before the plaintiff purchased, but as it uses anthracite coal it has never caused any annoyance. The rental value of the plaintiff's house has been injured by the use of soft coal by the defendant to the extent of $800, and he has incurred expense for cleaning rugs to the extent of $18 more.

The court, after repeating as conclusions of law its findings of fact in relation to reasonable and necessary use, further found as conclusions of law that "the defendant should be enjoined, restrained and forbidden from burning soft coal on its said plant in the village of Saratoga Springs, New York, for the purpose of generating steam," and that "the plaintiff herein is entitled to the sum of $818.00 damages and is also entitled to the costs of the action." Upon appeal to the Appellate Division the judgment was modified by deducting from the damages awarded the sum of $18.00 as of the date when the judgment was entered, and, as so modified, the judgment was unanimously affirmed.

The action of the courts below withdraws the evidence from our view, except for the consideration of exceptions relating thereto, and leaves but one question upon the merits for us to decide and that is whether the facts found support the conclusions of law? In other words, in a country district suitable for country homes, does the use of soft coal in a factory so situated that thick, black smoke therefrom, great in volume and dense in quality, envelopes and discolors a neighboring dwelling house, causing much discomfort and some financial loss to the occupants, constitute a nuisance, when such use of soft coal is not necessary for the practical running of the plant and is not a reasonable use of the manufacturer's property?

The principles governing the decision of that question are neither recent in origin nor doubtful in application. The ancient maxim of *sic utere tuo ut alienum non laedas* is the foundation of the well-established rule that no one may make an unreasonable use of his own premises to the material injury of his neighbor's premises, and if he does the latter has a right of action even if he is not driven from his dwelling, provided the enjoyment of life and property is materially lessened. Campbell v. Seaman, 63 N.Y. 568, 20 Am.Rep. 567; Cogswell v. New York, New Haven & Hartford R.R. Co., 103 N.Y. 10, 8 N.E. 537, 57 Am.Rep. 701; Bohan v. Port Jervis Gas Light Co., 122 N.Y. 18, 25 N.E. 246, 9 L.R.A. 711; Morton v. Mayor, etc., of N.Y., 140 N.Y. 207; Garvey v. Long Island R.R. Co., 159 N.Y. 323, 54 N.E. 57, 70 Am.St.Rep. 550; Bly v. Edison Electric Illuminating Co., 172

N.Y. 1, 64 N.E. 745, 58 L.R.A. 500; Pritchard v. Edison El. Ill. Co., 179 N.Y. 364, 72 N.E. 243.

The law relating to private nuisances is a law of degree and usually turns on the question of fact whether the use is reasonable or not under all the circumstances. No hard and fast rule controls the subject, for a use that is reasonable under one set of facts would be unreasonable under another. Whether the use of property to carry on a lawful business, which creates smoke or noxious gases in excessive quantities, amounts to a nuisance depends on the facts of each particular case. Location, priority of occupation and the fact that the injury is only occasional are not conclusive, but are to be considered in connection with all the evidence and the inference drawn from all the facts proved whether the controlling fact exists that the use is unreasonable. If that fact is found, a nuisance is established and the plaintiff is entitled to relief in some form. Unless that fact is found, or it is an inference of law from other facts found, no nuisance is established, even if the plaintiff shows that he has suffered some damage, annoyance and injury. Those evils are at times incidental to civilized life and the sufferer finds compensation in the arts and agencies of civilized society. (Campbell v. Seaman, *supra*.) What is reasonable is sometimes a question of law and at others a question of fact. When it depends upon an inference from peculiar, numerous or complicated circumstances it is usually a question of fact. Whether the use of property by one person is reasonable, with reference to the comfortable enjoyment of his own property by another, generally depends upon many and varied facts; such as location, nature of the use, character of the neighborhood, extent and frequency of the injury, the effect on the enjoyment of life, health and property and the like. Such was the nature of the question in this case which, we think, is one of fact.

The case last cited involved injury to ornamental shrubbery on land adjacent to a village, from the noxious gases of a brick factory, which dug the clay on its own premises, and the exhaustive opinion of Judge Earl holds, with the concurrence of all the judges, that articles of luxury are as much under the protection of the law as articles of necessity; that it is immaterial that the injury is only occasional; that the right to an injunction is not affected by the fact that the brick kiln was used before the plaintiff purchased his land and that if the use is such "as to produce a tangible and appreciable injury to neighboring property, or such as to render its enjoyment specially uncomfortable or inconvenient" it constitutes a nuisance.

In the well-known *Cogswell Case* (*supra*) a railroad company had erected an engine house near a dwelling house in a city and the smoke, cinders and coal dust, carried by the winds, filled the house, injured articles therein and rendered the air offensive and the house uncomfortable. It was held that the "engine house, as used, was within every definition a nuisance, for which, as between individuals, an action would lie for damages and for which a court of equity would afford a remedy by injunction." All the judges united with Judge Andrews in saying: "However necessary it may be for the defendant that its engine house should be located where it is, this constitutes no justification for the injury suffered by the plaintiff, nor is it any answer to the action that it exercises all practicable care in its management. It may have the right, which it claims, to acquire land by purchase for the accommodation of its business, but it must secure such a location as will enable it to conduct its operations without violating the just rights of others. Public policy, indeed, requires that in adjusting the mutual relations between railroads and individuals, courts should not stand upon the assertion of extreme rights for either side, but in this case the facts leave no room for doubt that the plaintiff has suffered a substantial and unauthorized injury."

The *Bohan Case* (*supra*) involved the comfortable enjoyment of neighboring property owing to noxious odors from gas works carried on by a corporation organized under the general statute. The court charged the jury that the question for them to determine was: "Did the odor pollute the air so as to substantially render plaintiff's property unfit for comfortable enjoyment?" The jury found for the plaintiff and the court held that the act complained of constituted a nuisance *per se*. The court refused to charge "that unless the jury should find that the works of the defendant were defective, or that they were out of repair, or that the persons in charge of manufacturing gas at these works were unskillful and incapable, their verdict should be for the defendant." It further refused to charge "that if the odors which affect the plaintiff are those that are inseparable from the manufacture of gas with the most approved apparatus and with the utmost skill and care and do not result from any defects in the works or from want of care in their management, the defendant is not liable." Both requests were refused and the exceptions to the rulings were held to raise no error. The thorough review of all the prior cases makes it unnecessary for us to mention them, and an able dissenting opinion added emphasis to the decision, for it showed that nothing had been overlooked and that no argument was left unused.

The leading authorities in all jurisdictions hold that the question is whether the defendant makes a reasonable or, as some judges express themselves, a proper use of his own property? Sometimes negligence is referred to as an element in the question. Judge Landon once pointedly said: "A lawful business negligently conducted is not a lawful business lawfully conducted," but, as the quotation implies, since a negligent use of one's own property to the injury of another is an unreasonable use, the ultimate question after all is whether the use is reasonable. Negligence, wrong business methods, improper appliances and the like may bear upon but do not control the question of reasonable use. If the use is reasonable there can be no private nuisance, but if the use is unreasonable and results in substantial injury, an actionable nuisance exists. Trifling results are disregarded, for the courts proceed with great caution and will not interfere with the use of property by the owner thereof unless such use is unreasonable, the injury material and actual, not fanciful or sentimental. *Lex non faxet votis delicatorum.*

The defendant's business is lawful and not a nuisance *per se*, although it has been found that as carried on it is a nuisance in fact. The extent more than the nature of the injury, the *quantum*, rather than the *damnum*, constitutes the nuisance. Some smoke is generally created by the natural and ordinary use of land near a village or city, and while this may sometimes be annoying to neighbors it is part of the price paid for living where there are neighbors. But when the smoke is so unusual and excessive as to materially interfere with the ordinary comfort of human existence, the trier of the facts, taking into account all the circumstances, such as public utility, locality, immediate surroundings and the like, may find the use unreasonable. This is not a case where the defendant cannot carry on its business without injury to neighboring property, for all damage can be avoided by the use of hard coal, as is done by one of its competitors in the same kind of business in the same locality, or possibly by the use of some modern appliance such as a smoke consumer, although either would involve an increase in expense. It is better, however, that profits should be somewhat reduced than to compel a householder to abandon his home, especially when he did not "come to the nuisance," but was there before. "The safety of property generally is superior in right to a particular use of a single piece of property by its owner. It renders the enjoyment of all property more secure by preventing such use of one piece by one man as may injure all his neighbors." Sullivan v. Dunham, 161 N.Y. 290, 300, 55 N.E. 923, 47 L.R.A. 715, 76 Am.St.Rep. 274.

The use made of property may be unpleasant, unsightly or, to some extent, annoying and disagreeable to the occupants of neighboring property without creating a nuisance. When, however, it not only interferes materially with the physical comfort of persons in their own homes, but also causes some financial injury to the owner, it constitutes a nuisance. That is this case, and the facts found compel an affirmance except in one particular.

The conclusion of law that the defendant should be enjoined from burning soft coal on its premises to make steam is too broad, for it is unlimited as to time or circumstances, and the judgment follows the conclusion. If the defendant, by the use of some appliance now known or which may become known hereafter, can burn soft coal in its factory without injury to the plaintiff, it cannot lawfully be deprived of that right. If the plaintiff should convert his house into a factory, using soft coal, he would not be entitled to an injunction. The defendant, therefore, should be permitted to apply at Special Term, upon proper notice at any time, for a modification of the decree at the foot thereof, permitting it to burn soft coal, upon proof of such a change of facts as to make such use of its property no longer unreasonable. Subject to this modification the judgment should be affirmed, with costs.

O'BRIEN, J. (dissenting). The plaintiff recovered a judgment in this case, enjoining the defendant from the transaction of business on its own land. Damages have also been awarded to the plaintiff as compensation for the injury complained of. The question arising upon the appeal is whether the facts found in the case sustain the conclusion of law.

The act of the defendant, which is the basis of the recovery, is that it is burning soft coal to generate steam in the manufacture of natural carbonic gas. The plaintiff has no right to complain of the manner in which the defendant is transacting its business unless it is in violation of some legal right which he may assert against the defendant. It is important, therefore, to state the facts which the court found, and which it is contended support the judgment. The claim of the plaintiff is that his dwelling house, in consequence of the business which the defendant is engaged in, has been rendered uncomfortable. It is found that this dwelling house is situated in a district so sparsely settled that it may properly be called neither a residence, factory nor business neighborhood. It is a country district near the village of Saratoga, which is appropriate for country homes, although not as yet so appropriated by others than the plaintiff himself. The defendant is and has been for some time engaged in the manufacture and development of natural carbonic gas, maintaining a plant with buildings and machinery thereon for that purpose upon lands adjoining the plaintiff's premises. This plant is operated by steam power used to compress natural gas extracted from mineral springs into semi-solid form convenient for shipment to the market. There are several frame buildings, an iron gasometer and two ninety-feet smokestacks. These smokestacks are eight hundred and forty feet distant from the plaintiff's residence. Soft coal is used in the boilers to generate the steam for the purpose of operating the plant, and from about two and one-half to four tons of soft coal are used daily by the defendant corporation. It may, I think, be assumed, although the fact is not found distinctly, that the defendant's business must be carried on, if at all, in the vicinity of mineral springs, and hence the defendant's plant was located with reference to that fact.

Of course volumes of smoke are emitted from the smokestacks produced by the use of soft coal, especially when the fires are freshened, as they are twice an hour. It is also found that there are times when the direction of the wind is such that the smoke blows down upon the plaintiff's house, and at other times when the atmosphere is dense and the wind right that clouds of smoke proceeding from the chimneys gather and settle about the plaintiff's house, sometimes obscuring it from view. This annoyance it seems is not continuous, but exists when the wind is in the right direction and the atmosphere is dense. The language of the finding on this subject is this: "That said smoke when the wind is in the proper direction and the condition of the atmosphere is right comes down and around plaintiff's house and premises." That the smoke and soot emitted from the chimneys has caused the exterior of the plaintiff's house to become discolored and has caused plaintiff and his family discomfort and annoyance and some financial injury, and that this is all caused by the use of soft coal. It is also found that the defendant could obviate this inconvenience or annoyance by the use of anthracite coal in its plant and would obtain the same result in manufacture, although at greater expense, and, hence, that the present use of soft coal is not a necessary use for the practical management and running of its plant.

The court in its findings expressly negatived some facts which the plaintiff sought to establish. It is found that no injury has been occasioned by the use of soft coal by the defendant to the trees or shrubbery of the plaintiff; that the use of soft coal by the defendant has not caused any injury to the health of the plaintiff or his family for which damages could be recovered; that there is nothing to show that plaintiff's house would not by this time require washing and painting even if it had not been soiled by the smoke from the defendant's plant; that no permanent injury has been done by the use of soft coal by the defendant to the plaintiff's furniture or to the interior decorations of his house. As a conclusion of law the court held and decided that the use of soft coal by the defendant in the operation of its plant is not a reasonable or necessary use, and that the discomfort and damage to the plaintiff are occasioned by the unreasonable use by the defendant of its property, and, therefore, that the defendant should be enjoined, restrained and forbidden from burning soft coal in the operation of its plant for the purpose of generating steam. There is no finding in the record that the defendant was guilty of any negligence in the operation of its plant or the conduct of its business, nor is there any finding that the use of soft coal as described in the findings referred to is *per se* a nuisance. The appeal, therefore, presents the single question whether upon the facts found there is any support for the judgment.

The principal authority upon which the learned counsel for the plaintiff relies in support of the judgment is the case of Bohan v. Port Jervis G.I., Co., 122 N.Y. 18, 25 N.E. 246, 9 L.R.A. 711. It seems to me that there is a very material distinction between that case and the one at bar. The act there complained of was the use of naphtha in the manufacture of gas. The defendant erected a tank on its own premises, the southern side of which was within a few feet of plaintiff's premises. It was found that naphtha is an offensive, noxious, unhealthy and sickening mineral substance, destructive to the health and comfort of those required to be and remain in close proximity to it; that the defendant's tank was erected and is maintained in a negligent and unskillful manner and by reason of the negligence and want of care upon the part of the defendant in the construction, use of and maintenance of said tank, and the negligent and unskillful manufacture of gas from naphtha, the defendant maintains a nuisance injurious to the comfort and enjoyment of the plaintiff and to the rental value of his premises. So that there was an allegation in that case, not only of negligence on the part of the defendant, but it was charged with maintaining a nuisance; and the character of naphtha as described in the allegation is widely different from anything that may be said in regard to the emission of smoke resulting from the use of soft coal. Moreover, the location of the tank within a few feet of the plaintiff's premises was an important element in the case which is absent from the case at bar. That case was tried before a jury and a general verdict rendered in favor of the plaintiff, so that all the facts alleged in the complaint must be deemed to have been found by the jury against the defendant. In the case at bar the trial was before the court and the judgment rests upon distinct findings of fact. The findings in this case practically negatived all the facts which were the basis of the recovery in the case referred to. . . .

. . . In the earlier case of Campbell v. Seaman, 63 N.Y. 568, 20 Am.Rep. 567, the rule was stated by Judge Earl in language somewhat different, but to the same effect: "It is a general rule that every person may exercise exclusive dominion over his own property and subject it to such uses as will best subserve his private interests. Generally, no other person can say how he shall use or what he shall do with his property. But this general right of property has its exceptions and qualifications. *Sic utere tuo ut alienum non laedas* is an old maxim which has a broad application. It does not mean that one must never use his own so as to do any injury to his neighbor or his property. Such a rule could not be enforced in civilized society. Persons living in organized communities must suffer some damage, annoyance and inconvenience from each other. For these they are compensated by all the advantages of civilized society. If one lives in the city he must expect to suffer the dirt, smoke, noisome odors, noise and confusion incident to city life."

The contention of the plaintiff in the present case is that the defendant in the operation of its manufacturing plant should have used anthracite coal instead of soft coal. It is found that this change must involve an additional expense upon the defendant. The amount of that additional expense has not been found, but it is found that in order to conduct the defendant's business from two and one-half to four tons of coal per day must be burned. The defendant cannot carry on its business without observing due economy in its management. If it can be compelled by the plaintiff for his own comfort to impose additional burdens upon the business, the result may be the loss of reasonable profits, and it may be in the destruction of the business entirely. If the plaintiff can legally demand that the defendant must use anthracite coal instead of soft coal, there is no reason why he may not demand other changes that would enhance his own comforts or enjoyment of his property. It is fair to assume from the findings that the defendant consumes on an average of three tons of coal per day. In the course of a year it is necessary, therefore, to burn about a thousand tons, and as the cost of hard coal would be about two dollars per ton more than that of soft coal, it would require the defendant to increase the expense of operating its plant in the sum of about two thousand dollars annually. There is nothing in the record to show that the business which the defendant is conducting is a very profitable one. It may well be that the business has not yet produced any profit whatever, and such an increase in the expense might not only absorb the profits, but result in a loss. It has been said that the power to tax includes the power to destroy, and if the plaintiff or other parties similarly situated, armed with the decree of the court, can compel the defendant to make the changes suggested by the judgment in this case for his own comfort, the application of such a principle might go far to render the defendant's property and business worthless.

It is quite difficult, if not impossible, to state from the findings, with any degree of accuracy, just what the legal injury is of which the plaintiff complains. No injury has been suffered from the use of soft coal to the trees, shrubbery or the grounds of the plaintiff, nor to his health or that of his family. The smoke and dust have not injured his house either in the interior or exterior, or the furniture or decorations. It was not shown or found that the conduct of the defendant's business discolored the plaintiff's house in any way. The present condition in that respect, whatever it is, is due to ordinary use and the lapse of time. The judgment must stand, if at all, upon that vague and somewhat fanciful claim that his home is not as comfortable as it would have been if the defendant's business was not carried on at all, or carried on in some different manner, or by the use of other materials at greater expense. No tangible *legal right* of the plaintiff as against the defendant has been or is violated, since whatever effect the operation of the defendant's business and the use of its own property has upon that of the plaintiff in diminishing his personal comfort is one of the results or incidents of residing in a locality where manufacturing is lawfully and necessarily carried on. All the cases hold that the plaintiff or other parties similarly situated must endure some inconvenience or some degree of discomfort, and I am unable to see why the facts of this case as found do not bring it within the operation of that principle.

We are not making law for this case merely. A legal principle is involved of far-reaching importance. Whatever we decide in this case must apply to every manufactory or manufacturing establishment in the state. It is a question of comfort on the part of the plaintiff. On the part of the defendant it may be a question of life or death, and it certainly is a question of the right to conduct a business such as that which the defendant is engaged in with good judgment and reasonable economy. There is no question such as was involved in the *Bohan* case, of noxious smells and poisonous vapors due to the use of naphtha, which it was alleged and found was detrimental to health. In the present case it is a question as to how far the defendant may be compelled to increase the expenses of its business in order to secure greater comfort for the plaintiff in the enjoyment of his home. Has he a legal right to demand that his property shall be exempt from smoke, dust or cinders on certain occasions when the wind is in the right direction, or the atmosphere in the right condition to produce the discomforts of which the plaintiff complains? Unless such a legal right exists the judgment in this case is wrong, since it imposes a burden upon the defendant's business greatly in excess of any monetary or other loss resulting from the use of soft coal. It seems to me that within the principles announced by this court and which have been stated, that no such legal right exists and, hence, the judgment should be reversed and a new trial granted, costs to abide the event.

GRAY, WERNER, WILLARD, BARTLETT and CHASE, JJ., concur with VANN, J.; O'BRIEN, J., reads dissenting opinion; CULLEN, Ch. J., absent.

Judgment accordingly.

NOTES

1. According to the Restatement (Second) of Torts § 822 (1977), for conduct to constitute a nuisance it must invade an interest in the private use and enjoyment of land. If the invasion is *unintentional*, the landowner can prevail only if he can demonstrate that the offender's conduct is negligent, reckless or constitutes an abnormally dangerous activity. If the invasion is *intentional*, the landowner will prevail if he can demonstrate that the offender's conduct was "unreasonable." Section 826(a) provides that an intentional invasion is "unreasonable" if the "gravity of the harm outweighs the utility of the actor's conduct." Sections 827 and 828, respectively, list the factors to be weighed in determining the gravity of harm and the utility of the offender's conduct:

§ 827(a) The extent of the harm involved;

(b) the character of the harm involved;

(c) the social value that the law attaches to the type of use or enjoyment invaded;

(d) the suitability of the particular use or enjoyment invaded to the character of the locality; and

(e) the burden on the person harmed of avoiding the harm.

§ 828(a) The social value that the law attaches to the primary purpose of the conduct;

(b) the suitability of the conduct to the character of the locality; and

(c) the impracticability of preventing or avoiding the invasion.

Did *McCarty* apply the gravity-utility balance? If so, did it weigh the relevant factors correctly?

Section 826(b) defines unreasonable conduct somewhat differently: "the harm caused by the conduct is serious and the financial burden of compensating for this and similar harm to others would not make the continuation of the conduct not feasible." Section 829A provides that "An intentional invasion of another's interest in the use and enjoyment of land is unreasonable if the harm resulting from the invasion is severe and greater than the other should be required to bear without compensation." What does section 826(b) add to the formula prescribed in section 826(a)? What does section 829A add to section 826 generally? Would *McCarty* have been decided differently if one formula rather than another had been applied?

2. *Visually Offensive Uses.* Noisy or noisome activities are frequently held to be actionable nuisances. Is there any reason to treat activities that offend a landowner's sense of sight differently from those that offend her sense of hearing or smell? The general approach to visually offensive land uses has been to excuse them, and to exclude from nuisance awards any elements of damage attributable to the unsightly appearance of the offending use. See for example, Houston Gas & Fuel Co. v. Harlow, 297 S.W. 570 (Tex.Civ.App. 1927). There may be an underlying concern that a rule against visual affronts would entangle courts in difficult free speech questions under the First Amendment.

Courts occasionally depart from the general rule. In Puritan Holding Co., Inc. v. Holloschitz, 82 Misc.2d 905, 372 N.Y.S.2d 500 (Sup.Ct.1975), the court awarded $30,000 nuisance damages against defendant, whose abandoned apartment building "had deteriorated, become unsightly and been taken over by derelicts. The building's condition has caused a deterioration in values on the block." Plaintiff's neighboring building had allegedly declined in value by $30,000 to $35,000 as a result. See generally, Note, A Nuisance Law Approach to the Problem of Housing Abandonment, 85 Yale L.J. 1130 (1976).

How can the general rule excusing visual affronts be reconciled with nuisance law's overriding concern to balance the utility of the offender's conduct against the gravity of harm to the offended landowner? Is the problem that the damages caused by visual affronts are too speculative to be measured? To be believed? If objective measurement of harm is the concern, does *Holloschitz* suggest a desirable way out, treating decline in land value as an objective measure of subjective reactions to unsightly surroundings?

For a pioneering effort in the area, see Noel, Unaesthetic Sights as Nuisances, 25 Cornell L.Q. 1 (1939). See also Note, Aesthetic Nuisance: An Emerging Cause of Action, 45 N.Y.U.L.Rev. 1075 (1970).

3. *Interferences With Light, Air or View.* As a general rule, a landowner has no action against a neighbor whose buildings or other improvements interfere with his light, air or view. The reason traditionally given for the rule is that, by encouraging land development, it leads to a more productive use of land. The principal exception to the rule is that spite fences or other structures erected for the sole, or at least primary, purpose of obstructing light, air and view, are actionable as nuisances. The reason for this exception is that spite fences are not productive uses of land.

Apparently one state high court believes it would be better to abandon the *per se* rule on light, air and view, and replace it with nuisance law's traditional balancing act—weighing the relative costs and benefits of the neighbors' activities. In Prah v. Maretti, 108 Wis.2d 223, 321 N.W.2d 182 (1982), the Wisconsin Supreme Court ruled that plaintiff, owner of a solar-heated residence, could state a cause of action for nuisance against defendant, whose proposed construction of a residence on an adjacent parcel would obstruct plaintiff's access to sunlight.

The Wisconsin Supreme Court noted that the reasons traditionally given for the *per se* rule were, "First, the right of landowners to use their property as they wished, as long as they did not cause physical damage to a neighbor, was jealously guarded. Second, sunlight was valued only for aesthetic enjoyment or as illumination . . . . Third, society has a significant interest in not restricting or impeding land development." In the court's view "these three policies are no longer fully accepted or applicable. They reflect factual circumstances and social priorities that are now obsolete. First, society has increasingly regulated the use of land by the landowner for the general welfare. Second, access to sunlight has taken on a new significance in recent years. In this case the plaintiff seeks to protect access to sunlight, not for aesthetic reasons or as a source of illumination but as a source of energy . . . . Third, the policy of favoring unhindered private development in an expanding economy is no longer in harmony with the realities of our society. The need for easy and rapid development is not as great today as it once was, while our perception of the value of sunlight as a source of energy has increased significantly." 108 Wis.2d at 235–237, 321 N.W.2d at 189–190.

Justice Callow dissented. First, "the majority has failed to convince me that these policies are obsolete . . . . The majority cites two zoning cases to support the conclusion that society has increasingly regulated private land use in the name of public welfare. The cases involving the use of police power and eminent domain are clearly distinguishable from the present situation as they relate to interference with a private right solely for the *public* health, safety, morals, or welfare. In the instant case, we are dealing with an action which seeks to restrict the defendant's private right to use his property, notwithstanding a complete lack of notice of restriction to the defendant and the defendant's compliance with applicable ordinances and statutes." 108 Wis.2d at 243–246, 321 N.W.2d at 193–194.

Second, "the majority concludes that sunlight has not heretofore been accorded the status of a source of energy, and consequently it has taken on a new significance in recent years. Solar energy for home heating is at this time sparingly used and of questionable economic value because solar collectors are not mass produced, and consequently, they are very costly. Their limited efficiency may explain the lack of production. Regarding the third policy the majority apparently believes is obsolete (that society has a significant interest in not restricting land development), I concede the law may be tending to recognize the value of aesthetics over increased volume development and that an individual may not use his land in such a way as to harm the *public*. The instant case, however, deals with a *private* benefit." 108 Wis.2d at 247, 321 N.W.2d at 194–195.

Justice Callow relied in part on "the frequently cited and followed case," Fontainebleau Hotel Corp. v. 4225 Inc., 114 So.2d 357 (Fla.App. 1959). Plaintiff there, owner of the Eden Roc Hotel, sought to enjoin defendant from building a fourteen-story addition to its neighboring Fontainebleau Hotel. The trial court entered a temporary injunction, finding that during the winter months the addition would block the sunlight from plaintiff's swimming and sunbathing areas for a substantial part of the day, and that there was "evidence indicating that the construction of the proposed annex by the Fontainebleau was malicious or deliberate for the purpose of injuring the Eden Roc . . . ." The appellate court reversed. Its principal objection was to the lower court's application of the maxim, *sic utere tuo ut alienum non laedas:* "This maxim does not mean that one must never use his own property in such a way as to do any injury to his neighbor. It means only that one must use his property so as not to injure the lawful *rights* of another."

See Comment, Obstruction of Sunlight as a Private Nuisance, 65 Calif.L.Rev. 94 (1977).

4. Could *McCarty* have been decided on a trespass rather than a nuisance theory? Although nuisance and trespass protect different interests—nuisance, the landowner's interest in using his land, and trespass, his interest in possessing it—the same interference will fre-

quently support either action. As a result, the landowner can weigh the tactical advantages of one cause of action over the other. Nuisance requires a showing of substantial harm, while trespass requires none, beyond the rule *de minimis non curat lex;* trespass typically requires that the landowner demonstrate a perceptible, physical invasion of his land, while nuisance is not nearly so insistent on showings of palpable intrusion; trespass is essentially a *per se* rule, while nuisance makes intentional invasions actionable only if they are unreasonable; only the holder of a present possessory interest has standing to bring an action for trespass, while holders of other than presently possessory interests may proceed against nuisances that diminish the value of these interests.

There has been a discernible trend to expand trespass doctrine to cover activities that formerly were the province of nuisance alone. In Martin v. Reynolds Metals Co., 221 Or. 86, 342 P.2d 790 (1959), the Oregon Supreme Court ruled that defendant's discharge of imperceptible fluoride gases and particulates onto plaintiff's land constituted a trespass entitling plaintiff to recover under the six-year statute of limitations for trespass rather than the two-year nuisance statute. Rejecting defendant's argument that, at most, the plaintiff stated a claim for nuisance, the court defined trespass as "any intrusion which invades the possessor's protected interest in exclusive possession, whether that intrusion is by visible or invisible pieces of matter, or by energy which can be measured only by the mathematical language of the physicist." 221 Or. at 94, 342 P.2d at 794.

After *Martin*, would the Oregon Supreme Court find a trespass when fire spread from a railroad's right of way onto plaintiff's land? See Martin et ux. v. Union Pacific Railroad Co., 256 Or. 563, 474 P.2d 739 (1970) (yes). When defendant aimed allegedly vile and obscene words and gestures at his mother-in-law while she was in her house? See Wilson v. Parent, 228 Or. 354, 361, 365 P.2d 72, 75 (1961) ("the ether waves moving from the hands of the defendant to the eyes of plaintiff and the sound waves from his vocal chords to her ears do not constitute trespass to land.")

5. Since *McCarty* was decided, zoning has overtaken nuisance law as the principal device for ordering land use. In place of judicial decisions balancing the economic interests of neighbors, zoning law introduced a system of local legislative and administrative decision-making motivated as much by politics as by economics, and taking the larger community as its arena for allocating specific land uses. In a word, zoning has substituted public choice for private choice respecting desirable land uses.

Which of these two systems of land use control—zoning or nuisance—is preferable, and in what circumstances? Zoning often regulates amenities, such as light, air, and view that lie outside the scope of modern nuisance law. Is it best to leave decisions on these matters to local politicians and administrators, or should nuisance law be expanded to cover them? One perceived advantage of nuisance law is that, by balancing the utility of the offender's conduct against the gravity of the victim's harm, courts are likely to reach results that will lead to the most productive use of land. Further, when the nuisance rule does not itself reach this result, private bargains can often be expected to set the proper balance. Does zoning afford any such opportunities for closely focused balancing and for private bargains to replace undesirable rules? Which system operates better when the community's interest needs to be weighed more heavily than the interest of neighbors, or when private bargains will be monetarily or morally too costly? For a penetrating analysis of these and related issues, see Ellickson, Alternatives to Zoning: Covenants, Nuisance Rules, and Fines as Land Use Controls, 40 U.Chi.L.Rev. 681 (1973).

Since both zoning and nuisance are here to stay, the more immediate question for public policy is how each should be adjusted to the other. For example, in determining whether an offender's conduct constitutes a private nuisance, courts must often determine whether, and how heavily, to weigh a local zoning ordinance that permits the offending use. As a general rule, courts take the zoning classification as some evidence that the use is reasonable in the circumstances. A few courts, and at least one statute, have gone further, excusing the offensive activity if it is permitted by a local zoning ordinance. See e.g., Bove v. Donner-Hanna Coke Corp., 236 App.Div. 37, 258 N.Y.S. 22 (1932) (alternative ground). West's Ann.Cal.Code Civ.Proc. § 731(a) (immunizing the offender so long as there is no evidence of "the employment of unnecessary and injurious methods of operation").

There is another, more subtle, relationship between zoning and nuisance law. Zoning ordinances typically divide a community's land into industrial, commercial and residential areas. As a result of this segregation there are fewer conflicts between competing uses and, therefore, fewer nuisance lawsuits. Also, by seeking to harmonize visual amenities and uses of light and air and other resources not traditionally covered by nuisance law, zoning ordinances have reduced the pressures for nuisance law to expand in these directions. In light of these developments, what kinds of nuisance lawsuits are likely to arise today in communities that have been comprehensively zoned? Are actions brought by angry or spiteful neighbors likely to overshadow actions brought in the pursuit of rational and productive land uses? How conducive are such actions to negotiated settlements at economically desirable prices?

b. REMEDIES

BOOMER v. ATLANTIC CEMENT CO., INC.

Court of Appeals of New York, 1970.
26 N.Y.2d 219, 309 N.Y.S.2d 312, 257 N.E.2d 870.

BERGAN, Judge.

Defendant operates a large cement plant near Albany. These are actions for injunction and damages by neighboring land owners alleging injury to property from dirt, smoke and vibration emanating from the plant. A nuisance has been found after trial, temporary damages have been allowed; but an injunction has been denied.

The public concern with air pollution arising from many sources in industry and in transportation is currently accorded ever wider recognition accompanied by a growing sense of responsibility in State and Federal Governments to control it. Cement plants are obvious sources of air pollution in the neighborhoods where they operate.

But there is now before the court private litigation in which individual property owners have sought specific relief from a single plant operation. The threshold question raised by the division of view on this appeal is whether the court should resolve the litigation between the parties now before it as equitably as seems possible; or whether, seeking promotion of the general public welfare, it should channel private litigation into broad public objectives.

A court performs its essential function when it decides the rights of parties before it. Its decision of private controversies may sometimes greatly affect public issues. Large questions of law are often resolved by the manner in which private litigation is decided. But this is normally an incident to the court's main function to settle controversy. It is a rare exercise of judicial power to use a decision in private litigation as a purposeful mechanism to achieve direct public objectives greatly beyond the rights and interests before the court.

Effective control of air pollution is a problem presently far from solution even with the full public and financial powers of government. In large measure adequate technical procedures are yet to be developed and some that appear possible may be economically impracticable.

It seems apparent that the amelioration of air pollution will depend on technical research in great depth; on a carefully balanced consideration of the economic impact of close regulation; and of the actual effect on public health. It is likely to require massive public expenditure and to demand more than any local community can accomplish and to depend on regional and interstate controls.

A court should not try to do this on its own as a by-product of private litigation and it seems manifest that the judicial establishment is neither equipped in the limited nature of any judgment it can pronounce nor prepared to lay down and implement an effective policy for the elimination of air pollution. This is an area beyond the circumference of one private lawsuit. It is a direct responsibility for government and should not thus be undertaken as an incident to solving a dispute between property owners and a single cement plant—one of many—in the Hudson River valley.

The cement making operations of defendant have been found by the court at Special Term to have damaged the nearby properties of plaintiffs in these two actions. That court, as it has been noted, accordingly found defendant maintained a nuisance and this has been affirmed at the Appellate Division. The total damage to plaintiffs' properties is, however, relatively small in comparison with the value of defendant's operation and with the consequences of the injunction which plaintiffs seek.

The ground for the denial of injunction, notwithstanding the finding both that there is a nuisance and that plaintiffs have been damaged substantially, is the large disparity in economic consequences of the nuisance and of the injunction. This theory cannot, however, be sustained without overruling a doctrine which has been consistently reaffirmed in several leading cases in this court and which has never been disavowed here, namely that where a nuisance has been found and where there has been any substantial damage shown by the party complaining an injunction will be granted.

The rule in New York has been that such a nuisance will be enjoined although marked disparity be shown in economic consequence between the effect of the injunction and the effect of the nuisance.

The problem of disparity in economic consequence was sharply in focus in Whalen v. Union Bag & Paper Co., 208 N.Y. 1, 101 N.E. 805. A pulp mill entailing an investment of more than a million dollars polluted a stream in which plaintiff, who owned a farm, was "a lower riparian owner". The economic loss to plaintiff from this pollution was small. This court, reversing the Appellate Division, reinstated the injunction granted by the Special Term against the argument of the mill owner that in view of "the slight advantage to plaintiff and the great loss that will be inflicted on defendant" an injunction should not be granted (p. 2, 101 N.E. p. 805). "Such a balancing of injuries cannot be justified by the circumstances of this case", Judge Werner noted (p. 4, 101 N.E. p. 805). He continued: "Although the damage to the plaintiff may be slight as compared with the defendant's expense of abating the condition, that is not a good reason for refusing an injunction" (p. 5, 101 N.E. p. 806).

Thus the unconditional injunction granted at Special Term was reinstated. The rule laid down in that case, then, is that whenever the damage resulting from a nuisance is found not "unsubstantial", viz., $100 a year, injunction would follow. This states a rule that had been followed in this court with marked consistency (McCarty v. Natural Carbonic Gas Co., 189 N.Y. 40, 81 N.E. 549; Strobel v. Kerr Salt Co., 164 N.Y. 303, 58 N.E. 142; Campbell v. Seaman, 63 N.Y. 568).

There are cases where injunction has been denied. McCann v. Chasm Power Co., 211 N.Y. 301, 105 N.E. 416 is one of them. There, however, the damage shown by plaintiffs was not only unsubstantial, it was non-existent. Plaintiffs owned a rocky bank of the stream in which defendant had raised the level of the water. This had no economic or other adverse consequence to plaintiffs, and thus injunctive relief was denied. Similar is the basis for denial of injunction in Forstmann v. Joray Holding Co., 244 N.Y. 22, 154 N.E. 652 where no benefit to plaintiffs could be seen from the injunction sought (p. 32, 154 N.E. 655). Thus if, within Whalen v. Union Bag & Paper Co., *supra* which authoritatively states the rule in New York, the damage to plaintiffs in these present cases from defendant's cement plant is "not unsubstantial", an injunction should follow.

Although the court at Special Term and the Appellate Division held that injunction should be denied, it was found that plaintiffs had been damaged in various specific amounts up to the time of the trial and damages to the respective plaintiffs were awarded for those amounts. The effect of this was, injunction having been denied, plaintiffs could maintain successive actions at law for damages thereafter as further damage was incurred.

The court at Special Term also found the amount of permanent damage attributable to each plaintiff, for the guidance of the parties in the event both sides stipulated to the payment and acceptance of such permanent damage as a settlement of all the controversies among the parties. The total of permanent damages to all plaintiffs thus found was $185,000. This basis of adjustment has not resulted in any stipulation by the parties.

This result at Special Term and at the Appellate Division is a departure from a rule that has become settled; but to follow the rule literally in these cases would be to close down the plant at once. This court is fully agreed to avoid that immediately drastic remedy; the difference in view is how best to avoid it.*

One alternative is to grant the injunction but postpone its effect to a specified future date to give opportunity for technical advances to permit defendant to eliminate the nuisance; another is to grant the injunction conditioned on the payment of permanent damages to plaintiffs which would compensate them for the total economic loss to their property present and future caused by defendant's operations. For reasons which will be developed the court chooses the latter alternative.

If the injunction were to be granted unless within a short period— e.g., 18 months—the nuisance be abated by improved methods, there

---

* Respondent's investment in the plant is in excess of $45,000,000. There are over 300 people employed there.

would be no assurance that any significant technical improvement would occur.

The parties could settle this private litigation at any time if defendant paid enough money and the imminent threat of closing the plant would build up the pressure on defendant. If there were no improved techniques found, there would inevitably be applications to the court at Special Term for extensions of time to perform on showing of good faith efforts to find such techniques.

Moreover, techniques to eliminate dust and other annoying by-products of cement making are unlikely to be developed by any research the defendant can undertake within any short period, but will depend on the total resources of the cement industry nationwide and throughout the world. The problem is universal wherever cement is made.

For obvious reasons the rate of the research is beyond control of defendant. If at the end of 18 months the whole industry has not found a technical solution a court would be hard put to close down this one cement plant if due regard be given to equitable principles.

On the other hand, to grant the injunction unless defendant pays plaintiffs such permanent damages as may be fixed by the court seems to do justice between the contending parties. All of the attributions of economic loss to the properties on which plaintiffs' complaints are based will have been redressed.

The nuisance complained of by these plaintiffs may have other public or private consequences, but these particular parties are the only ones who have sought remedies and the judgment proposed will fully redress them. The limitation of relief granted is a limitation only within the four corners of these actions and does not foreclose public health or other public agencies from seeking proper relief in a proper court.

It seems reasonable to think that the risk of being required to pay permanent damages to injured property owners by cement plant owners would itself be a reasonably effective spur to research for improved techniques to minimize nuisance.

The power of the court to condition on equitable grounds the continuance of an injunction on the payment of permanent damages seems undoubted.

The damage base here suggested is consistent with the general rule in those nuisance cases where damages are allowed. "Where a nuisance is of such a permanent and unabatable character that a single recovery can be had, including the whole damage past and future resulting therefrom, there can be but one recovery" (66 C.J.S. Nuisances § 140, p. 947). It has been said that permanent damages are allowed where the loss recoverable would obviously be small as compared with the cost of removal of the nuisance.

The present cases and the remedy here proposed are in a number of other respects rather similar to Northern Indiana Public Service Co. v. W. J. & M. S. Vesey, 210 Ind. 338, 200 N.E. 620 decided by the Supreme Court of Indiana. The gases, odors, ammonia and smoke from the Northern Indiana company's gas plant damaged the nearby Vesey greenhouse operation. An injunction and damages were sought, but an injunction was denied and the relief granted was limited to permanent damages "present, past, and future" (p. 371, 200 N.E. 620).

Denial of injunction was grounded on a public interest in the operation of the gas plant and on the court's conclusion "that less injury would be occasioned by requiring the appellant [Public Service] to pay the appellee [Vesey] all damages suffered by it . . . than by enjoining the operation of the gas plant; and that the maintenance and operation of the gas plant should not be enjoined" (p. 349, 200 N.E. p. 625).

The Indiana Supreme Court opinion continued: "When the trial court refused injunctive relief to the appellee upon the ground of public interest in the continuance of the gas plant, it properly retained jurisdiction of the case and awarded full compensation to the appellee. This is upon the general equitable principle that equity will give full relief in one action and prevent a multiplicity of suits" (pp. 353–354, 200 N.E. p. 627).

It was held that in this type of continuing and recurrent nuisance permanent damages were appropriate. See, also, City of Amarillo v. Ware, 120 Tex. 456, 40 S.W.2d 57 where recurring overflows from a system of storm sewers were treated as the kind of nuisance for which permanent depreciation of value of affected property would be recoverable.

There is some parallel to the conditioning of an injunction on the payment of permanent damages in the noted "elevated railway cases" (Pappenheim v. Metropolitan El. Ry. Co., 128 N.Y. 436, 28 N.E. 518 and others which followed). Decisions in these cases were based on the finding that the railways created a nuisance as to adjacent property owners, but in lieu of enjoining their operation, the court allowed permanent damages.

Judge Finch, reviewing these cases in Ferguson v. Village of Hamburg, 272 N.Y. 234, 239–240, 5 N.E.2d 801, 803, said: "The courts decided that the plaintiffs had a valuable right which was being impaired, but did not grant an absolute injunction or require the railway companies to resort to separate condemnation proceedings. Instead they held that a court of equity could ascertain the damages and grant an injunction which was not to be effective unless the defendant failed to pay the amount fixed as damages for the past and permanent injury inflicted."

Thus it seems fair to both sides to grant permanent damages to plaintiffs which will terminate this private litigation. The theory of damage is the "servitude on land" of plaintiffs imposed by defendant's nuisance. (See United States v. Causby, 328 U.S. 256, 261, 262, 267, 66 S.Ct. 1062, 90 L.Ed. 1206, where the term "servitude" addressed to the land was used by Justice Douglas relating to the effect of airplane noise on property near an airport.)

The judgment, by allowance of permanent damages imposing a servitude on land, which is the basis of the actions, would preclude future recovery by plaintiffs or their grantees.

This should be placed beyond debate by a provision of the judgment that the payment by defendant and the acceptance by plaintiffs of permanent damages found by the court shall be in compensation for a servitude on the land.

Although the Trial Term has found permanent damages as a possible basis of settlement of the litigation, on remission the court should be entirely free to re-examine this subject. It may again find the permanent damage already found; or make new findings.

The orders should be reversed, without costs, and the cases remitted to Supreme Court, Albany County to grant an injunction which shall be vacated upon payment by defendant of such amounts of permanent damage to the respective plaintiffs as shall for this purpose be determined by the court.

JASEN, Judge (dissenting).

I agree with the majority that a reversal is required here, but I do not subscribe to the newly enunciated doctrine of assessment of permanent damages, in lieu of an injunction, where substantial property rights have been impaired by the creation of a nuisance.

It has long been the rule in this State, as the majority acknowledges, that a nuisance which results in substantial continuing damage to neighbors must be enjoined. To now change the rule to permit the cement company to continue polluting the air indefinitely upon the payment of permanent damages is, in my opinion, compounding the magnitude of a very serious problem in our State and Nation today.

In recognition of this problem, the Legislature of this State has enacted the Air Pollution Control Act (Public Health Law, Consol.Laws, c. 45, §§ 1264 to 1299–m) declaring that it is the State policy to require the use of all available and reasonable methods to prevent and control air pollution (Public Health Law § 1265).

The harmful nature and widespread occurrence of air pollution have been extensively documented. Congressional hearings have revealed that air pollution causes substantial property damage, as well as being a contributing factor to a rising incidence of lung cancer, emphysema, bronchitis and asthma.

The specific problem faced here is known as particulate contamination because of the fine dust particles emanating from defendant's cement plant. The particular type of nuisance is not new, having appeared in many cases for at least the past 60 years. It is interesting to note that cement production has recently been identified as a significant source of particulate contamination in the Hudson Valley. This type of pollution, wherein very small particles escape and stay in the atmosphere, has been denominated as the type of air pollution which produces the greatest hazard to human health. We have thus a nuisance which not only is damaging to the plaintiffs, but also is decidedly harmful to the general public.

I see grave dangers in overruling our long-established rule of granting an injunction where a nuisance results in substantial continuing damage. In permitting the injunction to become inoperative upon the payment of permanent damages, the majority is, in effect, licensing a continuing wrong. It is the same as saying to the cement company, you may continue to do harm to your neighbors so long as you pay a fee for it. Furthermore, once such permanent damages are assessed and paid, the incentive to alleviate the wrong would be eliminated, thereby continuing air pollution of an area without abatement.

It is true that some courts have sanctioned the remedy here proposed by the majority in a number of cases, but none of the authorities relied upon by the majority are analogous to the situation before us. In those cases, the courts, in denying an injunction and awarding money damages, grounded their decision on a showing that the use to which the property was intended to be put was primarily for the public benefit. Here, on the other hand, it is clearly established that the cement company is creating a continuing air pollution nuisance primarily for its own private interest with no public benefit.

This kind of inverse condemnation may not be invoked by a private person or corporation for private gain or advantage. Inverse condemnation should only be permitted when the public is primarily served in the taking or impairment of property. The promotion of the interests of the polluting cement company has, in my opinion, no public use or benefit.

Nor is it constitutionally permissible to impose servitude on land, without consent of the owner, by payment of permanent damages where the continuing impairment of the land is for a private use. This is made clear by the State Constitution (art. I, § 7, subd. [a]) which provides that "[p]rivate property shall not be taken for *public use* without just compensation" (emphasis added). It is, of course, significant that the section makes no mention of taking for a *private* use.

In sum, then, by constitutional mandate as well as by judicial pronouncement, the permanent impairment of private property for private purposes is not authorized in the absence of clearly demonstrated public benefit and use.

I would enjoin the defendant cement company from continuing the discharge of dust particles upon its neighbors' properties unless, within 18 months, the cement company abated this nuisance.

It is not my intention to cause the removal of the cement plant from the Albany area, but to recognize the urgency of the problem stemming from this stationary source of air pollution, and to allow the company a specified period of time to develop a means to alleviate this nuisance.

I am aware that the trial court found that the most modern dust control devices available have been installed in defendant's plant, but, I submit, this does not mean that *better* and more effective dust control devices could not be developed within the time allowed to abate the pollution.

Moreover, I believe it is incumbent upon the defendant to develop such devices, since the cement company, at the time the plant commenced production (1962), was well aware of the plaintiffs' presence in the area, as well as the probable consequences of its contemplated operation. Yet, it still chose to build and operate the plant at this site.

In a day when there is a growing concern for clean air, highly developed industry should not expect acquiescence by the courts, but should, instead, plan its operations to eliminate contamination of our air and damage to its neighbors.

Accordingly, the orders of the Appellate Division, insofar as they denied the injunction, should be reversed, and the actions remitted to Supreme Court, Albany County to grant an injunction to take effect 18 months hence, unless the nuisance is abated by improved techniques prior to said date.

FULD, C.J., and BURKE and SCILEPPI, JJ., concur with BERGAN, J.

JASEN, J., dissents in part and votes to reverse in a separate opinion.

BREITEL and GIBSON, JJ., taking no part.

In each action: Order reversed, without costs, and the case remitted to Supreme Court, Albany County, for further proceedings in accordance with the opinion herein.

SPUR INDUSTRIES, INC. v. DEL E. WEBB DEVELOPMENT CO.

Supreme Court of Arizona, 1972.
108 Ariz. 178, 494 P.2d 700.

CAMERON, Vice Chief Justice.

From a judgment permanently enjoining the defendant, Spur Industries, Inc., from operating a cattle feedlot near the plaintiff Del E. Webb Development Company's Sun City, Spur appeals. Webb cross-appeals. Although numerous issues are raised, we feel that it is necessary to answer only two questions. They are:

1. Where the operation of a business, such as a cattle feedlot is lawful in the first instance, but becomes a nuisance by reason of a nearby residential area, may the feedlot operation be enjoined in an action brought by the developer of the residential area?

2. Assuming that the nuisance may be enjoined, may the developer of a completely new town or urban area in a previously agricultural area be required to indemnify the operator of the feedlot who must move or cease operation because of the presence of the residential area created by the developer?

The facts necessary for a determination of this matter on appeal are as follows. The area in question is located in Maricopa County, Arizona, some 14 to 15 miles west of the urban area of Phoenix, on the Phoenix-Wickenburg Highway, also known as Grand Avenue. About two miles south of Grand Avenue is Olive Avenue which runs east and west. 111th Avenue runs north and south as does the Agua Fria River immediately to the west. See Exhibits A and B below.

Farming started in this area about 1911. In 1929, with the completion of the Carl Pleasant Dam, gravity flow water became available to the property located to the west of the Agua Fria River, though land to the east remained dependent upon well water for irrigation. By 1950, the only urban areas in the vicinity were the agriculturally related communities of Peoria, El Mirage, and Surprise located along Grand Avenue. Along 111th Avenue, approximately one mile south of Grand Avenue and 1½ miles north of Olive Avenue, the community of Youngtown was commenced in 1954. Youngtown is a retirement community appealing primarily to senior citizens.

In 1956, Spur's predecessors in interest, H. Marion Welborn and the Northside Hay Mill and Trading Company, developed feedlots, about ½ mile south of Olive Avenue, in an area between the confluence of the usually dry Agua Fria and New Rivers. The area is well suited for cattle feeding and in 1959, there were 25 cattle feeding pens or dairy operations within a 7 mile radius of the location developed by Spur's predecessors. In April and May of 1959, the North-

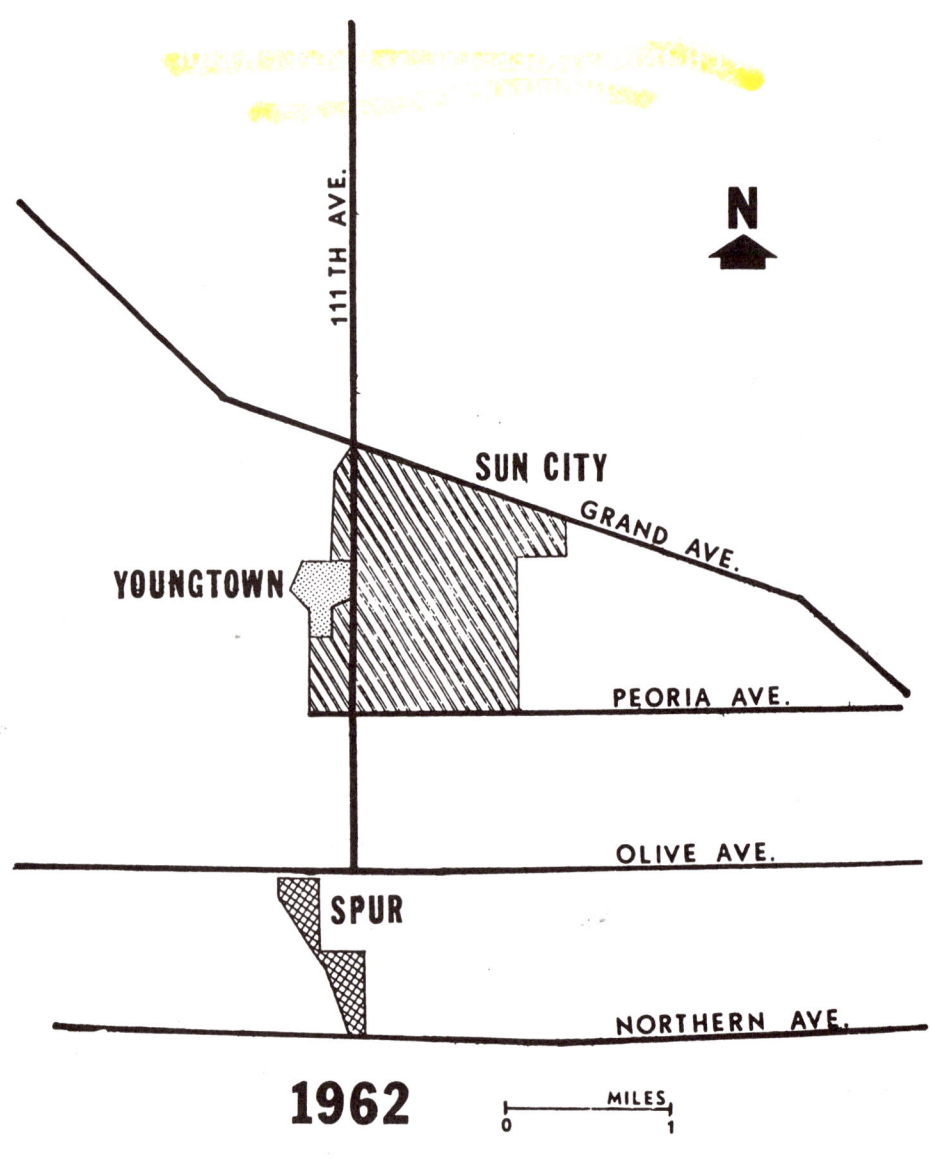

EXHIBIT A

side Hay Mill was feeding between 6,000 and 7,000 head of cattle and Welborn approximately 1,500 head on a combined area of 35 acres.

In May of 1959, Del Webb began to plan the development of an urban area to be known as Sun City. For this purpose, the Marinette and the Santa Fe Ranches, some 20,000 acres of farmland, were purchased for $15,000,000 or $750.00 per acre. This price was considerably less than the price of land located near the urban area of Phoenix, and along with the success of Youngtown was a factor influencing the decision to purchase the property in question.

WHY PROPERTY?

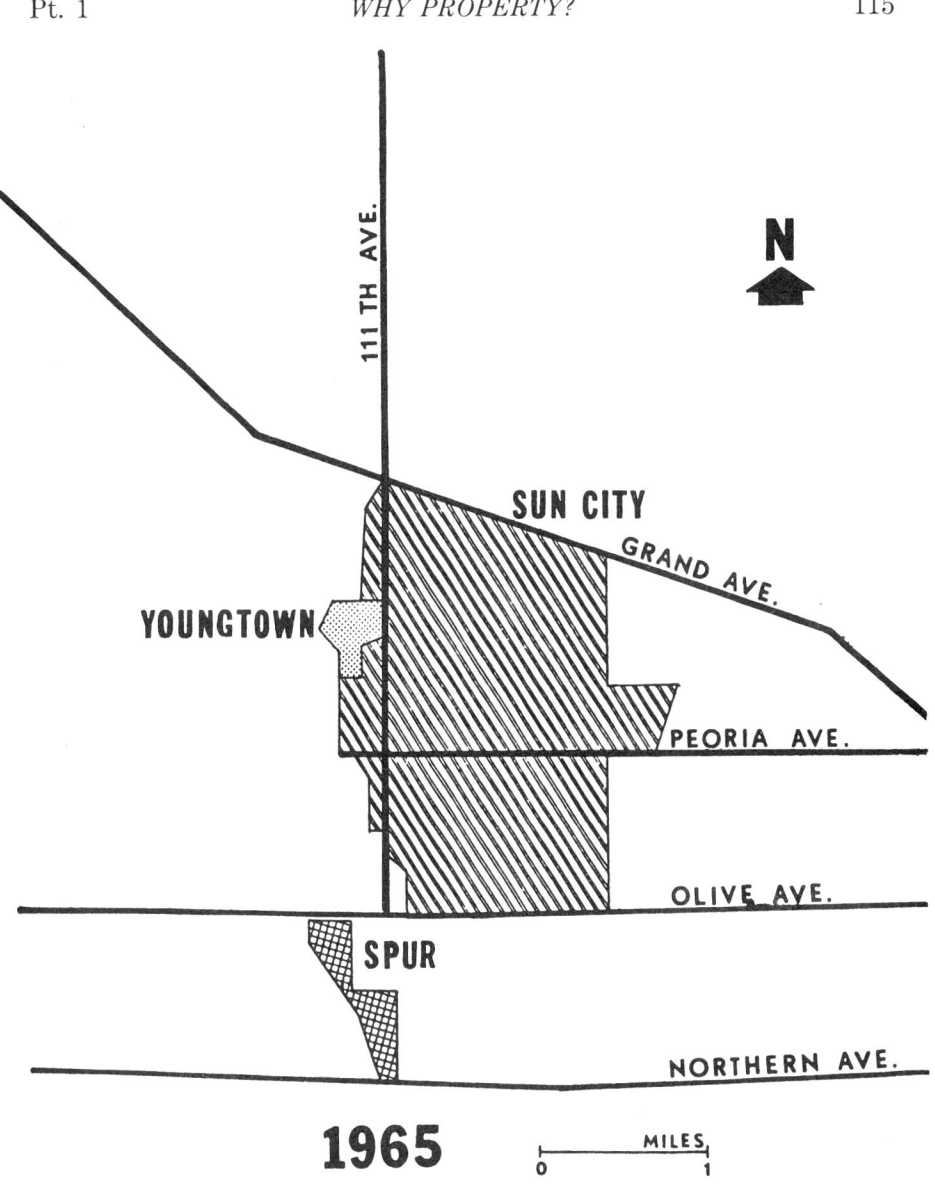

EXHIBIT B

By September 1959, Del Webb had started construction of a golf course south of Grand Avenue and Spur's predecessors had started to level ground for more feedlot area. In 1960, Spur purchased the property in question and began a rebuilding and expansion program extending both to the north and south of the original facilities. By 1962, Spur's expansion program was completed and had expanded from approximately 35 acres to 114 acres. See Exhibit A above.

Accompanied by an extensive advertising campaign, homes were first offered by Del Webb in January 1960 and the first unit to be completed was south of Grand Avenue and approximately 2½ miles north of Spur. By 2 May 1960, there were 450 to 500 houses completed or under construction. At this time, Del Webb did not consider odors from the Spur feed pens a problem and Del Webb continued to develop in a southerly direction, until sales resistance became so great that the parcels were difficult if not impossible to sell. Thomas E. Breen, Vice President and General Manager of the housing division of Del Webb, testified at deposition as follows:

"Q Did you ever have any discussions with Tony Cole at or about the time the sales office was opened south of Peoria concerning the problem in sales as the development came closer towards the feed lots?

"A Not at the time that that facility was opened. That was subsequent to that.

"Q All right, what is it that you recall about conversations with Cole on that subject?

"A Well, when the feed lot problem became a bigger problem, which, really, to the best of my recollection, commenced to become a serious problem in 1963, and there was some talk about not developing that area because of sales resistance, and to my recollection we shifted—we had planned at that time to the eastern portion of the property, and it was a consideration.

"Q Was any specific suggestion made by Mr. Cole as to the line of demarcation that should be drawn or anything of that type exactly where the development should cease?

"A I don't recall anything specific as far as the definite line would be, other than, you know, that it would be advisable to stay out of the southwestern portion there because of sales resistance.

"Q And to the best of your recollection, this was in about 1963?

"A That would be my recollection, yes.

. . .

"Q As you recall it, what was the reason that the suggestion was not adopted to stop developing towards the southwest of the development?

"A Well, as far as I know, that decision was made subsequent to that time.

"Q Right. But I mean at that time?

"A Well, at that time what I am really referring to is more of a long-range planning than immediate planning, and I think it was the case of just trying to figure out how far you could go with it before you really ran into a lot of sales resistance and found a necessity to shift the direction.

"Q So the plan was to go as far as you could until the resistance got to the point where you couldn't go any further?

"A I would say that is reasonable, yes."

By December 1967, Del Webb's property had extended south to Olive Avenue and Spur was within 500 feet of Olive Avenue to the north. See Exhibit B above. Del Webb filed its original complaint alleging that in excess of 1,300 lots in the southwest portion were unfit for development for sale as residential lots because of the operation of the Spur feedlot.

Del Webb's suit complained that the Spur feeding operation was a public nuisance because of the flies and the odor which were drifting or being blown by the prevailing south to north wind over the southern portion of Sun City. At the time of the suit, Spur was feeding between 20,000 and 30,000 head of cattle, and the facts amply support the finding of the trial court that the feed pens had become a nuisance to the people who resided in the southern part of Del Webb's development. The testimony indicated that cattle in a commercial feedlot will produce 35 to 40 pounds of wet manure per day, per head, or over a million pounds of wet manure per day for 30,000 head of cattle, and that despite the admittedly good feedlot management and good housekeeping practices by Spur, the resulting odor and flies produced an annoying if not unhealthy situation as far as the senior citizens of southern Sun City were concerned. There is no doubt that some of the citizens of Sun City were unable to enjoy the outdoor living which Del Webb had advertised and that Del Webb was faced with sales resistance from prospective purchasers as well as strong and persistent complaints from the people who had purchased homes in that area.

Trial was commenced before the court with an advisory jury. The advisory jury was later discharged and the trial was continued before the court alone. Findings of fact and conclusions of law were requested and given. The case was vigorously contested, including special actions in this court on some of the matters. In one of the special actions before this court, Spur agreed to, and did, shut down its operation without prejudice to a determination of the matter on appeal. On appeal the many questions raised were extensively briefed.

It is noted, however, that neither the citizens of Sun City nor Youngtown are represented in this lawsuit and the suit is solely between Del E. Webb Development Company and Spur Industries, Inc.

MAY SPUR BE ENJOINED?

The difference between a private nuisance and a public nuisance is generally one of degree. A private nuisance is one affecting a single individual or a definite small number of persons in the enjoyment of private rights not common to the public, while a public nuisance is one affecting the rights enjoyed by citizens as a part of the public. To constitute a public nuisance, the nuisance must affect a considerable number of people or an entire community or neighborhood.

Where the injury is slight, the remedy for minor inconveniences lies in an action for damages rather than in one for an injunction. Moreover, some courts have held, in the "balancing of conveniences" cases, that damages may be the sole remedy. See Boomer v. Atlantic Cement Co., 26 N.Y.2d 219, 309 N.Y.S.2d 312, 257 N.E.2d 870, 40 A.L.R.3d 590 (1970), and annotation comments, 40 A.L.R.3d 601.

Thus, it would appear from the admittedly incomplete record as developed in the trial court, that, at most, residents of Youngtown would be entitled to damages rather than injunctive relief.

We have no difficulty, however, in agreeing with the conclusion of the trial court that Spur's operation was an enjoinable public nuisance as far as the people in the southern portion of Del Webb's Sun City were concerned.

§ 36–601, subsec.A reads as follows:

" § 36–601. Public nuisances dangerous to public health

"A. The following conditions are specifically declared public nuisances dangerous to the public health:

"1. Any condition or place in populous areas which constitutes a breeding place for flies, rodents, mosquitoes and other insects which are capable of carrying and transmitting disease-causing organisms to any person or persons."

By this statute, before an otherwise lawful (and necessary) business may be declared a public nuisance, there must be a "populous" area in which people are injured:

". . . [I]t hardly admits a doubt that, in determining the question as to whether a lawful occupation is so conducted as to constitute a nuisance as a matter of fact, the locality and surroundings are of the first importance. (citations omitted) A business which is not per se a public nuisance may become such by being carried on at a place where the health, comfort, or convenience of a populous neighborhood is affected. . . . What might amount to a serious nuisance in one locality by reason of the density of the population, or character of the neighborhood affected, may in another place and under different surroundings be deemed proper and unobjectionable. . . . ." MacDonald v. Perry, 32 Ariz. 39, 49–50, 255 P. 494, 497 (1927).

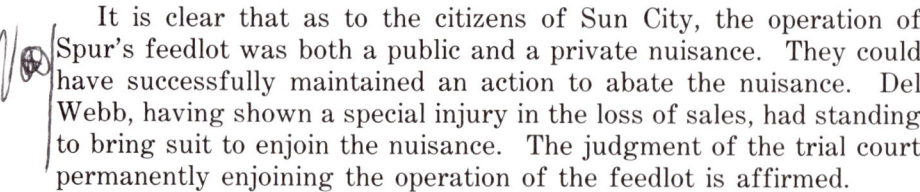

It is clear that as to the citizens of Sun City, the operation of Spur's feedlot was both a public and a private nuisance. They could have successfully maintained an action to abate the nuisance. Del Webb, having shown a special injury in the loss of sales, had standing to bring suit to enjoin the nuisance. The judgment of the trial court permanently enjoining the operation of the feedlot is affirmed.

MUST DEL WEBB INDEMNIFY SPUR?

A suit to enjoin a nuisance sounds in equity and the courts have long recognized a special responsibility to the public when acting as a court of equity:

> § 104. Where public interest is involved.
>
> "Courts of equity may, and frequently do, go much further both to give and withhold relief in furtherance of the public interest than they are accustomed to go when only private interests are involved. Accordingly, the granting or withholding of relief may properly be dependent upon considerations of public interest. . . ." 27 Am.Jur.2d, Equity, page 626.

In addition to protecting the public interest, however, courts of equity are concerned with protecting the operator of a lawfully, albeit noxious, business from the result of a knowing and willful encroachment by others near his business.

In the so-called "coming to the nuisance" cases, the courts have held that the residential landowner may not have relief if he knowingly came into a neighborhood reserved for industrial or agricultural endeavors and has been damaged thereby:

> "Plaintiffs chose to live in an area uncontrolled by zoning laws or restrictive covenants and remote from urban development. In such an area plaintiffs cannot complain that legitimate agricultural pursuits are being carried on in the vicinity, nor can plaintiffs, having chosen to build in an agricultural area, complain that the agricultural pursuits carried on in the area depreciate the value of their homes. The area being *primarily agricultural*, any opinion reflecting the value of such property must take this factor into account. The standards affecting the value of residence property in an urban setting, subject to zoning controls and controlled planning techniques, cannot be the standards by which agricultural properties are judged.
>
> "People employed in a city who build their homes in suburban areas of the county beyond the limits of a city and zoning regulations do so for a reason. Some do so to avoid the high taxation rate imposed by cities, or to avoid special assessments for street, sewer and water projects. They usually build on improved or hard surface highways, which have been built either at state or county expense and thereby avoid special assessments for these improvements. It may be that they desire to get away from the congestion of traffic, smoke, noise, foul air and the many other annoyances of city life. But with all these advantages in going beyond the area which is zoned and restricted to protect them in their homes, they must be prepared to take the disadvantages."

Dill v. Excel Packing Company, 183 Kan. 513, 525, 526, 331 P.2d 539, 548, 549 (1958).

And:

". . . a party cannot justly call upon the law to make that place suitable for his residence which was not so when he selected it. . . ." Gilbert v. Showerman, 23 Mich. 448, 455, 2 Brown 158 (1871).

Were Webb the only party injured, we would feel justified in holding that the doctrine of "coming to the nuisance" would have been a bar to the relief asked by Webb, and, on the other hand, had Spur located the feedlot near the outskirts of a city and had the city grown toward the feedlot, Spur would have to suffer the cost of abating the nuisance as to those people locating within the growth pattern of the expanding city:

"The case affords, perhaps, an example where a business established at a place remote from population is gradually surrounded and becomes part of a populous center, so that a business which formerly was not an interference with the rights of others has become so by the encroachment of the population . . . ." City of Ft. Smith v. Western Hide & Fur Co., 153 Ark. 99, 103, 239 S.W. 724, 726 (1922).

We agree, however, with the Massachusetts court that:

"The law of nuisance affords no rigid rule to be applied in all instances. It is elastic. It undertakes to require only that which is fair and reasonable under all the circumstances. In a commonwealth like this, which depends for its material prosperity so largely on the continued growth and enlargement of manufacturing of diverse varieties, 'extreme rights' cannot be enforced. . . ." Stevens v. Rockport Granite Co., 216 Mass. 486, 488, 104 N.E. 371, 373 (1914).

There was no indication in the instant case at the time Spur and its predecessors located in western Maricopa County that a new city would spring up, full-blown, alongside the feeding operation and that the developer of that city would ask the court to order Spur to move because of the new city. Spur is required to move not because of any wrongdoing on the part of Spur, but because of a proper and legitimate regard of the courts for the rights and interests of the public.

Del Webb, on the other hand, is entitled to the relief prayed for (a permanent injunction), not because Webb is blameless, but because of the damage to the people who have been encouraged to purchase homes in Sun City. It does not equitably or legally follow, however, that Webb, being entitled to the injunction, is then free of any liability to Spur if Webb has in fact been the cause of the damage Spur has sustained. It does not seem harsh to require a developer, who has taken advantage of the lesser land values in a rural area as well as the availability of large tracts of land on which to build and develop a new town or city in the area, to indemnify those who are forced to leave as a result.

Having brought people to the nuisance to the foreseeable detriment of Spur, Webb must indemnify Spur for a reasonable amount of the cost of moving or shutting down. It should be noted that this relief to Spur is limited to a case wherein a developer has, with foreseeability, brought into a previously agricultural or industrial area the population which makes necessary the granting of an injunction against a lawful business and for which the business has no adequate relief.

It is therefore the decision of this court that the matter be remanded to the trial court for a hearing upon the damages sustained by the defendant Spur as a reasonable and direct result of the granting of the permanent injunction. Since the result of the appeal may appear novel and both sides have obtained a measure of relief, it is ordered that each side will bear its own costs.

Affirmed in part, reversed in part, and remanded for further proceedings consistent with this opinion.

HAYS, C.J., STRUCKMEYER and LOCKWOOD, JJ., and UDALL, Retired Justice.

NOTES

1. Was the decision in *Boomer* correct? The court there seemed to be saying that the balance between the gravity of harm to plaintiff and the utility of defendant's conduct needs to be struck twice in nuisance cases: first, in determining whether a nuisance exists and second, if a nuisance exists, in determining whether plaintiff should be entitled to an injunctive decree or limited to an award of permanent damages. Is it likely that courts barred from balancing interests at the second step would strike the balance differently at the first step? For example, if the New York legislature had adopted an absolute rule that an injunction must be allowed once a nuisance is found, is it likely that the court would have found that Atlantic's conduct did not constitute a nuisance?

What are *Boomer's* probable effects on bargaining between polluters and their victims? What are the likely effects of a rule that would automatically entitle a victim to injunctive relief once she has proved a nuisance? Would injunctive relief enable the victim to "extort" the polluter and, if so, is the result necessarily undesirable? Say, for example, that the *Boomer* plaintiffs suffered $10,000 permanent damages as a result of Atlantic's operation, and that Atlantic would lose $100,000 if its operations were enjoined and shut down. Presumably, Atlantic would be willing to pay the *Boomer* plaintiffs any amount up to $100,000—say $99,000—to forestall its shutdown, even though their damage was only $10,000. Will a rule requiring Atlantic to pay $99,000 necessarily lead to a less productive use of land than a rule requiring it to pay only $10,000? Under the facts of the case, would transaction costs likely have disabled agreement even on these terms?

Say that, after entry of the decree in *Boomer*, Atlantic doubled its emissions. Would the *Boomer* plaintiffs be entitled to a new award of permanent damages? After the decree, would Atlantic have any incentive to *reduce* its emissions? Say that, after the decree, the federal government enforced an ambient air standard requiring Atlantic to cut its emissions by half. Could Atlantic successfully claim that the government had unconstitutionally deprived it of the property interest created by the decision in Boomer v. Atlantic Cement? Would Atlantic be entitled to compensation from the *Boomer* plaintiffs? Will *Boomer* encourage, discourage, or have no effect on, investment in research and development aimed at producing more effective pollution control devices? What effects, if any, are decisions like *Boomer* likely to have on decisions by industries and residents as to where they locate their factories and homes?

What difference, if any, is there between the result in *Boomer* and the result in Somerville v. Jacobs, p. 60 above? How appealing was Boomer's claim that its property was being unconstitutionally taken for a private rather than a public purpose? If an injunction had issued, would Atlantic have had a claim that *its* property had been taken, without any compensation at all? Would it have been better for the court to go one step further and hold that the *Boomer* plaintiffs could obtain an injunction by paying Atlantic the difference between Atlantic's cost of complying with the injunction and the permanent damages that were awarded? See Ellickson, Alternatives to Zoning: Covenants, Nuisance Rules, and Fines as Land Use Controls, 40 U.Chi.L.Rev. 681, 748 (1973). Was this the result reached in *Spur*?

For a careful analysis of the assumptions underlying *Boomer* and the arguments of its supporters, see Polinsky, Resolving Nuisance Disputes: The Simple Economics of Injunctive and Damage Remedies, 32 Stan.L.Rev. 1075 (1980).

2. Was *Spur* correct to give Webb an action even though it "came to the nuisance"? Section 840D of the Restatement (Second) of Torts (1977), headed "Coming to the Nuisance," provides that "the fact that the plaintiff has acquired or improved his land after a nuisance interfering with it has come into existence is not in itself sufficient to bar his action, but it is a factor to be considered in determining whether the nuisance is actionable." According to Comment *b*, the restatesmen thought that coming to the nuisance should not be an absolute bar because otherwise "the defendant by setting up an activity or a condition that results in the nuisance could condemn all the land in his vicinity to a servitude without paying any compensation, and so could arrogate to himself a good deal of the value of the adjoining land."

Do you agree? Was there a nuisance before Webb came to Spur's area? What cause of action, if any, did Spur have to prevent Sun City from expanding in its direction? Are you satisfied with the position that a prior user such as Spur should lose whenever a later user can demonstrate that the social value of the later use is greater than the social value of the earlier use? That the later user's cost of locating elsewhere is greater than the first user's cost of relocating? Applying the Coase theorem, p. 89 above, is there any reason to prefer a rule of liability over a rule of no liability in these circumstances? What are the likely effects of a decision either way on a first user's locational decisions? See generally, Wittman, First Come, First Served: An Economic Analysis of "Coming to the Nuisance," 9 J. Legal Studies 557 (1980).

3. On the assumption that *Spur* was correct to find a nuisance under the facts, was the court correct to charge Webb with the costs of Spur's relocation? If the court had found that Spur's activities did not constitute a nuisance as against Webb, what kind of bargain, if any, would Spur and Webb likely have struck between themselves? Would the terms of the bargain differ from the terms that the court imposed in requiring Webb to indemnify Spur? Would they be preferable? Is it desirable to separate the question, who has a *right* as against whom, from the question, who has what *remedy* as against whom?

Spur was anticipated in a very important law review article published that same year, Calabresi & Melamed, Property Rules, Liability Rules, and Inalienability: One View of the Cathedral, 85 Harv.L. Rev. 1089, 1105–1124 (1972). Calabresi and Melamed would ask, first, whether the offender or the victim is entitled to prevail and, second, whether the prevailing party—victim or offender—should be protected under a "property rule" (entitling him to an injunction) or a "liability rule" (entitling him only to damages). Thus, if the victim is entitled to prevail and is protected by a property rule, he can obtain an injunction against the offending use; a liability rule will, as in *Boomer*, give the victim damages only. If the offender is entitled to prevail—*i.e.*, there is no nuisance—and is protected by a property rule, the victim must, to stop the offender, pay the offender's price; a liability rule in this case will, as in *Spur*, give the victim an injunction against the offending use, but only if he compensates the offender for the offender's costs of complying. Would any of the first three alternatives be preferable to the resolution reached in *Spur*? See also, Rabin, Nuisance Law: Rethinking Fundamental Assumptions, 63 Va.L.Rev. 1299 (1977).

Calabresi and Melamed also formulated an "inalienability rule," disentitling the prevailing party from transferring his right either consensually or through court-ordered damages. Why do you suppose writers on the economics of nuisance law generally ignore this third rule in their analysis of remedial alternatives?

4. *Boomer* and *McCarty* involved claims of *private* nuisance. By contrast, a *public* nuisance is conduct that unreasonably interferes with the public's interest in health, safety, or general convenience. Unsanitary eating places, unsafe storage of explosives, and obstruction of highways, are just a few examples of public nuisances that have been made punishable at common law or by statute.

As a general rule, actions against public nuisances can be brought only by the appropriate public official. Thus, if *A*'s fallen tree blocks a public highway, no user of the highway, however inconvenienced, has an action against *A* for damages or for the tree's removal. One exception to the general rule is that the injured party, *B*, can recover damages if she suffers special injuries that differ in kind from those suffered by the public at large—if, for example, the obstruction keeps customers away from her business. And, if the conduct that constitutes a public nuisance also unreasonably interferes with *B*'s use of her land—if, for example, insects from the fallen tree begin to infest trees on *B*'s land—*B* may have an action for private nuisance. In this last example, *B* could probably proceed on a theory of either private nuisance or public nuisance with unique injury, or on both theories. Dean Prosser has observed that "the action founded on the public nuisance may sometimes be preferable, because it is well settled that prescriptive rights, laches and the statute of limitations do not run against it." W. Prosser, Torts, 589 (4th Ed. 1971).

Do you agree with *Spur*'s reasoning on the public nuisance point? If, in fact, Spur's activities constituted a public nuisance with respect to the Sun City Development, is it clear that Del Webb suffered the special sort of injury that entitles a property owner to bring an action against a public nuisance? What was Webb's special injury? How can loss of sales—to individuals who, if they became homebuyers would themselves have, at best, a private action against Spur—qualify as special injury?

5. A suit by over four hundred property owners in the Del Webb Development was pending against Spur at the time the Arizona Supreme Court decided Spur v. Webb. After the decision in *Spur*, Spur filed a third party complaint against Webb demanding that Webb indemnify it for damages for which it might be held liable to the plaintiff property owners. The third party complaint was dismissed by the trial court and Spur appealed.

In Spur Feeding Co. v. Superior Court of Maricopa County, 109 Ariz. 105, 505 P.2d 1377 (1973), the court held that the previous holding in Spur v. Webb was not *res judicata* as to the facts of the instant case. The court stated that Spur v. Webb only concerned itself with two questions: whether Spur's operations should be enjoined and, if so, who was going to pay for the cost of moving. In contrast, the present case was concerned with "1. whether each of the over 400 plaintiffs have sustained any damages as a result of Spur's previous operation, and 2. if so, whether Webb's conduct as to each of the individual plaintiffs is such that Webb should be required to indemnify Spur as to any damages that the court might find that the plaintiffs are entitled to receive." 109 Ariz. at 107, 505 P.2d at 1379. The court reversed the trial court's dismissal of Spur's third party complaint against Webb.

After Spur v. Webb, on what theory could Spur recover in its third-party action?

6. *Damages.* The basic measure of damages for nuisance is the difference in the land's value before and after the nuisance. Special damages may be recovered for injury to crops or business operations as well as for physical suffering. Some courts have held that plaintiff may recover for mental suffering even absent physical injury: "It is settled that, regardless of whether the occupant of land has sustained physical injury, he may recover the damages for the discomfort and annoyance of himself and the members of his family and for mental suffering occasioned by fear for the safety of himself and his family when such discomfort and suffering has been proximately caused by a trespass or a nuisance." Acadia California, Ltd. v. Herbert, 54 Cal.2d 328, 337, 5 Cal.Rptr. 686, 691, 353 P.2d 294, 299 (1960).

After the trial on the *Boomer* remand, two of the three still pending actions against Atlantic were settled. In the third action, Kinley v. Atlantic Cement, plaintiff argued for measuring damages against a more generous standard than fair market value—either "special market value" ("based on inflated prices paid by defendant for other properties in the neighborhood") or "contract price" ("the amount that a private corporation would have to pay where it needs such servitude to continue in operation as against a seller who was unwilling to sell his land.") In the court's view, "while the fair market value rule may not be the sole criterion, it does serve as a restraining influence on the possible excessiveness of the so-called 'special' market value, and as a sure check on the subjective and speculative nature of the so-called 'contract price.'" Finding that the value of plaintiff's land without the nuisance was $265,000, and with the nuisance was $125,000, the court concluded that the plaintiff had suffered $175,000 permanent damages. Boomer v. Atlantic Cement Co., 72 Misc.2d 834, 340 N.Y.S.2d 97 (Sup.Ct., Albany Cty. 1972), affirmed sub nom Kinley v. Atlantic Cement Co., 42 A.D.2d 496, 349 N.Y.S.2d 199 (3d Dept. 1973). According to the Appellate Division, the $35,000 difference between the damages ($175,000) awarded and the diminished value of the property ($265,000–$125,000, or $140,000) reflected "temporary damages . . . for the period October 1, 1962 to June, 1967, based upon the testimony at the prior trial and in accordance with the directive from the Court of Appeals." 42 A.D.2d at 498, 349 N.Y.S.2d at 201.

7. *Self Help Abatement.* Can a landowner employ self-help to abate a nuisance? According to the general view, "Whenever one experiences the kind and quantity of interference from a public or

private nuisance that would entitle him to damages at law, he is generally permitted to enter peaceably upon the land which bears the harmful condition and to contain or destroy such condition in a prompt and a reasonable manner." 6–A American Law of Property, § 28.34 (A.J. Casner, ed. 1952).

There are limits to the self-help remedy. Before attempting to abate the nuisance, the victim must usually give the offender notice and the opportunity to correct the problem himself. Also, the victim must move promptly: "where there is time and the opportunity for the interposition of an adequate legal remedy, which may be effectual, the law will not justify a summary resort to force." Martin v. Martin, 246 S.W.2d 718, 720 (Tex.Civ.App.1952). And, of course, the abater must use ordinary care not to inflict any more damage on the offender's property than is necessary to abate the nuisance.

Doubtless the most substantial curb on the abater's freedom to act is the risk of being wrong. If it is subsequently determined that the abated conduct did not constitute a nuisance, or that the abater gave insufficient notice, took an unreasonably long time to proceed, or caused unnecessary damage, he may face liability to his neighbor for property damages and also criminal liability for breach of the peace.

In what class of cases is abatement by self-help likely to commend itself to a nuisance victim? In what class of cases is it commendable as a matter of public policy?

2. LATERAL AND SUBJACENT SUPPORT

WARFEL v. VONDERSMITH

Supreme Court of Pennsylvania, 1954.
376 Pa. 1, 101 A.2d 736.

HORACE STERN, Chief Justice.

While there does not appear to be any precedent in Pennsylvania controlling the decision of the present appeal an application of the established principles governing other aspects of the problem supports the view taken by the court below and calls for an affirmance of its order.

The facts are these: Plaintiff, a general contractor, entered into a contract with Lancaster Newspapers, Inc., to demolish old structures and erect a new building on property belonging to it in the City of Lancaster. The new building was of heavy construction and required excavation for foundations and cellar to a depth of from 16 to 20 feet below the street level. Defendants are the owners of a property adjoining that of the Newspapers, and on it was erected a two-story brick store building together with a one-story structure used as a store room. These buildings were situated along the boundary line between the two properties; neither of them had a cellar or basement, but they rested on foundations which in general extended not more than 3 or 4 feet below the surface of the ground.

Plaintiff's plans called for an excavation along the boundary line for a distance of approximately 160 feet. Before starting operations he notified defendants of his intentions and that they should take all necessary measures to support their buildings. After some consultation and negotiations which proved abortive, defendants employed another contractor who undertook to protect their buildings from collapse by erecting certain temporary roof props or cribbing inside their buildings. Plaintiff notified defendants that in his opinion these precautions were wholly inadequate, but defendants refused to do any underpinning or shoring outside or under their buildings. Thereupon, allegedly in order to prevent interference with his work and injury to his workmen or other persons, plaintiff proceeded to underpin defendants' buildings at a cost of $3,572.37. Defendants had given plaintiff permission to enter upon their premises for that purpose but made no promise, express or implied, to pay the cost. Plaintiff brought the present action to recover the cost of the work. Defendants not only denied any obligation on their part to make such payment but filed a counterclaim for alleged damage to their property due to blasting and other operations conducted by plaintiff. The jury returned a verdict for plaintiff in the sum of $3,183.05, apparently the full amount of the claim less part of the counterclaim. Defendants moved for a new trial which the court granted solely on the ground that in its opinion defendants were not liable to pay plaintiff for the work done to support their buildings; the counterclaim, however, made it impossible to enter a judgment n.o.v. Plaintiff appeals from the granting of the new trial.

As far as the rights and obligations of one excavating on his own property are concerned the law is so well established as to require no citations of the multitude of authorities. At common law an owner of land is entitled to have it supported in its natural condition by the land of the adjoining proprietor. This right to lateral support is a natural right, not simply an easement but an incident to the land—a right of property attached to and passing with the soil. If the adjoining owner by excavation removes such support, thereby causing the land to fall, he is responsible in damages without regard to his degree of care or to the fact that the excavation may have been performed by an independent contractor. The right to lateral support, however, does not extend to structures erected on the property which materially increase the lateral pressure and therefore contribute to the subsidence of the land. As far as such structures are concerned an owner may lawfully excavate on his land although he injures them; in the absence of negligence (which varies with the circumstances) he is not obliged to underpin or otherwise support them and he incurs no liability for damage which may be caused them by the excavation. His only duty is to give notice to the adjoining owner of his intention to excavate and thus afford the latter an opportunity of protecting his buildings from all likely injury.

So much as to the well recognized rights and duties of the excavating owner. But when we come to a consideration of the rights and obligations of the adjoining owner we find a marked dearth of authoritative judicial decision. True, it is generally held that *if* such owner wishes to protect his buildings from collapse it is for him to take the necessary measures at his own expense. But is he *obliged*, as a duty to the excavating owner or contractor, to underpin and shore up his buildings, and, if he refuses so to do after having been properly notified, can the excavating owner or contractor thereupon perform that work and compel him to pay the cost thereof? The weight of existing authority is to the effect that his failure to support his building does *not* authorize the excavating owner or contractor to do so at the adjoining owner's expense.

. . . In Weisberger v. Maurer, 153 A. 626, at page 628, 9 N.J. Misc. 117, at page 120, affirmed 109 N.J.L. 273, 160 A. 634, the court said: "I am impressed by the argument in defendant's brief, that 'if I own a shack worth less than the cost of protecting it, it seems very high handed to allow the adjoining owner to protect it regardless of cost, at my expense. It may fall and do no damage. It may not fall at all.'" It was there accordingly held that the plaintiff could not recover for expenditures made by him in shoring up the adjoining owner's property after notice to the latter and failure by him to do the work himself.

In Korogodsky v. Chimberoff, 256 Ill.App. 255, at page 258, it was said: "If the owner of adjacent improved property does not see fit to protect himself and injury is sustained by him by reason of an excavation which is done with all reasonable care and skill, then he cannot recover, but the other person has no right to compel him to shore his own property. The one making the improvement has a commonlaw right to go upon the premises of the other for the purpose of shoring such building in order to protect property, when it is necessary, to prevent damage by reason of an excavation, but this is done at his own expense and cost."

In Braun v. Hamack, 206 Minn. 572, at pages 573, 575, 289 N.W. 553, at pages 553, 555, 129 A.L.R. 618, it was said: "The question presented is: Can an excavating land owner recover from the owner of adjoining burdened land sums expended by the former to brace and shore the latter's property when excavation could not be safely carried on without such precautions and when after having been given notice of the plan to excavate, the owner of the burdened land has refused to provide necessary protection? . . . One in the position of plaintiff, having the remedies mentioned and perhaps others, cannot, we feel, prevail in an action to recover money which he was under no legal or moral obligation to expend. True, it is alleged that he was required to brace and shore defendant's property in order safely to proceed with building operations. But no such action would have been required if plaintiff had not insisted on proceeding with such operations. Can he now base a claim for recovery on a necessity caused in part at least by himself? We think not. The money was expended without legal compulsion and in the absence of an unavoidable urgency. Therefore, plaintiff acted as a volunteer and we know of no legal principle upon which to premise an obligation, contractual or otherwise, on the part of defendant to reimburse him."

As against these authorities there are a few—none of a court of final jurisdiction—which hold otherwise, but which, in our opinion, are not well considered. As already stated the question has never apparently arisen for decision in Pennsylvania.[1] In our opinion, while, as previously stated, the excavating owner is under no duty to shore up, underpin or otherwise protect buildings on adjoining land, and, if the adjoining owner desires such protection he must himself take the necessary measures for that purpose, such adjoining owner is not *obliged* to take such action but may, if he so chooses, allow his building to remain in the condition resulting from the work of excavation in the neighboring property. If, on the other hand, the excavating owner or his contractor deems it necessary for purposes of their own to shore up or underpin buildings on the adjoining land they may themselves perform such work but at their own expense.

Apart from all that has thus been said concerning defendants' liability as adjoining owners it is extremely questionable, to say the least, whether, in any event, plaintiff, who is not the excavating owner but merely the contractor employed by him, can maintain any such right of action as is here asserted against the defendants inasmuch as there is no privity or other legal relation whatever between them.

The order of the court granting defendants a new trial is affirmed.

1. It may be of interest to note that by the Act of June 8, 1893, P.L. 360, § 8, it was provided, as to Philadelphia, that when the owner of property wished to excavate to a depth not exceeding 10 feet below the top of the curb line and the owner of adjoining land refused to underpin or protect any party or other walls wholly or partly thereon after notice from the Bureau of Building Inspection so to do, the inspector might enter upon the premises and take the necessary steps to make the same safe and secure at the expense of the owner of said wall or building of which it was a part. If, however, any owner desired to excavate to a greater depth than 10 feet it was his obligation to protect and underpin the wall of any adjoining structure at his own expense. These provisions were not to apply to buildings then erected or to dwelling houses. This Act was repealed by the Act of May 1, 1929, P.L. 1063, which, in section 1807, 53 P.S. § 5648, made it the duty of the owner excavating to a depth below the bottom of any party or other walls on the adjoining property to protect and underpin such walls and the buildings of which they formed a part. Upon refusal to do this after notification an inspector could have the work done at the expense of the excavating owner. This Act was repealed in turn by the Act of April 14, 1937, P.L. 313, 53 P.S. § 2224 et seq., which gave authority to the municipalities therein enumerated to govern and regulate by ordinance the construction and repair of all buildings.

FRIENDSWOOD DEVELOPMENT CO. v. SMITH-SOUTHWEST INDUSTRIES, INC.

Supreme Court of Texas, 1978.
576 S.W.2d 21.

DANIEL, Justice.

The question in this case is whether landowners who withdrew percolating ground waters from wells located on their own land are liable for subsidence which resulted on lands of others in the same general area.

Smith-Southwest Industries and other landowners located in the Seabrook and Clear Lake area of Harris County brought this class action in 1973 against Friendswood Development Company and its corporate parent, Exxon Corporation, alleging that severe subsidence of their lands was caused by the defendants' past and continuing withdrawals of vast quantities of underground water from wells on defendants' nearby lands. Friendswood, alleged to be the operator of the wells, joined as third party defendants numerous parties alleged to be withdrawing ground water in the same general area. Friendswood and Exxon moved for a summary judgment against the plaintiffs, and it was granted by the trial court along with denial of relief in the third party actions.

The trial court followed a long-established common law rule that, in the absence of willful waste or malicious injury, a landowner has the right to withdraw ground waters from wells located on his own land without liability for resulting damage to his neighbor's land. The Court of Civil Appeals reversed and remanded, holding that plaintiffs' petition stated a cause of action in nuisance and negligence and that the summary judgment record raises genuine issues of material fact with regard thereto. 546 S.W.2d 890. We reverse the judgment of the Court of Civil Appeals and affirm the judgment of the trial court.

Our decision results from what we conceive to be our duty to apply a rule of property law as it existed during the time of the actions complained of in this suit, even though we disagree with certain aspects of the existing rule. As to future subsidence caused by wells hereinafter drilled or produced, this Court, in the manner hereinafter set forth, will recognize and apply the law of negligence along with willful waste and malicious injury as limitations on the present rule applicable to subsidence resulting from withdrawal of underground waters.

Allegations and Summary Judgment Proof

The petition of Smith-Southwest, the name by which all of the plaintiffs will be identified, recites that plaintiffs are landowners in the area of Seabrook and Clear Lake, and as a class include all owners of fee simple and leasehold estates along the west bank of Galveston Bay from the north dike of the Houston Yacht Club, following the shore line south to the mouth of Clear Creek and inclusive of the entire shore line of Clear Lake, Armand's Bayou, and Taylor Bayou from the shore line to a contour line with elevation 15 feet above the shore line, except the land owned by the defendants.

The trial court had before it depositions, interrogatories, affidavits and exhibits which showed rather clearly that Friendswood had pumped large amounts of subsurface waters from its own property for sale primarily to industrial users in the Bayport industrial area developed by Friendswood and Exxon. These wells were drilled from 1964 through 1971, even though previous engineering reports to defendants showed that production therefrom would result in a certain amount of land subsidence in the area. Plaintiffs alleged that the wells were negligently spaced too close together, too near the common boundary of lands owned by plaintiffs and defendants, and that excessive quantities were produced with knowledge that this would cause subsidence and flooding of plaintiffs' lands. Plaintiffs alleged that this extensive withdrawal of ground water proximately caused the sinking and loss of elevation above mean sea level of their property and the property of others similarly situated along the shores of Galveston Bay and Clear Lake, resulting in the erosion and flooding of their lands and damage to their residences, businesses and improvements. Plaintiffs further allege that the manner in which Friendswood Development Company continues to use its property for the withdrawal and sale of large amounts of fresh water to commercial users on other lands constitutes a continuing nuisance and permanent loss and damage to their property.

The defendants, Friendswood Development Company and its parent company, Exxon, are sought to be held jointly liable for the damages alleged in this case on the theory that they jointly planned and pursued the operations complained of. Among other defenses, Friendswood and Exxon contend that subsidence was a problem in the area before their operations began and that owners of other water wells throughout Harris and Galveston Counties caused or contributed to the subsidence. Friendswood's third party action for contribution and indemnity was filed against twenty-two companies and municipalities in Harris and Galveston Counties, alleging that they contributed to any existing subsidence by pumping large quantities of ground water from the common aquifers underlying the lands in question. Plaintiffs concede that subsidence in the area complained of was known to be a "potential problem" before defendants' operations began, but they allege that Friendswood and Exxon knew that the problem "would be severely aggravated" by the withdrawals which the companies contemplated. There was summary judgment proof of such knowledge and aggravation.

Reports in the record and publications of official agencies reflect that land subsidence in Harris County is not peculiar to or confined within the Galveston Bay and Clear Creek areas described in plaintiffs' petition. Rather it is a problem which has existed for many years in Harris and Galveston Counties. Harris County alone had 2,635 ground water wells in the inventory compiled by the U.S. Geological Survey in cooperation with the Texas Water Development Board in 1972. The Chicot and Evangeline aquifers underlie the Houston-Galveston region, which includes all of Harris and Galveston Counties and parts of adjacent counties. These two aquifers furnish all of the ground water pumped in the Houston-Galveston region, according to the U.S. Geological Report prepared by R.K. Gabrysch and C.W. Bonnet in 1974. This report states that water level declines of as much as 200 feet have resulted in wells completed in the Chicot aquifer and as much as 325 feet in the Evangeline aquifer during 1943–73, and "the declines in artesian pressures have resulted in a pronounced regional subsidence of the land surface." It states that the area in which there has been subsidence of one foot or more has increased from 350 square miles in 1954 to about 2,500 square miles in 1973. The contour lines of this area encompass practically all of Harris and Galveston Counties and include all of the principal areas of ground water withdrawals. Maps in the report indicate that the land and wells involved in this suit are in or near the "Johnson Space Center Area," where the land surface subsided about 2.12 feet between 1964 and 1973.

The general and widespread problem of subsidence in Harris and Galveston Counties has been considered in numerous other writings, and more notably by action of the Legislature, which created the Harris-Galveston Coastal Subsidence District in 1975.[7] This is a comprehensive measure "to provide for the regulation of the withdrawal of ground water within the boundaries of the district for the purpose of ending subsidence which contributes to or precipitates flooding, inundation, or overflow of any area within the district . . . ." It includes all of Harris and Galveston Counties and provides for a board of fifteen members with the power to grant or decline permits for new wells, regulate spacing and production, require metering devices, and adopt any rules necessary to prevent further subsidence.[8]

The magnitude of the problem has been reviewed in depth because it is relevant to our determination of whether existing rules of law are applicable and appropriate, or whether new rules should be adopted by this Court or recommended for consideration by the Legislature.

7. Chap. 284, 64th Legislature, Reg. Sess., effective April 23, 1975. See Beckendorff v. Harris-Galveston Coastal Subsidence District, 558 S.W.2d 75 (Tex.Civ. App.1977, writ ref'd n.r.e.), a case which upheld the constitutionality of the Act.

8. Id., Sec. 1a; Secs. 19–24; and Secs. 28–30.

Nature of Plaintiffs' Action

Plaintiffs have alleged an action in tort based upon the general rule that a landowner has a duty not to use his property so as to injure others—*sic utere tuo ut alienum non laedas*. Storey v. Central Hide & Rendering Co., 148 Tex. 509, 226 S.W.2d 615 (1950); Turner v. Big Lake Oil Co., 128 Tex. 155, 96 S.W.2d 221 (1936); Gulf, C. & S.F. Ry. Co. v. Oakes, 94 Tex. 155, 58 S.W. 999 (1900). The Court of Civil Appeals cited the above cases and this general rule of tort law in holding that plaintiffs were entitled to a trial on the allegations of nuisance and negligence. The problem is that those cases, none of which related to ground water withdrawals, involved liability for the *unreasonable use* of correlative property rights or the balancing of legal and equitable rights between property owners. This is a concept which was deliberately rejected with respect to withdrawals of underground water when this Court adopted the common law rule that such rights are not correlative, but are absolute, and thus are not subject to the conflicting "reasonable use" rule. Houston & T.C. Ry. Co. v. East, 98 Tex. 146, 81 S.W. 279 (1904).

Plaintiffs insist that this is not a case involving conflicting claims to the ownership or nontortuous use of water and that, therefore, the "archaic and awkward" common law rule adopted in *East* as to "absolute" ownership should not insulate the defendants from damages due to nuisance in fact or negligence in the manner by which they made use of their property. This is, in effect, a contention that the "reasonable use" doctrine should apply to ground water the same as it does to other real property.

The plaintiff in *East* argued for the "reasonable use" rule in that case, and it was adopted by the Court of Civil Appeals. East v. Houston & T.C. Ry. Co., 77 S.W. 646 (Tex.Civ.App.1903, error granted). In that case the railroad company, with full knowledge of the long existence of Mr. East's small shallow well on his homestead, dug a well twenty feet in diameter and 66 feet deep on its own adjacent property, from which it pumped 25,000 gallons of water per day. This resulted in lowering the water level on plaintiff's land and drying up his well. The trial court found that the railroad's well was not a reasonable use of its property, and that plaintiff *and his land* had sustained damage in the sum of $206.00. Nevertheless, the trial court granted judgment for the railroad. The Court of Civil Appeals reversed and rendered judgment in favor of East. It followed what has since become known as the "reasonable use" or "American rule" as set forth in Bassett v. Salisbury Mfg. Co., 43 N.H. 569, 82 Am.Dec. 179 (1862), which held that the right of a landowner to draw underground water from his land was not absolute, but limited to the amount necessary for the reasonable use of his land, and that the rights of adjoining landowners are correlative and limited to reasonable use. The court also noted the contrary English doctrine laid down in Acton v. Blundell, 12 M. & W. 324, 152 E.R. 1223 (Ex.1843), that, "if a man digs a well on his own field and thereby drains his neighbor's, he may do so unless he does it maliciously." The court said that "to apply that rule under the facts shown here would shock our sense of justice."

Adoption of the Common Law Rule of Absolute Ownership

Thus, on the appeal of the *East* case to this Court, the conflicting aspects of the "reasonable use" rule and the common law rule, later referred to as the "English rule" or "absolute ownership rule," were clearly presented. This Court discussed both rules and made a deliberate choice of the common law rule as announced in Acton v. Blundell, *supra*, reciting that it had been followed since 1843 in the courts of England "and probably by all the courts of last resort in this country before which the [subject] has come, except the Supreme Court of New Hampshire." Houston & T.C. Ry. Co. v. East, 98 Tex. 146, 81 S.W. 279, 280 (1904). In reversing the Court of Civil Appeals and rejecting the "reasonable use" rule, this Court adopted the absolute ownership doctrine of underground percolating waters. It cited approvingly the language of the Supreme Court of Ohio in Frazier v. Brown, 12 Ohio St. 294 (1861): "In the absence of express contract and a positive authorized legislation, as between proprietors of adjoining land, the law recognizes no correlative rights in respect to underground water percolating, oozing, or filtrating through the earth; and this mainly from considerations of public policy . . . ." [9]

In holding that the owner may withdraw water from beneath his land without liability for lowering the water table and thus damaging his neighbor's well and land, the Court mentioned only waste and malice as possible limitations to the rule. Absent these, the Court clearly embraced the doctrine stated in Acton v. Blundell, *supra*, that this type of damage "falls within the description *damnum absque injuria*, which cannot become the ground of action." This legal maxim denotes a loss without injury in the legal sense, that is, without the invasion of a legal right or the violation of a legal duty. Langbrook Properties, Ltd. v. Surrey County Council, 3 ALL E.R. 1424 (Ch.1969). In *Langbrook*, which was an action for subsidence caused by withdrawal of ground water, the court held that the law of negligence and nuisance did not apply under the English rule because pumping of the water was lawful and there was no duty to protect against the injury. We have been cited no case from a jurisdiction

---

9. The public policy considerations were said to be (1) "because the existence, origin, movement and course of such waters, . . . are so secret, occult and concealed that an attempt to administer any set of legal rules in respect to them would be involved in hopeless uncertainty, and would, therefore, be practically impossible"; and (2) "because any such recognition of correlative rights would interfere, to the material detriment of the commonwealth, with drainage and agriculture, mining, ..." etc. 81 S.W. 279 at p. 281. For criticisms of the reasons for the rule see note 17, infra.

which adheres to the English rule in which actions in tort for subsidence have been recognized.

The English rule of so-called "absolute ownership" was applied by this Court in Texas Co. v. Burkett, 117 Tex. 16, 296 S.W. 273 (1927), which held that a landowner has the absolute right to sell percolating ground water for industrial purposes off the land. At a time when the trend in other jurisdictions was away from the English rule and toward the "reasonable use" rule, the English rule was reaffirmed by this Court in City of Corpus Christi v. City of Pleasanton, 154 Tex. 289, 276 S.W.2d 798 (1955). The Court said:

> "With both rules before it, this Court in 1904, adopted, unequivocally, the 'English' or 'Common Law' rule. Houston & T.C.R. Co. v. East, 98 Tex. 146, 81 S.W. 279, 280, 66 L.R.A. 738, 107 Am.St.Rep. 620. The opinion in the case shows quite clearly that the court weighed the merits of the two rules—'The practical reasons upon which the courts base their conclusions [applying the "English" rule] fully meet the more theoretical view of the New Hampshire Court [applying the "American" rule] and satisfy us of the necessity of the doctrine'—and, whether wisely or unwisely, made a deliberate choice. . . .
>
> ". . .
>
> "Having adopted the 'English' rule it may be assumed that the Court adopted it with only such limitations as existed in the common law. What were these limitations? About the only limitations applied by those jurisdictions retaining the 'English' rule are that the owner may not maliciously take water for the sole purpose of injuring his neighbor, wantonly and willfully waste it. 56 Am.Jur., sec. 119, p. 602. . . ." [10]

For similar recognition that percolating ground waters belong to the landowner and may be produced by him at his will, absent waste or malice, see Pecos County Water Control & Imp. Dist. No. 1 v. Williams, 271 S.W.2d 503 (Tex.Civ.App.1954, writ ref'd n.r.e.), which was pending in this Court simultaneously with the *Corpus Christi* case, *supra.* See also Brown v. Humble Oil & Ref. Co., 126 Tex. 296, 83 S.W.2d 935 (1935), one of the basic cases recognizing private ownership of oil and gas in place, which cites *East* as the earliest case establishing the "law of capture" in Texas. Other writers have traced both the Texas ownership and capture theories to the English rule relating to underground percolating waters, and it is interesting to note in this connection that the courts did not attempt to afford protection against the rule of capture of oil and gas until the Legislature enacted policy guidelines for the prevention of waste and protection of correlative rights. By the same token, it has been suggested that

---

10. In Bradford Corp. v. Pickles, 1 Ch. 145 (1895), aff'd H.L. [1895–99] ALL E.R. 984, and subsequent English cases, doubt was cast as to whether malicious injury was a limitation on the English rule. No doubt on this limitation has been expressed by this Court. We reaffirm the limitation in this opinion.

regulation of ground water production is primarily a legislative, not a judicial problem.

As heretofore mentioned in 1975 the Legislature undertook to retard further subsidence in Harris and Galveston Counties by creating a subsidence district with power to prevent future well spacing and excessive pumping of the nature alleged to have occurred in this case. Previously, in 1949 the Legislature provided for the creation of districts for the purpose of "conservation, preservation, protection, recharging, and prevention of waste of underground water . . . ."[13] In 1973, the Legislature added to such purposes the authority "to control subsidence caused by withdrawal of water . . . ."[14]

It is of some importance to note that in the laws authorizing these regulatory Underground Water Districts and the Harris-Galveston Coastal Subsidence District, the Legislature specifically confirmed private ownership of underground water. It provided: "The ownership and rights of the owner of land and his lessees and assigns in underground water are hereby recognized, and nothing in this Act shall be construed as depriving or divesting the owner or his lessees and assigns of the ownership or rights . . . .," subject only to the regulatory rules to be promulgated by the districts. See Vernon's Tex. Water Code Ann. § 52.002 and Sec. 29, Ch. 284, Acts 64 Leg. 1975.

Subsidence Cases Under the Common Law Rule

Although the *East, Corpus Christi*, and *Williams* cases involved damages to wells and lands of the plaintiffs because the water tables beneath their lands were lowered by ground water withdrawals of the defendants, none of these nor any other Texas case has dealt specifically with land subsidence resulting from such pumping of underground waters. In other jurisdictions adhering to the English ground water rule, liability for neighboring land subsidence has been denied. Langbrook Properties, Ltd. v. Surrey County Council, [1969] 3 ALL E.R. 1424 (Ch.1969); New York Continental Jewell Filtration Co. v. Jones, 37 App.D.C. 511 (D.C.Cir.1911); English v. Metropolitan Water Board, 1 K.B. 588 (1907); Elster v. City of Springfield, 30 N.E. 274 (Ohio 1892); Popplewell v. Hodgkinson, [1861–73] ALL E.R. 996 (Ex. 1869). See also Finley v. Teeter Stone, Inc., 251 M.D. 428, 248 A.2d 106 (1968), in which the same holding was made in a jurisdiction which follows the reasonable use rule.

On the basis of the earlier decisions cited above, the Restatement of Torts § 818 (1939), adopted the following rule:

13. Ch. 306, Acts 51st Leg.1949, p. 559, codified as Ch. 52 of Vernon's Texas Water Code.

14. Ch. 598, Acts 63rd Leg.1973, p. 1641, codified in Sec. 52.021 of the Texas Water Code.

" § 818. WITHDRAWING SUBTERRANEAN WATER.

To the extent that a person is not liable for withdrawing subterranean waters from the land of another, he is not liable for a subsidence of the other's land which is caused by the withdrawal."

The foregoing statement in § 818 fairly represents the law on the subject as pronounced in common law jurisdictions. In 1840, Texas adopted the common law of England, with exceptions not relevant here. Our present Article 1, Texas Revised Civil Statutes, reads:

> "The common law of England, so far as it is not inconsistent with the Constitution and laws of this State, shall together with such Constitution and laws, be the rule of decision, and shall continue in force until altered or repealed by the Legislature."

We have found nothing in our Constitution, laws, or decisions inconsistent with the common law rule. On the contrary, our decisions in *East, City of Pleasanton,* and *Williams*, denying liability for damages to neighboring property because of lowering the water tables beneath neighboring lands, are consistent with the rule as stated above. It has been suggested, but not by respondents, that another rule applicable to destruction of subjacent land support caused by withdrawal of minerals should be applied in this case. We disagree, because the common law has recognized a clear distinction between subsidence caused by withdrawal of water and that caused by withdrawal of minerals, especially when solid minerals were involved. Restatement of Torts § 820 (1939), relating to withdrawal of subjacent support, reflects this distinction by a specific exception of water withdrawals referred to in § 818, *supra*, as follows:

" § 820. WITHDRAWING NATURALLY NECESSARY SUBJACENT SUPPORT.

> (1) Except as stated in § 818, a person who withdraws the naturally necessary subjacent support of land in another's possession or the support which has been substituted for the naturally necessary support is liable for a subsidence of such land of the other as was naturally dependent upon the support withdrawn, in the absence of a superseding cause or other reason for relieving him."

Although a tentative revision of § 818 was adopted by the American Law Institute in 1969, which would completely reverse this rule, it is important to our decision in this case that the Restatement of Torts rule as quoted above was in effect, without any tentative change, from 1939 to 1969.[15] The defendants began drilling and production from their wells in 1964 and the majority of their wells were completed by 1969.

The facts and legal issues in *Langbrook, supra,* were most similar to those in the instant case. In *Langbrook*, the plaintiffs alleged nui-

---

15. The tentative change of § 818 from non-liability to strict liability, with the addition of other substances, reads as follows:

sance and negligence in an action for damages to their property due to subsidence alleged to have been caused by defendants in the manner by which they withdrew underground water from their own nearby property. The only question before the court was whether plaintiffs' suit, cast in nuisance and negligence, stated a cause of action. The court, after an exhaustive review of the English cases, held that the law of nuisance and negligence was not applicable in the case by reason of the acts complained of because there was no duty to take care against the resulting damage and no unlawful act of interference with lawful rights of the plaintiffs. The court said:

> "The authorities cited on behalf of the defendants in my judgment establish that a man may abstract the water under his land which percolates in undefined channels to whatever extent he pleases, notwithstanding that this may result in the abstraction of water percolating under the land of his neighbour and, thereby, cause him injury. In such circumstances the principle of *sic utere tuo ut alienum non laedas* [use your property so as not to injure the property of another] does not operate and the damage is *damnum sine injuria* [damages suffered without the invasion of a legal right or the violation of a legal duty].
>
> "Is there then any room for the law of nuisance or negligence to operate? In my judgment there is not . . . if there were, it seems to me highly probable that the courts would already have said so, and yet I have not been referred to any case in which that was done." [1969] 3 ALL E.R.Rep. at 1439–40.

The above holding is in accord with Texas rules of tort law that (1) in order to create liability for the maintenance of a nuisance, the act complained of must in some way constitute an unlawful invasion of the right of another, and (2) for redress in negligence actions there must be a violation of a legal right and the breach of a legal duty.

Stare Decisis

We agree that some aspects of the English or common law rule as to underground waters are harsh and outmoded, and the rule has been severely criticized since its reaffirmation by this Court in 1955.

" § 818. WITHDRAWING SUBTERRANEAN SUBSTANCES.

One who is privileged to withdraw subterranean water, oil, minerals or other substances from under the land of another is not for that reason privileged to cause a subsidence of the other's land by such withdrawal."

The proceedings of the American Law Institute reflect that this change was proposed by the Reporter, Dean Prosser, in what he termed "a rather bob-tailed session," with the explanation that instead of fixing liability, this revision of § 818 would simply "knock out the absolute privilege to withdraw water without liability for the consequences." 1969 Proceedings of the American Law Institute 268, 273. The Reporter's *Note to Institute* appended to the tentative draft states that "[t]he Advisors and the Council, meeting the problem for the first time, are in some doubt, but express themselves as willing to follow the majority of the cases." [Most of which related to substances other than water.] See tentative draft proposal # 15, Restatement (Second) of Torts § 818, Ch. 39.

Most of the critics, however, recognize that it has become an established rule of property law in this State, under which many citizens own land and water rights. The rule has been relied upon by thousands of farmers, industries, and municipalities in purchasing and developing vast tracts of land overlying aquifers of underground water. Approximately 50,000 wells are used to irrigate 2,800,000 acres in the thirteen county High Plains area of West Texas. As shown in the official reports cited earlier in this opinion, over 2,600 water wells have been drilled in Harris County alone while this rule of immunity from liability was in effect. The very wells which brought about this action were drilled after the English rule had been reaffirmed by this Court in 1955.

On this subject, we are not writing on a clean slate. Even though good reasons may exist for lifting the immunity from tort actions in cases of this nature, it would be unjust to do so retroactively. The doctrine of *stare decisis* has been and should be strictly followed by this Court in cases involving established rules of property rights. It is for this reason that, as to past actions complained of in this case, we follow the English rule and Restatement of Torts § 818 (1939) in holding that defendants are not liable on plaintiff's allegations of nuisance and negligence. The same reasoning applies to plaintiffs' other allegations in tort (wrongful diversion of surface waters onto and across plaintiffs' lands and wrongful taking and conversion of plaintiffs' property), which the Court of Civil Appeals did not reach. We have considered all of plaintiffs' points of error in the Court of Civil Appeals complaining of the trial court's judgment and find them to be without merit.

As To Future Wells and Subsidence

As heretofore mentioned, the Legislature has entered the field of regulation of ground water withdrawals and subsidence. This occurred after geologists, hydrologists, and engineers had developed more accurate knowledge concerning the location, source, and measurement of percolating underground waters, and after legislators became aware of the potential conflicts inherent in the unregulated use of ground water under the English rule of ownership. With a rule that recognizes ownership of underground water by each individual under his own land, but with no limitation on the manner and amount which another individual landowner might produce (absent willful waste and malicious malice), legislative action was essential in order to provide for conservation and protection of public interests.

The legislative policy contained in Chapter 52 of the Texas Water Code is designed to limit the exercise of that portion of the English rule which has been interpreted as giving each landowner the right to take all the water he pleases without regard to the effect on other lands in the same area. For instance, § 52.117 of the Water Code, applicable to Underground Water Conservation Districts, provides:

"§ 52.117. REGULATION OF SPACING AND PRODUCTION.

"In order to minimize as far as practicable the drawdown of the water table or the reduction of artesian pressure, to control subsidence, or to prevent waste, the district may provide for the spacing of water wells and may regulate the production of wells."

Ten of these Underground Water Conservation Districts are active in an area embracing much of West Texas. The need for additional legislation for creation of districts to cover unregulated ground water reservoirs and to solve other conflicts which may arise in this area of water law and subsidence seems to be inevitable. Providing policy and regulatory procedures in this field is a legislative function. It is well that the Legislature has assumed its proper role, because our courts are not equipped to regulate ground water uses and subsidence on a suit-by-suit basis.

This case, however, gives the Court its first opportunity to recognize, and to encourage compliance with, the policy set forth by the Legislature and its regulatory agencies in an effort to curb excessive underground water withdrawals and resulting land subsidence. It also affords us the opportunity to discard an objectionable aspect of the court-made English rule as it relates to subsidence by stating a rule for the future which is more in harmony with expressed legislative policy. We refer to the past immunity from negligence which heretofore has been afforded ground water producers solely because of their "absolute" ownership of the water.

As far as we can determine, there is no other use of private real property which enjoys such an immunity from liability under the law of negligence. This ownership of underground water comes with ownership of the surface; it is part of the soil. Yet, the use of one's ground-level surface and other elements of the soil is without such insulation from tort liability. Our consideration of this case convinces us that there is no valid reason to continue this special immunity insofar as it relates to future subsidence proximately caused by negligence in the manner which wells are drilled or produced in the future. It appears that the ownership and rights of all landowners will be better protected against subsidence if each has the duty to produce water from his land in a manner that will not negligently damage or destroy the lands of others.

Therefore, if the landowner's manner of withdrawing ground water from his land is negligent, willfully wasteful, or for the purpose of malicious injury, and such conduct is a proximate cause of the subsidence of the land of others, he will be liable for the consequences of his conduct. The addition of negligence as a ground of recovery shall apply only to future subsidence proximately caused by future withdrawals of ground water from wells which are either produced or drilled in a negligent manner after the date this opinion becomes final.

While this addition of negligence as a ground of recovery in subsidence cases applies to future negligence in producing water from existing wells and those drilled or produced in a negligent manner in the future, it has been suggested that this new ground of recovery should be applied in the present cause of action. This is often done when a court writes or adds a new rule applicable to personal injury cases, but seldom when rules of property law are involved. This is because precedent is necessarily a highly important factor when problems regarding land or contracts are concerned. In deeds, property transactions, and land developments, the parties should be able to rely on the law which existed at the time of their actions. For the power of the courts in this regard, see Great Northern Ry. Co. v. Sunburst Oil and Refining Co., 287 U.S. 358, 53 S.Ct. 145, 77 L.Ed. 360 (1932).

Judgment

Accordingly, the judgment of the Court of Civil Appeals is reversed and the judgment of the trial court is affirmed.

Dissenting Opinion by POPE, J., in which SAM D. JOHNSON, J., joins.

CHADICK, J., not sitting.

POPE, Justice, dissenting.

I respectfully dissent. The court has decided this cause upon the mistaken belief that the case is governed by the ownership of ground water. Plaintiffs assert no ownerships to the percolating waters pumped and extracted from the ground by defendants. They make no complaint that their own wells have been or will be pumped dry. They seek no damages for the defendants' sale of the water. Plaintiffs' action calls for no change in nor even a review of the English rule of "absolute ownership" of ground water, the American rule of "reasonable use" of ground water, nor the Texas rule of "nonwasteful" use of ground water. They claim no correlative rights in the water. The Texas law of percolating waters is not put in issue by this suit, and there is no occasion to overrule that law either now or prospectively. There is a question whether this court can or ought to do so after the Texas legislature has so often and so recently stated its intent that the law of ground waters should be respected.

Plaintiffs' complaint is that defendants are causing subsidence of their land. They assert an absolute right to keep the surface of their land at its natural horizon. The landowners' right to the subjacent support for their land is the only right in suit, and this is a case of original impression. Other areas of the law should not be disturbed, but the majority opinion needlessly does so. It is no more logical to say that this is a case concerning the right to ground water than it would be correct in a case in which an adjoining landowner removed lateral support by a caterpillar to say that the case would be governed by the law of caterpillars. In making this decision about one's right to subjacent support, I would use as analogies other kinds of cases concerning support, such as the right to lateral support.

A landowner's right to lateral support for his land is an absolute right. The instrument employed in causing land to slough off, cave in or wash away is not the real subject of inquiry. The inquiry is whether the adjoining owner actually causes the loss of support. Whether the support is destroyed by excavation, ditching, the flowing of water, the pumping of water, unnatural pressure, unnatural suction, or explosives, the right to support is the same, and it is an absolute right. It was said in San Jacinto Sand Co. v. Southwestern Bell Tel. Co., 426 S.W.2d 338, 345 (Tex.Civ.App.—Houston [14th Dist.] 1968, writ ref'd n.r.e.), in a case that concerned both the lateral and subjacent right to support for a utility easement: "[T]he existence of the right to lateral support is an absolute right and is not subordinate to any right of the *adjoining* proprietor." And again, the opinion stated, "Whether we say that necessary lateral and subjacent support of the easement here involved is an incident of appellee's right to the complete enjoyment of the easements, or whether lateral and subjacent support is a separate right of property makes little practical difference."

Respectable American authority supports the rule that a landowner has the right to the support afforded by subterranean waters.

A second analogous rule which protects one's subsurface from damage by an operator on other lands is found in Gregg v. Delhi-Taylor Oil Corp., 162 Tex. 26, 33, 344 S.W.2d 411, 416 (1961). Mr. Gregg, in the development of his mineral lease, was preparing to use a sand fracturing technique to open cracks and veins extending some distance from his lease and to alter the substructure of neighboring land. By use of hydraulic pressure the ruptures of the subsurface formations would free greater quantities of gas. The rupture beneath the Delhi-Taylor's lands would create only small veins about one-tenth of an inch in diameter. This court regarded the creation of fissures on another's land as an invasion of property rights. "The invasion alleged is direct and the action taken is intentional. . . . While the drilling bit of Gregg's well is not alleged to have extended into Delhi-Taylor's land, the same result is reached if in fact the cracks or veins extend into its land and gas is produced therefrom by Gregg." This court denied one landowner the right to interfere with the subsurface of lands beyond his own lease boundaries. The same principle was applied in Gregg v. Delhi-Taylor Oil Corp., 162 Tex. 38, 344 S.W.2d 419 (1961), and in Delhi-Taylor Oil Corp. v. Holmes, 162 Tex. 39, 344 S.W.2d 420 (1961).

In my judgment, the examples are indistinguishable from the present case. The geologic changes that the defendants are creating beneath the surface of the plaintiffs' land in the instant case are more severe than in the *Gregg* and *Holmes* cases. The plaintiffs made summary judgment showing that the defendants squeeze the water from the clay beneath plaintiffs' lands, and the clay is then compressed and compacted so that the layers become thinner. The subterranean strata beneath plaintiffs' land is wholly altered by the process. The process is permanent and irreversible. If one may not use pressure that alters the geologic status of one's subsurface estate, how can we approve a process which reduces the pressure and which more grievously alters the subsurface estate? With respect I suggest, had we used the same argument in the *Gregg* and *Holmes* cases that is today employed, we would have approached the problem by looking at *Gregg's* and *Holmes's* right to capture the oil through its wellbore on its own lease. Once we determine that they had the right to capture and own the oil, we would have ruled that the case was solved. In *Gregg* and *Holmes*, we correctly looked at the damage to the neighbors' subsurface estate that was threatened by one who had a complete legal right to capture from a wellbore on his own land the oil from beneath another's land. The right of capture did not carry with it the right to destroy or interfere with the geology beneath another's land.

Elliff v. Texon Drilling Co., 146 Tex. 575, 210 S.W.2d 558, 4 A.L.R. 2d 191 (1948), was another example in which this court looked at the damage done a neighbor's subsurface estate by an oil driller who had the right to capture oil through the wellbore on his own lease. This court expressly rejected holdings by the Louisiana Supreme Court which held that an adjoining owner has no action against one who negligently destroys a reservoir. This court also rejected the defense that one's right to capture the oil rendered him immune from damages for his negligence in wasting it.

We thus reach the end result. Under our prior holdings compared with today's one who mines for oil may not destroy his neighbor's subjacent geology; but the right to pump water, we inconsistently say, is the right to destroy the subsurface geology, the subjacent support and even the surface of the land. Defendants may pump the plaintiffs' land to the bottom of Galveston Bay.

There is a third analogous area which has rejected the approach and result of today's decision. This area of the law is one in which one party actually contracts with another that the latter may remove the minerals beneath his surface estate. This area of the law presents the contest between the rights of the servient surface estate and the dominant mineral estate. This court has already held that the owner of the dominant estate may not exercise his rights to the point of destruction. In Acker v. Guinn, 464 S.W.2d 348, 352 (Tex. 1971), we wrote that the grant of a right to mine for substances does not contemplate "that the utility of the surface for agricultural or grazing purposes will be destroyed or substantially impaired." Even when the right to mine had been granted by contract, we rejected a practice that would consume or destroy the surface estate. Consistent with that trend to avoid the destruction of the surface estate, we also made our decision in Getty Oil Co. v. Jones, 470 S.W.2d 618 (Tex. 1971). In *Getty Oil,* we protected the servient surface estate from the dominant mineral estate which did no more than interfere with an automatic irrigation system. If, therefore, this court will protect a servient estate in its operation of a watering system, surely we will protect an owner of an absolute property right to subjacent support from a neighbor whose practice is thrusting his land beneath the sea.

The error of the majority is its narrow focus upon the right of the defendants to pump ground water. We should enlarge our vision so we can see what this lawsuit is about. I do not believe it is sound law that the right to pump water is the power to destroy the surface of surrounding landowners. If defendants argue that they have an absolute right to pump groundwater, plaintiffs reply that they too have an absolute right to the support of their natural surface. According to some of the summary judgment proofs, the defendants with knowledge have destroyed and are destroying the natural surface estate of the plaintiffs. The summary judgment proofs include showings that the plaintiffs own lands that were originally seven feet above sea level; today their land is flooded or subject to periodic flooding and the situation is getting worse. The natural shoreline banks which once protected lands from Galveston Bay and Clear Lake have now fallen below sea level. Lands are inundated. More lands will be inundated in the future. Lands that were once above sea level are now under salt water.

There is yet another legal principle that we should observe. Many things, though lawful, when done to excess, become remediable. Church bells may toll the knell of parting day or announce the time for solemn services, but when bells continuously clang without interruption for many days, the rights of others spring into being. What we do cannot be understood except in relation to those we touch. We have in this case the pleadings and showing that the defendants have abused their right to pump water to the point that property and the rights of others are ignored and destroyed.

Plaintiffs asserted their action upon theories of negligence, intentional tort, nuisance, and a taking of their property. In my opinion, subject to proof, they have an action on the first three theories.

I therefore dissent from this court's treatment of this case as one which concerns ownership of ground water. I dissent from this court's endorsement of English water cases that have been rejected in this country. I dissent from this court's adherence to the Restatement of Torts § 818. As discussed above, Texas has its own developed and developing law in this area of the law that is fair and equitable. The members of the Restatement Committee are neither legislators nor members of the Congress, and we do not need their help in this instance.

I dissent from the court's holding that this case is governed by the stare decisis of ground water cases. There has not previously been a case like this in Texas and there is no stare decisis applicable. Damages for subsidence was not the issue when courts were writing City of Corpus Christi v. City of Pleasanton, 154 Tex. 289, 276 S.W.2d 798 (1955), and Texas Co. v. Burkett, 117 Tex. 16, 296 S.W. 273 (1927), and Houston & T.C. Ry. Co. v. East, 98 Tex. 146, 81 S.W. 279 (1904). The parties in these cases were fighting over water rights. Nor was that the issue in Acton v. Blundell, 12 Meeson & Welsby 324, 152 Eng.Rep. 1223 (Ex.1843). The law stated by those cases need not and should not be disturbed by today's opinion. Because there is no stare decisis, I also dissent from the court's holding that plaintiffs can have no remedy except by a retroactive application of the law. The defendants, according to some of the summary judgment proofs, had knowledge from expert opinions that their course of action would cause subsidence. When the defendants, after warning, elect to take their risks in an area in which there are no precedents, I see no reason to apply our holding prospectively. No property law had attached in this instance. I dissent from the court's dicta that the legislature has in some fashion recognized or legislated about the defendants' immunity. Where is that legislation found?

Finally, and importantly, I dissent from the majority's holding that landowners in the future may prosecute a suit for damages for the destruction of their property if, and only if the action is one for negligence, wilful waste, or malicious injury. I rather assume that pumpers of ground water will carefully do so, will not waste their water, and will bear no ill will toward those whose property they are destroying. In fact, pumpers more probably will feel benignly toward those who regrettably must suffer the loss of their lands under the law of Friendswood Development Company v. Smith-Southwest Industries, Inc.

I would hold that an owner of land may assert an action against one who destroys the lateral or subjacent support to his land in its natural state when: (1) he engages in conduct knowing that it will cause damages to another's land by loss or destruction of the subjacent support, or (2) the plaintiff proves negligence, or (3) the plaintiff proves a nuisance, and here a balancing will be a factor. Justice Williams, the author of *East* also wrote Gulf, C. & S.F. Ry. Co. v. Oakes, 94 Tex. 155, 58 S.W. 999 (1900), and accepted this reasonable solution to the resolution of the conflict between two property rights:

> It is a general principle of the law that the owner of property may use it as he chooses in any lawful way; but another maxim, in general terms, requires him to so use it as not to injure another . . . . Since the owner may use his land as he chooses, if he

does not violate any law, and is not to be substantially deprived of its use or of the ordinary pursuit of his own interests, but, at the same time, is required in its use to avoid injury to another, it at once follows that he may be required to forego a particular use when it is not essential to the substantial enjoyment of his property, and is fraught with unreasonable loss to his neighbor. On the other hand, the particular use may be so important to the owner, and the loss or inconvenience to his neighbor so slight compared to his, were he forbidden to so employ his property, that it would be unreasonable and unjust to impose such a restriction. In such cases, it is evident that all of the circumstances of the situation must be taken into consideration. The importance of the use to the owner, as well as the extent of the damage to be inflicted upon his neighbor, and the rights of the parties, are to be adjusted in a practical way; the question being whether or not the proposed use is a reasonable one, under all the circumstances . . . . As is said in some of the authorities, there must, in such inquiries where rights and interests seem to conflict, be a balancing of them. Id. at 1000–01.

The balancing of lawful but competing property rights has been the rule previously approved by our Texas courts. We wrote in Elliff v. Texon Drilling Co., 146 Tex. 575, 584, 210 S.W.2d 558, 563 (1948), "In the conduct of one's business or in the use and exploitation of one's property, the law imposes upon all persons the duty to exercise ordinary care to avoid injury or damage to the property of others." That rule is fair. It has often been applied in Texas as appears from the citations above and there are many others.

I also dissent from the court's denial of rights to the plaintiffs, while acknowledging that future landowners may have an action at least in negligence. This court, in recent years, has recognized a number of new actions, and each time, the successful party was allowed the victory. In my opinion, it is basically unfair to treat the plaintiffs in this case unequally by recognizing that they possess an action, but by denying them the remedy.

I would affirm the judgment of the court of civil appeals.

SAM D. JOHNSON, J., joins in this dissent.

NOTES

1. When are absolute rules like trespass preferable to balancing rules like nuisance? Into which category does the law of lateral support fall? The law entitling a landowner to the subjacent support provided by underlying soil and other solids? The law disentitling landowners from the subjacent support provided by water and other liquids? What social preferences respecting resource use underlie the rules on lateral and subjacent support? Are these preferences likely to change over time and from place to place? When private

and public preferences respecting the use of these resources diverge, how likely is it that landowners will be able to contract around the rule of law? Are private agreements respecting lateral and subjacent support more or less likely to be entered into than private agreements respecting trespass? Nuisance?

What kind of conduct is the rule in Warfel v. Vondersmith likely to encourage? If you were counselling an excavating landowner after that decision, are there any conditions under which you would recommend that she shore up her neighbor's building?

Is the rule of Warfel v. Vondersmith inconsistent with the general rule entitling a landowner to abate a nuisance through self-help?

2. Solids tend to stay in place. The starting point for the rule entitling landowners to the support of underlying solids is that their unauthorized removal constitutes trespass. Does the trespass rule necessarily follow from the impacted nature of solids? Does the rule of liability respecting subjacent support necessarily follow from the rule of trespass?

Liquids tend to be fugitive. The starting point for the rule disentitling landowners from support of underlying liquids is that their unauthorized removal is permitted under the rule of capture. Does the rule of nonliability respecting subjacent support necessarily follow from the rule of capture? Is the rule of capture a good rule, as measured by its effects on the timing and extent of resource use? Recall Hardin's observations on the tragedy of the commons, p. 6 above. Does the rule excusing liquid withdrawals from liability for subjacent support improperly magnify the effects of the rule of capture? What would be the effect of disconnecting the two rules?

The rule of trespass means that mineral excavators must obtain the surface owner's consent; the duty of support can at this time be altered by language to that effect in the grant of the mineral estate. Does this suggest that the rule of liability matters less in subjacent solid cases than it does in subjacent liquid cases where it is far more difficult for the interested parties to identify their appropriate contract partners?

Why is absolute liability for lateral support confined to land in its natural state and not extended to structures on the land? Would the result of a contrary rule necessarily be to encourage the overdevelopment of land by enabling each improving landowner to impose the cost of support on his neighbor? As a general rule, subsurface excavators are liable for damages only to surface improvements that existed at the time they obtained their subsurface estate. Does the rule excusing them from liability for later-added improvements make more or less sense than the rule excusing lateral excavators from all liability for non-negligent damage to improvements? What preventive steps can an excavator of subsurface solids take to support the overlying surface? What preventive steps can a withdrawer of subsurface liquids take to support the overlying surface?

3. *Remedies.* The remedies for withdrawal of lateral and subjacent support are substantially similar. Injunctions, rarely allowed against either form of entry, are only given on a showing that "the damages threatened cannot be measured by any pecuniary standard, the excavator is insolvent and consequently incapable of responding in damages, or the comparative injury to which the injunction would subject the supporting estate is small compared with the benefit it would afford to the estate supported." 6-A American Law of Property § 28.53 (A.J. Casner ed.1952).

As a general rule, courts in these cases award damages measured by the lesser of the diminution in the value of the injured land and the cost of restoring the land to its original condition. For example, in Knapp v. Cirillo, 133 N.Y.S.2d 356 (Sup.Ct. Westchester Cty. 1954), defendants undercut and removed a stone retaining wall between the plaintiff's and defendant's properties in the course of building a new garage, causing slides, slippages and a sharp drop between the two parcels. The court granted plaintiff $500 for the diminution in property value. Testimony had established that the cost of restoration was much greater than the diminution of market value, and the court held that the "law requires that only the lesser amount as between cost of restoration and diminution of market value be awarded." 133 N.Y.S.2d at 358. Is this rule consistent with the purported absolute nature of the right being protected?

In some states, defendant must pay the cost of restoration unless it exceeds the value of plaintiff's property before the injury, in which case plaintiff will recover only for the diminution in her land's value. And, some states will occasionally award both restoration expenses and an allowance for diminution in value. The court in Grant v. Leith, 67 Wn.2d 234, 407 P.2d 157 (1965), gave plaintiff restoration expenses for his land and improvements, which were far less than the original value of the property, but also allowed a recovery of $5,600 for permanent, irreparable damage—cracks in the foundations and walls that reduced the value of the property.

How well would a *Spur*-type remedy work in any of these cases?

4. The common law rules on lateral and subjacent support were formed within the setting of a predominantly agrarian economy. Statutes in several states and ordinances in many municipalities have altered the common law rules in an effort to encourage more productive land uses in urban land areas. The principal method of this legislation is to impose a duty to support neighboring improvements under specified conditions. New York City Admin. Code, § C26–385.0 is typical:

> § C26–385.0 Excavations affecting adjoining structures.—a. Excavations more than ten feet deep.—Whenever an excavation is carried to a depth of more than ten feet below the curb, the person who causes such excavation to be made shall, if afforded the license necessary to enter the adjoining premises, at all times and

at his own expense, preserve and protect from injury any structure the safety of which may be affected by such part of the excavation as extends more than ten feet below the curb, and such person shall support the adjoining structure by proper foundations, whether or not such structure is more than ten feet below the curb. If the necessary license is not afforded to the person causing the excavation to be made, it shall be the duty of the owner who fails to afford such license to make the structure safe, and to support such structure by proper foundations, and such owner shall, if it is necessary for such purpose, be afforded the license necessary to enter the premises where such excavation is to be made.

b. Excavations ten feet or less in depth.—The owner of any structure, the safety of which may be affected by an excavation, shall preserve and protect such structure from injury and shall support such structure by proper foundations, except as otherwise provided in subdivision a of this section and shall, if it is necessary for such purpose, be afforded the license necessary to enter the premises where the excavation is to be made.

c. Support of party walls.—In case an adjoining party wall is intended to be used by the person who causes an excavation to be made, and such party wall is in good condition and sufficient for the uses of the existing and proposed buildings, such person shall, at his own expense, preserve such party wall from injury and support it by proper foundations, so that it shall be and remain practically as safe as it was before the excavation was commenced.

d. Weather protection.—Where permission has been given under this section to any person to enter any adjoining structure, such person shall provide for such adjoining structure adequate protection against any danger of injury due to the elements which may result from such entry.

How are landowners and land developers likely to behave under this statute? How does this behavior differ from their behavior under the common law rule?

5. *Personal Property: Wild Animals and the Rule of Capture.* Can the rule of capture, alluded to in *Friendswood*, be applied to determine ownership of wild animals? For example, how would the rule of capture resolve a dispute between A, whose dogs flushed a game bird, B, who shot the bird, C who retrieved the bird, and D who removed the bird from C's knapsack and cooked it for dinner? How would it resolve a dispute between E and F when E shoots a bear on F's land, where the bear kept its cave?

As a general rule, the law focuses on possession, giving complete ownership rights in the wild animal—fish, fowl or beast—to the first person who takes possession of it. The principal question raised in these cases is which of two or more competing claimants was the first to reduce the animal to possession. Pierson v. Post, 3 Cai.R. 175

(N.Y.Sup.Ct.1805), is the classic case. According to the declaration in the case, "Post, being in possession of certain dogs and hounds under his command, did, 'upon a certain wild and uninhabited, unpossessed and waste land, called the beach, find and start one of those noxious beasts called a fox,' and whilst there hunting, chasing and pursuing the same with his dogs and hounds, and when in view thereof, Pierson, well knowing the fox was so hunted and pursued, did, in the sight of Post, to prevent his catching the same, kill and carry it off." The question to be decided was whether Post, "by the pursuit with his hounds in the manner alleged in his declaration, acquired such a right to, or property in, the fox as will sustain an action against Pierson for killing and taking him away?" 3 Cai.R. at 177.

The court answered that he did not. Justice Tompkins, writing for the court, relied on the "ancient writers" for the principle that "pursuit alone vests no property or right in the huntsman; and that even pursuit, accompanied with wounding, is equally ineffectual for that purpose, unless the animal be actually taken." Further, the court was "the more readily inclined to confine possession or occupancy of beasts *ferae naturae* within the limits prescribed by the learned authors above cited, for the sake of certainty, and preserving peace and order in society. If the first seeing, starting, or pursuing such animals, without having so wounded, circumvented or ensnared them, so as to deprive them of their natural liberty, and subject them to the control of their pursuer, should afford the basis of actions against others for intercepting and killing them, it would prove a fertile source of quarrels and litigation." 3 Cai.R. at 179.

Justice Livingston dissented. First, Livingston observed that the issue before the court involved a "knotty point," and "should have been submitted to the arbitration of sportsmen, without poring over Justinian, Fleta, Bracton, Puffendorf, Locke, Barbeyrac, or Blackstone, all of whom have been cited; they would have had no difficulty in coming to a prompt and correct conclusion. In a court thus constituted, the skin and carcass of poor reynard would have been properly disposed of, and a precedent set, interfering with no usage or custom which the experience of ages has sanctioned, and which must be so well known to every votary of Diana."

Second, because a fox is "a wild and noxious beast," Livingston thought "that our decision should have in view the greatest possible encouragement to the destruction of an animal, so cunning and ruthless in his career. But who would keep a pack of hounds; or what gentleman, at the sound of the horn, and at peep of day, would mount his steed, and for hours together, '*sub jove frigido*,' or a vertical sun, pursue the windings of this wily quadruped, if, just as night came on, and his stratagems and strength were nearly exhausted, a saucy intruder, who had not shared in the honors or labors of the chase, were permitted to come in at the death, and bear away in triumph the object of pursuit?" 3 Cai.R. at 180–181.

With whom do you agree, Justice Tompkins or Justice Livingston? What result would obtain under either position if the events had occurred not upon a wild and uninhabited wasteland, but on Blackacre, a privately owned and occupied farm? See R. Brown, Law of Personal Property § 2.4 (W. Raushenbush 3d ed.1975) ("if a trespasser captures wild beasts on the land of another, the title to the same may be in the landowner and not in the captor").

Why *should* possession of an unowned object constitute ownership? For some thoughtful reflections on the question, see Epstein, Possession as the Root of Title, 13 Ga.L.Rev. 1221 (1979).

II. LAND TRANSFER AND FINANCE

A. A TYPICAL LAND SALE

Buying land is no simple matter. Whether it is a one-family house or a 200-store shopping center, buyer and seller will typically find it necessary to execute several documents and to employ the services of many specialists. All purchase transactions, residential or commercial, rest on the same fundamental principles and usually follow roughly the same steps.

Steps in the Sale of Land. As an initial step, an owner who wishes to sell her home, will usually hire a real estate broker who, in return for a commission on sale—commonly 5% to 7% of the sale price—will agree to show the property to prospective buyers. Often this broker will enlist the aid of other brokers in the community to solicit buyers and to help close the transaction.

Once a willing buyer has been found and the terms of the purchase have been negotiated, the parties will execute a sales contract obligating the seller to convey title, and obligating the buyer to pay the purchase price, on the closing date, typically 30 or 60 days from the date the contract was signed. Seller's performance under the contract will usually be conditioned only on the buyer's payment of the purchase price. The buyer, however, will typically condition his performance on seller's ability to convey clear title and on the availability of a mortgage loan to finance his purchase.

During the executory period, the buyer will pursue the applications and inquiries required by the contract conditions. Often he will rely on the real estate broker to help him arrange the needed financing with a local institutional lender such as a bank or savings and loan association. In some locales the buyer's lawyer will order a search of the land title records, review the search report and then advise the buyer on whether the seller has good title; in other locales, the buyer will ask a title insurance company to perform the title search and, if the search discloses that title is good, to issue an insurance policy to that effect.

If the institutional lender refuses to make the requested loan, or if the title search reveals that the seller's title is not good, the buyer will be excused from performing the contract. If, however, all conditions have been met, the buyer will tender the purchase price and the seller will tender a deed conveying title to the property. The contract will close when the seller receives the money and the buyer receives the deed which he will then promptly record in the county recorder's office. (As part of the closing, the institutional lender will simultaneously receive a note or bond and mortgage or deed of trust from the buyer, and will promptly record the mortgage or deed of trust.)

The Causes of Complexity. Why are land transfers so complex? Why can a transfer of land not be accomplished as simply as the sale of a light bulb or a pound of butter? One reason is that a single parcel of real property is almost infinitely divisible into separate ownership—mining rights, surface rights and air rights, easements for rights of way or public utility lines, and security for mortgage loans, taxes and judgments. The buyer must, before closing, discover each such interest that will encumber his ownership. Since, unlike most other objects of ownership, land endures, these interests endure as well and, accumulating over time, increase a buyer's costs of search and negotiation as each day goes by.

Another reason for complexity is historical. Conveyancing rules were originally designed to meet needs quite different from those that dominate today's real estate marketplace, and law reform has not kept pace with economic and social change. Early English conveyancing law required—if this can be imagined—an actual, physical delivery of the land itself. The principal method of land transfer in feudal times was feoffment with livery of seisin: A and B, transferor and transferee, would travel to the land to be conveyed and, in the presence of assembled neighbors, A would orally convey title and possession to B, symbolizing the transfer by handing over a twig or clump of earth. If the land was particularly valuable, or the terms of the transfer complex, the conveyance might also be evidenced by a written charter or deed, but a writing was neither necessary nor sufficient to accomplish the conveyance. (Less substantial interests in land, such as right of way easements, could, however, be transferred by a writing alone.)

The Statute of Uses, enacted in 1535, made it possible for A to convey title to B by a written instrument alone, thus avoiding the inconvenience of feoffment with livery of seisin. And the Statute of Frauds, enacted in 1677, made it *mandatory* for A to use a written instrument. Thus, by the late seventeenth century, execution and delivery of a deed replaced the ceremony of livery of seisin as the central requirement for land transfers in England. See generally, A. Simpson, An Introduction to the History of the Land Law 112–115, 163–183 (1961).

The American colonists drew selectively from English conveyancing practice, adapting some elements, discarding others, to fit the needs of a society in which land was viewed as an item of commerce and not as a dynastic base, and in which free and easy transfers were preferred to highly formalized ceremonies. Although land in America was sometimes conveyed by feoffment with livery of seisin, transfer by delivery of a written deed was by far the more common practice. And, over time, the deeds themselves took increasingly shorter and more simplified forms. See generally, L. Friedman, History of American Law 54–55, 207–208, 376–379 (1973).

The evolution of conveyancing practice, both in England and America, produced an almost total dependence on written instruments, and on the paper record of those instruments, as the basis for land transfer. Although this new reliance on documentary evidences of title succeeded in adapting transfer formalities to post-feudal commercial needs, it also produced several new problems. Paper is cheap and easily transmitted—attributes that facilitate not only legitimate land transfers but unintended transactions as well. New formalities—seal, acknowledgement, delivery—were adopted to minimize the risk of a forged or other unintended transfer.

A still greater problem created by the new reliance on documentary transfers was that it enabled secret, multiple conveyances of the same piece of land to unsuspecting conveyees. Given several blank deed forms and a disposition to fraud, A, who had once conveyed Blackacre to B, could subsequently convey it, all over again, to C, D, E and countless others. In England, the Statute of Enrollments, enacted at the same time as the Statute of Uses, sought to reduce fraud by exposing conveyances on the public record; however, large loopholes in the statute doomed it to failure. Recording acts innovated in the New England colonies were far more successful and set the pattern for recording systems that, used in all American states today, almost entirely eliminate the opportunity for fraudulent or mistaken multiple transfers.

The recording acts, in turn, created yet another conveyancing dilemma. Because the efficacy of the recording system depends on the permanence of its underlying records, land titles will over time become tangled and encrusted with records of transactions dating back decades and even centuries; as a result, the speed and security of title searches decline as each year passes.

The Costs of Complexity. The total bill rendered by conveyancing professionals such as abstracters, appraisers, brokers, conveyancing lawyers, escrow agents, house inspectors, surveyors, and title companies is not small. According to a 1972 study, prepared by the United States Department of Housing and Urban Development and the Veterans Administration from a nationwide sample of more than 50,000 FHA and VA loan applications, total settlement costs average roughly 10% of the contract sale price—$1,937 on the sale of a $19,937 home. The study's breakdown of average total settlement costs reveals that brokers' fees accounted for 3.2% ($626) of sales price;[a] prepaid items such as insurance and taxes, for 1.5% ($299);

---

[a]. Because the breakdown is of *average* settlement costs, the underlying computations valued instances in which no fee was paid at $0. Thus, $626 is not the average commission paid by all sellers who incurred broker charges. The average fee, where a fee was charged, was $1,019.

loan discount payment for 2.3% ($454); and loan origination fee for 1% ($178). Title related costs (title examination, title insurance, attorneys' fees, closing fees) amounted to $254, or 1.3% of sales price—about 12% of total settlement costs. Department of Housing and Urban Development and Veteran's Administration, Mortgage Settlement Costs: Report to Sen.Comm. on Banking, Housing & Urban Affairs 35 (Comm. Print 1972).

Reformers have argued that these costs are too high, citing the wide disparities in average state closing costs as evidence. If average costs are $56 in North Dakota and $480 in New York, and if the average of the five lowest cost states is $84 and of the five highest cost states $418, the people in these last five states, it is argued, must be paying too much to close their home purchases. See Whitman, Home Transfer Costs: An Economic and Legal Analysis, 62 Geo.L.J. 1311, 1329 (1974). One obvious, but frequently overlooked, reason for the disparity is that buyers and sellers in high-cost states are paying for more, or higher quality, services such as more complete title searches and surveys. Thus, it is not uncommon in New York for buyer, seller and lender each to be represented by his or her own attorney; in other states, one lawyer may attempt to serve all three, and in still others, like California, lawyers rarely become involved at all in negotiating or closing residential sales.

Congress has sought to reduce closing costs by increasing the price information available to consumers, thus presumably increasing competition among suppliers. The Real Estate Settlement Procedures Act, 12 U.S.C.A. §§ 2601 et seq., passed in 1974 and substantially revised in 1976, requires mortgage lenders to provide borrower-homebuyers with an itemized statement of closing costs in advance of the closing. RESPA also outlaws rebates in the industry and directs the Department of Housing and Urban Development to sponsor further research into the causes and cures of high closing costs. See generally, Field, RESPA in a Nutshell, 11 Real Prop., Prob. & Tr.J. 447 (1976).

State legislatures have been less forthcoming. Although in 1977 the National Conference of Commissioners on Uniform State Laws promulgated a Uniform Simplification of Land Transfers Act aimed at, among other objects, reducing the costs of title examination and the risks of title defects, states have not rushed to adopt it. See generally, Maggs, Land Records of the Uniform Simplification of Land Transfers Act, 1981 So.Ill.L.J. 491 (1981); Pedowitz, Uniform Simplification of Land Transfers Act—A Commentary, 13 Real Prop., Prob. & Tr.J. 696 (1978).

Why do conveyancing costs matter? Put in the arid terms of economic analysis, they matter because they are transaction costs and, if too high, will prevent otherwise interested individuals from reaching efficient arrangements for land ownership and use. Put in more concrete terms, conveyancing costs matter because, if they are too high, an otherwise financially able and interested family may be unable to buy the home that it wants. Either way, conveyancing costs deserve your close attention. As you read the materials in this section, you may want to consider how conveyancing costs can be reduced without sacrificing desirable levels of quality in conveyancing services. What are desirable levels of quality? How much choice should consumers have in deciding the mix of cost and quality that is appropriate for them?

1. ARRANGING THE SALE

a. The Lawyer's Role

AMERICAN BAR ASSOCIATION, RESIDENTIAL REAL ESTATE TRANSACTIONS: THE LAWYER'S PROPER ROLE—SERVICES—COMPENSATION

3–9 (1978).

A. *The Brokerage Contract*

Initially a seller will enter into a brokerage contract with a real estate agent. In many jurisdictions this contract is not required to be in writing with all of the usual dangers of unwritten contracts. A special peril faced by sellers who have not had the advantage of legal counsel is that they may employ more than one broker and, in the absence of a clear understanding concerning the conditions under which the brokerage fee is earned, the seller may become liable to pay more than one fee.

In practice, a high percentage of brokerage contracts are in writing. A common assumption is that the contract is simple and standardized. In fact, a properly drawn contract will anticipate a number of legal problems of some complexity, such as the right of the seller to negotiate on the seller's own behalf, the effect of multiple listings, the disposition of earnest money if the buyer defaults, the rights of the broker if the seller is unable to proffer a marketable title, the duration of any exclusive listing and, as already brought out, the point at which the brokerage fee is earned. Most of the terms are negotiable and, in theory, a new contract should be drawn each time a broker is employed.

Standardized forms, where carefully drawn, have certain advantages. There are no objections to form contracts per se, as used by either brokers or other participants in the land transfer transaction. The objections to form contracts are that they may be inappropriate to the particular transaction, badly drawn initially or incorrectly filled in.

Any seller signing such a contract should have it approved by the seller's lawyer before signing. The seller should have the lawyer explain its meaning and be on hand to see that it is properly executed. (It is presumed that if the seller consults a lawyer, the lawyer will advise against entering into any oral agreement.) In other words, the seller needs the traditional legal services embraced in the expression "advice, representation and drafting." The broker needs similar services at one time or another and receives them from the broker's own lawyer as needed. In routine transactions the broker is sufficiently familiar with the details to be able to handle the matter without resort to professional assistance.

B. *The Preliminary Negotiations*

When the broker has found a potential buyer, negotiations between the buyer and the seller will begin, with the broker acting in the role of intermediary. In some cases the seller will leave to the broker all the work of negotiation and will merely ratify the agreement reached with the buyer.

It is generally thought that neither the buyer nor the seller needs a lawyer in the course of the negotiations. In theory this assumption is correct because neither party is bound until a written sales contract is signed. In fact, a great deal of trouble can be avoided if both the buyer and the seller consult their own lawyers during the course of the negotiations. If they are to make a proper bargain, they must know what to bargain about.

Aside from the the question of price, which seems paramount in the minds of both parties, they should consider such problems as the mode of paying the purchase price and the tax consequences resulting therefrom, the status of various articles as fixtures or personal property, the time set for occupancy and the effect of loss by casualty pending the closing.

They can make whatever agreement they want, but they should anticipate all important questions and be certain a complete understanding has been reached. Failure to do so in the preliminary negotiations may mean, at the time for signing a contract, that they will have to start negotiations all over again. Worse, they may enter into a contract highly disadvantageous to one or the other, so uncertain as to require litigation to determine its meaning, or so ambiguous as to be void for indefiniteness.

C. *The Commitment for Financing*

Before entering into a sales contract, it would be desirable for the buyer to obtain as much of a commitment as possible for necessary financing.

Many lenders, however, refuse to make the necessary inspections, appraisals and credit investigations to make such a commitment until the buyer can exhibit a signed purchase and sale agreement, and many buyers are reluctant to risk losing the property to a higher offer by deferring the execution of the purchase and sale agreement. All of this leads to the common practice of including in the agreement a "subject to financing" clause which should be examined by the lawyers for the parties before the contract is signed.

Finding a willing lender is not part of a lawyer's professional duties. In practice a lawyer, being a person of affairs, may be able to render this service. Legal expertise is exercised when the lawyer advises the buyer about problems the buyer should anticipate in coming to terms with the lender. By way of illustration, the buyer will seldom have any understanding of the potential effect of an acceleration clause. The buyer should know what the legal and practical consequences of such a clause will be. The buyer should also obtain an estimate of the closing costs that will have to be paid and should obtain legal advice as to all items found in the estimate.

The commitment contract between the lender and buyer will normally be prepared by the lender's lawyer. Before it is accepted, the buyer's lawyer should ascertain that it properly anticipates all important contingencies, comports with the oral agreement previously reached and binds the lender.

Normally the lender has much greater financial expertise than the buyer. This advantage may not have been of as much importance formerly as it is today, because the financing of homes has in many instances become extremely complex. For this reason, when dealing with the lender the buyer is in need of legal assistance.

D. *The Contract of Sale*

Once an informal agreement has been reached, the buyer and the seller will enter into a formal contract of sale. The importance of this document cannot be overemphasized. Once it is signed, the rights and obligations of the parties are fixed. Each transaction is unique and, in theory, a contract should be specially drafted for each.

The interested parties are the broker, the buyer and the seller. The contract should contain an appropriate provision with regard to the broker's commission. The buyer and the seller want assurance that the writing reflects their understanding. If they have not received legal advice during the preliminary negotiations, they will need to know what questions should have been anticipated and whether firm and advantageous provisions are found in the document. When the instrument is executed, their lawyers should be present to assure that the proper formalities are observed to make it binding. Here again the parties need legal services in the form of drafting, advice, and representation.

This need is not avoided by the use of forms. Even if the form is properly drawn, the printed portion may not adequately express the particular agreement made between the parties, or the words used in filling in blanks may distort its effectiveness. As a matter of practice standardized forms are widely used, and it is recognized that this practice likely will continue. It is recommended that local bar associations draft standard forms of sales agreements, and that joint seminars with real estate brokers and others regarding residential real estate transactions be held regularly. Whenever forms are used, any insertion should be carefully checked by the buyer's and seller's lawyers, and the appropriateness of the form for the particular transaction should be determined by the buyer's and seller's lawyers. The buyer and the seller are often unaware of what the contract means, what they should anticipate, and what steps are needed to make the instrument binding. They should be advised by their own legal counsel.

Prior to the time the contract is signed, the buyer and the seller should have detailed advice about many legal aspects of the transaction. For example, they may not be aware of the need to anticipate the question of who bears the loss of damage to, or destruction of, buildings on the premises between the time the contract is signed and the time of closing. They also may be unaware of the existence of such problems as whether the contract so changes the interest of the seller as to affect insurance policies; whether either the buyer or seller, or both, should execute new wills; whether federal and state gift and death tax matters are involved; whether joint tenancies or tenancies by the entireties will be affected; and the like.

E. *Determining the Status of the Title*

After the contract of sale is executed, the state of the seller's title must be determined to the satisfaction of both the buyer and the lender. This is generally the most important legal work connected with the transaction. The initial examination will be made by the lawyer for the buyer, the seller, the lender, or the title insurer, relying upon the official land title records or an abstract thereof, or a title plant maintained by a title insurance company. Where a lawyer's certificate is relied upon, either the lender or the buyer, or both, may desire additional protection in the form of a title insurance policy.

Whoever makes the title examination, the buyer's lawyer should inform the buyer of the limitations, if any, which impair the title. The buyer should also receive formal protection by a written opinion from the lawyer, an owner's title insurance policy, or both. If the buyer applies for title insurance, the buyer's lawyer should negotiate the provisions to be included or excluded from the policy. The lawyer should also make clear to the buyer what the policy means. In particular, the exceptions to coverage contained in the policy should be explained.

The use of standardized exceptions is common to title insurance. They are complex and restrictive and are frequently not understood by the layman.

Each title insurance policy is unique in that it may contain exceptions peculiar to that individual title. The buyer must first be made aware of the existence of these exceptions and must then be made to understand them. If the exception is to a $10,000 mortgage and the buyer sees the provision, the buyer will probably not mistake its meaning. But if the exception is to "all of the conditions and restrictions found in deed of X to Y, recorded in the office of the clerk of the court of Z County, in Deed Book 309 at page 873," the buyer will not, in the first place, realize that the exception is important, or, if the buyer does, will not understand its meaning without assistance from the lawyer.

F. *The Survey*

Survey problems arise in many transactions, and the lawyers for all parties should inform their clients of such problems. At some time prior to the approval of title the buyer, the lender, or the title insurance company may demand a survey. The primary purpose of the survey will be to find whether the legal description of the land conforms to the lines laid down on the ground. An additional purpose may be to determine whether structures on the premises violate restrictive covenants or zoning ordinances or constitute an encroachment. When the survey has been completed, the parties should have their lawyers advise them about any legal implications of the surveyor's findings and the scope and extent of the surveyor's certification.

G. *Curative Action*

In some cases curative action is needed to make titles marketable. Any such curative action should be carried out by a lawyer for the seller, the buyer, or the lender. If the curative action is carried out by the lawyer for the seller, it should be checked for sufficiency by the lawyers for the buyer and lender; if by the lawyer for the buyer, by the lawyer for the lender; and if by the lawyer for the lender, by the lawyer for the buyer.

H. *Termite Inspection*

In jurisdictions where a termite inspection must be made and a certificate given to the buyer, showing that the premises are free of infestation or damage by termites, the certificate may be ordered by the broker, lender or the lawyer for any of the parties.

In jurisdictions where such certificates are not required, a provision should be added to the contract requiring the seller to provide a current termite certificate by a licensed pest control agency. If there is infestation or damage, the cost of treatment and the cost of necessary repairs of termite-caused damage usually are borne by the seller. The contract should spell out the seller's obligation. A termite clause should be included in all standard form contracts.

I. *Drafting Instruments*

Before closing, a lawyer should draft the deed, mortgage and the bond or note secured by the mortgage. As a matter of convenience these papers are commonly drafted by the mortgagee's attorney, although the representative of either of the other parties is equally qualified. Whoever does the work, the product should be examined by lawyers for each of the other two parties and the title insurance company, and they should be advised whether the instruments are effective and create the interests intended.

The drafting of these instruments is sometimes considered merely routine work. This is not true. For example, the description of the parties must be so phrased as to prevent confusion, and the description of the land must be complete and accurate. The importance of the form of warranties is often overlooked. By way of illustration, if the title is encumbered by equitable covenants or utility easements, either or both may be acceptable to the buyer and lender, but they should be excepted from the warranty.

How title is to be taken should have been provided in the initial contract between the buyer and the seller, and the buyer should be advised as to the tax and other effects of the manner in which title is taken.

Of equal importance are other special agreements reached earlier in the transaction. The controlling law may provide that the deed supersedes prior understandings so that if they are not embraced in the deed they are nullified. Each deed must therefore be examined to determine whether it carries out what has been agreed upon.

J. *Incidental Paper Work*

The Real Estate Settlement Procedures Act requires the preparation of a settlement statement in virtually all residential real estate transactions. In addition, the Truth-In-Lending form must be filled in and executed. If the mortgage loan is to be insured by FHA, VA or by a private mortgage insurance company, more paper work is required. The required documents are standardized and can be completed without resort to legal expertise. They are part of the financing, rather than the legal aspects of the sale and mortgage. Nevertheless, lawyers are frequently called upon to do this work. With a few exceptions, the government has taken the position that whoever performs these services shall receive no compensation therefor.

K. *Obtaining Title Insurance*

Where a title insurance policy for the buyer is based on the certificate of a lawyer not employed by a title insurance company, the lawyer may make an application for the initial binder and, after closing, send in a final certificate and procure a policy. This is work for which the lawyer normally, and properly, should be paid by the client to the extent the lawyer is not paid for these services as the agent of the title company. The lawyer should not accept compensation from a title insurance company solely for referring business to that company. This is, of course, clearly improper and contrary to the recorded position of the American Bar Association. The Real Estate Settlement Procedures Act specifically prohibits the acceptance of any "kickbacks" from the title insurance company.

L. *Closing*

A closing statement is generally prepared prior to final closing. The statement may take various forms and is designed to indicate the allocation of debits and credits to the various parties. In some cases it is prepared by a layman, in others by a lawyer. The buyer's and seller's lawyers should make certain their clients understand the nature and amount of all closing costs. The American Bar Association supported the adoption of legislation requiring a uniform closing statement in all government-related mortgage transactions. In addition it is recommended that local bar associations draft uniform closing statement forms for use in all other real estate transactions. Even a standard closing form in itself is not sufficient, unless the parties are assured by their own lawyers of the appropriateness of each item.

Unless there is an escrow closing, a further check of title should be made immediately prior to closing. If this check is not made, it is possible that the parties will be unaware that the title has been impaired between the time of the original examination and the closing date. This further check will generally be carried out by the lawyer, abstracter or title insurance company certifying or insuring title.

The closing is the proceeding at which the parties exchange executed instruments, make required payments, and conclude the formal aspects of the transaction. At this point the buyer, the seller, and the lender should be represented by their own lawyers. They require advice and may need representation if a disagreement arises. They should be assured that the legal documents they exchange create the interests intended, that they receive the protection to which they are entitled and that correct payments have been made to those entitled to receive them.

As a part of the closing, arrangements must be made for insurance, taxes, and other incidents of ownership. Instruments must be recorded and a final check of title made. Disbursements must be made and documents distributed to the parties entitled to receive them. Title insurance policies, where called for, must be procured. If a lawyer handles the closing, the lawyer will attend to all or virtually all of these details.

The Conflicts of Interest

At every step set out above it has been said that buyers and sellers should have representation, advice and draftmanship. This is to say, each needs separate legal representation and should not rely on services rendered by a lawyer for some other party. Why, it will be asked, is so much legal service needed to consummate a routine, uncontested transaction? No two transactions are identical, and none is simple. Because of the complexity of property law a "minor" slip may cause great expense and inconvenience. To the buyer, at least, the purchase of a house may be the most important legal and financial transaction of a lifetime.

All of the parties have conflicting interests. Some of them have wide experience with land transfers. To others the transaction may be a once-in-a-lifetime event. Houses are bought and sold by the inexperienced as well as by the sophisticated. The buyer and seller, without representation, will usually not have as much knowledge of conveyancing as the other parties. Only their own attorneys will be motivated to explain fully the transaction.

It is sometimes said the parties require disinterested advice. This misstates the case. Instead of disinterested advice, each requires the assistance of someone dedicated to that person's interests and equipped with sufficient skill to protect that person. The escrow company used in some sections of the country is theoretically disinterested. Actually its primary loyalty usually is to the institutions which are the sources of its business.

AMERICAN BAR ASSOCIATION, CODE OF PROFESSIONAL RESPONSIBILITY (1980)

CANON 5 [b]

A Lawyer Should Exercise Independent Professional Judgment on Behalf of a Client

ETHICAL CONSIDERATIONS

Interests of Multiple Clients

EC 5–14 Maintaining the independence of professional judgment required of a lawyer precludes his acceptance or continuation of em-

[b]. "The Canons are statements of axiomatic norms, expressing in general terms the standards of professional conduct expected of lawyers in their relationships with the public, with the legal system, and with the legal profession. They embody the general concepts from which the Ethical Considerations and the Disciplinary Rules are derived.

"The Ethical Considerations are aspirational in character and represent the objectives toward which every member of the profession should strive. They constitute a body of principles upon which the lawyer can rely for guidance in many specific situations.

"The Disciplinary Rules, unlike the Ethical Considerations, are mandatory in

ployment that will adversely affect his judgment on behalf of or dilute his loyalty to a client. This problem arises whenever a lawyer is asked to represent two or more clients who may have differing interests, whether such interests be conflicting, inconsistent, diverse, or otherwise discordant.

EC 5–15 If a lawyer is requested to undertake or to continue representation of multiple clients having potentially differing interests, he must weigh carefully the possibility that his judgment may be impaired or his loyalty divided if he accepts or continues the employment. He should resolve all doubts against the propriety of the representation. A lawyer should never represent in litigation multiple clients with differing interests; and there are few situations in which he would be justified in representing in litigation multiple clients with potentially differing interests. If a lawyer accepted such employment and the interests did become actually differing, he would have to withdraw from employment with likelihood of resulting hardship on the clients; and for this reason it is preferable that he refuse the employment initially. On the other hand, there are many instances in which a lawyer may properly serve multiple clients having potentially differing interests in matters not involving litigation. If the interests vary only slightly, it is generally likely that the lawyer will not be subjected to an adverse influence and that he can retain his independent judgment on behalf of each client; and if the interests become differing, withdrawal is less likely to have a disruptive effect upon the causes of his clients.

EC 5–16 In those instances in which a lawyer is justified in representing two or more clients having differing interests, it is nevertheless essential that each client be given the opportunity to evaluate his need for representation free of any potential conflict and to obtain other counsel if he so desires. Thus before a lawyer may represent multiple clients, he should explain fully to each client the implications of the common representation and should accept or continue employment only if the clients consent. If there are present other circumstances that might cause any of the multiple clients to question the undivided loyalty of the lawyer, he should also advise all of the clients of those circumstances.

DISCIPLINARY RULES

DR 5–105 Refusing to Accept or Continue Employment if the Interests of Another Client May Impair the Independent Professional Judgment of the Lawyer.

(A) A lawyer shall decline proffered employment if the exercise of his independent professional judgment in behalf of a client will be or is likely to be adversely affected by the acceptance of the proffered character. The Disciplinary Rules state the minimum level of conduct below which no lawyer can fall without being subject to disciplinary action."

employment, or if it would be likely to involve him in representing differing interests, except to the extent permitted under DR 5–105(C).

(B) A lawyer shall not continue multiple employment if the exercise of his independent professional judgment in behalf of a client will be or is likely to be adversely affected by his representation of another client, or if it would be likely to involve him in representing differing interests, except to the extent permitted under DR 5–105(C).

(C) In the situations covered by DR 5–105(A) and (B), a lawyer may represent multiple clients if it is obvious that he can adequately represent the interest of each and if each consents to the representation after full disclosure of the possible effect of such representation on the exercise of his independent professional judgment on behalf of each.

(D) If a lawyer is required to decline employment or to withdraw from employment under a Disciplinary Rule, no partner, or associate, or any other lawyer affiliated with him or his firm, may accept or continue such employment.

IN RE LANZA

Supreme Court of New Jersey, 1974.
65 N.J. 347, 322 A.2d 445.

PER CURIAM.

The Bergen County Ethics Committee filed a presentment with this Court against respondent, Guy J. Lanza, who has been a practicing member of the bar of this State since 1954.

The Committee specifically found that respondent's conduct violated DR 5–105. This Disciplinary Rule forbids an attorney to represent adverse interests, except under certain very carefully circumscribed conditions.

In April or May of 1971, Elizabeth F. Greene consulted respondent with respect to the sale of her residence property in Palisades Park, New Jersey. Mr. Lanza agreed to act for her. In due course a contract, apparently prepared by a broker, was signed by Mrs. Greene as seller as well as by the prospective purchasers, James and Joan Connolly. The execution and delivery of the contract took place in Mr. Lanza's office, although he seems to have played little or no part in the negotiation of its terms. By this time he had agreed with the Connollys that he would represent them, as well as Mrs. Greene, in completing the transaction. The testimony is conflicting as to whether or not Mrs. Greene had been told of this dual representation at the time she signed the contract. Mr. Lanza says that she had been told, but according to her recollection she only learned of this at a later date from Mrs. Connolly. In any event it is quite clear that respondent agreed to act for the purchasers before discussing the question of such additional representation with Mrs. Greene.

The contract as originally drawn provided for a closing date in late July, 1971. At Mrs. Greene's request this date was postponed to September 1. A short time later, circumstances having again changed, Mrs. Greene found that she would now prefer the original date. This proved satisfactory to the purchasers but Mr. Connolly told Mrs. Greene that at this earlier date he would not have in hand funds sufficient to make up the full purchase price of $36,000. Of this sum he would lack $1,000. He suggested, however, that the parties might close title upon the earlier date if Mrs. Greene would accept, as part of the purchase price, a check for $1,000 postdated approximately 30 days. Mrs. Greene was personally agreeable to this. She consulted respondent who advised her that he saw no reason why she should not follow this course.

The closing accordingly took place late in July and in accordance with the foregoing arrangement, Mrs. Greene received, as part of the purchase price, Mr. Connolly's check in the sum of $1,000 dated August 31, 1971. Shortly after this latter date she deposited the check for collection and it was returned because of insufficient funds. When questioned, Mr. Connolly said that after he and his wife had taken possession of the property they discovered a serious water condition in the cellar. He added that Mrs. Greene had made an explicit representation that the cellar was at all times dry. For this reason he refused to make good the check, saying that it would cost him $1,000 to rectify the condition in the cellar. Mrs. Greene denied that she has ever made any representation whatsoever. She immediately got in touch with respondent who did nothing effective on her behalf. She then retained other counsel and has subsequently initiated legal proceedings against the Connollys.

We find respondent's conduct to have been unprofessional in two respects. In the first place, the way in which he undertook the dual representation failed to meet the standards imposed upon an attorney who elects to follow such a course. In the second place, after the latent conflict of interests of the two clients had become acute, he nevertheless continued to represent both parties. At that point, rather than going forward with the matter as he did, he should have withdrawn altogether.

Mr. Lanza first undertook to act for the seller, Mrs. Greene. This immediately placed upon him an obligation to represent her with undivided fidelity. Despite this obligation, he later agreed, without prior consultation with Mrs. Greene, to represent Mr. and Mrs. Connolly, whose interest in the matter was of course potentially adverse to that of his client. He should not have undertaken to represent the purchasers until he had initially conferred with Mrs. Greene. He should have first explained to her all the facts and indicated in specific detail all the areas of potential conflict that foreseeably might arise. He should also have made her aware that if indeed any of these contingencies should thereafter eventuate and not prove susceptible of ready solution in a manner fair and agreeable to all concerned, it would then become his professional duty immediately to cease acting for all parties. Only after such a conference with his client, and following her informed consent, would he have been at liberty to consider representing the purchasers. They, too, were entitled to the same explanation as is set forth above, as well as being told of respondent's existing attorney-client relationship with the seller.

The second instance of misconduct arose after respondent learned that the purchasers would not be able to pay the full purchase price in cash at the time of closing title. At that point adequate representation of the seller required that her attorney first strongly insist on her behalf that cash be forthcoming. Failing this, and if the seller persisted in her wish to close upon the earlier date, her attorney should have vigorously urged the execution and delivery to her of a mortgage from the purchasers in the amount of $1,000, or of other adequate security, in order to protect her interest pending receipt of the full cash payment. We think it fair to assume that had respondent not found himself in a position of conflicting loyalties, his representation of the seller would have taken some such course. Had the purchasers persisted in their unwillingness to pay the full amount in cash at the time of closing and had they also refused to execute and deliver a mortgage or other security, respondent should have immediately withdrawn from the matter, advising both parties to secure independent counsel of their respective choosing. At that point in time it would have clearly been impossible for any single attorney adequately and fairly to represent both sides.

This case serves to emphasize the pitfalls that await an attorney representing both buyer and seller in a real estate transaction. The Advisory Committee on Professional Ethics, in its Opinion 243, 95 N.J.L.J. 1145 (1972) has ruled that in all circumstances it is unethical for the same attorney to represent buyer and seller in negotiating the terms of a contract of sale. Here the respondent did not enter into these negotiations so he does not come under the ban of this rule. Canon 6 declared, however, that "[i]t is unprofessional to represent conflicting interests, except by express consent of all concerned given after a full disclosure of the facts." DR 5-105 is at least as strict in the requirements it lays down and in subparagraph (C) carries forward the injunction quoted above by prohibiting multiple representation unless "each [party] consents to the representation after full disclosure of the facts and of the possible effect of such representation on the exercise of his [the attorney's] independent professional judgment on behalf of each."

The extent of the necessary disclosure is what is important. As Opinion 243, supra, makes clear, this is a question that must be conscientiously resolved by each attorney in the light of the particular facts and circumstances that a given case presents. It is utterly insufficient simply to advise a client that he, the attorney, foresees no conflict of interest and then to ask the client whether the latter will consent to the multiple representation. This is no more than an empty form of words. A client cannot foresee and cannot be expected to foresee the great variety of potential areas of disagreement that may arise in a real estate transaction of this sort. The attorney is or should be familiar with at least the more common of these and they should be stated and laid before the client at some length and with considerable specificity. Of course all eventualities cannot be foreseen, but a great many can. Here respondent was representing Mrs. Greene, a seller of property. Generally a seller who has entered into a mutually binding contract of sale is principally interested in securing the full purchase price to which he or she is entitled. As counsel experienced in this field of practice well know, to allow a purchaser to take possession of the premises in question before the entire consideration has been received, either in the form of cash or purchase money mortgage, will often prove contrary to the seller's best interests. So it was here.

For the reasons set forth above, we deem respondent's conduct to merit censure. He is hereby reprimanded.

For reprimand: Chief Justice HUGHES and Justices JACOBS, HALL, MOUNTAIN, SULLIVAN, PASHMAN and CLIFFORD–7.

Opposed: None.

PASHMAN, J. (concurring).

. . .

It is virtually impossible for one attorney in any manner and under any circumstances to faithfully and with undivided allegiance represent both a buyer and seller. This concurrence, therefore, stands for the position of the majority and further holds that dual representation in a buyer-seller situation should be totally forbidden. The reasons for this seem to me fairly obvious. In this type of transaction, it is most certainly in the public interest to safeguard and protect both parties from any abuses, whether they be ill-advised or inadvertent. The potential conflict in home buying or selling may never come to fruition. However, when it does surface, both sides explode in anger and accusations. The attorney will then withdraw, leaving the situation no better than when it occurred and, for that matter, probably a bit worse. This is not fair to either party.

It is my contention that neither buyer nor seller can ever possibly fully appreciate all the complexities involved. That is precisely the reason why full disclosure and informed consent are illusory. What most people typically do is rely upon the representation of their attorney when he reassures them that everything will be properly handled. However, the attorney is, unfortunately, not a clairvoyant who can foresee problem areas, although he realizes that there is certainly the potential for genuine conflict. Even where his motives are of the highest, as they usually are, and in good faith believes that he can effect a meeting of the minds, he really is not sure. Because of that dangerous uncertainty, I believe attorneys would, generally, welcome this prohibition against potential conflict.

Numerous situations like the present instance require affirmative legal action and demand an attorney's undivided loyalty. If two separate attorneys were individually retained, both parties would be sure that they were receiving the best possible legal attention. If and when a conflict developed, they would be duly represented, instead of deserted. The inconvenience in retaining separate attorneys is minimal when weighed against the dangers involved, and the cost differential in the final analysis would be inconsequential.

NOTES

1. What amount of disclosure would *Lanza* require for informed consent? If you had been the lawyer in that transaction, what would you have thought to disclose to Mrs. Greene and the Connollys? Would you have anticipated the specific problem that subsequently arose? Would you have felt comfortable referring to the problem in general terms—"Disagreements may arise between you about how payment is to be made"? Form of payment is one of the more easily disclosed areas of potential dispute in land transactions. How would you have explained such harder, more slippery issues as the nature of the title defects that would excuse buyer from performing the contract?

2. The ideal world depicted by the ABA pamphlet, excerpted above, is not commonly realized in practice. Individual representation of all parties is the exception rather than the rule in residential transactions. According to an American Bar Foundation study, in only 40% of the estimated 5.5 million residential purchases made every year, will the purchaser consult a lawyer. Curran, Survey of the Public's Legal Needs, 64 A.B.A.J. 848 (1978).

One reason for the lack of individual representation is that the parties may perceive the residential sale to be sufficiently complex, and their investment sufficiently large, to warrant one lawyer, but not sufficiently large or complex to warrant two. They may also suspect that the expense of two lawyers will be more than twice the expense of one; time must be spent, and statements rendered, for the resolution of conflicts or potential conflicts that a single lawyer would probably glide over. Yet lawyers' fees in fact represent a far smaller part of total settlement costs than the fees charged by other conveyancing professionals such as real estate brokers. While brokers commonly get 5–7% of the sale price, lawyers commonly get no more than 1%. See U.S. Department of Housing & Urban Development and Veterans Administration, Mortgage Settlement Costs: Report to Sen. Comm. on Banking, Housing & Urban Affairs 35 (Comm. Print 1972).

What would happen if lawyers conscientiously followed the rule proposed in Justice Pashman's *Lanza* concurrence which would allow attorneys to represent no more than one party to a residential sale? Is it likely that each party would secure individual counsel? Is it likely that some or all parties would go without any legal advice at all? Is Pashman saying that no representation is preferable to representation shared with a potential adversary?

3. Individual representation is no guarantee of *good* representation. A survey of eight law firms conducted by the Wall Street Journal to determine the ability of lawyers to spot several defects in a proposed residential real estate sale contract, produced some unsettling results. In the judgment of the Journal's panel of real estate experts, none of the eight attorneys spotted every defect he or she should have. Two of the lawyers did "dangerously bad" jobs and four got "low marks" on either or both of the major problem areas. Lancaster, Rating Lawyers, Wall Street Journal, 1 (July 31, 1980).

These survey results should, however, be kept in perspective. The survey was "admittedly unscientific." Six of the eight firms were "advertised as, or appeared to be," legal clinics. And, probably most important, the survey was conducted in California where lawyers only rarely represent parties to residential transactions and thus have little of the experience that is so common to general practitioners elsewhere in the country. (Inexperience does not, however, excuse bad advice. As one member of the panel observed, the correct approach for several of these attorneys would have been to refer the client to a real estate specialist.)

Pt. 1   *LAND TRANSFER AND FINANCE*   171

b. THE BROKER'S ROLE

EXCLUSIVE RIGHT TO SELL LISTING AGREEMENT

EQUAL HOUSING OPPORTUNITY

REALTOR®

NOTICE TO HOMEOWNERS

The Secretary of State, State of New York, requires that the following explanation be given homeowners and acknowledged by them in the listing of property:

An "exclusive right to sell" listing means that if you, the owner of the property, find a buyer for your house, or if another Broker finds a buyer, you must pay the agreed commission to the present Broker.

An "exclusive agency" listing means that if you, the owner of the property, find a buyer, you will not have to pay a commission to the Broker. However, if another Broker finds a buyer, you will owe a commission to both the selling Broker and your present Broker.

SELLER'S REPRESENTATION REGARDING INSULATION

____ Urea-Formaldehyde Foam Insulation was installed on _____
(DATE)

____ Urea-Formaldehyde Foam Insulation was installed on _____
(DATE)

but was removed on _____
(DATE)

__X__ Urea-Formaldehyde Foam Insulation has not been installed, or

____ Seller has no knowledge regarding the presence or absense of Urea-Formaldehyde Foam Insulation, but it has not been installed since _____
(DATE)

Signed _____
HOMEOWNER OR HOMEOWNER'S AGENT

Photographer's Direction Information

Address __23 Oak Street__ TWP __Amherst__ District __450__

Near __Elm Street__ Lot Size __65 x 140__

Broker __Hardsell Realty, Inc.__ Code __4033__ Phone __555-1212__

Type __Ranch__ Const __Brick & Frame__ Age __20__ yrs.

Garage Att __1__ Det _____ None _____

White copy to Board Office
Gold (4th) copy to Board Office
Yellow copy retained by Listing Office
Pink copy to seller

ML10 2-83

[D514]

EXCLUSIVE RIGHT TO SELL LISTING CONTRACT

TO <u>Hardsell Realty, Inc.</u>   <u>July 1, 1983</u>
        REALTOR   DATE LISTED

GRANT OF EXCLUSIVE RIGHT TO SELL AND ITS TERMS.

In consideration of your agreement to list promptly through the Multiple Listing Service (MLS) of the Greater Buffalo Board of Realtors, Inc. the within described property at <u>23 Oak Street, Amherst, New York</u>

I(We) hereby grant to you, a Member of said Multiple Listing Service, for the term of <u> six months </u> from the date hereof, the exclusive right and privilege to sell, exchange, and/or lease said property for the sum of $<u>67,000.00</u> or at such other price or terms to which I(We) may consent. I(We) agree to pay you a commission of <u> 7 </u>% of the sale or lease price, providing such property is sold, exchanged, and/or leased before the expiration of this authority, whether such a sale or lease is made by you or by Me(Us) or by any Member of said Multiple Listing Service or by anyone else. Such compensation shall be paid if property is sold, conveyed or otherwise transferred within <u> 10 </u> days after the termination of this authority or any extension thereof to anyone who received information about the property prior to final termination, provided I(We) have received in writing, including the names of the prospective purchasers, before or upon termination of this agreement or any extension thereof. However I(We) shall not be obligated to pay such compensation if a valid listing agreement is entered into during the term of such protection period with another licensed real estate broker and a sale lease or exchange of the property is made during the term of said protection period.

SUBMISSION OF PURCHASE AND LEASE OFFERS.

I(We) understand that an option is given Me(Us) to have negotiated offers to purchase or lease residential property submitted to Me(Us) through either the listing Broker or the selling Broker but I(We) elect that any such offers to purchase or lease be submitted jointly by the listing and selling Brokers unless by mutual agreement of the Brokers one of the participating Brokers waives the right to be present at such submission.

OBLIGATIONS OF OWNER(S).

In the event of sale I(We) agree to furnish a fully guaranteed tax and title search and a new survey and tender to the purchaser a good and marketable title. I(We) understand that there may be a seller's mortgage loan fee. I(We) agree to furnish all information necessary to purchasers' mortgage processing.

AUTHORITY TO PUBLISH PROPERTY DATA.

You are hereby authorized to photograph said property and use such photographs in promoting the sale or lease and also to distribute sales and lease data.

I(We) hereby acknowledge receipt of a copy of this contract and a copy of the Multiple Listing Service membership roster.

Signed <u>Hardsell Realty, Inc.</u> Signed <u>   </u>
              REALTOR   OWNER

By <u>   </u> Signed <u>   </u>
     Harry Hardsell, Pres.   OWNER

OWNER MUST RECEIVE A COPY OF THIS CONTRACT AT TIME OF SIGNATURE

[D515]

FORBIS v. HONEYCUTT

Supreme Court of North Carolina, 1981.
301 N.C. 699, 273 S.E.2d 240.

CARLTON, Justice.

Plaintiffs bring this action seeking specific performance of an exclusive listing contract for certain real property. In their complaint, plaintiffs allege that defendants are the owners of the property, and that on or about 13 July 1979 the defendants signed an exclusive listing agreement whereby the land was listed for sale with Kiser Beaver Real Estate, Inc.

Plaintiffs further allege that they executed a written offer to purchase the property for the price quoted in the listing agreement, and delivered that offer to Kiser Beaver Real Estate, Inc., together with earnest money of $600.00. Plaintiffs sold their home in anticipation of buying the subject real property from the defendants. Plaintiffs also stand ready, willing and able to fulfill the terms of their offer, but defendants refuse to convey the property. Plaintiffs pray that defendants be required to execute a general warranty deed to them conveying the subject property.

Defendants answered, alleging as a first defense that plaintiffs' complaint failed to state a claim upon which relief could be granted. Subsequently, defendants filed a separate motion to dismiss under G.S. 1A-1, Rule 12(b)(6) which, following a hearing, was granted by the trial court. Plaintiffs appealed to the Court of Appeals and that court affirmed the trial court. . . .

Turning to the question whether plaintiffs' complaint states a claim upon which relief can be granted against defendants, we agree with the Court of Appeals that the dispositive substantive question is whether the listing agreement vested in the real estate agent the authority to enter into a contract binding on defendants to convey the subject property. If it did, plaintiffs' pleadings are "legally sufficient" to proceed to trial. If it did not, there appears "an absence of law to support a claim of the sort made" and "an insurmountable bar to recovery" appears on the face of the complaint.

We join the majority of jurisdictions and hold that a real estate listing agreement such as the one in question here does not confer on the real estate agent authority to enter into a contract binding the owners to convey.

The key provisions of the listing agreement here are as follows:

> The Owner hereby gives to the Agent the exclusive right to sell the property hereinafter listed at the price and upon the terms set forth below or at such other price as the parties hereto may agree upon. This listing contract shall continue until midnight, the last hour of 13 October 1979.

Property to be sold: 1616 Longbow Drive, Kannapolis, North Carolina 28081 Sale Price: Sixty two thousand five hundred dollars Dollars ($62,500.00).

. . .

If the property is sold, leased, transferred or exchanged by the Owner or by any other party before the expiration of this listing, at any terms accepted by the Owner or within three months thereafter to any purchaser with whom the Agent or Owner negotiated during the listing, or if a ready, willing and able purchaser is procured, the Owner agrees to pay the Agent's commission. The Agent's commission for his services shall be *SIX* percent (6.0%) of the gross sales price.

. . .

It is understood and agreed that if the property is sold during the period set forth herein, Owner will execute and deliver a fee simple deed with the usual covenants of warranty, subject only to current ad valorem taxes (which are to be prorated on the calendar year basis to the date of closing the transaction), existing easements, rights-of-way, and restrictive covenants, if any, and the following encumbrances, (if none, so state).

1st Mortgage—Citizens S & L, Kannapolis Bal. 24,500.00 Payment 266.00 PIT 9% loan.

Owner agrees to give a purchaser possession of the property by at the time of final settlement.

The Owner agrees to enter into contract of sale with and to convey said property by good and sufficient deed with usual warranties to such ready, willing and able purchaser for the price and on the terms and conditions herein stated: or if the stated price cannot be obtained, in the alternative, for such other price or on such other terms and conditions as the Owner may approve. This property which is the subject matter of this agreement is offered without respect to race, creed, color or national origin.

As the Court of Appeals recognized, the question here presented is one of first impression in this State. Case law from other jurisdictions, though, establishes the majority rule that a real estate broker listing agreement such as the one in this case does not confer on a real estate broker authority to enter into a binding contract to convey the disputed property.

It is well settled that in the absence of special authority, the agent who is authorized by his principal to negotiate the sale of real estate has no power to bind his principal to a contract to convey. An agent's authority from his principal to sell real estate is not to be readily inferred, but exists only where the intention of the principal to give such authority is plainly manifest.

Of course, a real estate agent *may* be vested with authority to enter into a contract of sale binding on the owner. But such authority must be expressly conferred upon the agent or necessarily implied from the terms of the particular contract.

> However, language relied upon to confer such authority must be specific, adequate, and appropriate to express an intention to create such power, in addition to the limited power inherent in the conventional relationship of owner and broker, merely to find a purchaser with whom the owner may negotiate with the object of entering into a contract of sale.

12 Am.Jur.2d, Brokers, § 71.

Applying the foregoing to the case *sub judice,* we first note that plaintiffs pled only the agreement between the defendants and the broker as a basis for finding the requisite contractual power in the agent. Our inquiry, then, is limited to the question whether as a matter of law this agreement gave the defendants' agent authority to contractually bind the defendants. We hold that it did not.

While the listing agreement states that the agent shall have an exclusive "right to sell" the property, such a provision does not imply authority to enter into a contract binding on the owners for the sale of the property. When used in contracts between real estate agents and owners of land, the term "to sell" is generally given the restricted meaning of power to find a purchaser, and alone is not sufficient to empower a real estate agent to enter into a contract of sale. Restatement 2d, Agency, § 53 interprets the terms "to buy" and "to sell" as meaning that the agent shall (a) find a seller or purchaser from whom or to whom the principal may buy or sell; (b) make a contract for purchase or sale; or (c) accept or make a conveyance for the principal. Comment (b) under this section says:

> *Land.* Unless the price and other terms have been completely stated by the principal, it is the normal inference that an agent employed "to buy" or "to sell" land and not given a formal power of attorney is authorized merely to find a seller or a purchaser with whom the principal is to conduct the final negotiations. *This inference is strengthened if the agent is a broker who ordinarily merely solicits; even where the complete terms have been set out, it is ordinarily inferred that such a person is employed merely to find a customer.* Authority to accept or to make a conveyance of land for the principal is found only if clearly expressed in the authorization or clearly indicated by the circumstances. (Emphasis added.)

Under the quoted language of the Restatement, plaintiffs' claim is not persuasive merely because the listing agreement here sets a sales price, fixes a commission and provides an expiration date for the exclusive listing. The agent was not given a power of attorney, nor any authority to contract on behalf of defendants. We see nothing in this agreement to defeat the normal inference that the agent was employed solely to find a buyer.

Our decision that the authority of the agent did not include the power to contract under the facts of this case is also supported by practical reasons and the inherent relationship of the parties. The decision whether to sell the land, on what terms, and to whom, involves complex questions which should not be deemed readily entrusted to an agent. Where several offers are received by an agent, they may vary not only as to price but also as to terms, financing, date of possession or numerous other factors. A decision on such matters would normally be for the owners of real estate, not their agents. Under the terms of the agreement set out above, we do not believe defendants intended to vest this agent with authority beyond that of finding willing purchasers. The decision of the Court of Appeals is

Affirmed.

TRISTRAM'S LANDING, INC. v. WAIT

Supreme Court of Massachusetts, 1975.
367 Mass. 622, 327 N.E.2d 727.

TAURO, Chief Justice.

This is an action in contract seeking to recover a brokerage commission alleged to be due to the plaintiffs from the defendant. The case was heard by a judge, sitting without a jury, on a stipulation of facts. The judge found for the plaintiffs in the full amount of the commission. The defendant filed exceptions to that finding and appealed.

The facts briefly are these: The plaintiffs are real estate brokers doing business in Nantucket. The defendant owned real estate on the island which she desired to sell. In the past, the plaintiffs acted as brokers for the defendant when she rented the same premises.

The plaintiffs heard that the defendant's property was for sale, and in the spring of 1972 the plaintiff Van der Wolk telephoned the defendant and asked for authority to show it. The defendant agreed that the plaintiffs could act as brokers, although not as exclusive brokers, and told them that the price for the property was $110,000. During this conversation there was no mention of a commission. The defendant knew that the normal brokerage commission in Nantucket was five per cent of the sale price.

In the early months of 1973, Van der Wolk located a prospective buyer, Louise L. Cashman (Cashman), who indicated that she was interested in purchasing the defendant's property. Her written offer of $100,000, dated April 29, was conveyed to the defendant. Shortly thereafter, the defendant's husband and attorney wrote to the plaintiffs that "a counter-offer of $105,000 with an October 1st closing" should be made to Cashman. Within a few weeks, the counter offer was orally accepted, and a purchase and sale agreement was drawn up by Van der Wolk.

The agreement was executed by Cashman and was returned to the plaintiffs with a check for $10,500, representing a ten per cent down payment. The agreement was then presented by the plaintiffs to the defendant, who signed it after reviewing it with her attorney. The down payment check was thereafter turned over to the defendant.

The purchase and sale agreement signed by the parties called for an October 1, 1973, closing date. On September 22, the defendant signed a fifteen day extension of the closing date, which was communicated to Cashman by the plaintiffs. Cashman did not sign the extension. On October 1, 1973, the defendant appeared at the registry of deeds with a deed to the property. Cashman did not appear for the closing and thereafter refused to go through with the purchase. No formal action has been taken by the defendant to enforce the agreement or to recover damages for its breach, although the defendant has retained the down payment.

Van der Wolk presented the defendant with a bill for commission in the amount of $5,250, five per cent of the agreed sales price. The defendant, through her attorney, refused to pay, stating that "[t]here has been no sale and consequently the 5% commission has not been earned." The plaintiffs then brought this action to recover the commission.

In the course of dealings between the plaintiffs and the defendant there was no mention of commission. The only reference to commission is found in the purchase and sale agreement signed by Cashman and the defendant, which reads as follows: "It is understood that a broker's commission of five (5) per cent on the said sale is to be paid to . . . [the broker] by the said seller." The plaintiffs contend that, having produced a buyer who was ready, willing and able to purchase the property, and who was in fact accepted by the seller, they are entitled to their full commission. The defendant argues that no commission was earned because the sale was not consummated. We agree with the defendant, and reverse the finding by the judge below.

1. The general rule regarding whether a broker is entitled to a commission from one attempting to sell real estate is that, absent special circumstances, the broker "is entitled to a commission if he produces a customer ready, able, and willing to buy upon the terms and for the price given the broker by the owner." Gaynor v. Laverdure, ___ Mass. ___, ___, 291 N.E.2d 617 (1973), quoting Henderson & Beal, Inc. v. Glen, 329 Mass. 748, 751, 110 N.E.2d 373 (1953). In the past, this rule has been construed to mean that once a customer is produced by the broker and accepted by the seller, the commission is earned, whether or not the sale is actually consummated. Furthermore, execution of a purchase and sale agreement is usually seen as conclusive evidence of the seller's acceptance of the buyer.

Despite these well established and often cited rules, we have held that "[t]he owner is not helpless" to protect himself from these consequences. "He may, by appropriate language in his dealings with the broker, limit his liability for payment of a commission to the situation where not only is the broker obligated to find a customer ready, willing and able to purchase on the owner's terms and for his price, but also it is provided that no commission is to become due until the customer actually takes a conveyance and pays therefor." Gaynor v. Laverdure, *supra*, at __ - __, 291 N.E.2d at 622.

In the application of these rules to the instant case, we believe that the broker here is not entitled to a commission. We cannot construe the purchase and sale agreement as an unconditional acceptance by the seller of the buyer, as the agreement itself contained conditional language. The purchase and sale agreement provided that the commission was to be paid "on the said sale," and we construe this language as requiring that the said sale be consummated before the commission is earned.

. . . In two of the more recent cases where we were faced with this issue, we declined to follow the developing trends in this area, holding that the cases presented were inappropriate for that purpose. See LeDonne v. Slade, 355 Mass. 490, 492, 245 N.E.2d 434 (1969); Gaynor v. Laverdure, __ Mass. __, __ - __, 291 N.E.2d 617. We believe, however, that it is both appropriate and necessary at this time to clarify the law, and we now join the growing minority of States who have adopted the rule of Ellsworth Dobbs, Inc. v. Johnson, 50 N.J. 528, 236 A.2d 843 (1967).[6]

In the *Ellsworth* case, the New Jersey court faced the task of clarifying the law regarding the legal relationships between sellers and brokers in real estate transactions. In order to formulate a just and proper rule, the court examined the realities of such transactions. The court noted that "ordinarily when an owner of property lists it with a broker for sale, his expectation is that the money for the payment of commission will come out of the proceeds of the sale." *Id.* at 547, 236 A.2d at 852. It quoted with approval from the opinion of Lord Justice Denning, in Dennis Reed, Ltd. v. Goody, [1950] 2 K.B. 277, 284–285, where he stated: "When a house owner puts his house into the hands of an estate agent, the ordinary understanding is that the agent is only to receive a commission if he succeeds in effecting a sale . . . . The common understanding of men is . . . that the agent's commission is payable out of the purchase price. . . . The

---

6. Both Kansas and Oregon have adopted the *Ellsworth* rule in its entirety. See Winkelman v. Allen, 214 Kansas 22, 519 P.2d 1377 (1974); Brown v. Grimm, 258 Or. 55, 59–61, 481 P.2d 63 (1971). Additionally, Vermont, Connecticut and Idaho have cited the case with approval. See also Potter v. Ridge Realty Corp., 28 Conn.Supp. 304, 311, 259 A.2d 758 (1969); Rogers v. Hendrix, 92 Idaho 141, 438 P.2d 653 (1968); Staab v. Messier, 128 Vt. 380, 384, 264 A.2d 790 (1970). Other States and the District of Columbia also have similar, but more limited, rules which were adopted prior to the *Ellsworth* case. See generally Gaynor v. Laverdure, __ Mass. __ n. 2, 291 N.E.2d 617 (1973).

house-owner wants to find a man who will actually buy his house and pay for it. He does not want a man who will only make an offer or sign a contract. He wants a purchaser 'able to purchase and able to complete as well.'" *Id.* at 549, 236 A.2d at 853.

The court went on to say that the principle binding "the seller to pay commission if he signs a contract of sale with the broker's customer, regardless of the customer's financial ability, puts the burden on the wrong shoulders. Since the broker's duty to the owner is to produce a prospective buyer who is financially able to pay the purchase price and take title, a right in the owner to assume such capacity when the broker presents his purchaser ought to be recognized." *Id.* at 548, 236 A.2d at 853. Reason and justice dictate that it should be the broker who bears the burden of producing a purchaser who is not only ready, willing and able at the time of the negotiations, but who also consummates the sale at the time of closing.

Thus, we adopt the following rules: "When a broker is engaged by an owner of property to find a purchaser for it, the broker earns his commission when (a) he produces a purchaser ready, willing and able to buy on the terms fixed by the owner, (b) the purchaser enters into a binding contract with the owner to do so, and (c) the purchaser completes the transaction by closing the title in accordance with the provisions of the contract. If the contract is not consummated because of lack of financial ability of the buyer to perform or because of any other default of his . . . there is no right to commission against the seller. On the other hand, if the failure of completion of the contract results from the wrongful act or interference of the seller, the broker's claim is valid and must be paid." *Id.* at 551, 236 A.2d at 855.

Accordingly, we hold that a real estate broker, under a brokerage agreement hereafter made, is entitled to a commission from the seller only if the requirements stated above are met. This rule provides necessary protection for the seller and places the burden with the broker, where it belongs. In view of the waiver of the counts in quantum meruit, we do not now consider the extent to which the broker may be entitled to share in a forfeited deposit or other benefit received by the seller as a result of the broker's efforts.

We recognize that this rule could be easily circumvented by language to the contrary in purchase and sale agreements or in agreements between sellers and brokers. In many States a signed writing is required for an agreement to pay a commission to a real estate broker. See Restatement 2d: Contracts, 418, 420 (Tent. drafts Nos. 1-7, 1973). Such a requirement may be worthy of legislative consideration, but we do not think we should establish such a requirement by judicial decision. Informal agreements fairly made between people of equal skill and understanding serve a useful purpose. But many sellers, unlike brokers, are involved in real estate transactions infrequently, perhaps only once in a lifetime, and are thus unfamiliar with their legal rights. In such cases agreements by the seller to pay a commission even though the purchaser defaults are to be scrutinized carefully. If not fairly made, such agreements may be unconscionable or against public policy.

Exceptions sustained.

Judgment for the defendant.

NOTES

1. There are four basic types of broker listing agreement: exclusive right to sell; exclusive agency; open; and net. *Exclusive right to sell* contracts are the most favorable to the listing broker, giving her the right to a commission if the property is sold by anyone, even the owner, during the term of the listing agreement. *Exclusive agency* contracts entitle the broker to a commission if she or any other broker sells the property, but not if the property is sold through the efforts of the owner. In an *open*, or *nonexclusive*, listing agreement, the broker is entitled to a commission only if she is the first to procure a ready, willing and able buyer; if the owner, or anyone else for that matter, finds a buyer first, the broker has no claim. In a *net* listing contract, the owner agrees to accept a specific price for the property and the broker receives any amount paid in excess of that price.

Which of these four types of agreements do you suppose the National Association of Realtors—the largest national organization of real estate professionals—encourages its members to employ? See Nat'l Assoc. of Realtors, Code of Ethics, Art. 6 (1976) ("To prevent dissension and misunderstanding and to assure better service to the owner, the Realtor should urge the exclusive listing of property unless contrary to the best interest of the owner.") See generally, D.B. Burke, Law of Real Estate Brokers (1982).

2. Even the most commonly used broker-drafted forms are not free from ambiguity, and courts are sometimes called on to determine what type of listing agreement broker and seller made. For example, in Holiday Homes of St. Johns, Inc. v. Lockhart, 678 F.2d 1176 (3rd Cir.1982), the form agreement specified an "Exclusive Right to Sell Basis," but also provided that the commission would be payable only upon the broker's procurement of a ready, willing and able buyer. The court seized on this ambiguity to hold that an exclusive right to sell agreement had not been created.

Courts generally construe ambiguous agreements against the broker on the ground that brokers have superior bargaining power, greater expertise, and are responsible for selecting the form of listing agreement. See Bourgoin v. Fortier, 310 A.2d 618 (Me.1973).

Are there any ambiguities in the Buffalo Board of Realtors form agreement, above? Re-read the sentence in the second full paragraph beginning, "Such compensation shall be paid . . . ." How is "final" termination different from "termination"? What will have been "received in writing . . . including the names of the prospective purchasers . . .."? In the preceding sentence of the form, how is a "lease price" to be determined for purposes of computing the 7% commission?

3. *Forbis* held that, absent an express grant of authority, real estate brokers are not empowered to enter into sales contracts on behalf of their clients. Does it follow that sellers will not be bound by *any* of the broker's representations to prospective buyers? For example, if a buyer relied on a representation in the broker's listing form that the lot size was 65 × 140 feet and the house 20 years old, would he have an action against the seller if it later turned out that the parcel was only 50 × 120 feet and the house was 35 years old? Should the seller be liable if she disclosed all relevant facts to the broker, but the broker did not disclose them to the buyer? See Crum v. McCoy, note 7, below.

4. A broker's duties to the listing seller are governed by a fiduciary standard. The standard is usually applied strictly. For example, in Cogan v. Kidder, Matthews & Segner, Inc., 97 Wn.2d 658, 648 P.2d 875 (1982), the broker's failure to inform the seller that it was acting as a dual agent, and also represented the buyer, was held to bar the broker from recovering the $19,000 commission that seller had agreed to pay, even though the nondisclosure caused seller only $660 damages, at most.

Is it realistic to apply such a strict fiduciary standard to the broker's relationship with the land seller? What implications does this standard have for the broker's behavior in presenting to the seller an offer that falls below the seller's asking price? Is it relevant that, because the broker will characteristically be working on a commission basis and will be paid only if a deal is concluded, she will be inclined to favor a sure deal at a lower price over the risk of no deal at the listing price?

Should the broker's fiduciary obligation to the seller change with the kind of listing agreement involved? For example, should a higher duty be imposed under an exclusive right to sell listing than under an exclusive agency or open listing? In borderline cases like *Cogan*, above, would it be preferable to allow the faithless broker to recover the agreed-upon commission with a set-off for any damages suffered by the seller as a consequence of the broker's breach?

5. Note that *Tristram's Landing* does not entirely relieve the seller of the duty to pay a commission on an aborted sale. Rather it allocates liability according to fault. If it was the seller's fault that the sale did not go through, the seller remains liable for the commission; if it was the buyer's fault, the seller is not liable.

Who should bear the risk when the sale fails to close through the fault of no one? In Hecht v. Meller, 23 N.Y.2d 301, 296 N.Y.S.2d 561, 244 N.E.2d 77 (1968), broker was awarded her commission even though the contract of sale had been rescinded because the property had been substantially destroyed by fire before the closing. The court rested its decision squarely on the traditional view that a broker's right to a commission attaches when she procures a ready, willing and able buyer. Would a court following *Tristram's Landing* reach a different result? The Buffalo Board of Realtors form listing agreement, above, obligates the seller to tender a "good and marketable title." If seller's title proves to be unmarketable, and buyer consequently rescinds, is the broker nonetheless entitled to her commission?

Tristram's Landing's interpretational presumption—no closing, no commission—has been widely followed by contemporary courts that have considered the issue. Ellsworth Dobbs, Inc. v. Johnson, 50 N.J. 528, 236 A.2d 843 (1967), the landmark decision relied on in *Tristram's Landing*, announced a second rule that has, by contrast, won few adherents. The rule is one of contract illegality rather than interpretation. According to the court, whenever "there is substantial inequality of bargaining power" between broker and seller, a clause entitling the broker to a commission on the contract signing, is "so contrary to the common understanding of men, and also so contrary to fairness, as to require a court to condemn it as unconscionable." 50 N.J. at 555, 236 A.2d at 857.

6. *The Multiple Listing Service.* Multiple listing services are local clearinghouses that regularly inform their broker members of all new listings in the community. The MLS is usually sponsored by the local real estate board, and access to the service is commonly conditioned on membership in the board. In the typical MLS, a broker submits each exclusive listing she obtains to the service. Once the listing is submitted to the service, every other broker member can try to sell the listed property by procuring a buyer. The commission from such "cooperative" sales is divided between the listing and the selling brokers. In a voluntary MLS, members can choose which listings they will submit to the service. In a mandatory service, members must submit all their listings.

Multiple listing services have been accused of abetting anticompetitive practices among brokers. One observer has argued that the forced sharing of information reduces quality-of-search competition among local board members and that the MLS also creates the ability to coordinate price-fixing. Owen, Kickbacks, Specialization, Price Fixing, and Efficiency in Residential Real Estate Markets, 29 Stan.L.Rev. 931, 947 (1977). Further, by imposing onerous membership requirements, and thus excluding new entrants from access to the MLS, local boards have succeeded in eliminating potential competitors from their localities.

See generally, Erxleben, In Search of Price and Service Competition in Residential Real Estate Brokerage: Breaking the Cartel, 56

Wash.L.Rev. 179 (1981); Trombetta, The MLS Access Issue: A Rule of Reason Analysis, 11 Seton Hall L.Rev. 396 (1981).

7. *Broker's Duties to Buyer.* Under traditional doctrine, the listing broker, who is retained by the seller, is the seller's agent and consequently has no duties, fiduciary or otherwise, to the buyer. Traditional doctrine also holds that an MLS member who shows a house listed by the seller's broker acts as the subagent of the listing broker and is thus under the same fiduciary duties to the seller as is the listing broker.

Traditional doctrine obviously ignores the new realities and expectations created by multiple listing services. A prospective buyer commonly approaches a broker who may have been recommended to him and describes his housing needs and financial capabilities to the broker. This broker will show the buyer all the listings in the current MLS book, take him on a tour of possibly interesting properties and, eventually, present the buyer's offer and negotiate on his behalf for the chosen property. After all this, what reasonable buyer will not assume that the broker is *his* agent and expect the broker to represent *his* interests in the negotiations? And, what seller can comfortably rely on the undivided loyalty of the broker in this position?

Although the broker's fiduciary duties are to the seller, an injured buyer is not entirely without remedy. Broker fraud is the claim most frequently litigated, with actions brought directly against the broker or against the seller as a principal responsible for her agent's conduct. In Crum v. McCoy, 41 Ohio Misc. 34, 322 N.E.2d 161 (Mun.Ct. 1974), sellers had told their broker about hidden defects in their water supply system. Although the broker had noted the defects on his listing form, he failed to include them in the Multiple Listing Service card because "there was not enough room." Buyers saw the MLS card and inspected the house. The court ruled that buyers had met their duty of diligent inspection and that sellers had committed constructive fraud because their broker-agents, acting within the scope of their authority, had failed to disclose a known latent defect. The court entered judgment for the buyers against the sellers and for the sellers, as third-party plaintiffs, against their brokers, as third-party defendants.

Another route to buyer recovery, available when the sale is negotiated by seller's listing broker and a broker chosen by the buyer, is simply to disregard the dogma that the broker chosen by the buyer is the seller's subagent, and to treat her as the buyer's agent instead. The Alabama Supreme Court took this innovative approach in Cashion v. Ahmadi, 345 So.2d 268 (Ala.1977), in which the buyer, on discovering a periodic water problem in the basement, abandoned the house and sued the seller and the two real estate firms that had brokered the transaction, claiming that all had known of the defect. Affirming the lower court judgment for the seller and the listing broker on strict *caveat emptor* grounds, the court reversed the judgment for the broker chosen by the buyer, holding that, as to him, a jury could find an agency relationship with the buyer and, consequently, a duty to disclose his knowledge of the defect. Among the facts to be considered on remand were whether the broker's statements indicated a belief that he was primarily representing buyer or seller. For a thoughtful comment on *Cashion,* see Payne, Broker's Liability for Nondisclosure of Known Defects in Sale Property—Caveat Emptor Still Applies, 6 Real Estate L.J. 341 (1978).

8. *Buyer's Duties to Broker.* Do the new realities and expectations created by multiple listing services also give brokers rights against buyers who have maneuvered them out of their commissions or prevented the deal from closing? Traditionally, brokers had little need for such rights since their client—seller—was liable for the commission at the moment the broker presented a ready, willing and able buyer. But with more recent decisions like *Tristram's Landing,* brokers must look to the defaulting buyer for relief.

Ellsworth Dobbs, relied on in *Tristram's Landing,* sought to protect the broker in these situations by enlarging the occasions for buyer liability: "when a prospective buyer solicits a broker to find or to show him property which he might be interested in buying, and the broker finds property satisfactory to him which the owner agrees to sell at the price offered, and the buyer knows the broker will earn a commission for the sale from the owner, the law will imply a promise on the part of the buyer to complete the transaction with the owner." 50 N.J. at 559, 236 A.2d at 859. At least one state court has followed *Ellsworth Dobbs'* implied promise theory, Donnellan v. Rocks, 22 Cal. App.3d 925, 99 Cal.Rptr. 692 (1972), and two have rejected it, Rich v. Emerson-Dumont Distributing Corp., 55 Mich.App. 142, 222 N.W.2d 65 (1974); Professional Realty Corp. v. Bender, 216 Va. 737, 222 S.E.2d 810 (1976).

Ellsworth Dobbs itself was limited by the New Jersey Supreme Court in Rothman Realty Corp. v. Bereck, 73 N.J. 590, 376 A.2d 902 (1977). Buyers in that case suffered a sudden stock market reversal, making it impossible for them to come up with the cash needed to close the purchase of a house. The court held that buyers' "implied promise to the broker to complete the transaction did not encompass a failure to close where they had acted in good faith, and the inability to consummate the deal . . . was due to a circumstance beyond their control." The court distinguished *Ellsworth Dobbs* on the ground that the buyer there was engaged in a commercial enterprise; the "bargaining power and expertise of such buyers are far superior to those of the average home purchaser." 73 N.J. at 602, 603, 376 A.2d at 908, 909.

9. *Unauthorized Practice of Law.* How far can real estate brokers go in conducting the negotiations that bring buyer and seller together, and in filling out the form of agreement that will keep them together, without engaging in the unauthorized practice of law? Because residential transactions are pervaded by legal issues and are heavily papered with legal instruments, the work performed by these nonlawyers unavoidably borders on the practice of law.

In one major case, State Bar of Arizona v. Arizona Title & Trust Co., 90 Ariz. 76, 366 P.2d 1 (1961), the Arizona Supreme Court took an unusually hard line against unauthorized practice, ruling that brokers may not advise or assist in the preparation of documents that affect, alter or define legal rights. The court's proscription encompassed even the filling in of blanks on printed forms. The brokers petitioned for a rehearing but ultimately enjoyed greater success by obtaining 107,420 signatures on an initiative petition for an amendment to the state constitution, giving real estate brokers and salespeople the right "to draft or fill out and complete, without charge, . . . preliminary purchase agreements . . . deeds, mortgages, leases . . . contracts of sale." The proposed amendment passed by a margin of almost 4 to 1. Arizona Const. Art. XXVI § 1.

The brokers' victory in Arizona was not costless. In 1976 an Arizona appellate court ruled that the constitutional amendment created not only new rights, but also new duties, and held that a broker breached his duty to seller by failing to explain the possible consequences of accepting buyer's promissory note in which one key phrase—"This note is secured by a mortgage on real property"—had been stricken. The action was precipitated by the buyer's default on the note. Morley v. J. Pagel Realty & Insurance, 27 Ariz.App. 62, 550 P.2d 1104 (1976).

For background on brokers' unauthorized practice in Arizona and elsewhere, see Marks, The Lawyers and the Realtors: Arizona's Experience, 49 A.B.A.J. 139 (1963); Riggs, Unauthorized Practice and the Public Interest: Arizona's Recent Constitutional Amendment, 37 S.Cal.L.Rev. 1 (1964); Note, 19 DePaul L.Rev. 319 (1969).

186 *THE REAL PROPERTY SYSTEM* Pt. 1

2. THE CONTRACT OF SALE

©BAR ASSOCIATION OF ERIE COUNTY and GREATER BUFFALO BOARD OF REALTORS, INC.
Form No. 1 (1982)

Published by David F. Williamson Co., Inc.
Buffalo, New York

of Erie County

This form not recommended for the sale of a condominium and/or real property which includes an interest in a homeowners' association.

CONTRACT OF SALE

CAUTION: IT IS RECOMMENDED THAT ANY PERSON NAMED IN THIS CONTRACT CONSULT HIS OR HER ATTORNEY BEFORE SIGNING IT.

Date _____ July 18 _____, 19 83 _____ Seller and Purchaser agree as follows:

Seller: ROBERT W. JONES and MARY RUTH JONES, his wife
Address: 23 Oak Street, Amherst, New York 14221

Purchaser: JOHN J. SMITH and KATHERINE ANN SMITH, his wife
Address: 49 Willow Street, Buffalo, New York 14202

1. **AGREEMENT.** Seller shall sell and Purchaser shall buy on the terms stated in this contract.
2. **PROPERTY.** The Property is described as follows:
   Street Address __23 Oak Street__
   ~~City/Village~~ Town of __Amherst__ County of Erie, _____, State of New York.
   Additional description:

   Being a three bedroom ranch with an attached garage, situated on a lot 65 feet front and rear and approximately 140 feet in depth as an accurate search and survey will show and more fully described in the deed.

   (If legal description, subdivision lot number or dimensions and location with distance from nearest intersecting street are not available, use tax bill number and description set forth on tax bill.)

   Purchaser will accept title to the Property subject to restrictions of record providing they have not been violated, unless their enforcement is barred by law; water lines, sanitary sewer, drainage, gas distribution line and main, electrical and telephone easements and rights-of-way of record provided they are or may be used to service the Property and provided buildings and other improvements on the Property are not on the easements; and also _____

3. **THE SALE INCLUDES** (a) all buildings and improvements on the Property and all rights of Seller to all streets, highways, alleys, driveways, easements and rights-of-way relating to the Property.
   (b) the following items, if any, belonging to the Seller and now on the Property: all heating, plumbing, lighting fixtures and bulbs, all flowers, shrubs, trees, linoleum, window shades, venetian blinds, curtain rods, traverse rods, storm windows and storm doors, screens, awnings, exterior T.V. antennas and rotor motor and controls, water softeners, sump pumps, bathroom fixtures, weather vanes, window boxes, fences, chandeliers, flag poles, fire place screens and equipment, wall to wall carpeting and runners, garbage disposals, garage door openers including hand-held units, and also (unless such items are free standing) all cabinets, mirrors, dishwashers, ovens, shelving, exhaust fans and hoods, trash compactors, air conditioning (except window) units, humidifiers and dehumidifiers, gas operated post-type outdoor grills, and swimming pools and all related equipment; and also _____

   Seller will maintain all heating, plumbing and lighting fixtures, and all appliances and other electrical devices in the same condition as they exist as of the date of this contract, reasonable wear and tear excepted.
   EXCLUDED FROM THIS SALE ARE: furniture and household furnishings; and also _____

4. **PRICE.** The purchase price is $ __67,000.00__ payable as follows:
   - When Purchaser signs this contract *(deposit)* .... $ __100.00__
   - When Seller signs this contract *(additional deposit)* within 3 days thereafter .... $ __4,900.00__
   - On delivery of deed .... $ __12,000.00__ *
     (*purchase price less deposits and less approximate mortgage amount, if any, to be assumed by Purchaser, subject to closing adjustments and exact balance at time of closing of assumed mortgage, if any.)
   - By assuming and agreeing to pay according to its terms the principal balance of the mortgage held by _____ in the approximate amount of .... $ __None__
     payable $ _____ monthly, interest rate _____ %.
     Monthly payments include _____
     The mortgage ☐ has no "balloon" payment provision ☐ has a "balloon" payment due _____
     A "balloon" payment is a required payment in full by a specified date of all unpaid principal and interest.
     Monthly payments include _____
     If mortgage holder's consent to assume this mortgage is required and not obtained by the _____ day of _____, 19 _____, either Purchaser or Seller shall have the right to cancel this contract by written notice to the other. If by the above date, consent for assumption is given only at an interest rate in excess of ____% per annum, Purchaser shall have the right to cancel this contract by written notice to Seller.
     Purchaser will pay mortgage holder's assumption fee.
   - By giving Seller a purchase money note and mortgage (in statutory form) in the amount of ... $ __50,000.00__
     which shall be a __first__ lien on the property payable as follows:
     $ __553.10__ monthly including principal and interest (interest rate __13__ %),
     monthly payment is based as if payments were made over __30__ years, but entire unpaid balance is due at end of __30__ years, with no penalty for prepayment.
     Such mortgage ☐ will ☒ will not be assumable without the consent of the Seller. Purchaser will pay a late charge of 2% of any payment not made within 15 days of the date due.
     (add any additional terms)

[D510]

Pt. 1 LAND TRANSFER AND FINANCE 187

5. **ADJUSTMENTS AT CLOSING.** There shall be prorated and adjusted, as of 12:00 midnight prior to delivery of the deed, rents, fuel oil, mortgage interest non-delinquent taxes and assessments appearing on current tax bills computed on a fiscal year basis, water and sewer charges and the following items: *(list insurance, or other items to be adjusted)* _____

   Purchaser will accept title to the Property subject to, and will pay, all assessments and installments of assessments for special or local improvements not payable as of the closing date, provided they appear on the current tax rolls.

   When a mortgage is assumed, Seller shall furnish to Purchaser at closing a statement by the mortgage holder stating the unpaid balance, interest due and terms of payment and shall transfer to Purchaser all money held in escrow by the mortgage holder and Purchaser shall pay that amount to Seller.

6. **SEARCH AND SURVEY.** Seller shall delivery to Purchaser's attorney at least 15 days before the date of closing a fully guaranteed tax and title search (which covers the property only) dated after this contract and a local tax certificate, where not covered by search, and a survey dated after this contract, prepared and certified according to Bar Association of Erie County standards, showing the Property and the location of all buildings, other structures, and improvements affecting it. If vacant land, the Property is to be staked.

7. **DEED.** At closing, Seller shall deliver to Purchaser a warranty deed (or fiduciary deed where appropriate) with lien covenant giving good and marketable title in fee simple, free and clear of all encumbrances except as stated in this contract.

8. **INSPECTION.** Before closing, Purchaser shall have the right to inspect the Property on reasonable notice to Seller.

9. **POSSESSION.** Purchaser shall have possession and occupancy of the Property and Seller shall be out of the Property at or prior to the time of the delivery of the deed except as follows: *(List all tenants, rents, leases if any, and security deposits.)*

10. **MORTGAGE COMMITMENT.** Purchaser shall apply for a _____ year (insert conventional fixed rate, adjustable rate, etc., FHA, VA) _____ mortgage loan in the amount of $ _____
    The ☐ initial ☐ fixed interest rate will not exceed _____ % per annum except that if the Purchaser accepts a mortgage commitment permitting the rate to be changed prior to closing, or if Purchaser's mortgage commitment expires before closing and will be renewed only at a changed interest rate, Purchaser will be bound by such change provided such change is to a rate of not more than _____ % per annum.
    Purchaser's application shall be made promptly and in good faith. If a commitment for this mortgage is not obtained by the _____ day of _____, 19 _____, either Purchaser or Seller may cancel this contract by written notice to the other and the entire deposit shall be returned. The same shall apply if the commitment is granted but later cancelled without fault of Purchaser.

    If Purchaser applies for an F.H.A. mortgage, the following applies: "It is expressly agreed that, notwithstanding any other provisions of this contract, the purchaser shall not be obligated to complete the purchase of the property described herein or to incur any penalty by forfeiture of earnest money deposits or otherwise, unless the seller has delivered to the purchaser a written statement issued by the Federal Housing Commissioner setting forth the appraised value of the property (excluding closing costs) of not less than $ _____ which statement the seller hereby agrees to deliver to the purchaser promptly after such appraised value statement is made available to seller. The purchaser shall, however, have the privilege and option of proceeding with the consummation of the contract without regard to the amount of the appraised valuation made by the Federal Housing Commissioner. The appraised valuation is arrived at to determine the maximum mortgage the Department of Housing and Urban Development will insure. HUD does not warrant the value or the condition of the property. The purchaser should satisfy himself/herself that the price and condition of the property are acceptable."

    If Purchaser applies for V.A. mortgage, the following applies: "It is expressly agreed that, notwithstanding any other provisions of this contract, the purchaser shall not incur any penalty by forfeiture of earnest money, or otherwise, or be obligated to complete the purchase of the property described herein, if the contract purchase price or cost exceeds the reasonable value of the property established by the Veterans Administration. The purchaser shall, however, have the privilege and option of proceeding with the consummation of the contract without regard to the amount of reasonable value established by the Veterans Administration."

11. **MORTGAGE LOAN FEE.** *(Complete if applicable.)*
    Seller shall pay loan fee of not more than _____ % of mortgage.
    Purchaser shall pay loan fee of not more than _____ % of mortgage.

12. **COSTS.** Seller shall pay for tax and title search to date of closing and for survey, transfer tax stamps and the special additional mortgage tax if it applies. Purchaser shall pay mortgage tax and for recording deed and mortgage.

13. **OBJECTION TO TITLE AND TITLE INSURANCE.** If Purchaser finds valid objections to Seller's title which make it unmarketable, both Seller and Purchaser have the right to cancel this contract on written notice, and the full deposit shall be returned. However, if Seller is able, within a reasonable time, to cure the objection or if thereafter either Seller or Purchaser obtain a committment for fee title insurance at standard rates covering the objection, Seller shall pay the cost of it and this contract shall remain in effect. Purchaser will pay for title insurance required by lender.

14. **IMPROVEMENT VIOLATIONS.** Purchaser intends to use the property for single family residence or *(insert other use if applicable)* _____

    The Seller shall apply for and supply to Purchaser any certificate normally required by current government regulations showing that the Property complies with any law, ordinance, regulation or code, including County Health Department approval of non-public sewage disposal system and water supply. Seller shall pay any cost in applying for such certification(s).

    If Purchaser makes valid objection to the legal status of the improvements on the Property or to the Property itself or if Seller is unable to obtain the certifications mentioned above without cost, except for application fees, the Seller has the choice of cancelling the contract on written notice to the Purchaser and returning the full deposit or correcting at Seller's expense the problem(s) which caused the objection within a reasonable time so that the certifications may be obtained.

15. **CLOSING.** This contract shall be closed at the County Clerk's Office at 10:00 A.M. on the __1st__ day of __September__, 19 __83__, or at whatever other date and time Purchaser and Seller later agree upon.

16. **BROKER'S COMMISSION.** Seller and Purchaser agree that __Hardsell Realty, Inc.__ brought about this sale and the Seller agrees to pay the entire broker's commission. The deposit(s) shall be held in escrow by __Hardsell Realty, Inc.__

17. **ENTIRE AGREEMENT.** This contract of sale with (insert "no" or number) _____ Riders contains the entire agreement between the Seller and Purchaser and nothing is binding on either of them which is not contained in this contract. This contract is intended to bind the Seller and Purchaser and those who succeed to their interests.

18. **SIGNATURES.** Unless all of the persons whose names appear at the beginning of the contract sign it on or before the __1st__ day of __July__, 19 __83__, this contract shall not become effective.

Seller	Date	Purchaser	Date
Robert W. Jones	7/18/83	John J. Smith	7/18/83
Mary Ruth Jones	7/18/83	Katherine Ann Smith	7/18/83

RECEIPTS

Received the Initial deposit of $ __100.00__ on account from purchaser.
Additional deposit of $ _____

Dated: __July 18__, 19 __83__   Received by: __Hardsell Realty, Inc.__

[0511]

QUESTIONS

Representing sellers or buyers, what changes would you try to make in the form of contract of sale, above, before advising your clients to sign? As you read the cases and materials in this section, you may want to refer back to this form to see how, if at all, it resolves several recurrent problems:

1. Is the form of contract sufficiently complete to satisfy the statute of frauds? For example, does the description appearing in Paragraph 2 identify the parcel with sufficient precision to distinguish it from all other parcels? At the time of signing, what can the parties do to obtain a more complete, legal description of the parcel?

2. Representing buyers, would you feel comfortable letting your clients commit themselves to accept title to the property "subject to restrictions of record"? Before a title report is ordered and received, you will probably not know whether those restrictions include prohibitions making the land unusable for your clients' purposes. For example, the title report may disclose a recorded restriction against altering any architectural features of the house or against installing a swimming pool in the yard. Are you comforted by the fact that Paragraph 7 obligates the seller to convey "good and marketable title"? (Note that this title is to be free and clear of all encumbrances, "except as stated in this contract.") Are you comforted by the provision in Paragraph 13 that if your client "finds valid objections to Seller's title which make it unmarketable," both seller and purchaser may cancel the contract? Will the validity of any such objection be measured by the terms of Paragraph 2?

3. Since, under Paragraph 4, the sellers are to finance the purchase, the buyers need not obtain mortgage financing from an institutional lender. Representing the buyers, should you be concerned that this might operate to your clients' disadvantage, depriving them of the objective—indeed fish-eyed—appraisal that institutional lenders conduct before committing themselves to make a mortgage loan? If instead the contract called for the buyers to obtain financing from an institutional lender, would you, representing the sellers, be concerned that the buyers might manipulate the clause into an escape hatch to ease themselves out of the contract for any reason, or for no reason at all?

4. Representing buyers or sellers, are you certain that you know what the form means when it refers in Paragraph 14 to buyer making "valid objection . . . to the Property itself"?

5. Representing buyers or sellers, do you know what remedies will obtain if any of the conditions, representations or obligations specified in the contract are not met? For example, are the provisions of Paragraph 2 subject to the remedies respecting marketable title in Paragraph 13? What remedies will the buyers have if the "search and survey" contemplated by Paragraph 2 reveals that the

lot is smaller than 140' x 65'? Rescission and return of the $5,000 deposit? Damages? If the survey shows that the lot is larger than 140' x 65', will the sellers be entitled to rescind? Will the buyers be entitled to rescission, damages, both or neither if sellers breach Paragraph 3's obligation to maintain all fixtures and appliances in the condition they were in at the date the contract was entered into, reasonable wear and tear excepted?

6. What are the rights and remedies of buyers and sellers if, through the fault of neither, the house at 23 Oak Street is destroyed or damaged by fire or other cause before the closing date, September 1, 1983?

a. THE STATUTE OF FRAUDS

BALILES v. CITIES SERVICE CO.
Supreme Court of Tennessee, 1979.
578 S.W.2d 621.

COOPER, Justice.

This is an action for specific performance of a contract for the sale of real property or, in the alternative, for damages for its breach. The chancellor decreed specific performance on completion of a condition precedent. The Court of Appeals reversed the chancellor's decree and dismissed the action.

Certiorari was granted to review the determination by the Court of Appeals that the written memorandum of an agreement to sell real estate was not sufficient to comply with the statute of frauds (T.C.A. § 23–201(4)); and that neither the doctrine of part performance nor estoppel was effective to take the transaction out of the statute of frauds.

In July 1974, the respondent Cities Service Company orally agreed to sell one of its employees, Dewey M. Newman, Jr., lots 99 and 100 in the Cherokee Hills Subdivision. It became necessary for Mr. Newman to borrow money from the local bank to cover costs of the construction planned for lots 99 and 100. An official of the bank requested a letter from respondents setting forth its commitment to sell lots 99 and 100 to Mr. Newman. On July 23, 1974, respondent sent the following letter to the bank, addressed to Mr. Newman:

> Cities Service Company has agreed to sell to you lots 99 and 100 in Cherokee Hills for residential purposes.
>
> As soon as residences are well under construction deeds to these lots will be delivered to you.

. letter

On receipt of the letter, the bank loaned Mr. Newman $5,000.00. Mr. Newman then began construction of a residence on lot 100. He completed the foundation and the outer walls of the ground-level basement before encountering financial difficulties.

In the summer of 1975, being in financial difficulty and realizing that he had no chance to build a second house, Mr. Newman went to respondent's offices and released lot 99 to respondent. It also appears that he requested a deed to lot 100, but was refused "until the house was in the dry."

On August 25, 1975, Mr. Newman assigned his interest in lots 99 and 100 to petitioner, Billy D. Baliles, for $6,500.00, the approximate value of the labor and materials expended in improving lot 100.

Petitioner wrote respondent on December 14, 1975, informing it that he had acquired Mr. Newman's interest in lot 100. By letter, dated December 16, 1975, respondent took the position that the agreement between it and Mr. Newman was not assignable.

Thereafter petitioner filed a complaint in the Chancery Court of Polk County, Tennessee, seeking specific performance of the agreement between respondent and Mr. Newman or, in the alternative, damages for its breach.

Cities Service Company defended the action on the grounds (1) the written memorandum signed by respondent was not sufficient to comply with the statute of frauds; (2) the agreement was not assignable by Mr. Newman to a non-employee; and (3) that petitioner was not entitled to a deed to lot 100 since the condition precedent of having the residence "well under construction" had not been met.

The chancellor found the memorandum of the agreement for the sale of lots 99 and 100 met the requirements of the statute of frauds. He further found that the assignment by Mr. Newman of his rights in lot 100 under the contract to petitioner was valid and would be enforceable when the residence on lot 100 was "well under construction"—which the chancellor concluded to be when the residence was "under roof." The chancellor then ordered respondent to execute a deed to petitioner for lot 100 when the residence was put "under roof."

The chancellor also found that the assignment by Mr. Newman to petitioner of his rights to lot 99 was ineffectual, as Mr. Newman had returned that lot to defendant before the assignment was executed.

Respondent appealed from that part of the chancellor's decree that affected lot 100. The Court of Appeals reversed the chancellor, holding that the memorandum of the agreement between respondent and Mr. Newman does not comply with the requirements of the statute of frauds. The Court of Appeals further held that part performance would not take the contract in question out of the operation of the statute of frauds, and that plaintiff could not rely upon the doctrine of equitable estoppel under the circumstances of this case. The Court of Appeals also noted that even if the agreement to sell lot 100 was not within the statute of frauds the petitioner was not entitled to a deed to the property because a condition precedent to receiving a deed—that is, to have the residence under roof—had not been met.

The applicable section of the statute of frauds, T.C.A. § 23-201, provides that:

> No action shall be brought: . . . (4) upon a contract for the sale of lands . . . [u]nless the promise or agreement upon which such action shall be brought or some memorandum or note thereof, shall be in writing, and signed by the party to be charged therewith, or some other person by him thereunto lawfully authorized.

The purpose of the statute of frauds "is to reduce contracts to a certainty, in order to avoid perjury on the one hand and fraud on the other." Price v. Tennessee Products & Chemical Corporation, 53 Tenn.App. 624, 385 S.W.2d 301 (1964). Consequently, to comply with the statute of frauds, a memorandum of an agreement to sell must show, with reasonable certainty, the estate intended to be sold.

> Where the instrument is so drawn that upon its face it refers necessarily to some existing tract of land, and its terms can be applied to that one tract only, parol evidence may be employed to show where the tract so mentioned is located. But, where the description employed is one that must necessarily apply with equal exactness to any one of an indefinite number of tracts, parol evidence is not admissible to show that the parties intended to designate a particular tract by the description." Dobson v. Litton, 45 Tenn. 616. See also Dry Goods Co. v. Hill, 135 Tenn. 60, 185 S.W. 723 (1916).

The memorandum relied on by petitioner as written evidence of the agreement to sell, and which is set out above, does not locate the Cherokee Hills Subdivision by county or state. Neither does it contain any information which would tend to locate the subdivision. Further, the description of the specific property that is the subject of the oral agreement is by lot numbers only. There is no recorded plat to show the location of lot 100 within the subdivision, nor its dimensions or calls.

In Kirshner v. Feigenbaum, 180 Tenn. 476, 176 S.W.2d 806 (1944), it is pointed out that a memorandum of an agreement for the transfer of an interest in real property which fails to designate the county and state where the land is located is insufficient under the statute of frauds, unless the description of the property as set out in the memorandum is otherwise so definite and exclusive that "it does not reasonably appear that the description given would fit equally any other tract, then parol proof is admissible to locate and designate the tract intended."

We think it evident, and we agree with the Court of Appeals, that the description in the memorandum does not describe the tract of land with reasonable certainty, that the description is of no material aid in locating the property that is the subject of the agreement to sell, and consequently does not satisfy the requirements of the statute of frauds.

Petitioner insists that even though the memorandum of the agreement to sell is insufficient to meet the requirements of the statute of frauds, the agreement should be enforced on the basis of part performance, or by the application of the doctrine of estoppel.

The appellate courts of this state consistently have refused to enforce an oral contract for the sale of land on the basis of part performance alone. And, it is now a rule of property in this state that part performance of a parol contract for the sale of land will not take the agreement out of the statute of frauds. The harshness of this rule has been mitigated by the application of the doctrine of equitable estoppel in exceptional cases where to enforce the statute of frauds would make it an instrument of hardship and oppression, verging on actual fraud.

> "Equitable estoppel, in the modern sense, arises from the 'conduct' of the party, using that word in its broadest meaning, as including his spoken or written words, his positive acts, and his silence or negative omission to do any thing. Its foundation is justice and good conscience. Its object is to prevent the unconscientious and inequitable assertion or enforcement of claims or rights which might have existed, or been enforceable by other rules of law, unless prevented by an estoppel; and its practical effect is, from motives of equity and fair dealing, to create and vest opposing rights in the party who obtains the benefit of the estoppel." Evans v. Belmont Land Co., 92 Tenn. 348, 365, 21 S.W. 670, 673–674 (1893).

We think this is such a case. In dealing with Mr. Newman, respondent not only placed him in possession and permitted him to construct improvements on lot 100, but took affirmative action thereafter to aid Mr. Newman to secure a $5,000.00 loan—this latter action being taken with the knowledge that the proceeds of the loan were to be used in the construction of a dwelling on lot 100. In the face of this affirmative action by respondent, to allow it to set up the statute of frauds as bar to enforcement of the agreement to sell lot 100 to Mr. Newman, and thus secure to itself the improvements on lot 100 would be a gross injustice and moral fraud on Mr. Newman.

Petitioner had no direct dealings with respondent relative to lot 100, except to give notice of the assignment executed by Mr. Newman. However, by virtue of the assignment, petitioner acquired all the rights and remedies possessed by Mr. Newman under the agreement to sell, and took the contract subject to the same restrictions, limitations, and defenses as it had in the hands of Mr. Newman. It follows that since it is unconscionable to allow respondent to set up the statute of frauds as a bar to enforcement of the agreement to sell lot 100 to Mr. Newman, it would be unconscionable to permit the defense to be interposed in this action brought by Mr. Newman.

Respondent argues that the agreement to sell lot 100 was not assignable—that it was a special kind of contract entered into only with respondent's employees. We find nothing in the record to indicate that the agreement was not assignable. To the contrary, the representative of respondent who made the agreement testified that there was nothing to prevent an employee from taking a lot, putting up a house, and then selling it to someone who was not an employee.

The Court of Appeals pointed out in its opinion that even if the agreement to sell lot 100 is enforceable, respondent [sic] is not now entitled to a deed to the property because a condition precedent to receiving a deed—that is, to have the residence under roof—has not been met. The chancellor also recognized that the condition precedent had not been met by petitioner at the time of trial of the cause. He also noted the practical difficulty, or dilemma, faced by petitioner in expending additional monies on the residence to place it under roof in the face of the insistence of respondent that Mr. Newman's rights in lot 100 were not assignable, and absent a judicial declaration of the efficacy of the agreement between Mr. Newman and respondent. In resolving this dilemma, the chancellor pointed out that the action brought by petitioner "conforms to a certain extent to a declaratory judgment." The chancellor then undertook to declare the rights of the parties in the agreement. He held the agreement to sell was enforceable, the assignment was valid, and that petitioner would be entitled to a deed to lot 100 when he had the residence under roof. We think the chancellor's findings were correct and that his declaration of petitioner's right to a deed to lot 100, when the condition precedent is met, was timely and proper.

The judgment of the Court of Appeals is reversed. The judgment of the chancellor is affirmed. Costs of the cause are adjudged against respondent.

FONES, BROCK, and HARBISON, JJ., and ALLISON B. HUMPHREYS, Special Judge, concur.

QUESTIONS

1. Most American statutes of frauds are closely patterned after the original English Statute of Frauds, 29 Car. II c. 3 (1677), and require not only that deeds conveying an interest in land be in writing and signed by the grantor, but also that land sale contracts be in writing and signed by the parties. Should the writing requirement for contracts be applied less stringently than the writing requirement for deeds? Note that deeds form links in a parcel's chain of title that must be relied upon to identify the parcel and its owner decades, and even centuries, later, when all witnesses to the transaction have disappeared and a prospective buyer is seeking to determine whether his seller has good title. Sales contracts, by contrast, have short lives—typically 45 or 60 days at most—and are rarely recorded; once the executory period expires, they are not relied on by anyone for any purpose.

2. *Baliles* lies somewhere between the two polar American views on the adequacy of descriptions in land sale contracts. At one pole, some courts treat contract descriptions far more liberally than deed descriptions. See for example, Stachnik v. Winkel, 50 Mich.App. 316, 213 N.W.2d 434 (1973), *reversed on other grounds* 394 Mich. 375, 230 N.W.2d 529 (1975) (contract for "your [seller's] property located in Glen Arbor Twp. Lee Lanau Co. situated on Wheeler Rd.," sufficiently definite; external evidence showed that this was the only property that the sellers owned in Lee Lanau County). At the other extreme, a few courts insist that the contract description contain all of the detail required for deeds. See, for example, Martin v. Seigel, 35 Wn.2d 223, 212 P.2d 107 (1949) (specific performance refused even though contract identified parcel by street address, city, county and state, and even though parol evidence further provided the parcel's lot and block numbers).

3. Was *Baliles* overly rigorous in holding that part performance alone will not take an oral contract out of the statute of frauds? Many courts are less exacting. Some hold that the buyer's entry onto the parcel under an oral contract will suffice. Others require possession accompanied by some payment to the seller. Others require possession and the construction of valuable improvements. And still others require possession and proof that removal will cause irreparable injury. See 3 American Law of Property § 11.7 (A.J. Casner ed. 1952).

4. Are there better devices than the present statutes of frauds "to avoid perjury on the one hand and fraud on the other"? The Uniform Land Transactions Act, approved in 1975 by the National Conference of Commissioners on Uniform State Laws, represents a comprehensive effort to harmonize, simplify and modernize state law governing land transactions. Its provisions paralleling the statutes of frauds appear in § 2–201:

> (a) Notwithstanding agreement to the contrary and except as provided in subsection (b), a contract to convey real estate is not enforceable by judicial proceeding unless there is a writing signed by the party against whom enforcement is sought or by the party's representative which:
>
> (1) contains a description of the real estate that is sufficiently definite to make possible an identification of the real estate with reasonable certainty;
>
> (2) except as to an option to renew a lease, states the price or a method of fixing the price; c and

c. What *was* the agreed-on price in *Baliles?* Ed.

(3) is sufficiently definite to indicate with reasonable certainty that a contract to convey has been made by the parties.

(b) A contract not evidenced by a writing satisfying the requirements of subsection (a), but which is valid in other respects, is enforceable if:

(1) it is for the conveyance of real estate for one year or less;

(2) the buyer has taken possession of the real estate, and has paid all or part of the contract price;

(3) the buyer has accepted a deed from the seller;

(4) the party seeking to enforce a contract, in reasonable reliance upon the contract and upon the continuing assent of the party against whom enforcement is sought has changed his position to his detriment to the extent that an unjust result can be avoided only by enforcing the contract; or

(5) the party against whom enforcement is sought admits in his pleading, testimony, or otherwise in court that the contract for conveyance was made.

Commissioners' Comment 4 adds that "Failure to satisfy the requirements of this section does not render the contract void for all purposes, but merely prevents it from being judicially enforced in favor of a party to the contract. For example, a buyer who takes possession of real estate as provided in an oral contract which the seller has not meanwhile repudiated, is not a trespasser. Nor would the statute of frauds provisions of this section be a defense to a third person who wrongfully induces a party to refuse to perform an oral contract, even though the injured party cannot maintain an action for damages against the party so refusing to perform."

Although the U.L.T.A. is frankly modeled on the Uniform Commercial Code, it is unlikely to win the same widespread adoption that the U.C.C. has enjoyed. For some reasons why, see Bruce, Mortgage Law Reform Under the Uniform Land Transactions Act, 64 Geo.L.J. 1245 (1976). On the U.L.T.A., generally, see Maggs, Remedies for Breach of Contract Under Article Two of the Uniform Land Transactions Act, 11 Ga.L.Rev. 275 (1977); Kratovil, Uniform Land Transactions Act: A First Look, 49 St. Johns L.Rev. 460 (1975); Kuklin & Balbach, Uniform Land Transactions Act, 11 Real Prop., Prob. & Tr. J. 1 (1976).

b. CONDITIONS

i. Marketable Title

CONKLIN v. DAVI

Supreme Court of New Jersey, 1978.
76 N.J. 468, 388 A.2d 598.

MOUNTAIN, J.

Plaintiffs contracted to sell and convey to defendants a residential property in Ridgewood. The purchasers refused to consummate the sale, alleging defects in title and misrepresentations on the part of the sellers. Plaintiffs instituted an action for specific performance; defendants counter-claimed for rescission. Before the trial commenced, plaintiffs abandoned their claim for specific performance, and the case proceeded solely as an action on the counterclaim of the defendants-purchasers, seeking rescission, in effect to secure the return of the down payment. . . .

It would appear that the validity of the title to a portion of the premises in question is sought to be sustained by the sellers upon a claim of adverse possession. The purchasers take the position that this being so, they were justified in repudiating the agreement; that the sellers could not force such a title upon them, but should have perfected the record title prior to the date of closing. This, they add, should have been done either by securing a deed from the present record title holder, or by means of an action to quiet title. While we readily concede that the sellers would have been well advised to have followed such a course, we do not agree that their failure to do so imperiled their position to the extent urged by the purchasers.

When a prospective seller's title is grounded upon adverse possession, or contains some apparent flaw of record, he has a choice of options. He may at once take whatever steps are necessary to perfect the record title, including resort to an action to quiet title, an action to cancel an outstanding encumbrance, or whatever other appropriate step may be necessary to accomplish the purpose. In the alternative he may, believing his title to be marketable despite the fact that it rests on adverse possession or is otherwise imperfect of record, choose to enter into a contract of sale, hoping to convince the purchaser or, if necessary, a court, that his estimate of the marketability of his title is justified. That is the course the sellers seem to have followed here. It must be borne in mind that this latter course is available only where the contract of sale does not require the vendor to give a title valid of record, but provides for a less stringent requirement, such as marketability or insurability. Such is the case here. Of course "[a] buyer is entitled to the kind of title stipulated for in the contract of sale." *Friedman, Contracts and Conveyances of Real Property* (3rd ed. 1975) § 4.2, p. 259; Lounsbery v. Locander, 25 N.J.Eq. 554 (E. & A.1874). Here the contract contained the following provision:

> Title to be conveyed shall be marketable and insurable at regular rates, by any reputable title insurance company licensed to do business in the State of New Jersey, subject only to the encumbrances hereinabove set forth.

It will be seen at once that while the title for which the purchasers have contracted must be marketable and insurable, there is no requirement that it be a perfect title of record. Many titles, imperfect of record, are nonetheless marketable. Justice Cardozo, then Chief Judge of the New York Court of Appeals, observed:

> The law assures to a buyer a title free from reasonable doubt, but not from every doubt. . . . If "the only defect in the title" is "a very remote and improbable contingency," a "slender possibility only," a conveyance will be decreed. . . . [Norwegian Evangelical Free Church v. Milhauser, 252 N.Y. 186, 169 N.E. 134, 135 (1929)]

Incidentally, the law will imply that title must be marketable, even where the contract is silent upon the point. The purchasers are accordingly in error in insisting that nothing less than a good record title will suffice. A title that is marketable and insurable, though imperfect of record, will meet the terms of the contract.

Having thus chosen to rely upon marketability of the title to so much of their land as they claim by adverse possession, and upon it clearly appearing that the purchasers would not, under such conditions, perform the contract, sellers instituted an action for specific performance. As we have seen, purchasers answered and filed a counterclaim for relief by way of rescission, seeking the return of their down payment as well as damages and attorneys' fees. Thereafter, as we have also noted, the sellers abandoned their suit for specific performance, leaving for trial only the issue raised by the purchasers' counterclaim for rescission. Purchasers assert that they have been in some way improperly prejudiced by the sellers having abandoned their suit for specific performance. We fail to see how this can be. The criterion, in a case such as this, is the same whether the seller seeks specific performance or the purchaser sues for the return of his deposit. The determinative issue in each case is whether or not the seller had marketable title.

> The criterion of a marketable title does not vary with the form of action in which it is an issue. In a situation wherein title is sufficiently doubtful to impel a court of equity to deny specific performance to the seller, the buyer may recover his downpayment in an action at law. [*Friedman, supra,* § 4.1, p. 258]

The purchasers also advance the contention that the validity of the title must be assessed as of the specified closing date, and not at some later time. But established doctrine refutes this contention. Where, because of an alleged title defect, vendor and vendee litigate the issue, it will be the title as it exists at the time of final decree or judgment that will control, not the title the vendor may have had when the suit was commenced.

> In all cases where the vendor seeks to force a title upon the vendee, it is the latter's position, not at the commencement of the suit, but at its termination, which is to be regarded. The question is, not what kind of a title the vendor has, but what kind of a title the vendee will get if the court of chancery or the court of errors and appeals, after reviewing the decree of the court of chancery, forces the offered title upon him. [Barger v. Gery, 64 N.J.Eq. 263, 268, 53 A. 483, 485. (Ch. 1902)]

In the last-cited case Vice Chancellor Stevenson went on to say,

> Where the alleged doubt in regard to the offered title relates to a matter of law, a decision of the court in the suit for specific performance undertaking to establish what the law is must, of necessity, have some effect either to strengthen or dispel the doubt. [*Id.*]

There the court granted specific performance, but noting that most of the evidence in support of complainant's otherwise defective title had been first brought forward during the trial, it denied complainant his costs.

> In this case the evidence to support the offered title was not presented by the vendor to the vendee; a very important part of it was obtained by the vendor after this suit was commenced. [*Id.* at 277, 53 A. at 488.]

RULE

To recapitulate, in an action for specific performance by a vendor or for rescission by a vendee, where the issue is marketability of title, the vendor is entitled to a judgment if, at the conclusion of the suit, the court holds title to be marketable, even though the decision in favor of marketability rests upon facts adduced for the first time at trial or upon legal rulings made during the course of the proceedings.

The purchasers have also advanced the contention that they were entitled to rescind the contract because, contrary to the contractual proviso, title was not insurable by a reputable title insurance company. Generally, provisions requiring title insurance as a condition precedent to acceptance of title are enforceable. This condition may already have been satisfied, for a Vice-President of New Jersey Realty Title Insurance Company testified to a willingness to insure the purchasers' possession against claims of third persons. Under these circumstances it would appear that the contractual condition had probably been met, but the point can be fully explored at the retrial.

As we have said, we agree with the Appellate Division that the trial court erred in granting the sellers' motion at the conclusion of the purchasers' case. The purchasers had shown that the sellers did not have record title to one tract of the entire parcel. The contract of sale provided that title must be marketable and insurable. It did not provide, however, as many such agreements do, that the sellers would be required to produce a clear title of record, without reliance upon adverse possession. It is well settled in New Jersey that title resting in adverse possession, if clearly established, will be held marketable. This rule represents the great weight of authority. Accordingly, if the sellers could prove that they did in fact hold title to the tract in question by virtue of adverse possession, they would have met their contractual obligation, at least insofar as marketability is concerned. Although the trial judge indicated that he believed the sellers could readily establish title by adverse possession, they had not yet done so. Therefore their motion should have been denied and they should have been directed to go forward with their proofs.

We note that it is not necessary for the sellers to join as parties all possible claimants with outstanding interests, as would be the case in an action to quiet title. In many, if not most, cases of this sort the claimants who may hold adverse interests are not joined; very often they are not known. It follows, as the purchasers here correctly point out, that a judgment in the action will not be *res judicata* as to such claimants. And yet virtually all courts agree that in such a suit there may be, and often is, a judgment of marketability leading to affirmative relief by way of specific performance or to a denial of a vendee's claim to rescind. This result has been reached in a number of reported cases in this state. In order to reach this result the court must conclude (1) that the outstanding claimants could not succeed were they in fact to assert a claim, and (2) that there is no real likelihood that any claim will ever be asserted. Such a conclusion leads to a determination of marketability.

Although there are statements in some of the cases to the contrary, we think that in a suit such as this, where the purchaser seeking rescission has shown that record title is outstanding in some person other than the seller, the burden should then shift to the seller to establish his title by adverse possession.

The judgment of the Appellate Division entering judgment in favor of the purchasers is reversed and the cause is remanded to the Superior Court, Chancery Division for a new trial in accordance with what has been said above.

For reversal and remandment: Chief Justice HUGHES and Justices MOUNTAIN, PASHMAN, CLIFFORD, SCHREIBER and HANDLER–6.

For affirmance: None.

ii. Financing

BUSHMILLER v. SCHILLER

Court of Appeals of Maryland, 1977.
35 Md.App. 1, 368 A.2d 1044.

MELVIN, Judge.

The dispute in this case is over which of the parties to a real estate contract is entitled to a $13,000 deposit initially received by the seller (appellant) from the buyer (appellee) as part payment of the $130,000 purchase price for a residential property located in Baltimore County. By suit and counter-suit, each party sought judgment against the other for the amount of the deposit. After a bench trial in the Circuit Court for Baltimore County (Proctor, J.), the buyer and original plaintiff, Mrs. Eunice Myrta Schiller, emerged victorious with a judgment for $13,000 against the seller and original defendant, Mr. Joseph Bushmiller. Judgment was also entered against Mr. Bushmiller in his counter-suit. Aggrieved by the results, Mr. Bushmiller has appealed to us to set aright what he perceives as a wrong decision by the trial court.

The dispute over the deposit had its genesis when Mrs. Schiller won "a million dollar lottery" in the Maryland State Lottery, entitling her to receive $50,000 a year for 20 years. Not long after this fortuitous happening, she entered into a written contract with Mr. Bushmiller, dated 25 July 1975, to purchase his house for $130,000. The contract provided for the payment of a deposit of $13,000 to be applied as part payment of the purchase price. Settlement was to be within 45 days and "[i]f the Purchaser . . . fail[ed] to make full settlement", the deposit was to be "forfeited at the option of the Seller, in which event the Purchaser shall be relieved from further liability . . . ."

The contract further provided that,

"This contract is subject to the ability of the Purchaser to secure [within 10 days], a written commitment for . . . [a] first mortgage secured on said premises in the amount of $100,000, for a term of Twenty (20) years, and bearing interest at the rate of prevailing per annum [sic].

"Purchaser utilizing a loan agrees to make application immediately and file all necessary papers that are required to complete processing, including resubmission and appeal where necessary, and agrees that failure so to do shall give the Seller the right to declare the deposit forfeited . . . ."

In her suit to recover the deposit Mrs. Schiller alleged that she "was unable to obtain the necessary financing and advised the Defendants and each of them and demanded the refund of the deposit monies and . . . . Defendants have failed and refused to return said monies". The gravamen of Mr. Bushmiller's counter-suit was that Mrs. Schiller "was obligated under the terms of the aforesaid Contract to act in good faith in securing a written commitment for a first mortgage within ten (10) days from the date of the Contract, and said Counter-Defendant wholly failed and refused to act in good faith to secure the said mortgage commitment, notwithstanding that mortgage monies on the terms required under the contract were readily available to the Counter-Defendant". By a "Stipulation of Counsel" filed prior to trial, Mr. Bushmiller's damages against Mrs. Schiller were "limited to the sum of Thirteen Thousand Dollars ($13,000.00)", the amount of the deposit that had been paid into court by Bushmiller's agent who had originally received it from Mrs. Schiller.

The Evidence

The pertinent facts as found by the trial judge can be summarized as follows:

Mrs. Schiller became interested in buying Mr. Bushmiller's property. Before submitting an offer she telephoned the Equitable Trust Bank on Wednesday 23 July 1975 to inquire about the possibility of a mortgage loan. She talked to a Mrs. Davis who was a mortgage loan officer for Equitable. Mrs. Davis advised her that a mortgage loan would in all probability be favorably considered on the basis of a 20-year mortgage with "ballooning" at the end of five years. Mrs. Schiller did not understand what the term "ballooning" meant and at that time made no effort to find out. The next day, 24 July, Mrs. Schiller filled out a formal application for a mortgage loan of $97,500.00, to be repaid in "300 months" (25 years). On the same day, Mrs. Schiller signed an undated contract of sale prepared by her agent, a Mr. Collins of Century 21, a real estate brokerage firm. Mrs. Schiller then left the Baltimore area to visit her sister in Connecticut.

On Friday, 25 July 1975, Mr. Collins submitted the contract offer to Mr. Bushmiller. As prepared by Mr. Collins, the contract provided that the time within which the purchaser was to secure a written commitment for the mortgage loan was 30 days. Mr. Bushmiller wanted that time period reduced to 10 days. Mr. Collins telephoned Mrs. Schiller in Connecticut and Mrs. Schiller agreed to the change by a telegram dated 25 July 1975. The change was made in the contract itself and initialed by Mr. Collins as agent for Mrs. Schiller. As thus amended, the contract was dated and executed by Mr. Bushmiller on 25 July 1975.

On Sunday 27 July, Mrs. Schiller left Connecticut and went to New Hampshire to visit her son. As found by the trial judge, "when she gets to her son's her eyes are opened, first, as to what balloon mortgage financing means, and secondly, as to the problems involved in a large expensive house. She immediately calls off the Equitable Trust Company loan, and then does nothing more." The record shows that Mrs. Schiller telephoned Equitable from New Hampshire on either 28 July, 29 July, or 30 July (probably 29 July) and cancelled her loan application. There is no indication in the record that she notified Mr. Bushmiller of the cancellation.

Mrs. Schiller returned to Baltimore in the late evening of 5 August, eleven days after the date the contract was executed. On 6 August, Mr. Bushmiller's agent contacted Mrs. Schiller. The agent's testimony (which the trial court found to be uncontradicted) concerning her conversation with Mrs. Schiller was as follows:

> "Then Mrs. Schiller told me that when she was in New Hampshire and talked to her son, he told her that it was unwise for her to buy this house. She said, ['] I cannot afford it; this is ridiculous. He's shown me that I will have to pay capital gains on my house,['] which was not true because she was reinvesting the money; and I tried to explain this to her. She said, ['] [W]ell, it doesn't—I just can't afford the house;['] and she said ['] [I]t doesn't matter.[']. And when we mentioned the means of financing that we had available and the fact that it was savings and loans money available at the terms that she wanted, she said ['] [T]hat doesn't matter, I'm not interested in buying the house; I can't afford it; my son has advised me against it.[']"

It appears that on 6 August, the day after her return to Baltimore, Mrs. Schiller also contacted Mrs. Davis of Equitable and told her she did not want a "balloon" mortgage. On 7 August Mrs. Davis wrote to Mrs. Schiller as follows:

"Dear Mrs. Schiller:

Pursuant to our telephone conversation of August 6, 1975, I must issue a letter of decline in answer to your mortgage request.

When I was first approached by Mrs. Spilman of Piper & Co. concerning financing for you, I told her that it would appear Equitable Trust would help you based on a $100,000.00 loan written for 5 years based on a 20 year payout. The interest rate would be determined when the loan was presented for approval. Since, on your application, you have specifically requested a straight 25 year mortgage loan and are not willing to consider a five year loan with a balloon payment, I must decline your loan request.

Thank you for the opportunity to be of service to you.

Very truly yours,

/s/Verna Q. Davis

Mortgage Officer"

Also on 7 August, Mrs. Schiller's attorney wrote to Mr. Bushmiller's agent and to Mr. Collins as follows:

"Dear Sir & Madam:

Our office represents E. Myrta Schiller and have had referred to it, for attention, the contract for the captioned property dated July 25, 1975.

As both of you know, Mrs. Schiller promptly made application for a mortgage loan with The Equitable Trust Company in the amount of $100,000.00 for a term of twenty years, repayable in monthly installments of principal and interest only.

We regret to advise that The Equitable Trust Company has turned down the application and was only willing to grant a 20 year amortization plan with a 5 year balloon.

As the balloon provision is unacceptable, I must advise that the purchaser was unable to secure a written commitment for the first mortgage described in the contract within ten days from the date of the contract.

Please, therefore, promptly return the $13,000.00 being held by you to the writer.

If there are any further negotiations to be conducted under a new contract between the seller and my client, I would appreciate your clearing the same through this office. I am enclosing herewith, for your records, a copy of the letter received from The Equitable Trust Company indicating that they would only write the mortgage loan under a balloon clause.

Very truly yours,

THEODORE C. DENICK"

The record reveals no further contact between the parties until 13 October 1975. On that date Mr. Bushmiller's attorney wrote to Mrs. Schiller's attorney as follows:

"Dear Mr. Denick:

As you know, this office represents Joseph Bushmiller, the owner and seller of the property known as 401 Falls Road. The seller's position remains unchanged, in that he is still ready, willing and able to convey the property to Mrs. Schiller under the contract of sale dated July 25, 1975.

It is our belief that Mrs. Schiller's failure to consummate this contract constitutes a breach of the contract; and we intend to hold Mrs. Schiller's deposit of $13,000.00, and we further intend to hold her liable for any damages which we sustain on resale of the property. We presently have two buyers who have offered $100,000.00 for the purchase of the property. Although we feel the property is worth more than $100,000.00, neither of the prospective buyers will offer more. Accordingly, we may be constrained to accept a $100,000.00 offer and look to Mrs. Schiller for the balance. The market conditions continue to deteriorate because of tight money and the approaching winter months. The seller has a second mortgage which falls due in early November and we have been advised that foreclosure proceedings will be instituted immediately if the entire mortgage balance is not paid when due.

If Mrs. Schiller is willing to proceed under her contract, I am confident that we can obtain financing for her at the prevailing interest rates. Please let me hear from you if Mrs. Schiller is willing to proceed with the contract; however, I shall notify you in any event of the execution of a new contract by the seller.

Very truly yours,

J. Earle Plumhoff"

Mrs. Schiller's response to this letter was her suit, filed 24 October 1975, to recover the $13,000 deposit.

Decision

It is clear that the requirement of obtaining mortgage financing as a condition in a contract for the sale of realty must be given effect unless the condition has been altered by the parties or waived by the one for whose benefit the condition was made. In this case, the obligations of Mrs. Schiller to buy and Mr. Bushmiller to sell were each conditioned upon Mrs. Schiller's ability to secure within ten (10) days of the contract date (July 25, 1975) a written commitment for a mortgage loan in the amount of $100,000, for a term of twenty (20) years at the "prevailing" interest rate. The burden of satisfying this condition was placed squarely upon Mrs. Schiller. By the terms of the contract she was obligated "to make application immediately and file all necessary papers that are required to complete processing, including resubmission and appeal where necessary." To these express requirements are added the further implied requirement that she take "bona fide, reasonable and prompt action to obtain the financing specified." Traylor v. Grafton, *supra*, 273 Md. at 689, 332 A.2d at 675.

The trial judge found that Mrs. Schiller did not know what "balloon" financing meant when she discussed the subject of a mortgage with Mrs. Davis of Equitable on 24 July and that it was not until Sunday 27 July when she visited her son in New Hampshire that she learned the meaning of the term. We cannot say that these factual findings were clearly erroneous. Nor do we find erroneous the judge's finding that upon learning the meaning of a "balloon" mortgage and upon being persuaded by her son "as to the problems involved in a large expensive house, [s]he immediately calle[d] off the Equitable Trust Company loan, and then does nothing more". We do not agree, however, that the inaction on her part satisfied the requirement of good faith efforts to obtain the financing specified by the contract. The judge felt that her inaction was justified and comported with good faith because ". . . even if she had probably made up her mind that she still wanted the house, it would almost certainly have been impossible for her in that very brief period of time to arrange for a written commitment for a loan in the amount of $100,000."

While it is undoubtedly true that it may have been difficult to obtain a loan commitment within the ten-day limitation, patently it would not have been "impossible". In any event, we cannot equate "no" efforts with "reasonable" efforts to obtain the specified financing. Moreover, there is no indication in the record that Mrs. Schiller's failure to proceed with further efforts to obtain financing within the allotted time was due in the slightest degree to any thought or knowledge on her part that it could not be obtained within the ten-day period. The conclusion is inescapable that after talking with her son on 27 July she decided she no longer wanted Mr. Bushmiller's "large expensive house", that she could not afford it, and that she wanted "out" of her contractual obligations, and that it was for these reasons alone that she ceased any further efforts to obtain the necessary financing. This conclusion is fortified by her refusal to even consider the offer of Mr. Bushmiller's agent to obtain financing for her that was "available at the terms that she wanted". It is true that this offer was made after the ten-day period, and had Mrs. Schiller made good faith efforts within the 10-day period to obtain financing and been unsuccessful, she would have been justified in not accepting the offer. Under the circumstances here, however, we think the refusal of the offer has significance as bearing on the question of Mrs. Schiller's good faith efforts to satisfy the condition precedent in the contract.

In the circumstances we hold that the trial judge was clearly erroneous in his finding that Mrs. Schiller's efforts to obtain financing were made in good faith. It follows that the judgments below must be reversed and the case remanded for entry of judgment for costs in favor of Mr. Bushmiller in the original suit filed by Mrs. Schiller, and for entry of a judgment for $13,000, plus costs and interest from date of entry in his counter-suit against Mrs. Schiller.

Judgments reversed. Case remanded for entry of judgments as directed by this opinion. Costs to be paid by appellee.

NOTES

1. The typical land sale contract contains several conditions that must be met or waived for the sale to close. Conditions are essentially substitutes for information—information about the seller's title, the premises, local land use regulations and the home finance market. Conditions effectively postpone contract performance to a point at

which this information can be obtained—through a title report, housing inspection, land use regulation review and institutional lenders' response to the buyer's loan application. Some conditions, such as marketable title, will be implied; others, such as the availability of financing, must be expressed.

Bushmiller v. Schiller graphically illustrates the pitfalls that surround real estate contract conditions. However carefully they are drafted, and however explicitly the parties' duties respecting their fulfillment are prescribed, contract conditions can still be used as an escape hatch, enabling buyer or seller to renege for reasons totally unrelated to the condition—at least if he or she is more circumspect than Mrs. Schiller about revealing the true motives for backing out of the contract. (Representing Mrs. Schiller, and with the benefit of hindsight, could you have improved on Mr. Denick's effort, in his August 7 letter, to state Mrs. Schiller's position in a noncompromising manner?)

One problem in drafting contract conditions is that the more precisely they are worded, the more likely it is they will not be met. For example, a financing condition that prescribes a twenty year, level payment mortgage at an interest rate of 11.75%, with no points and no prepayment penalties after five years, can easily be employed to excuse performance if interest rates move up a fraction or if market conditions operate to vary some other term. Yet, if the parties seek to close this loophole by phrasing the financing condition more generally—for example, "buyer must be able to obtain financing at prevailing market terms"—they run the risk that the contract will be held too indefinite to be enforced. And if fulfilling the condition is left to the exclusive control of one of the parties there is the added problem of illusoriness or lack of mutuality of obligation.

2. *"Reasonableness" and "Good Faith."* To what extent can concepts of reasonableness and good faith be used to patch over the dilemmas that inhere in drafting real estate contract conditions? Courts today will sometimes fill in incomplete financing clauses by looking to the circumstances surrounding the contract, including the prevailing money market conditions, that presumably reflect the parties' original expectations. See Lien v. Pitts, 46 Wis.2d 35, 174 N.W.2d 462 (1970). See also Uniform Land Transactions Act § 1–301 ("Every contract or duty governed by this Act imposes an obligation of good faith in its performance or enforcement.")

Did Mrs. Schiller act in bad faith by applying for a 25-year mortgage for $97,500 when the contract specified a 20-year mortgage for $100,000? Did the contract condition contemplate a fully amortized mortgage and, if so, would the proffered "balloon" feature have been sufficient to excuse her performance? Under a fully amortized mortgage, the borrower completely repays the principal—here, $100,000—over the mortgage term—here, 20 years. Under a balloon mortgage, no principal payments are made until the end of the term, when the entire principal—the "balloon"—becomes payable. The instrument offered by Equitable Trust to Mrs. Schiller was a hybrid: for the first five years, the mortgage would be amortized on the basis of a 20-year term; but, at the end of five years, the entire remaining principal would be fully payable.

3. *Title*. Is *Conklin* a good decision? One effect of the decision is to require buyers who have not contracted for record title to keep the funds for their share of the purchase price liquid, and to keep their institutional lender's commitment to finance the remainder of the purchase price alive, throughout the months and possibly years that it will take for litigation to resolve the status of seller's title. As a practical matter it will be virtually impossible for a residential buyer to persuade an institutional lender to extend its financing commitment indefinitely. Commercial buyers may have greater success in obtaining extensions, but at considerable expense.

Obviously, the buyer can protect himself against these consequences if he is aware of the *Conklin* rule *and* if in the negotiations leading up to the contract of sale he can get the seller to agree to convey valid title of record on the date of closing. Is it fair or efficient to place this negotiating burden on the buyer? As between seller and buyer who is better placed to acquire information respecting title expeditiously?

Absent an implied condition of good record title, and absent a willingness on the part of sellers to promise good record title expressly, the parties may compromise by agreeing on insurable title. Will a buyer always be better off with insurable title than with marketable title? Say that, although some defect makes title unmarketable, a title company is willing to insure against the defect because the company determines that it is unlikely that a claim based on the defect will ever be made. By accepting title insurance instead of marketable title, the buyer is effectively accepting a promise of cash payment from the title company as a substitute for the land itself in the event the claim is ever made.

4. *What is Marketable Title?* Courts in all states will imply a covenant or condition of marketable title into contracts for the sale of land. The definitions they give for marketable title are almost invariably circular and thus of little help in predicting results: "A marketable title has been defined as one that may be freely made the subject of resale. It is one which can be readily sold or mortgaged to a person of reasonable prudence, the test of the marketability of a title being whether there is an objection thereto such as would interfere with a sale or with the market value of the property," Regan v. Lanze, 40 N.Y.2d 475, 481–482, 387 N.Y.S.2d 79, 83, 354 N.E.2d 818, 822 (1976). Or, a marketable title is one "which at all times, and under all circumstances, may be forced upon an unwilling purchaser," Pyrke v. Waddington, 10 Hare 1, 68 Eng.Rep. 813 (Chancery 1852). The main reason the formula is so loose is that courts have stretched

it to encompass two essentially different problems affecting marketability—chain of title defects and encumbrances.

Chain of title defects affect ownership. For example, seller or one of seller's predecessors in title may have obtained title through a fraudulent transfer. There may have been an irregularity in the conduct of a mortgage foreclosure, tax sale or probate proceeding, or a technical error or omission in a prior conveyance, such as a misspelling in the name of a party, a misdescription of the parcel or the absence of a proper acknowledgement.

Every state has remedial statutes aimed at curing chain of title defects—curative acts, statutes of limitations and marketable title acts. These remedial statutes can be consulted to distinguish with some confidence between those title defects that have been cured with the passage of time and those that continue to impair title. While these statutes are not directly concerned with resolving contract disputes over marketable title, they do provide an independent and objective basis for determining the sort of title that seller A may be allowed to force upon buyer B and, by implication, the sort of title that buyer B will in the future be allowed to force upon his buyer C. A title with a defect that has been cured by passage of the statutory period, or by the occurrence of the statutorily-prescribed events, is not only good in some abstract sense; it is also marketable in the sense that, as a matter of public policy, the legislature has determined that in acquiring this title a buyer should feel confident that he can later sell it without fear that it will then be held unmarketable.

Encumbrances reduce the value of land in ways that fall short of breaks in the chain of title. Mainly they take the form of security interests, possessory interests and nonpossessory interests. Mechanics liens, mortgage liens and judgment liens are typical security interests. Leases typify possessory encumbrances. And right of way or utility easements and restrictive covenants prohibiting specified land uses are typical nonpossessory encumbrances.

Unlike chain of title defects, for which remedial statutes provide an objective benchmark of marketability, encumbrances must be measured on an entirely subjective, case-by-case basis. Whether and to what extent a right of way impairs a parcel's value will vary from time to time, from parcel to parcel, and from owner to owner. A restrictive covenant prohibiting the parcel's use for commercial purposes will be of no great concern to A who plans to put the parcel to residential use, but it will be of great concern to B who wants to operate a gas station on the parcel. As a result, the correct resolution between one buyer and seller may not be the correct resolution between another buyer and seller or, more important, between the present buyer and some future buyer from him.

See generally, M. Friedman, Contracts and Conveyances of Real Property 325–356 (3rd ed. 1975).

5. *Zoning and Other Land Use Controls.* Say that B contracts to buy an undeveloped parcel, Blackacre, from A, intending to build and operate a gas station on the parcel; after executing the contract, but before the closing, B discovers that a local zoning ordinance bars commercial uses such as gas stations in the neighborhood. Absent a specific provision in the contract governing the point, can B rescind the contract and recover his deposit? Is it relevant that if it were not a zoning ordinance, but rather a restrictive covenant, that barred B's commercial use, B might be able to rescind on the ground that title was unmarketable?

In deciding whether to excuse contract performance on the ground that a preexisting public land use regulation, such as a zoning ordinance, will interfere with buyer's plans, courts almost universally reject the analogy to private land use controls such as easements and covenants. As a general rule, "building and zoning laws in existence at the time a land contract is signed are not treated as encumbrances, and the purchaser has no recourse against the vendor by virtue of restrictions imposed by such laws on the use of the property purchased." Dover Pool & Racquet Club, Inc. v. Brooking, 366 Mass. 629, 631, 322 N.E.2d 168, 169 (1975). The position apparently rests on the rule that contracts are subject to all laws in force at the time they are made. See Josefowicz v. Porter, 32 N.J.Super. 585, 108 A.2d 865 (1954).

Courts divide on whether land use ordinances enacted *during* the executory period should be treated similarly. *Dover Pool* excused buyer performance in this situation. Other courts take the view that buyers should bear the risk of changes in the law. See, for example, DiDonato v. Reliance Standard Life Insurance Co., 433 Pa. 221, 225, 249 A.2d 327, 330 (1969).

Courts also split on whether the buyer should be excused when the land use being made at the time the contract of sale is signed violates an applicable regulation. One line of authority treats these violations like encumbrances and places their burden on seller. For example, in Lohmeyer v. Bower, 170 Kan. 442, 227 P.2d 102 (1951), buyers were granted rescission when, after signing the contract, they discovered that the house violated not only deed restrictions but also a local zoning ordinance. For the opposing view, that existing violations do not excuse buyer performance, see Gnash v. Saari, 44 Wn.2d 312, 267 P.2d 674 (1954).

6. *Financing.* If the financing condition in a land sale contract specifies not only the terms of an acceptable mortgage loan but also the particular institution that is to make the loan, will the buyer be excused if that institution rejects the loan application, but some other institutional lender agrees to make the loan on the terms specified? What if no institutional lender will make the loan, but the seller agrees to finance the transaction herself?

In Kovarik v. Vesely, 3 Wis.2d 573, 89 N.W.2d 279 (1958), buyers' performance was conditioned on financing through a "$7,000 purchase money mortgage from the Fort Atkinson Savings and Loan Ass'n." One week after unsuccessfully applying to Fort Atkinson Savings & Loan, the buyers were told that the sellers would be willing to take back a purchase money mortgage on the terms and conditions specified in the buyers' application to Fort Atkinson. The buyers declined and brought suit to recover their down payment. Holding for the sellers, the court agreed with the trial court's finding that the "buyers were interested in financing a Seven Thousand Dollar mortgage and not in any particular loaning agency." It rejected buyers' argument that, because their contract specified Fort Atkinson Savings & Loan, good faith did not require them to accept financing from the sellers. 3 Wis.2d at 581, 583, 89 N.W.2d at 284, 285.

Was *Kovarik* correctly decided? Why should a buyer care about the source of his funds? Justice Fairchild, dissenting, offered two possible reasons: "the buyer will feel more confident of his own judgment of the price he is to pay if a lending institution is willing to make a loan" and "the buyer would rather have the matter, in the event of default, in the hands of an established lending institution than in the hands of an individual who might be less able, if not less willing, to adjust matters reasonably." 3 Wis.2d at 583, 89 N.W.2d at 286.

7. *Is Time of the Essence?* If on the date set for closing seller fails to tender a deed, or buyer fails to tender the purchase price, is the other party discharged from the obligation to perform? The answer will turn on whether the action is in law or in equity. When a legal remedy is sought, performance on the closing date will be considered essential unless the contract discloses a contrary intent. In actions for an equitable remedy, time is not of the essence unless the contract or surrounding circumstances indicate that it should be. These rules apply not only to closing dates, but also to other deadlines specified in the contract such as the deadline for obtaining a financing commitment. See Kakalik v. Bernardo, 184 Conn. 386, 439 A.2d 1016 (1981).

In Limpus v. Armstrong, 3 Mass.App.Ct. 19, 322 N.E.2d 187 (1975), the contract of sale, dated September 16, called for a closing on or before November 25. After a series of missed telephone calls between buyer and seller, and buyer's failure to perform by November 25, seller on November 29 wrote buyer that the contract was no longer in force and that his $100 deposit was forfeited. Reversing a decision for seller, the court ruled that plaintiff buyer was entitled to specific performance. "The mere fact that the agreement specified a date for closing did not make time of the essence." Further, the court noted, both parties had it within their power to make time of the essence even after they entered into the contract of sale. "Since both the plaintiff and the defendants had failed to perform within the time specified for conveyance, either, by notice to the other upon unreasonable or unnecessary delay by the latter, might have been assigned a reasonable time for the completion of the transaction, thereby making performance within that time of the essence of the contract." 3 Mass.App.Ct. at 24, 322 N.E.2d at 190.

The Uniform Land Transactions Act goes beyond present law by rejecting the rule that time is of the essence in actions at law, and substituting for it a rule under which one party's delay in performance past a specified date discharges the other only if the delay amounts to a "material breach." ULTA § 2-302(b)(1). The provision is, however, hedged by limitations. For example, under section 2-302(d) one party can, by giving notice to the other before the date set for closing, "specify effectively that failure to perform on the specified date will discharge him from his own duties under the contract." Under ULTA § 2-302(a), if the contract does not specify a closing date, the time for performance is "a reasonable time after the making of the contract." Further, "either party may fix a time for performance if the time is not unreasonable and is fixed in good faith."

8. *Whose Condition Is It?* It is sometimes unclear whether the parties intended a particular condition to benefit buyer, seller, or both. For example, a financing condition requiring that the mortgage loan be obtained from a specified institutional lender is commonly intended to benefit the buyer, who may be relying on that lender's expertise. In fact, however, the condition may have been included for the benefit of the seller. If the specified institutional lender holds the existing mortgage on the property, the buyer's agreement to assume the obligations of this mortgage may be the only way the seller can avoid the heavy prepayment penalties often charged in the early years of a loan.

The question of who was intended to benefit from a particular condition is obviously important, for only the intended beneficiary can waive the condition. Nonetheless, even well-counselled buyers and sellers often fail to indicate which of them was intended to benefit from the specified conditions.

In Bushmiller v. Schiller, which party—buyer or seller—was the intended beneficiary of the financing condition? Of the ten-day time limit on performance of the condition? In a similar case, Loda v. H.K. Sargeant & Associates, Inc., 188 Conn. 69, 448 A.2d 812 (1982), the Connecticut Supreme Court upheld a lower court finding that the financing condition was intended to benefit the buyer while the time limit on performance was intended to benefit the seller who did not wish to keep his property tied up by a buyer who had no prospects of obtaining the needed financing. Note, though, that in discussing the offer by seller Bushmiller to obtain financing for buyer Schiller after the ten-day performance period had expired, the court observed that "had Mrs. Schiller made good faith efforts within the 10-day period to obtain financing and been unsuccessful, she would have been justified in not accepting the offer." 35 Md.App. at 6, 368 A.2d at 1049.

c. REMEDIES

A buyer whose seller has breached their contract for the sale of land has four possible remedies. The buyer can obtain a decree of specific performance, ordering seller to convey title to him in return for payment of the purchase price. He can obtain damages measured by the difference between the parcel's market value at the date of breach and the contract price, together with any incidental expenses and losses incurred. He can obtain rescission and recover any deposits made. Finally—although this remedy is not much used—the buyer has a lien (called a "vendee's lien") on seller's legal title, securing the seller's obligation to refund the buyer's deposit in the event the seller breaches; the lien can be foreclosed and the land sold to satisfy this obligation if the seller fails to refund the deposit.

A seller whose buyer has breached their contract for the sale of land also has four remedies, each closely paralleling the remedies available to buyer. The seller can obtain a decree of specific performance requiring buyer to pay the purchase price in return for the seller's conveyance of title. The seller can obtain damages measured by the difference between the contract price and the parcel's market value at the date of breach, together with incidental expenses and losses. She can obtain rescission, entitling her to retain any deposits made by the buyer on account. Finally, seller has a lien (called a "vendor's lien") on buyer's equitable title, securing the buyer's obligation to pay the purchase price; if buyer fails to perform, the lien can be foreclosed and the land sold to satisfy the buyer's obligation.

These remedial alternatives are limited only by the requirement that buyer and seller elect between those remedies that affirm the contract and those that disaffirm it. The affirming remedies of specific performance and damages may not be sought together with rescission, which disaffirms. Some aspects of these remedies are considered in the two cases below. The notes that follow explore each of the principal remedies more closely.

SMITH v. WARR

Supreme Court of Utah, 1977.
564 P.2d 771.

WILKINS, Justice:

This appeal involves a breach of contract for the sale of real estate.

On August 20, 1973, buyer (appellant) contracted with sellers (respondents) to purchase the property in question. The Uniform Real Estate Contracts they executed provided that title was to be passed by special warranty deed upon full payment. Within four months of the signing, an action in adverse possession was initiated by plaintiffs below (not parties to the present appeal) to quiet title against sellers. On June 16, 1975, plaintiffs joined buyer as a party defendant in said action. In his answer, buyer filed a cross complaint against sellers for breach of contract. Buyer, however, continued to make payments on the contract, throughout the adverse possession proceeding.

The District Court of Salt Lake County entered judgment in favor of the plaintiffs, the adverse possessors. Subsequently, on January 16, 1976, the Court ruled in favor of buyer on his cross complaint against sellers. Damages were awarded, however, only in the amount of buyer's out-of-pocket loss, and both attorney's fees and costs were denied. Buyer is appealing from the judgment in his favor below claiming that the court erred in awarding him only his out-of-pocket loss, rather than the larger amount of the benefit-of-the-bargain damages, i.e., the market value of the property at the time of the breach less the amount of the unpaid purchase money (as part of the contract price had been paid).

The issue on appeal, therefore, is whether the correct measure of damages for a breach of contract for the sale of real property in the State of Utah is out-of-pocket loss or benefit-of-the-bargain damages.

There is a split of authority among the states as to which measure of damages is appropriate for a breach of contract for the sale of land. Some states award benefit-of-the-bargain damages only if the breach was committed in bad faith. Others consistently award benefit-of-the-bargain damages, whether or not the breaching party had good faith cause for failing to convey.

Sellers argue that, although Utah has never expressly articulated which of these two positions it adheres to, case law in this state indicates that the good faith-bad faith distinction is required, and that only out-of-pocket loss is to be awarded in the case of good faith breach. Since the District Court made a finding of good faith on sellers' part, sellers contend it would then follow that out-of-pocket loss would be the correct measure of damages.

Sellers' contention that benefit-of-the-bargain damages have only been awarded in this state when the breach was in bad faith, however, is not well-founded. Sellers rely, for example, on Bunnell v. Bills, 13 Utah 2d 83, 368 P.2d 597 (1962). In that case the seller had contracted to sell to the buyer property that he did not yet own, but which he had contracted to buy. The seller was financially unable to proceed with the purchase of the property, and his contract with the owner was consequently rescinded, whereupon the buyer sued for breach of contract. There is no mention of bad faith in this Court's decision in *Bunnell*, nor is bad faith apparent from the facts of the case, yet this Court stated there:

> The measure of damages where the vendor has breached a land sale contract is the market value of the property at the time

of the breach less the contract price to the vendee. *Id.* 368 P.2d at 601.

Other cases cited by sellers in support of their position that Utah has implicitly followed the rule that awards benefit-of-the-bargain damages only in case of a bad faith breach are similarly unconvincing. In Dunshee v. Geoghegan, 7 Utah 113, 25 P. 731 (1891), for example, where bad faith was apparent, the court awarded benefit-of-the-bargain damages and then stated by way of dictum: "and it does not excuse the vendor that he may have acted in good faith . . .." *Id.* 25 P. at 732. Sellers also cited good faith cases, in which only out-of-pocket loss was awarded the buyer. In these cases, however, the buyers had only sought out-of-pocket losses, and the court expressly recognized that damages on the contract would also have been an available remedy.

The rule followed by Utah is that benefit-of-the-bargain damages are to be awarded for breach of contract for the sale of real estate, regardless of the good faith of the party in breach. We therefore reverse, and remand to the District Court for a determination of damages consistent with this opinion, for an award of reasonable attorney's fees as required by the contract, and for costs below in the discretion of the Court. Costs on appeal to Buyer-Appellant Warr.

ELLETT, C.J., and CROCKETT and MAUGHAN, JJ., concur.

FRANK v. JANSEN

Supreme Court of Minnesota, 1975.
303 Minn. 86, 226 N.W.2d 739.

KNUTSON, Justice.

This is an appeal from a judgment entered in favor of plaintiffs for $232.27 and from an order denying their motion for amended findings of fact and conclusions of law. Plaintiffs base their right to recover upon a breach of contract for the sale of real estate.

On July 20, 1970, plaintiffs, Daniel R. and Ethel D. Frank, entered into an agreement to sell their residence at 575 Mt. Curve Boulevard, St. Paul, to defendants, Paul W. and Betty L. Jansen, for the sum of $48,500. A neighbor of the Franks prepared the purchase agreement, using a Miller-Davis printed form. The purchase agreement, which is the vital evidence in this case, is reproduced below.

Pt. 1 — LAND TRANSFER AND FINANCE — 215

Plt. Exhibit B

Form 1762   Miller-Davis Co., Minneapolis

$2,000.00

July 20, 1970

Received of PAUL W. JANSEN and BETTY LOU JANSEN

Two Thousand and no/100 Dollars as a guarantee of good faith accompanying offer of $48,500.00 on terms as follows: $11,500 on or before Nov 1, 1970, and the balance of $35,000 to be paid in 180 equal monthly installments together with interest at 8% per annum commencing Dec 1, 1970 _____ for the purchase of 575 MT. CURVE BLVD.

Buyer shall have prepayment privilege.

This offer is subject to owner's approval; if accepted, the above amount will apply as a part of purchase price and if refused the above amount will be refunded _____ will be forfeited to _____

If offer is accepted and purchaser refuses to fulfill the above stated conditions the $ _____

I HEREBY MAKE THIS OFFER

Paul W. Jansen PURCHASER
Betty Lou Jansen

I HEREBY ACCEPT THIS OFFER

_____ SELLER

BY _____ AGENTS

The reverse side of the purchase agreement provided:
Items to be included without additional charge:
WASHER & DRYER
FREEZER
WINDOW AIR CONDITIONER
PING PONG TABLE
ALL DRAPES & CURTAINS
STOVE & REFRIG.
CALCINATOR
FIREPLACE FIXTURES
GARAGE OPERATORS
BED SPREADS
NOT INCLUDED:
TO BE REMOVED BY PRESENT OWNER
DINING ROOM AND MASTER BDRM. LIGHT FIXTURE.

Real estate taxes due and payable in 1970 to be paid by seller.
/s/Paul W. Jansen
/s/Ethel D. Frank

It will be noted that the purchase agreement recites that $2,000 has been received from defendants as a "guarantee of good faith." The clause in the printed contract calling for a forfeiture of a sum of money in case the purchaser refuses to fulfill the contract was left blank.

On October 23, 1970, defendants advised plaintiffs that they did not intend to purchase the property. The payment due on November 1, 1970, was not made.

In October 1970, defendants assisted plaintiffs in an unsuccessful attempt to resell the property without the aid of a realtor. The property was listed with Jambor Realty of St. Paul on November 14, 1970, and relisted with Rubin Realty Company of St. Paul on April 20, 1971. During the period from October 24, 1970, to July 23, 1971, extensive efforts were made to resell the property but no offers were received.

On July 24, 1971, James L. Diedrich offered to purchase the property, and on the following day Diedrich and plaintiffs entered into a purchase agreement for the sum of $43,700.

Prior to learning that defendants did not intend to go through with the purchase agreement, plaintiffs leased an apartment to which they moved on November 8, 1970. The Mt. Curve property remained vacant during the attempts to sell it. During the time the premises were vacant, plaintiffs continued to pay the real estate taxes, utilities, snow removal services, and insurance. They also incurred expenses for abstracting fees and newspaper advertisements connected with the attempts to resell the property. They also claim the right to recover legal fees in connection with the transaction with the Jansens.

The trial court held that the downpayment of $2,000 paid by defendants and retained by plaintiffs constituted liquidated damages. It also held that plaintiffs were entitled to recover abstracting fees and sums expended for newspaper advertisements, but allowed no other damages. In addition to finding that the downpayment of $2,000 constituted liquidated damages and that plaintiffs were entitled to recover the abstracting fees and cost of advertising, the court found as a fact that the purchase price of the realty was $48,500 and that the fair market value of the property at the time of the breach by defendants was $43,700.

Plaintiffs' motion for amended findings of fact and conclusions of law, in which they sought to increase the damages, was denied on September 25, 1973, judgment was entered on November 2, 1973, and this appeal followed.

Two issues are presented on this appeal, namely: (1) Does the evidence sustain the court's finding that the $2,000 downpayment made by defendants and retained by plaintiffs constituted liquidated damages? (2) Was the court correct in holding that only the abstracting fees and the cost of newspaper advertisements in an attempt to mitigate damages were recoverable? . . .

In Schutt Realty Co. v. Mullowney, 215 Minn. 340, 346, 10 N.W.2d 273, 276 (1943), we quoted with approval the following from 15 Am. Jur., Damages, § 240, the substance of which is now found in 22 Am. Jur.2d, Damages, § 212:

> "The term 'liquidated damages' signifies the damages the amount of which the parties to a contract stipulate and agree, when the contract is entered into, shall be paid in case of breach. It is well settled that the parties to a contract may stipulate in advance as to the amount to be paid in compensation for loss or injury which may result in the event of a breach of the agreement. A stipulation of this kind is enforceable, at least in those cases where the damages which result from a breach of the contract are not fixed by law or are in their nature uncertain and where the amount stipulated does not manifestly exceed the injury which will be suffered."

In Zirinsky v. Sheehan, 413 F.2d 481, 485 (8 Cir.1969), certiorari denied, 396 U.S. 1059, 90 S.Ct. 754, 24 L.Ed.2d 753 (1970), the Court of Appeals, in discussing Minnesota law, said:

> "In Minnesota, as elsewhere, a provision for liquidated damages is generally held to be a convenient substitute as a reasonable forecast of general damages."

Our attention has been called to Witt v. John Blomquist, Inc., 249 Minn. 32, 34, 81 N.W.2d 265, 267 (1957), where we said:

> "Our conclusion is not in conflict with the rule that, where earnest money has been paid to an agent by a purchaser of real estate pursuant to the terms of a contract which provides that the earnest money shall be forfeited to the vendor in the event the purchaser fails to perform the contract, and where such provision cannot be construed as a penalty, the vendor is entitled to retain such earnest money as liquidated damages if the purchaser does fail to complete the transaction."

It is true that the reference to liquidated damages in the above quotation might indicate that where the seller retains the downpayment of a purchaser it is to be considered as liquidated damages in all cases. However, that construction of the language we used is misleading. The case did not involve the question of liquidated damages as does the case now before us, only the right to retain the downpayment upon a breach of contract.

In the case of Costello v. Johnson, 265 Minn. 204, 121 N.W.2d 70 (1963), the buyers raised a contractual provision calling for forfeiture of earnest money as a defense in a seller's action for actual damages. We followed the language of Higbie v. Farr, [28 Minn. 439 (1881)] looking at the language of the contract, to determine whether the parties had actually intended the retention of earnest money to deprive the seller of all other remedies or whether he had a right to elect remedies. The relevant contractual provision in Costello was as follows:

> "Time is of the essence hereof, and *if such purchaser shall fail to perform this contract within the time herein limited, said seller or his agent shall retain the earnest money hereof as a part of his just compensation for such failure, and may declare this contract terminated and proceed for damages, or specific performance against such purchaser.*" 265 Minn. 206, 121 N.W.2d 73.

We held that this provision did not constitute an agreement for liquidated damages and would not bar the seller's action for actual damages. We said:

> "However, since defendants have not appealed from the damages awarded, which exceeded the earnest money payment, we must assume that the provision for retention of the downpayment upon breach by defendants was not intended by the parties as an anticipatory agreement for liquidated damages. The contract provision permitting plaintiffs to declare the contract terminated upon defendants' default and thereafter to proceed for damages also indicates that the parties did not intend to contract with respect to liquidated damages." 265 Minn. 210, 121 N.W.2d 75.

From these authorities we conclude that a provision in a contract of this kind calling for a forfeiture of the downpayment upon a breach of the contract will not of itself establish the fact that it is to be considered as liquidated damages. Whether the parties have stipulated for liquidated damages must be gleaned from the contract and all of the facts pointing to the intention of the parties. Before there can be a finding of liquidated damages, there must be evidence to support a finding that the parties intended the stipulated amount to be *in lieu of compensatory damages.* There is no such evidence in this case. As a matter of fact, what evidence there is points the other way. The provision in the printed contract which was used, pertaining to a forfeiture upon failure to fulfill the conditions of the contract, was left blank by the parties. Nor did defendants claim at the outset, or in their pleadings, that the downpayment was intended to constitute liquidated damages. In their answer and counterclaim they seek rescission of the contract and a return of the downpayment on the grounds of misrepresentation of the facts by plaintiffs. There is no evidence in the record that would establish the fact that the parties ever intended the downpayment to constitute liquidated damages. Furthermore, the court's holding that the downpayment was intended to be liquidated damages is inconsistent with the court's finding allowing plaintiffs to recover the abstracting fees and advertising expenses as compensatory damages. If the parties intended the downpayment to constitute liquidated damages, payment of that amount, which no one disputes, would end the matter. There cannot be both liquidated damages and compensatory damages.

In 22 Am.Jur.2d, Damages, § 235, we find the following:

"The effect of a clause for stipulated damages in a contract is to substitute the amount agreed upon as liquidated damages for the actual damages resulting from breach of the contract, and thereby prevents a controversy between the parties as to the amount of damages. If a provision is construed to be one for liquidated damages, the sum stipulated forms, in general, the measure of damages in case of a breach, and the recovery must be for that amount. No larger or smaller sum can be awarded even though the actual loss may be greater or less."

We recognize the rule that the findings of the trial court trying a case without a jury should not be disturbed on appeal if there is credible evidence to support them. But this rule is inapplicable where the findings of the court are not compatible with applicable law or where the evidence so clearly fails to sustain the court's findings. We are convinced that the court's finding that the downpayment made on this contract constitutes liquidated damages cannot stand.

2. We go then to the question of whether the court was correct on the issue of recoverable compensatory damages.

The general rule respecting the proper measure of damages in a case of this kind is easily stated, but sometimes not so easily applied.

In the case of Wilson v. Hoy, 120 Minn. 451, 454, 139 N.W. 817, 819 (1913), which involved an action to recover damages for an alleged breach of contract to purchase real estate, we said:

> "The proper measure of damages for a breach by the purchaser of a contract of purchase is the difference between the contract price and the actual or market value of the property at the time of the breach, including any expenses necessarily incurred by the vendor in his effort to carry out the contract."

In the case of Home Counsellors, Inc. v. Folta, 246 Minn. 481, 484, 75 N.W.2d 417, 420 (1956), which also involved a contract for the purchase of real estate, we said:

> ". . . The measure of damages for a breach by the purchaser of a contract of purchase is the difference between the contract price and the actual or market value of the property at the time of the breach, including any expenses necessarily incurred by the vendor in his effort to carry out the contract, minus any sums paid by the purchaser on the contract price."

In Costello v. Johnson, *supra*, we followed the same rule, citing and approving the above two cases.

Defendants' attempt to assist plaintiffs in reselling the property in mitigation of their damages is inconsistent with their present claim that their downpayment constituted liquidated damages. If the parties had intended the downpayment to constitute liquidated damages, defendants would have no interest in assisting plaintiffs in reselling the property. No one disputes the fact that the downpayment was actually made and retained by plaintiffs. That would have ended the matter as far as defendants' liability is concerned. In Paine v. Sherwood, 21 Minn. 225, 232 (1875), we find the following:

> "The rule of common law is that where a party sustains a loss by reason of a breach of contract, he is, so far as money can do it, to be placed in the same situation, with respect to damages, as if the contract had been performed."

We gather from Graves v. Moses, 13 Minn. 307, 335 (1868), that plaintiffs are entitled to recover such damages as are the natural and proximate consequences of the breach. The rule of Paine v. Sherwood, *supra*, is modified by the old rule of Hadley v. Baxendale, 154 Eng.Rep. 145 (Ex.1854), which is still followed in this state holding that damages which one party to a contract ought to receive in respect to a breach of it by the other are such as (1) either arise naturally, that is, in the usual course of things, from the breach itself, or (2) such as may reasonably be supposed to have been contemplated by the parties, when making the contract, as a probable result of breach.

It is the duty of the seller in a contract of this kind, upon a breach by the buyer, to use reasonable diligence to minimize his damages.

Thus, it follows that in this case the measure of damages is the difference between what defendants agreed to pay for the property and the actual market value at the time of defendants' breach plus such expenses as plaintiffs reasonably incurred in attempting to mitigate their damages less the amount they have already received as a downpayment. Applying this rule to the facts in this case, we find that the court was in error in denying at least some of the expenses incurred by plaintiffs. At the time of the breach, in reliance upon the contract, plaintiffs had altered their position by renting and moving into an apartment. The residence they had agreed to sell defendants remained vacant during the time they attempted to resell it. Had they remained in use and possession of the property, there is no doubt that some of these expenses would be offset against the reasonable value of the use, but here these expenses were incurred in an attempt to mitigate the general damages flowing from defendants' breach. Had plaintiffs failed to insure the property and a loss resulted as a result thereof, they could easily have been chargeable with failure to carry such insurance. The same is true with respect to the cost of heating the premises. In this climate it could hardly be expected that plaintiffs would leave the property vacant without heat or light, and the same is true with respect to snow removal. With respect to the payment of the property taxes, had defendants performed according to their agreement, the taxes due in 1971 would have been paid by the purchaser, but as a result of the breach of the contract by defendants plaintiffs were obligated to pay these taxes before they could resell the property to someone else. The right to recover attorneys' fees depends on proof that such fees were incurred in plaintiffs' effort to minimize their damages. If they were simply incurred as part of plaintiffs' original attempt to sell the property, they would not be recoverable. We fail to see any difference between these expenses if incurred in any effort to minimize plaintiffs' damages and the expenses of abstracting and newspaper advertising, which the court did allow.

It is argued by defendants that plaintiffs probably secured a benefit from payment of the taxes on their income tax. This might be true, but it does not justify denial of at least that part of the taxes which were not offset by the benefit plaintiffs received on their income taxes.

In light of the fact that we are convinced the court was in error in holding the downpayment made by defendants constituted liquidated damages, we are of the opinion that the case should be remanded for retrial on the issue of damages so that the court may determine what expenses were actually incurred by plaintiffs in an effort to mitigate their damages. Apparently the court was of the opinion that some of these expenses were included within the amount which it found constituted liquidated damages.

The case is, therefore, remanded to the trial court for a trial and determination on the issue of damages not inconsistent with this opinion.

Reversed and remanded.

NOTES

1. *Specific Performance.* Both buyer and seller are entitled as a matter of course to a decree of specific performance in the event of default by the other. Buyer is entitled to a decree requiring seller to convey title to him in return for payment of the purchase price. Seller is entitled to a decree requiring buyer to pay the purchase price in return for the conveyance of title. The standard rationale for giving buyers specific performance is that land is unique; having bargained for a specific parcel, the buyer is entitled to be made whole through a decree ordering its conveyance to him. The standard rationale for giving sellers specific performance is mutuality of remedy. "Where an equitable remedial right in the vendee is recognized, a corresponding remedial right should be admitted in favor of the vendor." J. Pomeroy, 5 Equity Jurisprudence and Equitable Remedies 4877 (1919).

Courts will often refuse to specifically enforce a contract if it only barely complies with the statute of frauds and is not complete in all material respects. For example, in Phillips v. Johnson, 266 Or. 544, 514 P.2d 1337 (1973), the Oregon Supreme Court upheld the trial court's specific enforcement of an earnest money receipt even though questions existed concerning the accuracy with which the instrument described the parcel to be conveyed and whether the instrument was anything more than an "agreement to agree." The court held, however, that the terms by which seller agreed to finance the purchase were too ambiguous to be specifically enforced. The court further held that since the instrument gave buyer an election to purchase outright for cash, the contract could be enforced on the condition that buyer made this election.

2. *Is Land Unique?* Should courts withhold specific performance when the property in question—a new tract home in a subdivision containing hundreds of identical houses—has few if any unique attributes? In Centex Homes Corp. v. Boag, 128 N.J.Super. 385, 320 A.2d 194 (Ch.Div.1974), the developers of a high rise condominium sought specific performance against defendants who had reneged on their contract to purchase a condominium unit. Noting that "the mutuality of remedy concept has been the prop which has supported equitable jurisdiction to grant specific performance in actions by vendors of real estate," and that "mutuality of remedy is not an appropriate basis for granting or denying specific performance," the court concluded that "the disappearance of the mutuality of remedy doctrine from our law dictates the conclusion that specific performance relief should no longer be automatically available to a vendor of

real estate, but should be confined to those special instances where vendor will otherwise suffer an economic injury for which his damage remedy at law will not be adequate, or where other equitable considerations require that relief be granted." 128 N.J.Super. at 390–393, 320 A.2d at 197–98.

The *Centex* court went on to observe that "the subject matter of the real estate transaction—a condominium apartment unit—has no unique quality but is one of hundreds of virtually identical units being offered by a developer for sale to the public." In view of the court's holding, was this observation gratuitous, or does it imply that in an action by the buyers the court would also have withheld specific performance? See also Suchan v. Rutherford, 90 Idaho 288, 410 P.2d 434 (1966).

Why should land's uniqueness justify the buyer remedy of specific performance? After all, a parcel's unique appeal to a particular buyer can always be reduced to dollars and cents—specifically, the amount the buyer would accept to give up his right to the parcel. The real reason courts order specific performance as a matter of course in land contract cases may well be the concern that juries making damage awards will systematically refuse to compensate buyers for losses based on valuations substantially in excess of "reasonable market value."

3. *Damages.* A land buyer whose seller has breached their contract is entitled to recover the difference between the market value of the property at the time of breach and the agreed-upon purchase price, together with consequential damages, if any, and return of any deposit paid on account. A seller whose buyer has breached is entitled to recover the difference between the contract price and the market value of the property at the time of breach, less any amounts paid by buyer on account, together with consequential damages and incidental expenses, if any, incurred in mitigating damages.

Is it fair to measure seller's damages from the date of breach, rather than from the date the seller resells the property to a second buyer? The rule has been criticized on the ground that because land, unlike fungible goods, is not readily disposable, considerable time may pass between the breach and a good faith sale to a second buyer. In a falling market—and buyers rarely breach in rising markets—the seller will be forced to bear the loss represented by any decline in value between the date of breach and the date of resale. "A more logical approach," it has been argued, "is to measure the vendor's damages by the excess of the contract price over the resale price of the land, if the resale was effected under certain conditions, such as with notice to the defaulting purchaser, in a reasonable manner, and within a reasonable time, together with any incidental damages." Note, Damages: The Illogical Differences in Measuring Breach of Contract Damages When the Contract Involves Land Rather than Goods, 26 Okla.L.Rev. 277, 278 (1973).

Do you agree with this criticism? Is it relevant that land sellers have alternative remedies at their disposal—remedies not generally available to sellers of fungible goods? The land seller who faces a long delay in a declining market before resale can try to make herself whole by obtaining a specific performance decree requiring that buyer pay the full contract price. And, even resale in a declining market will often make the seller whole: the resale price is good, and sometimes *prima facie*, evidence of the land's value at the time of breach, particularly if the sale was made at arm's length and shortly after the breach. See Costello v. Johnson, 265 Minn. 204, 121 N.W.2d 70 (1963). Consequential damages will also help to make the seller whole if she can introduce evidence that the land's value at the time of breach was depressed by the dissemination of information about the broken contract. Finally, in many cases, seller's retention of the buyer's deposit will more than compensate her for her loss.

4. The rule rejected in Smith v. Warr—that a buyer can recover benefit of bargain damages only if the seller's breach is in bad faith—continues to enjoy substantial support in other jurisdictions. The rule, which traces to Flureau v. Thornhill, 96 Eng.Rep. 635 (1776), has by recent count been expressly adopted in at least fifteen states. "Good faith" breaches characteristically arise from title defects. At the time *Flureau* was decided, land records were in such poor condition that it was thought to be unfair to burden a seller with damages unless she in fact knew that her title was defective. Does it make sense to continue following *Flureau* when contemporary American title institutions have dramatically improved the quality of title records and reduced the costs of searching them?

5. *Earnest Money Deposits and Liquidated Damages.* It is customary, on the execution of a land sale contract, for buyer to give seller an earnest money deposit securing his performance. The deposit, which commonly ranges from 1% to 10% of the purchase price, may be held by the seller, the broker or the escrow agent. The question that these deposits most frequently raise is whether the seller may retain the earnest money in the event of the buyer's breach, or must return it in whole or in part. The rule in most states is that the seller may keep a breaching buyer's deposit even though the contract nowhere expressly entitles her to do so and even though the forfeited sum exceeds the seller's provable damages. See generally, M. Friedman, Contracts and Conveyances of Real Property 777–782 (3rd ed. 1975).

A few jurisdictions allow the land seller to keep only as much of the deposit as is necessary to cover her damages, and require her to return the surplus to the buyer. Because, however, the buyer has the heavy burden of proving that the deposit exceeds seller's damages, sellers will, even in these states, probably be able to retain the entire deposit. For an example of the difficulties buyers encounter in discharging this burden of proof, see Zirinsky v. Sheehan, 413 F.2d

481 (8th Cir.1969), cert. denied 396 U.S. 1059, 90 S.Ct. 754, 24 L.Ed.2d 753.

Sellers can also try to forestall claims that they will be unjustly enriched if allowed to retain buyer's deposit by characterizing the deposit as liquidated damages. But liquidated damages clauses have their own requirements. To be upheld, the liquidated sum must be reasonably proportioned to the contract price and must represent a reasonable forecast of compensation for the harm caused by the breach. Further, the harm caused by the breach must be of the sort that is difficult to estimate accurately. See, for example, Johnson v. Carman, 572 P.2d 371 (Utah 1977) (to allow the seller to retain $34,596.10 paid by buyer when seller's actual damages were only $25,650.00 would be "grossly excessive and disproportionate to any possible loss"; court upholds order requiring seller to return the approximate difference, $8,845.00, to buyer).

As indicated in Frank v. Jansen, the principal strategic difference between treating a deposit as earnest money and treating it as liquidated damages is that earnest money leaves the seller free to pursue the full range of remedies, while liquidated damages bar the compensatory damages route. Say that Frank and Jansen had expressly agreed that the $2,000 "guarantee of good faith" should be treated as liquidated damages. Would it have been appropriate for the court to void the clause on the ground that it would grossly undercompensate the seller?

6. *Rescission.* Mutual rescission doubtless represents the most common resolution of land sale contract breaches, at least in the residential setting. By agreeing on rescission, buyer and seller can avoid the expense, delay and uncertainty of litigation and can, through the seller's return of part or all of the buyer's down payment, reach some rough justice between themselves. Mutual rescission creates problems only in retrospect, when one side tries to avoid the asserted rescission, and a court must determine whether rescission has in fact occurred. (*B* writes to *S*, "this whole deal is really a bad idea"; *S* responds, "I guess you could say so".) And even if a court can piece together an intent to rescind from ambiguous words and conduct, the question remains how the *status quo ante* is to be restored.

Unilateral rescission, in which buyer or seller declares that the other's conduct constitutes grounds for terminating the contract, contains more than the usual hazards of self-help. Pitfalls surround the requirements that the rescission be effected by notice and that the notice be timely. (What constitutes effective notice? At what point does notice become untimely?) There is also the risk that the asserted misconduct does not in fact constitute ground for termination. A seller wishing to rescind when her buyer fails to perform on the closing date must consider the possibility that time will be held not of the essence. A buyer who wishes to rescind when his seller contracts to sell the land to someone else must consider the possibility that the subsequent buyer will be held not to qualify as a bona fide purchaser who can defeat the original buyer's claims. An added cost of guessing wrong about the effect of the other side's conduct may be a finding that the rescinding party anticipatorily repudiated the contract.

7. *ULTA.* The Uniform Land Transactions Act's major remedial innovations are in seller's remedies. Section 2–504 aims to correct the perceived unfairness of measuring seller damages from the time of breach rather than resale by providing that if the seller resells the land reasonably and in good faith, she may recover the difference between the contract price and the resale price and any incidental and consequential damages, less expenses avoided because of the buyer's breach. At the same time, the Act curtails the general availability of specific performance. Section 2–506(b) would give seller specific performance only if she "is unable after reasonable effort to resell . . . at a reasonable price or the circumstances reasonably indicate the effort will be unavailing." Taken together, will sections 2–504 and 2–506 produce results any different from those produced by specific performance and damages under existing law?

The ULTA is less adventurous in its treatment of buyer remedies. Specific performance is still generally allowed. Loss of bargain damages are provided ("difference between the fair market value at the time for conveyance and the contract price") together with any incidental and consequential damages, reduced by "expenses avoided by the seller's breach." The rule of Flureau v. Thornhill is embodied in the provision that if seller is unable to convey because of a title defect unknown to her, "the buyer is entitled only to restitution of any amounts paid on the price and incidental damages." ULTA §§ 2–509–2–515.

d. RISK OF LOSS

SKELLY OIL CO. v. ASHMORE

Supreme Court of Missouri, 1963.
365 S.W.2d 582.

HYDE, Judge.

This suit for specific performance was transferred by Division Two to the Court en Banc because of the dissent of one of the Judges. We adopt the statement of facts, the statement of the contentions of the parties and the ruling on the validity of the contract involved from the Divisional opinion as hereinafter set out without quotation marks.

This is a suit by the purchaser, Skelly Oil Company, a corporation, against the vendors, Tom A. Ashmore and Madelyn Ashmore, husband and wife, in two counts. Count One is for the specific performance of a contract to sell the north half of a certain described southwest corner lot (fronting 97½ feet on Main and 195 feet on 42nd Streets) in that part of Joplin lying in Newton County. Count Two seeks an abatement in the purchase price of $10,000, being the proceeds received by the vendors under an insurance policy on a building on the property, which building was destroyed by fire in the interim between the execution of the contract of sale and the time for closing of said sale by the exchange of the $20,000 consideration for the deed to the property. The case was tried in Jasper County upon a change of venue granted from Newton County. The trial court found the issues in favor of the purchaser, decreed specific performance, and applied the $10,000 insurance proceeds on the $20,000 purchase price. The vendors have appealed.

The vendors acquired this property about 1953, and operated a grocery store in the concrete block building, with fixtures and furniture, and a one story frame "smoke house" thereon. Deeds of trust on the property, securing notes of the vendors to the Bank of Neosho were of record. At all times here material and up to September 30, 1961, the property was leased to Don Jones at a rental of $150 a month. The vendors had a fire insurance policy, with a standard mortgage clause in favor of the Bank of Neosho attached, on the buildings and fixtures, issued February 8, 1958, for a term of one year.

Joe Busby, of the Kansas City office of the Skelly Oil Company real estate department, and Mr. Ashmore conducted the negotiations resulting in the contract of sale. The Ashmores lived in Lawton, Oklahoma. Mr. Ashmore had engaged in the real estate business since 1951. Busby secured the execution of a Skelly printed form of option by the vendors, dated July 31, 1957, for Skelly "to purchase" for the sum of $20,000, "payable in cash upon delivery of deed" said property, "together with the buildings, driveways, and all construction and equipment thereon, at any time before" August 31, 1957. The words "and equipment" were "x-ed" out on said option. The option provided in typewriting (referring to the Jones lease): "Purchaser agrees to honor present lease on above property until expiration." The option originally lapsed August 31, 1957. Busby had an agreement for the mutual cancellation of the lease prepared by Skelly's legal department for execution by the Ashmores and Jones, and on August 20 took up securing a cancellation of the lease and possession with Ashmore and his lawyer, Mr. Foulke. Mr. Foulke did not know how long this would take and the option was extended to January 1, 1958. Busby knew Ashmore filed an ejectment suit against Jones, was "patiently waiting" to hear from Mr. Foulke, and on trips to Joplin would inquire if any headway was being made on securing possession. On December 30, the option was extended to March 1, 1958. Skelly's legal department concluded this lease entitled Jones to possession until September 30, 1961. Skelly acquired the property immediately south of the Ashmore property, continued the operation of a service station thereon, and decided to go ahead and exercise the Ashmore option with Jones in possession under his lease and later combine the two properties and erect a service station that required more area than the Ashmore property.

Busby and Ashmore met in Joplin on February 25. Busby informed Ashmore Skelly had decided to purchase under its option with Jones in possession under his lease. The parties orally agreed to certain details, some being mentioned hereinafter in connection with the contract of sale. Busby also informed Ashmore Skelly could not complete the transaction by March 1, and the Ashmores extended the option from March 1 to March 10, 1958. No consideration passed for any extension of the option.

The Bank of Neosho forwarded the abstract of title to Skelly.

The option provided it could be accepted "by giving written notice" to the vendors. By letter to the Ashmores under date of March 4, 1958, Skelly explicitly stated: "This letter is to inform you that Skelly Oil Company does hereby exercise its option to purchase the above described property for the sum of $20,000.00, subject to all the terms and conditions of the above referred to option, and with" further understandings, among others, to the effect: The fixtures and equipment in the store building were to remain the property of the Ashmores; the Ashmores were to assign the Jones lease to Skelly and Skelly was to remit to the Ashmores $5.00 a month for Jones' use of said fixtures and equipment; the Ashmores were to remove said fixtures and equipment within sixty days after the termination of said lease by lapse of time or otherwise, Skelly assuming no responsibility for the repair or physical condition of said fixtures and equipment. The letter also stated that upon approval of the title and the obtaining of necessary permits "we will get in touch with you further toward closing." Immediately following the signature of the purchaser on said letter appears: "ACKNOWLEDGED and AGREED TO This 7th day of March, 1958, Tom A. Ashmore Madelyn Ashmore." The vendors mailed the original thereof to the purchaser.

The latter part of March Busby telephoned to Ashmore in Lawton and they agreed to meet in Joplin on April 16, 1958, to close the transaction.

The concrete block building, furniture and fixtures were destroyed by fire on April 7, 1958, without fault of either party.

Skelly's Kansas City headquarters advised Busby, who was in St. Joseph, on April 7 of the fire. The next day Busby telephoned Ashmore from Kansas City. In this conversation Ashmore said he had insurance on the building and fixtures, naming the company in Kansas City carrying it. Asked on cross-examination whether he told Ashmore the fire would have no effect on the deal, Busby answered: "I told him absolutely not, we would go through with our deal. Q. Just like it was? A. Sure, just like this contract, sir, we're obligated, we can't get out of it." Busby called the insurance company and was informed there was $10,000 insurance on the building and $4,000 on the fixtures. He reported this to the purchaser's legal department. Then, after research, the legal department concluded that Skelly was entitled to have the insurance on the building applied on the purchase price. The closing papers were prepared accordingly.

The closing of the transaction was considered by the parties on April 15, 16 and 17. Busby and Ashmore met on the evening of the 15th. Mr. Winbigler of Skelly's legal department arrived on the 16th. They informed Ashmore they were there to close the purchase of the property; that Skelly thought it was entitled to the insurance proceeds on the building and would like an assignment of the insurance proceeds. When Ashmore disagreed, they informed him Skelly would close the deal and pay him the contract price but would not waive its rights to the insurance proceeds in so doing. Ashmore would not agree to this. They then went to Mr. Foulke's office and informed him of the situation. Mr. Foulke told them he needed time to check into the matter before he could advise his client. Busby and Winbigler returned to Kansas City.

By letter dated April 26, 1958, the Ashmores notified Skelly that the "option agreement" was rescinded "because it was given without consideration and is therefore not binding on us and for the further reason that you have refused to complete the purchase unless we reduce the agreed price, which constitutes a breach of the terms of the agreement."

A month or so later the Phoenix Insurance Company, under the standard mortgage clause, paid the Bank of Neosho the balance due on the vendors' notes, $7,242.46, and $2,757.54, the balance of the $10,000 insurance on the building, to the vendors, and also paid the vendors the $4,000 insurance carried on the furniture and fixtures.

This purchaser's claims are founded on the contract of sale in its letter of March 4, 1958, and the option therein referred to, which letter was "acknowledged and agreed to" by the vendors. Said claims are not based on a mere option to purchase where the improvements on the property were damaged prior to the purchaser's exercise of the option.

The vendors say that the letter and option were prepared by the purchaser and ambiguities and doubts therein are to be resolved in favor of the vendors; that the purchaser paid no consideration for the option or the three extensions; that specific performance will result in inequity, hardship or loss to vendors and that the trial court's decree of specific performance constitutes an abuse of discretion. It is stated that, since there was no binding contract between the parties prior to the letter of March 4, this letter was only an offer to purchase under the terms and conditions in the original option and said letter, which vendors could accept or reject; that the vendors retained possession and the option contained four or more conditions and the letter added others, and because of these "suspensive conditions" the plain intention of the parties was that the purchaser was not to be bound until all these contingencies were met and no specifically enforceable contract existed on April 7, the date of the fire.

We are not impressed with the vendors' broad position that no valid enforceable contract ever existed. The principal suspensive conditions under the option authorized the purchaser to withdraw its acceptance of the option "before the consummation of purchase by payment of the full purchase price" if, sufficiently stated, the purchaser be unable to secure the proper licenses, consents or permits for the erection, maintenance and operation of a service station of a type and according to a ground plan of its choice on the premises, or if any such licenses, consents or permits be revoked, or if the purchaser be enjoined from erecting and operating a service station on said premises. The option called for an abstract showing a merchantable title in the vendors, and the letter of March 4 stated: "Upon approval of title by our Legal Department and our obtaining all necessary permits, we will get in touch with you further toward closing." There was no objection to this condition in the letter and the parties made it definite by orally agreeing the last part of March upon April 16 for the closing date. Under the mentioned suspensive conditions, as well as others of less importance, when the vendors "acknowledged and agreed to" the contract of sale, the purchaser could not act arbitrarily, capriciously or in bad faith in invoking said provisions of the contract; and in consideration of the mutual promises a mutually enforceable contract of sale arose. None of the suspensive conditions entered into the vendors' failure to close the sale on April 16 or their rescission of the contract on April 26. The vendors' only objection to completing the transaction was, as stated in their letter of rescission, "that you have refused to complete the purchase unless we reduce the agreed price," which, of course, refers to the purchaser's claim to the $10,000 insurance proceeds. Mr. Ashmore testified that the only thing that held up the closing of the transaction was Skelly Oil Company's claim to the insurance proceeds. . . .

The contract of sale here involved contained no provision as to who assumed the risk of loss occasioned by a destruction of the building, or for protecting the building by insurance or for allocating any insurance proceeds received therefor. When the parties met to close the sale on April 16, the purchaser's counsel informed vendors and their attorney he was relying on Standard Oil Co. v. Dye, 223 Mo. App. 926, 20 S.W.2d 946, for purchaser's claim to the $10,000 insurance proceeds on the building. Purchaser made no claim to the $4,000 paid vendors for the loss of the furniture and fixtures. It is stated in 3 American Law of Property, § 11.30, p. 90, that in the circumstances here presented at least five different views have been advanced for allocating the burden of fortuitous loss between vendor and purchaser of real estate. We summarize those mentioned: (1) The view first enunciated in Paine v. Meller (Ch. 1801, 6 Ves.Jr. 349,

31 Eng. Reprint 1088, 1089) is said to be the most widely accepted; holding that from the time of the contract of sale of real estate the burden of fortuitous loss was on the purchaser even though the vendor retained possession. (2) The loss is on the vendor until legal title is conveyed, although the purchaser is in possession, stated to be a strong minority. (3) The burden of loss should be on the vendor until the time agreed upon for conveying the legal title, and thereafter on the purchaser unless the vendor be in such default as to preclude specific performance, not recognized in the decisions. (4) The burden of the loss should be on the party in possession, whether vendor or purchaser, so considered by some courts. (5) The burden of loss should be on the vendor unless there is something in the contract or in the relation of the parties from which the court can infer a different intention, stating "this rather vague test" has not received any avowed judicial acceptance, although it is not inconsistent with jurisdictions holding the loss is on the vendor until conveyance or jurisdictions adopting the possession test. As to the weight of the authority, see also 27 A.L.R.2d 448; Tiffany, Real Property, 3rd ed., § 309.

We do not agree that we should adopt the arbitrary rule of Paine v. Meller, supra, and Standard Oil Co. v. Dye, supra, that there is equitable conversion from the time of making a contract for sale and purchase of land and that the risk of loss from destruction of buildings or other substantial part of the property is from that moment on the purchaser. Criticisms of this rule by eminent authorities have been set out in the dissenting opinion of STORCKMAN, J., herein and will not be repeated here.

We take the view stated in an article on Equitable Conversion by Contract, 13 Columbia Law Review 369, 386, Dean Harlan F. Stone, later Chief Justice Stone, in which he points out that the only reason why a contract for the sale of land by the owner to another operates to effect conversion is that a court of equity will compel him specifically to perform his contract. He further states: "A preliminary to the determination of the question whether there is equitable ownership of land must therefore necessarily be the determination of the question whether there is a contract which can be and ought to be specifically performed *at the very time when the court is called upon to perform it.* This process of reasoning is, however, reversed in those jurisdictions where the 'burden of loss' is cast upon the vendee. The question is whether there shall be a specific performance of the contract, thus casting the burden on the vendee, by compelling him to pay the full purchase price for the subject matter of the contract, a substantial part of which has been destroyed. The question is answered somewhat in this wise: equitable ownership of the vendee in the subject matter of the contract can exist only where the contract is one which equity will specifically perform. The vendee of land is equitably entitled to land, therefore the vendee may be compelled to perform, although the vendor is unable to give in return the performance stipulated for by his contract. The *non sequitur* involved in the proposition that performance may be had because of the equitable ownership of the land by the vendee, which in turn depends upon the right of performance, is evident. The doctrine of equitable conversion, so far as it is exemplified by the authorities hitherto considered, cannot lead to the result of casting the burden of loss on the vendee, since the *conversion depends upon the question whether the contract should in equity be performed.* In all other cases where the vendee is treated as the equitable owner of the land, it is only because the contract is one which equity first determines should be specifically performed.

"Whether a plaintiff, in breach of his contract by a default which goes to the essence, as in the case of the destruction of a substantial part of the subject matter of the contract, should be entitled to specific performance, is a question which is answered in the negative in every case except that of destruction of the subject matter of the contract. To give a plaintiff specific performance of the contract when he is unable to perform the contract on his own part, violates the fundamental rule of equity that . . . *equity will not compel a defendant to perform when it is unable to so frame its decree as to compel the plaintiff to give in return substantially what he has undertaken to give* or to do for the defendant.

"The rule of casting the 'burden of loss' on the vendee by specific performance if justifiable at all can only be explained and justified upon one of two theories: first, that since equity has for most purposes treated the vendee as the equitable owner, it should do so for all purposes, although *this ignores the fact that in all other cases the vendee is so treated only because the contract is either being performed or in equity ought to be performed;* or, second, which is substantially the same proposition in a different form, the specific performance which casts the burden on the vendee is an incident to and a consequence of an equitable conversion, whereas in all other equity relations growing out of the contract, the equitable conversion, if it exists, is an incident to and consequence of, a specific performance. Certainly nothing could be more illogical than this process of reasoning." (Emphasis ours.)

For these reasons, we do not agree with the rule that arbitrarily places the risk of loss on the vendee from the time the contract is made. Instead we believe the Massachusetts rule is the proper rule. It is thus stated in Libman v. Levenson, 236 Mass. 221, 128 N.E. 13, 22 A.L.R. 560: When "the conveyance is to be made of the whole estate, including both land and buildings, for an entire price, and the value of the buildings constitutes a large part of the total value of the estate, and the terms of the agreement show that they constituted an important part of the subject matter of the contract . . . the contract is to be construed as subject to the implied condition that it no longer shall be binding if, before the time for the conveyance to be made, the buildings are destroyed by fire. The loss by the fire falls upon the vendor, the owner; and if he has not protected himself by insurance, he can have no reimbursement of this loss; but the contract is no longer binding upon either party. If the purchaser has advanced any part of the price, he can recover it back. If the change in the value of the estate is not so great, or if it appears that the buildings did not constitute so material a part of the estate to be conveyed as to result in an annulling of the contract, specific performance may be decreed, *with compensation for any breach of agreement*, or relief may be given in damages." (Emphasis ours.) An extreme case, showing the unfairness of the arbitrary rule placing all loss on the vendee, is Amundson v. Severson, 41 S.D. 377, 170 N.W. 633, where three-fourths of the land sold was washed away by the Missouri River (the part left being of little value) and the vendor brought suit for specific performance. Fortunately for the vendee, he was relieved by the fact that the vendor did not have good title at the time of the loss, although the vendor had procured it as a basis for his suit. However, if the vendor had then held good title even though he did not have the land, the vendee would have been required to pay the full contract price under the loss on the purchaser rule. (Would the vendee have been any better off if the vendor had good title from the start but did not have the land left to convey?) The reason for the Massachusetts rule is that specific performance is based on what is equitable; and it is not equitable to make a vendee pay the vendor for something the vendor cannot give him.

However, the issue in this case is not whether the vendee can be compelled to take the property without the building but whether the vendee is entitled to enforce the contract of sale, with the insurance proceeds substituted for the destroyed building. We see no inequity to defendants in such enforcement since they will receive the full amount ($20,000.00) for which they contracted to sell the property. Their contract not only described the land but also specifically stated they sold it "together with the buildings, driveways and all construction thereon." While the words "Service Station Site" appeared in the caption of the option contract and that no doubt was the ultimate use plaintiff intended to make of the land, the final agreement made by the parties was that plaintiff would take it subject to a lease of the building which would have brought plaintiff about $6,150.00 in rent during the term of the lease. Moreover, defendants' own evidence showed the building was valued in the insurance adjustment at $16,716.00 from which $4,179.00 was deducted for depreciation, making the loss $12,537.00. Therefore, defendants are not in a very good position to say the building was of no value to plaintiff. Furthermore, plaintiff having contracted for the land with the building on it, the decision concerning use or removal of the building, or even for resale of the entire property, was for the plaintiff to make. Statements were in evidence about the use of the building and its value to plaintiff made by its employee who negotiated the purchase but he was not one of plaintiff's chief executive officers nor possessed of authority to bind its board of directors. The short of the matter is that defendants will get all they bargained for; but without the building or its value plaintiff will not.

We therefore affirm the judgment and decree of the trial court.

EAGER, LEEDY and HOLLINGSWORTH, JJ., concur.

STORCKMAN, J., dissents in separate opinion filed.

WESTHUES, C.J., and DALTON, J., dissent and concur in separate dissenting opinion of STORCKMAN, J.

[The opinion of STORCKMAN, J., dissenting, is omitted.]

NOTES

1. *Allocation of Risk of Loss.* The rule of Paine v. Meller, 6 Ves.Tr. 349 (Ch.1801), making buyer bear the risk of loss during the executory interval, made practical sense in the early agrarian environment that spawned it. Because in an agrarian economy it was land, not buildings, that presumably formed the object of sale, fortuitous destruction of the buildings would not prevent the buyer from getting what he had bargained for and, so it was thought, should not be allowed to excuse his performance.

Although the rule of Paine v. Meller represents the majority position in the United States today, there is a growing trend to replace it with a rule that allocates risk of loss to the party—whether seller or buyer—in possession at the time the premises are destroyed. The technical rationale for this newer, minority rule is almost as formalistic as the rationale given for the majority rule: "the purchaser in possession is substantial owner of the property and should bear the burdens of ownership, while the purchaser out of possession is not substantial owner." 3 American Law of Property § 11.30 (A.J. Casner, ed. 1952). The better reason for the rule is that the party in possession is best placed to guard against the hazards of destruction, to insure the premises, and to conserve any evidence bearing on destruction.

Which of these two rules—majority or minority—makes more sense today? Should the answer depend on whether urban or rural land is involved? On whether the contract involves commercial or residential property? Whichever rule is adopted, should it be applied differently depending on whether the loss arose from destruction of the premises by natural causes, such as fire, or arose from government's condemnation of the land under the eminent domain power?

The most striking aspect of both the majority and minority rules is that there should be any need for them at all. They are rules of implication, not rules of law, and can be easily altered by contract terms expressly allocating the risk of loss. ("Buyer shall not be obligated to perform if, during the executory period and before Buyer takes possession, the premises are substantially or entirely destroyed by natural causes or if, during the executory period, and without regard to whether Buyer was in possession, the premises are substantially or entirely taken by eminent domain.") Why do you suppose residential buyers and sellers, and their lawyers and brokers, are so reluctant to address and resolve the question of loss during the executory term?

For background on equitable conversion and allocation of risk of loss during the executory interval, see Dunham, Vendor's Obligation as to Fitness of Land for a Particular Purpose, 37 Minn.L.Rev. 108 (1953); Note, Equitable Conversion and its Effect on Risk of Loss in Executory Contracts for the Sale of Real Property, 22 Drake L.Rev. 626 (1973); Lewis & Reeves, How the Doctrine of Equitable Conversion Affects Land Sale Contract Forfeitures, 3 Real Est.L.J. 249 (1975).

2. *Allocation of Insurance Proceeds.* American courts, which have widely followed the English rule of Paine v. Meller on risk of loss during the executory interval, have not followed the English position on a related question: who is entitled to the proceeds paid on the seller's insurance policy? The English rule, formulated in Rayner v. Preston, 18 Ch.Div. 1 (1881), is that the seller is entitled to retain the proceeds free of any claim by the buyer. American courts generally hold that the buyer is entitled to the insurance proceeds, chiefly to avoid giving the seller a windfall (the full purchase price plus the full insurance proceeds). See, for example, Berlier v. George, 94 N.M. 134, 607 P.2d 1152 (1980). It would appear to follow under the American approach that if a state adopts the minority rule on risk of loss and, as a consequence, allocates that risk to seller rather than to buyer, the seller will be entitled to retain the insurance proceeds. *Id.*

The English rule rests on the perception that the insurance policy is strictly a personal contract between the seller and her insurer, and its benefits do not pass with the land into the buyer's hands. American courts justify their position on three closely connected grounds: the insurance proceeds are held by the seller in trust for the purchaser; since, under equitable conversion, the buyer is considered to be equitable owner of the land, he should also be considered the equitable owner of the insurance proceeds which stand in place of the land; and since insurance is customarily considered to be for the benefit of the property rather than the person insured the proceeds should go with the land. 3 American Law of Property § 11.31 (A.J. Casner, ed. 1952).

3. Did the court in Skelly v. Ashmore in fact do what it claimed to have done—reject the Paine v. Meller rule which "arbitrarily places the risk of loss on the vendee from the time the contract is made"? Can the court's holding be explained by any rule *other* than Paine v. Meller? Recall that the American rule allocating seller's insurance proceeds to buyer rests entirely on the assumption that buyer bears the risk of loss; if seller bears the risk of loss, the American rule will give the insurance proceeds to seller rather than to buyer. The Massachusetts rule, which the court purported to adopt, squarely places risk of loss on seller, rather than buyer; it thus offers no basis for the court's decision awarding the insurance proceeds to the buyer.

Nor can the court's result be rationalized in terms of the Massachusetts rule that if the destruction is not great and "the buildings did not constitute so material a part of the estate as to result in an annulling of the contract, specific performance may be decreed, with compensation for any breach of agreement, or relief may be given in damages." As Judge Storckman observed in his dissent, "defendants' evidence tended to prove that the real estate was worth more as a site for a service station after the fire than before and that the value of the real estate after the fire was in excess of $20,000." 365 S.W.2d 582. As a result, Skelly apparently suffered no damages that could be set off against the purchase price.

4. *The UVPRA and the ULTA.* The Uniform Vendors and Purchasers Risk Act would alter the majority American rule by placing risk of loss from destruction or condemnation on buyer only if he has taken possession or title; otherwise seller bears the risk. The brain child of Professor Samuel Williston, the UVPRA was promulgated by the National Conference of Commissioners on Uniform State Laws in 1935. At last count, the Act has been adopted in ten states: West's Ann.Cal.Civ. Code § 1662; Hawaii Rev.Stat. § 508–1; Illinois—S.H.A. ch. 29, ¶¶ 8.1–8.3; Michigan Comp. Laws Ann. §§ 26.676(1) et seq.; New York—McKinney's Gen.Oblig. Law § 5–1311; North Carolina Gen.Stat. §§ 39–37 through 39–39; 16 Oklahoma Stat.Ann. §§ 201–203; Oregon Rev.Stat. 93.290; South Dakota Comp. Laws 43–26–5 through 43–26–8; Wisconsin Stat.Ann. 235.72.

Almost all these statutes track the language of the original Uniform Act. The Illinois version differs in one detail—assigning special consequence to passage of title through escrow. The New York act makes two changes. It states that its terms are not intended to deprive the seller or buyer of any right to recover damages against the other for breach of contract occurring prior to the destruction or condemnation. And it provides that if buyer has taken neither possession nor title, and an "immaterial part" is destroyed or taken, neither seller nor buyer "is thereby deprived of the right to enforce the contract; but there shall be, to the extent of the destruction or taking, an abatement of purchase price."

ULTA § 2–406, dealing with destruction of premises, modifies the approach taken by the UVPRA. Section 2–406(c)(2) adopts the Illinois rule on sales closed through escrow, and section 2–406(b)(2)(i) incorporates the New York approach respecting abatement of purchase price for nonmaterial diminutions in value. Also, in the event "the loss or taking results in a substantial failure of the real estate to conform to the contract," section 2–406(b)(1) gives the buyer the option of cancelling the contract and recovering any down payment or enforcing the contract and accepting the property with a "reduction of the contract price for the loss or taking." Can you think of situations in which it would be plainly unfair to require the seller to give up her property in return for a sharply reduced price?

3. CLOSING THE CONTRACT: THE DEED

WARRANTY DEED

Warranty Deed with Lien Covenant
Laws of 1917, Chap. 681, Laws of 1954

880½

David F. Williamson Co., Inc., Publishers
Buffalo, New York

This Indenture,

Made the 1st day of September, Nineteen Hundred and eighty-three (1983)

Between Robert W. Jones and Mary Ruth Jones, his wife, residing at 23 Oak Street, Amherst, New York 14221

Grantor(s), and

John J. Smith and Katherine Ann Smith, his wife, residing at 49 Willow Street, Buffalo, New York 14202

[PREMISES]

Witnesseth, that the said Grantor(s), in consideration of ---------- ONE & MORE ---------- Dollars ($1.00 & More ----------) lawful money of the United States, paid by the Grantee(s), do hereby grant and release unto the Grantee(s), their heirs and assigns forever.

All that Tract or Parcel of Land, situate in the Town of Amherst, County of Erie and State of New York, being part of Lot Number 45, Township 11 and Range 7 of the Holland Land Company's Survey and according to a Subdivision Map filed in the Erie County Clerk's Office under Cover Number 922 is known and distinguished as Subdivision Lot Number 117.

TOGETHER with the appurtenances and all the estate and rights of the Grantor(s) in and to the said premises.

TO HAVE AND TO HOLD, the above granted premises unto the said Grantee(s).

AND the said Grantor(s) do covenant with said Grantee(s) as follows:

FIRST.—That the Grantee(s) shall quietly enjoy the said premises.

SECOND.—That the Grantor(s) will forever **WARRANT** the title to said premises.

THIRD.—Subject to the trust fund provisions of section thirteen of the lien law.

havendum [HABENDUM]

IN WITNESS WHEREOF, The said Grantor(s) have hereunto set their hands and seals the day and year first above written.

IN PRESENCE OF

_____ [L.S.]   _____ [L.S.]
ROBERT W. JONES   MARY RUTH JONES

_____ [L.S.]   _____ [L.S.]

[EXECUTION CLAUSE]

STATE OF NEW YORK) ss.   On this 1st day of September,
COUNTY OF ERIE   )   Nineteen Hundred and eighty-three (1983)

before me, the subscriber(s), personally appeared Robert W. Jones and Mary Ruth Jones, his wife,

to me personally known and known to me to be the same persons described in and who executed the within instrument, and they acknowledged to me that they executed the same.

_____
notary public

STATE OF NEW YORK) ss.   On this   day of
COUNTY OF   )   Nineteen Hundred and

before me, the subscriber(s), personally appeared

to me personally known and known to me to be the same person described in and who executed the within instrument, and he acknowledged to me that he executed the same.

[ACKNOWLEDGMENT CLAUSE]

[D513]

NOTES

1. There is a modern trend to simplify the form and content of real property deeds. Many states have enacted short form deed statutes, prescribing language that eliminates many of the customary redundancies and flourishes. The Jones-Smith deed, above, reflects the contemporary trend toward simplification. Even so, the deed contains all of the basic elements that have traditionally been employed since the earliest English deeds.

The portion of the Jones-Smith deed beginning with "This indenture . . ." and ending with the line, "Together with . . .," constitutes the *premises* of the deed—the names of grantor and grantee; the words of grant; background facts and purposes; consideration; and the legal description of the parcels conveyed.

The next portion of the deed, beginning with the line, "To have and to hold," and ending with the third covenant, is the *habendum,* which describes the interest taken by the grantee, any conditions on the grant and any covenants of title (these last are sometimes said to comprise the *warranty clause).*

The *execution clause* begins with the phrase, "In Witness Whereof," and contains the grantors' signatures, their seal, and the date of the deed. (In states that require the deed to be witnessed, the signatures of the witnesses would also appear in the execution clause.) Finally, beneath the grantors' signatures is the *acknowledgement,* in which a public officer, typically a notary, attests to the execution.

2. *Formalities Required.* Apart from a written instrument signed by the grantor, most states today require few formalities for a deed to be effective. The deed must name the grantor and grantee; it must contain express words of grant; and it must describe the parcel conveyed to the exclusion of all other parcels in the world.

3. *Formalities Not Required. Consideration.* Although consideration is required for the grantee to be a "purchaser for value," and thus protected under the recording acts, it is not required for the deed to be effective as between the parties. Nonetheless, deeds will commonly refer to the consideration given, frequently in some such mysterious terms as "One and More Dollars," or "Ten Dollars and other Valuable Consideration." Why the secrecy? One reason is that deeds, once recorded, are public documents, and a recital of the owner's true purchase price might give an undesired bargaining advantage to some future purchaser from the owner. (Prospective purchasers will sometimes try to pierce this veil and calculate the seller's purchase price by counting the documentary tax stamps affixed to the deed; since, at the time of purchase the owner is required to buy stamps in proportion to the actual purchase price of the parcel, the number of stamps might be thought to indicate the purchase price. But sellers are clever, too, and, anticipating the future purchaser's

strategy, will sometimes buy more stamps than are required, thus indicating a higher price than was actually paid.)

Seal. It was once commonly required that for a deed to be effective it had to be sealed—stamped with the grantor's mark. Most states have since eliminated the requirement. And, even in those states that still impose the requirement, it is easily met—through use of the written word, "Seal," or, as in the Jones-Smith deed, through use of the initials "L.S.," (signifying *locus sigilli*, or "the place of the seal").

Acknowledgement. Only a small number of states require an acknowledgement for a deed to be effective as between the parties. Acknowledgement is, however, required for a deed to be legally recorded. Acknowledgement has traditionally conferred two other benefits. It makes the deed admissible into evidence without further proof of execution, and it creates a presumption that the deed is genuine. For an exhaustive analysis of acknowledgement requirements and related formalities see Brussack, Reform of American Conveyancing Formality, 32 Hastings L.J. 561 (1981).

4. *The Cost of Formalities.* One obvious and oft-lamented cost of formal requirements is that, by invalidating imperfect transfers, they penalize grantors and grantees who retained inept lawyers or no lawyers at all. Formal rules respecting deed drafting, descriptions and delivery, considered in the pages that follow, can have a similarly harsh effect.

Formal requirements have another, possibly more substantial cost. By inducing grantees and grantors to reduce their transactions to writing and to have these writings acknowledged, delivered and recorded, the American conveyancing system also induces future grantees to rely on the paper record as perfectly evidencing the current state of title. Unfortunately, even the most perfect-appearing paper record is sometimes flawed. A swindler can easily forge a deed conveying Blackacre from the current record owner to himself. By forging a notarial seal and acknowledgement, he can easily record the deed and, once having recorded it, can easily sell the land to some unsuspecting buyer.

Can you think of ways to reduce the incidence or cost of fraud without sacrificing the efficiencies of a paper record?

a. Deed Construction

BARRIER v. RANDOLPH

Supreme Court of North Carolina, 1963.
260 N.C. 741, 133 S.E.2d 655.

The hearing below was on plaintiffs' motion for judgment on the pleadings, which consist of the complaint, a copy of the deed attached thereto as Exhibit A and by reference made a part thereof, and the answer.

The facts alleged by plaintiffs and admitted by defendants, summarized except when quoted, are as follows:

The deed of which Exhibit A is a copy, referred to in the opinion as the Randolph-Austin deed, is dated March 24, 1950, and recorded in Book 1432, Page 93, Mecklenburg Registry. By the terms thereof, the present defendants and others conveyed to David Blair Austin and wife, Marian Robinson Austin, a tract of land in Sharon Township, Mecklenburg County, North Carolina, described by metes and bounds, containing 7.51 acres. The granting, habendum and warranty clauses are in terms of a conveyance in fee simple.

After the description, but before the habendum and warranty clauses, this provision is set forth: "And this Deed is made subject to the following conditions, reservations, and restrictions which constitute covenants running with the land and binding upon the parties hereto, their heirs and assigns, to wit": The conditions, reservations and restrictions are then set forth *in extenso* in eleven separate (numbered) paragraphs. They include, *inter alia*, restrictions that the property shall be used only for residential purposes, restrictions as to the size of lots in the event of subdivision, restrictions as to the location, cost and composition of any residence constructed thereon, etc. Too, they include reservations of rights of way for the installation of power and telephone lines.

Thereafter, through mesne conveyances, the 7.51-acre tract was conveyed to plaintiffs herein.

Plaintiffs allege that defendants claim an interest or estate adverse to plaintiffs in the said 7.51-acre tract based on the restrictions and easements set forth in Exhibit A, but that said restrictions and easements purport to limit the estate of plaintiffs "contrary to the granting clause and the habendum and the warranties" in Exhibit A and therefore are invalid and of no effect. Plaintiffs prayed that they be adjudged the owners in fee simple of the said 7.51-acre tract free and clear of any right or claim of defendants on account of the restrictions and easements set forth in Exhibit A.

Defendants denied the legal conclusions alleged by plaintiffs and asserted the restrictive covenants set forth in Exhibit A were and are valid and presently enforceable. Defendants prayed that plaintiffs' action be dismissed and that they recover their costs.

After hearing, the court, by order dated April 25, 1963, denied plaintiffs' motion for judgment on the pleadings. Plaintiffs excepted and appealed.

BOBBITT, Justice.

There has been no adjudication of the rights of the parties. The court did not enter final judgment but simply denied plaintiffs' motion for judgment on the pleadings. It is well established that an appeal does not lie from a denial of a motion for judgment on the pleadings. The proper practice was for plaintiffs to except to the court's denial of their said motion and bring forward this exception in the event of their appeal from an adverse final judgment.

Plaintiffs' appeal must be dismissed as fragmentary and premature. Even so, in the exercise of our discretionary power we deem it appropriate to express an opinion upon one, but only one, of the questions plaintiffs have attempted to raise by their fragmentary and premature appeal.

The one question we consider is that raised by plaintiffs' contention that *all* the "conditions, reservations and restrictions" set forth in the Randolph-Austin deed are repugnant to the granting, habendum and warranty clauses of said deed and therefore are surplusage and void *ab initio*. Plaintiffs base this contention upon Oxendine v. Lewis, 252 N.C. 669, 114 S.E.2d 706, asserting in their brief that "the Oxendine Case is determinative of the controversy herein."

The rule applied in Oxendine v. Lewis, supra, and in decisions cited therein, is stated by Parker, J., as follows: "We have repeatedly held that when the granting clause, the *habendum*, and the warranty in a deed are clear and unambiguous and fully sufficient to pass immediately a fee simple estate to the grantee or grantees, that a paragraph inserted between the description and the *habendum*, in which the grantor seeks to reserve a life estate in himself or another, or to otherwise limit the estate conveyed, will be rejected as repugnant to the estate and interest therein conveyed."

"In the interpretation of a deed, the intention of the grantor or grantors must be gathered from the whole instrument and every part thereof given effect, unless it contains conflicting provisions which are irreconcilable or a provision which is contrary to public policy or runs counter to some rule of law." Lackey v. Hamlet City Board of Education, 258 N.C. 460, 462, 128 S.E.2d 806, 808.

The sufficiency of the Randolph-Austin deed as a conveyance in fee simple of said 7.51-acre tract is not controverted. There is no contention it conveyed a life estate or other estate less than a fee simple.

In express terms, the Randolph-Austin deed provides that it is made subject to the conditions, reservations and restrictions therein set forth and that such conditions, reservations and restrictions constitute covenants. Indeed, the portion of the deed in which these conditions, reservations and restrictions are set forth constitutes the greater part of the entire (including description) deed. The intention of the grantors that such conveyance is made subject to such conditions, reservations and restrictions is manifest. Moreover, "(i)t is a settled principle of law that a grantee who accepts a deed poll containing covenants or conditions to be performed by him as the consideration of the grant, becomes bound for their performance, although he does not execute the deed as a party." Maynard v. Moore, 76 N.C. 158, 165.

In Lackey v. Hamlet City Board of Education, supra, this Court, in an opinion by Denny, C.J., while recognizing and restating the rule applied in Oxendine v. Lewis, supra, held it did not apply to the deed then under consideration. The granting clause of that deed was in terms of a fee simple conveyance. Immediately after the description, this paragraph appeared: "It is also made a part of this deed that in the event of the school's disbandonment (failure) that this lot of land shall revert to the original owners, to wit: The said E.A. Lackey and wife, Ella M. Lackey, or their legitimate heirs, but it is also agreed that any and all improvements therein shall remain the property of the town of Hamlet, N.C." The habendum clause read as follows: "TO HAVE AND TO HOLD the aforesaid lot or parcel of land, and all privileges and appurtenances thereto belonging, to the said parties of the second part, their successors and assigns, to their only use and behoof forever, for school purposes." The validity of the quoted reversion clause was upheld by this Court and was the basis of decision.

In Guilford County v. Porter, 167 N.C. 366, 83 S.E. 564, the purpose of the action (treated as an action for declaratory judgment) was, in the language of Brown, J., "to get rid of these restrictions upon the use of the property . . . ." The deed(s) under consideration, sufficient as conveyances in fee simple, contained this clause: "*Provided, however,* and it is understood and agreed that the said lot herein conveyed shall be used by the said parties of the second part as a public square and be forever kept open for that purpose, and should any building or structure of any character inconsistent with said purpose be erected thereon, the said party of the first part, his heirs or assigns may enter upon the land herein conveyed and abate and remove any and all buildings or parts of buildings inconsistent with its use as aforesaid." The quoted provision in said deed(s) was between the habendum and warranty clauses. The validity of this provision as a restrictive covenant was upheld. The contention that it was repugnant to the estate in fee simple already granted and therefore should be rejected and treated as surplusage was made, expressly considered by this Court and rejected.

The foregoing impels us to express the view that Oxendine v. Lewis, supra, does not control decision and that the conditions, reservations and restrictions set forth in the Randolph-Austin deed are not void *ab initio* on the ground they are repugnant to the granting, habendum and warranty clauses of said deed. We express no opinion as to whether these conditions, reservations and restrictions or any of them are void on *other grounds*. Neither do we express any opinion as to whether these conditions, reservations and restrictions, or any of them, are presently enforceable by defendants herein or other persons. These matters are for determination in the first instance in the superior court. Upon further hearing, all factual matters relevant to a proper decision should be brought to the attention of the court.

Appeal dismissed.

NOTE

Courts called on to construe real property deeds typically start from the proposition noted in Barrier v. Randolph that "the intention of the grantor or grantors must be gathered from the whole instrument and every part thereof given effect . . . ." If, however, the deed contains "conflicting provisions which are irreconcilable," courts will employ one or more standard interpretational canons to resolve the conflict or ambiguity.

For example, if there is an irreconcilable conflict between the granting clause and the habendum, it is generally said that the granting clause will control. And, "so long as they do not conflict, written and printed parts are of equal force; when inconsistent, printed parts must give way to typed or written words, and, between the latter two, written words give a stronger indication of intention than typed words. When contradictory, general words must usually give way to specific words. Where a recital and an operative part of the deed come in conflict, it is the latter which prevails. And it is a general rule, subject to all those just considered, that when two repugnant clauses cannot be reconciled, the earlier of the two will stand. Another rule, not to be applied until all others fail to reconcile a conflict, and only when there is a real ambiguity or uncertainty, is that a deed will be construed most strongly against the grantor, or against the grantee when the instrument was drafted by him." 3 American Law of Property § 12.90 (A.J. Casner ed. 1952).

It is the rare deed dispute in which some of these canons cannot be asserted on one side, and some on the other. Would these canons help you in giving a title opinion on an ambiguous deed executed thirty or forty years earlier? Consider whether you would feel more or less comfortable with your opinion, knowing that, in addition to these canons of construction, a court interpreting the deed will often look to "all the attendant circumstances as to situation of the parties, relationship, object of the conveyance, person who drew the deed, and all surrounding situations which may throw light on the meaning which the parties attached to ambiguous or inconsistent portions of the instruments. And unless forbidden by some rule of law, the courts will follow the construction given a deed by the parties themselves as shown by their subsequent admissions or conduct." 3 American Law of Property § 12.91 (A.J. Casner ed. 1952).

Given a choice, is it preferable for a court construing a deed to attempt to discern the actual, subjective intent of the original grantor and grantee, or to refuse to look outside the deed's four corners? Which rule will better promote certainty among title examiners and their clients over the long term?

b. Description of the Land Conveyed

C. BROWN, BOUNDARY CONTROL AND LEGAL PRINCIPLES*

9–11, 14–17 (2d ed. 1969).

1.6. WRITTEN PERIMETER DESCRIPTIONS

Land can be described by a sequence of courses, and where the sequence of courses has a direction of travel around a perimeter and has calls for adjoiners, the description is said to be by *metes and bounds*. Mete means to measure or to assign by measure, and *bounds* means the boundary of the land or the limits and extent of a property. Within the generally accepted usage of the term metes and bounds it is not necessary to recite measures of a property as implied by the word metes. A parcel of land can be described without a single measurement being given: "Beginning at an oak tree blazed on the north; thence to a large boulder located on the bank of Lake Washington; thence along the lake to . . ., etc." Usually metes and bounds descriptions are described by successive courses, said courses being fixed by adjoiners, monuments, direction, distance, or all four.

Bounds descriptions are perimeter descriptions, but they do not have a direction of travel: "All of that land bounded on the north by Thelma Lane; bounded on the south by Rodger River; bounded on the west by the land of Thomas L. Brown; and bounded on the east by the land of Ruth Almstead." The sequence of reciting the bounds is immaterial; the description has no mandatory direction of travel.

Metes descriptions are perimeter descriptions described by measurements, have a direction of travel, and recite no bounds (adjoiners). Often a metes description is included within the common usage of the term metes and bounds. . . .

1.9. CALLS IN DESCRIPTIONS

In litigation and in surveying the terms *deed calls* and *running out the calls* are commonly used. According to *Websters International Dictionary* in American land law a call is a "reference to, or statement of, an object, course (meaning direction), distance, or other matter of description in a survey or grant . . . ." The calls of a surveyor's field notes are for the objects and measurements noted. A call, as commonly used, can be a phrase in a land description: "thence to a blazed oak tree." This call tells the surveyor to go thence (from the last place mentioned) in a straight line to a blazed oak tree. Other examples of calls are N 10° 15′ E, 327.62′, along Red

---

* Copyright © 1957, 1969 by John Wiley & Sons, Inc. Reprinted by permission of John Wiley & Sons, Inc.

River, due north, along the center line of B Street, to the Santa Fe Railroad tracks . . . ..

DIRECTION OF TRAVEL

True metes and bounds descriptions and many quasi-metes and bounds descriptions have a direction of travel. A bearing may be stated in either of two directions on a map or plat but only one can be used in a written perimeter description. In Fig. 1.11b, starting at the point of beginning, the direction of travel is to the southeast, making the first written bearing in the description S 45° 00′ E, not N 45° 00′ W. Because the relationship of one line to another is shown by the plotting of the lines in Fig. 1.11b, it is immaterial whether the bearing on the plat is written S 45° 00′ E or N 45° 00′ W.

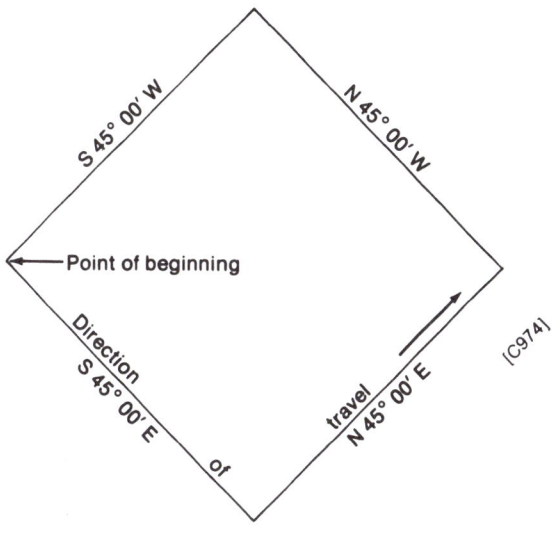

Figure 1.11b

MONUMENTS

Monuments are classified as either *natural, artificial, record,* or *legal.* Naturally occurring monuments such as rivers, lakes, oceans, bays, sloughs, cliffs, trees, hills, and large boulders are permanent objects found on the land as they were placed by nature and are usually considered controlling over *artificial monuments* (man-made) such as iron stakes, wooden stakes, rock mounds, stones, and wooden fences, but, if the writings clearly indicate a contrary intent, especially where the lines of a survey are called for, the control might be reversed. Some man-made monuments, because of the certainty of location, visibility, stability, and permanence, are considered equal in rank to natural monuments. In this classification would fall sidewalks, street paving, curbs, wells, canals, concrete buildings, and concrete fences.

RECORD MONUMENTS OR BOUNDARIES

These exist because of a reference to them in a deed or legal description; thus, "to Brown's property line" is a call for a record monument (Brown's property). Record monuments may or may not be marked upon the ground by artificial or natural monuments. Where a deed reads "to the side line of the street," the call is for the boundary of a record monument (street) which could be marked by stakes, improvements, fences, or all three, or not marked at all. A call for any record monument is a call for all the monuments, or considerations, that establish the location of the record monument. If a monument is controlling in a legal description, it is often classified as a *legal monument*. "To a stone" is a call for a legal artificial monument; "to Brown's property line" is a call for a legal record monument. The words record monument and legal monument are sometimes used synonymously. Because of the confusion over the various meanings of the term "legal," the words legal monument should be avoided.

Courts may refer to record monuments as natural monuments. The boundaries of a street are marked by man, but the dirt composing the street is naturally occurring, and, in this sense, the street is a natural monument. It is an unfortunate classification. In the order of importance of conflicting elements within deeds, natural monuments are normally considered superior to artificial monuments. A call for a record monument, where no senior right is interfered with, is normally subordinate to a call for an artificial monument. If record monuments are classified as natural monuments, the statement that natural monuments control artificial monuments is not exactly true.

Adjoiners, streets, and parcels of land differ from rivers, lakes, and the like, in that man marks and defines these boundary divisions. Waters and creeks always have visible boundaries, whereas a parcel of land may not be physically marked at all. A deed call for an adjoiner is a call for a monument in the form of a parcel of land that has size, shape, and location, but there is poor foundation for classifying the monument as a natural monument. Since the limits of a parcel of land must be marked by man, why not classify the call for an adjoiner as a call for an artificial monument? Because adjoiners to a conveyance are mainly dependent upon the record for their existence and because they may have invisible lines marking their limits, the classification "record monument" is preferred. The term "natural monument" as used herein is exclusive of record monuments.

PROPERTIES OF MONUMENTS

A good monument should possess the quality of being easily visible, certain of identification, stable in location, permanent in character, and nondependent upon measurement for its location. An artificial monument possesses the qualities of a natural monument to a lesser degree. Thus a stake placed in the ground will rust or rot with time and is less permanent than a naturally occurring large boulder. A stake is easier to move than a boulder and is therefore less stable. The visibility of record monuments is wholly dependent upon the natural or artificial monuments (fences, stakes, cultivation, plantings, and the like) that mark the limits of the record monument.

STRAIGHT LINES

A line in a description is assumed to be the shortest horizontal distance between the points called for unless the contrary is indicated by the writings. To be absolutely correct, a straight line curves with the surface of the earth; but the curvature is so slight that it is not considered in land descriptions. A line to be identified must have a definition of its start, direction, and length. *Free lines* are not terminated by an adjoiner or monument as "beginning at a 2-inch iron pipe; thence N 60° 00' W, 200.00 feet." If the same phrase were reworded "beginning at a 2-inch iron pipe; thence N 60° 00' W, 200.00 feet to a blazed sycamore tree," the terminus of the line is fixed by the tree; the line is not free. Many of the lines described in deeds are dependent upon monuments and are not free lines.

A bearing quoted for a line defines it as a straight line. If a line is defined by monuments, without bearing or distance, the words "in a straight line" or "in a direct line" are sometimes added to emphasize the presumed fact that the line is straight.

DIRECTION

As commonly practiced in this country, direction is defined by either a call for monuments or a bearing; but azimuth, deflection angle, or coordinate may be used. If a deed is written "commencing at a blazed sycamore tree located approximately 100 feet west of Jones' well; thence to a blazed white oak, etc.," the direction is clearly defined. It is very desirable to quote the bearing of the line for plotting purposes, but it is not essential to the legality of the conveyance. Bearings are always read in degrees and minutes (plus seconds if fractions of a minute are involved) from the *north* point or from the *south* point. *Never* from the east or west points . . . . The direction of a line is dependent upon [at] which end of the line you are standing; thus on a northwesterly line the direction would be SE if you were at the northerly terminus of a line, whereas it would be NW if you were at the southerly terminus of the same line. On a map it is immaterial which bearing you write, since the drawing shows the relationship of one line to another; but in a written metes and bounds description the exact direction of travel of the line being described must be stated.

CUNNYNGHAM, MAKING LAND SURVEYS AND PREPARING DESCRIPTIONS TO MEET LEGAL REQUIREMENTS

19 Missouri Law Review 234, 236–238 (1954).

[Metes and bounds] is the method used in most of the world, including 19 of the American States (Texas, and the states in, or carved out of the original Thirteen Colonies—Maine, New Hampshire, Vermont, Massachusetts, Rhode Island, Connecticut, New York, Pennsylvania, New Jersey, Delaware, Maryland, Virginia, West Virginia, Kentucky, North Carolina, Tennessee, South Carolina, and Georgia).

Land descriptions in the other 29 states are generally much simpler. Most of the lands in these states were at one time owned by the Federal Government. The disposition of such a vast acreage presented a major problem in identification and description. The fertile imagination and inventive genius of Thomas Jefferson worked out a plan for dividing the public lands into a gigantic checkerboard of uniform square tracts each measuring one mile (80 chains) on its sides, and containing 640 acres. These "sections" are divided into "quarters" of 160 acres each, ½ mile (40 chains) on a side; and may be still further subdivided into "quarter-quarter-sections" ($\frac{1}{16}$-section) of 40 acres, ¼ mile on each side etc. The boundaries of these sections were to be a series of parallel north-south lines one mile apart, and east-west lines, also one mile apart.

A square of 36 sections constitutes a "township" six miles on each side. The sections in a township are numbered from 1 to 36, starting at the north-east, and proceeding west and then east alternately to the 36th section in the south-east corner. Townships are identified by assigning to each a number which will show how many other townships intervene between the particular township and (1) a certain east-west line on its north or south (called the *"base line"*), and (2) east or west from one of the north-south lines (called the *"principal meridian"*). Under this system it should be possible to describe almost any tract in the 29 states so surveyed, by the simple statement that it is, for example: The (a) north-east one-fourth of the (b) south-east one-fourth of (c) Section 6 in (d) Township 44 north of the Little Rock, Arkansas, Base Line and Range 3 east of the Fifth Principal Meridian, in (e) St. Louis County, (f) State of Missouri, (g) containing 40 acres, more or less. This may be shortened to: A tract of land in St. Louis County, Missouri, being the NE¼, SE¼. Sec. 6, T. 44 N., R. 3 E., containing 40 acres, more or less.

However, in actual practice and for many reasons, sections will not always be found to fit into such a scheme with perfect uniformity. If two lines, drawn exactly one mile apart at the Base Line, are projected due north, they must approach closer together each mile as they proceed north, until they will have merged into a single point at the North Pole.

There are also mechanical and human surveying errors in determining bearings and distances in the east-west, as well as the north-south, lines. We should remember that some of the first surveys were made 150 years ago through almost impenetrable wildernesses, over wild land of little value, perhaps under harassment from hostile Indians, by contract surveyors sometimes interested only in collecting their pay for as little time and effort as possible, using crude instruments and methods (e.g., reputedly measuring distance by counting revolutions of a cartwheel with a rag tied around the rim or by a hemp rope dragged on horse back). Even with the most modern transit, the magnetic needle is not supported to a point toward true north, but toward a "magnetic" north which is continually shifting and changing the magnetic "declination". Local ore deposits, metal objects, and power lines affect the needle. "It (the magnetic compass) is an instrument helpful for finding general directions but not reliable when accuracy is required, nor is it used except for checking purposes in surveys." [4] When using the transit for turning angles from a base line, the finest gradation on the horizontal circle may be one degree, or on the more expensive instruments with vernier attachments, one-half minute.

C. BROWN, BOUNDARY CONTROL AND LEGAL PRINCIPLES*

10–11, 27–29 (2d ed. 1969).

1.8. DESCRIPTIONS BY REFERENCE

The simplest form for writing a land description is by reference to a map or plat as: Lot 1, Block 49 of La Jolla Park, City of San Diego, California. See Fig. 1.8. . . .

---

4. Henrie v. Hyer, 92 Utah 530, 70 P.2d 154, 158 (1937).

* Copyright © 1957, 1969 by John Wiley & Sons, Inc. Reprinted by permission of John Wiley & Sons, Inc.

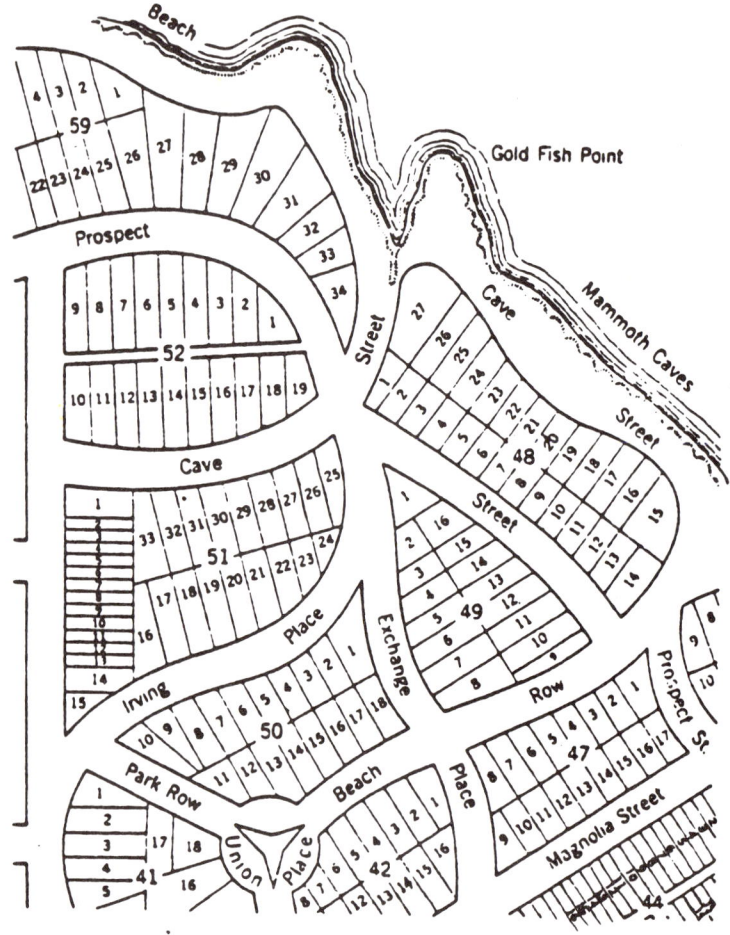

Figure 1.8 La Jolla Park.

[C976]

1.13. SUBDIVISION DESCRIPTIONS

If a map of parcels of land is filed with a public agency and the parcels thereon are designated by number or letters, the map is commonly referred to as a subdivision map. The precise meaning of the term subdivision varies from state to state, and the meaning within a given state is whatever the law defines it as being within that state. In a number of states the law authorizing preparation of subdivision maps is sometimes called a *platting* act instead of *subdivision* act.
. . .

From the standpoint of the retracement surveyor the important features of a map are the following

1. What monuments were set or found?

2. What are the record sizes and locations of the lots and blocks?

From the standpoint of the scrivener, subdivision maps offer the simplest means of describing land since they present the maximum of information and the minimum of words. "Lot 40 of La Mesa Colony, according to Map 346 as filed in the Office of the Recorder, San Diego County, Calif." or "Sec. 16, T15N, R20E, Principal Meridian" or "Lot 2 according to the partition map filed in Superior Court Case 17632" form complete descriptions of land that can be identified from all other parcels of land. The simplicity of the title wording does not mean that a lot and block description of a section of land is easier to survey than is a parcel of land described by a metes and bounds conveyance. Certainty and ease of location are totally unrelated to the length of the deed describing the land.

Most subdivision laws require that, previous to filing a map, survey markers must be established on the land. Many older maps, made before the passage of such laws, were "office maps" made from the record without benefit of survey. . . .

Early subdivisions executed by private interests were poorly regulated by law, and any sheet of paper presented as a subdivision map to the land or recorder's office was filed upon payment of the filing fee. Occasionally, maps failed to show street widths, lot sizes, and what was being subdivided. The map of La Jolla Park was compiled with undimensioned lots and undimensioned curved streets laid out with a varying radius french curve (see Fig. 1.8). On old maps the surveyor or engineer rarely made a statement describing what monuments he found or set. How could a later surveyor, ignorant of what markers were originally set, retrace a subdivision? Most modern subdivisions are regulated by rigid laws, which have corrected many of the conditions mentioned. . . .

1.14. PARCELS CREATED BY PROTRACTION

Parcels of land or lots drawn upon a subdivision map but not monumented on the ground by an original survey are said to be created by protraction. If a surveyor divides a parcel of land into blocks 200 × 300 feet by setting monuments at each block corner and then draws 12 lots in each block of his map, the lots are said to be protracted. In the sectionalized land system sections are created by prior survey and monumentation; parts of sections are created by protraction (SW¼ of NE¼ of Section 10). The words "protracted lots" or "protracted parcels" imply "created on paper without the benefit of an original survey." If several parcels or lots are protracted on the same map, all are simultaneously created at the moment of approval of the map; no parcel or lot has senior rights over an adjoiner.

In New York the date of sale determines prior rights; this is an exception to the general rule.

WALTERS v. TUCKER

Supreme Court of Missouri, 1955.
281 S.W.2d 843.

HOLLINGSWORTH, Judge.

This is an action to quiet title to certain real estate situate in the City of Webster Groves, St. Louis County, Missouri. Plaintiff and defendants are the owners of adjoining residential properties fronting northward on Oak Street. Plaintiff's property, known as 450 Oak Street, lies to the west of defendants' property, known as 446 Oak Street. The controversy arises over their division line. Plaintiff contends that her lot is 50 feet in width, east and west. Defendants contend that plaintiff's lot is only approximately 42 feet in width, east and west. The trial court, sitting without a jury, found the issues in favor of defendants and rendered judgment accordingly, from which plaintiff has appealed.

The common source of title is Fred F. Wolf and Rose E. Wolf, husband and wife, who in 1922 acquired the whole of Lot 13 of West Helfenstein Park, as shown by plat thereof recorded in St. Louis County. In 1924, Mr. and Mrs. Wolf conveyed to Charles Arthur Forse and wife the following described portion of said Lot 13:

> "The West 50 feet of Lot 13 of West Helfenstein Park, a Subdivision in United States Survey 1953, Twp. 45, Range 8 East, St. Louis County, Missouri, ...''

Plaintiff, through mesne conveyances carrying a description like that above, is the last grantee of and successor in title to the aforesaid portion of Lot 13. Defendants, through mesne conveyances, are the last grantees of and successors in title to the remaining portion of Lot 13.

At the time of the above conveyance in 1924, there was and is now situate on the tract described therein a one-story frame dwelling house (450 Oak Street), which was then and continuously since has been occupied as a dwelling by the successive owners of said tract, or their tenants. In 1925, Mr. and Mrs. Wolf built a 1½-story stucco dwelling house on the portion of Lot 13 retained by them. This house (446 Oak Street) continuously since has been occupied as a dwelling by the successive owners of said portion of Lot 13, or their tenants.

Despite the apparent clarity of the description in plaintiff's deed, extrinsic evidence was heard for the purpose of enabling the trial court to interpret the true meaning of the description set forth therein. At the close of all the evidence the trial court found that the description did not clearly reveal whether the property conveyed "was to be fifty feet along the front line facing Oak Street or fifty feet measured Eastwardly at right angles from the West line of the property . . . ."; that the "difference in method of ascertaining fifty feet would result in a difference to the parties of a strip the length of the lot and approximately eight feet in width"; that an ambiguity existed which justified the hearing of extrinsic evidence; and that the "West fifty feet should be measured on the front or street line facing Oak Street." The judgment rendered in conformity with the above finding had the effect of fixing the east-west width of plaintiff's tract at about 42 feet.

Plaintiff contends that the description in the deed is clear, definite and unambiguous, both on its face and when applied to the land; that the trial court erred in hearing and considering extrinsic evidence; and that its finding and judgment changes the clearly expressed meaning of the description and describes and substitutes a different tract from that acquired by her under her deed. Defendants do not contend that the description, on its face, is ambiguous, but do contend that when applied to the land it is subject to "dual interpretation"; that under the evidence trial court did not err in finding it contained a latent ambiguity and that parol evidence was admissible to ascertain and determine its true meaning; and that the finding and judgment of the trial court properly construes and adjudges the true meaning of the description set forth in said deed.

Attached hereto is a reduced copy of an unchallenged survey of Lot 13, as made by plaintiff's witness, Robert J. Joyce, surveyor and graduate (1928) in civil engineering at Massachusetts Institute of Technology, for use in this litigation. Inasmuch as the two properties here in question front northward on Oak Street, the plat is made to be viewed from the bottom toward the top, which in this instance is from north to south:

254 · THE REAL PROPERTY SYSTEM · Pt. 1

WEST HELFENSTEIN PARK

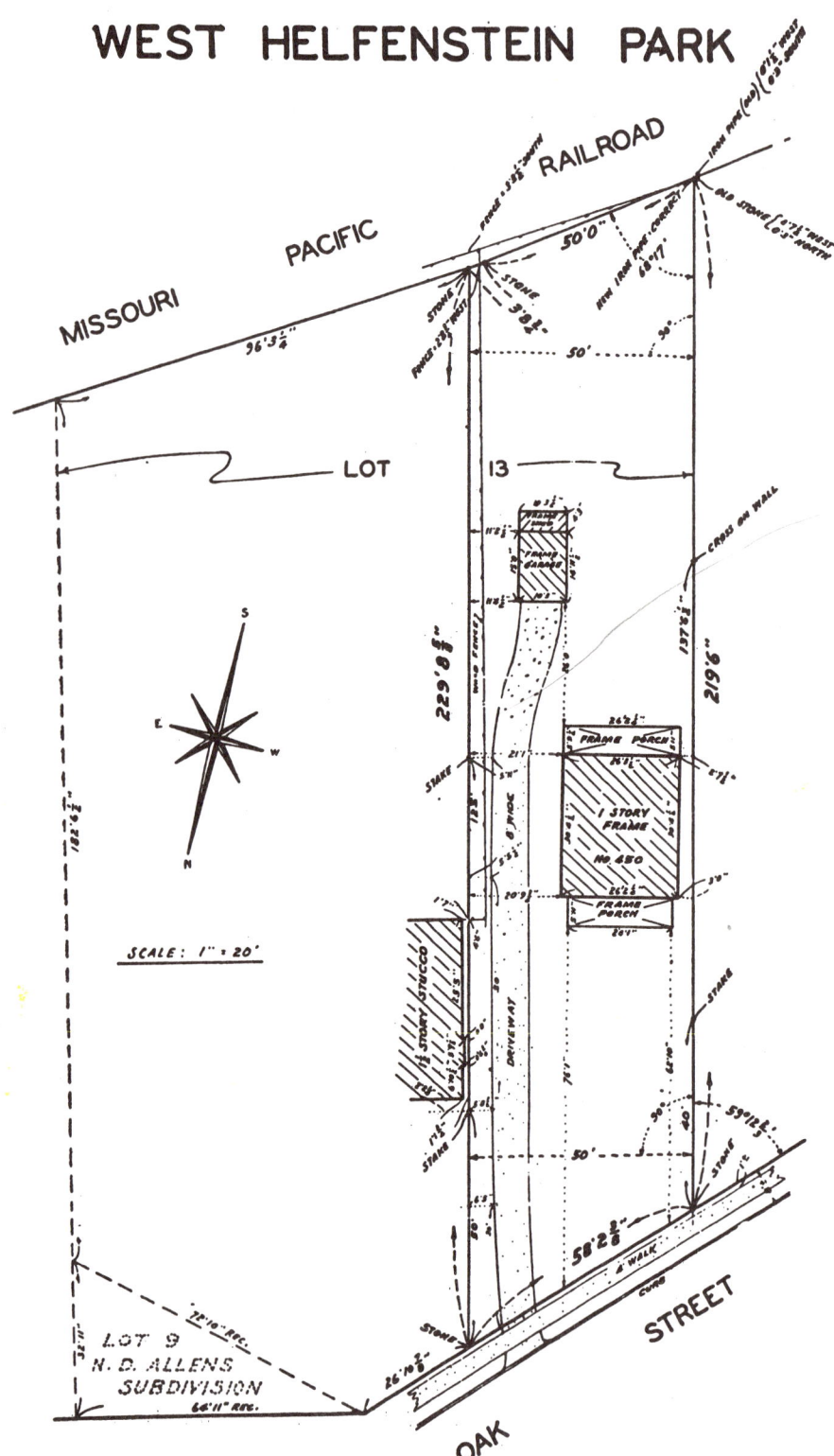

It is seen that Lot 13 extends generally north and south. It is bounded on the north by Oak Street (except that a small triangular lot from another subdivision cuts off its frontage thereon at the northeast corner). On the south it is bounded by the Missouri Pacific Railroad right of way. Both Oak Street and the railroad right of way extend in a general northeast-southwest direction, but at differing angles.

Joyce testified: The plat was a "survey of the West 50 feet of Lot 13 of West Helfenstein Park". In making the survey the west boundary line of Lot 13 was first established. Lines 50 feet in length (one near the north end and one near the south end of the lot, as shown by the plat) were run eastwardly at right angles to the west line of the lot, and then a line was run parallel to the west line and 50 feet, as above measured, from it, intersecting both the north and south boundaries of the lot. This line, which represented 50 feet in width of Lot 13, made a frontage of 58 feet, $2^3/_8$ inches, on Oak Street, and 53 feet, $8^3/_4$ inches, on the railroad right of way. The line, as thus measured, comes within 1 foot, $1^3/_4$ inches, of the west front corner of the stucco house (446 Oak Street), within 1 foot, 7 inches, of the west rear corner thereof, and within less than 1 foot of a chimney in the west wall.

The trial court refused to permit the witness to testify, but counsel for plaintiff offered to prove that, if permitted, witness would testify that the methods used by him in making the survey were in accordance with the practices and procedures followed in his profession in determining the boundaries of lots such as was described in the deed. The witness further testified that the method used by him was the only method by which a lot such as that described in the deeds in question could be measured having precisely and uniformly a width of 50 feet; and that a 50 foot strip is a strip with a uniform width of 50 feet.

Defendants also introduced in evidence a plat of Lot 13. It was prepared by Elbring Surveying Company for use in this litigation. August Elbring, a practicing surveyor and engineer for 34 years, testified in behalf of defendants: "In view of the fact that the deed (to the west 50 feet of Lot 13) made reference to the western 50 feet, and in view of the fact that the line which would have been established construing the dimension to be 50 feet at right angles, coming within a foot or so of an existing building (the stucco house), we felt that the line was intended to have been placed using the frontage of 50 feet on Oak Street and thence running the line (southward) parallel to the western line of Lot 13." The line so run, as being the east line of plaintiff's tract, was 8.01 feet west of the northwest corner of the stucco house and 8.32 feet west of its southwest corner. The Elbring plat does not show the actual width of plaintiff's tract as thus measured. But, concededly, there is no point on it where it approximates

50 feet in width; and, while it "fronts" 50 feet on Oak Street, its actual width is between 42 and 43 feet.

Both plats show a concrete driveway 8 feet in width extending from Oak Street to plaintiff's garage in the rear of her home, which, the testimony shows, was built by one of plaintiff's predecessors in title. The east line of plaintiff's tract, as measured by the Joyce (plaintiff's) survey, lies 6 or 7 feet east of the eastern edge of this driveway. Admittedly, the driveway is upon and an appurtenance of plaintiff's property. On the Elbring (defendants') plat, the east line of plaintiff's lot, as measured by Elbring, is shown to coincide with the east side of the driveway at Oak Street and to encroach upon it 1.25 feet for a distance of 30 or more feet as it extends between the houses. Thus, the area in dispute is essentially the area between the east edge of the driveway and the line fixed by the Joyce survey as the eastern line of plaintiff's tract.

Plaintiff adduced testimony to the effect that she and several of her predecessors in title had asserted claim to and had exercised physical dominion and control over all of the 50 feet in width of Lot 13, which included the concrete driveway and 6 or 7 feet to the east thereof. Defendants adduced testimony to the effect that they and their predecessors in title had asserted claim to and had exercised physical dominion and control over all of Lot 13 east of the driveway. The view we take of this case makes it unnecessary to set forth this testimony in detail.

The description under which plaintiff claims title, to wit: "The West 50 feet of Lot 13 . . . .", is on its face clear and free of ambiguity. It purports to convey a strip of land 50 feet in width off the west side of Lot 13. So clear is the meaning of the above language that defendants do not challenge it and it has been difficult to find any case wherein the meaning of a similar description has been questioned.

The law is clear that when there is no inconsistency on the face of a deed and, on application of the description to the ground, no inconsistency appears, parol evidence is not admissible to show that the parties intended to convey either more or less or different ground from that described. But where there are conflicting calls in a deed, or the description may be made to apply to two or more parcels, and there is nothing in the deed to show which is meant, then parol evidence is admissible to show the true meaning of the words used. "The office of extrinsic evidence as applied to the description of a parcel is to explain the latent ambiguity or to point out the property described on the ground. *Such evidence must not contradict the deed, or make a description of other land than that described in the deed.*" (Emphasis ours.) Thompson on Real Property, Vol. 6 § 3287, p. 468.

No ambiguity or confusion arises when the description here in question is applied to Lot 13. The description, when applied to the ground, fits the land claimed by plaintiff and cannot be made to apply to any other tract. When the deed was made, Lot 13 was vacant land except for the frame dwelling at 450 Oak Street. The stucco house (446 Oak Street) was not built until the following year. Under no conceivable theory can the fact that defendants' predecessors in title (Mr. and Mrs. Wolf) thereafter built the stucco house within a few feet of the east line of the property described in the deed be construed as competent evidence of any ambiguity in the description. Neither could the fact, if it be a fact, that the Wolfs and their successors in title claimed title to and exercised dominion and control over a portion of the tract be construed as creating or revealing an ambiguity in the description.

Whether the above testimony and other testimony in the record constitute evidence of a mistake in the deed we do not here determine. Defendants have not sought reformation, and yet that is what the decree herein rendered undertakes to do. It seems apparent that the trial court considered the testimony and came to the conclusion that the parties to the deed did not intend a conveyance of the "West 50 feet of Lot 13", but rather a tract fronting 50 feet on Oak Street. And, the decree, on the theory of interpreting an ambiguity, undertakes to change (reform) the description so as to describe a lot approximately 42 feet in width instead of a lot 50 feet in width, as originally described. That, we are convinced, the courts cannot do.

The judgment is reversed and the cause remanded for further proceedings not inconsistent with the views expressed.

All concur.

NOTES

1. *Ambiguous Descriptions in Deeds.* Traditionally, for a deed to be valid it had to describe the parcel conveyed to the exclusion of all other parcels in the world. Contemporary courts have relaxed this requirement somewhat by resorting to parol evidence—oral statements, extrinsic writings, the physical condition of the land and improvements—in order to cure omissions or ambiguities within the deed's four corners.

Colman v. Butkovich, 556 P.2d 503, 504–505 (Utah 1976), typifies the modern trend. In an action to quiet title, the question arose whether a deed description—"All unplatted land in this Block (29 P.C.) and all land West of this Blk: and Pt. Lot 1: Pt. Lot A"—was sufficient. Upholding the deed, the court observed:

> It is not to be questioned that in order to be valid, a deed must contain a sufficiently definite description to identify the property it conveys . . . . The problem lies in ascertaining the intent with which it was executed. It should be resolved, if possible, by looking to the terms of the instrument itself and any reasonable inferences to be drawn therefrom; and if there then remains any

uncertainty or ambiguity, it can be aided by extrinsic evidence. If from that process the property can be identified with reasonable certainty, the deed is not invalid for uncertainty.

Doubtless the main reason courts are so reluctant to invalidate deeds like the one in *Colman* is that the grantor, although she may have been less than clear in describing the parcel conveyed, has been crystal clear in expressing an intent to convey *something* to the grantee; if parol evidence will resolve the ambiguity and make the deed enforceable, it should be admitted.

Which will better serve an efficient conveyancing system: a rule that validates the deed by focusing on buyer's and seller's actual intent or one that invalidates the deed if that intent has not been expressed clearly in the written instrument? Is the threat of invalidation likely to spur buyers and sellers to draft clear descriptions? For some thoughtful reflections along these lines, see Note, The Use of Extrinsic Evidence to Interpret Real Property Conveyances: A Suggested Limitation, 65 Cal.L.Rev. 897 (1977).

For background on property description and surveys generally, see, in addition to the works excerpted above, J. Grimes, A Treatise on the Law of Surveying and Boundaries (4th ed.1976); 1 R. Patton & C. Patton, Land Titles (2d ed.1957); Keith, Government Land Surveys and Related Problems, 38 Iowa L.Rev. 86 (1952); Boyd & Uelmen, Resurveys and Metes and Bounds Descriptions, 1953 Wis.L.Rev. 657.

2. *Construing Deed Descriptions.* Ambiguity, even though not fatal to a real property deed, must still be cured if the deed is to be given force as between two or more neighbors, each of whom claims that the ambiguity should be resolved in favor of enlarging his parcel. Although parol evidence can help to resolve ambiguity, it will not always be available or, when available, dispositive. Thus, courts construing ambiguous or conflicting descriptions will often resort to any one or more of several canons of construction.

Some of these canons can be quite helpful in divining the seller's and buyer's intent. One canon states that, in case of a conflict between the various indicators and measures used in a description, "monuments control distances and courses; courses control distances; and quantity is the least reliable guide of all." The canon presumably corresponds with the expectations of seller and buyer: "most monuments would be difficult to mistake so they are probably identified correctly. A course, 'northerly at a 90° angle' is more certain than a distance 'thence 80 ft.,' since most people cannot measure distances with any degree of accuracy with the naked eye." Distance is also subject to the hazards of uneven terrain. J. Cribbet, Principles of the Law of Property 169–171 (2d ed.1975).

Another helpful canon is that, when "a tract of land is bounded by a monument which has width, such as a highway or a stream, the boundary line extends to the center, provided the grantor owns that far." Again, the canon presumably reflects the parties' original expectations—in this case, that the grantee would receive the grantor's entire interest in the parcel. To mark the boundary at the near edge of the highway or stream would mean that if the highway is later abandoned, or the stream diverted, the grantor would have title to the strip between the edge and the center. *Id.*

As Professor Cribbet acknowledges, however, other canons are simply conclusional, explaining rather than predicting results. Among these are, "extrinsic evidence will be allowed to explain a latent ambiguity but a patent ambiguity must be resolved within the four corners of the deed." (What is patent? What is latent?) "Useless or contradictory words may be disregarded as mere surplusage." (Which of two conflicting words is "useless"? Which of two antithetical terms is "contradictory"?) And, "particular descriptions control over general descriptions, although a false particular may be disregarded to give effect to a true general description." (?!?) See also, Note, Operation and Construction of Deeds, 6 St. Mary's L.J. 806 (1975).

Do you agree with the court's construction of the deed in Walters v. Tucker?

3. **Increasingly, surveyors are being held to account for their errors.** Breach of contract, the traditional ground for recovery on a faulty survey or description, has now been joined by the tort of negligent misrepresentation. Because it is a tort, and has no privity requirement, negligent misrepresentation can give relief to distant purchasers as well as to the buyer or developer who first contracted with the surveyor. Liability is also being extended by the "discovery" rule under which the statute of limitations for negligent misrepresentation does not begin to run until the misrepresentation has been, or should have been, discovered.

Rozny v. Marnul, 43 Ill.2d 54, 250 N.E.2d 656 (1969), reflects the modern trend. Defendant had prepared an inaccurate parcel survey for a builder. A legend appearing on the face of the survey stated that the "survey carries our absolute guarantee for accuracy." Plaintiffs, who bought the parcel from the builder, sought damages when they discovered that, relying on markers placed in accordance with the faulty survey, they had constructed improvements that encroached on an adjacent lot. Holding for plaintiffs, the Illinois Supreme Court reversed the appellate court's decision that plaintiffs' action was barred for lack of contractual privity. The Supreme Court chose instead to follow the warranty theory adopted in the Restatement of Torts, Second § 402B (1965): "The Restatement uses the language of misrepresentation to make it clear that the basis of liability is tort and expressly states that the privity of contract requirement is not applicable."

The court rejected the claim that its ruling would expose surveyors to unlimited liability. First, since defendant "admitted he knew the plats were customarily used by lending agencies and others," he could have reasonably foreseen that the plat would be "relied on to his damage by a third party [plaintiffs] in connection with the financing and purchase of the surveyed property." Second, the situation is "not one fraught with such an overwhelming potential liability as to dictate a contrary result, for the class of persons who might foreseeably use this plat is rather narrowly limited, if not exclusively so, to those who deal with the surveyed property as purchasers or lenders. Injury will ordinarily occur only once and to the one person then owning the lot." 43 Ill.2d at 66, 250 N.E.2d at 662.

Finally, the court rejected defendant's contention that the five year statute of limitations period began to run when the plat was delivered to the builder who ordered it or, at the latest, from the time the plaintiffs relied on the guarantee. Instead, the court held that the statute of limitations should not begin to run until the misrepresentation had been, or should have been, discovered: "Where the passage of time does little to increase the problems of proof, the ends of justice are served by permitting plaintiff to sue within the statutory period computed from the time at which he knew or should have known of the existence of the right to sue." 43 Ill.2d at 70, 250 N.E.2d at 664.

c. DELIVERY

SHROYER v. SHROYER

Supreme Court of Missouri, 1968.
425 S.W.2d 214.

HOUSER, Commissioner.

Bill in equity to cancel a warranty deed on the ground of nondelivery and for an accounting of royalties received from the operation of a stone quarry on the land, an 80-acre farm in Mercer County. Plaintiff is Jessie Shroyer, mother of the defendants J. Wesley and Wayne Shroyer. The trial chancellor cancelled the deed and ordered the grantees to pay $1,392.82 in royalties. Defendants appealed.

The common source of title is Jennie Peters, a widow, who acquired the farm by deed in 1935. Jennie's brother, Virgil Shroyer, helped her run the farm for many years, until his death in July, 1960. At the time of Virgil's death Jennie's family consisted of her brother George Shroyer and his wife Beulah, Virgil's widow (Jessie Shroyer, plaintiff herein), and Jessie's five daughters and two sons (Wayne and Wesley, defendants herein). On October 15, 1960 Jennie made and executed a will, properly witnessed, leaving the 80-acre farm to Virgil's widow, Jessie Shroyer, reciting that Virgil had kept up the farm for 30 years and that Jessie, his wife, "has been more than a sister to me in that time and all without compensation of any kind." (At that time Jessie owned or had an interest in farms totalling 663 acres, and a house in Mercer, subject to a mortgage of between $10,000 and $11,000, facts of which Jennie was aware.)

Jennie Peters was a strong-willed woman with a mind of her own. "You just didn't tell her what to do." She was generous with her relatives and from time to time made gifts to or paid bills for them. She gave one of her nieces $500 when the niece's husband died. She gave Wesley Shroyer $240 to pay for new dentures. She was "in the habit of making up deeds" and would dispose of her property, change her mind and make another disposition of her property, then change her mind again. In the six years before her death she made three different dispositions of her property. Jennie preferred secrecy about her property affairs and wanted to keep peace in the family. After executing the will dated October 15, 1960 Jennie turned it over to her niece Betty Daily with the request that Betty put it in her bank box and "not ever say anything about it." Jennie said she thought it would "keep down trouble in the family" if nobody knew about it. The will remained in Betty's safety deposit box in Peoples Bank of Mercer until Jennie died. After giving Betty possession of the will Jennie did not thereafter discuss the will with Betty, or request of Betty that she return the will or destroy it. After Virgil's death Wayne and Wesley would come out to Jennie's farm about once a week. They would chop ice and perform other chores, such as throwing hay down for the cattle, cleaning out the barn, repairing fences, etc.

Robert and Rachel Jones were close neighbors with whom Jennie had almost daily discussions about her business. For a period of 3 or 4 months prior to December 1, 1964 Jennie discussed with the Joneses the deeding of the 80-acre farm to Wayne and Wesley Shroyer. She stated that she wanted to deed the property to them; that "she wanted Wayne and Wesley to have the farm and that was her intentions." Jennie told the Joneses during this period that Betty Daily (sister of Wesley and Wayne) had asked Jennie to deed the farm to her since she (Betty) was the one who was taking care of her mother Jessie, but that Jennie had refused to do so. Robert Jones suggested that Jennie get a lawyer to prepare the deed but she wanted him to prepare it, so finally he "gave up" and he and his wife prepared the deed. Jennie made it known to Jones that the purpose of preparing the deed was "to pass title before she died so it wouldn't be probated as a part of her estate." Jones explained that Jennie was "a saving sort of person" and that she did not want too much property to "go through Probate Court." When asked whether she had any other papers "out" Jennie answered that all of her papers had been brought back to her and "everything was destroyed"—that there was no will or "anything else of that matter"; that her wills "had been destroyed" and "there is no other." In their discussions Jennie stated that she wanted to make sure that the farm stayed with one or the other of the boys; that if either wanted to sell, the other should have first chance to buy. The deed was drawn to make such a provision.

{ She did not want it known that she was deeding the farm to the boys. She wanted "to keep it quiet," and said "I just don't want trouble, Bob, in the family." She felt that the others in the family would be disturbed if they knew that she intended Wesley and Wayne to have the farm. The deed to Wesley and Wayne bears date December 1, 1964. It was notarized on December 8, 1964. Wayne Shroyer told the notary public that Jennie wanted her to come out to notarize some papers. The notary refused to drive out to the farm because of bad weather conditions. Wayne then offered to drive her out and bring her back, to which she consented. When the notary first saw the paper to be notarized it was lying on a table in the kitchen. Jennie asked the notary if she would notarize her signature "on that." The notary surmised that it was a warranty deed. Jennie folded it so that the notary could not see whose names were on the deed. Jennie did not identify the grantee. The notary considered that Jennie knew what she was doing but that for some reason Jennie wanted to keep the name of the grantee to herself. Only Jennie and the notary were in the room when the paper was notarized. Wayne was in another part of the house. The deed was not handed to Wayne in the notary's presence. It was lying on the table when the notary left.

[margin: notarization]

{ Afterward Jennie told the Joneses that she had signed the deed; that she had conveyed the farm to Wayne and Wesley and that they were the owners; that "it belonged to the boys"; that she had consulted with them about selling the farm; that she did not want them to ever sell the farm and told them that "if it were she, she would not sell." In the weeks and months that followed and up until the time of her death Jennie "conveyed the attitude" to the Joneses "that the boys were the owners of the farm."

[margin: Strong proof]

George Shroyer testified that about six months before Jennie's death he had a conversation with her at her home in which she told him that she had deeded the farm to Wayne and Wesley, and that "she told Wayne to take that deed and read it and he took it . . ."; that she "actually gave" the deed to Wayne and "told him it was his, but she wanted to keep it in her possession until she died"; that "she was going to keep the deed until she died"—"she was going to keep it in a safe place." When asked whether she told him why she didn't want Wayne to take the deed and put it of record he testified, "She wanted to keep it in the safety—to save any more trouble." Jennie did not say whether she might want to change the deed again. With reference to the will he testified that Jennie told him she had given Betty a will to keep; that the will was put in a bank box and kept for some time and that the will was outstanding, but "it was to be destroyed." She did not tell George that she had asked for the return of the will or had taken any steps on her own to see that the will was destroyed. Neither Wesley nor Wayne ever said anything to George Shroyer to indicate that they were making claim to the land.

[margin: testimony for Δ]

Mrs. Shroyer testified that Jennie told her that she had made the deed to Wesley and Wayne; that it was her intention that Wesley and Wayne have the farm; that she (Jennie) considered that the boys were owners of the farm, and that she did not want them to sell it; that Jennie told her that the previous will to Jessie Shroyer had been destroyed. Mrs. Shroyer also testified that Jennie said that Betty "was supposed to see that it was destroyed"; and that Jennie told her and George at the hospital that she was not going to live and that she wondered what the others would say when the deed was presented.

The lessee who quarried rock on the farm heard that Jennie had deeded all of her property to Wayne Shroyer. Concerned about his lease, he went to Jennie in July, 1966 and asked whether the land had been deeded to Wayne. She said "yes" but assured him that the deed was made after the lease and that she had "included the lease" in the deed. Jennie continued to live on the 80-acre farm and to collect royalties from the rock quarry until her death. She kept and retained the money for herself.

On July 5, 1966 Jennie wrote an unwitnessed and therefore ineffective "will" in her own handwriting, stating that she wanted to make known her wishes as to the disposal of her home and belongings. She recited that she had been alone, without financial help; that Virgil had always seen to it that she was comfortable; that since his passing his family had been wonderful to her; that his boys Wesley and Wayne "have been so helpful & still think of me first. To them I have deeded my home of 80 acres. Not much for all they have done for me But it is my life's work having lived here alone for 30 years. They shall have a good deed to farm subject to a lease contract with Stark & Cole Inc. for the production of road rock & lime for which I get .06¢ per ton for all material sold This contract along with deed being part and parcel of farm shall go with the deed to Wesley & Wayne My royalty of .06¢ per ton shall be used until all my obligations are taken care of same consisting of a nice funeral Noel Moss put my brother away beautifully I should like the same . . . . My heartfelt wish is that my estate being small as it is shall not need court action of any kind I have asked Bob Jones and Rachel to just take over when I pass on he said he would but without pay But I would prefer pay—and generous as they have been so helpful to me in those last years." Following her signature there were a number of specific bequests. She made this further statement:

"To Robert and Rachel Jones as Administrators

"My royalty payments check shall be deposited in the Peoples bank for my use until all accounts are settled when the deed to farm and lease contract including royalty payments (same being part and parcel of farm) shall be turned over to owners of farm Wesley and Wayne Shroyer. At my passing Robert Jones shall have full charge such as paying claims and distribution of funds he shall sign all papers and none shall be honored without the Peoples Bank O K"

After this statement she named those to whom should be given her father's picture; her bed; steer calf; reclining chair; range, big mirror, red rug, etc.

Jennie died in a hospital October 3, 1966. Two or three weeks before her death, just before going to the hospital for her final illness, Jennie obtained her "papers" from a bank box. At Jennie's instance the Joneses bought a metal strongbox for Jennie. Jennie put her papers in it and handed the box to Robert Jones, asking him to keep it while she was in the hospital. Jones refused to take the key to the strongbox, preferring not to have access to the box. Jennie did not give Jones instructions as to what to do with the metal box other than to keep it—she did not instruct him to deliver it to anyone else. Specifically, she did not tell the Joneses to give the deed to defendants in case she died. Jones would have redelivered the box to Jennie at her request. The box stayed in the possession of the Joneses at their house until Jennie's death and was not opened by them. After Jennie's death the Joneses took the locked box to the probate office at Princeton.

On the night of Jennie's death Wesley Shroyer stated that he did not know anything about the Jennie Peters estate; that he did not know anything about a deed. Asked later if he knew anything about Jennie's business Wesley stated that he didn't know anything about it.

After Jennie's death Betty Daily took Jennie's will dated October 15, 1960 out of her bank box and turned it over to Wesley Shroyer. Wesley said nothing to Betty about a deed, made no claim that the land had been deeded to his brother and him, and promised that he would take the will to the probate court the next morning. When the family assembled at the probate court the probate judge said there was no valid will. Betty got up and said there was a valid will and that it was in Wesley's possession. Wesley "reluctantly" produced the will and handed it to the probate judge. At that time neither Wesley nor Wayne Shroyer made any mention of a deed conveying the property to them. At a second meeting Wesley and Wayne, who were designated as "administrators" in the will of October 15, 1960, qualified as co-executors. A search was made at Jennie's home for the keys to the box. Mrs. Jones found the keys in a vase on Jennie's dresser. Wayne and Wesley opened the metal strongbox at the time of the making of the inventory, took out the deed of December 1, 1964 and had it filed for record on October 15, 1966. Later they went to Jessie and told her that there was a deed in the box made out to them, "so, therefore, the farm was theirs." The box and contents, including "General Warranty Deed," were listed in the estate inventory and appraisement. . . .

The only question is whether there was a delivery of the deed. The controlling element in determining this question, a mixed question of law and fact, is the intention of the parties, particularly the intention of the grantor. The vital inquiry with respect to the grantor is whether she intended a complete transfer; whether she parted with dominion over the instrument with the intention of relinquishing all dominion and control over the conveyance and of making it presently effective and operative as a conveyance of the title to the land. It is not necessary, in order to constitute a delivery of a deed, that the instrument actually be handed over to the grantee, or to another person for the grantee. There may be a delivery notwithstanding the deed remains in the custody of the grantor. A valid delivery once having taken place is not rendered ineffectual by the act of the grantee in giving the deed into the custody of the grantor for safekeeping. It is all a question of the intention of the parties, which may be manifested by words or acts or both.

The burden of proof of nondelivery of a deed is upon the party who seeks to invalidate the conveyance on the ground of nondelivery. In this case plaintiff, Jessie Shroyer, has the burden of proof of nondelivery.

Appellants-grantees claim the benefit of a presumption of delivery arising out of the fact that the deed was acknowledged, under § 490.410, RSMo 1959, V.A.M.S. and cases holding that under the statute the certificate of acknowledgment takes the place of proof that the deed was signed and delivered, and is prima facie evidence that the deed was duly executed, i.e., that it was signed and delivered. There is no such presumption in this case. "If there were nothing shown but the deed, duly acknowledged, and the fact that it was recorded and in possession of the defendant, the rule would settle the case in defendant's favor; but the plaintiff showed at the outset that the deed was not in possession of the defendants at the death of the grantor, but in possession of the grantor and placed among his other papers." Harrison v. Edmonston, Mo.Sup., 248 S.W. 586, 588. This deed was not recorded at the time of the grantor's death. The circumstances that the instrument was not recorded and was in the grantor's possession at the time of her death, unless explained, are deemed "conclusive that the parties did not intend a complete transfer." Phillips v. Phillips, 50 Mo. 603, 606.

Appellants further claim a presumption of delivery from their showing that the deed was in the possession of the grantees. Such a presumption arises where there is an unequivocal showing that grantee was given possession of the deed. The showing is equivocal in this case, for here the evidence indicates that grantor handed it to one of the two grantees momentarily, for the purpose of reading it, and that at grantor's direction it was immediately taken back into grantor's possession, to be kept by her until her death. A presumption of delivery does not arise under these circumstances.

On the contrary, there is a presumption in this case in favor of respondent, not appellants. There is a presumption of *nondelivery*, in view of the conceded fact that the deed was in grantor's possession at the time of her death and that the deed was not then recorded. "By the introduction of testimony substantially tending to show that the deed was in the grantor's possession, in his safety deposit box, at the time of his death, the plaintiffs made a prima facie case; for, if unrecorded and in the grantor's possession, the nondelivery of the deed is presumed." 26 C.J.S. Deeds § 184.

This showing placed upon grantees, defendants Wesley and Wayne Shroyer, the burden of going forward with the evidence to rebut plaintiff's prima facie case. To sustain this burden defendants introduced George and Beulah Shroyer's testimony.

In reviewing the evidence in this case we are conscious of the fact that the determination of delivery *vel non* depends to a large extent upon the credibility of George and Beulah Shroyer and the interpretation of their testimony. In weighing their testimony as well as all of the rest of the testimony in the case, and in making our own independent findings, we are aided and assisted by the findings and judgment of the chancellor, who heard and observed the demeanor of the witnesses and was in by far the best position to judge of their credibility and reliability. So armed and informed, and with due deference to the chancellor's findings, it is our conclusion that grantees-defendants Wesley and Wayne Shroyer have not met and sustained the burden of rebutting plaintiff's prima facie case of nondelivery.

We find that Jennie, under the false impression that her will of October 15, 1960 had been destroyed, made a warranty deed on December 1, 1964 and executed it one week later, by which she intended and undertook to convey her 80-acre homeplace to her nephews Wesley and Wayne Shroyer, but that she did not deliver, or intend to deliver, the deed to Wayne with the intention of relinquishing all dominion and control over the conveyance or of transferring title to Wesley and Wayne *in praesenti*; that in December, 1964 she wanted her nephews to eventually become the owners of the farm; that her attempts to effect such a transfer of title by the deed in question were ineffective for lack of delivery; that the deed never became operative and was properly cancelled and set aside by the chancellor and defendants properly called to account for the royalties received from the operation of the rock quarry. We are impelled to these findings by all of the evidence considered in its totality, being especially persuaded by the following facts: The deed did not reserve a life estate to Jennie. Such a reservation would have raised a strong presumption that she intended that title should immediatley vest in the grantees. Grantor retained possession of the deed until the date of her death. Grantees had no access to and no permission from grantor to take possession of the deed. It was found in her strongbox, which she had placed in the temporary custody of her trusted friends and neighbors, Robert and Rachel Jones. Grantor retained the keys and had the right to call for the return of the strongbox and its contents, including the deed in question, at any time. Grantor did not place the deed in the possession of her banker, the notary, the Joneses, her brother George (in whom she confided in business matters), or anyone else, with directions to deliver the deed to the grantees. Grantor had a penchant for changing her mind about the disposition of her property, and frequently did so. Nondelivery would make it possible for her to destroy the deed and otherwise dispose of the farm if she later decided to do so. The secrecy employed in the transaction is consistent with nondelivery and retention of control over the deed. Nondelivery would make it less likely that the transaction would come to the attention of the other members of the family than delivery. When the deed was found, after grantor's death, it had not been recorded. Grantor's retention of the unrecorded deed, in a place under her control, was consistent with her previous history of change in the disposition of her property. The significance grantor's manual handing of the deed to Wayne (if this actually happened) might otherwise have had is overcome by the fact that the deed was never recorded. The failure to record is consistent with the conclusion that grantor did not intend to pass to the grantees any present title, and no title at all until her death.

George Shroyer's testimony that Jennie told him that she handed the deed to Wayne is not conclusive that delivery was intended. What Jennie is supposed to have said at the time is not necessarily indicative of that intent but is subject to the interpretation that she was merely exhibiting the deed to Wayne to inform him of the fact that she intended the boys to have the farm at her death and to permit him to read the instrument, but that she was reserving control over the deed. It is a reasonable inference that if she handed the deed to Wayne it was ". . . merely for temporary convenience at the time, and [her] continued possession of the instrument afterwards indicated an intention to retain control of it." Harrison v. Edmonston, Mo.Sup., 248 S.W. 586, 588.

That she intended to retain control over the farm is confirmed by her subsequent exercise of acts of ownership over the farm, continuing to live there and operate it, and receiving and keeping the royalty payments for her own use and benefit. The fact that defendants were not placed in possession of the farm is yet another indication that Jennie did not intend to pass title presently.

George Shroyer's testimony relative to Jennie's exhibition of the deed to Wayne, and the theory of delivery, is detracted from by the testimony suggesting that neither Wesley nor Wayne, prior to Jennie's death, seemed to know anything about Jennie's estate or of the existence of a deed, and that after Jennie's death, when the family gathered at the probate office for the reading of the will, Wesley and

Wayne did not speak up, or claim the property by virtue of a deed, or suggest the existence of a deed from Jennie to them.

In addition to the foregoing reasons, the conclusion that the deed was not delivered at the time it was executed and acknowledged is buttressed by the writing of July 5, 1966 (some 19 months after the deed was executed) in which Jennie by a purported will in her own handwriting plainly demonstrated that she did not consider that the deed had been delivered so as to pass title in December, 1964. Although she recited that she *had deeded* her home of 80 acres to the boys, and gave her reasons, the wording used strongly indicates her intention that they were to take in the future. The boys *"shall* have a good deed to the farm." The rock contract *"shall* go with the deed to Wesley and Wayne." The royalties were to be used to pay her funeral expenses and other obligations (still retaining control over the proceeds of the quarry) and *after all accounts are settled* the deed and lease *"shall* be turned over to the owners of the farm Wesley and Wayne Shroyer." (Our emphasis.) This is not the language of a grantor who considered that she had previously transferred and relinquished all right, title and interest in a farm, by making and delivering a deed to the grantees. This "voice from the grave," so to speak, weighs heavily in our determination that Jennie did not deliver the deed, and that as late as approximately three months prior to her death Jennie did not consider that she had already delivered the deed and given up the property to her intended beneficiaries, but rather considered it yet necessary to make a will providing for the postmortem delivery of the deed.

The judgment is affirmed.

WELBORN and HIGGINS, CC., concur.

PER CURIAM:

The foregoing opinion by HOUSER, C., is adopted as the opinion of the court.

All of the Judges concur.

FERGUSON v. CASPAR

District of Columbia Court of Appeals, 1976.
359 A.2d 17.

REILLY, Chief Judge:

One of the most formal transactions known to the law is the transfer of title to real estate. In order to insure finality to such transactions, the practice in this jurisdiction is for the contracting parties, including the lienors and lienees, after they are satisfied with the report on title search, to meet with one another in the office of a title company, agree on the apportionment of outstanding taxes and other charges, and execute and deliver the conveyances (deeds) necessary to close the transaction. Such a meeting, popularly called a "closing" or a "settlement", precedes the transmission by the title company of the conveyancing instruments to the Recorder of Deeds for permanent entry into the official land records.

Although hundreds of such settlements occur every year in the District of Columbia, it is seldom indeed that the parties conduct themselves in such a way as to taint the finality of the "closing." The case before us stems from one of these uncommon situations and raises the question as to what point in a settlement proceeding finality attaches.

This is an appeal from a judgment and order of the trial court dismissing an amended complaint and granting judgment in favor of the appellees after trial by the court without a jury in an action brought by the contracting purchasers—appellants—for a declaratory judgment and for specific performance of a contract for the sale of real property in this city. To bring the issues in this controversy into perspective, a brief resume of the salient facts is in order.

Appellee Mrs. Ida Caspar was the owner of an unrestored row house in the Capitol Hill area. On November 18, 1972, she entered into a contract for the sale of the premises to the appellants for the sum of $23,000.00, payment of the purchase price to be made in cash at the time of settlement. Settlement was to be made at the office of the Lawyers Title Insurance Corporation on or before February 1, 1973. The contract of sale included a provision that the seller would convey the premises free of all notices of municipal violations existing at the date of the contract, such provision to survive the delivery of the deed.[2] On October 13, 1972, Mrs. Caspar had been personally served with a deficiency notice by a District of Columbia housing inspector informing her that there existed 126 Housing Code violations upon the premises and calling for their correction within 60 days. Subsequently, Mrs. Caspar, upon her written request, obtained an extension of time for compliance to January 25, 1973.

Early in January, 1973, the appellants became aware of the existence of the Housing Code violations but did not bring this matter to the attention of the seller. Instead, they obtained an estimate of $6,125.00 from a housing contractor as the cost of correcting the deficiencies. The notice of violations was still outstanding at the time of settlement.

By agreement, the parties met at the office of the Lawyers Title Insurance Corporation for settlement on the afternoon of February 1, 1973. Mrs. Caspar was attended by her son and daughter who assisted their mother in business matters. The appellants were present

---

2. The printed clause in the contract provided:

All notices of violations of Municipal orders or requirements noted or issued by any department of the District of Columbia, or prosecutions in any of the courts of the District of Columbia on account thereof against or affecting the property at the date of this contract shall be complied with by the seller and the property conveyed free thereof. This provision shall survive the delivery of the deed hereunder.

with their attorney. The settlement officer, an employee of the title company, prepared settlement statements for the respective parties which each of them signed. In addition, the parties signed the requisite District of Columbia tax recordation forms. Mrs. Caspar executed and delivered her deed to the property to the settlement officer. The purchasers delivered to the settlement officer the personal check of Mr. Ferguson in the sum of $12,924.42 payable to the order of the title company, representing the balance due as set forth in the settlement statement.

After the documents had been delivered to the settlement officer and as the parties were rising to leave, the attorney for the appellants handed separate letters to the settlement officer and to Mrs. Caspar's son. The letter addressed to the title company, after referring to the clause in the contract of sale requiring Mrs. Caspar to convey the premises free of any municipal violation notices, advised the title company that as of January 26, 1973, the outstanding Housing Code violations had not been corrected and that the purchasers had obtained an estimate in the amount of $6,125.00 to bring the premises into compliance. The letter concluded by stating:

> This is to put you on notice that purchasers are paying $6,125.00 of the purchase price to you as escrow agent to hold until seller has complied with the outstanding violation notices on this property. Written notice signed by the purchaser shall be sufficient to discharge you from any further obligations with respect to this sum.

The letter directed to Mrs. Caspar informed her of the existence of the notice of the Housing Code violations and her obligation under the agreement to comply with the notice. It went on to state that the Fergusons had obtained an estimate of approximately $6,125.00 as the cost of repairing the premises and concluded as follows:

> This is to advise you that Fergusons intend to enforce the requirement that these violations be corrected. Accordingly, I have written Lawyers Title requesting that they withhold the above amount from the purchase price in an escrow account until you and the Fergusons have reached a final understanding as to the cost of making these corrections.

Upon receiving the letter directed to the title company, the settlement officer advised the parties that the company could not record the deed or withhold any funds without formal authority to hold any funds in escrow. He informed the parties that he could not proceed with the settlement since the contract of sale provided for payment in cash and there was no provision for withholding any funds in escrow. Mrs. Caspar's son suggested that the parties complete the settlement, have the deed recorded, and thereafter "work out or litigate" the question of the Housing Code violations. The attorney for the appellants recommended that Mrs. Caspar seek the advice of an attorney. The parties then dispersed without the matter being resolved.

On February 13, 1973, not having received any further word or instructions from the parties, the settlement officer wrote to the Fergusons, returning the personal check which had been presented at the settlement and informing them that the deed could not be recorded in view of their attorney's letter directing the title company to withhold certain monies in escrow. Two days later, the Fergusons' attorney replied, returning the personal check to the settlement officer and insisting that the deed be recorded. This letter was received by the title company on February 16 and on the same day, the deed executed by Mrs. Caspar was returned to her son. On February 17, Mrs. Caspar signed a contract of sale for the premises to the appellees, John and Mary McAteer, and her deed to them was executed and recorded on February 23.

On February 21, 1973, appellants filed a complaint against Mrs. Caspar seeking a declaratory judgment and specific performance of the contract of sale entered into between the parties. Subsequently, the complaint was amended to include the McAteers as parties-defendant. In her answer to the amended complaint, Mrs. Caspar alleged *inter alia* that the appellants had breached the contract of sale and were not entitled to specific performance. The case was tried before the court without a jury. At the close of all the evidence, the court granted appellees' motion to dismiss the complaint on the ground that the plaintiffs, by imposing conditions on their tender of payment of the purchase price, had failed to make an unconditional tender of full performance of the contract on their part and had forfeited their right to specific performance. On June 15, 1973, the trial court entered its Judgment and Order of Dismissal setting forth its Findings of Fact and Conclusions of Law.

On this appeal, appellants' principal contentions are that legal title to the property in question passed to them upon the settlement between the seller and purchasers and that the trial court erred in concluding that the appellants were not entitled to specific performance of the contract of sale by reason of their failure to tender the full purchase price for the property as required by the contract. We agree with the determination of the trial court and affirm.

The initial contention of appellants is based upon the erroneous conclusion that legal title to the property in question passed to them when the settlement statements were signed by the respective parties, the seller's deed delivered to the settlement officer, and the personal check of the purchasers for the balance due delivered to the settlement officer. In this conclusion, appellants misconstrue the nature and effect of the settlement proceedings engaged in between the various parties at the meeting. In their briefs on appeal, the appellants and appellees both infer that under the circumstances of this case the title company's position in the transaction was that of an escrow agent. Our study of the contract of sale and the proceedings which ensued at the settlement meeting confirms our understanding that, as is the usual and customary practice in real estate transactions in the District of Columbia where the parties employ a third party to accept their respective tenders of performance under the contract, a valid escrow arrangement is created and the title company serves in the capacity of an escrow agent in the transaction.

Generally, an escrow agreement is created in a formal contract between the parties, setting forth the conditions and contingencies under which the instruments deposited in escrow are to be delivered and to take effect. However, no precise form of words is necessary to create an escrow but it must appear from all the facts and circumstances surrounding the execution and delivery of the instruments that they were not to take effect until certain conditions are performed.

A valid escrow agreement is a triangular arrangement. First there must be a contract between the seller and the buyer agreeing to the conditions of a deposit, then there must be delivery of the items on deposit to the escrow agent, and he must agree to perform the function of receiving and dispersing the items. The agreement by the seller and buyer to all the terms of the escrow instructions and the acceptance by the escrow agent of the position of depository create the escrow.

In the case at bar, the seller and the purchasers agreed to make full settlement in accordance with the terms of the contract of sale at the office of Lawyers Title Insurance Corporation, the title company searching the title, and that ". . . deposit with the Title Company . . . of the purchase money, the deed of conveyance for execution and such other papers as are required of either party by the terms of this contract shall be considered good and sufficient tender of performance of the terms hereof." Significantly, the deed executed by the seller was delivered to the settlement officer. The purchasers' personal check, which included the balance of the purchase price, was made payable to the title company and delivered to the settlement officer. The deed was deposited with the settlement officer as an escrow agent with the implied understanding that delivery to the purchasers was not to be effected until the purchasers had complied with their obligation under the contract of sale to pay the amount due the seller as purchase money. On the other hand, the settlement officer was not free to disburse any of the funds deposited by the purchasers until the title company was assured that the seller's deed conveyed title "good of record and in fact". Thus, the settlement meeting was only the initial step in the transaction and until all the conditions of the contract had been fulfilled, the settlement was not complete.[9]

---

9. The customary practice in settlements of this nature is for the title company to deposit the purchaser's check to assure that the check is honored. After the check clears and before recording the deed, the title company brings the title down to date by making a continuation title search from the date of its initial

Where a deed is deposited as an escrow, title does not pass to the grantee unless and until the condition of its delivery is performed. Although the purchasers tendered their personal check for the balance due from them at the settlement in ostensible payment of the purchase price, their subsequent direction to the title company to withhold from the seller a substantial portion of the purchase money to which she was entitled created a deviation from the condition upon which delivery of the deed to them could be effected. The settlement officer informed the purchasers that the settlement could not be completed and the deed could not be recorded. Since the condition precedent to the delivery of the deed had not been fulfilled, legal title to the property did not pass to the purchasers.

Appellants point to the fact that settlement statements were signed by the respective parties as indicative that settlement between the parties had been completed. Each of these statements was a separate and distinct document, one being the seller's statement establishing the "AMOUNT TO BE PAID SELLER" and the other, the purchasers' statement indicating the "BALANCE REQUIRED TO COMPLETE SETTLEMENT." The seller's statement contained an itemization of charges to be borne by the seller, including a charge for the apportionment of unpaid taxes, the brokerage fee to be paid to the real estate broker, disbursements to be paid to the broker for the costs of evicting the tenants, one-half of the recordation tax, and a charge of $50 to be held for water charges. These charges and anticipated disbursements were applied against the purchase price of the property and a balance struck, establishing the net amount which would be paid to the seller by the title company as the proceeds of the sale after the disbursements had been made and the settlement completed. The seller's signature on the statement noted her approval and acceptance of the statement as correct.

The purchasers' statement itemized the credits to their account, consisting of a credit for apportionment of unpaid taxes, the amount deposited with the broker as earnest money, and a credit to the purchasers of the sum to be received by the title company as the proceeds of the refinancing of other property owned by the purchasers. Against these credits, the purchasers were charged with the purchase price of the property and miscellaneous closing costs to be paid by them, including examination of title, title insurance, settlement fee, conveyancing fees, recording fees, and their share of the recordation tax. Offsetting the credits against the charges established a balance to be paid by the purchasers to the title company at settlement.

We do not attribute to these documents the significance which appellants attach to them. In effect, the seller's statement merely indicated what the seller would receive as the net proceeds of the sale after the settlement had been fully completed. The purchasers' search to the date of recordation of the deed to assure that no liens or encumbrances have been filed against the property in the interim.

statement was a statement of account of what remained to be paid by the purchasers to the title company, including the closing costs to be paid to the title company, after crediting the purchasers for the earnest money paid to the real estate broker and the sum anticipated to be received from the refinancing settlement. The incidental charges set forth on each statement were the concern solely of the party charged. Neither party bound himself to the settlement statement of the other. Neither statement constituted an acknowledgment that either the seller or the title company had received the purchase money which the purchasers were obligated to pay. The individual settlement statements were in effect an account stated separately between the title company and the seller and between the title company and the purchasers. Thus we reject the contention that the signing of the individual settlement statements by each of the parties signified that the transaction had been completed.

The appellants, contending that the settlement proceeding was completed, argue further that when the legal title to the premises passed to them the title to the purchase money vested in the seller and the subsequent demand by the purchasers that the title company withhold a portion of the seller's money was a "legal nullity" and "obviously unenforceable". In an escrow arrangement, the escrow holder is the dual agent of both parties until the performance of the conditions of the escrow agreement, whereupon he becomes the agent of each of the parties to the transaction in respect to those things placed in escrow to which each party has thus become entitled. Thus, when the conditions specified in the escrow agreement have been fully performed, the title to the premises passes to the purchaser and title to the purchase money passes to the seller. Thereupon, the escrow holder becomes the agent of the purchaser as to the deed and of the seller as to the money. However, as we have pointed out *supra*, the settlement was not completed and since the conditions upon which the seller's deed was to be delivered to the purchasers had not been performed, legal title to the property did not pass to the purchasers and title to the purchase money deposited with the settlement officer did not vest in the seller.

Furthermore, we find it difficult to comprehend appellants' present contention that their written demand upon the title company was a "legal nullity" in view of their contrary position at the settlement meeting. Upon receipt of the written demand from appellants' attorney, the settlement officer notified the parties that under the circumstances he could not proceed with the settlement. At the same time, Mrs. Caspar's son suggested that the appellants permit the settlement to proceed and that thereafter the parties "work out" the question of the Housing Code violations. Nevertheless, the appellants persisted in their demand that a portion of the purchase money be retained in escrow by the title company. The impasse was not resolved and the meeting broke up. By making the demand upon the title company, appellants placed the company in the difficult position of having to determine the rights of the respective parties. If the company honored appellants' demand, the seller could complain that the company had breached its duty to her. If the company refused to comply with the demand, the appellants would charge the title company with having disbursed the purchase money contrary to their express direction. In either event, the title company would have risked being subject to legal action by the party aggrieved. After waiting a reasonable period for the parties to adjust their differences and not having received any further word from either of them, the title company terminated its escrow agency and returned the escrow instruments to the respective parties. This turn of events was brought about by appellants' actions in serving the demand upon the title company and in persisting in their position. They cannot escape the consequences of their action by now claiming that their demand was a "nullity."

There is no dispute that a substantial number of violations of Housing Code regulations were duly noted against the premises and were in existence at the time the contract of sale was executed. Nor is there any dispute that Mrs. Caspar, as record owner of the property, was officially notified of the violations. Prior to the time for settlement, none of these violations had been corrected. Under these circumstances, the purchasers could have refused to consummate settlement and then have brought an action at law against the seller for such damages as they may have sustained. Alternatively, the purchasers could have elected to complete the settlement, and under the survival provisions of the contract, could have sued to recover from the seller such damages as they may have sustained by reason of her failure to correct the outstanding violations. The appellants here made no effort to rescind the contract but instead gave every indication of their intention to go forward with the transaction. Thus, despite the breach of the contract by the seller, the purchasers elected to proceed with the contract and obligated themselves to continue their performance of its terms.

To sustain the right to specific performance of their contract, the purchasers must show that they have performed or have offered to perform all of the obligations required of them by the contract.

It is the fundamental doctrine upon which the specific enforcement of contracts in equity depends, that either of the parties seeking to obtain the equitable remedy against the other must, as a condition precedent to the existence of his remedial right, show that he has done or offered to do, or is then ready and willing to do, all the essential and material acts required of him by the agreement at the time of commencing the suit, and also that he is ready and willing to do all such acts as shall be required of him in the specific execution of the contract according to its terms. [J.N. Pomeroy, Specific Performance of Contracts § 322 (3d ed.1926)].

Thus, where the purchaser under a contract for the sale of property instructed the escrow agent to hold the purchase money deposited with it until further notice and not to pay out any money to the seller, it was held that the purchaser had failed to perform his obligation under the contract to pay the purchase price to the seller and hence was not entitled to specific performance. And where an escrow contract required the purchaser to deposit a specific sum for the account of the vendor, a deposit of such sum with conditions that it could not and would not be paid to the seller did not constitute compliance with the contract. Similarly, where the purchase money was paid into escrow by the purchaser with instructions not agreed to by the seller, and which instructions went beyond reasonable requirements for securing the concurrent exchange of the deed for the purchase price, it was held that there was not a sufficient tender of performance on the part of the purchaser. A tender of performance by the purchaser which contains conditions other than those specified in the contract between the parties is ineffectual, and a tender of payment by the purchaser is ineffective where the purchaser has made arbitrary deductions therefrom for unliquidated claims against the seller.

In the case at bar, the trial court concluded that the appellants ". . . were not ready or willing to perform in accordance with the terms of the agreement . . ." and that their ". . . effort to impose conditions other than those specified in the contract resulted in a breach of their contractual duty, and a forfeiture of their right to specific performance of the contract." Appellants dispute this conclusion, pointing to the delivery of their personal check in the amount found to be due in accordance with the settlement sheet signed by them as proof that they were in fact ready and willing to perform their obligations under the contract. However, the evidence of record belies their contention. Appellants appeared at the settlement meeting armed with the letter demanding that a substantial portion of the purchase money be withheld from the seller. This was not a happenstance or a subsequently-formed decision but a preconceived plan by them to compel the seller to accept a lesser sum in payment for the property. The delivery of their check in ostensible payment of the amount due was a mere pretense since appellants never intended to have the seller receive the full amount due her upon settlement. The conclusion that appellants were not ready or willing to perform their obligation under the contract to pay the purchase price in cash is adequately supported by the record. By their own conduct, the appellants precluded their right to obtain specific performance of the contract.

Affirmed.

NOTES

1. A deed does not effectively transfer title to an interest in land until it is delivered. A will does not effectively transfer title to an

interest in land until the death of the individual who made the will. This means that if Jennie Peters' December 1, 1964 deed to Wesley and Wayne Shroyer had been delivered to the brothers before Jennie's death, the farm would have been theirs, and it would not have been hers to transfer by will. As a result, the two brothers would have prevailed over their mother, Jessie, whose only claim was under Jennie's October 15, 1960 will.

Delivery does *not* mean physical transfer of a deed from grantor to grantee. Rather, delivery is entirely a state of mind and occurs at the moment the grantor forms an intent presently to transfer an interest in land to the grantee, and the grantee forms the intent to accept the interest.

Intent to deliver may be proved or disproved by parol. Thus, grantor *A*'s failure to transfer the deed to grantee *B* will not defeat delivery if parol evidence indicates that the requisite intent is present. ("I am transferring Blackacre to you now, but will hold the deed for you until you reach the age of 18.") Similarly, even if *A* hands the deed to *B*, delivery will not occur if parol evidence indicates that the requisite intent is missing. ("I am giving you this deed to hold for safekeeping in the event I later decide to convey Blackacre to you.")

Making the question of delivery turn on intent raises few problems when the dispute is between the immediate grantor and grantee, *A* and *B*. But the rule becomes problematic when it is applied in disputes affecting third parties who had no means for discovering the absence of delivery in the original transaction. For example, say that *A* hands a deed, but does not deliver title, to *B*, so that *A* still holds title. *B*, having possession of the deed, records it. Twenty years later, *C*, relying on *B*'s recorded deed and lacking any knowledge—or means of acquiring knowledge—of *A*'s parol statement negating delivery, pays *B* consideration for what he expects is a conveyance of good title to Blackacre. Most courts would hold for *A* over *C* on the ground that, because *A* never delivered title to *B*, *B* had nothing to convey to *C*.

Obviously a system that rests title on something so ephemeral as intent can hardly be expected to promote faith in the paper record or in land transactions generally. Thus, it is no surprise that in the example just given some courts would give title to *C*, at least if he can show that it was negligent of *A* to have allowed *B* to come into possession of the deed. See 8 G. Thompson, Commentaries on the Modern Law of Real Property § 4236 (1963). Courts have also developed presumptions bringing delivery rules into line with the reasonable expectations of title searchers. Thus, while physical transfer does not constitute delivery, it is widely held to create a presumption of delivery. (Conversely, failure to transfer the deed creates a presumption of nondelivery.) Other acts creating a presumption of delivery are recordation of the deed and the deed's acknowledgment. See generally, 6A R. Powell, The Law of Real Property, § 891 (1982).

What other mechanisms might be employed to reduce the risks associated with nondelivery? Will *B*, who occupies Blackacre under an undelivered deed, eventually gain title by adverse possession? Will title insurance protect against losses resulting from nondelivery? See pages 373–378 below.

2. *Acceptance*. In order for a deed to be effectively delivered, the grantee must accept the delivery. In most cases, because the grant will benefit the grantee, acceptance will be presumed. However, courts will not presume acceptance if the conveyance might be disadvantageous to the grantee. And, even if the conveyance will be advantageous, courts will allow the presumption of acceptance to be rebutted by evidence that the grantee did not in fact wish to accept title to the land.

In Hood v. Hood, 384 A.2d 706 (Me.1978), plaintiff grantor, in her mid-eighties, had entered a hospital for surgery "from which she believed she might not recover." While in the hospital, she executed a deed to her farm, upon which she and her son Kenneth lived, to Kenneth. The attorney who drew up the deed recorded it the next day. According to the facts, "Kenneth E. Hood had no knowledge of the transaction until sometime later, when he visited his mother in the hospital. After she told him what she had done, her son informed her he wanted no part of the property, and he requested his mother to 'take it right back' to herself. Mrs. Hood subsequently attempted to contact the attorney who had drawn the deed, but was unsuccessful because he was on vacation. Kenneth E. Hood died on May 9, 1974, holding record title to the farm."

Mrs. Hood subsequently brought an action against Kenneth's surviving daughters, and their husbands, to declare the conveyance void. The Maine Supreme Court affirmed the trial court's judgment for Mrs. Hood. Rejecting defendants' argument that "delivery was completed when the Plaintiff gave the deed to the attorney for recording, thus relinquishing the right to recall the deed," the court observed that "Maine has traditionally followed what appears to be the majority rule that delivery of a deed is a consensual act. Thus, effective delivery of a deed requires the correlative act of acceptance by the grantee. The rationale for such a rule is that an estate cannot be thrust upon a person against his will, even if done gratuitously."

Do you think that the court would—or should—have reached the same result if Kenneth had survived his mother? What sentiments do you suppose prompted Kenneth's remark to his mother that "he wanted no part of the property," and his request that she "take it right back" to herself?

3. *Escrows*. The use of escrows has virtually eliminated delivery as an issue when land is being transferred for consideration. (Delivery continues to raise problems in donative settings like *Shroyer* and *Hood*.) Yet, as indicated by Ferguson v. Caspar, escrows themselves are not problem-free. When problems arise it is usually because the

parties have failed to be sufficiently explicit or objective in drafting the escrow instructions. Since an escrow agent should act strictly as an automaton and without discretion, escrow instructions will be inadequate if they fail to specify the agent's conduct under every conceivable contingency.

Practices vary from region to region as to who serves the escrow function: lawyer, broker, lender, title insurance company or independent escrow company. Overall closing costs may vary as a result. A comprehensive study of closing costs compared average title costs in the counties of Denver ($137), King (Seattle) ($291) and Los Angeles ($436), and concluded that one reason for Denver's lower charges was that escrow services there were performed by the lender and the broker, whose charges were included in the lender's origination fee and the broker's commission. By contrast, in King and Los Angeles Counties, independent escrow agents performed these services, at fees averaging $135 and $148, respectively. Dept. of Housing and Urban Development and Veteran's Administration, Mortgage Settlement Costs, Report to Sen.Comm. on Banking, Housing and Urban Affairs, 25–28 (Comm. Print 1972).

Escrow agents in King and Los Angeles Counties performed tasks that went well beyond the usual shuffling of papers. According to the HUD/VA study, they also initiated title searches, secured earnest money deposits and balance due statements on existing loans, drew up the grant deeds, computed prepaid items to be paid at closing, arranged financing, recorded instruments, disbursed funds to the seller and the broker, and furnished buyer and seller with statements of charges and disbursements made in the escrow. Such activities sometimes involve escrow agents in the unauthorized practice of law. See, for example, Bennion, Van Camp, Hagen & Ruhl v. Kassler Escrow, Inc., 96 Wn.2d 443, 635 P.2d 730 (1981) (escrow agent's selection, preparation and completion of documents and instruments in real estate transaction constitutes unauthorized practice of law).

4. LIABILITIES THAT SURVIVE THE DEED

Under the traditional doctrine of merger, a deed conveying real property supersedes any conflicting terms in the contract of sale and becomes the sole measure of the parties' rights and liabilities as between themselves and others. This means that even if the A–B contract of sale contains an express or implied covenant that A will deliver marketable title on closing, B's acceptance of the deed will bar B from an action against A if title later proves to be unmarketable—except to the extent that the deed itself contains express warranties of title.

In practice, merger doctrine is not nearly so clear-cut, nor B's prospects so bleak. First, merger is a rule of construction, not a rule of law and, when the interests of third parties will not be prejudiced, courts will weigh parol evidence in interpreting the deed. Also, just as the deed may specify obligations not mentioned in the contract, so the contract may effectively provide that the contract, and not the deed, is to control certain obligations. And, although most courts will not imply covenants respecting title into deeds, many courts today will imply covenants respecting the fitness of the premises. See generally, Dunham, Merger by Deed—Was it Ever Automatic?, 10 Ga.L.Rev. 419 (1976).

Also, merger does not affect seller liability for fraud. Before and after closing, the buyer who can prove seller fraud can obtain rescission and, in some cases, damages. Liability for fraud basically turns on buyer's and seller's relative access to pertinent information—what each knew or should have known about the purported defect. While the trend has been away from *caveat emptor*, and toward imposing a higher duty of disclosure on the seller, courts continue to burden buyers with some duty to inquire. For example, the buyer will be presumed to have exercised due diligence in examining the premises and title to the land.

The Uniform Land Transactions Act abolishes the doctrine of merger. Section 1–309 adopts a general rule that "acceptance by buyer or a secured party of a deed or other instrument of conveyance is not of itself a waiver or renunciation of any of his rights under the contract under which the deed or other instrument of conveyance is given and does not of itself relieve any party of the duty to perform all his obligations under the contract." Elsewhere, the ULTA allows the buyer to revoke his acceptance of real estate if seller committed a substantial breach and the buyer accepted on seller's assurance that the breach would be cured or, if buyer had not discovered the breach before his acceptance, he "reasonably relied upon the seller's representation that the real estate conformed to the contract or . . . the breach was one he could not reasonably have discovered before acceptance." § 2–402.

The ULTA also implies a wider array of warranties into the deed itself. Section 2–306 follows the approach of state "short form" deed statutes, providing that a "seller who executes a deed that does not provide to the contrary impliedly warrants that: (1) the real estate is free from all encumbrances; (2) the buyer will have quiet and peaceable possession of or right to enjoy the real estate conveyed; (3) the seller has the power and right to convey the title which he purports to convey; and (4) the seller will defend the title to the real estate conveyed against all persons lawfully claiming it." ULTA §§ 2–308 and 2–309, respectively, specify the conditions for finding express and implied warranties of quality. See generally, Note, Warranties in the Uniform Land Transactions Act of 1975—Progression or Retrogression for Pennsylvania?, 49 Temp.L.Q. 162 (1975).

What implications do these ULTA provisions on post-closing rights have for pre-closing behavior? The orthodox doctrine of merger gives the buyer an incentive during the executory period to make cer-

a. FITNESS OF THE PREMISES

WAWAK v. STEWART

Supreme Court of Arkansas, 1970.
247 Ark. 1093, 449 S.W.2d 922.

GEORGE ROSE SMITH, Justice.

The defendant-appellant Wawak, a house builder, bought a lot in North Little Rock in the course of his business, built a house on it, and sold it to the appellees Stewart for $28,500. The heating and air-conditioning ductwork had been embedded in the ground before the concrete-slab floor was poured above that ductwork. Some months after the Stewarts moved into the house a serious defect manifested itself, in that heavy rains caused water and particles of fill to seep into the ducts and thence through the floor vents into the interior of the house, with consequent damage that need not be described at the moment.

The Stewarts brought this action for damages. The great question in the case, overshadowing all other issues, is whether there is any implied warranty in a contract by which the builder-vendor of a new house sells it to its first purchaser. The trial court sustained the theory of implied warranty and awarded the Stewarts damages of $1,309.

The trial court was right. Twenty years ago one could hardly find any American decision recognizing the existence of an implied warranty in a routine sale of a new dwelling. Both the rapidity and the unanimity with which the courts have recently moved away from the harsh doctrine of caveat emptor in the sale of new houses are amazing, for the law has not traditionally progressed with such speed.

Yet there is nothing really surprising in the modern trend. The contrast between the rules of law applicable to the sale of personal property and those applicable to the sale of real property was so great as to be indefensible. One who bought a chattel as simple as a walking stick or a kitchen mop was entitled to get his money back if the article was not of merchantable quality. But the purchaser of a $50,000 home ordinarily had no remedy even if the foundation proved to be so defective that the structure collapsed into a heap of rubble.

Several law review articles, of which the earliest was published in 1952, forecast the new developments. Their titles suggest their contents: Dunham, Vendor's Obligation as to Fitness of Land For a Particular Purpose, 37 Minn.L.Rev. 108 (1952); Bearman, Caveat Emptor in Sales of Realty—Recent Assaults Upon the Rule, 14 Vanderbilt L.Rev. 541 (1961); Haskell, The Case For an Implied Warranty of Quality in Sales of Real Property, 53 Georgetown L.J. 633 (1965); Roberts, The Case of the Unwary Home Buyer: The Housing Merchant Did It, 52 Cornell L.Q. 835 (1967). In 1963 a new edition of Williston's Contracts added its weight to the movement, pointing out a practical advantage in the new point of view: "It would be much better if this enlightened approach were generally adopted with respect to the sale of new houses for it would tend to discourage much of the sloppy work and jerry-building that has become perceptible over the years." Williston, Contracts, § 926A (3d ed.1963).

In the past decade six states have recognized an implied warranty—of inhabitability, sound workmanship, or proper construction—in the sale of new houses by vendors who also built the structures. Carpenter v. Donohoe, 154 Colo. 78, 388 P.2d 399 (1964); Bethlahmy v. Bechtel, 91 Idaho 55, 415 P.2d 698 (1966); Schipper v. Levitt & Sons, 44 N.J. 70, 207 A.2d 314 (1965); Waggoner v. Midwestern Dev. Co., S.D., 154 N.W.2d 803 (1967); Humber v. Morton, Texas, 426 S.W.2d 554, 25 A.L.R.3d 372 (1968); House v. Thornton, Wash., 457 P.2d 199 (1969). The near unanimity of the judges in those cases is noteworthy. Of the 36 justices who made up the six appellate courts, the only dissent noted was that of Justice Griffin in the Texas case, who dissented without opinion.

A few excerpts from those recent opinions will illustrate what seems certain to be the accepted rule of the future. In the *Schipper* case the New Jersey court had this to say:

> The law should be based on current concepts of what is right and just and the judiciary should be alert to the never-ending need for keeping its common law principles abreast of the times. Ancient distinctions which make no sense in today's society and tend to discredit the law should be readily rejected . . . . We consider that there are no meaningful distinctions between Levitt's [a large-scale builder-seller] mass production and sale of homes and the mass production and sale of automobiles and that the pertinent overriding considerations are the same.
>
> . . .
>
> *Caveat emptor* developed when the buyer and seller were in an equal bargaining position and they could readily be expected to protect themselves in the deed. Buyers of mass produced development homes are not on an equal footing with the builder vendors and are no more able to protect themselves in the deed than are automobile purchasers in a position to protect themselves in the bill of sale. Levitt expresses the fear of "uncertainty and cha-

os" if responsibility for defective construction is continued after the builder vendor's delivery of the deed and its loss of control of the premises, but we fail to see why this should be anticipated or why it should materialize any more than in the products liability field where there has been no such result.

A similar point of view was expressed in the *House* case by the Washington Supreme Court:

> As between vendor and purchaser, the builder-vendors, even though exercising reasonable care to construct a sound building, had by far the better opportunity to examine the stability of the site and to determine the kind of foundation to install. Although hindsight, it is frequently said, is 20–20 and defendants used reasonable prudence in selecting the site and designing and constructing the building, their position throughout the process of selection, planning and construction was markedly superior to that of their first purchaser-occupant. To borrow an idea from equity, of the innocent parties who suffered, it was the builder-vendor who made the harm possible. If there is a comparative standard of innocence, as well as of culpability, the defendants who built and sold the house were less innocent and more culpable than the wholly innocent and unsuspecting buyer. Thus, the old rule of caveat emptor has little relevance to the sale of a brand-new house by a vendor-builder to a first buyer for purposes of occupancy.
>
> We apprehend it to be the rule that, when a vendor-builder sells a new house to its first intended occupant, he impliedly warrants that the foundations supporting it are firm and secure and that the house is structurally safe for the buyer's intended purpose of living in it. Current literature on the subject overwhelmingly supports this idea of an implied warranty of fitness in the sale of new houses. . . .

As might be expected, we have been presented with the timeworn, threadbare argument that a court is legislating whenever it modifies common-law rules to achieve justice in the light of modern economic and technological advances. That same argument was doubtless made in a famous case that parallels this one: MacPherson v. Buick Motor Co., 217 N.Y. 382, 111 N.E. 1050, Ann.Cas.1916C, 440, L.R.A.1916F, 696 (1916). There the court, with respect to the sale of automobiles, abolished a requirement of privity of contract that was just as firmly embedded in the common law as is the rule that we are now re-examining. Yet the doctrine of the *MacPherson* case is now accepted as commonplace throughout the nation. We have no doubt that the modification of the rule of *caveat emptor* that we are now considering will be accepted with like unanimity within a few years.

After the case at bar had been submitted to the court we invited the filing of *amici curiae* briefs, to avoid the possibility that persuasive arguments might be overlooked. The only brief that urges adherence to the old rule was filed by counsel for the Arkansas Home Builders Association.

The AHBA brief makes one point that merits comment. Counsel state that the AHBA "recognizes the need for the imposition of a warranty upon new construction." To that end the Association included a one-year warranty requirement in a bill that it sponsored, unsuccessfully, in the 1967 and 1969 sessions of the legislature. The main purpose of the bill, however, was to regulate the homebuilding industry by the creation of a governing board and the imposition of licensing requirements upon those engaged in the business.

We are not impressed by the AHBA's suggestion that we await legislative action, even though the Association concedes that some form of warranty is needed. To begin with, the General Assembly's repeated refusal to enact the proposed law hardly gives assurance that it will be passed in the near future. Furthermore, whatever decision we reach in this case can have no effect upon the General Assembly's freedom to change the law as it sees fit. To the contrary, a judicial decision may focus legislative attention upon the problem. See, for example, Act 165 of 1969, which was a prompt legislative reaction to our decision in Parish v. Pitts, 244 Ark. 1239, 429 S.W.2d 45 (1968).

To sum up, upon the facts before us in the case at bar we have no hesitancy in adopting the modern rule by which an implied warranty may be recognized in the sale of a new house by a seller who was also the builder. That rule, however, is a departure from our earlier cases; so, to avoid injustice, we adhere to the doctrine announced in Parish v. Pitts, *supra*, by which the new rule is made applicable only to the case at hand and to causes of action arising after this decision becomes final.

There are three subordinate points that require discussion. First, Wawak insists that all warranties, express or implied, were negatived by this paragraph in the offer-and-acceptance agreement that preceded the execution of a warranty deed when the sale was consummated:

> Buyer certifies that he has inspected the property and he is not relying upon any warranties, representations or statements of the Agent or Seller as to age or physical condition of improvements.

Even if we assume that the preliminary contract was not merged in the warranty deed, we think it plain that the quoted paragraph did not exclude an implied warranty with respect to the particular defect now in question, which lay beneath the concrete floor and could not possibly have been discovered by even the most careful inspection. The quoted paragraph does not purport to exclude all warranties. It merely states that the buyer has inspected the property and is not *relying* on any warranties as to the age or physical condition of the improvements. Construing the printed contract against the seller, who evidently prepared it, we hold that the clause applies only to defects that might reasonably have been discovered in the course of an inspection made by a purchaser of average experience in such matters.

Secondly, the trial court's judgment for $1,309 was composed of the following items of damage to the house and its furnishings, none of which the Stewarts had yet paid:

To clean rug	$ 75.00
To paint house (interior)	235.00
To clean furniture	22.00
To replace lamp shades	35.00
To clean duct system	200.00
To replace draperies	300.00
Minor repairs	22.00
Drain tile to correct leakage	420.00
	$1,309.00

Wawak insists that the recovery of the foregoing items is barred by the rule that a plaintiff must use reasonable care to mitigate his damages and that if the damages could have been avoided at reasonable expense then the measure of damages is the amount of such expense.

The pertinent facts are these: The subterranean ductwork radiates from a metal chamber or plenum, which sits under the heating and air-conditioning units. When Wawak and his ductwork subcontractor, Plummer, were first notified by Stewart of the seepage, they siphoned off the water through the plenum. They next installed drain tile and gravel along two sides of the house, but those measures failed to correct the trouble. In the meantime Stewart bought a sump pump at a cost of $12.50. Whenever rains caused seepage in the ductwork Stewart would place his pump in the plenum, about two hours after the water had accumulated, and pump the duct system dry. Under that procedure some of the seepage got into the house and caused most of the damage that we have itemized above.

Soon after the difficulty first arose Wawak and Plummer proposed the installation of an automatic sump pump, which cost $76 or $78. Their plan was to dig out the floor of the plenum so that the automatic pump would be below the level of the ducts. Whenever the water at the site of the pump rose to a depth of three quarters of an inch the pump would start automatically and pump out the water. Thus the water would never rise high enough to overflow the floor vents and damage the interior of the house. Wawak and Plummer do not contend that their plan would have corrected the subterranean defect. From Wawak's testimony: "I figured if we could get the pump in there to pump it out, then we could continue to try to find out where [the water] was coming from. It wasn't our intention to just leave it." Wawak stated that when he offered to put in the automatic pump there was no damage to the house except some staining of the draperies, which were cleaned at Wawak's expense.

Stewart refused to allow the automatic pump to be installed, insisting that he wanted to know where the water was coming from and would accept nothing less. When the proffer of the pump was refused, Wawak and Plummer abandoned their efforts to correct the trouble. Thereafter Stewart used his own pump in the manner that we have described, with attendant damage to the house and its furnishings. A period of two years or more elapsed before this action was finally brought.

In the main Wawak is correct in his argument that the Stewarts should have mitigated their damages by permitting the installation of the automatic pump. On the record made below it is an undisputed fact that such a pump would have avoided practically all the itemized damages that were allowed by the trial court.

The pump, however, would not have corrected the basic defect, nor does Wawak so contend. Stewart testified without contradiction and without objection that a man named Gordon could remedy the defect by installing drain tile along the remaining two sides of the house at a cost of $425. That corrective measure would not have been rendered unnecessary by the installation of the automatic pump; so the Stewarts' duty to mitigate their damages does not involve that item. The amount of the Stewarts' judgment will therefore be reduced to $420—the amount allowed by the trial court for the one item of damage that we find to be recoverable.

Thirdly, Wawak argues that he is entitled to judgment over against the appellee Plummer, who installed the ductwork under a subcontract with Wawak. It cannot be said as a matter of law, however, that Plummer was at fault, because the slab floor above the ducts was poured by another subcontractor. Upon this point the trial court's judgment is sufficiently supported by the proof.

Finally, what we have said also disposes of the appellees' cross appeal, by which they contend that the court erred in not allowing them the full amount of some of their itemized claims. In any event recovery upon the cross appeal would have to be denied under the rule established in Fulbright v. Phipps, 176 Ark. 356, 3 S.W.2d 49 (1928), and the cases that have followed it, holding that the verdict need not correspond in amount to the proof adduced by either party.

The judgment as modified is affirmed.

HARRIS, C.J., and FOGLEMAN and BYRD, JJ., dissent.

[The opinions of FOGLEMAN, J., dissenting in part and concurring in part, and BYRD, J., dissenting, are omitted.]

BLAGG v. FRED HUNT CO., INC.

Supreme Court of Arkansas, 1981.
272 Ark. 185, 612 S.W.2d 321.

DUDLEY, Justice.

The appellee, Fred Hunt Company, Inc., a house builder, bought a lot in the Pleasant Valley Addition to Little Rock, built a house on it, and sold it to the Dentons on October 9, 1978. The Dentons sold the house to the American Foundation Life Insurance Company, which on June 29, 1979, sold the house to appellants, J. Ted Blagg and Kathye Blagg. This purchase by appellants was made a few days less than 9 months after the date of the original sale. The appellants filed a two-count complaint alleging that after they purchased the home a strong odor and fumes from formaldehyde became apparent. They traced this defect to the carpet and pad which was installed by appellee. A motion to dismiss was filed by the appellee and the trial court granted the motion on count one of the complaint, the implied warranty count, on the basis of lack of privity. The court denied the motion on count two, which is framed in terms of strict liability.

When considering a motion to dismiss a complaint pursuant to Arkansas Rules of Civil Procedure, Rule 12(b)(6), on the ground that it fails to state a claim on which relief can be granted, the facts alleged in the complaint are treated as true and are viewed in the light most favorable to the party seeking relief.

Count one of the complaint is based upon an implied warranty. The trial judge dismissed this count because the appellants are not in privity with the appellee. This court, in Wawak v. Stewart, 247 Ark. 1093, 449 S.W.2d 922 (1970), abandoned the doctrine of caveat emptor and took the view that a builder-vendor impliedly warranted the home to the first purchaser. The issue of first impression in this case is whether the liability of the builder-vendor should be extended to a second or third purchaser.

Since *Wawak*, the original homebuyer has been able to place reliance on the builder-vendor's implied warranty. This has protected that investment which, in most instances, represents the family's largest single expenditure.

We find no reason that those same basic concepts should not be extended to subsequent purchasers of real estate. This is an area of the law being developed on a case by case basis. Our ruling is based on the complaint before us and involves a home which had a defect that became apparent to the third purchasers, the appellants, within 9 months of the original sale date. Obviously, there is a point in time beyond which the implied warranty will expire and that time should be based on a standard of reasonableness.

We hold that the builder-vendor's implied warranty of fitness for habitation runs not only in favor of the first owner, but extends to subsequent purchasers for a reasonable length of time where there is no substantial change or alteration in the condition of the building from the original sale. This implied warranty is limited to latent defects which are not discoverable by subsequent purchasers upon reasonable inspection and which become manifest only after the purchase. Wyoming adopted this rule in a well reasoned opinion. Moxley v. Laramie Builders, Inc., 600 P.2d 733 (Wyo.1979).

Appellants next contend that even if the implied warranty extends to subsequent purchasers, we should affirm the trial court as there is an express warranty which is exclusive. We do not consider this argument as the complaint does not allege an express warranty, and the sufficiency of the complaint is all that is tested.

We hold that count one of the complaint should not have been dismissed.

Appellee, in its cross-appeal, contends that the trial judge committed error in not dismissing count two of the complaint, the claim for damages under strict liability. We affirm the trial judge's ruling.

Our strict liability statute, Ark.Stat.Ann. § 85–2–318.2 (Supp.1979) is as follows:

> Liability of Supplier—Conditions.—A supplier of a product is subject to liability in damages for harm to a person or to property if:
>
> (a) the supplier is engaged in the business of manufacturing, assembling, selling, leasing or otherwise distributing such product;
>
> (b) the product was supplied by him in a defective condition which rendered it unreasonably dangerous; and
>
> (c) the defective condition was a proximate cause of the harm to person or to property. [Acts 1973, No. 111, § 1, p. 331.]

This 1973 act broadens somewhat § 402(A) of the Restatement, Second, Torts (1965). . . .

Our first issue is whether this strict liability statute encompasses count two of the complaint. It is an oversimplification, but correct, to state that the construction of the word "product" is determinative. To decide the proper construction we have examined the few cases in other jurisdictions and various treatises.

Judge Henry Woods in The Personal Injury Action in Warranty—Has the Arkansas Strict Liability Statute Rendered it Obsolete?, 28 Ark.L.R. 335 (1974), gives a most perceptive preview of the real issue. He notes that we must choose between the persuasive reasoning of two outstanding jurists—Chief Justice Traynor in Seely v. White Motor Company, 63 Cal.2d 9, 403 P.2d 145, 45 Cal.Rptr. 17 (1965), and Justice Francis in Santor v. A & M Karagheusian, Inc., 44 N.J. 52, 207 A.2d 305 (1965). If the Traynor view is adopted, the implied warranty will be very much alive when a purchaser is suing for purely economic loss from a defective product. His view, as stated in *Seely*, supra, is that when economic losses result from commercial transactions, as here, the parties should be relegated to the law of sales:

> Although the rules governing warranties complicated resolution of the problems of personal injuries, there is no reason to conclude that they do not meet the "needs of commercial transactions." The law of warranty "grew as a branch of the law of commercial transactions and was primarily aimed at controlling the commercial aspects of these transactions." . . .
>
> Although the rules of warranty frustrate rational compensation for physical injury, they function well in a commercial setting.

Justice Francis, in *Santor*, supra, prophetically extended the doctrine in a case involving carpeting that developed a defect, a purely economic loss, not a personal injury. In applying the doctrine of strict liability for purely economic loss he said:

> The obligation of the manufacturer thus becomes what in justice it ought to be—an enterprise liability, and one which should not depend on the law of sales. . . .

After lengthy consideration, we choose to adopt the views of Justice Francis. We find no valid reason for holding that strict liability should not apply to property damage in a house sold by a builder-vendor. Accordingly, in construing the Arkansas strict liability statute, we hold that the word "product" is as applicable to a house as to an automobile.

Reversed and remanded on direct appeal; affirmed on cross-appeal.

NOTE, THE HOME OWNERS WARRANTY PROGRAM: AN INITIAL ANALYSIS, 28 STAN.L.REV. 357–363 (1976): After thoroughly inspecting a newly constructed house and finding no defects, a family makes what is probably the biggest purchase of a lifetime and moves into the home. A few months later, they discover numerous defects including chipped and peeling paint, inadequate heating, guttering, and draining systems, a leaking carport and even a defective fireplace. Except for its disappointment and frustration, this family's problems may be remedied if its new house is enrolled in the Home Owners Warranty (HOW) Program.

"The HOW Program, adopted in September 1973 by the National Association of Home Builders (NAHB), is a potentially comprehensive industry-sponsored mechanism designed to prevent and resolve disputes arising out of new home purchases. Patterned after the warranty insurance program of the National House-Building Council (NHBC) of Great Britain, HOW provides a 10-year warranty and insurance protection package for new owner-occupied single-family houses, townhouses and condominiums. A 2-tiered complaint settlement mechanism complements the warranty and insurance coverage. . . .

I. THE HOME OWNERS WARRANTY PROGRAM

A. *Administration*

Prompted in part by fear of federal preemption in the homeowner protection field and by a purported subscription to the belief that "good consumerism means good business," the Board of Directors of the NAHB, whose members construct about one-half of all new houses in the United States, adopted the Home Owners Warranty Program. Participating builders must register with HOW and agree to observe HOW's approved construction and performance standards. The Home Owners Warranty Corporation, a wholly owned subsidiary of the NAHB, administers the program, licenses and monitors the performance of local warranty councils, and maintains a registry of the participating builders. These local councils register the local participating builders, enroll new units, adopt local builder performance and building quality standards, monitor local inspection procedures, and arrange for conciliation and arbitration of claims. Only those builders constructing homes in an area served by a local warranty council can participate in the program.

A HOW-registered builder contracts with home buyers to cover faulty workmanship and defective materials, as well as major construction defects during the first year. Additionally, during the first 2 years the builder guarantees plumbing, heating, electrical, and cooling systems and repair of major construction defects. During the third through tenth years of the warranty, the unit is protected against major construction defects through private insurance coverage arranged by HOW. The insurance company further underwrites the builder's performance during the first 2 years, with a right of subrogation, if for any reason the builder cannot or will not meet his warranted responsibilities.

To cover the expenses of the program, a one-time fee of $2 per $1,000 of the closing price is charged and is presumably incorporated into the cost of the unit. One-half of this amount is used to pay for the insurance premium; the other half is earmarked for administration and promotion of the program by the national and local councils. All builders registering with HOW pay an initial registration fee and an annual reregistration fee, both of which are set and collected by the local councils.

B. *Conciliation and Arbitration*

If the buyer is not satisifed with the builder's response to his written complaint, he may request conciliation administered by the local warranty council. A person selected by the council investigates the complaint and meets with the buyer and builder in an effort to reach a mutually satisfactory solution. If conciliation fails, either party may request binding arbitration conducted by the American Arbitration Association or a comparable organization.

Although either party may secure a lawyer to represent its interest at either the conciliation or arbitration stage, it is anticipated that the presence of lawyers, except when a significant defect is the matter in dispute, will be the exception. Notwithstanding the dispute settlement mechanism incorporated in HOW, the buyer retains all rights to initiate litigation.

NOTES

1. *Incidence of Housing Defects*. A government study, based on a sample of new housing built in 1977 and 1978, revealed that 79% of new housing buyers had at least one complaint about housing quality. Seventy-five percent of the problems were discovered in the first six months of ownership, and ninety-three percent in the first year. On receiving complaints, builders were most ready to correct defects in plumbing, cooling and heating systems, in major appliances and in interior electrical work. Builders were less willing to correct problems with yard drainage, roofs, foundations and driveways and improperly fitted doors and windows. Seven percent of buyers reported that they consulted a lawyer about the problem and four percent retained lawyers. U.S. Dept. of Housing & Urban Development and Federal Trade Commission, A Survey of Homeowner Experience with New Residential Housing Construction iii-viii, 10–29 (1980).

2. The implied warranty of fitness represents the main avenue today for buyers of defective housing to recover from their builder-sellers. With roots in both contract and tort theory, the warranty of fitness has made substantial inroads on *caveat emptor*, giving disappointed buyers an easier and more complete remedy than fraud or negligence. By recent count, forty-two states imply a warranty into new housing sales, variously calling it a warranty of "quality," "habitability," "good workmanship," or "fitness." See Shedd, The Implied Warranty of Habitability: New Implications, New Applications, 8 Real Estate L.J. 291 (1980).

Like *Wawak*, most courts that have implied a warranty of fitness into sales of new housing have reasoned by analogy to the warranty of fitness implied into sales of personal property. Are there any differences between real and personal property that make the analogy inapt? See generally, Rabin & Grossman, Defective Products or Realty Causing Economic Loss: Toward a Unified Theory of Recovery, 12 Southwestern Univ.L.Rev. 5 (1981). At the least, should courts take care to discriminate between real and personal property in determining what kinds of defects will breach the warranty? Justice Fogelman, dissenting in part and concurring in part in *Wawak*, objected to the majority's failure to address the question whether the warranty in fact had been breached. Noting that the implied warranty "does not impose upon the builder an obligation to deliver a perfect house," he concluded that the evidence "simply does not show the breach of any implied warranty." 247 Ark. at 1101, 449 S.W.2d at 930.

For an excellent analysis of the history and doctrinal implications of seller liability for housing defects, see Roberts, The Case of the Unwary Home Buyer: The Housing Merchant Did It, 52 Cornell L.Q. 835 (1967). For general background, see Bearman, Caveat Emptor in Sales of Realty—Recent Assaults Upon the Rule, 14 Vand.L.Rev. 541 (1961); Bixby, Let the Seller Beware: Remedies for the Purchase of a Defective Home, 49 J. of Urb.L. 533 (1971); Haskell, The Case for an Implied Warranty of Quality in Sales of Real Property, 53 Geo.L.J. 633 (1965); McNamara, The Implied Warranty in New-House Construction: Has the Doctrine of Caveat Emptor Been Abolished?, 1 Real Est.L.J. 43 (1972); McNamara, The Implied Warranty in New-House Construction Revisited, 3 Real Est.L.J. 136 (1974).

3. *Used Housing*. Most residential sales involve used rather than new housing. Should buyers of used housing be able to recover for latent defects against either the original builder or their immediate seller? Tort actions based on a strict liability theory are usually fruitless because, most commonly, only unrecoverable economic damages are alleged. Warranty actions brought against homebuilders by second and subsequent buyers are usually dismissed for lack of privity. Warranty actions against the immediate seller, with whom the second or subsequent buyer is in privity, are usually dismissed on the ground that there is no inequality of bargaining power or expertise between buyer and seller.

As indicated in *Blagg*, the barriers to recovery by distant buyers against developers are beginning to break down. Product liability law's requirement that plaintiff demonstrate personal injury in order to recover was the first barrier to crumble. In Kriegler v. Eichler Homes, Inc., 269 Cal.App.2d 224, 74 Cal.Rptr. 749 (1969), a California Court of Appeal imposed strict liability for defects causing economic injury. Eichler's faulty installation of a radiant heating system in a house that plaintiff had bought from its original buyer eventually caused the system to fail, reducing the value of the house by over $5,000. Holding for plaintiff homeowners, the court noted that "at the time of the installation of the heating system in the Kriegler home," the building industry "had knowledge of methods by which the injury could reasonably have been avoided." A short while later, another California Court of Appeal relied on *Eichler* to impose strict liability for damages to a house and lot caused by the improper compaction of fill and other errors in the developer's preparation of the soil. Avner v. Longridge Estates, 272 Cal.App.2d 607, 77 Cal.Rptr. 633 (1969).

More recently, the privity bar to warranty actions has begun to give way. Representing a developer, would you be comfortable with

Blagg's extension of the implied warranty "for a reasonable length of time"? Other courts extending the warranty have been similarly uninstructive about the duration of the builder's exposure. See, for example, Redarowicz v. Ohlendorf, 92 Ill.2d 171, 65 Ill.Dec. 411, 441 N.E.2d 324 (1982). Can a developer protect herself against warranty liability to second and successive purchasers by obtaining from her immediate buyer an express disclaimer of any implied warranties? Is indeterminate liability likely to induce developers to build houses that are more durable—and probably more expensive—than their immediate buyers might desire?

See generally, Note, Builders' Liability for Latent Defects in Used Homes, 32 Stan.L.Rev. 607 (1980).

4. *Disclaimers.* Most courts that imply a warranty of fitness into the sale of new housing will also allow seller and buyer to contract around the implied warranty. Yet, there is a general disposition to construe disclaimers and "as is" provisions against builder-sellers. *Wawak* is typical in holding that, strictly construed, the disclaimer clause did not exclude an implied warranty with respect to latent defects—"the clause applies only to defects that might reasonably have been discovered in the course of an inspection made by a purchaser of average experience in such matters."

Other courts have reached the same result by holding that, to be enforced, a disclaimer clause must be expressed in clear and unambiguous language and that seller has the burden of proving that buyer knowingly made the disclaimer. See, for example, Crowder v. Vandendeale, 564 S.W.2d 879, 881 n. 4 (Mo.1978) ("One seeking the benefit of such a disclaimer must not only show a conspicuous provision which fully discloses the consequences of its inclusion but also that such was *in fact* the agreement reached. The heavy burden thus placed on the builder is completely justified, for by his assertion of the disclaimer he is seeking to show that the buyer has relinquished protection afforded him by public policy. A knowing waiver of this protection will not be readily implied.").

5. *Statutory Developments.* State warranty legislation ranges from statutes like Maryland's Code of Real Property, §§ 10–201 *et seq.* (1981), which follow the general contours of the common law implied warranty, to New Jersey's far more ambitious New Home Warranty and Builder's Registration Act, N.J.Stat.Ann. 46:3B–1 *et seq.* (1977).

The Maryland statute implies into sales of improved residential real property a warranty that the improvement (defined as a newly constructed private dwelling unit), is habitable, free from faulty materials and constructed according to sound engineering standards in a workmanlike manner. The warranty lasts for one year after closing and excludes any defect that inspection by a reasonably diligent first buyer would have disclosed. The warranty may be waived or modified only through a writing signed by the purchaser that specifically describes the warranty waived and the terms of the new agreement. The statute implies a warranty of fitness for a particular purpose, and also provides that an express warranty is created by a written affirmation of fact or promise, a written description of the improvement, or a sample model that is part of the basis of the bargain.

The New Jersey statute directs the Commissioner of the Department of Community Affairs to prescribe home warranties incorporating quality standards for construction materials and methods. The warranty's duration will depend on its subject matter—one year for defects caused by a specified class of faulty installation of plumbing, electrical, heating and cooling systems, and ten years for major construction defects including damages due to soil subsidence. The builder's liability extends not only to the initial buyer but also to any subsequent buyer whose claim arises during the applicable warranty period. The ceiling on liability is the purchase price of the home in the first good faith sale.

A builder must register with the Department to build houses in New Jersey. One condition of registration is that the builder participate in a warranty security fund, established by the Act, or an approved alternative fund. The fund provides a back-up source of compensation when fund participants have not themselves made good on valid homeowner claims. Before making a claim against the fund, a homeowner must notify the builder of the defects and allow a reasonable time for their repair. Once a claim is made against the fund, it is reviewed through a conciliation or arbitration procedure administered by the Department. If a defect is found, the builder is ordered to correct it and, failing that, the owner is allowed to recover from the fund. While the Act does not preempt private law remedies, it does require the homeowner to elect between statutory and common law relief.

6. *Liability of Brokers, Lenders and Architects*. Buyers disappointed with the quality of their housing may seek relief not only against the builder but also against the broker who arranged the sale, the lender who financed it and the architect who designed the house. Broker liability rests almost exclusively on fraud and typically arises when the seller mentions some material defect to the listing broker who then fails to disclose it to the unsuspecting buyer.

Although actions against lenders have generally been unavailing, buyers enjoy occasional success. For example, in Connor v. Great Western Savings & Loan Association, 69 Cal.2d 850, 858, 73 Cal.Rptr. 369, 377, 447 P.2d 609, 617 (1968), a lender which had not only financed a housing development, but also exercised substantial control over its construction and design, was held liable to homebuyers for damages resulting from faulty foundations: "privity of contract is not necessary to establish the existence of a duty to exercise ordinary care not to injure another, but such duty may arise out of a voluntarily assumed relationship if public policy dictates the existence of such a duty." *Connor* has since been substantially limited by statute in California, West's Ann.Cal.Civ. Code § 3434, and has been rejected or distinguished in other states. See, for example, Wierzbicki v. Alaska Mutual Savings Bank, 630 P.2d 998 (Alaska 1981). Would buyer have a stronger case if he could demonstrate that the contract under which he purchased the house included a "subject to financing" clause, that the bank to which he had applied for a loan had inspected the house before agreeing to make the loan, and that he had closed the contract relying on the bank's implicit approval of the house's condition? See Jeminson v. Montgomery Real Estate & Co., 396 Mich. 106, 240 N.W.2d 205 (1976).

Architects have only recently been made liable to third parties injured as a consequence of negligently prepared plans. Until the middle 1950's the general rule was that an architect's liability to individuals other than his client evaporated at the moment the client accepted the completed building. There were early exceptions to the rule—for willful negligence and latent dangerous conditions—but the rule itself did not begin to collapse until the 1950's. Architects are now widely held liable for design defects ranging from soil and foundation failures to improper windows, insulation and roofing. For a thorough analysis of architect liability, with proposals for reform, see Comment, Architect Tort Liability in Preparation of Plans and Specifications, 55 Cal.L.Rev. 1361 (1967). See also, Note, Architectural Malpractice: A Contract-Based Approach, 92 Harv.L.Rev. 1075 (1979); Note, 60 Kentucky L.J. 462 (1972).

b. Title

Before paying the purchase price and accepting seller A's deed, buyer B will want assurance that A's title is good—that no fraud or formal defect clouds her ownership and that there are no outstanding conditions or encumbrances that might interfere with B's ownership or use of the land. B can get this assurance in part by searching A's record title and updating this search down to the moment of closing. If the search discloses a material defect, the covenant of marketable title in the parties' contract will excuse B from performing and entitle him to the return of his deposit. But, if the search discloses no such defect B will, as required by the contract, accept A's deed and pay the price.

Since some title defects will not be disclosed by a record search, B may want additional assurances that A's title is good. One form that these assurances commonly take is covenants—promises—respecting title made by A and incorporated in her deed to B. Title covenants can be shaped to meet any specific need—that title is good as against a neighbor claiming adverse possession, that a disputed mortgage has been paid off, or that a troublesome relative in fact has no interest in the land. In addition to such custom-crafted covenants are six standard title covenants that have been in common use since at least the seventeenth century in England:

Covenant of Seisin. This covenant is the grantor's promise that she owns at least the interest in land that she is purporting to convey to the grantee. (Thus, if A's deed purports to give B complete ownership of Blackacre, but at the time of the conveyance A had only a twenty-year lease to Blackacre, the covenant would be breached.)

Covenant of the Right to Convey. Here the grantor covenants that she has full power to transfer the interest that the deed purports to convey. This covenant substantially overlaps the covenant of seisin, but provides protection in occasional circumstances where the covenant of seisin does not. For example, the fact that X is in adverse possession of Blackacre at the time A conveys to B does not affect A's ownership of the parcel and, thus, does not breach her covenant of seisin; it would, however, give B an action against A for breach of the covenant of the right to convey.

Covenant Against Encumbrances. This is the grantor's promise that no outstanding encumbrances affect ownership or use of the land. Mortgages, leases, unpaid taxes and judgment liens are typical encumbrances affecting ownership. Easements, building restrictions and rights in third parties to remove minerals or other resources from the land are typical encumbrances affecting use.

Covenant of Warranty. This is the single most frequently used covenant in the United States. It obligates the grantor to compensate the grantee for any losses when the title conveyed falls short of the title that the deed purports to convey. A covenant of *general warranty* encompasses all defects in title and shortages in the area conveyed, regardless of the reason for the defect or shortage. Covenants of *special warranty* limit the defects covered; they may, for example, cover only those defects that arose while the grantor owned the land.

Covenant of Quiet Enjoyment. Under this covenant, the grantor promises that the grantee's possession will not be disrupted either by the grantor or by anyone with a lawful claim superior to the grantor. (The covenant does not, however, protect against intrusions by trespassers.) Courts in the United States generally treat the covenant for quiet enjoyment as equivalent to the covenant of warranty.

Covenant for Further Assurances. Rarely used in the United States, the covenant for further assurances obligates the grantor to take such further reasonable steps as are necessary to cure defects in the grantee's title. For example, the grantor might be required to obtain the release of an encumbrance or to buy off an adverse possessor. Unlike the covenant of warranty, which gives the grantee damages for the land he has lost, the covenant for further assurances enables the grantee to remain in possession of the land—a particularly valuable right when the land has substantially appreciated in value.

The first three covenants—seisin, right to convey and freedom from encumbrances—are commonly called *present covenants* because they make representations respecting the condition of title at the time the deed is delivered to the grantee. As a consequence, these covenants are breached only if the defect they cover exists at the time of delivery, and the statute of limitations for breach begins to run from that time. The second set of three covenants—warranty, quiet enjoyment and further assurances—are called *future covenants* because they protect against interferences with possession occurring at some future time, and obligate the grantor to take steps to correct the interference at that time. As a consequence, the statute of limitations for their breach begins to run not from the moment of delivery, but rather from the moment at which the grantee or his successor is first evicted from possession.

Deeds sometimes spell out each of the agreed-upon covenants in detail. Many states, however, have eliminated the need for full explication by providing that a deed's use of a single key word or phrase will automatically incorporate specified covenants in the deed unless the deed expressly excludes them. For example, in Alabama use of the word "grant," "bargain" or "sell" will imply covenants of seisin, freedom from encumbrances created by the grantor, and quiet enjoyment. Ala. Code 1975 § 35–4–271.

BROWN v. LOBER

Supreme Court of Illinois, 1979.
75 Ill.2d 547, 27 Ill.Dec. 780, 389 N.E.2d 1188.

UNDERWOOD, Justice:

Plaintiffs instituted this action in the Montgomery County circuit court based on an alleged breach of the covenant of seisin in their warranty deed. The trial court held that although there had been a breach of the covenant of seisin, the suit was barred by the 10-year statute of limitations in section 16 of the Limitations Act (Ill.Rev.Stat. 1975, ch. 83, par. 17). Plaintiffs' posttrial motion, which was based on an alleged breach of the covenant of quiet enjoyment, was also denied. A divided Fifth District Appellate Court reversed and remanded. We allowed the defendant's petition for leave to appeal.

The parties submitted an agreed statement of facts which sets forth the relevant history of this controversy. Plaintiffs purchased 80 acres of Montgomery County real estate from William and Faith Bost and received a statutory warranty deed containing no exceptions, dated December 21, 1957. Subsequently, plaintiffs took possession of the land and recorded their deed.

On May 8, 1974, plaintiffs granted a coal option to Consolidated Coal Company (Consolidated) for the coal rights on the 80-acre tract for the sum of $6,000. Approximately two years later, however, plaintiffs "discovered" that they, in fact, owned only a one-third interest in the subsurface coal rights. It is a matter of public record that, in 1947, a prior grantor had reserved a two-thirds interest in the mineral rights on the property. Although plaintiffs had their abstract of title examined in 1958 and 1968 for loan purposes, they contend that until May 4, 1976, they believed that they were the sole owners of the surface and subsurface rights on the 80-acre tract. Upon discovering that a prior grantor had reserved a two-thirds interest in the coal rights, plaintiffs and Consolidated renegotiated their agreement to provide for payment of $2,000 in exchange for a one-third interest in the subsurface coal rights. On May 25, 1976, plaintiffs filed this action against the executor of the estate of Faith Bost, seeking damages in the amount of $4,000.

The deed which plaintiffs received from the Bosts was a general statutory form warranty deed meeting the requirements of section 9 of "An Act concerning conveyances" (Ill.Rev.Stat.1957, ch. 30, par. 8). That section provides:

> "Every deed in substance in the above form, when otherwise duly executed, shall be deemed and held a conveyance in fee simple, to the grantee, his heirs or assigns, with covenants on the part of the grantor, (1) that at the time of the making and delivery of such deed he was lawfully seized of an indefeasible estate in fee simple, in and to the premises therein described, and had good right and full power to convey the same; (2) that the same were then free from all incumbrances; and (3) that he warrants to the grantee, his heirs and assigns, the quiet and peaceable possession of such premises, and will defend the title thereto against all persons who may lawfully claim the same. And such covenants shall be obligatory upon any grantor, his heirs and personal representatives, as fully and with like effect as if written at length in such deed." Ill.Rev.Stat.1957, ch. 30, par. 8.

The effect of this provision is that certain covenants of title are implied in every statutory form warranty deed. Subsection 1 contains the covenant of seisin and the covenant of good right to convey. These covenants, which are considered synonymous assure the grantee that the grantor is, at the time of the conveyance, lawfully seized and has the power to convey an estate of the quality and quantity which he professes to convey.

Subsection 2 represents the covenant against incumbrances. An incumbrance is any right to, or interest in, land which may subsist in a third party to the diminution of the value of the estate, but consistent with the passing of the fee by conveyance.

Subsection 3 sets forth the covenant of quiet enjoyment, which is synonymous with the covenant of warranty in Illinois. By this covenant, "the grantor warrants to the grantee, his heirs and assigns, the possession of the premises and that he will defend the title granted by the terms of the deed against persons who may lawfully claim the same, and that such covenant shall be obligatory upon the grantor, his heirs, personal representatives, and assigns." Biwer v. Martin (1920), 294 Ill. 488, 497, 128 N.E. 518, 522.

Plaintiffs' complaint is premised upon the fact that "William Roy Bost and Faith Bost covenanted that they were the owners in fee simple of the above described property at the time of the conveyance to the plaintiffs." While the complaint could be more explicit, it appears that plaintiffs were alleging a cause of action for breach of the covenant of seisin. This court has stated repeatedly that the covenant of seisin is a covenant *in praesenti* and, therefore, if broken at all, is broken at the time of delivery of the deed.

Since the deed was delivered to the plaintiffs on December 21, 1957, any cause of action for breach of the covenant of seisin would have accrued on that date. The trial court held that this cause of action was barred by the statute of limitations. No question is raised as to the applicability of the 10-year statute of limitations (Ill.Rev. Stat.1975, ch. 83, par. 17). We conclude, therefore, that the cause of action for breach of the covenant of seisin was properly determined by the trial court to be barred by the statute of limitations since plaintiffs did not file their complaint until May 25, 1976, nearly 20 years after their alleged cause of action accrued.

In their post-trial motion, plaintiffs set forth as an additional theory of recovery an alleged breach of the covenant of quiet enjoyment. The trial court, without explanation, denied the motion. The appellate court reversed, holding that the cause of action on the covenant of quiet enjoyment was not barred by the statute of limitations. The appellate court theorized that plaintiffs' cause of action did not accrue until 1976, when plaintiffs discovered that they only had a one-third interest in the subsurface coal rights and renegotiated their contract with the coal company for one-third of the previous contract price. The primary issue before us, therefore, is when, if at all, the plaintiffs' cause of action for breach of the covenant of quiet enjoyment is deemed to have accrued.

This court has stated on numerous occasions that, in contrast to the covenant of seisin, the covenant of warranty or quiet enjoyment is prospective in nature and is breached only when there is an actual or constructive eviction of the covenantee by the paramount titleholder.

The cases are also replete with statements to the effect that the mere existence of paramount title in one other than the covenantee is not sufficient to constitute a breach of the covenant of warranty or quiet enjoyment: "[T]here must be a union of acts of disturbance and lawful title, to constitute a breach of the covenant for quiet enjoyment, or warranty . . . ." (Barry v. Guild (1888), 126 Ill. 439, 446,

18 N.E. 759, 761.) "[T]here is a general concurrence that something more than the mere existence of a paramount title is necessary to constitute a breach of the covenant of warranty." (Scott v. Kirkendall (1878), 88 Ill. 465, 467.) "A mere want of title is no breach of this covenant. There must not only be a want of title, but there must be an ouster under a paramount title." Moore v. Vail (1855), 17 Ill. 185, 189.

The question is whether plaintiffs have alleged facts sufficient to constitute a constructive eviction. They argue that if a covenantee fails in his effort to sell an interest in land because he discovers that he does not own what his warranty deed purported to convey, he has suffered a constructive eviction and is thereby entitled to bring an action against his grantor for breach of the covenant of quiet enjoyment. We think that the decision of this court in Scott v. Kirkendall (1878), 88 Ill. 465, is controlling on this issue and compels us to reject plaintiffs' argument.

In *Scott*, an action was brought for breach of the covenant of warranty by a grantee who discovered that other parties had paramount title to the land in question. The land was vacant and unoccupied at all relevant times. This court, in rejecting the grantee's claim that there was a breach of the covenant of quiet enjoyment, quoted the earlier decision in Moore v. Vail (1855), 17 Ill. 185, 191:

> " 'Until that time, (the taking possession by the owner of the paramount title,) he might peaceably have entered upon and enjoyed the premises, without resistance or molestation, which was all his grantors covenanted he should do. They did not guarantee to him a perfect title, but the possession and enjoyment of the premises.' " 88 Ill. 465, 468.

Relying on this language in *Moore*, the *Scott* court concluded:

> "We do not see but what this fully decides the present case against the appellant. It holds that the mere existence of a paramount title does not constitute a breach of the covenant. That is all there is here. There has been no assertion of the adverse title. The land has always been vacant. Appellant could at any time have taken peaceable possession of it. He has in no way been prevented or hindered from the enjoyment of the possession by any one having a better right. It was but the possession and enjoyment of the premises which was assured to him, and there has been no disturbance or interference in that respect. True, there is a superior title in another, but appellant has never felt 'its pressure upon him.' " 88 Ill. 465, 468–69.

Admittedly, *Scott* dealt with surface rights while the case before us concerns subsurface mineral rights. We are, nevertheless, convinced that the reasoning employed in *Scott* is applicable to the present case. While plaintiffs went into possession of the surface area, they cannot be said to have possessed the subsurface minerals. "Possession of the surface does not carry possession of the minerals

. . . . [Citation.] To possess the mineral estate, one must undertake the actual removal thereof from the ground or do such other act as will apprise the community that such interest is in the exclusive use and enjoyment of the claiming party." Failoni v. Chicago & North Western Ry. Co. (1964), 30 Ill.2d 258, 262, 195 N.E.2d 619, 622.

Since no one has, as yet, undertaken to remove the coal or otherwise manifested a clear intent to exclusively "possess" the mineral estate, it must be concluded that the subsurface estate is "vacant." As in *Scott*, plaintiffs "could at any time have taken peaceable possession of it. [They have] in no way been prevented or hindered from the enjoyment of the possession by any one having a better right." (88 Ill. 465, 468.) Accordingly, until such time as one holding paramount title interferes with plaintiffs' right of possession (*e.g.*, by beginning to mine the coal), there can be no constructive eviction and, therefore, no breach of the covenant of quiet enjoyment.

What plaintiffs are apparently attempting to do on this appeal is to extend the protection afforded by the covenant of quiet enjoyment. However, we decline to expand the historical scope of this covenant to provide a remedy where another of the covenants of title is so clearly applicable. As this court stated in Scott v. Kirkendall (1878), 88 Ill. 465, 469:

> "To sustain the present action would be to confound all distinction between the covenant of warranty and that of seizin, or of right to convey. They are not equivalent covenants. An action will lie upon the latter, though there be no disturbance of possession. A defect of title will suffice. Not so with the covenant of warranty, or for quiet enjoyment, as has always been held by the prevailing authority."

The covenant of seisin, unquestionably, was breached when the Bosts delivered the deed to plaintiffs, and plaintiffs then had a cause of action. However, despite the fact that it was a matter of public record that there was a reservation of a two-thirds interest in the mineral rights in the earlier deed, plaintiffs failed to bring an action for breach of the covenant of seisin within the 10-year period following delivery of the deed. The likely explanation is that plaintiffs had not secured a title opinion at the time they purchased the property, and the subsequent examiners for the lenders were not concerned with the mineral rights. Plaintiffs' oversight, however, does not justify us in overruling earlier decisions in order to recognize an otherwise premature cause of action. The mere fact that plaintiffs' original contract with Consolidated had to be modified due to their discovery that paramount title to two-thirds of the subsurface minerals belonged to another is not sufficient to constitute the constructive eviction necessary to a breach of the covenant of quiet enjoyment.

Finally, although plaintiffs also have argued in this court that there was a breach of the covenant against incumbrances entitling them to recovery, we decline to address this issue which was argued for the first time on appeal. It is well settled that questions not raised in the trial court will not be considered by this court on appeal.

Accordingly, the judgment of the appellate court is reversed, and the judgment of the circuit court of Montgomery County is affirmed.

Appellate court reversed; circuit court affirmed.

QUESTIONS

Was it fair in *Lober* for plaintiffs' action on the covenant of seisin to be barred by the statute of limitations? For plaintiffs' action on the covenant of quiet enjoyment to be dismissed on the ground that the covenant had not yet been breached? What, if anything, could plaintiff have done to precipitate a constructive eviction and hence a breach of the covenant of quiet enjoyment? How would you advise a client caught between one title claim that is not yet ripe and another that is overripe? Can you draft a covenant that would cover the situation that arose in *Lober*?

Should plaintiffs have been barred on the alternative ground that, at the time they accepted delivery they knew or should have known of the outstanding mineral interest? As a general rule, a buyer's actual or constructive knowledge of a title defect or encumbrance will not defeat his action on a covenant that covers the defect or encumbrance. See Jones v. Grow Investment & Mortgage Co., 11 Utah 2d 326, 358 P.2d 909 (1961) ("The very purpose of the covenant is to protect a grantee against defects and to hold that one can be protected only against unknown defects would be to rob the covenant of most of its value. If from the force of the covenant it is desired to eliminate known defects, or to limit the covenant in any way, it is easy to do so.").

How effective are title covenants in guaranteeing not the quality of title, but rather the quantity of land conveyed? Consider the next principal case.

MAXWELL v. REDD

Supreme Court of Kansas, 1972.
209 Kan. 264, 496 P.2d 1320.

KAUL, Justice:

This action was brought by plaintiffs-appellees to recover damages from defendant-appellant on the theory that defendant breached covenants of title in a deed for conveyance to plaintiffs. The controversy arose when it was discovered, after an exchange of one-half quarter sections of land, that defendant did not own the one-half of the quarter section which he conveyed but only 76.5 acres thereof, which was described in metes and bounds. The contract and deeds effecting the exchange were executed on January 10, 1968. In their brief plaintiffs state that upon discovery that defendant owned only part of the tract involved they immediately requested that defendant either restore the parties to their original position by mutual reconveyances of the exchanged lands, or that the balance of the tract be acquired at defendant's expense, or that defendant pay damages to plaintiffs for the loss sustained. Defendant refused and plaintiffs filed suit.

In his answer to plaintiffs' petition defendant admitted that he owned only the metes and bounds description set out in plaintiffs' petition, but alleged that the facts were either known to plaintiffs or in the exercise of due care should have been known to them and that, in spite of such knowledge or access thereto, plaintiffs proceeded with the trade. Defendant further alleged that the market value of the land received by plaintiffs was in excess of the market value of the land received by him; that the parties exchanged land in gross; and that the exact acreage was of no consequence. Requests for admissions by defendant were filed, and on October 31, 1969, a pretrial conference was had. The pretrial order reflects facts agreed upon as follows:

"(2) Facts agreed upon by the parties: That plaintiffs and defendant are Reno county residents; that in the spring of 1968, plaintiffs deeded to defendant the South Half of the Southwest Quarter of section 17, Township 24 South, Range 7 West, in Reno county, Kansas; and in return defendant deeded to plaintiffs the West Half of the Southeast Quarter of section 30, Township 23 South, Range 6 West, in Reno county, Kansas; that subsequently it was ascertained the defendant did not have merchantable title to all of the land he deeded to plaintiffs."

Plaintiffs filed a motion for summary judgment on the issue of liability upon which the trial court ruled as follows:

"THIS matter comes before the court upon the plaintiffs' motion for summary judgment with respect to the question of the defendant's liability to plaintiffs only. Case files to date, and KSA 60–236, are made a part of this memorandum opinion by reference. Arguments and admissions are presented by counsel.

"From the pleadings it is conceded that on Janury 10, 1968, plaintiffs entered into a written contract with the defendant whereby plaintiffs would convey by warranty deed the $S^1/_2$ of the $SW^1/_4$ of 17–24–6, in Reno County, Kansas, to said defendant, and in turn, said defendant would convey by warranty deed to plaintiffs the $W^1/_2$ of the $SE^1/_4$ of 30–23–6, in Reno County, Kansas; that said warranty deeds were so given; that subsequently it was discovered defendant did not have good and merchantable title to all of the realty described in said deed given plaintiffs but only owned that portion as set forth in paragraph 5 of plaintiffs' petition.

"In addition to the foregoing, the court finds that there was a partial failure of title and a breach of warranty with respect to the deed given plaintiffs by the defendant.

"Accordingly, partial summary judgment in favor of plaintiffs and against defendant with reference to all questions of liability only is hereby granted.

"This matter will be set for trial during the January 1970 term of court with reference to the matters of damages, if any."

A jury was waived and the issue of damages was tried to the court on June 10, 1970.

The trial court filed a memorandum opinion which we quote in part as follows:

"A point to be remembered: had the defendant owned merchantable title to all of the West Half of the Southeast Quarter of Section 30, Township 23 South, Range 6 West, in Reno County, Kansas, then whether or not same contained 80 acres or 76.5 acres would have been immaterial. However, the contract and deed called for conveyance by defendant to plaintiffs of the above described land to which defendant only had partial title.

"From the evidence presented the court finds: that as of January 10, 1968, the value of the West Half of the Southeast Quarter of Section 30, Township 23 South, Range 6 West, in Reno County, Kansas, was $365.00 per acre; that according to the government survey said West Half of the Southeast Quarter of Section 30, Township 23 South, Range 6 West, in Reno County, Kansas, consists of 80 acres; and that there was a shortage of 3.5 acres in the quantity of land as described in the defendant's deed of conveyance to the plaintiffs and the amount to which the defendant actually had merchantable title.

"Accordingly, judgment is given plaintiffs against the defendant in the sum of $1277.50, ($365 per acre $\times$ 3.5 acres), with interest at 8% per annum from January 10, 1968. Costs are assessed against the defendant."

Judgment was entered in accord with the trial court's opinion and this appeal followed.

On appeal, as in the trial court, the main thrust of defendant's argument is that the parties dealt in gross rather than on an acreage basis, and thus plaintiffs are not entitled to damages for a 3.5 deficiency in acreage which defendant says is inconsequential.

In his brief defendant states his position in these words:

". . . Where it [a sale] is by the tract, the courts have, in the absence of fraud, either refused altogether to grant relief for a mistake, even though the mistake results in a large excess or deficiency, or have limited relief to situations where the deficiency is so great as to warrant the conclusion that the parties would not have contracted had the truth been known, or where the extent of the discrepancy warrants the presumption of fraud." (citing 1 A.L.R.2d, Anno. § 6, p. 18.)

Defendant cites a number of our cases holding in accord with his position. (Pickering v. Hollabaugh, 194 Kan. 804, 401 P.2d 891; Martin v. Ott, 114 Kan. 419, 219 P. 275; and Maffet v. Schaar, 89 Kan. 403, 131 P. 589.) The cases mentioned demonstrate the distinction between a sale on an acreage basis, as in *Maffet*, and a sale in gross, as described in the *Martin* case, or an exchange in gross, as described in the *Pickering* case. The law is succinctly summed up by Justice Dawson speaking for the court in Martin v. Ott, supra:

"The law on this subject is really simple. Where a farm is sold as a represented number of acres, the vendor is liable for a deficiency in the acreage. Where a farm is sold in gross—that is, for a lump sum regardless of the acreage—the vendor is not liable for any deficiency in the acreage except for fraud which exception raises a question of fact, and in this case that question has been fairly determined against the plaintiff . . . ." (114 Kan. p. 424, 219 P. p. 277.)

In the *Maffet*, *Martin* and *Pickering* cases, although there was a deficiency in acreage, the vendors in each instance owned all the property described in the respective conveyances. In *Maffet* the total consideration was arrived at on a price per acre basis, and recovery was predicated on the fact that the vendee had contracted on the basis of a specified number of acres which did not in fact exist within the description. In *Martin* and *Pickering* the transactions were in gross, and since the vendors in each instance were seized of all the property described, recovery was denied vendees in each case—the court holding that the recital of acreage in each case was for identification purposes and not a warranty of acreage. None of the cases mentioned were actions brought for a breach of any warranty of title.

Obviously, the transaction in the instant case was an exchange in gross. However, the trouble with defendant's position is that the rule dealing with acreage deficiencies in the case of a transfer in gross presupposes that the sale or exchange in gross transfers to the purchaser all of the description contracted for. As we held in *Martin* a party contracting on an acreage basis for a specified tract at an agreed price per acre is entitled to recover the difference between the purchase price and the actual acreage times the price per acre. It is equally obvious that, in the absence of fraud or mutual mistake of fact, a party who exchanges or buys in gross by described boundaries or government survey rather than on an acreage basis has no claim for damages if he receives a good title to the entire tract described, notwithstanding it contains less acreage than expected by him. So in the instant case if plaintiffs, as purchasers of the west half of the quarter section in question, had discovered it contained less than eighty acres by reason of a correction line or was a short eighty because of some other similar reason, they could not demand a proportionate refund of the purchase price for a sale in gross as long as they received title to the entire west half of the southeast quarter. Instead of the west half of the southeast described in the deed, and for which they bargained, plaintiffs received only a tract 78 rods by 160 rods by 75 rods by 160 rods situated in the west half of the southeast quarter. The paramount title of the remainder of the west half of the quarter section was admitted to be in parties other than defendant. In the deed to plaintiffs, defendant, together with the usual warranties, specifically covenanted that—

". . . he is lawfully seized in his own right, of an absolute and indefeasible estate of inheritance, in fee simple, of and in all and singular the above granted and described premises . . . ."

When the defendant refused to restore the parties by mutual reconveyance or to pay plaintiffs damages for their loss this action was instituted to recover damages for breach of covenant of title, or more specifically the covenant of seisin.

The guarantee of a covenant of seisin is that the grantor, at the time of the conveyance, was lawfully seized of a good, absolute and indefeasible estate of inheritance, in fee simple, and had power to convey the same. Where a grantor did not have title to a part of the land conveyed there was a breach of the covenant.

The ordinary remedy for breach of a covenant of title in a conveyance of land is an action at law for damages.

The applicable rule is stated in these terms in 7 Thompson on Real Property [1962 Replacement], Covenants in Deeds, § 3180, p. 248:

". . . The grantee may recover for a breach of a covenant of seisin though the seisin fails as to a part only of the land conveyed by a deed . . . .

"If at the time of the conveyance the grantee finds the land in the possession of one claiming paramount title, the covenant of seisin is broken. Proof of eviction is not necessary in order to sustain an action for breach of covenant of seisin; it is sufficient to negative the covenant and prove that the grantor did not have title to the land at the time of the conveyance." (p. 249.)

An action for damages is recognized as the remedy afforded a grantee for breach of a covenant of seisin in this state. The time limitation in which such an action on a covenant of seisin may be brought is specifically prescribed in K.S.A.1971 Supp. 60–511(2).

Defendant argues that our holding in the case of Brewer v. Schammerhorn, 183 Kan. 739, 332 P.2d 526, requires that plaintiffs here must have relied upon a specified acreage in order to recover. The *Brewer* case involved conveyances of tracts from a "long" quarter section which, as a whole, contained slightly more than 163½ acres. The original owner first conveyed the "North 80 acres *pre-*

cisely" thus there remained the South 83½ acres. The owner then conveyed the remainder of the quarter section, describing it as the south one-half, together with one-half of another quarter section, included with the descriptions was the phrase *"containing 160 acres, more or less."* The successors in title to the original grantees of the long quarter became involved in a boundary dispute involving the 3.5 acres which gave rise to the litigation. Parol evidence was admitted to explain the ambiguity. On appeal this court, relying heavily on the presumption that the grantor intended to convey everything remaining, held that the deed conveying the south half took with it the extra acreage not included in the "precise North 80 acres" previously conveyed.

The *Brewer* case is not applicable to the issue here. It involved no breach of covenant and there was no question raised concerning a deficiency of title to the property conveyed. The controversy there involved ownership of land apparently not conveyed and the construction of an ambiguous description. There is no evidence here, such as in the *Brewer* case, which indicated an intention of the parties contrary to what was expressed in the deed. The only evidence bearing on the subject was the testimony of plaintiff Ernest A. Maxwell who was called as a witness by defendant. Mr. Maxwell testified that he was not familiar with the boundaries of the tract prior to the conveyance; that he was trading for the west half of the quarter section, and entered into the exchange on that basis; that he was bargaining for and would receive such tract, which was what the contract called for. As narrated in the record, he testified:

". . . [T]hat there is a hedge row in the land, but it is not a boundary line; that driving by the land you would naturally think that it was a boundary line; that he traded for the W/2 of that quarter section; . . . ."

Defendant makes no claim that the hedge row constituted an agreed boundary line, nor was there any evidence offered to that effect. This action was neither pleaded nor tried as a boundary line dispute but as an action for breach of warranty of title and defended on the theory of an exchange in gross.

In view of what has been said the order of the trial court granting judgment to plaintiffs on the issue of liability must be affirmed.

We turn next to defendant's complaints concerning the measure of damages adopted by the trial court.

The trial court found as follows:

". . . [T]he measure of damages for the partial breach of a covenant of warranty in a deed is the relative value which the part of the real estate as to which the title failed bears to the purchase price or consideration of the whole estate. The parties are further instructed that upon the partial breach of a covenant of title, and where the land to which the title has failed in part was conveyed in exchange for other land without a stipulated or agreed value, the plaintiffs' recovery should be the proportionate part of the value of such other land rather than the value of the land to which title failed. For example, if the value of the portion of the land to which title failed represented $1/20$th of the whole value of the entire tract conveyed to the plaintiffs, then the plaintiffs would be entitled to recover a sum equal to $1/20$th of the value of the land conveyed to the defendant in exchange."

The trial court then proceeded to find from the evidence presented that the value per acre of the west one-half deeded to plaintiffs was $365.00 which was multiplied by 3.5, resulting in the judgment of $1,277.50. There was no variance in the per acre value of the 3.5 acres.

There was evidence to support the findings and we believe the proper measure of damages was applied with respect to a partial breach of the covenant of seisin. The applicable rule is set forth in 20 Am.Jur.2d, Covenants, Conditions, Etc., § 144, p. 701:

> ". . . Thus, in the case of a partial breach of a covenant of warranty by reason of a failure of title to a portion of the estate conveyed resulting in eviction from that portion of the premises, the measure of damages is the relative value which the part as to which the title failed bears to the purchase price or consideration of the whole estate. A similar rule applies where the action is based upon the covenant of seisin or right to convey; in such case the covenantee recovers pro tanto only . . . ." (pp. 702–703.)

The rule stated is followed in this jurisdiction. In the early case of Dale v. Shively, 8 Kan. 276, the court dealt specifically with a breach of covenant of seisin. At page 279 we find this statement:

> "As to the measure of damages: The consideration money, with interest, is the extent to which the damages can, under any circumstances, be recovered upon this covenant, upon a total breach; but where there is a partial breach, the grantee may recover *pro tanto* . . . ."

Although there was testimony that the lands exchanged were of approximately equal value, notwithstanding the deficiency of 3.5 acres in the tract deeded them, plaintiffs were entitled to the benefit of their bargain and they bargained for the land described in the deed. This was not an action for the breach of a contract to exchange land. The contract had long since been performed. The lands had been described, the deeds executed and delivered and possession transferred, all in accord with the provisions of the contract. When the deficiency of defendant's title was discovered there was no remedy left to plaintiffs except an action on the covenants of the deed.

We have carefully examined authorities cited by defendant on the measure of damages and the application thereof. The cases cited by defendant deal with the measure of damages as applied to actions for breach of contract or with actions where the deficiency was a shortage of the acreage represented to be within the land described, not with a situation where the grantor did not own what was conveyed as in the instant case.

Finally, defendant complains concerning the trial court's allowance of interest at eight percent per annum from the date of the contract, January 10, 1968. Defendant makes a two-pronged attack on the trial court's ruling. Defendant claims first that damages were unliquidated and totally unascertainable prior to trial and thus no interest prior to judgment should have been allowed. Second, defendant argues that if interest prior to judgment is allowed then the rate can only be six percent for that period. We believe both contentions have merit. With respect to defendant's second contention, K.S.A. 16–201 provides in substance that the legal rate of interest shall be six percent per annum, when no other interest is agreed upon. Prior to July 1969, K.S.A. 16–204 provided that all judgments shall bear interest at the rate of six percent per annum from the date rendered. Effective July 1, 1969, K.S.A. 16–204 [now 1971 Supp.], was amended to provide for eight percent. We have held the amendment to have only prospective application. K.S.A. 16–201 was not amended, thus in no event could more than six percent per annum be allowed prior to the date of judgment on June 10, 1970.

Turning next to defendant's argument on his first point with respect to the allowance of interest. We are cognizant that the basic measure of damages generally adopted for a breach of covenants of warranty in a suit by grantee against grantor, is the value of the land at the time of the conveyance, which is the consideration agreed upon by the parties, with interest and costs. The transaction in the instant case, however, was an exchange of lands. There was no value or consideration fixed by the parties in either the contract or deeds; neither is there any evidence that the parties at any time during negotiations fixed a value for the lands either on a lump sum or per acre basis. In other words, the claim of plaintiffs was not only unliquidated but as a practical matter it was unascertainable prior to determination at trial.

Under the particular facts and circumstances appearing in the instant case, we hold that the allowance of interest from the date of the deed, January 10, 1968, to the date of the judgment, June 10, 1970, should be deleted from the judgment which is in all respects affirmed.

FONTRON, J., concurs in the result.

B. TITLE ASSURANCE

1. THE RECORD SYSTEM

The aim of the record system in America is to protect a buyer of land against the possibility that his seller, or some predecessor in interest to his seller, previously conveyed away all or part of the interest that the buyer has contracted to buy.

At early common law, when land was transferred by the ceremony of feoffment with livery of seisin, the possibility of such multiple transfers was small. The required presence of witnesses disciplined landowners from trying to sell the same parcel twice. But, with the growth of documentary transfers after the Statute of Uses, and with the proliferation of interests such as covenants, easements and tax and mortgage liens that could simultaneously coexist in a single parcel, it became increasingly probable that a scheming or forgetful grantor would fail to inform her grantee of some prior, adverse transfer respecting the land. Covenants of title partially protected grantees who obtained less than they bargained for. Covenantors could not always be found, however, and, if found, often lacked the resources to make good on their promises. A rule was needed to determine the rights of competing grantees fairly and efficiently.

The common law responded with a simple rule for determining who should prevail when grantor A conveyed the same interest in land to two grantees, B and C: *first in time, first in right*. The rule worked fairly and efficiently when the first grantee, B, went into immediate possession of the land. A quick inspection by C before accepting and paying for the deed from A, would disclose that someone other than A was in possession. C's inquiry of B as to why B rather than A was in possession would disclose that B's possession was under a prior deed from A. C could then rescind the contract with A and recover any deposit paid. But the rule of first in time, first in right was neither efficient nor fair when, as often happened, B did not go into possession. C, seeing either A or no one in possession, would have no reason to inquire into the possibility that anyone other than A had title. C, having paid the purchase price, would then lose his interest when B later asserted his prior rights.

The first recording acts were passed to resolve this shortcoming. The American acts replaced the common law rule of first in time, first in right with an equally simple, but fairer and more efficient prescription: *first to record, first in right*. By providing a place to record instruments effecting transfers of real property—typically county recorders' offices—and by providing that an instrument of transfer will be valid as against subsequent, competing instruments only if it is recorded, the American record system provided a comparatively cheap and certain method for C not only to determine whether A was conveying good title to him, but also to assure himself that title, once conveyed to him, would not be lost to any subsequent competing grantee.

The system enabled C to determine the status of A's title by conducting a record search in the county where the land was situated. Under the system, if prior grantee, B, was not in possession, C would nonetheless discover the conveyance to B if B had recorded it. The title search would fail to disclose the A–B transfer only when B had failed to record the instrument. But, if B had failed to record, his interest would be invalid against C under a first to record, first in right regime—so long as C promptly recorded *his* instrument of transfer. And by promptly recording, C would gain priority not only over all earlier grantees who failed to record, but against all grantees subsequent to him who, by definition, will have recorded later.

The genius of the American recording system is that it operates almost entirely on individual initiative. A buyer who follows the steps prescribed by the system can almost always assure himself of good title. Although American recording acts take different forms, all assure the buyer that his interest will be secure as against both earlier and later grantees if he follows the standard operating procedure of searching title down to the moment of closing, rejecting title at that point if it is unmarketable, and, if title is marketable, recording his interest at the moment of closing.

Because recording acts of one kind or another have been enacted in every state, and because they so completely dominate the conveyancing system, it is easy to overlook the fact that the recording acts have only partially preempted the common law rule of first in time, first in right, with the result that, in situations to which the recording acts do not apply, the common law priorities still govern in every state.

When will the common law priority, rather than the recording act priority apply? One recurrent situation arises when the interest that A conveyed to B is one for which the local recording act does not require recordation. Because the recording act does not apply, and the party first in time is first in right, B, who is first, but has not recorded, will prevail over C, even though C made a title search and recorded promptly. This poses no problem for C in states that give an all-encompassing description of recordable instruments. Arizona, for example, makes any "instrument affecting real property" recordable, Ariz.Rev.Stat.Ann. § 33–411 (1956). Most states, however, specify several exceptions. Some eastern states exempt leases of less than seven years from recording requirements, while western states traditionally except leases of one year or less. Compare Mass. Gen. Laws Ann. c. 183, § 4 (1977) with West's Ann.Cal.Civ. Code

§ 1214. Buyers in these states face the risk of taking subject to prior unrecordable interests.

Under modern recording acts, *C* faces other extra-record risks as well. Virtually no state today will protect *C* against prior grantee *B*, even though *B* had not recorded, if a reasonable inspection of the land by *C* would have disclosed *B*'s prior interest. Further, *C*'s title search, no matter how diligently conducted, will not uncover rights acquired by adverse possession. Nor will it disclose the possible fact that a deed in the chain of title was forged, undelivered or executed by an incompetent. For a hair-raising catalogue of extra-record risks to title, see Straw, Off-Record Risks for Bona Fide Purchasers of Interests in Real Property, 72 Dick.L.Rev. 35 (1967).

Should recording acts be revised to completely preempt the common law priority and be conclusive as to the current state of title? If you were a residential tenant under a short term lease, would you be happy knowing that, under such a regime, your lease could be terminated at any time by a grantee from your landlord unless you had recorded it? Will your answer depend on how easily and cheaply recording can be accomplished?

For a provocative analysis of some of these points, see Baird & Jackson, Information, Uncertainty and the Transfer of Property, 13 J. Legal Stud. 331 (1984).

WILSON v. SCHNEITER'S RIVERSIDE GOLF COURSE

Supreme Court of Utah, 1974.
523 P.2d 1226.

TUCKETT, Justice:

The plaintiffs initiated these proceedings in the district court seeking a decree quieting their title to certain land in Weber County. The defendant counterclaimed praying that the title to the disputed area be quieted in it. The trial court found the issues in favor of the defendant and ordered the title be quieted in the defendant. The plaintiffs are here seeking a reversal.

On March 19, 1965, the plaintiffs entered into a real estate contract with one Lillie Sherwood whereby they agreed to purchase a tract of unoccupied land. The contract and a warranty deed were deposited with an escrow. On April 9, 1965, the plaintiffs recorded a notice of their purchase in the County Recorder's office.

The defendant had entered into a real estate contract with Lillie Sherwood whereby they undertook to purchase a tract of land adjacent to that involved in the Wilsons' contract. There was an overlap in the descriptions of the property sold to the Wilsons and the defendant that affected 2.39 acres which is the subject matter of these proceedings. During November 1965 the defendant received information of the plaintiffs' recorded notice of their purchase and thereafter paid off the balance due under its purchase contract and recorded the deed from Lillie Sherwood.

In July 1970 the plaintiffs became aware of the defendant's claim of ownership. The plaintiffs continued to make the payments and in July 1972 they paid the balance due under the contract. Plaintiffs were concerned that should they fail to make the payments their interest in the property would be forfeited under the provisions of the contract. The trial court found that the plaintiffs were not bona fide purchasers for value inasmuch as they had paid the balance due under their purchase contract after they had learned of defendant's claim of ownership of the tract of land in question. It should be noted that the defendant likewise paid off the balance due under its contract after it had notice both actual and constructive of the claimed interest of the plaintiffs. It would thus appear that the claims of the plaintiffs and the defendant are on equal footing.

The provisions of Section 57-3-2, U.C.A.1953, are governing in this case and are herein set out:

> Every conveyance, or instrument in writing affecting real estate, executed, acknowledged or proved, and certified, in the manner prescribed by this title, and every patent to lands within this state duly executed and verified according to law, and every judgment, order or decree of any court of record in this state, or a copy thereof, required by law to be recorded in the office of the county recorder shall, from the time of filing the same with the recorder for record, impart notice to all persons of the contents thereof; and subsequent purchasers, mortgagees and lien holders shall be deemed to purchase and take with notice.

Plaintiffs having recorded their notice of purchase prior to the recording of the defendant's deed, the defendant becomes the subsequent purchaser and is deemed to take with notice of the plaintiffs' interest. The sufficiency of the notice recorded by the plaintiffs was not an issue in the court below and we do not deal with it here.

The decision of the court below is reversed and that court is directed to enter a decree quieting title to the land in question in the plaintiffs. Appellants are entitled to costs.

CALLISTER, C.J., and CROCKETT, J., concur.

HENRIOD, J., concurs in the result.

ELLETT, Justice: (dissenting).

I am unable to concur in the main opinion for the following reasons:

The sequence of events which lead up to this lawsuit is as follows:

Schneiter bought on contract 40 acres of land, including the disputed strip, from Sherwood under date of April 2, 1962. Wilson bought on contract 64.42 acres of land from Sherwood, also including the disputed land, under date of March 19, 1965. Wilson did not record his contract but did record notice of his purchase on April 9, 1965. Schneiter first learned of Wilsons' interest and paid off the balance due on its contract and recorded the deed on November 12, 1965. Wilsons learned of Schneiter's claim in July, 1970, at which time they still owed $24,000 on their contract out of the original purchase price of $29,768.00. They paid the balance due, received their deed, and recorded it July 25, 1972, over six years after the deed to Schneiter had been recorded.

It is to be noted that each party here had only an equity in and to the disputed piece of ground prior to the time he received his deed.

Schneiter's equitable interest dated from April 2, 1962, while that of the Wilsons dated from March 19, 1965. The legal title was in Sherwood until November 12, 1965, when Schneiter got possession of its deed.

The law is well settled that where there is a conflict of equitable interests, the oldest equity has priority. The following statements in 55 Am.Jur., Vendor and Purchaser, are to the point:

> Sec. 693: The interest of a purchaser of real estate before a conveyance is a mere equitable interest, and is not sufficient to afford the purchaser protection against an earlier equal equity. Moreover, it is held in many cases that whatever a vendee who holds a mere equitable interest does to perfect his title after notice does not entitle him to protection as a bona fide purchaser, that the holder of a junior equitable interest who has knowledge of a superior equitable interest does not, by acquiring the legal title, cut off the outstanding equitable interest, and that although the purchaser may have made his contract to purchase and paid the purchase money before he has notice of the outstanding equity, yet if he receives notice before his own equity is clothed with the legal title, he takes subject to the prior equity. A similar rule has been applied to a prior unrecorded interest to which the purchaser has been held to take subject where he receives notice thereof before his purchase is completed by a conveyance of the legal title . . . ..

> Sec. 682: The interest of a purchaser of real estate before a conveyance is a mere equitable interest, and is not sufficient to afford the purchaser protection against an earlier equal equity . . . ..

> Sec. 678: The general rule that where the equities are otherwise equal, the older in point of time prevails, is applicable to the purchaser of an equitable interest in real estate. The equities being otherwise equal, nothing but the legal title will give priority to the equity junior in point of time. Hence, the protection afforded a bona fide purchaser of real estate extends, as a general rule, only to persons purchasing and acquiring the legal title, and not to

the purchaser of an equitable interest. Where the purchase is only of an equitable title, it is ordinarily taken with all its imperfections and outstanding equities, notwithstanding a valuable consideration may have been given, and there may have been no notice of the equity or defense against the title. In such case, the purchaser takes the place of the person from whom he purchases. . . .

As to who is a bona fide purchaser entitled to protection against a prior unrecorded conveyance or encumbrance, 66 Am.Jur.2d, Records and Recording Laws, Sec. 163, states the law in these words:

. . . The words "bona fide purchaser," therefore when introduced into the recording acts, were intended to be in accordance with the established meaning. To entitle one to the protection provided for bona fide purchasers by the recording acts, it has been held to be essential: (1) that he be the purchaser of the legal as distinguished from an equitable title . . . ..

If it be assumed that the purchaser of an equitable interest in land is a *purchaser* under the statute, then the Wilsons are not helped because the statute by its terms imparts notice to *subsequent purchasers*, etc. Schneiter was not a subsequent purchaser, but rather it was a prior purchaser; and when it purchased, there was nothing of record to show any conflicting interest at all.

The statute quoted in the prevailing opinion provides that every instrument in writing, affecting real estate, executed, acknowledged or proved, and certified, in the manner prescribed by this title, imparts notice from the time it is recorded, etc. The instrument recorded by the Wilsons was not an instrument affecting realty as contemplated by the statute. It was merely a notice to whom it may concern that they were purchasing certain land. They did not record their contract, which they should have done if they expected to be protected against *subsequent purchasers*, assuming that equitable interests are within the meaning of the statute.

If a purchaser of land fails to record his deed, he is not given the statutory protection to subsequent innocent purchasers, and the recording of a notice that he has purchased the land does not comply with the statute and, therefore, is of no force and effect so far as those who do not have actual knowledge is concerned.

It may well be that one who reads the notice may be alerted so as to have the equivalent of actual notice, and to this extent the filing of the notice may be of some value to the purchaser. In this case Schneiter never knew of the Wilson notice until November, 1965.

While this latter proposition was not urged in the brief of respondent, it is material to a proper determination of this case, because we are permitted to consider matters which are not urged when it will affirm the ruling of the trial court.

I think the judgment should be affirmed and respondent awarded costs.

QUESTIONS

Both the majority and dissenting justices in *Wilson* appeared to agree that defendant had an equitable interest in the land from April 2, 1962, when it signed the contract with Sherwood, until November 12, 1965, when it obtained and recorded a deed to the property, and that plaintiffs had an equitable interest in the property from March 19, 1965, when they signed their contract with Sherwood, until July 25, 1972, when they obtained and recorded a deed to the property. Although it should be obvious that neither party received legal title to the disputed strip before obtaining a deed from Sherwood, do you understand why each had equitable title before then? The answer lies in the rule of equitable conversion: at the moment a contract for the sale of real property is signed, equitable title passes to the buyer. (You have already seen the doctrine applied in allocating risk of accidental loss as between buyer and seller during the executory period, page 234 above.)

Which party would have prevailed under the facts of this case if no recording act had been in force, and the common law rule of first in time, first in right applied? If only equitable titles were compared, defendant would clearly prevail because it acquired its equitable interest before plaintiffs acquired theirs. If only legal titles were compared, defendant would again prevail because it acquired legal title before plaintiffs.

How did Utah's recording act alter these priorities? Was it correct to hold against defendant on the ground that, at the time it acquired legal title, it had constructive notice of plaintiff's prior equity embodied in the recorded "notice of purchase"? (Is it pertinent that when the plaintiffs acquired legal title *they* had notice of defendant's equitable and legal title?) Of what did defendant have constructive notice? Note that in the view of the dissenting justice, the "notice of purchase was not an instrument affecting realty as contemplated by the statute," and thus was neither recordable nor capable of imparting constructive notice. The majority sidestepped the point of recordability because it was "not in issue in the court below and we do not deal with it here."

As a practical matter what could defendant, as owner of an equitable interest on April 2, 1962, have done to protect itself against the possibility that a subsequent buyer would acquire an interest in the same parcel and record that interest before defendant acquired legal title? With the benefit of hindsight, it seems evident that defendant should have recorded a notice of its purchase on April 2, 1962, thus effectively putting any subsequent purchaser of equitable or legal title on notice of its interest. Yet, it is far from clear that on April 2,

1962, or at any time before the *Wilson* decision, any land buyer in Utah would have reasonably believed that a "notice of purchase" was a recordable interest, capable of imparting constructive notice.

a. Types of Recording Acts

JOHNSON, PURPOSE AND SCOPE OF RECORDING STATUTES

47 Iowa Law Review 231–233 (1962).

A basic policy question is whether emphasis should be upon penalizing those who fail to record or upon protecting those who deserve protection. Conceivably, strict adherence to the penalty approach could lead to requiring recordation as essential to the validity of a deed, even as to the grantor, in addition to the requirements of delivery and writing. On the other hand, it would be consistent with the protection approach to regard unrecorded deeds void only as to those who actually examine the records and who substantially change their positions in reliance thereon. No modern recording act (excluding Torrens acts) goes to either of these extremes. Rather, the impact of both policies—penalty and protection—may be observed in the acts now in force. How these seemingly inconsistent policies have been accommodated is a major question to be considered in this review of the salient features of land recording acts.

I. BASIC TYPES OF STATUTES

Recording acts typically are classified as (1) race, (2) notice, or (3) race-notice. If conveyees are allowed a specified period of time within which to record—a feature which may be added to any of the above types of acts but which is not common today—the statute is also categorized as a "period of grace" act. A recent survey placed the recording acts of only two states, Louisiana and North Carolina, in the race category generally, and those of three other states in that category as to some instruments—mortgages in Arkansas, Ohio, and Pennsylvania (except for purchase money) and oil and gas leases in Ohio. Most states have acts either of the notice or race-notice type, each type having about an equal following.

Of these types, the race statute is most consistent with the penalty principle. The North Carolina act provides: "No conveyance of land . . . shall be valid to pass any property, as against lien creditors or purchasers for a valuable consideration . . . but from the time of registration thereof . . . ." ² Under this act, as construed, an unrecorded conveyance is void even as to a subsequent purchaser who knew of its existence, and a subsequent bona fide purchaser gains no priority over the earlier unrecorded instrument unless he records first. Thus, priority is determined by a race to the records. Of course, an unrecorded conveyance would be valid as to the grantor, his heirs, devisees, donees, and anyone else other than "lien creditors or purchasers for a valuable consideration." The North Carolina act is very similar to the Colonial prototypes. While there are many factors which may have shaped the early acts, it has been asserted that the most significant was a desire to provide a substitute for the publicity afforded by livery of seisin, which had been discarded as a mode of conveyance. In this context there would be a tendency to look upon recording acts as an additional conveyancing formality and to emphasize what was to be required of the grantor rather than what should be the qualifications of those to be protected. Subsequently, probably as a result of experience with actual cases, attention shifted to the latter and to "the view generally accepted in America today that the Recording Acts are an extension of the equitable doctrine of notice." ⁷

In some of its applications the race statute seems unfair and out of harmony with the stated objectives of recordation. But instances in which bad faith purchasers are benefited and good faith purchasers are harmed are probably infrequent, and can be almost eliminated by prompt recording. Indeed, the threat of such dire consequences may provide added incentive to prompt recordation. The best argument in favor of the race statute, however, is that it enables the title searcher to rely upon the records without the substantial risk under other types of acts that one will have constructive notice of unrecorded instruments.

A representative "notice" type act is the Iowa statute, which provides: "No instrument affecting real estate is of any validity against subsequent purchasers for a valuable consideration, without notice, unless filed in the office of the recorder of the county in which the same lies, as hereinafter provided." ⁸ California's act is an example of the "race-notice" type: "Every conveyance of real property . . . is void as against any subsequent purchaser or mortgagee of the same property, or any part thereof, in good faith and for a valuable consideration, whose conveyance is first duly recorded . . . ." ⁹ Both acts give priority over unrecorded instruments to subsequent purchasers only if they are without notice, and the California act also requires the bona fide purchaser to record first. The latter is an obvious compromise of the objectives of penalizing non-recordation and

2. N.C.Gen.Stat. § 47–18 (Supp.1959).

7. Bordwell, Recording of Instruments Affecting Land, 2 Iowa L.Bull. 51, 52 (1916).

8. Iowa Code § 558.41 (1958).

9. Cal.Civ.Code § 1214.

protecting those who are likely to rely upon the records. By withholding protection from one who has not himself obeyed the statutory mandate to record, the race-notice act may be thought to have the merit of fairness and to encourage recording to a greater extent than would the notice act. But the seeming fairness of putting beyond the pale of the act both non-recorders is quite superficial, since only one has caused harm. It is also extremely doubtful that recording is actually stimulated by acts of the race-notice type, since even in a state having a notice type statute failure to record makes those protected by the act vulnerable to subsequent claims.

RECORDING ACTS

RACE TYPE

GENERAL STATUTES OF NORTH CAROLINA (1976).

§ 47–18. Conveyances, Contracts to Convey, Options and Leases of Land

(a) No (i) conveyance of land, or (ii) contract to convey, or (iii) option to convey, or (iv) lease of land for more than three years shall be valid to pass any property interest as against lien creditors or purchasers for a valuable consideration from the donor, bargainor or lessor but from the time of registration thereof in the county where the land lies, or if the land is located in more than one county, then in each county where any portion of the land lies to be effective as to the land in that county.

(b) This section shall not apply to contracts, leases or deeds executed prior to March 1, 1885, until January 1, 1886; and no purchase from any such donor, bargainor or lessor shall avail or pass title as against any unregistered deed executed prior to December 1, 1885, when the person holding or claiming under such unregistered deed shall be in actual possession and enjoyment of such land, either in person or by his tenant, at the time of the execution of such second deed, or when the person claiming under or taking such second deed had at the time of taking or purchasing under such deed actual or constructive notice of such unregistered deed, or the claim of the person holding or claiming thereunder.

NOTICE TYPE

ANNOTATED LAWS OF MASSACHUSETTS c. 183 (1977)

§ 4. Effect of Unrecorded Deed, Lease for More than Seven Years, or Assignment of Rents or Profits

A conveyance of an estate in fee simple, fee tail or for life, or a lease for a term of seven years, or an assignment of rents or profits from an estate or lease, shall not be valid as against any person, except the grantor or lessor, his heirs and devisees and persons having actual notice of it, unless it, or an office copy as provided in section thirteen of chapter thirty-six, or, with respect to such a lease or an assignment of rents or profits, a notice of lease or a notice of assignment of rents or profits, as hereinafter defined, is recorded in the registry of deeds for the county or district in which the land to which it relates lies. A "notice of lease", as used in this section, shall mean an instrument in writing executed by all persons who are parties to the lease of which notice is given and shall contain the following information with reference to such lease:—the date of execution thereof and a description, in the form contained in such lease, of the premises demised, and the term of such lease, with the date of commencement of such term and all rights of extension or renewal. A "notice of assignment of rents and profits", as used in this section, shall mean an instrument in writing executed by the assignor and containing the following information:—a description of the premises, the rent or profits of which have been assigned, adequate to identify the premises, the name of assignee, and the rents and profits which have been assigned. A provision in a recorded mortgage assigning or conditionally assigning rents or profits or obligating the mortgagor to assign or conditionally assign existing or future rents or profits shall constitute a "notice of assignment of rents or profits".

RACE-NOTICE TYPE

NEW YORK REAL PROPERTY LAW

§ 291. Recording of Conveyances

A conveyance of real property, within the state, on being duly acknowledged by the person executing the same, or proved as required by this chapter, and such acknowledgment or proof duly certified when required by this chapter, may be recorded in the office of the clerk of the county where such real property is situated, and such county clerk shall, upon the request of any party, on tender of the lawful fees therefor, record the same in his said office. Every such conveyance not so recorded is void as against any person who subsequently purchases or acquires by exchange or contracts to purchase or acquire by exchange, the same real property or any portion thereof, or acquires by assignment the rent to accrue therefrom as provided in section two hundred ninety-four-a of the real property law, in good faith and for a valuable consideration, from the same vendor or assignor, his distributees or devisees, and whose conveyance, contract or assignment is first duly recorded, and is void as against the lien upon the same real property or any portion thereof arising from payments made upon the execution of or pursuant to the terms of a contract with the same vendor, his distributees or devisees, if such contract is made in good faith and is first duly recorded.

NOTE

Although race statutes and notice statutes rest on sharply divergent conceptual bases, their practical operation is much the same. Whether Blackacre is in a race or a notice jurisdiction, B, who is about to acquire the parcel, will be well advised to conduct a thorough title search before paying A and accepting a deed. In a race jurisdiction, only a title search can inform B whether there is an outstanding interest adverse to his that has been recorded first. In a notice jurisdiction, a title search will inform B of any recorded, adverse interest that will operate to defeat his title under the doctrine of constructive notice. Similarly, once B acquires Blackacre, he is well advised, whether in a race or notice jurisdiction, to record his instrument promptly—in a race jurisdiction, in order to win the race to the recorder's office as against any subsequent grantee; in a notice jurisdiction, to give any subsequent grantee constructive notice of his claim.

As a practical matter, race and notice systems differ only in the additional search burden that notice statutes impose on the buyer. Under a race statute, B need do no more than search record title. In a notice jurisdiction, B must not only search title, but must also inspect Blackacre for physical evidence of title defects or encumbrances, such as possession by someone other than A, putting him on inquiry notice of an adverse claim.

Which system, race or notice, is more efficient? More fair? As a legislator forced to choose between the two, which would you pick? Do race-notice statutes offer a desirable compromise, or do they only compound the individual defects of race and notice systems?

b. STATUTORY CONDITIONS OF PROTECTION

i. Purchaser Without Notice

MISTER DONUT OF AMERICA, INC. v. KEMP

Supreme Court of Massachusetts, 1975.
368 Mass. 220, 330 N.E.2d 810.

BRAUCHER, Justice.

The principal question before us is whether a "notice of lease" recorded in a registry of deeds under G.L. c. 183, § 4, must refer to an option to purchase contained in the lease. We hold that such an option is not a right of "extension or renewal" and need not be referred to in the notice of lease. The recorded notice in this case was therefore in statutory form and was sufficient to give constructive notice of the option to the defendants, as persons not having "actual notice" of it.

The plaintiff lessee, Mister Donut of America, Inc., is the assignee of a lease made by Ernest Webby, Joseph E. Webby, and John J. Webby as lessors. The lease contains an option to purchase, and the lessee seeks specific performance of the option against the defendants Kemp, a grantee of the lessors, and Plymouth-Home National Bank, a mortgagee from Kemp. The facts are stipulated except as to the defendants' actual notice of the option, which was the subject of testimony. A judge of the Superior Court filed a memorandum of findings, rulings and order for decree granting specific performance, but after further hearing he vacated that memorandum and filed a second memorandum ordering a decree for the defendants. A decree was entered dismissing the bill in equity, and the plaintiff appealed to the Appeals Court. We granted the plaintiff's application for direct appellate review pursuant to G.L. c. 211A, § 10(A).

We summarize the judge's second memorandum, which he adopted as a report of material facts. The lease ran for twenty years from March 22, 1961, and was not recorded. Paragraph eleven gave the lessee the option to purchase the premises during the sixth to twentieth year for $53,000. A pasted overlay strip containing a substitute paragraph ten, unless lifted, hid most of paragraph eleven from view. A notice of lease in statutory form, recorded March 31, 1966, included the following: "Rights of extension and renewal, if any: *None.*"

On July 15, 1971, Kemp and the Webbys and attorneys for them and for the bank were present in the office of the bank's attorney when Kemp took title to the premises from the Webbys. The Webbys told Kemp the original of the lease had been stolen, and gave him a photocopy and a written representation and warranty that the lease was as shown on the copy. The copy contained a legible reproduction of a portion of the option paragraph, containing clues pointing to a passage of title to real estate. Kemp acted in good faith; the bank attorney knew of the recorded notice but did not read the photocopy. Neither Kemp nor the bank had actual knowledge of the option. They were put on sufficient notice to warrant further inquiry, which would have revealed the option, but the circumstances were not sufficient to constitute "actual notice" under the statute.

1. *Actual notice.* Under G.L. c. 183, § 4,[2] "actual notice" is ordinarily a question of fact, and a person claiming that another is not a

2. As amended by St.1941, c. 85: ". . . a lease for more than seven years from the making thereof shall not be valid as against any person, except the . . . lessor, his heirs and devisees and persons having *actual notice* of it,

good faith purchaser has the burden of proof. Knowledge of facts which would ordinarily put a party on inquiry is not enough. We are not prepared to relax our strict construction of the requirement, and therefore we uphold the judge's finding that the defendants had no actual notice of the option.

2. *Constructive notice.* The judge ruled "that a fair reading of the statute would require reference to the option in the notice following the legend 'rights of extension or renewal' in order to give constructive notice of the option to Kemp and the Bank," citing for comparison Universal Container Corp. v. Cambridge, 278 N.E.2d 727 (1972). In that case we said (278 N.E.2d at 729) "The recorded notice of lease is in the statutory form, and is sufficient to give the city constructive notice of the petitioner's interest." The interest in question was the tenant's right to share in damages for a taking by eminent domain; it depended in part on a provision of the lease not referred to in the statutory form.

Rights of "extension or renewal" have a settled meaning. Mutual Paper Co. v. Hoague-Sprague Corp., 297 Mass. 294, 299, 8 N.E.2d 802, 806 (1937): "An option for renewal implies the giving of a new lease upon the same terms as the old lease, whereas an option for extension contemplates a continuance of the old lease for a further period." Under our decisions such rights affect "the term during which the land which a purchaser had bought could be kept from his possession by the holder of an unrecorded lease." Toupin v. Peabody, 162 Mass. 473, 477, 39 N.E. 280, 281 (1895). An option to purchase is quite different; it does not contemplate either the giving of a new lease or the continuance of the old one. The statute does not require the notice of lease to refer to an option to purchase.

The plain object of the statute is to place recording of a notice of lease in statutory form on the same footing as recording of the entire lease, and to place both on the same footing as actual notice of the lease. If recording of a notice of lease were given a lesser effect, its utility would be largely lost, since those concerned would be well advised not to use it. The prospective purchaser of the lessor's interest can fully protect himself by examining the original lease or by consulting the lessee. Hence we hold that the defendants had constructive notice of the plaintiff's option to purchase.

3. *Consequences of notice.* The parties have assumed that if the defendants had actual or constructive notice of the lessee's option

. . . or, with respect to such a lease, a notice of lease, as hereinafter defined, is recorded in the register of deeds . . .. A 'notice of lease', as used in this section, shall mean an instrument in writing executed by all persons who are parties to the lease of which notice is given and shall contain the following information with reference to such lease:— the date of execution thereof and a description, in the form contained in such lease, of the premises demised, and the term of such lease, with the date of commencement of such term and all *rights of extension or renewal*" (emphasis supplied). The amendment made by St.1973. c. 205, is not pertinent.

to purchase they took subject to it. No contention is made that the option was independent of the lease rather than incidental to it.

4. *Disposition.* The decree is reversed and the case is remanded to the Superior Court for further proceedings consistent with this opinion.

So ordered.

GAGNER v. KITTERY WATER DISTRICT

Supreme Court of Maine, 1978.
385 A.2d 206.

McKUSICK, Chief Justice.

The Kittery Water District (District), a defendant in the action below, appeals from the York County Superior Court's ruling that it has no valid easement as against the plaintiffs for maintenance of a water main claimed by the District. We sustain the appeal.

In 1969 Warren's Realty, Inc. (Realty) conveyed to the plaintiffs, Raymond and Beatrice Gagner, by warranty deed, certain realty abutting Route 1 in Kittery, Maine. The Gagners commenced the present action against their seller in 1971 for breach of covenant of warranty against encumbrances, having discovered shortly after taking the deed that a water main, owned by the District and serving the Portsmouth Naval Shipyard, traversed the property. Realty then brought a third-party complaint against the plaintiffs' attorney, who, in addition to having represented both the Gagners and Realty in the land transfer, had also searched the title for the plaintiffs and certified it to be free and clear of all encumbrances.[1] The plaintiffs later amended their complaint to join the District as an additional party defendant. With the case thus postured, the Superior Court issued a pre-trial order severing for hearing the issue of the validity of the District's easement. After a hearing limited to that issue, the Superior Court ruled that "there is no valid easement as against plaintiffs in this case for the maintenance of the water main claimed by the Kittery Water District." The District appealed the final judgment entered against it below.

The validity of the District's unrecorded water pipe easement as against the Gagners depends upon our applying to the facts of this

---

[1]. At the time of the attorney's title search in 1969, the District owned an unrecorded water pipe easement over the property that the Gagners purchased. The easement was not recorded until December 13, 1973. All parties agree that the District's act of recordation has no bearing upon the outcome of the present litigation.

case the governing Maine recording statute, 33 M.R.S.A. § 201 (1964), providing in pertinent part that:

"*[n]o conveyance* of an estate in fee simple, fee tail or for life, or lease for more than 2 years or for an indefinite term *is effectual against any person except* the grantor, his heirs and devisees, and *persons having actual notice thereof unless* the deed or lease is acknowledged and *recorded* in the registry of deeds within the county where the land lies . . . ." (Emphasis added).

This court has in the past had occasion to define the term "actual notice" as used in the recording act.

"Actual notice and actual knowledge are not necessarily synonymous expressions. Actual notice is that which gives actual knowledge, or the means to such knowledge. It is a warning brought directly home to one whom it concerns to know. Actual notice may be either express or implied. It is express when established by direct proof. It is implied when inferable as a fact by proof of circumstances. 'Express actual notice' is, perhaps, its own best definition. Implied actual notice is that which one who is put on a trail is in duty bound to seek to know, even though the track or scent lead to knowledge of unpleasant and unwelcome facts." Hopkins v. McCarthy, 121 Me. 27, 29, 115 A. 513, 515 (1921).

Elaborating more particularly on the concept of "implied actual notice," we earlier said in Knapp v. Bailey, 79 Me. 195, 204, 9 A. 122, 124 (1887), that:

"The doctrine of actual notice implied by circumstances (actual notice in the second degree) necessarily involves the rule that a purchaser before buying, should clear up the doubts which apparently hang upon the title, by making due inquiry and investigation. If a party has knowledge of such facts as would lead a fair and prudent man, using ordinary caution, to make further inquiries, and he avoids the inquiry, he is chargeable with notice of the facts which by ordinary diligence he would have ascertained. He has no right to shut his eyes against the light before him. He does a wrong not to heed the 'signs and signals' seen by him. It may be well concluded that he is avoiding notice of that which he in reality believes or knows. Actual notice of facts which, to the mind of a prudent man, indicate notice is proof of notice."

The Superior Court found in the present case that the plaintiffs had no notice, actual or implied, of the existence of the Kittery Water District's water line crossing their property. To the contrary, we conclude that in the circumstances of this case the plaintiffs, through their attorney and title searcher, were put on inquiry notice of the District's easement, but the inquiries made by them did not, as a matter of law, constitute the due diligence required to prevent the enforcement of the District's unrecorded easement against them.[3]

While examining the chain of title to the property at the York County Registry of Deeds in 1969, the Gagners' attorney noticed language in several earlier deeds, first appearing in 1922, stating that the conveyance was made "subject to the rights of the Kittery Water District to maintain a line of water pipes across said premises, as set forth in [a release from Joseph H. Blaisdell] to said Water District." The attorney searched the Registry records for the above-mentioned release, but, as it was then yet unrecorded, he found no such instrument. From the face of the deeds, the attorney also learned that the property which the Gagners desired to purchase had once formed part of a single larger parcel. In 1943 Warren Wurm and his wife had purchased that parcel "subject to" the rights of the District. In 1953 and 1958, the Wurms by two separate conveyances transferred title to the entire parcel to Realty, the Wurms' corporation. Only that part of the land conveyed by the 1953 deed was, however, conveyed "subject to" the rights of the District. Realty later conveyed that first parcel to a third party by a deed containing no reference to any rights of the Kittery Water District. The parcel that the Gagners purchased was identical to that which the Wurms had conveyed to Realty in 1958 without any "subject to" language.

At the hearing the Gagners' attorney acknowledged that what he actually saw in the deeds put him on inquiry as to the existence of the District's water line. Thus alerted, he contacted Warren Wurm representing Realty, the seller, and asked him whether the District owned any rights in the property. Wurm assured him in the negative. As the attorney testified:

> "Mr. Wurm was very anxious to close, have a closing as soon as possible, and I had to go back a second time to the Registry of Deeds because of my concern about this easement. To my best recollection, Mr. Wurm came into my office, I believe it was in my office, he came in a couple of times regarding the closing and selling this parcel to Mr. Gagner, and I asked him about the water, the water easement, which was mentioned, and he assured me that it did not concern the Gagner parcel."

In addition, Mr. Gagner personally inspected the property prior to the purchase and was told by Warren Wurm that a water hydrant located immediately adjacent to the highway supplied water to the property. Mr. Gagner's inspection of the premises revealed no evidence of any other water main crossing the property. According to the attorney's testimony,

> "At the time, not finding any recorded easement, and being assured by Mr. Wurm that it did not affect the premises, coupled

---

3. In view of our conclusion that the facts in this case add up to actual notice, we need not in addition inquire whether "constructive," or record, notice also existed.

with the fact that the deed, the prior deed of the premises being conveyed, made no mention of the right of way, it seemed to me I had done as much as was necessary . . . ."

The foregoing summary represents the sum total of the steps taken by the plaintiffs, through their attorney, to determine whether the District in fact owned any interest in the property they were purchasing. At no time was any attempt made to contact the District to inquire of *it* whether any such interest existed. In view of all the facts the plaintiffs are charged with knowing, the failure to do so constituted a fatal omission in executing their duty of reasonable inquiry.

The plaintiffs' attorney knew from the record that Joseph H. Blaisdell had once given a release to the District to maintain a line of water pipes at some location across the larger tract of which the Gagners were buying a portion. He admitted that the clause in the deeds put him on notice of a possible claim of the District in the property. What inquiry of the seller will satisfy the purchaser's duty of due diligence is in every case a question of fact. When the facts known to the purchaser cast doubt upon the very existence of the seller's title, he is bound to inquire of him whether he has any real title or not. The plaintiffs, by their attorney, recognized a duty to inquire of the seller, but upon receiving a false answer did nothing to check with the Kittery Water District, the named holder of the unrecorded interest. Knapp v. Bailey, *supra*, cannot be read to hold that inquiry of the seller will in all instances satisfy a purchaser's duty to inquire. Clearly, more could easily have been done here, and equally clearly, the true facts would have then been revealed.

The District, named as grantee of the interest, had its office in the same town where the subject property was located, and, as an active public utility, could be expected to maintain at a readily available office comprehensive maps and records relating to the easements for its mains. Under these circumstances, the purchasers were bound to inquire of the District, as the most reliable source of information, whether it still claimed the rights referred to in the deeds. Under all the circumstances, the failure to seek an explanation beyond that given by Warren Wurm, who, as the principal of the corporate seller, had an obvious interest in nondisclosure, can only be viewed as a failure of due inquiry. The Gagners are "chargeable with notice of the facts which by ordinary diligence [they] would have ascertained." Knapp v. Bailey, *supra*, 79 Me. at 204, 9 A. at 124.

The entry must be:

Appeal sustained.

Judgment reversed.

MILLER v. GREEN

Supreme Court of Wisconsin, 1953.
264 Wis. 159, 58 N.W.2d 704.

CURRIE, Justice.

Defendants Hines claim that their title under their deed is superior to the land contract interest of the plaintiffs inasmuch as their deed was recorded first. Section 235.49, Stats., provides as follows:

> "Every conveyance of real estate within this state hereafter made (except patents issued by the United States or this state, or by the proper officers of either) which shall not be recorded as provided by law shall be void as against any subsequent purchaser in good faith and for a valuable consideration of the same real estate or any portion thereof whose conveyance shall first be duly recorded."

The question at issue on this appeal is whether the defendants Hines qualify under the foregoing statute as subsequent purchasers *"in good faith"*. Plaintiffs contend that the defendants Hines do not so qualify because the plaintiffs were in possession of the premises on November 29, 1950, when the defendant W.E. Hines paid Mrs. Green $500 toward the purchase price of the farm, and that such possession constituted constructive notice of the plaintiffs' rights under their land contract. This makes it necessary to review the evidence bearing on such possession by the plaintiffs, or either of them.

Approximately 40 acres of the 63-acre tract was cultivated land and the remainder was pasture and woods. The buildings on the farm consisted of a small log house, a barn, and some sheds, which were in a dilapidated condition; the house was unlivable; and such buildings had not been used for many years. The plaintiff Eugene M. Miller had leased the entire 63-acre tract for the crop season of 1950 and had grown crops on the cultivated 40 acres and had grazed livestock on the remaining portion. The crop had been harvested prior to November, 1950, and the livestock had been removed when cold weather came about November 22, 1950. However, starting November 4, 1950 (the date that the Millers contracted to purchase this farm tract), Miller's father, in behalf of the Millers, hauled between 59 and 60 loads of manure to the farm. First the manure was spread over the land, but then after a snowstorm came it was piled on a pile about 100 feet from the road, such pile being about 60 feet long and several feet high. Such hauling of manure was taking place on November 29, 1950 (the date that the defendants Hines made the $500 down payment on the purchase price), and continued until about December 8 or 9, 1950. Also in November, prior to the snowstorm, approximately 2 acres of land had been plowed by Miller, which plowed land was plainly visible from the abutting highway before the snowstorm.

The Hines farm was located about one half mile from this 63-acre tract, although the distance by highway was about one and one half miles. Part of the tract was visible from the Hines home. The defendant W.E. Hines testified that he knew that the plaintiff Eugene M. Miller had leased the tract for the crop season of 1950, but denied that he drove past the tract on the abutting highway during November, 1950, and denied having seen the plowing of the land, the hauling of the manure, or the manure pile on the land, although he admitted finding the manure pile there the following spring.

The general rule is that possession of land is notice to the world of whatever rights the possessor may have in the premises. The reason underlying this rule is well stated in Pippin v. Richards, 1911, 146 Wis. 69, 74, 130 N.W. 872, 874:

"The theory of the law is that the person in possession may be asked to disclose the right or title which he has in the premises, and the purchaser will be chargeable with the actual notice he would have received, had he made inquiry. In Frame v. Frame, 32 W.Va. [463], at page 478, 9 S.E. [901] at page 907 (5 L.R.A. 323), the court said: 'The earth has been described as that universal manuscript, open to the eyes of all. When, therefore, a man proposes to buy or deal with realty, his first duty is to read this public manuscript; that is, to look and see who is there upon it, and what are his rights there. And, if the person in possession has an equitable title to it, he is as much bound to respect it, as if it was a perfect legal title evidenced by a deed duly recorded.'"

An apt statement of this general principle of possession being constructive notice is stated in State v. Jewell, 1947, 250 Wis. 165, at page 171, 26 N.W.2d 825, at page 828, 28 N.W.2d 314:

"The possession of real estate is generally considered constructive notice of rights of the possessor, whether the possession is sought to be used for the purpose of charging a purchaser with notice of an outstanding equity, or whether it is sought to charge a subsequent purchaser with notice of an unrecorded instrument and thereby defeat his right to protection under the recording acts. It is so held in the United States courts and in 28 states of the Union."

The rule with respect to possession of a tenant constituting notice of any rights claimed by such tenant is stated in 5 Tiffany, Real Property, Third Ed., p. 73, sec. 1291:

"It has been decided in a number of states that, by the possession of a tenant under a lease, a purchaser is chargeable with notice, not only of the tenant's rights under the lease, but also of any right which he may have not under the lease, as, for instance, under an agreement by the lessor to sell the property to him."

The authorities generally hold that in order that possession may constitute constructive notice such possession must be "open, visible, exclusive and unambiguous". Ely v. Wilcox, 20 Wis. 523; Wickes v. Lake, 25 Wis. 71; and 55 Am.Jur., Vendor and Purchaser, p. 1090, sec. 716. It will thus be seen that the requirements as to the type of possession that will constitute constructive notice are practically identical with the requirements of the type of possession necessary to constitute adverse possession. In view of the fact that the farm buildings were unusable, the plowing of the 2 acres of land after November 4, 1950, and the hauling of the manure practically every day throughout November were acts which not only were "open and visible", but also "exclusive and unambiguous". They were the customary acts of possession which could be exercised as to unoccupied farm lands at such time of year. Surely they would have been sufficient to have constituted acts of adverse possession, and it would appear that the rule as to acts of possession necessary to constitute constructive notice to a purchaser is no more strict. Wickes v. Lake, supra, is authority for the principle that actual residence on the land is not required in order to have sufficient possession to constitute constructive notice.

In George v. Stansbury, 1922, 90 W.Va. 593, 111 S.E. 598, both the plaintiff and defendants claimed title to a city lot. The plaintiff, during 1919, had maintained a garden on the lot, and the following year, although he did not have a garden there, he permitted the owner of a nearby lot who was excavating for a building to haul a large quantity of dirt from the excavation and dump it on the lot so as to fill a low place. It was during this second year that the defendants purchased the premises and obtained a deed which they recorded, while the plaintiff's title was not recorded. The West Virginia court held that the gardening during the one season, followed by the permitting of the dirt to be hauled in and dumped the second year, constituted sufficient possession to be constructive notice to the defendants of plaintiff's rights, and plaintiff was held to have the superior title. If hauling dirt onto a vacant lot constitutes sufficient possession to be constructive notice to a subsequent purchaser, surely hauling manure onto farm land, as in the instant case, should be held to be equally effective to constitute constructive notice.

In Lyman v. Russell, 1867, 45 Ill. 281, plaintiff purchased some farm land but did not record his deed. The defendants claimed under a subsequent mortgage executed by plaintiff's vendor. The question was whether there was such "actual, open, notorious and visible possession" of the lands by plaintiff as to constitute constructive notice to the subsequent mortgagees. Plaintiff's act of possession consisted of plowing some of the land in view of all who passed along the adjoining highway. The Illinois court held that the plaintiff's possession was sufficient notice to put a subsequent purchaser on inquiry, and should operate as notice of plaintiff's rights.

The learned trial court in the instant case apparently was of the opinion that, in order for the plaintiff Eugene M. Miller's possession of the premises to have been constructive notice to the defendants Hines that Miller claimed rights of ownership therein, there must have been some change in the type of his possession after November 4, 1950 (the date the Millers entered into the contract to purchase), and his possession prior thereto. This is very apparent from finding No. 5 of the findings of fact made by the trial court, such finding reading as follows:

"That the plaintiff, Eugene M. Miller, continued in possession of said premises, and continued to pasture livestock thereon until about November 22, 1950, when it was necessary to remove them because of the weather, and continued to make such use of the tillable land on said premises as the weather permitted during the month of November, 1950. That the defendant, W.E. Hines knew at that time of the oral lease between the plaintiff, Eugene M. Miller, and the defendant, Mary Green, for the 1950 season. That there was nothing in the use to which the land was put by the plaintiff, Eugene M. Miller, to indicate to the defendant, W.E. Hines, that there had been a change in the status of said plaintiff with relation to said land."

In other words the trial court found that there was possession of the premises by Millers from November 4, 1950, through to the end of that month, but there was no change in the type of possession. Apparently it was the theory of the trial court that the defendants Hines could assume, because of such lack of change in the character of possession, that the possession after November 4, 1950, was that of a tenant and not of a purchaser. The authorities, however, clearly establish that no such change in the character of possession is necessary.

8 Thompson on Real Property (Permanent Edition), p. 413, sec. 4516, states:

"If the tenant changes his character by taking an agreement to purchase, or he has this right under his lease and exercises his option to purchase, his possession amounts to notice of his equitable title as purchaser."

To the same effect see Anderson v. Brinser, 1889, 129 Pa. 376, 404, 11 A. 809, 18 A. 520, 521, 6 L.R.A. 205, wherein the Pennsylvania court stated:

"Knowledge of the existence of a lease will, of course, give constructive notice of all its provisions; but the possession, apart from the lease, we think, should be treated as notice of the possessor's claim of title, whatever that claim may be, for the lease may be but the first of two or more successive rights acquired by the tenant. While in the occupancy under a lease for years, the tenant may have purchased under articles, and entitled himself to an equity; or, indeed, he may have purchased the legal estate in fee, and failed to record his deed. Would it be supposed that a knowledge of the precedent lease would dispense with the duty of inquiry, and entitle a subsequent grantee to the protection of an innocent purchaser? . . . In Sugden on Vendors, (volume 1, 6th Amer., from 10th London, Ed., p. 265, § 22,) it is expressly stated, and numerous authorities are cited in support of the statement, that if a tenant, during his tenancy, changes his character by having agreed to purchase the estate, his possession amounts to notice of his equitable title as purchaser."

It is our considered judgment that the acts of possession on the part of the plaintiff Eugene M. Miller throughout the remainder of the month of November, 1950, following the purchase of the tract by the Millers on November 4, 1950, constituted constructive notice to all the world which required a subsequent purchaser to make inquiry as to what rights, if any, the plaintiff Eugene M. Miller claimed to have in the premises. Subsequent purchasers could not safely assume, without inquiry, as did the defendants Hines, that, because Miller had theretofore been a tenant for the season, there had been no subsequent change in his rights from that of a tenant to that of a purchaser.

Judgment reversed and cause remanded with directions to enter judgment as prayed for in plaintiffs' complaint.

GEHL, Justice (dissenting).

The majority say in effect that as a matter of law any entry upon land and its occupation, no matter that the acts of entry may be infrequent and the occupation may be for short interrupted periods, constitutes such possession as to put a purchaser upon inquiry as to the rights of the person so occupying; that possession, regardless of its nature or extent, serves as notice to put the prospective buyer upon inquiry.

That is erroneous. Possession to constitute notice is that which is *required by law*, and is defined in Ely v. Wilcox, 20 Wis. 523:

"The next question is, whether there was such possession by *Ely* at the date of the deed to the appellant as to be constructive notice to him of the plaintiff's title. The burden of proof was on the plaintiff to prove such possession. He has failed to prove that either he or any one under him was in actual possession of the premises or any part of them at the date of the deed. The rule is, that possession, to be notice, must be open, visible, exclusive, and unambiguous; not liable to be misunderstood or misconstrued. Patten v. Moore, 32 N.H. [382] 384, and authorities there cited. The plaintiff had no such possession."

In Wickes v. Lake, 25 Wis. 71, the court restated the rule in the same language. Both cases have been considered and cited by this court numerous times.

Not all of the latter cases have dealt with the precise question here involved; they are referred to only as indicating that it is quite likely that the court has not overlooked the rule there stated. It has never, so far as I have been able to find, been held by this court that possession to be constructive notice, may be of a nature different from that there defined. The majority cite a number of cases dealing with situations similar to that presented in the instant case. The court in those cases described the possession upon which the party relied in opposition to the contention of one claiming as *bona fide* purchaser in terms different from those used by the court in the two earlier cases. But a reading of those cases will disclose that the possession there found was such as to meet the requirements of the earlier definition.

The rule as it is stated in the Ely case, supra, and the Wickes case is in substance identical with that stated in 55 Am.Jur. 1090:

"In order that possession of real estate may constitute notice to a purchaser of the rights of the party in possession or by virtue of which the possession is held, such possession must be visible, open, clear, full, notorious, unequivocal, unambiguous, inconsistent with or adverse to the title or interest of the vendor, and not likely to be misunderstood or misconstrued, but, to the contrary, sufficient to put the purchaser on his guard."

The issue presented is one of fact, and the court's finding should not be disturbed. That a finding has force is indicated quite clearly in First Nat. Bank v. Savings L. & T. Co., 207 Wis. 272, 240 N.W. 381, 384, a case involving similar issues where the court in discussing a finding that one claiming to be a *bona fide* purchaser did not have sufficient notice to put him upon inquiry said:

"It is not at all clear that this court could have disturbed a contrary finding . . . ."

It was the burden of the plaintiffs to establish that Hines was not a *bona fide* purchaser. The court found that they had not met the burden. The fact that some of the land had been plowed, that a water tank and a pile of manure were left upon the farm (neither of which circumstances is evidence of possession inconsistent with the right of possession of Mrs. Green, and neither of which is a circumstance which would necessarily suggest that Miller rather than Mrs. Green or some one else acting for or under her had left the tank and manure upon the premises and had plowed the land), considered with the fact that the buildings were unoccupied and that the crop season for which period Miller had rented the farm had ended, are not such as to permit us to hold that the court's findings are contrary to the great weight and clear preponderance of the evidence. Certainly we should not say that under those circumstances the court erred in its finding that plaintiffs had failed to meet the burden to establish that their possession of the farm was "open, visible, exclusive and unambiguous; not liable to be misunderstood or misconstrued."

The trial judge made no specific finding that the possession of Miller was not that required by law to put Hines on inquiry. He did find that "there was nothing in the use to which the land was put by the plaintiff Eugene M. Miller, to indicate to the defendant W.E. Hines that (there had) been a change in the status of said plaintiff with relation to said land," which I construe as a finding that Miller's occupancy of the land was not such as is required by law to put Hines on inquiry. In any event, the omission, if there were such, to make the specific finding, one which is necessary to support the judgment, is equivalent to a finding against the contention of the plaintiffs.

I am authorized to state that BROADFOOT and BROWN, JJ., join in this dissent.

NOTES

1. Three forms of notice will operate to defeat subsequent purchasers under notice and race-notice statutes:

(a) *Actual notice* (the notice given by the subsequent purchaser's actual knowledge of the prior transfer);

(b) *Inquiry notice*, sometimes called *implied actual notice* (the notice given by the subsequent purchaser's actual knowledge of facts that, if reasonably inquired into, would produce actual knowledge of the prior transfer);

(c) *Constructive notice* (the notice given by a transfer's recordation in the public title records in such a way that the subsequent purchaser, conducting a reasonable title search, would obtain actual knowledge of the transfer).

These three forms of notice effectively prescribe the standard operating procedure that a purchaser in notice and race-notice jurisdictions should follow before paying the purchase price and accepting a deed: (a) search files, desk drawers and memory for any facts or communications that might have given actual knowledge; (b) inspect the land for physical evidence of an interest in someone other than the immediate seller; and (c) conduct a title search for documentary evidence of an interest in someone other than the immediate seller. (A purchaser in a race jurisdiction need only conduct a title search to determine whether anyone has beaten him, or any predecessor in title, to the recorder's office.)

There is some interplay between the three forms of notice. For example, it is generally held that recordation of an unrecordable instrument, such as an unacknowledged deed, will not give constructive notice of the instrument's contents; yet the instrument will give *actual* notice to a title examiner who comes upon the recordation in the course of his or her search. As a matter of standard operating procedure, buyers will almost invariably order title searches before paying the purchase money. Thus, as a practical matter they will, in the course of reviewing their examiner's title report, obtain actual notice of recorded, but unrecordable, instruments.

Would you ever advise a client *not* to order a title search on the off-chance that he can thus avoid learning of an earlier transaction embodied in a recorded but unrecordable instrument?

2. To what extent will a recorded instrument trigger a duty of further inquiry? The question arises when a recorded instrument has obviously been altered or phrased in an unusual manner, or when a title search reveals only a partial conveyance to the purchaser's grantor or some predecessor in title, and no indication as to whether, or to whom, the other parts were conveyed. Courts generally hold purchasers to notice of all facts that they could have discovered through reasonable inquiry into the discrepancy.

The same question arises when an instrument that is disclosed by the title search refers to an instrument that is not disclosed, as happens when a deed recites that the property is subject to a mortgage and the mortgage is unrecorded. Here, too, courts impose a duty of reasonable inquiry. Many legislatures, however, have acted to relax the duty. Massachusetts, for example, requires that a reference be "definite" in order to put purchasers on notice. An "indefinite reference" is one that recites interests created by unrecorded or improperly recorded documents, ambiguous descriptions of the interest, indications that the holder of the interest is a "trustee" when the trust is not of record, or any references that do not disclose where the instrument is recorded. Mass.Gen.Laws Ann. c. 184, § 25 (1977).

Is the Massachusetts Supreme Court opinion in *Kemp* consistent with these principles? After *Kemp*, would you ever allow a client to buy land subject to a lease without first obtaining and reading the entire lease? Say your client is planning to buy a large shopping center or apartment house occupied by 250 tenants. Will it be necessary for him to review each of the 250 leases?

3. *Inquiry Notice.* One fact that is universally held to put a purchaser on inquiry notice is possession by someone other than his seller. Often in these circumstances the possessor will be a tenant, and the purchaser will thus be placed on notice not only of the tenant's rights under its lease, but of any other rights, such as an option to purchase the property. Occasionally the possessor will claim ownership of the land through adverse possession or through a prior deed from the present seller or some other owner. See Bump v. Dahl, 26 Wis.2d 607, 133 N.W.2d 295 (1965) (grading, sodding, planting and landscaping of parcel gave subsequent purchaser inquiry notice of prior purchaser's possessory claim).

Nonpossessory interests are more problematic. Will manhole covers suffice to put a purchaser on inquiry notice of an easement for an underlying sewer line? Compare Lake Meredith Development Co. v. City of Fritch, 564 S.W.2d 427 (Tex.Civ.App.1978) (yes) with Fanti v. Welsh, 152 W.Va. 233, 161 S.E.2d 501 (1967) (no). Wolek v. Di Feo, 60 N.J.Super. 324, 159 A.2d 127 (1960), found no basis for inquiry notice against an easement holder's argument that "in the quiet hours of the evening" the purchaser "must have heard the rush of water through the underground pipes." Even nonpossessory interests offering more clearly visible clues, such as power lines and support poles installed pursuant to a public utility easement, have been treated differently within the same jurisdiction. Compare Florida Power & Light Co. v. Rader, 306 So.2d 565 (Fla.App.Dist. 4 1975) with McDaniel v. Lawyers' Title Guaranty Fund, 327 So.2d 852 (Fla.App. Dist. 2 1976).

Do you agree with the result in Miller v. Green? Can a buyer avoid inquiry notice by simply not viewing the land? The answer, obviously, is that he cannot. All purchasers are presumed to have inspected the land they are about to buy, and to have seen all inquiry-provoking facts that such an inspection would have disclosed.

4. Information uncovered in the course of a title search will give actual notice to the client who ordered the search, either because the searcher will communicate the information to the client or, absent such communication, because the agency relationship between searcher and client will impute the searcher's knowledge to the client. This latter rule is a frequent source of problems. For example, in Farr v. Newman, 14 N.Y.2d 183, 250 N.Y.S.2d 272, 199 N.E.2d 369 (1964), plaintiff, who had entered into, but not recorded, a contract to purchase a parcel for $3,000, sought specific performance against defendant who purchased the parcel for $4,000 before plaintiff's contract was to close, but not before plaintiff informed defendant's attorney of plaintiff's outstanding contract. Holding for plaintiff, the court of appeals noted first that "[e]ven if the plaintiff had not affirmatively relied upon the agency of the attorney by giving notice, and the attorney had merely discovered plaintiff's equity in the course of his title investigation, the principal would still be bound by such knowledge. A conflict of interest does not avoid the imputation of knowledge." 14 N.Y.2d at 190, 250 N.Y.S.2d at 278, 199 N.E.2d at 373.

Did the attorney who represented both buyer and seller in Gagner v. Kittery Water District properly resolve the potential conflict of interest arising from that dual representation? What kind of disclosure should the attorney have made to buyer and seller? Compare In re Lanza, page 165, above. How could the attorney have properly served the interests of these two clients once having been told by seller's representative, Warren Wurm, that the Water District had no rights in the property and knowing also that "Mr. Wurm was very anxious to close" and that a far more reliable answer could be provided by the District?

5. What policies would be served, and what policies would be disserved, if states were to drop the inquiry notice bar? The actual notice bar? Representing a buyer, how comfortable would you feel knowing that every tramped-down footpath or half-remembered conversation may later form the basis for a finding of inquiry or actual

notice? In terms of fairness or efficiency, what is wrong with a pure race regime?

ii. Purchaser for Value

LOWN v. NICHOLS PLUMBING AND HEATING, INC.
Supreme Court of Alaska, 1981.
634 P.2d 554.

MATTHEWS, Justice.

In February 1978, the appellee, Nichols Plumbing and Heating, Inc. sued to quiet title to a parcel of land in the Chilkat Acres subdivision, located at Swanson Harbor, twenty-six miles west of Juneau. Appellant Robin Lown answered and counterclaimed, asserting that he was the fee simple owner of the land in question. The parties moved for summary judgment and the court ruled in favor of Nichols. Lown has appealed. We affirm.

On January 1, 1965, Walter and Carol Reams executed a promissory note to the Coast Small Business Investment Company, a California corporation. On December 14, 1965, as security for this note, the Reams signed a deed of trust covering several parcels of land, including the parcel at issue. Although this land lies within the Juneau recording district, the deed of trust was originally recorded in Petersburg, and was not correctly recorded in Juneau until May 1967.

Eight days after he executed the deed of trust, Walter Reams executed and recorded a deed conveying the land to J.J. Lown, appellant's father. However, Reams did not tell J.J. Lown about this conveyance until early 1966. Shortly thereafter, the two visited the property. According to Lown, Reams told him that he had deeded Lown the property to induce him to build a lodge on it, so that the surrounding parcels retained by Reams would be saleable as cabin sites. Lown stated that he decided to accept the conveyance and to proceed with the lodge project in the summer of 1966.

On a second trip to Swanson Harbor that summer, Reams and Lown set up a wall tent on the land deeded to Lown. This tent was to be used in the initial stages of the lodge construction. Because they were unable to come up with construction money, however, nothing further was done in 1966.

In June 1967, Lown and Laura Bailey moved to Swanson Harbor and undertook construction of a 48′ × 64′ lodge. Their building and living supplies were paid for by Reams and delivered by him by boat from Juneau. However, neither Lown nor Bailey were paid for their work. After Reams' death in the summer of 1968 Lown and Bailey were forced to abandon construction because of their lack of money and inability to get supplies.

In July of 1967, Coast began non-judicial foreclosure pursuant to the terms of the deed of trust. Notice of Reams' default was mailed to Lown at his Juneau address, but he evidently did not receive this notice, although Reams had apparently been bringing his mail to Swanson Harbor. Reams was served personally with the notice of default, but never told Lown about it. The foreclosure sale took place on November 7, 1967, and Coast bought all the property listed in the deed of trust for the amount owed by Reams.

In December 1967, Lown, at the instigation of Bailey, finally asked Reams to deliver the deed to the property. Reams did so and explained to Lown that he had taken a loan on the rest of the property, but that the section deeded to Lown was unencumbered. Reams did not mention that the foreclosure sale had already occurred.

Lown deeded the land to Bailey and his son Robin in 1969. In 1975, Bailey deeded her interest in the land to Robin. Coast conveyed its interest to Nichols in April 1976, about two years before commencement of this action.

AS 34.15.290, provides:

Invalidity of unrecorded conveyance. A conveyance of real property in the state hereafter made, other than a lease for a term not exceeding one year, is void as against a subsequent innocent purchaser or mortgagee in good faith for a valuable consideration of the property or a portion of it, whose conveyance is first duly recorded. An unrecorded instrument is valid as between the parties to it and as against one who has actual notice of it.

The question in this case is whether J.J. Lown was, to use the terms of the statute, an innocent purchaser in good faith for a valuable consideration, before Coast's deed of trust was properly recorded in Juneau in May of 1967. If he was not, Robin Lown cannot claim priority of title under this statute. Instead, the general rule that a "purchaser at a deed of trust sale takes land subject only to those encumbrances which were created before execution of the trust deed . . . ." [1] governs.

J.J. Lown was initially a donee rather than a purchaser. By working to build a lodge on the property he substantially relied on his grant. Arguably, he may be said to have then given valuable consideration and perhaps should be considered to be a purchaser for the purposes of AS 34.15.290 as of the time of his substantial reliance. If so, the statute cannot be construed to protect him because his substantial reliance did not take place until June of 1967, after Coast's deed of trust was properly recorded.

This result is well supported by authority. Where a purchase is made, but the purchaser does not give substantial consideration until

---

1. Alaska Laborers Training Fund v. P & R Enterprises, Inc., 583 P.2d 825, 826 (Alaska 1978) *quoting* Lynch v. McCann, 478 P.2d 835, 836–37 (Alaska 1970).

after a prior conveyance is recorded, the purchaser takes subject to the prior conveyance.

This does not mean, as the dissent suggests, that one making installment payments must check the title at the recording office before making each payment. All that is required is an initial payment of substantial consideration, or a promise to pay which has been relied upon by a third person. Part of the policy of the rule is based on a change of position in reliance on the absence of record or actual notice. As the court stated in La Fon v. Grimes:

> The principle upon which the doctrine of innocent purchaser for value rests, like equitable principles in general, is not a hard and fast rule of narrow application, but one to be liberally and equitably applied. Under it relief is denied to a purchaser without notice who has not paid value, on the ground that his equity arises, not out of his mere lack of notice, but out of injury to him, through an innocent change of position to his prejudice. It is therefore denied where the matter of the payment remains executory between purchaser and seller, and there is no irrevocable change of position. It is granted where either the buyer has paid the purchase price or has entered with third persons into a binding obligation with regard to it, whether the obligation arises out of the execution or the assumption of negotiable promissory notes, or other form of undertaking which the buyer is able to perform, and from which he cannot in law withdraw.

86 F.2d 809, 812–13 (5th Cir.1936).

Since J.J. Lown, at best, stood in the position of a subsequent purchaser for valuable consideration only after Coast's deed of trust was properly recorded, the deed of trust had priority over his deed.

Accordingly, the judgment is affirmed.

RABINOWITZ, C.J., dissenting.

COMPTON, J., not participating.

RABINOWITZ, Chief Justice, dissenting.

The superior court relied upon three separate grounds in granting summary judgment in Nichols' favor and in this appeal Nichols has presented a fourth theory on which the summary judgment may be upheld. I conclude that summary judgment was inappropriate on all four grounds.

The superior court found that there was no delivery of the deed by Reams to J.J. Lown until December of 1967, by which point Nichols' interest had become paramount by virtue of the recording of Coast's deed of trust in May of 1967; that the deed from Reams to J.J. Lown on December 22, 1965 was fraudulent in that it was an effort to hinder or defraud the creditor in whose favor Reams had made the deed of trust just eight days earlier, and as such was void under AS 34.40.010; and that the subsequent foreclosure of the deed of trust effectively transferred to Nichols' predecessor all the interest that Reams had in the property on December 14, 1965, when the deed of trust was made. Under any of these theories, the superior court rules, Nichols would prevail; the issues of fact raised by Lown were immaterial to all three conclusions.

On appeal, Nichols has presented a new theory on the basis of which, it argues, the superior court's ruling can be upheld: that J.J. Lown had not tendered any consideration to Reams before he was put on constructive notice of Coast's interest in the land by the May, 1967, recordation in Juneau, and that therefore Coast's deed of trust, the first executed by Reams, is determinative of ownership. I will discuss these theories seriatim . . . .

Nichols' new theory is that Lown's invocation of AS 34.15.290 cannot be sustained on these facts because, even assuming arguendo that the deed had been "delivered" in 1966, J.J. Lown had given no consideration until he started building the lodge in June of 1967; Coast Small Business Investment had recorded in May of 1967; since J.J. Lown should have checked the title records before parting with consideration, he is chargeable with the knowledge of that deed of trust and thus he is not entitled to the protection of AS 34.15.290.

There is no doubt that this would be the correct ruling had J.J. Lown received actual notice of the deed of trust in May of 1967—*i.e.*, had Coast Small Business Investment, which should have found the Reams-Lown deed at the time it recorded the deed of trust, immediately informed Lown of the deed of trust—because then J.J. Lown would have lost the status of innocent purchaser in good faith for valuable consideration, as to any consideration he transferred after the date of that actual notice (which, in this case, would mean all of the consideration). The statute itself specifies that "[a]n unrecorded instrument is valid as between the parties to it and as against one who has actual notice of it." AS 34.15.290. There is no dispute that such actual notice was not given to J.J. Lown; Nichols urged the court to reach the same conclusion, however, on theories of constructive notice and of inquiry notice.

Under the constructive notice theory, Nichols urges adoption of a rule that "a title search is necessary through the date when full consideration is paid in order to qualify the transferee as an innocent purchaser for a valuable consideration without notice." Were this rule adopted it is clear that Nichols would prevail here, since it recorded its deed of trust a month before the initial transfer of consideration, and long before full payment (which, indeed, never occurred, as the lodge remains uncompleted).

However, I find that a rule holding that the status of "innocent purchaser in good faith for a valuable consideration" can be destroyed by subsequent constructive notice, as well as subsequent actual notice, of a prior unrecorded third party interest, would be essentially unworkable. In most such transfers of land, including this one, consideration is conveyed over a long period of time. The general rule is that when the purchaser receives actual notice of a third party's prior unrecorded interest, the purchaser has the status of "innocent purchaser in good faith for a valuable consideration" only to the extent of payments made before he becomes "infected" with notice, and is entitled only to a lien on the land as security for reimbursement for those payments. Were this rule extended to constructive notice, a purchaser would have to re-check the title records before each and every payment to insure that he was still "in good faith" in making that payment. I regard this as unduly burdensome.

A less restrictive rule would require an additional search only before the initial transfer of consideration. However, I see no valid reason for imposing such a duty absent unusual circumstances. Where, as here, a third party tardily records an instrument between the time of delivery of the subsequent purchaser's deed and the first transfer of consideration under that subsequent conveyance, I think it is more reasonable to place the burden on that third party to provide the purchaser with actual notice, thereby destroying the purchaser's status as an "innocent purchaser in good faith for a valuable consideration," rather than requiring that purchaser to re-check for constructive notice.

Although I realize that "on this question different conclusions have been reached," Annot., 109 A.L.R. 163, 172 (1937), I am persuaded by the reasoning in Lowden v. Wilson, 233 Ill. 340, 84 N.E. 245 (1908), which was decided under a race-notice statute like Alaska's. In that case, as here, the grantor made two conveyances; the prior grantee initially failed to record the deed; the subsequent grantee received and recorded the deed; then the prior grantee tardily recorded his deed, after the recordation of the subsequent conveyance, but before consideration had been transferred under that subsequent conveyance. There, as here, the subsequent grantee had no actual notice, and thus the prior grantee was forced to argue that the subsequent purchaser had to show that he paid the entire purchase price before receiving constructive notice of the prior conveyance. The court rejected this argument, emphasizing that one of the purposes of the recording statute was to protect subsequent purchasers against prior deeds or mortgages not recorded, and that a recordation could function as constructive notice only to those who subsequently acquired some interest in the property, not to those who had acquired their interest and recorded their conveyance previously. I also think it significant that AS 34.15.290 requires actual notice in providing that an unrecorded instrument can be valid as to one not a party to the conveyance in that instrument.

Perhaps realizing the difficulties inherent in the constructive notice argument, Nichols' counsel at oral argument relied much more heavily on the inquiry notice argument. He argued that the strange circumstances of the transfer, as explained to J.J. Lown in 1966, should have prompted some inquiry whether there were underlying reasons for the recordation of the deed prior to the property's actually having been offered to J.J. Lown.

I have reservations whether this would be sufficient to trigger inquiry notice. The case at bar does not present a situation as compelling as that in Modrock v. Marshall, 523 P.2d 172 (Alaska 1974), in which we held that a purchaser was put on inquiry notice by the fact that the seller's ex-husband was still living in the house which the wife was selling. Especially since the superior court made no ruling on this point, I cannot say that there was no genuine issue whether the manner of the conveyance was unusual enough to have put J.J. Lown on inquiry notice.

However, I need not express any opinion as to whether the circumstances should have triggered inquiry notice. If that was the case, then J.J. Lown was put on inquiry notice as of early 1966, the point at which Reams explained to him the terms of the conveyance. J.J. Lown would then have been chargeable with whatever the title records revealed at that time; but, as Nichols' counsel conceded at oral argument, the title records at that time would have shown only the conveyance from Reams to Lown, not the Coast Small Business Investment deed of trust:

> [Inquiry] notice may be found where the later conveyee knew of facts or circumstances which should have induced further investigations, which investigations, if prosecuted, would have produced actual knowledge of the prior conveyance. When the facts suffice to impose the duty of investigation, the purchaser is charged with notice of what a proper investigation would have discovered, whether the investigation was, or was not, made. It follows that there is no 'notice' when either a reasonable inquiry reveals nothing, or a search, though not conducted, was certain to be futile.

6A R. Powell, The Law of Real Property 916, at 289–90 (Rohan rev. ed.1968) (footnotes omitted). Here, since the search of the title records in Juneau, although not conducted, was certain to be futile, any triggering of inquiry notice does not change my analysis of the case.

Since I am convinced that there are genuine issues of material fact which must be resolved in this case, I would reverse the grant of summary judgment.

NOTE

Almost all states today require that, to be protected, a subsequent grantee must be a purchaser for value. In most states the requirement appears in the recording act. In a few it has been added by judicial gloss. Courts generally agree that the required value need not approximate the property's market value but must represent more than merely nominal consideration. See generally, 6A R. Powell, The Law of Real Property ¶ 904[2][a] (1982).

What interests does the purchaser for value requirement serve? Do the requirement's benefits outweigh the costs created by uncertainty respecting whether a purchaser gave the requisite value? How should the requirement be coordinated with the notice bar when, as in *Lown*, the grantee first gives value sometime after he acquires the interest in land? Who was better placed to discover the other's interest—Coast, when it re-recorded in Juneau in May 1967, or Lown, when he and Laura Bailey began construction in June 1967?

2. THE SYSTEM AT WORK: THE TITLE SEARCH

a. THE INDICES

NOTE, THE TRACT AND GRANTOR–GRANTEE INDICES, 47 IOWA L.REV. 481–482 (1962): A practical and convenient means of locating records which an owner of property must rely upon to prove his title and which a prospective purchaser must depend upon when making a title search is an indispensable part of a workable system of recordation. Therefore, it is not surprising to discover that statutory provisions providing for some system of indexing which affords a history of the ownership of land and which discloses instruments or encumbrances affecting title to real property have been enacted in every state. There are currently two types of indices in use: (1) the grantor-grantee index, and (2) the tract index. This should not be interpreted as meaning that a dual system of indexing has always been present in the United States, for under the land owned by the English, French, Mexican, and Spanish governments on the North American Continent, there were no numbered tract systems in existence which could serve as a basis for land description. This was, of course, directly related to the fact that a competent survey had never been made of the land owned by these countries. Under these circumstances, even tax levies had to be against the owners of the land rather than against the land itself. Therefore, it was only logical that when some system of indexing was finally adopted the alphabetical or grantor-grantee system of indexing was selected. Nevertheless, even after the United States Government acquired the land formerly held by foreign countries in what is now the United States and adequate Government surveys had been undertaken and completed, the grantor-grantee system of indexing was still retained as the basis of land description. However, it was gradually discovered that the grantor-grantee system of indexing was inadequate in many respects. This led several states to enact statutes establishing a tract or numerical system of indexing. Nevertheless, even those states which adopted the tract system of indexing retained the alphabetical system of indexing which they had established at an earlier date.

Under the grantor-grantee or alphabetical index, pages are assigned in the index to each letter of the alphabet. As an instrument is received at the recorder's office, it is first recorded and then indexed under the name of the granting party on the appropriate page of the index. In addition, the county recorder is usually required to make notations on the grantor's page which disclose the name of the other party to the transaction, the book and page of the record where this particular transaction can be found, a description of the property, the date when the instrument was executed, the date when the instrument was filed for recordation, and the nature of the instrument. These same notations are then made as the transaction is indexed under the name of the grantee or the receiving party. After both steps have been completed, the instrument is considered to have been properly indexed.

Under the tract indexing system each parcel of land in a certain area is assigned a separate page in the index and every subsequent transaction affecting this property will be noted thereon. Under the tract system of indexing, a "parcel of land" means any geographical unit of land which has been surveyed and platted, such as sections, blocks, and lots. In addition to describing the property, the tract index also discloses the character of the instrument which affects the title to the property, the date of the execution of the instrument, the date of the filing of the instrument for recordation, and the names of the parties to the transaction. Under this system, therefore, *all* the instruments which affect the title to a particular parcel of realty will be noted on one page of the index. For this reason and innumerable others, the uniform adoption of the tract index has been urged by many legal scholars. However, the reaction of the respective state legislatures to this proposal apparently has not been enthusiastic.

E. BADE, CASES AND MATERIALS ON REAL PROPERTY AND CONVEYANCING

237–238 (1954).

INDICES OF RECORDS

The most widely required forms of indices for real estate records are grantor and grantee indices. In the grantor index, all conveyances are indexed alphabetically and chronologically under the initial letter of the grantor's surname. In the grantee index, a like index is made of conveyances under the initial letter of the grantee's surname. In running these indices the title searcher may begin with a known owner, A, at a stated time. He traces this name in the grantor index from the time A became an owner until he finds A made a conveyance of his title to another—B. The index will give the name of the grantee and other particulars such as the date of the instrument, date of recording, kind of instrument, and place where recorded in extenso. At this point he drops A and turns to B in the grantor index and traces B's name from the *date of the deed* to him (not from the date of recording) until he finds a conveyance of the title from B to C. He repeats this operation for each successive owner in the chain of title. The grantor-index search for each is bounded in time by the date of *acquisition* and the date *of record* of his conveyance out.

Normally, the title search begins with the grantee index. Z, who claims to be the fee owner, is proposing to sell the land to a prospective purchaser. The intending buyer, or his agent, will go to the grantee index and beginning in point of time *presently* where the page is still blank, he will trace back in point of time to see when, if ever, Z became a grantee of the land. If he finds Z's name, the index will tell him the name of Z's grantor, Y, the date of recording, the date of the deed together with the same information contained in the grantor index.

The title searcher now drops his search for Z in the grantee index and turns to Y. He now searches the grantee index to see when Y became a grantee. In point of time, the search for Y as a grantee begins at the date of *the record* of the deed to Z and proceeds backward in time until Y's name is found. In this way the title is traced back link by link. Both indices must be traced to complete the search.

To illustrate the matter for one step or link. When the searcher finds Y was the grantor of Z the searcher will then trace the grantee index to find when Y became a grantee. He will then want to know whether Y at any time since the *date of the deed* (not the date of its record) to him, made any conveyance out. Hence he traces Y in the grantor index from the *date of the deed* to Y down to the point where Y granted all his interest in the land to Z. The search at this point continues to the *date of record* of the deed from Y to Z. This is done because if Z did not record promptly, in notice and notice-race jurisdictions, Y may have made a subsequent conveyance to a bona fide purchaser for value who may have recorded his conveyance first, cutting off Z's rights. In notice jurisdictions, of course, Z's rights could be cut off without a prior recording.

In following this procedure, it will be apparent that if Y made a conveyance of the land before the date of the deed to him and which was recorded before the date of the deed to him, it would not be found. It will be outside the chain of title. So also it will be evident that a serious discrepancy in the name of a person who is a grantor and grantee or a misdescription of the property may break the thread of search.

The other type of index is variously known as a tract index, block index, and numerical index; most commonly as a tract index. Under this type of index a line or column is assigned to conveniently sized tracts. It may be a section, quarter section, platted blocks or lots. Under that land description, every conveyance of any interest in that land is indexed chronologically. Hence all conveyances affecting the title to that land will appear there. It will appear there no matter who made it, whether he is a stranger to the title or not. Consequently, if a tract index is a required record, purchasers should be, and usually are charged with constructive notice of all conveyances indexed there.

Most abstractors prepare abstracts of title from tract indices. If an abstract so prepared refers to a conveyance outside the chain of title, and is examined by the prospective purchaser or by his agent or attorney, is he put on inquiry even though a tract index is not a required index in the jurisdiction?

HANSON v. ZOLLER

Supreme Court of North Dakota, 1971.
187 N.W.2d 47.

ADAM GEFREH, District Judge.

In this action the plaintiff seeks to foreclose a certain mortgage given by John Zoller and Martha Zoller, husband and wife, pertaining to the South Half of the Northeast Quarter (S½ NE¼) of Section Twenty-six (26), Township One Hundred Thirty-nine (139), Range Eighty (80), Burleigh County, North Dakota, and other land not involved in this action.

In addition to John Zoller and Martha Zoller, other subsequent purchasers, encumbrancers and lienholders were made defendants to the foreclosure action.

The defendants, James P. Zoller and Alice R. Zoller, husband and wife; Eugene V. Binder and Gloria A. Binder, husband and wife; Paul M. Breene and the State of North Dakota, are purchasers subsequent to the mortgage in question, and The Dakota National Bank of Bismarck, and Gate City Savings and Loan Association, are holders of mortgages subsequent to the plaintiff's mortgage. Defendants James P. and Alice R. Zoller, and Gate City Savings and Loan Association; Eugene V. and Gloria A. Binder and The Dakota National Bank of Bismarck, as third-party plaintiffs in separate actions impleaded The North Dakota Guaranty and Title Company as third-party defendant.

In the District Court, judgment was granted in favor of the plaintiff as against John and Martha Zoller, the Credit Bureau, Inc., of Bismarck, Max D. Rosenberg, trustee of State Acceptance Corporation, a bankrupt, and Atlas, Inc., who did not answer the complaint and were in default, and in favor of all the named defendants and against the plaintiff. Since judgment was granted in favor of defendants and third-party plaintiffs in the foreclosure action, the third-par-

LAND TRANSFER AND FINANCE

ty complaint against The North Dakota Guaranty and Title Company was dismissed. After the plaintiff, Clifford P. Hanson, had filed his notice of appeal the defendants and third-party plaintiffs filed appeals from the orders dismissing their third-party complaints against the third-party defendant. All the parties demanded a Trial De Novo in the Supreme Court.

The mortgage being foreclosed is dated May 16, 1962, and was filed for record in the office of the Register of Deeds of Burleigh County, North Dakota, on March 6, 1963, at 10:30 A.M., and was subsequently recorded in Book 358 of Mortgages on Page 108.

The record shows that in July of 1964, John Zoller and Martha Zoller, the mortgagors, caused part of the land described in the mortgage to be subdivided into Tracts A, B, and C, and other parcels which subdivision plat was filed on November 5, 1964, in Plat File Z with the Register of Deeds. Subsequent to the date and recording of plaintiff's mortgage, James P. and Alice R. Zoller acquired title to Tract A, Eugene V. and Gloria A. Binder acquired title to Tract B, and Paul M. Breene acquired title to Tract C and also other lands, all by warranty deeds from John and Martha Zoller. Thereafter, James P. and Alice R. Zoller mortgaged their tract to Gate City Savings and Loan Association, and Eugene V. and Gloria A. Binder mortgaged their tract to The Dakota National Bank of Bismarck, which mortgages were filed for record subsequent to the recording of the plaintiff's mortgage.

Additionally, the State of North Dakota acquired by condemnation part of the property in the South Half of the Northeast Quarter ($S^1/_2$ $NE^1/_4$) of Section Twenty-six (26), described in the plaintiff's mortgage subsequent to the recording of plaintiff's mortgage.

The record further shows that abstracts of title were obtained from the North Dakota Guaranty and Title Company for Tracts A, B, and C, and the State of North Dakota had obtained a Title Certificate from a title insurance company. The abstracts of title pertaining to Tracts A, B, and C, did not show the mortgage from John and Martha Zoller to the plaintiff. The Title Insurance Certificate to the State of North Dakota also did not make reference to the plaintiff's mortgage. It is undisputed that all of the defendants named had no actual knowledge of the existence of plaintiff's mortgage from John and Martha Zoller.

At the trial of the action, James Horner and Mildred Benesh, employees of the North Dakota Guaranty and Title Company, the firm that prepared the abstracts to Tracts A, B, and C, testified that the abstracts they prepared were prepared from the information derived from the tract index pertaining to the land in question and at the time the abstracts were prepared plaintiff's mortgage was not indexed under the South Half of the Northeast Quarter ($S^1/_2$ $NE^1/_4$) of Section Twenty-six (26), Township One Hundred Thirty-nine (139), Range Eighty (80). James Horner, further testified that sometime during

September of 1966, he found the plaintiff's mortgage indexed in the tract index against either the northwest or southwest quarter of the northwest quarter. Mildred Benesh, also testified that on March 29, 1967, when she prepared the abstract of title for plaintiff pertaining to land embraced in his mortgage, the tract index showed the mortgage indexed against the South Half of the Northeast Quarter of Section 26, but subsequent to March 29, 1967, when she had an occasion to check the grantor-grantee and grantee-grantor indexes they still showed the property indexed as part of the Northwest Quarter. During the course of the trial all of the records from the register of deeds office, the reception book, tract index, grantor and grantee indexes and Page 108 of Book 358 of Mortgages were introduced as evidence.

The District Court, upon conclusion of the trial, found that the Hanson mortgage was originally indexed insofar as the property in question was concerned as part of the Northwest Quarter of Section 26, rather than the Northeast Quarter; that alterations in the records in the register of deeds office were made subsequent to the recording of the conveyances to the defendants, and held that the recording of the plaintiff's mortgage in the manner it was recorded did not comply with our recording statute and therefore it did not constitute constructive notice to third persons, and that the defendants were purchasers or encumbrancers for value without any notice, actual or constructive.

An examination of Page 108 of Book 358 of Mortgages, being Defendant's Exhibit "V—1," shows that when the mortgage was copied the portion pertaining to the description in question read: "The South one-half of the North one-quarter of Section 26, Township 139, Range 80, County of Burleigh, State of North Dakota." A correction with different type was made by inserting the word "east" below the word "one" in the phrase "North one-quarter." In the original instrument which was introduced in evidence, a similar correction appears, but the correction is made in ink and the word "east" is above the "one" in the "North one-quarter" phrase . . ..

We have examined all of the exhibits relevant to the issues and have reviewed the transcript of the testimony adduced at the trial and agree with the findings of the trial court, that the original records in the office of the register of deeds incorrectly described the property in question, in the reception book, tract index, grantor and grantee indexes, and that certain corrections and alterations were subsequently made, and that these corrections and alterations were made subsequent to the conveyances of the defendants in this action.

The trial court concluded that proper indexing is an essential part of the recording process and unless the indexes correctly reflect the existence and contents of an instrument, the instrument will not impart constructive notice to subsequent purchasers and encumbrancers.

The issues presented in this appeal as they relate to the action between the plaintiff and defendants are:

(1) Does an instrument that is erroneously indexed under the wrong description in the tract index constitute constructive notice of its execution and contents to subsequent purchasers and encumbrancers?

(2) Does a prospective purchaser or encumbrancer ordinarily have a duty to consult the reception book, grantor and grantee indexes, that if consulted would contain sufficient information to put a prudent person upon inquiry?

(3) If both questions are answered in the negative, should the consequence of the failure of the register of deeds to correctly index the mortgage in the tract index fall upon the plaintiff or the defendant?

The plaintiff argues that his mortgage was deposited with the register of deeds for recording and that the mortgage was subsequently accurately copied in the book of mortgages, and therefore pursuant to Sections 47-19-45, 47-19-08 and 47-19-19 of the N.D. C.C. this constituted constructive notice to subsequent purchasers and encumbrancers.

The sections referred to read as follows:

> The depositing with the proper officer for record of any instrument shall be constructive notice of the execution of such instrument to all purchasers and encumbrancers subsequent to such depositing, if such instrument is subsequently recorded. All instruments entitled to record, the record of all instruments, or a duly certified copy of such record, shall be admissible in evidence in all the courts of this state and may be read in evidence in all of the courts of this state without further proof.

Sec. 47-19-45, N.D.C.C.

> An instrument is deemed to be recorded when, whether entitled to record or not, it is deposited with the proper officer for record, if such instrument is subsequently recorded.

Sec. 47-19-08, N.D.C.C.

> The record of any instrument shall be notice of the contents of the instrument, as it appears of record, as to all persons.

Sec. 47-19-19, N.D.C.C.

The plaintiff further contends that an instrument is recorded within the meaning of these sections quoted when it is transcribed in the proper book in the register of deeds' office.

The defendants argue that an instrument cannot be deemed recorded so as to constitute constructive notice to third persons until all the steps required by the statutes pertaining to the register of deeds have been completed, and that would include correct indexing in the tract index book.

The following sections pertain to the duties of the register of deeds . . . .

The register of deeds shall keep a separate tract index of the deeds, contracts, and other instruments which are not merely liens and a separate tract index of the mortgages and other liens affecting or relating to the title to real property. Such indexes shall be in substantially the following forms: . . . (Forms omitted)

Sec. 11–18–07, N.D.C.C.

The register of deeds shall keep separate grantor and grantee indexes of the deeds, contracts, and other instruments not merely liens and separate grantor and grantee indexes of the mortgages and other instruments which are liens affecting or relating to the title to real property . . . .

We do not believe that all of the sections pertaining to the duties of the register of deeds in recording instruments have to be complied with in order for an instrument to impart constructive notice to subsequent purchasers and encumbrancers. We believe only those sections or steps that pertain to the aspect of notice must be substantially complied with.

The fundamental purpose of the recording statutes is to protect potential purchasers of real property against the risk that they may be paying out good money to someone who does not actually own the property that he is purporting to sell. The recording acts operate by making the history of the title involved in a real estate transaction readily available to a prospective purchaser, and by providing that the history so disclosed by the record is binding upon a prospective purchaser whether he consults the record or not.

At the time North Dakota adopted its recording acts, many states were still utilizing only grantor-grantee indexes as the chief aids in title search. This is a cumbersome way of digging out the history of the title to a given tract of land.

Our recording acts date back to the territorial code of 1877, which in turn were adopted from the California Civil Code of 1875. Several of the midwestern and western states adopted similar statutes patterned after the California statutes.

The territorial code of 1877 provided for a more modern recording procedure and provided for a numerical tract index in lieu of the grantor-grantee index.

Chapter 21, Counties and County Officers, Sec. 58, Rev. Code Dakota 1877, reads as follows:

> The registers of deeds shall prepare from the records of their offices respectively, and shall hereafter keep a numerical index of the deeds, mortgages, and other instruments of record in their respective offices affecting or relating to the title to real property, in lieu of the indexes by names of grantors and grantees, as now kept.

Apparently it was the intention of the Territorial Legislature to only require the register of deeds to keep a tract index. However, for whatever the reason may have been, the provision for also requiring grantor-grantee indexes was added in 1887, and both provisions became a part of our law from the time of statehood. Since the original adoption of these recording acts by the several states, all have undergone some changes in order to make them more applicable to the specific needs of each state.

Although this court over the years has had to interpret several sections of our recordings laws, the precise question that is now before us as to what constitutes sufficient compliance with the recording statutes so as to give constructive notice has never been decided.

We believe, however, that some of our prior decisions are relevant to the issue before us and do provide a direction in what we believe to be the correct interpretation of our recording statutes.

This court in Northwestern Improvement Company v. Norris, 74 N.W.2d 497, answered the argument that the mere depositing of an instrument with the register of deeds for recording would thereafter constitute notice to subsequent purchasers, by holding that Section 47–19–08 and Section 47–19–45, quoted earlier, must be construed together, and stated:

> Their proper construction is that an instrument gives only temporary constructive notice of its contents when deposited in the office of the register of deeds and that when the instrument is recorded the record for purposes of constructive notice relates back to the date of deposit and as of that time is constructive notice of the contents actually and correctly recorded.

The same principle was reaffirmed in Northern Pacific Railway Co. v. Advance Realty, 78 N.W.2d 705.

There can no longer be any doubt that in order for an instrument to impart constructive notice to the public it must actually be recorded in the books required to be kept by the register of deeds. Must an instrument be also indexed?

The existence of a tract index, which not only makes all instruments equally accessible to reasonable search, but which has its primary focus upon tracts of land rather than upon grantors and grantees, makes the concept of "chain of title" as developed in relation to the old grantor and grantee type index inapplicable. The fact that in our state we have developed a recording system by counties, and which consequently results in many thousands of instruments being recorded annually in some counties, makes it totally impractical for anyone to make a title search by means of grantor-grantee indexes.

In our state, today, the tract index is the only practical index through which instruments on record can be located. It would be a prohibitive burden to locate instruments on record without a tract index. It would certainly be a travesty of justice to hold that prospective purchasers are bound by the record, if for all practical purposes the record cannot be located.

The practice today by abstracters, attorneys, and others making title searches is to use the tract index rather than by the old means of the grantor-grantee indexes. Although the register of deeds still has to keep all the indexes, the grantor-grantee index is actually a carry over from the old system, and is only an additional tool available to title searchers for other purposes.

Under the tract index system the title is traced by searching the tract index for instruments pertaining to the tract to be searched. The names of the grantor and grantee are not material to this search.

We have considered several decisions from other jurisdictions that appear to have recording statutes similar to ours and which have held that an instrument will not give constructive notice of its contents unless it has been recorded in substantial compliance with their recording statutes, and that failure to properly index an instrument does not constitute substantial compliance with the recording statutes.

We have also noted cases that are holding contrary to the cases cited above. However, in analyzing these cases we are inclined to believe that the rule or principle that they asserted was more applicable to the old grantor-grantee type recording systems than to the tract index system that we have in our state.

After considering all the statutes and all of the authorities cited in this opinion, and considering the practice in use by lawyers, lending agencies and abstracters, we conclude that a prospective purchaser cannot be deemed to have constructive notice of instruments that are not indexed in the tract index under the specific tract of real estate to which they pertain. We conclude that there must be substantial compliance with those sections of the recording laws that pertain to the matter of notice in order to give constructive notice. Failure to index an instrument in the tract index does not constitute such compliance.

The appellant also argues that if the error by the register of deeds in indexing the instrument under the wrong description deprives the instrument of giving constructive notice, the entries in the reception book, and in the grantor-grantee index books, would constitute sufficient notice to put a prudent person upon inquiry. The plain fact is that the reception book and grantor and grantee indexes only serve very limited purposes. The reception book would only be consulted for the purpose of determining whether there are any instruments on deposit with the register of deeds that have not yet been fully recorded, or to determine priorities between instruments if priority becomes an issue.

Under the statute and our holdings in Northwestern Improvement Co. v. Norris, *supra*, the actual instrument deposited with the register of deeds accords constructive notice of its execution only from the

Pt. 1 *LAND TRANSFER AND FINANCE* 353

time of its deposit until the recording has been completed. After recording, the actual record made constitutes constructive notice. The reception book, therefore, is primarily being consulted by a title searcher for the limited purpose of determining whether there are any unrecorded instruments in the hands of the register of deeds. The tract index which contains a record of every instrument that has ever been filed pertaining to any tract of land in the county is the composite index that directs a title searcher to all the instruments on record that affect each specific tract of land. A prospective purchaser or encumbrancer searching the records has a right to assume that the register of deeds has performed his duties correctly and has indexed every instrument correctly in the tract index. The ordinary prudent person searching the record to determine the title status to a specific tract of land would have no need to consult the grantor-grantee indexes, because the tract index discloses the names of the grantors and grantees of the instruments that pertain to a certain tract of land.

We see no material difference between the principle of substantial compliance with the recording sections pertaining to notice to constitute constructive notice, and the principle of sufficient information in the records to cause or require a person to make inquiry so as to be considered having actual notice of the instruments on record. The same standard should apply, since it is immaterial whether a subsequent purchaser looks at the record or not, he is bound by the record which he has a duty to search, and if such record is such that a person searching it should find the instrument, then the record is also such that it will give constructive notice. Statutes should receive a reasonable interpretation that is consonant with what the actual practice is among those to whom the statute has application.

We therefore conclude that under our modern practice of recording real estate transactions, there is no duty upon a prospective purchaser in so far as constructive notice is concerned to consult the grantor-grantee indexes or the reception book beyond the extent of determining whether there are any unrecorded instruments in the hands of the register of deeds that may not yet have been recorded and indexed. To require a person to check the grantor-grantee indexes and go through the entire reception book to determine whether all the instruments on record have been properly recorded and indexed would be to completely nullify the use of the tract index which is the modern tool used by anyone making a title search. Therefore, the defendants cannot be charged with information that may have been obtained from consulting the reception book or grantor-grantee indexes.

The plaintiff also contends that the abstracter had knowledge of the erroneous indexing within a couple of months after the mortgage was recorded, which knowledge of the abstracter must be imputed to the defendants, and therefore they cannot be considered encumbrancers without notice.

We can not agree with this contention. The relationship between an abstracter and persons who come into possession of an abstract prepared by an abstracter is not an agency type relationship. The liability of an abstracter is contractual in nature, in addition to the statutory liability imposed upon him. There is no evidence in this case to support a principal-agency relationship, and consequently any knowledge that employees of the abstracting firm may have acquired during the course of their work is not imputable to the defendants in this case.

Having concluded that appellants' mortgage as recorded did not give constructive notice, or any other notice of the execution of the instrument to the defendants, upon whom should the consequences of the failure of the register of deeds to properly index the instrument fall?

In Northwestern Improvement Co. v. Norris, *supra*, this court held that it was the duty of the grantor in a conveyance to protect his interest against any subsequent purchaser in good faith by making certain that the reservation and exception of minerals therein was properly recorded. The holding in effect is that the beneficiary of any interest in any real estate conveyance has a duty to protect his interest against subsequent purchasers by making certain that the instrument conveying his interest is properly recorded, because he is the only person that by exercising some diligence can discover errors in the recording which a subsequent purchaser even by the exercise of the greatest diligence could not possibly do.

It is well recognized that every major lending agency operating in the state today will require an abstract of title continued to include all the instruments necessary to give it good title to the interest conveyed before it will release any money. Had the appellant followed this well established practice he would have promptly discovered the error of the register of deeds and could have had it corrected.

Plaintiff has cited Atlas Lumber Company v. Canadian-American Mortgage and Trust Company, 36 N.D. 39, 161 N.W. 604, in support of his contention that errors of the register of deeds should not be visited upon the persons leaving an instrument for recording. The facts in the present case are materially different from the facts in that case. In that case the clerk of court erroneously showed the wrong lien as having been satisfied. There was no question but that the lien so erroneously satisfied had been properly filed and recorded. The principle of law stated in that case has no application to the case under consideration.

The facts in Northwestern Improvement Co. v. Norris, *supra*, are more analogous to the present case and the principle established in that case has application here. The principle is fully in accord with the general principle of law which appears to prevail in the majority of jurisdictions and stated in Section 64, Vol. 1, Patton on Titles, P. 218:

> However, the majority rule is that, except as the existence of error is apparent on the face of the record, a subsequent purchaser is bound by what appears upon the record only, regardless of the contents of the original instrument. This rule places the loss upon the beneficiary in the instrument in the transcribing of which the error was made. As between him and the subsequent purchaser, he is the only one who had it in his power to make comparison and to have the error corrected, and upon him devolved the duty, not merely of filing his instrument for record, but of having it correctly recorded.

For the reasons stated we affirm the decision of the trial court and the judgments entered by the trial court.

Since we have affirmed the trial court in the principal action, the issues raised in the appeal between the third party plaintiffs and third party defendant have become moot.

TEIGEN, J., and C.F. KELSCH, District Judge, concur.

KNUDSON and PAULSON, JJ., dissent.

NOTE

Some form of indexing is obviously required by the tremendous volume of recorded instruments. According to one report, approximately 7,000 instruments are recorded each month in Suffolk County, Massachusetts (Boston); about 15,000 documents are recorded each month in Cook County, Illinois (Chicago) and 5,000–6,000 instruments are recorded each day in Los Angeles. Basye, A Uniform Land Parcel Identifier—Its Potential for All Our Land Records, 22 Am.U.L. Rev. 251 (1973).

Even the best official indexing systems are incomplete. One limitation of contemporary indexing systems is that they do not tell title examiners how far back in a chain of title they must search in order to identify an indisputable source of title. This limitation is not particularly burdensome when a tract index is used because the tract index accumulates all transactions, including the first, on consecutive pages. The limitations can, however, prove costly when only grantor and grantee indices are available, particularly if the searcher must trace title all the way back to the original grant from the sovereign.

Many transactions affecting title will be revealed by neither the grantor-grantee index nor the tract index, no matter how far back title is traced. An examiner searching title in Erie County, New York on behalf of Mr. and Mrs. Smith must consult, among other sources, the indices of wills and administration of decedents' estates in the office of the county surrogate; the index of bankrupts in local federal court; local judgment dockets and dockets of federal tax liens. One limitation of these other sources is that they were designed for purposes other than facilitating title searches. For example, because neither grantor-grantee nor tract indices refer to land transfers effected by will or intestacy, a title examiner will quickly conclude that if these indices reveal a gap in ownership it is because the land at that point passed by devise or descent. But it will take considerable sleuthing to bridge that gap since probate registers are indexed alphabetically by the name of the decedent and not by the name of the estate's recipient—the only name that the examiner knows.

Although tract indices suffer many of the same limitations in breadth as grantor-grantee indices, they are clearly superior on other relevant criteria: depth, speed and accuracy of search. Why, then, have tract indices not been widely adopted across the country? The simple answer is that they have—although not as official public indices, but rather as unofficial private indices maintained as "title plants" by examiners, abstracters and title insurance companies. Recognizing the superiority of tract indices, title examiners long ago began compiling them on their own. Each time an examiner searched title to a parcel, she would place a copy of the search in her files, indexed by reference to the parcel; the next time the examiner was retained to search title to that parcel, she had only to pull the relevant file and update her last search to the present. Title plants represent valuable assets and many, if not most, have been purchased by title insurance companies, enabling them quickly to establish themselves and their services in new locales. See generally, Cook, Land Law Reform: A Modern Computerized System of Land Records, 38 U.Cin.L.Rev. 385 (1969); Cook, Land Data Systems: The Next Steps, 43 U.Cin.L.Rev. 527 (1974); Jensen, Computerization of Land Records by the Title Industry, 22 Am.U.L.Rev. 393 (1973).

b. Extent of Search

MORSE v. CURTIS

Supreme Court of Massachusetts, 1885.
140 Mass. 112, 2 N.E. 929.

MORTON, C.J. This is a writ of entry. Both parties derive their title from one Hall. Hall mortgaged the land to the demandant, August 8, 1872. On September 7, 1875, Hall mortgaged the land to one Clark, who had notice of the earlier mortgage. The mortgage to Clark was recorded January 31, 1876. The mortgage to the demandant was recorded September 8, 1876. On October 4, 1881, Clark assigned his mortgage to the tenant, who had no notice of the mortgage to the demandant. The question is, which of these titles has priority? The same question was distinctly raised and adjudicated in the two cases of Connecticut v. Bradish, 14 Mass. 296, and Trull v.

Bigelow, 16 Mass. 406. These adjudications establish a rule of property which ought not to be unnoticed, except for the strongest reasons. It is true that in the late case of Flynt v. Arnold, 2 Metc. 614, Chief Justice SHAW expresses his individual opinion against the soundness of these decisions; but in that case the decision of the court was distinctly put upon that ground, and his remarks can be only considered in the light of *dicta*, and not as overruling the earlier adjudications.

Upon careful consideration, the reasons upon which the earlier cases were decided seem to us the more satisfactory because they follow the spirit of our registry laws and the practice of the profession under them. The earliest registry law provides that no conveyance of land shall be good and effectual in law "against any other person or persons but the grantor or grantors, and their heirs only, unless the deed or deeds thereof be acknowledged and recorded in manner aforesaid." St.1783, c. 37, § 4. Under this statute the court, at an early period, held that the recording was designed to take the place of the notorious act of livery of seizin, and that though by the first deed the title passed out of the grantor as against himself, yet he could, if such deed was not recorded, convey a good title to an innocent purchaser who received and recorded his deed. But the court then held that a prior unrecorded deed would be valid against a second purchaser who took his deed with a knowledge of the prior deed, thus ingrafting an exception upon the statute. 3 Mass. 575; Marshall v. Fisk, 6 Mass. 24. This exception was adopted on the ground that it was a fraud in the second grantee to take a deed if he had knowledge of the prior deed. As Chief Justice SHAW forcibly says in Lawrence v. Stratton, 6 Cush. 163, the rule is "put upon the ground that a party with such notice could not take a deed without fraud; the objection was not to the nature of the conveyance, but to the honesty of the taker, and therefore, if the estate had passed through such taker to a *bona fide* purchaser without fraud, the conveyance was held valid." This exception by judicial exposition was afterwards ingrafted upon the statute, and somewhat extended by the legislature. Rev.St. 59, p. 28; Gen.St. c. 59, § 31; Pub.St. c. 120, § 4. It is to be observed that in each of these revisions it is provided that an unrecorded prior deed is not valid against any person except the grantor, his heirs and devisees, "and persons having actual notice of it." The reason why the statutes require actual notice to a second purchaser, in order to defeat his title, is apparent; its purpose is that his title shall not prevail against the prior deed if he has been guilty of a fraud upon the first grantee, and he could not be guilty of such fraud unless he had actual notice of the first deed.

Now, in the case before us, it is found as a fact that the tenant had no actual knowledge of the prior mortgage to the demandant at the time he took his assignment from Clark. But it is contended that he had constructive notice, because the demandant's mortgage was recorded before such assignment. It was held in Connecticut v.

Bradish, supra, that such record was evidence of actual notice, but was not of itself enough to show actual notice, and to charge the assignee of the second deed with a fraud upon the holder of the first unrecorded deed. This seems to us to accord with the spirit of our registry laws, and the uniform understanding of and practice under them by the profession. These laws not only provide that deeds must be recorded, but they also prescribe the method in which the records shall be kept and indexes prepared for public inspection and examination. There are indexes of grantors and grantees, so that, in searching a title, the examiner is obliged to run down the list of grantors or run backward through the list of grantees. If he can start with an owner who is known to have a good title, as in the case at bar he could start with Hall, he is obliged to run through the index of grantors until he finds a conveyance by the owner of the land in question. After such conveyance the former owner becomes a stranger to the title, and the examiner must follow down the name of the new owner to see if he has conveyed the land, and so on. It would be a hardship to require an examiner to follow in the index of grantors the name of every person who at any time, through, perhaps, a long chain of title, was the owner of the estate.

We do not think this is the practical construction which lawyers and conveyancers have given to our registry laws. The inconvenience of such a construction would be much greater than would be the inconvenience of requiring a person who has neglected to record his prior deed for a time, to record it, and to bring a bill in equity to set aside the subsequent deed, if it was taken in fraud of his rights. The better rule, and the least likely to create confusion of titles, seems to us to be that if a purchaser, upon examining the registry, finds a conveyance from the owner of the land to his grantor which gives him a perfect record title, complete by what the law at the time it is recorded regards as equivalent to a livery of seizin, he is entitled to rely upon such recorded title, and is not obliged to search the record afterwards made, to see if there has been any prior unrecorded deed of the original owners.

This rule of property, established by the early case of Connecticut v. Bradish, supra, ought not to be departed from unless conclusive reasons therefor can be shown. We are therefore of opinion that in the case at bar the tenant has the better title. Verdict set aside.

SABO v. HORVATH

Supreme Court of Alaska, 1976.
559 P.2d 1038.

BOOCHEVER, Chief Justice.

This appeal arises because Grover C. Lowery conveyed the same five-acre piece of land twice—first to William A. Horvath and Barbara J. Horvath and later to William Sabo and Barbara Sabo. Both conveyances were by separate documents entitled "Quitclaim Deeds." Lowery's interest in the land originates in a patent from the United States Government under 43 U.S.C. § 687a (1970) ("Alaska Homesite Law"). Lowery's conveyance to the Horvaths was prior to the issuance of patent, and his subsequent conveyance to the Sabos was after the issuance of patent. The Horvaths recorded their deed in the Chitna Recording District on January 5, 1970; the Sabos recorded their deed on December 13, 1973. The transfer to the Horvaths, however, predated patent and title, and thus the Horvaths' interest in the land was recorded "outside the chain of title." Mr. Horvath brought suit to quiet title, and the Sabos counterclaimed to quiet their title.

In a memorandum opinion, the superior court ruled that Lowery had an equitable interest capable of transfer at the time of his conveyance to the Horvaths and further said the transfer contemplated more than a "mere quitclaim"—it warranted patent would be transferred. The superior court also held that Horvath had the superior claim to the land because his prior recording had given the Sabos constructive notice for purposes of AS 34.15.290. The Sabos' appeal raises the following issues:

1. Under 43 U.S.C. § 687a (1970), when did Lowery obtain a present equitable interest in land which he could convey?

2. Are the Sabos, as grantees under a quitclaim deed, "subsequent innocent purchaser[s] in good faith"?

3. Is the Horvaths' first recorded interest, which is outside the chain of title, constructive notice to Sabo?

We affirm the trial court's ruling that Lowery had an interest to convey at the time of his conveyance to the Horvaths. We further hold that Sabo may be a "good faith purchaser" even though he takes by quitclaim deed. We reverse the trial court's ruling that Sabo had constructive notice and hold that a deed recorded outside the chain of title is a "wild deed" and does not give constructive notice under the recording laws of Alaska.[2]

The facts may be stated as follows. Grover C. Lowery occupied land in the Chitna Recording District on October 10, 1964 for purposes of obtaining Federal patent. Lowery filed a location notice on February 24, 1965, and made his application to purchase on June 6, 1967 with the Bureau of Land Management (BLM). On March 7, 1968, the BLM field examiner's report was filed which recommended that patent issue to Lowery. On October 7, 1969, a request for survey was made by the United States Government. On January 3, 1970, Lowery issued a document entitled "Quitclaim Deed" to the Horvaths; Horvath recorded the deed on January 5, 1970 in the Chitna Recording District. Horvath testified that when he bought the land from Lowery, he knew patent and title were still in the Unit-

---

2. Because we hold Lowery had a conveyable interest under the Federal statute, we need not decide issues raised by the parties regarding after-acquired property and the related issue of estoppel by deed.

ed States Government, but he did not rerecord his interest after patent had passed to Lowery.

Following the sale to the Horvaths, further action was taken by Lowery and the BLM pertaining to the application for patent and culminating in issuance of the patent on August 10, 1973.

Almost immediately after the patent was issued, Lowery advertised the land for sale in a newspaper. He then executed a second document also entitled "quitclaim" to the Sabos on October 15, 1973. The Sabos duly recorded this document on December 13, 1973.

Luther Moss, a representative of the BLM, testified to procedures followed under the Alaska Homesite Law [43 U.S.C. § 687a (1970)]. After numerous steps, a plat is approved and the claimant notified that he should direct publication of his claim. In this case, Lowery executed his conveyance to the Horvaths after the BLM field report had recommended patent.

The first question this court must consider is whether Lowery had an interest to convey at the time of his transfer to the Horvaths. Lowery's interest was obtained pursuant to patent law 43 U.S.C. § 687a (1970) commonly called the "Alaska Homesite Law". Since Lowery's title to the property was contingent upon the patent ultimately issuing from the United States Government and since Lowery's conveyance to the Horvaths predated issuance of the patent, the question is "at what point in the pre-patent chain of procedures does a person have a sufficient interest in a particular tract of land to convey that land by quitclaim deed." Willis v. City of Valdez, 546 P.2d 570, 575 (Alaska 1976). . . .

In Willis v. City of Valdez, *supra* at 578, we held that one who later secured a patent under the Soldiers' Additional Homestead Act had an interest in land which was alienable at the time that he requested a survey. Here, Lowery had complied with numerous requirements under the Homesite Law including those of occupancy, and the BLM had recommended issuance of the patent. Since 43 U.S.C. § 687a (1970) does not prohibit alienation, we hold that at the time Lowery executed the deed to the Horvaths he had complied with the statute to a sufficient extent so as to have an interest in the land which was capable of conveyance.

Since the Horvaths received a valid interest from Lowery, we must now resolve the conflict between the Horvaths' first recorded interest and the Sabos' later recorded interest.

The Sabos, like the Horvaths, received their interest in the property by a quitclaim deed. They are asserting that their interest supersedes the Horvaths under Alaska's statutory recording system. AS 34.15.290 provides that:

> A conveyance of real property . . . is void as against a subsequent innocent purchaser . . . for a valuable consideration of the property . . . whose conveyance is first duly recorded.

An unrecorded instrument is valid . . . as against one who has actual notice of it.

Initially, we must decide whether the Sabos, who received their interest by means of a quitclaim deed, can ever be "innocent purchaser[s]" within the meaning of AS 34.15.290. Since a "quitclaim" only transfers the interest of the grantor, the question is whether a "quitclaim" deed itself puts a purchaser on constructive notice. Although the authorities are in conflict over this issue, the clear weight of authority is that a quitclaim grantee can be protected by the recording system, assuming, of course, the grantee purchased for valuable consideration and did not otherwise have actual or constructive knowledge as defined by the recording laws. We choose to follow the majority rule and hold that a quitclaim grantee is not precluded from attaining the status of an "innocent purchaser."

In this case, the Horvaths recorded their interest from Lowery prior to the time the Sabos recorded their interest. Thus, the issue is whether the Sabos are charged with constructive knowledge because of the Horvaths' prior recordation. Horvath is correct in his assertion that in the usual case a prior recorded deed serves as constructive notice pursuant to AS 34.15.290, and thus precludes a subsequent recordation from taking precedence. Here, however, the Sabos argue that because Horvath recorded his deed prior to Lowery having obtained patent, they were not given constructive notice by the recording system. They contend that since Horvaths' recordation was outside the chain of title, the recording should be regarded as a "wild deed".

It is an axiom of hornbook law that a purchaser has notice only of recorded instruments that are within his "chain of title." If a grantor (Lowery) transfers prior to obtaining title, and the grantee (Horvath) records prior to title passing, a second grantee who diligently examines all conveyances under the grantor's name from the date that the grantor had secured title would not discover the prior conveyance. The rule in most jurisdictions which have adopted a grantor-grantee index system of recording is that a "wild deed" does not serve as constructive notice to a subsequent purchaser who duly records.

Alaska's recording system utilizes a "grantor-grantee" index. Had Sabo searched title under both grantor's and grantee's names but limited his search to the chain of title subsequent to patent, he would not be chargeable with discovery of the pre-patent transfer to Horvath.

On one hand, we could require Sabo to check beyond the chain of title to look for pretitle conveyances. While in this particular case the burden may not have been great, as a general rule, requiring title checks beyond the chain of title could add a significant burden as well as uncertainty to real estate purchases. To a certain extent, requiring title searches of records prior to the date a grantor acquired title would thus defeat the purposes of the recording system. The records as to each grantor in the chain of title would theoretically have to be checked back to the later of the grantor's date of birth or the date when records were first retained.

On the other hand, we could require Horvath to rerecord his interest in the land once title passes, that is, after patent had issued to Lowery. As a general rule, rerecording an interest once title passes is less of a burden than requiring property purchasers to check indefinitely beyond the chain of title.

It is unfortunate that in this case due to Lowery's double conveyances, one or the other party to this suit must suffer an undeserved loss. We are cognizant that in this case, the equities are closely balanced between the parties to this appeal. Our decision, however, in addition to resolving the litigants' dispute, must delineate the requirements of Alaska's recording laws.

Because we want to promote simplicity and certainty in title transactions, we choose to follow the majority rule and hold that the Horvaths' deed, recorded outside the chain of title, does not give constructive notice to the Sabos and is not "duly recorded" under the Alaskan Recording Act, AS 34.15.290. Since the Sabos' interest is the first duly recorded interest and was recorded without actual or constructive knowledge of the prior deed, we hold that the Sabos' interest must prevail. The trial court's decision is accordingly.

Reversed.

NOTES

1. Would and should the result in Morse v. Curtis have been different if demandant had gone into possession of the property? If the Massachusetts legislature had mandated use of an official tract index? If Massachusetts had a race-notice statute? A race statute? The rule of Morse v. Curtis has been rejected in a minority of states. See, for example, Woods v. Garnett, 72 Miss. 78, 16 So. 390 (1894). As a title examiner in one of these minority jurisdictions, is it likely that the cost of your search will be much higher than it would be in a majority jurisdiction? Needlessly so? Will your answer depend on whether you have ready access to a private title plant indexing all land transfers in your county by reference to the tract involved?

After the decision in Sabo v. Horvath, would the Horvaths have an action against Lowery to recover the value they paid for the land? Note that although the Lowery-Horvath conveyance was by quitclaim deed, the trial court found that "the transfer contemplated more than a 'mere quitclaim'—it warranted patent would be transferred."

2. If Lowery had not subsequently executed a deed to the Sabos, the Horvaths would clearly have prevailed in a quiet title action against Lowery under the venerable doctrine of "estoppel by deed." This doctrine holds that if *A*, not owning Blackacre, purports to con-

vey Blackacre to *B* by warranty deed, then if *A* later acquires title to Blackacre, her title will automatically pass to *B* under the terms of the deed. The rationale for the doctrine is that *A*, as grantor under a deed to *B*, is representing that she owns the land, and thus will be estopped from later denying the effectiveness of that deed. Should the doctrine's force depend on whether *A* transferred by warranty deed or quitclaim deed?

What effect will estoppel by deed have on a subsequent purchaser *C* who had no notice of the *A* to *B* deed? Although the *Sabo* court expressly sidestepped consideration of the issue (559 P.2d 1039 n. 2), other courts have confronted it directly. For example, in Breen v. Morehead, 104 Tex. 254, 136 S.W. 1047 (1911), McKelligon, who had possession of, but not title to, a piece of land, deeded the property to Breen, who promptly recorded. About two years later, McKelligon acquired title to the parcel from the state and subsequently deeded it to Kern who had no knowledge of the earlier transfer to Breen. Other things being equal, the doctrine of estoppel by deed would have given title to Breen. But, of course, other things were not equal, for Kern, a bona fide purchaser for value, had intervened. The Texas Supreme Court held for Kern on the ground that if he were required to look beyond the origin of the title under which he was purchasing, "there could be no limit short of the vendor's life, and such requirement of purchasers would involve land titles in such uncertainty that it would be impracticable to rely on any investigation."

The court concluded: "We believe that the rule stated above that the date when the title originated in McKelligon marked the limit of investigation for previous sales or encumbrances of that tract of land by McKelligon should be applied here. It would be unreasonable to suppose that a man who had just received a title from the state had previously made a transfer of that land. That ordinary care and caution which the subsequent purchaser must exercise would not suggest an investigation for conveyances made before acquisition of title. It follows that the record of Breen's deed in El Paso county gave no notice to the subsequent purchasers from McKelligon who had no actual notice and paid a valuable consideration for the land." 104 Tex. at 258, 136 S.W. at 1049.

A few states reject the rule followed in Breen v. Morehead. See, for example, Tefft v. Munson, 57 N.Y. 97 (1874). After Morse v. Curtis, would you expect Massachusetts to follow or to reject the rule? The surprising answer is that Massachusetts has rejected the rule. See Knight v. Thayer, 125 Mass. 25 (1878). Can you reconcile Knight v. Thayer with Morse v. Curtis?

3. Abstracts, Opinions and Title Insurance

Using the public records or his own title plant, a title examiner will first search back to a parcel's root of title—when the parcel was last made the subject of an undisputed transfer—and he then will

search forward, tracing all subsequent transfers to the present. The examiner will then prepare an abstract of title summarizing all transfers beginning with the first and indicating all other matters of record affecting the title. Characteristically, the abstract will conclude with the examiner's certification respecting the periods and records covered by his search.

Next, the abstract will be analyzed. Cancelled mortgages and other liens will be eliminated as will interests barred by the statute of limitations, reducing the abstract to the few surviving interests that continue to encumber or otherwise affect title. This analysis may be performed by a lawyer and embodied in a lawyer's opinion on title rendered to the buyer. Alternatively, a title insurance company may perform the analysis, stating the results in a policy of title insurance that guarantees good title except with respect to specified encumbrances or defects. (The lawyer's opinion will commonly read, "I have examined the abstract of title attached hereto, and from it find that on said date marketable title of record was vested in seller, free from encumbrances or defects, except as follows . . . ." The title company's guarantee will typically read, "The following estates, interests, defects, objections to title, liens and encumbrances and other matters are excepted from the coverage of this policy . . . .")

Although the steps from search to abstract to title opinion or title policy might seem entirely mechanical, they in fact often call for the most meticulous judgment. "Such questions as the following may be involved: whether a recorded conveyance should be questioned which does not have a notary's seal, or does not have a statement of the date on which the notary's commission expires; or, if a conveyance is made by a corporation, whether it should be questioned because there is no resolution on record showing the action of the corporation to make the conveyance, or showing whether the people who executed it as officers were in fact such officers at the time. As to these matters some title examiners may reach one conclusion and others the opposite conclusion . . . . If the practice of conveyancers is not uniform, the tendency always is for the standards of the overmeticulous conveyancer to determine the standards of all conveyancers. Lawyer *A* feels that a title should be passed even though there are certain defects in the recorded acknowledgment, and he realizes that the majority of experienced, competent conveyancers would agree with him. But he also knows that Lawyer *B* would refuse to pass the title and would require a quiet title suit. Since Lawyer *A* is aware that his client may some day wish to sell the land to someone who employs Lawyer *B* to pass on the title, he will be inclined to impose the same overmeticulous standard as Lawyer *B*. Like Gresham's law, the result will be that bad title standards drive out good standards." L. Simes & C. Taylor, Model Title Standards, 2–3 (1960).

One solution, noted by Simes and Taylor and followed in many states, is for state bar associations to promulgate uniform title standards: "Although Lawyer A may not dare to approve a title solely on his individual judgment, the situation is different if his judgment is backed by the official action of a bar association. If the official standards are supported by the great majority of competent, experienced conveyancers, and the prestige of the bar association is high, overmeticulous conveyancers may well follow these standards. Or even if a few do not, the conveyancer who does follow them can justify his position to his client by pointing out that he has followed officially approved standards." *Id.*

The sources of title services have changed dramatically over the past one hundred years. Originally lawyers conducted the title searches, prepared the abstract, and rendered the opinion based on the abstract. Although, in some places, lawyers continue to discharge all these functions, they have in most communities been partially or completely displaced by abstract and title companies. An abstract company may perform the search and compile the abstract while a lawyer selected by the buyer will review and opine on the abstract. Increasingly, title insurance companies are serving all these functions—conducting the search, preparing the abstract and issuing a title policy insuring the accuracy of the search. Lawyers in many communities have responded to these incursions by setting up title insurance companies of their own. "By 1976, over 10,000 lawyers in nineteen states were organized in nine separate bar-related companies, with assets in excess of $18 million." Roussel & Rosenberg, Lawyer-Controlled Title Insurance Companies: Legal Ethics and the Need for Insurance Department Regulation, 48 Fordham L.Rev. 25, 28 (1979).

Lawyers have also responded by charging that title companies engage in the unauthorized practice of law, largely in connection with preparing deeds and title reports and obtaining affidavits of title. See State Bar of Arizona v. Arizona Land Title and Trust Co., page 185, above. But see, State Bar of New Mexico v. Guardian Abstract & Title Co., 91 N.M. 434, 440, 575 P.2d 943, 949 (1978) ("We first must consider the paramount interest of the public in determining who should perform the service of completing the forms. There was no convincing evidence that the massive changeover in the performance of this service from attorneys to the title companies during the past several years has been accompanied by any great loss, detriment or inconvenience to the public.").

In several parts of the country, title companies and bar associations have worked out their differences through treaties. See generally, Brossman & Rosenberg, Title Companies and The Unauthorized Practice Rules: The Exclusive Domain Reexamined, 83 Dick L.Rev. 437 (1979). For an excellent study of title insurance and the title insurance industry, see Johnstone, Title Insurance, 66 Yale L.J. 492 (1957).

a. ABSTRACTS AND LAWYERS' OPINIONS

WILLIAMS v. POLGAR

Supreme Court of Michigan, 1974.
391 Mich. 6, 215 N.W.2d 149.

WILLIAMS, Justice (To Affirm).

While important, the issue in this case is a relatively narrow one.

Michigan already permits a buyer of property who has relied on a faulty abstract to his detriment to recover from the abstracter, even though there is no clear contractual privity between them, if the abstracter in fact knew the buyer would rely on the abstract.

This case presents the issue whether a faulty abstracter should likewise be liable to a buyer *he should have foreseen would rely* on the abstract as well as to the buyer *he knew would rely* on it. The question boils down to whether there should be liability for *foreseeable* as well as *known* reliance.

This Court has answered that question affirmatively in a related fact situation, and in categorical terms relieved Michigan jurisprudence of the restrictions of "privity." In this opinion, we reaffirm our general decision eliminating privity and specifically apply it to abstracters.

There is a second issue in this case. When does liability accrue and what statute of limitations applies.

I—FACTS

Plaintiffs Williams purchased certain property situated in the City of Warren, Macomb County, from defendants Polgar on a land contract dated August 1, 1959. At the time of purchase, as provided in the land contract, defendants furnished to plaintiffs an abstract of title certified to July 15, 1959 by Abstract and Title Guaranty Company. This abstract was originally issued on February 4, 1926 by the Macomb County Abstract Company and was extended by said company in 1936, 1937, 1943, 1944, 1945, 1946, 1948, 1951, and 1952. Defendant American Title Insurance Company is the successor in interest to Macomb County Abstract Company.

The abstract of title failed to include a deed dated May 1, 1926 which was recorded on May 24, 1926 in Liber 242 of Deeds at page 174 of Macomb County records. This deed conveyed the southerly 60 feet of the property in question to the Macomb County Board of Road Commissioners.

After execution of the land contract on August 1, 1959, plaintiffs learned, allegedly for the first time, of the existence of this omitted deed. As the result thereof, plaintiffs claim they were required to completely remove a building and that certain other damages were incurred.

Plaintiffs filed this action on April 21, 1971. All defendants filed motions for accelerated judgment based on the statute of limitations. The trial court held that plaintiffs' cause of action accrued no later than the execution of the land contract on August 1, 1959. Thus accelerated judgment was granted defendants. Plaintiffs were nonsuited. The Court of Appeals reversed and remanded. Defendant American Title Insurance Company requested leave to appeal to this Court which was granted on December 12, 1972.

II—EFFECT OF ACCELERATED JUDGMENT

Under a motion for accelerated judgment by defendants the facts well pleaded by plaintiffs and the reasonable inferences therefrom must be considered most favorably towards plaintiffs. As the complaint adequately alleges the title company's negligent misrepresentation in the abstract, plaintiffs' reliance thereon and the damage caused thereby as well as the other matters appearing in the above statement of facts, this case presents at this point no dispute as to facts.

Where there is a person negligently injured by another, normally there is recovery therefor. *Ubi injuria, ibi remedium.*

Defendant title company here, however, seeks immunity from liability for the injury it caused plaintiff buyers, pleading two defenses. First, defendant pleads it is immune from suit because it is not in contractual privity with plaintiffs. Second, defendant pleads it is immune from suit because of the statute of limitations. We disagree.

III—DEFENSE OF PRIVITY

A. Cessante Ratione Legis, Cessat et Ipsa Lex

The early common law rule restricting liability to those in contractual privity with an abstracter was based on a system where abstracts would only be used by real estate owners.

As time went on the actual usage of abstracts and the class of people relying on them expanded . . . .

Responding to the actual change in use of abstracts and the additional classes of persons relying on them, at least six general court-created exceptions have been grafted onto the supposed common law requirement of strict contractual privity. These exceptions include:

(1) abstracter's fraud or collusion,

(2) theory of third-party beneficiary contracts,

(3) theory of foreseeability of use by a third-party,

(4) actual knowledge or notice of third-party,

(5) agent for disclosed or undisclosed principal contracting with an abstracter, and

(6) re-issuance or recertification of an abstract.

Whereas the common law rule limiting abstracter liability provided immunity from all who were injured by a faulty abstract except those in actual contractual privity, of the 35 jurisdictions (outside of Michigan) addressing themselves to this matter only seven retain a rule of strict contractual privity: Arizona, California, Florida, Illinois, Ohio, Texas and Wisconsin. On the other hand, 11 extend liability to known third-parties relying thereon: Alabama, District of Columbia, Hawaii, Idaho, Indiana, Maryland, Missouri, New Jersey, New York, Pennsylvania and Tennessee. Two jurisdictions have allowed recovery by undiscovered principals: Iowa and Washington. Fourteen purport to extend liability by statute to "any person" relying on the abstract: Arkansas, Colorado, Kansas, Minnesota, Montana, Nebraska, Nevada, New Mexico, North Dakota, Oklahoma, Oregon, South Dakota, Utah and Wyoming. And one jurisdiction extends liability to foreseeable relying third-parties by court decision: Louisiana.

B. Michigan Has Abolished Privity Requirement

Michigan ended the last century and began this one firmly wed to the rule of contractual privity immunizing abstracters. By the end of the second decade it reluctantly broke away from strict privity in favor of a known third-party beneficiary. Beckovsky v. Burton Abstract & Title Co., 208 Mich. 224, 175 N.W. 235 (1919). Michigan thereby joined a category of 11 other jurisdictions just noted who had opened recovery to parties the abstracter knew would rely on the abstract. In *Beckovsky*, the plaintiff buyer actually accompanied the seller to the office of defendant title company and said he wanted an abstract but the contract in all truth was between the seller and the title company with the seller paying the title company for its work, although in order to avoid the title company's defense of privity, the trial court graciously put that question to the jury.

So *Beckovsky* extends liability to the faulty abstracter who knows a third-party beneficiary will rely on its abstract. The question remains, will liability likewise apply to the faulty abstracter who can reasonably foresee reliance by a third-party.

. . .

C. Privity Conclusion

Michigan's own jurisprudence records the categorical elimination of privity. This Court had previously extended abstracter liability consonant with the historical growth in reliance and use of abstracts and the corresponding changes in the law to known relying third-parties. Confronted now as of first impression with the question of abstracter liability to foreseeable relying third-parties, we have but to apply our own persuasive precedent of categorical elimination of privity to an analogous situation, and we do so.

IV—ABSTRACTER LIABILITY IN TORT FOR NEGLIGENT MISREPRESENTATION

. . .

With respect to the particular type of tort action arising from breach of an abstracter's contractual duty, we hold it to be an action in negligent misrepresentation. Numerous cases and law review articles have debated the precise tort cause of action most appropriate in this context. The theories of fraud, deceit, warranty, and strict liability have all been the subject of extensive discussion with respect to professional misrepresentations of this sort. None of these theories has been found to adequately deal with this particular problem; negligent misrepresentation, on the other hand, precisely fits this situation.

The obvious difficulty with a fraud or deceit action is the requisite element of scienter. The issue we are dealing with in the instant case does not, on the pleadings, involve *intentional* misrepresentation. To supply the element of intent constructively is to do great violence to existing law on the subject of fraud.

. . .

Further, to treat this cause of action as sounding in warranty or strict liability might serve to extend an abstracter's duty beyond the duty anticipated by the original contract. It is important to repeat that the tort cause of action created by an abstracter's nonfeasance or misfeasance stems from the contractual duty originally imposed and does not render an abstracter liable for action beyond such contractually-imposed duty, i.e., to perform in a diligent and reasonably skillful workmanlike manner.

Thus, we adopt the tort action of negligent misrepresentation in this context. It should be noted that this action is premised on negligence in title search; an abstracter is not converted into a title insurer by virtue of our decision today. We repeat that the only liability an abstracter has to an injured third-party is with respect to negligent performance of his or her contractual duty.

. . .

This cause of action arising from breach of the abstracter's contractual duty runs to those persons an abstracter could reasonably foresee as relying on the accuracy of the abstract put into motion. The particular expert-client relationship accruing to a professional contract to certify the condition of the record of title reposes a peculiar trust in an abstracter which runs not only to the original contracting party. There is a clearly foreseeable class of potential injured persons which would obviously include grantees where his or her grantor or any predecessor in title of the grantor has initiated the contract for abstracting services with the abstracter.

V—DEFENSE OF STATUTE OF LIMITATIONS

Defendants below were granted accelerated judgments on the basis of a plea of statute of limitations bar to this action. There is some textbook authority to the effect that the statute of limitations in an abstracter liability action begins to run from the date the abstract was furnished rather than from the time of the discovery of the error.

But the textbook authority referred to is predicated upon an action *in contract* not an action *in tort*. Consider for example, part of the applicable section in American Jurisprudence:

". . . the statute of limitations begins to run from the time of the occurrence of the breach of duty . . .." 1 Am.Jur.2d 245.

While such a breach of duty creating a cause of action *in a contract action* would date from the actual act of omission or misrepresentation, the cause of action *in a tort action* runs from the date the tort was committed, not the date the actor put his or her force wrongfully into motion.

. . .

VI—CONCLUSION

For the reasons outlined above, we hold that there is a valid tort cause of action in the nature of negligent misrepresentation arising from a contract for an abstracter's services in favor of a non-contracting damaged third-party whose reliance on the abstract could be foreseen. In a tort action of this nature, the statute of limitations begins running from the date the injured party knew or should have known of the existence of the negligent misrepresentation, a date not clearly in evidence in this case. The accelerated judgment granted by the trial court was thus improper.

The judgment of the Court of Appeals is affirmed. This case is remanded to Macomb County Circuit Court for further proceedings not inconsistent with this opinion. Costs to the appellees.

T.M. KAVANAGH, C.J., and LEVIN, COLEMAN, BRENNAN, T.G. KAVANAGH, and SWAINSON, JJ., concur.

. . .

COLEMAN, Justice (dissenting).

Although it characterizes plaintiff's cause of action as "arising from breach of an abstracter's contractual duty", the majority opinion adopts a "tort action of negligent misrepresentation in this context". The effect and purpose of this adoption is to delay the running of the statute of limitations.

I cannot agree with the theory or the result.

I agree with the majority that plaintiff's action is premised on a breach of contractual duty. M.C.L.A. § 600.5807, M.S.A. § 27A.5807 says:

"No person may bring or maintain any action to recover damages or sums due for breach of contract . . . unless, after the claim first accrued to himself or to someone through whom he claims, he commences the action within the periods of time prescribed by this section:

. . .

(8) The period of limitations is 6 years for all other actions to recover damages or sums due for breach of contract."

When did plaintiff's claim accrue? The answer is found in M.C. L.A. § 600.5827, M.S.A. § 27A.5827 which provides, insofar as applicable to these facts,

"[T]he claim accrues at the time the wrong upon which the claim is based was done regardless of the time when damage results."

Plaintiff's claim thus accrued, at the very latest, in 1959, although no specific date was alleged. Suit was not filed until 1971.

. . .

I would reverse the Court of Appeals and affirm the circuit court's grant of accelerated judgment.

NOTES

1. Abstracters and lawyers are liable for defects in their work product—abstracters for errors and omissions in compiling the abstract, lawyers for errors in analyzing the abstract and opining on title. Although buyers can pursue both contract and tort theories against the lawyer who represented them, tort theory represents their primary route for recovery against an abstracter with whom they will commonly not be in contractual privity.

Should buyers have a tort action against abstracters? If *Polgar* had gone the other way, is it likely that Michigan buyers would in the future protect themselves against title defects by insisting that their sellers give them warranty deeds? (Note that if a buyer recovers against his seller on a title covenant, the seller can then proceed on a contract theory against the abstracter with whom she will be in privity.) Is there any material difference in the damages a buyer will recover by proceeding against the seller under a covenant theory and proceeding against the abstracter under a tort theory? If, as often happens, the property appreciates in value between the time the buyer acquires it and the time he discovers the title defect, which theory—tort or contract—is more likely to make the buyer whole?

2. Many states, most of them situated west of the Mississippi, have enacted licensing laws for abstracters and abstracting firms.

Among the statutory requirements are maintenance of an adequate title plant and bonding to cover liability for errors and omissions in compiling abstracts. See, for example, Colo.Rev.Stat.1973, 12-1-101 *et seq.* Most of these states require abstracting companies to employ at least one licensed abstracter who has successfully completed a state-administered exam.

3. Lawyers who search or analyze title for their clients are held to the traditional negligence standard of reasonable care and skill. Malpractice claims most often involve the failure to note an encumbrance or to determine the property's true owner or proper location. Good faith errors in judgment are excused, and the lawyer is not considered to have guaranteed that title is perfect—unless, of course, he or she specifically makes such a guarantee.

While reasonable care will be measured by the skills possessed, and the customs ordinarily followed, by lawyers in the community, custom will not excuse grossly unreliable practices. In Gleason v. Title Guarantee Co., 300 F.2d 813 (5th Cir.1962), a title company sued for damages arising from defendant attorney's erroneous opinion that certain titles were clear when in fact they were encumbered by outstanding mortgages. The attorney had certified to having made a personal examination of the relevant records but had in fact reviewed neither the records nor the abstracts, relying instead on information received by telephone from the abstract company. In response to the attorney's argument that this method of obtaining title information was standard practice in that part of Florida, the court held that an improper custom, no matter how widely practiced, could not reduce the attorney's duty of care. Damages were awarded for the losses suffered by the title company.

4. How much liability can a lawyer disclaim? In Owen v. Neely, 471 S.W.2d 705 (Ky.1971), defendant attorney, employed to "do the title work," gave plaintiffs a certificate of clear and merchantable title containing the standard disclaimer that the certificate was "subject to any information that would be revealed by an accurate survey . . . ." In making the certificate, the attorney had used a description prepared by a surveyor. The lawyer later admitted that he had noticed discrepancies between the deed description and the survey description. In fact, the survey was erroneous, and the house the clients thought they were buying was not situated on the land that they bought. Acknowledging that reservations and disclaimers expressly set forth in the certificate of title will generally be enforced, the court ruled that if an attorney examining title receives information that would give him or her grounds to suspect a defect, the attorney owes the client a duty of investigation that cannot be disclaimed.

b. TITLE INSURANCE

TITLE INSURANCE POLICY

THE TITLE GUARANTEE COMPANY
and
TICOR TITLE INSURANCE COMPANY

THE TITLE GUARANTEE COMPANY, a New York Corporation, and **TICOR TITLE INSURANCE COMPANY**, A California Corporation, jointly and severally, together herein called "the Company," in consideration of the payment of its charges for the examination of title and its premium for insurance, insures the within named insured against all loss or damage not exceeding the amount of insurance stated herein and in addition the costs and expenses of defending the title, estate or interest insured, which the insured shall sustain by reason of any defect or defects of title affecting the premises described in Schedule A or affecting the interest of the insured therein as herein set forth, or by reason of unmarketability of the title of the insured to or in the premises, or by reason of liens or incumbrances affecting title at the date hereof, or by reason of any statutory lien for labor or material furnished prior to the date hereof which has now gained or which may hereafter gain priority over the interest insured hereby, or by reason of a lack of access to and from the premises, excepting all loss and damage by reason of the estates, interests, defects, objections, liens, incumbrances and other matters set forth in Schedule B, or by the conditions of this policy hereby incorporated into this contract, the loss and the amount to be ascertained in the manner provided in said conditions and to be payable upon compliance by the insured with the stipulations of said conditions, and not otherwise.

In Witness Whereof, the companies have caused their corporate names and seals to be hereunto affixed by their duly authorized officers.

TICOR TITLE INSURANCE COMPANY   **THE TITLE GUARANTEE COMPANY**

CONDITIONS OF THIS POLICY

Section 1 — DEFINITIONS

(a) Wherever the term "insured" is used in this policy it includes those who succeed to the interest of the insured by operation of law including, without limitation, heirs, distributees, devisees, survivors, personal representatives, next of kin or corporate successors, as the case may be, and those to whom the insured has assigned this policy where such assignment is permitted by the terms hereof, and whenever the term "insured" is used in the conditions of this policy it also includes the attorneys and agents of the "insured."

(b) Wherever the term "this company" is used in this policy it means The Title Guarantee Company and Ticor Title Insurance Company.

(c) Wherever the term "final determination" or "finally determined" is used in this policy, it means the final determination of a court of competent jurisdiction after disposition of all appeals or after the time to appeal has expired.

(d) Wherever the term "the premises" is used in this policy, it means the property insured herein as described in Schedule A of this policy including such buildings and improvements thereon which by law constitute real property.

(e) Wherever the term "recorded" is used in this policy it means, unless otherwise indicated, recorded in the office of the recording officer of the county in which property insured herein lies.

Section 2 — DEFENSE AND PROSECUTION OF SUITS

(a) This company will, at its own cost, defend the insured in all actions or proceedings founded on a claim of title or incumbrance not excepted in this policy.

(b) This company shall have the right and may, at its own cost, maintain or defend any action or proceeding relating to the title or interest hereby insured, or upon or under any covenant or contract relating thereto which it considers desirable to prevent or reduce loss hereunder.

(c) In all cases where this policy requires or permits this company to prosecute or defend, the insured shall secure to it the right and opportunity to maintain or defend the action or proceeding, and all appeals from any determination therein, and give it all reasonable aid therein, and hereby permits it to use therein, at its option, its own name or the name of the insured.

(d) The provisions of this section shall survive payment by this company of any specific loss or payment of the entire amount of this policy to the extent that this company shall deem it necessary in recovering the loss from those who may be liable therefor to the insured or to this company.

Section 3 — CASES WHERE LIABILITY ARISES

No claim for damages shall arise or be maintainable under this policy except in the following cases:

(a) Where there has been a final determination under which the insured may be dispossessed, evicted or ejected from the premises or from some part or undivided share or interest therein.

(b) Where there has been a final determination adverse to the title, upon a lien or incumbrance not excepted in this policy.

(c) Where the insured shall have contracted in good faith in writing to sell the insured estate or interest, or where the insured estate has been sold for the benefit of the insured pursuant to the judgment or order of a court and the title has been rejected because of a defect or incumbrance not excepted in this policy and there has been a final determination sustaining the objection to the title.

(d) Where the insurance is upon the interest of a mortgagee and the mortgage has been adjudged by a final determination to be invalid or ineffectual to charge the insured's estate or interest in the premises, or subject to a prior lien or incumbrance not excepted in this policy; or where a recording officer has refused to accept from the insured a satisfaction of the insured mortgage and there has been a final determination sustaining the refusal because of a defect in the title to the said mortgage.

(e) Where the insured shall have negotiated a loan to be made on the security of a mortgage on the insured's estate or interest in the premises and the title shall have been rejected by the proposed lender and it shall have been finally determined that the rejection of the title was justified because of a defect or incumbrance not excepted in this policy.

(f) Where the insured shall have transferred the title insured by an instrument containing covenants in regard to title or warranty thereof and there shall have been a final determination on any of such covenants or warranty, against the insured, because of a defect or incumbrance not excepted in this policy.

(g) Where the insured estate or interest or a part thereof has been taken by condemnation and it has been finally determined that the insured is not entitled to a full award for the estate or interest taken because of a defect or incumbrance not excepted in this policy.

No claim for damages shall arise or be maintainable under this policy (1) if this company, after having received notice of an alleged defect or incumbrance, removes such defect or incumbrance within thirty days after receipt of such notice; or (2) for liability voluntarily assumed by the insured in settling any claim or suit without the written consent of this company.

Section 4 — NOTICE OF CLAIM

In case a purchaser or proposed mortgage lender raises any question as to the sufficiency of the title hereby insured, or in case actual knowledge shall come to the insured of any claim adverse to the title insured hereby, or in case of the service on or receipt by the insured of any paper, or of any notice, summons, process or pleading in any action or proceeding, the object or effect of which shall or may be to impugn, attack or call in question the validity of the title hereby insured, the insured shall promptly notify this company thereof in writing at its main office and forward to this company such paper or such notice, summons, process or pleading. Delay in giving this notice and delay in forwarding such paper or such notice, summons, process or pleading shall not affect this company's liability if such failure has not prejudiced and cannot in the future prejudice this company.

Section 5 — PAYMENT OF LOSS

(a) This company will pay, in addition to the loss, all statutory costs and allowances imposed on the insured in litigation carried on by this company for the insured under the terms of this policy. This company shall not be liable for and will not pay the fees of any counsel or attorney employed by the insured.

(b) In every case where claim is made for loss or damage this company (1) reserves the right to settle, at its own cost, any claim or suit which may involve liability under this policy; or (2) may terminate its liability hereunder by paying or tendering the full amount of this policy; or (3) may, without conceding liability, demand a valuation of the insured estate or interest, to be made by three arbitrators or any two of them, one to be chosen by the insured and one by this company, and the two thus chosen selecting an umpire. Such valuation, less the amount of any incumbrances on said insured estate and interest not hereby insured against, shall be the extent of this company's liability for such claim and no right of action shall accrue hereunder for the recovery thereof until thirty days after notice of such valuation shall have been served upon this company, and the insured shall have tendered a conveyance or assignment of the insured estate or interest to this company or its designee at such valuation, diminished as aforesaid. The foregoing option to fix a valuation by arbitration shall not apply to a policy insuring a mortgage or leasehold interest.

(c) Liability to any collateral holder of this policy shall not exceed the amount of the pecuniary interest of such collateral holder in the premises.

(d) All payments made by this company under this policy shall reduce the amount hereof pro tanto except (1) payments made for counsel fees and disbursements in defending or prosecuting actions or proceedings in behalf of the insured and for statutory costs and allowances imposed on the insured in such actions and proceedings, and (2) if the insured is a mortgagee, payments made to satisfy or subordinate prior liens or incumbrances not set forth in Schedule B.

(e) When liability has been definitely fixed in accordance with the conditions of this policy, the loss or damage shall be payable within thirty days thereafter.

CONDITIONS CONTINUED ON INSIDE BACK COVER

CONDITIONS CONTINUED FROM INSIDE FRONT COVER

Section 6   **COINSURANCE AND APPORTIONMENT**

(a) In the event that a partial loss occurs after the insured makes an improvement subsequent to the date of this policy, and only in that event, the insured becomes a coinsurer to the extent hereinafter set forth.

If the cost of the improvement exceeds twenty per centum of the amount of this policy, such proportion only of any partial loss established shall be borne by the company as one hundred twenty per centum of the amount of this policy bears to the sum of the amount of this policy and the amount expended for the improvement. The foregoing provisions shall not apply to costs and attorneys' fees incurred by the company in prosecuting or providing for the defense of actions or proceedings in behalf of the insured pursuant to the terms of this policy or to costs imposed on the insured in such actions or proceedings, and shall apply only to that portion of losses which exceed in the aggregate ten per cent of the face of the policy.

Provided, however, that the foregoing coinsurance provisions shall not apply to any loss arising out of a lien or incumbrance for a liquidated amount which existed on the date of this policy and was not shown in Schedule B; and provided further, such coinsurance provisions shall not apply to any loss if, at the time of the occurrence of such loss, the then value of the premises, as so improved, does not exceed one hundred twenty per centum of the amount of this policy.

(b) If the premises are divisible into separate, independent parcels, and a loss is established affecting one or more but not all of said parcels, the loss shall be computed and settled on a pro rata basis as if this policy were divided pro rata as to value of said separate, independent parcels, exclusive of improvements made subsequent to the date of this policy.

(c) Clauses "(a)" and "(b)" of this section apply to mortgage policies only after the insured shall have acquired the interest of the mortgagor.

(d) If, at the time liability for any loss shall have been fixed pursuant to the conditions of this policy, the insured holds another policy of insurance covering the same loss issued by another company, this company shall not be liable to the insured for a greater proportion of the loss than the amount that this policy bears to the whole amount of insurance held by the insured, unless another method of apportioning the loss shall have been provided by agreement between this company and the other insurer or insurers.

Section 7   **ASSIGNMENT OF POLICY**

If the interest insured by this policy is that of a mortgagee, this policy may be assigned to and shall inure to the benefit of successive assignees of the mortgage without consent of this company or its endorsement of this policy. Provision is made in the rate manual of New York Board of Title Underwriters filed with the Superintendent of Insurance of the State of New York on behalf of this and other member companies for continuation of liability to grantees of the insured in certain specific circumstances only. In no circumstance provided for in this section shall this company be deemed to have insured the sufficiency of the form of the assignment or other instrument of transfer or conveyance or to have assumed any liability for the sufficiency of any proceedings after the date of this policy.

Section 8   **SUBROGATION**

(a) This company shall to the extent of any payment by it of loss under this policy, be subrogated to all rights of the insured with respect thereto. The insured shall execute such instruments as may be requested to transfer such rights to this company. The rights so transferred shall be subordinate to any remaining interest of the insured.

(b) If the insured is a mortgagee, this company's right of subrogation shall not prevent the insured from releasing the personal liability of the obligor or guarantor or from releasing a portion of the premises from the lien of the mortgage or from increasing or otherwise modifying the insured mortgage provided such acts do not affect the validity or priority of the lien of the mortgage insured. However, the liability of this company under this policy shall in no event be increased by any such act of the insured.

Section 9   **MISREPRESENTATION**

Any untrue statement made by the insured, with respect to any material fact, or any suppression of or failure to disclose any material fact, or any untrue answer by the insured, to material inquiries before the issuance of this policy, shall void this policy.

Section 10   **NO WAIVER OF CONDITIONS**

This company may take any appropriate action under the terms of this policy whether or not it shall be liable hereunder and shall not thereby concede liability or waive any provision of this policy.

Section 11   **POLICY ENTIRE CONTRACT**

All actions or proceedings against this company must be based on the provisions of this policy. Any other action or actions or rights of action that the insured may have or may bring against this company in respect of other services rendered in connection with the issuance of this policy, shall be deemed to have merged in and be restricted to its terms and conditions.

Section 12   **VALIDATION AND MODIFICATION**

This policy is valid only when duly signed by a validating officer or agent. Changes may be effected only by written endorsement. If the recording date of the instruments creating the insured interest is later than the policy date, such policy shall also cover intervening liens or incumbrances, except real estate taxes, assessments, water charges and sewer rents.

ENDORSEMENTS

Name of Insured JOHN J. SMITH AND
KATHERINE ANN SMITH,
his wife

Policy No. T50-83-00849

Amount of Insurance $ 67,000.00

Date of Issue September 1, 1983

The estate or interest insured by this policy is **fee simple** vested in the insured by means of

Warranty Deed made by Robert W. Jones and Mary Ruth Jones, his wife, to the insured, dated September 1, 1983 and recorded on September 1, 1983, in Liber 9236 of Deeds at page 166.

SCHEDULE "B"

The following estates, interests, defects, objections to title, liens and incumbrances and other matters are excepted from the coverage of this policy:

1. *Defects and incumbrances arising or becoming a lien after the date of this policy, except as herein provided.*
2. *Consequences of the exercise and enforcement or attempted enforcement of any governmental, war or police powers over the premises.*
3. *Any laws, regulations or ordinances (including, but not limited to zoning, building, and environmental protection) as to use, occupancy, subdivision or improvement of the premises adopted or imposed by any governmental body, or the effect of any noncompliance with or any violation thereof.*
4. *Judgments against the insured or estates, interests, defects, objections, liens or incumbrances created, suffered, assumed or agreed to, by or with the privity of the insured.*
5. *Title to any property beyond the lines of the premises, or title to areas within or rights or easements in any abutting streets, roads, avenues, lanes, ways or waterways, or the right to maintain therein vaults, tunnels, ramps, or any other structure or improvement, unless this policy specifically provides that such titles, rights, or easements are insured. Notwithstanding any provisions in this paragraph to the contrary, this policy, unless otherwise excepted, insures the ordinary rights of access and egress belonging to abutting owners.*
6. *Title to any personal property, whether the same be attached to or used in connection with said premises or otherwise.*
7. Rights and claims of parties in possession not shown of record.
8. Future installments of special assessments for improvements payable with County Taxes.
9. Easement as set out in Quit Claim Deed made by County of Erie to John Daley, Jr., by instrument recorded in Liber 4709 of Deeds at page 226 on May 18, 1950.
10. Exceptions as disclosed by Survey No. 117,186 LL. 270 made by Krause & Gantzer dated February 25, 1983, as follows:-

    (1) Variation between the line of fence and the westerly line of record title.

SCHEDULE "B" OF THIS POLICY CONSISTS OF [2] SHEET(S).

THE TITLE GUARANTEE COMPANY and TICOR TITLE INSURANCE COMPANY [D518]

Policy No. T50-83-00849

SCHEDULE "B" (continued)

11. Mortgage for $50,000.00 and interest, made by John J. Smith and Katherine Ann Smith, his wife, to Robert W. Jones and Mary Ruth Jones, his wife, dated September 1, 1983, and recorded on September 1, 1983, in Liber 8655 of Mortgages at page 197.

THE TITLE GUARANTEE COMPANY and TICOR TITLE INSURANCE COMPANY

[D519]

Policy No. T50-83-00 849

SCHEDULE "A"
(Continued)

The land referred to in this Policy is described as follows:

ALL THAT TRACT OR PARCEL OF LAND, situate in the Town of Amherst, County of Erie and State of New York, being part of Lot 45, Township 11 and Range 7 of the Holland Land Company survey and according to a Subdivision Map filed in the Erie County Clerk's Office under Cover No. 922, known and distinguished as Subdivision No. 117.

THE TITLE GUARANTEE COMPANY and TICOR TITLE INSURANCE COMPANY

[D520]

SHOTWELL v. TRANSAMERICA TITLE INSURANCE CO.

Supreme Court of Washington, 1978.
91 Wn.2d 161, 588 P.2d 208.

STAFFORD, Justice.

Petitioner Transamerica Title Insurance Co. seeks review of the Court of Appeals decision in Shotwell v. Transamerica Title Ins. Co., 16 Wash.App. 627, 558 P.2d 1359 (1976). We affirm the Court of Appeals, but on narrower grounds.

In 1974 respondents Shotwell purchased unimproved property bordering upon the west bank of the Elwah River. It was described in their conveyance as:

> The Northwest Quarter of the Northwest Quarter, Section 34, Government Lot 4, Section 27; Government Lot 1, Section 28; all in Township 31 North, Range 7 West W.M., *EXCEPT right of way for existing roads.* Situated in Clallam County, State of Washington.

(Italics ours.) Prior to the purchase, Transamerica issued respondents a preliminary commitment for title insurance in which it agreed to issue its policy subject only to exceptions listed in the commitment and in the policy form. The commitment excepted from title protection: "2. Right of way for existing roads."

Subsequently, Transamerica issued its title policy insuring respondents against loss or damage sustained by reason of:

> Any defect in, or lien or encumbrance on, said title existing at the date hereof, *not shown in Schedule B* . . . .

(Italics ours.) Schedule B lists five specific exceptions and contains four general exception clauses. Of the five specific exceptions only No. 2 is relevant. It reads "2. Right of way for existing roads." Of the four general exception clauses, only two are relevant. They read:

> 1. . . . public or private easements, streets, roads, alleys or highways, *unless disclosed of record by* . . . *decree of a Court of record* . . . .
>
> 2. . . . rights or claims based upon instruments or upon facts *not disclosed by the public records but of which* rights, claims, instruments or facts *the insured has knowledge.*

(Italics ours.) Both the preliminary commitment and title policy described the property insured in language identical to that contained in respondents' conveyance.

At the time respondents purchased the property a narrow road and a dike were located thereon. The road was between 10 and 15 feet wide and began near the southwest corner of the property. From there, the road, insofar as visible, traversed the property in a northeasterly direction but terminated 200 feet short of the Elwah River.

At each end of this visible road the county had erected markers to identify it as belonging to the county. The dike began at the northeasterly terminus of the visible road, as indicated by the county markers, and continued to the property's border on the Elwah River. At the time of purchase respondents were aware of the visible road, the county markers, and the dike.

Following respondents' purchase of the property and the issuance of Transamerica's title policy, respondents learned Clallam County had title to a right-of-way across the property. The county's title had been established in 1944 by decree entered in Clallam County Cause No. 9075. This county right-of-way transected the *entire* property and was *40 feet* in width.

Upon learning of the 1944 decree, respondents filed this action claiming coverage under the title policy. They alleged that the existence of the county right-of-way constituted an encumbrance for which insurance was provided. It was respondents' theory that the policy's failure to specifically refer to either the 1944 decree or to the county right-of-way entitled them to recover losses sustained by reason of the county's right-of-way.

At trial it was established that the 10–15 foot wide road was "generally" located within the county right-of-way. Further, respondent Jonathan Shotwell was found to have considerable experience in real estate matters, roads, easements and rights-of-way, although neither he nor his wife were found to have had knowledge of the right-of-way established by the 1944 decree when they purchased the property.

The trial court entered two conclusions of law in support of its judgment dismissing the complaint. First, the court held that the preliminary commitment and title policy specifically excepted the county right-of-way for the "existing public road." Second, the trial court concluded that the existence of the visible road and county markers together with the specific exception of the "right of way for existing roads" in the legal description, preliminary commitment, and title policy were sufficient to put a reasonable person on notice of the existence of the full 40-foot right-of-way.

Respondents appealed. The Court of Appeals sua sponte held (1) that Transamerica had a duty to conduct a reasonable search which arose by implication from the insurance contract; and (2) that a policyholder has a reasonable expectation that he will be specifically informed of title defects revealed by such a search even though he has or should have had knowledge of the general nature of the defect. The Court of Appeals determined that Transamerica had breached this duty, reversed the trial court and remanded the cause with directions to ascertain respondents' damages.

Transamerica petitioned this court for review asserting that a duty to search and specifically disclose title defects imposed burdens upon it not contemplated by the insurance contract. We granted review because of the novel approach adopted sua sponte by the Court of Appeals.

We recognize such a "duty" might arise from the combined expectations of a title policy applicant and the service to be performed by title insurance companies. See Williams v. Polgar, 43 Mich.App. 95, 204 N.W.2d 57 (1973) . . . . However, even assuming such a "duty" might conceivably be warranted, there are several reasons for declining to impose one here. First, neither party submitted a brief on the issue. The absence of full adversary review of an issue warrants caution when considering such a departure from long-established precedent. Further, under the facts and the law governing this case, there is no need to impose such a "duty." Thus, we treat the appeal as if it had been addressed to us originally.

The question is solely one of law involving the correct interpretation to be given the *exclusionary phrase* "right of way for existing roads." Transamerica, relying on the language "right of way," contends the exclusionary phrase excludes the county's 40-foot right-of-way established by the 1944 decree. On the other hand, respondents emphasize the language "existing roads" in support of their contention that the exclusionary phrase excludes a right-of-way the same width and length as the existing road, *i.e.*, the visible road.

We note that each party places undue emphasis upon isolated portions of the exclusionary phrase. Insurance contracts should be interpreted in light of the actual language used and with respect to the policy as a whole, not in terms of isolated segments. However, a review of the unchallenged facts and the entire insurance policy reveals the reason for the parties' differing constructions of the same language.

Initially, we contrast the 1944 decree with the exclusionary phrase "right of way for existing roads." The 1944 decree established a *county* right-of-way *40* feet in width, transecting the *entire* property. The decree describes the right-of-way by metes and bounds. In stark contrast, Transamerica's policy *lacks any specificity* whatsoever in its attempt to exclude the same right-of-way. The policy is vague in three material respects: (1) it fails to legally describe the right-of-way; (2) it fails to incorporate the 1944 decree by reference or *otherwise;* and (3) it gives the policyholder no indication that the right-of-way, which Transamerica attempts to exclude, is a public one. In the place of precision based upon facts disclosed by the public records, the policy merely excludes a "right of way for existing roads" yet the only road "existing" is 10–15 feet wide extending between the county markers.

Partially because of the vague exclusionary language, there is no way to determine whether Transamerica was in fact referring to the county right-of-way established by the 1944 decree. This is particularly true in light of the general exception clauses also contained in Schedule B. Both subsections (1) and (2), by negative implication, provide coverage for public easements, streets, roads, alleys, highways, rights or claims which *are disclosed* by public record. Here, the county's right-of-way was disclosed by public record and thus under the *policy's own language* arguably is *completely insured.*

Finally, another disparity arises if we examine the road as it actually was located on the property. The only road actually *existing* on the property was between 10 and 15 feet in width extending over only a portion of the property. Yet, Transamerica now claims the exclusionary language covers the full 40 feet in width plus an additional 200 feet in length upon which no road in fact ever existed.

In light of the policy's ambiguity and the factual disparity, we must interpret the exclusionary language most favorably for the insured. Where a provision of a policy of insurance is capable of two meanings, or is fairly susceptible of two constructions, the meaning and construction most favorable to the insured must be employed, even though the insurer may have intended otherwise. This rule applies with added force in the case of exceptions and limitations to a policy's coverage. Further, the language of an insurance contract must be interpreted as it would be understood by the average person purchasing insurance.

Reviewing the language of the instant policy in light of the foregoing rules, we find it hard to believe an *average* person purchasing this type of insurance would contemplate that a 40-foot right-of-way extending over his entire property would have been excluded from policy coverage. Had the insurance company intended such an exclusion, it could easily have referred specifically to the 1944 decree known to it *or* legally described the right-of-way pursuant to that decree. Under the circumstances it is entirely understandable that an average person purchasing this insurance would be expected to conclude that the right-of-way excluded from coverage consisted solely of the right-of-way upon which there was in fact an *existing* road. Further, the average person purchasing such insurance would be expected to consider the exclusion in terms of its ordinary meaning, *i.e.,* in terms of an *existing road* as opposed to a *partially invisible* right-of-way. *Webster's Third New International Dictionary* (1966) defines the term "exist" at page 796 as having "actual or real being whether material or spiritual . . . [having] been in space and time . . . ." Here, the only right-of-way clearly *existing in actual fact* was that right-of-way extending the width and length of the existing road as indicated by the county road markers. Such construction must be adopted where the policy is, on its face, arguably subject to two interpretations.

The policy is ambiguous as a matter of law. Thus, we hold the trial court erred in adopting the construction most favorable to the *insurer* when it concluded that the county right-of-way established in 1944 was specifically excepted from policy coverage. The policy excepts only a right-of-way extending the width and length of the existing road as indicated by the county road markers. Any *right-of-way* owned by the county beyond the actual width of the *existing road* or *beyond the county markers upon which there was no existing road* is not excluded from policy coverage. This is not only a logical construction but also is the one most favorable to the insured. Further, the construction also reflects what an average purchaser would have understood. Thus, it must be adopted.

Transamerica also argues that it cannot be held to have insured against the county right-of-way because respondents acquired no title to the right-of-way from their grantor. Transamerica relies upon the fact that the description of *property insured* in its policy was identical to the grantor's description of *property conveyed.* In essence, Transamerica urges us to interpret the property description actually used in the title policy as an exclusion from policy coverage. However, as indicated earlier, the language does not exclude the *entire* county right-of-way. Rather, it excludes only that part upon which the existing road was in fact located. Further, petitioner's argument confuses the law of conveyancing with the principles of title *insurance.* As stated in San Jacinto Title Guar. Co. v. Lemmon, 417 S.W.2d 429, 431–32 (Tex.Civ.App.1967) in addressing the same argument raised here:

> The description of the property in the policy is identical with and obviously copied from the description in the warranty deed by which appellees acquired title. . . . Unquestionably, the reference in the warranty deed to the recorded map or plat contemplated the purposes of the deed. *The description of the land in the policy was for the purpose of identifying the land covered by the policy and not, as appellant contends, for the purpose of limiting the insurance protection purchased.* In our opinion, this was the clear and unambiguous meaning of the policy. To hold otherwise would, in effect, require appellees, who have purchased title insurance, to be their own insurer in so far as their title to the land, in the respect here under consideration, is concerned. Such a result would not be in keeping with the principal purpose of the policy . . .

(Italics ours.) In construing a policy of insurance the rules of conveyancing do not necessarily apply.

We turn finally to the trial court's conclusion that the road, gates, specific policy exception, and the policy's legal description were sufficient to put a reasonable person on notice that "a right-of-way for public roads existed on and across said real property."

The conclusion is susceptible of two interpretations relevant to an action upon the insurance policy. If interpreted to permit a policyholder's negligence to bar an action on the policy, the conclusion is erroneous. As stated in Maggio v. Abstract Title & Mort. Corp., 277 App.Div. 940, 98 N.Y.S.2d 1011, 1013 (1950):

> In the case of a title insurance policy, the insurer undertakes to indemnify the insured if the title turns out to be defective. That is the purpose of procuring the insurance and knowledge of defects in the title by the insured in no way lessens the liability of the insurer. The doctrine of skill or negligence has no application to a contract of title insurance.

Further, if the conclusion is intended to cover the interpretation given the policy by an average policyholder, we have already held such interpretation to be erroneous.

Thus, we find it unnecessary to reach the issue of whether a "duty to search and specifically disclose" exists. Nevertheless, we affirm the Court of Appeals insofar as it reversed the trial court and remanded the cause. The trial court is directed to ascertain respondents' damages in light of our opinion.

ROSELLINI, HAMILTON, UTTER, HOROWITZ and HICKS, JJ., concur.

WRIGHT, Chief Justice (dissenting).

I dissent in part from the views of the majority. I take the view the words "EXCEPT right of way for existing roads" means exactly what it says. The majority says correctly that in case of an ambiguity the policy of title insurance (as with any insurance policy) shall be construed in favor of the insured. I do *not* agree, however, that any ambiguity exists, except possibly as to the approximately 200 feet beyond the existing road. As to that 200 feet, I am willing to accept the view of the majority.

As to the distance upon which a road actually existed, that is clearly within the exception.

The term "right-of-way" has several meanings in different contexts. The meaning involved here refers to a strip or tract of land within the confines of which some facility such as a road, highway, railroad, pipe line, electric transmission line or other similar thing is located. The right-of-way is generally greater in width than the part actually used for the facility.

The legislature has long recognized the rights-of-way for county roads. Laws of 1937, chapter 187, section 14 provided the right-of-way for any county road should be 30 feet on each side of the center line of the roadway unless the board of county commissioners should specifically designate a different width. The section also provided for additional width as needed for cuts and fills. That section has been substantially carried into the present laws as RCW 36.86.010, which reads as follows:

> From and after April 1, 1937, the width of thirty feet on each side of the center line of county roads, exclusive of such additional

width as may be required for cuts and fills, is the necessary and proper right-of-way width for county roads, unless the board of county commissioners, shall, in any instance, adopt and designate a different width. This shall not be construed to require the acquisition of increased right-of-way for any county road already established and the right-of-way for which has been secured.

It is a matter of common knowledge that the traveled portion of few county roads are 60 feet in width. The legislative intent is plain that the right-of-way shall be greater in width than the actual road.

There are comparatively few judicial definitions of the term "right-of-way" in the context here relevant. One case in which the term is defined is St. Louis, Kansas City and Colorado Railroad Company v. Wabash Railroad Company and the City of St. Louis, 217 U.S. 247, 253, 30 S.Ct. 510, 513, 54 L.Ed. 752 (1910) wherein it is said:

> "The ordinary signification of the term 'right-of-way,' when used to describe land which a railroad corporation owns or is entitled to use for railroad purposes, is the entire strip or tract it owns or is entitled to use for this purpose, and not any specific or limited part thereof upon which its main track or other specified improvements are located. . . ."

In the instant case, the right-of-way granted by judicial decree was 40 feet in width. Given what I consider to be the appropriate definition of right-of-way, it was, and is, the right-of-way for an existing road. Thus, by clear and unambiguous language, this entire right-of-way is excepted from the coverage of the policy of title insurance. I would, therefore, reverse the Court of Appeals and reinstate the judgment of the trial court in so far as the same relates to the existing road.

DOLLIVER and BRACHTENBACH, JJ., concur.

NOTES

1. Although title insurance policies almost always follow a standard form, considerable room exists for the knowledgeable attorney to negotiate additional protection for his or her client, by persuading the insurer to delete one or more exceptions or by purchasing additional coverage through endorsements designed to resolve particular title problems.

As a starting point, though, the lawyer should carefully study the proffered form itself to make certain that he or she fully understands the policy's basic coverage and terms. For example, of what relevance is it that Section 1(a) of N.Y.B.T.U. Form 100E, above, provides that "whenever the term 'insured' is used in the conditions of this policy, it also includes the agents and attorneys of the 'insured'"? When taken together with Section 9, dealing with misrepresentations by the 'insured', what duties does this definition place on the lawyer who, before the policy issues, learns of a condemnation proceeding affecting access to the parcel to be insured? Consider L. Smirlock Realty Corp. v. Title Guarantee Co., 52 N.Y.2d 179, 437 N.Y.S.2d 57, 418 N.E.2d 650 (1981) (insured under no duty to disclose known fact of pending condemnation to insurer, since the fact was also a matter of public record, and hence readily discoverable by the insurer). What are the "ordinary rights of access and egress" referred to in Paragraph 5 of Schedule B?

Under Section 1(a), do "those who succeed to the interest of the insured by operation of law" include anyone who later acquires title to the parcel through adverse possession? To whom does the policy permit assignment? Can the insured effectively transfer the benefits of the policy by giving a full warranty deed to her future buyer, knowing that she always can bring an action against the insurer on the policy if and when her buyer proceeds against her for breach of warranty? See Section 3(f).

What protection, if any, would the N.Y.B.T.U. Form 100E policy have provided against the right of way involved in Shotwell v. Transamerica Title? Against a misdescription or surveyor error that results in the insured's house encroaching on a neighbor's parcel? That results in a neighbor's house encroaching on the insured's parcel? Against a subsequent buyer's refusal to perform his purchase contract with the insured on the ground of unmarketable title? Against a forged deed in the insured's chain of title? An undelivered deed? Against a wild deed, appearing outside the insured's chain of title? Compare Ryczkowski v. Chelsea Title & Guaranty Co., 85 Nev. 37, 449 P.2d 261 (1969) (easement, granted by insured's predecessor in title, and recorded before grantor had acquired patent from state, was outside chain of title and thus excluded from coverage since policy did not insure against loss by reason of easements or claims of easements not shown by public records). Is it relevant that most, if not all, title companies have private title plants, indexed by reference to tract rather than by reference to grantor and grantee?

See generally, Rooney, Title Insurance: A Primer for Attorneys, 14 Real Prop., Prob. & Tr.J. 608 (1979); Taub, Rights and Remedies Under a Title Policy, 15 Real Prop., Prob. & Tr.J. 422 (1980).

2. Like fire, theft and accident insurance, title insurance serves two functions. It spreads casualty losses among many policyholders, and it seeks to reduce the risk that the covered casualty will occur. Title insurance differs from these other forms of insurance by effectively reducing risk almost to a point at which no casualty element remains. By maintaining a complete and current title plant, conducting careful title searches, and analyzing title meticulously, the company can hope to reduce its risk of loss on title claims to almost zero. This explains why title policies, unlike more typical casualty policies, call for a comparatively modest one-time premium, payable at the time of closing.

Can a buyer who has relied on a title insurer to perform its usual, careful search, prevail in a tort action against the company when it conducts that search negligently? Although an apparent majority of states hold that he can, a substantial minority limit the buyer to the terms of the insurance contract. See, for example, Horn v. Lawyers Title Insurance Corp., 89 N.M. 709, 711, 557 P.2d 206, 208 (1976) ("The rights and duties of the parties are fixed by the contract of title insurance . . . . Hence, any duty on the part of defendant to search the records must be expressed in or implied from the policy of title insurance . . . . Defendant clearly had no duty under the policy to search the records, and any search it may have actually undertaken, was undertaken solely for its own protection as indemnitor against losses covered by its policy").

When will a buyer prefer tort to contract theory in an action against a title insurer? If the land has appreciated in value, tort recovery will be more likely to make the buyer whole than will recovery limited to the face amount of the policy. Also, tort theory enables recovery of consequential damages. And, of course, if the buyer relied on his seller's title insurance policy, rather than on a title policy he purchased for himself, tort will be the only available theory of recovery. Compare Williams v. Polgar, page 366 above.

3. As title insurance companies have grown and expanded into new territories they have inevitably encountered state regulation. Although patterns vary from state to state, two concerns predominate: the price and quality of insurance, and the insurer's solvency. In Washington, for example, title insurers must file their rates with the state insurance commissioner who "may order the modification of any premium rate or schedule of premium rates found by him after a hearing to be excessive, or inadequate, or unfairly discriminatory." West's Rev.Code Wash.Ann. 48.29.140(3) (1961).

Most states require specified reserve funds and capitalization levels to assure the ability of title companies to pay off claims against them. New York, with one of the more extensive and detailed statutes, calls, among other things, for a "loss reserve at least equal to the aggregate estimated amounts due or to become due on account of all such unpaid losses and claims . . . ." N.Y.—McKinney's Ins.Law § 434. Some states require a cash deposit with the insurance commissioner and prohibit the issuance of any policy exposing the insurer to loss liability for more than fifty percent of its total capital and surplus. See, e.g., Hawaii Rev.Stat. § 432–3 (1976).

On regulatory issues, see Quiner, Title Insurance and the Title Insurance Industry, 22 Drake L.Rev. 711 (1973).

4. REFORMING THE TITLE ASSURANCE SYSTEM

a. Marketable Title Acts, Statutes of Limitations, Curative Acts

L. SIMES AND C. TAYLOR, IMPROVEMENT OF CONVEYANCING BY LEGISLATION
3–5, 17–19, 37, 41–43 (1960).

MARKETABLE TITLE ACTS

No other remedial legislation which has been enacted or proposed in recent years for the improvement of conveyancing offers as much as the marketable title act. It may be regarded as the keystone in the arch which constitutes the structure of a modernized system of conveyancing.

Without doubt the chief impetus for such legislation has been the increasing length of the record of instruments which must be examined before a land title can be approved. As is well known, the practice still prevails in a very large number of states to trace title back to a grant from the United States or from a state. The period of search thus becomes longer and longer as time goes on; and eventually this practice will have to be abandoned and the period restricted.

There is, of course, nothing new about limiting the period of search to a certain number of years. Obviously, in England, where there is no such thing as tracing land titles back to the government, the practice has long obtained of a vendee requiring title deeds to show a chain of title only for a fixed period of years. In some way this period seems to have been found by using the analogy of the longest period named in statutes of limitations with respect to actions for the recovery of real property. At the present time the period accepted is thirty years, and this practice is embodied in a statute. Similar practices have developed in some of the eastern states, where chains of title may be centuries long and are not traceable to the government.

But these practices of the bar in which titles are traced back only for an agreed period of years are unlike marketable title acts in one important respect. The bar practices leave the risk of loss, by reason of a defect in the title prior to the named period, on the purchaser. But under a marketable title act defects in the title prior to the named period are, by operation of the statute, extinguished.

Sometimes the modern American marketable title act is phrased like a statute of limitations; sometimes it may be analogized to a curative act. But in fact it is neither; and indeed it is definitely unique. Instead of interests being cut off because a claimant failed to sue, as would be the case if a statute of limitations were involved, the claimant's interest is extinguished because he failed to file a notice. In a sense the marketable title act may impose upon an owner a small additional burden, analogous to the burden of recording which was imposed when recording acts were first passed. Thus, before the recording acts, a prior conveyance from an owner of land was unimpeachable. But under recording acts, the grantee in the prior conveyance may lose his if he fails to record. Likewise, under a marketable title act, a claimant under a recorded deed may be required to file a notice in order to protect his title.

The essence of the Model Marketable Title Act which follows is simply this: If a person has a record chain of title for forty years, and no one else has filed a notice of claim to the property during the forty-year period, then all conflicting claims based upon any title transaction prior to the forty-year period are extinguished.

In one sense, the operation of the statute is all inclusive. It cuts off all interests, subject to a few exceptions unlikely to be encountered, which arise from title transactions prior to the forty-year period. It can extinguish ancient mortgages, servitudes, easements, titles by adverse possession, interests which are equitable as well as legal, future as well as present.

Yet in another sense, as a practical matter, the statute will probably cut off nothing at all, because there are no valid outstanding claims. It has been the experience of states with long-term marketable title acts that few if any notices of claim are ever filed, thus indicating that few claims actually exist. Indeed, the very fact that in some states title examination for only a thirty- or forty-year period is commonly accepted, without any legislation so providing indicates that there are in fact no enforceable claims adverse to the thirty- or forty-year chain of title.

It must not be assumed that the enactment of the Model Marketable Title Act will necessarily usher in an era of forty-year abstracts of title. The very fact that there are exceptions in the statute means that a title examiner will have to look back of the forty-year period to find instruments which may include the exceptions. But a competent title examiner will be able to see at a glance that most of the instruments do not concern the exceptions, and thus his task will be definitely lightened.

An important feature of the operation of the statute, however, is its curative effect. Ancient defects, which do not in fact give rise to substantial claims, but which may be the basis of a refusal to approve a title, are completely wiped out if they appear in the record more than forty years back. Even though the title examiner looks at the entire record from the government down to the present time, he is still greatly aided by the fact that he can ignore ancient defects . . . ."

CURATIVE ACTS

A curative act is one which reaches back and corrects an error made in the past. As applied to conveyancing, it provides that certain prior failures to comply with the requirements for the execution or recording of an instrument, or for the transfer of an interest in land, shall be disregarded. Thus, a statute may provide that, after a defectively acknowledged instrument has been on record for two years, it shall be treated for all purposes as if it had been properly acknowledged at the time of its recording.

The permissible scope of curative legislation obviously is limited. Courts have said that one person's property may not be taken away from him and given to another as of a prior date. In general, curative statutes may be said to deal with matters of a formal character and to carry out the intentions of the parties which may otherwise have been frustrated by their failure to comply with formal requirements. Since the legislature could do away with such requirements, and since, quite commonly, the parties could be relieved of the requirements in the particular case by a judicial proceeding, retroactive statutes may be passed relieving the parties of these formal requirements as of a prior time.

In spite of their limitations, curative acts have been in operation since colonial times. They have dealt with a variety of situations, such as the following: absence of a seal; defective acknowledgments; failure to include any acknowledgment; defective conveyances under powers of attorney; defectively executed deeds of corporations; defective records of judicial sales.

The rational basis for the curative act may be stated as follows: Since human nature is fallible, people do make mistakes in executing legal instruments. There is no way to keep mistakes from creeping into the conveyancing process. But after defective instruments have been left standing for a certain period of time, justice is generally secured by providing that the defects are then to be ignored. Thus, the basic intent of the parties will be effectuated. Just where the line is to be drawn between those objectives which can be accomplished by curative acts and those which cannot, will be discussed more fully in connection with the subject of constitutionality of such legislation. Certainly no single formula can be found which will enable us to draw the line. We must, however, recognize that curative legislation has traditionally been approved in certain areas, that it tends to further the intent of the parties, and that it will not be approved to deprive innocent third parties of their property.

If the error to be corrected by curative legislation is of sufficiently long standing, it can equally well be corrected by a marketable title act. The great advantage of having curative acts in addition to a marketable act is that the curative acts become operative, in justice to all concerned, at the expiration of a much shorter period of time than the period of a marketable title act. Hence, curative legislation, when it is used at all to clear land titles, should provide for a relatively short period after which the defect is cured.

A curative statute may take at least three possible forms. First, it may have a continuous and delayed operation, so that it will continue to cure the named defects after a certain period has elapsed. An example has already been given of a statute which continues to cure defective acknowledgments after they have been on record for two years. Second, the statute may name a particular date in the past, and be designed to cure defects in all instruments executed or recorded prior to that date. Thus, a statute might provide that all defectively acknowledged instruments which were recorded prior to January 1, 1954, shall be treated for all purposes, as if properly acknowledged at the time of their recording. The disadvantage of such a form of statute is that, as time passes, the period prior to which instruments are cured becomes longer, and it soon is necessary to enact a new statute naming a later date.

This second form of statute may, however, be desirable when it accompanies a change in legislative policy. Thus, the legislature may have repealed a requirement that instruments of conveyance be sealed. Thereafter, a statute may be enacted curing all unsealed instruments executed prior to the date of the repeal. Thus, the curative provision merely has the effect of making retroactive the statute abolishing the use of seals on instruments of conveyance. The policy in this legislation is not merely to correct the frailty of human nature, but to make retroactive a change of legislative policy.

Or, third, there may be a change in legislative policy with respect to certain formal requirements for conveyancing, and as a part of this legislation, or contemporaneous with it, a curative statute is enacted, immediately effective as to all instruments. Thus, in connection with the abolition of the requirement of a seal for instruments of conveyance, it may be enacted that, from and after the effective date of the act, all instruments of conveyance heretofore executed shall be valid without being sealed . . . ..

STATUTES OF LIMITATIONS

Essentially, statutes of limitations fix a time beyond which ancient disputes, claims and matters can no longer be brought forth for judicial determination. Simply by withdrawing the privilege to litigate and denying the aid of the courts in asserting claims and interests of ancient origin, they effectuate a number of important public policies. Further, although the application of a rigidly fixed time limitation in a particular case may appear arbitrary, no one doubts that, in general, they tend to promote justice as between parties to controversies.

But they also perform other important functions, entirely apart from affecting the course of any actual litigation; and nowhere are such functions more important than in the law of conveyancing . . . .

Statutes limiting recovery of real property commonly have three weaknesses as devices to cure defective titles: (1) the time when the period ends is uncertain due to provisions for extension by reason of disabilities and other facts; (2) adverse possession for the statutory period is outside the record and is often difficult to prove; (3) the statutes do not bar future interests. An ideal statute should go as far as possible to obviate these weaknesses.

As to disabilities, the type of statute which merely states an additional period after disabilities have terminated is undesirable. If the disability is insanity, there is no way to determine how long the period may last. It is preferable to name an overall period, which is the maximum regardless of disabilities. Thus, in the model statute the periods are extended by disabilities, but in no case are they extended beyond twenty years from the time the right of recovery first accrued. Furthermore, if the person subject to the disability is under guardianship, it is provided that there is no extension for disability during the period of guardianship. All these provisions as to disabilities are based on precedents in existing legislation, as is indicated in the comment . . . .

It is important, however, to have provisions in the statute naming a short period where there is color of title of record. This results in the clearing of a record title, and does not lead to a title based solely on extrinsic facts. It is here, no doubt, that the statute will have its greatest value for the title man. The Model Act states a period of five years for title by adverse possession with color of title consisting of recorded instruments.

However, we still are faced with the question: How do we prove adverse possession for the statutory period? Various attempts have been made by legislation to avoid the necessity of direct proof of possession. Thus, in some states payment of taxes for the statutory period is made the equivalent of possession for that period. One difficulty with that solution is that payment of taxes is a matter to be determined by tax records and not by title records, and also, tax records may not show who paid the taxes or be available for the requisite period. If it cannot be determined that the person claiming adversely paid the taxes, the payment is of uncertain significance. On the other hand, there is no reason why payment of taxes for the statutory period may not constitute prima facie evidence of adverse possession, and the Model Act so provides. It also provides that present possession together with a recorded instrument of title for the statutory period is prima facie evidence of adverse possession.

MARSHALL v. HOLLYWOOD, INC.
Supreme Court of Florida, 1970.
236 So.2d 114.

CARLTON, Justice.

We now review an application of the Marketable Record Titles to Real Property Act, Chapter 712, Florida Statutes. The District Court of Appeal, Fourth District, has certified that its decision in this cause, reported at 224 So.2d 743, is one which passes upon a question of great public interest. The District Court held, in effect, that the Act confers marketability to a chain of title arising out of a forged or a wild deed, so long as the strict requirements of the Act are met. We affirm this decision.

The complex facts involved in this case have been presented extensively and with clarity in the opinion of the District Court. We will only briefly summarize these facts. In 1912 Mathew Marshall and Carl Weidling owned a large tract of land in South Florida. In 1913 they organized and incorporated the Atlantic Beach Company. They transferred their property interests in the large tract to the Company, and in return they received two-thirds and one-third, respectively, of the Company's total authorized and issued stock, in direct proportion to their initial ownership interests in the tract. Marshall and Weidling were the sole officers of the Company and they alone participated in its stock.

Mr. Marshall died in December 1923, leaving Louise Marshall as his widow and sole surviving heir. Mrs. Marshall was totally unaware of her husband's interests in the Company, and within a month after his passing, she left the State without ever returning. After her departure, a man named Frank M. Terry, apparently aided and abetted by certain associates, set into motion a clever scheme calculated to defraud the Marshall estate of all interests in the Company and its property. Although there is some question as to exactly who played what part in this scheme, for purposes of this opinion we shall ascribe all responsibility to Mr. Terry.

Within a few days after Mrs. Marshall's departure, Terry forged her name to an Application for Letters of Administration concerning Mathew Marshall's estate. Letters were subsequently issued by the County Judge, Dade County, to Mrs. Marshall and Terry received them. About this same time, Terry wrote up certain "Minutes of Dissolution of Atlantic Beach Company" and he also prepared a deed conveying all of the Company's property to himself and others residing out of the State, who were alleged in the spurious Minutes to be the remaining stockholders of the Company. Thereafter, these Minutes were purportedly acknowledged, and the deed conveying all of the Company's property was executed by those who were alleged to be the stockholders.

Next, Terry prepared a petition seeking an Order dissolving the Company which was then filed in Circuit Court, Broward County, along with the Minutes of Dissolution. The Court granted the petition since it appeared in order, and a decree dissolving the Company was entered in February 1924. The day before this petition was filed, Terry and the other grantees under the deed from the Company joined in executing a deed conveying the tract to Hollywood Realty Company, a Florida corporation. This deed was recorded in April 1924. In August 1924 Hollywood Realty in turn executed a deed conveying this same property to Homeseekers Realty Company, which was recorded August 22, 1924.

All of the foregoing transactions are alleged by petitioner to have been part of a scheme to defraud the Mathew Marshall estate. The record is silent as to why Carl Weidling, initially owner of a one-third undivided interest in the tract, and subsequently holder of one-third of the Atlantic Beach Company stock, never raised any objections or questions. Mr. Weidling died in 1963; his interests are not represented in this suit. Mrs. Marshall died in 1945 without ever having learned of her husband's interests in the Company. The Company itself was never legally dissolved until September 14, 1936, when it was dissolved by proclamation of the Governor on account of failure to pay capital stock tax.

Homeseekers Realty Company disposed of approximately one-third of the initial Atlantic Beach Company tract through sales before it lost its control over the remainder by forced sheriff's sale in 1929. In that year, the Highway Construction Company of Ohio, Inc., obtained a judgment against Homeseekers and caused the sale at which Highway purchased the remaining unsold two-thirds of the initial tract. A sheriff's deed evidencing the judgment sale was recorded December 30, 1930. Highway Construction Company then conveyed its interests in the tract to respondent Hollywood, Inc., and this deed was recorded on February 21, 1931.

Respondent Hollywood, Inc., still retains title to the two-thirds of the original Atlantic Beach tract which was conveyed to it as a result of the forced sheriff's sale. The other respondents are those numerous persons, or their successors, who derived title to parcels on the one-third portion of the original tract from Homeseekers Realty prior to the 1929 judgment sale. Diagrammed, the chain of title to the property involved in this suit, insofar as it is relevant to the issues involved here, looks like this:

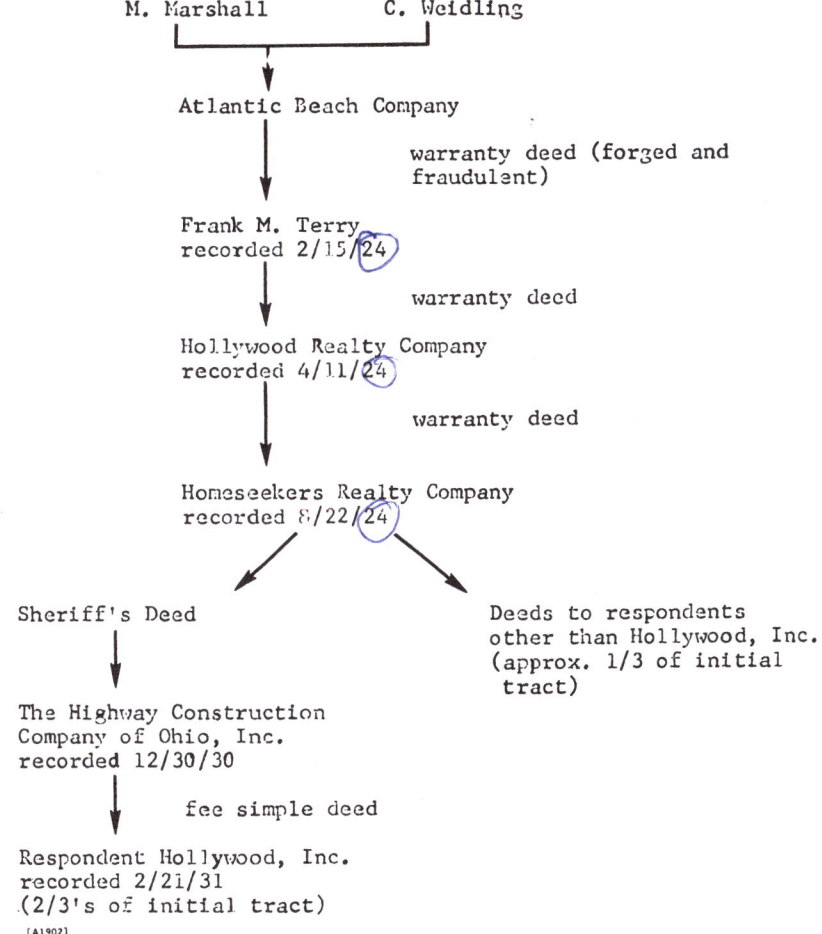

It was not until November 1966, that petitioner, a brother of Mathew Marshall, uncovered Terry's actions. Petitioner obtained appointment as Administrator of the Marshall estate, and subsequently, in his capacity as Administrator, he filed his initial complaint on July 13, 1967. An amended complaint was filed on April 5, 1968. The amended complaint sought a decree establishing the equitable interest of petitioner in the tract initially belonging to the Atlantic Beach Company, confirmation of the ownership of Atlantic Beach stock by petitioner, and also the appointment of a trustee for the Company who could convey legal title to the interest in the original tract to the heirs of Marshall.

Upon respondents' motion, the amended complaint was dismissed by final judgment with prejudice. The order of dismissal stated that petitioner's amended complaint failed to state a cause of action because the estate's claims were barred by operation of the Marketable Record Title Act, Ch. 712, F.S. The dismissal was appealed to the District Court. The issue framed on appeal was whether or not the

Act applied to the claim of title asserted in petitioner's amended complaint in a manner which would extinguish the claim.

. . .

. . . The most persuasive argument of petitioner is that the Marketable Record Title Act preserves case law which is inconsistent with dismissal of petitioner's amended complaint. F.S. § 712.07, F.S.A. states:

"Nothing contained in this Act shall be construed to extend the period for the bringing of an action or for the doing of any other act required under any statute of limitations or to affect the operation of any statute governing the effect of the recording or the failure to record any instrument affecting land. This law shall not vitiate any curative act."

Petitioner asserts that by preserving the operation of statutes of limitations, and curative and recording acts, the Legislature intended that the Act must be construed in a manner consistent with these previous enactments and all case law interpreting them. In cases dealing with wild or forged deeds under these various acts, it has consistently been held, according to petitioner, that such deeds are void and of no effect even though they may have been recorded. Therefore petitioner suggests that the Act cannot bar a complaint which demonstrates that the chain of title involved in a cause initiated out of a forgery or a wild deed, even though the forgery or the wild deed came into being more than thirty years before marketability was being determined.

The answer to this argument is simply that the Act in question goes beyond previous enactments and is in a category of its own. We quote with approval the following commentary. Boyer & Shapo, Florida's Marketable Title Act: Prospects and Problems, 18 U.Miami L.Rev. 103, 104:

"The Marketable title concept is simple, although it has fathered many variations in draftsmanship. The idea is to extinguish all claims of a given age (thirty years in the Florida Statute) which conflict with a record chain of title which is at least that old. The act performs this task by combining several features, which generally, are singly labeled as 'statutes of limitations,' 'curative acts,' and 'recording acts.'

"The new act is in fact all of these: It declares a marketable title on a recorded chain of title which is more than thirty years old, and it nullifies all interests which are older than the root of title. This nullification is subject to a group of exceptions—including interests which have been filed for record in a prescribed manner.

"The act is also more: It goes beyond the conventional statute of limitations because it runs against persons under disability. It is broader than the kind of legislation generally described as a curative act, because it actually invalidates interests instead of simply 'curing' formal defects. It also differs from a recording act by requiring a rerecording of outstanding interests in order to preserve them."

. . .

In view of the special nature of this Act and its special purpose the assertion that its construction and application must be bound by precedents relating to less comprehensive acts does not make good sense and cannot make good law. The clear Legislative intention behind the Act, as expressed in F.S. § 712.10, F.S.A., was to simplify and facilitate land title transactions by allowing persons to rely on a record title as described by F.S. § 712.02, F.S.A., subject only to such limitations as appear in F.S. § 712.03, F.S.A. To accept petitioner's arguments would be to disembowel the Act through a case dealing with a factual situation of a nature precisely contemplated and remedied by the Act itself. This we cannot do.

In summary, although the Atlantic Beach Company/Terry deed initiating the chain of title involved here was forged, this deed formed but one link in the chain coming *before* the effective roots of title in this case as defined by the Act, i.e., transactions with either The Highway Construction Company or the Homeseekers Realty Company as grantors. Claims arising out of transactions, whether based upon forgeries or not, predating the effective roots of title are extinguished by operation of the Act unless claimants can come in under any of the specified exceptions to the Act. In this case, petitioner fails to qualify under any of the exceptions to the Act, and therefore, petitioner's claims are barred.

The certified question involved in this cause was, in effect, whether the Marketable Record Titles to Real Property Act, Ch. 712, F.S., confers marketability to a chain of title arising out of a forged or wild deed, so long as the strict requirements of the Act are met. This question is answered in the affirmative.

The decision of the appellate court here reviewed having properly affirmed the decree of the lower court, the writ heretofore issued in this cause should be and it is hereby discharged.

It is so ordered.

ERVIN, C.J., ROBERTS, DREW, ADKINS and BOYD, JJ., and VANN, Circuit Judge, concur.

b. Title Registration

C. FLICK, 1 ABSTRACT AND TITLE PRACTICE

188–190, 192–194 (2d ed. 1958).

The certificate system is in world-wide use for the purpose of showing ownership of merchant vessels. Every ship is listed in a national registry. A page in the Register is devoted to each ship and on that page there appears its name and description, the name of the owner, and any encumbrances. A duplicate of this page in the form of a certificate is given to the owner and is his evidence of ownership no matter where he may be. It is usually kept on the ship and accordingly is frequently spoken of in literature as the "ship's papers." Any lien or claim against a ship is required to be noted on the original register page so that it is possible for any interested person to tell at a glance exactly the condition of the title. To make a transfer, the owner assigns the certificate which he has and takes it to the registry office whereupon the old certificate is cancelled, the old page is closed, a new page is opened, and a duplicate certificate of the new page is given to the new owner.

In fact the Torrens system grew out of the fact that its originator, Robert R. Torrens, had been connected with the shipping industry for a number of years before he was appointed Registrar General of the Province of South Australia and given charge of registering all instruments affecting the title to real estate in that province. His experience in his former office led him to speculate on the subject of why the title to a tract of land could not be registered with the same simplicity as the title to a ship. He demonstrated that this was entirely possible and the system for which he drafted the law in Australia has proven to be a very efficient method of keeping track of the ownership of real property and of simplifying every transaction concerned with transferring the title or of using that type of property as security.

Torrens Acts have been passed in California, 1897; Colorado, 1903; Illinois, 1895, declared invalid and new act passed in 1897; Massachusetts, 1898; Minnesota, 1901; Mississippi, 1913; New York, 1908; North Carolina, 1913; Ohio, 1896, declared invalid and new act passed in 1913; Oregon, 1901; Washington, 1907; Hawaii, 1903; and the Phillippines, 1902.

The only acts of this nature which have been declared unconstitutional were the first acts of Ohio and Illinois. Neither of those provided for a decree of court before there could be registration, and in each state a later act was passed, which did so provide . . ..

Upon each voluntary transfer by deed, and upon each involuntary transfer by deed, decree, descent, devise, or otherwise when accompanied by a court order directing it, the registrar cancels the old certificate and its duplicate and enters a new certificate and delivers an owner's duplicate to the new owner—all much the same as in the case of a transfer of corporation stock. It is the registration of a conveyance which is the operative act of transfer to a new owner. Prior to registration, a deed of registered land, like a fulfilled contract for a deed under the recording system, creates merely a right to the title as between the parties and is of no effect as to a bona fide purchaser from the registered owner.

From the foregoing it will be apparent that a report as to ownership may be made, and can only be made, from an examination, direct or indirect, of the original certificate of title on file in the office of the registrar. The certificate will usually be found to be in such definite and certain terms that no construction is required; when this is not the case the principles which govern the construction of deeds also apply to certificates of title. The reliability of an examiner's report will necessarily depend upon the conclusiveness of the certificate of title. This may vary slightly in the different states, but the variation is confined almost entirely to the difference in periods of limitation and periods allowed for appeal, or to reopen, as to a case upon the final order in which a certificate depends. After allowing for these, and for such exceptions as are expressly provided for in the registration statutes, the certificate creates an indefeasible title in the registered owner as against every one else, free from all claims and incumbrances except those noted on the certificate of title. Examination of the certificate alone is all that is necessary to determine ownership of the legal title.

Loss or destruction of duplicates occasionally occurs, and the registration acts all make provision for issuance of a new duplicate. In some states this is only after notice and hearing by the court, in others upon proof of loss and identity to the registrar, but in all states under very careful safeguards. Neither the public nor the owner is subject to any danger of loss from forged deeds so long as the latter safeguards his duplicate with the same care that he keeps any other valuable paper. If he is careless in the matter of to whom he entrusts it, there exists, except for the owner's signature card on file with the registrar, the same danger that exists with unregistered titles—with the loss, however, if not payable from an assurance fund, upon the negligent owner rather than upon an innocent purchaser or mortgagee.

In furtherance of the theory that everything regarding a present title should be ascertainable from the certificate on file in the office of the Registrar of Titles, the statutes provide that no title to registered land in derogation of that of the registered owner may be acquired by prescription or by adverse possession and, in the main, that the time-honored doctrine in most states of constructive notice by reason of occupancy does not prevail. This is the only change in substantive principles, though there are necessarily some changes in purely statutory principles, such as the nonapplicability of the recording act, the inception of judgment liens and other matters.

ECHOLS v. OLSEN

Supreme Court of Illinois, 1976.
63 Ill.2d 270, 347 N.E.2d 720.

WARD, Chief Justice.

What the facts are in this case is not in dispute. Vernal Echols, the petitioner, and her husband Valentine were joint owners of a lot in Chicago that was registered under "An Act concerning land titles" (Ill.Rev.Stat.1973, ch. 30, pars. 45–148) (hereafter cited as the Torrens Act). On September 29, 1966, the circuit court of Cook County entered a decree of divorce in a suit that had been brought by the petitioner. Under the terms of the decree, the petitioner was required to pay her former husband $2,000 and he, in turn, was required to execute a quitclaim deed in her favor surrendering his interest in the lot. The petitioner's attorney recorded the quitclaim deed in the office of the Cook County Recorder of Deeds on October 18, 1966, but he failed at that time to register the deed with the Cook County Registrar of Titles (Registrar).

The Independence Bank of Chicago (the Bank) obtained in 1969 an *ex parte* judgment in the amount of $1,058.67, against Valentine Echols. On January 21, 1971, the Bank had the judgment memorialized on the duplicate Torrens certificate that is maintained in the Registrar's office. As the petitioner had not registered the quitclaim deed, the duplicate certificate had shown Valentine and Vernal Echols as joint owners of the lot. On February 24, 1971, Vernal Echols filed a petition in the circuit court requesting the court to direct the Registrar to remove the Bank's memorial and to issue a new certificate showing title to be in the petitioner alone. Both the Bank and the Registrar were named as respondents.

The Bank moved to dismiss the petition contending that under the Torrens Act a judgment creditor who memorializes his judgment after the judgment debtor has conveyed his interest in property acquires an interest superior to that of a prior transferee who failed to register his deed. On August 4, 1971, the court ordered the Registrar to issue a new certificate of title showing title to be in the petitioner alone but showing that her interest was subject to the Bank's registered judgment.

The petitioner filed a notice of appeal to the appellate court on September 17, 1971, but she served a copy of it only upon the Bank. The petitioner and the Bank briefed and orally argued the case and the court reversed the trial court, holding that the Bank did not acquire an interest in the property since Valentine Echols had conveyed his interest to the petitioner before the judgment was memorialized.

On learning of the decision, the Registrar moved the appellate court to dismiss the appeal for failing to provide him with notice of the appeal, or, in the alternative, to have the court withdraw its opinion and to permit him to file a brief and to argue his position, which was the same as the Bank's. The court did not withdraw its opinion but it did allow the Registrar to file a brief. After oral argument on June 4, 1975, by the petitioner and the Registrar, the appellate court on June 9, 1975, announced this order:

"On our own motion we allowed a rehearing. We have again allowed oral argument and considered the briefs that were filed. We find no merit in the request and we dismiss the appeal. After thoroughly reviewing the case again, we are of the opinion our original decision was correct and we so hold. It is hereby ordered the rehearing is dismissed."

We granted the Registrar's petition for leave to appeal under our Rule 315.

. . .

We must now consider whether under the Torrens Act, as the Registrar contends, a judgment creditor who has registered his judgment after the judgment debtor has conveyed his interest in the property acquires an interest superior to that of a prior grantee from the debtor who did not register his deed. The principal objective of the Torrens Act is "to provide an independent system of registration, whereby an intending purchaser of land can determine from the register the condition of the title." While generally it has been held that to achieve this all matters affecting title to registered property should be either registered or memorialized so that the Registrar's duplicate certificate will indicate to all interested parties the status of the title, we have held that the provisions of the Act must be construed in light of the established law of property and that the register of title will not always be considered conclusive.

The language of the Torrens Act does not provide any direct answer to the Registrar's contention; nor has the contention been considered in any reported decision in Illinois. The Registrar urges that in order to serve the objective of the Act, that is, to enable an intending purchaser to determine the condition of title from the register we should read into the Act a provision similar to section 30 of "An Act concerning conveyances" (Ill.Rev.Stat.1973, ch. 30, par. 29) (hereafter the Conveyance Act). Section 30 provides that a judgment creditor, as well as a *bona fide* purchaser, who records his judgment in accordance with the provisions of the Conveyance Act acquires rights superior to those of the holder of a prior unrecorded interest. It is only because of this statute that a judgment creditor will prevail over the holder of a prior but unrecorded interest. The plea of the Registrar that we read into the Torrens Act what section 30 of the Conveyance Act provides cannot be allowed. To do so would be an egregious intrusion upon the legislative authority. The Torrens Act was designed by the legislature to protect intending purchasers and has never been considered to extend the preference to judgment creditors. Judgment creditors under section 30 are preferred to holders of prior but unrecorded interests only because of that statute. Section 30 existed prior to the Torrens Act and it is not unreasonable to say that had the legislature intended that judgment creditors receive under the Torrens Act the priority and preference they are given under Section 30 it would have inserted a provision in the Torrens Act similar to section 30.

The Torrens Act provides that in disputes under it, courts should be guided by the provisions of the Act, of course, and by general principles of equity. The holder of an unregistered interest has strong claims to equitable consideration, especially when, as here, the holder of an interest claiming preference (here, the Bank) did not rely upon the absence of a registration. We said in Kostelny v. Peterson, 19 Ill. 2d 480, 484, 167 N.E.2d 203, 205 that:

"Whereas at common law a deed took effect upon delivery without regard to recordation, under the Torrens Act it is the registration itself which completes the conveyance of legal title.

"This does not mean, however, that under the registration statute [Ill.Rev.Stat.1973, ch. 30, par. 98] an unfiled deed must be considered as a mere executory contract. Rather, as was pointed out in Klouda v. Pechousek, 414 Ill. 75, 110 N.E.2d 258, and Naiburg v. Hendriksen, 370 Ill. 502, 19 N.E.2d 348, a deed to Torrens property may take effect in equity upon delivery to the grantee so as to immediately pass the equitable title."

Too, it has been held that a judgment creditor's lien extends under section 30 only to the actual interest of the judgment debtor in the property and that this interest will not be extended to allow him to claim property of another in satisfaction of his lien in the absence of a statute specifically giving him this right. It was said in East St. Louis Lumber Co. v. Schnipper, 310 Ill. 150, 156, 141 N.E. 542, 544, that a judgment creditor cannot attach his judgment to a "mere naked legal estate when the entire equitable estate is vested in some third person."

When Valentine Echols quitclaimed his interest to the petitioner in September of 1966, he relinquished all equitable rights in the property. The Bank could not attach its judgment to the legal interest which remained in his name only because the petitioner had not registered the quitclaim deed. The trial court erred in not ordering the Registrar to remove the Bank's memorial.

We do not accept the Registrar's additional argument that since it was the petitioner's neglect that led the Bank to memorialize its judgment, the judgment creditor should prevail as a matter of equity. The force that this argument would have in the case of a *bona fide* purchaser for value who without notice purchased property relying on the state of the registered title of the property or the case of a mortgagee who made a loan because of a similar reliance does not extend to a judgment creditor who has not acted to his prejudice in reliance on the registered state of title.

. . .

For the reasons given the judgment of the appellate court is affirmed.

Judgment affirmed.

KLUCZYNSKI, J., dissenting:

I must respectfully dissent from the majority's opinion.

The issue presented in this appeal is whether a judgment lien, properly memorialized under the Torrens Act, attaches to the legal title of a registered owner after he has executed an unregistered deed of his entire interest to another. The Torrens Act contains a number of provisions relevant to this issue. Section 46 of the Act (Ill. Rev.Stat.1973, ch. 30, par. 90) provides that the bringing of land under the Act, or any dealings with land registered thereunder, implies an agreement that the land be subject to the terms of the Act, i.e., the holders of title take registered property "subject to all of the rights, privileges and obligations of such registration and the law applicable thereto," and are "presumed to know all of its terms".

Section 54 states that a "deed . . . purporting to convey . . . registered land . . . shall take effect only by way of contract . . . and as authority to the registrar to register the transfer . . . ." and that only "on the completion of such registration [does] the land . . . become transferred . . . according to the . . . terms of the deed . . . ." (Ill.Rev.Stat.1973, ch. 30, par. 98.) Accordingly, petitioner's quitclaim deed from her husband was only a contract purporting to convey whatever interest he possessed in the joint tenancy at the time the transfer was completed upon registration. Under the present factual situation, at the time the transfer was completed by registration, the interest of petitioner's husband was already subject to the judgment lien. Since section 45 (Ill. Rev.Stat.1973, ch. 30, par. 89) provides that a lien properly memorialized shall be carried forward until cancelled according to the Act, it necessarily follows that a lien memorialized before land is transferred by registration must be carried forward.

This court has previously held section 54 not determinative in a number of cases, some cited by the majority, on the ground that an unregistered deed is effective to transfer the equitable title. None of these cases, however, involved the rights of a party who duly registered an interest from or through a registered owner as against the rights of another who claimed under a prior unregistered instrument.

. . .

In the present case while petitioner received equitable title at the time of execution of the quitclaim deed from her husband, until she registered her interest, her husband had the power to encumber or transfer, voluntarily or involuntarily, his interest. Until it was registered petitioner's equitable title was subject to divestment. Had the petitioner's husband voluntarily transferred his registered interest to another who was not a party to fraud, the latter would take the interest free of any claim by the petitioner. The Torrens Act provides no basis for distinguishing in this regard between voluntary or involuntary conveyances, or between those who take by judgment lien, purchase or otherwise. The Act is very explicit:

"Except in case of fraud and except as herein otherwise provided, *no person* taking a transfer of registered land, or *any* estate or interest therein, or of *any charge* upon the same from the registered owner shall be held to inquire into the circumstances under which, or the consideration for which such owner or any previous registered owner was registered, or be affected with notice, actual or constructive, of *any unregistered* trust, lien, *claim*, demand or *interest;* and the knowledge that *any unregistered* trust, lien, *claim*, demand or interest is in existence shall not of itself be imputed as fraud." (Emphasis added.) Ill.Rev.Stat.1973, ch. 30, par. 86.

Section 84 of the Act (Ill.Rev.Stat.1973, ch. 30, par. 121) states that no civil action affecting registered land shall be deemed *lis pendens* or notice to any person unless a certificate of the pendency of such action is filed with the Registrar and memorialized. Since petitioner's divorce action involved her interest in the land and resulted in a decree requiring the execution of a quitclaim deed, it was a suit affecting registered land. Had the action been memorialized according to the provisions of section 84, it would have provided notice to the Bank before it registered its judgment lien.

By virtue of section 30 of the Conveyance Act, a judgment creditor may have priority over the holder of a prior unrecorded interest in the same land. The opinion maintains that "[s]ection 30 existed prior to the Torrens Act and it is not unreasonable to say that had the legislature intended the judgment creditors receive under the Torrens Act the priority and preference they are given under section 30 it would have inserted a provision in the Torrens Act similar to section 30." The defect in this reasoning, however, is that it assumes the Torrens and the recording systems are comparable, while, in fact, the theoretical basis for each system and its practical operations are quite different.

Under the recording system, the legal title and the title of record may be completely different. A party who acquires an interest in land by deed under the recording system may or may not record this instrument. If the interest is not recorded, the party who takes under it faces the risk that a subsequent purchaser entitled to the protection of the recording act may, by virtue of that act, acquire priority. In Illinois, a subsequent purchaser is entitled to the Act's protection if he is a purchaser in good faith, without notice of the prior unrecorded instrument, pays value and records first. The recording of an instrument imparts constructive notice and prevents subsequent purchasers from taking without notice. Under the recording acts of most jurisdictions, judgment creditors are not protected by the acts because they are not considered to be purchasers or are not considered to have paid value within the meaning of those acts. Thus, the necessity of a section 30 is apparent to place judgment creditors at some level of priority.

The Torrens system of registration is an almost completely different system in both theory and practical operation. Under Torrens, the title itself is registered, not merely the evidences thereof. "The Torrens Act differs in many material respects from the usual method of transferring title and the requirement for recording instruments affecting title. In respect to property not registered under the Torrens Act, title is transferred by the delivery of a deed from the owner to the grantee. The recording of such instrument is not necessary to the validity of the transfer." People v. Mortenson, 404 Ill. 107, 111, 88 N.E.2d 35, 38.

The goal of the Torrens system is to make the public record in the Registrar's office and the actual title one and the same.

Unlike the recording system, the Torrens system does not operate by conferring priorities upon those who qualify as protected parties. The latter system operates by making record title in the register and actual title virtually identical, thus enabling anyone to ascertain the true state of the title by only examining the certificate in the register and ordering a tax lien search. Under the Torrens system, questions of good faith (except in cases of fraud), notice, reliance and payment of value are immaterial. (Ill.Rev.Stat.1973, ch. 30, par. 86.) Therefore, it was unnecessary for the legislature to make a special provision for judgment lienors in the Torrens Act similar to section 30 of the Conveyance Act . . . ..

. . .

The opinion attempts to distinguish the present factual situation involving a judgment creditor from one involving a *bona fide* purchaser or a mortgagee. The distinction, it maintains, is that the latter parties would have detrimentally relied upon the state of the registered title, while the judgment creditor has not so relied. This view overlooks the obvious fact that had the judgment creditor not relied upon the condition of the registered title, it would not have memorialized its judgment. As previously stated, the Torrens Act was designed to encourage reliance on the state of the registered title. Between two innocent parties, the judgment creditor and the petitioner herein, the consequences of the petitioner's failure to register her title should be borne by her.

In view of the above-stated considerations, I would affirm the judgment of the circuit court.

UNDERWOOD and CREBS, JJ., join in this dissent.

NOTE

Although as many as twenty-one states had at one time authorized the registration of title to real property, the number has since dwindled to twelve—Colorado, Georgia, Hawaii, Illinois, Massachusetts, Minnesota, New York, North Carolina, Ohio, Oregon, Virginia, and Washington. See Fiflis, English Registered Conveyancing: A Study in Effective Land Transfer, 59 N.W.L.Rev. 468 (1964). And, even in these states, landowners only infrequently resort to title registration. According to Fiflis, "In Hawaii, perhaps one-third of all transactions are under the title registration system. In Cook County, Illinois, about 15% of all transactions are in registered land. Except in these states, and Massachusetts, Minnesota and perhaps Ohio, the system is virtually unused." Id. n. 1. The history of state adoption of Torrens is summarized in 6A R. Powell, The Law of Real Property ¶ 908 (1982).

This general rejection of title registration contrasts sharply with the claims for its superiority made in the literature. See for example, Janczyk, An Economic Analysis of the Land Title Systems for Transferring Real Property, 6 J. Legal Stud. 213, 215 (1977) ("The results of this paper indicate that the cost of transferring a title in the Torrens [system] is approximately $100 less than in the recording system, and further, that Cook County could save $76 million by adopting the Torrens system; some other counties could also realize a substantial savings.").

Why has title registration failed to take hold in the United States? Blame is most commonly placed on the title insurance companies: "The chief, major, proximate, and direct cause of the non-use of, or of the public 'disinclination' to use, the Torrens system has been the bitter, multi-form opposition—lobbying against any reform, wounding statutes when enactment is inevitable, conspiring with lending agencies, spreading adverse publicity, and so forth—of title companies and title lawyers." McDougal & Brabner-Smith, Land Title Transfer: A Regression, 48 Yale L.J. 1125, 1147 (1939). Do you understand why title companies can be expected to oppose title registration? Why should industry opposition alone have succeeded in sinking the concept? What reasons do consumers have to switch from title insurance to title registration, which is initially more costly?

The fight over title registration has produced some of the sharpest scholarly debates in real property law. Compare, for example, R. Powell, Registration of the Title to Land in the State of New York (1938), with McDougal & Brabner-Smith, Land Title Transfer: A Regression, 48 Yale L.J. 1125 (1939). Proposals for the adoption of title registration continue to be made. See, for example, Note, The Torrens System of Title Registration: A New Proposal for Effective Implementation, 29 U.C.L.A.L.Rev. 661 (1982) (also contains footnote references to most of the major literature in the area); Lobel, A Proposal for a Title Registration System for Realty, 11 U.Rich.L.Rev. 471 (1977).

See generally, B. Shick & I. Plotkin, Torrens in the United States (1978).

C. LAND FINANCE

Virtually every developed piece of land in America has, at one time or another, been pledged as security for a loan. The pledge may have taken one of several forms. It may have taken the form of a *mortgage* given by the landowner, as *mortgagor*, to the lender, as *mortgagee*, to secure the landowner's obligation to pay a debt, evidenced by a *bond* or *promissory note*. It may have taken the form of a *deed of trust*, executed by landowner, as *trustor* to some third party as *trustee*, to hold title for the benefit of lender, as *beneficiary*, to secure payment of a bond or note. Or it may have taken the form of an *installment land contract*, structured much like the usual land sale contract but having a much longer executory period—20 or 30 years rather than 30 or 60 days—so that, during the executory period, the buyer in possession who makes monthly payments to the seller is effectively the homeowner, and the seller is effectively the lender, with the contract itself representing both the security instrument and the promise to repay.

These land finance arrangements can be used for many purposes. They can, as in the Jones-Smith transaction, be used to finance the acquisition of a house or an undeveloped parcel of land, in which case the instrument is typically called a *purchase money mortgage* or a *purchase money deed of trust*. They may be used to finance the construction of improvements on land, or activities totally unconnected to land, such as a vacation trip or a child's college education. Land finance is not limited to the needs of residential homeowners. Every day, loans for millions of dollars are given on the security of shopping centers, apartment houses and office buildings. Both residential and commercial real estate loans come from a variety of sources—savings and loan associations, savings banks, commercial banks, life insurance companies, pension funds, real estate investment trusts and, as in the Jones-Smith transaction, from the sellers themselves.

Because land is such a central and productive asset in American life, the law and institutions of land finance unavoidably mirror the nation's economic and social history. The cycles of agricultural bust and boom throughout the nineteenth century can be traced in laws enacted in the farming states, first enlarging the rights of farmer-mortgagors to redeem their property from foreclosing bank-mortgagees and then, when farming conditions improved, reducing mortgagors' redemption rights in order to stimulate increased lending activity. See generally, Skilton, Developments in Mortgage Law and Practice, 17 Temp.Univ.L.Q. 315, 326–331 (1943).

The depression of the 1930's produced even more dramatic upheavals in the law and practice of land finance. The principal change was the federal government's effort, through direct intervention in land finance markets, to increase the opportunities for financing housing purchases and to create a national market for the purchase and sale of mortgage loans. The Federal Housing Administration, created by the National Housing Act in 1934, was given authority to insure home mortgage loans made by private lenders. The FHA not only stimulated private lending but also, through its underwriting requirements, effectively altered the prevailing real estate loan from a short term instrument with the principal fully payable at maturity, to far more affordable and stable long-term instruments—typically 25- or 30-year mortgages, with principal repayments, or amortization, spread out over the entire period. The Federal National Mortgage Association was chartered by the FHA in 1938 to create a secondary market for FHA-insured mortgages, buying these instruments when credit was tight and selling them when funds for housing finance were abundant. The Federal Home Loan Bank System, created by the Federal Home Loan Bank Act in 1932 and modelled after the Federal Reserve System, was intended to give credit to member institutions engaged in mortgage lending, taking some of the members' mortgages as collateral. See generally, Dept. of Housing & Urban Development, "Housing in the Seventies," Hearings before the Subcomm. on Housing of the House Comm. on Banking & Currency, Part 3, 93rd Cong. 1st Sess. 2024, 2059–2070 (1973).

Spiraling inflation and the credit crunch of the 1970's and 1980's tested the ability of land finance institutions to respond to a different social and economic development: the collapse of the American dream that anyone who worked hard enough could, in time, afford the down payment and monthly installments needed to acquire a home. The private and governmental responses were mixed. Government lifted usury limits, reopening finance markets that had frozen shut once interest rates exceeded the statutory ceiling. See generally, Ewing & Vickers, Federal Preemption of State Usury Laws Affecting Real Estate Financing, 47 Mo.L.Rev. 171 (1982). To combat higher interest costs, many state courts outlawed due-on-sale clauses by which institutional lenders prohibited borrowers from passing on their old, low-interest loans to their buyers. Lenders offered a new array of mortgage instruments designed to reconcile consumer needs with the capacities of capital markets. Many of the new instruments were only dressed-up versions of pre-Depression devices, but all got snappy new names—variable rate mortgages, renegotiable rate mortgages, reverse annuity mortgages and shared appreciation mortgages, to name just a few.

The materials in this section touch only on the fundamentals of land finance. They focus almost exclusively on home finance, rather than on more complex commercial land transactions, and leave to other courses and other casebooks consideration of the intricate planning strategies that pervade land finance. See, for example, P. Goldstein, Real Estate Transactions: Cases and Materials on Land Transfer, Development and Finance (1980). The standard treatise is G. Osborne, G. Nelson & D. Whitman, Real Estate Finance Law (1979).

N.Y. Bond (Note) and Mortgage
Plain Language format; 11/78
895 A½ P.L.
David F. Williamson Co., Inc., Publishers
, Bflo., N.Y. 14203

This Bond and Mortgage

Date

Made the 1st day of September , Nineteen Hundred and eighty-three (1983)

Parties

BETWEEN: John J. Smith and Katherine Ann Smith, his wife, residing at 49 Willow Street, Buffalo, New York 14202
Mortgagor (Borrower)

Mortgagee (Lender) Robert W. Jones and Mary Ruth Jones, his wife, residing at
Address   23 Oak Street, Amherst, New York 14221

Promises, Amount of Debt and payments

Mortgagor promises to pay to Mortgagee the principal sum of ----------------------------
--FIFTY THOUSAND and 0/100----------dollars ($ 50,000.00 ------) in lawful money of the United States, plus interest of   13% per year from the date above until paid in full as follows: The sum of $553.10 on the first day of October, 1983, and a like sum of $553.10 on the first day of each and every month thereafter to and including the first day of September, 2013, when the balance of the principal sum then remaining unpaid shall become due and payable, each of said monthly payments to be applied first to interest at the rate of thirteen (13%) percent per annum from the date hereof, computed monthly on all sums from time to time remaining unpaid, and the balance of each of said monthly payments to be applied to the principal sum; the mortgagors to have the privilege of making additional payments in multiples of $553.10 or paying the whole of said principal sum remaining unpaid on any of the aforesaid payment dates.

Property Mortgaged

The property mortgaged is: ALL THAT TRACT OR PARCEL OF LAND, situate in the Town of Amherst, County of Erie and State of New York, being part of Lot Number 45, Township 11 and Range 7 of the Holland Land Company's Survey and according to a Subdivision Map filed in the Erie County Clerk's Office under Cover Number 922 is known and distinguished as Subdivision Lot Number 117.

This mortgage may not be assumed without the prior written consent of the mortgagees nor shall premises be the subject of an Installment Land Contract or Lease with Option to Purchase without the prior written consent of the mortgagees.

In the event that any sum payable shall become past due for a period of fifteen (15) days, a "late charge" of two cents for each dollar ($1.00) so past due may be charged by the mortgagees for the purpose of defraying the expenses incident thereto.

It is agreed by the mortgagors that on the foreclosure of this mortgage, there shall be included in the computation of the amount due the amount of the fee for attorney's services in the foreclosure proceedings as well as all disbursements, allowances, additional allowances and costs provided by law.

It is agreed that the whole of said principal sum and interest remaining unpaid shall immediately become due and payable at the option of the mortgagees at any time if title to said premises is no longer vested in the mortgagors herein.

This mortgage is given to secure the payment of a part of the purchase price of the above-described premises.

That premises described herein are improved by a one or two-family dwelling only.

That the mortgagors will provide fire insurance on premises to protect the mortgagees to the extent of the unpaid principal balance of the mortgage.

[D508]

And, the Mortgagor promises the Mortgagee as follows:

Payments 1. That the Mortgagor will pay the indebtedness as hereinbefore provided to the Mortgagee at the above address.

Insurance 2. That the Mortgagor will keep the buildings on the premises insured against loss by fire for the benefit of the Mortgagee; that he will assign and deliver the policies to the Mortgagee; and that he will reimburse the Mortgagee for any premiums paid for insurance made by the Mortgagee on the Mortgagor's default in so insuring the buildings or in so assigning and delivering the policies.

Alteration 3. That no building on the premises shall be removed or demolished without the consent of the Mortgagee.

Default - Failure to pay on time or other reasons 4. That the whole said of said principal sum and interest shall become due at the option of the Mortgagee: after default in the payment of any installment of principal   or of interest for   days, or after default in the payment of any tax, water rate or assessment for   days after notice and demand; or after default after notice and demand either in assigning and delivering the policies insuring the buildings against loss by fire or in reimbursing the Mortgagee for premiums paid on such insurance, as hereinbefore provided; or after default upon request in furnishing a statement of the amount due on the Bond and Mortgage and whether any offsets or defenses exist against the Mortgage Debt, as hereinbefore provided.

Receiver 5. That the holder of this Bond and Mortgage, in any action to foreclose the Mortgage, shall be entitled to the appointment of a receiver.

Taxes, etc. 6. That the Mortgagor will pay all taxes, assessments or water rates, and in default thereof, the Mortgagee may pay the same.

Statement of amount due 7. Within five days after request in person or within ten days after request by mail, Mortgagor shall give to Mortgagee a signed statement of the amount due on this Bond and Mortgage and whether there are any offsets or defenses against the Debt.

Notices 8. That notice and demand or request may be in writing and may be served in person or by mail.

Title 9. That the Mortgagor warrant the title to the premises.

Lien Law Section 13 10. That the Mortgagor will receive the advances secured by this Mortgage and will hold the right to receive such advances as a trust fund to be applied first for the purpose of paying the cost of improvement, and will apply the same first to the payment of the cost of improvement before using any part of the total of the same for any other purpose.

Sale or assignment 11. That in the event the premises covered by this Mortgage are sold without the written consent of the Mortgagee, or should the Mortgagor make a voluntary assignment for the benefit of creditors, the whole amount of principal and interest hereby secured shall become immediately due and payable at the option of the Mortgagee.

Changes 12. This Bond and Mortgage cannot be changed or ended except in writing signed by Mortgagee.

Rights 13. Mortgagee shall have all the rights set forth in Section 254 of the New York Real Property Law in addition to Mortgagee's rights set forth in this Bond and Mortgage, even if the rights are different from each other.

Parties Bound 14. If there are more than one Mortgagor each shall be separately liable. The words "Mortgagor" and "Mortgagee" shall include their heirs, executors, administrators, successors and assigns. If there are more than one Mortgagor or Mortgagee the words "Mortgagor" and "Mortgagee" used in this Mortgage includes them.

Signatures IN WITNESS WHEREOF, this Bond and Mortgage has been duly signed and sealed by the Mortgagor as of the date at the top of the first page.

WITNESS

MORTGAGOR

John J. Smith [L.S.]

Katherine Ann Smith [L.S.]

STATE OF NEW YORK, COUNTY OF   ss.:
On   19   , before me personally came   to me known, who, being by me duly sworn, did depose and say that deponent resides at No.   deponent is   of   the corporation described in and which executed, the foregoing instrument; deponent knows the seal of said corporation; that the seal affixed to said instrument is such corporate seal; that it was so affixed by order of the Board of Directors of said corporation; that deponent signed deponent's name thereto by like order.

STATE OF NEW YORK, COUNTY OF   ERIE   ss.:
On   September 1   19 83, before me personally came   John J. Smith and Katherine Ann Smith, his wife

to me known to be the individualS described in, and who executed the foregoing instrument, and acknowledged that they executed the same.

notary public

[D509]

NOTE

What effect does a mortgage have on title to the underlying land? Many states continue to follow the "title theory" of mortgages, clinging to the early common law view that the mortgagee holds title from the moment the mortgage is executed to the time that the underlying obligation is paid or the mortgage is foreclosed. A majority of states, however, now follow the "lien theory," under which the mortgagee has only a lien on the property to secure the mortgagor's performance.

The basic distinction between the two theories lies in the right to possession. In title theory states the mortgagee has the right, rarely exercised, to possess the land from the moment the mortgage is given. In lien theory states the mortgagor has the right to possession unless and until foreclosure occurs. In a third group of states, following the "intermediate theory," the mortgagor has the right to possession until default on the underlying obligation.

Though much written about, the distinctions between these three theories have little practical consequence since title and intermediate states effectively clothe the mortgagor with virtually all of the attributes of ownership. Further, the distinctions are easily circumvented by agreement between borrower and lender. See generally, G. Osborne, G. Nelson, & D. Whitman, Real Estate Finance Law §§ 4.1–4.3 (1979).

1. THE FORMS OF LAND FINANCE

B. RUDDEN & H. MOSELEY, AN OUTLINE OF THE LAW OF MORTGAGES
3–6, 8 (1967).

1. THE MORTGAGE AT COMMON LAW

Mortgages of land were made in England long before there was any system of law common to the whole country. There are records of mortgages in Anglo-Saxon days, and at the period immediately after the Conquest when Domesday Book was being compiled. But there was no effective common law over the whole of England until the first half of the 12th century, and it is therefore impossible to state the doctrines of the law concerning mortgages before that time. Even then the practice is obscure, but it is clear that lending money at interest was both a moral wrong and a crime against the usury laws. Even a feudal economy, however, could not flourish without some means of financing development, and so the earliest transactions had to provide both security to the lender and some means of enabling him to obtain a return on his loan in lieu of the forbidden interest. So the lender took a lease of the land, went into possession, and farmed or otherwise managed it, using the profits to pay off the principal—in which case the transaction was called a "live pledge" (in Norman French, *vif gage*). Alternatively, in the harsher type of deal, the lender used the profits of the land for his own gain, leaving the principal advance still owing. This was the "dead pledge" or *mort gage*. The disadvantage of this situation from the point of view of the lender was that, being a mere tenant, he was not, at that time, well protected by the courts. In particular, if he were evicted, his only remedy was damages; so the whole value of the arrangement was lost to him, as he could not be sure of keeping his hands on the land itself. To be absolutely secure he had to be able to show that he was a *freeholder*. Consequently, by the end of the 15th century, most lenders insist that the land be conveyed to them *in fee simple*, in return for the loan. The transaction is still a mortgage, of course, not an out-and-out sale, and so the fee simple is transferred subject to a condition that, if the loan is repaid on the date agreed, the borrower may re-enter the land and claim the fee simple. As a further precaution, and to provide documentary evidence that the borrower has repaid the loan and redeemed the land, the lender covenants that, on repayment, he will re-convey the fee simple.

This gives the lender a great deal of security and, as the usury laws after 1545 allowed interest to be charged (subject to maximum rates), there was not the same need for the lender to go into possession to disguise interest as profits. Consequently, the practice grew of leaving the borrower in possession. In a case in 1620 we find a proviso "that the mortgagee, his heirs and assigns shall not intermeddle with the actual possession of the premises or perception of the rents until default of payment" and after the Restoration this practice became a commonplace.

The lender could afford to leave the borrower in possession since, from the former's point of view, the transaction is simply an investment of money and since he could, if necessary, evict the borrower at once.

Thus the later mortgage at common law consisted of a conveyance of his estate by the borrower (who was, and is, called the mortgagor) to the lender (the mortgagee) as security for the debt or loan owing to or advanced by the latter. The conveyance was a transfer of the fee simple, as a vendor might convey it to a purchaser; but it contained the "proviso for redemption", i.e., a stipulation that, if the mortgagor should repay the debt with a certain rate of interest upon it, *at an agreed date* (usually six months hence) the mortgagee would reconvey the fee simple to the mortgagor.

The common law enforced strictly the proviso for redemption— after all, said the judges, that was what the parties had agreed. Consequently the borrower had one chance *and one only* to redeem his property—on the agreed date. If he did not do so then, at common law, the lender's estate was absolute and could never be redeemed. The transaction was regarded primarily as a bargain between the parties; and, as in the case of any other bargain, the law would enforce it according to its terms . . . .

The above is a description of the classical form of the mortgage— a form which it retained until 1925, a form which determines the present appearance of a mortgage deed, and a form which is one long lie. The reason for this is the intervention of equity.

2. THE MORTGAGE IN EQUITY

We have seen that the mortgagor whose date for redemption had passed could not approach the common law courts and ask them to make the lender re-convey the land on receipt of the money. But if the mortgagor petitioned the Court of Chancery he might well succeed . . . .

It will be obvious that the mortgage was a fertile field for the growth of the Chancellor's powers. Up to the early 17th century, he would give relief only in special cases as where there was some fraud on the part of the lender, or the borrower's inability to repay on the exact date arose through some accident. After that time, however, Chancery took the view that *all* mortgages were no more than a borrowing upon security, and it became settled that the mortgagor was entitled to redeem at any time, notwithstanding that the date on which he had promised to do so was long past. If the lender refused to allow redemption, Chancery would order him to reconvey the estate . . . .

It is most important—even today—to understand this dual nature of the mortgage, which resulted from the fact that the transaction could come before two separate courts. The common law court would do nothing unless the borrower repaid the loan on the agreed date; and, since the lender already had the fee simple conveyed to him by the mortgage, on default in repayment by the mortgagor he was, at common law, the absolute owner. Equity, however, would still intervene, treating the *borrower* as the owner, and confining the mortgagee's rights to those necessary to secure his advance. This affected profoundly the rights of the parties. The practice grew of stipulating in the mortgage deed that the loan should be repaid in six months' time. Usually, of course, both parties expected the loan to be outstanding for a much longer time—after all, it is an investment by the lender. The date was put in, however, so that the mortgagee could, if necessary, call in his loan at any time thereafter; and, as will be shown, he has several remedies to enforce his right to the money. As far as the borrower is concerned, he has two rights to redeem: the *contractual right* on the date specified in the deed, and the *equitable right* to redeem *at any time* thereafter, on paying principal, interest and costs and giving proper notice to the mortgagee.

This equitable right to redeem could be ended by the court itself in an application by the mortgagee—for what the Chancellor had created, he could end. This process of curtailing the equitable right to redeem and so leaving the mortgagee with a fee simple absolute both at law and in equity, is known as *foreclosure*.

SEBASTIAN v. FLOYD

Supreme Court of Kentucky, 1979.
585 S.W.2d 381.

AKER, Justice.

This case presents the question whether a clause in an installment land sale contract providing for forfeiture of the buyer's payments upon the buyer's default may be enforced by the seller.

The movant, Jean Sebastian, contracted on November 8, 1974, to buy a house and lot situated in Covington, Kentucky, from Perl and Zona Floyd, respondents in this motion for review. Sebastian paid $3,800.00 down and was to pay the balance of the $10,900.00 purchase price, plus taxes, insurance, and interest at the rate of $8^1/_2\%$ per annum, in monthly installments of $120.00. A forfeiture clause in the contract provided that if Sebastian failed to make any monthly payment and remained in default for 60 days, the Floyds could terminate the contract and retain all payments previously made as rent and liquidated damages.

During the next 21 months, Sebastian missed seven installments. Including her down payment, she paid the Floyds a total of $5,480.00, rather than the $6,320.00 which was called for by the terms of the contract. Of this amount, $4,300.00, or nearly 40% of the contract price, had been applied against the principal.

The Floyds brought suit in the Kenton Circuit Court against Sebastian in August, 1976, seeking a judgment of $700.00 plus compensation for payments for taxes and insurance, and seeking enforcement of the forfeiture clause. Sebastian admitted by her answer that she was in default but asked the court not to enforce the forfeiture clause. Sebastian counterclaimed for all payments made pursuant to the contract. On advice of counsel, Sebastian ceased to make payments after the institution of this law suit.

The case was referred to a master commissioner for hearing. The commissioner recommended termination of the land sale contract and enforcement of the forfeiture clause. The Kenton Circuit Court entered a judgment adopting the commissioner's recommendations. On appeal, the Court of Appeals affirmed. We granted discretionary review to consider the validity of the forfeiture clause. We reverse.

When a typical installment land contract is used as the means of financing the purchase of property, legal title to the property remains in the seller until the buyer has paid the entire contract price or some agreed-upon portion thereof, at which time the seller tenders a deed to the buyer. However, equitable title passes to the buyer when the contract is entered. The seller holds nothing but the bare legal title, as security for the payment of the purchase price.

There is no practical distinction between the land sale contract and a purchase money mortgage, in which the seller conveys legal title to the buyer but retains a lien on the property to secure payment. The significant feature of each device is the seller's financing the buyer's purchase of the property, using the property as collateral for the loan.

Where the purchaser of property has given a mortgage and subsequently defaults on his payments, his entire interest in the property is not forfeited. The mortgagor has the right to redeem the property by paying the full debt plus interest and expenses incurred by the creditor due to default. In order to cut off the mortgagor's right to redeem, the mortgagee must request a court to sell the property at public auction. From the proceeds of the sale, the mortgagee recovers the amount owed him on the mortgage, as well as the expenses of bringing suit; the mortgagor is entitled to the balance, if any.

The modern trend is for courts to treat land sale contracts as analogous to conventional mortgages, thus requiring a seller to seek a judicial sale of the property upon the buyer's default. It was stated in Skendzel v. Marshall, 261 Ind. 226, 301 N.E.2d 641, 648 (1973):

> "A conditional land contract in effect creates a vendor's lien in the property to secure the unpaid balance owed under the contract. This lien is closely analogous to a mortgage—in fact, the vendor is commonly referred to as an 'equitable mortgagee.' . . . In view of this characterization of the vendor as a lienholder, it is only logical that such a lien be enforced through foreclosure proceedings."

We are of the opinion that a rule treating the seller's interest as a lien will best protect the interests of both buyer and seller. Ordinarily, the seller will receive the balance due on the contract, plus expenses, thus fulfilling the expectations he had when he agreed to sell his land. In addition, the buyer's equity in the property will be protected.

This holding comports with our decision in Real Estate and Mortgage Co. of Louisville v. Duke, 251 Ky. 385, 65 S.W.2d 81 (1933), wherein it was stated at page 82 of 65 S.W.2d:

> "The forfeiture clause was intended simply as a security for the payment of the purchase price. In these circumstances the forfeiture provided for by the contract will be disregarded . . . ."

Respondents contend the preponderance of Kentucky cases permits enforcement of forfeiture clauses in land sale contracts. However, installment land contracts were not involved in two of the cases cited in respondents' brief. In Ward Real Estate v. Childers, 223 Ky. 302, 3 S.W.2d 601 (1928), and Graves v. Winer, Ky., 351 S.W.2d 193 (1961), this court permitted retention by the sellers of "earnest money" deposited pursuant to an executory deposit receipt agreement. The ordinary short-term real estate contract presents a situation very different from the case at bar. Such an agreement generally provides that in the event the buyer fails to perform the contract, the seller may retain the down payment (usually no more than ten per cent of the contract price) as liquidated damages. In *Ward*, supra, and *Graves*, supra, the sum specified as liquidated damages clearly bore a reasonable relation to the actual damages suffered by the seller, which damages would be difficult to ascertain. Our holding therefore has no bearing on the typical earnest money deposit.

Respondents also cite Maschinot v. Moore, 275 Ky. 36, 120 S.W.2d 750 (1938). Their reliance on that case is misplaced, however, because there the court dealt with the question whether the vendor could maintain an action in ejectment against the vendee under a land sale contract; the court did not address the issue of the enforceability of a forfeiture clause such as that in the instant case.

In Miles v. Proffitt, Ky., 266 S.W.2d 333 (1954), we held that a party to an installment land sale contract who had advanced money in part performance and then failed to make further payments was not entitled to recover any of the money so advanced. The court relied on Kravitz v. Grimm, 273 Ky. 18, 115 S.W.2d 368 (1938), as authority for its holding in *Miles*. To the extent *Miles* and *Kravitz* uphold the validity of forfeiture clauses in installment land sale contracts, they are overruled. The seller's remedy for breach of the contract is to obtain a judicial sale of the property.

The judgment of the trial court and the opinion of the Court of Appeals are reversed and the case remanded for further proceedings consistent with this opinion.

All concur except STERNBERG, J., who did not sit.

KOENIG v. VAN REKEN

Court of Appeals of Michigan, 1979.
89 Mich.App. 102, 279 N.W.2d 590.

V.J. BRENNAN, Presiding Judge.

In October of 1974, plaintiff Helen Koenig brought suit in Oakland County Circuit Court to have a warranty deed executed by her to defendants Van Reken declared an equitable mortgage. The original complaint was later supplemented to add a count against the defendants for unjust enrichment. The defendants moved for a summary judgment under GCR 1963, 117.2(1) claiming that the plaintiff failed to state a claim upon which relief could be granted. The plaintiff appeals by right the lower court's granting of the defendants' motion, but contests only the dismissal of the equitable mortgage count. Our review is thus limited to the question of whether the trial court under GCR 1963, 117.2(1) properly dismissed the action regarding the imposition of an equitable mortgage. . . .

In 1970, plaintiff owned a home in Oakland County with a market value of $60,000 that was encumbered by three mortgages totaling $25,933.26. The real estate taxes on plaintiff's home had become delinquent and foreclosure proceedings had begun on one of the mortgages. Plaintiff was then approached by defendant, Stanley Van Reken, who proposed that for a fee of 10% he would "service" the mortgages and pay the delinquent taxes. Subsequently, on June 16, 1970, plaintiff and defendant Stanley Van Reken executed three documents that form the basis of this action.

The first of these documents, entitled "AGREEMENT", stated that plaintiff desired to prevent the loss of her home and provided that defendant Stanley Van Reken purchase the property, redeem it from tax sale and mortgage foreclosure, and give plaintiff an exclusive right to repurchase according to the terms of a lease-option agreement that was also executed between the parties.

The second document was a warranty deed which conveyed the property from plaintiff to defendants for a stated consideration of $28,600. Plaintiff alleges that the deed was silent as to consideration when she signed it, that the figure of $28,600 was added subsequently, and that she never received any such consideration.

The third document provided that Stanley Van Reken was to lease the premises to plaintiff for a 3-year period at a fixed monthly rent of $300. Plaintiff was also to receive an exclusive option to repurchase the premises during the term of the lease for a price of $32,318.79, with a downpayment of $3,500 and monthly payments of $300 which were to include taxes, insurance, principal and interest.

At no time during the negotiations that led to the execution of these documents was plaintiff represented by an attorney, and all three documents were prepared by Stanley Van Reken.

The parties operated under the lease from June 16, 1970, to February, 1972, and during this time plaintiff made total payments of $5,800. In February, 1972, plaintiff defaulted in a monthly rental payment. Plaintiff was thereupon evicted from the home.

The defendants argue on appeal that the subject transaction cannot be deemed to create an equitable mortgage since it has not been alleged that the deed was given to secure an obligation owed by the plaintiff to the defendants. The defendants contend that the "obligation owed" is a necessary requisite to establish an equitable mortgage "as a matter of law".

The defendants' argument not only shows a lack of understanding of the nature and purpose of equitable relief but overlooks well-established Michigan case law on point. The court of equity protects the necessitous by looking through form to the substance of the transaction. Although no set criterion has been established, the controlling factor in determining whether a deed absolute on its face should be deemed a mortgage is the intention of the parties. Such intention may be gathered from the circumstances attending the transaction including the conduct and relative economic positions of the parties and the value of the property in relation to the price fixed in the alleged sale. Under Michigan law, it is well settled that the adverse financial condition of the grantor, coupled with the inadequacy of the purchase price for the property, is sufficient to establish a deed absolute on its face to be a mortgage. Ellis v. Wayne Real Estate Co., 357 Mich. 115, 97 N.W.2d 758 (1959).

In *Ellis, supra*, the plaintiffs initially sought a loan from defendant to save their home from forfeiture. After hurried negotiations, the plaintiffs executed a quit claim deed to defendant and simultaneously entered into a land contract under which the plaintiffs were to repurchase the property. The defendant then satisfied a default and paid the delinquent taxes. In noting the discrepancy between the price paid by the defendant and the value of the property, the Court held that the transaction constituted a loan by defendant secured by a mortgage on the property.

In taking the plaintiff's well-pleaded facts in the present case as true, there is a close parallel with *Ellis, supra.* Here the plaintiff, while in financial distress, sought help from the defendants in saving her home from foreclosure. Although plaintiff was not desirous of selling her home, she entered into a transaction which conveyed her equity worth over $30,000 for less than $4,000. While financial embarrassment of the grantor and inadequacy of consideration do not provide an infallible test, they are an indication that the parties did not consider the conveyance to be absolute. We note that the leaseback arrangement entered into by the parties effectively circumvented the right to redeem, which is designed to protect purchasers such as plaintiff in times of financial crisis. In applying these facts to the aforementioned case law, it could be found without difficulty that the subject transaction constituted a mortgage to secure a loan in the amount of defendants' initial expenditure.

We reverse the order granting summary judgment in favor of the defendant on the equitable mortgage count and remand for trial on this issue.

NOTES

1. A financing arrangement arises any time one person provides part or all of the capital needed to support another's activities in return for repayment of the capital, plus consideration, over a period of time. Although mortgages and deeds of trust are the instruments most popularly associated with land finance, many other arrangements also qualify. Installment land contracts like the one in *Sebastian* are often used to finance the acquisition of housing or of undeveloped land. Leases are also financing arrangements. The leased premises represent the asset lent by the landlord to the tenant; in return, the tenant pays rent for use of the premises. (If, as sometimes happens, the lease gives the tenant an option to buy the premises at the end of the term at a specified price, the lease begins to look much more like an installment land contract or even a purchase money mortgage or deed of trust given by buyer to seller.)

Lawyers structuring real estate transactions must help to select the financing form that will best accommodate the parties' interests. One pitfall to be avoided is the ever-present risk that the form the parties select will later be judicially recast into some other form, as happened in both *Sebastian* and *Koenig*. Judicial recharacterization of a financing arrangement will obviously disrupt the expectations of the immediate parties; it may unsettle the expectations of third parties as well. If Van Reken had recorded his putative deed from Koenig and then sold the premises to a third party who had no notice of the underlying transaction, would—and should—the third party be bound by the deed's later recharacterization as an equitable mortgage? For a court to protect the third party purchaser in this situation will only encourage grantee-lenders to record and dispose of their putative interests as quickly as they can, leaving the original grantor with only a personal action. See generally, Cunningham & Tischler, Disguised Real Estate Security Transactions as Mortgages in Substance, 26 Rutgers L.Rev. 1 (1972).

2. The Uniform Land Transactions Act (1978) has sought to consolidate the various forms of land finance into a unified structure. Article 3, entitled "Secured Transactions," aims "to provide a simple and unified structure within which the immense variety of financing secured by real estate can go forward with greater certainty and less transaction cost. Under this Article the traditional distinctions among security interests based largely on form or whether the creditor had 'title' to the real estate collateral are not retained. The Article applies to all transactions intended to create a security interest in real estate regardless of form"—including mortgages, deeds of trust, land sales contracts, leases intended as security, and assignments of leases or rents intended as security. Introductory Comment to Article 3.

3. Probably the most important distinction between the different forms of real property security is their contemplated method of foreclosure and sale. Unless a mortgage provides otherwise, the mortgagee must resort to judicial proceedings in order to foreclose the mortgagor's equity of redemption and obtain a sale of the property to satisfy the debt. However, if the mortgage contains a *power of sale,* expressly giving the mortgagee the power to conduct the foreclosure sale herself, and if local statutes do not bar this self help procedure, judicial proceedings are unnecessary and the mortgagee can foreclose simply by public sale after notice to all interested parties.

Lenders in several states have traditionally preferred the deed of trust to the mortgage with power of sale. Like the mortgage with power of sale, the deed of trust enables sale of the encumbered property without resort to judicial process. The deed of trust differs in that, where the mortgage involves two parties—mortgagor and mortgagee—the deed of trust involves three: the borrower ("trustor") conveys title to a third party ("trustee") as security for the trustor's performance of its debt obligation to the lender ("beneficiary"). If the trustor defaults, and if the beneficiary so requests, the trustee will arrange a public nonjudicial sale of the land to satisfy the debt.

For lenders, the original advantage of the deed of trust over the mortgage with power of sale was the freedom that it gave them to bid at the foreclosure sale. Since the sale under a mortgage with power of sale was conducted by the mortgagee, courts and legislatures, concerned about the possibility of self-dealing, barred mortgagees from bidding at their own sales. Because the sale under a deed of trust was conducted by a third party trustee, lawmakers saw no conflict of interest. (This clearly represents form triumphing over substance: more often than not, the third party trustee is the nominee or alter ego of the beneficiary.) Statutes today have eliminated most of the differences between deeds of trust and mortgages with power of sale, and have generally removed the restriction on the mortgagee's ability to bid at her own foreclosure sale. The two forms of security are for this reason treated interchangeably throughout this chapter.

4. *The "Credit Quartet."* All land finance arrangements can be reduced to four variables: interest rate; rate of amortization (the rate at which the loan principal is paid off); length of loan term; and loan-to-value ratio (the ratio between the amount of the loan and the value of the property securing it; thus an $80,000 loan on a property appraised at $100,000 has an 8:10 loan to value ratio, sometimes simply called an 80% loan to value ratio). Each variable can be adjusted to meet the particular needs of borrower and lender. For example, a borrower might agree to a shorter loan term, thereby reducing the lender's exposure and risk, in return for a lower interest rate, a slower amortization rate, or a higher loan to value ratio.

The most dramatic, systemic shift in the orientation of these four variables occurred as a result of the Depression of the 1930's. The standard pre-Depression mortgage instrument had a short-term (typically 5 years); low loan to value ratio (typically 50%); and no amortization (the entire principal was payable as a "balloon" at the end of the term). New Deal programs introduced a strikingly different instrument and encouraged its adoption with the lure of FHA insurance. The new instrument had a much longer term (20 to 30 years); a higher loan to value ratio (typically 80%); and complete amortization over the life of the loan. Most instruments of this period were so-called "level payment" mortgages, calling for an identical monthly payment covering interest and reduction in principal throughout the loan term. Level payment mortgages are still widely used. In the loan's early years, most of the level payment goes toward interest payments and only a small amount toward reduction of principal. But, as principal is reduced, the interest payments on the principal outstanding become smaller and reductions in principal become consequently larger, producing still smaller interest payments and still larger reductions in principal, until the loan is completely paid off.

5. *The "New" Mortgages.* By the mid-1970's, the long-term fixed rate mortgage had become increasingly unattractive to lenders and borrowers alike. With interest rates constantly rising, lenders were reluctant to tie up their capital over a long period at interest rates that they believed would soon fall short of their own cost of

capital. Borrowers disliked the higher interest rates, shorter terms, and lower loan to value ratios that lenders began to require in return for their own diminished prospects. This shared dilemma produced a burst of "creative financing" that often resembled, and bore many of the hazards of, pre-Depression real estate finance. Among the more prominent arrangements proffered were:

(a) *Variable Rate Mortgage.* In a VRM, the interest rate paid by the borrower varies over the life of the loan according to a designated index reflecting current market rates. Since the common wisdom during the 1970's was that interest rates would rise over the long term, VRMs were attractive to lenders because they protected against inflation, and were attractive to borrowers who might thus obtain a lower initial interest rate than under a fixed rate mortgage. Borrowers' concerns that interest increases might exceed increases in their income, thus jeopardizing their ability to make the monthly mortgage payment, were assuaged by legislated limits on the frequency and amount by which interest rates could be increased.

(b) *Renegotiable Rate Mortgage* (also called a "rollover" mortgage). The RRM is a series of renewable short term loans—usually for 3, 4 or 5 years—secured by a long term mortgage—of up to 30 years—with principal fully amortized over the longer term. At the end of each short term loan period, the borrower can choose between "rolling over" into a new loan, or paying off the loan; if the borrower rolls over, all terms of the new loan, except interest rate, will be identical to those of the old; the interest rate is negotiable within prescribed limits.

(c) *Graduated Payment Mortgage.* The GPM is a long-term, fixed rate mortgage whose monthly payment gradually increases over the life of the loan. Although payments in the early years of the loan will be insufficient to amortize the principal, or even to pay all of the interest on the loan, the increased payments in the loan's later years are calculated to make up for the difference. The GPM was designed to meet the needs of younger borrowers who cannot initially afford the monthly payments required by a conventional fixed rate mortgage, but who expect their income to increase over the years to a point at which they can afford to pay more than the fixed monthly rate. (Does the GPM expose lenders to the risk that, if the borrower defaults in the early years of the loan, the outstanding debt will exceed the value of the property, with the result that the lender is undersecured? Can the loan-to-value variable be manipulated to avoid this result?)

(d) *Shared Appreciation Mortgage.* A SAM is usually a short term—5 to 10 year—mortgage in which the interest rate is reduced below market levels in return for the lender's right to receive a predetermined portion of the property's increase in value—if any—over the life of the loan. (In a typical SAM, the interest rate would be reduced by about ⅓ in exchange for ⅓ of the property's appreciation.)

(e) *Reverse Annuity Mortgages.* RAMs are aimed at the plight not of young, first-time homebuyers, but rather of older homeowners on fixed incomes who find it increasingly difficult to make ends meet. Essentially, the RAM is designed to enable these homeowners to draw cash out of the accumulated equity in their homes, without the bother or dislocation of selling the house itself. The typical RAM enables the homeowner effectively to use the equity in her home as security for an annuity, giving her monthly payments over her lifetime or some predetermined period. With each monthly payment from the lender, the borrower's debt to the lender, secured by the house, increases. In the usual RAM, the entire debt is to be repaid at the earlier of 10 years from the beginning of the loan, or the death of the borrower, with funds to come from the sale of the property or probate of the homeowner's estate.

See generally, Comment, The New Mortgages: A Functional Legal Analysis, 10 Fla.St.U.L.Rev. 95 (1982); Izeman, Alternative Mortgage Instruments: Their Effect on Residential Financing, 10 Real Est.L.J. 3 (1981).

2. OBLIGATIONS OF DEBTOR

DAUGHARTHY v. MONRITT ASSOCIATES

Supreme Court of Maryland, 1982.
293 Md. 399, 444 A.2d 1030.

DAVIDSON, Judge.

In recent years, the wrap-around mortgage has achieved widespread use in the financing of real estate transactions. This case concerns the application of principles of real property law to wrap-around mortgages. More particularly, this case presents a question concerning the circumstances under which an assumption of the obligation to pay a debt embodied in a pre-existing deed of trust will be implied when a buyer has executed a subsequent deed of trust providing that it is "subject to and wraps around" the pre-existing deed of trust.

In 1977, the appellants, Alan L. Daugharthy and Elizabeth Daugharthy, sold certain real property to the appellee, Monritt Associates, a Maryland Limited Partnership, for $200,000.00. At settlement, Monritt gave the appellants a promissory note and a deferred purchase money deed of trust dated 21 September 1977 (pre-existing 1977 deed of trust) securing the principal sum of $163,036.00 with interest at the rate of $8^{1}/_{2}\%$ per annum. The pre-existing 1977 deed of trust provided in pertinent part:

"The parties agree that the said deferred purchase price Deed of Trust *shall be assumable by a later purchaser*, should grantor herein sell the property to a third party, provided, however, that the note holders, or assignee or assignees, shall have the right to change the rate of interest to a prevailing rate of interest as of the time of such assumption." (Emphasis added.)

In 1980, Monritt (seller) sold the property to Joseph Gerald Kurtinitis and Sandra Kurtinitis (buyers) for $275,000.00. At settlement, the buyers gave the seller a promissory note and a deferred purchase money wrap-around deed of trust (1980 wrap-around deed of trust) securing a principal sum of $235,000.00 with interest at the rate of 10% per annum. The 1980 wrap-around deed of trust provided in pertinent part:

"This Deed of Trust *is subject to and 'WRAPS AROUND' that certain Deed of Trust dated September 21, 1977* and recorded in Liber 5035 at Folio 135 of the Land Records of Montgomery County, Maryland. The unpaid principal balance of the indebtedness secured by said Deed of Trust, as of January 21, 1980, is approximately $158,347.00 and that amount is *included* in the indebtedness of $235,000.00 secured hereby. *The holder* of the promissory note secured hereby, *in accepting monthly payments* hereunder, *agrees to pay from such payments the monthly payments as required by the terms of the aforementioned Deed of Trust* as such payments become due and payable on the Note secured by said Deed of Trust dated September 21, 1977 and recorded in Liber 5035 at Folio 135. *In the event the holder* of the promissory note secured hereby *fails to make the payments* as required under the terms of the above referred 'WRAPPED AROUND' Deed of Trust *the grantor herein shall be entitled to pay such installment due on said 'WRAPPED AROUND' Deed of Trust* and to apply such payment as a credit against the next installment due under the promissory note secured hereby.

"The grantor further agrees to comply with all of the terms, covenants and conditions of said 'WRAPPED AROUND' Deed of Trust, *other than with respect to the liability for the payment of the principal sum and/or the payment of the monthly installments of principal and interest due under said Deed of Trust.* In the event the grantor shall fail to so comply with any of the terms, provisions and conditions of said 'WRAPPED AROUND' Deed of Trust and such failure shall result in a default thereunder, *except with respect to the payment of the monthly pay-*

ments of principal and interest and the liability for the payment of the principal sum, such failure on the part of the grantor herein shall automatically constitute a default under this Deed of Trust . . . ." (Emphasis added.)

The settlement sheet applicable to this transaction showed the $235,000.00 indebtedness under the 1980 wrap-around deed of trust as a debit to the seller against the $275,000.00 purchase price.

In 1980, the appellants notified the buyers and the seller that they viewed the 1980 wrap-around deed of trust as an assumption of the pre-existing 1977 deed of trust and were electing to increase the rate of interest on the obligation embodied in the pre-existing 1977 deed of trust from 8½% per annum to 14% per annum. The buyers responded that they had taken the property "subject to" the pre-existing 1977 deed of trust and that the transaction did not involve an assumption of the debt embodied in that pre-existing encumbrance. Thereafter, the appellants notified the seller that they were demanding the unpaid balance and accrued interest outstanding on the pre-existing 1977 deed of trust and that failure to respond within 10 days would result in the immediate institution of foreclosure proceedings.

On 31 March 1980, in the Circuit Court for Montgomery County, the seller filed a Bill of Complaint for Declaratory Judgment and For Injunction to Stay Foreclosure. The complaint requested a declaration that the seller was not in default under the pre-existing 1977 deed of trust and that it was not liable for payment of an increased rate of interest. The complaint also sought an injunction against the appellants prohibiting them from instituting a foreclosure proceeding.

After a hearing on cross motions for summary judgment, the trial court found that the 1980 wrap-around deed of trust embodied an express agreement that the buyers had not assumed the obligation to pay the debt arising from the pre-existing 1977 deed of trust. The trial court granted the seller's motion for summary judgment and denied the appellants' motion for summary judgment. On 9 February 1981, the trial court entered a decree declaring that the seller was not in default of payments due under the pre-existing 1977 deed of trust. The trial court's order enjoined the appellants from accelerating the sum due under the pre-existing 1977 deed of trust, from increasing the rate of interest under that encumbrance, and from instituting foreclosure proceedings.

On 23 February 1981, the appellants filed an appeal to the Court of Special Appeals. On 9 April 1981, they filed a petition for a writ of certiorari to this Court. We issued a writ of certiorari before consideration by that Court.

Here, as in the trial court, the appellants' basic contention is that the buyers assumed the obligation to pay the pre-existing 1977 deed of trust. This position is premised upon three factors. Relying on

Brice v. Griffin, 269 Md. 558, 307 A.2d 660 (1973), the appellants initially assert that an assumption must be implied because the settlement sheet reflects that the buyers elected to deduct the amount due on the pre-existing 1977 deed of trust from the purchase price. The appellants further assert that an assumption must be implied because the buyers are in fact making the payments due under the pre-existing 1977 deed of trust. In support of this position, they point out that the 1980 wrap-around deed of trust expressly provides that the seller must make the monthly payments due under the pre-existing 1977 deed of trust from monthly payments made by the buyers under the 1980 wrap-around deed of trust. Additionally, the appellants allege that an assumption must be implied because the pre-existing 1977 deed of trust requires a subsequent purchaser to assume the obligations of that encumbrance. In support of this position, they point out that the pre-existing 1977 deed of trust expressly provides that that encumbrance "shall be assumable by a later purchaser." The appellants conclude that because the buyers assumed the obligations of the pre-existing 1977 deed of trust, the appellants were justified in demanding a change in the rate of interest. We do not agree.

In Maryland, there is a distinction between the sale of property "subject to" an existing mortgage or deed of trust and such a sale with an assumption of an existing mortgage or deed of trust. Ordinarily, when there is a sale of property subject to an existing mortgage or deed of trust, the purchaser does not become personally responsible for payment of the obligation. However, when there is an assumption of an existing mortgage or deed of trust, the buyer undertakes personal responsibility for the payment of the obligation arising under the existing encumbrance. The purchase of property subject to a specified encumbrance is not an agreement to assume and pay the encumbrance. In order to establish that an assumption has occurred, there must be an agreement, express or implied, written or parol, incorporated in or separate from the deed conveying the property. Such an agreement may be shown so long as it does not tend to vary or contradict the material terms of the deed. In the absence of an express contrary agreement, an assumption will be implied when the amount due under the trust obligation has been deducted from the purchase price.

These principles were most recently articulated in *Brice*. There, the sellers sold the buyers a building for $64,221.23. The buyers were to take title "subject to a first and second deed of trust." The settlement statement showed the amounts due under the first and second trust, as debits against the purchase price indicating that the buyers had elected to deduct the amounts due under the first and second trust from the purchase price.

This Court held that in the absence of an express contrary agreement the buyers' election to deduct from the purchase price the amounts due under the pre-existing deeds of trust constituted an agreement to assume the obligation to pay the amounts due under the pre-existing deeds of trust. In reaching this result, this Court said:

> "The law is clear in this State that the mere purchase of a property subject to an existing mortgage or deed of trust does not create a personal obligation on the part of the purchaser to pay it. But, the law here is equally clear, if the purchaser assumes the payment of an existing mortgage or deed of trust as a part of the purchase price of the property, then, in that event, it becomes his duty to satisfy the obligation, and to protect his vendor against any demands that may be made for payment of the debt it secures. *Whether the purchaser as between a vendor and vendee assumes the payment of such an existing obligation is a matter for agreement, which may be either express or implied, written or parol, and even separate from the deed conveying the property; but, in the absence of an express contrary agreement, an assumption will be implied when, as here, the amount then due under the trust obligation has been deducted from the purchase price.*
>
> "In this case, the appellants contracted to take title to the apartment property 'subject to the first and second deed of trust.' Standing alone, and without relating it to the agreed upon purchase price, that language would mean that Brice and Gaddis acquired only the equity of redemption and thereby assumed no personal responsibility to pay the obligations created by the existing deeds of trust. But here, as the settlement sheet demonstrates, instead of paying the purchase price in full, appellants elected to deduct from that price the sums due under the two existing trusts. . . . "

Here, unlike *Brice*, there was an express agreement between the buyers and seller governing, as between them, the obligation to pay the amount due under the pre-existing 1977 deed of trust. The 1980 wrap-around deed of trust provides that it is "subject to" the pre-existing 1977 deed of trust. It states that the balance of the indebtedness secured by the pre-existing 1977 deed of trust is included in the amount of indebtedness secured by the 1980 wrap-around deed of trust. It further states that the seller, who receives the buyers' monthly payments under the 1980 wrap-around trust, agrees to pay monthly payments to the appellants under the pre-existing 1977 deed of trust. It additionally states that in the event of the seller's default, the buyers are entitled, but not obligated, to make monthly payments due under the pre-existing 1977 deed of trust to the appellants. Finally, the 1980 wrap-around deed of trust expressly provides that the buyers are not personally liable for the payment of the amounts due under the pre-existing 1977 deed of trust.

The language of the 1980 wrap-around deed of trust is plain and unambiguous. It establishes the seller's obligation to pay the amount due under the pre-existing 1977 deed of trust. More important, it negates an intention on the part of the buyers to assume personal responsibility to pay the obligations arising under the pre-existing 1977 deed of trust. In light of the express language embodied in the 1980 wrap-around deed of trust governing the obligations of the buyers and the seller to pay the amounts due under the pre-existing 1977 deed of trust, we can only conclude that the buyers did not agree to assume personal responsibility to pay the obligations arising under that pre-existing encumbrance.

Under the circumstances here, the seller was not in default of payments due under the pre-existing 1977 deed of trust. The trial court did not err in enjoining the appellants from accelerating the sum due under the pre-existing 1977 deed of trust, from increasing the rate of interest under that encumbrance, and from instituting foreclosure proceedings. Accordingly, we shall affirm the judgment of the trial court.

Judgment affirmed.

NOTES

1. A mortgagee typically has two avenues of relief against a defaulting mortgagor. She may proceed against the mortgagor personally on his promise, embodied in his note or bond, to repay the mortgage debt. And she may proceed against the land securing the promise by foreclosure and sale, using the sale proceeds to satisfy the personal debt.

Relief becomes a bit more complicated when the mortgagor has transferred the encumbered land. If the transferee has *taken subject to* the mortgage, the mortgagee will have no recourse against the transferee personally but can, as before, obtain relief against the mortgagor personally or against the land through foreclosure. If the mortgagee chooses to proceed against the mortgagor personally, the mortgagor, once having paid the debt, becomes subrogated to the mortgagee's rights against the land and can thus obtain reimbursement from the land itself through foreclosure, sale and satisfaction of the debt out of the sale proceeds.

If, by contrast, the transferee has *assumed* the mortgagor's personal liability for the debt, the mortgagee will be able to obtain relief not only from the mortgagor and from the land, but also from the transferee personally. If the mortgagee elects to proceed against the mortgagor personally, the mortgagor can obtain reimbursement by proceeding both against the transferee on his promise and against the land, which remains the primary security for the debt. See generally, G. Osborne, G. Nelson, D. Whitman, Real Estate Finance Law §§ 5.2–5.11 (1979).

2. Why did *Brice*, discussed in *Daugharthy*, attach so much weight to whether the parties initially stated the unencumbered value

of the parcel and then subtracted the outstanding mortgage, or simply stated the value of the parcel as encumbered—implying an assumption of the mortgage in the first situation, but not in the second? Although several courts follow the *Brice* approach, many reject it, as do most of the commentators, principally because it attaches too much consequence to a purely formal distinction. See, for example, Warm, Some Aspects of the Rights and Liabilities of Mortgagee, Mortgagor and Grantee, 10 Temp.L.Q. 116, 119–121 (1936).

3. *Due on Sale Clauses.* Lenders frequently require that their loan instruments include a due on sale clause, accelerating the loan and making it fully payable upon the borrower's sale of the land, and effectively preventing the new buyer from either assuming or taking subject to his seller's mortgage. One traditional justification for due on sale clauses is that they protect the lender against the possibility that the new owner will be less creditworthy or less inclined to maintain the premises than the original borrower, thus increasing the prospect of default and impairing the security for the loan.

The dramatically increasing interest rates of the 1970's supplied an additional reason for due on sale clauses: by enforcing a due on sale clause and requiring the original borrower to pay off a loan that had been made when interest rates were low, the lender could recapture funds for relending at the higher, prevailing market rates. (As a lender, how would you feel about holding a 30-year, $100,000 note with fixed interest of 6% and 20 years to run, in a market in which interest rates are 12% and rising?) Sellers obviously disliked due on sale clauses because, without one, a seller could transfer her property subject to a mortgage bearing a below market interest rate and obtain from her buyer, as additional consideration for the property, the capitalized value of the difference between the interest rate on the existing mortgage and the interest that the buyer would have to pay at current market rates. (As a buyer, how much would you pay your seller for the right to have $100,000 for 20 years at 6% interest rather than at 12% interest?)

This economic conflict between lenders and borrowers inevitably led to a rash of litigation challenging due on sale clauses. Courts in several states invalidated the clauses in whole or in part on the ground that, by inhibiting the original borrower's ability to sell her property, they constituted an unlawful restraint on alienation. For example, in Wellenkamp v. Bank of America, 21 Cal.3d. 943, 148 Cal. Rptr. 379, 582 P.2d 970 (1978), the California Supreme Court rejected the "contention that the lender's interest in maintaining its loan portfolio at current interest rates justifies the restraint imposed by exercise of a due-on clause upon transfer of title in an outright sale," and held that "a due-on clause contained in a promissory note or deed of trust cannot be enforced upon the occurrence of an outright sale unless the lender can demonstrate that enforcement is reasonably necessary to protect against impairment to its security or the risk of default." 21 Cal.3d at 952–953, 148 Cal.Rptr. at 385–386, 582 P.2d at 976–977.

The wave of controversy surrounding the due on sale issue carried it into both the Supreme Court and the Congress. In Fidelity Federal Savings & Loan Association v. De La Cuesta, 458 U.S. 141, 102 S.Ct. 3014, 73 L.Ed.2d 664 (1982), the Court held that a regulation promulgated by the Federal Home Loan Bank Board permitting federal savings and loan associations to exercise due on sale clauses in their mortgages preempted conflicting state law. And the Garn-St. Germain Depository Institutions Act of 1982, Pub.L. 97–320, 96 Stat. 1469, preempts state law prohibitions of due on sale clauses, generally, for transfers occurring after October 15, 1982. Under the Act, the rights and remedies of lender and borrower are to be governed exclusively by the terms of the loan instrument. Recognizing that a "blanket federal preemption of state restrictions on the enforcement of due-on-sale clauses would, however, have an unfair impact on those homebuyers who, despite the contractual terms of their mortgage contracts, relied on state due-on-sale restrictions and reasonably believed they had assumable loans," the Act carved out a "window period" exception "for mortgages made or assumed after state action prohibited the enforcement of due-on-sale clauses." Report of Sen. Comm. on Banking, Housing and Urban Affairs, to Accompany S. 2789, 97th Cong. 2d Sess. p. 22, Sen.Rep. No. 97–536 (1982).

See generally, Note, Due-On-Sale: Recent Developments Affecting the Future of Due-On-Sale Litigation, 59 N.D.L.Rev. 57 (1983); A.B.A.Comm. on Real Estate Financing, Enforcement of Due-on-Transfer Clauses, 13 Real Prop., Prob. & Tr.J. 891 (1978); Dunn & Nowinski, Enforcement of Due-On-Transfer Clauses: An Update, 16 Real Prop., Prob. & Tr.J. 291 (1981) (contains appendix with state-by-state listing of principal due-on-sale cases).

4. *Waste.* Before agreeing to make a home loan, an institutional lender will typically examine the borrower's resources and job prospects in order to assure itself that the borrower will be able to make the mortgage payments over the life of the loan. The lender will also appraise the house and land to assure itself that, in the event of default, the property will, on foreclosure, produce sufficient cash to pay off the outstanding debt. Once the loan is made, there is obviously little the lender can do to keep the borrower gainfully employed. However, the lender can, by appropriate provisions in the mortgage instrument, require that the house and land be kept in good condition so that the loan security remains unimpaired.

Absent an express agreement on the subject between mortgagor and mortgagee, courts will impose a duty on the mortgagor not to waste the premises. (The common law of waste generally is considered at pages 549 to 563 below.) Does the availability of relief for waste, and the fact that mortgagor and mortgagee can by contract increase the mortgagor's duties respecting maintenance of the premises, remove one justification—avoiding impairment of the security—that lenders commonly give for insisting on due on sale clauses?

See generally, Leipziger, The Mortgagee's Remedies for Waste, 64 Calif.L.Rev. 1086 (1976).

3. DEFAULT

CORNELISON v. KORNBLUTH

Supreme Court of California, 1975.
15 Cal.3d 590, 125 Cal.Rptr. 557, 542 P.2d 981.

SULLIVAN, Justice.

In this action for damages for the breach of covenants contained in a deed of trust and for damages for waste, brought by the beneficiary against the trustors and their successors in interest, plaintiff Mary Cornelison appeals from a summary judgment entered in favor of defendant John Kornbluth and against plaintiff. As will appear, we have concluded that upon the record presented, the summary judgment was properly granted and should be affirmed.

On July 15, 1964, plaintiff sold a single-family dwelling in Van Nuys, California, to Maurice and Leona Chanon, taking back a promissory note in the sum of $18,800 secured by a first deed of trust on the property. The deed of trust, recorded on August 21, 1964, contained the following covenants: that the Chanons would pay the real property taxes and assessments against the property; that they would care for and maintain the property; and that if they resold the property, the entire unpaid balance would become immediately due and payable.

On December 10, 1964, the Chanons conveyed the property to defendant by grant deed. On September 6, 1968, defendant sold the property to Richard Larkins. In January 1969 the county health department condemned the house as unfit for human habitation. The Chanons being in default on the promissory note, plaintiff caused the property to be sold at a trustee's sale. Plaintiff purchased the property at the sale for the sum of $21,921.42, that being an amount equal to the balance due on the note plus foreclosure costs.

Plaintiff then brought the instant action for damages, her amended complaint (hereafter "complaint") filed March 24, 1970, setting forth two causes of action, one for breach of contract and one for damages for waste. The first cause of action alleged in substance that defendant "agreed in writing to be bound by and to perform all of the covenants contained in the Note and Deed of Trust theretofore executed by defendants Maurice L. Chanon and Leona Chanon"; and that defendants breached these covenants (a) by selling the property to Larkins, (b) by failing to pay property taxes, (c) by failing to make payments on the note, and (d) by failing to properly care for and maintain the premises.

The second cause of action, after incorporating by reference the material allegations of the first cause of action, alleged in substance that defendant owed a duty to properly and adequately care for the property and that defendant negligently failed to fulfill this duty, thereby causing plaintiff to be damaged in specified particulars and amounts by reason of the loss of improvements to the real property as well as by reason of the loss of its use. On the first cause of action plaintiff prayed for damages in the sum of $18,169.66, and on the second cause of action for damages in the sum of $20,000 plus the reasonable rental of the property, and in addition for $45,000 punitive damages.

Defendant's answer admitted that he purchased the property from the Chanons and sold it to Larkins, but denied all other allegations for lack of information or belief. Defendant then moved for summary judgment. His declaration in support of the motion states in substance that he purchased the subject real property from the Chanons, that at the time of the purchase he knew it was encumbered by the deed of trust in favor of plaintiff as beneficiary, that he never assumed either orally or in writing the indebtedness secured by the deed of trust, and that no such assumption was contained in the deed conveying the property to him. The declaration attaches and incorporates by reference a copy of the grant deed which confirms the last statement.

Defendant also filed in support of the motion the declaration of one of his attorneys stating in substance that plaintiff regained possession of the subject property by purchasing it for $21,921.42 at the foreclosure sale conducted on June 4, 1969, said purchase having been effected "by a full credit bid resulting in the full satisfaction of the remaining indebtedness secured by the deed of trust . . . ." The declaration attaches and incorporates by reference a copy of the "trustees deed upon sale" which confirmed the statements of the declaration. Plaintiff filed no counteraffidavits. The court granted defendant's motion and entered judgment accordingly. This appeal followed.

Plaintiff contends that the court erred in granting summary judgment because the "complaint is regular on its face and raises issues of fact." . . .

. . . For present purposes, we need be concerned only with the following rule: "Summary judgment is proper only if the affidavits in support of the moving party would be sufficient to sustain a judgment in his favor and his opponent does not by affidavit show such facts as may be deemed by the judge hearing the motion sufficient to present a triable issue." (Stationers Corp. v. Dun & Bradstreet, Inc. (1965) 52 Cal.2d 412, 417, 42 Cal.Rptr. 449, 452, 398 P.2d 785, 788.)

Applying the foregoing rule we are satisfied that defendant's declaration is sufficient to support a summary judgment on the first cause of action for breach of contract. As previously stated, the basic theory of this cause of action is that defendant had a duty to comply with the covenants contained in the deed of trust given plaintiff by the Chanons since the document was recorded and its covenants ran with the land. Plaintiff's legal premise is completely erroneous. Upon the transfer of real property covered by a mortgage or deed of trust as security for an indebtedness, the property remains subject to the secured indebtedness but the grantee is not personally liable for the indebtedness or to perform any of the obligations of the mortgage or trust deed unless his agreement to pay the indebtedness, or some note or memorandum thereof, is in writing and subscribed by him or his agent or his assumption of the indebtedness is specifically provided for in the conveyance. (Civ.Code, § 1624, subd. 7; Snidow v. Hill (1948) 87 Cal.App.2d 803, 806–807, 197 P.2d 801.) Defendant's declaration states positively that he never assumed either orally or in writing the indebtedness secured by the Chanon deed of trust and that no such assumption was contained in the deed by which the Chanons conveyed the property to him. An examination of a copy of the deed attached to the declaration confirms this. Plaintiff filed no counterdeclaration denying these allegations and as a consequence raised no triable issue of fact. Contrary to plaintiff's contention, a triable issue of fact cannot be raised by the allegations of her complaint. (Coyne v. Krempels, *supra*, 36 Cal.2d 257, 262, 223 P.2d 244.) Accordingly, summary judgment on the first cause of action was properly granted.

We now proceed to determine whether defendant's declarations are sufficient to support the summary judgment on the second stated cause of action for waste. On this issue we may outline the positions of the parties as follows: Defendant contends that since, as set forth in his attorney's declaration, plaintiff purchased the property for a full credit bid an action for waste is thereby precluded both by reason of the antideficiency legislation (Code Civ.Proc., §§ 580b, 580d; Schumacher v. Gaines (1971) 18 Cal.App.3d 994, 96 Cal.Rptr. 223) and by reason of the extinguishment of the security interest through a full credit bid at the trustee's sale. (Duarte v. Lake Gregory Land and Water Co. (1974) 39 Cal.App.3d 101, 105, 113 Cal.Rptr. 893.) Plaintiff on the other hand contends that an action for waste may be maintained independently of the antideficiency provisions of sections 580b and 580d of the Code of Civil Procedure.

In order to resolve this issue it is necessary to first define, and trace the history of an action for waste and secondly to analyze the impact of the antideficiency legislation induced by the depression of the 1930's upon this traditional action.

Section 2929 of the Civil Code provides: "*Waste.* No person whose interest is subject to the lien of a mortgage may do any act which will substantially impair the mortgagee's security." This section, enacted in 1872, codified a portion of the common law action for waste, as developed in England and adopted in earlier California cases. "[W]aste is conduct (including in this word both acts of commission and of omission) on the part of a person in possession of land which is actionable at the behest of, and for protection of the reasonable expectations of, another owner of an interest in the same land . . . .. Thus, waste is, functionally, a part of the law which keeps in balance the conflicting desires of persons having interests in the same land." (5 Powell on Real Property (1974) § 636, pp. 5–6.) . . .

Over a century ago this court in Robinson v. Russell (1864) 24 Cal. 467, 472–473, relying upon *Van Pelt*, declared that an action on the case could be maintained by the mortgagee of real property for damages for injuries done to the property which impaired the mortgage security and that action for an injunction would lie to restrain the commission of waste on the premises. It was this cause of action that was codified in 1872 as Civil Code section 2929.

Section 2929 of the Civil Code, though referring only to "the lien of a *mortgage*" (italics added) and to the impairment of "the *mortgagee's* security," (italics added) applies equally to a deed of trust, since a mortgage with power of sale and a deed of trust are treated similarly in California and both are considered as security interests protected from impairment. (Hetland, Cal. Real Estate Secured Transactions (Cont.Ed.Bar 1970) § 2.7, pp. 11–12; see American Sav. & Loan Assn. v. Leeds, *supra*, 68 Cal.2d 611, 614, fn. 2, 68 Cal.Rptr. 453, 440 P.2d 933; United States Financial v. Sullivan, *supra*, 37 Cal.App.3d 5, 15, 112 Cal.Rptr. 18.) The statute imposes a duty not to commit waste upon any "person whose interest is subject to the lien." Although a nonassuming grantee of mortgaged property is not personally liable on the debt, his interest in the property is subject to the lien (Braun v. Crew (1920) 183 Cal. 728, 731, 192 P. 531; Hibernia Sav., etc., Soc. v. Dickinson (1914) 167 Cal. 616, 621, 140 P. 265) and therefore he is under a duty not to impair the mortgagee's security. Defendant as a nonassuming grantee of the property subject to plaintiff's deed of trust was under a duty not to commit waste.

Defendant contends, however, that assuming arguendo that he was under a duty not to commit waste and that his acts or omissions constituted waste by so materially impairing the value of the property as to render it inadequate security for the mortgage debt, nevertheless plaintiff is not entitled to recover because such recovery for waste would amount to a deficiency judgment proscribed by sections 580b [5] and 580d [6] of the Code of Civil Procedure. In order to resolve

---

5. Section 580b provides in relevant part: "No deficiency judgment shall lie in any event after any sale of real property for failure of the purchaser to complete his contract of sale, or under a deed of trust, or mortgage, given to the vendor to secure payment of the balance of the purchase price of real property, or

6. See note 6 on page 434.

this contention it is necessary to briefly summarize the array of legislation in the field of secured transactions in real property spawned by the depression of the 1930's.

Prior to 1933, a mortgagee of real property was required to exhaust his security before enforcing the debt or otherwise to waive all right to his security (§ 726; see Walker v. Community Bank (1974) 10 Cal.3d 729, 733–734, 111 Cal.Rptr. 897, 518 P.2d 329). However, having resorted to the security, whether by judicial sale or private nonjudicial sale, the mortgagee could obtain a deficiency judgment against the mortgagor for the difference between the amount of the indebtedness and the amount realized from the sale. As a consequence during the great depression with its dearth of money and declining property values, a mortgagee was able to purchase the subject real property at the foreclosure sale at a depressed price far below its normal fair market value and thereafter to obtain a double recovery by holding the debtor for a large deficiency. (Roseleaf Corp. v. Chierighino (1963) 59 Cal.2d 35, 40, 27 Cal.Rptr. 873, 378 P.2d 97; see Glenn, Mortgages (1943) § 156, pp. 857–861.) In order to counteract this situation, California in 1933 enacted fair market value limitations applicable to both judicial foreclosure sales (§ 726) [7] and private foreclosure sales (§ 580a) [8] which limited the mortgagee's deficiency judg-

under a deed of trust, or mortgage, on a dwelling for not more than four families given to a lender to secure repayment of a loan which was in fact used to pay all or part of the purchase price of such dwelling occupied, entirely or in part, by the purchaser."

Hereafter, unless otherwise noted, all section references are to the Code of Civil Procedure.

6. Section 580d provides: "No judgment shall be rendered for any deficiency upon a note secured by a deed of trust or mortgage upon real property hereafter executed in any case in which the real property has been sold by the mortgagee or trustee under power of sale contained in such mortgage or deed of trust. . . ."

7. Section 726 provides in part: "In the event that a deficiency is not waived or prohibited and it is decreed that any defendant is personally liable for such debt, then upon application of the plaintiff filed at any time within three months of the date of the foreclosure sale and after a hearing thereon at which the court shall take evidence and at which hearing either party may present evidence as to the fair value of the property or the interest therein sold as of the date of sale, the court shall render a money judgment against such defendant or defendants for the amount by which the amount of the indebtedness with interest and costs of sale and of action exceeds the fair value of the property or interest therein sold as of the date of sale; provided, however, that in no event shall the amount of said judgment, exclusive of interest from the date of sale and of costs exceed the difference between the amount for which the property was sold and the entire amount of the indebtedness secured by said mortgage or deed of trust."

8. Section 580a provides: "Whenever a money judgment is sought for the balance due upon an obligation for the payment of which a deed of trust or mortgage with power of sale upon real property or any interest therein was given as security, following the exercise of the power of sale in such deed of trust or mortgage, the plaintiff shall set forth in his complaint the entire amount of the indebtedness which was secured by said deed of trust or mortgage at the time of sale, the amount for which such real property or interest therein was sold and the fair market value thereof at the date of sale and the date of such sale. Upon the application of either party made at least ten days before the time of trial the court shall, and upon its own motion the court at any time may, appoint one of the inheritance tax appraisers provided for by law to appraise the property or the interest therein sold as of the time of sale. Such appraiser shall file his appraisal with the clerk and the same shall be ad-

ment after exhaustion of the security to the difference between the fair value of the property at the time of the sale (irrespective of the amount actually realized at the sale) and the outstanding debt for which the property was security. Therefore, if, due to the depressed economic conditions, the property serving as security was sold for less than the fair value as determined under section 726 or section 580a, the mortgagee could not recover the amount of that difference in his action for a deficiency judgment.

In certain situations, however, the Legislature deemed even this partial deficiency too oppressive. Accordingly, in 1933 it enacted section 580b (see fn. 5, *ante*) which barred deficiency judgments altogether on purchase money mortgages. "Section 580b places the risk of inadequate security on the purchase money mortgagee. A vendor is thus discouraged from overvaluing the security. Precarious land promotion schemes are discouraged, for the security value of the land gives purchasers a clue as to its true market value. [Citation.] If inadequacy of security results, not from overvaluing, but from a decline in property values during a general or local depression, section 580b prevents the aggravation of the downturn that would result if defaulting purchasers were burdened with large personal liability. Section 580b thus serves as a stabilizing factor in land sales." (Roseleaf Corp. v. Chierighino, *supra*, 59 Cal.2d 35, 42, 27 Cal.Rptr. 873, 877, 378 P.2d 97, 101; see also Spangler v. Memel (1972) 7 Cal.3d 603, 612, 102 Cal.Rptr. 807, 498 P.2d 1055; Bargioni v. Hill (1963) 59 Cal.2d 121, 123, 28 Cal.Rptr. 321, 378 P.2d 593.)

Although both judicial foreclosure sales and private nonjudicial foreclosure sales provided for identical deficiency judgments in non-purchase money situations subsequent to the 1933 enactment of the fair value limitations, one significant difference remained, namely property sold through judicial foreclosure was subject to the statutory right of redemption (§ 725a), while property sold by private foreclosure sale was not redeemable. By virtue of sections 725a and 701,

missible in evidence. Such appraiser shall take and subscribe an oath to be attached to the appraisal that he has truly, honestly and impartially appraised the property to the best of his knowledge and ability. Any appraiser so appointed may be called and examined as a witness by any party or by the court itself. The court must fix the compensation of such appraiser, not to exceed five dollars per day, and expenses for the time actually engaged in such appraisal, which may be taxed and allowed in like manner as other costs. Before rendering any judgment the court shall find the fair market value of the real property, or interest therein sold, at the time of sale. The court may render judgment for not more than the amount by which the entire amount of the indebtedness due at the time of sale exceeded the fair market value of the real property or interest therein sold at the time of sale with interest thereon from the date of the sale; provided, however, that in no event shall the amount of said judgment, exclusive of interest after the date of sale, exceed the difference between the amount for which the property was sold and the entire amount of the indebtedness secured by said deed of trust or mortgage. Any such action must be brought within three months of the time of sale under such deed of trust or mortgage. No judgment shall be rendered in any such action until the real property or interest therein has first been sold pursuant to the terms of such deed of trust or mortgage, unless such real property or interest therein has become valueless."

the judgment debtor, his successor in interest or a junior lienor could redeem the property at any time during one year after the sale, frequently by tendering the sale price. The effect of this right of redemption was to remove any incentive on the part of the mortgagee to enter a low bid at the sale (since the property could be redeemed for that amount) and to encourage the making of a bid approximating the fair market value of the security. However, since real property purchased at a private foreclosure sale was not subject to redemption, the mortgagee by electing this remedy, could gain irredeemable title to the property by a bid substantially below the fair value and still collect a deficiency judgment for the difference between the fair value of the security and the outstanding indebtedness.

In 1940 the Legislature placed the two remedies, judicial foreclosure sale and private nonjudicial foreclosure sale on a parity by enacting section 580d (see fn. 6, *supra*). Section 580d bars "any deficiency judgment" following a private foreclosure sale. "It seems clear that section 580d was enacted to put judicial enforcement on a parity with private enforcement. This result could be accomplished by giving the debtor a right to redeem after a sale under the power. The right to redeem, like proscription of a deficiency judgment, has the effect of making the security satisfy a realistic share of the debt. [Citation.] By choosing instead to bar a deficiency judgment after private sale, the Legislature achieved its purpose without denying the creditor his election of remedies. If the creditor wishes a deficiency judgment, his sale is subject to statutory redemption rights. If he wishes a sale resulting in nonredeemable title, he must forego the right to a deficiency judgment. In either case the debtor is protected." (Roseleaf v. Chierighino, *supra*, 59 Cal.2d 35, 43–44, 27 Cal.Rptr. 873, 878, 378 P.2d 97, 102.)

In the case at bench, we are now called upon to determine the effect of this antideficiency legislation upon the statutory action for waste. (Civ.Code, § 2929.) It will be recalled that damages in an action for waste are measured by the amount of injury to the security caused by the mortgagor's acts, that is by the substantial harm which "impair[s] the value of the property subject to the lien so as to render it an inadequate security for the mortgage debt." (Robinson v. Russell, *supra*, 24 Cal. 467, 473.) A deficiency judgment is a personal judgment against the debtor-mortgagor for the difference between the fair market value of the property held as security and the outstanding indebtedness. (§ 726.) It is clear that the two judgments against the mortgagor, one for waste and the other for a deficiency, are closely interrelated and may often reflect identical amounts. If property values in general are declining, a deficiency judgment and a judgment for waste would be identical up to the point at which the harm caused by the mortgagor is equal to or less than the general decline in property values resulting from market conditions. When waste is committed in a depressed market, a deficiency judgment, although reflecting the amount of the waste, will of course exceed it if the decline of property values is greater. However, when waste is committed in a rising market, there will be no deficiency judgment, unless the property was originally overvalued; in this event, there would be no damages for waste unless the impairment due to waste exceeded the general increase in property values.

Mindful of the foregoing, we now proceed to arrive at an assessment of the effect of sections 580b and 580d upon an action for waste. First, we examine the 580b proscription of a deficiency judgment after any foreclosure sale, private or judicial, of property securing a purchase money mortgage. The primary purpose of section 580b is "in the event of a depression in land values, to prevent the aggravation of the downturn that would result if defaulting purchasers lost the land and were burdened with personal liability." (Bargioni v. Hill, *supra*, 59 Cal.2d 121, 123, 28 Cal.Rptr. 321, 322, 378 P.2d 593, 594.) It is clear that allowing an action for waste following a foreclosure sale of property securing purchase money mortgages may often frustrate this purpose. Damages for waste would burden the defaulting purchaser with both loss of land and personal liability and the acts giving rise to that liability would have been caused in many cases by the economic downturn itself. For example, a purchaser caught in such circumstances may be compelled in the normal course of events to forego the general maintenance and repair of the property in order to keep up his payments on the mortgage debt. If he eventually defaults and loses the property, to hold him subject to additional liability for waste would seem to run counter to the purpose of section 580b and to permit the purchase money lender to obtain what is in effect a deficiency judgment. It is of course true that not all owners of real property subject to a purchase money mortgage commit waste solely or primarily as a result of the economic pressures of a market depression; indeed many are reckless, intentional, and at times even malicious despoilers of property. In these latter circumstances to which we shall refer for convenience as waste committed in bad faith, the purchase money lender should not go remediless since they do not involve the type of risk intended to be borne by him in promoting the objectives of section 580b alluded to above.

Accordingly, we hold that section 580b should apply to bar recovery in actions for waste following foreclosure sale in the first instance but should not so apply in the second instance of "bad faith" waste. We further hold that it is within the province of the trier of fact to determine on a case by case basis to what, if any, extent the impairment of the mortgagee's security has been caused (as in the first instance) by the general decline of real property values and to what, if any, extent (as in the second instance) by the bad faith acts of the mortgagor, such determination, in either instance, being subject to review under the established rule of appellate review.

We now turn to assess the effect upon an action for waste of section 580d which applies to a nonpurchase money mortgage. We are satisfied that a different analysis must be pursued. It will be recalled from our earlier discussion that the Legislature intended to establish parity between judicial foreclosure and private foreclosure by denying a deficiency judgment subsequent to a private sale. Under a judicial foreclosure, the mortgagee is entitled to a deficiency judgment, but must bear the burden of a statutory redemption; under a private sale the mortgagee need not bear the burden of redemption, but cannot recover any deficiency judgment. If following a nonjudicial sale the mortgagee were allowed to obtain a judgment for damages for waste against the mortgagor, he would have the double benefits of an irredeemable title to the property and a personal judgment against the mortgagor for the impairment of the value of the property. This would essentially destroy the parity between judicial foreclosure and private foreclosure in all instances where the waste is actually caused by general economic conditions, since as we have explained, such recovery is in effect a deficiency judgment. If, however, the recovery is limited to waste committed in "bad faith," then the personal judgment would be entirely independent of the problems encompassed by the antideficiency legislation and would not affect the parity of remedies. Accordingly, we hold that in situations arising under section 580d, recovery for waste against the mortgagor following nonjudicial foreclosure sale is barred by the section's proscription against deficiency judgments when the waste actually results from the depressed condition of the general real estate market but not when the waste is caused by the "bad faith" acts of the mortgagor. . . .

While our foregoing conclusion may expose defendant to liability on the basis of having committed "bad faith" waste, the question need not be resolved. We have further concluded that even assuming that defendant is liable on such basis, nevertheless plaintiff cannot recover since she purchased the subject property at the trustee's sale by making a full credit bid. As stated previously, the measure of damages for waste is the amount of the impairment of the security, that is the amount by which the value of the security is less than the outstanding indebtedness and is thereby rendered inadequate. (Robinson v. Russell, *supra*, 24 Cal. 467, 473.) The point of defendant's argument is that the mortgagee's purchase of the property securing the debt by entering a full credit bid establishes the value of the security as being equal to the outstanding indebtedness and ipso facto the nonexistence of any impairment of the security. As applied to the factual context of the instant case, the argument is that the purchase by plaintiff-vendor-beneficiary of the property covered by the purchase money deed of trust pursuant to a full credit bid made and accepted at the nonjudicial foreclosure sale resulted in a total satisfaction of the secured obligation. We agree. . . .

. . . If the beneficiary or mortgagee at the foreclosure sale enters a bid for the full amount of the obligation owing to him together with the costs and fees due in connection with the sale he cannot recover damages for waste, since he cannot establish any impairment of security, the lien of the deed of trust or mortgage having been theretofore extinguished by his full credit bid and all his security interest in the property thereby nullified. If, however, he bids less than the full amount of the obligation and thereby acquires the property valued at less than the full amount, his security has been impaired and he may recover damages for waste in an amount not exceeding the difference between the amount of his bid and the full amount of the outstanding indebtedness immediately prior to the foreclosure sale.

Plaintiff complains that it is difficult to calculate precisely the amount of damages recoverable for waste so as to determine the proper amount which the beneficiary or mortgagee should bid at the foreclosure sale; therefore, she urges, it is unfair to impose such a burden on the beneficiary or mortgagee. Suffice it to say that no complicated calculations are necessary. The beneficiary or mortgagee need only enter a credit bid in an amount equal to what he assesses the fair market value of the property to be in its condition at the time of the foreclosure sale. If that amount is below the full amount of the outstanding indebtedness and he is successful in acquiring the property at the foreclosure sale, he may then recover any provable damages for waste.

To recapitulate, we conclude that the trial court properly granted summary judgment in favor of defendant and against plaintiff (1) as to the first cause of action for breach of contract since defendant at no time assumed the underlying indebtedness; and (2) as to the second cause of action for waste since, although defendant as a nonassuming grantee could be held liable for waste if proved to have been committed in bad faith, nevertheless plaintiff can establish no impairment of security, having acquired the property at the foreclosure sale by making a full credit bid.

The judgment is affirmed.

WRIGHT, C.J., and McCOMB, TOBRINER, MOSK, CLARK and RICHARDSON, JJ., concur.

CENTRAL FINANCIAL SERVICES, INC. v. SPEARS

Supreme Court of Mississippi, 1983.
425 So.2d 403.

SUGG, Presiding Justice, for the Court:

The question in this case is whether a mortgagee, who purchases the mortgaged property at a foreclosure sale must account to the mortgagor for the surplus arising from a sale of the property by the mortgagee within two weeks for two and one-half times the amount bid by the mortgagee at the foreclosure sale.

Marshall Spears borrowed $1250 from Central Financial Services, Inc. (CFS), and executed a promissory note and financial disclosure statement along with his wife, Esther Spears. They also executed a deed of trust covering certain real property described therein to secure the debt. The total amount secured was $1797.30 which included principal, interest, insurance and fees.

Spears gave his son $625 or half the amount of the principal and expected him to assist in paying back the loan. They could not agree on an arrangement so payments on the promissory note fell into arrears. CFS advertised the property for sale under the terms of the deed of trust, but stopped the advertisement when Spears paid the amount in arrears including cost of the foreclosure proceedings. Spears and his son still could not agree upon how they could make payments on the note, so once again it became delinquent. On October 12, 1979, after advertising the sale in accord with section 89–1–55 Mississippi Code Annotated (1972), the sale was conducted and CFS bid $1458.86, the amount of the indebtedness then due plus costs of foreclosure. There were no other bidders. Two days later, Spears was notified by an agent for CFS that he would have to vacate the premises. Spears claimed that this was the first time he was aware of the second sale and that he offered to pay the amount of the delinquency, but was told it was too late for that.

On October 24, 1979, CFS sold the property to Joe Stewart and Earl Aycock for $4,000. CFS then paid a $30 judgment lien on the property and realized a profit of $2481.14. Aycock and Stewart sold the property to Roger C. Henderson on February 19, 1980 for $6,500. Henderson then made improvements to the property.

On March 11, 1980, Spears filed a bill of complaint in the Chancery Court of Lauderdale County which named CFS, Thomas B. Bourdeaux, Trustee, Joe Stewart, Earl Aycock and Roger Henderson as defendants. The bill prayed that the second foreclosure sale be set aside, alleging violation of Spears' constitutional rights, inadequate sale price and prayed for an injunction and other relief. The demurrer of the defendants was sustained and Spears appealed to this Court.

The appeal was submitted on March 3, 1981, and, in an unpublished opinion we held, "On the face of the complaint, taking as true Spears' allegation that the fair market value was $7,000, the consideration of $1458.86 was so grossly inadequate as to shock the conscience of this Court." We reversed and remanded for a trial on the merits because of the gross inadequacy of consideration alleged on the face of the complaint.

The chancellor dismissed the case as against the trustee, Aycock, Stewart and Henderson, but found that the sale price at the second foreclosure sale was so inadequate that it shocked the conscience of the court. He determined from the evidence presented that the property had a fair market value of $6,000 at the time of the sale and ordered CFS to respond in damages based on the difference between fair market value and the price paid at the foreclosure sale. CFS appealed. Spears did not cross-appeal so the dismissal of the action against the trustee, Aycock, Stewart and Henderson is not at issue.

We have reviewed our cases involving adequacy of consideration as a ground for setting aside a foreclosure sale.[1] These cases do not address the issue involved in this case but do lay down the general rule that mere inadequacy of price [2] is not sufficient to set aside a foreclosure sale unless the price is so inadequate as to shock the conscience of the court. These cases, except Federal Credit Co. v. Boleware, do not involve a resale by the mortgagee of property purchased by it at a foreclosure sale. We also note that most of the cases cited in footnote 1 involved sales during a time of economic depression and, as stated in Hardin v. Grenada Bank, supra, many of the sales were deemed adequate because the entire country "was in the throes of a depression."

In this case, the chancellor found that the sale price was so inadequate it shocked his conscience. This finding is amply supported by

---

1. Myles v. Cox, 217 So.2d 31 (Miss.1968); Triplett v. Bridgforth, 205 Miss. 328, 38 So.2d 756 (1949); Harris v. Bailey Avenue Park, Inc., 202 Miss. 776, 32 So.2d 689 (1947); Home Owners Loan Corp. v. Wiggins, et al., 188 Miss. 750, 196 So. 240 (1940); Anthony v. Bank of Wiggins, 183 Miss. 885, 184 So. 626 (1938); Hardin v. Grenada Bank, 182 Miss. 689, 180 So. 805 (1938); Blacketor v. Cartee, 172 Miss. 889, 161 So. 696 (1935); Wheeler v. Cleveland State Bank, 174 Miss. 542, 164 So. 400 (1935); First [sic] Credit Co. v. Boleware, 163 Miss. 830, 142 So. 1 (1932); Hesdorffer v. Welsh, 127 Miss. 261, 90 So. 3 (1921); and Weyburn v. Watkins, 90 Miss. 728, 44 So. 145 (1907).

2. Criticism from many sources has been leveled against the foreclosure sales procedure in Mississippi because the true market value of the property is seldom bid at such sales.

For example, Professor Guthrie T. Abbott, in an article in 50 Mississippi Law Journal, page 665, discussed some of the reasons for inadequate bids in the following language.

It has been the experience of this author that most power of sale foreclosures in Mississippi produce little, if any, bidding at the sale. The vast majority of such sales results in the beneficiary under the deed of trust being the only bidder, and the successful bid by the beneficiary is usually for the amount of the indebtedness or less. It is almost impossible to succeed in having such a sale set aside on the basis of an inadequate sale price because the test is that the inadequacy from such a forced sale must be so gross as to shock the conscience of the court or to amount to fraud. This stringent standard should require that every possible safeguard be built into the power of sale foreclosure procedure to ensure as high a sales price as possible, but this is certainly not the case in Mississippi. The notice requirements, as discussed above, do the very minimum to notify the debtor(s), much less to notify prospective bidders. One of the classic modes by which a junior lienor may protect his interest is to bid at the foreclosure sale so as either to obtain the property or to guarantee a sale at close to market price. However, in Mississippi, the junior lienor will often only obtain knowledge of the sale after it has concluded. The advertisements required by statute are buried in the legal notices section of the newspaper, and with the exception of the beneficiary's bid up to the amount of the indebtedness, the sale must be made for cash to be paid in full at the time of the sale. The cumulative effect of the deficient sales procedures described above is to ensure a severely depressed sales price at most Mississippi power of sale foreclosures. [50 M.L.J. at 680–81 (1979)].

the evidence because CFS bid only $1458.86 at the foreclosure sale and twelve days later sold the property for $4,000. We hold that a sale of mortgaged property within twelve days of the foreclosure sale at a price two and one-half times the bid of the mortgagee is so inadequate, it would be "impossible to state it to a man of common sense without producing an exclamation at the inequality of it."[4] The chancellor did not set the sale aside; instead, he fashioned a remedy with which we agree in principle.

CFS was in compliance with the statutory law pertaining to the advertisement and sale of real property under deeds of trust. However, the sale of the property by CFS twelve days later resulted in a windfall to it of approximately $2,500. We deem this windfall to be unjust. If CFS had bid $4,000 at the foreclosure sale it would have been entitled to recover the amount of its indebtedness plus the expense of the sale, with the surplus being payable to Spears. Certainly a sale twelve days later for $4,000 enabled CFS to recover $2500 more than it risked in the transaction it made when it advanced $1250 to Spears.

We agree with the chancellor that the sale price was so inadequate that it shocks the conscience of this Court. However, we are of the opinion that the decree should be modified to reduce the amount of recovery against CFS.

The chancellor ordered the difference between the fair market value, which he fixed at $6,000, and the amount bid by CFS be returned to Spears. CFS should not be required to suffer any pecuniary loss, which it would do under the decree of the chancellor. There is no evidence of any conspiracy between appellant and its vendees to defraud appellee by fixing the sales price below market value; rather, the sale was an arms length transaction. We are of the opinion, and hold, that the difference between the amount bid and the $4,000 received by CFS at the private sale twelve days later should be used in computing the amount due Spears.

The record shows that the total amount of the indebtedness due at the time of the foreclosure sale was $1,458.86. Interest on this amount at the rate fixed in the note for twelve days amounts to $13.51. CFS also paid off a $30 judgment lien against the property and is entitled to credit for the judgment lien. We therefore, reduce the chancellor's award to $2,497.63, computed as follows:

Sale price of the property to Aycock and Stewart		$4,000.00
LESS:		
Amount of indebtedness	$1,458.86	
Judgment paid by CFS	30.00	
Twelve days interest	13.51	1,502.37
		$2,497.63

Affirmed as Modified.

4. Federal Credit Co. v. Boleware, 163 Miss. at 835, 142 So. at 2.

PATTERSON, C.J., WALKER, P.J., and BROOM, ROY NOBLE LEE, BOWLING, HAWKINS, DAN M. LEE and PRATHER, JJ., concur.

NOTES

1. *Remedies on Default*. Mortgagees have historically been able to terminate the defaulting mortgagor's interest, and recover the land or its cash equivalent, through one or more of four methods.

The oldest method, *strict foreclosure,* was commonly employed in England and the American colonies through the end of the seventeenth century. Strict foreclosure simply terminated the mortgagor's equity of redemption and, without a sale or further proceeding, vested title to the property in the mortgagee. The mortgagee would enjoy a windfall—and the mortgagor would suffer a loss—to the extent that the value of the land exceeded the amount of the debt outstanding. Strict foreclosure has been abolished in all but a small handful of states. See, for example, Conn.Gen.Stat.Ann. § 49–15 (1982); 12 Vt.Stat.Ann. § 4531 (1983). Illinois, another state allowing strict foreclosure, imposes three requirements designed to safeguard the mortgagor and prevent unjust enrichment to the mortgagee: the property's value cannot exceed the debt; a deficiency judgment cannot be recovered; and the mortgagor must be insolvent. See generally, Tefft, The Myth of Strict Foreclosure, 4 U.Chi.L.Rev. 575 (1937).

By the early nineteenth century, courts in England and courts and legislatures in the United States had replaced strict foreclosure with *judicial foreclosure*. Although judicial foreclosure eliminated the possibility of unjust enrichment by requiring that the excess of the property's value over the outstanding debt be returned to the mortgagor, the method could benefit mortgagees in another respect: if the value of the property fell below the amount of the debt, the mortgagee could as part of the foreclosure proceeding obtain a judgment against the mortgagor for the difference. Then, as now, the "number of steps necessary to consummate foreclosure by court process naturally results in delay, considerable court costs and a fairly large attorney's fee"; the typical proceeding "involves a preliminary title search, to determine all parties in interest; the filing of a *lis pendens,* summons or complaint; service of the process; a time for a hearing, if necessary; the decree or judgment; the delivery to the sheriff of papers authorizing him to sell; notice of sale and service of notice; the actual sale and the issuance of a certificate of sale; and the sheriff's report." Skilton, Developments in Mortgage Law and Practice, 17 Temp.Univ.L.Q. 315, 320 (1943).

By the last quarter of the nineteenth century, mortgagees commonly resorted to *nonjudicial foreclosure*, authorized by their deeds of trust or mortgages with power of sale, in order to avoid the expense and delay of judicial foreclosure. Nonjudicial foreclosure required only two steps: notice and sale. One observer, writing in 1877, noted that the use of deeds of trust and mortgage with power of sale "has rapidly extended, so that in some states the use of any other form is exceptional. The validity of these powers of sale is everywhere recognized, and the use of them, either in mortgages or trust deeds, is becoming general." Jones, Power of Sale Mortgages and Trust Deeds, 3 So.L.Rev. 703, 708 (1877). Does nonjudicial foreclosure deprive mortgagors of property without due process of law? Most federal and state courts reviewing power of sale foreclosures have found no violation of due process guarantees, principally because they could find no state action. See, for example, Levine v. Stein, 560 F.2d 1175 (4th Cir. 1977), cert. denied, 434 U.S. 1046, 98 S.Ct. 891, 54 L.Ed.2d 797. But see, Turner v. Blackburn, 389 F.Supp. 1250 (W.D.N.C.1975).

When it is clear to the mortgagor that a foreclosure sale will not yield proceeds in excess of the debt, and it is clear to the mortgagee that an action on the note will either be barred by antideficiency rules or unavailing because the mortgagor has no resources, the two may agree on a *deed in lieu of foreclosure* under which the mortgagor simply conveys the land to the mortgagee. Although this simple solution may be best for both sides, it is surrounded by legal pitfalls. Courts will invalidate the transfer if there is any hint of fraud or overreaching by the mortgagee, and will sometimes recharacterize the deed as an equitable mortgage.

2. California's foreclosure scheme, outlined in *Cornelison*, embodies virtually all of the techniques that states across the country employ to protect mortgagors from price inadequacy in mortgage foreclosure sales. In addition to an outright prohibition on deficiency judgments, a state may limit mortgagor liability by imposing fair value restrictions, statutory redemption periods or procedural safeguards on sale. The California scheme is unusual only in that it combines so many rules and policies in a single system.

When, if ever, would it make sense for a California institutional lender, foreclosing on a loan it had made for a home purchase, to proceed by judicial rather than nonjudicial foreclosure, with its added delay, expense and the hurdle of statutory redemption? To be sure, West's Ann.Cal. Civil Code § 580d prohibits deficiency judgments after nonjudicial foreclosure. But will section 580b allow the lender to obtain a deficiency judgment in these circumstances after judicial foreclosure?

Cornelison also exposes the variety of policies that lie behind these various debtor-protection schemes. One policy is to protect homeowners against the immediate burdens of economic collapse. Another is to spread the risk of decline in real property values between property owners and secured lenders. Do you agree with these policies? Do you agree with the more specific policies behind section 580b—for example, prohibiting deficiency judgments when the seller has financed the purchase? Does it make sense to apply section 580b's bar not only to financing sellers but also to third-party lenders?

3. *Statutory Right to Redeem.* In nearly half of the thirty-three states that provide for statutory redemption periods, the debtor is unconditionally allowed to remain in possession of the land. In others, he is allowed to stay on only under special conditions, such as that the land is a homestead or is used for farming. See, for example, West's Rev. Code Wash.Ann. 6.24.210 (Supp.1983). In a few states, the purchaser is allowed to occupy the land during the redemption period but is generally required to credit any rents received against the amount the debtor must pay to redeem. See, for example, N.H.Rev.Stat.Ann. 529:26 (1974).

Ironically, the statutory right to redeem—ostensibly a debtor-protection provision—will effectively depress the price obtained at a foreclosure sale since during a redemption period, which may be as long as a year or more, it clouds the purchaser's title with the prospect that the mortgagor will retake his title through redemption.

On the causes and cures of price inadequacy, see generally, Washburn, The Judicial and Legislative Response to Price Inadequacy in Mortgage Foreclosure Sales, 53 S.Cal.L.Rev. 843 (1980).

4. *One-Action Rules*. Can an undersecured mortgagee circumvent a state's fair value or antideficiency rule by proceeding first against the mortgagor personally on the note and then, to the extent the personal judgment is unsatisfied, by foreclosing on the real property security and applying the sales proceeds to the remainder of the debt?

This strategy affronts the notion, held by some state legislatures, that creditors who seek collateral for their loan should be required to proceed first against the collateral. Five states require the mortgagee to proceed against the real property securing the debt before obtaining a final judgment in a personal action on the note. West's Ann.Cal.Code Civ.Proc. § 726; Idaho Code § 6–101 (1979); Mont. Code Ann. 71–1–222 (1981); Nev.Rev.Stat. 40.430 (1979); Utah Code Ann. 78–37–1 (1977). If the mortgagor fails to raise the requirement as a defense on the note, he will suffer a personal judgment. He can, however, later prevent a foreclosure proceeding against the real property on the ground that, by proceeding first on the note, the mortgagee effectively elected that as his exclusive remedy. See Walker v. Community Bank, 10 Cal.3d 729, 111 Cal.Rptr. 897, 518 P.2d 329 (1974).

D. FEDERAL INCOME TAXATION

1. PROPERTY USED AS A PERSONAL RESIDENCE

The federal income tax law offers substantial incentives to homeownership. Internal Revenue Code sections 163 and 164, respectively, allow the taxpayer to deduct payments for mortgage interest (but not mortgage amortization) and real property taxes—the two largest items of homeownership expense. Section 165 similarly allows deductions from taxable income for losses caused by such casualties as flood, earthquake and explosion. Section 262, however, bars deductions for other ownership-related costs—repairs, depreciation, insurance—on the ground that they are "personal, living, or family expenses." 26 U.S.C.A. §§ 163, 164, 165, 262 (1976).

The Internal Revenue Code further pampers homeowners by forgiving or postponing tax liability for two property-related items of income. First, the Code does not tax the homeowner on the imputed income represented by the value of his occupancy—a value that can be approximated by determining the amount for which the owner could rent the premises to someone else. (Note that if the homeowner *were* to rent the premises to someone else the net rental income would be taxable.) "In practice, to tax this form of imputed income, however desirable it might be from the standpoint of equity or of obtaining neutrality between owning and renting, would severely complicate tax compliance and administration. Because the owner-occupier does not explicitly make a rental payment to himself, the value of the current use of his house is not revealed." One consequence of the "incentive for home ownership that results from including net income from rental housing in the tax base while excluding it for owner-occupied housing" is "a distortion from the pattern of consumer housing choices that would otherwise prevail." United States Dept. of Treasury, Blueprints for Basic Tax Reform 86 (1977).

Second, the Code postpones taxation of increases in the property's value from the year in which the increase occurs to the year in which the taxpayer sells or otherwise disposes of the property. Thus, although the Smiths' house may have increased in value from $67,000 to $71,000 between September 1, 1983, when they acquired the house from the Joneses, and December 31, 1983, the end of the tax year, their income tax bill for 1983 will not reflect this $4,000 increase in their personal wealth. The Smiths will pay tax on any appreciation in the value of their home only when they dispose of the property. Thus, if the Smiths sell the house in 1988 for $91,000, they would in that year be liable for tax on a capital gain of $24,000 (the difference between the amount realized, $91,000, and their cost, or "basis," $67,000). Although tax liability is thus only postponed and not forgiven, the Code's treatment of capital appreciation does confer two benefits on the homeowner: During the years over which tax liability is postponed, the homeowner has the use of money that he would otherwise have paid in taxes. And gain, when finally recognized, will be taxed not at the "ordinary income" rate (for which the highest marginal tax rate is 50%), but rather at the considerably lower "long term capital gains" rate (measured as 40% of the taxpayer's marginal tax rate).

The Code offers still other opportunities for tax postponement or forgiveness. Under section 1034, if a taxpayer sells his "principal residence" and, within two years before or after the sale, acquires another principal residence, any gain from sale of the old residence will be recognized only to the extent that the sales price of the old residence exceeds the cost of the new residence. (Thus, if in 1988 the Smiths sell their house at 23 Oak Street for $91,000 and buy another principal residence for $103,000, their $24,000 gain on the sale of 23 Oak Street [$91,000 sales price minus $67,000 basis] will go untaxed that year since the sales price of the old residence is less than the purchase price of the new residence.) Since section 1034(e) requires the taxpayer to reduce his basis in the new residence by the amount of untaxed gain realized on the sale of the old residence, section 1034 effectively postpones tax on gain. (The basis of the Smiths' new home would be $79,000 [$103,000 cost minus $24,000 gain untaxed on the sale of 23 Oak Street]. If the Smiths in 1991 sold their new home for $116,000, their taxable gain on sale—assuming they did not buy another, more expensive home—would be $37,000 [$116,000, amount realized, minus $79,000 adjusted basis], representing the $24,000 gain during their 1983–1988 ownership of 23 Oak, and the $13,000 gain during their ownership of the subsequently acquired home between 1988–1991.)

One rationale behind section 1034 is that homeowners typically "trade up," purchasing bigger and more expensive homes as their families and incomes grow. Since the series of residences they buy can be viewed as a single, growing asset, recognition of gain can plausibly be postponed until the point at which they "trade down" or leave the home ownership market entirely—typically when their children have left home or they are planning to retire. By this point, considerable, untaxed capital gains will likely have accrued and a whopping capital gains tax will come due. To soften the blow, and to encourage homeowners to trade down when their housing needs diminish, section 121 allows taxpayers age 55 or older to exclude from tax up to $125,000 of any gain realized on the sale of their principal residence; they can, however, take advantage of this exclusion only once.

The comparative tax advantages of homeownership have led some policymakers to propose legislation that would reduce the perceived disparity between owners and renters by allowing tenants to deduct from taxable income that portion of their rent that goes to pay state and local property taxes, or by eliminating the homeowner's deductions for real property taxes and mortgage interest. See, for example, Congressional Record, Senate, Sept. 23, 1976, S. 16483–16489; United States Dept. of Treasury, Blueprints for Basic Tax Reform 86–89 (1977). Is there in fact an economic disparity between homeowners and renters? It is not at all clear that landlords pass the full cost of real property taxes on to their tenants. See generally, Netzer, The Incidence of the Property Tax Revisited, 26 Nat'l. Tax J. 515 (1973); H. Aaron, Who Pays the Property Tax? A New View (1975). Further, the direct subsidies that the federal government gives to many low- and moderate-income rental housing projects may partially balance the indirect subsidies that homeowners get through tax deductions for interest and property taxes. And landlords, permitted under the Internal Revenue Code to accelerate the deductions that they take for the depreciation of their buildings, may pass some of these savings on to their tenants in the form of lowered rent. Estimates of this reduction in average rentals range between 11% and 17%, depending on the landlord's tax bracket. See Hellmuth, Homeowner Preferences, in Comprehensive Income Taxation 163 (J. Pechman, ed. 1977).

2. PROPERTY HELD FOR INVESTMENT, INCOME OR BUSINESS PURPOSES

The Internal Revenue Code also offers substantial incentives to the ownership of real property for investment, income or business purposes. Indeed, there are some commercial real estate transactions whose structure can be explained only in terms of the tax benefits that it produces. Like the owner of a personal residence, the owner of an investment or business property can deduct interest expense and real property taxes; unlike the homeowner, she can also take deductions for repairs, maintenance and insurance and for depreciation of any improvements on the land. 26 U.S.C.A. §§ 162, 167, 212. Like the homeowner, the commercial owner can postpone the payment of tax on gains from the time the gains occur to the time the property is sold or otherwise transferred; unlike the homeowner, she can also deduct any loss realized on disposition of the property. And, like the homeowner, the commercial owner is given the opportunity to postpone the recognition of gain even beyond the date of sale or other disposition. 26 U.S.C.A. §§ 453, 1031.

The Code rests the availability of particular deductions, and of capital gain or loss treatment, on how the real property is classified—as property held for investment or production of income, as property used in the taxpayer's trade or business, or as property held primarily for sale to customers in the ordinary course of trade or business.

Property held for investment or production of income. Property held for investment or production of income qualifies as a capital asset under section 1221, and all gains or losses realized on its sale or exchange are taxed as capital gains or losses. Under section 212, which allows deductions for "the management, conservation, or maintenance of property held for the production of income," the property owner can deduct the expenses of real property taxes, interest, maintenance and repairs. Under § 167 the taxpayer can also take a deduction for the depreciation of any improvements situated on the land. Section 1031, if its criteria for tax-free exchanges are met, will postpone recognition of gain or loss on transfer of the property.

Property used in the taxpayer's trade or business. Section 1221 expressly excludes a taxpayer's "real property used in his trade or business" from its definition of capital asset. While capital asset treatment is thus lost to this class of real estate investment, greater tax advantages are created under the terms of section 1231. Gain on the disposition of trade or business property is taxed as capital gain, while loss is treated as ordinary loss which can be offset against ordinary income. Section 1231 property is entitled to all of the expense deductions, including depreciation deductions, allowed for section 1221 property, and similarly qualifies for deferred recognition of gain and loss under section 1031.

Property held primarily for sale to customers in the ordinary course of trade or business. Section 1221 excludes from its definition of capital asset, and section 1231 excludes from its definition of trade or business property, "property held by the taxpayer primarily for sale to customers in the ordinary course of his trade or business." Gains or losses on sales or exchanges of property in this category are treated as ordinary income and ordinary loss rather than as capital gains and losses. Further, property in this class does not qualify for deferred recognition of gain or loss under section 1031.

As should be evident, the lines between these three categories will often be difficult to draw. Is an apartment house, rented out by the taxpayer for fifteen years, § 1221 property, so that loss on sale will be treated as a capital loss, or is it § 1231 property, so that loss on sale will be treated as an ordinary loss? When the owner converts the apartment house to a condominium and sells off the individual units, one by one, is she now holding the property primarily for sale to customers in the ordinary course of trade or business, so that any gain on sale will be treated as ordinary income rather than capital gain? These linedrawing difficulties are no doubt increased by taxpayers' unremitting efforts to structure their transactions to fall on the most advantageous side of the line.

Probably the single greatest boon—some would say boondoggle—available to owners of income or business property is the depreciation deduction. Unlike the deductions for interest, real property taxes and maintenance, each of which reflects an equivalent cash outlay by the taxpayer, section 167's depreciation provisions enable taxpayers to take deductions without any matching cash outlay. So long as depreciation deductions (tax deductions without corresponding cash expenditures) exceed amortization of any debt on the property (cash expenditures without corresponding tax deductions), the investment will provide a "tax shelter" for the taxpayer's income.

The taxpayer's first step in computing her depreciation deduction is to identify the part of her basis in the real property that is properly allocable to a depreciable asset. (Assume that, of the taxpayer's $650,000 basis in the property, $200,000 is allocable to land, which is not depreciable, and $450,000 is allocable to a building on the land, which is depreciable.) Next, the taxpayer must assign a useful life to the improvements (assume 20 years) and a salvage value for the improvements at the end of their useful life (assume $50,000). By subtracting salvage value from total improvement value ($450,000 minus $50,000), the taxpayer arrives at the depreciable basis that she can write off over the period of the asset's useful life. (Thus, in the example given, the taxpayer can take depreciation deductions totaling $400,000 over 20 years.) The taxpayer's next step is to choose a depreciation method. The most conservative method, "straight line" depreciation, will prorate the improvement's depreciable basis equally over its useful life. (In the example given, this means $400,000 divided by a 20-year useful life, or a $20,000 depreciation deduction each year.)

The taxpayer may seek to increase her tax advantages by using an accelerated method of depreciation such as "double declining balance." Under the double declining balance method, a constant rate (twice the straight line rate) is applied each year to a decreasing depreciable basis that consists of the original depreciable basis, diminished each year by the total amount of depreciation taken in the preceding years. While salvage value is, for these purposes, included in depreciable basis, the improvement cannot be depreciated below its salvage value. (In the example given, the straight line rate is 1/20, or 5%. Thus under the double declining balance method, twice that rate, or 10%, is applied to $450,000 in order to determine the first year's depreciation—$45,000. In the second year, depreciation is [$450,000 minus $45,000] × 10% or $40,500; in the third year it is [$405,000 minus $40,500] × 10% or $36,450.) Use of a 175% declining balance method entails only a change in the number by which the straight line rate is multiplied, from 2 to 1.75.

Because depreciation deductions are subtracted from the property's basis, they will be partially offset by an increase in the gain realized when the property is disposed of. (Thus, in the example just given, the taxpayer, having taken a total of $121,950 in depreciation deductions [$45,000 + $40,500 + $36,450] over three years, must reduce her basis by that amount, leaving a basis of $528,050 [$650,000 − $121,950]. If the taxpayer sold the property at the end of the third year for no more than the $650,000 she paid for it, she would still have to pay tax on a capital gain of $121,950—the difference between amount realized, $650,000, and adjusted basis, or $528,050.) Thus, as a general matter, the depreciation deduction's real advantage to the taxpayer is that it gives her the economic benefit of present deductions against ordinary income while requiring only that she pay for this benefit by recognizing future gains taxed at the more favorable capital gains rate.

Congress has, over time, variously expanded and contracted the depreciation tax shelter. After a series of reforms curtailing the availability and benefits of accelerated depreciation, The Economic Recovery Tax Act of 1981, P.L. 97-34, 95 Stat. 172, dramatically increased the available depreciation deductions by introducing an accelerated cost recovery system (ACRS) applicable to property placed in service on or after 1 January 1981. ACRS allows depreciable real property to be depreciated over a 15-year period (as compared with useful lives ranging generally between 40 and 60 years under previous I.R.S. guidelines). Under the Act, taxpayers may elect a 35- or 45-year recovery period instead. The Act allows the taxpayer to choose between straight line and accelerated methods of depreciation; while straight line can be used in connection with the 15-, 35- or 45-year recovery period, the accelerated depreciation method can be used only in connection with the 15-year recovery period. Further, the taxpayer who opts for accelerated depreciation must calculate depreciation on the basis of tables that approximate 175 percent declining balance or, if the real property is a qualifying subsidized housing project, that approximate double declining balance. However, if the taxpayer employs an accelerated depreciation method, her depreciation deductions will be "recaptured" at the time of disposition and taxed at ordinary income rates. The extent of recapture will turn on whether the property is residential or nonresidential real estate. If it is residential real estate, such as an apartment building, only depreciation taken in excess of the amount that would have been taken under the straight line method will be recaptured and taxed as ordinary income. By contrast, if it is nonresidential property such as a factory or warehouse, gain on disposition will be treated as ordinary income to the extent of *all* depreciation taken, and not just depreciation in excess of the amount that would have been taken under the straight line method.

Depreciation tax shelters are most advantageous to taxpayers who finance their acquisition of the depreciable property. Because the amount of mortgage financing will be included in the taxpayer's depreciable basis, it represents a tax-free method of inflating the depreciation deduction—a phenomenon called "leveraged depreciation." Thus, the taxpayer in the preceding example may have financed her purchase of the $650,000 parcel with a $600,000 mortgage loan, putting up only $50,000 of her own cash. As a result, for a total investment of $50,000, the taxpayer using the straight line method is able to write off $20,000 in depreciation deductions each year for 20 years;

if she is in the 50% bracket, this means an extra $10,000 cash in her pocket every year for 20 years. Use of the double declining balance method will enable the taxpayer to write off $45,000—almost her complete investment—in the first year.

The taxpayer need not be personally obligated on the debt encumbering her property for the debt to be included in her basis. Crane v. Commissioner, 331 U.S. 1, 67 S.Ct. 1047, 91 L.Ed. 1301 (1946). This rule, which is particularly congenial to the real estate market where so much financing is nonrecourse, may lead to abuses. Consider the following example: Taxpayer acquires an office building and underlying land with an aggregate market value of $2,500,000 ($500,000 allocable to land, $2,000,000 allocable to the improvement). She buys the land for $1,000,000, giving seller a 10-year, interest-only purchase money mortgage, at 5% interest, with a $1,000,000, balloon at the end. She acquires the building in fee for $5,000,000, giving the seller a purchase money mortgage for that amount. The mortgage is for ten years, is nonrecourse, interest only, with an interest rate of 5% and a $5,000,000 balloon payment of principal at the end of ten years. The taxpayer's net income from the property is $300,000, just enough to cover her mortgage payments. Because these payments are fully deductible, this aspect of the transaction is a wash. If the building has a twenty-five year useful life and no salvage value, the taxpayer, using straight line depreciation, will have an annual depreciation deduction available for setoff against other income of $200,000 ($5,000,000/25). This is two and one-half times the deduction she would have had if she had given a mortgage not for $5,000,000, but for the building's market value of $2,000,000. Presumably the taxpayer will default and abandon the property just as the mortgage principal becomes due, leaving the seller with his security, worth $2,500,000 (assuming no change in market value), and, for having participated in the charade, receipt over the ten years of an above-market return on his mortgages.

Will such an abuse be tolerated? In *Crane* the Supreme Court expressly noted that "if the value of the property is less than the amount of the mortgage, a mortgagor who is not personally liable cannot realize a benefit equal to the mortgage. Consequently, a different problem might be encountered where a mortgagor abandoned the property or transferred it subject to the mortgage without receiving boot. That is not this case." 331 U.S. at 14 n. 37, 67 S.Ct. at 1054 n. 37. How should such a mortgage debt be accounted for? Is it really debt? These questions are considered, respectively, in the next two cases.

COMMISSIONER OF INTERNAL REVENUE v. TUFTS

Supreme Court of the United States, 1983.
___ U.S. ___, 103 S.Ct. 1826, 75 L.Ed.2d 863.

Justice BLACKMUN delivered the opinion of the Court.

Over 35 years ago, in Crane v. Commissioner, 331 U.S. 1, 67 S.Ct. 1947, 91 L.Ed. 1301 (1947), this Court ruled that a taxpayer, who sold property encumbered by a nonrecourse mortgage (the amount of the mortgage being less than the property's value), must include the unpaid balance of the mortgage in the computation of the amount the taxpayer realized on the sale. The case now before us presents the question whether the same rule applies when the unpaid amount of the nonrecourse mortgage exceeds the fair market value of the property sold.

I

On August 1, 1970, respondent Clark Pelt, a builder, and his wholly owned corporation, respondent Clark, Inc., formed a general partnership. The purpose of the partnership was to construct a 120-unit apartment complex in Duncanville, Tex., a Dallas suburb. Neither Pelt nor Clark, Inc., made any capital contribution to the partnership. Six days later, the partnership entered into a mortgage loan agreement with the Farm & Home Savings Association (F & H). Under the agreement, F & H was committed for a $1,851,500 loan for the complex. In return, the partnership executed a note and a deed of trust in favor of F & H. The partnership obtained the loan on a nonrecourse basis: neither the partnership nor its partners assumed any personal liability for repayment of the loan. Pelt later admitted four friends and relatives, respondents Tufts, Steger, Stephens, and Austin, as general partners. None of them contributed capital upon entering the partnership.

The construction of the complex was completed in August 1971. During 1971, each partner made small capital contributions to the partnership; in 1972, however, only Pelt made a contribution. The total of the partners' capital contributions was $44,212. In each tax year, all partners claimed as income tax deductions their allocable shares of ordinary losses and depreciation. The deductions taken by the partners in 1971 and 1972 totalled $439,972. Due to these contributions and deductions, the partnership's adjusted basis in the property in August 1972 was $1,455,740.

In 1971 and 1972, major employers in the Duncanville area laid off significant numbers of workers. As a result, the partnership's rental income was less than expected, and it was unable to make the payments due on the mortgage. Each partner, on August 28, 1972, sold his partnership interest to an unrelated third party, Fred Bayles. As consideration, Bayles agreed to reimburse each partner's sale expenses up to $250; he also assumed the nonrecourse mortgage.

On the date of transfer, the fair market value of the property did not exceed $1,400,000. Each partner reported the sale on his federal income tax return and indicated that a partnership loss of $55,740 had been sustained.[1] The Commissioner of Internal Revenue, on audit, determined that the sale resulted in a partnership capital gain of approximately $400,000. His theory was that the partnership had realized the full amount of the nonrecourse obligation.[2]

Relying on Millar v. Commissioner, 577 F.2d 212, 215 (CA3), cert. denied, 439 U.S. 1046, 99 S.Ct. 721, 58 L.Ed.2d 704 (1978), the United States Tax Court, in an unreviewed decision, upheld the asserted deficiencies. 70 T.C. 756 (1978). The United States Court of Appeals for the Fifth Circuit reversed. 651 F.2d 1058 (1981). That court expressly disagreed with the *Millar* analysis, and, in limiting Crane v. Commissioner, *supra*, to its facts, questioned the theoretical underpinnings of the *Crane* decision. We granted certiorari to resolve the conflict. 456 U.S. 960, 102 S.Ct. 2034, 72 L.Ed.2d 483 (1982).

II

Section 752(d) of the Internal Revenue Code of 1954, 26 U.S.C. § 752(d), specifically provides that liabilities incurred in the sale or exchange of a partnership interest are to "be treated in the same manner as liabilities in connection with the sale or exchange of property not associated with partnerships." Section 1001 governs the determination of gains and losses on the disposition of property. Under § 1001(a), the gain or loss from a sale or other disposition of property is defined as the difference between "the amount realized" on the disposition and the property's adjusted basis. Subsection (b) of § 1001 defines "amount realized": "The amount realized from the sale or other disposition of property shall be the sum of any money received plus the fair market value of the property (other than money) received." At issue is the application of the latter provision to the disposition of property encumbered by a nonrecourse mortgage of an amount in excess of the property's fair market value.

1. The loss was the difference between the adjusted basis, $1,455,740 and the fair market value of the property, $1,400,000. On their individual tax returns, the partners did not claim deductions for their respective shares of this loss. In their petitions to the Tax Court, however, the partners did claim the loss.

2. The Commissioner determined the partnership's gain on the sale by subtracting the adjusted basis, $1,455,740, from the liability assumed by Bayles, $1,851,500. Of the resulting figure, $395,760, the Commissioner treated $348,661 as capital gain, pursuant to § 741 of the Internal Revenue Code of 1954, 26 U.S.C. § 741, and $47,099 as ordinary gain under the recapture provisions of § 1250 of the Code. The application of § 1250 in determining the character of the gain is not at issue here.

A

In Crane v. Commissioner, *supra*, this Court took the first and controlling step toward the resolution of this issue. Beulah B. Crane was the sole beneficiary under the will of her deceased husband. At his death in January 1932, he owned an apartment building that was then mortgaged for an amount which proved to be equal to its fair market value, as determined for federal estate tax purposes. The widow, of course, was not personally liable on the mortgage. She operated the building for nearly seven years, hoping to turn it into a profitable venture; during that period, she claimed income tax deductions for depreciation, property taxes, interest, and operating expenses, but did not make payments upon the mortgage principal. In computing her basis for the depreciation deductions, she included the full amount of the mortgage debt. In November 1938, with her hopes unfulfilled and the mortgagee threatening foreclosure, Mrs. Crane sold the building. The purchaser took the property subject to the mortgage and paid Crane $3,000; of that amount, $500 went for the expenses of the sale.

Crane reported a gain of $2,500 on the transaction. She reasoned that her basis in the property was zero (despite her earlier depreciation deductions based on including the amount of the mortgage) and that the amount she realized from the sale was simply the cash she received. The Commissioner disputed this claim. He asserted that Crane's basis in the property, under § 113(a)(5) of the Revenue Act of 1938, 52 Stat. 490 (the current version is § 1014 of the 1954 Code, as amended, 26 U.S.C. § 1014 (1976 ed. and Supp. V)), was the property's fair market value at the time of her husband's death, adjusted for depreciation in the interim, and that the amount realized was the net cash received plus the amount of the outstanding mortgage assumed by the purchaser.

In upholding the Commissioner's interpretation of § 113(a)(5) of the 1938 Act,[3] the Court observed that to regard merely the taxpayer's equity in the property as her basis would lead to depreciation deductions less than the actual physical deterioration of the property, and would require the basis to be recomputed with each payment on the mortgage. The Court rejected Crane's claim that any loss due to depreciation belonged to the mortgagee. The effect of the Court's ruling was that the taxpayer's basis was the value of the property undiminished by the mortgage.

The Court next proceeded to determine the amount realized under § 111(b) of the 1938 Act, 52 Stat. 484 (the current version is § 1001(b)

---

3. Section 113(a)(5) defined the basis of "property . . . acquired by . . . devise . . . or by the decedent's estate from the decedent" as "the fair market value of such property at the time of such acquisition." The Court interpreted the term "property" to refer to the physical land and buildings owned by Crane or the aggregate of her rights to control and dispose of them. 331 U.S., at 6, 67 S.Ct., at 1050.

of the 1954 Code, 26 U.S.C. § 1001(b)). In order to avoid the "absurdity," see 331 U.S., at 13, 67 S.Ct., at 1054, of Crane's realizing only $2,500 on the sale of property worth over a quarter of a million dollars, the Court treated the amount realized as it had treated basis, that is, by including the outstanding value of the mortgage. To do otherwise would have permitted Crane to recognize a tax loss unconnected with any actual economic loss. The Court refused to construe one section of the Revenue Act so as "to frustrate the Act as a whole." *Ibid.*

Crane, however, insisted that the nonrecourse nature of the mortgage required different treatment. The Court, for two reasons, disagreed. First, excluding the nonrecourse debt from the amount realized would result in the same absurdity and frustration of the Code. Second, the Court concluded that Crane obtained an economic benefit from the purchaser's assumption of the mortgage identical to the benefit conferred by the cancellation of personal debt. Because the value of the property in that case exceeded the amount of the mortgage, it was in Crane's economic interest to treat the mortgage as a personal obligation; only by so doing could she realize upon sale the appreciation in her equity represented by the $2,500 boot. The purchaser's assumption of the liability thus resulted in a taxable economic benefit to her, just as if she had been given, in addition to the boot, a sum of cash sufficient to satisfy the mortgage.[4]

In a footnote, pertinent to the present case, the Court observed:

"Obviously, if the value of the property is less than the amount of the mortgage, a mortgagor who is not personally liable cannot realize a benefit equal to the mortgage. Consequently, a different problem might be encountered where a mortgagor abandoned the property or transferred it subject to the mortgage without receiving boot. That is not this case." *Id.*, at 14, n. 37, 67 S.Ct., at 1054–55, n. 37.

B

This case presents that unresolved issue. We are disinclined to overrule *Crane*, and we conclude that the same rule applies when the unpaid amount of the nonrecourse mortgage exceeds the value of the property transferred. *Crane* ultimately does not rest on its limited theory of economic benefit; instead, we read *Crane* to have approved the Commissioner's decision to treat a nonrecourse mortgage in this

---

4. Crane also argued that even if the statute required the inclusion of the amount of the nonrecourse debt, that amount was not Sixteenth Amendment income because the overall transaction had been "by all dictates of common sense . . . a ruinous disaster." Brief for Petitioner in Crane v. Commissioner, O.T.1946, No. 68, p. 51. The Court noted, however, that Crane had been entitled to and actually took depreciation deductions for nearly seven years. To allow her to exclude sums on which those deductions were based from the calculation of her taxable gain would permit her "a double deduction . . . on the same loss of assets." The Sixteenth Amendment, it was said, did not require that result. 331 U.S., at 15–16, 67 S.Ct., at 1055.

context as a true loan. This approval underlies *Crane's* holding that the amount of the nonrecourse liability is to be included in calculating both the basis and the amount realized on disposition. That the amount of the loan exceeds the fair market value of the property thus becomes irrelevant.

When a taxpayer receives a loan, he incurs an obligation to repay that loan at some future date. Because of this obligation, the loan proceeds do not qualify as income to the taxpayer. When he fulfills the obligation, the repayment of the loan likewise has no effect on his tax liability.

Another consequence to the taxpayer from this obligation occurs when the taxpayer applies the loan proceeds to the purchase price of property used to secure the loan. Because of the obligation to repay, the taxpayer is entitled to include the amount of the loan in computing his basis in the property; the loan, under § 1012, is part of the taxpayer's cost of the property. Although a different approach might have been taken with respect to a nonrecourse mortgage loan, the Commissioner has chosen to accord it the same treatment he gives to a recourse mortgage loan. The Court approved that choice in *Crane*, and the respondents do not challenge it here. The choice and its resultant benefits to the taxpayer are predicated on the assumption that the mortgage will be repaid in full.

When encumbered property is sold or otherwise disposed of and the purchaser assumes the mortgage, the associated extinguishment of the mortgagor's obligation to repay is accounted for in the computation of the amount realized. Because no difference between recourse and nonrecourse obligations is recognized in calculating basis,[7] *Crane* teaches that the Commissioner may ignore the nonrecourse nature of the obligation in determining the amount realized upon disposition of the encumbered property. He thus may include in the amount realized the amount of the nonrecourse mortgage assumed by the purchaser. The rationale for this treatment is that the original inclusion of the amount of the mortgage in basis rested on the assumption that the mortgagor incurred an obligation to repay. Moreover, this treatment balances the fact that the mortgagor originally received the proceeds of the nonrecourse loan tax-free on the same assumption. Unless the outstanding amount of the mortgage

---

7. The Commissioner's choice in *Crane* "laid the foundation stone of most tax shelters," Bittker, Tax Shelters, Nonrecourse Debt, and the *Crane* Case, 33 Tax.L.Rev. 277, 283 (1978), by permitting taxpayers who bear no risk to take deductions on depreciable property. Congress recently has acted to curb this avoidance device by forbidding a taxpayer to take depreciation deductions in excess of amounts he has at risk in the investment. Pub.L. 94–455, § 204(a), 90 Stat. 1531 (1976), 26 U.S.C. § 465; Pub.L. 95–600, §§ 201–204, 92 Stat. 2814–2817 (1978), 26 U.S.C. § 465(a) (1976 ed., Supp. V). Real estate investments, however, are exempt from this prohibition. § 465(c)(3)(D) (1976 ed., Supp. V). Although this congressional action may foreshadow a day when nonrecourse and recourse debts will be treated differently, neither Congress nor the Commissioner has sought to alter *Crane's* rule of including nonrecourse liability in both basis and the amount realized.

is deemed to be realized, the mortgagor effectively will have received untaxed income at the time the loan was extended and will have received an unwarranted increase in the basis of his property.[8] The Commissioner's interpretation of § 1001(b) in this fashion cannot be said to be unreasonable.

C

The Commissioner in fact has applied this rule even when the fair market value of the property falls below the amount of the nonrecourse obligation. Treas.Reg. § 1.1001–2(b), 26 CFR § 1.1001–2(b) (1982); Rev.Rul. 76–111, 1976–1 Cum.Bull. 214. Because the theory on which the rule is based applies equally in this situation, we have no reason, after *Crane*, to question this treatment.[11]

---

8. Although the *Crane* rule has some affinity with the tax benefit rule, see Bittker, *supra*, at 282; Del Cotto, Sales and Other Dispositions of Property Under Section 1001: The Taxable Event, Amount Realized and Related Problems of Basis, 26 Buffalo L.Rev. 219, 323–324 (1977), the analysis we adopt is different. Our analysis applies even in the situation in which no deductions are taken. It focuses on the obligation to repay and its subsequent extinguishment, not on the taking and recovery of deductions. See generally Note, 82 Colum.L.Rev., at 1526–1529.

11. Professor Wayne G. Barnett, as *amicus* in the present case, argues that the liability and property portions of the transaction should be accounted for separately. Under his view, there was a transfer of the property for $1.4 million, and there was a cancellation of the $1.85 million obligation for a payment of $1.4 million. The former resulted in a capital loss of $50,000, and the latter in the realization of $450,000 of ordinary income. Taxation of the ordinary income might be deferred under § 108 by a reduction of respondents' bases in their partnership interests.

Although this indeed could be a justifiable mode of analysis, it has not been adopted by the Commissioner. Nor is there anything to indicate that the Code requires the Commissioner to adopt it. We note that Professor Barnett's approach does assume that recourse and nonrecourse debt may be treated identically.

The Commissioner also has chosen not to characterize the transaction as cancellation of indebtedness. We are not presented with and do not decide the contours of the cancellation-of-indebtedness doctrine. We note only that our approach does not fall within certain prior interpretations of that doctrine. In one view, the doctrine rests on the same initial premise as our analysis here—an obligation to repay—but the doctrine relies on a freeing-of-assets theory to attribute ordinary income to the debtor upon cancellation. According to that view, when nonrecourse debt is forgiven, the debtor's basis in the securing property is reduced by the amount of debt canceled, and realization of income is deferred until the sale of the property. Because that interpretation attributes income only when assets are freed, however, an insolvent debtor realizes income just to the extent his assets exceed his liabilities after the cancellation. Similarly, if the nonrecourse indebtedness exceeds the value of the securing property, the taxpayer never realizes the full amount of the obligation canceled because the tax law has not recognized negative basis.

Although the economic benefit prong of *Crane* also relies on a freeing-of-assets theory, that theory is irrelevant to our broader approach. In the context of a sale or disposition of property under § 1001, the extinguishment of the obligation to repay is not ordinary income; instead, the amount of the canceled debt is included in the amount realized, and enters into the computation of gain or loss on the disposition of property. According to *Crane*, this treatment is no different when the obligation is nonrecourse: the basis is not reduced as in the cancellation-of-indebtedness context, and the full value of the outstanding liability is included in the amount realized. Thus, the problem of negative basis is avoided.

Respondents received a mortgage loan with the concomitant obligation to repay by the year 2012. The only difference between that mortgage and one on which the borrower is personally liable is that the mortgagee's remedy is limited to foreclosing on the securing property. This difference does not alter the nature of the obligation; its only effect is to shift from the borrower to the lender any potential loss caused by devaluation of the property.[12] If the fair market value of the property falls below the amount of the outstanding obligation, the mortgagee's ability to protect its interests is impaired, for the mortgagor is free to abandon the property to the mortgagee and be relieved of his obligation.

This, however, does not erase the fact that the mortgagor received the loan proceeds tax-free and included them in his basis on the understanding that he had an obligation to repay the full amount. When the obligation is canceled, the mortgagor is relieved of his responsibility to repay the sum he originally received and thus realizes value to that extent within the meaning of § 1001(b). From the mortgagor's point of view, when his obligation is assumed by a third party who purchases the encumbered property, it is as if the mortgagor first had been paid with cash borrowed by the third party from the mortgagee on a nonrecourse basis, and then had used the cash to satisfy his obligation to the mortgagee.

Moreover, this approach avoids the absurdity the Court recognized in *Crane*. Because of the remedy accompanying the mortgage in the nonrecourse situation, the depreciation in the fair market value of the property is relevant economically only to the mortgagee, who by lending on a nonrecourse basis remains at risk. To permit the taxpayer to limit his realization to the fair market value of the property would be to recognize a tax loss for which he has suffered no corresponding economic loss.[13] Such a result would be to construe "one section of the Act . . . so as . . . to defeat the intention

---

12. In his opinion for the Court of Appeals in *Crane*, Judge Learned Hand observed:

"[The mortgagor] has all the income from the property; he manages it; he may sell it; any increase in its value goes to him; any decrease falls on him, until the value goes below the amount of the lien . . . . When therefore upon a sale the mortgagor makes an allowance to the vendee of the amount of the lien, he secures a release from a charge upon his property quite as though the vendee had paid him the full price on condition that before he took title the lien should be cleared . . . ." 153 F.2d 504, 506 (CA2 1945).

13. In the present case, the Government bore the ultimate loss. The nonrecourse mortgage was extended to respondents only after the planned complex was endorsed for mortgage insurance under §§ 221(b) and (d)(4) of the National Housing Act, 12 U.S.C. § 1715*l*(b) and (d)(4) (1976 ed. and Supp. V). After acquiring the complex from respondents, Bayles operated it for a few years, but was unable to make it profitable. In 1974, F & H foreclosed, and the Department of Housing and Urban Development paid off the lender to obtain title. In 1976, the Department sold the complex to another developer for $1,502,000. The sale was financed by the Department's taking back a note for $1,314,800 and a nonrecourse mortgage. To fail to recognize the value of the nonrecourse loan in the amount realized, therefore, would permit respondents to compound the Government's loss by claiming the tax benefits of that loss for themselves.

of another or to frustrate the Act as a whole." 331 U.S., at 13, 67 S.Ct., at 1054.

In the specific circumstances of *Crane*, the economic benefit theory did support the Commissioner's treatment of the nonrecourse mortgage as a personal obligation. The footnote in *Crane* acknowledged the limitations of that theory when applied to a different set of facts. *Crane* also stands for the broader proposition, however, that a nonrecourse loan should be treated as a true loan. We therefore hold that a taxpayer must account for the proceeds of obligations he has received tax-free and included in basis. Nothing in either § 1001(b) or in the Court's prior decisions requires the Commissioner to permit a taxpayer to treat a sale of encumbered property asymmetrically, by including the proceeds of the nonrecourse obligation in basis but not accounting for the proceeds upon transfer of the encumbered property. . . .

IV

When a taxpayer sells or disposes of property encumbered by a nonrecourse obligation, the Commissioner properly requires him to include among the assets realized the outstanding amount of the obligation. The fair market value of the property is irrelevant to this calculation. We find this interpretation to be consistent with Crane v. Commissioner, 331 U.S. 1, 67 S.Ct. 1047, 91 L.Ed. 1301 (1947), and to implement the statutory mandate in a reasonable manner.

The judgment of the Court of Appeals is therefore reversed.

It is so ordered.

Justice O'CONNOR, concurring.

I concur in the opinion of the Court, accepting the view of the Commissioner. I do not, however, endorse the Commissioner's view. Indeed, were we writing on a slate clean except for the *Crane* decision, I would take quite a different approach—that urged upon us by Professor Barnett as *amicus*.

Crane established that a taxpayer could treat property as entirely his own, in spite of the "coinvestment" provided by his mortgagee in the form of a nonrecourse loan. That is, the full basis of the property, with all its tax consequences, belongs to the mortgagor. That rule alone, though, does not in any way tie nonrecourse debt to the cost of property or to the proceeds upon disposition. I see no reason to treat the purchase, ownership, and eventual disposition of property differently because the taxpayer also takes out a mortgage, an independent transaction. In this case, the taxpayer purchased property, using nonrecourse financing, and sold it after it declined in value to a buyer who assumed the mortgage. There is no economic difference between the events in this case and a case in which the taxpayer buys property with cash; later obtains a nonrecourse loan by pledging the property as security; still later, using cash on hand, buys off the mortgage for the market value of the devalued property; and finally sells the property to a third party for its market value.

The logical way to treat both this case and the hypothesized case is to separate the two aspects of these events and to consider, first, the ownership and sale of the property, and, second, the arrangement and retirement of the loan. Under *Crane*, the fair market value of the property on the date of acquisition—the purchase price—represents the taxpayer's basis in the property, and the fair market value on the date of disposition represents the proceeds on sale. The benefit received by the taxpayer in return for the property is the cancellation of a mortgage that is worth no more than the fair market value of the property, for that is all the mortgagee can expect to collect on the mortgage. His gain or loss on the disposition of the property equals the difference between the proceeds and the cost of acquisition. Thus, the taxation of the transaction *in property* reflects the economic fate of the *property*. If the property has declined in value, as was the case here, the taxpayer recognizes a loss on the disposition of the property. The new purchaser then takes as his basis the fair market value as of the date of the sale.

In the separate borrowing transaction, the taxpayer acquires cash from the mortgagee. He need not recognize income at that time, of course, because he also incurs an obligation to repay the money. Later, though, when he is able to satisfy the debt by surrendering property that is worth less than the face amount of the debt, we have a classic situation of cancellation of indebtedness, requiring the taxpayer to recognize income in the amount of the difference between the proceeds of the loan and the amount for which he is able to satisfy his creditor. 26 U.S.C. § 61(a)(12). The taxation of the financing transaction then reflects the economic fate of the loan.

The reason that separation of the two aspects of the events in this case is important is, of course, that the Code treats different sorts of income differently. A gain on the sale of the property may qualify for capital gains treatment while the cancellation of indebtedness is ordinary income, but income that the taxpayer may be able to defer. Not only does Professor Barnett's theory permit us to accord appropriate treatment to each of the two types of income or loss present in these sorts of transactions, it also restores continuity to the system by making the taxpayer-seller's proceeds on the disposition of property equal to the purchaser's basis in the property. Further, and most important, it allows us to tax the events in this case in the same way that we tax the economically identical hypothesized transaction.

Persuaded though I am by the logical coherence and internal consistency of this approach, I agree with the Court's decision not to adopt it judicially. We do not write on a slate marked only by *Crane*. The Commissioner's longstanding position, Rev.Rul. 76–111, 1976–1 C.B. 214, is now reflected in the regulations. Treas.Reg. § 1.1001–2, 26 CFR § 1.1001–2 (1982). In the light of the numerous cases in the lower courts including the amount of the unrepaid proceeds of the mortgage in the proceeds on sale or disposition, it is difficult to conclude that the Commissioner's interpretation of the statute exceeds the bounds of his discretion. As the Court's opinion demonstrates, his interpretation is defensible. One can reasonably read § 1001(b)'s reference to "the amount realized *from* the sale or other disposition of property" (emphasis added) to permit the Commissioner to collapse the two aspects of the transaction. As long as his view is a reasonable reading of § 1001(b), we should defer to the regulations promulgated by the agency charged with interpretation of the statute. Accordingly, I concur.

ESTATE OF FRANKLIN v. COMMISSIONER OF INTERNAL REVENUE

United States Court of Appeals, Ninth Circuit, 1976.
544 F.2d 1045.

SNEED, Circuit Judge:

This case involves another effort on the part of the Commissioner to curb the use of real estate tax shelters.[1] In this instance he seeks to disallow deductions for the taxpayers' distributive share of losses reported by a limited partnership with respect to its acquisition of a motel and related property. These "losses" have their origin in deductions for depreciation and interest claimed with respect to the motel and related property. These deductions were disallowed by the Commissioner on the ground either that the acquisition was a sham or that the entire acquisition transaction was in substance the purchase by the partnership of an option to acquire the motel and related property on January 15, 1979. The Tax Court held that the transaction constituted an option exercisable in 1979 and disallowed the taxpayers' deductions. Estate of Charles T. Franklin, 64 T.C. 752 (1975). We affirm this disallowance although our approach differs somewhat from that of the Tax Court.

The interest and depreciation deductions were taken by Twenty-Fourth Property Associates (hereinafter referred to as Associates), a California limited partnership of which Charles T. Franklin and seven other doctors were the limited partners. The deductions flowed from

1. An early skirmish in this particular effort appears in Manuel D. Mayerson, 47 T.C. 340 (1966), which the Commissioner lost. The Commissioner attacked the substance of a nonrecourse sale, but based his attack on the nonrecourse and long-term nature of the purchase money note, without focusing on whether the sale was made at an unrealistically high price. In his acquiescence to *Mayerson*, 1969–2 Cum.Bull. xxiv, the Commissioner recognized that the fundamental issue in these cases generally will be whether the property has been "acquired" at an artificially high price, having little relation to its fair market value. "The Service emphasizes that its acquiescence in *Mayerson* is based on the particular facts in the case and will not be relied upon in the disposition of other cases except where it is clear that the property has been acquired at its fair market value in an arm's length transaction creating a bona fide purchase and a bona fide debt obligation." Rev.Rul. 69–77, 1969–1 Cum.Bull. 59.

the purported "purchase" by Associates of the Thunderbird Inn, an Arizona motel, from Wayne L. Romney and Joan E. Romney (hereinafter referred to as the Romneys) on November 15, 1968.

Under a document entitled "Sales Agreement," the Romneys agreed to "sell" the Thunderbird Inn to Associates for $1,224,000. The property would be paid for over a period of ten years, with interest on any unpaid balance of seven and one-half percent per annum. "Prepaid interest" in the amount of $75,000 was payable immediately; monthly principal and interest installments of $9,045.36 would be paid for approximately the first ten years, with Associates required to make a balloon payment at the end of the ten years of the difference between the remaining purchase price, forecast as $975,000, and any mortgages then outstanding against the property.

The purchase obligation of Associates to the Romneys was nonrecourse; the Romneys' only remedy in the event of default would be forfeiture of the partnership's interest. The sales agreement was recorded in the local county. A warranty deed was placed in an escrow account, along with a quitclaim deed from Associates to the Romneys, both documents to be delivered either to Associates upon full payment of the purchase price, or to the Romneys upon default.

The sale was combined with a leaseback of the property by Associates to the Romneys; Associates therefore never took physical possession. The lease payments were designed to approximate closely the principal and interest payments with the consequence that with the exception of the $75,000 prepaid interest payment no cash would cross between Associates and Romneys until the balloon payment. The lease was on a net basis; thus, the Romneys were responsible for all of the typical expenses of owning the motel property including all utility costs, taxes, assessments, rents, charges, and levies of "every name, nature and kind whatsoever." The Romneys also were to continue to be responsible for the first and second mortgages until the final purchase installment was made; the Romneys could, and indeed did, place additional mortgages on the property without the permission of Associates. Finally, the Romneys were allowed to propose new capital improvements which Associates would be required to either build themselves or allow the Romneys to construct with compensating modifications in rent or purchase price.

In holding that the transaction between Associates and the Romneys more nearly resembled an option than a sale, the Tax Court emphasized that Associates had the power at the end of ten years to walk away from the transaction and merely lose its $75,000 "prepaid interest payment." It also pointed out that a *deed* was never recorded and that the "benefits and burdens of ownership" appeared to remain with the Romneys. Thus, the sale was combined with a leaseback in which no cash would pass; the Romneys remained responsible under the mortgages, which they could increase; and the

Romneys could make capital improvements.[2] The Tax Court further justified its "option" characterization by reference to the nonrecourse nature of the purchase money debt and the nice balance between the rental and purchase money payments.

Our emphasis is different from that of the Tax Court. We believe the characteristics set out above can exist in a situation in which the sale imposes upon the purchaser a genuine indebtedness within the meaning of section 167(a), Internal Revenue Code of 1954, which will support both interest and depreciation deductions. They substantially so existed in Hudspeth v. Commissioner, 509 F.2d 1224 (9th Cir. 1975) in which parents entered into sale-leaseback transactions with their children. The children paid for the property by executing non-negotiable notes and mortgages equal to the fair market value of the property; state law proscribed deficiency judgments in case of default, limiting the parents' remedy to foreclosure of the property. The children had no funds with which to make mortgage payments; instead, the payments were offset in part by the rental payments, with the difference met by gifts from the parents to their children. Despite these characteristics this court held that there was a bona fide indebtedness on which the children, to the extent of the rental payments, could base interest deductions. See also American Realty Trust v. United States, 498 F.2d 1194 (4th Cir. 1974); Manuel D. Mayerson, 47 T.C. 340 (1966).

In none of these cases, however, did the taxpayer fail to demonstrate that the purchase price was at least approximately equivalent to the fair market value of the property. Just such a failure occurred here. The Tax Court explicitly found that on the basis of the facts before it the value of the property could not be estimated. 64 T.C. at 767–768.[4] In our view this defect in the taxpayers' proof is fatal.

---

2. There was evidence that not all of the benefits and burdens of ownership remained with the Romneys. Thus, for example, the leaseback agreement appears to provide that any condemnation award will go to Associates. Exhibit 6–F, at p. 5.

4. The Tax Court found that appellants had "not shown that the purported sales price of $1,224,000 (or any other price) had any relationship to the actual market value of the motel property . . . .." 64 T.C. at 767.

Petitioners spent a substantial amount of time at trial attempting to establish that, whatever the actual market value of the property, Associates acted in the good faith *belief* that the market value of the property approximated the selling price. However, this evidence only goes to the issue of sham and does not supply substance to this transaction. "Save in those instances where the statute itself turns on intent, a matter so real as taxation must depend on objective realities, not on the varying subjective beliefs of individual taxpayers." Lynch v. Commissioner, 273 F.2d 867, 872 (2d Cir. 1959).

In oral argument it was suggested by the appellants that neither the Tax Court nor they recognized the importance of fair market value during the presentation of evidence and that this hampered the full and open development of this issue. However, upon an examination of the record, we are satisfied that the taxpayers recognized the importance of presenting objective evidence of the fair market value and were awarded ample opportunity to present their proof; appellants merely failed to present clear and admissible evidence that fair market value did indeed approximate the purchase price. Such evidence of fair market value as was relied upon by the appellants, *viz.* two appraisals, one completed in 1968

Reason supports our perception. An acquisition such as that of Associates if at a price approximately equal to the fair market value of the property under ordinary circumstances would rather quickly yield an equity in the property which the purchaser could not prudently abandon. This is the stuff of substance. It meshes with the form of the transaction and constitutes a sale.

No such meshing occurs when the purchase price exceeds a demonstrably reasonable estimate of the fair market value. Payments on the principal of the purchase price yield no equity so long as the unpaid balance of the purchase price exceeds the then existing fair market value. Under these circumstances the purchaser by abandoning the transaction can lose no more than a mere chance to acquire an equity in the future should the value of the acquired property increase. While this chance undoubtedly influenced the Tax Court's determination that the transaction before us constitutes an option, we need only point out that its existence fails to supply the substance necessary to justify treating the transaction as a sale *ab initio*. It is not necessary to the disposition of this case to decide the tax consequences of a transaction such as that before us if in a subsequent year the fair market value of the property increases to an extent that permits the purchaser to acquire an equity.[5]

Authority also supports our perception. It is fundamental that "depreciation is not predicated upon ownership of property *but rather upon an investment in property.* Gladding Dry Goods Co., 2 BTA 336 (1925)." *Mayerson,* supra at 350 (italics added). No such investment exists when payments of the purchase price in accordance with the design of the parties yield no equity to the purchaser. In the transaction before us and during the taxable years in question the purchase price payments by Associates have not been shown to constitute an *investment in the property.* Depreciation was properly disallowed. Only the Romneys had an investment in the property.

Authority also supports disallowance of the interest deductions. This is said even though it has long been recognized that the absence

and a second in 1971, even if fully admissible as evidence of the truth of the estimates of value appearing therein, does not require us to set aside the Tax Court's finding. As the Tax Court found, the 1968 appraisal was "error-filled, sketchy" and "obviously suspect." 64 T.C. at 767 n. 13. The 1971 appraisal had little relevancy as to 1968 values. On the other side, there existed cogent evidence indicating that the fair market value was substantially less than the purchase price. This evidence included (i) the Romneys' purchase of the stock of two corporations, one of which wholly-owned the motel, for approximately $800,000 in the year preceding the "sale" to Associates ($660,000 of which was allocable to the sale property, according to Mr. Romney's estimate), and (ii) insurance policies on the property from 1967 through 1974 of only $583,200, $700,000, and $614,000. 64 T.C. at 767–768.

Given that it was the appellants' burden to present evidence showing that the purchase price did not exceed the fair market value and that he had a fair opportunity to do so, we see no reason to remand this case for further proceedings.

5. These consequences would include a determination of the proper basis of the acquired property at the date the increments to the purchaser's equity commenced.

of personal liability for the purchase money debt secured by a mortgage on the acquired property does not deprive the debt of its character as a bona fide debt obligation able to support an interest deduction. *Mayerson*, supra at 352. However, this is no longer true when it appears that the debt has economic significance only if the property substantially appreciates in value prior to the date at which a very large portion of the purchase price is to be discharged. Under these circumstances the purchaser has not secured "the use or forbearance of money." Nor has the seller advanced money or forborne its use. Prior to the date at which the balloon payment on the purchase price is required, and assuming no substantial increase in the fair market value of the property, the absence of personal liability on the debt reduces the transaction in economic terms to a mere chance that a genuine debt obligation may arise. This is not enough to justify an interest deduction. To justify the deduction the debt must exist; potential existence will not do. For debt to exist, the purchaser, in the absence of personal liability, must confront a situation in which it is presently reasonable from an economic point of view for him to make a capital investment in the amount of the unpaid purchase price. Associates, during the taxable years in question, confronted no such situation. Compare Crane v. Commissioner, 331 U.S. 1, 11–12, 67 S.Ct. 1047, 91 L.Ed. 1301 (1947).

Our focus on the relationship of the fair market value of the property to the unpaid purchase price should not be read as premised upon the belief that a sale is not a sale if the purchaser pays too much. Bad bargains from the buyer's point of view—as well as sensible bargains from buyer's, but exceptionally good from the seller's point of view—do not thereby cease to be sales. We intend our holding and explanation thereof to be understood as limited to transactions substantially similar to that now before us.

Affirmed.

BIBLIOGRAPHIC NOTE

In addition to the standard tax treatises and textbooks, you may find the following sources helpful: P. Anderson, Tax Factors in Real Estate Operations (5th ed. 1978); P. Anderson, Tax Planning of Real Estate (7th ed. 1977); I. Faggen, et al., Federal Taxes Affecting Real Estate (5th ed. 1981); M. Levine, Real Estate Transactions: Tax Planning and Consequences (3d ed. 1981); G. Robinson, Federal Income Taxation of Real Estate (3rd ed. 1979). The Journal of Real Estate Taxation, published quarterly, is an excellent source of articles on currently important tax topics.

Part Two

PRIVATE ARRANGEMENTS FOR POSSESSION AND USE

I. POSSESSORY INTERESTS: PRESENT, FUTURE, CONCURRENT

A. THE ESTATES SYSTEM

The estates system represents one way to divide interests in land, defining ownership in terms of possession and time. *A* may own an estate entitling her to possess Blackacre forever. She can, if she chooses, part with possession of Blackacre for a specified period, such as by renting the land to *B* for ten years, giving *B* the present right to possess the land for ten years, and leaving herself with a future interest—the right to regain possession at the end of ten years. *A* could alternatively convey present possession to her husband for his lifetime, with possession to pass upon his death to their child, *C*.

In addition to enabling the division of the right to possession over time, the estates system provides the labels to be applied to each possessory interest created. In the examples just given, *A*'s original estate is called a *fee simple absolute*, connoting the right to possess the land in perpetuity. In the first example, *A* transferred a *term of years* estate to *B*, retaining a future interest, specifically a *reversion* in fee simple absolute, to herself. In more familiar terms, *A* is a landlord and *B* is her tenant. In the second transfer, *A*'s husband received a *life estate*, and their child, *C*, received a future interest, called a *remainder*, in fee simple absolute. The number of estates is limited to a bare handful, and each estate has its own attributes. Although private choice is thus somewhat constrained, the estates system aims to promote certainty and simplicity by limiting transfers to a few well-established forms with well-established consequences.

All of this just skims the surface, though, for the modern system of estates in land represents only one phase in an evolutionary process that dates back more than nine hundred years and that, doubtless, still has some distance to go. The relationship between landlord and tenant today offers only the faintest reflection of the bonds of blood, loyalty and service that tied tenant to lord in feudal England when land was the central form of wealth and source of power, and when the division of interests in land always implied the subordination of some tenant to some lord and formed the effective basis for government and politics. Several doctrines that were first shaped to resolve the peculiar tensions of feudal society have survived to the present, and the law of estates is still in the process of shedding anachronistic encumbrances.

The historical background is relevant to the practice of law today. Lawyers should be prepared to show legislatures and courts which of the old rules are no longer useful and which, although ancient, nonetheless serve contemporary interests in efficient land transfer. Lawyers must also be familiar with each stage in the slow evolution of real property law in their state. One set of rules may have controlled the disposition of a parcel in 1870, another set in 1900 when the parcel was next conveyed, and still another set in 1970 when it was last conveyed. In order for a lawyer reviewing that parcel's chain of title to give an opinion on the state of title today, he or she must know the law that governed each transaction in the chain.

1. The Feudal Period: From 1066–1290. One of the first steps that William of Normandy took after the victory at Hastings in 1066 established his right to the Crown of England was to position himself as the sole owner of all land in the country. He conveyed vast tracts of land to his followers and confirmed ownership in those Englishmen who were willing to pay the price—cash and a vow of loyalty to the King. The genius of William's system was that each grantee held his land not as an outright owner but rather as a tenant whose continued possession depended upon his loyalty and delivery of prescribed services to the King.

Another striking feature of the system was that it readily lent itself to replication. The tenants who held directly of the King (tenants in chief, or *in capite*) parcelled out some of their lands to other tenants, who in turn conveyed some of their lands to still other tenants. A tenant in chief whose right to possession was conditioned on providing military service to the King might divide his land into several parcels, occupying one and granting the others to tenants who would agree to render military service or other consideration such as food or labor. These tenants would then make conditional transfers to other tenants, and these to others. At the bottom of the pyramid was the tenant *in demesne*, the only one of these tenants actually in possession of the land. Above the tenant in demesne were the *mesne* lords and at the very top, of course, was the King.

Three features dominated each level of this hierarchy. One was the personal bond between tenant and lord, expressed in the ceremony of doing homage. According to Littleton's treatise, *Of Tenures*:

> When the tenant shall make homage to his lord, he shall be ungirt, and his head uncovered, and his lord shall sit, and the tenant shall kneel before him on both his knees, and hold his hands jointly together between the hands of his lord, and shall say thus: I become your man from this day forward [of life and limb, and of earthly worship], and unto you shall be true and faithful, and bear to you faith for the tenements that I claim to hold of you, saving the faith that I owe unto our sovereign lord the king; and then the lord, so sitting, shall kiss him. Book II, c. 1 (1481).

The second major feature of the feudal hierarchy was the requirement that the tenant render specified services to his lord in return for possession of the land and for the lord's protection. The third feature was the payment of incidents—essentially feudal taxes. It was these last two features, services and incidents, that eventually gave shape to the common law system of estates.

a. *Tenures and Services.* William and his successors needed three things to keep government going. On earth they needed the security offered by a standing army. In heaven they needed the support of the Church. And, at table they needed the supplies provided by agricultural enterprise. The so-called "free tenures" were devised to secure these needs. They were, respectively, the military tenures, frankalmoign tenure and socage tenure.

i. *Military Tenures.* Of the military tenures, the tenancy by knight service was the most important. The tenancy by knight service required the tenant to provide a designated number of knights for a specified period, sometimes as brief as forty days each year. Although the King could assemble as many as 5,000 knights this way, their service was discontinuous, making the army far less effective than a full time army of mercenaries. But, to hire mercenaries, the King needed money. By 1166 he was encouraging his tenants in chief to substitute money payments (called *scutages*, or shield money) for their fixed quota of warriors. The tenants in chief raised this money by exacting scutages from their tenants, and these tenants by exacting scutages from theirs.

ii. *Frankalmoign.* Frankalmoign tenure involved the grant of lands to religious institutions or officials in return for their performance of spiritual—and occasionally more worldly—services on behalf of the grantor.

iii. *Socage.* Socage was the great residual class of free tenures. If a free tenure was not a military tenure or frankalmoign tenure, it was considered to be socage tenure. The services required under socage tenure usually involved the provision of labor or agricultural goods, or, eventually, their money equivalent. Sometimes the service was only nominal, such as giving a peppercorn or a rose at midsummer, for the purpose of providing continuing evidence that the land was held of the lord.

iv. *The Nature of Services.* Although there were only a few types of tenures, the required services took a wide variety of forms shaped to meet the lord's needs or whims. In addition to the substantial economic services that could be exacted from tenants holding by military or socage tenure were such services as training hounds and hawks for the lord's use on hunts, assisting the King when travel across the Channel made him seasick and, as in the case of the unfortunate Rolland, the obligation every Christmas day to make a leap, a whistle and a fart for the amusement of the King. All these services had two things in common: virtually all—including Rolland's—were eventually converted into money payments, and all served to document the fact that the land was held of a lord, to whom were due the increasingly important incidents. See generally, A.W.B. Simpson, An Introduction to the History of the Land Law 1–14 (1961).

b. Incidents. Together with homage, fealty and services, each form of tenure except frankalmoign carried specified incidents. Among the more important were *aids* (money contributions to the lord on the knighting of his eldest son, on the marriage of his eldest daughter, and on his capture by enemies if a ransom was required); *relief* (payment by the tenant's heir on the tenant's death) and *escheat* (the land's reversion to the lord if the tenant died without heirs).

In addition, the military tenures carried the incidents of *wardship* and *marriage*. If a tenant died and his heir was a minor, wardship gave the lord custody of the heir and of the tenant's lands, entitling the lord to receive, and not be accountable for, their rents and profits. Marriage gave the lord the right to choose his ward's marriage partner—and the right to compensation from the ward who, unhappy with the lord's choice, decided to look elsewhere for a spouse.

Incidents flourished long after the tenures and services to which they were attached lost their substance and value. Reliefs effectively became inheritance taxes. Wardships and marriage, with their guaranteed stream of income, were traded like securities. The principal reason for the continued vitality of incidents was that, unlike services which had a fixed value, incidents were essentially inflation-proof, fluctuating with the value of the land to which they were annexed.

c. Copyhold. The elaborate feudal edifice, with all of its channels of duty, privilege and protection, and its network of service and incident, could not obscure a simple fact: for the system to run, someone had to work the land. The task fell to *villeins* agricultural laborers who lived on the lord's manor, providing food for the lord and his entourage for a week or a month every year, receiving in return shelter and use of the parcel for their own family needs. The villein's economic position improved over time. By the fourteenth century, fixed money payments replaced the obligation to provide food and labor. (The lord used this money to employ hired help.) By the sixteenth century, the real value of these fixed payments had slipped substantially and tenants were soon paying lump sums to buy out their rental obligations.

The villein's legal position also improved dramatically over this period, from a status in which he held at the will of his lord, to one approximating outright ownership. First, the workers were given a copy (hence the term "copyhold") of manorial court records reflecting not only their obligations to the lord but also their rights. These rights were gradually expanded and solidified to reflect the custom of the manor and, by the fifteenth century, copyholders had gained access to the King's courts for protection against the lord's infringement of their rights. One opinion of the period went so far as to suggest that a lord who wrongfully ejected his copyholder could be sued for trespass. Thus, copyhold tenure came to possess the security and dignity of socage tenure in all respects but one: freehold status was not conferred until the Law of Property Act of 1922.

d. **The Rise of the Fee.** William's primary concern was that his tenants, particularly those who held by knight service, remain loyal and able, and he was careful to provide that each tenant held only for the tenant's life; no interest in land passed to the tenant's heir, whose loyalty and ability to discharge his father's obligations were unknown. Tenants in chief and mesne lords imposed the same limit on their grants. Soon, however, land was commonly allowed to pass from father to son upon payment of relief and, in the case of the military tenures, subject to wardship and marriage. Heirs early pressed for legal recognition of this customary claim and, by 1100, a hereditary principle was recognized for lands held by tenants in chief and, soon after, for lands held of mesne lords, again subject to all of the feudal incidents.

Recognition of heirs' claims meant that the tenant's ability to transfer his land was doubly constrained, requiring the consent both of his heir apparent and of his lord. In 1225, D'Arundel's Case, Bracton's Notebook, pl. 1054, lifted the first constraint, holding that a tenant could make an inter vivos transfer free of his heir's claims. As a result, the heir would acquire the land only if his predecessor died without having transferred it in his lifetime.

Efforts to remove the second constraint culminated in 1290 with the statute, *Quia Emptores,* a major turning point in the development of the principle of free marketability and, as it turned out, in the decline of the feudal system. Before *Quia Emptores*, tenants could transfer their estates either by substitution or subinfeudation. In a transfer by substitution, *B*, who held as the tenant of *A*, would convey to *C*, who would be substituted for *B* in the relationship with *A*. Because the services to *A* would now be owed by someone other than his original tenant, *A*'s consent to the transfer was required. By contrast, *A*'s consent was probably not required for subinfeudation, in which *B*'s transfer to *C* effectively added a level to the feudal hierarchy, making *C* the tenant of *B*, while *B* remained the tenant of *A*. Although subinfeudation would not disturb the services due to *A*, it could substantially undermine the incidents which were measured by the value of *B*'s estate. If *B* conveyed to *C* in return for a substantial money payment at the outset, and the periodic delivery of a peppercorn or a red rose at midsummer, it was the periodic payment that determined—and thus trivialized—the value of *B*'s estate, and it was only this value that *A* would receive in the event of escheat, relief, wardship or marriage.

Quia Emptores represented a compromise between the major lords and the lower tenants: transfers by substitution would be freely permitted, without any requirement of the lord's consent; but transfer by subinfeudation in fee simple would henceforth be prohibited. Some of the Statute's consequences, such as the free marketability of land, were immediate. Others became apparent only later. Over time, with escheats and forfeitures, many mesne lordships dropped out, substantially collapsing the feudal structure. It would not be until 1660, however, that the military tenures, and with them the bulk of feudal incidents, were abolished. Also, because the Statute's prohibition on subinfeudation was confined to fee simple transfers, tenants were free to carve out other estates—the fee tail, life estates, terms of years, and defeasible fees such as determinable fees and fees on condition subsequent.

2. *The Evolution of Estates: From 1290 On.* As tenures and services declined, greater importance began to attach to estates, the vehicles through which private grantors carved out their commercial and dynastic designs. There was also a new insistence on precision in wording. After D'Arundel's Case and *Quia Emptores*, *A*'s conveyance "to *B and his heirs*" would be held to transfer a fee simple to *B*. After the statute, *De Donis Conditionalibus* (1285), another piece of Edwardian legislation, use of the language "to *B and the heirs of his body*" would be held to create a fee tail in *B*, essentially a string of life estates in *B*'s lineal descendants. Failure to use the formulaic "and his heirs" or "heirs of his body" language meant that *B* would acquire no more than a life estate.

The fee simple, fee tail and life estate were called *freehold* estates, signaling their normal use within the traditional feudal tenures, and distinguishing them from villeinage and copyhold as well as from the term of years estate which originated as a device for evading the prohibition against usury. (To the medieval mind, these latter estates were inferior to the freehold estates even though the tenant's possession might last longer—a term of years, for example, frequently outlasting a life estate.) The principal distinction between nonfreehold and freehold estates was that the owner of a nonfreehold estate was entitled to occupancy, while the owner of a freehold estate was entitled to something subtly greater—*seisin*, meaning very roughly, possession. The distinction made a difference in terms of the remedies available to the possessor against intruders on his land.

3. Tenure and Estates in America. By the time England settled the American colonies, the feudal tenures were clearly in decline. Yet, as William Vance has observed, "The first royal grants of vacant lands in the New World were made during the critical period when the Stuarts were struggling to re-establish the waning feudal powers of the Crown." Subinfeudation, outlawed at home, was expressly permitted in the colonies. And, it "was but natural that patents were in feudal form, the land to be held in free and common socage, reserving some nominal services, like the annual render of two beaver skins or 'an Indian arrow of these parts.'" Vance, The Quest for Tenure in the United States, 33 Yale L.J. 248, 256 (1924). Services also often involved money payments, called quit rents, and it was these, with their implicit message of subordination to the sovereign's will, that most angered the colonists. Not surprisingly, quit rents quickly disappeared almost everywhere when the Revolution ended all tenurial ties to the Crown.

Holding title to a vast, vacant domain, the new federal government faced the same challenge and opportunity as William of Normandy seven centuries earlier: to dispose of its land in a way that would best secure the interests of the sovereign. The objects and methods chosen contrasted sharply with William's. Instead of subordinating landholders to state ownership, the government sought through its sales and grants of land to promote economic and political independence among its settlers. The government's sales program first focused on sales of large tracts of land but, by 1832, it reduced the minimum saleable tract to 40 acres and reduced the price per acre as well. The Homestead Act, passed in 1862, gave land free to those who would settle and work it. 12 Stats. 392 (Act of May 20, 1862). Other grants were fashioned to serve more specific objects. For example, the Morrill Act of 1862, 12 Stats. 503 (Act of July 2, 1862) gave land to individual states to support agricultural colleges. Other grants sought to encourage entrepreneurs to build railroads spanning the country.

Although the tenurial system never obtained a substantial or lasting hold in America, the English system of estates did. *De Donis*, *Quia Emptores* and the distinctions between freehold and nonfreehold estates were received into state law almost everywhere. The validity and efficacy of the fee simple, fee tail and life estate were widely acknowledged. Although some doubt was expressed about the validity of fees simple determinable and fees simple subject to condition subsequent, these, too, were soon accepted into American conveyancing practice.

4. *The Legacy of Tenures and Estates.* The long history of tenures and estates in England reveals a single, driving force toward the freer marketability of land. The commutation of services into cash obligations and the free trade in feudal incidents were the beginnings of a trend. D'Arundel's Case, freeing tenants from the claims of their heirs, and *Quia Emptores*, freeing them from the claims of their lord, were only the most salient milestones along the way. Judicially-evolved rules of interpretation and privately designed legal mechanisms also pressed in the same direction. As you will soon see, American courts were quick to pick up the trend, amplifying it and eventually elevating it to an explicit, overarching and operative policy favoring the free marketability of land.

Although this policy is sometimes said to favor free *alienability*, it should be clear that alienability and marketability are different, often opposite, concepts. Free alienability means that a landowner can in disposing of his lands impose whatever conditions he wishes, for as long as he wishes—for example, it might please A to convey Blackacre to B "for life, then to such children of C as shall survive B, so long as no such survivor shall consume alcoholic beverages, and failing that condition, to D or D's heirs in fee." Free marketability means that interests in land should be readily saleable—an object defeated by the conveyance in the preceding example because the contingent nature of many of the interests created, and the fact that considerable time must elapse before all the interest holders can be identified, means that it would be highly impractical, if not impossible, for one person to try to buy Blackacre by identifying all interest holders and obtaining conveyances from them.

NOTES

1. Estates in land are unknown outside the common law system. In the civil law world, encompassing most of western Europe, Central and South America and parts of Asia and Africa, ownership, not estate, is the operative concept. Unlike common law estates, which contemplate Blackacre's division into present and future interests, civilian ownership is indivisible: one, and only one, person can at any time be said to own a particular piece of land. Thus, in Italy, a typical civil law jurisdiction, it would be unthinkable to say that the transfer, "A to B for life" created a freehold estate in B equal in dignity to A's reversion. Rather, A alone would be said to own the land, subject to an "usufrutto," giving B certain rights, but no part of the

land's ownership. Similarly, a lease from *A* to *B* in Italy gives *B* general contract rights but no property interest, and *A* remains the exclusive owner.

As a general matter, the civil law concept of indivisible ownership offers the landowner less flexibility in carving up his interests than does the common law. The differences between civil and common law systems should not, however, be exaggerated. Similar economic and social pressures in both systems often produce results that in practice are much alike. Thus, there are many more similarities than differences between the actual positions of a life tenant and the holder of an usufrutto for life. And in landlord-tenant disputes, the Italian and American practices are gradually approaching each other—as the Italians devise special rules to meet the unique needs of the lease arrangement, and as the Americans introduce general contract rules into the landlord-tenant relationship.

For an excellent, brief comparison of the common law and civil law property systems, see Merryman, Ownership and Estate (Variations on a Theme by Lawson), 48 Tul.L.Rev. 916 (1974).

2. England, the birthplace of estates in land, has to a significant degree become a final resting place as well. The 1925 Law of Property Act, 15 & 16 Geo. V, c. 20, abolished all *legal* estates other than the fee simple absolute and term of years. Grantees of any other interest—life tenancies, defeasible fees, remainders, executory interests, reverters and reversions—can hold these only as *equitable* estates with legal title to the fee vested in a trustee.

The Act's principal aim was to increase the marketability of land titles by enabling a single, readily identifiable person—the trustee—to convey fee title unencumbered by future interests. Before the Act, title to land held, "to *B* for life, remainder to her surviving children," would have been unmarketable in *B*'s lifetime because a buyer could not possibly identify *B*'s surviving children in order to buy out their interests. After the Act, *B*, or some independent trustee, has legal title to the land in fee simple absolute and the children have equitable remainders. Having a legal fee simple absolute, *B* or the independent trustee can freely sell or otherwise dispose of the land. The purchase money—presumably the cash equivalent of the land's value—will be held by *B* or the independent trustee for distribution according to the terms of the original conveyance—income to *B* for life, and principal to the equitable remaindermen who survive her.

Bordwell, English Property Reform and Its American Aspects, 37 Yale L.J. 1, 179 (1927) and Schnebly, "Legal" and "Equitable" Interests in Land Under the English Legislation of 1925, 40 Harv.L.Rev. 248 (1926), offer contemporary American views on the English reforms. See also Maudsley, Escaping the Tyranny of Common Law Estates, 42 Mo.L.Rev. 355 (1977).

1. CLASSIFICATION OF ESTATES IN LAND

The estates system, consisting of present possessory interests and their companion future interests, has evolved to the following point today:

Present Interest	Future Interest	
	In Grantor	In Transferee
Fee simple absolute	None	None
Fee simple determinable	Possibility of reverter	None
Fee simple subject to a condition subsequent	Right of entry	None
Fee simple subject to an executory limitation	None	Executory interest
Fee tail	Reversion	Remainder
Life estate	Reversion	Remainder
Term of years	Reversion	Remainder
Periodic tenancy	Reversion	Remainder
Tenancy at will	Reversion	Remainder

Standard form language has evolved for the creation of each of these present and future interests, and litigation involving freehold estates today focuses principally on determining the intent of grantors who failed to use the prescribed form. The answer can be crucial, for the attributes of one present or future interest will often differ from those of another. The methods employed in classifying present freehold interests are considered in this section; the methods for classifying future interests are considered in the next.

a. THE FEE SIMPLE

RESTATEMENT OF PROPERTY

(1936).

§ 14. Estate in Fee Simple.

An estate in fee simple is an estate which

(a) has a duration

(i) potentially infinite; or

(ii) terminable upon an event which is certain to occur but is not certain to occur within a fixed or computable period of time or within the duration of any specified life or lives; or

(iii) terminable upon an event which is certain to occur, provided such estate is one left in the conveyor, subject to defeat upon the occurrence of the stated event in favor of a person other than the conveyor; and

(b) if limited in favor of a natural person, would be inheritable by his collateral as well as by his lineal heirs.

NOTES

1. At common law, it was essential to the creation of a fee simple by inter vivos transfer that the conveyance be worded "to B and his (or her) heirs." Form prevailed over A's express statements of intent such as, "A to B to hold forever," or even "A to B in fee simple absolute." Failure to use the talismanic words, "and his heirs," meant that B received only a life estate and A retained the reversion. The rule was not, however, applied to testamentary transfers. A will would be held to transfer a fee estate even absent the "and his heirs" language so long as the testator's intent to create a fee was evident.

Most states have abolished the "and his heirs" requirement by statute, with the result that a conveyance worded, "to B forever," or "to B in fee simple," will today be held to transfer A's fee simple estate. See, e.g., West's Ann.Cal.Civ.Code § 1072; N.Y.—McKinney's Real Prop. Law § 240(1). Statutes in these states also typically go one step further, providing that every conveyance of land is presumed to transfer the grantor's entire fee simple estate. See, e.g., West's Ann.Cal.Civ.Code § 1105; N.Y.—McKinney's Real Prop. Law § 245. Thus, if A, owning a fee simple absolute, conveys to B with the words, "A hereby conveys to B," B will take a fee simple absolute unless it is clearly demonstrated that A's intent was to transfer some lesser estate.

In some states it was courts, not legislatures, that abandoned the common law requirement. In Dennen v. Searle, 149 Conn. 126, 176 A.2d 561 (1961), the state supreme court reasoned that its usual rule of construction was to enforce the expressed intent of the parties, that it did not require the "and his heirs" language for fee transfers by will, and that it could find no good reason to impose the requirement on inter vivos transfers in which the grantor's intent was otherwise clear. Although earlier cases had assumed that the common law requirement was applicable, "in no case, have we directly so held." 149 Conn. at 137, 176 A.2d at 568.

What if the words, "A hereby conveys in fee to B," appeared in a deed delivered before the effective date of the state statute providing that the "and his heirs" language is unnecessary to the creation of a fee? Would it be appropriate to apply the statute retroactively? Would it be constitutional? Should rules that purport to effectuate a grantor's intent be treated differently for these purposes from rules that invalidate the grantor's intended disposition? Should the constitutional result be any different if, instead of applying a statute retroactively, a court, as in Dennen v. Searle, simply declares that it has *always* been the law in the state that the "and his heirs" language is unnecessary to transfer a fee?

2. *Heirs.* What interest, if any, do the heirs obtain if a grantor *does* (and many still do) use the phrase, "to B and his heirs"? At one time, heirs, or at least the eldest surviving son, obtained something like a remainder interest. But in 1225, D'Arundel's Case established that B could entirely defeat this interest by an inter vivos transfer. Thus, early on, the heirs' interest was reduced to a bare expectancy that they would take the land in the event B died without having transferred the land in his lifetime.

Heirs are not, as is sometimes thought, those who take under a will. Nor are heirs necessarily the decedent's children. Nor are heirs ascertainable during the decedent's lifetime. Heirs are simply those individuals who, under the applicable state statute of descent, are entitled to take the property of an intestate—someone who dies without a valid will. The prescribed order of descent varies from state to state, but it is not unusual to find statutes dividing an intestate's property first between the surviving spouse and the intestate's descendants (children, grandchildren, and so on); then, if there is no surviving spouse or descendant, to the intestate's parents, brothers and sisters, or descendants of the brothers and sisters; if none of these survives, then to the intestate's grandparents and their descendants; then to great-grandparents and to their descendents; then to the intestate's nearest remaining kindred (such as cousins many times removed). See, e.g., Ill.—S.H.A., Probate ch. $110\frac{1}{2}$, ¶ 2–1 (1982).

What if there are no heirs at all? In that case, the intestate's property typically passes—escheats—to the state in which the property is situated.

3. Courts and lawyers often use the terms, "words of purchase" and "words of limitation" in cases involving estates. Words of purchase identify *who* takes the estate. Words of limitation identify *what* that estate is. Thus, in the transfer, "A to B and her heirs," the words, "to B" are words of purchase because they identify B as taker. (B is a "purchaser" for conveyancing purposes whether or not she gave consideration for the transfer.) The words "and her heirs" are words of limitation, defining B's estate as a fee simple.

i. Fee Simple Absolute

WHITE v. BROWN

Supreme Court of Tennessee, 1977.
559 S.W.2d 938.

BROCK, Justice.

This is a suit for the construction of a will. The Chancellor held that the will passed a life estate, but not the remainder, in certain realty, leaving the remainder to pass by inheritance to the testatrix's heirs at law. The Court of Appeals affirmed.

Mrs. Jessie Lide died on February 15, 1973, leaving a holographic will which, in its entirety, reads as follows:

"April 19, 1972

"I, Jessie Lide, being in sound mind declare this to be my last will and testament. I appoint my niece Sandra White Perry to be the executrix of my estate. I wish Evelyn White to have my home to live in and not to be sold.

"I also leave my personal property to Sandra White Perry. My house is not to be sold.

Jessie Lide"
(Underscoring by testatrix).

Mrs. Lide was a widow and had no children. Although she had nine brothers and sisters, only two sisters residing in Ohio survived her. These two sisters quitclaimed any interest they might have in the residence to Mrs. White. The nieces and nephews of the testatrix, her heirs at law, are defendants in this action.

Mrs. White, her husband, who was the testatrix's brother, and her daughter, Sandra White Perry, lived with Mrs. Lide as a family for some twenty-five years. After Sandra married in 1969 and Mrs. White's husband died in 1971, Evelyn White continued to live with Mrs. Lide until Mrs. Lide's death in 1973 at age 88.

Mrs. White, joined by her daughter as executrix, filed this action to obtain construction of the will, alleging that she is vested with a fee simple title to the home. The defendants contend that the will conveyed only a life estate to Mrs. White, leaving the remainder to go to them under our laws of intestate succession. The Chancellor held that the will unambiguously conveyed only a life interest in the home to Mrs. White and refused to consider extrinsic evidence concerning Mrs. Lide's relationship with her surviving relatives. Due to the debilitated condition of the property and in accordance with the desire of all parties, the Chancellor ordered the property sold with the proceeds distributed in designated shares among the beneficiaries.

I.

Our cases have repeatedly acknowledged that the intention of the testator is to be ascertained from the language of the entire instrument when read in the light of surrounding circumstances. But, the practical difficulty in this case, as in so many other cases involving wills drafted by lay persons, is that the words chosen by the testatrix are not specific enough to clearly state her intent. Thus, in our opinion, it is not clear whether Mrs. Lide intended to convey a life estate in the home to Mrs. White, leaving the remainder interest to descend by operation of law, or a fee interest with a restraint on alienation. Moreover, the will might even be read as conveying a fee interest subject to a condition subsequent (Mrs. White's failure to live in the home).

In such ambiguous cases it is obvious that rules of construction, always yielding to the cardinal rule of the testator's intent, must be employed as auxiliary aids in the court's endeavor to ascertain the testator's intent.

In 1851 our General Assembly enacted two such statutes of construction, thereby creating a statutory presumption against partial intestacy.

Chapter 33 of the Public Acts of 1851 (now codified as T.C.A. §§ 64–101 and 64–501) reversed the common law presumption that a life estate was intended unless the intent to pass a fee simple was clearly expressed in the instrument. T.C.A. § 64–501 provides:

"Every grant or devise of real estate, or any interest therein, shall pass all the estate or interest of the grantor or devisor, unless the intent to pass a lesser estate or interest shall appear by express terms, or be necessarily implied in the terms of the instrument."

Chapter 180, Section 2 of the Public Acts of 1851 (now codified as T.C.A. § 32–301) was specifically directed to the operation of a devise. In relevant part, T.C.A. § 32–301 provides:

"A will . . . shall convey all the real estate belonging to [the testator] or in which he had any interest at his decease, unless a contrary intention appear by its words and context."

Thus, under our law, unless the "words and context" of Mrs. Lide's will clearly evidence her intention to convey only a life estate to Mrs. White, the will should be construed as passing the home to Mrs. White in fee. "'If the expression in the will is doubtful, the doubt is resolved against the limitation and in favor of the absolute estate.'" Meacham v. Graham, 98 Tenn. 190, 206, 39 S.W. 12, 15 (1897) (quoting Washbon v. Cope, 144 N.Y. 287, 39 N.E. 388).

Several of our cases demonstrate the effect of these statutory presumptions against intestacy by construing language which might seem to convey an estate for life, without provision for a gift over after the termination of such life estate, as passing a fee simple instead. In Green v. Young, 163 Tenn. 16, 40 S.W.2d 793 (1931), the testatrix's disposition of all of her property to her husband "to be used by him for his support and comfort during his life" was held to pass a fee estate. Similarly, in Williams v. Williams, 167 Tenn. 26, 65 S.W.2d 561 (1933), the testator's devise of real property to his children "for and during their natural lives" without provision for a gift over was held to convey a fee. And, in Webb v. Webb, 53 Tenn.App. 609, 385 S.W.2d 295 (1964), a devise of personal property to the testator's wife "for her maintenance, support and comfort, for the full period of her natural life" with complete powers of alienation but without provision for the remainder passed absolute title to the widow.

II.

Thus, if the sole question for our determination were whether the will's conveyance of the home to Mrs. White "to live in" gave her a life interest or a fee in the home, a conclusion favoring the absolute estate would be clearly required. The question, however, is complicated somewhat by the caveat contained in the will that the home is "not to be sold"—a restriction conflicting with the free alienation of property, one of the most significant incidents of fee ownership. We must determine, therefore, whether Mrs. Lide's will, when taken as a whole, clearly evidences her intent to convey only a life estate in her home to Mrs. White.

Under ordinary circumstances a person makes a will to dispose of his or her entire estate. If, therefore, a will is susceptible of two constructions, by one of which the testator disposes of the whole of his estate and by the other of which he disposes of only a part of his estate, dying intestate as to the remainder, this Court has always preferred that construction which disposes of the whole of the testator's estate if that construction is reasonable and consistent with the general scope and provisions of the will. A construction which results in partial intestacy will not be adopted unless such intention clearly appears. It has been said that the courts will prefer any reasonable construction or any construction which does not do violence to a testator's language, to a construction which results in partial intestacy.

The intent to create a fee simple or other absolute interest and, at the same time to impose a restraint upon its alienation can be clearly expressed. If the testator specifically declares that he devises land to A "in fee simple" or to A "and his heirs" but that A shall not have the power to alienate the land, there is but one tenable construction, viz., the testator's intent is to impose a restraint upon a fee simple. To construe such language to create a life estate would conflict with the express specification of a fee simple as well as with the presumption of intent to make a complete testamentary disposition of all of a testator's property. By extension, as noted by Professor Casner in his treatise on the law of real property:

> "Since it is now generally presumed that a conveyor intends to transfer his whole interest in the property, it may be reasonable to adopt the same construction, [conveyance of a fee simple] even in the absence of words of inheritance, if there is no language that can be construed to create a remainder." 6 American Law of Property § 26.58 (A.J. Casner ed. 1952).

In our opinion, testatrix's apparent testamentary restraint on the alienation of the home devised to Mrs. White does not evidence such a clear intent to pass only a life estate as is sufficient to overcome the law's strong presumption that a fee simple interest was conveyed.

Accordingly, we conclude that Mrs. Lide's will passed a fee simple absolute in the home to Mrs. White. Her attempted restraint on alienation must be declared void as inconsistent with the incidents and nature of the estate devised and contrary to public policy.

The decrees of the Court of Appeals and the trial court are reversed and the cause is remanded to the chancery court for such further proceedings as may be necessary, consistent with this opinion. Costs are taxed against appellees.

COOPER and FONES, JJ., concur.

HARBISON, Justice, dissenting.

With deference to the views of the majority, and recognizing the principles of law contained in the majority opinion, I am unable to agree that the language of the will of Mrs. Lide did or was intended to convey a fee simple interest in her residence to her sister-in-law, Mrs. Evelyn White.

The testatrix expressed the wish that Mrs. White was "to have my home to live in and *not* to be *sold*". The emphasis is that of the testatrix, and her desire that Mrs. White was not to have an unlimited estate in the property was reiterated in the last sentence of the will, to wit: "My house is not to be sold."

The testatrix appointed her niece, Mrs. Perry, executrix and made an outright bequest to her of all personal property.

The will does not seem to me to be particularly ambiguous, and like the Chancellor and the Court of Appeals, I am of the opinion that the testatrix gave Mrs. White a life estate only, and that upon the death of Mrs. White the remainder will pass to the heirs at law of the testatrix.

The cases cited by petitioners in support of their contention that a fee simple was conveyed are not persuasive, in my opinion. Possibly the strongest case cited by the appellants is Green v. Young, 163 Tenn. 16, 40 S.W.2d 793 (1931), in which the testatrix bequeathed all of her real and personal property to her husband "to be used by him for his support and comfort during his life." The will expressly stated that it included all of the property, real and personal, which the testatrix owned at the time of her death. There was no limitation whatever upon the power of the husband to use, consume, or dispose of the property, and the Court concluded that a fee simple was intended.

In the case of Williams v. Williams, 167 Tenn. 26, 65 S.W.2d 561 (1933), a father devised property to his children "for and during their natural lives" but the will contained other provisions not mentioned in the majority opinion which seem to me to distinguish the case. Unlike the provisions of the present will, other clauses in the *Williams* will contained provisions that these same children were to have "all the residue of my estate personal or mixed of which I shall die possessed or seized, or to which I shall be entitled at the time of my decease, to have and to hold the same to them and their executors and administrators and assigns forever."

Further, following some specific gifts to grandchildren, there was another bequest of the remainder of the testator's money to these same three children. The language used by the testator in that case was held to convey the fee simple interest in real estate to the children, but its provisions hardly seem analogous to the language employed by the testatrix in the instant case.

In the case of Webb v. Webb, 53 Tenn.App. 609, 385 S.W.2d 295 (1964), the testator gave his wife all the residue of his property with a clear, unqualified and unrestricted power of use, sale or disposition. Thereafter he attempted to limit her interest to a life estate, with a gift over to his heirs of any unconsumed property. Again, under settled rules of construction and interpretation, the wife was found to have a fee simple estate, but, unlike the present case, there was no limitation whatever upon the power of use or disposition of the property by the beneficiary.

On the other hand, in the case of Magevney v. Karsch, 167 Tenn. 32, 65 S.W.2d 562 (1933), a gift of the residue of the large estate of the testator to his daughter, with power "at her demise [to] dispose of it as she pleases . . . ." was held to create only a life estate with a power of appointment, and not an absolute gift of the residue. In other portions of the will the testator had given another beneficiary a power to use and dispose of property, and the Court concluded that he appreciated the distinction between a life estate and an absolute estate, recognizing that a life tenant could not dispose of property and use the proceeds as she pleased. 167 Tenn. at 57, 65 S.W.2d at 569.

In the present case the testatrix knew how to make an outright gift, if desired. She left all of her personal property to her niece without restraint or limitation. As to her sister-in-law, however, she merely wished the latter have her house "to live in", and expressly withheld from her any power of sale.

The majority opinion holds that the testatrix violated a rule of law by attempting to restrict the power of the donee to dispose of the real estate. Only by thus striking a portion of the will, and holding it inoperative, is the conclusion reached that an unlimited estate resulted.

In my opinion, this interpretation conflicts more greatly with the apparent intention of the testatrix than did the conclusion of the courts below, limiting the gift to Mrs. White to a life estate. I have serious doubt that the testatrix intended to create any illegal restraint on alienation or to violate any other rules of law. It seems to me that she rather emphatically intended to provide that her sister-in-law was not to be able to sell the house during the lifetime of the latter—a result which is both legal and consistent with the creation of a life estate.

In my opinion the judgment of the courts below was correct and I would affirm.

I am authorized to state that Chief Justice HENRY joins in this opinion.

QUESTIONS

Would, and should, the Tennessee Supreme Court's decision have been different if the disputed language had appeared in an inter vivos transfer rather than in a will? In an inter vivos transfer, a life estate in Mrs. White would have implied a reversion in fee in Mrs. Lide. Should the presumption against partial intestacy be any stronger than the presumption, stated in Tenn.Code Ann. § 64–501 (1976), that every grant or devise of real estate "shall pass all the estate or interest of the grantor or devisor"?

Would, and should, the decision have been different if Mrs. Lide had children who, had they survived, would have been her heirs at law?

Should the court have given greater weight to the express restraint on alienation? Should an interpretation that gives effect to all of a will's provisions be preferred to one that requires the invalidation of some part of a will? Is it at least equally plausible that the testatrix's injunction against sale of the house was directed at the executrix, and not at Mrs. White? Did the Chancellor's decree, ordering that the property be sold, violate this injunction? Who, if anyone, had standing to enforce the restraint? The rules governing restraints on alienation are considered at pages 587 to 598.

What do *you* think was Mrs. Lide's intent?

ii. Defeasible Fees

OLDFIELD v. STOECO HOMES, INC.

Supreme Court of New Jersey, 1958.
26 N.J. 246, 139 A.2d 291.

BURLING, J.

This is a proceeding in lieu of prerogative writ. Suit was instituted by plaintiffs, residents and taxpayers of the City of Ocean City, with the object of having several resolutions of the City of Ocean City extending the time for performance of certain conditions in a deed declared invalid, and for the further relief of having lands owned by the defendants forfeited and returned to the city. The parties defendants are Stoeco Homes, Inc., the purchaser from Ocean City, Workshop, Inc., a subsequent grantee of a portion of the land from Stoeco, and Seaboard Fidelity Company, Workshop's mortgagee, and the City of Ocean City.

From an adverse determination in the Superior Court, Law Division, plaintiffs prosecuted an appeal. Prior to hearing in the Appellate Division, we certified the cause on our own motion.

The facts are not in dispute and have been stipulated by the parties. This stipulation, together with the exhibits and the additional testimony of three witnesses, the mayor of Ocean City, a city commissioner and a corporate officer (secretary) and stockholder of Stoeco comprise the evidence in the case.

In 1951 Ocean City held title to a large number of lots of undeveloped land in a low lying area of the city. The locale of the lots is roughly divisible into two large segments, with Bay Avenue forming a dividing line between east and west. The western segment, in which the city owned several hundred lots, extends from Bay Avenue on the east to the bay thorofare on the west from 18th Street on the north to 24th Street on the south. The eastern segment, in which the city owned some 653 lots, is bounded by Bay Avenue on the west, Haven Avenue on the east, 20th Street on the north and 34th Street on the south. It is the lots in the eastern segment which are the subject matter of this litigation.

The topography of the entire area is an essential factor in this case. What little there is in the record concerning the western segment indicates that, although it was below grade and required fill, it was generally higher and necessitated less fill in order to raise the grade to the existent levels in the remainder of the city than the eastern segment. It was also situated nearer the bay and conceded to be commercially more valuable.

The eastern tract consisted largely of mosquito breeding swamp and meadow lands with salt ponds interspersed and required extensive filling and grading before the land could be utilized for residential or other productive uses.

Stoeco was desirous of acquiring the lots owned by the city in the western segment, and as part of a general plan of redevelopment it conceived of the idea of acquiring the lots owned by the city in the eastern segment also. Ocean City, recognizing that an extensive redevelopment of these swampy areas would benefit the community, indicated its willingness to sell the lots, with the exception of 226 lots in the eastern tract which it desired to retain.

After receiving minimum bids for the two groups of lots, Ocean City advertised both tracts of land for public sale on February 14, 1951, setting forth in the advertisement various terms and conditions with which the vendee was to comply. At the sale Stoeco was the only and therefore the highest bidder for both the eastern and western groups of lots, bidding $10,525 for the former and $100,000 for the latter. The sales were duly confirmed by two resolutions of the municipality dated February 16, 1951, and final settlement was made on both sales on June 29, 1951. Throughout the sales were treated as separate transactions and no question is raised in this case concerning Stoeco's performance of the conditions imposed by the deeds to the lots on the western side.

While the deed from Ocean City to Stoeco contained various conditions and restrictions, the core provisions around which this dispute centers are:

"(a) Within one (1) year from the date of this Deed, the party of the second part shall fill all of the following listed lots of land now owned by the party of the first part and which are not being conveyed.

(Here follows a list of lots by lot number and block number.)

. . .

"(b) Within one (1) year following the date of this Deed, the party of the second part shall fill all of the lots of land sold to said party of the second part as a result of this sale."

"(d) All such lands shall be filled to at least the now established and existing grades of the City of Ocean City, New Jersey for the areas and lots to be filled."

"The City of Ocean City reserves the right to change or modify any restriction, condition or other requirements hereby imposed in a manner agreeable to or as permitted by law.

"A failure to comply with the covenants and conditions of paragraphs (a), (b) and (d) hereof will automatically cause title to all lands to revert to the City of Ocean City; and a failure of any other restrictions and covenants may cause title to revert to the

City as to any particular land, lot or lots involved in any violation."

Thus, Stoeco was required to fill and grade not only the lots sold to them by the city, but also the lots retained by the city.

Some of the blocks did not contain all the lots making up the block, so that in order to complete its holdings Stoeco purchased between February and November of 1951, 137 lots from various individuals for a total price of $20,020. Shortly after settlement Stoeco entered into a contract with the Hill Dredging Company to hydraulically fill the two areas purchased by Stoeco. With materials dredged from two new lagoons on the west side, the Dredging Company between September and December of 1951 filled hydraulically a large portion of the west side and a small portion of the east side. At this stage serious difficulties were encountered by Stoeco in the performance of its undertakings. Stoeco's original scheme contemplated that five lagoons located on the west side should be dredged and the materials removed would be employed to fill the eastern side of Bay Avenue. It quickly became apparent however, that the material dredged from the lagoons was not of sufficient quality to be used as fill; it contained too high a quantity of mud and silt. In fact, Stoeco was compelled to acquire an island from a private source to use as a spill area in order to dispose of the substandard substances dredged from the lagoons. These unfavorable dredging conditions, not originally contemplated, created serious engineering and financial problems for Stoeco.

By June 29, 1952, one year after obtaining the deed, Stoeco had still not completed the substantial portion of filling and grading, nor had it done so by February of 1953. Ocean City, more interested in redevelopment than declaring a default, passed a resolution on February 20, 1953 to change and modify the terms and conditions of the sale of land. The city relied upon N.J.S.A. 40:60–51.2 and N.J.S.A. 40:60–51.5 as the wellspring of its authority, following the procedure as to publication of notice, public hearing and passage outlined. Plaintiffs were not present at the Commissioners' meeting to object to the passage of the resolution.

The general import of the resolution was that Stoeco was to be given until December 31, 1954 to complete the filling and grading of all lots purchased between Bay and Haven Avenues and 20th and 24th Streets. The resolution further provided that Stoeco was to fill to city grade all the lots in the area retained by the city, and that Stoeco was to execute and deliver a deed to be held in escrow on the conditions set forth in the resolution.

The deed concluded:

"If the purchaser is not in default on December 31st, 1954, the City may consider, by any method then permitted by law, the terms and conditions by which the purchaser may be permitted to retain title to the lots between 24th and 34th Street and the plan of filling and development of the lots therein;"

Thereafter on March 6, 1953 Stoeco conveyed the lots in the area between Bay and Haven Avenues and 20th and 22nd Streets to Workshop, Inc. Workshop trucked in fill for the area at a cost of approximately $58,000. Thereafter Workshop, under an agreement with Stoeco, erected 23 homes on the tract it had acquired. All these homes were sold, the sales prices totalling $262,100. The stipulation of facts contains the following recital:

> "None of the individuals who purchased homes from Workshop, Inc. have been made parties to this litigation and it is agreed that any judgment of the court should not affect the rights of any of these individuals."

Workshop, in order to finance the construction, mortgaged a portion of the tract it had received from Stoeco to defendant Seaboard Fidelity Company, for $82,000.

Ocean City, by December 31, 1954, accepted the filling of the area between Bay and Haven Avenues and 20th and 24th Streets as substantially completed. On December 30, 1954, Ocean City passed the second of the disputed resolutions, again following the procedures as to publication of notice, public hearing and passage provided by N.J. S.A. 40:60–51.2 and N.J.S.A. 40:60–51.5. This resolution extended the time for performance of the original conditions of the sale as to land between 24th and 30th Streets until January 1, 1958, and as to the lots between 30th and 34th Streets until January 1, 1960. The resolution further provided for destruction of the deed executed by Stoeco under the 1953 resolution and required that Stoeco execute and deliver two new deeds to be held in escrow by the city clerk on the terms and conditions set forth.

Plaintiffs were present at the commissioners' meeting of December 30, 1954, when the second resolution was adopted, and voiced their objections. Some time later, on October 3, 1955, plaintiffs instituted the instant in lieu proceeding attacking the two resolutions and seeking a forfeiture of all the lands to Ocean City for failure to comply with the original one year time limitation.

The legal issues projected by the pleadings and pre-trial order were: (1) whether the deed from Ocean City to Stoeco created an estate in fee simple subject to a condition subsequent or an estate subject to a limitation (a fee simple determinable, Restatement, Property, § 44 (1936)); (2) whether the resolutions extending the time for performance were without consideration and void because in violation of N.J.Const.1947, Art. VIII, Sec. III, par. 3, which provides:

> "No donation of land or appropriation of money shall be made by the State or any county or municipal corporation to or for the use of any society, association or corporation whatever."

(3) whether the resolutions were *ultra vires*; (4) whether the proceeding was barred because of the application of doctrines of waiver or estoppel or because not instituted within the 30-day limitation contained in R.R. 4:88–15(a), as that rule read at the time of commencement of this action.

The court below held that the nature of the defeasible estate created was one in fee simple, subject to a condition subsequent; that the resolutions were neither unconstitutional nor *ultra vires*, and that the proceeding was barred on all the grounds advanced. The issues raised below are again urged on appeal.

First, we consider the issue relating to the nature of the estate created. It is said that a fee simple determinable differs from a fee simple subject to a condition subsequent in that, in the former, upon the happening of the stated event the estate *"ipso facto"* or "automatically" reverts to the grantor or his heirs, while in the latter the grantor must take some affirmative action to divest the grantee of his estate. The interest remaining in the grantee in a fee simple determinable has been denominated a possibility of reverter, while the interest remaining in the grantee of a fee simple subject to a condition subsequent, i.e., the right to re-enter upon the happening of the prescribed contingency, has been denominated a power of termination.

It is further alleged that a fee simple determinable estate is more onerous than an estate in fee simple subject to condition subsequent in that the defenses of waiver and estoppel which are applicable to the latter are unavailing in the former. We can assume, without deciding the point, that such a distinction exists between the two estates, for the reason that, as will be hereafter developed, the estate created in the instant case was one subject to a condition subsequent.

The reverter clause in the deed bears repetition at this point:

> "A failure to comply with the covenants and conditions of paragraphs (a), (b) and (d) hereof will automatically cause title to all lands to revert to the City of Ocean City; and a failure of any other restrictions and covenants may cause title to revert to the City as to any particular land, lot or lots involved in any violation."

Plaintiffs assert that the language of automatic reverter in the deed indicates beyond cavil that the estate created was a fee simple determinable and that therefore the municipality's effort to waive the breach of performance was ineffectual.

While language is the primary guide for the ascertainment of whether a given deed attempts to condition or limit an estate, still it is the instrument as a whole, and not a particular phrase aborted from the context which provides the basis for the attainment of our ultimate task which is to effectuate the intention of the parties. The particular words, upon which are predicated the right, or lack of it, to a forfeiture are often emphasized. Thus, it has been said that such words as "so long as," "until" or "during," followed by words of reverter, are appropriate to create a fee simple determinable, whereas such words as "upon condition that" or "provided that" are usual indicators of an estate upon condition subsequent. But that particular forms of expression standing alone and without resort to the purpose of the instrument in question are not determinative is at once apparent to a discerning surveyor of the case authorities. A comparison of the language utilized with the constructional result reached in the New Jersey cases demonstrates this proposition. In Cornelius v. Ivins, 26 N.J.L. 376 (Sup.Ct.1857), the following language was construed as a condition subsequent:

> ". . . the said party of the second part, their heirs or assigns shall at any time hereafter wholly cease to use the said rail or tramway for the purpose of transportation or conveyance, or suffer the same to go entirely out of repair, and to become unfit for use, or cease to use the same for transportation or conveyance for the space of five whole years, that then, or in either of the said cases, or on failure of any of the said conditions, or either of them, this deed and the estate hereby granted shall cease, determine, and become utterly void, anything herein contained to the contrary notwithstanding; and the said premises shall revert to the said party of the first part, their heirs and assigns, and re-vest in them, in as full and ample manner as if this deed had not been made; and they shall be entitled to demand of the said party of the second part a re-conveyance thereof, if they shall desire the same;" (at pages 380–381)

While in Pamrapau Corporation v. City of Bayonne, 126 N.J.Eq. 479, 8 A.2d 835 (Ch.1939), motion denied 126 N.J.Eq. 478, 8 A.2d 908 (Ch. 1939), affirmed 127 N.J.Eq. 340, 12 A.2d 860 (E. & A.1940), motions denied 129 N.J.Eq. 3, 17 A.2d 544 (Ch.1941), affirmed 129 N.J.Eq. 586, 19 A.2d 877 (E. & A.1941) and 130 N.J.Eq. 240, 21 A.2d 863 (E. & A. 1941), the following language was construed as a special limitation:

> ". . . and if at any time hereafter any conveyance is made to any person or corporation of the premises aforesaid now owned by the city . . . then this grant shall end and determine and the said lands under water, and all the rights and privileges shall revert to and belong to the state, free and clear of any claim or claims under or by virtue of this grant." (126 N.J.Eq., at page 481, 8 A.2d at page 836)

The ancient land law imputed a thaumaturgic quality to language. If the judicial eye in scanning the instrument chanced upon a pet phrase the inquiry was ended without resorting to the arduous effort of reconciling evident inconsistencies therein. The universal touchstone today is the intention of the parties to the instrument creating the interest in land.

If the four corners of the deed provide a coherent expression of the parties' intent, we need search no further, but if an ambiguity or a reasonable doubt appears from a perusal of the particular symbols of expression our horizons must be broadened to encompass the circumstances surrounding the transaction. To the foregoing must be added certain constructional biases developed in a hierarchical fashion and predicated upon the proposition that the law abhors a forfeiture. Thus, if the choice is between a condition subsequent and a restrictive covenant, the former is preferred. And where the choice is between an estate in fee simple determinable and an estate on condition subsequent, the latter is preferred.

To focus attention solely on the words "automatically cause title to revert" is to ignore and refuse effect to the following provisions:

> "This conveyance is also subject to the following *conditions*, requirements, reservations, covenants and restrictions:" (Emphasis supplied.)

and

> "A failure to comply with the *covenants* and *conditions of paragraphs (a), (b) and (d) hereof* . . . ." (Emphasis supplied.)

Moreover, the deed contained the following clause:

> "The City of Ocean City reserves the right to change or modify any restriction, condition or other requirements hereby imposed in a manner agreeable to or as permitted by law."

The repeated use of the word "condition" and the provision reserving the right to alter the arrangement in the clauses are sufficient to cast a reasonable doubt upon what was intended. Accordingly, we shall consider the surrounding circumstances in order to ascertain the intention of the parties in creating the estate.

Before proceeding to a determination of this question, however, it is well to keep in mind what condition in the deed was violated. The plaintiffs treat the condition as to the grading and filling within one year as a single condition. Thus, they contend that since by June 1952 the grading and filling was not complied with, the city, even if the clause be construed as a condition subsequent, had a right to reenter and terminate the estate. This power of termination for breach of a condition subsequent is in New Jersey an assignable and hence a saleable property interest. They therefore conclude that to extend the time for performance was in essence to donate a valuable property right to Stoeco without consideration. But the fault in analysis is that the language imposing the duty upon the municipality is in reality two conditions and not one. First Stoeco was to fill and grade according to specifications the various lots and secondly, they were to do it within one year. It is this latter condition which was modified by the city. There is a distinction recognized in the cases between a waiver of the time for performance and a waiver of the performance itself. It may be that had the municipality waived the performance such action would be violative of the constitutional proscriptions. But that question is not before us. All the municipality did was to modify the original time for performance.

With this in mind, we proceed to a determination of whether the limitation as to time was a condition subsequent which could be waived by the city in its discretion or a limitation (fee simple determinable).

To hold that the condition as to time was so essential to the scheme of the parties that to violate it by a day would result in an immediate and automatic forfeiture of the estate is to distort beyond recognition what the parties intended. There is no indication that time was of the essence of the agreement. Ocean City was to receive two substantial considerations by this agreement. First, the 226 lots owned and retained by it were to be filled and graded, and hence their value greatly enhanced. Secondly, and perhaps more important, a large tract of land, hitherto the breeding place for mosquitos, was to be developed for productive use. Indeed, an initial *quid pro quo* has already been received in the erection of 23 dwelling units in the area. No immediacy or sense of urgency in relation to the time within which this development was to take place is apparent. It may be fairly inferred that the one-year limitation was originally put in because Stoeco conceived that the fill from the drained lagoons on the west side would be of sufficient quantity and quality that the task could easily be completed within one year. But, as is often the case, difficulties were encountered with the plan, and at last it had to be discarded in favor of alternative and more expensive methods of grading and filling than was originally contemplated. In light of this impediment, the parties renegotiated for the time in which performance was to be made. To say that the parties intended a forfeiture irrespective of future contingencies impeding the original scheme is to ignore and refuse legal efficacy to the following language previously referred to in the resolutions and deed:

> "The City of Ocean City reserves the right to change or modify any restriction, condition or other requirements hereby imposed in a manner agreeable to or as permitted by law."

A certain amount of flexibility is inherent among such large scale undertakings as the one under consideration. We might add here that the more one probes into the essence of this arrangement the more it becomes apparent that although deeds were utilized as the devices to accomplish the ultimate desired results, the transaction bears a closer resemblance to the law of contract than of real property.

It is our conclusion that the parties contemplated that the estate created was not to expire automatically at the end of a year and that therefore it is one subject to a condition subsequent.

The remaining questions asserted need not long detain us. Plaintiffs argue that the city has no statutory power to alter or modify the terms and conditions of performance and hence that the resolutions are *ultra vires*. Defendants, on the other hand, rely upon the power conferred by N.J.S.A. 40:60–26 which reads that a municipality in selling realty may impose ". . . any other conditions of sale in the manner and to the same extent as any other vendor of real estate, . . .", or alternatively upon N.J.S.A. 40:60–51.2 and N.J.S.A. 40:60–51.5. R.S. 40:60–51.2, N.J.S.A., provides in part:

> "Any municipality is authorized and empowered, by resolution of the governing body thereof, to waive, release or modify any covenants, conditions or limitations as to the erection of buildings or any other use to be made of land heretofore imposed by said municipality in sales and conveyances of land by such municipality at public or private sale made prior to July 1, 1956, ..."

We need not consider whether the waiver of the time for performance is contemplated in the language of N.J.S.A. 40:60–51.2. The power to alter or modify the time for performance of a condition is clearly inherent in the power to create such conditions on the sale of realty in the first instance. Thus, N.J.S.A. 40:60–26 supplies the basic statutory power, as stated by the court in Hendlin v. Fairmount Construction Co., 8 N.J.Super. 310, at page 339, 72 A.2d 541, at page 556 (Ch. Div.1950):

> "R.S. 40:60–26 N.J.S.A. provides that municipalities may impose conditions and restrictions on the use to be made of lands sold by it 'in the manner and to the same extent as any other vendor of real estate.' Implicit in this power to impose restrictions is the necessarily related power of altering, relaxing or waiving such restrictions. . . . Conditions change and policies must be revised in the interest of the public good. If such covenants must remain perpetually rigid and unchangeable and the municipality completely paralyzed with respect to a needed change, considerable property will be so encumbered and circumscribed as to interfere with the public good."

One last point remains, *i.e.*, whether the instant in lieu proceeding was brought within the time limitations of R.R. 4:88–15(a). At the time of the commencement of this suit R.R. 4:88–15(a) provided:

> "(a) No proceedings for review, hearing and relief in lieu of prerogative writs shall be commenced, unless it shall be commenced within 30 days of the accrual of the right to such review, hearing, or relief . . .."

Defendants contended that since the plaintiffs waited over seven months before initiating action they are barred by the rule. But even under the rule prior to its recent amendment exceptions to the stringent time limitations within which action could be commenced existed. The issues raised by this case fall within those exceptions, *i.e.*, constitutional questions, and consideration of whether the resolutions were *ultra vires*. In this connection we might note that the recent amendment to R.R. 4:88–15, *i.e.*, subparagraph (c) provides more flexible criteria for determining when such actions, when not brought within the time limitation of subparagraph (a) (45 days) may nonetheless be heard.

The judgment appealed from is affirmed.

For affirmance: Chief Justice WEINTRAUB and Justices WACHENFELD, BURLING, JACOBS, FRANCIS and PROCTOR—6.

For reversal: None.

CAPITOL FEDERAL SAVINGS & LOAN ASSOCIATION v. SMITH

Supreme Court of Colorado, 1957.
136 Colo. 265, 316 P.2d 252.

KNAUSS, Justice.

For convenience we shall refer to the parties to this writ of error as they appeared in the trial court, where defendants in error were plaintiffs and plaintiffs in error were defendants.

Two claims were stated in plaintiffs' amended complaint, one for a decree quieting title to real property, a second to obtain a declaratory judgment. Plaintiffs alleged that they were the owners of and in possession of certain lots in Block 6 Ashley's Addition to Denver and that on May 9, 1942 certain owners of lots in said Block, including plaintiffs' predecessors in title, entered into an agreement among themselves that the lots owned by them should not be sold or leased to colored persons and providing for forfeiture of any lots or parts of lots sold or leased in violation of the agreement to such of the then owners of other lots in said block who might place notice of their claims of record. Plaintiffs further alleged that they were colored persons of negro extraction and that any interest, or claim of any interest of defendants, under said agreement was without foundation of right and in violation of the Constitution of the United States and that said agreement was a cloud on plaintiffs' title which should be removed. Plaintiffs prayed for a complete adjudication of the rights of all parties to the action. Defendants placed of record in the office of the Clerk and Recorder of the City and County of Denver a Notice of Claim asserting that they were owners of lots in said Block 6 embraced in the agreement above mentioned and asserted title to the property which is the subject matter of the complaint by virtue of said agreement. By their answer and counterclaim defendants alleged that they were the owners and entitled to the possession of the real estate described in the complaint by virtue of the forfeiture provisions in the above mentioned agreement, and prayed for a complete adjudication of the rights of all parties and a decree quieting their title to the property in question.

All facts were stipulated and trial was to the court.

The trial court entered a decree and Declaratory Judgment pursuant to Rules 105 and 57, R.C.P.Colo. The court found that the plaintiffs were the owners in fee simple of the property described in the complaint and quieted their title thereto free and clear of any right of enforcement or attempted enforcement of the restrictive covenant or the Notice of Claim filed by defendants. The court further adjudged and decreed that the restrictive covenant "may not be enforced by this court as a matter of law, as to enforce same by this court would be a violation of the equal protection clause of the Fourteenth Amendment of the United States Constitution, and the enforceability of same is hereby removed as a cloud upon the title of plaintiffs . . .." From the judgment and decree so entered the defendants bring the case here on writ of error.

The covenant or agreement under consideration was dated May 9, 1942 and the several signatories to the contract agreed for themselves, their heirs and assigns "not to sell or lease the said above described lots and parcels of land owned by them respectively . . . to any colored person or persons, and covenant and agree not to permit any colored person or persons to occupy said premises during the period from this date to January 1, 1990." It further provided that if any of said property "shall be conveyed or leased in violation of this agreement" the right, title or interest of the owner so violating the agreement "shall be forfeited to and rest in such of the then owners of all of said lots and parcels of land not included in such conveyance or lease who may assert title thereto by filing for record notice of their claim . . .."

The agreement also provided for an action to recover damages against any person or persons who violated the restriction, "or such owners may jointly or severally enforce or have their rights hereunder enforced by an action for specific performance, abatement, ejectment, or by injunction or any other proper judicial proceedings, which right shall be in addition to any and all right to the interest so conveyed or leased in violation of this agreement."

It is contended by counsel for defendants that the Supreme Court of the United States in Shelley v. Kraemer, 334 U.S. 1, 68 S.Ct. 836, 92 L.Ed. 1161, McGhee v. Sipes, 334 U.S. 1, 68 S.Ct. 836, 92 L.Ed. 1161 and Barrows v. Jackson, 346 U.S. 249, 73 S.Ct. 1031, 97 L.Ed. 1586, did not have before it an agreement "for automatic forfeiture, nor did any of them create a future interest in the land." Counsel assert that they have no quarrel with these decisions stating that the Supreme Court "has been concerned solely with the question of judicial enforcement of restrictive covenants by injunction or by damages."

Covenants such as the one here considered whether denominated "executory interests" or "future interests", as urged by counsel for defendants, cannot change the character of what was here attempted.

Counsel for defendants contend that the agreement in question entered into by the predecessors in interest of plaintiffs and defendants did not create a "private antiracial restrictive covenant." Instead they claim that it created a future interest in the land known as an executory interest. They assert "Such interest vested automatically in the defendants upon the happening of the events specified in the original instrument of grant, and the validity of the vesting did not in any way depend upon judicial action by the courts. The trial court's failure and refusal to recognize the vested interest of the defendants, and its ruling that the defendants have no title or interest in or to the property, deprived the defendants of their property without just compensation and without due process of law." We cannot agree.

In the amended complaint numerous persons, firms and corporations were named as defendants, but in designating the record to be filed in this court only the amended complaint, the answer and counterclaim of the defendants Whitney J. Armelin, Carmelita Armelin and Capitol Federal Savings and Loan Association, together with plaintiff's reply thereto, the stipulation of facts together with the judgment and decree of the trial court, are specified. The record was amended on motion of Midland Federal Savings and Loan Association to include its answer in which the allegations of the amended complaint were admitted and said association prayed that plaintiffs be awarded the relief demanded in their amended complaint. We are not advised as to pleadings filed by the other defendants, including Robert E. Lee, Public Trustee and the City and County of Denver, who with the Midland Federal Savings and Loan Association are named as defendants in error in the instant case.

We are unable to rid ourselves of a strong impression that this writ of error is being prosecuted in the interest of title examiners, rather than in that of the property owners in Block 6 Ashley's addition to Denver. In the brief of counsel for plaintiffs in error we find this significant language: "Title examiners are in constant apprehension as to whether a title may be passed where these restrictive covenants prevail, and we feel that we should call upon this Honorable Body as to the doubts of this decision."

No matter by what ariose terms the covenant under consideration may be classified by astute counsel, it is still a racial restriction in violation of the Fourteenth Amendment to the Federal Constitution. That this is so has been definitely settled by the decisions of the Supreme Court of the United States. High sounding phrases or outmoded common law terms cannot alter the effect of the agreement embraced in the instant case. While the hands may seem to be the hands of Esau to a blind Isaac, the voice is definitely Jacob's. We cannot give our judicial approval or blessing to a contract such as is here involved.

In Shelley v. Kraemer, supra [334 U.S. 1, 68 S.Ct. 845], the Supreme Court of the United States said:

"We hold that in granting judicial enforcement of the restrictive agreements in these cases, the States have denied petitioners the equal protection of the laws and that, therefore, the action of the state courts cannot stand. We have noted that freedom from discrimination by the States in the enjoyment of property rights was among the basic objectives sought to be effectuated by the framers of the Fourteenth Amendment. That such discrimination has occurred in these cases is clear. Because of the race or color of these petitioners they have been denied rights of ownership or occupancy enjoyed as a matter of course by other citizens of different race or color. The Fourteenth Amendment declares 'that all persons, whether colored, or white, shall stand equal before the laws of the States, and, in regard to the colored race, for whose protection the amendment was primarily designed, that *no discrimination shall be made against them by law because of their color.*'" (Emphasis supplied.)

Because the language of the United States Supreme Court suggested that private racially restrictive covenants were not invalid per se, it was believed for some time that an action for damages might lie against one who violated such a covenant. A number of state courts adopted this position, and awarded damages against those who, contrary to their agreements, had made sales of property to negroes or other persons within the excluded classes. This problem came to the attention of the Supreme Court of the United States in Barrows v. Jackson, 346 U.S. 249, 253–254, 258, 259, 73 S.Ct. 1031, 97 L.Ed. 1586, where it was held that although such a grantor's constitutional rights were not violated, nevertheless the commodious protection of the Fourteenth Amendment extended to her and she could not be made to respond in damages for treating her restrictive covenant as a nullity.

Because the United States Supreme Court has extracted any teeth which such a covenant was supposed to have, no rights, duties or obligations can be based thereon.

The judgment is affirmed.

FRANTZ, J., not participating.

NOTES

1. If you were counsel for Ocean City in 1941, when the deeds to Stoeco were being drafted, would you have written the operative language any differently in order to transfer a fee simple determinable? After *Stoeco*, what language would you use to be certain you had created a fee simple determinable? After *Stoeco*, what result would the New Jersey Supreme Court reach in the following case: *A* conveys land to his 22-year old grandson *B*, in fee, so long as he graduates from law school before reaching the age of 26. Because of aca-

demic difficulties, B is in the middle of his second year at law school at the time of his 26th birthday and his grandfather declares a forfeiture. Do you think the *Stoeco* court would have found a fee simple determinable if, at the end of the period specified for performance, the city had declared a forfeiture?

2. Fees simple defeasible may, like the fee simple absolute, last forever. Their duration, however, is indeterminate rather than infinite. A defeasible estate will terminate, and its connected future interests will become possessory, if and when the event specified in the conveyance occurs. Defeasible fees differ among themselves in terms of the nature of the condition or event that will terminate the fee and in terms of the identity of the future interest holder and the nature of her interest.

a. *Fee Simple Determinable* (also sometimes called a *fee simple on a special limitation*, a *base fee*, or a *qualified fee*). A fee simple determinable ends—determines—automatically upon the occurrence of the specified event. Thus, if A, who owns Blackacre conveys it "to B so long as alcoholic beverages are not sold on the premises," B or his successors will automatically lose their right to the land if and when alcohol is sold. (Note that, because it is the estate that is limited, the prohibition binds not only B, the immediate grantee, but also anyone who subsequently acquires the estate.)

The future interest that follows a fee simple determinable is always held by the grantor and her successors and is called a *possibility of reverter*. In the example above, a court would imply a possibility of reverter in A on the ground that A, who originally owned a fee simple absolute, conveyed away less than her full bundle of interests and therefore retained any interest not transferred—in this case, the future interest entitling her to possess the land in the event that alcohol is sold. (Can determinable fees be reconciled with *Quia Emptores*, p. 471 above? Although a technical argument can be made that they violate the Statute, courts everywhere have accepted the estate's validity.)

Durational language, like "so long as," is usually accepted as evidence that a fee simple determinable was intended. Other durational terms commonly used to signify a fee simple determinable are "until" ("until alcohol is sold on the premises"), "while" ("while alcohol is not sold on the premises") and "during" ("during the time that alcohol is not sold on the premises").

b. *Fee Simple Subject to Condition Subsequent.* In the example above, A could have created a fee simple subject to condition subsequent rather than a fee simple determinable by wording her conveyance, "A to B on the condition that alcohol not be sold on the premises, and in the event of such sale, then A may enter and re-take the premises." The main consequential difference is that B's estate would terminate, not upon the sale of alcoholic beverages, but rather when *A* or her successors exercise their right to enter for breach of condition.

The future interest in the grantor following a fee simple subject to condition subsequent is called a *right of entry* (or sometimes, *power of termination*), and will often, as in the example just used, be expressly reserved. If the grantor fails to reserve the right of entry expressly, the court may imply one, but only if it is clear that the grantor's intent was in fact to create a fee simple subject to a condition subsequent.

Conditional rather than durational language usually signals the intent to create a fee simple subject to condition subsequent. "On the condition that," or "on the express condition that," are just two examples. Other conditional phrases include "but if" ("but if alcoholic beverages are sold on the premises . . ."), and "provided, however" ("provided, however, that alcohol not be sold on the premises . . .").

c. *Fee Simple Subject to Executory Limitation* (sometimes called a *fee simple subject to an executory interest*). Like the fee simple determinable, and unlike the fee simple subject to condition subsequent, the fee simple subject to executory limitation terminates automatically upon the occurrence of the specified event. Unlike both these other estates, whose future interests are always held by the grantor, the fee simple subject to executory limitation is always followed by a future interest—called an executory interest—in someone other than the grantor. Thus, *A* could convey Blackacre "to *B* until alcohol is sold on the premises, and then to *C*," or "to *B*, but if alcohol is sold on the premises, then to *C*." In both examples, *B*'s interest is a fee simple subject to an executory limitation, and *C*'s is an executory interest. How would you characterize the interest created by the conveyance, "*A* hereby conveys to *B* the right to possess Blackacre upon *B*'s successful completion of law school"?

3. In practice, the fee simple determinable and the fee simple subject to condition subsequent are not as different as the distinction between automatic and elective forfeiture might make them appear. The holder of the possibility of reverter must usually bring an action to obtain possession after occurrence of the determining event; the same action brought by the right of entry holder after breach of the specified condition will typically provide the required evidence of her election to terminate. And the statute of limitations for the action on both interests will often be the same and will often have the same starting point—the occurrence of the defeasing event. See generally, Dunham, Possibility of Reverter and Powers of Termination—Fraternal or Identical Twins? 20 U.Chi.L.Rev. 215 (1953).

4. *Presumptions.* Stoeco correctly stated the general interpretational presumption that if there is doubt whether a fee simple determinable or a fee simple subject to condition subsequent was intended, the doubt should be resolved in favor of the fee simple

subject to condition subsequent. This interpretational presumption is one of several that seek to avoid the forfeiture of fee interests in order to promote their freer marketability. At least at the time the policy against forfeitures was being formulated, the fee simple on condition subsequent was the less forfeitable of the two estates since the right of entry holder's failure to exercise her right could eventually bar the right through equitable estoppel or laches, allowing the possessory estate to ripen into a fee simple absolute.

Stoeco erred, however, in its assertion that "if the choice is between a condition subsequent and a restrictive covenant, the former is preferred." Faced with this choice, courts generally favor the restrictive covenant, which poses no risk of forfeiture at all. Thus, finding a restrictive covenant in the language, "*B*, as a condition, expressly undertakes for himself, his heirs, successors and assigns, that no alcoholic beverages shall be sold on the premises," will give *B* a fee simple absolute and *A* and her successors only an action for damages or injunction in the event that the covenant is breached. Covenants are considered at pages 719 to 787, below.

Similarly, faced with a choice between a covenant, which binds not only *B* but also his successors to Blackacre, and a contract, which binds *B* only, courts prefer the contract interpretation. (A court would probably find a contract rather than a covenant in the language, "*B* expressly undertakes that no alcoholic beverages shall be sold," in part because no reference is made to binding *B's* successors.) And, given a choice between a contractual undertaking and a precatory indication of purpose with no operative consequence at all, courts prefer the latter. ("*A* conveys to *B*, and *B* understands that it is *A's* desire in making this conveyance that alcoholic beverages not be sold on the premises.")

5. Did *Capitol Federal* hold that the automatic vesting of the neighbors' interests constituted state action, like the judicial enforcement of covenants in Shelley v. Kraemer? If so, do you agree? If not, how else can the court's decision be reconciled with the Fourteenth Amendment's requirement of state action? Can you think of any ground on which the court could have reached the same result without raising the constitutional issue? Would the interpretational presumptions against forfeitable estates have helped? Would reliance on these presumptions have satisfied the title examiners, in whose interests the court thought the appeal was possibly being prosecuted?

6. *Capitol Federal* is just one chapter in the long history of efforts to segregate neighborhoods along racial lines. Earlier, the Supreme Court's decision in Buchanan v. Warley, 245 U.S. 60, 38 S.Ct. 16, 62 L.Ed. 149 (1917), that racially restrictive zoning ordinances violated the Fourteenth Amendment, spurred the creation of private discriminatory schemes, using contracts, covenants, conditions or some combination of these devices. Although some states invalidated

these restrictions as unlawful restraints on alienation, the Supreme Court's decision in Corrigan v. Buckley, 271 U.S. 323, 46 S.Ct. 521, 70 L.Ed. 969 (1926), was widely viewed as settling the constitutionality of judicial enforcement of racially restrictive covenants. See generally, McGovney, Racial Residential Segregation by State Court Enforcement of Restrictive Agreements, Covenants or Conditions in Deeds is Unconstitutional, 33 Calif.L.Rev. 5 (1945).

The Supreme Court's decisions in Shelley v. Kraemer and Barrows v. Jackson established that racially restrictive covenants cannot be enforced by injunction or damages, but left open the question whether automatic forfeitures, not directly implicating state action, were similarly proscribed. *Capitol Federal* answered that they were. But another state supreme court said that they were not. Charlotte Park & Recreation Commission v. Barringer, 242 N.C. 311, 322, 88 S.E.2d 114, 123 (1955) (the "operation of this reversion provision is not by any judicial enforcement by the State Courts of North Carolina and Shelley v. Kraemer has no application"). The Supreme Court denied certiorari, 350 U.S. 983, 76 S.Ct. 469, 100 L.Ed. 851 (1956).

The pressure for a Supreme Court decision on the issue has since abated. One reason is that legislative and administrative developments appear to have overtaken the field. Several state legislatures have expressly invalidated racial restrictions affecting the transfer of real estate. The Fair Housing Act, Title VIII of the Civil Rights Act of 1968, 42 U.S.C.A. §§ 3601, *et seq.*, and the Supreme Court's decision in Jones v. Alfred H. Mayer Co., 392 U.S. 409, 88 S.Ct. 2186, 20 Ed.2d 1189 (1968), interpreting 42 U.S.C.A. § 1982, stake out the federal position on housing discrimination. The creation of any racially restricted interest in property would appear to be prohibited under *Jones* as an act of private racial discrimination. And a 1969 letter from the Department of Justice to eighteen major title insurance companies stated that the 1968 Act "broadened the *Shelley* prohibition to cover not only judicial enforcement of such covenants, but also their inclusion in public documents such as deeds or insurance policies." The "Department informed the companies that they were violating the law by their practice of reporting the existence of racial restrictions appearing in the records of title on property for which they were issuing title insurance policies. All eighteen title companies replied that in future policies they would eliminate any reference to such restrictions." Meyers v. Ridley, 465 F.2d 630, 649 (1972) (Wilkey, J. concurring).

b. THE FEE TAIL

The history of the fee tail graphically illustrates the continuing cycle of conflict between the desire to impose perpetual restraints on land ownership and the desire for free marketability. The history begins in 1225 with D'Arundel's Case striking a blow for free marketability by confirming that the language, "*A* to *B* and his heirs," created no interest in the heirs and that *B* was able to convey free of their claims. Shortly after, grantors began to use the phrase, "to *B* and the heirs of his body," to signify their intent to create no more than a life estate in *B* with a succession of life estates in *B*'s heirs—under primogeniture, the eldest surviving son in each succeeding generation—unless and until the line of descent failed, at which point the land would return to *A* or his successors.

The next blow for free marketability was struck some time before 1250, with courts interpreting the phrase, "and the heirs of his body," to impose no more than a condition that *B* have issue; upon the birth of a child, *B* could convey a fee simple, free of any claims by his heirs, or by *A*. The new estate was called a fee simple conditional. Next came the statute, *De Donis Conditionalibus*, 13 Edw. I, c. 1 (1285), which effectively overturned the fee simple conditional and required courts to enforce these conveyances according to the grantor's original intent, "so that they to whom the land was given under such condition shall have no power to alien the land so given, but that it shall remain unto the issue of them to whom it was given after their death, or shall revert unto the giver or his heirs if issue fail either by reason that there is no issue at all, or if any issue be, it fail by death, the heir of such issue failing." The estate was soon called the fee tail (from the French, "tailler," meaning to cut up or to carve) reflecting the grantor's intent to carve out a series of succeeding estates.

It was almost two centuries before lawyers managed to circumvent *De Donis* through the *common recovery*, a web of lies and fictions so preposterous that it worked. The elements necessary for the common recovery, apart from adept lawyers and an indulgent court, were: a tenant in tail, *A*, who wished to convert his fee tail in Blackacre into a fee simple absolute; two straw men, *B* and *C*, one of whom had to be judgment proof; and two rules of law—one holding that a tenant in tail could convey his estate in fee simple so long as he replaced it with an asset of equal value, and a second rule holding that a judgment for land of equal value qualified as such an asset.

Taking these elements together, *A*, *B* and *C* would stage a collusive lawsuit. *B* would bring an action against *A*, falsely claiming fee title to Blackacre and demanding its recovery. *A* would respond, falsely asserting that he had acquired his title from *C*, and that *C* had warranted and promised to defend the title. *A* would then call on *C* to defend *A*'s title and would demand that, in the event *C* should fail in his defense, *A* should have judgment to recover lands of equivalent value from *C*. Next, in the action *B* v. *A*, *C* would falsely admit his conveyance and warranty to *A* and would suffer a default in favor of *B*; *A*, complying with the judgment, would convey Blackacre to *B*. *C* would also suffer a default in *A*'s action against him to recover lands of equal value, and *A* would use this judgment against *C* to replace the entailed estate; the judgment would, of course, be worthless because *C* was judgment proof. Finally, by prearrangement, *B* would convey his fee simple absolute in Blackacre to *A*.

Taltarum's Case, Y.B. 12 Edw. IV, 19 (1472), was the first decision to validate the common recovery, and this device, together with another collusive practice, the *fine*, was widely employed in England until the Fines and Recoveries Act, 3 & 4 Will. IV, c. 74 (1833), replaced them with a far more direct method: simply by conveying his estate to another, a tenant in tail who was in possession could convert it into a fee simple absolute. Thus, *A*, holding as a tenant in tail, could, by conveying "to *B* and his heirs," give *B* a fee simple. If the parties desired, *B* could then reconvey the fee simple absolute to *A*. On the evolution of the fee tail and disentailment devices, see generally, J. Williams, Principles of the Law of Real Property 124–153 (R. Eastwood, 24th ed. 1926).

American states have taken five approaches to eliminating or reducing the effects of fees tail:

(1) Some states abolish the fee tail. See, e.g., Vernon's Ann. Texas Const. Art. I, § 26. What is the effect in these jurisdictions of language in a deed, "*A* to *B* and the heirs of his body"? The apparent constructional preference is to find a fee simple in *B*. See Restatement of Property § 104 (1936).

(2) Other states preserve the fee tail for one generation. In these states, the phrase "*A* to *B* and the heirs of his body" will give a fee tail to *B* and a fee simple to his issue. See, e.g., Conn.Gen.Stat.Ann. § 47-3 (1978).

(3) Several states will find a life estate in *B* with a remainder in fee in his issue. See, e.g., Colo.Rev.Stat.1973, 38-30-106.

(4) Many states provide that the language, "to *B* and the heirs of his body," creates a fee simple absolute in *B*, and no interest at all in the issue. See, e.g., West's Ann.Cal.Civil Code § 763.

(5) Other states permit the estate tail but, as in England since 1833, allow *B* to disentail by conveying a fee simple absolute. See, e.g., Mass.Gen.Laws Ann. c. 183, § 45 (1977). See generally, Morris, Primogeniture and Entailed Estates in America, 27 Colum.L.Rev. 24 (1927).

Long v. Long, the next principal case, explores some issues raised by contemporary use of the fee tail in America. As in so many other estates cases, the facts are complex and the reasoning is sometimes intricate. It may help you to understand the case if you first read through it quickly to get a feel for the facts and issues rather than a close understanding of the court's reasoning and result; a diagram appearing at the end of the case may help you to keep the facts in place. Then, read the case a second time for reasoning and resolution.

LONG v. LONG

Supreme Court of Ohio, 1976.
45 Ohio St.2d 165, 343 N.E.2d 100.

Appeal from the Court of Appeals for Darke County.

Plaintiff-appellees herein, Howard W. Long and Paul H. Olinger, the grandsons of Henry Long, commenced a declaratory judgment action in the Court of Common Pleas of Darke County, Probate Division, against the defendant-appellant herein, Bessie Long, the widow and beneficiary of Eugene Long, the deceased brother of appellee, Howard W. Long, to determine the ownership of certain real property.

The undisputed facts are as follows:

On April 2, 1919, Henry Long conveyed three separate tracts of land in fee tail to each of his three children, Jesse Long, Edward W. Long and Emma Long Olinger. The latter two were survived by living children who took their respective tracts in fee simple, pursuant to R.C. § 2131.08. Their parcels are not involved in the present controversy.

The granting clause in the deed from Henry Long to Jesse Long, which is similar to those conveying the other parcels to the other children, reads, in part:

". . . to . . . Jesse S. Long, and the children of his body begotten, and their heirs and assigns forever . . .."

Henry Long died testate in August 1932. His will contained no general residuary clause, but provided in Item IV, as follows:

"At the decease of my wife I will and direct that my executor sell all my real estate, at public or private sale as deemed best at the time, and reduce all my personal estate into money, and from said funds then pay,—1st to my then living grand-children the sum of Three Thousand Dollars ($3,000.00) to be divided equally among such grand-children and the residue to my three children, or their issue, if any be deceased with issue—if any of my children at the time of such division, be deceased, leaving no issue, no part of said funds shall pass to the estate of such deceased."

Edward Long died intestate in March 1946, survived by his wife, Emma, and sons, Howard and Eugene. Emma Long died testate on July 3, 1964, survived by Howard and Eugene. Her will contained a clause dividing her residuary estate equally between her sons. Eugene died testate in October 1966 without issue, and was survived by his wife, Bessie Long. His will made Bessie Long his sole beneficiary and specifically mentioned the real estate in controversy.

Emma Long Olinger was predeceased by her husband and died intestate on October 19, 1954, survived by a son, Paul H. Olinger.

In 1945, Jesse Long executed a quitclaim deed conveying whatever interest he had in the property in question to Rosella Long, who died testate and made Marie Ethel Brown and her husband, John Brown, her sole beneficiaries. The Browns subsequently executed a quitclaim deed conveying whatever interest they had in the property to Howard W. Long and his wife, Esther Naomi Long.

Jesse Long died intestate on March 4, 1974, without issue.

The appellant, Bessie Long, maintains that, "where a grantor deeds real estate to his son and to the children of his body begotten, their heirs and assigns forever, and such son dies without having sired a child, a possibility of reverter remains in the original grantor of such fee tail estate which is a descendible, devisable estate at the death of the original grantor of the estate tail." Appellant contends that, from the time Henry Long conveyed the fee tail estate to Jesse Long, there remained in him, as the grantor, a "possibility of reverter." Appellant argues that this "possibility of reverter" was a descendible, devisable interest and, therefore, passed at the grantor's death to his heirs existing at that time. Appellant contends that Item IV of Henry Long's will expressed an intention to convey the residue of his estate only to those surviving children who had issue and, therefore, Jesse Long's conveyance was ineffective. Appellant maintains that the possibility of reverter following Jesse Long's fee tail descended or was devised, one-half to Edward Long and one-half to Emma Long Olinger.

Appellant claims, through her deceased husband, Eugene Long, a one-fourth interest in the property from Edward's portion. Appellant also maintains that Howard W. Long received the other one-fourth interest from Edward's portion and that Paul Olinger, Emma Long Olinger's son, received, by descent, Emma's one-half interest in the possibility of reverter.

The Probate Court determined that a possibility of reverter is not an estate of inheritance and that, upon the happening of the contingency, the grantee's death without issue, the property passes to the next of kin and heirs at law of the grantor then living—in the present case the appellees, Howard Long and Paul Olinger.

The Court of Appeals affirmed the judgment of the Probate Court, one judge dissenting.

The cause is now before this court pursuant to the allowance of appellant's motion to certify the record.

CORRIGAN, J.

I.

The unique issue in this case concerns the nature of the interest remaining in the grantor, Henry Long, after the creation by deed of a fee tail estate which was conveyed by the grantor to his son "Jesse S.

Long, and the children of his body begotten, and their heirs and assigns forever."

The parties agree that the estate created by the grantor was a fee tail. Pollock v. Speidel, 17 Ohio St. 439 (1867).

Appellant maintains that the interest remaining in the grantor is a "possibility of reverter" which is a descendible, devisable estate at the death of the original grantor of the estate tail. Appellant contends that, upon the death of the first donee in tail without issue, the interest then passes to the heirs of the grantor living at his death, and to their descendants.

The appellees, too, maintain that the interest remaining in the grantor of a fee tail estate is a possibility of reverter. Appellees contend, however, that this possibility of reverter was not of sufficient quality to descend to an heir until the donee in tail dies without issue. At this point, appellees argue, the possibility ripens into a fee simple estate in the grantor and, where he has predeceased the donee in tail, the estate then passes by the law of intestate succession to his heirs living at the time of the ripening of the possibility.

II.

Considerable confusion exists in the present case because of the term used to designate the nature of the grantor's future interest in the property conveyed.

At early common law, prior to the enactment of the Statute of Westminster, 13 Edward I, Chapter 1, *De Donis Conditionalibus*, in 1285, the transfer of a fee restrained to some particular heirs exclusive of others, *e.g.*, to the heirs of a man's body, created an estate designated a fee simple conditional.

The future interest in the grantor of a conditional fee at common law was generally called a possibility of reversion or right of reverter. The usual practice at common law, however, was for the tenant in tail to alien the land conveyed and afterward repurchase, taking an absolute estate in the land which would descend to his heirs generally and prevent any reversion to the donor. To prevent this practice, the statute *de donis* was enacted, imposing a restraint upon the power of alienation by the tenant in tail. Prior to the enactment of the statute, a fee simple conditional became absolute upon the birth of issue. By operation of the statute the tenant now held an estate tail and the donor had a reversion of fee simple expectant on the failure of the issue in tail. The tenant could no longer alien, upon his having issue, but the feud (estate) was to remain to the issue according to the form of the gift, *i.e.*, the issue of the donee in tail took *per formam doni* (by the form of the gift) or from the grantor rather than through any particular tenant in tail. The statute preserved the estate for the benefit of the issue of the grantee and the reversion for the benefit of the donor and his heirs by declaring that the intention of the donor manifestly expressed according to the form of the deed should be observed.

The real source of the title was the donor, himself, who always retained a reversion expectant upon the failure of issue. Pollock v. Speidel, supra; Richardson v. Cincinnati Union Stockyard Co., 8 N.P. 213, 11 O.D. 367 (1901); Gibson v. McNeely, 11 Ohio St. 131 (1860).

It should be noted that the statute *de donis* did not create the estate tail but rather gave it perpetuity.

More importantly, for purposes of the present case, the statute *de donis* converted the donor's bare possibility of reversion or right of reverter into a reversion or fee simple expectant upon failure of issue. This distinction is important because a reversion in fee is a vested interest or estate and is descendible, alienable or assignable by deed or conveyance, and is also devisable.

A reversion is the residue of an estate left in the grantor or other transferor, to commence in possession after the determination of some particular estate transferred by him. A reversion arises only by operation of law and is a vested right.

A reversion arises whenever a person having a vested estate transfers to another a lesser vested estate. Since the reversion is the undisposed of portion of a vested estate, it follows that all reversions are vested interests. A reversion is said to be vested because there is no condition precedent to the taking effect in possession other than the termination of the preceding estates. This does not mean, however, that every reversion is certain to take effect in possession and enjoyment. The distinguishing feature of the reversion is that it is not subject to a condition precedent to its taking effect in possession, and all other conditions defeating a reversion are regarded as conditions subsequent.

A reversion is historically distinguishable from a possibility of reverter in that a reversion arises when the estate transferred is of a lesser quantum than the transferor owns. A possibility of reverter arises when the estate conveyed is of the same quantum as the transferor owns.

III.

In Ohio, the term "possibility of reverter" is used to denominate the future interest remaining in the transferor of a "qualified fee."

Ohio cases have held that this interest is not an estate but only the possibility of having an estate at a future time, and that the estate is vested in the grantee, subject to divestment at a future time.

The possibility of reverter is regarded as a lesser interest than the reversion because of the nature of the fee transferred. The term "qualified fee" is used to designate those fees which descend as fees simple but which will, or may, terminate or be subject to termination upon the occurrence of a stated event. Such fees include fees simple determinable, fees simple subject to condition subsequent, fees simple subject to executory limitation and conditional fees, in those jurisdictions in which the fee tail has been completely abolished and the predecessor conditional fee is still recognized. Qualified fees do not include the fee simple absolute or the fee tail.

Possibilities of reverter and the right of entry for condition broken following a fee simple condition subsequent were not alienable *inter vivos* or devisable prior to the enactment of R.C. § 2131.04 (G.C. § 10512–4) in 1932. Both, however, appear always to have been capable of descent, and either interest might be released to the holder of the possessory interest in the land. These interests are clearly distinguishable in their incidents from the reversion which is a vested estate, descendible, alienable, assignable and devisable.

There appears to be a disparity of views on the descendibility of possibility of reverters as to the time that the heirs are determined, whether at the grantor's death or at the time of the happening of the contingency. These views are cited and discussed by the parties in the present case, but since they relate to possibilities of reverter and not to reversions, they are not relevant. The important point in this discussion is that the future interest remaining in the grantor of a common-law fee tail estate is an estate designated a reversion and not a possibility of reverter or right of entry.

IV.

The only remaining issue to consider is whether the Ohio enactment of 1811 (10 Ohio Laws 7),* modifying fee tail estates, has had any effect on the reversionary interest in the grantor.

In Pollock v. Speidel, *supra* (17 Ohio St. 439), this court recognized the continued existence of estates tail in Ohio, subject to the statutory modification enacted in 1811, and now embodied in R.C. § 2131.08, which converted estates tail into fees simple in the hands of the issue of the first donee in tail. Subsequent decisions, in Harkness v. Corning, 24 Ohio St. 416 (1873); Broadstone v. Brown, 24 Ohio St. 430 (1873); and Dungan v. Kline, 81 Ohio St. 371 (1910), made it clear that the statutory enactment did not change the nature of the estate tail in the donee in tail from an inheritable estate to an estate for life merely but restricted the entailment to the immediate issue of such donee.

---

* "AN ACT to restrict the entailment of real estate.

"Sect. 1 Be it enacted by the General Assembly of the state of Ohio. That from and after the taking effect of this act, no estate in fee simple, fee tail, or any lesser estate in lands or tenements, lying within this state, shall be given or granted by deed or will to any person or persons, but such as are in being, or to the immediate issue or descendants of such as are in being at the time of making such deed or will, and that all estates given in tail shall be and remain an absolute estate in fee simple to the issue of the first donee in tail.

"This act to take effect and be in force from and after the first day of June next.

". . .

"December 17, 1811."

Ohio courts have also recognized the existence of a reversion in the grantor of an estate tail.

In Gibson v. McNeely, the court held that there was a reversion in fee simple expectant on the failure of an estate tail before its conversion into a fee by operation of the Act to restrict the entailment of real estate. The court, in *Gibson*, held specifically that this reversion expectant on the failure of issue, undisposed of by the will of the testator, passed at his death to his heirs at law then living. The court determined further that the reversion descended through the testator's heirs living at his death to their lineal descendants who took a possessory interest in the devised property on the failure of issue. Clearly, this decision recognized the existence of the common-law reversion as it existed after the statute *de donis*, and the vested nature of the interest in the grantor and his heirs.

In Richardson v. Cincinnati Union Stockyard Co., *supra*, the Superior Court of Cincinnati recognized the existence of the fee tail estate in the same form as it existed after the statute *de donis*, subject only to the limitation created in the Act of 1811, which enlarged the estate tail into a fee simple in the hands of the issue of the first donee in tail. All three judges concurred in the conclusion that the reversion following the fee tail which a testator devised to his daughter after the life estate devised to her mother was a descendible, assignable interest. The court held that the reversion had, in fact, descended to the testator's heirs and had been assigned by some of them to the Cincinnati Union Stockyard Company. The case was complicated by ambiguous language in the will to the effect that, upon the death of the life tenant, if the donee in tail had predeceased the testator without issue, then the property would devolve upon the testator's surviving children. Two judges held that this condition should be interpreted to mean that the testator's daughter took a fee tail estate and the heirs of the testator took by descent a reversion in the estate upon the testator's death, which reversion was subject to divestment by the donee in tail's death with surviving issue or if children of the testator survived him. The remaining judge decided that the only estate created in the daughter was a fee tail estate and that the testator died intestate in regard to the reversion. Neither theory in regard to the condition was relevant in that the donee in tail was an aged woman with no natural children and was the sole surviving child of the testator. The court held that the testator's reversion arising from the creation of the fee tail estate had descended at his death to his children then living and vested in them. Since the reversion was vested, those children who had assigned the reversion to the Cincinnati Union Stockyard Company had made effective conveyances.

Clearly, both the *Gibson* and *Richardson* decisions have upheld the existence of a descendible, devisable, assignable and alienable reversion as it existed at common law following the enactment of the statute *de donis*. Common-law fee tail estates and their incidents subsisted in full force in the United States prior to the Revolution and still exist in those states where they have not been abolished, including Ohio.

In accordance with the undisputed authority that the interest created in the grantor of a common-law fee tail estate is a vested reversion, and in view of the decisions to the effect that the Ohio enactment restricting fee tail estates does not alter the fundamental nature of the estate tail in the first donee in tail, we hold that such reversions are vested estates fully descendible, devisable and alienable *inter vivos*.

As a result, in the present case, the series of conveyances begun by Henry Long's deceased son, Jesse Long, were effective to convey his one-third reversionary interest in the property to appellee Howard W. Long, and Esther Naomi Long, one-sixth to each.

As to Henry Long's son, Edward Long, who died intestate, his one-third reversionary interest in the property descended, one-half or a one-sixth share to his son, appellee Howard W. Long, and the other one-half interest or one-sixth share to his other son, Eugene Long. Eugene Long died testate in 1966, specifically devising his estate including the one-sixth share of the reversion to his wife, appellant Bessie Long.

As to Henry Long's daughter, Emma Long Olinger, who died intestate, her one-third share of the reversion descended to her son, appellee Paul H. Olinger.

The present ownership of the realty in question rests, therefore, in the following undivided interests:

1. Esther Naomi Long, wife of Howard W. Long .....one-sixth (from Jesse's portion)
2. Howard W. Long (Appellee) ....one-sixth (from Jesse's portion)
   and ....one-sixth (from Edward's portion)
   Howard W. Long's Total Interest is .... one-third
3. Bessie Long (Appellant) .... one-sixth (from Edward's portion)
4. Paul H. Olinger ......one-third (Emma Long Olinger's portion)

It should be noted that this distribution is consistent with that expressed in the minority opinion of the Court of Appeals for Darke County, written by Judge Sherer. It is not the precise distribution contended for by the appellant. The appellant urged that, although Henry Long's will contained no general residuary clause, Item IV thereof evidences a clear intention on the part of the testator that no part of the residue of his estate, including the reversion in the fee tail estate granted to Jesse Long, should pass to any of his children unless that child had issue. Appellant maintains, therefore, that Jesse Long did not qualify and no part of the reversion passed to him but passed, one-half to Emma Long Olinger and by descent to her son, appellee Paul H. Olinger, one-half to Edward Long, one-fourth descending to Howard W. Long and one-fourth descending to Eugene Long, devised by him to his surviving spouse, appellant Bessie Long. For reason of the foregoing, this contention has no merit. The Probate Court and Court of Appeals are correct in the holding that Item IV does not constitute a general residuary clause capable of transferring any of Henry Long's interest in the property in question.

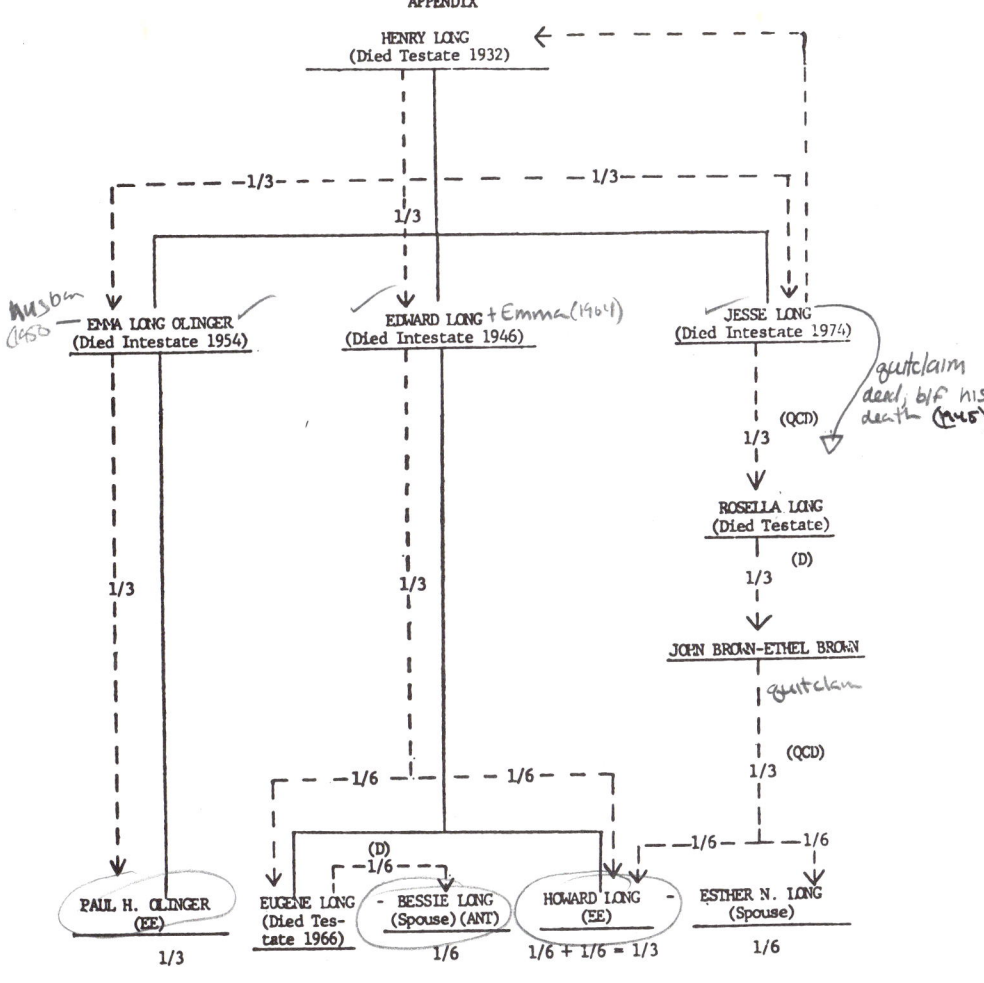

c. THE LIFE ESTATE

DICKSON v. ALEXANDRIA HOSPITAL, INC.

United States Court of Appeals, Fourth Circuit, 1949.
177 F.2d 876.

BARKSDALE, District Judge.

This is an action instituted by plaintiff, Paulette Louise B. Dickson, against Alexandria Hospital, Inc., a beneficiary under the will of Virginia Simpson, deceased, and the First National Bank of Alexandria, her executor, alleging that, as sole beneficiary under the will of plaintiff's deceased husband, French Cameron Simpson, she was entitled to a share of the estate of George L. Simpson, deceased, which said Virginia Simpson had disposed of by her will. Upon the motion of defendants, the district court dismissed the complaint as failing to state a claim against the defendants upon which relief could be granted, and from the dismissal of her complaint, the plaintiff has appealed.

On this appeal, two minor questions are presented, one of them being the question of the jurisdiction of the district court. While it is true that federal courts have no jurisdiction to probate wills or administer estates, this is an action by a nonresident against residents of this State, to establish a claim to property not in the custody of the State court, and the jurisdictional amount being present, there is no doubt that the district court had jurisdiction, notwithstanding the fact that the real question here presented is the construction of a will.

The other minor question presented is the determination of the effect of certain probate proceedings purportedly under the authority of Section 5439, Code of Virginia. We do not find that a consideration of this question is at all necessary to our decision, and therefore express no opinion on it.

The real question in the case is the construction of the holographic will of George L. Simpson, formerly a resident of Alexandria, Virginia, who died on April 20, 1907, survived by his widow, Virginia Simpson, and two sons, George Robbins Simpson and French Cameron Simpson, which will is as follows:

"I, Geo. L. Simpson, being of sound mind do hereby make this my last will and testament; first I do not wish any appraisment of my estate; Secondly I do not wish my wife Virginia Simpson, whom I appoint my executrix, to give any security; Thirdly, I give to my wife

Virginia Simpson, my property on Cameron and Columbus Streets, including furniture and contents of my home. Fourthly I give to each of my boys Geo. Robbins Simpson and French Cameron Simpson, the sum of ten thousand dollars, this money to be paid over to them when Geo. Robbins Simpson shall have reached the age of twenty-five years and when French Cameron Simpson shall have reached the age of twenty-five years. *The remainder of my property to go to my wife Virginia Simpson as long as she remains my widow. In the event of her marrying then said remainder of my property is to be equally divided between my sons Geo. Robbins and French Cameron Simpson.*

"Feb. 13, 1903.

"Geo. L. Simpson." (Italics supplied.)

Promptly after the death of George L. Simpson, his will was admitted to probate, and his widow, Virginia Simpson, qualified as his executrix, giving bond in the penalty of $35,000 without security. George Robbins Simpson died intestate and unmarried on August 24, 1934. French Cameron Simpson died January 27, 1940, leaving a will whereby he devised and bequeathed his entire estate to his widow, plaintiff in the district court and appellant here. Virginia Simpson, widow of George L. Simpson, died March 19, 1944, without having remarried, and left a will whereby she appointed appellee, First National Bank, as her executor, and the Bank duly qualified as such. Virginia Simpson left a substantial estate, and by her will, after making numerous specific bequests and establishing a trust fund, left her entire residuary estate to Alexandria Hospital, Inc., after the termination of the trust. Prior to the institution of this action, her executor had paid over to Alexandria Hospital, Inc., all the residue of the estate of Virginia Simpson, deceased.

Plaintiff's contention is, that by his disposition of the residuum of his estate, as follows: "The remainder of my property to go to my wife Virginia Simpson so long as she remains my widow. In the event of her marrying, then said remainder of my property is to be equally divided between my sons Geo. Robbins and French Cameron Simpson."—testator created a defeasible life estate in Virginia Simpson, one-half of which, at the death of Virginia Simpson, passed to her, the plaintiff, as sole beneficiary under the will of her deceased husband, French Cameron Simpson.  Plaintiff alleges that the First National Bank, as executor, and Alexandria Hospital, Inc., as beneficiary, have refused to pay her the share to which she claims she is entitled, and therefore she instituted this action.

On the other hand, defendants contend that the above quoted language of George L. Simpson's will created a defeasible fee simple in Virginia Simpson, and said Virginia Simpson having died without remarrying, a fee simple title to the residuum passed to them by her will. Thus, the question of whether the above quoted sentences created a defeasible life estate in Virginia Simpson, or whether thereby she took a defeasible fee simple, was squarely presented to the district court. The district court held that Virginia Simpson took a defeasible fee simple estate, which became absolute when she died without having remarried, and dismissed the complaint. We hold that the conclusion reached by the district court was right.

There is no question about the fact that Virginia law controls the decision of this case. No Virginia statute is directly applicable, so we must look to the common law as declared by the Virginia courts in the light of Virginia statutes which have a bearing on the question.

Appellant relies heavily on Blackstone's Commentaries, Minor's Institutes, and Minor on Real Property (Bl.Com. 121, 2 Minor's Insts., 3rd Ed., 99, 100, and 1 Minor on Real Property, 2d Ed., par. 199.3). The statement of the law relied on by appellants is thus phrased by Mr. Raleigh Minor (1 Minor on Real Property, 2d Ed., par. 199.3):

"*Estates Not Expressly for Life, but which May Last for Life.*"

"Such estates do not include estates *expressly for life, but liable to be prematurely defeated* by the happening of a *condition subsequent*. Here, as in the case of a *fee qualified* and elsewhere, care must be taken to distinguish between an estate *upon condition subsequent* and an estate upon *special limitation*.

"It is the latter class of estates we are now to consider. Thus, a conveyance 'during coverture', or 'until marriage', or 'durante viduitate', or 'as long as Z resides abroad', creates an estate of this character. But a conveyance 'to A for life, but if he marries X, his estate to cease and determine' is an *express life estate* upon *condition subsequent*, and does not belong to the class of life estates we are now considering."

It is to be noted, however, that the paragraph above quoted is primarily a statement of a type of life estate occurring in a chapter entitled, "Life Estates in General", which contains no discussion of the specific question here presented.

By the common law, words of inheritance were absolutely necessary for the creation of a fee simple estate by *deed*, and even in a *devise* of land, words such as "issue", "descendants", "offspring", or the like, showing the intent that the land shall descend in indefinite succession, were necessary if the technical word "heirs" was not used. Under these rules of the common law, it would seem clear that, under the language in the will here under consideration, Virginia Simpson could not possibly have taken a fee simple title. But, for many years, by statute, words of inheritance have not been necessary to create a fee simple title by either deed or will in Virginia. The statute is as follows: "Where any real estate is conveyed, devised, or granted to any person without any words of limitation, such devise, conveyance, or grant shall be construed to pass the fee simple or other whole estate or interest which the testator or grantor had power to dispose of in such real estate, unless a contrary intention shall appear by the will, conveyance, or grant." Sec. 5149, Code of Virginia 1942.

In discussing the distinction between conditions subsequent and conditions in law, or common law (or special) limitations, Mr. Minor says (1 Minor on Real Property, 2d Ed., par. 525): "Common law or special limitations are created by such words as 'while,' 'during', 'as long as', 'until', etc. Thus, a grant to A *until* Z returns from abroad; to a woman *while* she remains a widow, or *during* widowhood (durante viduitate), or during coverture; to D and his heirs *as long as* Y has heirs of the body (a fee qualified);—all these are special limitations, and not conditions subsequent."

In discussing the distinction between a "fee qualified" and a "fee upon condition", he says (1 Minor on Real Property, 2d Ed., par. 165):

"A special limitation is created by the use of such words as 'until', or 'as long as', or 'while', or 'during', etc. To this latter class belong *fees qualified*.

"Thus, a conveyance of land 'to A and his heirs *as long as* they remain citizens of Virginia' is a fee qualified in A, which may last forever, but terminates at any time not only by the exhaustion of A's heirs, but by their ceasing to be citizens of Virginia. On the other hand, a conveyance 'to A and his heirs (in fee simple), *but if* they should cease to be citizens of Virginia, the estate to *terminate*', creates a fee simple in A *upon condition subsequent*."

It would seem that a conveyance "to A and his heirs as long as A remains unmarried", would stand exactly in the same category as a conveyance of land "to A and his heirs, as long as they remain citizens of Virginia", both being conveyances upon special limitation. Mr. Minor says that the form of conveyance last quoted creates a fee qualified. Inasmuch as by the statute above quoted, Section 5149, Code of Virginia 1942, words of inheritance are no longer necessary in Virginia, it would seem that Mr. Minor might consider a conveyance "to A as long as A remains unmarried" to create a fee qualified in A.

The textwriters quoted by appellant in her brief as tending to support her contention that under the will here in controversy Virginia Simpson took only a determinable life estate, generally indicate the importance of looking to the whole will, to determine the intention of the testator, in construing such a provision as is here under consideration. From the earliest times, Virginia courts have considered the intention of the testator of paramount importance in the construction of wills. In the very early case of Kennon v. McRoberts, 1 Wash. 96, 97, 102, 1 Am.Dec. 428, the court said: "That the intention of the testator is to give the rule of construction, is declared by all the judges both ancient and modern. Ld. Holt and some others more modern, emphatically call that intention, the Polar Star, which is to guide our decision—and in a late case of Hodgson v. Ambrose, Dougl. 323, the court says, that this is the governing rule, to which all other rules of construction must yield."

And later, in Conrad v. Conrad's Ex'r, 123 Va. 711, 716, 97 S.E. 336, 338, the court said: "The rule is elementary that the intention of the testator is the polar star which is to guide in the interpretation of all wills, and, when ascertained, effect will be given to it unless it violates some rule of law, or is contrary to public policy."

The District Judge was of the opinion that within the four corners of the will, the intention of the testator that his widow should have a fee simple, defeasible only by her remarriage, was apparent. A careful consideration of the will gives strong support to this view. At the beginning of the will here in controversy, which testator himself wrote, he did four things: (1) he provided that there be no appraisement, (2) he appointed his wife his executrix, (3) he provided that she give no security, and (4) he devised to his wife, in fee simple, his residence, including its furniture and contents. He would hardly have provided that there be no appraisement if he had wished his wife to be accountable to his sons for the residuum of his estate. The fact that he appointed her his executrix, without security, and gave her outright his home with all its contents, strongly indicates not only his love for her, but his trust in her loyalty and good judgment. The testator then made specific devises of $10,000.00 to each of his sons, payable to them when they reached the age of twenty-five. This would seem to indicate that it was the testator's intention to give each son $10,000.00 with which to start his business career, and rely upon his wife to make such provision for them from the residuary estate as in her judgment might be wise and proper. In the event of a diversion of her affections by remarriage, the testator specifically provided that the residuum of his estate should go to his sons.

A consideration of the Virginia cases leads us to the conclusion that the disputed language in the will under Virginia law created a defeasible fee simple estate in testator's widow. In the case of Vaughan v. Vaughan's Ex'x, 97 Va. 322, 33 S.E. 603, 604, the court was called upon to construe the following provision of a will: "I do hereby bequeath to my wife, Emma Lee Vaughan, and to my children, all my property, of every kind, real and personal, and do hereby appoint my wife my sole executrix, without security, as long as she shall remain my lawful widow. Should she marry again, the minor children to choose guardians, and my wife in that event to take a child's part, to be hers as long as she lives, and at her death to be distributed amongst my children then living. I further request that no appraisement or other expense be made."

The court held that the widow took the entire estate in fee simple, defeasible only in the event she married again, in which event she would take a child's part for her life. The court said, 97 Va. at page 325, 33 S.E. at page 604: "The only harmonious construction to be drawn from all the provisions and words of the will, considered together, is that the testator intended to give to her the entire estate, but, if she married again, then she was only to have a child's part for her life."

The leading case, and the one which we believe to be decisive of the question here presented, is Trice v. Powell, 168 Va. 397, 191 S.E. 758, 759. The provision of the will there under consideration was as follows: "That I give and bequeath to my sister, Nannie Goodwin, all money & bonds and the entire landed estate to do as she thinks proper, so long as she remains single, but if she marries it is to be sold and divided between the heirs of body of Julia D. Kuper, Mattie W. Powell & Robert Goodwin, and she to retain one-fourth of said sale, and in the event of her death intestate, it is to be divided as above stated."

The court cited Vaughan v. Vaughan's Ex'x, supra, considered Minor on Real Property (Sections 168 and 540, 1st edition, which are Sections 165 and 525, 2nd edition), and quoted from 69 Corpus Juris, "Wills", as follows:

"A devise to a testator's widow, which is absolute except for a provision terminating the estate, or providing for a gift over, in the event of her remarriage, creates a defeasible fee subject to be defeated by her remarriage." (Section 1557).

"It is generally held that, where an estate has been devised in fee, subject to be defeated by the happening of some future event or contingency, if the happening of such event or contingency becomes impossible of occurrence, the defeasible fee becomes a fee simple absolute. A defeasible fee will be enlarged into a fee simple absolute upon the death of the first devisee prior to the happening of the event or contingency by which alone his estate can be defeated, and which event or contingency cannot possibly occur after his death." (Section 1559).

In considering the clause of the will, "That I give and bequeath to my sister, Nannie Goodwin, all money & bonds and the entire landed estate to do as she thinks proper, . . .", the court said: "We then arrive at the conclusion that whether we end the clause after the word 'estate,' or after the word 'proper,' a fee-simple estate is conveyed subject only to such limitation as is placed thereon by the language 'so long as she remains single,' annexed thereto. These latter words mark out the utmost period during which the estate conveyed to her may endure. The clause 'but if she marries,' is but another expression confining the disposition of the estate to a period 'so long as she remains single.' Both clauses, 'but if she marries,' and 'in the event she dies intestate', are words of defeasance with a meaning so clear and distinct that little doubt can be entertained that they established a special limitation upon the fee simple."

The court held that Nannie Goodwin took "a qualified or defeasible fee in the estate devised, which became an absolute fee upon her death, unmarried and testate." . . .

It is therefore our conclusion that the last two sentences of the will created a defeasible fee simple title to the residuum in the widow, Virginia Simpson, which became a fee simple absolute when she died without having remarried. It therefore follows that the decision of the district court will be

Affirmed.

LONG v. SHORT

Court of Appeals of Kentucky, 1977.
553 S.W.2d 297.

PARK, Judge.

Under the provisions of two separate deeds from their parents, Ray Long and Alvis Long possessed life estates in two tracts of land. Following the death of Ray Long, a dispute arose with respect to the ownership of the two tracts. Alvis Long contended that he possessed a life estate in the whole property following the death of Ray. On the other hand, the heirs of Ray Long contended that their undivided one-half remainder interest in the property became possessory immediately upon Ray Long's death. The Cumberland Circuit Court upheld the claim of the heirs of Ray Long adjudging that they owned an undivided one-half interest free of any claim of Alvis Long. The trial court further ordered a partition of the larger tract and a sale of the smaller tract for purposes of partition. Alvis Long appeals, contending that he possesses a life estate in the whole property following the death of Ray Long, and that as a result it was error for the trial court to order a partition and division of the property.

The property was conveyed to Ray Long and Alvis Long by deeds from their father and mother, I.N. Long and Ellen Long. The first deed, dated July 19, 1934, conveyed a tract of approximately 125 acres. Immediately following the description of the property and immediately preceding the habendum clause, the first deed provided:

> "It is further stated that the party of the first part [I.N. Long] is to have full control of said described land as long as he lives and at his death his wife Ellen Long is to have a one-third interest in said described land as long as she lives and at her death to go to her two sons Ray Long and Alvis Long and it is further stated that Alvis Long is to have full control/management of said described land and *at their death* said described land is to go *to their heirs*." (Emphasis added)

The second deed, dated June 20, 1934, conveyed a smaller tract of 20 acres. Following the description of the 20 acre tract and immediately before the habendum clause, the second deed provided:

> "It is further agreed that the party of the first part [I.N. Long] is to have full control of said described land as long as he lives and said described land is to go to the heirs of the second party [Ray Long and Alvis Long] *at their death.*" (Emphasis added)

Alvis Long contends that the heirs of Ray Long were to have no possessory interest until the death of both life tenants.

When deeds, wills or other instruments create two or more life estates and there is no express provision governing the disposition of the property following the death of the first life tenant to die, the courts have adopted a number of different constructions. In some cases, cross-remainders have been implied in favor of the surviving life tenants. Alvis Long urges this construction of the two deeds. In a second line of cases, similar instruments have been construed to create estates pur autre vie, that is, an estate for the life of the survivor of the income beneficiaries. Under such a construction, Ray Long would have possessed a right to one-half of the income from the property for the remainder of the life of Alvis Long, and at his death, such interests would have passed as personal property to the personal representative of Ray Long. This construction was adopted in Anderson v. Simpson, 214 Ky. 375, 283 S.W. 941 (1926), but neither party urges this construction in this case. In a third line of cases, courts have rejected any construction that the remainder becomes possessory only at the termination of all of the life interests. The trial court accepted the argument of the heirs of Ray Long and adopted this last construction. For a thorough discussion of the construction problem presented, see 5 American Law of Property § 21.35 (1952); 2 Powell on Real Property § 324 (Rohan Ed. 1977); Annotation, 140 A.L.R. 841 (1941), supplemented 71 A.L.R.2d 1332 (1960).

No hard or fast rule can be adopted. The particular language used in each instrument must be considered in adopting the proper construction. The phrase "at their death" used in the two deeds is ambiguous. It can be construed to mean at "their respective deaths" or it can be construed to mean "at the death of the last survivor." If the deeds are construed to mean "at their respective deaths," the one-half remainder interest of Ray's heirs would become possessory immediately on his death. On the other hand, if the phrase is construed to mean "at the death of the last survivor," this court must still determine whether a cross-remainder is to be implied in favor of Alvis Long or whether Ray Long possessed an estate pur autre vie which passed to his personal representative.

We conclude that the trial court was correct in construing the language in question to mean "at their respective deaths." There is nothing in the deeds which indicates that I.N. Long intended that either of his two sons receive more than one-half of the income from the property during his life. It is true that Alvis Long was granted full management and control of the 125 acre tract. However, according to the testimony of Alvis Long, his brother Ray was not capable of managing the farm. With the death of Ray Long, the reason for granting Alvis Long management and control of the larger tract also ceased. The provision for the management and control of the 125 acre tract does not indicate an intention to confer any special benefit or interest on Alvis Long. Had Alvis Long been the first to die, there is nothing in the deeds to indicate that the remainder interest of his heirs should not become possessory until the death of Ray.

In support of his contention that a cross-remainder should be implied, Alvis Long relies upon the decision in McCallister v. Folden's Assignee, 110 Ky. 732, 62 S.W. 538 (1901). However, that decision involved a special rule of construction applicable only to conveyances of life estates to a husband and wife. Based upon the questionable theory that a husband and wife are but one grantee, the survivor was held to hold a life estate in the whole property following the death of the other spouse. This rule of construction would have no application to a deed to two brothers.

For the foregoing reasons, the judgment of the circuit court is affirmed.

All concur.

NOTES

1. Do you agree that George L. Simpson intended to give his wife a defeasible fee simple rather than a defeasible life estate? The words "as long as she remains my widow" certainly could have been read to mean Virginia's lifetime instead of her widowhood. Why would George have intended the estate to go to his sons in the event of Virginia's remarriage but not in the event of her death? Were the policy pressures favoring the fee simple stronger or weaker in *Dickson* than they were in White v. Brown, page 479, above?

How would you have drafted George L. Simpson's will to create a defeasible fee? A defeasible life estate? How would you have drafted the deeds in Long v. Short to make the parents' judicially-discerned intent more explicit?

2. Life estates are transferable inter vivos. B, who holds a life estate under the conveyance, "A to B for life, remainder to C," can sell, lease, mortgage or otherwise dispose of her interest—*if* she can find someone to pay for an interest that will evaporate on her death. If B conveys her interest to X, (or if A had conveyed "to X for the life of B,") X's right to possess Blackacre until B's death is called a life estate *pur autre vie*.

3. *Trusts.* The estates created by the deeds in Long v. Short— legal life estates under which the sons had legal title to their interest and the remaindermen had legal title to theirs—have a history that traces to the years just after the Conquest. However well-suited the legal life estate was to the dynastic needs of an earlier day, it puts too many impediments in the way of efficient land transfers to be a useful device in modern times. As a practical matter, if B has a life estate and A has the reversion or C has the remainder, anyone wishing to acquire fee title to the land, or even to lease the land, must acquire not only B's interest, but also the interest of A or C. The

transaction will frequently be complicated by the fact that the reversion or remainder is held by many people, some of whom may not be readily ascertainable.

These difficulties prompted the English to abolish the legal life estate in 1925, and to allow the creation only of equitable life estates. See page 475, note 2 above. Roughly the same result is achieved in this country through a private arrangement called a trust: the trustee holds legal title to Blackacre in fee simple absolute for the benefit of the life tenant, B—who is said to have an equitable life estate entitling him to possession or income from Blackacre during his life—and for the benefit of the equitable remainderman, C, or equitable reversioner, A, who will receive Blackacre or its equivalent upon B's death. Anyone who wishes to acquire Blackacre in fee, or to take a mortgage or lease on it, need deal only with the trustee. Under the terms of the trust instrument, or local law, the trustee will be required to invest the proceeds of any such transaction for the benefit of the life tenant and the remainderman or reversioner. The comparative advantage of the trust in facilitating land transfers explains why equitable life estates are so popular today, and legal life estates so rarely used. The modern trust is considered further at page 525.

2. FUTURE INTERESTS

Every present possessory interest other than the fee simple absolute will be accompanied by one or more future interests. The future interest may be reserved to the grantor ("A to B for life, then to A"); it may be created in someone other than the grantor ("A to B for life, then to C"); or it may be divided between the two ("A to B for life, remainder to C if she survives B, otherwise to A"). The grantor may retain present possession to himself while creating a future interest in another ("A to B, B to take possession on the occasion of her graduation from law school"). The chart at page 476 displays the various future interests together with their companion present interests.

The first and most important step in dealing with future interests is to classify them correctly. Thus, in the first example, it is important to characterize A's interest as a *reversion* (the name given to the grantor's future interest following a life estate) rather than as a *possibility of reverter* (the grantor's future interest following a fee simple determinable) or some other future interest, because the rules governing the enforceability and transferability of reversions often differ from those governing other future interests. It is also important to characterize C's interest in the conveyance, "A to B for life, then to C," as a *remainder* (the third-party future interest following a life estate) to distinguish it from the *executory interest* (the future interest following a fee simple subject to executory limitation).

Second, all interests must be accounted for. If A started with a fee simple absolute, the interests he conveyed or reserved must add up to a fee simple absolute. Thus, in the conveyance, "A to B for life," courts will say that B has an estate for her life and that A has impliedly retained a reversion in fee simple absolute for himself. Taken together, the life estate and reversion add up to the fee simple absolute with which A began. Similarly, C's interest in the conveyance, "A to B for life, then to C," is a remainder in fee simple absolute.

The classification and arithmetic of estates were as important to early common law conveyancing as they are today. There were, however, fewer classes of permissible future interests. The reversion and remainder were probably in use by the late thirteenth century and, as the fee simple determinable and the fee simple subject to condition subsequent evolved, future interests approximating today's possibility of reverter and right of entry came with them. But, interests equivalent to today's executory interests were forbidden at early common law, and any attempt to create them was given no effect. Thus, in A's conveyance, "to my oldest son B and his heirs, but if B acquires more than 100 acres of my other lands at any time, then to my second son, C and his heirs," C's interest (which today would be an executory interest) would be invalidated on the ground that it was a *shifting interest* in a stranger that unlawfully cut short B's freehold estate. B would be held to have a fee simple absolute. Similarly, in the conveyance, "A to X and his heirs upon X's marriage to A's daughter, D," X's future interest (which today would be an executory interest) would be invalidated on the ground that it was an unlawful *springing interest*, a freehold estate intended to spring up out of the grantor at some point in the future. A would be held to have a fee simple absolute.

The great political and legal upheavals that eventually led to the validation of shifting and springing interests brought other, major changes as well. The revolution centered on the institution of the *use*.

a. *Uses.* The common law's refusal to recognize shifting and springing interests hampered early efforts at estate planning and commercial transactions. A may have wanted to avoid the effects of primogeniture by having his second son, C, take the land in the event that A's death left the oldest son, B, adequately provided for. A, whose daughter was planning to marry X, would not want X to have control of the marriage parcel until the knot was actually tied. As early as the twelfth century, grantors sought to avoid the common law rule by leaving the legal fee title intact, and charging the title with a use. Thus, in the last example, A (the *feoffor*) would convey legal fee title to T, a trusted friend of both A and X, "to the use of X and his heirs when X should marry A's daughter, D." A would continue in possession until the marriage, at which point *T*, the *feoffee to uses*, would convey legal title to *X*.

Since common law courts would not enforce uses, only *T*'s steadfastness guaranteed his performance. See Helmholz, The Early Enforcement of Uses, 79 Colum.L.Rev. 1503 (1979). Soon, though, grantors looked to the church courts to enforce uses as a matter of moral obligation. By the mid-fifteenth century, grantors regularly turned for relief to Chancery, with its burgeoning jurisdiction, its sweeping equitable powers of injunction and imprisonment—and its freedom from the common law rules against shifting and springing interests. Although the Chancellor could not render judgment on legal title—strictly a matter for the common law courts—he could, by recognizing equitable interests, effectuate the grantor's plans. Thus, Chancery would hold that if the conveyance, "*A* to *T* and his heirs to the use of *X* and his heirs when *X* should marry *D*," gave *T legal title* in fee simple absolute, then *A* held *equitable title* in fee simple subject to an equitable executory interest in *X*. *T* could enforce his interest at law, and *A* and *X* could enforce their interests at equity.

Uses enabled more than just the circumvention of common law rules against shifting and springing interests. Grantors could also employ uses to avoid the common law requirement that freehold estates be transferred only through an elaborate public ceremony, called livery of seisin, requiring *A*, as seller, and *B*, as buyer, to travel to the parcel where *A* would convey title and possession by handing a twig or a clod of earth to *B* while speaking the words of conveyance. To avoid this bother and the attendant publicity, *A* and *B* might instead enter into a bargain and sale agreement which, if it recited consideration paid by *B*, would be treated by Chancery as vesting equitable title in *B* on the theory that equity views as done that which should be done. The agreement effectively made *A* a feoffee to the use of *B*. *A* still had legal title and *B* had equitable title in fee simple absolute.

Uses were probably most popular as a vehicle for testamentary transfers. *A* was not at this time allowed to transfer a common law estate in land by will. But, through the device of the use, *A* could in his lifetime convey legal title to *T* in fee simple, to be held by *T* to *A*'s use in fee simple, and on *A*'s death, *T* to convey legal title to such persons, in such proportions, as *A* shall designate by will. If *T* failed to perform, *A*'s devisees could petition the Chancellor to order the conveyance according to the terms of the use and the will. Alternatively, since uses—unlike legal estates—were devisable, *A* could simply devise the use to the objects of his desires.

b. The Statute of Uses. Shifting and springing interests, secret conveyances, and testamentary transfers of land—all made possible by the use—substantially undercut the common law scheme. Even more unsettling, particularly to the King, was the extent to which the use enabled landowners to avoid the important, revenue-raising feudal incidents—wardship, marriage, relief—that became due when property descended on death. The principal tax avoidance technique was for *A* to enfeoff as joint tenants a large number of feoffees to the use of *A*. On *A*'s death, the use would pass by will or intestacy. Since it was an equitable, not a legal, interest that passed, there was no occasion for the assessment of feudal incidents. At the same time, the death of any one or more of the joint tenants holding legal title would not result in the imposition of incidents because, under the rules applicable to joint tenancies, the interest of one joint tenant accrues on his death to the remaining joint tenants and does not descend to his heirs. When the number of surviving joint tenants began to dwindle, it was easy enough for the equitable titleholder to ask the remaining feoffees to enfeoff additional younger joint tenants. The effect was that legal title never descended and the feudal incidents never came due.

Although piecemeal efforts were made to correct the situation, it was left to a financially strapped Henry VIII to end the charade entirely in 1535 with the Statute of Uses, 27 Hen. VIII, c. 10. The Statute, which came into effect on May 1, 1536, provided that whenever one or more individuals (*T*) are seised to the use of another (*A*), the beneficiary of the use (*A*) shall have a legal estate of the same character as the equitable estate that he held under the use. Simply, the Statute transformed ("executed") equitable estates into their corresponding legal estates. Thus, the effect of the Statute on the conveyance, "*A* to *T* and his heirs to the use of *A* and his heirs," was to convert *A*'s equitable title in fee simple absolute into legal title in fee simple absolute, and to deprive *T* of any title at all.

Although it might at first appear that the Statute did little more than place *A* back in his original position, the consequences were in fact enormous:

Executory Interests. "*A* to *T* and his heirs to the use of *X* and his heirs upon *X*'s marriage to *D*." The Statute converted *A*'s equitable fee simple subject to a springing executory interest into a legal fee simple subject to a springing executory interest and converted *X*'s equitable springing executory interest into a legal springing executory interest. In a word, the Statute validated legal executory interests. (Because the Statute only executed uses, and did not directly validate executory interests, it was necessary, in order to create a legal executory interest, to couch the conveyance in terms of a use that could then be executed. This extra step is unnecessary today and, under modern practice, *A* would simply convey "to *X* upon the occasion of his marriage to *D*.")

Inter Vivos Transfers. The Statute's effect on bargain and sale agreements between *A* as seller and *B* as buyer was to convert *B*'s equitable title into legal title and to convert *A*'s legal title into no title at all. Thus, in a stroke, the Statute enabled the transfer of legal title without resort to the cumbersome and public formalities of livery of seisin. The change also facilitated secret transfers, and it was to prevent these that Parliament enacted the Statute of Enrollments, 27 Hen. VIII c. 16 (1536), providing that a freehold conveyance would be ineffective unless it was recorded—enrolled—in one of the King's courts of record within six months of its execution. Although the Statute of Enrollments was poorly drawn and was quickly circumvented by ingenious lawyers, it was the precursor of the modern recording acts in force and universally honored throughout the United States.

Testamentary Transfers. However great a boon it was to *inter vivos* transfers, the Statute of Uses appeared to eliminate testamentary land transfers entirely, forcing estate planners back to the unsatisfactory, pre-use alternatives of inter vivos transfers or reliance on the laws of descent. Strong public pressure for change led to the Statute of Wills, 32 Hen. VIII c. 1 (1540), permitting landowners to devise two-thirds of any land held in knight service and all lands held in socage tenure. Devisees were, however, liable for the feudal incidents to the same extent as if they had taken by descent.

The Statute of Uses has generally been adopted in the United States—in some states as part of the received common law, in others through express statutory confirmation, and in others through the enactment of legislation approximating the Statute. The Statute was repealed in England as part of the Law of Property Act of 1925, 15 Geo. V, Ch. 5, 7th Sched.

c. *Uses after the Statute.* The Statute of Uses did not execute all uses. Doubtless the most significant exception carved out by courts involved the so-called active use in which A conveyed to T for the use of B, imposing on T the duty to actively manage the property for the benefit of B. The active use is the direct forerunner of the modern trust in which A transfers real or personal property, or both, to T, as trustee, to hold and manage for the trust beneficiary, B. As in the use, T has legal title to the trust assets and B has equitable title. T's basic obligation is to manage the trust assets faithfully and prudently according to the terms of the trust and applicable local law, selling the trust assets when appropriate, reinvesting the proceeds, and paying the income to the beneficiary.

NOTE

Uses were just one technique through which landowners sought to avoid the imposition of feudal incidents. Another ploy was to take advantage of the fact that incidents were payable not on death but on descent. If A conveyed to B in fee simple absolute, and B died intestate, B's heirs would be liable for the feudal incidents. But, if A conveyed "to B for life, remainder to the heirs of B," A could hope to get the land into the heirs' hands without the payment of incidents since the heirs would succeed to *B*'s estate by purchase rather than descent. Similarly, instead of *A* conveying "to *B* for life," leaving *A* with a reversion in fee that would pass to *A*'s heirs by descent, *A* could convey "to *B* for life, remainder to the heirs of *A*." Courts were quick to stymie both these efforts at medieval tax avoidance— the first through what became known as the Rule in Shelley's Case, and the second through the Doctrine of Worthier Title.

The Rule in Shelley's Case. At least as early as 1366, it was held that the conveyance, "*A* to *B* for life, remainder to the heirs of *B*," gave *B* not only the life estate, but the remainder in fee as well, thus effectively recasting the conveyance as, "to *B* for life, remainder to *B* in fee simple." Provost of Beverley's Case, Y.B. 40 Edw. III, 9 (1366). [The Rule takes its name from the case that gave it its most famous exposition, Wolfe v. Henry Shelley, 1 Co.Rep. 93, 76 Eng. Reps. 206 (K.B.1581).] Because the life estate and the remainder were held by a single individual, *B*, the doctrine of merger converted them into a single fee simple absolute in *B*'s hands. If *B* died without having disposed of the fee inter vivos, it would descend to his heirs who would then become liable for the feudal incidents.

Early received into American common law, the Rule in Shelley's Case has since been abolished by statute or judicial decision in the great majority of states.

The Doctrine of Worthier Title. The Doctrine of Worthier Title (also called the Rule Forbidding Remainders to the Grantor's Heirs) holds that, in the conveyance, "*A* to *B* for life, remainder to the heirs of *A*," the grantor's attempt to create a remainder in her own heirs is void, thus leaving an implied reversion in the grantor. As a result, if *A*'s heirs were to take at all, they would take by descent rather than as purchasers. (The doctrine got its name—its misnomer, really— from a connected rule that, if *A* attempts to devise by will the same freehold estate that the devisee would have taken by descent if *A* had died intestate, then the estate passes by descent, rather than by devise, because descent represents the source of "worthier title.")

The Doctrine of Worthier Title is followed in many states today, although predominantly as a rule of construction rather than as a rule of law. A New York decision, Doctor v. Hughes, 225 N.Y. 305, 122 N.E. 221 (1919), pioneered the doctrine's use as a rule of construction, holding that in the conveyance, "*A* to *B* for life, then to the heirs of *A*," *A* will be presumed to have retained a reversion in herself, and it is up to the heirs to prove affirmatively that she intended them to have a remainder. It is one thing to announce a rule of construction and another to apply it. "Just how bad the situation has become in New York is reflected by the divergent results of the reported decisions. In forty cases decided in New York since Doctor v. Hughes, the box score is twenty-five reversions, fifteen remainders. However, these forty cases have produced fifty-seven reported decisions, and the box score for all decisions is thirty-four reversions, twenty-three remainders. The count at the court of appeals level is eight remainders, five reversions. Of the thirteen court of appeals cases decided since Doctor v. Hughes, eight reversed lower court decisions, five affirmed." Johanson, Reversions, Remainders, and the Doctrine of Worthier Title, 45 Tex.L.Rev. 1, 12–13 (1966).

NOTE: THE VALUATION OF PRESENT AND FUTURE INTERESTS

Future interests always have present value. The value may be substantial and certain, as in the case of A's reversion following a four-year estate for years in B. Or it may be no more than the value of a lottery ticket, as the interest of A and his successors in the possibility of reverter following an estate "to B so long as no alcoholic beverages are consumed on the premises." Real estate lawyers encounter problems involving the valuation of future interests in a wide range of settings: in litigation, like White v. Brown, p. 479 above, in which a parcel is ordered to be sold and the proceeds divided between present and future interest holders; in counseling clients interested in buying up outstanding future interests in order to make title marketable; and in negotiating for the acquisition of the reversionary interest in an income-producing property.

The same fundamental principles apply to all these valuation contexts. To start with a highly simplified example, suppose that A owns Blackacre in fee simple absolute, an interest worth $100,000 on today's market. She gives her son, B, an estate for four years in Blackacre, retaining the reversion to herself. B's estate is clearly not worth $100,000 for all he has is the use of Blackacre for four years. Nor is A's reversion worth $100,000, for she only has the right to receive the parcel four years from today, and valuation of her interest must account for the lost use of $100,000 over four years. It is clear, however, that, taken together, A's interest and B's add up to $100,000, the amount they would receive if they joined in a conveyance of the fee.

The first step in valuing A's reversion at the time of the conveyance is to recognize that the present value of the right to receive $100,000 four years hence is not $100,000, but rather a lesser sum—an amount that, invested today at a specified interest rate, would equal $100,000 four years from today. The next steps are to select an interest rate—say 5% compounded annually—and then to determine what amount, invested today at 5% interest compounded annually, will total $100,000 four years from today. The answer—$82,270—represents the present value of A's reversion and is easily ascertainable from a present value table, available in basic banking and finance handbooks. The closer A gets to the actual reversion date, the greater the value of her reversion. Thus, at the end of three years into B's term, A's reversion will be worth $95,238, the amount that, if invested at 5%, would total $100,000 at the end of the year.

The value of B's estate is most easily figured by subtracting the value of A's reversion from $100,000 ($100,000 − $82,270 = $17,730, the present value of B's four-year estate). A conceptually clearer way to express this result is to say that the value of B's estate is the present value of the right to receive $5,000 (5% × $100,000) per year for four years. (Obviously, the amount is something less than $20,000, for the present value of the right to receive $5,000 at the end of each of the succeeding four years will be successively less than $5,000.) The question to ask, then, is, what sum, if invested at 5% interest, will pay $5,000 a year and be exhausted at the end of four years? The answer, readily ascertainable from an annuity table, is, not surprisingly, $17,730.

The valuation principles would be the same if A gave B not a term of years, but a life estate. The value of B's interest would be the present value of the right to receive $5,000 per year over the course of his lifetime, and the value of A's reversion would be the present value of the right to receive $100,000 upon the death of B. The only complicating factor—that the length of B's life is unknown—is resolved through the use of mortality tables that calculate average life expectancies. If at the time of valuation B was a 33 year old male, his life expectancy would be approximately 40 years, and the value of his estate would be $85,795 (the present value of the right to receive $5,000 a year over 40 years). The value of A's reversion would be $14,205 (the present value of the right to receive $100,000 40 years hence).

a. CLASSIFICATION

As a first step in classification, future interests are divided into those that are retained by the grantor or his successors ("A to B for life, *then back to A*"), and those that are created in transferees ("A to B for life, *then to C*"); the second step is to determine whether the future interest is "vested." The distinction between future interests retained by the grantor and those created in transferees is crucial, as is the determination whether a particular future interest is vested. As you will see in the three cases that follow this introduction, the validity, transferability and enforceability of a future interest will often turn on how it is classified and on whether it is vested or not.

Future Interests Retained by the Grantor. The future interests retained by the grantor are subclassified as the *reversion* (the future interest in the grantor following a life estate, fee tail, or term of years), the *possibility of reverter* (the future interest in the grantor following a fee simple determinable), and the *right of entry* (the future interest in the grantor following a fee simple subject to condition subsequent).

Future Interests in Transferees. Future interests in transferees are subclassified into remainders and executory interests. While grantor future interests can be easily subclassified by referring to the possessory estates that they follow, the proper subclassification of transferee future interests requires deeper probing into the circumstances under which the future interest will become presently possessory. A transferee future interest is a remainder only if "it can become a present interest upon the expiration of all prior interests simultaneously created, and cannot divest any interest except an interest left in the transferor." Restatement of Property § 156 (1936). Thus, in the conveyance, "*A* to *B* for life, then to *C* and his heirs," *C's* interest is a remainder because it becomes possessory upon the expiration of *B's* estate; since *B's* estate ended with her death, *C's* interest is viewed as succeeding it, rather than as divesting it.

If the transferee future interest does not qualify as a remainder, it is an executory interest. Thus in the conveyance, "*A* to *B* so long as no house over two stories is built on the premises, then to *C*," *C's* interest is an executory interest because it divests *B's* preceding fee estate. Another way to put the proposition is that if a transferee future interest follows a fee simple estate, it must be an executory interest, for remainders can never follow a fee simple. At early common law it was thought that the fee interest was so substantial that, once it was created, there was not enough left for the creation of a remainder in a third person. (Recall the force behind the statute, *Quia Emptores*, and recall that, until the Statute of Uses, executory interests could not be created at law.)

Vesting. In classifying and enforcing future interests, it often becomes important to determine whether the interest is *vested in interest.* A future interest is vested in interest if, (a) there is no contingency that must be met before the interest can become presently possessory and, (b) the person or persons who will be entitled to possession are immediately ascertainable. Under this definition, executory interests are typically not vested in interest since some contingency must be met before they can become possessory. Thus, in the conveyance, "*A* to *B* so long as alcohol is never sold on the premises, then to *C*," *C's* executory interest is not vested in interest because it is not certain that alcohol will ever be sold on the premises, and thus it is uncertain that *C*, his assigns, devisees or heirs will ever take possession.

When will a remainder be vested in interest? In the conveyance, "*A* to *B* for life, remainder to *C*," *C's* remainder is vested (specifically, it is an *indefeasibly vested remainder*) because (a) *C's* interest is certain to become possessory, since *B* must die at some point, and (b) it has been created in an ascertainable person or persons—*C*. By contrast, in the conveyance, "*A* to *B* for life, then to the heirs of *C*," if *C* was alive at the time of the conveyance, the remainder in her heirs is not vested since the heirs are not ascertainable in her lifetime. (The heirs' interest is called a *contingent remainder*.) In the conveyance, "*A* to *B* for life, then to *C* if she survives *B*, otherwise to *D*," *C*'s remainder, if *B* is still alive, is a contingent, rather than a vested, remainder since it is uncertain whether she will survive *B*. *D*'s interest is an *alternative contingent remainder*.

How should *C*'s remainder be classified in the conveyance, "*A* to *B* for life, then to *C*, but if *C* shall not survive *B*, then to *D*"? Substantively, *C*'s remainder might appear to be identical to the contingent remainder created in the last example. Nonetheless, *C*'s interest will be called a vested remainder, specifically, a *remainder vested subject to complete defeasance*. What is the difference between the two? Only syntax. In the earlier example, the condition was inserted *before* the language creating an otherwise vested remainder, thus indicating that, as a condition precedent to taking the land, *C* had to survive *B*. In the present example, the condition appears *after* the language creating a vested remainder, indicating that, upon *B*'s death, *C* will become automatically entitled to possess the land but that, as a condition subsequent, she will lose the right to possession if she does not survive *B*. Having classified *C*'s interest in this last example as a remainder vested subject to complete defeasance, *D*'s interest cannot be an alternative contingent remainder because it can become possessory only by divesting *C*'s remainder in fee. Thus *D*'s interest here is an executory interest.

FLETCHER v. HURDLE

Supreme Court of Arkansas, 1976.
259 Ark. 640, 536 S.W.2d 109.

FOGLEMAN, Justice.

This action originated as a suit in ejectment brought by Nash Fletcher, Gerald Fletcher, Bruce Fletcher, Rose Fletcher Crabtree and Joann Fletcher States against James Hurdle and Shirl Hurdle, the co-executors of the will of Betty Roach deceased and her only devisees. These defendants, appellees here, claimed title to the real property involved under their decedent's will. They asserted that she had title by the virtue of a warranty deed executed by Barbara Jean Stephens, the sister of the plaintiff-appellants. These parties, along with Barbara Jean Stephens, were heirs of Asbury Fletcher, who died intestate. The Asbury Fletcher heirs, who originated the suit, will hereafter be referred to as the plaintiff-appellants. Barbara Jean Stephens will be referred to as Barbara Jean. The appellees, who cross-appealed on the dismissal of a third party complaint against the executor of the estate of Barbara Jean will be referred to as the Hurdles.

Babe Fletcher, the brother of Asbury Fletcher, intervened, claiming that he was the owner of an undivided one-half interest in the lands in question in fee simple as a residual devisee under the will of

I.N. Fletcher, deceased, the father of Asbury and Babe Fletcher. At the time of the trial, the plaintiff-appellants took the position that they were the owners in fee simple of an undivided five-twelfths interest in the land in question. On the basic issue the positions of the plaintiff-appellants and the intervenor-appellant are identical.

I.N. Fletcher was the common source of title claimed by all parties. He died on September 20, 1950. The issues turn upon the proper construction of his will and of a deed executed by the plaintiff-appellants to their sister Barbara Jean. The pertinent provisions of the will of I.N. Fletcher are:

> 3. I devise and bequeath to my granddaughter, Barbara Jean Fletcher, for and during her natural life, then to the heirs of her body, if any, and if not then to Asbury Fletcher his heirs and assigns, the following described real estate situated in Craighead County, Arkansas to-wit: [describing the lands in controversy].
>
> . . .
>
> 7. After payment of all specific bequests and devises herein, I hereby devise and bequeath the entire residue of my estate, real, personal, or mixed to my two sons Asbury Fletcher and Babe Fletcher in equal parts.

Asbury Fletcher died October 11, 1956, leaving the plaintiff-appellants and Barbara Jean as his surviving heirs at law. Barbara Jean claimed title as an heir of her father Asbury Fletcher and by virtue of a quitclaim deed executed by the plaintiff-appellants on December 6, 1956. Barbara Jean died without issue in March of 1974, having conveyed the lands in controversy to Betty Roach by warranty deed dated September 12, 1968. The appellants contend that paragraph three of I.N. Fletcher's will created a life estate with alternative contingent remainders, so that the testator retained a divestible reversion which, when Barbara Jean died without having heirs of her body, but surviving her father Asbury, vested the fee title in the appellants by virtue of the residuary clause of I.N. Fletcher's will. On the other hand, the Hurdles contend that their title comes through Asbury Fletcher as a contingent remainderman under the will of I.N. Fletcher, but that his heirs took as remaindermen, and the interest of all the heirs merged in Barbara Jean through the quitclaim deed to her in December, 1956. That deed was entitled "Quitclaim Deed" and by it the plaintiff-appellants did thereby "grant, sell and quitclaim unto the said Barbara Jean . . . the following lands," to wit:

> All of our interest and possibility of remainder by reason of the will of our Grandfather, recorded in Probate Record Book 1, at page 116, Records of Craighead County Lake City District, as to [the lands in controversy].

The appellees alleged, but did not prove, that at the time of the deed to Barbara Jean, her grantors knew that she was incapable of bearing children. Jury trial was waived and the cause was submitted to the court on the pleadings, stipulations of counsel and oral testimony. The circuit judge found that appellants had no interest in the land in controversy and dismissed the complaint and intervention. The judgment was based upon oral findings of the circuit judge. Among other things, he found that:

> I.N. Fletcher, by specifically listing and naming the subject property, attempting to convey it to his granddaughter Barbara Jean, for her life, then to her children, and if no children, to Asbury Fletcher and his heirs, did divest himself of the subject property to the heirs of Asbury Fletcher in fee, whether by a vested remainder or to the heirs of Asbury Fletcher, or his devisee, of the reversionary interest to the heirs of Asbury Fletcher. I.N. Fletcher intended to, and did, divest himself of the property by paragraph three of his will and the property did not constitute a part of the residual estate disposed of in paragraph seven.

We agree with appellants that the circuit court erred in treating paragraph three of the will as creating a vested remainder, either in Asbury Fletcher, who predeceased the life tenant, or in his heirs. Of course, the devise to Barbara Jean Fletcher for life, "then to the heirs of her body, if any," vested only a life estate in Barbara Jean, with remainder to the heirs of her body. The words, "if any," are certainly indicative that any remainder in the heirs of the body of Barbara Jean was contingent, if there could otherwise have been any doubt about the matter.

A remainder is contingent when the remainderman cannot be ascertained until the death of the life tenant and no title passes until the happening of the contingency, i.e., the death of the life tenant. Where the estate in remainder is limited to take effect either to a dubious or uncertain person or upon a dubious and uncertain event, the remainder is contingent. Where the right of the remainderman to succeed to the enjoyment of the estate depends upon some contingency which may never arise or where the person who is entitled to succeed to possession is not, and may never be, ascertained or is not in being, the remainder is contingent. Hurst v. Hilderbrandt, 178 Ark. 337, 10 S.W.2d 491; Wise v. Craig, 216 Ark. 144, 226 S.W.2d 347. It is the uncertainty of the right of enjoyment and not the uncertainty of actual enjoyment that renders a remainder contingent. Where the persons who may take under a will are uncertain and cannot be ascertained until the life tenant dies, the remainder is contingent.

The distinction between contingent and vested remainders is well made by a quotation from 23 RCL 500, § 32, in Hurst v. Hilderbrandt, supra, viz:

> The fundamental distinction between the two kinds of remainders is that in the case of a vested remainder, the right to the estate is fixed and certain, though the right to possession is deferred to some future period, while, in the case of a contingent remainder, the right to the estate as well as the right to the pos-

session of such estate is not only deferred to a future period, but is dependent on the happening of some future contingency. The broad distinction between vested and contingent remainders is this: In the first there is some person in esse known and ascertained who, by the will or deed creating the estate, is to take and enjoy the estate, and whose right to such remainder no contingency can defeat. In the second it depends upon the happening of a contingent event, whether the estate limited as a remainder shall ever take effect at all. The event may either never happen, or it may not happen until after the particular estate upon which it depended shall have been determined, so that the estate in remainder will never take effect.

That the remainder to the heirs of the body of Barbara Jean was contingent is beyond cavil. Appellees do not contend otherwise.

Turning then to the subsequent clause in paragraph three of the will, and applying the well-established rules of property distinguishing between vested and contingent remainders, we come to the inevitable conclusion that any remainder in Asbury Fletcher was a contingent remainder, because the remainder could not possibly have vested unless Barbara Jean predeceased him without having heirs of her body. Any estate in Asbury Fletcher was necessarily dependent upon the happening of this contingency. The remainder was obviously to a dubious or uncertain person or upon a dubious and uncertain event. The person or persons who might take under this clause of the will were uncertain and could not be ascertained until the death of the life tenant. If Barbara Jean had left an heir of her body, the remainder over would have been gone forever, insofar as Asbury Fletcher or his heirs are concerned. That contingency would have defeated any remainder in Asbury Fletcher and no estate would ever have vested in him. In the absence of any showing to the contrary there is a presumption that a woman may have issue so long as life continues. As previously pointed out, there was no evidence to indicate that Barbara Jean was incapable of bearing children.

If there were any lingering doubt about the contingency of the remainder to Asbury Fletcher, the use of the word "then" immediately following the creation of the life estate in Barbara Jean denotes the time the fee would vest, i.e., at the time of Barbara Jean's death. Where the interest of a remainderman is contingent upon his surviving the life tenant and he dies during the continuance of the life estate, he takes no interest in the land under the remainder and no interest devolves upon his heirs. It is clear that the interest of Asbury Fletcher was contingent upon his surviving Barbara Jean.

Appellees argue, however, that the contingent remainder to Asbury Fletcher descended to his heirs at law. In advancing this argument, they attempt to distinguish Wise v. Craig, supra. But the rules there announced clearly apply in this case.

Appellees seize upon 33 Am.Jur. 618, § 152, for a qualification of the general rule that a contingent remainder does not pass by descent. The application of the principle espoused by appellees depends, however, upon the certainty of the person who is to take and the lack of necessity for his surviving some particular time or event as a part of the contingency upon which the remainder is intended to take effect. It is unnecessary for us to pass on the validity of the rule for which appellees contend, because the clear language of the will required that Asbury Fletcher survive his daughter Barbara Jean before any estate vested in him. A contingent remainder can hardly become vested in a person who is not in being. The only way that any contrary intention could be found in this clause of the will would be by resort to an impermissible construction of the words "his heirs and assigns" following the naming of Asbury Fletcher. Of course, these words cannot be more than words of limitation. It is presumed that the word "heir" is used in its primary legal sense, i.e., as a word of limitation, in the absence of qualifying or explanatory words which are repugnant to the acceptance of the word in its strict legal sense. In determining the intention of the testator, the question is not what the testator meant, but it is the meaning of his words. The addition of the words, "and assigns," is merely declaratory of the power of alienation which the taker possesses without them and they cannot operate to enlarge the grant or defeat its express limitations. The words "heirs and assigns" are to be taken in their technical sense to denote the character of the estate or the extent of the interest to be taken by a named devisee and, as such, are words of limitation, and cannot be words of substitution. The rule in Shelley's case has such an impact in Arkansas that it is to be applied, regardless of the intention of a testator or grantor, who cannot disavow the rule, even in express words. In other words, this language cannot be taken as a substitution of the heirs and assigns of Asbury Fletcher, for him, as a remainderman, if he should not be living at the time of the death of Barbara Jean without heirs of her body.

We find nothing in Ark.Stat.Ann. § 61–101 (1947)[1] to support the argument of appellees. The definition of real estate in Ark.Stat.Ann. § 61–120 (1947)[1] eliminates any such possibility. One cannot be "seized or possessed" of a contingent remainder as is required when those two sections are read together. Furthermore, Ark.Stat.Ann. § 61–137 (Repl.1971) is inapplicable to this situation because it was not in effect at any time critical to the issues here.

The characterization of the interest remaining after the death of Barbara Jean and its disposition remain to be determined. It is quite clear that under Arkansas law a grant to one for life with remainder to the heirs of his body leaves a divestible reversion in the grantor, which would remain in him if the grantee should die without bodily heirs during the lifetime of the grantor.

1. Now repealed.

But here we have alternative remainders. Alternative remainders, limited upon a single precedent estate, are always contingent. It would be helpful to examine the nature of a reversion, as distinguished from a remainder, and to consider the effect of the failure of alternative contingent remainders. The distinction was clearly made in Wilson v. Pharris, 203 Ark. 614, 158 S.W.2d 274. There we pointed out that a remainder is an estate limited to take effect in possession immediately after the expiration of a prior estate created at the same time and by the same instrument. We also pointed out that a reversion is the residue of an estate left in the grantor to commence in possession after the determination of some particular estate granted out by him and that, unlike a remainder, which must be created by deed or devise, a reversion arises only by operation of law. Furthermore, in quoting from 23 RCL p. 111, Reversions, we said:

. . . At common law, if a man seised of an estate limits it to one for life, remainder to his own right heirs, they take not as remaindermen, but as reversioners; and it will be, moreover, competent for him, as being himself the reversioner, after making such a limitation, to grant away the reversion. The same result is reached when an ultimate remainder in fee is contingent. Until it vests there is a reversion in the grantor or devisor and his heirs.

By application of the rules of property hereinabove set out, I.N. Fletcher created a life estate in Barbara Jean, alternative contingent remainders to the heirs of the body of Barbara Jean and Asbury Fletcher and left in himself a reversion. Such a reversion is divestible and may pass by deed or inheritance and, in the absence of a grant by deed in the lifetime of the creator, it will pass by will, and in the absence of a specific devise, will pass under the residuary clause of the will of the holder of the reversion. Thus, the reversionary interest in I.N. Fletcher passed under the residuary clause in the will to Babe Fletcher and Asbury Fletcher. This made Babe Fletcher the holder of an undivided one-half interest in fee upon the death of Barbara Jean. Consequently, the holding of the circuit court was erroneous as to him.

The reversionary interest in I.N. Fletcher could not possibly have passed to Asbury Fletcher under paragraph three of the will because to so hold would mean that no remainder, contingent or otherwise, was created in Asbury Fletcher by paragraph three. The basis of the trial court's holding in this respect was that, by making the devise to Asbury Fletcher and his heirs, the testator divested himself of the property to the heirs of Asbury Fletcher in fee, regardless of whether the interest was a vested remainder or a reversionary interest. The fallacy of this holding has been pointed out in our treatment of the significance of the word "heirs" in paragraph three.

We cannot agree, however that the plaintiff-appellants are not bound by their quitclaim deed to their sister Barbara Jean. It is true that ordinarily a contingent remainder cannot be conveyed by deed.

On the other hand, the conveyance by the plaintiff-appellants of all their interest as to the property would carry the reversionary interest, even if they didn't realize they had it. Although we would agree that the interest passed to the plaintiff-appellants by descent from Asbury Fletcher, we do not agree with these appellants that the words "by reason of the will of our grandfather" limit the words "all of our interest." The limitation is upon the possibility of remainder. This divestible reversion was a present and not a prospective interest held by the plaintiff-appellants. So even if the limitation is upon "our interest," the result is the same. In this respect, the holding of the circuit judge was correct, and his judgment should be affirmed to that extent . . . . .

The judgment of the circuit court is affirmed on direct appeal as to the plaintiff-appellants and reversed and remanded for the entry of a judgment in favor of appellant Babe Fletcher consistent with this opinion.

HARRIS, C.J., and JONES and BYRD, JJ., dissent.

BYRD, Justice (dissenting).

The majority somewhat syllogistically reasons that since the testator gave alternative contingent remainders under paragraph three of his will then it follows that Asbury Fletcher had to survive the life tenant before his interest under paragraph three could pass by descent to his children. At page six of the majority opinion, they state "the clear language of the will required that Asbury Fletcher survive his daughter Barbara Jean before any estate vested in him." Both suppositions are erroneous. The will of I.N. Fletcher, in so far as here pertinent provides:

"KNOW ALL MEN BY THESE PRESENTS:

That I, I.N. Fletcher, of Craighead County, Arkansas, being of sound mind and disposing memory and above the age of twenty-one years, do hereby make, publish and declare this to be my last will and testament, and do hereby revoke all other Wills or codicils thereto heretofore by me made, that is to say:

1. I direct that as soon after my death as practicable all of my just debts, including burial expense be paid.

2. I here devise to my son, Asbury Fletcher, in fee simple, the following described real estate situated in Craighead County, Arkansas, to-wit:

The Southwest Quarter ($SW^{1}/_{4}$) of the Northeast Quarter ($NE^{1}/_{4}$) Section Eight (8), Township Fourteen (14), North, Range Six (6) East and also the South Three (3) acres of the Northwest Quarter ($NW^{1}/_{4}$) of the Northeast Quarter ($NE^{1}/_{4}$) of said Section Eight (8).

3. I devise and bequeath to my granddaughter, Barbara Jean Fletcher, for and during her natural life, then to the heirs of her

body, if any, and if not then to Asbury Fletcher his heirs and assigns, the following described real estate situated in Craighead County, Arkansas, to-wit:

All that part of the West Half of the Southeast Quarter (SE¼) of Section Five (5), Township Fourteen (14) North, Range Six (6) East which lies South of Thompson Creek Drainage Ditch containing approximately Eighteen (18) acres and Twenty (20) acres in the Northwest Quarter (NW¼) of the Northeast Quarter (NE¼) of Section Eight (8), Township Fourteen (14) North, Range Six (6) East bounded on the West by the west line of said Northwest Quarter (NW¼) of Northeast Quarter (NE¼) of Section Eight (8) and on the South by the North line of the three (3) acre tract described in Paragraph number two (2).

4. I hereby devise to my son Babe Fletcher, in fee simple, the following described real estate situated in Craighead County, Arkansas, to-wit:

All that part of the North Half (N½) of the Northeast Quarter (NE¼) of Section Eight (8), Township Fourteen (14) North, Range Six (6) East of which I am the owner at the date of this Will, except that portion devised to Barbara Jean Fletcher under paragraph Three (3).

Said North Half (N½) of Northeast Quarter (NE¼) of said Section Eight (8) is an Eighty (80) acre tract of which I originally owned Seventy-eight (78) acres, a Mr. Gipson now owns one and one-half (1½) acres and Charles McDuffee Three (3) acres, leaving Seventy-three and a half (73½) acres, more or less, of which I am the owner, but of which I have devised Twenty (20) acres to my Granddaughter, Barbara Jean Fletcher as shown above. I also devise to my son Babe Fletcher the fractional North Half (N½) of Northwest Quarter (NW¼), Section Nine (9) containing Thirty-three and ninety hundredths (33.90) acres, more or less, and the North four and Sixty-five hundredths 4.65 acres of the Southwest Quarter (SW¼) of the Northwest Quarter (NW¼) of said Section Nine (9), both in Township Fourteen (14) North, Range Six (6) East.

5. I hereby bequeath to my daughter, Mattie Velma McDuffee, the sum of Three Thousand and No/100 ($3,000.00) Dollars.

6. It is intended and I so direct that if at my death any liens exist upon any of the real estate herein devised, then that said liens be released and discharged by payment of the amounts owing so that title in fee simple, free and clear of all encumbrance will vest in the devisees; and that such payments be made by my Executors out of the residue of my estate.

7. After payment of all specific bequests and devises herein, I hereby devise and bequeath the entire residue of my estate, real,

personal, or mixed to my two sons Asbury Fletcher and Babe Fletcher in equal parts.

. . ."

That the intention of the testator is of prime importance in determining the rights of the parties under the provisions of a will can be seen in Cox v. Danehower, 211 Ark. 696, 202 S.W.2d 200 (1947), cited and relied upon by the majority, which states:

"At the outset we are confronted with the fact that an interpretation of only one item of a will is sought by the parties and the whole will is not before us. The entire will is not set forth in the pleadings and does not appear in the record. One of the cardinal rules in the construction of wills is that it is the court's duty to ascertain the intent of a testator, and in doing so such intent is not to be determined by one clause only, but must be gathered from a full consideration of the entire will. In the case at bar, however, the parties seem willing to assume that a consideration of the other portions of the will would not aid their respective contentions, and are content to rest their case upon the devise above quoted. Acting upon this assumption, we proceed to determine whether the language of this devise alone supports the conclusion reached by the chancellor."

When we remember that Barbara Jean Fletcher is the daughter of Asbury Fletcher, it is at once obvious to me that the testator wanted the land given to Barbara Jean to go back to Asbury if she should die without heirs of her body. There is nothing in any clause of the will that requires Asbury to survive Barbara Jean. Any assertion by the majority to the contrary is unsupported by provisions of the will.

There is nothing in Wise v. Craig, 216 Ark. 144, 226 S.W.2d 347 (1949), that supports the majority view that Asbury must survive his daughter. The will in the *Craig* case specifically provided what would happen if the remaindermen did not survive the life tenant, in the following words:

"In case any of my said nephews and nieces are dead at the time of the death of my daughter Sallie, then the descendants of such deceased devisee shall take such share as would have gone to such nephew or niece if living."

The real issue in the instant case is whether the interest of Asbury Fletcher is inheritable since he did not survive the life tenant. I think there is no question that it is. In L. Simes and A. Smith, *The Law of Future Interests*, § 135 (2d ed. 1956), in a discussion on whether survivorship is a condition precedent, it is stated:

"In a large number of cases in which the discussion proceeds as if the problem were merely whether the remainder is vested or contingent, the real question involved is simply whether there is a requirement that a certain devisee must survive until his interest becomes possessory; it being conceded that he has not so survived. In many of such cases the whole discussion of the distinction is irrelevant, because exactly the same result would be reached if the remainder in question were treated as contingent or as vested subject to complete defeasance on the death of the remainderman before the termination of the particular estate. Thus, in a limitation to A for life and then to B and his heirs if he survives A, the interest of B ends when he predeceases A, whether we classify the interest as contingent or as vested subject to complete defeasance. More dangerous are the cases in which it does make a difference how the interest is classified and in which the courts get involved in a peculiar mingling of fallacies concerning the meaning of the terms 'vested' and 'contingent.' On the one hand, these cases seem to assume that if there is no condition precedent of survivorship, the remainder is necessarily vested (thus purporting to give the term 'vested' the meaning: 'not subject to a condition precedent of survivorship'). On the other hand, they assume that all contingent remainders are necessarily subject to a condition precedent of survivorship. Both of these assumptions are invalid and do not conform to the normal meanings of the two terms in question. As to the first, it is true that if there is a condition precedent of survivorship, the remainder in question is contingent, but the converse is not true. If survivorship is not a requisite, it does not follow that the remainder is vested. A remainder may be subject to some other condition precedent which renders it contingent, even though there is no condition that the devisee must survive until the termination of the preceding estate.

The second assumption—that all contingent remainders are subject to an implied condition of survivorship—is equally invalid. While it is true that the courts will sometimes imply a condition precedent of survivorship (and thus make the remainder contingent), it is also true that some contingent remainders are inheritable, and thus capable of transmission even though the holder thereof does not survive until the interest becomes possessory.

These cases represent an area of the law which engenders confusion because of the narrow meaning which is given to the term 'vested' and because of a failure to appreciate that the question of whether there is a requirement of survivorship is not synonymous with the question of whether the remainder is vested or contingent."

In 23 Am.Jur.2d Descent and Distribution § 32 (1965), we find, contrary to the suggestion of the majority opinion in the second full paragraph on page six, the following statement:

"As a general rule, a contingent remainder passes under the statute of descent and distribution. Similarly, in the case of an executory interest, where the fee is limited to commence in the future upon a contingency, the fee passes, until the contingency happens, in the usual course of descent to the heirs at law.

. . .

. . . While contingent interests have sometimes been considered as subject to an implied condition of the donee surviving the particular estate, seemingly just because they are subject to *some* condition precedent, this is not logically sound where the contingency refers only to the time of enjoyment and possession and not to the time for the title to pass or for the determination of the person taking."

That it was not necessary for Asbury Fletcher to survive the life tenant is eminently supported by Black v. Todd, 121 S.C. 243, 113 S.E. 793 (1922). In that case the will devised the property to Corrinna Mystis Harris for life, the remainder to her children, if any, and if no children then to Mary Brown for life with remainder to her children, if any, and if none then to Samuel P. Black. Corrinna Mystis Harris outlived both Mary Brown and her children, all of whom died without issue. After the death of Corrinna Mystis Harris without children, the court held that a conveyance from the children of Mary Brown was valid as against the claims of Samuel P. Black.

For the reasons stated, I respectfully dissent.

HARRIS, C.J., and JONES, J., join in this dissent.

BROWNING v. SACRISON

Supreme Court of Oregon, 1974.
267 Or. 645, 518 P.2d 656.

O'CONNELL, Chief Justice.

This is a suit in which plaintiff seeks to have a provision in the will of Kate Webb construed. The question presented is whether the remainder devised to plaintiff's husband, Franklin Browning, now deceased, and his brother, Robert Sacrison, the defendant, was vested or contingent at the time of Mrs. Webb's death. The trial court found the remainder to be contingent. Plaintiff appeals.

Kate Webb was the maternal grandmother of Franklin Browning and Robert Sacrison. Her will, executed in 1943, when Franklin was 20 and Robert 13, contained the following provision (paragraph III):

"I give and devise to my daughter, Ada W. Sacrison, a life estate for the term of her natural life in and to all real property belonging to me at the time of my death, excepting only the residence property at Pilot Rock described in paragraph II of this will, with remainder over at the death of the said Ada W. Sacrison, share and share alike, to my grandsons, Francis Marion Browning [1] and Robert Stanley Browning,[2] or, if either of them be dead,

---

1. Francis Marion Browning is the same person as Franklin M. Browning.

2. Robert Stanley Browning is the same person as Robert Stanley Sacrison.

then all to the other, subject to a like condition as to the use of the same or any portion of the proceeds thereof for Clyde Browning, as mentioned in paragraph II of this my last will."³

Kate Webb died in 1954. She was survived by her daughter, Ada, and grandchildren Franklin and Robert. At the time of her death, Mrs. Webb owned 960 acres of farmland in Umatilla County. This is the land devised by paragraph III of the will. Franklin died in 1972 without issue. He did not survive the life tenant Ada, who is still alive.

Plaintiff takes the position that the language in paragraph III of the will, creating an interest in the two grandsons "or, if either of them be dead, then all to the other" refers to the death of the testatrix not the death of their mother Ada, the life tenant. Thus, she argues the estate vested at the time of Mrs. Webb's death.

Conversely, defendant contends that the grandsons each took a remainder contingent upon surviving the life tenant.

Plaintiff relies upon the constructional preference favoring the early vesting of estates. It cannot be denied that there is considerable case support, including our own cases, for the view that the law favors the early vesting of estates. And it is clear that at an earlier day the rule was widely, if not universally accepted. The policy reason for this preference is that it "quickens commerce in the ownership of property by facilitating alienability to a considerable degree." ⁶ But with the passage of time the rule was eroded by exceptions and by a closer analysis of the rationale for the early vesting preference, until today that constructional preference probably no longer represents the prevailing view.⁷ The most severe criticism of the constructional preference for vesting is found in V American Law of Property, § 21.3 at 130 (Casner ed. 1952), where it is said:

> "The preference for vested interests undoubtedly originated in connection with conveyances of interests in land and at a time in feudal England when contingent interests in land had not attained a dignified stature. Under such conditions, it may be reasonable to attribute to a transferor the intention to give the transferee an estate of recognized quality. Today, however, unfortunate tax consequences may follow a determination that an interest is vested and most transferors who consider all the consequences which

---

3. This condition was "that no portion of the property or proceeds thereof shall ever go to or be used for the benefit of their father, Clyde Browning." For further discussion of the effect of this condition see *infra*.

6. Dean et al. v. First Nat'l Bank et al., 217 Or. 340 at 361, 341 P.2d 512 at 522 (1959).

7. "It is the peculiar genius of the common law that rarely is an outmoded rule suddenly repudiated. Usually, it is gradually eroded by exceptions that ultimately form a new rule; what remains of the old rule becomes the exception. Most of the exceptions to the rule favoring the vesting of estates have not been explicitly recognized as such. Nevertheless, exceptions exist and are becoming more common." Rabin, The Law Favors the Vesting of Estates. Why?, 65 Colum.L.Rev. 467, 473 (1965).

attach to a vested interest are inclined to postpone vesting until the time set for enjoyment of the interest in possession. Thus continued adherence to this preference in modern times is at least of doubtful validity in many situations."

The foregoing critique has in turn been criticized for being a "harsh, unbalanced assessment of the rule, . . . as unfortunate as the more common tendency to accept the rule uncritically." [9] Thus a middle position has evolved which urges that "what is needed is a more discriminating evaluation rather than outright rejection of the rule." [10]

We adopt this latter approach. It is true that the reasons which prompted the creation of the rule favoring early vesting no longer obtain. Nevertheless, early vesting still may be desirable for other reasons which have application today.[11] On the other hand, the factors supporting early vesting must compete against other factors favoring the postponement of vesting. All of the factors "must be given their respective weights in the ultimate determination of the judicially ascertained intent of the conveyor." [12]

In the present case, competing with the constructional preference for early vesting is the preference for that construction which conforms more closely to the intent commonly prevalent among conveyors similarly situated than does any other possible construction.[13] In modern law it is felt that when a devise is made to a life tenant with a remainder conditioned upon an ambiguous form of survivorship, the intent "commonly prevalent among conveyors similarly situated" [14] is deemed to require that the remainderman survive the life tenant rather than the testator. The application of this constructional preference would make Franklin's interest subject to the condition that he survive his mother Ada, as the trial court held.

The trial court based its decision in part upon a comparison of the language in other parts of the will with the language in paragraph III. For example, paragraph II provided as follows:

> "I give and devise to my grandsons, Francis Marion Browning and Robert Stanley Browning, share and share alike, the real property owned by me in the Town of Pilot Rock, in Umatilla

---

9. Rabin, *supra* note 7 at 479.

10. *Ibid.*

11. ". . . Nevertheless the early vesting of interests is still regarded as very desirable from the viewpoint of public interest. Construing an interest as vested may reduce the number of persons having interests in the affected thing and thus makes it easier to secure a conveyance of the ownership of such thing. Also such construction tends to reduce the uncertainties as to the created interest and hence results in a readier market for it. Thus earlier vesting still facilitates alienability to a considerable degree. Furthermore the rule against perpetuities operates more destructively as to interests subject to a condition precedent than as to interests vested subject to complete defeasance." 3 Restatement, Property, § 243 at 1217–18 (1940).

12. 3 Restatement, Property, § 243 at 1209 (1940).

13. 3 Restatement, Property, § 243 at 1208 (1940).

14. *Ibid.*

County, Oregon, subject to the condition that no portion of said property or the proceeds thereof shall ever go to or be used for the benefit of their father, Clyde Browning, and if either of said grandchildren be not living at the time of my death, then the other shall take all of such property, subject to said condition."

In this paragraph the testatrix expressly designates that the time for vesting of the Pilot Rock property in the survivor shall be "at the time of my death." The trial court reasoned that "it must be assumed that when these specific words were not used [in paragraph III] after the estate of Ada Sacrison, but the words, 'or, if either of them be dead, then to the other,' the testatrix intended that the interest become vested at the time of the death of the life tenant, and not at the date of her death."

The principle employed by the trial court is well recognized as one of the canons of construction. However, it loses some of its force here because the disposition in paragraph II, being directly to the devisees or the survivor without the intervention of a life estate, would necessarily have to vest, if it were going to vest at all, upon the death of the testatrix and therefore the survivorship provision could not relate to any other person's death insofar as it affected the vesting of the estate. This factor, standing alone, therefore would not justify the trial court's decision.

The trial court did, however, point to another factor which we think is more significant in ascertaining the testatrix's intent. The trial court noted that "all provisions of the will specifically excluded Clyde Browning from sharing in any interest in the estate." The court then concluded that "[i]f the construction propounded by the plaintiff were to be followed, the grandsons of Kate Webb would have had a vested transferable interest at the death of Kate Webb, and had they died intestate without issue prior to the death of the life tenant, their father, Claude (sic) Browning would have shared in his interest to the estate of Kate Webb as an heir of his child, contrary to the testatrix' specific wishes."

To strengthen this conclusion, the trial court could have pointed out that at the time the will was executed in 1943 Robert was only 13, Franklin was 20, and neither of them was married. (Indeed, neither had married by 1954 when the testatrix died.) There was, then, at least in the case of Robert, a rather long period of time during which a beneficiary might die intestate and before marriage and/or the birth of issue could divert the estate from vesting in whole or in part in Clyde Browning. It must be noted, of course, that even if the estate is regarded as vesting only upon the death of Ada, the life tenant, the survivor who outlived Ada might not have married or had issue, in which case Clyde would share in the estate upon his son's death. Moreover, if a grandson did have issue and predeceased the life tenant, treating the vesting event as the death of Ada would result in the disinheritance of the grandson's issue. However, we can only indulge in assumptions as to her possible objectives. We think that the assumption made by the trial court, supported by the preference for the construction which more closely conforms to the intent commonly prevalent among testators similarly situated, is the most reasonable.

The decree of the trial court is affirmed.

Affirmed.

ABO PETROLEUM CORP. v. AMSTUTZ

Supreme Court of New Mexico, 1979.
93 N.M. 332, 600 P.2d 278.

PAYNE, Justice.

This action was brought in the District Court of Eddy County by Abo Petroleum and others against the children of Beulah Turknett Jones and Ruby Turknett Jones to quiet title to certain property in Eddy County. Both sides moved for summary judgment. The district court granted Abo's motion, denied the children's motion, and entered a partial final judgment in favor of Abo. The children appealed, and we reverse the district court.

James and Amanda Turknett, the parents of Beulah and Ruby, owned in fee simple the disputed property in this case. In February 1908, by separate instruments entitled "conditional deeds," the parents conveyed life estates in two separate parcels, one each to Beulah and Ruby. Each deed provided that the property would remain the daughter's

> during her natural life, . . . and at her death to revert, vest in, and become the property absolute of her heir or heirs, meaning her children if she have any at her death, but if she die without an heir or heirs, then and in that event this said property and real estate shall vest in and become the property of the estate of . . . [her], to be distributed as provided by law at the time of her death . . . .

At the time of the delivery of the deed, neither daughter was married, nor were any children born to either daughter for several years thereafter.

In 1911, the parents gave another deed to Beulah, which covered the same land conveyed in 1908. This deed purported to convey "absolute title to the grantee . . . ." In 1916, the parents executed yet another deed to Beulah, granting a portion of the property included in her two previous deeds. A second deed was also executed to Ruby, which provided that it was a "correction deed" for the 1908 deed.

After all the deeds from the parents had been executed, Beulah had three children and Ruby had four children. These children are the appellants herein.

Subsequent to the execution of these deeds, Beulah and Ruby attempted to convey fee simple interests in the property to the predecessors of Abo. The children of Beulah and Ruby contend that the 1908 deeds gave their parents life estates in the property, and that Beulah and Ruby could only have conveyed life estates to the predecessors in interest of Abo. Abo argues that the 1911 and 1916 deeds vested Beulah and Ruby with fee simple title, and that such title was conveyed to Abo's predecessors in interest, thereby giving Abo fee simple title to the property.

We begin our inquiry by examining the nature of the estates James and Amanda Turknett conveyed in the 1908 deeds.

First, the deeds gave each of the daughters property "during her natural life." As Abo apparently concedes, these words conveyed only a life estate.

Second, each deed provided that upon the daughter's death, the property would pass to her "heir or heirs," which was specifically defined as "her children if she have any at her death." Because it was impossible at the time of the original conveyance to determine whether the daughters would have children, or whether any of their children would survive them, the deeds created contingent remainders in the daughters' children, which could not vest until the death of the daughter holding the life estate.

Third, each deed provided that if the contingent remainder failed, the property would become part of the daughter's estate, and pass "as provided by law at the time of her death." The effect of this language would be to pass the property to the heirs of the daughter upon the failure of the first contingent remainder. Because one's heirs are not ascertainable until death, the grant over to the daughter's estate created a second, or alternative, contingent remainder.

The only issues that remain are whether the parents retained any interest, whether by their subsequent deeds to their daughters they conveyed any interest that remained, and whether those conveyances destroyed the contingent remainders in the children.

The grantor-parents divested themselves of the life estate and contingent remainder interests in the property upon delivery of the first deed. Because both remainders are contingent, however, the parents retained a reversionary interest in the property.

Abo's position is that by the subsequent conveyances to the daughters, the parents' reversionary interest merged with the daughters' life estates, thus destroying the contingent remainders in the daughters' children and giving the daughters fee simple title to the property. This contention presents a question which this Court has not previously addressed—whether the doctrine of the destructibility of contingent remainders is applicable in New Mexico.

This doctrine, which originated in England in the Sixteenth Century, was based upon the feudal concept that seisin of land could never be in abeyance. From that principle, the rule developed that if the prior estate terminated before the occurrence of the contingency, the contingent remainder was destroyed for lack of a supporting freehold estate. The one instance in which this could happen occurred when the supporting life estate merged with the reversionary interest.

Although New Mexico has adopted the common law of England by statute, § 38–1–3, N.M.S.A.1978, it has been repeatedly held that "if the common law is not 'applicable to our condition and circumstances' it is not to be given effect." Flores v. Flores, 84 N.M. 601, 603, 506 P.2d 345, 347 (Ct.App.1973), *cert. denied*, 84 N.M. 592, 506 P.2d 336 (1973). *See also* Hicks v. State, 88 N.M. 588, 544 P.2d 1153 (1975). In *Hicks* this Court held that sovereign immunity—another doctrine of the common law—could be "put to rest by the judiciary" once it had reached a point of obsolescence. *Id.* at 590, 544 P.2d at 1155.

The doctrine of destructibility of contingent remainders has been almost universally regarded to be obsolete by legislatures, courts and legal writers. It has been renounced by virtually all jurisdictions in the United States, either by statute or judicial decision, and was abandoned in the country of its origin over a century ago. Section 240 of the Restatement of Property (1936) takes the position that the doctrine is based in history, not reason. Comment (d) to § 240 states that "complexity, confusion, unpredictability and frustration of manifested intent" are the demonstrated consequences of adherence to the doctrine of destructibility. Furthermore, because operation of the doctrine can be avoided by the use of a trust to support the contingent remainder, the doctrine places a premium on the drafting skills of the lawyer.

The only tenable argument in support of the doctrine is that it promotes the alienability of land. It does so, however, only arbitrarily, and oftentimes by defeating the intent of the grantor. Land often carries burdens with it, but courts do not arbitrarily cut off those burdens merely in order to make land more alienable.

Because the doctrine of destructibility of contingent remainders is but a relic of the feudal past, which has no justification or support in modern society, we decline to apply it in New Mexico. As Justice Holmes put it:

> It is revolting to have no better reason for a rule of law than that so it was laid down in the time of Henry IV. It is still more revolting if the grounds upon which it was laid down have vanished long since, and the rule simply persists from blind imitation of the past.

Holmes, The Path of the Law, 10 Harv.L.Rev. 457 at 469 (1897).

We hold that the conveyances of the property to the daughters did not destroy the contingent remainders in the daughters' children. The daughters acquired no more interest in the property by virtue of the later deeds than they had been granted in the original deeds. Any conveyance by them could transfer only the interest they had originally acquired, even if it purported to convey a fee simple. Cook v. Daniels, 306 S.W.2d 573 (Mo.1957).

The summary judgment and partial final judgment entered in favor of Abo are reversed, and the cause is remanded for further proceedings consistent with this opinion.

It is so ordered.

SOSA, C.J., and FELTER, J., concur.

NOTES

1. The common law rules respecting the destructibility of contingent remainders are now followed in only a handful of states. See 2A R. Powell, Real Property ¶ 314 (1981). In the states where they are still enforced, these rules offer one important reason for distinguishing between vested and contingent remainders and between contingent remainders and executory interests. Only contingent remainders are destructible. Vested remainders and executory interests, as well as future interests retained by the grantor, are categorically exempt.

The common law rules will destroy contingent remainders in either of two contexts. First, a contingent remainder will be destroyed unless it has vested at the time the preceding freehold estate terminates. For example, in the conveyance, "A to B for life, then to C when she turns 21," C's remainder will be destroyed if it does not vest at or before B's death—if, for example, C predeceases B before turning 21 or if, at B's death, C has not yet reached 21. As a result, C will take no interest at all—even if she subsequently turns 21—and the next vested estate—in this case A's implied reversion—will become possessory immediately upon B's death.

Second, as was argued in Abo v. Amstutz, a contingent remainder can be destroyed through merger. The doctrine of merger provides that when a person holding one interest in land acquires another interest in the same land, the two interests merge if no other interest stands between them. Thus for example, if after the conveyance, "A to B for life, then to C when she reaches 21," A conveys his reversion to the life tenant, B, before C reaches 21, A's estate and B's will be held to merge, giving B a fee simple absolute. What of C's interest? Since it had not vested at the time of A's transfer of his reversion to B, it was not sufficiently strong to stave off merger and was thus destroyed.

Does either of these two rules make more practical sense than the other? Does *Abo*, which held against the second rule, stand as authority against the first? *Abo* is discussed in Cohen, Contingent Remainders—Rule of Destructibility Abolished in New Mexico, 10 N.M. L.Rev. 471 (1980).

2. Proper classification is sometimes crucial to determining whether a future interest enjoys the very important attribute of alienability inter vivos. At common law, only reversions and vested remainders could be transferred inter vivos. Possibilities of reverter, rights of entry, contingent remainders and executory interests were held to be inalienable inter vivos on the theory that they were too insubstantial or speculative to qualify as true interests in land that were capable of transfer.

In sharp contrast to the common law position, most states today hold that all future interests are freely alienable inter vivos as well as devisable and descendible. A few states, however, continue to treat executory interests and contingent remainders as inalienable. Some states also treat possibilities of reverter and rights of entry as inalienable.

Of all future interests, the right of entry retains the strongest ties to the common law rule of inalienability inter vivos. Indeed, a dwindling handful of states hold that any effort to transfer the right of entry inter vivos will destroy it. In Pickens v. Daughterty, 217 Tenn. 349, 397 S.W.2d 815 (1965), grantor, Gregg, had conveyed one-half acre, out of a 149-acre parcel, to the county, retaining a right of entry in the event the parcel was not used for school purposes. On Gregg's death, his executor conveyed by a deed that purported to transfer the entire 149-acre parcel and that made no reference to the school lot. Defendants, who had through mesne conveyances succeeded to the retained parcel, went into possession of the 148.5 acres. When the one-half acre school site was abandoned, defendants sought its possession, too, on the theory that the executor's deed had given them the right of entry respecting that lot. Gregg's heirs objected, claiming that the right of entry was inalienable inter vivos and thus had passed to them by descent. Defendants responded that, if the right of entry was inalienable, it had been extinguished by the attempted transfer, leaving the heirs with no interest on which to base their claim.

The Tennessee Supreme Court found for Gregg's heirs, ruling that, although the right of entry was not transferable inter vivos, the attempted conveyance did not destroy the interest: "How can it be said the right of re-entry upon condition broken is inalienable but an attempt to convey it destroys the right altogether? How can it be said that which does not pass does not remain?" 217 Tenn. at 355–6, 397 S.W.2d at 818. Concluding that the rule contended for was "unsound and illogical," the court expressly overruled an earlier decision, Humphreys County Board of Education v. Baker, 124 Tenn. 39, 134 S.W. 863 (1911), which had approved the extinguishment rule.

What reason is there today for distinguishing between rights of entry and possibilities of reverter for purposes of determining whether the interest is transferable inter vivos? Recall, from Oldfield v. Stoeco Homes, page 485 above, that it is frequently difficult to determine whether the grantor intended to create a fee simple on condition subsequent, or a fee simple determinable. Is it appropriate to make such an important attribute of the future interest turn on the grantor's presumed intent respecting the present possessory estate he created? Do these rules on the alienability and extinguishment of rights of entry suggest that the constructional preference for a fee simple on condition subsequent does not, as is often thought, advance the free marketability of interests in land?

What reason is there today not to make all these future interests freely alienable? It is possible that the pressures for free alienability have been weakened by the fact that present and future interests are characteristically created in trust under which full fee title can always be effectively transferred by the trustee.

b. Rights of Future Interest Holders: Waste

DORSEY v. SPEELMAN
Court of Appeals of Washington, 1969.
1 Wn.App. 85, 459 P.2d 416.

JAMES, Chief Judge.

Defendants (appellants) leased an 80-acre dairy farm from the plaintiffs (respondents) for a period of five years. After the expiration of the lease, plaintiffs brought this action for damages to the real property, alleging waste committed thereon. For a number of the items, plaintiffs sought treble damages under RCW 64.12.020, which provides in part:

> If a . . . tenant . . . of real property commit[s] waste thereon, any person injured thereby may maintain an action at law for damages therefor against such tenant . in which action, if the plaintiff prevails, there shall be judgment for treble damages, ...

The trial was without a jury. The trial judge found that the defendants had both "committed" and "permitted" waste. Finding of fact No. 4 describes 10 items of damage; five are categorized as commissive waste. For these items the judge awarded treble damages.

The only error urged by defendants is the award of treble damages. Their argument is that exemplary or punitive damages are not favored in the law and that a statute which permits them must be strictly construed. Defendants find support for this contention in DeLano v. Tennent, 138 Wash. 39, 47, 244 P. 273, 276, 45 A.L.R. 766 (1926) wherein it is stated:

> This court, early in its history, announced the doctrine that the rule allowing recovery of exemplary and punitive damages was unsound in principle, and held that such damages were not recoverable in this jurisdiction unless expressly so provided by statute.

> . . . [T]he statute permits recovery in treble damages only where the waste is willful and wanton, ...

The statute referred to in *DeLano* was the precursor of RCW 64.12.020. It was amended in 1943. Prior to amendment, the statute provided that for waste committed by a tenant, there *may* be judgment for treble damages. The effect of the amendment was determined in Graffell v. Honeysuckle, 30 Wash.2d 390, 401, 191 P.2d 858, 865 (1948).

> In our opinion, the legislature, in enacting the amendatory act of 1943 Rem.Supp.1943 § 938, intended to provide, and did provide, that where a . . . tenant . . . of real property *commits* waste thereon, that is, does some voluntary destructive act, the person injured thereby may maintain an action for damages against the offending party; and if the injured party prevails in such action the judgment *shall be* for treble damages, ...

(Italics in original.)

The court in *Graffell*, at 398, 191 P.2d at 863, also defined "waste" as contemplated by the statute and discussed the distinction between "commissive" and "permissive":

> "Waste," as understood in the law of real property and as variously defined by this court, is an unreasonable or improper use, abuse, mismanagement, or omission of duty touching real estate by one rightfully in possession which results in its substantial injury. It is the violation of an obligation to treat the premises in such manner that no harm be done to them, and that the estate may revert to those having an underlying interest undeteriorated by any willful or negligent act.
>
> Waste may be either voluntary or permissive. Voluntary waste, sometimes spoken of as commissive waste, consists of the commission of some deliberate or voluntary destructive act, such as pulling down a house, or removing things fixed to and constituting a material part of the freehold. Permissive waste implies negligence or omission to do that which will prevent injury, as, for instance, to suffer a house to go to decay for want of repair or to deteriorate from neglect.

It is defendants' contention that the evidence upon which the trial judge based his finding that the defendants "committed" rather than "permitted" waste does not satisfy the standard of strict statutory construction. The largest separate item for which there was an award of treble damages involved a small cabin near the farm house occupied by the defendants. The trial judge's finding concerning the cabin was as follows:

> That during defendants' use and occupancy of the premises, they did commit and permit numerous acts of waste to and upon

the premises, consisting of the following and for which the court finds plaintiffs have been damaged in the following amounts:

> (a) By destroying the interior of a small house located upon said premises, tearing out walls and ceilings, destroying cabinets and ripping out wiring, and other acts of damage therein to the extent that said house was damaged and would require $1,366.00 to repair, exclusive of roof damage caused by a windstorm, and the court further finds said damage constitutes commissive waste and awards treble damages therefor in the amount of $4,008.00. [sic] That casualty damage to the roof and interior of said house, as a result of wind and rain, was minimal and is felt by the court to be covered by the allowance of $75.00 which was testified to as the cost of repairing the said roof.

Except for one witness who testified that he saw a relative of defendants throw materials out of a broken window of the small house, there was no direct evidence as to the identity of the person or persons who actually perpetrated the destruction found by the trial judge to constitute commissive waste. But the trial judge found that the circumstantial evidence strongly suggested that the destruction in each case was either the act of the defendants or was committed with their knowledge and approval. With reference to the small house, the trial judge made this observation in his oral opinion:

> I cannot believe that sort of damage was caused by a windstorm. . . . [T]he type of damage that appears in Plaintiffs' 13 and 14 is just plain malicious damage. . . .

> While I do not believe that Speelman is [defendants are] responsible for windstorm damage to the roof, it is a little hard to believe that a windstorm took out all of the windows and window sashes. It just doesn't ring true. I can't believe that a water tank could be ripped out, or cupboards torn off the walls by anything other than a person deliberately doing it.

In his written memorandum opinion following argument of the motion for a new trial, the trial judge referred to the damage to the small house as follows:

> The court is firmly convinced (with the exception of some minor storm damage to the cabin roof) the destruction of the cabin interior was wilful, intentional and voluntary. It would be impossible to conclude that a water tank could be ripped out, walls completely torn down, cupboards torn off the wall, wiring stripped out of the building, sink torn out and the other extensive damage be done by other than voluntary, wilful, and intentional acts of some person or persons.

These observations were typical of the judge's comments concerning other items of damage which he found to be commissive.

Defendants argue that the damage could have been done by third persons without defendants' knowledge. This contention the trial judge disposed of with the following language in his written memorandum:

> Furthermore, the cabin was but a short distance from the house and also a very short distance from the barn and other outdoor buildings used by the defendants every day of the year.
>
> If the defendants are to be believed about the time they spend working in and about the farm and the barns (near the cabin), the court must find they were probably in the area of the cabin approximately 365 days out of the year during the entire term of the lease.
>
> The type of damage that was done to the cabin could not have gone unnoticed by anyone in the vicinity of the cabin. The damage was so extensive that it would have caused considerable noise to carry out and would have required too much effort on the part of some person or persons to do it secretly or unnoticed. Furthermore, one witness testified he saw a relative of the defendants throwing things (of the kind with which we are here concerned) out a broken window of the cabin.
>
> It is not logical to assume the defendants did not know of the destruction going on. It was too extensive and of such a nature that a person who was in the vicinity for 365 days a year would be compelled to know, unless they intentionally sought to ignore what was going on.

In each instance in which the trial judge awarded treble damages, he found that the damage was the result of something more than neglect. The concept of "commissive" waste does not require proof of a solitary personal performance by the tenant in possession. A perpetrator of waste can act through an agent or participate as an aider and abettor. The judge's finding that the waste was "committed" either by the defendants or with their knowledge, encouragement or consent, is supported by substantial evidence. It will not be disturbed.

The judgment is affirmed.

FARRIS and SWANSON, JJ., concur.

MELMS v. PABST BREWING CO.

Supreme Court of Wisconsin, 1899.
104 Wis. 7, 79 N.W. 738.

Action by Franz Melms and others against the Pabst Brewing Company. From a judgment dismissing the complaint, plaintiffs appeal. Affirmed.

This is an action for waste, brought by reversioners against the defendant, which is the owner of an estate for the life of another quarter of an acre of land in the city of Milwaukee. The waste claimed is the destruction of a dwelling house upon the land, and the grading of the same down to the level of the street. The complaint demands double damages, under section 3176, Rev.St.1898. The quarter of an acre of land in question is situated upon Virginia Street, in the city of Milwaukee, and was the homestead of one Charles T. Melms, deceased. The house thereon was a large brick building, built by Melms in the year 1864, and cost more than $20,000. At the time of the building of the house, Melms owned the adjoining real estate, and also owned a brewery upon a part of the premises. Charles T. Melms died in the year 1869, leaving his estate involved in financial difficulties. After his decease, both the brewery and the homestead were sold and conveyed to the Pabst Brewing Company, but it was held in the action of Melms v. Brewing Co., 93 Wis. 140, 66 N.W. 244, that the brewing company only acquired Mrs. Melms' life estate in the homestead, and that the plaintiffs in this action were the owners of the fee, subject to such life estate. As to the brewery property, it was held in an action under the same title, decided at the same time, and reported in 93 Wis. 153, 66 N.W. 518, that the brewing company acquired the full title in fee. The homestead consists of a piece of land 90 feet square, in the center of which the aforesaid dwelling house stood; and this parcel is connected with Virginia street on the south by a strip 45 feet wide and 60 feet long, making an exact quarter of an acre. It clearly appears by the evidence that after the purchase of this land by the brewing company the general character of real estate upon Virginia street about the homestead rapidly changed, so that soon after the year 1890 it became wholly undesirable and unprofitable as residence property. Factories and railway tracks increased in the vicinity, and the balance of the property was built up with brewing buildings, until the quarter of an acre homestead in question became an isolated lot and building, standing from 20 to 30 feet above the level of the street, the balance of the property having been graded down in order to fit it for business purposes. The evidence shows without material dispute that, owing to these circumstances, the residence, which was at one time a handsome and desirable one, became of no practical value, and would not rent for enough to pay taxes and insurance thereon; whereas, if the property were cut down to the level of the street, so that it was capable of being used as business property, it would again be useful, and its value would be largely enhanced. Under these circumstances, and prior to the judgment in the former action, the defendant removed the building, and graded down the property to about the level of the street, and these are the acts which it is claimed constitute waste. The action was tried before the court without a jury, and the court found, in addition to the facts above stated, that the removal of the building and grading down of the earth was done by the defendant in 1891 and 1892, believing itself to be the owner in fee simple of the property, and that by said acts the estate of the plaintiffs in the property was substantially increased, and that the plaintiffs have been in no way injured thereby. Upon these findings the complaint was dismissed, and the plaintiffs appeal.

WINSLOW, J. (after stating the facts). Our statutes recognize waste, and provide a remedy by action, and the recovery of double damages therefor (Rev.St.1898, § 3170 et seq.); but they do not define it. It may be either voluntary or permissive, and may be of houses, gardens, orchards, lands, or woods (Id. § 3171); but, in order to ascertain whether a given act constitutes waste or not, recourse must be had to the common law as expounded by the text-books and decisions. In the present case a large dwelling house, expensive when constructed, has been destroyed, and the ground has been graded down, by the owner of the life estate, in order to make the property serve business purposes. That these acts would constitute waste under ordinary circumstances cannot be doubted. It is not necessary to delve deeply into the Year Books, or philosophize extensively as to the meaning of early judicial utterances, in order to arrive at this conclusion. The following definition of "waste" was approved by this court in Bandlow v. Thieme, 53 Wis. 57, 9 N.W. 920: "It may be defined to be any act or omission of duty by a tenant of land which does a lasting injury to the freehold, tends to the permanent loss of the owner of the fee, or to destroy or lessen the value of the inheritance, or to destroy the identity of the property, or impair the evidence of title." In the same case it was also said: "The damage being to the inheritance, and the heir of the reversioner having the right of action to recover it, imply that the injury must be of a lasting and permanent character." And in Brock v. Dole, 66 Wis. 142, 28 N.W. 334, it was also said that "any material change in the nature and character of the buildings made by the tenant is waste, although the value of the property should be enhanced by the alteration." These recent judicial utterances in this court settle the general rules which govern waste without difficulty, and it may be said, also, that these rules are in accord with the general current of the authorities elsewhere. But, while they are correct as general expressions of the law upon the subject, and were properly applicable to the cases under consideration, it must be remembered that they are general rules only, and, like most general propositions, are not to be accepted without limitation or reserve under any and all circumstances. Thus the ancient English rule which prevented the tenant from converting a meadow into arable land was early softened down, and the doctrine of meliorating waste was adopted, which, without changing the legal definition of waste, still allowed the tenant to change the course of husbandry upon the estate if such change be for the betterment of the estate. Again, and in accordance with this same principle, the rule that any change in a building upon the premises constitutes waste has been greatly modified, even in England; and it is now well settled that, while such change may constitute technical waste, still it will not be enjoined in equity when it clearly appears that the change will be, in effect, a meliorating change, which rather improves the inheritance than injures it. Following the same general line of reasoning, it was early held in the United States that, while the English doctrine as to waste was a part of our common law, still that the cutting of timber in order to clear up wild land and fit it for cultivation, if consonant with the rules of good husbandry, was not waste, although such acts would clearly have been waste in England. These familiar examples of departure from ancient rules will serve to show that, while definitions have remained much the same, the law upon the subject of waste is not an unchanging and unchangeable code, which was crystallized for all time in the days of feudal tenures, but that it is subject to such reasonable modifications as may be demanded by the growth of civilization and varying conditions. And so it is now laid down that the same act may be waste in one part of the country while in another it is a legitimate use of the land, and that the usages and customs of each community enter largely into the settlement of the question. This is entirely consistent with, and in fact springs from, the central idea upon which the disability of waste is now, and always has been, founded, namely, the preservation of the property for the benefit of the owner of the future estate without permanent injury to it. This element will be found in all the definitions of waste, namely, that it must be an act resulting in permanent injury to the inheritance or future estate. It has been frequently said that this injury may consist either in diminishing the value of the inheritance, or increasing its burdens, or in destroying the identity of the property, or impairing the evidence of title. The last element of injury so enumerated, while a cogent and persuasive one in former times, has lost most, if not all, of its force, at the present time. It was important when titles were not registered, and descriptions of land were frequently dependent upon natural monuments, or the uses to which the land was put; but since the universal adoption of accurate surveys, and the establishment of the system of recording conveyances, there can be few acts which will impair any evidence of title. But the principle that the reversioner or remainder-man is ordinarily entitled to receive the identical estate, or, in other words, that the identity of the property is not to be destroyed, still remains, and it has been said that changes in the nature of buildings, though enhancing the value of the property, will constitute waste if they change the identity of the estate. This principle was enforced in the last-named case, where it was held that a tenant from year to year of a room in a frame building would be enjoined from constructing a chimney in the building against the objection of his landlord. The importance of this rule to the landlord or owner of the future estate cannot be denied. Especially is it valuable and essential to the protection of a landlord who rents his premises for a short time. He has fitted his premises for certain uses. He leases them for such uses, and he is entitled to receive them back at the end of the term still fitted for those uses; and he may well say that he does not choose to have a different property returned to him from that which he leased, even if, upon the taking of testimony, it might be found of greater value by reason of the change. Many cases will be found sustaining this rule; and that it is a wholesome rule of law, operating to prevent lawless acts on the part of tenants, cannot be doubted, nor is it intended to depart therefrom in this decision. The case now before us, however, bears little likeness to such a case, and contains elements so radically different from those present in Brock v. Dole that we cannot regard that case as controlling this one.

There are no contract relations in the present case. The defendants are the grantees of a life estate, and their rights may continue for a number of years. The evidence shows that the property became valueless for the purpose of residence property as the result of the growth and development of a great city. Business and manufacturing interests advanced and surrounded the once elegant mansion, until it stood isolated and alone, standing upon just enough ground to support it, and surrounded by factories and railway tracks, absolutely undesirable as a residence, and incapable of any use as business property. Here was a complete change of conditions, not produced by the tenant, but resulting from causes which none could control. Can it be reasonably or logically said that this entire change of condition is to be completely ignored, and the ironclad rule applied that the tenant can make no change in the uses of the property because he will destroy its identity? Must the tenant stand by, and preserve the useless dwelling house, so that he may at some future time turn it over to the reversioner, equally useless? Certainly, all the analogies are to the contrary. As we have before seen, the cutting of timber, which in England was considered waste, has become in this country an act which may be waste or not, according to the surrounding conditions and the rules of good husbandry; and the same rule applies to the change of a meadow to arable land. The changes of conditions which justify these departures from early inflexible rules are no more marked nor complete than is the change of conditions which destroys the value of residence property as such, and renders it only useful for business purposes. Suppose the house in question had been so situated that it could have been remodeled into business property; would any court of equity have enjoined such remodeling under the circumstances here shown, or ought any court to render a judgment for damages for such an act? Clearly, we think not. Again, suppose an orchard to have become permanently unproductive through disease or death of the trees, and the land to have become far more valuable, by reason of new conditions, as a vegetable garden or wheat field, is the life tenant to be compelled to preserve or renew the useless orchard, and forego the advantages to be derived from a different use? Or suppose a farm to have become absolutely unprofitable by reason of change of market conditions as a grain farm, but very valuable as a tobacco plantation, would it be waste for the life tenant to change the use accordingly, and remodel a now useless barn or granary into a tobacco shed? All these questions naturally suggest their own answer, and it is certainly difficult to see why, if change of conditions is so potent in the case of timber, orchards, or kind of crops, it should be of no effect in the case of buildings similarly affected. It is certainly true that a case involving so complete a change of situation as regards buildings has been rarely, if ever, presented to the courts, yet we are not without authorities approaching very nearly to the case before us. Thus, in the case of Doherty v. Allman, before cited, a court of equity refused an injunction preventing a tenant for a long term from changing storehouses into dwelling houses, on the ground that by change of conditions the demand for storehouses had ceased, and the property had become worthless, whereas it might be productive when fitted for dwelling houses. Again, in the case of Sherrill v. Connor, 107 N.C. 630, 12 S.E. 588, which was an action for permissive waste against a tenant in dower, who had permitted large barns and outbuildings upon a plantation to fall into decay, it was held that, as these buildings had been built before the Civil War to accommodate the operation of the plantation by slaves, it was not necessarily waste to tear them down, or allow them to remain unrepaired, after the war, when the conditions had completely changed by reason of the emancipation, and the changed methods of use resulting therefrom; and that it became a question for the jury whether a prudent owner of the fee, if in possession, would have suffered the unsuitable barns and buildings to have fallen into decay, rather than incur the cost of repair. This last case is very persuasive and well reasoned, and it well states the principle which we think is equally applicable to the case before us. In the absence of any contract, express or implied, to use the property for a specified purpose, or to return it in the same condition in which it was received, a radical and permanent change of surrounding conditions, such as is presented in the case before us, must always be an important, and sometimes a controlling, consideration upon the question whether a physical change in the use of the buildings constitutes waste. In the present case this consideration was regarded by the trial court as controlling, and we are satisfied that this is the right view. This case is not to be construed as justifying a tenant in making substantial changes in the leasehold property, or the buildings thereon, to suit his own whim or convenience, because, perchance, he may be able to show that the change is in some degree beneficial. Under all ordinary circumstances the landlord or reversioner, even in the absence of any contract, is entitled to receive the property at the close of the tenancy substantially in the condition in which it was when the tenant received it; but when, as here, there has occurred a complete and permanent change of surrounding conditions, which has deprived the property of its value and usefulness as previously used, the question whether a life tenant, not bound by contract to restore the property in the same condition in which he received it, has been guilty of waste in making changes necessary to make the property useful, is a question of fact for the jury under proper instructions, or for the court where, as in the present case, the question is tried by the court. Judgment affirmed.

NOTES

1. The rules on waste are rules of implication and will be applied only if the parties have not themselves expressed the level of use and care to be exercised by the party in possession of the land. The level of use and care may be expressed in the instrument creating the present and future interests ("A to B for life, then to C, and B shall maintain casualty insurance on the premises") or in a separate instrument between the interest holders ("B and C hereby agree that B shall maintain casualty insurance").

If the parties have not expressly agreed on the present possessor's duties, or on the remedies for their breach, courts will determine (a) whether the nature of the future interest justifies the application of waste doctrine; and, if waste rules apply, (b) whether the present possessor's conduct violates the applicable standard; and, if it does, (c) what remedy or remedies should be given. Answers to the three questions will be determined primarily by the relative economic stake that the present and future interest holders have in the land: if the future interest holder has a certain and substantial interest, such as a vested remainder following a life estate, he will be more likely to obtain the full battery of remedies against even the slightest deviation by the present possessor than if he held a less certain or substantial interest. The three notes that follow discuss each of these three questions.

2. *Nature of the Present and Future Interests.* The aim of waste doctrine is to give effect to the original parties' presumed intent that the future interest holder receive the land in substantially its condition at the time the present possessor took possession. Reversioners and indefeasibly vested remaindermen, who are certain to take at some future time, will almost invariably be given monetary and injunctive relief against conduct of the present possessor that substantially alters the land or improvements. If, however, the future interest holder is uncertain to take possession, he will be denied such complete relief. Holders of contingent or defeasibly vested remainders cannot get damages since they can prove no certain damage to themselves. They can, however, obtain injunctive relief to preserve the land for its eventual taker. On the same theory, damages will not be given to holders of possibilities of reverter, rights of entry and executory interests, and injunctive relief will be awarded only if they can demonstrate that the present possessor's conduct is extreme and that there is a real likelihood that their interest will become possessory.

Is the sharp distinction between vested and contingent remaindermen appropriate? If all contingent interest holders joined in the waste action, they would, together, have the same interest as the vested remaindermen and could apportion the damage award among themselves. What of an approach allowing damages and impounding the award for future distribution to those future interest holders who become entitled to possession? See Restatement of Property § 189(1)(c) (1936). Should a sharper distinction be made between contingent or defeasibly vested remainders, on the one hand, and possibilities of reverter, rights of entry and executory interests, on the other?

3. *Nature of Occupant's Conduct.* Waste can occur in any of three ways: (a) through acts of the present possessor that substantially impair the value of the land (*affirmative, voluntary* or *commissive* waste); (b) through substantial impairment of the land's value as a result of the present possessor's failure to act (*permissive* waste); and (c) through acts of the present possessor that, although they do not impair the value of the land, will change its identity (*ameliorative* waste). The rules governing these three forms of waste are all aimed at securing the future interest holder's right to receive the land in substantially the same condition as when the present holder took possession. For an excellent overview, see 5 R. Powell, Real Property ¶ 640 (1981).

(a) *Affirmative Waste.* While cases like Dorsey v. Speelman sometimes arise, most litigation respecting affirmative waste involves claims that the tenant in possession was taking resources from the land to such an extent that the land would be substantially depleted by the time it came into the hands of the future interest holder. Courts have enjoined a tenant's removal of topsoil, manure or hay as waste, but have also shown some inclination to allow the removal when it is consistent with local custom—either on the theory that the grantor formed his original intent respecting permissible use of the land in light of local custom, or on the theory that local custom provides good evidence of what constitutes reasonable use. Reasonableness and the grantor's presumed intent have also played an important part in the modification of the strict common law rule prohibiting tenants from cutting timber for other than immediate household or agricultural uses. American courts have allowed extensive lumbering activities on the theory that they constitute good husbandry or are consistent with use of the land at the time of conveyance. Similarly, tenants have generally been allowed to work mineral reserves—including oil and gas—that had already been opened at the time of the conveyance.

(b) *Permissive Waste.* What efforts and expenditures must a tenant undertake in order to avoid a finding of permissive waste? The general rule is that "the life tenant must keep the premises in as good repair as they were when the life tenancy began"; further, the life tenant "is not expected to make repairs until the necessity of doing so arises." In re Stout's Estate, 151 Or. 411, 424, 50 P.2d 768, 773 (1935). City of New York v. United States, 97 F.Supp. 808, 818 (Ct.Cl.1951) offers some examples: "a tenant for years . . . must therefore keep the premises wind and water tight; and is bound to make fair and tenantable repairs, such as the keeping of fences in order, or replacing doors and windows that are broken, during his occupation . . . . But he is not bound to rebuild premises which have accidentally become ruinous during his occupation, unless he is under a covenant to rebuild. Neither is he liable for the ordinary wear and tear of the premises; nor answerable if they are accidentally burnt down; nor bound to rebuild a fallen chimney . . . to put a new roof on the building; or to make similar substantial and lasting repairs, such as are usually called general repairs."

The duty to pay taxes, mortgage interest and insurance premiums differs depending upon whether the occupant is a lessee or a life tenant. Lessees, at least under short term leases, typically have no obligation to pay these bills. Life tenants do: "In addition to the taxes, absent a different stipulation in the instrument creating the life estate, a life tenant owes a duty to the remainderman to pay the interest accruing during the period of his estate on a mortgage encumbrance given prior to the creation of the life estate and remainder or reversion, at least to the extent of the income or rental value of the property." But, the "life tenant's only duty to the remainderman is to pay the interest. He is under no obligation to pay any part of the principal." Thompson v. Watkins, 285 N.C. 616, 620–621, 207 S.E.2d 740, 743–744 (1974).

(c) *Ameliorative Waste.* Probably the most surprising aspect of waste doctrine is the rule that present possessors can be enjoined from acts that increase, rather than decrease, the value of the land. The cases, however, are few—and for good reason. How often will a future interest holder complain of conduct that will increase the value of the land when it comes into his hands? What are a future interest holder's motives likely to be in bringing suit for ameliorative waste? As a matter of policy, are these motives that courts and legislatures should honor?

As indicated by Melms v. Pabst Brewing, these cases do arise. Although *Melms* held for the occupant, its holding may be limited by the facts that, at the time Pabst levelled the dwelling, it thought it owned the land in fee, and that "there has occurred a complete and permanent change of surrounding conditions, which has deprived the property of its value and usefulness as previously used." In Brokaw v. Fairchild, 135 Misc. 70, 237 N.Y.S. 6, 70, (Sup.Ct.1929), affirmed 231 App.Div. 704, 245 N.Y.S. 402 (1st Dept.1930), affirmed 256 N.Y. 670, 177 N.E. 186 (1931), a New York court seized on this last point to distinguish *Melms* and to enjoin a life tenant from razing a palatial residence on New York City's Fifth Avenue in order to erect a more profitable apartment building on the site. In the court's view, the dwelling was neither isolated nor undesirable as a residence, and construction of the apartment building "would change the inheritance or thing, the use of which was given to the plaintiff as tenant for life . . . ." 135 Misc. at 77, 237 N.Y.S. at 15.

In 1937 the New York Legislature partially altered the rule of Brokaw v. Fairchild by allowing life tenants and lessees to alter structures on specified conditions, including the giving of security if required by the future interest holders, and a demonstration that "the proposed alteration or replacement is one which a prudent owner of an estate in fee simple absolute in the affected land would be likely to make in view of the conditions existing on or in the neighborhood of the affected land" and that "the proposed alteration or replacement, when completed, will not reduce the market value of the interests in such land subsequent to the estate for life or for years." N.Y.—McKinney's Real Prop.Acts. & Proc.Law § 803.

4. *Nature of Remedies Sought.* Remedies will be modulated on the basis of both the nature of the plaintiff's future interest and the conduct about which he is complaining. Among the substantial minority of states with statutes that empower courts to declare the present holder's estate forfeited to the future interest holder in the event of waste, many limit this extraordinary remedy to claims by indefeasibly vested remaindermen and reversioners. See, for example, Wright v. Conner, 200 Ga. 413, 37 S.E.2d 353 (1946). Many also limit the remedy to cases of affirmative, or even wanton, waste. See, e.g., Minn.Stat.Ann. § 561.17 (1947). Similarly, statutes in the substantial minority of states that permit waste damages to be doubled or trebled usually restrict this extraordinary relief to cases of wanton conduct. See, e.g., Va. Code 55–214 (1981).

Forfeiture may also be expressly prescribed in the conveyance. In Conger v. Conger, 208 Kan. 823, 494 P.2d 1081 (1972), grantor had, by will, devised property to defendant for life, and then to plaintiff for life, imposing on each life tenant the duty to pay taxes, maintain insurance and keep the buildings in repair, and providing that, should either tenant fail to meet these duties, "then his estate and interest therein shall terminate on such default." Finding that defendant had failed to keep the premises insured and in repair, the court held that, under the will, defendant's estate terminated and the land passed to plaintiff, the second life tenant.

5. Since the purpose of the rules on waste is to give effect to the presumed intent of grantor and grantee, their rationale is the same as the rationale that underlies the enforcement of private agreements respecting land ownership and use generally—that the enforcement of private agreements will in the usual case lead to the most productive uses of land. The more specific rationale, and the reason the rules reconstruct the parties' intent as they do, is that present possessors of limited interests should be inhibited from conduct that,

though serving their own objects, will disserve the productive use of land over the longer run. A tenant occupying timberland will have every incentive to cut down all the trees on the parcel and will have no incentive to replace them with new trees that will first mature only after her term expires; a fee owner, with the longer range in view, would cut and reforest more judiciously. Similarly a tenant will be disinclined to make repairs that, though economical, will outlast her term. By giving an action to the ultimate fee owner, the rules on affirmative and permissive waste seek to counter these short term objectives and promote land uses that will benefit the land over the longer run.

Do the rules on waste in fact serve these economic objectives? What reason is there to give greater rights to indefeasibly vested remaindermen and reversioners than to holders of less certain or less readily identifiable interests? Since, unlike other future interest holders, the holders of indefeasibly vested interests are readily identifiable, can they not be expected to enter into private arrangements with present possessors at relatively low cost, thus obviating the need for an intrusive rule of law?

Although the problem of transaction costs may dictate the adoption of a rule of law when future interest holders—contingent remaindermen and the like—are not readily identifiable, is it clear that the rules adopted are appropriate? What reason is there to withhold damages from this class of interest holders, but to give them injunctive relief? Does the possible extortionate effect of the injunctive remedy give these individuals greater control over the present possessor's use than is proper? Would it be preferable to limit them to damages, discounted both to present value and to reflect the uncertainty of their ever taking possession?

What reason is there to distinguish between the remedies for affirmative and permissive waste—deterring the first, but not the second, through the prospect of double or treble damages and forfeiture? What reason is there to give injunctive relief against ameliorative waste, since limiting the future interest holders to actual damages (presumably none) will more accurately reflect their true injury?

Are rules on waste necessary? One rationale sometimes given for the law of waste is that a rule of law is needed because the difficulty of identifying all interested parties will make private agreements between present and future interest holders too costly to conclude. Yet, this rationale overlooks the fact that at one point—when the conveyance was originally made—there was ample and costless opportunity to prescribe the duties of the present possessor. Is it appropriate to presume that, in the unusual case where the parties did not prescribe these duties, they intended a standard conducive to the most productive use of land? Is it not at least equally plausible that they intended to give the present possessor free rein?

6. Rules on waste are sometimes applied to situations outside the estates context. A mortgagee-lender may have an action against a mortgagor-borrower whose conduct threatens to impair the mortgage security. And a buyer or optionee may have an action against a seller or optionor who threatens to injure the property.

7. Should a present possessor have an action for waste against future interest holders who refuse to join in a sale that will put the parcel to its highest and best use? Consider the next principal case.

BAKER v. WEEDON

Supreme Court of Mississippi, 1972.
262 So.2d 641.

PATTERSON, Justice:

This is an appeal from a decree of the Chancery Court of Alcorn County. It directs a sale of land affected by a life estate and future interests with provision for the investment of the proceeds. The interest therefrom is to be paid to the life tenant for her maintenance. We reverse and remand.

John Harrison Weedon was born in High Point, North Carolina. He lived throughout the South and was married twice prior to establishing his final residence in Alcorn County. His first marriage to Lula Edwards resulted in two siblings, Mrs. Florence Weedon Baker and Mrs. Delette Weedon Jones. Mrs. Baker was the mother of three children, Henry Baker, Sarah Baker Lyman and Louise Virginia Baker Heck, the appellants herein. Mrs. Delette Weedon Jones adopted a daughter, Dorothy Jean Jones, who has not been heard from for a number of years and whose whereabouts are presently unknown.

John Weedon was next married to Ella Howell and to this union there was born one child, Rachel. Both Ella and Rachel are now deceased.

Subsequent to these marriages John Weedon bought Oakland Farm in 1905 and engaged himself in its operation. In 1915 John, who was then 55 years of age, married Anna Plaxico, 17 years of age. This marriage, though resulting in no children, was a compatible relationship. John and Anna worked side by side in farming this 152.95-acre tract of land in Alcorn County. There can be no doubt that Anna's contribution to the development and existence of Oakland Farm was significant. The record discloses that during the monetarily difficult years following World War I she hoed, picked cotton and milked an average of fifteen cows per day to protect the farm from financial ruin.

While the relationship of John and Anna was close and amiable, that between John and his daughters of his first marriage was distant and strained. He had no contact with Florence, who was reared by Mr. Weedon's sister in North Carolina, during the seventeen years preceding his death. An even more unfortunate relationship existed between John and his second daughter, Delette Weedon Jones. She is portrayed by the record as being a nomadic person who only contacted her father for money, threatening on several occasions to bring suit against him.

With an obvious intent to exclude his daughters and provide for his wife Anna, John executed his last will and testament in 1925. It provided in part:

> Second; I give and bequeath to my beloved wife, Anna Plaxco Weedon all of my property both real, personal and mixed during her natural life and upon her death to her children, if she has any, and in the event she dies without issue then at the death of my wife Anna Plaxco Weedon I give, bequeath and devise all of my property to my grandchildren, each grandchild sharing equally with the other.
>
> Third; In this will I have not provided for my daughters, Mrs. Florence Baker and Mrs. Delette Weedon Jones, the reason is, I have given them their share of my property and they have not looked after and cared for me in the latter part of my life.

Subsequent to John Weedon's death in 1932 and the probate of his will, Anna continued to live on Oakland Farm. In 1933 Anna, who had been urged by John to remarry in the event of his death, wed J. E. Myers. This union lasted some twenty years and produced no offspring which might terminate the contingent remainder vested in Weedon's grandchildren by the will.

There was no contact between Anna and John Weedon's children or grandchildren from 1932 until 1964. Anna ceased to operate the farm in 1955 due to her age and it has been rented since that time. Anna's only income is $1000 annually from the farm rental, $300 per year from sign rental and $50 per month by way of social security payments. Without contradiction Anna's income is presently insufficient and places a severe burden upon her ability to live comfortably in view of her age and the infirmities therefrom.

In 1964 the growth of the city of Corinth was approaching Oakland Farm. A right-of-way through the property was sought by the Mississippi State Highway Department for the construction of U.S. Highway 45 bypass. The highway department located Florence Baker's three children, the contingent remaindermen by the will of John Weedon, to negotiate with them for the purchase of the right-of-way. Dorothy Jean Jones, the adopted daughter of Delette Weedon Jones, was not located and due to the long passage of years, is presumably dead. A decree pro confesso was entered against her.

Until the notice afforded by the highway department the grandchildren were unaware of their possible inheritance. Henry Baker, a native of New Jersey, journeyed to Mississippi to supervise their interests. He appears, as was true of the other grandchildren, to have been totally sympathetic to the conditions surrounding Anna's existence as a life tenant. A settlement of $20,000 was completed for the right-of-way bypass of which Anna received $7500 with which to construct a new home. It is significant that all legal and administrative fees were deducted from the shares of the three grandchildren and not taxed to the life tenant. A contract was executed in 1970 for the sale of soil from the property for $2500. Anna received $1000 of this sum which went toward completion of payments for the home.

There was substantial evidence introduced to indicate the value of the property is appreciating significantly with the nearing completion of U.S. Highway 45 bypass plus the growth of the city of Corinth. While the commercial value of the property is appreciating, it is notable that the rental value for agricultural purposes is not. It is apparent that the land can bring no more for agricultural rental purposes than the $1000 per year now received.

The value of the property for commercial purposes at the time of trial was $168,500. Its estimated value within the ensuing four years is placed at $336,000, reflecting the great influence of the interstate construction upon the land. Mr. Baker, for himself and other remaindermen, appears to have made numerous honest and sincere efforts to sell the property at a favorable price. However, his endeavors have been hindered by the slowness of the construction of the bypass.

Anna, the life tenant and appellee here, is 73 years of age and although now living in a new home, has brought this suit due to her economic distress. She prays that the property, less the house site, be sold by a commissioner and that the proceeds be invested to provide her with an adequate income resulting from interest on the trust investment. She prays also that the sale and investment management be under the direction of the chancery court.

The chancellor granted the relief prayed by Anna under the theory of economic waste. His opinion reflects:

> . . . [T]he change of the economy in this area, the change in farming conditions, the equipment required for farming, and the age of this complainant leave the real estate where it is to all intents and purposes unproductive when viewed in light of its capacity and that a continuing use under the present conditions would result in economic waste.

The contingent remaindermen by the will, appellants here, were granted an interlocutory appeal to settle the issue of the propriety of the chancellor's decree in divesting the contingency title of the remaindermen by ordering a sale of the property.

The weight of authority reflects a tendency to afford a court of equity the power to order the sale of land in which there are future interests. Simes, Law of Future Interests, section 53 (2d ed. 1966), states:

> By the weight of authority, it is held that a court of equity has the power to order a judicial sale of land affected with a future interest and an investment of the proceeds, where this is necessary for the preservation of all interests in the land. When the power is exercised, the proceeds of the sale are held in a judicially created trust. The beneficiaries of the trust are the persons who held interests in the land, and the beneficial interests are of the same character as the legal interests which they formally held in the land.

This Court has long recognized that chancery courts do have jurisdiction to order the sale of land for the prevention of waste. Kelly v. Neville, 136 Miss. 429, 101 So. 565 (1924). In Riley v. Norfleet, 167 Miss. 420, 436–437, 148 So. 777, 781 (1933), Justice Cook, speaking for the Court and citing *Kelly, supra,* stated:

> . . . The power of a court of equity on a plenary bill, with adversary interest properly represented, to sell contingent remainders in land, under some circumstances, though the contingent remaindermen are not then ascertained or in being, as, for instance, to preserve the estate from complete or partial destruction, is well established.

While Mississippi and most jurisdictions recognize the inherent power of a court of equity to direct a judicial sale of land which is subject to a future interest, nevertheless the scope of this power has not been clearly defined. It is difficult to determine the facts and circumstances which will merit such a sale.

It is apparent that there must be "necessity" before the chancery court can order a judicial sale. It is also beyond cavil that the power should be exercised with caution and only when the need is evident. Lambdin v. Lambdin, 209 Miss. 672, 48 So.2d 341 (1950). These cases, *Kelly, Riley* and *Lambdin, supra,* are all illustrative of situations where the freehold estate was deteriorating and the income therefrom was insufficient to pay taxes and maintain the property. In each of these this Court approved a judicial sale to preserve and maintain the estate. The appellants argue, therefore, that since Oakland Farm is not deteriorating and since there is sufficient income from rental to pay taxes, a judicial sale by direction of the court was not proper.

The unusual circumstances of this case persuade us to the contrary. We are of the opinion that deterioration and waste of the property is not the exclusive and ultimate test to be used in determining whether a sale of land affected by a future interest is proper, but also that consideration should be given to the question of whether a sale is necessary for the best interest of all the parties, that is, the life tenant and the contingent remaindermen. This "necessary for the best interest of all parties" rule is gleaned from Rogers, Removal of Future Interest Encumbrances—Sale of the Fee Simple Estate, 17 Vanderbilt L.Rev. 1437 (1964); Simes, Law of Future Interests, supra; Simes and Smith, The Law of Future Interests, § 1941 (1956); and appears to have the necessary flexibility to meet the requirements of unusual and unique situations which demand in justice an equitable solution.

Our decision to reverse the chancellor and remand the case for his further consideration is couched in our belief that the best interest of all the parties would not be served by a judicial sale of the entirety of the property at this time. While true that such a sale would provide immediate relief to the life tenant who is worthy of this aid in equity, admitted by the remaindermen, it would nevertheless under the circumstances before us cause great financial loss to the remaindermen.

We therefore reverse and remand this cause to the chancery court, which shall have continuing jurisdiction thereof, for determination upon motion of the life tenant, if she so desires, for relief by way of sale of a part of the burdened land sufficient to provide for her reasonable needs from interest derived from the investment of the proceeds. The sale, however, is to be made only in the event the parties cannot unite to hypothecate the land for sufficient funds for the life tenant's reasonable needs. By affording the options above we do not mean to suggest that other remedies suitable to the parties which will provide economic relief to the aging life tenant are not open to them if approved by the chancellor. It is our opinion, shared by the chancellor and acknowledged by the appellants, that the facts suggest an equitable remedy. However, it is our further opinion that this equity does not warrant the remedy of sale of all of the property since this would unjustly impinge upon the vested rights of the remaindermen.

Reversed and remanded.

RODGERS, P.J., and JONES, INZER, and ROBERTSON, JJ., concur.

B. PROMOTING ALIENABILITY AND MARKETABILITY

1. RULE AGAINST PERPETUITIES

HAGEMANN v. NATIONAL BANK & TRUST CO.

Supreme Court of Virginia, 1977.
218 Va. 333, 237 S.E.2d 388.

POFF, Justice.

In this appeal, we are asked to construe a will to determine whether the residuary clause violates the rule against perpetuities.

The will of Mildred Hart Woodward, executed January 15, 1971, was admitted to probate on March 16, 1971 and National Bank and Trust Company, the trustee named in the will, qualified as administrator, c.t.a. The testatrix was survived by her children, Anne Mutter Woodward Hagemann, Fletcher D. Woodward, Jr., and Malcolm P. Woodward, her sole heirs at law, all of whom were named as beneficiaries in her will.

Article Eight, the residuary clause of the will, creates two equal trust funds, one for Fletcher and his descendants and the other for Malcolm and his descendants. The clause contains eight paragraphs. Paragraph 1 provides that the son will receive the income so long as he lives and has living children under the age of 25 years and that, upon the son's death, the income shall be paid to his surviving wife and children for their "support, comfort and education"; paragraph 2 authorizes the trustee to invade the corpus for such purposes. Paragraph 3 provides:

> "3. When the youngest living child of such son of mine has reached age twenty-five years, that trust shall end and the fund shall be divided one-third to such son of mine and two-thirds equally to his then living descendants, *per stirpes*. Should such son of mine not then be living, the whole of the fund shall go to his then living descendants, *per stirpes*."

Under paragraph 4, if the last surviving child of one of the testatrix's sons dies before attaining the age of 25 years, the corpus will be paid on that date to that son, if living, and if not, will be added to the corpus of the other trust fund. Paragraphs 5, 6, and 7 are irrelevant to the issue at bar. The provisions of paragraph 8, however, considered in context with those of paragraph 3, are of crucial relevance:

> "8. Notwithstanding the foregoing, if any portion of my estate is in any contingency capable of being held in trust for a longer period than is permitted by the law of the state of my domicile, or if in any such contingency the vesting of any interest hereunder may occur after the expiration of such permissive period, then upon the happening of any such contingency such portion of my estate shall not be held in further trust, but shall rather be paid over absolutely to the person or persons to whom, and in the proportions in which, such portion would ultimately go under the provisions hereof."

Anne and Fletcher, complainants, filed a bill of complaint seeking construction of the will. The administrator-trustee, Malcolm, and infant beneficiaries, now born or as yet unborn, were named respondents. The chancellor appointed a guardian *ad litem* to represent the infant respondents and later joined Katherine D. Woodward, one of Fletcher's children who had attained her majority, as a party-respondent. Complainants prayed that the residuary clause "be declared null and void and of no effect as violating the rule against perpetuities, and that as a consequence thereof it be declared that the testatrix died intestate as to her residuary estate". Respondents answered, and the cause was heard on the pleadings, memoranda of law, and argument by counsel.

The chancellor found that, absent paragraph 8, the provisions of paragraphs 1 through 7 "may result in" a violation of the rule against perpetuities but that paragraph 8 "modified" those provisions. The chancellor decreed that the residuary clause, as modified, "is construed to provide that the trust for [each son] shall continue until his then youngest living child reaches the age of twenty-one years, at which time the trust will terminate and the corpus will vest absolutely as of that date". By final decree entered February 13, 1976, he upheld the residuary clause as so construed, denied the prayer of the bill, and struck the cause from the docket.

On appeal, all parties agree that under the rule against perpetuities as applied in this Commonwealth, the remainder interests granted the children (or descendants) of the testatrix's sons by paragraph 3 are void unless "saved" by paragraph 8. Complainants contend that paragraph 8 "saves" none of the interests granted by paragraph 3 and that the residuary estate must pass by the laws of descent and distribution in equal shares to the three children of the testatrix. Respondents argue that paragraph 8 "saves" the residuary clause in its entirety, or, in the alternative, that the rule invalidates only the remainder interests of the children (or descendants) of the sons but not the income or remainder interests of the sons.

The rule against perpetuities in Virginia voids a contingent remainder or executory interest, created *inter vivos* or by will, which may, by some possibility, however unlikely that possibility may be, vest beyond a life or lives in being at the effective date of the instrument creating the interest, plus 21 years and 10 months.

The effective date of the Woodward will is the date of Mrs. Woodward's death. In paragraph 3, she disposes of two-thirds of each of the two funds there created to the descendants of her sons living when the youngest living child of a son attains 25 years. The words "then living" create an express condition that a descendant, as a member of the class of descendants, must survive to the time at which the youngest child of the son attains 25 years of age. A contingent remainder is created in the class of "descendants".

By the familiar rule in Leake v. Robinson, 2 Mer. 363, 35 Eng.Rep. 979 (1817), generally followed in the United States and discussed in detail in Simes and Smith, The Law of Future Interests § 1265 (2d Ed.1956), a class must stand or fall as a unit when the rule against perpetuities is applied. If the interest of one member of that class could vest beyond the time permitted by the rule, the interests of all members of that class fail for remoteness. Here, it is possible that the sons could die survived by a child in gestation or by a child under the age of three years and two months. In such case the interest of descendants of the testatrix would vest upon the 25th birthday of that child which is beyond the time permitted by the rule. It is not *actuality* or *probability* but *possibility*, viewed from the effective date of the will, that actuates the rule against perpetuities.

Contrary to inadvertent dictum in Driskill v. Carwile, 145 Va. 116, 121–22, 133 S.E. 773, 774–75 (1926), which was later specifically rejected by this Court in White v. National Bank, *supra*, 212 Va. at 572, 186 S.E.2d at 24 (1972), there is no requirement in Virginia that members of a class must survive the closing date of the class and there is no presumption that such a requirement was intended. In paragraph 3 of the Woodward will, there is an *express* requirement of survivorship; the descendants take who are "then living" when the youngest child of a son attains 25 years of age.

In support of their position that the residuary clause is valid in its entirety, respondents rely upon two rationales. First, they urge us to approve the chancellor's holding that all residuary interests are saved by his construction of the clause as modified by paragraph 8; second, they ask us to construe the residuary clause "in a manner which upholds its validity while allowing a 'wait and see attitude' as to whether or not the savings clause has to be applied." We address the latter rationale first.

As respondents point out, these contingent remainders *could* vest before expiration of the term permitted by the rule upon the happening of any of several events. For example, the rule *could* be satisfied if the testatrix's son should die survived by children, none of whom are under the age of three years and two months and none of whom are in gestation at his death. There are other possibilities, even probabilities, of valid vesting. Respondents say, in effect, that we should so construe the will that the trustee will be allowed to "wait and see" whether any such future event occurs, and if not, then "upon the happening of any such contingency" which violates the rule, the trustee will be allowed to terminate the trust and distribute the corpus.

A statute embodying the "wait and see" doctrine has been adopted in England, Perpetuities and Accumulations Act, 1964, c. 55, § 3(1), and in some of the states, *see, e.g.*, Ky.Rev.Stat. § 381.216 (1972), Vt.Stat.Ann. Tit. 27, § 501 (1975). But a majority of the states, including Virginia, apply the common law rule in its orthodox form. As respondents tacitly acknowledge, the "wait and see" rule is actuated by the possibility of timeliness. The common law rule is actuated by the possibility of remoteness. Burruss v. Baldwin, 199 Va. at 887, 103 S.E.2d at 252. Absent statutory mandate, we reject the "wait and see" rule and adhere to the common law rule.

Turning to respondents' first rationale, we examine the chancellor's ruling that paragraph 8 "saved" the residuary clause.

The rule against perpetuities "is a rule adopted in furtherance of public policy to prevent excessive restraints or limitations upon the alienation of an estate." Burruss v. Baldwin, *supra*. The language of the Woodward will leaves nothing ambiguous about the possibility of remoteness or the thrust of testamentary intent. The testatrix intended to forbid alienation of her residuary estate until her youngest grandchild, living at the time of her death or later born, reached the age of 25 years. Nor can there be any doubt that she attempted to do so knowing that what she attempted posed the possibility of remoteness and constituted a violation of the rule as applied "in the state of [her] domicile". She knew, too, that what she attempted would succeed so long as her will was not challenged in court.

Against the hazard of such a challenge, she added a "savings clause". That clause provides that if "the vesting of any interest hereunder may occur after the expiration of . . . [the period permitted by the rule], then upon the happening of any such contingency such portion of my estate shall not be held in further trust but shall be paid over absolutely". Manifestly, the testatrix's deliberate purpose was to violate but, if possible, evade the effect of the rule against perpetuities, and if the rule were ever invoked, to rewrite the rule so that it would be actuated only upon the "happening" of an event which made remoteness an inevitability. But, as we have said, the rule is actuated by the *possibility* of remoteness, and that possibility must be determined as of the date of the testatrix's death.

The savings clause was patterned after a model form found in Rabkin & Johnson, 3 Current Legal Forms, Form 8.24(30). Indeed, with one exception, the language was identical. The Woodward clause provided that, upon the happening of a contingency that violated the rule against perpetuities, the corpus would be paid "to the person or persons to whom, and in the proportions in which, such portion would ultimately go under the provisions hereof"; the model form provided that in such event the corpus would be paid to those to whom "the income therefrom was then payable." While we do not decide what impact the model form might have had if its exact language had been employed in the Woodward will, we do note that the effect of such language is to fix the date for determining the remaindermen at a time within the term permitted by the rule against perpetuities. The language of the Woodward will, on the other hand, fixes the date at a time which could fall beyond the end of that term, for it identifies the remaindermen as those to whom the corpus "would ultimately go under the provisions hereof." Under the provisions of paragraph 3, the interests of the grandchild-remaindermen would be void for remoteness. A "savings clause" cannot save a void interest by adopting the very provisions which make it void.

Yet, insisting that we need not construe the language of paragraph 8 as adopting the provisions of paragraph 3, respondents rely upon Jewett v. Harvie, 183 Va. 734, 746–47, 33 S.E.2d 213, 218 (1945), where we said:

> "Where one construction of the will will be void because of perpetuity and another construction of the will is valid, the court sustains the construction which maintains the validity of the will."

Jewett did not adopt that language as a universal rule. It was applied specifically to uphold a remainder which was made contingent upon either of two events. The remainder had vested under one contingency, and we held that the vested estate could not be defeated by the fact that the other contingency might have violated the rule against perpetuities. Here, where there is but one contingency, and it violates the rule, that holding does not apply.

Invoking the principle that testamentary intent "is the 'Pole star' and 'sovereign guide' in construction of a will", respondents say that, even if the original testamentary design violated the rule, the "overriding" testamentary intent was to avoid a violation and that we should give effect to such intent in obedience to the maxim that the law does not favor intestacy. As we have indicated, we believe that the testatrix's dominant intent was to violate the rule against perpetuities with the hope that the violation would never be challenged and that the savings clause would never have to be applied.

The whole function of the rule is to defeat testamentary intent to violate its mandate.

> "The Rule against Perpetuities is not a rule of construction, but a peremptory command of law. It is not, like a rule of construction, a test, more or less artificial, to determine intention. Its object is to defeat intention. Therefore every provision in a will or settlement is to be construed as if the Rule did not exist, and then to the provision so construed the Rule is to be remorselessly applied." Gray, *The Rule Against Perpetuities* § 629 (4th Ed. 1942).

When the maxim that the law does not favor intestacy collides with the "public policy to prevent excessive restraints or limitations upon the alienation of an estate", Burruss v. Baldwin, *supra*, the former must yield.

Respondents cite several cases decided in other jurisdictions which uphold savings clauses. Those clauses and the testamentary gifts to which they were applied are wholly unlike those before us, and we neither endorse nor reject the reasoning applied or the result reached in those cases.

Nor do we intend to imply that all savings clauses are inherently ineffectual in Virginia. If the language of a will leaves it ambiguous whether there is a possibility of remoteness, then a savings clause may be effective. But where, as here, the language reasonably permits no construction but that remoteness is a possibility, the use of a savings clause only reinforces the conclusion that the paramount testamentary intent was to violate the very rule which condemns such intent.

Accordingly, we hold that paragraph 8 of the residuary clause in the Woodward will did not save the remainder interests granted by paragraph 3 to the children (or descendants) of the testatrix's sons.

Finally, we consider whether the failure of these interests caused the other interests created by the residuary clause to fail.

Arguing the negative, respondents cite White v. National Bank, 212 Va. 568, 186 S.E.2d 21 (1972). There, the will established a trust to terminate 25 years after the testatrix's death. If living on that date, John Henry White, one of the beneficiaries of the income, was to receive a share of the corpus; if not, his share was to be paid to "his heirs and distributees, per stirpes." We held that those heirs were to be determined as of the date of White's death (rather than the date of the termination of the trust) and that even if White should die before the trust terminated, their interests did not offend the rule. In the course of our opinion, we noted that both the income and remainder interests granted White "must necessarily vest in him, if at all, during the life of a 'life in being'" and that consequently both of his interests were valid. *Id.*, 212 Va. at 570–71, 186 S.E.2d at 23. Since neither White's interests nor those of his heirs violated the rule against perpetuities, it was not necessary to decide, and we did not decide, whether White's interests would have failed if the interests of the heirs had been void. The case does not, therefore, support respondents' argument.

Respondents also rely upon the following language from 61 Am. Jur.2d Perpetuities § 91:

"Where the devise or grant is in such terms as standing alone would convey a fee, but there is also an attempt to create a limitation over which is void for remoteness, the prior estate will take effect as a fee, divested of the void limitation, according to the terms of the devise or grant. For example, where a devise is made to a man and his heirs forever, and for want of such heirs then to a stranger in fee, the devise over to the stranger would be void for remoteness, and the first taker will have a fee simple absolute."

As respondents point out, the principle inherent in this language was applied in Rose v. Rose, *supra*, to a deed which conveyed property to "Otto R. Wachsman and his children and their children" and in Nixon v. Rose, 53 Va. (12 Gratt.) 425 (1855), where a will created a trust for "Emily Coupland or her heirs". The Woodward will makes no "devise . . . in such terms as standing alone would convey a fee" and the principle respondents invoke is altogether inapposite.

As authority for their position that the remote remainders invalidate the anterior estates, complainants rely upon Burruss v. Baldwin, *supra;* Prichard v. Prichard, 91 W.Va. 398, 113 S.E. 256 (1922); and

Closset v. Burtchaell, 112 Or. 585, 230 P. 554 (1924). But the critical inquiry in those cases was the possibility of remoteness in class gifts; the opinions did not address the question of the effect of a void remainder on an anterior estate. Complainants also cite Andrews v. Lincoln, 95 Me. 541, 50 A. 898 (1901), and Johnston's Estate, 185 Pa. 179, 39 A. 879 (1898). The latter decision has been harshly criticized as "difficult to maintain." Gray, *The Rule Against Perpetuities* § 249.2 (4th Ed. 1942). Apparently, the court in *Andrews* considered it was dealing with a class gift when, in fact, what was involved were successive interests. We find no guidance in these cases.

Indeed, neither party has cited a case we consider controlling. The cases discovered in our research are conflicting, but the conflicts result not so much from jurisprudential differences as from factual, syntactical, and statutory diversity. We have concluded that the most succinct exposition of the general rule is that found in 28 A.L.R. Prior Estate-Remainder Void for Remoteness 375, supp. 75 A.L.R. 124, 168 A.L.R. 321:

> "The general rule is that a remainder which is void because in violation of the rule against perpetuities does not necessarily render invalid the prior estate, but that the latter will be sustained notwithstanding the invalidity of the ulterior estate, where the two are not inseparable and dependent parts of a general testamentary scheme, and to uphold the one without the other would not defeat the primary or dominant purpose of the testator . . . ."

Unless infected by the invalidity of the ulterior estates, the anterior estates created by the residuary clause of the Woodward will are valid: the income interest of the son will vest, if at all, within his lifetime; the income interests of the "surviving wife" of the son and his children will vest, if at all, not later than the death of the son; and the son's interest in the corpus will vest, if at all, within his lifetime. Under the rule quoted above, these anterior estates are not infected by the invalidity of the ulterior estates when "the two are not inseparable and dependent parts of a general testamentary scheme, and to uphold the one without the other would not defeat the primary or dominant purpose" of the testatrix.

As reflected in the will as a whole, the testatrix's "general testamentary scheme" was to make roughly equivalent provision for her three children and their descendants. In Article Seven, she created a specific trust for the benefit of her daughter and her daughter's children, and in Article Eight she created residuary trusts for her two sons and their descendants. If the invalidity of the ulterior interests infects the anterior interests, the entire residuary estate will pass by intestacy. In such case, the daughter would receive a portion of the estate intended for the sons and their descendants. This would effectively thwart the general testamentary scheme and defeat what we perceive to be the primary or dominant purpose of the testatrix.

Clearly, with respect to her residuary estate, the testatrix's dominant purpose was to make available, during the critical period her grandchildren were to be reared and educated, not only the income from the trust but also such portion of the corpus as might be necessary for "support, comfort and education". Only after the expiration of that critical period was the corpus to be distributed and, then, only what had not been consumed.

We are of opinion that the anterior and ulterior estates were not "inseparable and dependent parts" of the general testamentary scheme and that to uphold the former would not defeat but, rather, would substantially promote the "primary or dominant purpose" of the testatrix.

We hold, therefore, that the anterior estates which, as we have said, will vest, if at all, within the term permitted by the rule against perpetuities, are not infected by the invalidity of the ulterior estates. We will reverse the final decree insofar as it upholds the remote remainders and affirm the final decree insofar as it upholds the other estates created by the residuary clause. And this cause will be remanded with instructions to restore it to the docket and enter a new decree consistent with this opinion.

Reversed in part, affirmed in part, and remanded.

PACE v. CULPEPPER

Supreme Court of Mississippi, 1977.
347 So.2d 1313.

SUGG, Justice, for the Court:

The appeal and cross appeal in this case are from a decree of the Chancery Court of Lauderdale County. The primary question is whether the rule against perpetuities applies to an option to purchase land.

On March 28, 1970 Mr. and Mrs. C.B. Walker conveyed by warranty deed 2.54 acres to James L. and Louise S. Culpepper for the consideration of $1,000 per acre. On the same date the Walkers and Culpeppers signed an option giving the Culpeppers the first option to purchase an additional .6 of an acre owned by the Walkers at $1,000 per acre.

On March 28, 1973, following the death of his wife, C.B. Walker conveyed by quitclaim deed the .6 of an acre covered by the option to his daughter, Doris Elizabeth Pace, who then conveyed an undivided one-half interest to her brother, James C. Walker on June 21, 1973. C.B. Walker died on June 30, 1973.

Doris Elizabeth Pace and James C. Walker filed suit in the Chancery Court against James Lamar Culpepper and wife, Louise Shirley Culpepper, seeking to set aside the option and warranty deed on the grounds that (1) the consideration was so inadequate as to shock the conscience, (2) the option was void because it violated the rule against perpetuities, (3) the option is void as a restraint upon the alienation of property, and (4) the option and the deed together form a single integral transaction and if the option is void and set aside the deed must also be set aside. The Culpeppers answered and denied the essential allegations of appellants' lawsuit and the matter was submitted to the chancery court without testimony based upon the pleadings and documents involved.

No proof was offered on the question of inadequacy of consideration so this question was not before the trial court and is not before this Court on appeal.

The chancery court held that the deed was valid but the option was void and should be cancelled. Complainants appealed from the holding that the warranty deed was valid and defendants cross appealed from the holding that the option was void.

At the outset the difference between an ordinary option and a pre-emptive right should be noted. In a typical option the optionee has the absolute right to purchase for a definite consideration. A pre-emptive right involves the creation of the privilege to purchase only on the formulation of a desire on the part of the owner to sell.

In considering whether the option violated the rule against perpetuities two questions are presented: (1) was the pre-emptive right granted the Culpeppers personal; namely, would it die with them and therefore not violate the rule against perpetuities; and (2) even if the pre-emptive right was not personal, did it violate the rule against perpetuities?

In considering the first question, we do not experience difficulty in concluding that the right was not personal because the option grants to the Culpeppers and "their heirs, executors, administrators and/or assigns the first option to purchase said .6 of an acre at the rate of $1,000 per acre." By the express terms of the option, the pre-emptive right to purchase extends not only to the Culpeppers but to their heirs, executors, administrators or assigns without limit as to time.

We have never decided whether the rule against perpetuities applies to options to purchase real estate; however, the Court has been confronted with the rule in other contexts. In Magee v. Magee's Estate, 236 Miss. 572, 111 So.2d 394 (1959), we held that a testamentary trust was not in violation of the rule against perpetuities and in so holding the following definition of the rule was given:

> 'The rule against perpetuities prohibits the creation of future interests or estates which by possibility may not become vested within a life or lives in being at the time of the testator's death or the effective date of the instrument creating the future interest, and twenty-one years thereafter, . . .' (236 Miss. at 591, 111 So.2d at 402).

In Carter v. Berry, 243 Miss. 321, 136 So.2d 871, sugg. of error, 140 So.2d 843 (1962), this Court stated:

> The rule against perpetuities is the law limiting the time within which future interests can be created. Gray, The Rule Against Perpetuities, Fourth Edition, Sec. 4, p. 4. It is stated as follows: 'No interest subject to a condition precedent is good, unless the condition must be fulfilled, if at all, within twenty-one years after some life in being at the creation of the interest.' And also: 'No interest is good unless it must vest, if at all, not later than twenty-one years after some life in being at the creation of the interest.' Sec. 201, p. 191, ibid. But, a true vested interest is never obnoxious to that Rule, while a contingent interest not only may be, but often is, violative of the Rule. Sec. 99, p. 88, ibid. And again, 'A vested interest is not subject to the Rule against Perpetuities.' Sec. 205, p. 194, ibid. See also 70 C.J.S. Perpetuities § 10, p. 585. (243 Miss. at 343, 136 So.2d at 875–876).

. . .

The rule against perpetuities is a rule invalidating interests which vest too remotely. It is not a rule against suspension of the power of alienation of property through the creation of interests in unborn or unascertained persons. It is not satisfied by the fact that there are persons in being who can together give a complete title to a purchaser. However, both principles stem from the general policy against withdrawal of property from commerce. In other words, an interest violating the rule against perpetuities fails because it vests too remotely; it may be, and usually is, freely alienable at all times. We are not concerned here with the 'succession of donees' statute. Miss. Code 1942, Rec., Sec. 838.

Applying our decisions to this case, it is readily apparent that the option violates the rule. At the time of its inception the option vested no immediate interest in the Culpeppers. To the contrary there was a mere possibility that the Culpeppers would ever acquire an interest to the .6 of an acre. This possibility depended on whether the Walkers, or their heirs, ever decided to sell the property. *Magee* and *Carter* are but two of our many cases holding that the rule does not apply to vested interests but does apply to future interests or estates which by possibility may not become vested within the time required.

It is not necessary for us to rely solely on the general rules announced by this Court to determine whether the option is void because there is an abundance of authority in other jurisdictions supporting the view that the rule against perpetuities is applicable to options to purchase real estate.

In 61 Am.Jur.2d, Perpetuities § 50 at 51 (1972), the rule is stated as follows:

> Options given to purchase real estate are regarded as having the effect of creating future interests depending on the contingen-

cy of the exercise of the option. Hence if there is a possibility that the option may not be exercised within the limits of time allowed by the rule against perpetuities, the option is void as a violation of this rule. Such is held to be the case where no time is fixed within which the option must be accepted. So, according to the generally prevailing view, an option to purchase real property, unlimited as to the time for its exercise, or extending beyond the period limited by the rule against perpetuities, violates such rule and is invalid.

The rationale behind this rule is explained in Morris and Leach, The Rule Against Perpetuities, Ch. 8, at 213 (1956):

> But it has been held both in England and the United States that an option to purchase land is too remote if it can be exercised beyond the perpetuity period. The reasoning by which this result was reached was as follows. An option to purchase land is specifically enforceable. This gives the option-holder an equitable interest in the land; this interest is contingent upon his election to exercise the option. Contingent interests in land are void unless they must vest (if at all) within the perpetuity period. Therefore an option to purchase which may be exercised beyond the perpetuity period is void to the extent that it creates an interest in land.

Pre-emptive rights to purchase real estate are subject to the rule against perpetuities. 61 Am.Jur.2d Perpetuities § 54 at 55 (1972), states the rule as follows:

> A pre-emptive right to purchase real estate, which right involves the creation of a privilege to buy only on the formulation of a desire by the owner to sell, as distinguished from an ordinary option giving the optionee the absolute right to buy for a definite consideration, is held to be subject to the rule against perpetuities. Thus it has been ruled that a contractual right, granted to A and his heirs and assigns, unlimited as to time, to purchase real estate upon the same terms as the owner could and would sell to a third person, is void. However, where a pre-emptive right option is personal to the parties and is not binding upon their heirs or assigns, it has been held not to violate the rule against perpetuities.

It has been said that, "A pre-emption of unlimited duration, requiring offer to the pre-emptioner for a specified sum of money, is the most objectionable type of pre-emption, and is void by the weight of authority." American Law of Property, Vol. VI, § 26.67, p. 510.

The option in the case before us created in the Culpeppers, the optionees, a pre-emptive right to purchase unlimited as to time and indefinite in duration. The option was not personal to the optionees, but created a future equitable interest in the .6 of an acre which was susceptible of inheritance. It violated the rule against perpetuities because there is a possibility that it may not become vested within the time required by the rule.

Option contracts such as the one involved in this case cannot be upheld because such contracts take property out of commerce and prevent land from answering to the needs of growing communities. No improvements can be made on land so encumbered because the land always remains subject to being taken under the option. It is not a matter which affects the rights of individuals only, but the welfare of the public is at stake. It was for the express purpose of destroying such hinderances to progress that the rule against perpetuities was brought forth.

The Culpeppers argue that we should apply the doctrine of equitable approximation and hold invalid that portion of the option which could extend beyond the lives of the Walkers. The rule of equitable approximation was defined by this Court in National Bank of Greece v. Savarika, 167 Miss. 571, 148 So. 649 (1933) as follows:

" 'At this point it should be observed that the cy pres practice is not to be confused with the equitable doctrine of approximation which has grown up in the judicial administration (as distinguished from judicial creation) of charitable trusts. The ecclesiastical rule of cy pres is one thing, and the equitable rule of approximation is distinctly another. Their purpose, and their application are entirely different. As said by the Alabama court (Lovelace v. Marion Institute et al., 215 Ala. 271, 110 So. 381), 'The appeal in this case is not to any cy pres power of the court, but to the equitable doctrine of approximation, in virtue of which the court of chancery exercises jurisdiction merely to vary the details of administration, in order to preserve the trust, and carry out the general purpose of the donor.' " (167 Miss. at 593, 148 So. at 654).

The equitable rule of approximation was applied in Carter v. Berry, *supra*, and In Re Estate of Kelly, 193 So.2d 575 (Miss.1967). In its final analysis the equitable rule of approximation is a rule of judicial construction, designed to aid the Court to ascertain and carry out, as nearly as may be, the intent of a donor or testator. It has been applied in this state to trusts and wills but has never been applied to options. In trusts and wills there is a vesting of property and the rule is applied to vary the details of administration to preserve the trust and to carry out the intention of the donor or testator, whereas in an option there is no vesting of property.

The complainants in their direct appeal argue that the deed executed by the Walkers to the Culpeppers, together with the option, constituted a single transaction and if the option fails the deed must also fail. They urge, under the holding of Carter v. Berry, *supra*, that the total plan of the parties to the deed and to the option is a part of a single transaction with each instrument inextricably tied to the other.

We reject this contention because the deed is valid and complete on its face. Full consideration was paid for the 2.54 acres conveyed by the deed. The deed does not contain any restriction or limitation.

It was not dependent upon the validity of the option and the Culpeppers by the option did not bind themselves to purchase the additional .6 of an acre. Cancellation of the option does not affect the validity of the deed.

Affirmed.

NOTES

1. The common law Rule Against Perpetuities is generally followed throughout the United States. In most states the rule is embedded in decisional law. In others it is restated or modified by statute. See, e.g., West's Ann.Cal.Civ.Code §§ 715 *et seq.;* N.Y.—McKinney's Est., Powers & Trusts Law 9–1.1 *et seq.* Although a number of states have at one time experimented with statutory modifications, several have since returned to the common law fold. See 6 American Law of Property, Part 25 (A.J. Casner ed. 1952).

The traditional formulation of the Rule reads: *No interest is good unless it must vest, if at all, not later than twenty-one years after some life in being at the creation of the interest.* J. Gray, The Rule Against Perpetuities § 201 (3rd ed. 1915). Put more plainly: *An interest is void if there is any possibility that it will vest more than twenty-one years after the end of some life in being at the creation of the interest.*

It is one thing to state the rule, quite another to apply it. As a starting point, it is important to bear in mind that the rule is concerned with *possibilities,* not *probabilities.* Thus, in the conveyance, "A to B until the snowfall in downtown Buffalo, N.Y. next exceeds eight inches, and then to C," C's interest is invalid because it is possible—even though improbable—that the defeasing event will first occur, and C's interest will first vest, outside the period of the Rule.

Second, the Rule is concerned with the possibility that a future interest will *vest* outside the prescribed period, not with the possibility that it will become *possessory* outside the period. So, for example, in the conveyance, "A to B for seventy years, then to C and her heirs," C's interest is valid under the rule even though it may become *possessory* more than twenty-one years after lives in being at the time of its creation. The crucial point is that C's interest was vested—specifically, it was vested in interest—at the very moment of the conveyance, thus excluding any possibility that it would first vest outside the period. For a refresher on the concept of vesting in interest, see pages 529 to 530, above.

Finally, it is necessary to parse the Rule. Which "interests" are covered by the Rule, and which fall outside its scope? What is the consequence of finding that an interest is "void" under the Rule? How rigorous is the Rule when it speaks of "any possibility"? What is the meaning of "vest" for purposes of the Rule? What lives qualify as "lives in being"? The five notes that follow amplify each of these operative terms. See generally, Featheringill, Understanding the Rule Against Perpetuities: A Step-by-Step Approach, 13 Cumb.L.Rev. 161 (1982).

2. *"An interest . . . ."*. Although, taken literally, the Rule Against Perpetuities covers all interests, it effectively governs only future interests. Interests that become presently possessory at the moment of the transfer are always valid under the Rule because they are immediately *vested in possession*, thus removing any possibility that they will first vest outside the perpetuities period. Thus, in the conveyances, "*A* to *B* for life, remainder to *C*," and "*A* to *B* so long as no house over two stories is built on the premises, then to *C*," *B*'s present possessory interest is valid under the Rule.

The Rule also excuses future interests held by the grantor or his successors—reversions, possibilities of reverter, rights of entry—on the theory that, though not vested in possession, they are inherently *vested in interest* from the moment of the transfer. Thus, in the conveyance, "*A* to *B* so long as no house over two stories is built on the parcel," *A*'s possibility of reverter is valid.

Can this exception be employed to circumvent the Rule's application to future interests created in transferees? For example, could you, using two pieces of paper instead of one, have employed this exception to effectuate the grantor's intent in the two principal cases, Hagemann v. National Bank and Pace v. Culpepper? What functional reason is there for excluding grantor future interests from the operation of the Rule? See generally, Chaffin, Reverters, Rights of Entry, and Executory Interests: Semantic Confusion and the Tying Up of Land, 31 Fordham L.Rev. 303 (1962).

3. *". . . is void . . . ."*. The effect of a finding that an interest is void under the Rule Against Perpetuities is to strike the interest from the conveyance and to treat the conveyance as if the interest had never been created.

What is the effect of an interest's invalidation on the remaining, otherwise valid interests? In part, the answer turns on the grantor's intent. If, as in *Hagemann*, enforcement of the remaining interest will not violate the grantor's overall purpose, it will be left intact. If, however, the voided interest was integral to the grantor's plan, the entire transfer will be voided. The answer also depends on the nature of the stricken interest and of the preceding estates. In the conveyance, "*A* to *B* for life, remainder to such of *B*'s children as shall reach 25," the remainder will be stricken for violating the Rule, and the preceding life estate will be kept intact, with a reversion following the life estate implied in *A* and his successors. See, e.g., Lovering v. Worthington, 106 Mass. 86 (1870).

What if an interest following a defeasible fee is stricken? In the conveyance, "*A* to *B* so long as no house over two stories is erected on the parcel, then to *C*," *C*'s interest will be stricken, *B* will be held to have a fee simple determinable, and *A* and her successors will be held to have an implied possibility of reverter. See, e.g., First Universalist Society of North Adams v. Boland, 155 Mass. 171, 29 N.E. 524 (1892). By contrast, in the conveyance, "A to B on the express condition that no house over two stories be erected on the parcel, and in that event to C," C's interest will be stricken, and B's interest will be characterized as a fee simple absolute with no future interest implied in A or her successors. See, e.g., Brattle Square Church v. Grant, 69 Mass. (3 Gray) 142 (1855). Why should B have a fee simple determinable under the first conveyance and a fee simple absolute under the second? The technical reason given is that in the first conveyance the determining event is part of the fee and remains with it when the executory interest is stricken, while in the second conveyance the condition subsequent is part of the executory interest, rather than the preceding fee, with the result that, when the executory interest falls, the condition falls with it. Does the distinction make any sense? Does it give proper effect to the general principle that, apart from the Rule's effect on proscribed interests, the grantor's intent is to be honored?

4. *". . . if there is any possibility . . . ".* If, at the time an interest is created, there is *any* possibility that the interest will vest outside the perpetuities period, the interest is void even though it probably would have vested or—viewed in retrospect—actually did vest within the period. Thus, if A devises Blackacre "to B for life, remainder to that son of B who first reaches the age of 30," and if at the time of the devise B has no son who has reached 30, the remainder is invalid—even though at B's death he has a son who is only one day short of his thirtieth birthday, even though the son will in all probability reach his thirtieth birthday, and even though, in retrospect, when the devise is first litigated, it is clear that the son had in fact reached thirty.

The Rule's rigorous insistence on considering even the most ludicrous possibilities in determining an interest's validity has been the object of widespread criticism and occasional reform. It has also produced some common law oddities—fertile octogenarians, unborn widows and slothful executors:

The Fertile Octogenarian. A devises Blackacre "to B [a widow, age 85, with three children] for life, then to B's children for their lives, remainder in fee to the children of B's children then living." The remainder to the grandchildren is invalid because the possibility exists that B will have yet another child—who, unborn at the time of A's death, when A's will first becomes effective, cannot be used as a measuring life—and the interest of this child's children could thus vest more than twenty-one years after the death of everyone alive at the time of A's death. See Jee v. Audley, 1 Cox Eq. Cases 324, 29 Eng.Rep. 1186 (Ch. 1787). Could the remainder be saved on the ground that, at the time of the devise, it was physically impossible for B to have any more children? On the ground that, recognizing this impossibility, *A* in using the phrase, "children of *B*," meant only *B*'s children then living? See In re Wright's Estate, 284 Pa. 334, 131 A. 188 (1925). How could *A* have redrafted his will to avoid this problem?

The Unborn Widow. *A* devises Blackacre "to *B* [a male, age sixty, with wife and children] for life, then to *B*'s widow for her life, remainder in fee to the children of *B* then living." The children's remainder is invalid because *B* might remarry and his new wife might not yet have been born at the time of *A*'s devise, thus disqualifying her as a life in being. The children's interest, since it is contingent on their surviving *B*'s widow, may thus vest outside the perpetuities period. How could *A* have redrafted his will to avoid this problem?

The Slothful Executor. *A* devises Blackacre "to *B* and her heirs on the admission of this will to probate." *B*'s executory interest is invalid because probate may still be incomplete after twenty-one years from the death of *A*, *B* and any other lives in being at the time of the devise, due to the executor's slowness. See Miller v. Weston, 67 Colo. 534, 189 P. 610 (1920). How could *A* have redrafted his will to avoid this problem?

5. "*. . . that the interest will vest . . .*". An interest can vest either in possession or in interest. An interest *vests in possession* when the person holding the interest first becomes entitled to possess the land. Thus, in the transfer, "*A* to *B* for life, remainder to *C* in fee," *B*'s interest became presently vested in possession at the moment of the conveyance; it is valid under the Rule since there is no possibility that it will first vest at some later point, outside the perpetuities period.

An interest *vests in interest* at the moment it is held by an ascertained person with no condition precedent to enjoyment of the interest. See pages 529 to 530 above. In the transfer, "*A* to *B* for life, remainder to *C* in fee," *C*'s interest became vested in interest at the moment of the transfer since there is doubt neither about the identity of the interest holder—*C*—nor about the fact that *C*'s interest will at some point vest in possession—since *B* will certainly die and her life estate end. *C*'s interest is thus valid under the Rule since there is no possibility that it will vest outside the perpetuities period. Similarly, in the devise from *A* "to *B* for life, then to *B*'s children for their lives, remainder to *C* in fee," *C*'s interest is valid even though it may not become possessory within the perpetuities period. (*B* may have a child subsequent to the devise with the result that *C* may not take possession for more than twenty-one years following some life in being at the time of the devise.) *C*'s interest is valid because it was vested in interest at the moment of the devise, and it was vested in interest because *C* was identified as the taker, and because it is certain that he or his estate will take the land at some future point—the death of all of *B*'s children.

When is an interest *not* presently vested in interest? In the transfer, "A to B for life, then to B's first-born child in fee," if B has no children at the time of the conveyance, the child's interest is not presently vested because the child is not ascertained at the moment of the transfer. The child's interest—a contingent remainder—is valid under the Rule, however, because there is no possibility that she will first become identified—and her interest first vest—outside the period of the Rule. Similarly, in the transfer, "A to B for life, remainder to the first child of B to complete nursing school," the child's interest is not presently vested because there is a condition precedent to her enjoying the interest. Because the condition precedent may first be met—and the presently unborn child's interest may first vest—outside the perpetuities period, the child's interest is invalid. Also, in the transfer, "A to B so long as the land is used for school purposes, then to C," C's executory interest is invalid because of the possibility that the condition precedent—use for other than school purposes—will occur too remotely.

6. *". . . more than 21 years after some life in being at the creation of the interest."* At common law, and sometimes by statute, the twenty-one year period is extended to include the period of gestation. Thus, in the transfer, "A to my brother B for life, remainder to such children of B as shall reach the age of twenty-one," the children's remainder would technically be invalid since B's wife might give birth to his child after his death, with the result that the child's interest would vest, if at all, more than twenty-one years after the end of all relevant lives in being. Since, however, periods of gestation are annexed to the rule's twenty-one year period, the gift over is valid.

Who can be counted as a life in being? Certainly anyone who is mentioned in the transfer will be included if he was alive at the time of the transfer. Lives will also be included if, though not mentioned, they are essential to the design of the transfer. Thus, in the devise from A, "to my grandchildren who shall reach the age of twenty-one," A's children can be counted as lives in being since, to have grandchildren, A must have children. Using A's children as measuring lives, the grandchildren's interest is valid, for A can have no more children after her death and all grandchildren must be born within the lives of these children.

In at least some jurisdictions, individuals whose lives operate as measuring lives need not be connected to the interests created. Thus, in a 1926 devise with a period of restriction defined as "the period ending at the expiration of 20 years from the day of the death of the last survivor of all the lineal descendants of Her Late Majesty Queen Victoria who shall be living at the time of my death," the lineal descendants—120 in all—were held to constitute valid measuring lives. In re Villar, Ch. 243 (1929).

7. Many states have partially blunted the rule's rigorous application through decision and statute. One technique is to construe ambiguous language to favor interests that comply with, rather than violate, the Rule. Even John Chipman Gray, the most ardent advocate of the Rule's remorseless application, allowed that, "When the expression which a testator uses is really ambiguous, and is fairly capable of two constructions, one of which would produce a legal result, and the other a result that would be bad for remoteness, it is a fair presumption that the testator meant to create a legal rather than an illegal interest." J. Gray, The Rule Against Perpetuities, § 633 (3rd ed. 1915).

The doctrines of *cy pres* and equitable reformation or approximation offer a somewhat more dramatic technique, reforming otherwise invalid interests so that they comply with the Rule. For example, in Berry v. Union National Bank, 262 S.E.2d 766 (1980), the West Virginia Supreme Court recognized that a private educational trust created by testatrix to last for twenty-five years after her death, with the principal to then go to certain named beneficiaries, clearly violated the Rule. Nonetheless, the court validated the future interest by adopting a doctrine of "equitable modification" to reduce the twenty-five year period to twenty-one years. The court imposed strict limits on the doctrine, requiring that four conditions be met before an instrument will be modified: "(1) the testator's intent is expressed in the instrument or can readily be determined by a court; (2) the testator's general intent does not violate the rule against perpetuities; (3) the testator's particular intent, which does violate the rule, is not a critical aspect of the testamentary scheme; and (4) the proposed modification will effectuate the testator's general intent, will avoid the consequences of intestacy, and will conform to the policy considerations underlying the rule." 262 S.E.2d at 771.

By far the most dramatic inroad on the Rule is the "wait-and-see approach," adopted in a handful of states and by the American Law Institute in Restatement of the Law Second, Property 2d (Donative Transfers) § 1.4 (1983). "Wait-and-see" validates interests that, *in fact*, vest within the perpetuities period even though, at the time of their creation, some possibility existed that they would vest too remotely. Thus, in the conveyance, "*A* to *B* so long as the land is used for school purposes, then to *C*," *C*'s executory interest is void under a strict application of the Rule. "Wait-and-see" would defer the determination of validity for twenty-one years after the death of all lives in being at the creation of the interest and if, within that period, the land ceased to be used for school purposes, *C*'s interest would be validated because it actually vested within the perpetuities period.

What are the disadvantages of an approach like "wait-and-see" that defers the determination of an interest's validity until well after its creation? Is *cy pres* preferable? See generally, Waggoner, Perpetuity Reform, 81 Mich.L.Rev. 1718 (1983).

8. Could the court in Pace v. Culpepper have construed the option as personal to the option holders, thus validating their interest on the theory that, as lives in being at the creation of the interest, they could not possibly have exercised the right outside the perpetuities period? Would an absolute, rather than a preemptive, option in *Culpepper* have been valid on the theory that it vested at the moment of its creation?

Should a lessee's option to purchase the leased premises be treated differently from other options? According to Professor Leach:

> In England it was held that an option to purchase by a lessee stood on the same footing as an option to purchase in gross: it was void if it could be exercised beyond the period of perpetuities. Thus an option to purchase at any time during a lease for 30 years failed. It was not observed that the situation was the exact opposite of that which exists where there is an option in gross. The improvement of the land is stimulated, not retarded, by the existence of an option in the lessee. If the lessee has an option to purchase he can safely improve; for, by the exercise of the option, he can preserve to himself the benefit of the improvement. If he has no option he cannot economically make an improvement which will still have a substantial value at the termination of the lease. Thus, a rule which invalidates options in lessees for the full term of their leases defeats the policy favoring free alienation and full use of property which the Rule against Perpetuities was designed to further. Several American jurisdictions have recognized this fact and have held valid such options; but the English cases still have some following in the United States.

Leach, Perpetuities in a Nutshell, 51 Harv.L.Rev. 638, 661 (1938).

Options are not the only trap that the Rule lays for the unwary business lawyer. Is a building lease, whose ten-year term is to commence "upon the completion of said building," valid under the Rule? The California Supreme Court has ruled that it is. Wong v. Di Grazia, 60 Cal.2d 525, 35 Cal.Rptr. 241, 386 P.2d 817 (1963). Recognizing that the Rule's literal application might invalidate the lease because of the possibility that it would first vest in possession outside the perpetuities period, the court ruled that the "nature of the circumstances of the transaction shows that the contemplated building was to be completed within a reasonable time and that such reasonable time was less than twenty-one years. Hence the interest would either vest or fail within the statutory period." 60 Cal.2d at 528, 35 Cal.Rptr. at 243, 386 P.2d at 819. Could the lease have been validated on the ground that, although not vested in possession, it had vested in interest at the moment of its execution? See Isen v. Giant Food, Inc., 295 F.2d 136 (D.C.Cir. 1961).

9. The Rule Against Perpetuities was first formulated in the Duke of Norfolk's Case, 3 Ch.Cas. 1, 22 Eng.Rep. 931 (1682). It has long been thought that the Rule originated as a weapon against re-

straints on alienation, designed to enable the late seventeenth-century's emerging mercantile class to trade freely in real property as well as goods. In fact, the Rule's origins, purposes and effects were quite different. According to Professor George Haskins, seventeenth-century England was dominated not by the emerging merchant class, but rather by "a landed class generally hostile to mercantile or capitalist ideas." This class viewed the Rule as a vehicle for enhancing rather than reducing their ability to tie up land ownership over time through carefully drawn conveyances. Haskins, Extending the Grasp of the Dead Hand: Reflections on the Origins of the Rule Against Perpetuities, 126 U.Pa.L.Rev. 19, 22 (1977).

10. To what extent does the Rule Against Perpetuities promote productive land use today? Professor Leach has observed, "practically anything a testator is likely to want can be done within the limits of the Rule Against Perpetuities. Wills fail because of inept work of lawyers, not because of excessive demands of testators." Leach, Perpetuities in a Nutshell, 51 Harv.L.Rev. 638, 669 (1938). If this is correct, is it appropriate for the Rule to serve only as a trap for the unwary or for those without the resources, or the wit, to hire experienced counsel?

To the extent that the Rule has substantive effect, does it in fact meet its avowed objective of promoting the free marketability of land? The future interests affected by the Rule will almost always be held beneficially under a trust in which the trustee has the full legal title in fee with the power to sell the property or put it to other productive use. Indeed, under modern doctrine, the trustee has not only the power, but also the duty, to manage the trust assets productively. Since the trustee enjoys the full power of transfer, and since unidentified or contingent future interest holders do not have to join to convey good title, what role, if any, does the Rule play today in advancing marketability?

2. RULE AGAINST RESTRAINTS ON ALIENATION

HANKINS v. MATHEWS

Supreme Court of Tennessee, 1968.
221 Tenn. 190, 425 S.W.2d 608.

BURNETT, Chief Justice.

The parties will hereinafter be referred to as they appeared in the trial court; that is, James A. Hankins, et al., complainants, and Virgil Mathews, et al., defendants.

We are asked on this appeal to ascertain the legal consequences of certain provisions contained in the will of one A. A. Hankins. Mr.

Hankins died testate on January 31, 1952, leaving a will, the pertinent provisions of which read as follows:

> "Second. In the event my wife, Sarah Elizabeth should survive me I give, devise and bequeath to her all of my personal property of every nature, description and wherever located and all of my real estate, particularly such real estate as is described in said deeds recorded in Deed Book 528, Page 275 and Deed Book 236, Page 339 and Deed Book 273, Page 440 to have and to hold during her natural life and at her death to go to the persons hereinafter described: . . .
>
> "Fourth. I give and bequeath to my nephew, Jim Grubb, at the death of my wife, Sarah Elizabeth Hankins all of my personal property that the said Elizabeth Hankins has not used during her life 'if she survives me' of every nature, description and wherever located. I further give and bequeath to my nephew the following real estate: One tract of land containing twenty five (25) acres more or less described in certain deed of P. H. Stanford and wife, Sally Stanford being deed dated March 18, 1914, recorded in Deed Book 273, Page 440 and a certain tract of land containing thirty acres more or less described in a certain deed dated June 17, 1914 from D. M. Roberts and wife, Mary S. Roberts, recorded in Deed Book 236, Page 339. The said Jim Grubb is to keep this property in his possession ten years before he is able to sell, mortgage or in any other manner incumber and dispose of the same, and if he should attempt to do so, then in this event the said tracts of land shall revert to the heirs at law of A. A. Hankins."

It appears from the record that the 25 acre tract of land mentioned above was acquired by the said A. A. Hankins and wife, Sarah Elizabeth Hankins, between the period of January 1, 1914, and April 16, 1919, which is commonly called the "hiatus" period, and was therefore owned by them as tenants in common. The other real estate with which we are concerned was owned outright by Mr. A. A. Hankins.

The will of the said Sarah Elizabeth Hankins with reference to her property, including her interest as tenant in common in the aforementioned 25 acre tract, provided as follows:

> "After the payment of my just debts, if any, and funeral expenses I will, devise and bequeath all of my property of every kind and character wherever found to JAMES A. GRUBB."

After the death of Sarah Elizabeth Hankins, and within the ten year period thereafter, Jim Grubb executed certain deeds and leases in which he transferred the property in question to the defendants.

The complainants then filed their original bill in the Chancery Court of Knox County, alleging that they are the sole heirs of A. A. Hankins and that by virtue of the attempted transfers from Jim Grubb to the defendants, the property, in accordance with the will of

A. A. Hankins, had reverted to them. The complainants prayed that they be declared to be the lawful owners in fee simple of the entire thirty acre tract and of a one-half undivided interest in the twenty-five acre tract; that the twenty-five acre tract either be partitioned or sold and the proceeds divided accordingly; that they be awarded certain rents and profits; that all the deeds to the defendants be declared void and removed as a cloud from the complainants' title and that the defendants be perpetually enjoined from setting up any claims with respect to the property.

The defendants demurred to the original bill on the ground that the restrictions placed by the testator on Jim Grubb's right to sell or otherwise encumber this real estate were "absolutely void as an illegal and unlawful attempt to restrain the alienation of said property."

The Chancellor overruled the demurrer and granted the defendants a discretionary appeal to this Court. Accordingly the only assignment of error before this Court is that the Chancellor erred in so doing.

The defendants insist that the testator, having given Jim Grubb a fee simple absolute estate in the property in one portion of his will, cannot subsequently divest said Grubb of important incidents of ownership such as the right to sell, mortgage or otherwise encumber the property. It is argued that these rights are inherent in a fee simple absolute estate in property and an attempt to take them away, even for a limited period, is an attempt to create an estate not recognized by the law.

The complainants insist, however, that the testator was only placing a reasonable restriction on the right of alienation, and that such reasonable restraints are in full accordance with the established law in this State.

After a thorough consideration of the problem we find ourselves inclined to agree with the propositions put forth by the defendants.

In Phillips' Pritchard Law of Wills, Vol. 1, § 161, the following statement is found:

> "The power of alienation is necessarily incident to every estate in fee, and a condition in a devise of lands in fee simple altogether preventing alienation, is repugnant to the estate and void. No one can create what is in the intendment of the law an estate in fee simple and at the same time deprive the owner of those rights and privileges which the law annexes to it. Hence, a condition in a devise in fee that the devisee shall make oath that he will not dispose of the estate during his life, is void. So is a condition that land devised to several shall not be divided until the death of certain persons . . . .. So are restrictions against sale until one of several devisees shall be twenty-five years old, . . ."

A leading annotation on the problem at hand uses the following language in relating the general rule:

"The doctrine of most jurisdictions, as shown by the numerous cases hereinafter cited, is that where land is granted or devised in fee, a provision of any sort that the taker shall not alienate, or shall not have power to alienate, is void, whether amounting to a mere naked prohibition or direction, or expressed or construed to be a condition, or conjoined with a limitation over in the event of alienation or attempt to alienate.

"It will not do for the grantor to create the highest estate known to the law and then, in the same instrument, say to his grantee that he does not possess the right of disposition." Annot. Restraint on Alienation—Validity, 42 A.L.R.2d 1243, 1265.

It is further stated in the above discussion that the reasoning usually assigned for the expressed rule is that the restraint is repugnant to the fee, and is void even though it is meant to last for a period of years.

It should be emphasized before proceeding further that we are herein dealing with a total restriction upon the right of alienation, even though such restriction is only to last for ten years. We are not confronted with a situation similar to that presented in the case of Overton v. Lea, 108 Tenn. 505, 68 S.W. 250 (1902). In that case it was provided in the testator's will that property left to the beneficiary was never to come into the possession of the testator's sister or the sister's husband or anyone bearing the name of Kelly. The Supreme Court allowed the provision to stand on the ground that it was not inconsistent with the reasonable enjoyment of the fee. It was emphasized that the result would have been different had the restriction been a total one.

The generally accepted rule of law is well stated in a leading work on the subject of real property:

"The fact that a restriction upon the right to alienate a vested estate in fee simple is to endure for a limited time only does not, by the weight of authority, render the restriction valid. But there are dicta and occasional decisions to the effect that a condition or limitation, looking to the divesting of the estate upon the making of a conveyance within a period named is valid, and in one state, Kentucky, the validity of a restriction for a 'reasonable time' is fully recognized." Tiffany on Real Property, 3rd Ed., Vol. 5, § 1346.

The complainants strongly insist that even though it be the minority rule, Tennessee law is that a grantor or testator may impose reasonable restraints for a period of years where the fee is conveyed or devised. In support of this proposition the case of Fowlkes v. Wagoner (Tenn.Ch.App.), 46 S.W. 586 (1898) is cited. In that case the testator gave land to a nephew and then said: "I further direct that he shall not sell or dispose of said land until after he arrives at the age of twenty-five years. . . ." The nephew, Fowlkes, attempted to convey before he reached the age of twenty-five. A bill was filed by the heirs at law of the testator to recover the land on the theory that it accrued to them upon violation of the clause restraining a sale by their father.

The court went into a detailed discussion of the common law and cited several authorities to the effect that conditions which prohibit the alienation to anyone are repugnant to the estate granted and are void. (The court was referring to a situation where the basic estate created was a fee simple absolute.) Thereafter, the court went into a detailed discussion of the difference between an estate upon a condition subsequent and a conditional limitation. Some statements were made to the effect that since there was no limitation over nor possibility of reverter provided for in the testator's will, that neither of the estates discussed was created and that therefore the restricting clause was only an attempt to control the use of the land and was void.

It is the opinion of this Court, as it has been the opinion of most leading writers on the subject of real property, that the dictum found in the case of Fowlkes v. Wagoner, supra, does not stand for the proposition advanced by the complainants. In the case of Keeling v. Keeling, 185 Tenn. 134, 203 S.W.2d 601 (1947), Mr. Justice Gailor stated:

> "We can find no exception to the rule that conditions subsequent preventing alienation of an estate in fee, even for a limited time, are universally held void as inconsistent with the incidents and nature of the estate devised and contrary to public policy."

Cited as authority for this statement is the case of Fowlkes v. Wagoner. There was discussion in that case about absolute restraints being reasonable in some cases. However, even a casual reading of the opinion reveals that the court was referring to conditions which were attached to equitable estates not greater than life estates. That is not the problem with which we are dealing in the case at bar.

In Andrews v. Hall, 156 Neb. 817, 58 N.W.2d 201 (1953), the Supreme Court of Nebraska discusses estates subject to conditions in language which we consider adequate. It is there stated:

> "We do not say that a testator may not create a vested fee simple estate subject to a condition subsequent, or a determinable or defeasible fee. What we do say is that a restriction against alienation of a vested fee simple estate is not any one of these, nor, since it is void, can it be used as the sole basis for the creation of any of these estates."

In our research we have found that the courts of practically all jurisdictions are in accord with the opinions expressed herein.

For the reasons discussed herein, we hold that the demurrer should be sustained and the case dismissed.

ALSUP v. MONTOYA

Supreme Court of Tennessee, 1972.
488 S.W.2d 725.

ERBY L. JENKINS, Special Justice.

This is an action brought by devisees under the will of W. C. Alsup to have certain lands devised under the will sold and the proceeds reinvested for the benefit of the life tenants and contingent remaindermen.

W. C. Alsup died, and his will was probated, in 1920. By that will he devised to each of his three daughters, for and during their lives, a farm of approximately two hundred acres. The will further provided that:

> "These tracts of land I devise to my daughters for and during the periods of their natural lives, and after their deaths, they are to go to their children, or the heirs of any child who may then be dead, the heirs of any child who may then be dead to represent its parent and take his or her share of said land. If either of my daughters should die leaving no children and no issue of their bodies, then the tract of land herein devised to her will go to her sisters, or the heirs of any sister who may then be dead, said heirs to represent said sister and take her share of said lands.
>
> "The land herein devised to my daughters shall not be sold or alienated *during their lives* and no court shall sell the same for reinvestment or alter the situation of said land as it exists today, it being my purpose that it shall not be sold in any way whatever." (Emphasis ours.)

The complainants in this case are the three daughters of W. C. Alsup. Also joined as complainants are the two adult children of one daughter, Mrs. Martha Virginia Alsup Ritland. The other two daughters, Susan Rebecca Alsup and Miriam Katherine Alsup, now sixty-two and fifty-seven years old respectively, are unmarried and have no issue. Joined as defendants are the minor children of Mrs. Ritland's daughters. The defendants are sued individually and as representatives of the class of possible remaindermen under the will.

The theory of the original complaint is that "due to material change in conditions, the restraint upon alienation . . . should be abrogated and set aside" under the inherent powers vested in a court of equity. By an amended complaint it is also contended that the restraint upon alienation was void ab initio.

The case was tried in the Chancery Court upon stipulations of fact. As fairly summarized in the complainants' brief, the stipulations show that since 1924 the entire family has lived in California.

The family did not inherit the testator's agricultural love. The land has been rented out or share-cropped for more than fifty years. For a long time a benevolent Federal Government had it in the "Soil Bank," allowing it to lie fallow, paying yearly "rent" thereon, a questionable practice not only for the economy of the country but also the morale of the people. The buildings are antiquated and would require extensive repair, and some of the fences are in need of rebuilding. Some of the land has been heavily cropped over the years and has deteriorated in fertility and productivity. The farms are located in a strictly agricultural section of the county and would sell, even in their present condition, for an amount considerably in excess of $100,000.00. The income to the life tenants is considerably less than a reasonable return based on the present market value of the land.

Upon hearing of the cause the Chancellor found there had been a material change in conditions which could not have been foreseen by Mr. Alsup at the time the will was executed; that due to this material change it was in the best interest of all the parties, especially the ultimate remaindermen, that the land be sold for reinvestment, and that, accordingly, this restraint on alienation was no longer valid. From the Chancellor's decree ordering a sale of the land the defendants bring this appeal.

The defendants, by their guardian ad litem, make essentially three contentions on appeal. First, that the restraint on alienation is valid; second, that the Chancery Court had no power to remove the restraint because of a change in conditions, or because it might be in the best interests of the life tenants or remaindermen; and, third, that there was in any event no evidence or stipulation of fact that the removal of the restraint on alienation would be in the best interest of the contingent remaindermen.

The defendants rely principally upon the case of Keeling v. Keeling, 185 Tenn. 134, 203 S.W.2d 601 (1947), for the proposition that the restraint upon alienation is valid. In that case the testatrix had devised a "little house" to her nephew and his children, providing further that the nephew was not to sell it, and that if he should not use it as a home, it was to be "rented and kept up and he and his children to have the rents therefrom." The Court held that the nephew took a life estate, and his children took vested remainders subject to partial divestment by afterborn children. The life estate, however, was to be held by the nephew "for the *use and benefit of himself and his children.*" 185 Tenn. at 143, 203 S.W.2d at 605 (emphasis added). The Court held the restraint on alienation to be valid, saying:

> "We can find no exception to the rule that conditions subsequent preventing alienation of an estate in fee, even for a limited time, are universally held void as inconsistent with the incidents and nature of the estate devised and contrary to public policy." [citing authorities]

"But restrictions by conditions subsequent or conditional limitation, even if they be absolute restraints upon alienation, are generally held valid if annexed to *an equitable estate not greater than a life estate.*" 185 Tenn. at 139, 203 S.W.2d at 603 (emphasis added).

It is clear that the Court in Keeling v. Keeling was dealing with the validity of a restraint upon alienation annexed to an equitable estate. The nephew held a legal life estate in the property, of course, but he held it as trustee for himself and his children. This is a situation clearly different from a similar restraint upon the alienation of a purely legal estate. The restraint upon the power to alienate the trust estate, while valid, was nevertheless subject to the well-recognized power of a court of equity to order a sale when circumstances unforeseen by the testator render it likely that otherwise the primary purpose of the trust would be defeated.

While there is no case in Tennessee directly passing upon the validity of a restraint upon alienation annexed to a legal life estate, the law generally is clear that any restraint which undertakes to wholly remove the power of a life tenant to alienate his estate is absolutely void.

We can see no reason to depart from this nearly unanimous view of the law. A testator, or the settlor of a nontestamentary trust, if he so desires, may still through the medium of a trust restrict the power of his trustee to sell or otherwise alienate the property which he has devised or given. And, in such a case, the devise or gift is subject to the constant supervision of courts of equity, which are empowered, if conditions so warrant, to decree a sale of the property when necessary to effectuate the intention of the testator.

The overriding issue is, what did the creator of this estate wish? What were his desires when the will was made, and what would his desires be under the conditions as exist today?

Although we do not necessarily concur, it has been written that "The only authentic evidence . . . which we have of the survival of life after death is the ability of the judges to read the intention of the testator long after he has been buried," and it may come to pass that a group of ghosts of dissatisfied testators may wait on the other side of the River Styx or on the Golden Shore to "receive" this and other courts who have construed their wills; however, under the circumstances, we cannot permit the writing of a dead hand of over fifty years, from the silent tomb, to control the action of this Court in this case.

When this will was made, the testator had three daughters, and three farms. His paramount desire, no doubt, as is the desire of so many men of wealth, was to protect his loved ones insofar as he could do so. But in trying he went too far. He could not look into the future and envision the changed conditions of over half a century. He desired to protect his children from all who descend upon those who come into wealth. He had made his living by farming and he felt that they would live on these farms, raise their children who would also be farmers.

Let us for a moment, in our mind's eye, witness his reaction to this situation, if he could be "materialized and view the present situation on his return to earth."

First of all, he would no doubt be disappointed that they all had forsaken the land and moved to far-away California, a place he had heard of, but probably never seen. Then, as he rides over his once fertile acres and takes a look at his once proud farms in their run-down condition, he probably would want to remake his will, but he cannot do that now. He sees once lush producing acres now grown up and cropped up to death, stately beautiful houses and great barns, falling in decay and disrepair. If he were not a very devout man, we can imagine some of his torrid words and exclamations.

Then, too, it would be hard for him, a rugged individualist, to understand the philosophy of a paternalistic government that pays a farmer not to farm under the guise of a soil bank, the only bank he ever heard of being one where money is kept.

And we can imagine, after surveying all that had happened, the condition that the land and the buildings are in, he would say, "Judge, times have changed. Do the best you can under the changed circumstances. I tried and made a mistake." And then, taking a last look around, he would mount his horse, and ride into the sunset and the great beyond, a land to where we are all hastening and where he has spent over half of a century, and as he rides off, we can hear him say, "I am better here."

We, therefore, hold the restraint upon alienation in his case to be invalid.

Although such a holding makes it unnecessary to discuss the other assignments of error made by the defendants, it cannot fully dispose of the case. The restraint being void, the life tenants are, of course, free to sell their estates. But the complainants have sought by this suit the sale of the entire fee, and not the sale of the life interests only.

Our law is clear, however, that a chancery court has wide discretion and the inherent power to order a sale for reinvestment, such as is being sought here, provided that the sale is manifestly advantageous to the interests of all the parties.

Although the chancellor's decree below was concerned with the avoidance of the restraint upon alienation, it was based on his finding that a sale of the property was "to the manifest interest of the parties and especially to the manifest interest of the ultimate remaindermen . . . ." This finding is in our opinion fully supported by the stipulated facts which were summarized above.

We, therefore, find that the decree for sale and reinvestment was proper, and the case must be in all respects affirmed.

DYER, C.J., and CHATTIN and McCANLESS, JJ., concur.

NOTES

1. The validity of restraints on the sale or other transfer of real property is traditionally measured in terms of three factors: the scope of the restraint, the method by which the restraint is enforced, and the nature of the interest restrained.

Scope of the Restraint. The restraint may be *total* or *partial*. While a total restraint prohibits all transfers, a partial restraint limits transfers with respect to time ("*A* conveys Blackacre to *B*, but *B* shall not transfer Blackacre until she reaches the age of 21"); with respect to manner ("*A* to *B*, but *B* may not transfer other than by warranty deed"); or with respect to transferees ("*A* to *B*, but *B* may not convey Blackacre to any member of the Grubb family"). Other things being equal, courts are more likely to uphold partial restraints than total restraints.

Was *Hankins* correct to characterize the restraint there as total? What reasons are there for treating total and partial restraints differently? For distinguishing among different forms of partial restraints? What result would the court have reached if A. A. Hankins had devised the land to Jim Grubb under a lease for ten years, with the fee to vest in Grubb if he remained in possession throughout the ten years?

Method of the Restraint. *Disabling* restraints withhold the power of alienation ("*A* to *B*, and any attempted transfer by *B* shall be void and of no effect"). *Forfeiture* restraints provide that the grantee will lose her interest on an attempted transfer ("*A* to *B* so long as *B* does not convey"). *Promissory* restraints expose the grantee to contract remedies in the event of an attempted transfer ("*A* to *B*, and *B* promises never to convey the lands").

In cases of ambiguity, courts prefer forfeiture restraints to disabling restraints, and promissory restraints to forfeiture restraints. Why?

Nature of the Interest Restrained. Restraints on the alienation of fee interests are generally invalid. However, the restraint has some chance of being upheld if it is only partial and promissory. Restraints on life estates will generally be upheld if they are promissory or forfeiture restraints, but not if they are disabling restraints. And, all forms of restraint are generally allowed in leases; the constructional preference, though, is for alienability.

2. What was the nature of the interest restrained in Alsup v. Montoya? What was the scope of the restraint? The method of the restraint? Reasoning backwards from the result in the case, it would appear that the court viewed the restriction as a disabling restraint

since forfeiture and promissory restraints on life estates are generally permitted. Would the court have better effectuated the testator's intent if it had applied the rule against restraints on alienation as a rule of construction, rather than as a rule of law, and had interpreted the language in W.C. Alsup's will as suggestive rather than mandatory? As a matter of policy, is it preferable to use the rule against restraints on alienation to invalidate conveyances or to construe them? What effect does the choice have on the marketability of title to land?

Should the court in *Montoya* have disposed of the case on a threshold, procedural ground? When a disabling, rather than a forfeiture or promissory restraint is created, who has standing to enforce the restraint? Should these parties have been represented in the proceeding? Were they? Who were the likely successors, if any, to W.C. Alsup's interest in enforcing the restriction? Was there any reason for the action on the restraint to have been brought or decided at all?

3. *Indirect Restraints.* Courts sometimes invalidate arrangements that, though not expressly restraining alienation, are perceived to do so indirectly. For example, some courts have voided mortgage clauses that require the landowner to pay off the note secured by the mortgage when he sells the land. Although these "due on sale" clauses do not expressly prohibit alienation, they may inhibit it if the sale produces insufficient cash for the landowner to pay off the note. See, for example, Wellenkamp v. Bank of America, 21 Cal.3d 943, 148 Cal.Rptr. 379, 582 P.2d 970 (1978). The problem, of course, is that *all* divisions of title to land necessarily restrain alienability to some degree because they multiply the number of interest holders with whom a buyer must deal. The difficulty of distinguishing unlawful indirect restraints from lawful estates transactions doubtless explains why the decisions in the area are so scattered, contradictory and confused.

The common thread that links the decisions is that courts appear to be using the rule against indirect restraints as a basis for voiding restrictions that, apart from their incidental effect on alienability, offend some independent notion of desirable public policy. The invalidation of due-on-sale clauses, for example, reflects the belief that lenders rather than borrowers should bear the risk of rising interest rates. Similarly, a requirement that the grantee occupy the land conveyed for a specified period and add the grantor's surname to his own legal name, has been invalidated on the ground that "a condition attached to a fee simple title which has for its purpose the satisfaction of a whimsical obsession or an expression of testator's vanity ought not be permitted as a fettering of a fee simple title." Cast v. National Bank of Commerce, Trust & Savings Association of Lincoln, 186 Neb. 385, 390, 183 N.W.2d 485, 489 (1971).

Do rules such as these, which inevitably turn on changing social values, in fact hinder rather than enhance marketability? If you were today reviewing a chain of title that contained a 1940 conveyance, "A to B in fee, so long as the owner of this parcel does not marry someone of another race or religion, or cohabit with an unrelated person of the same sex," how would you advise your client on the validity of the restriction and on the need to obtain a quitclaim from the owner of the possibility of reverter?

4. Why should restraints on alienation be invalidated at all? In a system that purports to honor private arrangements respecting land use, what good reason is there to invalidate these arrangements? Although, nominally, these restraints might appear to curtail marketability, is it clear that they do, in fact, have this effect? Under the traditional approach, the restraints that are most susceptible to invalidation are those that encumber fee and other vested interests. Is it any more difficult for prospective buyers to acquire the outstanding rights respecting these interests than it is for them to acquire the outstanding rights respecting other interests?

5. *Restraints on Marriage.* As a general rule at common law, provisions in deeds or wills restraining the grantee from marrying were void as against public policy. The general rule has since been eroded by several exceptions. Restraints on remarriage, which typically appear in the devise by one spouse to her survivor, are today upheld on the theory that, upon remarriage, the surviving spouse will no longer need the economic support provided by the land devised; at that point, if the testator so provided, the land will better go to others, typically the couple's children. A conveyance from parent to child until the child marries will often be upheld on the ground that, although the restriction may deter the child from marrying, it represents a reasonable effort to provide support until the child acquires a helpmate. Courts today also uphold marriage restraints that are limited in time, such as the restraint that the grantee not marry until he reaches a stated age, typically his majority.

Restatement of the Law Second, Property 2d (Donative Transfers) Parts II and III (1983), cover not only provisions restraining alienation or marriage, but also provisions encouraging separation or divorce and provisions concerning religion, personal habits, education and occupation.

3. STATUTORY LIMITATIONS

TRUSTEES OF SCHOOLS OF TOWNSHIP NO. 1 v. BATDORF

Supreme Court of Illinois, 1955.
6 Ill.2d 486, 130 N.E.2d 111.

SCHAEFER, Justice.

These two cases have been consolidated for opinion because they involve common questions of law and similar questions of fact. Both are actions to quiet title to certain school lands, and both are here upon direct appeal from decrees of the circuit court of St. Clair County which held unconstitutional the Reverter Act of 1947. Ill.Rev.Stat. 1953, chapter 30, pars. 37b to 37h.

One case involves the Batdorf school site, located on a one-half acre tract conveyed by warranty deed dated July 1, 1895, from John and Anna E. Batdorf to the Board of School Trustees and their successors for the purpose of "maintaining thereon a nonsectarian Free school according to the school laws of the State of Illinois, ... Provided however that in case the Directors of said District No. Six fail to maintain a school, or said school shall be discontinued or removed then the above half acre to revert to the tract from which it was taken."

The other case involves the one-acre Hertel school site, which was conveyed to the school trustees by a warranty deed, dated June 26, 1893, from Frederick and Dorothea Helms "to be used for a publick school building site, providing the same shall not be used for dwelling purposes, and further provided, that when the premises cease to be used as a publick school site, the land hereby conveyed shall revert back to the tract from which it is now taken. All property belonging to the School District may be removed within one year from the time the premises have ceased to be used as above specified."

On March 12, 1949, the school districts which had operated the Batdorf school and the Hertel school were taken over by the newly organized Community Consolidated School District No. 70 of St. Clair County, Illinois. Classes were held in the Batdorf school continuously from 1895 until sometime in October, 1946. Since then the building has been rented intermittently as a residence by District No. 70. The Hertel school operated continuously from 1893 until May 2, 1947. Since then the building has been vacant. No formal action has been taken at any time by District No. 70, or its predecessors, declaring either school site unsuitable, unnecessary, or inconvenient for a school. In 1951, however, the trustees of schools of the township anticipated the possibility of sale of the two sites, and brought these actions to have declared invalid, under the Reverter Act, any possibilities of reverter that might exist by reason of the deeds under which the school sites had originally been acquired.

The complaint in each case alleged that the plaintiff trustees held legal title to the school sites and the buildings thereon for the use and benefit of the plaintiff school districts; that the defendants claimed some interest because of the reversionary provision in each deed; that the defendants' claim was invalid by reason of the Reverter Act, and prayed that title be quieted in the plaintiffs.

The heirs of the respective grantors were made parties defendant in each of the cases. In the Batdorf case C. Don Donley and Jessie Donley filed a bill of interpleader which alleged that they were owners of the property by mesne conveyances from the original grantor; that school was no longer conducted in the building; that it was being rented for residential purposes, and prayed that they be decreed the owners. In the Hertel case Russell Classen and Alice Classen filed a joint answer and counterclaim which alleged that they were owners of 160 acres which included the one-acre school tract, by virtue of an award to them in kind in a partition suit; that they had been seized of an undivided one-tenth interest as heirs of the original grantor; that the tract had been abandoned for school purposes, and that as a consequence they were now its owners by way of reverter.

Each case was referred to a master, who recommended quieting title in the plaintiffs. In the Batdorf case the master held that the possibility of reverter was inalienable, that the evidence of abandonment of the site for school uses was insufficient, and that the possibility of reverter had been destroyed by the Reverter Act, regardless of whether there had been an abandonment or of whether such abandonment had occurred before or after July 21, 1947, the effective date of the act. In the Hertel case the master held the possibility of reverter invalid under the act without reaching the question of abandonment. The circuit court declined to follow the recommendations of the master and entered a decree in each case holding that the possibility of reverter was alienable, and that the Reverter Act was unconstitutional as being an *ex post facto* law and in violation of the due process clauses of the State and Federal constitutions. The decree in the Batdorf case found that C. Don Donley and Jessie Donley, his wife, as joint tenants, were the owners of the property, and in the Hertel case that Russell Classen and Alice Classen were the owners.

Before we reach the principal issues, two preliminary matters should be mentioned. The first relates to the language of the original conveyances. Each deed provided that in the event the premises therein described ceased to be used as a school, the land should "revert to the tract from which it was taken." This language is anomalous, but the parties have construed the instruments as effective to create valid possibilities of reverter in the grantors, and we accept their construction. The second concerns the right of the Donleys and the Classens, appellees here, to claim an interest by way of reverter. In each case the plaintiffs have challenged that right. Since the attempts to alienate did not destroy the possibilities of reverter, and since in each case the heirs of the original grantors were parties defendant, it is unnecessary to analyze the circumstances under which the claims of the appellees arose. The possibilities of reverter survived the attempts to alienate in any event, and under our conclusion upon the primary issues in the case it makes no difference whether that interest was in the heirs of the grantors or in the appellees.

Sections 4 and 5 of the Reverter Act, if valid, control the decision of this case. They are:

"§ 4. Neither possibilities of reverter nor rights of entry or re-entry for breach of condition subsequent, whether heretofore or hereafter created, where the condition has not been broken, shall be valid for a longer period than fifty years from the date of the creation of the condition or possibility of reverter. If such a possibility of reverter or right of entry or re-entry is created to endure for a longer period than fifty years, it shall be valid for fifty years.

"§ 5. If by reason of a possibility of reverter created more than fifty years prior to the effective date of this Act, a reverter has come into existence prior to the time of the effective date of this Act, no person shall commence an action for the recovery of the land or any part thereof based upon such possibility of reverter, after one year from the effective date of this Act. . . ." Ill.Rev.Stat.1953, chapter 30, pars. 37e and 37f.

Each of the deeds in these cases was executed more than fifty years before the effective date of the act, July 21, 1947. The trial court found that the two sites had been abandoned for school purposes, but made no finding as to when the abandonments occurred. Under the Reverter Act such a finding is not essential in this case. If the abandonment took place after July 21, 1947, the possibilities of reverter are invalid under section 4. If the abandonment took place before July 21, 1947, section 5 bars defendants from asserting any claim based on these possibilities of reverter in this suit which was filed nearly three years after the effective date of the act.

Defendants challenge the constitutionality of the statute on the ground that it impairs the obligation of contracts, is an *ex post facto* law, and deprives persons of their property without due process of law, in violation of both the Illinois and the United States constitutions.

Section 4 limits the duration of a possibility of reverter where the condition had not been broken prior to the adoption of the act to a period of fifty years from the date of its creation. Although a possibility of reverter can pass by descent, it is incapable of alienation, devise or partition. Until the limiting contingency occurs it is, as its name indicates, no more than an expectation,—a possibility that an interest in property may accrue in the future. Under the decisions of this court in Prall v. Burckhartt, 299 Ill. 19, 132 N.E. 280, 18 A.L.R. 992, and People ex rel. Franchere v. City of Chicago, 321 Ill. 466, 152 N.E. 141, 144, it is subject to change, modification or abolition by legislative action. These decisions involved statutes enacted to cut off litigation of the title to vacated streets by the scattered heirs of deceased dedicators. They provided that upon vacation title should go to the abutting owners, and their validity was sustained. The court stated in the City of Chicago case: "Prior to the act in question, after the executing and recording of a statutory plat and its acceptance by the municipality, nothing remained in the dedicator but a mere possibility of reverter. . . . This possibility, not being an estate, was not protected by any constitutional limitation, and it was competent for the Legislature to abolish this possibility of reverter or to change the devolution of the title upon the happening of the future contingency in any way it saw fit, and . . . any legislative enactment to that end is not unconstitutional."

The legislature has modified or abrogated property rights less remotely expectant than these possibilities of reverter, and its action has been sustained. So legislation was upheld which retroactively affected inchoate rights of dower and curtesy. Similarly the Contingent Remainder Act (Ill.Rev.Stat.1953, chapter 30, par. 40), which terminated the right of the life tenant and the remainderman to destroy contingent remainders, has been applied to deeds and wills effective prior to adoption of the act. In Butterfield v. Sawyer, 187 Ill. 598, 58 N.E. 602, 52 L.R.A. 75, a deed provided for a contingent remainder to the "heirs generally" of the life tenant, if she should die without issue. After the execution of the deed, the Adoption Act was amended to make an adopted child an heir. It was held that the interest of the heirs was contingent until the death of the life tenant, and that until that time the class could be enlarged by statute.

It has been said that the Reverter Act was passed in recognition of the operation of possibilities of reverter as "clogs on title, withdrawing property thus encumbered from the commercial mortgage market long after the individual, social or economic reason for their creation had ceased, and at a time when the heirs from whom a release could be obtained would be so numerous as to be virtually impossible to locate." Comment, 43 Illinois Law Rev. 90. The statute reflects the General Assembly's appraisal of the actual economic significance of these interests, weighed against the inconvenience and expense caused by their continued existence for unlimited periods of time without regard to altered circumstances. As a result of that appraisal, their potential duration has been limited to fifty years. A more sensitive treatment of the problem, perhaps by way of conferring equitable jurisdiction to extinguish such interests when they have ceased to serve any useful purpose, might be thought preferable. Our problem, however, is not that of choosing between alternative methods of handling the problems created by these interests, but the reasonableness of the method chosen by the General Assembly. We are unable to say that that method offends the constitutional provisions relied upon.

Section 5 of the Reverter Act deals with possibilities of reverter which had fallen in prior to the effective date of the act. It allows the holder of such an interest one year from the effective date to bring his action for recovery of the land. This section does not abolish or change any established or vested right. Rather it modifies the procedure for enforcing the right, by shortening the period of time in which suit may be brought. "The legislature may prescribe a limitation for the bringing of suits where none previously existed, as well as shorten the time within which suits to enforce existing causes of action may be commenced, provided, in each case, a reasonable time, taking all the circumstances into consideration, be given by the new law for the commencement of suit before the bar takes effect." Wheeler v. Jackson, 137 U.S. 245, 255, 11 S.Ct. 76, 78, 34 L.Ed. 659. In McQueen v. Connor, 385 Ill. 455, 53 N.E.2d 435, a statute reduced the time for filing will contests from one year to nine months. This court upheld the application of the act to an existing cause of action, where it was shown that plaintiff had more than eight months after the adoption of the act to file his suit. We think that the time allowed under section 5 of the Reverter Act was reasonable and afforded adequate opportunity to enforce rights which had vested prior to its enactment.

The decree in each case is reversed and the cause remanded, with directions to enter a decree as prayed for in the complaint.

Reversed and remanded, with directions.

NOTES

1. After *Batdorf*, could the Illinois Legislature constitutionally terminate contingent remainders fifty years after their creation? Remainders vested subject to complete or partial defeasance? Indefeasibly vested remainders? Reversions? Under the court's reasoning, what constitutional barrier, if any, is there to obliterating present possessory estates?

Legislatures have enacted title-clearing mechanisms less aggressive than the one involved in *Batdorf* and encountered greater constitutional resistance from the courts. In Board of Education of Central School District No. 1 v. Miles, 15 N.Y.2d 364, 259 N.Y.S.2d 129, 207 N.E.2d 181 (1965), the Court of Appeals invalidated portions of N.Y.—McKinney's Real Prop.Law § 345 that made rights of entry and possibilities of reverter unenforceable unless a declaration of intention to preserve the future interest was recorded and renewed within prescribed periods after the condition or restriction was created. The court said that § 345 was unconstitutional as applied to defendants because their "reverter had not matured at the time when the statute prescribed that it became barred, nor could anyone have known prior to the cut-off date who would be parties in interest at the time when the reverter took effect." 15 N.Y.2d at 373, 259 N.Y.S.2d at 134, 207 N.E.2d at 186.

Consider the constitutionality of the even less intrusive approach taken by so-called "marketable title acts" which extinguish any claims that conflict with a record chain of title if the record chain of title has existed for a specified period (typically 30 or 40 years) and no one has filed a notice of the conflicting claim within that period. What of statutes that authorize courts to invalidate a condition that has become "merely nominal and of no actual or substantial benefit to the transferor or other person in whose favor it is to be performed"? Wis.Stat.Ann. 700.15 (1981).

2. Many future interests, particularly those following defeasible fees, will be terminated by operation of the applicable statutes of limitations, since, by the time the defeasing event occurs and the cause of action accrues, the future interest holders will be too distant in time and place to know that they have an action. Rights of entry, because they become possessory only if their holders take affirmative steps to reenter, are particularly susceptible to the equitable defenses of estoppel, waiver and laches. The interest holder may, for example, be equitably barred if he knowingly lets the breach of the condition continue for an unconscionably long time, to the occupant's economic prejudice.

What if the future interest holder's perceived inequitable conduct occurs *off* the premises? In Brown v. Wrightman, 5 Cal.App. 391, 90 P. 467 (1907), plaintiff, Brown, owner of a fifteen-acre parcel on which he resided, conveyed an adjacent 45-acre parcel to defendant's predecessors upon the "expressed condition subsequent" that, among other things, should any "bawdy house, house of illfame or house of prostitution" ever be conducted on the premises, "this grant to cease and be void." Although at the time the conveyance was made the entire area was free of prostitution, Brown later sold or leased portions of his fifteen-acre tract without restriction to individuals who, with Brown's acquiescence, ran "houses of prostitution." When the defendant rented two cottages on the 45-acre parcel for the same purpose, Brown brought an action to have the court declare a forfeiture of title to the 45-acre parcel. Agreeing with the trial court that, by his own conduct, Brown had waived his right and was estopped to claim a forfeiture, the appellate court specifically rejected Brown's argument that "his conduct with reference to other lands can have nothing to do with his right to the lands conveyed upon condition."

The court apparently thought that the original purpose behind the condition subsequent was to preserve the neighborhood for residential use. Is it likely that Brown had some other, quite different purpose in mind?

3. What interests would be served by the statutory simplification of the estates system itself? Professor Lawrence W. Waggoner has offered one reformulation of the estates system aimed at promoting simplicity over complexity and substance over form. Waggoner, Re-

formulating the Structure of Estates: A Proposal for Legislative Action, 85 Harv.L.Rev. 729 (1972).

Specifically, Waggoner's proposal "is based on the premise that the only appropriate distinctions are between certainty and uncertainty as to the termination of possessory interests and between certainty and uncertainty as to the ultimate possession of future interests. Possessory interests, by the terms of the particular transfer, either will not terminate (fee simple absolute), will terminate (life estate or term of years), or will possibly terminate (defeasible interest). Future interests either will become possessory (indefeasibly vested), will become possessory but with a now uncertain number of takers (vested subject to open), or will possibly become possessory (contingent)."

Waggoner's reconstructed system would look like this:

Possessory Interests	Future Interests
Fee Simple Absolute	None permissible
Defeasible Fee Simple	Contingent
Life Estate (may or may not be defeasible)	Contingent (not certain to become possessory); Alternative Contingent Future Interest
	Vested Subject to Open; Contingent (in unborn class members)
	Indefeasibly Vested
Term of Years	Same as with Life Estate

85 Harv.L.Rev. 755–56. Compare this system with the system that presently obtains, page 476 above. What are the comparative advantages of the proposed system? The disadvantages? How substantially would the trimmed-down version constrict the range of private choice available to grantors and grantees? How would the common law Rule Against Perpetuities apply to the proposed future interests? See 85 Harv.L.Rev. 757–765.

4. Reverter acts, marketable title acts, re-recording acts, statutes of limitations and doctrines of waiver, estoppel and changed conditions, as well as other legislative and judicial measures, reveal a jumble of techniques aimed at making land more marketable. One technique is to increase certainty with respect to the validity of interests, thus enabling title companies, title examiners and lawyers to render cleaner opinions on title, and enabling sellers, buyers and lenders to calculate their risks more precisely. A second approach is to resolve the possible worthlessness of future interests and the difficulty of identifying their holders by requiring these interest holders to come forward and identify themselves as a condition to preserving their interests. Another technique is to remove identification problems and risk entirely, not by clarifying the nature and ownership of the interest, but by retrospectively outlawing the interest altogether. Yet another approach would simply limit the kinds of future interests

that can be created prospectively—the ultimate logic of which might be to outlaw future interests entirely.

Forced to choose, which technique or combination of techniques would you recommend as offering the best possibility for balancing interests in free marketability against interests in preserving private choice and expectation? How would you implement the technique to insure that the balance is struck properly?

C. SHARED OWNERSHIP

1. CONCURRENT ESTATES

The right to possess land can be divided not only consecutively, over time ("A conveys Blackacre to B for life, then to C"), but also concurrently, among individuals ("A conveys Blackacre to B and C in fee simple absolute). B and C in this last example are *cotenants*, holding a *concurrent estate* in Blackacre in fee. Cotenancies can be created in future interests as well as present interests, in less than fee estates, and in any number of individuals ("A to B for life, then to the children of B for their lives and, on the death of B's last surviving child, to C, D, E, F and G in fee").

The most striking feature of concurrent estates is their *indivisibility*, or *unity of possession*: each cotenant, no matter how small her interest, is entitled to possess the entire parcel. Thus, in the last example, C, D, E, F and G each have an undivided one-fifth interest in the remainder and, once the remainder becomes possessory, each will have the right to possess all of Blackacre. Indivisibility obviously creates great potential for conflict. If B and C are cotenants of Blackacre—a one-family house on a quarter-acre lot—and B exercises his right to possession by moving into the house with his family, how can C exercise *her* right to possession? Is C entitled to remove B by judicial process or self-help? If so, what substance is there to B's right of possession? If not, what substance is there to C's right of possession? These questions are considered in section b, below.

The common law today recognizes three concurrent estates: the *tenancy in common*, the *joint tenancy*, and the *tenancy by the entireties*. (At early common law, when heirs took equal undivided shares in land by descent from the same ancestor, they were said to take as *tenants in coparcenary*. Coparcenary has since been replaced by the tenancy in common.)

The main distinction between the modern forms of cotenancy lies in what happens to the cotenant's interest on death. A tenancy in common can be transferred not only inter vivos, but also by will or intestacy. (Thus, if B, C and D hold Blackacre as tenants in common, each having a one-third undivided interest, and B dies, devising "all of my real property to X," X, C and D will each hold a one-third undivided interest in Blackacre.) By contrast, on the death of a joint tenant or a tenant by the entireties, the decedent's interest passes instantly and automatically to the surviving cotenant, regardless of any attempted disposition by will. (Thus, if B, C and D own Blackacre as joint tenants, each holding a one-third undivided interest, and B dies, devising "all of my real property to X," X will take nothing, for B's interest passed instantaneously to his surviving cotenants, C and D, who each now hold a one-half undivided interest. If C then predeceases D, D, the final survivor, will take the entire interest in Blackacre.) The principal difference between a joint tenancy and a tenancy by the entireties is that a joint tenancy can be created between any two or more persons, while a tenancy by the entireties can only be created between a husband and wife.

When a conveyance is ambiguous, and the grantor's intent to create a tenancy in common, a joint tenancy or a tenancy by the entireties is unclear, which cotenancy should the court find? Which cotenancy will better serve interests in the free marketability of land? Interests in avoiding friction between cotenants respecting the right to possess Blackacre? These questions are considered next.

a. JOINT TENANCY OR TENANCY IN COMMON?

i. Classification

IN RE MICHAEL'S ESTATE

Supreme Court of Pennsylvania, 1966.
421 Pa. 207, 218 A.2d 338.

Opinion by Mr. Justice JONES, March 22, 1966:

This is an appeal from a decree of the Orphans' Court of Lycoming County entered in a proceeding brought under the Uniform Declaratory Judgments Act. The purpose of the proceeding was to obtain an interpretation and construction of a deed to determine whether the decedent, Bertha W. Michael, died owning any interest in realty located in Wolf and Moreland Townships, Lycoming County, known as "King Farm."

On February 24, 1947, Joyce E. King deeded certain real estate in Lycoming County, known as "King Farm", to Harry L. Michael and Bertha M. Michael,[1] his wife, and Ford W. Michael (son of Bertha and Harry L. Michael) and Helen M. Michael, his wife. The pertinent pro-

---

1. It is stipulated that Bertha M. Michael and Bertha W. Michael are one and the same person.

visions of the lawyer-drawn deed are as follows: "This Indenture Made the 24th day of February in the year of our Lord one thousand nine hundred forty-seven (1947).

"Between Joyce E. King, widow, of Milton, Northumberland County, State of Pennsylvania, party of the first part, Harry L. Michael and Bertha M. Michael, his wife, tenants by the entireties and Ford W. Michael and Helen M. Michael, his wife, as tenants by the entireties, *with right of survivorship*, of Hughesville, Lycoming County, Pennsylvania, parties of the second part." (Emphasis supplied).

". . . have granted, bargained, sold, aliened, enfeoffed, released, conveyed and confirmed and by these presents does grant, bargain, sell, alien, enfeoff, release, convey and confirm unto the said parties of the second part, their heirs and assigns.

. . .

"To Have and To Hold the said hereditaments and premises hereby granted or mentioned and intended so to be with the appurtenances unto the said parties of the second part, their heirs and assigns to and for the only proper use and behoof of the said parties of the second part, their heirs and assigns forever."

Harry L. Michael died prior to February 20, 1962 leaving to survive him his wife, Bertha W. Michael and two sons, Ford W. Michael, one of the grantees, and Robert C. Michael, the appellant.

Bertha W. Michael died testate, November 26, 1963, leaving to survive her two sons, Ford W. and Robert C. Michael. By her will dated February 20, 1962, she provided, inter alia, as follows: "Second. It is my sincere wish and I hereby direct that my Executors settle my estate in such way that my sons Ford W. Michael and Robert C. Michael each receive an equal share of the same. Because of the fact that a good portion of my estate may be in the form of real estate, my Executors shall use their own discretion in the matter of the method to be used to make the division. The following, however, are my desires in this matter and these desires follow closely the wishes of their father, namely: . . . (d) That my interest in the "King Farm" situate partly in Wolf and partly in Moreland Townships go to Robert C. Michael and the sum of $1,000.00, be paid to Ford W. Michael to balance this gift."

The two sons were appointed executors of their mother's estate. Soon thereafter a dispute arose as to what, *if any*, interest Bertha W. Michael had in the real estate known as "King Farm." The answer to this question turns on the construction of the language, above-quoted, contained in the deed of 1947. The court below held that the deed created a joint tenancy with right of survivorship between the two sets of husbands and wives.

The appellant urges that the deed created a tenancy in common as between the two married couples, each couple holding its undivided one-half interest as tenants by the entireties.² The appellees, conceding that the respective one-half interests were held by husband and wife as tenants by the entireties, contend, however, that *as to each other* the couples held as joint tenants with a right of survivorship. The lower court, predicating its decision on the use in the deed of the phrase "with right of survivorship", held that there was a clear expression of an intended right of survivorship between the two couples. To further support its decision, the court found it significant that the phrase was not used twice in modification of each husband-wife-grantee designation, but rather was utilized after both couples had been named and had been designated severally as tenants by the entireties.

At common law, joint tenancies were favored, and the doctrine of survivorship was a recognized incident to a joint estate. The courts of the United States have generally been opposed to the creation of such estates, the presumption being that all tenants hold jointly as tenants in common, unless a clear intention to the contrary is shown.

In Pennsylvania, by the Act of 1812,³ the incident of survivorship in joint tenancies was eliminated unless the instrument creating the estate expressly provided that such incident should exist. The Act of 1812 has been repeatedly held to be a statute of construction; it does not *forbid* creation of a joint tenancy if the language creating it *clearly* expresses that intent. Whereas before the Act, a conveyance or devise to two or more persons (not husband and wife or trustees) was presumed to create a joint tenancy with the right of survivorship unless otherwise clearly stated, the presumption is reversed by the Act, with the result that now such a conveyance or devise carries with it no right of survivorship unless clearly expressed, and in effect it creates, not a joint tenancy, but a tenancy in common.

Since passage of the Act of 1812, the question of survivorship has become a matter of intent and, in order to engraft the right of survivorship on a co-tenancy which might otherwise be a tenancy in common, the intent to do so must be expressed with sufficient clarity to overcome the statutory presumption that survivorship is not intend-

---

2. Appellant, in urging the creation of a tenancy in common, points to decedent's will (above-quoted in part) wherein she indicated that she expected her interest in the property to pass under her will. From this appellant argues that the interest was considered by the parties to be one of tenancy in common rather than joint tenancy. Such an argument is insufficient to establish the intention of the parties. The question must be answered solely by reference to the language employed in the conveying instrument.

3. Act of March 31, 1812, P.L. 259, 5 Sm.L. 395, § 1, 20 P.S. § 121. ". . . If partition be not made between joint tenants, whether they be such as might have been compelled to make partition or not, or of whatever kind the estates or thing holden or possessed be, the parts of those who die first shall not accrue to the survivors, but shall descend or pass by devise, and shall be subject to debts, charges, curtesy or dower, or transmissible to executors or administrators, and be considered to every other intent and purpose in the same manner as if such deceased joint tenants had been tenants in common: Provided always, that nothing in this act shall be taken to affect any trust estate."

ed. Whether or not survivorship was intended is to be gathered from the instrument and its language, but no particular form of words is required to manifest such intention. The incident of survivorship may be expressly provided for in a deed or a will or it may arise by necessary implication.

Applying the above-stated principles to the instant facts, we fail to find a sufficiently *clear* expression of intent to create a right of survivorship, as required by the case law, to overcome the presumption against such a right arising from the Act of 1812. Neither the research of the parties involved nor our own has yielded any case involving language or involving facts similar to that in the present litigation.

The lower court found that the use in the deed of the phrase "with right of survivorship" and the location of that phrase in such deed (see quoted provision of deed, supra) constituted a clear expression of an intended right of survivorship. The inherent difficulty with such an interpretation is that it is purely conjectural and finds certainty in a totally ambiguous phrase.

The phrase, "with right of survivorship", is capable, as appellant properly urges, of at least three possible interpretations: (1) explanatory of one of the incidents of the estate, known as tenancy by the entirety; (2) explanatory of the one tenancy by the entirety, the creation of which it follows or (3), as the appellee and the lower court contend, indicative of the creation of a right of survivorship as between the two sets of spouses. Any one of these interpretations is a *possibility* but deciding which was intended by the parties would involve nothing but a mere guess. Such ambiguous terminology falls far short of the *clear* expression of intent required to overcome the statutory presumption.

Nowhere in the deed is the term "joint tenants" employed. To create a right of survivorship the *normal* procedure is to employ the phrase "joint tenants, with a right of survivorship, and not as tenants in common" in describing the manner in which the grantees are to take or hold the property being conveyed or transferred.

The deed herein involved also uses the term "*their* heirs and assigns forever." (emphasis supplied). The use of the plural would tend to indicate a tenancy in common. If "*his* or *her*" heirs and assigns had been used a strong argument could be made that the grantor intended a right of survivorship and that the survivor of the four named grantees would have an absolute undivided fee in the property.

Both the Act of 1812 and our case law clearly dictate that joint tenancies with the incident right of survivorship are not to be deemed favorites of the law. We cannot find within the four corners of this deed a *clearly* expressed intention to create a joint tenancy with the right of survivorship. Having failed to find a *clear* intention to overcome the statutory presumption against such estates, the Act of 1812 compels us to find that the deed of 1947 created a tenancy in common as between the two sets of married couples, each couple holding its undivided one-half interest as tenants by the entireties.

Decree reversed. Each party to bear own costs.

Mr. Justice COHEN and Mr. Justice ROBERTS dissent.

ZOMISKY v. ZAMISKA

Supreme Court of Pennsylvania, 1972.
449 Pa. 239, 296 A.2d 722.

Opinion by Mr. Justice EAGEN, November 17, 1972:

Mike Zamiska and George Zamiska were father and son. On December 26, 1957, Mike Zamiska executed a deed conveying the title in certain land to Mike Zamiska and George Zamiska "as joint tenants and as in common with the right of survivorship." Upon his father's death (intestate) on July 18, 1970, George claimed complete title in the land. Other children and grandchildren of Mike Zamiska, claiming the 1957 deed created only a tenancy in common in the grantees, instituted an action in equity asking the court to declare that George's ownership was limited to an undivided one-half interest.[1] The court below ruled the deed created a joint tenancy in the grantees with the right of survivorship and entered a decree granting the defendants' motion for judgment on the pleadings. This appeal followed.

At common law joint tenancies were favored, and the doctrine of survivorship was a recognized incident to a joint estate. But the courts of the United States have generally been opposed to the creation of such estates, the presumption being that all tenants, who are not husband and wife, hold jointly as tenants in common, unless a clear intention to the contrary is shown.

In Pennsylvania, by the Act of March 31, 1812, P.L. 259, 5 Sm.L. 395, § 1, 20 P.S. § 121, the incident of survivorship in joint tenancies (except where the grantees or devisees are husband and wife) was eliminated unless the instrument creating the estate expressly provided that such incident should exist. . . .

Since the issue was decided on the pleading below, our inquiry is limited to whether the deed involved expressed the intent to create a joint tenancy with the right of survivorship with sufficient clarity to overcome the statutory presumption to the contrary. We conclude it did, as did the court below. Hence, we will affirm.

The pertinent phrase in the deed is: "Mike Zamiska and George Zamiska as Joint tenants and as in common with the right of survivorship." Appellants contend that the words "with the right of survi-

---

1. After his father's death, George Zamiska conveyed his interest in the land to himself and his wife, Elizabeth A. Zamiska; hence, she was named a defendant in the action.

vorship" conflict with the words "and as in common" and argue since they are part of the same phrase, said words are without sense or meaning. The phrase "with the right of survivorship", it is urged is not a clear expression of anything under the circumstances. Consequently, the deed fails to contain a clear expression of intention to create a joint tenancy with the right of survivorship, and instead creates by operation of law an equal tenancy in common between the two grantees. However, appellants' position would render the words "with the right of survivorship" meaningless and consequently give no expression to the intent of the parties. Since the question of survivorship is a matter of intent we must reject appellants' position and strive to give full effect to the intent of the parties: Pennsylvania Bank and Trust Company v. Thompson.* In that case the grantee clause was "to William J.M. Thompson and A.C. Thompson, . . . as 'tenants by the entireties'. . . ." The issue there was the same now presented, namely, determining the intention of the parties. Mr. Justice Roberts, speaking for the Court, stated that, "To interpret otherwise and hold that the addition of the words 'as tenants by the entireties' does not include the right of survivorship, would render those words meaningless." He went on to say at page 265: "Nor would it be proper to simply disregard the words 'tenants by the entireties' as meaningless. These words are an expression of some intent which cannot be ignored entirely."

While the term "entireties" is not an element instantly, the principle is clear we cannot disregard the words "with the right of survivorship" in the instant deed as meaningless. It is true that if we were to look merely to the words in the deed "as Joint tenants and as in common," we would have an ambiguity since joint tenancy implies the term "survivorship" and "in common" implies the opposite. However, the use of the words "Joint tenants" in connection with the operative words "with the right of survivorship" removes the ambiguity and makes it clear that the intention of the parties was to create a joint tenancy, with the passage of the title to the survivor upon the death of the other.

Appellants next contend the phrase "with the right of survivorship" is not a magic phrase and this Court recently saw fit to disregard it in Michael Estate, 421 Pa. 207, 218 A.2d 338 (1966). In that case the controversial language of the deed was: "'Between Joyce E. King, widow, of Milton, Northumberland County, State of Pennsylvania, party of the first part, Harry L. Michael and Bertha M. Michael, his wife, tenants by the entireties and Ford W. Michael and Helen M. Michael, his wife, as tenants by the entireties, *with the right of survivorship* . . .'" Id. at 208, 209. The issue was what type of tenure existed between the two sets of married couples inter se. The Court concluded that this language created a tenancy in common, relying on the Act of 1812 to resolve the ambiguity creat-

---

* 432 Pa. 262, 247 A.2d 771 (1968).

ed by the possible interpretation of the language "right of survivorship". This was a proper disposition since it was not clear whether "with the right of survivorship" applied to one couple or both. In the present case, however, it is abundantly clear that the designation "with the right of survivorship" applies to Mike and George Zamiska, father and son.

Lastly, appellants argue that in the deed, there are other expressions affirmatively indicating that a tenancy in common was intended to be created. They point in particular to the use of the words "their heirs and assigns" rather than "his heirs, and assigns". This Court answered this identical contention in Maxwell v. Saylor,* at page 97: "It is contended by plaintiffs that the phrase in the deed 'their heirs and assigns' is in conflict with, and serves to negative [sic] any presumed intention to create a right of survivorship; this argument fails, however, in view of the fact that 'their heirs and assigns' are not words of purchase but of limitation, such being their time-honored use for the purpose of conveying a fee simple title."

Decree affirmed. Each side to pay own costs.

NOTES

1. In most states, statutes and judicial decisions have reversed the common law presumption for joint tenancies in favor of a presumption for tenancies in common. A few states have enacted statutes that entirely abolish the joint tenancy, either directly or by eliminating the survivorship feature. See generally, 4A R. Powell, Real Property ¶ 602 (1982). Reread the Pennsylvania statute applied in *Michael* and consider whether it was intended to be a "statute of construction," as the court held, or was in fact intended to outlaw the joint tenancy. (One hint: the statute's title, omitted from the *Michael* opinion, is *"Land held by joint tenancy to descend as estates of tenants in common."*)

Although the trend is generally against joint tenancies, states have been curiously ambivalent in their choice of methods for curtailing the estate. Oregon's Revised Statutes 93.180 (1981), provides:

Tenancy in common, when created; joint tenancy abolished. Every conveyance or devise of lands, or interest therein, made to two or more persons, other than to executors or trustees, as such, creates a tenancy in common unless it is expressly declared in the conveyance or devise that the grantees or devisees take the lands as joint tenants. Joint tenancy is abolished and all persons having an undivided interest in real property are to be deemed and considered tenants in common.

How would you advise an Oregon client who wishes to create a joint tenancy? Compare Erickson v. Erickson, 167 Or. 1, 115 P.2d 172 (1941) (statute abolishes "joint tenancy at common law," but does not

---

* 359 Pa. 94, 58 A.2d 355 (1948).

prohibit "the right of survivorship if created by express words. Such right may exist without all of the incidents of technical joint tenancy"), with Halleck v. Halleck, 216 Or. 23, 337 P.2d 330 (1959) (construing *Erickson* to hold that statute abolishes joint tenancy *and* survivorship). See generally, O'Connell, Are Joint Tenancies Abolished in Oregon? 21 Or.L.Rev. 159 (1942). (This article, which sharply criticizes the *Erickson* decision, was written while its author was an Associate Professor of Law at the University of Oregon; Professor O'Connell later ascended to the Oregon Supreme Court, where he authored the opinion in *Halleck*.)

What justification is there for the shift in preference from joint tenancy to tenancy in common? Courts in the Middle Ages favored the joint tenancy because its survivorship feature consolidated ownership in a few individuals, making feudal services and incidents easier to enforce. With the decline in feudalism, courts began to object to survivorship's gambling aspect—"an 'odious thing' that too often deprived a man's heirs of their rightful inheritance." Hines, Real Property Joint Tenancies: Law, Fact, and Fancy, 51 Iowa L.Rev. 582, 585 (1966). Does the constructional preference for the tenancy in common serve or disserve contemporary interests in the free marketability of land?

2. Do you agree with *Michael* that, as employed, the phrase, "with right of survivorship," was open to at least three interpretations? If, to take the court's first possible interpretation, the phrase was intended only to explain the attributes of the tenancy by the entireties, why was it not placed *after* the language that created each of the two tenancies by the entireties? Or, to take the second possible interpretation, why would it be used to explain the second tenancy by the entireties and not the first? Is it plausible that the grantor chose not to use the phrase, "as joint tenants," in order to avoid confusing the intended two sets of tenancies by the entireties with two sets of unintended joint tenancies?

How would *you* have drafted the conveyance, employing the term, "joint tenants," if you had intended a joint tenancy between the two sets of tenants by the entireties? Can you reconcile *Michael's* treatment of the phrase, "their heirs and assigns," with *Zomisky's* treatment of the identical phrase?

3. It would be dangerous to assume that, just because courts and legislatures have treated the joint tenancy with increasing hostility, private landowners have done likewise. In a superb empirical study, based both on an analysis of over 10,000 deeds recorded in five Iowa counties during 1954, 1959 and 1964, and on interviews with local real estate specialists, Professor N. William Hines revealed that, starting "from a base of less than 1 per cent in 1933, the incidence of joint tenancy in Iowa rose to 6 per cent of all transfers in 1938, escalated to 10 per cent in 1940, and then rocketed to 31 per cent by 1944. The rate of increase slowed down somewhat during the next decade, but

by 1954 the 45 per cent level was reached in most of the counties. Between 1954 and 1964 the expansion in usage generally continued, and the latest figures show that in 1964 an average of 52 per cent of all Iowa land transfers created joint tenancies. Something of a leveling off does seem to have taken place in the last few years. However, when contrasted with the traditional slowness that has marked most changes in real property holding patterns, this record of growth in the use of joint tenancy over the past twenty-five years is nothing short of meteoric." Hines, Real Property Joint Tenancies: Law, Fact, and Fancy, 51 Iowa L.Rev. 582, 586–587 (1966).

What explains this meteoric growth? Hines suggests as one possibility that many deeds between 1935–1940 involved reconveyances of farmland by foreclosing mortgagees to husband and wife co-owners; lenders commonly used the joint tenancy in the hope that the survivorship right would avoid fragmentation in title. Tax reduction offers another possible explanation. "In searching for a way to minimize the increasing income tax burden, many people apparently settled upon the technique of splitting the income from income-producing property by dividing the ownership of the property within the family, chiefly between husband and wife. The joint tenancy form of holding presumably was chosen to assure that the artificially divided interests in the property would be reunited in the survivor on the death of either tenant." War bonds, with their survivorship feature, also helped to popularize the concept, contributing to the joint tenancy's reputation as a " 'poor man's will.' The possibility for persons with relatively small estates to avoid the time, trouble, and expense associated with estate administration is probably the primary reason for the choice to utilize joint tenancy in most cases." *Id.* 588–589, 596.

The study's most dramatic finding is that "joint tenancy today is almost exclusively a husband and wife holding. Joint tenancies between related persons other than husbands and wives are rare, survivorship arrangements between unrelated persons virtually nonexistent. Further, husband and wife joint tenancies dominate the whole area of cotenancy. If a cotenancy is created today, the chances are 9 out of 10 that it will be a marital joint tenancy. More important, husband and wife joint tenancies are widely used. Conveyances of realty to husband and wife joint tenants currently comprise the bulk of all land transfers. Properties of many types and in a wide range of values are taken by married joint tenants. Farms are taken in joint tenancy less frequently than urban property, higher value property is generally less often subjected to survivorship arrangements than lower value property, but in almost all classes husband and wife joint tenancies account for a significant proportion of the transfers. The preference for the marital joint tenancy has continued for over twenty years and shows little sign of reversing itself in the foreseeable future." *Id.* at 623.

Does the apparent predominance of joint tenancies suggest that, in the interest of efficiency, the modern presumption favoring tenancies in common should be reversed? Does the predominance of marital joint tenancies suggest that courts and legislatures should reshape existing joint tenancy rules to respond to the specific needs of husbands and wives? "Several of the strong objections commonly raised against joint tenancy have little application to husband and wife joint tenancies. For example, the possible prejudice to the heirs of the first tenant to die would seem to be outweighed by the strong policy in favor of assuring that adequate provision is made for a surviving spouse. Tax disadvantages are also appreciably less in marital joint tenancies. In addition, several of the advantages ordinarily associated with joint tenancy, such as rapid title clearance and avoidance of fragmented ownership, have particular importance in the husband and wife context." *Id.* at 623–624.

ii. Severance

TENHET v. BOSWELL

Supreme Court of California, 1976.
18 Cal.3d 150, 133 Cal.Rptr. 10, 554 P.2d 330.

MOSK, Justice.

A joint tenant leases his interest in the joint tenancy property to a third person for a term of years, and dies during that term. We conclude that the lease does not sever the joint tenancy, but expires upon the death of the lessor joint tenant.

Raymond Johnson and plaintiff Hazel Tenhet owned a parcel of property as joint tenants. Assertedly without plaintiff's knowledge or consent, Johnson leased the property to defendant Boswell for a period of 10 years at a rental of $150 per year with a provision granting the lessee an "option to purchase." [2] Johnson died some three months after execution of the lease, and plaintiff sought to establish her sole right to possession of the property as the surviving joint tenant. After an unsuccessful demand upon defendant to vacate the premises, plaintiff brought this action to have the lease declared invalid. The trial court sustained demurrers to the complaint, and plaintiff appealed from the ensuing judgment of dismissal. . . .

---

2. The lease did not disclose that the lessor possessed only a joint interest in the property. To the contrary, the "option to purchase" granted to the lessee, which might more accurately be described as a right of first refusal, implied that the lessor possessed a fee simple. It provided in part: "Lessee is given a first exclusive right, privilege and option to purchase the house and lot covered by this lease. . . . [¶] If so purchased, Lessor will convey title by grant deed on the usual form subject only to easements or rights of way of record and liens or encumbrances specifically agreed to by and between Lessor and Lessee. [¶] Lessor shall furnish Lessee with a policy of title insurance at Lessor's cost . . . ."

II

An understanding of the nature of a joint interest in this state is fundamental to a determination of the question whether the present lease severed the joint tenancy. Civil Code section 683 provides in part: "A joint interest is one owned by two or more persons in equal shares, by a title created by a single will or transfer, when expressly declared in the will or transfer to be a joint tenancy . . . ." This statute, requiring an express declaration for the creation of joint interests, does not abrogate the common law rule that four unities are essential to an estate in joint tenancy: unity of interest, unity of time, unity of title, and unity of possession.

The requirement of four unities reflects the basic concept that there is but one estate which is taken jointly; if an essential unity is destroyed the joint tenancy is severed and a tenancy in common results. Accordingly, one of two joint tenants may unilaterally terminate the joint tenancy by conveying his interest to a third person. Severance of the joint tenancy, of course, extinguishes the principal feature of that estate—the *jus accrescendi* or right of survivorship. Thus, a joint tenant's right of survivorship is an expectancy that is not irrevocably fixed upon the creation of the estate; it arises only upon success in the ultimate gamble—survival—and then only if the unity of the estate has not theretofore been destroyed by voluntary conveyance, by partition proceedings, by involuntary alienation under an execution, or by any other action which operates to sever the joint tenancy.

Our initial inquiry is whether the partial alienation of Johnson's interest in the property effected a severance of the joint tenancy under these principles. It could be argued that a lease destroys the unities of interest and possession because the leasing joint tenant transfers to the lessee his present possessory interest and retains a mere reversion. Moreover, the possibility that the term of the lease may continue beyond the lifetime of the lessor is inconsistent with a complete right of survivorship.

On the other hand, if the lease entered into here by Johnson and defendant is valid only during Johnson's life, then the conveyance is more a variety of life estate *pur autre vie* than a term of years. Such a result is inconsistent with Johnson's freedom to alienate his interest during his lifetime.

We are mindful that the issue here presented is "an ancient controversy, going back to Coke and Littleton." (2 Am.Law of Prop. (1952) § 6.2, p. 10.) Yet the problem is like a comet in our law: though its existence in theory has been frequently recognized, its observed passages are few. Some authorities support the view that a lease by a joint tenant to a third person effects a complete and final severance of the joint tenancy. Such a view is generally based upon what is thought to be the English common law rule.

Others adopt a position that there is a temporary severance during the term of the lease. If the lessor dies while the lease is in force, under this view the existence of the lease at the moment when the right of survivorship would otherwise take effect operates as a severance, extinguishing the joint tenancy. If, however, the term of the lease expires before the lessor, it is reasoned that the joint tenancy is undisturbed because the joint tenants resume their original relation. The single conclusion that can be drawn from centuries of academic speculation on the question is that its resolution is unclear.

As we shall explain, it is our opinion that a lease is not so inherently inconsistent with joint tenancy as to create a severance, either temporary or permanent.

Under Civil Code sections 683 and 686 a joint tenancy must be expressly declared in the creating instrument, or a tenancy in common results. This is a statutory departure from the common law preference in favor of joint tenancy. Inasmuch as the estate arises only upon express intent, and in many cases such intent will be the intent of the joint tenants themselves, we decline to find a severance in circumstances which do not clearly and unambiguously establish that either of the joint tenants desired to terminate the estate.

If plaintiff and Johnson did not choose to continue the joint tenancy, they might have converted it into a tenancy in common by written mutual agreement. They might also have jointly conveyed the property to a third person and divided the proceeds. Even if they could not agree to act in concert, either plaintiff or Johnson might have severed the joint tenancy, with or without the consent of the other, by an act which was clearly indicative of an intent to terminate, such as a conveyance of her or his entire interest. Either might also have brought an action to partition the property, which, upon judgment, would have effected a severance. Because a joint tenancy may be created only by express intent, and because there are alternative and unambiguous means of altering the nature of that estate, we hold that the lease here in issue did not operate to sever the joint tenancy.

III

Having concluded that the joint tenancy was not severed by the lease and that sole ownership of the property therefore vested in plaintiff upon her joint tenant's death by operation of her right of survivorship, we turn next to the issue whether she takes the property unencumbered by the lease.

In arguing that plaintiff takes subject to the lease, defendant relies on Swartzbaugh v. Sampson (1936) 11 Cal.App.2d 451, 54 P.2d 73. In that case, one of two joint tenants entered into lease agreements over the objection of his joint tenant wife, who sought to cancel the leases. The court held in favor of the lessor joint tenant, concluding that the leases were valid.

But the suit to cancel the lease in *Swartzbaugh* was brought during the lifetime of both joint tenants, not as in the present case after the death of the lessor. Significantly, the court concluded that "a lease to all of the joint property by one joint tenant is not a nullity but is a valid and supportable contract *in so far as the interest of the lessor in the joint property is concerned.*" (Italics added; *id.*, at p. 458, 54 P.2d at p. 77.) During the lifetime of the lessor joint tenant, as the *Swartzbaugh* court perceived, her interest in the joint property was an undivided interest in fee simple that encompassed the right to lease the property.

By the very nature of joint tenancy, however, the interest of the nonsurviving joint tenant extinguishes upon his death. And as the lease is valid only "in so far as the interest of the lessor in the joint property is concerned," it follows that the lease of the joint tenancy property also expires when the lessor dies.

This conclusion is borne out by decisions in this state involving liens on and mortgages of joint tenancy property. In Zeigler v. Bonnell (1942) 52 Cal.App.2d 217, 126 P.2d 118, the Court of Appeal ruled that a surviving joint tenant takes an estate free from a judgment lien on the interest of a deceased cotenant judgment debtor. The court reasoned that "The right of survivorship is the chief characteristic that distinguishes a joint tenancy from other interests in property. . . . The judgment lien of [the creditor] could attach only to the interest of his debtor . . . . That interest terminated upon [the debtor's] death." (*Id.* at pp. 219–220, 126 P.2d at p. 119.) After his death "the deceased joint tenant had no interest in the property, and his judgment creditor has no greater rights." (*Id.* at p. 220, 126 P.2d at p. 120.)

A similar analysis was followed in People v. Nogarr (1958) 164 Cal.App.2d 591, 330 P.2d 858, which held that upon the death of a joint tenant who had executed a mortgage on the tenancy property, the surviving joint tenant took the property free of the mortgage. The court reasoned (at p. 594, 330 P.2d at p. 861) that "as the mortgage lien attached only to such interest as [the deceased joint tenant] had in the real property[,] when his interest ceased to exist the lien of the mortgage expired with it."

As these decisions demonstrate, a joint tenant may, during his lifetime, grant certain rights in the joint property without severing the tenancy. But when such a joint tenant dies his interest dies with him, and any encumbrances placed by him on the property become unenforceable against the surviving joint tenant. For the reasons stated a lease falls within this rule.

Any other result would defeat the justifiable expectations of the surviving joint tenant. Thus if A agrees to create a joint tenancy with B, A can reasonably anticipate that when B dies A will take an unencumbered interest in fee simple. During his lifetime, of course, B may sever the tenancy or lease his interest to a third party. But to allow B to lease for a term continuing *after* his death would indirectly defeat the very purposes of the joint tenancy. For example, for personal reasons B might execute a 99-year lease on valuable property for a consideration of one dollar a year. A would then take a fee simple on B's death, but would find his right to use the property—and its market value—substantially impaired. This circumstance would effectively nullify the benefits of the right of survivorship, the basic attribute of the joint tenancy.

On the other hand, we are not insensitive to the potential injury that may be sustained by a person in good faith who leases from one joint tenant. In some circumstances a lessee might be unaware that his lessor is not a fee simple owner but merely a joint tenant, and could find himself unexpectedly evicted when the lessor dies prior to expiration of the lease. This result would be avoided by a prudent lessee who conducts a title search prior to leasing, but we appreciate that such a course would often be economically burdensome to the lessee of a residential dwelling or a modest parcel of property. Nevertheless, it must also be recognized that every lessee may one day face the unhappy revelation that his lessor's estate in the leased property is less than a fee simple. For example, a lessee who innocently rents from the holder of a life estate is subject to risks comparable to those imposed upon a lessee of joint tenancy property.

More significantly, we cannot allow extraneous factors to erode the functioning of joint tenancy. The estate of joint tenancy is firmly embedded in centuries of real property law and in the California statute books. Its crucial element is the right of survivorship, a right that would be more illusory than real if a joint tenant were permitted to lease for a term continuing after his death. Accordingly, we hold that under the facts alleged in the complaint the lease herein is no longer valid.

It is ordered that the judgment dated June 18, 1973, be and it is hereby amended to read as follows:

"It is ordered, adjudged and decreed that Defendant, W.W. Boswell, Jr., have judgment against Plaintiff of dismissal of said First, Second and Third Causes of Action of said Third Amended Complaint and the Plaintiff, with respect to said defendant, take nothing by said First, Second and Third Causes of Action of said Third Amended Complaint."

As amended, the judgment is reversed.

WRIGHT, C.J., and McCOMB, TOBRINER, CLARK and RICHARDSON, JJ., concur.

NOTES

1. *The "Four Unities."* As noted in *Tenhet*, the common law requires that four unities be present for a joint tenancy to exist. The

unities have not changed materially since Blackstone restated them over two centuries ago:

Unity of Interest. All the tenants "must have one and the same interest." Specifically, they must have equal undivided shares and identical estates; "one cannot be tenant for life, and the other for years: one cannot be tenant in fee, and the other in tail."

Unity of Title. All the joint tenants must acquire title by the same instrument or by the same act of adverse possession; "their estate must be created by one and the same act, whether legal or illegal; as by one and the same grant, or by one and the same disseisin. Joint tenancy cannot arise by descent or act of law . . . ."

Unity of Time. The interests of the joint tenants must vest at the same time. "As in the case of a present estate made to A and B; or a remainder in fee to A and B after a particular estate; in either case A and B joint-tenants of this present estate, or this vested remainder. But, if after a lease for life, the remainder be limited to the heirs of A and B; and during the continuance of the particular estate A dies, which vests the remainder of one moiety in his heir; and then B dies, whereby the other moiety becomes vested in the heir of B: now A's heir and B's heir are not joint tenants of this remainder, but tenants in common; for one moiety vested at one time, and the other moiety vested at another."

Unity of Possession. All the tenants must be entitled to possess the entire estate. Each has "the entire possession, as well as every parcel as of the whole. They have not, one of them a seisin of one half or moiety, and the other of the other moiety; neither can one be exclusively seised of one acre, and his companion of another; but each as an undivided moiety of the whole, and not the whole of an undivided moiety."

2 W. Blackstone, Commentaries Chap. XII, pp. 180–182 (Tucker ed. 1803). Only the last of these unities—unity of possession—is necessary to the creation of a tenancy in common. All four unities, plus a fifth—spousal unity—are necessary to the creation of a tenancy by the entireties.

2. The four unities requirement, when taken together with the common law delivery rule that one cannot transfer title to oneself, means that A, holding title to property, cannot effectively convey it to herself and to B as joint tenants. At most, the attempted conveyance would give B an undivided one-half interest, leaving A with one-half of the interest she started with. Because A and B thus took their interests at different times by different acts, the unities of time and title would be absent, and the two would be tenants in common. The situation is not at all unusual, for a wife or husband, owning real property individually, will often want to convert sole ownership into a joint tenancy with her or his spouse.

How then can *A* create a joint tenancy in herself and *B*? The obvious solution is for *A* to convey to a straw man *X*, and for *X* immediately to reconvey to *A* and *B* as joint tenants. Although in many states this is the only way in which *A* can create a joint tenancy in herself and another, a growing number of states have, by statute or judicial decision, removed the need for the straw man. Wis.Stat.Ann. 700.19(5) (1981) simply provides that the "common law requirements of unity of title and time for creation of a joint tenancy are abolished." Mass.Gen.Laws Ann. c. 184, § 8 (1977) takes an even more direct route: "Real estate, including any interest therein, may be transferred by a person to himself jointly with another person in the same manner in which it might be transferred by him to another person . . . ."

For an excellent discussion of common law and statutory developments in the area, see Note, The Creation of Joint Tenancies—Common Law Technicalities vs. The Grantor's Intent, 82 W.Va.L.Rev. 335 (1979).

3. **The four unities are required, not only for a joint tenancy to be created, but also for it to continue.** A joint tenant's transfer of his entire interest to a third party will, because it destroys the unities of title and time, sever the joint tenancy and convert it into a tenancy in common. Other acts that have been held to sever a joint tenancy include one joint tenant's execution of a contract of sale, or mortgage or deed of trust, and the forced sale of a joint tenant's interest by his creditors. See 4A R. Powell, Real Property ¶ 618 (1982). And, as recognized in *Tenhet*, some authorities hold that a lease by one joint tenant to a third person severs the joint tenancy.

On strictly technical grounds, was the court's decision in *Tenhet* correct? Was the court right to focus on the argument that a lease destroys the unities of *interest* and *possession*—rather than the unities of *title* and *time*? As a practical matter, would the expectations of all the parties have been better served by a finding of permanent severance? Of temporary severance? Does *Tenhet* contradict the purpose behind the modern constructional presumption favoring tenancies in common? Did the court misconstrue the purport of West's Ann. Civil Code §§ 683 and 686?

Should the statutory relaxation of the four unities required for the *creation* of a joint tenancy, Note 2 above, also control decisions on the *continuation* of joint tenancies? If a joint tenant's conveyance of his interest has historically been held to sever the joint tenancy because it destroys the unities of title and time, should severance be found in states that, like Wisconsin, have abolished the unities of title and time for purposes of creating a joint tenancy? Should courts in states that have relaxed the four unities validate one joint tenant's attempt to sever the joint tenancy by a conveyance to himself? See Krause v. Crossley, 202 Neb. 806, 277 N.W.2d 242 (1979) ("Here the cotenant, Fred Kleensang, attempted to sever the joint tenancy by a deed from himself as grantor to himself as grantee. We now hold that this act does not constitute a severance of the joint tenancy and that the right of survivorship at the time of the death of Fred Kleensang was in the plaintiff, Herbert Krause").

4. *Who Gets the Property When one Joint Tenant Murders her Cotenant?* Although the survivorship feature might appear to offer one joint tenant a unique incentive to murder her cotenant, the question usually arises in the setting of more generalized—typically interspousal—conflict. The principal approach today is to hold that when one joint tenant kills another, the joint tenancy is severed and a tenancy in common results. Nevada's "slayer statute," Nev.Rev.Stat. 111.067 (1979), provides: "No person convicted of the murder of a decedent is entitled to any of the decedent's share of a joint tenancy. If there is no other joint tenant, the tenancy becomes a tenancy in common and the share of the decedent becomes part of his estate."

A small number of states have taken either of two other approaches. One approach is to apply the survivorship attribute literally, allowing the killer to take all, at least where insanity or some other fact mitigates guilt. See Anderson v. Grasberg, 247 Minn. 538, 78 N.W.2d 450 (1956). Another approach is to impose a constructive trust on the decedent's share, or on both the decedent's and survivor's shares, for the benefit of the decedent's estate. Compare Sikora v. Sikora, 160 Mont. 27, 499 P.2d 808 (1972) (imposing constructive trust on decedent's share for benefit of his estate), with Hargrove v. Taylor, 236 Or. 451, 389 P.2d 36 (1964) (decedent's estate and survivor each entitled to one half of rents and profits during survivor's lifetime, after which entire property passes to decedent's estate).

5. *Simultaneous Deaths.* How should the survivorship feature be administered if it is impossible or impracticable to determine the order in which the joint tenants died? The question, which typically arises when joint tenants die in a common accident, is resolved in most states under the terms of Uniform Simultaneous Death Act § 3:

> Where there is no sufficient evidence that two joint tenants or tenants by the entirety have died otherwise than simultaneously the property so held shall be distributed one-half as if one had survived and one-half as if the other had survived. If there are more than two joint tenants and all of them have so died the property then distributed shall be in the proportion that one bears to the whole number of joint tenants.
>
> The term "joint tenants" includes owners of property held under circumstances which entitled one or more to the whole of the property on the death of the other or others.

6. Can a grantor who wishes to provide for survivorship overcome statutory presumptions and proscriptions against joint tenancies, as well as problems with the four unities, by creating a tenancy in common for the lives of the cotenants with a remainder in the sur-

viving cotenant? See Durant v. Hamrick, 409 So.2d 731 (Ala.1982) (conveyance to grantees "as tenants in common and with equal rights and interests for the period or term that the said Grantees shall both survive and unto the survivor of the said Grantees, at the death of the other . . ." held to create a tenancy in common for life with cross contingent remainders in fee, the contingency being survival).

One difference between a joint tenancy and a life tenancy in common with remainder in the survivor is that in the joint tenancy the survivorship feature can be unilaterally destroyed through severance, while the remainder following concurrent life estates can only be eliminated through agreement of all the remaindermen.

b. RIGHTS AND LIABILITIES OF COTENANTS

McKNIGHT v. BASILIDES

Supreme Court of Washington, 1943.
19 Wn.2d 391, 143 P.2d 307.

SIMPSON, Chief Justice.

This is an action for the partition of real estate and for an accounting of the income obtained by the defendant in possession.

Judgment of default was entered against defendant Ruth Allison.

At the conclusion of the trial, the court made findings of fact and conclusions of law, and entered its decree of partition. The decree provided (1) that each of plaintiffs had an undivided one-sixth interest in two pieces of real estate, one at 5203 First Avenue Northwest, known as the "Big House," and the other, at 326 West Forty-first street, known as the "Little House," both properties being situated in the city of Seattle; (2) that plaintiffs have judgment against Charles Basilides in the sum of $1,083.16 for their share of the rents and rental use of the property, and that the judgment was a lien upon the interest of Charles Basilides in the property; (3) that the house and lot at 5203 First Avenue Northwest be sold in the manner provided by law relative to partition and sale of real estate; (4) that the property at 326 West Forty-first street be not sold; (5) that plaintiffs be allowed an attorney's fee of $500 and that a like sum be allowed counsel for defendants. Both amounts were made a lien on the proceeds of the sale of the property at 5203 First Avenue Northwest.

The decree further provided for the appointment of a referee to sell the First avenue property. Defendant Charles Basilides appealed.

The assignments of error are in holding that possession of appellant was never at any time adverse to respondents and requiring appellant to make an accounting; in not allowing appellant a lien on the property for the taxes and assessments paid and improvements made; in ordering an accounting for rents and profits received more than three years prior to the beginning of the action; in not dismissing the action because of laches, bad faith and lack of equity on the part of respondents; and in giving respondents a lien on the interest of appellant in the property.

The facts are these:

In the year 1901 appellant married Alice King in the city of Chicago. At the time of her marriage to appellant, Mrs. King had two children by a former marriage, Alice, now Alice McKnight, and Fred W. King. Defendant Ruth Allison is the child of appellant and his wife Alice. During the year 1907 the family moved to Seattle where appellant engaged in business and acquired two pieces of real property, one known in the evidence as the "Little House," located at 326 West Forty-first street, and the other, known as the "Big House," located at 5203 First Avenue Northwest, both in the city of Seattle.

Alice Basilides died intestate, November 20, 1929, and the estate has never been probated. Appellant has been in possession of both pieces of property since the death of his wife, and has paid all the taxes and assessments levied against the property. In addition, he made certain improvements upon the real estate. He rented the "Little House" and occupied the "Big House" as his home. During the time from the death of his wife Alice until a few days prior to the beginning of this action, appellant never made any claim to respondents that he was the sole owner of the property, nor did respondents make any claim to the property during the same period of time.

The assignments of error present three questions for consideration:

First. Did appellant obtain title to the real estate by adverse possession?

Second. Should appellant be compelled to make an accounting of income from the property?

Third. Were respondents entitled to a lien upon appellant's interest in the property for the amount found due after accounting?

We will discuss the questions in the order set out above.

Appellant contends that the evidence shows him to have been in actual, uninterrupted, open, notorious, hostile and exclusive possession of the property under claim of right since November 20, 1929, and for that reason he has acquired title by adverse possession.

The general rule relative to securing title to property owned in common by adverse possession is found in the following comprehensive statements:

"Since acts of ownership which, in case of a stranger, would be deemed adverse and per se a disseisin, are, in cases of tenancies in common, susceptible of explanation consistently with the real title, they are not necessarily inconsistent with the unity of possession existing under a cotenancy. For this reason, whether the acts of ownership will be such as to break and dissolve the unity of possession, constitute an adverse possession as against the cotenants, and amount to a disseisin, depends upon the intent with which they are done, and upon their notoriety and essential character. Accordingly, it is a general rule that the entry of a cotenant on the common property, even if he takes the rents, cultivates the land, or cuts the wood and timber without accounting or paying for any share of it, will not ordinarily be considered as adverse to his cotenants and an ouster of them. Rather, such acts will be construed in support of the common title. Mere exclusive possession, accompanied by no act that can amount to an ouster of the other cotenant, or give notice to him that such possession is adverse, will not be held to amount to a disseisin of such cotenant. Mere intention, unannounced, is not sufficient to support a claim of adverse title. Although the exclusive taking of the profits by one tenant in common for a long period of time, with the knowledge of the other cotenant and without any claim of right by him, may raise a natural presumption of ouster upon which the jury may find the fact to exist, if it satisfies their minds, yet the law will not, from this fact, merely raise a presumption of such ouster.

"Generally, a cotenant's sole possession of the land becomes adverse to his fellow tenants by his repudiation or disavowal of the relation of cotenancy between them, and any act or conduct signifying his intention to hold, occupy, and enjoy the premises exclusively, and of which the tenant out of possession has knowledge, or of which he has sufficient information to put him upon inquiry, amounts to an ouster of such tenant. In other words, where one cotenant occupies the common property notoriously as the sole owner, using it exclusively, improving it and taking to his own use the rents and profits, or otherwise exercising over it such acts of ownership as manifest unequivocally an intention to ignore and repudiate any right in his cotenants, such occupation or acts and claim of sole ownership will amount to a disseisin of his cotenants, and his possession will be regarded as adverse from the time they have knowledge of such acts or occupation and of the claim of exclusive ownership. A writing is unnecessary, but the claimant must show a definite and continuous assertion of an adverse right by overt acts of unequivocal character clearly indicating an assertion of ownership of the premises to the exclusion of the right of the other cotenants." 1 Am.Jur., Adverse Possession § 54.

"It is a general rule that an entry upon real property by a tenant in common claiming an adverse possession against his cotenants can never become the foundation of such a title until such cotenants first have had actual knowledge of the repudiation of their rights. The law deems the possession to be amicable until the tenant out of possession has in some way been notified that it has become hostile." 1 Am.Jur., Adverse Possession, § 56. . . .

We therefore hold that the evidence in this case was not sufficient to establish the claim that appellant made any adverse claim to the property, and that the facts indicate that his actions in living in the "Big House" and collecting rents from the "Little House" were not such outward acts as would amount to adverse possession.

Appellant argues, however, that the action was not commenced within the time limited by law. There is no merit in this contention. The statute of limitations does not begin to run in cases of this character until notice has been made of an adverse holding or claim on the part of one seeking title by adverse possession, and there has been an ouster.

It is next claimed that respondents were guilty of laches which estopped them from claiming an interest in the property. Appellant argues that respondents deliberately delayed their action for fourteen years and concealed their claim in the hope of profiting by the delay and the ignorance of the claim on the part of appellant. He argues that the intent to delay on the part of respondents is proven by certain testimony given by Mrs. McKnight. About a year after appellant re-married in 1933 and after appellant had asked her to sign a quitclaim deed to the properties, Mrs. McKnight consulted a lawyer concerning her interest in the property. Her testimony relative to the visit to the attorney was as follows: "A. Yes, and I went to him and I says—After he looked it up to see if he had probated anything and there wasn't anything probated at all, he says, 'They can't do a thing. There won't be anything done until it is probated.' And he says, 'I wouldn't worry a thing about it until it is probated,' he says, 'Let them start probating and then it is time for you to start in.'"

He presents figures to prove that, if the estate had been probated, he would have received over $4,000 and the respondents about $400 each, but that, under the present judgment, he will receive approximately $200 and respondents over $3,000.

"Laches is a doctrine of equity. It does not arise from mere lapse of time alone, but arises upon lapse of time together with some intervening change in the condition or relation of the parties adversely affecting the rights of the party sought to be charged. To constitute laches, not only must there have been delay in the assertion of the claim, but some change of condition must have occurred which would make it inequitable to enforce the claim." Lindblom v. Johnston, 92 Wash. 171, 158 P. 972, 974. . . .

The lapse of time did not obscure any evidence in this case. All of the witnesses who could have testified relative to the situation and condition of the property in 1929 were available at the trial of this case, and there is no showing that any material documents were lost or destroyed. Appellant's argument that he would have received more from the property had the estate been probated promptly loses its force when we call to mind that he could have himself probated the estate immediately after the death of his wife in 1929. If there was any undue delay, he was a party to that delay and cannot now urge the defense of laches against his cotenants.

We hold that respondents were not estopped by their delay in instituting this action.

The trial court compelled appellant to make an accounting. In so doing, appellant was given credit for repairs, improvements, taxes and insurance in the amount of $4,753.46. He was then charged for the use of the properties between November 20, 1929, and May, 1943, in the total sum of $8,001. Respondents were given a judgment in the sum of $1,083.18 for their share of the rental use of the two properties, and the judgment was made a lien upon the interest that appellant owned in the properties. A portion of the income received consisted of rentals for the "Little House," which was sold, April 1, 1938, on a partial payment sales contract. Since the date of the sale, appellant was charged a reasonable value for its use. The charge for the use of the "Big House" was fixed at an amount which the court found from testimony to be the reasonable rental value thereof. The record discloses that the income was at all times sufficient to pay the taxes and other expenses. The improvements were of a minor nature and did not to any appreciable extent enhance the rental or sales value of the property.

Appellant was responsible for and was properly held to an accounting of the rents he received from the "Little House."

The charge for the occupancy of the "Big House" and the reasonable rental value of the "Little House" subsequent to its sale present a more difficult problem.

The general rule is stated as follows in 62 C.J., Tenancy in Common, p. 446, § 64:

"While there is some authority in the United States to the contrary, based apparently upon the assumption that the Statute of Anne has become a part of the common law of the particular jurisdiction and upon an interpretation of that statute at variance with that adopted by the English courts, the generally accepted rule is that at common law one tenant in common who occupies all or more than his proportionate share of the common premises is not liable, because of such occupancy alone, to his cotenant or cotenants for rent or for use and occupation. He may become liable therefor, however, because of an express or implied agreement or if he stands in a fiduciary relationship to his cotenant, or where he has ousted his cotenant and, in some jurisdictions, liability is placed on him by virtue of express statute or because of the interpretation placed upon statutes similar in their terms to that of the Statute of Anne. Notwithstanding the rule may prevail in the particular jurisdiction that a cotenant may be charged for the use and occupancy of more than his proportionate share of the common premises, the circumstances of the particular case may require a denial of the application of the rule as inequitable, as where the occupancy has been with the acquiescence of the cotenants or the other cotenants have abandoned the occupancy of the property and declined to occupy it. . . .

"If common property was unoccupied without the fault of any of the tenants in common then, on an accounting between them, none of them should be charged for the use of the property."

[*margin note: GEN RULE*]

This court has passed upon the question of an accounting by cotenants in possession in several cases to which we now call attention.

In Leake v. Hayes, 13 Wash. 213, 43 P. 48, 50, 52 Am.St.Rep. 34, Charles Washburn died in 1880, leaving a widow and minor children. He had executed a will leaving his property to his wife, but did not mention his children in the will. The probate court entered a decree which recited that the widow was the owner of the real estate. The land at that time was unproductive. Mrs. Washburn remarried, and she and her second husband improved the land until it reached a highly productive stage. One of her children instituted an action for partition. This court held that, if those in possession were ". . . liable at all for use and occupation, or rents and profits, their liability did not arise until after demand was made therefor by the respondent."

In Eckert v. Schmitt, 60 Wash. 23, 110 P. 635, it appears that individuals owned property as tenants in common. This court held that those not in possession were entitled to an accounting and partition.

The rule is restated in Daniel v. Daniel, 106 Wash. 659, 181 P. 215, 221, in the following words: "Where one tenant in common enters upon the common estate which in its then condition yields no profit, and so improves it as to make it productive, he is entitled to all of the profits produced by means of his improvements. And also when the profits are the result of the individual labors of the tenant in possession, and no demand for an accounting has been made, an accounting will not be decreed. But the general rule is to the contrary; the instances where an accounting is refused being exceptions to, and not expressive of, the general rule."

[*margin note: L' in WASH.*]

Appellant cites Womach v. Sandygren, 107 Wash. 80, 180 P. 922, as authority for the rule that accounting between cotenants will not be required until after demand or the owner in possession holds the property adversely. However, what was said about the requirement of a demand in cases in which there was no adverse possession was not necessary to a decision of that case and is therefore of no controlling influence.

The last expression of this court upon the question under discussion is found in In re Foster's Estate, 139 Wash. 224, 246 P. 290, 292. The facts in that case were that one John Foster was the owner of an undivided one-half interest in real estate upon which he made his home. The other half was owned by his children. After the death of his wife, Foster remarried and subsequently died. The surviving spouse brought an action against the children for taxes, insurance and improvements made upon the property. The evidence showed that the taxes and insurance had been paid by Foster, and that his widow had made a number of improvements on the property. The trial court denied the right to show the rental value of the use of the premises occupied by the widow from the time of the death of Foster. This court reversed the case and in so doing stated:

"Objection is also made that the court refused to allow recovery for the rental value of the premises occupied by Adeline Foster from the time of decedent's death. If it is sought to render a money judgment in favor of Adeline Foster for improvements made from her separate funds, there should be offset against this one-half of the reasonable rental value of the premises from the time of decedent's death. The court was of the opinion that the claim for rent should be filed in the matter of the estate. But the occupancy by Adeline Foster of the premises in question was not an occupancy as administratrix; it was personal. As to the one-half belonging to the estate she may be required at the time of her final account as administratrix to render an account as to its rental value if the circumstances justify, but, as to the one-half belonging to the other cotenant, her use is a personal one, which can be offset against any claim that she has against the cotenants.

"The cause is reversed, with instructions (1) to ascertain if the improvements made upon the premises were necessary, or to what extent they enhanced the value thereof; (2) to ascertain the reasonable value of the rental of the premises, and allow recovery for one-half of that amount."

It will be noted that the Leake case adheres to the general law which we have quoted, while the Eckert, Daniel and Foster cases adopt the principle that the cotenant in possession must account for his personal use of that portion of the property which he does not own. We are not disposed to follow the general rule laid down in 62 C.J., supra, for the reason that it is not an equitable one. There is no sound basis for the general rule of law. No practical or reasonable argument can be advanced for allowing one in possession to reap a financial benefit by occupying property owned in common without paying for his personal use of that part of the property owned by his cotenants. The fairest method in cases in which the cotenant occupies and uses common property, instead of renting it out, is to charge him with its reasonable rental value. Of course there would be an exception to this holding in cases where the income resulted from improvements placed upon the property by the cotenant in possession. Appellant used the "Big House" as a home for many years, and it was proper that he be charged with the reasonable rental value of that use and made to account to his cotenants for their share of that rental value. However, appellant should not be charged with the rental value of the "Little House" after its sale, for the reason that he did not receive any rent, nor did he occupy or use it in any way.

Appellant maintains that he should be allowed ten per cent interest on the amounts he paid for taxes and assessments, basing his contention upon the provisions of Rem.Rev.Stat. § 9415. He cites, as additional authority, Olson v. Chapman, 4 Wash.2d 522, 104 P.2d 344. Neither the statute nor the holding in the above-mentioned case have any application to the facts presented in the case at bar. The statute contemplates that a cotenant shall receive interest upon funds owned and advanced by him. In the instant case the amounts paid for taxes and assessments were less than the amounts of income from the property, and appellant's payments in fact amounted to payments from funds jointly owned. The facts in the cited case showed that the tenants paid the taxes from their own funds and not out of moneys derived from the property income.

The trial court ruled correctly in not allowing interest to appellant.

Finally, it is argued that the court erred in impressing a lien upon the interest which appellant owned in the property. It is true that no lien exists in favor of one cotenant against the share owned by the others. However, the court may, in the exercise of its equitable powers and in order to do full justice to all parties concerned, impose a lien upon the interest in the property owned by the one who has benefited by possession, and may provide for the payment of the judgment from the proceeds of the sale in a partition action.

The judgment will be modified by striking therefrom the charge for use of the "Little House" subsequent to the time it was sold.

In all other particulars the judgment will be affirmed.

MILLARD, BLAKE, and ROBINSON, JJ., concur.

MALLERY, Justice (dissenting).

"The generally accepted rule is that at common law one tenant in common who occupies all or more than his proportionate share of the common premises is not liable, because of such occupancy alone, to his cotenant or cotenants for rent or for use and occupation." 62 C.J. Tenancy in Common, P. 446, Sec. 64.

This rule accords well with the rule that in the absence of an ouster the cotenant's possession is not adverse. In the face of the presumption of permission, the hostile character of the possession must fail.

Therefore the majority opinion rightly holds that appellant's claim to title by adverse possession cannot prevail.

By the same token, since the adverse possession failed by reason of the permissive nature of his possession, he cannot be held liable for rent for the use of the "big house". His cotenants deliberately let him "carry the burden" during the depression years. They cannot now deny their permission without establishing his hostile possession. Of course the rentals for the "little house" were received in trust for his cotenants.

Appellant has been charged in the accounting with his share of $8,001 of the rental value on the "big house" for the period beginning

THREATT v. RUSHING

Supreme Court of Mississippi, 1978.
361 So.2d 329.

BROOM, Justice, for the Court:

Whether one whose interest in lands consists of (1) a life estate plus (2) an undivided one-fourth in the fee interest may, without consulting the cotenants, cut and sell timber is the chief issue of this cause appealed from the Chancery Court of Lauderdale County. Johnny Roy Rushing, Andrew Ray Rushing, and Mittie Edna Rushing Foster (appellees) sued appellant, Mittie Alice Cooper Rushing Threatt (Mrs. Threatt herein), Henry Cornish and Glen Cornish, seeking to enjoin Mrs. Threatt and the two Cornishes from cutting timber and seeking a judgment for timber already cut. The lower court granted the injunction and entered a money decree against Mrs. Threatt and the two Cornishes for $9,344.26. We affirm.

Mrs. Threatt owns a life estate in the timberlands in question, and an undivided one-fourth interest in the fee interest. She previously owned the lands in fee simple but later deeded the lands to her children (appellees), reserving a life estate. Afterward one of her daughters deeded back a one-fourth interest to her, leaving the three remaining children, Johnny Roy Rushing, Andrew Ray Rushing, and Mittie Rushing Foster owning an undivided one-fourth interest each. She attacked her deed to the children but this court upheld the deed in Threatt v. Rushing, 355 So.2d 1096 (Miss.1978), decided without a written opinion.[1] According to Mrs. Threatt's testimony, in 1976 she decided to "improve" the timber by cutting out mature trees, leaving a good stand "that could reseed," and employed Henry Cornish (one of appellants) to selectively cut the mature trees. Whether she notified her children (remainder cotenants, appellees) is disputed. Cornish agreed to pay her $100 per thousand feet for the pine and $60 per thousand for hardwood (clear to her). The children sued Mrs. Threatt in December 1976 and, pending trial, the parties entered an agreed order to the effect that timber cutting would cease, timber on the ground would be removed, and Mrs. Threatt and the two Cornishes (timber cutters) would account for the timber already dis-

---

1. When Mrs. Threatt arranged to have the timber cut, her attack on her deed to the children was on appeal here, rendering her interest in the land then unsettled. If said deed were held void she apparently would have been fee owner; otherwise, she would have owned a life estate plus one-fourth of the remainder.

posed of. Mrs. Threatt was to have two-fifths, and the children three-fifths of the proceeds.

Forester Goforth testified at trial that the lands had about 1,019,300 board feet of standing timber, of which 92,300 board feet of pine and 21,200 board feet of hardwood had been cut, the timber already cut being worth about $14,825.63. According to Goforth, the land was primarily used for growing timber and needed to be thinned or "you're taking a chance" on losing profit. Henry Cornish testified that his "thinning" made the smaller timber grow faster and improved the timber. Cornish explained that his method of timber removal did less damage than the method used by the big timber companies, but that his was more expensive. He admitted that the children had told him to quit cutting the trees. The timber (cut and standing) was checked and appraised by witness Goforth partly at the instance of appellees and additionally at the court's direction. Included in the money decree against Mrs. Threatt is $460 for the services of Goforth in estimating and appraising the timber.

Did Mrs. Threatt, the life tenant, waste the interests of the remaindermen (her children) by cutting the timber? The correct test may be stated thusly: Do the acts of the life tenant in cutting the timber damage or diminish the value of the chief inheritance? If so, such acts are actionable waste. This was the meaning of Learned v. Ogden, 80 Miss. 769, 32 So. 278 (1902), which stated that "the cutting down by the tenant of trees for sale is waste . . . an injury to the inheritance . . . ." Cannon v. Barry, 59 Miss. 289, 306 (1881), an earlier case, held that acts dictated by "good husbandry" are not in law waste. Under the common law, a life tenant (as is Mrs. Threatt) may cut growing timber for estovers, making necessary repairs, for fuel, or to pay taxes, but cannot "lessen the value of the inheritance." 1 Thompson on Real Property, § 104 (1964).

Here, Mrs. Threatt holds a life estate, and by virtue of the fact that one of the daughters had deeded back her (the daughter's) one-fourth interest, Mrs. Threatt holds a one-fourth of the remainder interest along with her other three children (appellees). We cannot agree, given the facts of this case, that the lower court erred in holding that Mrs. Threatt's undertaking to cut the mature timber (leaving enough for reseeding) was simply not "good husbandry." Testimony shows there was over one million board feet of mature timber on the lands; to cut such a large part of the timber would obviously reduce the value of the chief estate. The cutting of timber here was of great magnitude and not for "estovers" or merely for the purpose of improving or maintaining the estate, but was in a large measure a commercial operation of Mrs. Threatt for profit and constitutes waste.

The second proposition argued on behalf of Mrs. Threatt is that as a cotenant, i.e., owner of an undivided one-fourth interest in the lands, she has a right, acting unilaterally, to harvest one-fourth of the mature timber and retain the proceeds. Mr. Goforth, appellees' witness, indicated that Mrs. Threatt and the Cornishes had not cut one-fourth of the mature timber on the property in dispute, but only about 92,300 board feet of pine and 21,200 board feet of hardwood out of a total mature timber of 1,019,300 board feet.

There is conflict among authorities as to whether or not a cotenant may cut timber from common property without the consent of the other cotenant(s). 20 Am.Jur.2d Cotenancy and Joint Ownership § 36 (1965) appears to recognize the right of one cotenant to cut up to his fractional interest of such timber, but to the contrary is 86 C.J.S. Tenancy in Common § 54 (1954). This court has not, so far as we can find, clearly decided the issue but dealt with it to some extent in Leatherbury v. McInnis, 85 Miss. 160, 37 So. 1018 (1904). That dispute involved the defendant's boxing of trees for turpentine on a tract of 1,040 acres in which he owned an undivided one-half interest. He had boxed 120 acres of trees and expressed the intention of boxing trees on the whole property, which was valuable only for its pine timber. Appellees obtained an injunction restraining him from boxing any more trees, and the lower court overruled a motion to dissolve the injunction. On appeal this court held that the injunction was properly granted, but that it should have only restrained the appellants from boxing more than one-half of the trees in value and quantity.

The rule of foreign jurisdictions varies widely, as indicated by the contrasting views cited in 86 C.J.S. Tenancy in Common § 54 (1954). In Rhode Island, timber is treated like crop income from the land and thus may be sold without liability for waste. Conversely, in the State of Washington timber is considered part of the realty and thus subject to an action for waste. Rayonier, Inc. v. Polson, 400 F.2d 909 (9th Cir. 1968); Buchanan v. Jencks, 38 R.I. 443, 96 A. 307 (1916).

We held in Bernard v. Board of Supervisors, 216 Miss. 387, 62 So. 2d 576 (1953), that timber of commercial size is part of the realty (the same as in Washington, but the opposite of Rhode Island.) Our decision in Learned v. Ogden, *supra*, indicates that trees when severed from the soil become personal property of the "reversioners" (cotenant children here) who may maintain an action for possession. This is consistent with Shepard v. Pettit, 30 Minn. 119, 14 N.W. 511 (1883), where the Minnesota court said that timber, when severed, becomes the personal property of the cotenants. Each would own a proportionate share and be entitled to an accounting for his fair share upon conversion or sale.

The 9th Circuit, in construing the rights of an assignee of a cotenant to remove timber, in Rayonier, Inc. v. Polson, *supra*, stated:

> [O]ne cotenant of real property may use and enjoy the entire property to the fullest extent consistent with the ordinary manner of deriving profits from property of like character . . . and he may grant to other persons freely and without the necessity of the

> consent of his cotenants, his interest in the property and whatever rights he enjoys . . ..

But:

> Courts generally hold that a cotenant has no right to remove substantial amounts of timber from land having a value primarily for its timber and that to do so constitutes waste for which he is liable.

> In some jurisdictions a cotenant may cut his fractional share of the timber (not merely stumpage, but determined by commercial and other considerations) without consulting with or being accountable to the other cotenants. Such a rule seems to allow cotenants to vie or race with each other in the disposition of their estate, and could create a situation in which all the cotenants might descend on the property, taking what they individually seize upon so long as they limit themselves to their fractional share. How such a rule can be applied without pandemonium or chaos is not clear. We hold that the better rule which we now adopt is that a cotenant may not sever timber from the land without consent of the other cotenant(s). If a cotenant cannot obtain such consent, he may have to resort to partition proceedings or some other form of litigation, but he may not unilaterally partition the property himself by simply cutting timber, even though he cuts only his own fractional interest of timber ownership. Leatherbury v. McInnis, *supra*, has been interpreted to mean that a cotenant cannot complain if another cotenant cuts timber not in excess of his proportionate interest. Our decision there seems, however, to be limited to the extent that a cotenant may be enjoined from cutting timber where such cutting is "tending to the destruction of the chief value of the property." In the present case, it is obvious that Mrs. Threatt's timber cutting would likely damage the "chief property"—the value of the total estate—and to that extent *Leatherbury* is not authority to say that the injunction against Mrs. Threatt and the Cornishes was erroneously granted. Admittedly, the concluding language of *Leatherbury* is capable of being construed to mean that a cotenant may not be enjoined from cutting up to his fractional interest in the entire estate, but, to that extent, our decision there (if it be so understood) is modified.

> Mrs. Threatt contends that the court misapplied the doctrine of waste to the facts of the case, and that the record is undisputed that she observed "good husbandry" in cutting the timber. She argues that, in issuing the injunction, the trial court mistakenly assumed that any cutting of trees, even for the sake of "good husbandry," constituted waste. Here, however, the magnitude of the cutting operation of Mrs. Threatt was far beyond the bounds of "good husbandry," and it clearly appears that detriment was being done to the chief estate or inheritance. Our scrutiny of the record shows that the injunction was properly issued pursuant to Cannon v. Barry, 59 Miss. 289 (1881),

in which the assignee of the life tenant was enjoined from committing further "acts of voluntary waste to the detriment of the inheritance."

Finally it is argued that the trial court erred in holding liable Henry Cornish and Glen Cornish (the ones doing the actual cutting for Mrs. Threatt). We find no merit to that contention, and hold that no reversible error has been established.

Affirmed.

NOTES

1. Several rules have evolved for allocating rights and liabilities between cotenants. Some of these rules make sense. Others rest on distinctions that are often arbitrary and almost always confusing. One principal distinction is between items of cotenancy income and items of cotenancy expenditure. Some finer distinctions are drawn between different types of income and different types of expenditure. Thus courts will distinguish between whether the income in issue is cash income—represented by a third party's payment to one cotenant for the right to occupy the land, to harvest crops or to take off resources—or is imputed income—represented by the value to a cotenant of his own occupancy of the land or consumption of crops or resources. Courts will also distinguish between those expenditures that may be set off against cash income and those that may be set off against imputed income, as well as between "upkeep" expenditures and "improvement" expenditures. The various rules, explored at 4A R. Powell, Real Property ¶¶ 603–604 (1982) and 2 American Law of Property §§ 6.10–6.18 (A.J. Casner ed. 1952), are summarized here.

Income. In England before enactment of the Statute of Anne, 4 Anne, Ch. 16 § 27 (1705), a cotenant could occupy the entire property, or collect rent from a third person occupying the entire property, without being required to give his cotenant a share of the rental value or the rent received. Most American states today follow the approach introduced by the Statute of Anne and hold that while one cotenant is not liable to his cotenants for any part of the rental value he himself derives from possessing the whole, he must account to them for their proportional share of any rents he has received from a third-party occupant. A few states follow McKnight v. Basilides and require the cotenant to apportion not only rents received but also the rental value of his own occupancy.

The majority rules respecting income from crops generally follow the rules on income from occupancy. If one cotenant grows and harvests the crops herself, she will not be required to account to her cotenants for any part of their value, even though she may have realized cash profits from their sale. If, however, the cotenant leases the land to a third party for farming purposes, she must account to her cotenants for their fractional share of the rents received. When it is not crops, but depletable natural resources, such as minerals or timber, that are removed from the land, courts diverge in their results. Some courts will characterize any removal of depletable resources as waste and will enjoin it; others will allow the cotenant to remove up to her fractional share of the resources, without any duty to account; and still others will allow the cotenant to remove resources from the entire parcel in a reasonable manner, with a duty to account to her cotenants for their fractional share of the profits. If the cotenant instead leases out the property, and authorizes the lessee to remove depletable resources, some courts will nullify the lease and enjoin the removal as waste, while others will honor the lease but require the cotenant to account to her cotenants for their fractional share of the rents received.

Expenditures: Upkeep. As a general principle, a cotenant who pays for upkeep expenses such as maintenance, taxes, insurance and debt service, is entitled to have his cotenants contribute their fractional share. The general principle will be applied differently depending on whether the expenses are less or more than the rent or rental value the cotenant received.

If the expenses are *less than* the rent received from a third party, the cotenant who paid the expenses can effectively obtain contribution by setting expenses off against rent and disbursing only the net profits to his cotenants. Similarly, if expenses are less than rental value, an occupying cotenant who is liable to his cotenants for rental value—either because he has ousted them or because the minority, *McKnight* approach is followed—can deduct upkeep expenses from the rental value owed. However, an occupying cotenant who is not liable for rental value cannot charge his cotenants with any part of the upkeep expense. If upkeep expenses *exceed* rent or rental value received, the cotenant can bring an action for contribution against his cotenants, regardless of whether he would have been liable to them for any part of the rent or rental value received. However, the amount of contribution will be reduced by the rent or rental value received and not shared with the cotenants.

Expenditures: Improvements: In principle, a cotenant who authorizes and pays for improvements on the common property has no right to contribution from cotenants who did not authorize the improvement. This principle will, however, be affected by the context in which it is applied. If the question of liability arises not in an action for contribution brought by the improving cotenant, but rather in an action for partition brought by any cotenant, the improver will often recoup the complete value of the improvement because courts will typically partition the land in a way that gives the improver the part that has the improvement on it; if physical partition is impracticable and a sale is ordered, courts will usually give the improver not only her fractional share of the sale proceeds attributable to the value of the land, but also the full amount of the proceeds attributable to the improvement.

2. *Ouster.* McKnight v. Basilides offers the standard definition of ouster: "a cotenant's sole possession of the land becomes adverse to his fellow tenants by his repudiation or disavowal of the relation of cotenancy between them and any act or conduct signifying his intention to hold, occupy, and enjoy the premises exclusively, and of which the tenant out of possession has knowledge, or of which he has sufficient information to put him on inquiry . . . ." (quoting 1 Am. Jur., Adverse Possession, § 54.)

Ouster has two distinct consequences. First, upon proving that she has been ousted, the cotenant out of possession becomes entitled to recover her fractional share of the premises' rental value from the cotenant in possession. Second, ouster starts the statute of limitations running against the ousted cotenant, who must bring an action to establish her interest in the real property within the limitations period or else lose her interest by adverse possession. Should the rules that are employed to determine whether ouster has occurred differ depending on whether it is the first or the second issue that is to be resolved? Although courts do not expressly separate the two situations, the decisions suggest that a line is in fact being drawn.

Entitlement to Share of Rental Value. In Mastbaum v. Mastbaum, 126 N.J.Eq. 366, 369, 9 A.2d 51, 53 (1939), the question was whether an ouster had occurred entitling the cotenants out of possession to recover a fractional share of the rental value from the cotenants in possession. Under the facts, the premises, occupied by two of the cotenants, were too small to house the other cotenants. The court focused on whether, by his conduct, "the defendant in possession, while not claiming sole title . . . deprives his cotenant of all benefit from the premises," such as by refusing to join in an advantageous lease.

The court rested its holding that ouster had not occurred, and that the cotenants in possession were not liable to the cotenants out of possession for any part of the rental value, on the finding that the "only way in which all the tenants could obtain an equal benefit from the apartment was by renting it to a third party. This, through the instrumentality of the executor, they tried unsuccessfully to do. If defendants had obstructed a leasing so as to obtain for themselves the sole benefit, they would be liable to account for the rental value under the cases cited above, but they did not do so. They moved into the property because it was advantageous for them to do so and because complainants did not desire to live there. Unless defendants had moved in, none of the parties would have received any benefit from the property. Tenants in common are not required to let their property stand vacant under penalty of paying rent to their cotenants." 126 N.J.Eq. 373, 9 A.2d 55.

Adverse Possession. Courts determining whether ouster has occurred for purposes of adverse possession generally focus on whether the cotenant out of possession has received adequate notice of the adverse claim. For example, in Nedry v. Morgan, 284 Or. 65, 584 P.2d 1381 (1978), a cotenant with a one-half undivided interest in the property conveyed his interest to third-party transferees under a deed that purported to convey full title to the property. The transferor's cotenants brought suit after the transferees had been in exclusive possession of the property for twenty-five years, paying taxes, irrigating the land and cultivating it. The court concluded that the transferees' exclusive possession of the property sufficed to put the cotenants out of possession on notice that "persons other than the original cotenants were in possession." The transferees were not required to give actual notice of ouster in order to qualify as adverse possessors.

3. Since cotenants are entirely free to contract around any of the legal rules allocating their rights and liabilities *inter se,* the question naturally arises whether these rules matter. The answer is that they probably do. Although the number of cotenants will often be sufficiently small to enable them to contract with each other at comparatively low cost, circumstances will doubtless exist in which the large number of cotenants, or strategic behavior by one or more of them, will prevent all of the cotenants from reaching an agreement on rights and liabilities.

On the assumption that these rules matter, do they make sense? Say that the value of the occupying cotenant's use (as a warehouse) is $80 per month and that the market value of the premises is $100 per month, represented by a third party's willingness to pay that amount to use the premises as a retail store. It would seem that the majority rule requiring a cotenant to share any rental proceeds, but allowing him to occupy the land himself rent-free, results in land being put to less than its most productive use: the cotenant in possession will prefer $80 "free" rental to the $50 cash he would receive after being required to share the $100 rental proceeds with his cotenant.

Does the rule on ouster correct this discrepancy and assure that the land will be put to its most productive use? Recall that the refusal by a cotenant in possession to rent to a third party proposed by the cotenant out of possession constitutes ouster, making the cotenant in possession liable for one-half the premises' rental value. Thus, in the example given, the cotenant in possession, whose use is worth $80 per month, will be forced to disgorge $50 per month to the cotenant out of possession who finds a third-party tenant willing to pay $100 per month. The amount retained—$30 rental value per month—will be less than the amount—$50 cash per month—that the cotenant in possession would enjoy from renting the premises out to the third party. The ouster rule thus tends to assure that the land will be put to its most productive use. It will prod the cotenant in possession to rent to the more productive user proposed by his cotenant or to make the more productive use himself. If the cotenant in possession chooses the latter course, he can be expected to respond to his cotenant's offer of a third-party tenant with an offer to split the value of his use and pay the cotenant out of possession up to $50 per month.

Can the rules respecting the allocation of liabilities for the expense, upkeep, improvement and depletion of resources be rationalized in the same terms? In what ways will cotenants' behavior be affected by the fact that judicial partition and sale will always be available to any single dissatisfied cotenant, virtually on demand?

See generally, Berger, An Analysis of the Economic Relations Between Cotenants, 21 Ariz.L.Rev. 1015 (1979).

c. PARTITION

PENFIELD v. JARVIS

Supreme Court of Connecticut, 1978.
175 Conn. 463, 399 A.2d 1280.

COTTER, Chief Justice.

The plaintiff brought this action for a partition by sale of real property pursuant to § 52-500 of the General Statutes.[1] The court sustained the defendants' demurrer to the first prayer for relief sought in the complaint, and, on the plaintiff's failure to plead over, rendered judgment for the defendants, from which the plaintiff has appealed.

The validity of a court's ruling sustaining a demurrer is determined upon the basis of the facts which may properly be proved under the allegations demurred to; and such facts are to be given the same favorable construction that the trier would adopt in admitting evidence.

The amended complaint alleges the following: The plaintiff, Helen W. Penfield, and two of the defendants, Adeline P. Jarvis and William F. Jarvis, are tenants in common of life estates in six noncontiguous parcels of real property located in Portland, Connecticut. Adeline P. Jarvis also has a vested remainder in a portion of four of the parcels, while the remaining three defendants, Penfield Jarvis, Marshall N.

---

1. "[General Statutes] Sec. 52-500. Sale of real or personal property owned by two or more. Any court of equitable jurisdiction may, upon the complaint of any person interested, order the sale of any estate, real or personal, owned by two or more persons, when, in the opinion of the court, a sale will better promote the interests of the owners. The provisions of this section shall extend to and include land owned by two or more persons, when the whole or a part of such land is vested in any person for life with remainder to his heirs, general or special, or, on failure of such heirs, to any other person, whether the same, or any part thereof, is held in trust or otherwise. A conveyance made in pursuance of a decree ordering a sale of such land shall vest the title in the purchaser thereof, and shall bind the person entitled to the life estate and his legal heirs and any other person having a remainder interest in the lands; but the court passing such decree shall make such order in relation to the investment of the avails of such sale as it deems necessary for the security of all persons having any interest in such land.

Jarvis and Wallace F. Jarvis, hold vested remainders in all six parcels as tenants in common. The parties to the action hold varying fractional shares in these parcels both as to the life estates and the remainder interest;[2] and no persons other than the plaintiff and all defendants have any interest in the property. The complaint further alleges that an in-kind partition of the property would be impractical since the subject real estate is composed of six noncontiguous parcels of land each having a different size, potential use, topography and value and since the ownership of each is held in a variety of fractional shares. Moreover, a sale of the property would best promote the interests of the owners in view of the fact that the premises are not productive of income necessary to the support and maintenance of the plaintiff.

In her prayer for relief the plaintiff claimed, inter alia, "[a] decree pursuant to Section 52–500 of the Connecticut General Statutes ordering the sale of said premises." The defendants demurred to that prayer for relief on the grounds that the complaint did not allege "that any of the remaindermen are heirs of the plaintiff or that their interests are in any way concerned with a failure of her heirs." Thus, the specific issue raised by this appeal is whether, under our statute, a co-life tenant may maintain an action for partition by sale against remaindermen or against other life tenants so as to bind those holding future interests in the property, where the remaindermen are neither heirs of the plaintiff nor holders of interests in any way concerned with the failure of her heirs.

In view of the fact that the precise question raised by this appeal is one of first impression in this state, earlier cases decided by this court involving the right to partition are of limited value. Similarly, since the statutory right to partition by sale must be examined in light of the particular statute in effect, its language and historical derivation, the decisions of other jurisdictions are not helpful. An historical examination of the right to partition generally and its development under Connecticut law must, therefore, govern our determination of the issue raised in this appeal.

Compulsory partition procedures, which originated under early English law, were initially available only to coparceners—those who had become concurrent owners by way of descent and who, therefore, were never voluntary participants in the creation of the concurrent ownership. Freeman, Cotenancy & Partition (2d Ed., 1886) § 420. In

---

2. The life tenants own the various parcels in the following fractional shares:

	Parcels 1, 2	Parcels 3, 4, 5, 6
Helen Wilcox Penfield	1/2	1/4
Adeline Penfield Jarvis	1/4	5/8
William F. Jarvis	1/4	1/8

The interests of the remaindermen are held as follows:

	Parcels 1, 2	Parcels 3, 4, 5, 6
Penfield Jarvis	1/3	1/6
Marshall N. Jarvis	1/3	1/6
Wallace F. Jarvis	1/3	1/6
Adeline Penfield Jarvis	—	1/2

the sixteenth century, this right to partition in kind was, by statute, made available to joint tenants and tenants in common of estates of inheritance who had a present right to possession of the property. 31 Henry VIII, c. 1 (1539). In the following year, the remedy of partition was expressly extended to include those holding land in joint or common tenancy for life or for a term of years, provided that such partition would not be prejudicial to any person not a party to the action. 32 Henry VIII, c. 32 (1540). Shortly, thereafter, an equitable procedure for partition in kind evolved in the Courts of Chancery, and its demonstrated superiorities caused it rapidly to supplant the procedure initiated by a common-law writ.

Both at law and in equity, however, the general rule was—and is—that a joint tenant or tenant in common must have either actual possession or an immediate right to possession in order to maintain an action for partition. Such a rule is understandable in the context of the problem to which the remedy by partition was directed: avoiding the conflicts which might arise if each cotenant asserted the right to be in possession of every part of the lands of the cotenancy. Through the right to partition, "it was intended that the undivided possession should be severed, and that each person having the right to be in possession of the whole property should exchange that right for one more exclusive in its nature, whereby, during the continuance of his estate, he should be entitled to the sole use and enjoyment of some specific purparty." Freeman, op.cit. § 440, p. 582. Since those with no right to immediate possession would not be deprived of present use and enjoyment or inconvenienced by the undivided possession of the property by others, there was a logical basis for denying to tenants of estates in reversion or remainder the right to interfere with tenants in possession, and, correspondingly, for precluding tenants in possession from effecting a severance of estate in remainder or reversion. Possession or the right to immediate possession is, therefore, a general prerequisite to the maintenance of an action for partition.

In this country, each state now has a statute allowing for compulsory partition. These statutes are, in large measure, embodiments of the prior practices of the English courts. The first Connecticut statute providing an absolute right to partition by physical division was enacted in 1720; Statutes, 1796, p. 258; the substance of which has survived virtually intact to the present day with only insignificant changes in the wording of the original enactment. While there are numerous decisions by this court stressing that this statutory right to partition is absolute and that the difficulty of making partition and inconvenience to other tenants are not grounds for denying the remedy; we find no cases specifically treating the scope of a life tenant's right to partition under the statute: i.e., can a life tenant obtain partition against parties holding successive interests, and can a life tenant obtain partition binding beyond the duration of the life estate.

Despite the dearth of judicial authority regarding the full scope of this statutory remedy in Connecticut, a review of the traditional application of the partition remedy supports the conclusion that, under our statute, a party could obtain partition only to the extent of the interest actually held. Thus, for example, under the prevailing practice, a party possessing a life interest would be entitled to partition only for the duration of his life. Moreover, under the rule limiting the right to partition to concurrent owners with *present* possessory interests, the partition of successive interests was not permitted under the common law since the requisite unity of possession was absent. A sole life tenant, therefore, would not be allowed to maintain partition as against reversioners or remaindermen; and, similarly, reversioners or remaindermen were incapable of demanding partition against the possessory owners because they were not concurrent owners adversely affected by the undivided possession held by others. The enactment, in 1840, of a statute providing for only a limited right to partition successive interests [6] fortifies the proposition that, in this state, there was no *broad* right to partition of such interests.

As noted earlier, under the rule both at common law and in equity "[a] cotenant of an estate in possession less than in fee, although entitled to partition, cannot by his partition affect estates in reversion or remainder unless authorized to do so by statute." 30 Cyc.Law and Proc., Partition, p. 183 (1908); 1 Kerr, Real Property § 612 (1895). There is no Connecticut statute expressly extending this limited right of a cotenant holding a less-than-fee interest, nor is there judicial precedent construing the existing statute to convey such a right. If we decide on this basis that a co-life tenant can obtain partition only for the duration of the life estate, and further conclude that the right of a life tenant to obtain partition as against successive interests is severely restricted, then we are compelled to hold that, as a general rule in this state, a life tenant can bring an action for partition only against other parties holding present possessory interests, and that any resultant partition will have no binding effect upon those holding future interests in the property. Neither the statutory changes since 1720 nor decisions of this court give any indication that this general rule does not still apply today in actions for physical partition pursuant to § 52–495 of the General Statutes.

Due to the frequent impracticality inherent in actual division, however, all states, except Maine, have, by statute, expanded the right to partition to permit a partition by sale under certain circumstances. In Connecticut, an act extending the power of our courts to order a sale in partition proceedings was enacted in 1844. Public Acts 1844, c. XIII. Prior to that time, the court had no power to order a sale of lands held in common; if the parties could not agree to a voluntary division, the only remedy was physical partition by the court upon the

---

6. That statute, now § 52–496 of the General Statutes, authorizes partition by owners of future interests only where the future interest was created by the will of a deceased tenant in common, joint tenant or coparcener.

application of a party. The early decisions of this court dealing with the new statutory remedy of partition by sale emphasized that "[t]he statute giving the power of sale introduces . . . no new principle; it provides only for an emergency, when a division cannot be well made, in any other way." The statutory proceeding for sale is ancillary to that for partition by physical division. It is thus clear that the previously noted rules governing the right to compel physical partition likewise control the remedy of partition by sale. In the present case, the plaintiff, a cotenant holding less than a fee interest in the subject property, could not compel a *physical* partition against other co-life tenants so as to bind those holding future interests; correspondingly, under the original statutory provisions allowing partition by sale in this state, she would be similarly restricted, and a court could order a sale of the life estate only.

The right to partition by sale was extended by statute in 1876. The passage of this statute provides further support for our conclusions regarding the scope of the remedy of partition by sale and leads us to the further conclusion that the relief sought by the plaintiff in the present case is vulnerable to demurrer under the statute as it now exists.[7] The 1876 statute, now incorporated in § 52–500 of the General Statutes, provided, in part, that the right to partition by sale "shall extend to and include land owned by two or more persons when the whole or a part of such land is vested in any person for life with remainder to his heirs, general or special, or, on failure of such heirs, to any other person . . . [[a]nd] A conveyance made in pursuance of a decree ordering a sale of such land . . . shall bind the person entitled to the life estate and his legal heirs and any other person having a remainder interest in the lands." The plaintiff by suggesting that this additional provision simply provided a sole life tenant with the right to seek partition by sale as against remaindermen, has misconstrued the import of the statutory language.

As previously explained, prior to 1876, one holding a life estate was unable to compel a partition either by division or by sale binding beyond the duration of the life estate. The statute of 1876, however, specifically provided for a limited right to partition by sale of successive interests where land is "owned by two or more persons when the *whole or a part* of said lands is vested in any person for life." (Emphasis added.) From the language used, it is clear that this provision is intended to apply both to co-life tenants and to sole life tenants. Any other construction would amount to an impermissible disregard of the plain wording of the statute.

This right to compel a partition by sale against successive interests does not apply to all life tenants, however. The remedy is avail-

---

7. Chapter XL of the Public Acts of 1876 (see General Statutes § 1312 [Rev. 1888]) was, in 1902, combined with the existing statute (see General Statutes § 1307 [Rev.1888]) providing for the right to partition by sale. General Statutes § 1037 (Rev.1902). The present § 52–500 is virtually identical with § 1037.

able only when the life tenant holds the estate either in cotenancy or in severalty "with remainder to his heirs . . . or, on failure of such heirs, to any other person."⁹ The plaintiff's complaint does not allege that she falls within this narrow class covered by the statute. Since we have concluded that only those life tenants specifically described in the provisions of § 52-500 of the General Statutes have the right to compel a partition by sale against remaindermen or against co-life tenants so as to be binding beyond the term of the life estate, the plaintiff's complaint was properly demurrable.

It is important to note at this point that our decision in the present case is governed by a 100-year-old statute which we have construed in light of its history, language and apparent purpose, and with consideration for the circumstances surrounding its enactment. Although policy considerations may since have changed, and these restrictive partition provisions may be less desirable to our present society, this court is precluded from substituting its own ideas of what might be a wise provision in place of a clear expression of legislative will.

There is no error.

In this opinion the other Judges concurred.

---

9. The historical development of property law in this state during the 19th century provides a logical basis for the restrictiveness of this right.

In the case of partition by sale, the class of life tenants described in § 52-500 was most likely considered a special group by the legislature of 1876. Under the Rule in Shelley's Case; 1 Co.Rep. 104; if in a conveyance or a will a life estate was given to a person and in the same conveyance or will a remainder was limited to the heirs or the heirs of the body of that person, that person took both the life estate and the remainder. Bishop v. Selleck, 1 Day 299, 300. Such a person, possessing a fee-simple absolute under the application of the Rule, would unquestionably have been able to obtain a partition by sale of the entire fee under the law of this state. However, in 1821 the Rule in Shelley's Case was abrogated in Connecticut by statute; General Statutes title 57, c. 1 (Rev.1821); see Goodrich v. Lambert, 10 Conn. 447, 454; and those formerly considered to be owners of the entire fee were only life tenants, unable to compel partition beyond the duration of their life estates.

The fact that a physical partition will be binding only for the duration of the life estate of a person seeking partition will not seriously interfere with the life tenant's right to undisturbed use and enjoyment of a portion of the property. However, since a *life estate* is not a readily marketable commodity, the remedial alternative of partition by sale is seriously hampered by the inability of a court to order the sale of the entire fee interest and the rights of the party seeking partition are severely curtailed. See annot., 134 A.L.R. 661, 667. It is thus probable that the 1876 provision was intended to extend the right to partition by sale to those life tenants who, but for the abrogation of the Rule in Shelley's Case, would have been able to compel a partition binding beyond the duration of their own lives.

Although the above assumptions may not be entirely applicable to conveyances which contained a "failure of heirs" provision, i.e., "to A for life, remainder to A's heirs, or, on failure of such heirs, to B," this class of life tenants was presumably given the same extended right to a partition by sale because the contingent remainder to B was viewed as simply an expression of the grantor's intent to prevent escheat in the unlikely event that the life tenant died without any heirs.

In any case, the interests of the heirs and contingent remaindermen were adequately protected by postponing distribution of the remainder share of the proceeds of the sale until after the death of the life tenant.

QUESTIONS

As indicated in Penfield v. Jarvis, all, or virtually all, states today authorize courts to judicially partition lands held in cotenancy and to order sale of the lands and division of the proceeds. Although these statutes generally make partition available on demand by any cotenant entitled to possession, they attempt to limit forced sales to those situations in which division in kind would be impracticable. The attempt has not been particularly successful. According to one experienced observer, "division in kind has become actually infrequent of occurrence. Lip service is still given to the historical preference for physical division of the affected land, but sale normally is the product of a partition proceeding, either because the parties all wish it or because courts are easily convinced that sale is necessary for the fair treatment of the parties." 4A R. Powell, Real Property ¶ 612 (1982).*

What reason was there for the Connecticut legislature to so closely limit the application of its partition statute to future interests? Was the Connecticut Supreme Court correct to construe the statute as narrowly as it did? If sale and division of proceeds can be justified as a means for reducing friction and promoting fairness between cotenants, why can it not also be justified as a means for increasing efficiency and fairness by liquidating the interests of present and future interest holders generally? Would you support a statute that authorized a court, on petition of any present or future interest holder, and after notice to all affected parties, to order the sale of the land and order the proceeds paid in appropriate shares to all present and future interest holders or their representatives? How would this approach differ from private trust arrangements, page 525, above? From the approach taken by the 1925 English Law of Property Act, page 475 above?

2. PROPERTY RIGHTS OF HUSBAND AND WIFE

As a general rule, property belongs to the person who acquires it consensually from another. The wisdom of the general rule, self-evident in most cases, is sorely tested in others. Thus, in the case of wife and husband, one working at a salaried job and the other working without salary at managing a home, it is more than likely that the salaried partner will use his or her cash income to acquire property throughout the marriage, while the homemaker, having no cash income, will be unable to do so. Husband and wife might seek to reset the balance by contract, agreeing to divide all property acquired during the marriage equally, or assigning some dollar value to the homemaker's services and proportioning the property assignment to this

---

* Copyright 1982 by Matthew Bender & Co., Inc. and reprinted with permission from *Powell on Real Property*.

value. But, at least historically, the marriage relationship has not proved to be a conducive setting for reaching efficient results through contract arrangements.

The American states have taken two approaches to property rights of husband and wife. The common law system, adopted in forty-two states, takes as its starting point the proposition that each partner is entitled only to the property that he or she acquires individually. Thus, in the example just given, the wage earner would own all property acquired with his or her income and the homemaker would get none. By contrast, the community property system, adopted in eight states,[d] starts from the proposition that all property acquired during the marriage belongs half to husband and half to wife without regard to which of the two received the income used to acquire the property.

These are starting points only. In practice, and as the law has evolved through years of legislative and judicial modification, the two systems often approximate each other on all the points that matter: management and control of property during marriage, and disposition of the property on divorce or death. And, just as it is important not to overstate the differences between the common law and community property systems, it is crucial not to understate the differences between states within each group. Specific rules differ, often dramatically, among both common law states and community property states.

For excellent overviews of the two systems, and their moves toward resetting the property balance between husband and wife, see Johnston, Sex and Property: The Common Law Tradition, The Law School Curriculum, and Developments Toward Equality, 47 N.Y.U.L. Rev. 1033 (1972); Younger, Community Property, Women and the Law School Curriculum, 48 N.Y.U.L.Rev. 211 (1973); Kulzer, Law and the Housewife: Property, Divorce, and Death, 28 U.Fla.L.Rev. 1 (1975).

a. THE COMMON LAW SYSTEM

i. *Early Structures.* Throughout the feudal period, single women enjoyed essentially the same power to own, manage, and dispose of real property as did single men. Women lost these powers upon marriage. The feudal doctrine that sought to rationalize this result was *coverture:* "By marriage, the husband and wife are one person in law: that is, the very being or legal existence of the *woman* is suspended during the marriage, or at least is incorporated and consolidated into that of the husband . . . ." 1 Blackstone, Commentaries 442 (Chitty ed.1838) (emphasis added). Coverture meant that, during the marriage, the husband gained control of any

---

d. Arizona, California, Idaho, Louisiana, Nevada, New Mexico, Texas, and Washington.

freeholds that his wife owned at the time of marriage or later acquired. He had the exclusive right (his *jure uxoris*) to occupy these lands himself or to rent them; he had no duty to account for the profits; he could transfer this right to others; and the right could be reached by his creditors. If the wife brought any leasehold estates to the marriage, the husband was free not only to use these as he pleased, but also to sell them if he wished. Coverture also meant that the wife had no unilateral right to transfer her property during the marriage.

To justify the disabilities imposed by coverture, the common law gave the wife the right to her husband's support. It also gave her *dower*—the right, if she survived her husband, to a life estate in one-third of the lands that the husband had owned during the marriage. The right to dower attached at the moment of marriage and could not, without the wife's consent, be defeated by the husband's inter vivos or testamentary transfers. As a counterpart to dower, the common law gave the husband who survived his wife *curtesy*—a life estate in all her freehold lands. Unlike dower, curtesy was conditioned upon the birth of a child to the couple.

Eventually, equity offered prospective brides and their families devices to sequester the wife's estate from the husband's encompassing *jure uxoris*. One was the Chancellor's enforcement of antenuptial agreements, unenforceable at law, giving the wife the right to control, and to take the rents and profits from, the property that she brought to, or acquired during, the marriage. Another equitable device, the trust, enabled a concerned parent to place property in trust for the benefit of a married daughter and enabled the daughter, as beneficiary, to enjoy the income from the property and to enforce the terms of the trust against the trustee. The key advantage of these techniques was that, whether the wife obtained her equitable estate through contract or trust, she held it just as she would if she had been a single rather than a married woman.

ii. *Contemporary Developments.* The common law regime, subordinating the married woman's rights to her husband's *jure uxoris* finally gave way in the latter part of the nineteenth century. Legislative reform centered on the Married Women's Property Acts, adopted in virtually all of the common law states by the end of the century, giving the married woman full control over all of the property that she brought to, or acquired during, the marriage. But the reform was by no means complete. Well into the twentieth century, several states continued to disable the married woman from conveying her own land, or engaging in business, without her husband's consent.

Dower and curtesy also began to crumble during this period, largely because they hindered the free marketability of land. In their place, the rules on descent were altered to entitle husband and wife to a portion of the other's estate should she or he die intestate.

This change clearly prejudiced the homemaker, for the wage earner—typically at this time, the husband—could dispose of all of his property by will, thus depriving his widow of the portion that she would have taken under dower. The situation was partially corrected by legislation entitling the widow to choose between the amount, if any, that she was given under her husband's will, and a statutory "forced" share—typically the amount she would have taken had he died intestate. The husband could, of course, defeat these claims through inter vivos transfers.

iii. *Tenancy by the Entireties.* The common law fiction of spousal unity also underlies the tenancy by the entireties, a cotenancy between husband and wife resembling the joint tenancy, but with distinct attributes of its own. As in the joint tenancy, the surviving cotenant—husband or wife—takes the entire estate. Like the joint tenancy, the tenancy by the entireties requires the four unities of time, title, interest and possession. It also requires that the cotenants be married at the time of the transfer. Not only death, but divorce, will terminate the tenancy, converting the relationship between the former spouses into a tenancy in common.

As originally designed, the tenancy by the entireties also differed from other cotenancies by vesting the exclusive rights of possession and management in one cotenant—the husband—without any duty to account to the other for rents and profits. The wife's only right was to take the land in the event that she survived her husband. Although the husband's powers in a tenancy by the entireties closely paralleled those that he enjoyed as a consequence of his *jure uxoris*, the Married Women's Property Acts did not eliminate them as extensively as they did the *jure uxoris*. Three states held that since the Acts dealt only with separate property they had no effect on the unity of interest held by the entireties. At least nine states held that the Acts, having obliterated the concept of spousal unity, also effectively abolished the tenancy by the entireties. Seventeen states held that the Acts had in varying degrees reduced the exclusivity of the husband's power over property held by the entireties. See Phipps, Tenancy by Entireties, 25 Temp.L.Q. 24, 29–32 (1951).

The common law favored the tenancy by the entireties, erecting a strong presumption that any conveyance to husband and wife created a tenancy by the entireties rather than some other form of cotenancy. This common law presumption has since been reversed in favor of a presumption for a joint tenancy or tenancy in common, and in one state the statutory presumption favoring the tenancy in common has been held to abolish the tenancy by the entireties. Wilson v. Wilson, 43 Minn. 398, 45 N.W. 710 (1890). Originally adopted in all but three of the American common law jurisdictions, the tenancy by the entireties today is important in probably no more than twenty-two states. See 4A R. Powell, Real Property ¶ 621 (1981).

SAWADA v. ENDO

Supreme Court of Hawaii, 1977.
57 Hawaii 608, 561 P.2d 1291.

MENOR, Justice.

This is a civil action brought by the plaintiffs-appellants, Masako Sawada and Helen Sawada, in aid of execution of money judgments in their favor, seeking to set aside a conveyance of real property from judgment debtor Kokichi Endo to Samuel H. Endo and Toru Endo, defendants-appellees herein, on the ground that the conveyance as to the Sawadas was fraudulent.

On November 30, 1968, the Sawadas were injured when struck by a motor vehicle operated by Kokichi Endo. On June 17, 1969, Helen Sawada filed her complaint for damages against Kokichi Endo. Masako Sawada filed her suit against him on August 13, 1969. The complaint and summons in each case was served on Kokichi Endo on October 29, 1969.

On the date of the accident, Kokichi Endo was the owner, as a tenant by the entirety with his wife, Ume Endo, of a parcel of real property situate at Wahiawa, Oahu, Hawaii. By deed, dated July 26, 1969, Kokichi Endo and his wife conveyed the property to their sons, Samuel H. Endo and Toru Endo. This document was recorded in the Bureau of Conveyances on December 17, 1969. No consideration was paid by the grantees for the conveyance. Both were aware at the time of the conveyance that their father had been involved in an accident, and that he carried no liability insurance. Kokichi Endo and Ume Endo, while reserving no life interests therein, continued to reside on the premises.

On January 19, 1971, after a consolidated trial on the merits, judgment was entered in favor of Helen Sawada and against Kokichi Endo in the sum of $8,846.46. At the same time, Masako Sawada was awarded judgment on her complaint in the amount of $16,199.28. Ume Endo, wife of Kokichi Endo, died on January 29, 1971. She was survived by her husband, Kokichi. Subsequently, after being frustrated in their attempts to obtain satisfaction of judgment from the personal property of Kokichi Endo, the Sawadas brought suit to set aside the conveyance which is the subject matter of this controversy. The trial court refused to set aside the conveyance, and the Sawadas appeal.

I

The determinative question in this case is, whether the interest of one spouse in real property, held in tenancy by the entireties, is subject to levy and execution by his or her individual creditors. This issue is one of first impression in this jurisdiction.

A brief review of the present state of the tenancy by the entirety might be helpful. Dean Phipps, writing in 1951,[1] pointed out that only nineteen states and the District of Columbia continued to recognize it as a valid and subsisting institution in the field of property law. Phipps divided these jurisdictions into four groups. He made no mention of Alaska and Hawaii, both of which were then territories of the United States.

In the Group I states (Massachusetts, Michigan, and North Carolina) the estate is essentially the common law tenancy by the entireties, unaffected by the Married Women's Property Acts. As at common law, the possession and profits of the estate are subject to the husband's exclusive dominion and control. In all three states, as at common law, the *husband* may convey the entire estate subject only to the possibility that the wife may become entitled to the whole estate upon surviving him. As at common law, the obverse as to the wife does not hold true. Only in Massachusetts, however, is the estate in its entirety subject to levy by the husband's creditors. In both Michigan and North Carolina, the use and income from the estate is not subject to levy during the marriage for the separate debts of either spouse.

In the Group II states (Alaska, Arkansas, New Jersey, New York, and Oregon) the interest of the debtor spouse in the estate may be sold or levied upon for his or her separate debts, subject to the other spouse's contingent right of survivorship. Alaska, which has been added to this group, has provided by statute that the interest of a debtor spouse in any type of estate, except a homestead as defined and held in tenancy by the entirety, shall be subject to his or her separate debts.

In the Group III jurisdictions (Delaware, District of Columbia, Florida, Indiana, Maryland, Missouri, Pennsylvania, Rhode Island, Vermont, Virginia, and Wyoming) an attempted conveyance by either spouse is wholly void, and the estate may not be subjected to the separate debts of one spouse only.

In Group IV, the two states of Kentucky and Tennessee hold that the contingent right of survivorship appertaining to either spouse is separately alienable by him and attachable by his creditors during the marriage. The use and profits, however, may neither be alienated nor attached during coverture.

It appears, therefore, that Hawaii is the only jurisdiction still to be heard from on the question. Today we join that group of states and the District of Columbia which hold that under the Married Women's Property Acts the interest of a husband or a wife in an estate by the entireties is not subject to the claims of his or her individual creditors during the joint lives of the spouses. In so doing, we are placing our

---

1. Phipps, "Tenancy by Entireties," 25 Temple L.Q. 24 (1951).

stamp of approval upon what is apparently the prevailing view of the lower courts of this jurisdiction.

Hawaii has long recognized and continues to recognize the tenancy in common, the joint tenancy, and the tenancy by the entirety, as separate and distinct estates. See Paahana v. Bila, 3 Haw. 725 (1876). That the Married Women's Property Act of 1888 was not intended to abolish the tenancy by the entirety was made clear by the language of Act 19 of the Session Laws of Hawaii, 1903 (now HRS § 509-1). The tenancy by the entirety is predicated upon the legal unity of husband and wife, and the estate is held by them in single ownership. They do not take by moieties, but both and each are seized of the whole estate.

A joint tenant has a specific, albeit undivided, interest in the property, and if he survives his cotenant he becomes the owner of a larger interest than he had prior to the death of the other joint tenant. But tenants by the entirety are each deemed to be seized of the entirety from the time of the creation of the estate. At common law, this taking of the "whole estate" did not have the real significance that it does today, insofar as the rights of the wife in the property were concerned. For all practical purposes, the wife had no right during coverture to the use and enjoyment and exercise of ownership in the marital estate. All she possessed was her contingent right of survivorship.

The effect of the Married Women's Property Acts was to abrogate the husband's common law dominance over the marital estate and to place the wife on a level of equality with him as regards the exercise of ownership over the whole estate. The tenancy was and still is predicated upon the legal unity of husband and wife, but the Acts converted it into a unity of equals and not of unequals as at common law. No longer could the husband convey, lease, mortgage or otherwise encumber the property without her consent. The Acts confirmed her right to the use and enjoyment of the whole estate, and all the privileges that ownership of property confers, including the right to convey the property in its entirety, jointly with her husband, during the marriage relation. Jordan v. Reynolds, 105 Md. 288, 66 A. 37 (1907); Hurd v. Hughes, 12 Del.Ch. 188, 109 A. 418 (1920); Vasilion v. Vasilion, *supra;* Frost v. Frost, 200 Mo. 474, 98 S.W. 527 (1906). They also had the effect of insulating the wife's interest in the estate from the separate debts of her husband.

Neither husband nor wife has a separate divisible interest in the property held by the entirety that can be conveyed or reached by execution. Fairclaw v. Forrest, 76 U.S.App.D.C. 197, 130 F.2d 829 (1942). A joint tenancy may be destroyed by voluntary alienation, or by levy and execution, or by compulsory partition, but a tenancy by the entirety may not. The indivisibility of the estate, except by joint action of the spouses, is an indispensable feature of the tenancy by the entirety.

In Jordan v. Reynolds, *supra*, the Maryland court held that no lien could attach against entirety property for the separate debts of the husband, for that would be in derogation of the entirety of title in the spouses and would be tantamount to a conversion of the tenancy into a joint tenancy or tenancy in common. In holding that the spouses could jointly convey the property, free of any judgment liens against the husband, the court said:

"To hold the judgment to be a lien at all against this property, and the right of execution suspended during the life of the wife, and to be enforced on the death of the wife, would, we think, likewise encumber her estate, and be in contravention of the constitutional provision heretofore mentioned, protecting the wife's property from the husband's debts.

It is clear, we think, if the judgment here is declared a lien, but suspended during the life of the wife, and not enforceable until her death, if the husband should survive the wife, it will defeat the sale here made by the husband and wife to the purchaser, and thereby make the wife's property liable for the debts of her husband." 105 Md. at 295, 296, 66 A. at 39.

In Hurd v. Hughes, *supra*, the Delaware court, recognizing the peculiar nature of an estate by the entirety, in that the husband and wife are the owners, not merely of equal interests but of the whole estate, stated:

"The estate [by the entireties] can be acquired or held only by a man and woman while married. Each spouse owns the whole while both live; neither can sell any interest except with the other's consent, and by their joint act; and at the death of either the other continues to own the whole, and does not acquire any new interest from the other. There can be no partition between them. From this is deduced the indivisibility and unseverability of the estate into two interests, and hence that the creditors of either spouse cannot during their joint lives reach by execution any interest which the debtor had in land so held. . . . One may have doubts as to whether the holding of land by entireties is advisable or in harmony with the spirit of the legislation in favor of married women; but when such an estate is created due effect must be given to its peculiar characteristics." 12 Del.Ch. at 190, 109 A. at 419.

In Frost v. Frost, *supra*, the Missouri court said:

"Under the facts of the case at bar it is not necessary for us to decide whether or not under our married women's statutes the husband has been shorn of the exclusive right to the possession and control of the property held as an estate in entirety; it is sufficient to say, as we do say, that the title in such an estate is as it was at common law; neither husband nor wife has an interest in the property, to the exclusion of the other. Each owns the whole while both live and at the death of either the other continues to own the whole, freed from the claim of any one claiming under or through the deceased." 200 Mo. at 483, 98 S.W. at 528, 529.

We are not persuaded by the argument that it would be unfair to the creditors of either spouse to hold that the estate by the entirety may not, without the consent of both spouses, be levied upon for the separate debts of either spouse. No unfairness to the creditor is involved here. We agree with the court in Hurd v. Hughes, *supra:*

"But creditors are not entitled to special consideration. If the debt arose prior to the creation of the estate, the property was not a basis of credit, and if the debt arose subsequently the creditor presumably had notice of the characteristics of the estate which limited his right to reach the property." 12 Del.Ch. at 193, 109 A. at 420.

We might also add that there is obviously nothing to prevent the creditor from insisting upon the subjection of property held in tenancy by the entirety as a condition precedent to the extension of credit. Further, the creation of a tenancy by the entirety may not be used as a device to defraud existing creditors.

Were we to view the matter strictly from the standpoint of public policy, we would still be constrained to hold as we have done here today. In Fairclaw v. Forrest, *supra*, the court makes this observation:

"The interest in family solidarity retains some influence upon the institution [of tenancy by the entirety]. It is available only to husband and wife. It is a convenient mode of protecting a surviving spouse from inconvenient administration of the decedent's estate and from the other's improvident debts. It is in that protection the estate finds its peculiar and justifiable function." 130 F.2d at 833.

It is a matter of common knowledge that the demand for single-family residential lots has increased rapidly in recent years, and the magnitude of the problem is emphasized by the concentration of the bulk of fee simple land in the hands of a few. The shortage of single-family residential fee simple property is critical and government has seen fit to attempt to alleviate the problem through legislation. When a family can afford to own real property, it becomes their single most important asset. Encumbered as it usually is by a first mortgage, the fact remains that so long as it remains whole during the joint lives of the spouses, it is always available in its entirety for the benefit and use of the entire family. Loans for education and other emergency expenses, for example, may be obtained on the security of the marital estate. This would not be possible where a third party has become a tenant in common or a joint tenant with one of the spouses, or where the ownership of the contingent right of survivorship of one of the spouses in a third party has cast a cloud upon the title of the marital estate, making it virtually impossible to utilize the estate for these purposes.

If we were to select between a public policy favoring the creditors of one of the spouses and one favoring the interests of the family unit, we would not hesitate to choose the latter. But we need not make this choice for, as we pointed out earlier, by the very nature of the estate by the entirety as we view it, and as other courts of our sister jurisdictions have viewed it, "[a] unilaterally indestructible right of survivorship, an inability of one spouse to alienate his interest, and, importantly for this case, a broad immunity from claims of separate creditors remain among its vital incidents." In re Estate of Wall, 440 F.2d at 218 (D.C.Cir.1971).

Having determined that an estate by the entirety is not subject to the claims of the creditors of one of the spouses during their joint lives, we now hold that the conveyance of the marital property by Kokichi Endo and Ume Endo, husband and wife, to their sons, Samuel H. Endo and Toru Endo, was not in fraud of Kokichi Endo's judgment creditors.

Affirmed.

KIDWELL, Justice, dissenting.

This case has been well briefed, and the arguments against the conclusions reached by the majority have been well presented. It will not materially assist the court in resolving the issues for me to engage in an extensive review of the conflicting views. Appellants' position on the appeal was that tenancy by the entirety as it existed at common law, together with all of the rights which the husband had over the property of his wife by virtue of the common law doctrine of the unity of the person, was recognized by the early decisions, that the Married Women's Act of 1888 (now Ch. 573, HRS) destroyed the fictional unity of husband and wife; that the legislature has recognized the continuing existence of the estate of tenancy by the entirety, but has not defined the nature or the incidents of that estate, HRS § 509-1, 509-2; that at common law the interest of the husband in an estate by the entireties could be taken by his separate creditors on execution against him, subject only to the wife's right of survivorship; and that the Married Women's Act merely eliminated any inequality in the positions of the spouses with respect to their interests in the property, thus depriving the husband of his former power over the wife's interest, without thereby altering the nature and incidents of the husband's interest.

I find the logic of Appellant's analysis convincing. While the authorities are divided, I consider that the reasoning of the cases cited by Appellant best reconciles the Married Women's Act with the common law.

The majority reaches its conclusion by holding that the effect of the Married Women's Act was to equalize the positions of the spouses by taking from the husband his common law right to transfer his interest, rather than by elevating the wife's right of alienation of her interest to place it on a position of equality with the husband's. I disagree. I believe that a better interpretation of the Married Women's Acts is that offered by the Supreme Court of New Jersey in King v. Greene, 30 N.J. 395, 412, 153 A.2d 49, 60 (1959):

> It is clear that the Married Women's Act created an equality between the spouses in New Jersey, insofar as tenancies by the entirety are concerned. If, as we have previously concluded, the husband could alienate his right of survivorship at common law, the wife, by virtue of the act, can alienate her right of survivorship. And it follows, that if the wife takes equal rights with the husband in the estate, she must take equal disabilities. Such are the dictates of common equality. Thus, the judgment creditors of either spouse may levy and execute upon their separate rights of survivorship.

One may speculate whether the courts which first chose the path to equality now followed by the majority might have felt an unexpressed aversion to entrusting a wife with as much control over her interest as had previously been granted to the husband with respect to his interest. Whatever may be the historical explanation for these decisions, I feel that the resultant restriction upon the freedom of the spouses to deal independently with their respective interests is both illogical and unnecessarily at odds with present policy trends. Accordingly, I would hold that the separate interest of the husband in entireties property, at least to the extent of his right of survivorship, is alienable by him and subject to attachment by his separate creditors, so that a voluntary conveyance of the husband's interest should be set aside where it is fraudulent as to such creditors, under applicable principles of the law of fraudulent conveyances.

b. The Community Property System

The eight community property states fashioned their laws from institutions tracing back to Spanish and French civil law traditions. The central premise of community property systems is that husband and wife contribute equally to the material successes and failures of their marriage and thus should share equally in the property—called community property—acquired through the labors of either or both spouses. One corollary is that property that is not acquired through community effort—"separate property"—belongs exclusively to the partner who acquired it.

Although rules differ from state to state, sometimes on the most fundamental points, a few rough generalizations are possible. As a general rule, community property is defined as all income, and all assets acquired with income, earned by either spouse during the course of the marriage, as well as all income derived from the investment or sale of property thus acquired. Separate property generally consists of the property that either spouse owned before the marriage or acquired during the marriage by gift, inheritance or devise, together with all income derived from such property. Property acquired during marriage is presumed to be community, rather than separate, property.

Community property's sharing principle did not, historically, extend to questions of management and control. As in the common law states, the husband was traditionally vested with exclusive control not only of the community assets, but also of the wife's separate property. Although the husband could not transfer the wife's separate property without her consent, he could freely dispose of the community assets. The only legal limit on the husband's powers of management and control was that he not act in bad faith.

The Married Women's Acts partially curtailed the husband's management powers by giving wives full control over their separate property. But it was not until a century later, in the 1970s, that community property states first began to give wives an equal say in the management and control of community assets. California's legislation, passed in 1973, went as far as any, providing that, "either spouse has the management and control of the community personal property . . . with like absolute power of disposition, other than testamentary, as the spouse has of the separate estate of the spouse." West's Ann.Cal.Civ. Code § 5125. As to community real property, "either spouse has the management and control," but both spouses "must join in executing any instrument when such community real property or any interest therein is leased for a longer period than one year, or is sold, conveyed, or encumbered . . . ." West's Ann.Cal.Civ. Code § 5127.

Courts and legislatures continue to depart from the equal sharing principle on dissolution and death, with the result that community property dispositions often approximate those made in common law jurisdictions at these two critical points. Courts in most community property states have the power, frequently exercised, to divide community assets on dissolution in such proportions as are "just and equitable." In addition, they can award alimony. And, in some, a spouse can dispose of more than his or her half of the community assets by will, forcing the survivor to elect between taking the one-half statutory share or taking under the will.

IN RE MARRIAGE OF LUCAS

Supreme Court of California, 1980.
27 Cal.3d 808, 166 Cal.Rptr. 853, 614 P.2d 285.

MANUEL, Justice.

Gerald E. Lucas appeals from an interlocutory judgment dissolving his marriage to Brenda G. Lucas, awarding child custody, fixing spousal and child support and dividing property. Gerald contests only the trial court's determination of the parties' ownership interests in their residence and in a vehicle, both of which were purchased with a combination of community and separate funds. In this case we must resolve a conflict among the Courts of Appeal regarding the proper method of determining separate and community property interests in a single family dwelling acquired during the marriage with both separate property and community property funds.

Brenda and Gerald were married in March 1964 and lived together continuously until their separation in December 1976. At the time of their marriage Brenda was beneficiary of a trust. The trust corpus was distributed to her free of the trust in September 1964. She immediately established a revocable *inter vivos* trust of which she was trustor and beneficiary. The trust, conceded by Gerald to be Brenda's separate property, had a value of approximately $44,000 at the time of trial.

In November 1968, Brenda and Gerald bought a house for $23,300. Brenda used $6,351.57 from her trust for the down payment, and they assumed a loan of $16,948.43 for the balance of the purchase price. Title to the house was taken as "Gerald E. Lucas and Brenda G. Lucas, Husband and Wife as Joint Tenants." Brenda paid $2,962 from her trust funds for improvements to the property; the remainder of the expenses on the property was paid for with community funds. At the time of trial the residence had a fair market value of approximately $56,250 and a loan balance of approximately $14,600, leaving a net equity of approximately $41,650. The community had reduced the principal by $2,052.32 and paid $6,801.14 in interest and $5,146.20 for taxes.

The trial court findings describe the parties' intent regarding ownership of the residence as follows: "The only discussions with regard to taking joint tenancy title to the property related to wife's understanding that title would pass to husband upon her death and that the children would benefit from this result; further, the parties contemplated that taking title in this manner would result in favorable tax consequences due to husband's veteran status. Wife did not intend to make a gift to the husband of any interest in the home purchased with her separate funds, nor did she know of any other legal significance of taking title to real property in the manner it was taken. Neither did husband intend to make a gift to wife of the payments made on the home from community funds during the period of ownership."

Brenda testified that she and Gerald did not discuss where the down payment would come from except to the extent that the payments would be higher if they did not use her trust fund and instead took a second trust deed on the house. Brenda said they had no agreement regarding the manner in which she would be disposing of the trust funds and that they did not discuss keeping the funds separate or using them to exhaust community debts. Brenda also testified that it was her intention at the time of the purchase to acquire the house for herself but that she did not discuss this with her husband.

In the interlocutory judgment entered in April 1978, the trial court deducted Brenda's $2,962 payment for improvements from the equity of $41,650.50 and then awarded a community property interest in the residence of 24.42 percent with a value of $9,477.50.[1] A separate property interest of 75.58 percent with a value of $29,241 was confirmed to Brenda.

The Courts of Appeal have taken conflicting approaches to the question of the proper method for determining the ownership interests in a residence purchased during the parties' marriage with both separate and community funds. In In re Marriage of Bjornestad (1974) 38 Cal.App.3d 801, 113 Cal.Rptr. 576, the Court of Appeal allowed only reimbursement for separate property contributions to the down payment on the purchase of the parties' residence. In In re Marriage of Aufmuth (1979) 89 Cal.App.3d 446, 152 Cal.Rptr. 668, the Court of Appeal developed a scheme of pro rata apportionment of the equity appreciation between the separate and community property contributions to the purchase price. The Court of Appeal in In re Marriage of Trantafello (1979) 94 Cal.App.3d 533, 156 Cal.Rptr. 556, however, held that the residence was entirely community in nature in the absence of any evidence of an agreement or understanding between the parties to the contrary.

The beginning point of analysis in each case was the nature of title taken by the parties. In *Bjornestad* and *Trantafello*, title was taken by husband and wife as joint tenants; in *Aufmuth*, it was taken as community property. Until modified by statute in 1965, there was a rebuttable presumption that the ownership interest in property was as stated in the title to it. Thus a residence purchased with community funds, but held by a husband and wife as joint tenants, was presumed to be separate property in which each spouse had a half interest. The presumption arising from the form of title could be overcome by evidence of an agreement or understanding between the parties that the interests were to be otherwise. It could not be overcome, however, "solely by evidence as to the source of the funds used to purchase the property." (Gudelj v. Gudelj, 41 Cal.2d at p. 212, 259 P.2d at p. 662.) Nor could it "be overcome by testimony of a hidden intention not disclosed to the other grantee at the time of the execution of the conveyance." (*Ibid.*; Socol v. King, 36 Cal.2d at p. 346, 223 P.2d 627; Machado v. Machado, 58 Cal.2d at p. 506, 25 Cal.Rptr. 87, 375 P.2d 55.)

The presumption arising from the form of title created problems upon divorce or separation when title to the parties' residence was held in joint tenancy. (Review of Selected 1965 Code Legislation (Cont. Ed. Bar) p. 40; Final Rep. of Assem. Interim Com. on Judiciary

---

1. The amounts stated in the interlocutory judgment differ slightly from those stated in the findings. The figures given are those stated in the judgment.

Relating to Domestic Relations (1965) pp. 121–122, 2 Appen. to Assem. J. (1965 Reg.Sess.) hereafter referred to as Domestic Relations Rep.) Unless the presumption of separate property created by the form of title could be overcome by evidence of a common understanding or agreement to the contrary, a house so held could not be awarded to the wife as a family residence for her and the children. In 1965 the Legislature considered various proposals to remedy this problem. The Legislature also noted that "husbands and wives take property in joint tenancy without legal counsel but primarily because deeds prepared by real estate brokers, escrow companies and by title companies are usually presented to the parties in joint tenancy form. The result is that they don't know what joint tenancy is, that they think it is community property, and then find out upon death or divorce that they didn't have what they thought they had all along and instead have something else which isn't what they had intended." (Domestic Relations Rep., p. 124.)

In 1965, in an attempt to solve these problems, the Legislature added the following provision to Civil Code section 164: "[W]hen a single family residence of a husband and wife is acquired by them during marriage as joint tenants, for the purpose of the division of such property upon divorce or separate maintenance only, the presumption is that such single family residence is the community property of said husband and wife." (Stats.1965, ch. 1710, p. 3843; see now Civ.Code § 5110.)[2] The effect of this provision was to change the presumptive form of ownership to that more closely matching the intent and assumptions of most spouses who acquire and hold their residence in joint tenancy. There is no indication that the Legislature intended in any way to change the rules regarding the strength and type of evidence necessary to overcome the presumption arising from the form of title.

The presumption arising from the form of title is to be distinguished from the general presumption set forth in Civil Code section 5110 that property acquired during marriage is community property. It is the affirmative act of specifying a form of ownership in the conveyance of title that removes such property from the more general presumption. It is because of this express designation of ownership that a greater showing is necessary to overcome the presumption arising therefrom than is necessary to overcome the more general presumption that property acquired during marriage is community

---

2. Section 164 was repealed in 1969 in connection with the enactment of the Family Law Act. (Stats.1969, ch. 1608, § 3, p. 3313.) It was replaced by section 5110 which contains an almost identical provision: "When a single-family residence of a husband and wife is acquired by them during marriage as joint tenants, for the purpose of the division of such property upon dissolution of marriage or legal separation only, the presumption is that such single-family residence is the community property of the husband and wife."

Although section 164 was the applicable statute when the parties in this case purchased their house, as a matter of convenience, future references in this opinion will be to the current statute, section 5110.

property. In the latter situation, where there is no written indication of ownership interests as between the spouses, the general presumption of community property may be overcome simply by tracing the source of funds used to acquire the property to separate property. It is not necessary to show that the spouses understood or intended that property traceable to separate property should remain separate.

The rule requiring an understanding or agreement comes into play when the issue is whether the presumption arising from the form of title has been overcome. It is supported by sound policy considerations, and we decline to depart from it. To allow a lesser showing could result in unfairness to the spouse who has not made the separate property contribution. Unless the latter knows that the spouse contributing the separate property expects to be reimbursed or to acquire a separate property interest, he or she has no opportunity to attempt to preserve the joint ownership of the property by making other financing arrangements. The act of taking title in a joint and equal ownership form is inconsistent with an intention to preserve a separate property interest. Accordingly, the expectations of parties who take title jointly are best protected by presuming that the specified ownership interest is intended in the absence of an agreement or understanding to the contrary. We therefore resolve the conflict in Court of Appeal opinions by following *Trantafello* and disapproving *Aufmuth* and *Bjornestad* to the extent they are inconsistent with this opinion.

In the present case there is no evidence of an agreement or understanding that Brenda was to retain a separate property interest in the house. Nor is there any finding by the trial court on the question. The only findings in this regard are that neither party intended a gift to the other. Such evidence and findings are insufficient to rebut the presumption arising from title set forth in Civil Code section 5110. The trial court's determination must therefore be reversed.

Neither the parties nor the court applied the correct rules to this case, and it is possible that had they done so the proof might have been different. In the interest of justice, therefore, the matter of the community or separate property character of the residence must be remanded for reconsideration in light of these rules.

If on reconsideration the house is found to be entirely community in nature, Brenda would also be barred from reimbursement for the separate property funds she contributed in the absence of an agreement therefor. It is a well-settled rule that a "party who uses his separate property for community purposes is entitled to reimbursement from the community or separate property of the other only if there is an agreement between the parties to that effect." (See v. See, 64 Cal.2d at p. 785, 51 Cal.Rptr. at p. 893, 415 P.2d at p. 781; Weinberg v. Weinberg (1967) 67 Cal.2d 557, 570, 63 Cal.Rptr. 13, 432 P.2d 709; In re Marriage of Epstein (1979) 24 Cal.3d 76, 82–86, 154 Cal.Rptr. 413, 592 P.2d 1165.) While the parties are married and living together it is presumed that, "unless an agreement between the parties specifies that the contributing party be reimbursed, a party who utilizes his separate property for community purposes intends a gift to the community." (In re Marriage of Epstein, *supra*, 24 Cal.3d at p. 82, 154 Cal.Rptr. at p. 417, 592 P.2d at p. 1169.)

For guidance in the event that on reconsideration the court finds there was an understanding or agreement that Brenda was to retain a separate property interest in the residence, we discuss briefly the question of the proper method of calculating the community and separate interests. In these inflationary times when residential housing is undergoing enormous and rapid appreciation in value, we believe that the most equitable method of calculating the separate and community interests when the down payment was made with separate funds and the loan was based on a community or joint obligation is that set forth by Justice McGuire in In re Marriage of Aufmuth, *supra*, 89 Cal.App.3d at pp. 456–457, 152 Cal.Rptr. 668. In brief, the *Aufmuth* formula gives the spouse who made the separate property down payment a separate property interest in the residence in the proportion that the down payment bears to the purchase price; the community acquires that percentage of the residence which the community loan bears to the purchase price.[3]

If the trial court finds no agreement or understanding that Brenda was to retain a separate property interest in the residence, Brenda's contribution of $2,962 of separate funds for improvements should have no effect on the determination of the parties' interests, and the presumption of section 5110 is controlling. If there was an understanding that Brenda's separate interest should be maintained, but no separate understanding with respect to improvements, Brenda should receive no additional credit for her expenditure for improvements, for it may be presumed that she intended that they redound to both the community and her separate interest in the property.

---

3. The value of those interests is computed by first determining the amount of capital appreciation, which is computed by subtracting the purchase price from the fair market value of the residence. The separate property interest would be determined by adding the amount of capital appreciation attributable to separate funds to the amount of equity paid by separate funds. The community interest would be the amount of capital appreciation attributable to community funds plus the amount of equity paid by community funds; the amount of equity paid by community funds is represented by the amount by which the principal balance on the loan has been reduced.

These principles may be exemplified by considering a house purchased for $100,000, with the wife paying the entire down payment of $20,000 from separate property funds and the community contributing the rest of the purchase price in the amount of a loan for $80,000. There would be a 20 percent separate property interest and an 80 percent community property interest in the house. Assume that the fair market value of the house at the time of trial is $175,000, resulting in a capital appreciation of $75,000, and the mortgage balance at the time of separation was $78,000. The value of the separate property interest would be $35,000, which represents the amount of capital appreciation attributable to the separate funds (20 percent of $75,000) added to the amount of equity paid by separate funds ($20,000). The net value of the community property interest would be $62,000, which represents the amount of capital appreciation attributable to community funds (80 percent of $75,000) added to the amount of equity paid by community funds ($80,000 minus $78,000).

Gerald also challenges the trial court's determination that a 1976 Harvest Mini-Motorhome, purchased in January 1976 for a cash price of $10,388, was Brenda's separate property. A community property vehicle was traded in on the purchase for an allowance of $2,567. An additional cash payment of $100 was made on the purchase from community funds. The cost of insurance and license fees ($474) added to the cash price of the motorhome, less the trade-in allowance and cash down payment, left a total unpaid balance of $8,195. That sum was paid by check drawn on Brenda's separate checking account. The community contributed 24.6 percent of the cost and Brenda contributed 75.4 percent of the cost of the vehicle. The fair market value of it at the time of trial was $9,000.

The purchase contract was made out in the name of Gerald alone, but title and registration were taken in Brenda's name only. Brenda wished to have title in her name alone, and Gerald did not object. The motorhome was purchased for family use and was referred to and used by the parties as a "family vehicle."

The trial court confirmed the motorhome to Brenda as her separate property. The interlocutory judgment stated that Gerald "had a de minimus community property interest therein which was made a gift to respondent [Brenda] at the time of the purchase."

Contrary to Gerald's contention, the trial court's determination that he made a gift of his interest is supported by substantial evidence. Title was taken in Brenda's name alone. Gerald was aware of this and did not object. This evidence constitutes substantial support for the trial court's conclusion that Gerald was making a gift to Brenda of his community property interest in the motorhome.

The judgment is reversed insofar as it determines the respective interests of the parties in the residence and divides the community property. It is affirmed in all other respects.

BIRD, C.J., and TOBRINER, MOSK, CLARK, RICHARDSON and NEWMAN, JJ., concur.

c. Administering Marital Property Systems

The administration of common law and community property systems reveals many common problems. The solutions sometimes diverge widely, not only between the two systems, but also among the states that subscribe to each.

One problem is that although marital property rights might appear by definition to depend on the existence of a marital relationship, fairness and respect for the legitimate expectations of the parties may require that they attach as well to relationships that fall short of marriage—for example, where a marriage is invalid because one of the spouses failed to obtain the dissolution of a prior marriage. Some courts will honor these "putative" marriages, at least if one of the parties acted in good faith. What if the parties cohabit for an extended period without going through a marriage ceremony? Several states will find a common law marriage if the relationship continues long enough, and will assign property rights just as if it were a ceremonial marriage. Elsewhere, courts divide on whether in these circumstances a contract claim can lie for the recovery of a portion of the assets acquired during the relationship. Compare Marvin v. Marvin, 18 Cal.3d 660, 665, 134 Cal.Rptr. 815, 819, 557 P.2d 106, 110 (1976) (courts should enforce express and implied agreements "between nonmarital partners except to the extent that the contract is explicitly founded on the consideration of meretricious sexual services"), with Hewitt v. Hewitt, 77 Ill.2d 49, 66, 31 Ill.Dec. 827, 834, 394 N.E.2d 1204, 1211 (1979) ("plaintiff's claims are unenforceable for the reason that they contravene the public policy, implicit in the statutory scheme of the Illinois Marriage and Dissolution of Marriage Act, disfavoring the grant of mutually enforceable property rights to knowingly unmarried cohabitants").

Administration is also complicated by the fact that a couple may live in two or more states—common law and community property—over the course of their marriage, acquiring and disposing of assets in each. Presumably their expectations respecting these assets will be shaped by the law of the state in which they were domiciled when they acquired them. Can a court of one state, supervising the distribution of these assets at dissolution or death, disregard the laws of these other states without running afoul of the constitutional bar to the deprivation of property without due process? See In re Thornton's Estate, 1 Cal.2d 1, 33 P.2d 1 (1934). Can a state legislature circumvent this problem by recharacterizing the property interests in these assets for the limited purposes of dissolution or probate? See West's Ann.Cal. Civil Code § 4803; Addison v. Addison, 62 Cal.2d 558, 43 Cal.Rptr. 97, 399 P.2d 897 (1965).

The most frequent and difficult problems in the administration of common law and community property systems arise from the fact that husband and wife will invariably have economic relations and interests that exist apart from the marriage but that must be reconciled with the marital relation and interests. *Sawada* and *Lucas*, pages 650 and 657 above, illustrate two aspects of these problems. The next principal case, Marriage of Graham, illustrates another aspect.

IN RE MARRIAGE OF GRAHAM

Supreme Court of Colorado, 1978.
194 Colo. 429, 574 P.2d 75.

LEE, Justice.

This case presents the novel question of whether in a marriage dissolution proceeding a master's degree in business administration

(M.B.A.) constitutes marital property which is subject to division by the court. In its opinion in Graham v. Graham, Colo.App., 555 P.2d 527, the Colorado Court of Appeals held that it was not. We affirm the judgment.

The Uniform Dissolution of Marriage Act requires that a court shall divide marital property, without regard to marital misconduct, in such proportions as the court deems just after considering all relevant factors. The Act defines marital property as follows:

"For purposes of this article only, 'marital property' means all property acquired by either spouse subsequent to the marriage except:

"(a) Property acquired by gift, bequest, devise, or descent;

"(b) Property acquired in exchange for property acquired prior to the marriage or in exchange for property acquired by gift, bequest, devise, or descent;

"(c) Property acquired by a spouse after a decree of legal separation; and

"(d) Property excluded by valid agreement of the parties."

Section 14–10–113(2), C.R.S.1973.

The parties to this proceeding were married on August 5, 1968, in Denver, Colorado. Throughout the six-year marriage, Anne P. Graham, wife and petitioner here, was employed full-time as an airline stewardess. She is still so employed. Her husband, Dennis J. Graham, respondent, worked part-time for most of the marriage, although his main pursuit was his education. He attended school for approximately three and one-half years of the marriage, acquiring both a bachelor of science degree in engineering physics and a master's degree in business administration at the University of Colorado. Following graduation, he obtained a job as an executive assistant with a large corporation at a starting salary of $14,000 per year. The trial court determined that during the marriage petitioner contributed seventy percent of the financial support, which was used both for family expenses and for her husband's education. No marital assets were accumulated during the marriage. In addition, the Grahams together managed an apartment house and petitioner did the majority of housework and cooked most of the meals for the couple. No children were born during the marriage.

The parties jointly filed a petition for dissolution, on February 4, 1974, in the Boulder County District Court. Petitioner did not make a claim for maintenance or for attorney fees. After a hearing on October 24, 1974, the trial court found, as a matter of law, that an education obtained by one spouse during a marriage is jointly-owned property to which the other spouse has a property right. The future earnings value of the M.B.A. to respondent was evaluated at $82,836 and petitioner was awarded $33,134 of this amount, payable in monthly installments of $100.

The court of appeals reversed, holding that an education is not itself "property" subject to division under the Act, although it was one factor to be considered in determining maintenance or in arriving at an equitable property division.

I.

The purpose of the division of marital property is to allocate to each spouse what equitably belongs to him or her. The division is committed to the sound discretion of the trial court and there is no rigid mathematical formula that the court must adhere to. An appellate court will alter a division of property only if the trial court abuses its discretion. This court, however, is empowered at all times to interpret Colorado statutes.

The legislature intended the term "property" to be broadly inclusive, as indicated by its use of the qualifying adjective "all" in section 14-10-113(2). Previous Colorado cases have given "property" a comprehensive meaning, as typified by the following definition: "In short it embraces anything and everything which may belong to a man and in the ownership of which he has a right to be protected by law." Las Animas County High School District v. Raye, 144 Colo. 367, 356 P.2d 237.

Nonetheless, there are necessary limits upon what may be considered "property," and we do not find any indication in the Act that the concept as used by the legislature is other than that usually understood to be embodied within the term. One helpful definition is "everything that has an exchangeable value or which goes to make up wealth or estate." Black's Law Dictionary 1382 (rev. 4th ed. 1968). In Ellis v. Ellis, Colo., 552 P.2d 506, this court held that military retirement pay was not property for the reason that it did not have any of the elements of cash surrender value, loan value, redemption value, lump sum value, or value realizable after death. The court of appeals has considered other factors as well in deciding whether something falls within the concept, particularly whether it can be assigned, sold, transferred, conveyed, or pledged, or whether it terminates on the death of the owner.

An educational degree, such as an M.B.A., is simply not encompassed even by the broad views of the concept of "property." It does not have an exchange value or any objective transferable value on an open market. It is personal to the holder. It terminates on death of the holder and is not inheritable. It cannot be assigned, sold, transferred, conveyed, or pledged. An advanced degree is a cumulative product of many years of previous education, combined with diligence and hard work. It may not be acquired by the mere expenditure of money. It is simply an intellectual achievement that may potentially assist in the future acquisition of property. In our view, it has none of the attributes of property in the usual sense of that term.

II.

Our interpretation is in accord with cases in other jurisdictions. We have been unable to find any decision, even in community property states, which appears to have held that an education of one spouse is marital property to be divided on dissolution. This contention was dismissed in Todd v. Todd, 272 Cal.App.2d 786, 78 Cal.Rptr. 131 (Ct.App.), where it was held that a law degree is not a community property asset capable of division, partly because it "cannot have monetary value placed upon it." Similarly, it has been recently held that a person's earning capacity, even where enhanced by a law degree financed by the other spouse, "should not be recognized as a separate, particular item of property." Stern v. Stern, 66 N.J. 340, 331 A.2d 257.

Other cases cited have dealt only with related issues. For example, in awarding alimony, as opposed to dividing property, one court has found that an education is one factor to be considered. Daniels v. Daniels, 20 Ohio Op.2d 458, 185 N.E.2d 773 (Ct.App.). In another case, the wife supported the husband while he went to medical school. Nail v. Nail, 486 S.W.2d 761 (Tex.). The question was whether the accrued good will of his medical practice was marital property, and the court held it was not, inasmuch as good will was based on the husband's personal skill, reputation, and experience.

III.

The trial court relied on Greer v. Greer, 32 Colo.App. 196, 510 P.2d 905, for its determination that an education is "property." In that case, a six-year marriage was dissolved in which the wife worked as a teacher while the husband obtained a medical degree. The parties had accumulated marital property. The trial court awarded the wife alimony of $150 per month for four years. The court of appeals found this to be proper, whether considered as an adjustment of property rights based upon the wife's financial contribution to the marriage, or as an award of alimony in gross. The court there stated that ". . . [i]t must be considered as a substitute for, or in lieu of, the wife's rights in the husband's property . . .." We note that the court did not determine that the medical education itself was divisible property. The case is distinguishable from the instant case in that here there was no accumulation of marital property and the petitioner did not seek maintenance [alimony].

IV.

A spouse who provides financial support while the other spouse acquires an education is not without a remedy. Where there is marital property to be divided, such contribution to the education of the other spouse may be taken into consideration by the court. Here, we again note that no marital property had been accumulated by the parties. Further, if maintenance is sought and a need is demonstrated, the trial court may make an award based on all relevant factors. Section 14–10–114(2). Certainly, among the relevant factors to be considered is the contribution of the spouse seeking maintenance to the education of the other spouse from whom the maintenance is sought. Again, we note that in this case petitioner sought no maintenance from respondent.

The judgment is affirmed.

PRINGLE, C. J., and GROVES and CARRIGAN, JJ., dissent.

CARRIGAN, Justice, dissenting:

I respectfully dissent.

As a matter of economic reality the most valuable asset acquired by either party during this six-year marriage was the husband's increased earning capacity. There is no dispute that this asset resulted from his having obtained Bachelor of Science and Master of Business Administration degrees while married. These degrees, in turn, resulted in large part from the wife's employment which contributed about 70% of the couple's total income. Her earnings not only provided her husband's support but also were "invested" in his education in the sense that she assumed the role of breadwinner so that he would have the time and funds necessary to obtain his education.

The case presents the not-unfamiliar pattern of the wife who, willing to sacrifice for a more secure family financial future, works to educate her husband, only to be awarded a divorce decree shortly after he is awarded his degree. The issue here is whether traditional, narrow concepts of what constitutes "property" render the courts impotent to provide a remedy for an obvious injustice.

In cases such as this, equity demands that courts seek extraordinary remedies to prevent extraordinary injustice. If the parties had remained married long enough after the husband had completed his post-graduate education so that they could have accumulated substantial property, there would have been no problem. In that situation abundant precedent authorized the trial court, in determining how much of the marital property to allocate to the wife, to take into account her contributions to her husband's earning capacity. Greer v. Greer, 32 Colo.App. 196, 510 P.2d 905 (1973) (wife supported husband through medical school); In re Marriage of Vanet, 544 S.W.2d 236 (Mo.App.1976) (wife was breadwinner while husband was in law school).

A husband's future income earning potential, sometimes as indicated by the goodwill value of a professional practice, may be considered in deciding property division or alimony matters, and the wife's award may be increased on the ground that the husband probably will have substantial future earnings. Todd v. Todd, 272 Cal.App.2d 786, 78 Cal.Rptr. 131 (1969) (goodwill of husband's law practice);

Golden v. Golden, 270 Cal.App.2d 401, 75 Cal.Rptr. 735 (1969) (goodwill of husband's medical practice); Mueller v. Mueller, 144 Cal.App.2d 245, 301 P.2d 90 (1956) (goodwill of husband's dental lab); In re Marriage of Goger, 27 Or.App. 729, 557 P.2d 46 (1976) (potential earnings of husband's dental practice); In re Marriage of Lukens, 16 Wash.App. 481, 558 P.2d 279 (1976) (goodwill of husband's medical practice indicated future earning capacity).

Similarly, the wife's contributions to enhancing the husband's financial status or earning capacity have been considered in awarding alimony and maintenance. The majority opinion emphasizes that in this case no maintenance was requested. However, the Colorado statute would seem to preclude an award of maintenance here, for it restricts the court's power to award maintenance to cases where the spouse seeking it is unable to support himself or herself.

While the majority opinion focuses on whether the husband's master's degree is marital "property" subject to division, it is not the degree itself which constitutes the asset in question. Rather it is the increase in the husband's earning power concomitant to that degree which is the asset conferred on him by his wife's efforts. That increased earning capacity was the asset appraised in the economist's expert opinion testimony as having a discounted present value of $82,000.

Unquestionably the law, in other contexts, recognizes future earning capacity as an asset whose wrongful deprivation is compensable. Thus one who tortiously destroys or impairs another's future earning capacity must pay as damages the amount the injured party has lost in anticipated future earnings.

Where a husband is killed, his widow is entitled to recover for loss of his future support damages based in part on the present value of his anticipated future earnings, which may be computed by taking into account probable future increases in his earning capacity.

The day before the divorce the wife had a legally recognized interest in her husband's earning capacity. Perhaps the wife might have a remedy in a separate action based on implied debt, quasi-contract, unjust enrichment, or some similar theory. Nevertheless, the law favors settling all aspects of a dispute in a single action where that is possible. Therefore I would affirm the trial court's award.

I am authorized to state that Mr. Chief Justice PRINGLE and Mr. Justice GROVES join in this dissent.

II. NONPOSSESSORY INTERESTS: EASEMENTS, COVENANTS, SERVITUDES

Landowners sometimes acquire nonpossessory interests in their neighbors' lands. *A*, who owns Whiteacre, might purchase the right to cross neighbor *B*'s parcel, Blackacre, in order to swim in the lake that borders Blackacre. *A* might also obtain *B*'s promise to clear and maintain the path to the lake. *B* might undertake not to erect any structure on Blackacre that will interfere with *A*'s view of the lake or with the light and air available to Whiteacre. And, to preserve the neighborhood's residential character, *B* might promise *A* that no commercial venture will be operated on Blackacre. These are all nonpossessory, rather than possessory, interests because they give their holder, *A*, the right to use, but not to possess, some part of Blackacre—to cross over the pathway to the lake, for example, or to enjoy an unobstructed view through the airspace over Blackacre. It is important to distinguish among the different types of nonpossessory interests. Much will often turn on whether the nonpossessory interest is properly classified as an *easement*, a *covenant* or a *servitude* and, if an easement or a covenant, on whether it is *affirmative* or *negative*.

TYPES OF NONPOSSESSORY INTERESTS

Affirmative Easements. An affirmative easement entitles its holder to use another's land in a way that, absent the easement, would constitute a trespass or a nuisance. In the example above, *A*'s right to cross Blackacre is an affirmative easement. *A* would also have an affirmative easement in Blackacre if *B* had granted him the right to lay drainage pipe or utility lines, or to emit smoke or fumes over Blackacre.

What if *B* gives *A* the right not only to enter onto Blackacre but also to take some resource—timber, soil or minerals—off? Although some courts would call the arrangement a *profit à prendre*, others, following the American Law Institute, do not make the distinction and instead include profits in their definition of easements. Restatement of Property § 450 Comments f and g, (1944).

Negative Easements. A negative easement prohibits an otherwise lawful use of land. *B*'s undertaking not to build a structure that would block the light and air flowing onto Whiteacre is a classic negative easement because it prohibits *B* from developing her land in an otherwise lawful manner. Courts early limited the permissible forms of negative easements to a bare handful: easements for light and air, for subjacent and lateral support, and for the unimpeded flow of an artificial stream. Many courts today have expanded easements for light and air to include easements for view.

Affirmative Covenants. An affirmative covenant is a promise that a landowner will do something that she is otherwise not obligated to do. In the example above, *B*'s promise to clear and maintain the pathway is an affirmative covenant. *B* might also have covenanted to give *A* a right of first refusal on the sale of Blackacre, or to pay an annual maintenance fee to the association that manages the subdivision in which Blackacre and Whiteacre are situated.

Negative Covenants. Sometimes also called *restrictive covenants*, these are promises that a landowner will not do something that she is otherwise free to do—for example, a promise not to use Blackacre for other than residential purposes. Negative covenants are obviously similar to negative easements. Indeed, the two are sometimes indistinguishable. One difference is that while negative easements may be created by words of promise, negative covenants can only be created by words of promise. Another difference is that, while most courts confine negative easements to a small handful of traditional categories, they impose virtually no limit on the kinds of negative covenants that can be created.

Equitable Servitudes. Equitable servitudes are effectively negative covenants that are enforced by a court's equity side rather than by its law side. If *A* seeks a legal remedy—damages—for *B*'s violation of the residential restriction on Blackacre, he will proceed by calling the restriction a negative covenant. If, however, he seeks an injunction, he would properly characterize the restriction as an equitable servitude. The difference is more than nominal, for courts impose fewer requirements for enforcing equitable servitudes through injunctive relief than for enforcing negative covenants through damage awards.

Is there an equitable counterpart to *affirmative* covenants? Some courts have seized on the *real obligation* as an equitable means for repairing the breach of affirmative obligations, but the device has not proved to be nearly as popular as the equitable servitude.

Courts are not always consistent in the labels they use to distinguish between the different kinds of nonpossessory interests and, for example, will sometimes call an interest a negative covenant when they really mean a negative easement. Courts have even been known to confuse affirmative covenants with negative covenants. One remedy for the confusion is simply to abolish the distinctions between easements, covenants and servitudes, and to unify the three into a single, integrated interest in land. For some thoughtful views on unification, see Reichman, Toward a Unified Concept of Servitudes, and French, Toward a Modern Law of Servitudes: Reweaving the Ancient Strands, 55 So.Cal.L.Rev. 1177, 1261 (1982). Comments on these two articles are also included in this symposium issue. Whatever its merits, unification has not won acceptance in either the courts or the legislatures. For the present, confusion between easements, covenants and servitudes can best be reduced by careful attention to the common elements shared by all nonpossessory interests.

ELEMENTS OF NONPOSSESSORY INTERESTS

The elements of nonpossessory interests can be divided into four pairs:

Benefit and *Burden.* Every nonpossessory interest creates both a benefit and a burden. The benefit is the right to use land possessed by another. The burden is the corresponding restriction in the possessor's use of her land. *A* in the example above holds the benefit of a right of way easement over Blackacre; *B*, who owns Blackacre, bears the burden of having *A* go across her land. (When dealing with covenants and servitudes, courts typically say that one party has the benefit of the covenant or servitude and another has the burden. By contrast, when dealing with easements, courts often substitute the shorthand term, "easement," for the more precise term, "benefit of the easement." Thus, in the example just given, a court would likely say that *A* "owns an easement in Blackacre.")

What are the benefit and the burden of *B's* undertaking not to interfere with *A's* light and air? Of the affirmative covenant to clear and maintain the pathway? Of the negative covenant not to use Blackacre for commercial purposes?

Appurtenant and *In Gross.* These two terms are used to describe how the *benefit* of an easement, covenant or servitude is held. A benefit is appurtenant—it appertains to a parcel of land—if it is intended to benefit that parcel of land. A benefit is in gross if, instead of attaching to some parcel of land, it is intended to benefit an individual. If a benefit is appurtenant, it is enforceable by successors in interest to the benefited land. If it is in gross, it is enforceable by successors in interest to the benefited individual. (Courts dealing with easements often resort to shorthand and instead of saying that the benefit of the easement is appurtenant or in gross, will simply say that the easement is an "appurtenant easement" or an "easement in gross").

Where the parties have not clearly expressed their intent as to how the benefit should be held, courts will determine intent by looking to the purpose behind the nonpossessory interest. Thus, absent a contrary expressed intent, a court would probably hold that the benefit of the right of way easement over Blackacre is appurtenant to Whiteacre since it increases the utility of Whiteacre by giving its occupant access to a nearby lake. The benefit of the affirmative covenant giving *A* a right of first refusal to Blackacre might also be construed as appurtenant, but it would more likely be held to be in gross since it gives *A* an economic benefit that is independent of the ownership of Whiteacre. Courts are generally guided by a strong presumption favoring appurtenant benefits.

Servient Estate and *Dominant Estate.* The servient estate is the parcel that bears the burden of an easement, covenant or servitude. In the examples above, Blackacre is the servient estate. The dominant estate is the parcel that enjoys the benefit of the easement, covenant or servitude. Obviously, there will be a dominant estate only if the benefit is appurtenant. In the examples above involving appurtenant benefits, Whiteacre would be the dominant estate.

Does the Burden Run? Does the Benefit Run? Disputes between *A* and *B* over enforcement of the easements, covenants and servitudes created in the examples above could properly be resolved under general contract principles, without resort to special real property doctrines. In each case, *A* and *B* are in privity of contract, and contract law is all that is needed to interpret the agreements, to determine whether they have been breached, and to dispense the appropriate remedies.

But, what if *B* sells Blackacre to *Z* who refuses to honor *B's* undertakings: Does *A* have an action against *Z*? The answer under contract law is clearly no, for *A* and *Z* are not in privity of contract. *A* will, however, have an action against *Z* under real property doctrine if the burden of the particular interest "runs with the land," binding successors in interest to the servient estate. The burden will be held to run with the land only if specific requirements, different for each form of nonpossessory interest, are met.

If *A* sells Whiteacre to *Y*, can *Y* enforce the benefit against *B* or *Z*, with whom he is not in privity of contract? Again the answer under real property law is yes, but only if the benefit is appurtenant, so that it passes with the dominant estate to *Y, and* only if specific requirements are met for the benefit to "run with the land."

A. EASEMENTS

1. CREATION

a. BY INSTRUMENT

COVENANTS, CONDITIONS AND RESTRICTIONS FOR TANSI RESORT SUBDIVISION

CUMBERLAND PLATEAU RESORTS, INC. TO WHOM IT MAY CONCERN:

Restrictive Covenants, Limitations and Reservations on the Tansi Resort Sub-Division, Crossville, Tennessee.

Developed by Cumberland Plateau Resorts, Inc.

The following restrictive covenants and conditions shall be applicable to and binding upon those certain residential lots or parcels of land conveyed as residential lots by Cumberland Plateau Resorts, Inc., and shown on a certain plat or plats of TANSI RESORT Sub-Division, filed or to be filed for record in the Register's Office of Cumberland County, Crossville, Tennessee.

. . . 7. Cumberland Plateau Resorts, Inc., for itself, its successors, assigns and licensees reserves easements, as shown on said plats, over, through and upon said land for the installation of utilities and drains and the maintenance thereof. Cumberland Plateau Resorts, Inc., for itself, its successors, assigns and licensees also reserves the right to install and operate electric and telephone lines, poles and appurtenances thereto; gas and water mains and appurtenances thereto; sewer lines, culverts and drainage ditches, reserving also the rights of ingress and egress to above mentioned installations. Cumberland Plateau Resorts, Inc., for itself, its successors, assigns and licensees also reserves the right to locate and install drains where it deems necessary and to cause or permit drainage of surface waters over and/or through said land. The owners of said land shall have no cause of action against Cumberland Plateau Resorts, Inc., its successors, assigns, or licensees either at law or equity, excepting in cases of wilful negligence, by reason of any damages caused said land in installing, operation and maintaining above mentioned installations.

BASEBALL PUBLISHING CO. v. BRUTON

Supreme Court of Massachusetts, 1938.
302 Mass. 54, 18 N.E.2d 362.

LUMMUS, Justice.

The plaintiff, engaged in the business of controlling locations for billboards and signs and contracting with advertisers for the exhibition of their placards and posters, obtained from the defendant on October 9, 1934, a writing signed but not sealed by the defendant whereby the defendant "in consideration of twenty-five dollars . . . agrees to give" the plaintiff "the exclusive right and privilege to maintain advertising sign one 10' × 25' on wall of building 3003 Washington Street" in Boston, owned by the defendant, "for a period of one year with the privilege of renewal from year to year for four years more at the same consideration." It was provided that "all signs placed on the premises remain the personal property of the plaintiff." The writing was headed "Lease No. ___." It was not to be effective until accepted by the plaintiff.

It was accepted in writing on November 10, 1934, when the plaintiff sent the defendant a check for $25, the agreed consideration for the first year. The defendant returned the check. The plaintiff nevertheless erected the contemplated sign, and maintained it until February 23, 1937, sending the defendant early in November of the years 1935 and 1936 checks for $25 which were returned. On February 23, 1937, the defendant caused the sign to be removed. On February 26, 1937, the plaintiff brought this bill for specific performance, contending that the writing was a lease. The judge ruled that the writing was a contract to give a license, but on November 2, 1937, entered a final decree for specific performance, with damages and costs. The defendant appealed. It is stipulated that on November 3, 1937, the plaintiff tendered $25 for the renewal of its right for another year beginning November 10, 1937, but the defendant refused the money.

The distinction between a lease and a license is plain, although at times it is hard to classify a particular instrument. A lease of land conveys an interest in land, requires a writing to comply with the statute of frauds though not always a seal, and transfers possession. A license merely excuses acts done by one on land in possession of another that without the license would be trespasses, conveys no interest in land, and may be contracted for or given orally. A lease of a roof or a wall for advertising purposes is possible. The writing in question, however, giving the plaintiff the "exclusive right and privilege to maintain advertising sign . . . on wall of building," but leaving the wall in the possession of the owner with the right to use it for all purposes not forbidden by the contract and with all the responsibilities of ownership and control, is not a lease. The fact that in one corner of the writing are found the words, "Lease No. ___," does not convert it into a lease. Those words are merely a misdescription of the writing.

Subject to the right of a licensee to be on the land of another for a reasonable time after the revocation of a license, for the purpose of removing his chattels, it is of the essence of a license that it is revocable at the will of the possessor of the land. The revocation of a license may constitute a breach of contract, and give rise to an action for damages. But it is none the less effective to deprive the licensee of all justification for entering or remaining upon the land.

If what the plaintiff bargained for and received was a license, and nothing more, then specific performance that might compel the defendant to renew the license, leaving it revocable at will, would be futile and for that reason should not be granted. Specific performance that might render the license irrevocable for the term of the contract would convert it into an equitable estate in land, and give the plaintiff more than the contract gave. There can be no specific performance of a contract to give a license, at least in the absence of fraud or estoppel.

The writing in the present case, however, seems to us to go beyond a mere license. It purports to give "the exclusive right and privilege to maintain" a certain sign on the defendant's wall. So far as the law permits, it should be so construed as to vest in the plaintiff the right which it purports to give. That right is in the nature of an easement in gross, which, whatever may be the law elsewhere, is recognized in Massachusetts. We see no objection to treating the writing as a grant for one year and a contract to grant for four more years an easement in gross thus limited to five years. Similar writings have been so treated in other jurisdictions.

An easement, being inconsistent with seisin in the person owning it, always lay in grant and could not be created by livery of seisin. It is an interest in land within the statute of frauds and, apart from prescription, requires a writing for its creation. Indeed, the creation of a legal freehold interest in an easement, apart from prescription, requires a deed. And differing from a lease of land for not more than seven years, a grant of an easement for as short a term as five years apparently requires a deed in order to create a legal interest. But in equity a seal is not necessary to the creation of an easement. Since equity treats an act as done where there is a duty to do it enforceable in equity, or, as more tersely phrased, equity treats that as done which ought to be done, an enforceable unsealed contract such as the writing in this case, providing for the creation of an easement, actually creates an easement in equity.

There is no error in the final decree granting specific performance. The affirmance of this decree will not prevent an assessment of the damages as of the date of the final decree after rescript.

Interlocutory decree overruling demurrer affirmed.

Final decree affirmed, with costs.

STONER v. ZUCKER

Supreme Court of California, 1906.
148 Cal. 516, 83 P. 808.

HENSHAW, J. Plaintiff pleaded that defendants had entered upon his land in 1899, under license, and had constructed thereon and thereover a ditch for the carrying of water; that he never conveyed or agreed to convey to the defendants any right of way, easement, or interest in the land for the purpose, and their right to construct and maintain the ditch rested wholly upon this license; that in 1900 he served notice upon them that the license to construct and operate the ditch had been revoked and abrogated by him. Notwithstanding this notice of revocation and abrogation, the defendants, disregarding it, have continuously entered upon plaintiff's land, making repairs upon the ditch and restoring the same where it was broken and washed away, and defendants threaten to continue this trespass upon the lands of the plaintiff. Plaintiff therefore prayed that the defendants be adjudged trespassers and be enjoined from the use of the ditch or from in any manner entering upon the lands of the plaintiff to repair or otherwise maintain it. The evidence established, without controversy, that defendants constructed the ditch for the purpose of carrying water for irrigation to their own and other lands, and had expended upon the ditch the sum of seven thousand and more dollars. The court found that "a right of way for the construction and maintenance of the ditch for the purpose of taking water from Santa Ana river for use in connection with and upon defendants' lands was given and granted by the plaintiff to the defendants, and that the defendants are the owners of a right of way for said ditch for the purpose aforesaid." The court further found that there was a consideration for the "granting of said right of way, in that defendants contracted and agreed with the plaintiff to deliver to and for the use of the plaintiff on his land lying under said canal sufficient water to irrigate the land, and the defendants have at all times delivered said water so agreed to be delivered. This last finding derives no support from the evidence, and the first finding, to the effect that the plaintiff "granted" a right of way, can be supported only upon the understanding that the court by "grant" meant that "permission" was given to defendants for the construction and maintenance of the ditch. So construing the findings, the question is squarely presented as to the revocability or nonrevocability of an executed parol license, whose execution has involved the expenditure of money, and where, from the very nature of the license given, it was to be continuous in use.

Appellant contends that a parol license to do an act upon the land of the licensor, while it justifies anything done by the licensee before revocation, is revocable at the option of the licensor, so that no further acts may be justified under it, and this, although the intention was to confer a continuing right, and money has been expended by the licensor upon the faith of the license, and that such a license cannot be changed into an equitable right on the ground of equitable estoppel. To the support of this proposition is offered authority of great weight and of the highest respectability. The argument in brief is that a license in its very nature is a revocable permission, that whoever accepts that permission does it with knowledge that the permission may be revoked at any time; that the rule cannot be changed, therefore, because the licensee has foolishly or improvidently expended money in the hope of a continuance of a license, upon the permanent continuance of which he has no right in law or in equity to rely; that to convert such a parol license into a grant or easement under the doctrine of estoppel is destructive of the statute of frauds, which was meant to lay down an inflexible rule; and, finally, that there is no room or play for the operation of the doctrine of estoppel, since the licensor has in no way deceived the licensee by revocation, has put no fraud upon him, and has merely asserted a right which had been absolutely reserved to him by the very terms of his permission. No one has stated this argument more clearly and cogently than Judge Cooley, who, holding to this construction of the law, has expressed it in his work on Torts. Cooley, Torts (2d Ed.) 364. But that the same eminent jurist recognized the injustice and the hardship which followed such a conclusion is plainly to be seen from his opinion in Maxwell v. Bay City Bridge Co., 41 Mich. 453, 2 N.W. 639, where, discussing this subject, he says: "But the injustice of a revocation after the licensee, in reliance upon the license, has made large and expensive improvements, is so serious that it seems a reproach to the law that it should fail to provide some adequate protection against it. Some of the courts have been disposed to enforce the license as a parol contract which has been performed on one side." Indeed, the learned jurist, with equal accuracy, might have stated that the majority of courts have so decided, in accordance with the leading case of Rerick v. Kern, 14 Serg. & R. 267, 16 Am.Dec. 497. That case was carefully considered, and it was held that it would be to countenance a fraud upon the part of the licensor if he were allowed, after expenditure of money by the licensees upon the faith of the license, to cut short by revocation the natural term of its continuance and existence, and that under the doctrine of estoppel, the licensor would not be allowed to do this. The decision was that the licensor would be held to have conveyed an easement commensurate in its extent and duration with the right to be enjoyed. In that case there was a parol license without consideration to use the waters of a stream for a sawmill, and it was held it could not be revoked at the grantor's pleasure, where the grantee, in consequence of the license, had erected a mill. The court in that case says, after discussion: "It is to be considered as if there had been a formal conveyance of the right, and nothing remains but to determine its duration and extent. A right under a license, when not specifically restricted, is commensurate with the thing of which the license is an accessory." And the court said further: "Having in view an unlimited enjoyment of the privilege, the grantee has purchased by the expenditure of money, a right indefinite in point of duration, which cannot be forfeited by a nonuser unless for a period sufficient to raise the presumption of a release. The right to rebuild in case of destruction or dilapidation and to continue the business on its original footing may have been in fact as necessary to his safety, and may have been an inducement of the particular investment in the first instance."

It will not be necessary to multiply citations of authority upon this point. It is sufficient to refer to the very instructive comment of Prof. Freeman to the case of Rerick v. Kern, reported in 16 Am.Dec., at page 497. The learned author of the note concludes his review by saying, as he shows, that "it will be seen that the doctrine of the principal case, though not recognized in some of our state courts, is, nevertheless, expressive of the law as administered by the majority of them, and that the preponderance of recent judicial opinions is in harmony with the views of Judge Gibson." This court in the case of Flickinger v. Shaw, 87 Cal. 126, 25 Pac. 268, 11 L.R.A. 134, 22 Am.St. Rep. 234, discussed and approved the case of Rerick v. Kern, supra. It was not called upon there to pass upon the precise question here presented, because in that case defendant had entered and expended money upon a parol agreement to convey a right of way, and the court was called upon merely to decide in consonance with undisputed equitable principles that that parol agreement was enforceable, but in

Smith v. Green, 109 Cal. 234, 41 Pac. 1024, the exact principle here announced is distinctly recognized, and it is said: "The general rule, no doubt, is that one who rests his claim to an easement on a verbal contract alone, unexecuted and unaccompanied by any other facts, has no rights thereto which he can enforce. But there are many cases where a mere parol license which has been executed, and where investments have been made upon the faith of it, has been held irrevocable. Gould on Waters, §§ 232, 324." The recognized principle, therefore, is that where a licensee has entered under a parol license and has expended money, or its equivalent in labor, in the execution of the license, the license becomes irrevocable, the licensee will have a right of entry upon the lands of the licensor for the purpose of maintaining his structures or, in general, his rights under his license, and the license will continue for so long a time as the nature of it calls for. Thus, for example, where the license was to erect a lumber mill, the license came to an end when the timber available for use at that mill had been worked up into lumber. The same has been held as to a milldam, the right to maintain the dam continuing so long as there was use for the mill, and the right being lost by abandonment and disuse only when the nonuser had continued for a period sufficient to raise the presumption of release. In the case of irrigating ditches, drains, and the like, the license becomes, in all essentials, an easement, continuing for such length of time, under the indicated conditions, as the use itself may continue.

For these reasons the judgment and order appealed from are affirmed.

We concur: McFARLAND, J.; LORIGAN, J.

NOTES

1. Statutes commonly require that grants of easements comply with the same formalities as conveyances of possessory interests. The Statute of Frauds applies and is usually interpreted as requiring a written instrument that accurately identifies the servient and the dominant estates and the location and extent of the easement. The once standard requirement that an instrument be sealed in order to create an easement, covenant or servitude has today been almost universally eliminated. But see Alaska Stats. § 34.15.010 (1975).

Despite the statutory insistence on form, courts often in fact relax the formal requirements for easements. Martinez v. Martinez, 93 N.M. 673, 604 P.2d 366 (1979), is typical. Plaintiff, whose deed from defendant loosely "provided for rights of ingress and egress," sought to enforce a right of way easement across defendant's land. Holding that a "right of ingress and egress is descriptive of the easement right," and that "the language in this deed is certain and definite," the court concluded that plaintiff had an express easement to cross defendant's land in order to obtain access to his own land, and remanded for the trial court to locate the easement. Justice Payne, dissenting, objected that "the majority has read more into the deed than the law allows," as the language was not sufficiently definite to clearly show intent to grant an easement. In Payne's view the deed was fatally defective because "there is no mention in the deed of a particular road or way, nor is there mention of a servient estate supporting the easement." 93 N.M. at 676, 604 P.2d at 369.

Also, decisions that do invalidate express easements for failure to comply with statutory formalities should be taken with a grain of salt; invalidation of an express easement is sometimes only a prelude to implying an easement, typically on the ground of necessity. See page 684, below. See also, Oliver v. Ernul, 277 N.C. 591, 178 S.E.2d 393 (1971). The two principal cases, Baseball Publishing v. Bruton and Stoner v. Zucker, offer two other examples of judicial techniques for relaxing formalities.

Does Paragraph 7 of the Tansi Resort CC & Rs, set out at page 674 above, adequately describe the extent and location of the easements created there? Are the "rights" mentioned in the second sentence of Paragraph 7 governed by the limitation in the preceding sentence, ". . . as shown on said plats"? What of the "right to locate and install drains," reserved in the third sentence?

2. *Affirmative Easements.* Affirmative easements can, in subdivisions like the Tansi Resort, be used to assure residents access to parking lots, laundry areas, swimming pools, tennis courts, and other recreational facilities dispersed throughout the development. Right of way and utility easements can connect the owners of interior lots to public roads, sewers, power and telephone lines. In shopping centers, a Reciprocal Easement and Operating Agreement may give each tenant and its customers access to common facilities such as parking areas, entrances, exits, walkways, and commercial spaces; in larger centers, it is not unusual for the R.E.O.A. to run to 100 pages or more of closely drafted provisions.

Affirmative easements are limited only by the draftsman's imagination. In addition to subdivision and shopping center easements and to the garden variety right of way and utility easements, there are, to sample just a few: aviation easements, allowing aircraft to fly over the servient estate at low altitudes; encroachment easements, allowing terraces and window air conditioners from adjacent buildings to overhang the servient estate; pasture easements, allowing ranchers to graze their livestock on the servient estate; drainage or flowage easements allowing the owner of the dominant estate to divert flood waters over the surface of the servient estate; and pollution easements, allowing the discharge of contaminants over and onto the servient estate.

3. *Negative Easements.* Not nearly as much variety or innovation is permitted in negative easements—easements for light and air; for greater lateral and subjacent support than required by law; and for the unimpeded flow of an artificial stream across the dominant

estate. The common law has been slow to recognize new categories, apparently concerned that parties would too freely enter into restrictive land use arrangements that provide no countervailing social benefits. Expansion, when it occurs, is toward approval of easements that are closely analogous to the existing categories and that can be demonstrated to benefit an adjacent parcel. One such interest, accepted by some courts, is an easement that restricts the development of the servient estate to assure an attractive view from the neighboring dominant estate. Should the common law recognize conservation easements aimed at preserving scenic views from adjacent public highways and parks? What of landmark preservation easements, prohibiting changes in the exterior of historically important buildings?

4. *Solar Easements.* The newest negative easement is a statutory creation. At last count, more than a dozen states have enacted laws recognizing solar easements. The object of a solar easement is to prohibit any improvement on the servient estate that will prevent direct sunlight from reaching a solar collector situated on the dominant estate. The Colorado statute, Colo.Rev.Stat. § 38–32.5–102 (1982), is typical. Section 38–32.5–102 provides:

Contents. (1) Any instrument creating a solar easement shall include, but the contents shall not be limited to:

(a) A description of the vertical and horizontal angles, expressed in degrees together with any pertinent hourly, diurnal, or seasonal variations thereof, and measured from the site of the solar energy device, within which the solar easement extends over the real property subject to the solar easement, or any other description which defines the three-dimensional space or the place and time of day in which an obstruction to direct sunlight is prohibited or limited;

(b) Any terms or conditions or both under which the solar easement is granted or will be terminated;

(c) Any provisions for compensation of the owner of the property benefitting from the solar easement in the event of interference with the enjoyment of the solar easement or compensation of the owner of the property subject to the solar easement for maintaining the solar easement;

(d) The restrictions placed upon vegetation, structures, and other objects which would impair or obstruct the passage of sunlight through the easement.

Section 38–32.5–101 adds that solar easements "shall be created in writing and shall be subject to the same conveyancing and instrument recording requirements as other easements, except that a solar easement shall not be acquired by prescription."

See generally, Gergacz, Solar Energy Law: Easements of Access to Sunlight, 10 N.M.L.Rev. 121 (1979–80); Pfeiffer, Ancient Lights: Legal Protection of Access to Solar Energy, 68 A.B.A.J. 288 (1982);

Pedowitz, Solar Energy Easements, 15 Real Prop.Prob. & Trust J. 797 (1980). See also, Gaumnitz & Gergacz, How to Draft and Determine the Value of Express Solar Access Easements, 9 Real Est.L.J. 128 (1980–1981).

5. Compare *Stoner* with Nelson v. American Telephone & Telegraph Co., 270 Mass. 471, 170 N.E. 416 (1930), in which the Massachusetts Supreme Court ruled that defendant, AT & T, had obtained no rights under an unsealed and unacknowledged 1893 deed from plaintiff's predecessor purporting to grant AT & T, its successors and assigns, the right "to construct, operate and maintain its lines" over his property, even though AT & T had promptly installed thirty-two poles carrying thirty-four wires, and had maintained the installation for more than thirty years with the apparent acquiescence both of plaintiff's predecessor and of plaintiff. Reversing the lower court decree which had denied plaintiff's request for an injunction and had awarded him instead $400 damages "for the retention by the defendant of a permanent easement," the supreme court remanded for a determination of "the time within which the defendant shall remove its poles, wires, and other property and restore the plaintiff's land to a proper condition." 270 Mass. at 482, 170 N.E. at 420.

In the high court's view, "the defendant at all times must be held to have known that the instrument under which it was permitted to occupy and use the locus was a mere license which was revocable and gave it no estate or interest in the land. It was also bound to know when it entered upon and used the locus that the license was revocable not only at the will of the owner of the property on which it is to be exercised but by his death, by alienation, or demise of the land by him, and by whatever would deprive the original owner of the right to do the acts in question, or give permission to others to do them." 270 Mass. at 480, 170 N.E. at 420.

Which result is better, *Stoner* or *Nelson*? What could plaintiff have done to protect itself against the decision in *Stoner*? What could AT & T have done to protect itself against the decision in *Nelson*? Can the cases be distinguished on the basis of AT & T's presumed superior expertise and bargaining power? How would the *Stoner* court have treated an instrument that expressly limited an easement to some point short of its "natural life"? What limits are there to an "easement commensurate in its extent and duration with the right to be enjoyed"?

Should a distinction be drawn between cases in which the parties clearly intended a parol license and made no effort to execute an easement, and cases in which they did attempt an easement but failed for noncompliance with one or more formalities? If so, does the distinction suggest that both *Stoner* and *Nelson* were wrongly decided?

In *Nelson*, the Massachusetts Supreme Court was apparently not disturbed by the fact that plaintiff suffered only $400 "damage" from the poles and wires, while AT & T's cost of removing its lines and placing them elsewhere would exceed $5000. In the bargaining between Nelson and AT & T after the supreme court's decree, how little would Nelson be willing to accept, and how much would AT & T be willing to pay, to leave the poles and wires in place? From a policy viewpoint, can you comfortably say that one figure is preferable to the other?

Is *Nelson* still good law in Massachusetts after the Massachusetts Supreme Court's decision eight years later in Baseball Publishing v. Bruton? What relevant difference, if any, is there between an unsealed grant of an easement, and an unsealed contract that is treated as "a grant for a year and a contract to grant for four more years an easement in gross" if the parties in both cases invested in reliance on the underlying document?

6. *Licenses.* At any given moment, more people occupy land under license than under any other form of legal arrangement. For every one person in possession of land, there are probably thousands more exercising licenses to enter movie theatres, ball parks, museums, rock concerts, shops and restaurants. For every one who holds a right of way, there are probably tens of thousands licensed to enter the grounds of public schools, colleges, professional schools, hospitals, retirement homes, their places of work and those of their doctors, lawyers, accountants and auto mechanics.

Despite their widespread, indeed pervasive, use, licenses occupy only a small corner in real property law. The reason, of course, is that, because licenses can be revoked by either licensor or licensee at any time, they are too slender and fragile to support the kind of investment that is routinely made in easements, covenants and servitudes. Although the theatre owner who ejects a patron may be liable for breach of the contract implied in the ticket of admission, the patron's remedies are strictly contractual, for he has no enforceable interest in the land itself.

Stoner represents one of the two ways in which a revocable license may become an irrevocable easement. The other is the so-called license coupled with an interest which arises when A, the owner of Whiteacre, sells goods situated on Whiteacre to B, and expressly or impliedly gives B the privilege of collecting the goods or other chattels. B's privilege to go on Whiteacre becomes irrevocable for a reasonable period. Restatement of Property § 513 comment b, illustration 3 (1944) gives as an example, "A, the owner and possessor of Whiteacre, sells to B a car of coal already mined and standing on Whiteacre, which is owned and possessed by A. If there is an effective sale of the coal, B has a license coupled with an interest to get on Whiteacre to remove the coal." But if A instead grants B all the coal running through a specified vein in Whiteacre, so that B becomes the owner of the coal in place, "B has, as incidental to the ownership of the coal, an implied privilege to enter Whiteacre to sever and remove coal. This privilege is a part of an easement appurtenant to the coal *as land* and is *not* a license." § 513 comment b, illustration 1.

b. BY IMPLICATION AND NECESSITY

CHENEY v. MUELLER
Supreme Court of Oregon, 1971.
259 Or. 108, 485 P.2d 1218.

TONGUE, Justice.

Defendants appeal from a judgment granting to plaintiffs an easement by implied reservation across defendants' property.

Plaintiffs' complaint, after alleging the facts, asked that the deed from plaintiffs to defendants be reformed to include a reference to "existing rights of way for roads"; that defendants be enjoined from blocking the access road to a house subsequently sold by plaintiffs to a Mr. Hansen and "for such other and further relief as to the court seems just and equitable." Defendants' answer, in addition to a general denial, also asked for affirmative relief requiring plaintiffs to deliver a warranty deed subject only to easements of record, and thus excluding the disputed access road.

Since the granting of an easement by implied reservation depends primarily upon a determination of the intent of the parties, as reflected by their conduct and in the light of the particular facts and circumstances, the principal question in this case is one of fact.

In November 1958 [e] plaintiffs sold to defendants the property in question, consisting of a service station and trailer park near Prineville, Oregon. At that time plaintiffs also owned adjacent property on the west of the trailer court. Both tracts fronted to the south on a highway running west to Prineville. Plaintiffs also then owned property to the north of the trailer court and had previously owned property adjacent to it both on the west and the east. In selling the property to the east of the trailer court a road easement eight feet in width was provided, running north and south along the east side of the trailer court property so as to provide access to the purchasers of portions of the property northeast and east of it. The original tract owned by plaintiffs (before these sales) included 33 acres and was purchased by them in 1947.

At the time of the sale to defendants the plaintiffs owned two houses on the property immediately west of the trailer court, one of which also fronted on the highway. The other house (later sold to Mr. Hansen and called the "Hansen house" throughout this case) was built in 1948 by Mr. Cheney, who then lived in it for a time. At the time of the sale of the trailer court to defendants the "Hansen house" was occupied by a Mrs. Baker, who was employed by plaintiffs in

---

e. *Sic.* Should probably read, "November, 1967" or "August, 1968."

operating the trailer court. The access to that house is the problem in this case.

At that time, of course, there was no legal problem of access to the "Hansen house," since both that house and the adjacent property to the east, as well as to the south, were all owned by plaintiffs. As a practical matter, however, access to the car port on the east side of that house was provided by a roadway extending in a general easterly or southeasterly direction from that car port across the trailer park to the eight foot road easement extending along the east side of the trailer park property. At that time there was also a fence between plaintiffs' trailer park property and their adjacent property to the west, including the "Hansen house." However, a wire gate was provided in that fence for the roadway to that house at a point immediately opposite the entrance to the car port of that house. All previous occupants of the "Hansen house" used that roadway for access.

Prior to the sale to defendants a map had been prepared by a surveyor of the trailer park property and the property immediately north of it. That map also showed four tracts of property to the east of the trailer park, as previously sold by plaintiffs, together with a dotted line to show the location of the eight foot road easement extending along the east side of the trailer park property so as to provide access to three of such tracts. The map also included a metes and bounds description of that road easement, after which followed the words: "Subject to all existing easements and rights of way."

The map also showed a similar dotted line parallel to the north line of the trailer park property so as to indicate a strip of the same width extending along the north side of that tract and between it and the tract immediately north of the trailer court property. No metes and bounds description for that strip was shown on the map. The map did not show the location of the "Hansen house" or the gate opposite its car port. The surveyor who prepared that map testified that he added that "dotted line" at the request of Mr. Cheney after completing the remainder of the map and for that reason did not include a metes and bounds description of it. He also testified that the usual way to show an easement on a survey map is by dotted lines. He did not know whether the strip as shown by these dotted lines corresponded to any existing roadway. The evidence showed, however, that the west end of that strip terminated at or about the location of the gate opposite the "Hansen house" car port.

On the evening of Saturday, November 25, 1967, defendants came to look at the trailer park in response to an advertisement placed by plaintiffs and after corresponding with them. That same evening they also drove up to look at the "Hansen house," which was also for sale, Mr. Mueller having found out how to get to that house. In doing so, defendants drove through the trailer court and through the gate opposite the car port of that house, but said that they did not see the gate, which may have been open at that time.

The next day defendants also walked over the trailer court property. Meanwhile, there had been a light snow. They testified that they saw no car tracks in the snow leading across the trailer court property to the "Hansen house" (where they had driven the night before).

Defendants admitted that in showing them the trailer court property the next day Mr. Cheney showed them a map "like" the one which showed the "strip" by a dotted line running east and west along the north line of the trailer court property. Defendants also said that they asked if that map had been recorded, but did not rely on it. Defendants testified that there was no discussion of that "strip" or of any roadway or right of way to the "Hansen house." They also testified that there was no "defined roadway" at that time and that there could have been no roadway along the "strip" shown on the map because of a four foot "bank" at the west end of that "strip."

Plaintiffs testified, on the contrary, that in showing defendants the property they not only showed defendants the map in going over the property, but informed them of the roadway, although admitting that "nothing in particular" was said about it. Mr. Cheney also testified that the "tracks" on the roadway through the gate to the "Hansen house" were "plain" at that time. He also testified that he had previously put rock on that roadway.

After looking at the trailer court property, defendants decided also to buy the tract immediately north of it (and north of the "strip" as shown on the map along the boundary of that tract). A price was then agreed upon for both tracts and an earnest money contract was then prepared by plaintiffs' attorney and signed by both parties on November 28, 1967. A copy of the same survey map, showing the same "strip" in dotted lines, was referred to and attached, as well as a legal description, which included a metes and bounds description of the road easement along the east side of the property and also again added "subject to all existing easements and rights of way."

The attorney then prepared a formal contract, dated December 5, 1967, which included the same description, but added the words, "subject to other existing easements and rights of ways *now of record if any.*" Later, however, on payment of the contract, a deed was prepared by the same attorney and executed on August 15, 1968, with a description in substantially the same terms as the earnest money contract ("also subject to existing rights of way for roads"), but not including either the limitation "now of record if any" or reference to the word "easements," as included in the contract of sale.

After executing the earnest money receipt defendants returned to their home in Alaska and did not take possession of the property until March or April 1968. Meanwhile, Mrs. Baker operated the trailer court for them and continued to live in the "Hansen house" until July 1968. During that time she continued to use the same roadway for access to the house, without objection by defendants. At that time, however, she was still employed by them.

After Mrs. Baker moved out, the house was vacant until sold by plaintiffs to Mr. Hansen. On May 5, 1969, plaintiffs sold the "Hansen house" to Mr. Hansen, showed him the same map, and told him that there was an easement across the Mueller property to the roadway along the east side of that property. The contract of sale to Hansen made no reference to any access roadway or easement, but describes only the tract actually conveyed and which is adjacent to the trailer park on the west. That tract is also adjacent to plaintiffs' remaining property (and house), which was also adjacent to the trailer park on the west, but south of the "Hansen house" and between it and the highway.

Mr. Mueller also testified that he never heard of an easement to the "Hansen house" until after Mr. Hansen moved in; that he then went to see the attorney who prepared the deed, who told him there was no such easement, and that when he first talked to Mr. Hansen about it, Hansen agreed to find another way into the house, but wanted "a couple of weeks" to do so; that Mueller then waited several weeks and then put up a fence to close off the access to the "Hansen house" across his property. During that period, according to Mr. Mueller, the traffic to the "Hansen house" was getting "unbearable" and on one occasion a party at the house late at night kept the "whole trailer court awake." Defendants also complained of the dust and noise resulting from use of the roadway by Mr. Hansen as not good for the trailer court business and said that customers had complained to them.

According to Mr. Cheney, however, after defendants built the fence and blocked access to the "Hansen house," he went to see Mr. Mueller and said "don't you know the easement is there" and that Mr. Mueller said, "Well, yes, I know it's there," but "I don't know for what purpose." Mr. Cheney also testified that after the sale to Mr. Hansen, and apparently before that conversation, Mr. Mueller came to him and said that he was "fifty feet too far down the hill with the road easement" (the east-west "strip" in question) and that they then "chained" it together and found that it was "within one foot." He also testified that defendants then asked to move it four feet up the hill and that he said that he didn't think Mr. Hansen would object "as long as it's put on the map and you rebuild the road as it now is with rock on it."

Defendants denied any such conversation and denied that there was any rock on the roadway when they bought this property and said that the only measurement they made with Mr. Cheney was to find a stake on the east line of the property and that this was in 1968. Mrs. Mueller stated, however, that what they were objecting to was not the Hansens using the road, but the manner in which they used it, including use late at night.

Plaintiffs also offered evidence that, according to records showing the amounts of periodic gasoline and oil deliveries to defendants, their business increased in 1969 over 1968, showing that it had not been damaged by use of the roadway by Mr. Hansen.

It appears from the evidence that for some time after defendants built the fence Mr. Hansen was obliged to get to his house by driving across lands owned by a third party to the west of his house, but leading to the back door on the west side of the house, rather than to the car port on the east side of the house. It also appears from the evidence that other access to the highway would have required building a road directly to the south from the "Hansen house" across the lot retained by plaintiffs between the "Hansen house" and the highway, but this apparently would have required removal of a "rock house" building.

In addition, it appears that after purchasing the trailer court Mr. Mueller made some changes in the area immediately east of the Hansen car port and that the actual roadway leading to the "Hansen house" does not follow the exact location of the eight foot "strip" on the map, but proceeds from the car port in more of a southeasterly direction across defendants' property to the roadway along the east side of that property. The record also shows that the trial judge viewed the property and observed that it would not be practical to run a road "as shown on the map."

This court has previously recognized that an easement may be created by implication in favor of either the grantor or grantee. Rose et ux v. Denn, 188 Or. 1, 19, 212 P.2d 1077, 213 P.2d 810 (1950). It has also recognized, however, that implied easements are not favored by the courts and that a plaintiff has the burden of establishing such an easement. Dressler et al v. Isaacs et al, 217 Or. 586, 596, 343 P.2d 714 (1959).

In addition, this court in *Rose* and *Dressler* approved the rule as stated in 5 Restatement, Property § 476, setting forth the following factors as "important" in determining "whether the circumstances under which a conveyance of land (was) made imply an easement":

"(a) whether the claimant is the conveyor or the conveyee,

"(b) the terms of the conveyance,

"(c) the consideration given for it,

"(d) whether the claim is made against a simultaneous conveyee,

"(e) the extent of necessity of the easement to the claimant,

"(f) whether reciprocal benefits result to the conveyor and the conveyee,

"(g) the manner in which the land was used prior to its conveyance, and

"(h) the extent to which the manner of prior use was or might have been known to the parties."

As stated in Comment (a), under § 476, these facts are "variables rather than absolutes" and "None can be given a fixed value." The reason for considering these factors, as stated in *Dressler*, 217 Or. at 597, 343 P.2d at 719, is that:

> "At the time of the severance of the land the circumstances must be such as to permit an inference that had the grantor put his mind to the matter he would have intended the servitude to be created. . . ."

As also stated in *Dressler*, however, 217 Or. at p. 599, 343 P.2d at p. 720:

> "We think that the proper adjustment of the conflicting claims of the parties in this type of case can be arrived at more directly by attempting to determine what a reasonable grantee would be justified in expecting as a part of his bargain when he purchases land under the particular circumstances. . . ."

After considering the entire record in this case in the light of these various "factors," and also bearing in mind that while this is a suit in equity, determinations by the trial court based upon conflicting evidence are entitled to considerable weight, we have concluded that the trial court was correct in finding an easement by implied reservation in this case.

Of the various factors to be considered in reaching this result the following are controlling, in our opinion, under the facts of this case:

(1) *The terms of the conveyance.*

The terms of the conveyance by plaintiffs to defendants, while not alone sufficient to reserve such an easement, at least did not expressly warrant against any such easement and, on the contrary, included the words "also subject to existing rights of way for roads" and omitted the additional term "now of record," as used in the preceding contract.

(2) *The prior use of the roadway.*

Although prior use of a roadway on land subsequently conveyed, but while still also owned by the grantor, cannot of itself establish an easement, nevertheless, as stated in Comment i under § 476:

> "The inference of intention is strengthened by the extent to which the prior use has resulted in a physical adaptation of the premises to such use. . . ."

(3) *Extent of knowledge of prior use.*

While defendants in this case denied knowledge of the prior use of the easement in dispute by occupants of the "Hansen house," in walking over the trailer court property prior to its purchase they could hardly have failed to notice that the car port of that house faced the trailer court property, with an apparently open gate in front of the car port. Indeed, they had themselves driven to that house across the trailer court the night before. In addition, plaintiffs testified that on showing the property to defendants mention was made of the roadway to that house and that he showed them a map (later attached to the earnest money contract) on which an eight foot "strip" across the property at that approximate location was marked by dotted lines in the same manner as the admitted roadway easement along the east side of the property. As stated in Comment j, § 476:

"To draw such an inference the prior use must have been known to the parties at the time of the conveyance, or, at least, have been within the possibility of their knowledge at that time. Each party to a conveyance is bound not merely to what he intended, but also to what he might reasonably have foreseen the other party to the conveyance expected. Parties to a conveyance may, therefore, be assumed to intend the continuance of uses known to them which are in a considerable degree necessary to the continued usefulness of the land. . . . The degree of necessity required to imply an easement in favor of the conveyor is greater than that required in the case of the conveyee (see Comment c). Yet, even in the case of the conveyor, the implication from necessity will be aided by a previous use made apparent by the physical adaptation of the premises to it."

In addition, as stated in Comment i, § 476:

"The fact that a use has been made may justify the inference that it was intended to continue though the degree of necessity existing is less than would be required for the implication of an easement on the basis of necessity alone. . . ."

(4) *Extent of necessity for easement.*

This leaves for consideration the factor of "the extent of necessity of the easement to the claimant." We have previously held in Dressler v. Isaacs, *supra*, 217 Or. at 598, 343 P.2d at p. 720:

"Reasonable need for the use of an easement is a flexible concept which may be described by an infinite range of circumstances; at one extreme it could mean that without the claimed right no effective use could be made of the alleged dominant estate, and at the other extreme it could mean that the use of that estate would be less convenient only. . . ."

As also held by this court in Jack v. Hunt et ux, 200 Or. 263, 264 P.2d 461, 265 P.2d 251 (1953), at 269, 264 P.2d 461, at 464:

"We are of the opinion that in matters of this kind the rule should be less strict than that of absolute and indispensable necessity. However, such a rule of reasonable necessity should not be grounded in mere convenience, but rather in the necessity appearing from the apparent purpose, the adaptability, and the known use to which the property is to be put. This so that the court may say that the parties as reasonable men contemplated and duly considered the continued use of the quasi easement claimed as necessary to a reasonable enjoyment of the dominant estate at the time of conveyance."

We nevertheless recognize, as held in *Dressler,* 217 Or. at p. 603, 343 P.2d p. 722, that "Ordinarily, if the dominant land can be used without an easement by a reasonable expenditure the factor of necessity is lacking."

Although the extent of necessity for the easement in this case is not as strong as the other "factors" previously mentioned, we nevertheless feel constrained to agree that the fact of the previous use of the roadway, as testified to by plaintiffs' witnesses, and the fact that defendants knew of such use, according to such testimony, justifies the inference that the parties intended that the use of the roadway by the occupant of the "Hansen house" continue, even though not absolutely necessary. This inference is further strengthened by the testimony (although denied by defendants), that defendant Mueller, after the sale to Mr. Hansen, instead of immediately objecting to plaintiffs, stated only that the "strip" for the roadway as shown on the map appeared to be too far south. In addition, the alternate means of access would be expensive. Access across the land to the west would require its purchase from the owner of that land and access to the south would apparently require the moving of a building.

Accordingly, we find that the circumstances of this case are such as not only to "permit the inference that had the grantor put his mind to the matter he would have intended the servitude to be created," but also that this same result follows, under the facts of this case, when considered from the standpoint of "the reasonable expectations of a reasonable man receiving (such) conveyance of land" (to paraphrase Dressler, 217 Or. at pp. 597 and 600, 343 P.2d at pp. 719 and 721). We also agree with the trial judge, however, in holding that since an easement along the "strip" as shown on the map would be impractical, the easement should follow the traveled portion of the roadway to the easement along the east boundary of the Mueller property, with plaintiffs to pay the cost of any necessary survey.

Defendants contend that Jack v. Hunt, *supra,* is controlling and requires a contrary result, but we find the facts of that case to be quite different. We agree with defendants' further contention that there is a well defined distinction between an implied grant and an implied reservation and that the law will imply an easement in favor of a grantee more readily than in favor of a grantor. Whether the claimant is the grantor or grantee, however, is only one of the various factors to be considered under Restatement § 476, as previously approved by this court.

Defendants also contend that there was no clearly defined existing roadway, but there was a conflict of the testimony on that subject, just as there was with reference to the various conversations between the parties. We also reject defendants' contention that plaintiffs' proof was not sufficiently "clear and convincing," and hold that it was sufficient to establish that "the truth of the facts was highly probable," so as to satisfy the test of Cook v. Michael, 214 Or. 513, 514, 330 P.2d 1026 (1958).

Defendants' final contention is that since plaintiffs' complaint prayed for a reformation of the deed to include such an easement, the court erred in granting an easement on a theory of implied reservation. It appears from the record, however, that plaintiffs' complaint not only pleaded all of the facts necessary for relief on such a theory, but also included a prayer for "such other and further relief as to the court seems just and equitable." In addition, prior to resting their opening case, plaintiffs' counsel stated the contention that they were entitled to relief on a theory of a reservation of a quasi-easement by implication. Defendants made no claim of surprise, but proceeded with the trial without objection.

For all of these reasons, the judgment and decree of the trial court is affirmed, without costs to either party.

FINN v. WILLIAMS

Supreme Court of Illinois, 1941.
376 Ill. 95, 33 N.E.2d 226.

WILSON, Justice

February 16, 1895, Charles H. Williams owned a tract of land in Salisburg township, in Sangamon county, consisting of approximately 140 acres. On the day named, Williams conveyed 39.47 acres to Thomas J. Bacon. In 1937, the plaintiffs, Eugene E. Finn and Curtis Estallar Finn, acquired the title to this tract. The defendant, Zilphia Jane Williams, inherited the remaining 100 acres. By their complaint filed in the circuit court of Sangamon county, plaintiffs charge that the nearest and only available means of egress from and ingress to their land to a highway and to any market for their livestock and crops is by means of a right of way over defendant's tract immediately to the north; that their tract is not located or situated on any public highway and is entirely surrounded by land of strangers and the defendant's tract; that prior to and during all the time the 40 acres and the 100 acres constituted one tract and were owned by defendant's husband, the only means of ingress and egress to and from the single tract to a highway was by right of way in a northerly direction through a third tract of land north and adjacent to the present tract of defendant, and that this open road is still used by defendant as her only means of egress and ingress from and to the highway. The relief sought was the declaration of a right of way easement of necessity from the north line of plaintiffs' tract through the defendant's tract, to the beginning of the right of way road through the third tract mentioned. Answering, the defendant admitted that plaintiffs' land is not located or situated on any public highway but averred that since its severance from her land it is and has been located on a private road leading to the south to a public highway. This averment, plaintiffs denied. Evidence was heard, and a decree rendered adjudging the plaintiffs to be the owners of a right of way easement of necessity over defendant's 100 acres, as alleged. Defendant appeals directly to this court, a freehold being involved. . . .

Private permissive ways of ingress and egress over the land of strangers both to the east and to the south have been available to the successive owners, including plaintiffs, of the 40-acre tract since its severance from the 100-acre tract of the defendant in 1895, but each of the private ways over the lands of the adjoining strangers has been closed and, as defendant concedes, these permissive means of ingress and egress do not now exist. Two witnesses for defendant who had lived near the property in controversy for about sixty years testified to roads leading to the south and to the east from the 40-acre tract over the land of strangers. These roads were private roads over the property of strangers, and are now closed. Nathan Woodrum, defendant's son-in-law, testified that he had until recently lived on the 100-acre tract, and that a road through defendant's land connects with the road through the tract at the north, and that the road through this third tract is the only mode of access to the highway unless permission be obtained to go through the land of strangers. Since May, 1939, defendant has refused to permit plaintiffs to travel further over the right of way through her tract. As a result of defendant's action, the plaintiffs have been unable to take their livestock and farm products to market, have had no means of egress from or ingress to their 40 acres on which they live, and have had to walk to the township highway, a distance of about three-quarters of a mile, carrying such produce as they could.

The evidence does not sustain defendant's averment that plaintiffs have the use of a private road leading to the south to a public highway and defendant, by her concession that a present necessity exists, has apparently abandoned this claim. She maintains, however, that the necessity has arisen by reason of changed circumstances since the severance of the two tracts. Firmly established principles control. Where an owner of land conveys a parcel thereof which has no outlet to a highway except over the remaining lands of the grantor or over the land of strangers, a way by necessity exists over the remaining lands of the grantor. If, at one time, there has been unity of title, as here, the right to a way by necessity may lay dormant through several transfers of title and yet pass with each transfer as appurtenant to the dominant estate and be exercised at any time by the holder of the title thereto. Plaintiffs' land is entirely surrounded by property of strangers and the land of the defendant from which it was originally severed. A right of way easement of necessity was necessarily implied in the conveyance severing the two tracts in 1895, and passed by mesne conveyances to plaintiffs in 1937. The fact that the original grantee and his successors in interest have been permitted ingress to and egress from the 40 acres over the land owned by surrounding strangers is immaterial. When such permission is denied, as in the present case, the subsequent grantees may avail themselves of the dormant easement implied in the deed severing the dominant and servient estates.

The decree of the circuit court is right, and it is affirmed.

Decree affirmed.

NOTES

1. Would the *Cheney* court have found an implied easement if plaintiff had been unable to demonstrate *any* necessity to use the roadway across defendant's parcel? Can preexisting use alone support an inference that grantor and grantee intended the use to continue after the conveyance? Why was Cheney, whose parcel fronted on the east-west highway, the plaintiff in an action seeking an easement over Mueller's land to connect Hansen's lot to the eight foot road that connected to the east-west highway? One answer may be that the action was for reformation of the Cheney-Mueller deed. Another may be that Cheney's deed to Hansen warranted access to public roads, and that this suit was Cheney's way of making good on that promise. Yet another answer may be that Cheney was seeking to forestall an action by Hansen against him for declaration of an implied easement across Cheney's parcel.

If Cheney had failed in his action to establish an easement across Mueller's parcel, would Hansen have prevailed in a subsequent action for declaration of an easement across Cheney's parcel? The need for a right of way would certainly weigh in Hansen's favor, as would the fact that, when Hansen's parcel was split off, he was the grantee rather than the grantor. Weighing against Hansen would be the fact that there was no roadway in use over Cheney's parcel at the time of the conveyance. What do you suppose the parties intended at the time of the conveyance to Hansen? Would the case of Hansen v. Cheney look more like Cheney v. Mueller or Finn v. Williams?

Would Finn v. Williams have gone the same way if the court had applied the Restatement factors referred to in *Cheney*? Note that Restatement of Property § 476 focuses on "the circumstances under which a conveyance of land is made." What were the relevant circumstances surrounding the 1894 conveyance from Williams to Bacon? Is it likely that the parties intended the right of way to lie "dormant" through several transfers of title, passing with each transfer as appurtenant to the dominant estate? What if the Finns and their predecessors originally had received access to the parcel not by the permission of strangers, but rather from a public highway that was later closed? If the Finns had originally discharged their sewage through a private sewer facility that subsequently closed down, would they be entitled to connect into Williams' sewer lines? What limits, if any, are there to *Finn's* dormancy theory?

Was the *Finn* court enforcing the 1895 intent of the original parties, or was it enforcing its own 1941 notions respecting fairness and productive land use? Which approach better serves constitutionally protected expectations respecting land use? Which better serves interests in productive land use? Is there any way in which the *Finn* court could have compensated Williams for her lost use without acknowledging that its decision was depriving her of part of her interest in land?

2. "*Necessity.*" Necessity, although not the only fact from which intent to create an easement may be inferred, is certainly the central one. How much, and what kind, of necessity is needed to support the inference? Courts generally agree that "strict" or "absolute" necessity must be shown if the claimed easement was not being used at the time of the disputed conveyance; only "reasonable" or "some" necessity need be shown if there was a preexisting use at the time of the conveyance. But how strict is "strict" and how much less so is "reasonable"?

The Restatement conceptualizes strict necessity as characterizing an easement without which "the land cannot be effectively used," and the cases generally treat access to a landlocked parcel as meeting this criterion. Restatement of Property § 476, comment g (1944). But does the Restatement formula only beg the question? What *is* an "effective use"? To the neighbor of a landlocked parcel who desires peace and quiet, the parcel's most effective use may very well be as unoccupied open space. Is the real question whether the value of the adjoining parcels, taken together, will be greater with or without the use for which the easement is being sought?

You may find it helpful in answering these questions to compare decisions on implied easements with decisions on nuisances. The question in both contexts is whether one neighbor's unauthorized interference with another's land use should be permitted, and the implicit method in both is to attempt to reconstruct the agreement that the parties would have made had they expressly negotiated over the situation. The difference between the two contexts is that, while the law of implied easements looks to past necessity for evidence of the agreement that the parties would have made at the time of the original conveyance, the law of nuisance looks to present utilities in order to reconstruct the arrangement that the parties would have struck at the time of the lawsuit. How different is "necessity" from "utility"? Should implied easement cases discard their reliance on past intent and, like nuisance cases, focus on present utility? Is it a complete answer that the parties in implied easement cases will rarely face the problems of transaction costs that justify the imposition of nuisance rules?

Can Finn v. Williams be explained as relying on present utility rather than past necessity? Reliance on present utility in implied easement cases has respectable antecedents in early English practice. See, for example, Packer v. Welsted, 2 Sid. 39, 111, 82 Eng.Rep. 1244, 1284 (K.B.1658). See generally, Simonton, Ways By Necessity, 25 Colum.L.Rev. 571 (1925). For an excellent analysis of the shifting roles of the necessity requirement, see Glenn, Implied Easements in the North Carolina Courts: An Essay on the Meaning of "Necessary," 58 N.C.L.Rev. 223 (1979–1980).

3. In addition to weighing necessity and prior use, courts deciding whether to imply an easement will sometimes consider whether the claimed easement was created by grant or by reservation. An easement is implied by *grant* when A, who is using one part of his parcel to the benefit of another part, sells the part benefited (sometimes called the "quasi-dominant" estate) and retains the part burdened (the "quasi-servient" estate); the benefit is said to be granted along with the conveyance of the benefited parcel. An easement is implied by *reservation* when A conveys the quasi-servient estate and retains the quasi-dominant estate; the grantor is said to have reserved the benefit to himself.

Many, if not most states are more willing to imply an easement by grant than by reservation. Suffield v. Brown, 4 DeG.J. & S. 185 (Ch. 1864), the landmark case on the point, explains the principle behind the preference: "It seems to me more reasonable and just to hold that if the grantor intends to reserve any right over the property granted, it is his duty to reserve it expressly in the grant, rather than to limit and cut down the operation of a plain grant (which is not pretended to be otherwise than in conformity with the contract between the parties), by the fiction of an implied reservation." 4 DeG.J. & S. 190. Does this constructional principle accurately reflect modern conveyancing and title insurance practices under which the subject of easements is more likely to be the object of bargaining between grantor and grantee than of unilateral imposition by the grantor alone?

4. Cheney v. Miller and Finn v. Williams involved affirmative easements. Can a *negative* easement be implied by necessity? Say that A and B own adjoining lots acquired from common grantor O, and that B erects a ten-foot high wall, three inches within his boundary line, obstructing the passage of light and air through A's kitchen windows. Will A succeed in an action to have an easement of light and air implied into the conveyance from O, and requiring B as owner of the servient estate to remove the obstructing portion of the wall? In Maioriello v. Arlotta, 364 Pa. 557, 73 A.2d 374 (1950), the lower court decreed that the height of the wall be reduced from ten feet to six feet on the ground that, "because title to *both* premises had become vested in the same individual in 1916, and subsequently such owner conveyed the two properties separately, the grantor thereby created an easement of light and air, *by implication because of necessity.*" 364 Pa. at 559, 73 A.2d at 375.

The Pennsylvania Supreme Court reversed. Noting that an easement of light and air may be implied because of necessity, the court concluded that plaintiff's claim fell short in two respects. First, plaintiff had made no proofs respecting the sequence in which O had conveyed the two parcels. "In order that the defendant's lot should become servient to plaintiff's, the plaintiff must have acquired the servitude before the defendant bought. Then and only then would the defendant take title to his lot charged with the servitude." Second, "even if an easement of light and air would be *implied* in circumstances which reveal an absolute necessity, the finding of the learned Chancellor was that while a small amount of light and air was admitted into the kitchen, it was insufficient for the reasonable comfort, enjoyment and health of the plaintiff. This would constitute but a *partial* obstruction of light and air. But it was testified that a skylight can be placed in the ceiling of the kitchen, which would supply an ample amount of light and air. As it clearly appears that there exists no absolute necessity, no implied easement of light and air can be decreed." 364 Pa. at 559–561, 73 A.2d at 375–376.

5. *Statutory Solutions*. Several states have sought to remedy situations like those involved in *Cheney* and *Finn* through private condemnation statutes. For example, Wyo.Stat.1977, § 24–9–101 provides that "Any person whose land shall be so situated that it has no outlet to nor connection with a public road, may make application in writing to the board of county commissioners of his county at a regular session, for a private road leading from his premises to some convenient public road." Upon a finding of necessity, three appraisers are to be appointed by the board to "locate and mark out a private road in accordance with said application, not exceeding thirty (30) feet in width from a certain point on the premises of the applicant to some certain point on the public road, so as to do the least possible damage to the lands through which such private road is located, and they shall also at the same time assess the damages [to be paid by the applicant] sustained by the owner or owners over which such road is to be established . . . ." The Wyoming Supreme Court has interpreted the statute to allow landlocked owners to choose between pursuing the common law way of necessity and the statutory remedy. Walton v. Dana, 609 P.2d 461 (Wyo.1980). See generally, Note, Acquiring Access to Private Landlocked Tracts: Wyoming's Statutory Right-of-Way, 16 Land & Water L.Rev. 281 (1981).

Does the Wyoming statute violate the constitutional injunction against takings of property for other than a public purpose? In Estate of Waggoner v. Gleghorn, 378 S.W.2d 47 (Tex.1964), the Texas Supreme Court invalidated Vernon's Ann. Civil St., art. 1377b § 2, which gave the owner of land, wholly or partially surrounded by the land of another, the right to an ingress and egress easement over the surrounding land. Although the statute did not require that the surrounding landowner be fairly compensated for the easement, the Texas court made clear that this was not the statute's only constitutional defect: "the permanent appropriation of an easement for a right of way for travel across a tract of land constitutes a 'taking' within the purview of Article 1, Section 17 of the Constitution. In our opinion Article 1377b is unconstitutional and void to the extent that it purports to authorize the taking of private property for a private purpose." 378 S.W.2d at 50. How would the Texas court have decided Finn v. Williams?

c. By Prescription

PACE v. CARTER

Supreme Court of Maine, 1978.
390 A.2d 505.

GODFREY, Justice.

The parties to this action are abutting landowners. A dispute about the use of a driveway across the land of appellants Pace gave rise to the instant complaint, filed on August 19, 1974, in which the Paces sought an injunction against the Carters' further use of the driveway and compensation for water damage to the Paces' home alleged to have been caused by the Carters' grading and filling the driveway. The Carters denied liability for any damages and counterclaimed, seeking a declaration that they had acquired a prescriptive easement for use of the driveway.

By agreement with both parties reserving the right to object to the acceptance of a final report, the Superior Court ordered a referee to hear the case and make findings of fact and conclusions of law pursuant to Rule 53, M.R.Civ.P. After hearing the testimony of both sides, the referee concluded that the Carters had acquired a prescriptive easement in the disputed driveway. He also found that the evidence presented did not establish the claim that the Carters had caused damage to the Paces' home. From the Superior Court's adoption of the referee's report and from entry of judgment upon it the plaintiffs appealed.

From the evidence, the referee found the following facts: Until early 1953, the Carters had used the disputed driveway only casually and intermittently to reach their own lot, which they had acquired in 1936. In the spring of 1953, they began construction of a house on their lot and in the spring of 1954 their use of the driveway became intensive. In addition to the Carters' nearly daily use, trucks traversed the driveway to deliver building materials and haul out rocks and timber. Since the completion of their home in November, 1954, the Carters have used the driveway continuously as the primary means of access to their lot. Service trucks have been using the driveway to deliver oil, gas and firewood to the Carter home.

In 1954, the present Pace property was owned and occupied by a Mrs. Shepard, the Paces' predecessor in title. There was testimony that in the spring of 1954 Mr. Carter conceived the idea of relocating part of the driveway to make easier the passage of trucks delivering building material. The location of most of the driveway was to remain, and has remained, unchanged. Mr. Carter testified that although he had used the driveway under claim of right since 1936, he thought that before relocating a part of it which he and Mrs. Shepard both used, he should get the "permission" of Mrs. Shepard. Mr. Carter testified that when he presented his plan to Mrs. Shepard, she replied, in substance, "Do what you wish. It is your driveway." In his final report the referee, expressly finding that Mrs. Shepard had made such a reply, characterized her statement as a "parol grant to the defendants of the way as changed."

Since an oral grant of a permanent easement is unenforceable, the appellees did not base their right to use the driveway on an oral grant of an easement; instead, they based their claim on the existence of a prescriptive easement arising from their continuous, open, adverse use of the driveway under claim of right for over twenty years with the acquiescence of the owners.

In Jacobs v. Boomer, Me., 267 A.2d 376, 378 (1970), we reiterated the elements essential to the ripening of a prescriptive easement, quoting with approval from our opinion in Dartnell v. Bidwell, 115 Me. 227, 230, 98 A. 743, 744 (1916), as follows:

> "A prescriptive easement is created only by a continuous use for at least twenty years under a claim of right adverse to the owner, with his knowledge and acquiescence, or by a use so open, notorious, visible, and uninterrupted that knowledge and acquiescence will be presumed."

The owner's acquiescence in an adverse use is essential in Maine to the establishment of a prescriptive easement.[2] "Acquiescence" has been judicially defined as passive assent or submission to the use, as distinguished from the granting of a license or permission given with the intention that the licensee's use may continue only as long as the owner continues to consent to it.

The referee concluded that Mrs. Shepard's statement to appellee Carter amounted to a parol grant of the driveway "as changed." Mrs. Shepard's statement seems to suggest a belief on Mrs. Shepard's part that the Carters already had rights in the driveway and to indicate a purpose to grant rights of use that the Carters had not theretofore enjoyed. The referee's conclusion should perhaps be understood as relating to the relocated part of the driveway, to which any rights the Carters might have acquired by prior express grant or long continued use might not have extended. The referee's inference of a parol grant, whether applicable to all or only the relocated part of the driveway, was accompanied by a finding that the use had continued with the acquiescence of the appellants and their predecessors in title for more than twenty years, the appellants having made no objection until after the prescriptive period had elapsed. The referee

---

2. On this point, the acquisition of an easement by prescription differs, in Maine, from the acquisition of title by adverse possession. Dartnell v. Bidwell, 115 Me. 227, 98 A. 743 (1916). Sections 812 and 813 of title 14 of the Revised Statutes have no counterparts in the provisions bearing on acquisition of title by adverse possession. See 14 M.R.S.A. §§ 801–811, 814–816.

concluded that Mrs. Shepard's statement manifested her acquiescence in the Carters' use of the driveway as changed, as a matter of right, and that she was not permitting or licensing the use as a matter of grace.

To the extent that the Carters used all or any part of the driveway under a parol grant, their use was adverse to Mrs. Shepard and her successors in title. The fact that a parol grant is attempted may be probative of a landowner's state of mind at the time adverse use of his property is being made. A parol grant may manifest an intention on the part of the would-be grantor that the grantee is to enter the property under a claim of right based on the supposed grant, rather than pursuant to the grantor's permission or license. Likewise the grantee's use of the land pursuant to a parol grant may manifest a claim of right hostile to the grantor's full ownership of all rights in the property. For purposes of proving a prescriptive easement, evidence of an unenforceable parol grant of an easement tends to show the landowner's acquiescence in the use that the grantee makes of the land within the terms of the grant.

There was sufficient evidence to support the referee's finding that the Carters used the driveway under claim of right acquiesced in by the owners of the Shepard-Pace lot. That finding was supported by evidence and is not clearly erroneous. It must therefore stand.

Although the appellants acquired title to Mrs. Shepard's property by June 11, 1973, they did not attempt to bar the Carters' use of the driveway until June 15, 1974. This later date was approximately twenty years and one month after Mrs. Shepard acquiesced in the adverse use of the driveway as changed in the spring of 1954. The driveway passes within ten feet of the Pace home, and the appellants do not contend that they were unaware of the Carters' continuing use of the driveway from June, 1973, when the Paces purchased their home, until June, 1974, when they attempted to bar further use.

The record establishes that the Carters did not take up residence in their newly constructed home until November of 1954. Appellants urge this Court to hold, as a matter of law, that the use to which the driveway was put after November, 1954, was so different from its prior adverse use that it constituted a new kind of use necessitating the commencement of a new twenty-year period of prescription. Under this theory the period of prescription would have run until November, 1974, and appellants' action for trespass would have been instituted in time to defeat the ripening of an easement.

In support of their position the appellants cite numerous decisions holding that when an easement is obtained by adverse use alone, its extent must be measured by its use. The uses to which the driveway was put, before and after November, 1954, were not so dissimilar in purpose, burden and physical characteristics that the referee was obliged to treat them as legally distinct uses. Since the spring of 1953 the general purpose of the adverse use of the Pace driveway has remained vehicular access to the Carter lot. In the fall of 1954 the specific reason for vehicular access changed from construction of a home to maintenance and use of a home. Such a minor variation in purpose should not be of controlling importance.

The referee heard uncontroverted testimony that from the spring of 1954 to the fall of 1954 Mrs. Shepard's driveway, as changed, was used by the Carters on a daily basis as the primary means of access to the lot on which their house was being built. During that period numerous heavy vehicles, including a platform truck, traversed the drive in order to deliver building materials and to remove timber and earth. After November, 1954, the defendants used the driveway on a nearly daily basis as the primary means of access to the lot on which their home had been built. Since that time trucks have continued to use the driveway to make deliveries of oil, gas and firewood. The physical activities constituting the use, and the extent of the burden of the use, continuously imposed on the Pace-Shepard driveway have remained essentially unchanged since early 1954, and the referee did not err in deciding that they constituted a single continuous use. There being sufficient evidence in the record to establish the other essential elements of a ripened prescriptive easement, the referee's conclusion must be affirmed.

Appellants assert that the referee erred in concluding that they had failed to meet their burden of proving, by a fair preponderance of the evidence, that the damage to their basement resulted from the actions of the defendants. The referee considered testimony offered by both parties on this question. Tested by the appropriate standard of appellate review, the referee's finding of fact—*i.e.*, the absence of causation—was not clearly erroneous.

The entry is:

Appeal denied.

Judgment affirmed.

NOTES

1. To gain an easement by prescription, a claimant must show not only that his use was actual, continuous and exclusive, but also that it was without the neighbor's permission. Pace v. Carter suggests the difficult problems of proof and strategy that face the claimant who seeks to meet these requirements. One problem is that permission, or its absence, is inherently hard to prove. Words uttered and steps taken over a lengthy prescriptive period will often be ambiguous and contradictory at best.

Another strategic problem is to tread the line between acquiescence, which *Pace* requires for prescriptive use, and permission, which disqualifies the use. For example, *Pace* states that for "purposes of proving a prescriptive easement, evidence of an unenforceable parol grant of an easement tends to show the landowner's acquiescence in the use that the grantee makes of the land within the terms of the grant." Thus, if the claimant was using a right of way across his neighbor's land under an instrument that, but for some formal defect, would constitute an enforceable express easement, it would seem his use was under claim of right and was acquiesced in by the neighbor. But the faulty instrument might also be viewed as giving the claimant only permission to use the neighbor's land—a license revocable at any time.

As a matter of strategy, consider the plight of the claimant who seeks to establish a prescriptive easement, confident that he can demonstrate lack of permission, but less certain of his proofs on one or more of the other three requirements. Will success in disproving permission, but failure on some other requirement, bar him not only from a prescriptive easement, but also from an easement on the theory of Stoner v. Zucker? Recall that Stoner v. Zucker requires that permission be *proved*, rather than disproved, for an easement to be created. What inconsistencies of proof, if any, underlie the requirements for implying an easement by necessity and gaining one by prescription?

2. Easements by prescription bear many obvious similarities to titles by adverse possession. Yet, subtle differences, stemming primarily from the perceived difference between possession and use, separate the two bodies of law. (Adverse possession is considered at pages 24 to 60 above.) For a brief review of some historical differences between easements by prescription and title by adverse possession in England and the United States, see 2 American Law of Property, §§ 8.50–8.52 (A.J. Casner ed. 1952). See also, Simonton, Fictional Lost Grant in Prescription—A Nocuous Archaism, 35 W.Va. Law Q. 46 (1928).

a. Continuous. Continuity of possession is physically different from continuity of use. Claimant's house which encroaches on a neighbor's parcel will physically deprive the neighbor of possession throughout the limitations period. By contrast, claimant's use of a neighbor's pathway will characteristically be discontinuous, for there will be many times during the limitations period when the claimant is not actually present on the land; and, even when the claimant is present, his use will typically not exclude the neighbor's use and possession. As a result, courts have been far less rigorous in imposing the continuity requirement in prescriptive easement cases than in adverse possession cases.

What limits should be placed on this comparatively relaxed attitude? What if claimant uses two paths with identical terminal points, changing from one path to the other midway through the prescription period? See Speight v. Anderson, 226 N.C. 492, 39 S.E.2d 371 (1946) (Held: no prescriptive easement). What if claimant can only prove that he used one-half of a subsequently developed road? See Krencicki v. Petersen, 22 Ariz.App. 1, 522 P.2d 762 (1974) (Held: prescriptive easement limited to the one-half used).

b. *Hostile and Under Claim of Right*. The frequent discontinuity of prescriptive use also has implications for the requirement that the claimant's possession or use not be permissive since use is more likely than possession to be punctuated by shifts from permission to objection. In Simonsen v. Todd, 261 Iowa 485, 154 N.W.2d 730 (1967), A claimed a prescriptive right of way easement over B's land. From 1940 to 1957, B's predecessor in title expressly permitted A to cross his parcel. B bought the parcel in 1957 and in 1963 blocked A's access across B's property. The trial court held that, although the use was originally permissive, use as of right had continued for longer than the ten-year prescriptive period and had therefore ripened into an easement before B took title. The Iowa Supreme Court reversed, holding that a use that is originally permissive, and is not claimed as a right independent of permission, does not start the running of the prescriptive period.

c. *Known or Open and Notorious*. Because land uses are characteristically discontinuous, and often covert, courts have struck a distinctive balance between the user's interest in gaining prescriptive rights and his neighbor's interest in knowing of any conduct that will start the statute of limitations running against her. Actual knowledge, if shown, obviates proof that the use was open and notorious. Absent actual knowledge, the requisite notice will be implied if the claimant's use was sufficiently open and notorious to make a reasonable neighbor aware of it. See, for example, Hopkins v. Hill, 160 Neb. 29, 68 N.W.2d 678 (1955). Acquiescence will usually be presumed from the owner's failure to halt the use once she knows, or should know, of it. Pace v. Carter is unusual in its insistence on independent proof of the neighbor's acquiescence, and, as a general rule, it is not necessary for the claimant to demonstrate acquiescence independently of knowledge.

d. *Exclusive*. Like the adverse possessor, the prescriptive user must demonstrate that his use is exclusive. Exclusivity does not require use only by the claimant, but does mean that the claimant's right must not depend on a similar right in others. Thus, the claimant's use, along with use by the owner of the servient estate or by adjoining landowners will be exclusive so long as the use is based on an individual claim. For example, in Clayton v. Jensen, 240 Md. 337, 214 A.2d 154 (1965), use of a driveway in conjunction with neighbors did not fail the exclusivity test, and in Cramer v. Jenkins, 399 S.W.2d 15 (Mo.1966), A's use of a path in conjunction with a discrete, small number of adjoining landowners was held to be exclusive.

Claimant's use cannot, however, be in common with the public at large. In Scoville v. Fisher, 181 Neb. 496, 149 N.W.2d 339 (1967), B owned a lot, part of which was used by the public as a crossing and parking area and by adjoining commercial landowners for deliveries. When B walled in this part of the lot, adjoining landowner A sued, claiming a prescriptive easement for ingress, egress, and other purposes. The court held for *B* on the ground that, because *A's* use had been in conjunction with the public, it was not exclusive.

3. *Public Easements.* If public use will bar a private prescriptive easement, can it, nonetheless, form the basis for a public prescriptive easement? Public easements by prescription, though recognized, have not enjoyed the universal acceptance of private prescriptive easements. An alternative theory, dedication, has won substantial acceptance, and a third theory, custom, has been recognized in a small handful of states. All three theories were asserted in State ex rel. Haman v. Fox, 100 Idaho 140, 594 P.2d 1093 (1979), to support the claim that more than thirty years of public recreational use had given the public rights in private beach property on Lake Coeur d'Alene. The Idaho Supreme Court affirmed the trial court's decision for defendant property owners and rejected the theory of prescription. Although the court did accept the theories of dedication and custom, it found that the facts of the case did not fulfill the requirements of either theory.

Prescription. Acknowledging that other courts have recognized public easements by prescription, the *Fox* court took the view that the "'general public' or 'the people of the state of Idaho' as distinguished from specific individuals cannot, absent specific statutory authorization, acquire prescriptive rights to private property." 100 Idaho at 145, 594 P.2d at 1098. The court's principal reason lay in an analytical quandary: easements by prescription are based on the statute of limitations, and the statute of limitations bars actions only against those identifiable individuals who have met all of its requirements. But, in the case of public easements, "as against whom would the owner be barred? Only those who had actually made open, notorious, continuous, uninterrupted use, under a claim of right, with the knowledge of the owner, for the five year period. Those persons who had not made such use could be enjoined from further interfering with the owner's superior rights. . . . [T]he rights contended for here are in the nature of an easement in gross. Being a personal right, the rule is that one individual's prescriptive use cannot inure to the benefit of anyone else. Personal prescriptive rights are confined to the actual adverse user and are limited to the use exercised during the prescriptive period." 100 Idaho at 146, 594 P.2d at 1099.

Dedication. The *Fox* court did accept the closely analogous theory of dedication, under which a longstanding public use that is adverse, continuous and actually or constructively known to the owner is held to be evidence of the owner's implied offer to dedicate an easement to the public, entitling it to continue making the use. Long public use will also imply the public's acceptance of the owner's offer. Like prescription, dedication poses the difficult task of allocating property rights on the basis of chancy retrospective inferences about a landowner's state of mind over a lengthy period. In *Fox*, the court relied on evidence that the owner had at various times ousted unwelcome public users, and had removed trash cans put on the property by the city, to find that there was no intent to dedicate the property to the public.

Custom. A few states, joined by Idaho in *Fox*, have adopted the English doctrine of custom. This doctrine protects a longstanding public use by making it irrevocable but gives the public no interest in the underlying land. For a right to be acquired through custom, the use "must have continued from time immemorial, without interruption, and as of right." 3 H. Tiffany, Law of Real Property, § 935 (3d ed. 1939). Custom differs from prescription and dedication theory in that customary rights can be established without proof respecting the owner's state of mind. From the public's viewpoint, however, the theory has its own limitations. For example, in *Fox*, the supreme court agreed with the trial court that public use beginning in 1912 did not "constitute 'from time immemorial.' The second requirement, that the use must be uninterrupted, is not met because of the fact that respondents had personally and with police assistance removed members of the public from their land. Without further burdening this opinion, suffice it to say that of the seven essential elements of a customary right, the trial court found adversely to appellant on six of them. We find ample evidence in the record to support the findings, and we therefore affirm the district court's denial of any customary rights in this case." 100 Idaho at 148, 594 P.2d at 1101.

4. What is the extent of use permitted by a prescriptive easement? Aztec Ltd., Inc. v. Creekside Investment Co., 100 Idaho 566, 568, 602 P.2d 64, 66 (1979), states the general rule: "an easement acquired by prescription is confined to the right as exercised during the prescriptive period. It is limited by the purpose for which it is acquired and the use to which it is put." At the same time, the court reaffirmed "a single and narrow exception," stated in an earlier decision, Gibbens v. Weisshaupt, 98 Idaho 633, 639, 570 P.2d 870, 876, (1977): "some changes in the character of the dominant estate are foreseeable and will necessitate changes in the use of a prescriptive easement. We emphasize, however, that any changes in the use of a prescriptive easement cannot result in an unreasonable increased burden on the servient estate and that the increase in use must be reasonably foreseeable at the time the easement is established."

Applying the rule and its exception to the case before it, *Aztec* held that a prescriptive easement to use a twenty-foot roadway for access to and from three or four private homes could not be expanded to include access to 200 apartment dwelling units. The court also ruled that it was impermissible to widen the roadway: "any increase in width of a prescriptive easement would constitute an impermissible expansion even if a contemporaneous increase in traffic over the easement would not. An increase in width does more than merely increase the burden upon the servient estate; it has the effect of enveloping additional land." 100 Idaho at 569, 602 P.2d at 67.

Should the principles that are used to determine the extent of express easements also be used to determine the extent of prescriptive easements? Is it relevant that in one case the court is asked to interpret a written instrument and, in the other, to construe physical use over time?

5. *Doctrine of Ancient Lights; Spite Fences.* Does the requirement of actual or implied knowledge leave any room for prescriptive *negative* easements, such as an easement for light and air? Since negative easements involve no physical use of the servient estate, how could courts determine the extent of the prescriptive easement? What steps could a landowner take to prevent her parcel from becoming the servient estate burdened by a negative easement?

In England, the doctrine of ancient lights gives a landowner who has continuously received light and air from across his neighbor's land a prescriptive right, entitling him to an injunction against his neighbor's subsequent obstruction of the light and air reaching his windows. (The prescriptive right is not to completely unobstructed light and air, but rather to an amount just above the "grumble line"—the point at which a reasonable person would begin to complain.) The prescriptive period, originally "immemorial use"—"a time whereof the memory of man runneth not to the contrary"—was later fixed at twenty years by the statute of limitations and, later still, expanded to twenty-seven years by the Rights of Light Act, 7 & 8 Eliz. II, Ch. 56 (1959).

Although the doctrine of ancient lights enjoyed an early, tentative foothold in the United States, it was soon rejected throughout the country. "This doctrine was out of place—or so the courts thought—in a country bent on economic growth, trying to promote, not curb, the intensive use of land. Chancellor Kent thought the rule did not 'reasonably or equitably apply . . . to buildings on narrow lots in the rapidly growing cities in this country.' A Massachusetts statute of 1852 denied that the 'mere continuance of . . . windows' gave an easement 'of light and air' so as to keep an adjoining landowner from building on his land. By the late nineteenth century, every state except three had rejected the idea of this easement." L. Friedman, History of American Law 360 (1973).

How can an English landowner who presently is not interested in developing her land prevent her neighbor from obtaining a prescriptive easement for light and air? Until 1959, the only answer was to erect a wall for the sole purpose of obstructing the neighbor's light and air before the prescriptive period expired. (Under the 1959 Rights of Light Act, above, the landowner can achieve the same result by simply filing a notice opposing the prescription.) Recognizing that these walls represented the landowner's most expedient form of protection against the accrual of prescriptive rights, English courts refused to examine the motives behind them, even if it was evident that the landowner's only reason for erecting the wall or fence was to spite, annoy and injure her neighbor.

American courts, having rejected the doctrine of ancient lights, should not be inclined to approve of so-called spite fences. Nonetheless, a substantial number of American courts have refused to enjoin people from building walls purely for malicious reasons. A growing number, however, will inquire into motive, and enjoin spite fences. Compare Hornsby v. Smith, 191 Ga. 491, 499, 13 S.E.2d 20, 24 (1941) ("Thus it is our opinion that malicious use of property resulting in injury to another is never a 'lawful use', but is in every case unlawful"), with Letts v. Kessler, 54 Ohio St. 73, 82, 42 N.E. 765, 766 (1896) ("In this state a man is free to direct his moral conduct as he pleases, insofar as he is not restrained by statute. . . . It would be much more inequitable and intolerable to allow a man's neighbors to question his motives every time that he should undertake to erect a structure upon his own premises, and drag him before a court of equity to ascertain whether he is about to erect the structure for ornament or profit, or through motives of unmixed malice"). Several state legislatures have also responded. See, for example, West's Ann.Cal.Civ. Code § 841.4; New York—McKinney's Real Prop.Acts & Proc.Law § 843.

6. What steps short of filing a lawsuit can a landowner take to prevent an affirmative easement from arising by prescription, dedication or custom? Physical barriers such as fences may suffice, so long as they are not surmounted by the user. What of a sign, posted at the entrance to a pathway, reading: "Passage by Permission of Owner. Permission May Be Revoked At Any Time."?

2. ENFORCEMENT BY AND AGAINST SUCCESSORS IN INTEREST

a. Who Is Bound? Does the Burden Run?

If *B* has expressly, impliedly or prescriptively given *A* an easement to use Blackacre, *B* must, of course, honor *A*'s rights so long as she continues to own Blackacre. But when *B* conveys Blackacre to *Z*, will *Z* be bound by an easement to which she did not herself agree? As a general rule, the burden of an easement will run, and *Z* will be bound, only if two requirements are met: *A* and *B* must have intended that the burden run, and *Z*, the party against whom the easement is sought to be enforced, must have had notice of the easement at the time she acquired Blackacre.

Intent. In the case of express easements, courts will divine the necessary intent from the language of the instrument and from the nature of the easement. *B*'s express undertaking for herself, and "for her heirs, successors and assigns," clearly signifies an intent to bind successors. Also, if *A's* reasonable expectations, and the easement's utility, depend upon the easement's continued force, without regard to who owns the servient estate, courts are likely to infer an intent that the burden run. In the case of implied easements, a court, having construed the facts surrounding *B's* conveyance to *A* as implying an easement, will ask whether the facts also reflect a shared intent that the burden of the easement run. Intent that prescriptive easements run will be implied as a matter of law; because *A* and *B* never expressly or impliedly agreed on the easement, no basis exists for inferring intent from words or facts.

Notice. To be bound, Z or any other successor must have had actual, constructive or inquiry notice of the easement at the time she acquired the putative servient estate. *Actual notice* means that at the time Z acquired Blackacre she actually knew of the easement's existence; *B* may have told her of it or, more likely, she may have discovered a recorded instrument in the course of searching title before purchasing the parcel. But what if Z fails to make a title search? The recording act in her state will probably provide that she is on *constructive notice* of all instruments that a reasonable title search would have disclosed.

How will Z acquire notice of a prescriptive easement, an easement implied from necessity, or any other easement not created by a written instrument? Clearly, constructive notice will not work, for if there is no writing, there is nothing that can be recorded. Furthermore, *B*, who is trying to sell Blackacre to Z, cannot be expected to give Z actual notice by telling her of the encumbrance. But what if, on inspecting Blackacre, Z sees a roadway running through the parcel, or utility lines strung across the parcel, or manholes to a sewer line under the parcel? In all these cases, Z would probably be held to *inquiry notice*—notice of any easement that reasonable inquiry would have disclosed. The presence of the roadway, utility lines or manholes, should indicate to Z that *B* is sharing the use of Blackacre with someone else, and Z will be expected to ask *B*, *B's* neighbors and the utility company whether in fact an easement underlies their use. An affirmative answer will give Z actual notice of the easement. Note that Z will be bound to notice of these facts whether or not she makes the inquiry for, as with constructive notice, she will be held to have notice of everything that she would have discovered from a reasonable inspection of the land and a follow-up inquiry.

The notice requirement raises special problems in the context of easements by necessity. In Backhausen v. Mayer, 204 Wis. 286, 234 N.W. 904 (1931), *O*, who owned an eighty-acre parcel, had in 1885 sold *A's* father the north twenty-five acres, isolating this parcel from access to any public highways. *O* conveyed the south 55 acres to Z's predecessor, *B*. Z later purchased the south 55 acres and brought this action against *A* for trespass. *A* alleged a way of necessity. The court held that a way of necessity originally existed, but that, because Z had no notice of the easement, he was not bound by it.

Acknowledging that Z had no actual notice of the easement, A had also failed to demonstrate that Z had inquiry notice from the visible condition of the parcel. In addition A had failed to prove constructive notice. "An examination of the record would have revealed to [Z's predecessor] that his grantor at one time owned the north twenty-five acres and that he had conveyed it, but the record would not have advised him that it was conveyed to one who had no access to a highway. The most that might be said is that when the record revealed a former co-ownership by [the common] grantor of the dominant and servient estate, he was put upon inquiry to ascertain whether the severance of the ownership of the two estates was of such a nature as to give the owner of the dominant estate a way of necessity over the servient estate which he was then purchasing. Such a doctrine would be unreasonable." 204 Wis. 291, 234 N.W. 906.

b. Who Is Benefited? Does the Benefit Run?

DUNN BROS., INC. v. LESNEWSKY
Supreme Court of Connecticut, 1973.
164 Conn. 331, 321 A.2d 453.

HOUSE, C.J.

This is an appeal by the defendant from a judgment of the Superior Court which permanently enjoined her from interfering with the right of the three corporate plaintiffs to enjoy the use of a railroad spur track or siding running through her property. The court also awarded damages of $192 to the named plaintiff and refused the plaintiffs' prayer for a declaratory judgment.

The facts are not disputed. The three plaintiffs and the defendant each own one of four contiguous parcels of land in the town of South Windsor once belonging to a common grantor. A railway main line, formerly of the New York, New Haven and Hartford Railroad Company, now operated by the Penn Central Railroad Company, runs in a north-south direction parallel to the westerly boundary of the defendant's parcel. A spur track or siding runs from this main line in an easterly direction across the land of the defendant, through the land of the plaintiff Quinnipiac Industrial Corporation, north of and adjacent to land owned by the plaintiff Propane Gas Service, Inc., and thence through the land of the plaintiff Dunn Brothers, Inc. The siding had been in continuous use by the plaintiffs and their predecessors in title as an appurtenance to their respective parcels of land since at least 1915. In June, 1970, the defendant caused to be erected a barricade consisting of a fence and a locked gate over the track and thereby denied the plaintiffs use of the spur track and access by rail to their land.

Prior to 1956, Robert P. Clark, William O. Clark and George H. Clark were the owners as tenants in common of all the land now owned by the parties to this action. In 1956, the Clarks, by warranty deed, conveyed to the defendant a portion of the land adjacent to the main railroad line. This deed reserved several rights-of-way. Of importance to the present controversy is the following language: "Reserving the right to the use of the railroad track on the premises herein conveyed for and as an appurtenance to other land of the grantors adjoining on the east and the north of the above described premises." The "other land of the grantors" has passed by virtue of several deeds to the plaintiffs. Each such deed contained language conveying rights-of-way and appurtenances.

The trial court concluded that the plaintiffs owned an easement both by grant and by necessity to use the spur track running across the defendant's land and that the defendant, therefore, acted wrongfully in causing the barricade to be erected. Based on the limited evidence offered on the issue of damages, the court awarded damages only to the named plaintiff and in the amount of $192 but permanently enjoined the defendant from maintaining any barrier over the track and in any manner interfering with the right of each of the plaintiffs to use the track. Of the five assignments of error, the sole claim pressed on appeal and, therefore, the only claim considered by this court is that the trial court erred in concluding that the right to use the spur track reserved by the grantors in 1956 was appurtenant rather than, as the defendant claimed, in gross so that it did not pass to the plaintiffs.

The defendant claims that the language reserving the right-of-way "for and as an appurtenance to other land of the grantors" reserved merely a personal right in the grantors that was not, and could not be, transferred to subsequent owners. She relies on a presumption that in the absence of specific words of inheritance, as "heirs and assigns," the reservation of an easement should be construed to be personal in nature. She also argues that since another clause in the same deed to her granted a right-of-way over other land of the grantors to the "grantee, her heirs and assigns," the absence of reference to heirs and assigns in the siding reservation in issue indicated an intent that the reservation was to be merely personal. With these contentions we do not agree.

The question of whether an easement runs with the land or is merely personal "is to be resolved by seeking the intent of the parties as expressed in the deed, and this intent is to be ascertained by reading the words of the deed in the light of the attendant circumstances." Birdsey v. Kosienski, 140 Conn. 403, 410, 101 A.2d 274, 277. While it is true that the absence of words of inheritance may create a presumption that the easement was intended to be in gross; that presumption will be defeated if, "from all the surrounding circumstances, it appears that . . . [to create a permanent easement] was the intention of the parties. Knowlton v. New York, N.H. & H.R. Co., 72 Conn. 188, 192, 44 A. 8; Chappell v. New York, N.H.

& H.R. Co., 62 Conn. 195, 203, 24 A. 997." Birdsey v. Kosienski, supra.

This court has noted circumstances that may negate the force of the presumption. If the easement serves to enhance the value of the dominant estate, rather than merely to further the convenience of the grantor, the easement is generally considered to have been intended to be appurtenant. The trial court expressly found that the easement in issue here was of value to the land now owned by the plaintiffs.

A second significant test is whether the owner of the servient estate has recognized the right of subsequent owners of the dominant estate to exercise the easement. The findings in this case disclose no effort made by the defendant prior to 1970 to restrain the plaintiffs from using the track.

Finally, the language of the reservation itself strongly indicates that the easement was intended to run with the land: the easement was reserved "for and as an appurtenance to other land of the grantors," not just to the grantors themselves. The absence of words of inheritance assumes very little significance where the easement specifically is described as appurtenant to the land. The other rights-of-way created in the 1956 deed were either granted to "the grantee, her heirs and assigns," or reserved by the grantors for their use. No direct comparison of the language used in creating the easements, as urged by the defendant, serves to indicate that because of the inclusion of words of inheritance in one clause, and their omission in another, the intention of the parties was to create a purely personal right to use of the spur track. By definition, an appurtenant easement runs with the land rather than with any particular owner, and the phrase in a deed "with the appurtenances thereof" is sufficient to convey to a grantee rights-of-way appurtenant to the land conveyed.

We find no error in the conclusion of the trial court that the easement to use the railroad spur track which the grantors reserved in their deed to the defendant was an easement appurtenant to their land which ran with the land and passed to the plaintiffs and that they were entitled to the relief which the court granted.

There is no error.

In this opinion the other judges concurred.

STOCKDALE v. YERDEN

Supreme Court of Michigan, 1922.
220 Mich. 444, 190 N.W. 225.

WIEST, J. October 5, 1908, Arthur W. Harrington, owner of 101 acres of land in Allegan county, sold and conveyed the same to defendants grantors, excepting $19\frac{1}{3}$ acres at the rear, and reserved in the deed a right of way across the conveyed premises for the purpose of removing the timber on the land excepted, and gave to the grantees in the deed the right to use the $19\frac{1}{3}$ acres until flowed.

October 29, 1908, Mr. Harrington sold and conveyed the $19^1/_3$ acres of land to W.A. Foote, and in the deed made the following reservation:

"First party reserves the right to cut and remove the standing timber at any time before said premises are flowed by second party or his assigns, and he also reserves for himself or his assigns the right to pasture said premises when same are not flowed and he may remove any timber left by him within three years after said premises are flowed."

The plaintiff, about 10 years ago, without any writing, purchased from Mr. Harrington the timber then standing together with the right to remove the same within the time specified in the conveyance to Mr. Foote, and paid therefor the sum of $250. The premises have not yet been flowed. Plaintiff removed timber from the premises over the land of defendants for six years.

In September, 1921, plaintiff attempted to pass over defendants' land for the purpose of removing timber from the $19^1/_3$ acres and was stopped by defendants. Thereupon the bill herein was filed by plaintiff, and upon the hearing a decree was granted restraining defendants from interfering with plaintiff's right to cross over their premises for the purpose of removing the timber until three years after the flowing of the $19^1/_3$ acres.

Defendants insist that, at the most, Mr. Harrington possessed an easement in gross across their premises, limited in purpose and to a reasonable time, and as such it was not assignable to plaintiff.

Plaintiff contends that Mr. Harrington reserved the right of way in the deed for the purpose of removing the timber on the $19^1/_3$ acres and such reservation gave to Mr. Harrington, and to plaintiff the right to use the way for the purpose designated.

If the reservation in the deed from Mr. Harrington to defendants' grantors constituted an easement appurtenant, such easement passed with the dominant estate when it was conveyed to Mr. Foote.

Evidently Mr. Harrington at the time of selling the $81^2/_3$ acres to defendants' grantors contemplated the sale of the $19^1/_3$ acres with a reservation of the standing timber, as he made such sale within a few days. To permit him to remove the timber he provided for the right of passage over defendants' land. Having in mind the reservation in the deed and the manifest purpose thereof, the easement was not appurtenant to the dominant estate, but only an easement in gross. As an easement in gross it was not assignable to plaintiff.

The question is so well covered in Boatman v. Lasley, 23 Ohio St. 614, that we quote therefrom:

"Is a private right of way over the lands of another, in gross, such an interest or estate in land as may be cast by descent, or may be assigned by the grantee to one who has no interest in the land? . . .

"It is strongly insisted upon in argument that a right of way in gross may be conveyed to the grantee 'and to his heirs and assigns forever,' because an owner in fee may carve out of his estate any interest less than the whole and dispose of the less estate absolutely; and this because the power to dispose of the whole estate includes a power to dispose of any part of it.

"This argument assumes the affirmative of the very question in controversy, to wit, that such a right of way is an interest or estate in the land.

"A mere naked right to pass and repass over the land of another, a use which excludes all participation in the profits of the land, is not, in any proper sense, an interest or estate in the land itself. Such a right is in its nature personal; it attaches itself to the person of him to whom it is granted, and must die with the person.

"If such right be an inheritable estate, how will the heirs take? In severalty, in joint tenancy, in coparcenary, or as tenants in common? If not in severalty, how can their interests be severed?

"If it be assignable, what limit can be placed on the power of alienation? To whom and to how many may it be transferred? Why not to the public at large, and thus convert into a public way that which was intended to be a private and exclusive way only?

"Where the way is appendant or appurtenant to other lands, very different considerations arise. There the right attaches to the lands to which the way is appurtenant, because it is granted for the convenience of their occupation without respect to the ownership or number of occupants. In such case the right of way passes with the dominant estate as an incident thereto. A right of way appendant cannot be converted into a way in gross, nor can a way in gross be turned into a way appendant.

"A very marked distinction also exists between a way in gross and an easement of profit à prendre, such as the right to enter upon the lands of another, and remove gravel or other materials therefrom. The latter so far partakes of the nature of an estate in the land itself as to be treated as an inheritable and assignable interest. Post v. Pearsall, 22 Wend. 432. . . .

"Mr. Washburn in his work on Easements, p. 8, par. 11, states the law upon this subject as follows: 'A man may have a way in gross over another's land, but it must, from its nature, be a personal right not assignable or inheritable; nor can it be made so by any terms in the grant, any more than a collateral and independent contract can be made to run with the land.' See, also, Ackroyd v. Smith, 10 C.B. 164; Garrison v. Budd, 19 Ill. 558; Post v. Pearsall, 22 Wend. 432; Woolrych on Ways, 20; 2 Black.Com. 35, 3 Kent's Com. 420, 512."

In 9 R.C.L. p. 739, it is stated:

"Under the rule that there can be no easement without a distinct dominant tenement, there can, in strictness, be no such thing as an easement in gross. There is, however, a class of rights which are impressed upon the land of one person in favor of another person or other persons, and not in favor of another tract of land, and these rights are sometimes spoken of by courts and legal writers as 'easements in gross.' An easement in gross is defined as a mere personal interest in the real estate of another. The principal distinction between it and an easement appurtenant is found in the fact that in the first there is, and in the second there is not, a dominant tenement. The easement is in gross, and personal to the grantee, because it is not appurtenant to other premises. The great weight of the authorities supports the doctrine that easements in gross, properly so called because of their personal character, are not assignable or inheritable, nor can they be made so by any terms in the grant. Many cases which seem to be in conflict with this rule are reconcilable because under their facts the rights in question were profits à prendre, and not easements in gross."

Plaintiff has no right of way over the premises of defendants. The decree entered below is reversed, and one will be entered here dismissing the bill, with costs to defendants.

FELLOWS, C.J., and McDONALD and BIRD, JJ., concur with WIEST, J.

SHARPE, J. (concurring). By the reservation in his deed to defendants' grantors, Harrington created an easement in the $81^{2}/_{3}$ acres conveyed for the benefit of the $19^{1}/_{3}$ retained by him. This easement, an interest in land, even if not transferred by the deed to Foote, did not pass to plaintiff on his parol purchase of the standing timber. Such sale but amounted to a revocable license to remove the timber. The assignment of an easement must be in writing.

NOTE

Dunn v. Lesnewsky and Stockdale v. Yerden reflect some of the confusion that has grown up around a fairly simple question: Who can enforce the benefit of an easement? One source of the confusion is historical: there was a medieval English bias against easements in gross, and this bias has clearly infected contemporary American decisions on the question. Another source is the occasional misapprehension of easements' adverse effects on marketability. A brief summary of the governing principles should help you to keep the issues in their proper place.

1. *Who Holds the Benefit?*

   a. *Easements Appurtenant.* The determination that an easement is appurtenant, and thus attaches to the dominant estate, provides the starting point for determining who holds the benefit of the easement on the transfer of the dominant estate. Restatement of Property § 487 (1944) provides that, "Except as prevented by the terms of its transfer, or by the manner or the terms of the creation of the easement appurtenant thereto, one who succeeds to the possession of a dominant tenement thereby succeeds to the privileges of use of the servient tenement authorized by the easement."

But appurtenance is no more than a starting point; it triggers a presumption respecting who holds the benefit that may be rebutted by language in the conveyance from A, the owner of the dominant estate, to Y, his successor. If the conveyance expressly transfers the benefit to Y, or omits to mention it, Y will obtain the benefit as an incident of owning the dominant estate. But, what if A's conveyance to Y expressly reserves the benefit to A? For example, if the easement gave A, as owner of Whiteacre, the right to swim in the pond on Blackacre, A might expressly reserve this right when he transfers Whiteacre to Y. One possible result of this reservation is that A will retain the benefit, effectively converting the easement appurtenant into an easement in gross; A will be able to swim in the pond to the exclusion of Y. Another possible result is that A's attempted reservation will be given no effect and the easement will remain appurtenant; Y will be able to swim in the pond to the exclusion of A. The third possible result is that the attempted reservation will extinguish the easement; neither A nor Y will have the right to swim in the pond.

As between the first two possibilities, the result will turn on whether A and B intended, when they created the easement, that A could convert the appurtenant easement into an easement in gross. The general presumption is that they did not. Thus, if the easement does not clearly permit the conversion, A's attempted reservation will either be ineffective, passing the benefit to Y, or it will terminate the easement. As between these two possibilities, termination will result only if A, who is expressly or presumptively barred from reserving the benefit to himself in gross, makes it clear in his transfer to Y, that if A cannot have the benefit of the easement, then Y cannot have it either. See Restatement of Property § 487 Comment b (1944).

b. *Easements in Gross.* Easements in gross have no dominant estate and their benefits are held entirely apart from any other interest in land. The benefit of an easement in gross is freely assignable, and *Stockdale*, which says it is not, represents a minority position. The Restatement recognizes this principle but draws a distinction between "commercial easements in gross" and "noncommercial easements in gross." Under the Restatement, "Easements in gross, if of a commercial character, are alienable property interests." By contrast, "alienability of noncommercial easements in gross is determined by the manner or the terms of their creation." Restatement of Property §§ 489–491 (1944). Among the factors to be considered in determining whether *A* and *B* intended their noncommercial easement in gross to be alienable, Restatement § 492 cites as "important factors":

> (a) the personal relations existing at the time of creation between the owner of the easement and the owner of the servient tenement;
>
> (b) the extent of the probable increase in the burden on the servient tenement resulting from the alienability of the easement either by increasing the physical use of the land or by decreasing its value;
>
> (c) the consideration paid for the easement.

The principal problem with the Restatement approach is that the asserted distinction between commercial and noncommercial easements is artificial at best. According to the Restatement, an easement in gross "is of a commercial character when the use authorized by it results primarily in economic benefit rather than personal satisfaction." § 489, comment c. By contrast, noncommercial easements "contribute to pleasure rather than to financial well-being." § 491, comment a. Yet, a dollar value can be attached to personal pleasure, and personal pleasure can be measured as a function of economic benefit. Is it a commercial or a noncommercial easement when *B* grants to *A* the freely assignable right to cross Blackacre in order to swim in the pond on Blackacre? Will it alter the result if *B* charges everyone else a dollar a day for the same privilege? The consequences of the commercial-noncommercial distinction are not great, to be sure, for *A* and *B* can draft around the two presumptions to make a noncommercial easement freely assignable and a commercial easement not assignable.

The Restatement reflects what appears to be the majority position on the assignability of easements in gross. However, a substantial number of states take the position that, as a matter of law, these easements are not assignable. The Michigan Supreme Court, which took this position in Stockdale v. Yerden, later withdrew from it partially in Johnston v. Michigan Consolidated Gas Co., 337 Mich. 572, 60 N.W.2d 464 (1953). Relying in part on Restatement § 489, the court in that case upheld the assignment of the benefit of a pipeline easement, distinguishing *Stockdale* on the ground that "the easement there in question was only the right to pass over the lands of another. The easement in the instant case is of a very different nature, for here the right is to bury and install pipe lines which when installed use up a part of the land itself." 337 Mich. at 580, 60 N.W.2d at 468. Should the distinction make a difference?

Why have a substantial number of states prohibited the assignment of easements in gross and why have others erected a constructional preference against assignment? Charles Clark, probably the most vocal opponent of assignable easements in gross, argued that such easements, "usually of small value, and easily forgotten by the holder thereof, often are discovered many years later just at a time when they may hold up or prevent an advantageous sale of the servient estate . . . . Contrast this situation with that of an easement appurtenant to some dominant land. The latter is an interest hardly to be overlooked either upon death or removal elsewhere of the owner. Consequently it and the appurtenant easement will pass to some definitely ascertainable person." C. Clark, Real Covenants and Other Interests Which "Run with the Land" 73 (2d ed. 1947). Would it be better to permit the alienation of easements in gross and to devise rules that, over time, will weed out those that are unnecessarily burdensome?

Are the consequences of Clark's position, and the minority rule prohibiting assignments, even worse than the consequences of free assignability? The rule against assignment can be circumvented. One artifice is for utility companies to make easements in gross look like easements appurtenant by including language in their easement forms representing that the easement is for the benefit of some dominant tract of land. See Laird, Some Problems of Public Utilities in Acquiring and Maintaining Easements, 58 Ill.B.J. 832, 835 (1970). Circumvention is likely to cost more, both privately and socially, than assignability. Utility companies that cannot show a dominant estate to which the easement's benefit appertains may forego the easement approach entirely and instead acquire the strip underlying their poles and lines in fee simple absolute. Apart from being less desirable to the utility company and the landowner—who probably would have preferred an easement—the choice is more costly for society since, unlike easements, fees that have lost their usefulness cannot be terminated by abandonment or changed conditions.

2. *Is the Benefit Appurtenant or in Gross?* According to the Restatement of Property § 453 (1944), "An easement is appurtenant to land when the easement is created to benefit and does benefit the possessor of the land in his use of the land." Comment b adds that "the easement must in some degree benefit the possessor of the land in his physical use or enjoyment of the tract of land to which the easement is appurtenant. It is not sufficient to satisfy this requirement that he may, because of the easement, realize more revenue from his use of it." Restatement § 454 defines an easement in gross as the opposite of an easement appurtenant: "An easement is in gross when it is not created to benefit or when it does not benefit the possessor of any tract of land and his use of it as such possessor."

The question whether an easement is appurtenant or in gross essentially involves a determination of the intent of those who created the easement. In making this determination, courts indulge a strong constructional preference for easements appurtenant. So long as there is a dominant estate to which the easement can be said to appertain, and so long as grantor and grantee have not clearly demonstrated an intent that the easement be in gross, the court will probably find an easement appurtenant.

What has evolved in this country as a rule of construction originated in England as a rule of law. No matter how clear the parties' intent, easements there could not be created in gross. The English rule developed at a time when courts drew a sharp distinction between profits, which involved the removal of resources such as coal or water from the servient estate, and easements, which typically involved rights of way and rights to water. Profits characteristically were owned by individuals who possessed no land bordering the servient estate; as a result the law early assumed that they could be held in gross. By contrast, easements characteristically were held by neighbors and benefited the neighbor's use of his estate; thus it was assumed that they could only be held appurtenant. This habit of thought, buttressed by deference to Roman law principles, soon became a rule of law. "There can be no such thing according to our law, or according to civil law, as what I may term an easement in gross. An easement must be connected with a dominant tenement." Rangeley v. Midland Railway Co., 3 L.R. Ch. 306, 311 (1868). By the time the need arose for utility and other easements not directly benefiting an adjacent parcel, the English courts had already closed the doors of easement law.

Is there any contemporary justification for the English rule outlawing easements in gross? For the American presumption against them? Since the American rule of construction is just a reminder to parties and their lawyers that they must express their intent clearly if they wish to create an easement in gross, any mistakes in the underlying policy might be thought to have limited consequence. Yet policy has not been so confined. The same concerns that have led courts to prefer easements appurtenant to easements in gross, have led them to decisions like Stockdale v. Yerden, holding that the benefit of an easement in gross cannot be assigned. These preferences, and the doctrinal confusion they produce, are not, alas, confined to the law of easements. As you will soon see, they appear in the law of covenants, too. Can the benefit of a covenant be created in gross? If so, can it be assigned?

B. COVENANTS AND SERVITUDES

1. CREATION

a. By Instrument

COVENANTS, CONDITIONS AND RESTRICTIONS FOR TANSI RESORT SUBDIVISION

CUMBERLAND PLATEAU RESORTS, INC. TO WHOM IT MAY CONCERN:

Restrictive Covenants, Limitations and Reservations on the Tansi Resort Sub-Division, Crossville, Tennessee.

Developed by Cumberland Plateau Resorts, Inc.

The following restrictive covenants and conditions shall be applicable to and binding upon those certain residential lots or parcels of land conveyed as residential lots by Cumberland Plateau Resorts, Inc., and shown on a certain plat or plats of TANSI RESORT Sub-Division, filed or to be filed for record in the Register's Office of Cumberland County, Crossville, Tennessee.

1. Said lots shall be used exclusively for residential purposes.

2. Not more than one single family dwelling house may be erected on any one such residential lot, nor more than one other building for garage or storage purposes in connection therewith and provided further that such garage or storage building shall not be constructed prior to the dwelling house. No accessory or temporary building shall be used or occupied as living quarters. No building shall be constructed or erected on said lot unless built of solid or permanent material. Wood exteriors shall be stained or painted with at least two coats of stain or paint. No structure shall have tar paper, roll brick, siding or similar material on the outside wall. No tents, shacks or other structure shall at any time be erected on said property, no residence of less than 1200 sq. ft. of living space, exclusive of porch or car port area, shall be erected or constructed on lots designated as Class "A". No residence of less than 900 sq. ft. of living space, exclusive of porch or car port area, shall be erected or constructed on lots designated as Class "B". No residence of less than 600 sq. ft. of living space, exclusive of porch or car port area, shall be erected or constructed on lots designated as Class "D". No residence of less than 360 sq. ft. of living space, exclusive of porch or car port area, shall be erected or constructed on lots designated as Class "E". Lots

designated as "D" and "C" must also have a porch connected to the residence of not less than 100 sq. ft. Plans for buildings to be constructed or erected on said lots must be approved by Cumberland Plateau Resorts, Inc. or its assigns, before construction is started.

3. Trailers designed for living purposes shall only be brought upon the property when there shall be a certain specific area so designated as a trailer park area.

4. No porch or projection to any residence or appurtenant building thereto shall extend nearer than 40 feet from the front line of the property nor within 10 feet from the line of any abutting owner, except, where set-back lines appear on the plat, structures or appurtenant buildings thereto may be constructed within the described areas shown by such lines.

5. No outside toilets shall be allowed on said lots. No waste shall be permitted to enter Lake Tansi and all sanitary arrangements must be inspected and approved by local or state health officers before any septic tanks are installed or before other waste disposal systems shall be constructed. No drain field or other disposal system shall be allowed nearer than 50 feet from the high water mark of Lake Tansi.

6. No animals or fowl shall be kept or maintained on said lots except customary household pets. No signs of any kind shall be displayed on any lot without the written permission of Cumberland Plateau Resorts, Inc., or its successors and/or assigns . . . ..

8. No boat docks, floats or other structures extending into the lake shall be constructed or placed into or on said lake without prior written approval of Cumberland Plateau Resorts, Inc., its successors and/or assigns. No loud or annoying motors shall be permitted on the lake between the hours of 10:00 P.M. and 8:00 A.M.

9. No noxious or offensive activity shall be carried on on any lots, nor shall anything be done thereon which shall be or become an annoyance or nuisance to the neighborhood.

10. The purchaser or purchasers of said lots agrees not to sell, transfer or convey said lots to any person or persons who have not made application and been accepted as a member or members of the Tansi Resort Property Owners' Association.

11. These restrictions shall be considered as covenants running with the land, and shall bind the purchasers of all lots shown on the sub-division plat or plats hereinbefore referred to, recorded or to be recorded, their heirs, executors, administrators and assigns, and if said owners, or any of them, their heirs, executors, successors and assigns, shall violate or attempt to violate any of the covenants or restrictions herein contained, it shall be lawful for any person or persons owning any such lots in the sub-division in which said lot is situated to prosecute any proceeding at law or in equity against the person or persons violating or attempting to violate any such covenants

or restrictions and either to prevent him or them from so doing or to recover damages for such violation. Any invalidation of any one of these covenants and restrictions shall in no way affect any other of the provisions thereof which shall thereafter remain in full force and effect.

Executed this 5th day of April, 1963.

CUMBERLAND PLATEAU RESORTS, INC.

By <u>S. Henry Rodgers</u>
PRESIDENT

ANDREWS v. LAKE SERENE PROPERTY OWNERS ASSOCIATION, INC.

Supreme Court of Mississippi, 1983.
434 So.2d 1328.

ROBERTSON, Justice, for the Court:

I.

The meaning of the term "lot" in protective covenants, as amended, for Unit Two of the Lake Serene Subdivision in Lamar County, Mississippi, is at the core of this civil dispute.

William E. Andrews, III, and Kent F. Hudson own three lots which are part of a 15 lot resubdivision of the original Lots 83 and 84 of Unit Two of Lake Serene. Andrews and Hudson, Complainants below, are Appellants here. They contend that the protective covenants permit construction of a single dwelling on each such resubdivided lot, provided, of course, that all other protective and restrictive covenants are complied with.

The Lake Serene Property Owners Association, Inc., Appellee here, argues for a contrary construction of the covenants. The property owners association contends that the restriction of one single family dwelling per lot refers to the original Lots 83 and 84, not to the resubdivision which has brought into existence 15 smaller lots instead of two very large lots.

After plenary trial on the merits and a careful consideration of the issues involved, the Chancery Court found an "ambiguity" within the covenants relating to the minimum size of lots in Lake Serene, notwithstanding, the Chancery Court held that the covenants should be construed to provide that no more than one single family dwelling may be constructed on original Lot 83 and no more than one single family dwelling may be constructed on original Lot 84. Andrews and Hudson have appealed from this ruling. Believing that the Chancellor erred in his resolution of the underlying question of law involved in this case, we reverse. We hold that Lots 6, 7 and 13 of the Lakeview Subdivision are separate lots within the meaning of the restrictive covenants applicable thereto.

II.

Lake Serene is a residential subdivision located on Highway 98 a few miles west of Hattiesburg but in Lamar County, Mississippi. Unit Two of the entire Lake Serene Subdivision has its own separate plat and its own separate protective covenants. The original plat of Unit Two was filed for record in April of 1965. Lot 83 of Unit Two, as originally platted, consisted of 3.74 acres. Lot 84 of Unit Two consisted of 5.165 acres.

On June 3, 1965, the original protective covenants for Unit Two were filed for record. Those original covenants provided in pertinent part as follows:

> "3. LAND USE & BUILDING TYPE: No lot shall be used except for the construction of a dwelling. . . ."

> . . .

> "6. LOT AREA & WIDTH: No dwelling shall be erected or placed on any lot having a width of less than 50 feet at the minimum building setback line nor shall any dwelling be erected or placed on any lot having an area of less than 17,500 square feet."

The word "lot" was not specifically defined. Further, no provision of the protective covenants prohibited resubdivision of the original lots of Unit Two.

On April 25, 1968, the developers of Lake Serene conveyed original Lots 83 and 84 to one Herbert Slay. Less than four months later, on August 13, 1968, to be specific, Slay and his partner W.J. Mims caused to be duly filed for record a plat of the Lakeview Subdivision. This Lakeview Subdivision effected a resubdivision of Lots 83 and 84 of Unit Two. The two large lots were divided into 15 smaller lots, each still having an area of at least 20,000 square feet.

On May 2, 1973, the protective covenants for Unit Two of Lake Serene were amended. The pertinent provisions of the amended covenants are as follows:

> "1. Lots 1 through 11 inclusive and Lots 20 through 98 in said Unit Two of Lake Serene Subdivision shall be known and described as residential lots and no other structure shall be erected, altered or permitted to remain on any of said residential building lots other than one single family dwelling with appurtenant out buildings."

> . . .

> "5. LOT & AREA WIDTH: No single family dwelling shall be erected or placed on any lot having width of less than fifty feet (50′) at the minimum building setback line nor shall any dwelling

be erected or placed on any lot having an area less than twenty thousand square feet (20,000 sq. ft.)."

Once again, the protective covenants contained no prohibition against subdivision of lots.

By instrument dated May 2, 1973, and filed for record on June 12, 1973, the protective covenants on Unit Two were extended.[1] This instrument contained the following pertinent language:

> "The original protective covenants and building restrictions on Unit Two, Lake Serene Subdivision, Lamar County, Mississippi, shall be extended for a term of eight years and shall be covenants which are to run with the land. . . ."

On May 15, 1974, the State of Mississippi duly chartered a nonprofit organization denominated The Lake Serene Property Owners Association, Inc. The Association is a voluntary one composed of owners of property within Units 1, 2, 3, 4, 5 and 6 of the entire Lake Serene Development. This is the property owners association which is the appellee here.

This litigation involves only three of the 15 lots in the Lakeview Subdivision, which, as explained above, is a resubdivision of Lots 83 and 84 of Unit Two of Lake Serene. In November of 1977, these three lots were acquired by appellants Andrews and Hudson.

Prior to the advent of this civil action, a single family dwelling was constructed on Lot 1 of Lakeview Subdivision which is a part of the original Lot 84. Another single family dwelling was constructed on Lot 8 of Lakeview Subdivision which is carved out of the original Lot 83. Thus, in a very real sense, at the time the instant controversy arose, there was existing on the land, which was the original Lot 83, one single family residential dwelling. Similarly, there was one single family dwelling on original Lot 84.

Soon after acquiring Lots 6, 7 and 13 of the Lakeview Subdivision, Andrews and Hudson made known their intention to construct single family dwellings on each. Andrews and Hudson at all times have acknowledged their obligation to comply with all provisions of the protective covenants applicable to Unit Two, including the 20,000 square foot area requirement and the 50 foot minimum setback line requirement. Though they are concerned directly with only three lots of the Lakeview Subdivision, their position necessarily is that the covenants should be construed to allow ultimately construction of 15 single family dwellings, one per resubdivided lot.

1. The covenants further provide:

"These covenants are to run with the land and shall be binding on all parties and all persons claiming under them for a period of not to exceed eight years from the date these covenants are recorded, after which time said covenants shall be automatically extended for successive periods of eight years unless an instrument signed by a majority of the then owners of the lots has been recorded agreeing to change such covenants, in whole or in part." Without doubt the covenants, as amended, are still in full force and effect.

The Property Owners Association disputed this construction of the covenants. Adopting the civilized way of resolving their bona fide differences, the parties have submitted this controversy to the Chancery Court of Lamar County, Mississippi, which, as indicated above, held in favor of the Property Owners Association. Feeling aggrieved, Andrews and Hudson have asked this Court to review the questions of law ruled upon by the Chancery Court.

III.

A.

Andrews and Hudson own the fee to Lots 6, 7 and 13 of the Lakeview Subdivision, a resubdivision of Lots 83 and 84 of Unit Two of Lake Serene Subdivision, Lamar County, Mississippi. Ordinarily, that miniscule portion of this planet's soil as a person owns may be put to such use as that person desires. Andrews and Hudson desire to build three single family dwellings, one on Lot 6, one on Lot 7 and one on Lot 13.

Over the years our law has come to recognize the need, when properly called upon, to enforce certain types of limitations upon land use. Broadly speaking, these limitations fall into two categories by reference to their source and nature. First, there are those limitations created by the public law emanating from an identifiable sovereign, limitations such as zoning laws, building codes and fire codes. Second, private lawmaking, in accordance with the empowering and enabling rules of the sovereign, has given rise to such useful devices as licenses, easements, defeasible estates and protective covenants.

In this case, we are concerned with privately created restrictions upon land use. The land in question owned by Andrews and Hudson is subject to certain protective covenants, sometimes called restrictive covenants, which limit their use. This case turns on the construction given the term "lot" as that term has been used in the applicable covenants. Not surprisingly, each group of litigants has a different view.

We are aided by general rules of construction heretofore adopted by this Court. Indeed, in its less than serene history, Lake Serene has contributed to the development of these rules of construction, for in Kemp v. Lake Serene Property Owners Association, Inc., 256 So.2d 924 (Miss.1971), this Court stated:

> Generally courts do not look with favor on restrictive covenants. Such covenants are subject more or less to a strict construction and in the case of ambiguity, construction is most strongly against the person seeking the restriction and in favor of the person being restricted. 245 So.2d at 926.

This rule of construction had been established in this state long before Lake Serene and its litigious occupants began to make their presence felt.

An important corollary rule, however, is that the clear and unambiguous wording of protective covenants will not be disregarded merely because a use is prohibited or restricted. If the intent to prohibit or restrict be expressed in clear and unambiguous wording, enforcement is available in the courts of this state. In A.A. Home Imp. Co. v. Hideaway Lake, 393 So.2d 1333 (Miss.1981), this Court recognized that:

> In construing restrictive covenants the question is primarily one of intention, and the fundamental rule is that the intention of the parties as shown by the agreement governs, being determined by fair interpretation of the entire text of the covenant.

The intent must be clear. Still, clear restrictive language, manifesting a restrictive intent, and unambiguous on its face or in the factual context faced by the Court, will be enforced.

These rules of construction are helpful guidelines. Yet in no way do they establish a precise formula which, when applied to a given case, mechanically produce an unassailable result. Our touchstone remains the covenants themselves. For it is established in our law that clearly worded protective covenants, if lawfully made, are indeed enforceable as written.

B.

When formally approved and placed of record on June 3, 1965, the original Unit Two protective covenants provided (with exceptions not relevant here) that no lot could be used except for the construction of a dwelling. At that time the only reasonable construction of the word "lot" was by reference to those lots designated formally on the only existing plat. At that time Lot 83 was a lot—one lot, and Lot 84 was a lot—one lot.

Shortly over three years later, however, the two large lots, numbered 83 and 84, were redivided so that they became 15 smaller lots. They became then known as the Lakeview Subdivision lots. The protective covenants contained no prohibition against resubdivision. The formation of the Lakeview Subdivision and the creation of 15 lots where there had once been only two was within the lawful power of the then owners of Lots 83 and 84.

A critical question is whether, with the recording of the plat of the Lakeview Subdivision on August 13, 1968, the term "lot" in the original protective covenants continued to refer to the original Lots 83 and 84, or, whether the term "lot" thereafter referred to those newly created lots numbered one through 15 of the Lakeview Subdivision. To be sure, the draftsmen of the original protective covenants had the power to word those covenants so that "lot" continued, then and forever, to refer to the orginal plat. This, however, they did not do in the protective covenants under consideration here.

Law and its meanings are not static, as surely all are aware. This is true of all laws designed to last over time. It is true of terms and provisions in statutes enacted by a legislature, rules of law approved by courts and the privately made law found in covenants and contracts. Times change. Circumstances change. Those creating law, legislators, privately contracting parties, or whoever may and ought anticipate change and provide therefor. In the absence of such anticipatory provision, however, a wooden construction based on conditions no longer existing leads to folly and mischief.

The term lot in the original protective covenants in this case should be given no static definition—for it has been given none by its draftsmen. The term means each area of land designated as a lot on the day the definition is given. It refers to whatever was and is a *lawfully* designated "lot" on the day the definition is sought. After August 13, 1968, the three plots of land in issue here, Lots 6, 7 and 13, each became a lot. The owner of each such lot was after that date entitled to construct on each such lot one single family dwelling, provided, of course, that all provisions of the protective covenants were complied with.

C.

Nothing in the 1973 amendments to the protective covenants changes the conclusion we reach here. Construing the 1973 amendments favorably to the owners of Lots 6, 7 and 13 and strongly but fairly against those seeking to restrict use, we find that the amended covenants allow the construction on Lot 6 of the Lakeview Subdivision of one single family dwelling with appurtenant outbuildings, and a similar single family dwelling on Lot 7 and on Lot 13 each.

The language in Section 1 of the 1973 amendments must be read in light of conditions then existing. When the amendments provide for the single family dwelling limitation, they refer to:

"Lots 1 through 11 inclusive and Lots 20 through 89 in said Unit Two of Lake Serene Subdivision."

Sensibly construed, this means those areas as they *then* (in 1973) existed and were *then* subdivided. Applying the rules of construction stated and explained above, we hold that this language should be construed to read:

Lots 1 through 11 inclusive and Lots 20 through 89 [sic] (including the 15 lots of the resubdivision of Lots 83 and 84 into the Lakeview Subdivision) of said Unit Two of Lake Serene Subdivision.
. . .

The 1973 amendments described the land covered and affected by the covenants as:

Entire Unit 2 of Lake Serene Subdivision, Lamar County, Mississippi, as per map or plat thereof on file in the office of the Chancery Clerk, Lamar County, Plat Book 1 at page 103.

This refers to the original plat. But that plat had been amended in 1968 by the Lakeview Subdivision of Lots 83 and 84. Absent an express exclusion of the amendments, the above quoted language contained in the 1973 covenants should be read as though the words "as amended" were appended thereto.

Again, an express provision to the contrary was within the power of the makers of the 1973 amendments to adopt. Had such been adopted, no court of competent jurisdiction would hesitate to enforce it. In view of the rules of construction applicable to restrictive covenants, however, we find that the language employed falls far short of the degree of specificity and clarity necessary to undo the meaning of "lot" as it had existed from August 1968 until May of 1973 and restore to that term "lot" a reference to Lots 83 and 84 which had ceased to have any legal existence five years earlier.

We note that Section 5 of the 1973 amendments to the protective covenants permits the construction of a single family dwelling on any lot having an area of 20,000 square feet or more. According to the record before this Court, Lots 1, 2, 3, 4, 12, 13, 14 and 15 of the Lakeview Subdivision contain exactly 20,000 square feet. The other seven are even larger. Nothing in what Andrews and Hudson contemplate will violate this dominant provision of the covenants.

In this context, absent a far more express provision in the 1973 amendments to the protective covenants, it is difficult to discern any justice or legality in prohibiting Andrews and Hudson from using their miniscule portion of this earth's soil as they contemplate. There is no equity in prohibiting Andrews and Hudson from constructing a single family dwelling on each of their 20,000 square foot lots while allowing such on any other similarly sized lots within Unit Two.

Reversed and Rendered.

PATTERSON, C.J., WALKER and BROOM, P.JJ., and ROY NOBLE LEE, BOWLING, HAWKINS and DAN M. LEE, JJ., concur.

PRATHER, J., not participating.

NOTES

1. Real covenants can take a variety of forms. *B*, who owns Blackacre, may promise *A*, who owns neighboring Whiteacre, that she will erect and maintain a boundary wall running between the two parcels, or that she will not place any improvement on Blackacre that obstructs the scenic view from Whiteacre. *C*, a major department store tenant in a suburban shopping center, may promise the center's small retail tenants that it will actively conduct its business during regular shopping center hours, seven days a week; each tenant may in turn promise *C* and the other tenants not to sell competing lines of merchandise. Or, as in the Tansi Subdivision, each homebuyer may promise her neighbor, and each neighbor, in turn, may promise her

and each other, to occupy and maintain their lots in a prescribed manner.

The Tansi Covenants, Conditions and Restrictions (CC & Rs) only hint at the intricacy with which interdependent networks of negative and affirmative covenants, along with easements and sometimes conditions, can be fashioned to organize land use in a residential subdivision. There is no such thing as a "form" declaration of CC & Rs. An attorney should review any proposed declaration with a careful eye to the interests of his or her particular client—developer, homebuyer or homebuyer's lender.

Representing a homebuyer in the Tansi Subdivision, what questions would you have about Paragraph 1 of the CC & Rs? Is it a covenant or a condition? If it is a covenant, is it a negative covenant (prohibiting other than residential use) or an affirmative covenant (requiring residential use and effectively prohibiting the owner from letting her lot lie idle)? What is a residential use? What remedies will be available in the event the covenant is breached? Is Paragraph 10's restraint on alienation enforceable? Does it prohibit leasing as well as sale? Representing a lender from whom a homebuyer in the subdivision has sought a mortgage loan, would you feel uneasy about the prospect that, if the buyer later defaults and foreclosure ensues, Paragraph 10 will hamper the lender's efforts to sell the parcel at a foreclosure sale?

Would you feel comfortable buying a lot in a subdivision subject to restrictions such as those imposed by the Tansi CC & Rs? What difficulties are likely to surround attempts to change the CC & Rs in order to meet the special needs of individual homebuyers? How comfortable would you feel in subjecting yourself to the will of the Homeowner's Association, a private mini-government chartered by the CC & Rs to supervise and maintain roads, utilities, open spaces and other recreational amenities serving the subdivision, and to prescribe norms of conduct for life in the subdivision? Do CC & Rs offer more or less flexibility for these purposes than zoning regulations adopted by local governments?

2. Do you agree with the decision in *Lake Serene*? What do you think was intended by the term, "said residential building lots," in paragraph 1 of the 1973 amended CC & Rs? What was the "underlying question of law" on which the supreme court believed that the Chancellor erred? What reasons underlie the constructional preference against restrictive covenants? Do these reasons apply in a context like the Lake Serene subdivision in which the restrictive covenants are reciprocal, binding all of the parcels in the subdivision and presumably enhancing their aggregate value?

Representing the developer, how would you have drafted the 1965 CC & Rs to prohibit the kind of resubdivision that was complained of in *Lake Serene*? Representing the Property Owners Association after this lawsuit, what obstacles would you expect to encounter if the

Association sought to amend the CC & Rs once again, this time to prohibit more than one unit on each original subdivided lot?

3. Although covenants today bear many similarities to easements and, indeed, are sometimes used interchangeably with them, the historical sources of the two are widely separated. Easements sprang directly out of real property law and were considered to represent just another type of real property interest. Covenants, by contrast, developed out of contract law and first became associated with real property transfers in the form of the warranties of title and possession that a grantor made to his grantee. Since these covenants of warranty could be enforced, not only by the original grantee, but also by his heirs and any other successors to his estate, the notion developed that the benefit of the covenant attached to the estate and passed with the estate to successive owners. By the fourteenth century, it was recognized that other covenants could be attached to estates in the same fashion as warranties. A pioneering decision, Pakenham's Case, Y.B. 42 Edw. III, Hil f. 3, pl. 14 (1369), enforced defendant's promise to celebrate divine service in the chapel of plaintiff, a successor to the estate originally held by defendant's covenantee. See generally, A. Simpson, An Introduction to the History of the Land Law, 109–111 (1961).

4. History helps explain some differences in the formal requirements for the creation of covenants and easements. While easements were from the outset required to comply with the provisions of the Statute of Frauds governing the transfer of interests in land, covenants were viewed as subject only to the Statute's requirements respecting contracts. Although there is now a split of authority on the question, the modern trend is to view covenants as interests in land, and to treat them as coming within the Statute of Frauds provisions respecting land transfers. See generally, Stoebuck, Running Covenants: An Analytical Primer, 52 Wash.L.Rev. 861, 867–869 (1977).

A deed executed only by the grantor (called a *deed poll*) is by far the most common form of conveyance. (If the deed were executed by both grantor and grantee, it would be an *indenture*.) If A conveys Blackacre to B by a deed that obligates B to perform one or more covenants, will B be bound even though only A, the grantor, executed the deed? Most courts hold that B's acceptance of a deed poll obligates her to perform any covenant contained in the deed. See, for example, Johnston v. Michigan Consolidated Gas Co., 337 Mich. 572, 60 N.W.2d 464 (1953).

The rationales that courts employ to excuse the statutory formalities for covenants have a distinctive contract flavor. For example, in Remilong v. Crolla, 576 P.2d 461 (Wyo.1978), B, who owned two adjacent parcels, sold one to A, and retained title to the second. At the time, B orally agreed to remove all the mobile homes from the retained parcel before the sale of the other parcel closed, and not to place any mobile homes on the retained parcel thereafter. B did remove the mobile homes before the closing, but replaced them after the closing. A sued to enjoin the installation of any further mobile homes on the retained parcel and sought an order for the removal of those mobile homes installed after the closing. Recognizing that restrictive covenants create an interest in land and are therefore within the scope of the Statute of Frauds, the Wyoming Supreme Court held that an enforceable restrictive covenant was nonetheless created under the facts because *B's* removal of the mobile homes prior to the closing was sufficient to engage the doctrine of promissory estoppel, defeating the Statute of Frauds. Can you think of an easier way for the court to have reached the same result?

b. BY IMPLICATION

ARTHUR v. LAKE TANSI VILLAGE, INC.

Supreme Court of Tennessee, 1979.
590 S.W.2d 923.

BROOKS McLEMORE, Special Justice.

This case involves the question of whether there exist *implied* restrictive covenants running with the land which prohibit the defendant-respondent, hereinafter called the defendant, from removing or relocating certain recreational facilities, namely; (1) a marina which is to be relocated from the north shore of Lake Tansi, to the south shore, which would place a modern marina equipped to moor and service some 80 boats along a dam in close proximity to plaintiffs' property; (2) a sand beach which has been destroyed, but which according to the defendant's president, will be re-established near its original location; (3) a golf course, 13 holes of which are to be relocated; some of these are lakeside holes which are to be moved away from the lake; and, (4) an airstrip which was closed because of the inability of the defendant to meet FAA regulations in regard to its operation, as well as the defendant's failure to obtain air rights so takeoff and landings could be accomplished in both directions. The space made available by the relocation of 13 holes of the golf course and the abandonment of the air strip is to be subdivided and sold for homesites. The sand beach space is to be reserved for future development. There are no stated plans for the present marina site.

The trial court and the Court of Appeals both found in favor of the defendant.

Darrell Arthur, Jack Hickey, Charles Taylor, Sam Hambric and their wives, plaintiffs-petitioners, hereinafter called plaintiffs, petitioned this court and certiorari was granted to review that action. The suit was brought individually and not in a representative capacity.

We affirm the judgment of the Court of Appeals.

During a portion of the year 1963, and prior thereto, Cosby Harrison and wife operated considerable acreage including the Lake, then named Lake Harrison, in the business of renting property for transient guests. Harrison operated the property as a resort area and did not sell any homesite property as he was not interested in that type of development.

By deeds dated March 1, 1963, and September 2, 1963, Cumberland Plateau Resorts, Inc., a Tennessee corporation, the common grantor of all property which is the subject matter of this lawsuit, acquired approximately 2,660 acres of improved and unimproved property from Cosby Harrison and wife; this included among other things, Lake Harrison, a nine-hole golf course which was located partially along the shore of the lake, a marina, an airstrip and a sand beach.

Cumberland Plateau Resorts, Inc., whose main object was the sale of primary and secondary homesites, changed the name of the lake to Lake Tansi, platted a relatively small portion of the property and placed of record in the Cumberland County Register's Office various subdivision plats depicting certain portions of the property adjacent to and surrounding the lake. These subdivision plats depicted some of the various lots then for sale, parts of the original nine-hole golf course, the airstrip, the marina, and the general area for the proposed second nine holes of golf. The number of lots for sale in 1963 consisted of approximately 686 of which 133 were lake-front lots some of which were accessible only by boat. The property owned by plaintiffs is from this group of lots. Copies of these plats were in the sales office at Lake Tansi; however, none of plaintiffs' lots are shown on plats that show the recreation facilities mentioned.

Certain brochures describing and showing pictures of the recreational facilities at Lake Tansi were available in the sales office and were used in sales.

The plaintiffs acquired their respective homesites either directly or by succession of title from Cumberland during a period beginning on May 20, 1963, and ending March 30, 1968. From the deeds filed in the stipulation, it appears that all of the lots owned by plaintiffs except three, were conveyed by Cumberland either to the plaintiffs or others in their chain of title by August 22, 1963; the three lots were conveyed by Cumberland to Taylor by deed dated August 16, 1966. Though all the deeds are not in the record, it appears Arthur owns one and one-half lots, Hamrick owns two which adjoin, Hickey owns one and Taylor owns five in a block. All of plaintiffs' lots are in the same general area and all are lake-front lots. *None of these lots adjoin, touch or are close to, the marina, the airstrip, the sand beach or the golf course.*

Plaintiffs' deeds did not mention any of these facilities; however, they were permitted to use these facilities for an annual fee. Apparently, the general public could use all the facilities upon payment of appropriate charges. Later, Cumberland added the additional nine holes to the golf course; some of these holes were placed along the lake shore.

All the deeds filed in the stipulation concerning property purchased by the plaintiffs, except two, describe the property by lot number "as shown by plat no. 3 of Tansi Resort Sub-division, which plat is duly recorded in Plat Book No. 1, Page 169, Register's Office, Cumberland County, Tennessee." As to the two exceptions, one deed also refers to a revised plat found at Plat Book 1, Page 176 and a second deed refers to Plat Book 1, Page 194. All of the deeds recite that "this conveyance is made subject to restrictive covenants, limitations and conditions contained in the restrictive covenants in the Tansi Resort Sub-division, dated the 5th day of April, 1963, of record in Deed Book No. D-62, Page 30, Register's Office, Cumberland County, Tennessee." The recorded restrictions above mentioned are not a part of the record, although there are certain property reports made by the defendant pursuant to federal statute which do show restrictions as to Southlake 3, that portion of Lake Tansi Resort embracing plaintiffs' lots. The first restriction recites, "the lots shall be used exclusively for residential purposes except those lots designated as business or commercial areas."

In 1968, Lake Tansi Village, Inc., was incorporated in Tennessee; it then purchased on May 14, 1968, all of the Lake Tansi property from Cumberland except those lots sold to third persons like the plaintiffs and their predecessors. Thereafter, in December of 1971, new management assumed control when all the stock of Lake Tansi Village, Inc. was purchased by National American Corporation. By virtue of this stock purchase and a subsequent merger with an Alabama corporation, which was also a subsidiary of National American, the defendant became an Alabama corporation licensed to do business in Tennessee. Lake Tansi Village, Inc., is a wholly owned subsidiary of National American Corporation. An additional 1780 acres of land were acquired from third parties. Shortly thereafter, a land planner was hired and an overall plat was developed by the planner; this plat reflected, among other things, the planner's recommendation to relocate part of the existing 18 holes of golf and to eliminate the landing strip. The overall plat consists of 3,327.45 acres, subdivided into 9,655 residential lots and in addition, several hundred acres of recreational facilities. The overall plat is not recorded as one, but was recorded as approximately 50 smaller plats. The large plat was reduced to printing press size and distributed by the tens of thousands in 1974. An enlargement of the overall plat was, and still is, displayed in the Sales Office.

Beginning in 1972, the defendant filed several property reports under the Interstate Land Sales Full Disclosure Act. The report dated April 30, 1972, lists recreational facilities that were available at that time. This list included the 18-hole golf course, however, the landing strip was not listed as being available for use, nor was the sand beach or marina included among the facilities listed. This report contained the statement, "All presently contemplated facilities are complete." A second property report, effective on May 29, 1973, lists the same facilities as in the 1972 report and similarly does not mention a landing strip, sand beach and marina. This property report adds the following statements: "At present, there is a grass runway for small planes. Because of its infrequent use, seller plans to abandon such runway at a future date and add such land to its residential development . . . .. Sellers reserve the right to relocate certain holes of the golf course, however, such relocation will not take place until replacement holes have been constructed and ready for play." A report of July 10, 1973, listed the same facilities as did the second report and contained the above-quoted statements. The most recent property report, dated December 28, 1976, contains an expanded list of facilities available and proposed. It reports the plan to close the airstrip and it also contains a disclosure regarding the right to relocate various holes of the golf course, as well as the pro shop, and to develop the property where they exist. An assurance is given that an 18-hole golf course and pro shop will always be available for property owners. "Lake Tansi and boat marina" are listed; the sand beach is not.

On November 21, 1973, the defendant inserted an advertisement in a local newspaper describing certain of the facilities. The airstrip is not mentioned. This advertisement contained the following:

FOREVER IS A LONG TIME . . ..

But that's how long you & your family will be able to enjoy the facilities of Lake Tansi Village.

In the early part of 1977, the plaintiffs became aware of the defendant's intention to relocate certain holes of the golf course away from the lake and to abandon the present marina and build a new marina in close proximity to their lots. This suit for injunction, or in the alternative, damages, resulted. Plaintiffs have filed three assignments of error. They assign as error, first, that the evidence preponderates in favor of their insistence of implied covenants and second, that the defendant is estopped from denying the existence of such covenants. By their third assignment of error, plaintiffs insist that the Court of Appeals erred in holding that plaintiffs could not rely upon plats not referred to in their deeds to establish the existence of implied restrictive covenants.

Parenthetically, we note that it would be difficult to read this record without perceiving that the real concern of the plaintiffs is the relocation of the marina near their lots with all the attendant noise, wakes, pollution and impediment of their view of the lake.

In beginning our consideration of the assignments of error, we quote with approval from the Court of Appeals' opinion prepared by Judge Goddard:

> As a preliminary to addressing the assignments of error, we observe that although our courts recognize the validity of restrictive covenants they are not favored. This Court in a recent case, Waller v. Thomas, 545 S.W.2d 745, at page 747 (Tenn.App.1976), said:
>
>> Our courts have long recognized several established rules of construction regarding restrictive covenants, which can be stated as follows: Although the law recognizes the validity of restrictive covenants, they are not favored because such covenants are in derogation of the unrestricted enjoyment of the fee. Therefore, restrictive covenants are to be strictly construed and will not be extended by implication and any ambiguity in the restriction will be resolved against the restriction.
>
> With this background we turn to the assignments of error and conclude that insofar as implied covenants are concerned the plaintiff may prevail only on a showing of one of the following: (1) implication by necessity, (2) implication by conveying property with restrictions under a general plan or scheme of development, (3) implication by reference to a plat.
>
> As to the first, the plaintiffs rely upon a case decided by the Supreme Court of Texas, Danciger Oil & Refining Company of Texas v. Powell, 154 S.W.2d 632 (1941), which incidentally, did not find a restrictive covenant by implication. There the Court said (at page 635):
>
>> In the outset it should be noted that when parties reduce their agreements to writing, the written instrument is presumed to embody their entire contract, and the court should not read into the instrument additional provisions unless this be necessary in order to effectuate the intention of the parties as disclosed by the contract as a whole. An implied covenant must rest entirely on the presumed intention of the parties as gathered from the terms as actually expressed in the written instrument itself, and it must appear that it was so clearly within the contemplation of the parties that they deemed it unnecessary to express it, and therefore omitted to do so, or it must appear that it is necessary to infer such a covenant in order to effectuate the full purpose of the contract as a whole as gathered from the written instrument. It is not enough to say that an implied covenant is necessary in order to make the contract fair, or that without such a covenant it would be improvident or unwise, or that the contract would operate unjustly. It must arise from the presumed intention of the parties as gathered from the instrument as a whole. However, covenants will be implied in fact when necessary to give effect to

the actual intention of the parties as reflected by the contract or conveyance as construed in its entirety in the light of the circumstances under which it was made and the purposes sought to be accomplished thereby.

Upon viewing the conveyances we cannot say that the restrictions insisted upon by the plaintiffs were so clearly within the contemplation of the parties that they deemed it unnecessary to express them. Consequently, the plaintiffs may not prevail under this theory.

We believe that the foregoing rationale and statement of the law succinctly and adequately deals with the theory of implication by necessity as it applies to the instant case.

In assignment two, plaintiffs focus their argument upon the implication of restrictive covenants stemming from the defendant's development of this property along the lines of a general plan or scheme. Ways of establishing such a plan or scheme are discussed at 20 Am. Jur.2d, Covenants § 175 (1965):

> "One of the most common forms of imposing building restrictions is by the establishment of a general building plan of improvement or development covering a tract divided into a number of lots. Such a plan may be established in various ways, such as by express covenant, by implication from a filed map, or by parol representations made in sales brochures, maps, advertising, and oral statements on which the purchaser relied in making his purchase. It is said that the most complete way is by a reciprocal covenant whereby the grantor covenants to insert like covenants in all deeds out of the common development, and that other ways may consist of the grantor's selling the lots upon representations to the individual purchasers that like covenants will be inserted in the grantor's deeds to others, for the common benefit, or the grantor's pursuing a course of conduct indicating a neighborhood scheme, leading the several purchasers to assume its adoption and the adherence to it by such conduct.
>
> As heretofore shown, where such a plan is created, the conveyance of a lot or lots therein raises an implied covenant restricting the remaining lots . . . ."

The doctrine of reciprocal negative easements was recognized and applied by this court in Land Developers, Inc. v. Maxwell, 537 S.W.2d 904 (Tenn.1976). This doctrine involves the general plan or scheme of development theory. There, the restrictions all involved limiting the property previously conveyed to residential development.

The Court explains the manner in which negative reciprocal easements, a form of restrictive covenants, are to be applied. Justice Harbison speaking for the court said:

> ". . . the doctrine of negative reciprocal easements, while well recognized in the law of property, is to be applied with great care.

Thus the Court of Appeals of Kentucky, while recognizing the doctrine, stated:

> 'We think it quite apparent that the doctrine ought to be used and applied with extreme caution, for it involves difficulty and lodges discretionary power in a court of equity, in a degree, to deprive a man of his property by imposing a servitude through implication.' McCurdy v. Standard Realty Corp., 295 Ky. 587, 175 S.W.2d 28, 30 (1943).'"

If restrictive covenants enforceable by the plaintiffs prohibiting the abandonment of the air strip and the relocation of the marina, the sand beach and a portion of the golf course arising from a general plan of development do exist, these arose at the time the plaintiffs or their predecessors in title purchased their property. The Chancellor, rather than finding a plan in existence at the time plaintiffs purchased, found, "that the defendant, for the past several years has put into effect an overall development plan, which includes the alteration or relocation of certain golf holes, a sand beach, and a boat marina, together with the abandonment of a grass landing strip for small aircraft." The Court of Appeals found specifically that there was no general plan of development in the early stages when plaintiffs or their predecessors purchased. The statement of the Court of Appeals in part is, ". . . in the early stages the development was like Topsy and no real general plan emerged until after the merger was accomplished and a real estate consultant employed." We agree with this finding and therefore, plaintiffs can obtain no relief under this theory.

To aid in the disposition of plaintiffs' third assignment of error with respect to implication by reference to a plat, we quote with approval from the opinion of the Court of Appeals:

> "As to the last point, plaintiffs insist that because certain recorded plats show the facilities, they have acquired a property right in them under the authority of Moore v. Queener, 62 Tenn.App. 490, 464 S.W.2d 296 (1970). The problem with this theory however, is that the plats to which the plaintiffs' deeds refer are not a part of the record. Moreover, we gather from plaintiffs' briefs that the facilities are not shown upon these plats because counsel argues that the defendant should be bound by other plats which actually show the facilities. Plaintiffs maintain that this was necessary because the development is so large that it was impractical, if not impossible, to show all the various subdivisions comprising the resort on a plat the size of which is suitable for recording. We concede that this may be true. However, the rationale behind implying a property right in cases like *Moore* is because the plat is incorporated by reference in the deed of conveyance. Obviously a plat to which no reference is made cannot be incorporated in a deed."

Plaintiffs' third assignment of error in this court takes issue with the foregoing reasoning and holding of the Court of Appeals. Plaintiffs complain that the Court of Appeals has, in effect, held that the plaintiffs may not rely upon recorded plats showing the golf course, marina and air strip because plaintiffs' lots do not appear on the same plats. We find no merit to this assignment. As earlier stated, plaintiffs' lots do not appear on the plat with the recreational facilities mentioned and plaintiffs' deeds *do not refer* either to the facilities or the plats of record that show these facilities. The opposite is true in the case of McCleary et al. v. Lourie, 80 N.H. 389, 117 A. 730 (1922) upon which the plaintiffs heavily rely.

We interpret the holding of the Court of Appeals on this point to be that a plat may be utilized in establishing implied restrictive covenants if the deed of the party seeking to impose the restriction refers to the plat. This holding is in accord with established legal principles. See, *e.g.*, 25 Am.Jur.2d, Easements and Licenses § 26 (1966) where it is said:

> Generally, where property sold is described in the conveyance with reference to a plat or map on which streets, alleys, parks, and other open areas are shown, an easement therein is created in favor of the grantee . . . . But such an easement does not arise unless the conveyance refers to the map or plat which indicated the way, park, or other area in which an easement is claimed; *this requirement is not obviated by the fact that the way is shown on a recorded plat.* [Emphasis supplied.]

In Moore v. Queener, *supra*, plaintiffs' deed specifically referred to a plat upon which the easement he claimed appeared.

We find no merit to this assignment of error.

We turn now to plaintiffs' contention that the defendant is estopped from denying the existence of restrictive covenants.

Plaintiffs Arthur, Taylor and Hambric all testified that they saw the maps which depicted the golf course and the marina in the Sales Office prior to their purchase; however, the testimony as to plaintiffs' reliance on these maps and brochures is confusing. Hickey did not testify. There is no solid evidence of actual promises of permanency being made to plaintiffs by the original grantor or his agents. Plaintiffs contend that defendant's actions in distributing brochures, advertising in the newspaper, and making statements in its property reports all would estop the defendant, if not initially when plaintiffs purchased, then subsequently because of the improvements and maintenance of their property after such acts occurred. As to this contention, we point out as did the Court of Appeals, that the plaintiffs purchased their property long before the defendant ever assumed control of the resort and before it distributed brochures, advertised in the local newspaper, or filed its property reports, and there is no satisfactory proof that the improvements or continued maintenance were done in reliance upon any acts or statements of the defendant.

Therefore, an essential element of estoppel, action by one party in reliance upon misstatement by another to his detriment, is not present.

Estoppel *in pais* has been defined in this state as:

"Estoppel in pais is an estoppel that does not arise from a record or written instrument, but arises from the conduct or silence of a party and is sometimes referred to as equitable estoppel. In the true sense, all matters of estoppel arise in equity, for the purpose of the existence of the doctrine is to prevent inconsistency and fraud resulting in an injustice. When a man has been misled by the untruth propounded by another, *and acted to his detriment in reliance upon the misrepresentation*, the misleading party will be estopped to show that the true facts are contrary to those he first propounded." Duke v. Hopper, 486 S.W.2d 744, 748 (Tenn. App.1972). [Emphasis supplied.]

Even if implied restrictive covenants arose at the time of purchase, the restrictions cannot be imposed against the defendant, a purchaser for value, unless the evidence establishes that the defendant had notice of the restrictions. This general rule set forth in 28 Am.Jur.2d, Estoppel and Waiver, 117, page 776, is as follows:

As a general rule, an estoppel of a grantor runs against his grantee. Obviously, estoppels affecting grantees often involve the running and binding effect of covenants . . . . It has been held that where an estoppel works on an interest in land, it becomes a muniment of the title, and when the owner conveys it he necessarily does so subject to the estoppel in the hands of his grantee. Clearly, a grantee is in privity with his grantor to the extent that he is bound by an estoppel in pais against the grantor if he had notice of the facts from which the estoppel arose at the time of the grant, but, according to the prevailing rule, a bona fide purchaser for value and without notice of an estoppel against his grantor is not bound by the estoppel . . . .

In *Maxwell, supra,* this court, at page 913, said:

"Of course, it is well settled, in Tennessee as elsewhere, that an owner of land is not bound by covenants restricting the use of the land by his remote grantor, when such covenants do not appear in the owner's chain of title and when he had no actual notice of the alleged covenant at the time he acquired title."

Plaintiffs contend that because the facilities were present on the ground and in use, and because of brochures used by former owners, and because of the recorded plats previously mentioned, the defendant had notice of restrictive covenants.

When the history of this development is considered, knowledge by the defendant that there was in existence in 1972 a golf course, a marina, a sand beach and a landing strip, none of which adjoined or were close to plaintiffs' lots, would not put the defendant on notice that there were any agreements between the original grantor and the plaintiffs prohibiting the relocation of the facilities or the abandonment of the landing strip. The fact that a purchaser may know about certain characteristics of the land purchased will not necessarily impute knowledge as to any implied restrictions. In *Maxwell, supra,* it was found that the original grantor intended for all "Mimosa Heights" property to be residential and therefore, remaining property that had passed into the hands of others who were not purchasers for value was burdened by reciprocal negative easements, *i.e.,* they stood in the same position as would the original grantor. However, it was held that in the hands of a purchaser for value, a portion of the same remaining property would not be subject to the restrictions though the purchaser knew of the recorded restrictions as to property previously sold. The court found that such knowledge was a far cry from charging him with knowledge of unrecorded, oral, or implied easements or restrictions covering unsold acreage.

The record is devoid of any proof of actual knowledge of defendant of any implied restrictive covenants running with plaintiffs' lots when the defendant purchased the development. On the other hand, there is convincing evidence in the record that management as far back as the purchase by Cumberland Plateau Resorts, Inc., did consider, and "there was talk of," moving some of the holes on the golf course, moving the marina and abandoning the airstrip, and that management never knew of or considered that there was any prohibition, express or implied, against altering or relocating the facilities. We conclude that the defendant had no notice of implied restrictive covenants and is not estopped as far as plaintiffs are concerned.

For the foregoing reasons, all assignments of error are overruled and the judgment of the Court of Appeals is affirmed. Costs are taxed against plaintiffs, and sureties.

BROCK, C.J., and COOPER, HENRY and HARBISON, JJ., concur.

NOTES

1. In the typical case of covenants implied by reason of a general plan or common neighborhood scheme, *A* purchases Whiteacre subject to an express negative covenant, restricting Whiteacre to residential use, upon developer *B*'s representation that all other parcels in the subdivision will be subjected to the same restriction; when subdivision neighbor *Z*, who subsequently acquired Blackacre from *B* under a deed containing no such restriction, starts building a grocery store on Blackacre, *A* seeks an injunction. Do the facts in *Tansi* conform to this general pattern? Were plaintiffs there seeking to establish implied negative covenants or implied affirmative covenants? What was the claimed servient estate corresponding to Blackacre? On what theory could plaintiffs claim an original intent that their parcels were to benefit from the implied covenant? Why did the court

underscore the fact that "none of the lots adjoin, touch or are close to, the marina, the airstrip, the sand beach or the golf course"?

Does the court's discussion of plaintiffs' first theory—implication of a covenant by necessity—suggest that a lower degree of necessity is required to imply a covenant than to imply an easement? The court's test for covenants appears to be rooted in rules of contract interpretation, while the test for easements is rooted in the more rigorous standards for construing land conveyances. Does the court's test properly respond to the fact that covenants are interests in land and can affect land use and the marketability of titles to the same extent as easements?

In discussing plaintiffs' second and third theories—implication of a covenant by general plan and by reference to a plat—the court expressly relied on cases and commentaries dealing with easements, apparently on the assumption that the rules respecting the two forms of nonpossessory interests are interchangeable. If the rules are in fact interchangeable—and many courts act as if they are—should they be? Is it relevant that more substantial requirements must be met for the burden of a covenant to run with the land than for the burden of an easement to run? Are *A*'s, *B*'s and *Z*'s expectations likely to differ depending on whether they are thinking about covenant interests or easement interests?

Might plaintiffs have had a nuisance action against "the relocation of the marina near their lots with all the attendant noise, wakes, pollution and impediment of their view of the lake"? Do the CC & Rs provide any evidence respecting the relative gravity of plaintiffs' harm and utility of defendant's conduct?

Representing a subdivision homebuyer in Tennessee after *Tansi*, would you qualify your title opinions to include the possibility that a restrictive covenant might be implied? An affirmative covenant? Representing a subdivision developer after *Tansi*, would you seek to include any special protective language in your CC & Rs? At least one Tennessee lawyer now includes the following provision as a matter of course:

> These covenants and restrictions shall only apply to the property herein conveyed and shall not be construed as creating any requirement on the part of the grantor herein or his heirs or assigns to restrict any of the remaining property located within the original _____ acre tract, of which this property is a part, from being used for purposes other than residential, and from being conveyed subject to the same, similar, different, or any of the covenants and restrictions herein set out. No negative reciprocal covenants or implied or equitable covenants of any nature shall be deemed to arise or be created as to any of the remaining property owned by grantor in the aforementioned _____ acre tract by virtue of the property herein conveyed being subject to the foregoing cove-

nants; and, grantee(s) herein, their heirs and assigns, acknowledge and accept this provision in purchasing said property.

Letter from Thomas E. Looney, Esq., Crossville, Tennessee, July 24, 1981. See generally, Comment, A Survey of the Law of Restrictive Covenants That Run With the Land in Tennessee, 50 Tenn.L.Rev. 149 (1982).

2. In order to imply a covenant by reason of a common neighborhood plan, virtually all courts require that a uniform plan exist at the time the parcel sought to be burdened is first conveyed. Courts differ mainly on the level of proof required to establish a common neighborhood plan. Some courts hold that uniform restrictions appearing in deeds to a substantial number of lots in the subdivision will suffice. Others require additional direct evidence of intent—typically the subdivider's representation to homebuyers that the restrictions appearing in their deeds will also appear in the deeds to all other parcels in the subdivision. A few courts will not allow these representations to be proved by parol, such as oral statements or declarations in documents or maps, and require that the representation appear in the homebuyer's deed.

Consider which standard the court applied in Mid-State Equipment Co., Inc. v. Bell, 217 Va. 133, 225 S.E.2d 877 (1976). Eubank, owner of an 85-acre tract, subdivided part of the tract adjacent to his own home into numbered parcels, comprising the "Jefferson Manor Subdivision" and, shortly afterwards, sold the numbered parcels to homebuyers. The subdivision plat contained a residential use restriction that, though encumbering all of the numbered parcels, did not by its terms affect the adjacent Eubank house and lot. Through subsequent conveyances, the Eubank homesite came into the hands of Mid-State which proceeded to convert the dwelling into a sales office for its operations on the parcel. Neighbors in the subdivision sued to enforce the subdivision's residential restrictions.

Recognizing that the restrictive covenants in issue were not expressly or directly applicable to Mid-State's Property, and that covenants "restricting the free use of land are not favored and must be strictly construed," the court nonetheless implied and enforced the covenants against Mid-State. "First, the Eubanks' home was located on the 'James D. & Mary R. Eubank' parcel when the development began in 1960, and it was used for residential purposes by the Eubanks until they sold it in 1966. Second, we have the unchallenged testimony of Overstreet, the surveyor, that he was instructed by Eubank to 'leave out' of the platted area sufficient land for two residential lots . . . . It is apparent from this omission of numbered lots 11 and 12 that the 'James D. & Mary R. Eubank' parcel was intended to be residential lots 11 and 12. The conclusion is strengthened when we blend the foregoing facts with other circumstances, which standing alone may not be sufficient to establish intent. For example, the property is shown on the Overstreet 'Plat of Jefferson

Manor' as an unreserved delineated lot; the residential restriction on the face of the plat refers to '[a]ll lots in this subdivision', not all numbered lots; and when the 1966 conveyance to [Mid-State's predecessor] took place . . . the deed made specific reference to the Overstreet plat containing the restriction." 217 Va. at 142, 225 S.E.2d at 885.

Justice Cochran dissented. "The property in question was not included in the 'Description' found on the Overstreet Plat of Jefferson Manor Subdivision. Therefore, we are not dealing with the omission of restrictive covenants from a deed to a numbered lot in the subdivision, where the intent to apply such covenants to all numbered lots may be implied. The subdivider reserved an unnumbered lot adjoining the subdivision, and there is at least as strong an implication that there was a deliberate exclusion of this property from subdivision restrictions as that there was an intent to make the property subject to the restrictions." 217 Va. at 143, 225 S.E.2d at 886.

3. How can decisions that infer common neighborhood plans from such fugitive evidence as sales brochures and advertisements, and that imply restrictive covenants based on these plans into deeds absolute on their face, be reconciled with the policies behind the Statute of Frauds and the parol evidence rule? Would an absolute rule forbidding courts to imply covenants discourage sloppy draftsmanship, leaving it to dissatisfied buyers to bring actions against neglectful developers and their title or escrow companies?

Both sides of the question were closely explored in Riley v. Bear Creek Planning Committee, 17 Cal.3d 500, 131 Cal.Rptr. 381, 551 P.2d 1213 (1976), which held that plaintiff, who acquired a subdivision parcel through a deed containing no restrictions, was not bound by CC & Rs recorded for the subdivision nine months after the conveyance to him. The court reached this result even though extrinsic evidence "tended to prove that the grantor intended to convey and plaintiffs intended to purchase a parcel which both parties assume to be governed by building restrictions."

The court acknowledged that since 1919, when it held in Werner v. Graham, 181 Cal. 174, 183 P. 946 (1919), that such extrinsic evidence should be excluded, the parol evidence rule had been liberalized to a point at which it might allow such evidence to be used in construing the deed. Nonetheless, the court held that the continuing force of the Statute of Frauds required that the evidence be given no weight. "Any other rule would make important questions of the title to real estate largely dependent upon the uncertain recollection and testimony of interested witnesses. The rule of the *Werner* case is supported by every consideration of sound public policy which has led to the enactment and enforcement of statutes of frauds in every English-speaking commonwealth." 17 Cal.3d at 510, 551 P.2d at 1220. Can this view be reconciled with the court's concession that "From the recordation of the first deed which effectively imposes restrictions on the land conveyed and that retained by the common grantor, the restrictions are binding upon all subsequent grantees of parcels so affected who take with notice thereof notwithstanding that similar clauses have been omitted from their deeds"? 17 Cal.3d at 507, 551 P.2d at 1218.

Justice Tobriner dissented. "I believe, therefore, that in light of this court's modification of the parol evidence rule, Werner v. Graham is no longer a correct application of existing law and should be overruled. The question remains, however, whether, as the majority maintains, the policy underlying the statute of frauds provides an independent basis for rejecting the evidence offered by defendants. That policy, as the majority points out, is to prevent fraud and perjury with respect to certain types of transactions by requiring the most reliable evidence available, a written document. In the present case, however, insistence upon a writing signed by both grantor and grantee is not necessary to prevent fraud, and such a requirement should not be invoked to frustrate the intention of the parties." 17 Cal.3d at 517, 551 P.2d at 1225. Tobriner cited the deed poll as one example of the situations "in which circumstances surrounding a transaction render the production of a writing signed by both parties unnecessary and accordingly have established a number of exceptions to the application of the statute." Is the analogy sound?

After *Riley*, would plaintiff have been entitled to enforce the burden of the restrictions encumbering his neighbors' estates?

4. For *Z*, a successor in interest to the putative servient estate, to be bound by an implied covenant, she must have had notice of the covenant at the time she acquired the parcel. Courts in their occasional zeal to imply and enforce residential restrictive covenants sometimes overlook or distort the standard notice requirements.

Sanborn v. McLean, 233 Mich. 227, 206 N.W. 496 (1925), is an example. The court there enforced an implied residential covenant (which it mistakenly called a "reciprocal negative easement"), even though plaintiff had failed to demonstrate that defendant had actual notice of the covenant, and even though defendant had no constructive notice since, the covenant being implied, no instrument in defendant's chain of title referred to it. The court held that defendants had inquiry notice of the implied restriction. "Considering the [residential] character of use made of all the lots open to a view of Mr. McLean when he purchased, we think he was put thereby to inquiry, beyond asking his grantor whether there were restrictions. . . . he could not avoid noticing the strictly uniform residence character given the lots by the expensive dwellings thereon, and the least inquiry would have quickly developed the fact that lot 86 was subjected to a reciprocal negative easement . . . ." 233 Mich. at 232, 206 N.W. at 498.

Representing a subdivision lot buyer in Michigan after *Sanborn*, what steps would you take to protect your client against implied negative covenants, and yourself against giving an unqualified opinion on title? Will the absence of dogs in the subdivision put your client under a duty to inquire whether there is an implied covenant prohibiting dogs? Will the absence of large dogs create a duty to inquire about a covenant excluding large dogs only?

2. ENFORCEMENT BY AND AGAINST SUCCESSORS IN INTEREST

a. Who is Bound? Does the Burden Run?

English courts early allowed the *benefit* of a covenant to run to nonpromisees. They were reluctant, however, to allow the *burden* of a covenant to run to nonpromisors. In part, the reasons for this reluctance were connected to the common law intricacies of the warranties of title; in part they were connected to the belief that it is a larger step to impose the burden of promises on nonpromisors than to shower their benefits on nonpromisees. The single context in which English law developed an integrated system of running benefits and burdens was landlord-tenant law, and that development was largely statutory. The statute, 32 Henry VIII, c. 34 (1534), together with some earlier common law developments, charged successors to the tenant's estate and to the landlord's reversionary interest with both the benefits and the burdens of covenants undertaken by their predecessors.

The English heritage is evident in the reluctance with which modern American courts allow the burden of real covenants to bind nonpromising parties. Although American courts have been more generous than their English counterparts in allowing burdens to run outside the landlord-tenant relationship, they have succeeded only by replacing parsimony with prolixity. Piling requirement upon requirement for the burden to run, American courts have produced what one observer has characterized as "an unnecessarily complicated, cumbersome and unpredictable complex of rules." Berger, A Policy Analysis of Promises Respecting the Use of Land, 55 Minn.L.Rev. 167, 169 (1970). The Restatement of Property § 530 (1944), after stating the straightforward proposition that "the successors to land respecting the use of which the owner has made a promise become bound upon the promise as promisors," subjects the general rule to a series of exacting but inexactly worded requirements. It is some measure of the ingenuity of private lawyers, and of the limits of written law, that major land developments have been undertaken despite these hurdles, all on the assumption that the underlying covenant arrangements would be enforceable against successors in interest.

Apart from tradition, what reason is there to require anything more than intent and notice for the burden of a covenant to run? (These are, you will recall, the only requirements traditionally imposed to determine whether the burden of an easement runs.) Rigorous proof that *A* and *B* intended that the covenant burden *B*'s successors should suffice to demonstrate their seriousness of purpose in carving out an interest in land. Furthermore, the notice requirement assures that *B*'s successor, *Z*, will have had the opportunity to evaluate the cost of complying with the burden and to adjust her purchase price for Blackacre accordingly. And, since only a private arrangement is involved, *A* and *B*, or their successors, *Y* and *Z*, by executing a release, can undo the arrangement any time the cost of complying with the covenant exceeds its value. If transaction costs block the release, courts may lift the covenant through rules on abandonment and changed neighborhood conditions that seek to approximate the bargain that *Y* and *Z* would have made in the absence of transaction costs.

Clark, The American Law Institute's Law of Real Covenants, 52 Yale L.J. 699 (1943), offers a sharp critique of the Restatement position on covenants, and a rare glimpse into the politicking that can occur in the course of preparing a major restatement. Rundell, Judge Clark on the American Law Institute's Law of Real Covenants: A Comment, 53 Yale L.J. 312 (1944), is a reply from one of the Restatement's reporters. C. Clark, Real Covenants and Other Interests Which "Run with the Land" (2d ed. 1947), is an indispensable overview.

Among the more recent writings are Berger, A Policy Analysis of Promises Respecting the Use of Land, 55 Minn.L.Rev. 167 (1970); Browder, Running Covenants and Public Policy, 77 Mich.L.Rev. 12 (1978); and Stoebuck, Running Covenants: An Analytical Primer, 52 Wash.L.Rev. 861 (1977).

i. Intent and Notice

For the burden of a covenant to run, the promisee and promisor, *A* and *B*, must have intended that the burden run, and *B*'s successor, *Z*, who is sought to be charged with the burden, must have had notice of the covenant at the time she acquired the servient estate. The standard way to indicate the requisite intent is for *B* to promise, "for herself, her heirs, successors and assigns." But any clear expression of intent will do. And, if the parties do not express their intent, courts may infer it from the circumstances surrounding the covenant's creation.

It is clear that the notice required for the burden of a covenant to run may be actual, inquiry or constructive, as in the law of easements, and conveyancing generally. But notice of what? Although most covenants will explicitly prescribe the conduct they require, some subdivision covenants today will vest general rulemaking authority in a homeowner's association or architectural review board. Is the homeowner bound by rules that the association adopts after she acquired her parcel? In Davis v. Huey, 620 S.W.2d 561 (Tex.1981), plaintiff neighbors sought to enjoin defendants from building a house in a manner that violated standards adopted under the subdivision's architectural review covenant. The Texas Supreme Court ruled that defendants would be bound by discretionary site decisions only if they were part of a general development scheme, and only if they had notice of the scheme at the time they acquired their parcel. The court found that the limitations on defendants' use of their property "were not based on the restrictive covenants but rather on the voluntary decisions of neighboring lot owners who had the good fortune to construct their houses" before defendants. As defendants could not have discovered these decisions in the course of a title search, they "did not purchase with notice of the limitation sought to be imposed and their lot is not burdened by the placement restriction." 620 S.W.2d at 568.

ii. Privity

(A) "Horizontal" Privity

WHEELER v. SCHAD

Supreme Court of Nevada, 1871.
7 Nev. 204.

By the Court, LEWIS, C.J.:

On the fifth day of June, A.D. 1862, M.S. Hurd, Ferdinand Dunker and Peter Bossell, being the owners and in possession of a certain mill-site and water privilege, regularly conveyed to Charles Doscher, Charles Itgen, Charles D. McWilliams and William C. Duval a portion thereof, together with the water privilege connected therewith. The grantees entered into possession and erected a quartz mill on the premises thus conveyed. The stream was first conducted to the mill of Hurd and associates, and thence to that of their grantees. On the eleventh day of the same month, the respective parties entered into an agreement which, after reciting the necessity of constructing a dam across the river and a flume to conduct the water to their several mills, provided that the dam and flume should be constructed at their joint expense, Hurd and his associates, however, agreeing to pay five hundred dollars more than one half the cost, and the other parties the balance; the dam and flume, when completed, to be owned and enjoyed jointly in equal shares. It was also agreed that they should be kept in good order and repair at the joint and equal expense of the respective parties. Some time after the construction of these works, Wheeler succeeded to the interest of Bossell, and he, together with Hurd and Dunker, continued in the ownership and remained in possession of the first mill, known as the Eureka.

Doscher and his associates having mortgaged their mill some time between January and March, 1868, put the assignee of the mortgage (defendant) in possession, who continued to hold the property under the mortgage until he obtained the absolute title by virtue of foreclosure and sale under his mortgage, which occurred in October, A.D. 1868. Early in the year 1868, while the defendant was in possession under the mortgage, the dam and flume were damaged to such an extent that it became necessary to make extensive repairs upon them. Before proceeding with the work, the plaintiffs notified the defendant of their damaged condition; and requested him to unite with them in making the proper repairs. The defendant agreed that the work should proceed, and requested the plaintiff Wheeler to superintend it, and "take charge of the workmen." The repairs were made in due time, at an expense of three thousand five hundred dollars, one half of which is now sought to be recovered. Judgment for defendant; plaintiffs appeal; and it is argued on their behalf: first, that the defendant is liable on the agreement entered into between the defendant's grantors and the plaintiffs; and secondly, if not, that he is so upon his own agreement with the plaintiffs, authorizing the work to be done.

To maintain the first point, it is contended that the deed of conveyance of the mill-site to the grantors of the defendant, and the agreement referred to, should be held to be one instrument; that the stipulations of the latter should be engrafted upon the deed and held to be covenants running with the land. But nothing is clearer than that the two instruments are utterly disconnected, as completely independent of each other as they possibly could be. The deed was executed on the fifth day of June, at which time it does not appear that there was any thought of an agreement to construct or keep in repair any dam or flume. There is no evidence that such a project was in contemplation even by any of the parties, much less that any agreement of this character was in view. It was not, in fact, executed until six days afterwards, and there can be no presumption other than that it was not contemplated until such time. Had it entered into the transaction, had it been understood between the parties at the time of the conveyance that such contract should be executed, there might be some ground for the claim that the agreement and deed constituted but one transaction, and therefore should be construed as one instrument; but unfortunately for the appellants, there is no such showing in the case. If, in fact, the agreement did not enter into the conveyance, or was not contemplated at the time, it is of no consequence how soon afterwards it may have been executed; a day or an hour would as completely separate the instruments and make them independent of each other as a year. It is impossible, under the evidence in this case, to merge the deed and agreement into one instrument, and construe them as if executed simultaneously.

Unless they constituted one instrument or transaction, it cannot be claimed that the covenants run with the land so as to charge the grantee of the covenantor. To make a covenant run with the land, it is necessary, first, that it should relate to and concern the land; and secondly, a covenant imposing a burden on the land can only be created where there is privity of estate between the covenantor and covenantee. Whether a covenant for the benefit of land can be created where there is no privity is still questioned by some authorities; but it was held in *Packenham's case,* determined as early as the time of Edward III, that a stranger might covenant with the owner in such manner as to attach the benefit of a covenant to the land, and have it run in favor of the assignees of the covenantee; and the rule there established has since been frequently recognized at law, although questioned by text writers, and the broad doctrine sought to be maintained that privity of estate is absolutely essential in all cases, to give one man a right of action against another upon a covenant, when there is no privity of contract.

Whether the rule announced in *Packenham's case* be law or not, is not necessary to determine here, for all the courts hold that the burden of a covenant can only be imposed upon land so as to run with it when there is privity of estate between the covenantor and covenantee. It was said by Lord Kenyon, in Webb v. Russell, 3 Term, 393, that "it is not sufficient that a covenant is concerning the land, but in order to make it run with the land there must be a privity of estate between the covenanting parties." That was the law long prior to the time of Kenyon, and has never been doubted, although perhaps cases may be found where an erroneous application of the rule has been made. To render a covenant binding on the assignee of the covenantor, it must therefore not only be meant to bind his estate as well as his person, but the relation between the parties must be such as to render the intention effectual—that is, there must be privity of estate between the covenanting parties. To constitute such relation, they must both have an interest in the land sought to be charged by the covenant. It is said their position must be such as would formerly have given rise to the relation of tenure. A covenant real is, and can only be, an incident to land. It cannot pass independent of it. It adheres to the land, is maintained by it, is in fact a legal parasite, created out of and deriving life from the land to which it adheres. It follows, that the person in whose favor a covenant is made must have an interest in the land charged with it; for he can only get the covenant through, and as an incident to the land to which it is attached. Says Coke, 385, *(a):* "A. seized of the mannor of D., whereof a Chappell was parcell, a prior with the assent of his covent covenanteth by deed indented with A. and his heires to celebrate divine service in his said Chappell weekely, for the lord of the said Mannor and his servants, etc. In this case the assignees shall have an action of covenant, albeit they are not named, for that the remedie by covenant doth runne with the land, to give damages to the partie grieved, and was in a manner appurtenant to the Mannor. But if the covenant had beene with a stranger to celebrate divine service in the Chappell of A. and his heires, there the assignee shall not have an action of covenant; for the covenant cannot be annexed to the Mannor because the covenantee was not seized of the Mannor." So it is manifest this interest in the land sought to be charged with the covenant must exist at the time the covenant is made. It needs no argument to show that an interest acquired afterwards would not avail the covenantee.

Did the plaintiffs in this case have any estate in the land owned by the defendant at the time this agreement was entered into? It is not even claimed they had. Nor did the agreement itself create any such interest. There is no attempt in it to convey any estate to them, nor a word of grant in the whole instrument. It is a mere contract for the erection of a dam, which does not appear to be on the premises either of the plaintiffs or defendant, and a flume to conduct water to their respective mills, and to maintain them in good order. Suppose the grantors of the defendant had entered into an agreement binding themselves to build the dam and flume for the benefit of the plaintiffs, for a stipulated sum of money; will it be claimed that such an agreement could be held a covenant running with land owned by such grantors, and which was entirely distinct from that upon which the work was to be performed? We apprehend not. Where the distinction, as to its capacity to run with the land, between such a covenant and that entered into here, where instead of compensation in money the defendant's grantors were to receive a benefit from the improvement itself?

As the grantors had no estate in the land owned by the defendant when the agreement was entered into, but were mere strangers to it, the case comes directly within the rule announced by Lord Coke, and very uniformly followed both by the English and American courts since his time. . . .

There being no privity of estate, or of contract between the parties, it only remains to determine whether the defendant is holden on his own promise made to the plaintiffs. First, the action is not based on any such promise or contract. The complaint is framed with reference exclusively to the written agreement, and upon that alone relief is sought. Nothing is charged in the complaint tending to charge the defendant with any personal obligation, except that the repairs were made with his knowledge. As the complaint does not allege any personal promise or contract on the part of the defendant, it would hardly be conformable to the rules of law to award relief upon the assumption of its existence. No personal promise or agreement by the defendant could properly be proven under the complaint; for proof is only admissible to establish the case made by the allegations of the pleading.

But, again, if any such promise was made, it is undoubtedly barred by the statute of limitations, not being evidenced by writing. It cannot be said that the defendant adopted the written agreement as his own, and thereby bound himself to it, for it is not shown that he knew of its existence. But even if he knew of it, the only evidence of his obligation upon it was in parol, and therefore it cannot, with any degree of reason, be said that if he had directly adopted the contract by a parol promise, his obligation would not be barred by the limitation prescribed for parol contracts.

The judgment below must be affirmed.

(B) "Vertical" Privity

DUNLAP v. BULLARD

Supreme Court of Massachusetts, 1881.
131 Mass. 161.

COLT, J. This action is brought by the lessors upon a covenant to pay taxes contained in a lease given in 1855 for the term of twenty-two years, at a fixed rent payable quarterly. The whole interest of the original lessees was transferred by successive assignments to Shepherd Ostrom, who, in 1868, leased the premises with the buildings erected since the date of the original lease to Earl W. Johnson, to hold for a term equal to the whole of the unexpired term of the original lease, but at an increased rent payable monthly. The last-named lease also contained covenants on the part of the lessee to pay rent and taxes, and that the lessor might enter and take possession for breach of covenant, and that the lessee would quit and deliver up the premises to the lessor at the end of the term. This lease was assigned by Johnson to the defendant, who was in possession when the taxes sued for in this action were assessed.

The plaintiffs contend that privity of estate was created between them and the defendant, as assignee of Johnson, by which the defendant became bound in law to perform the covenant to pay taxes contained in the original lease. A covenant to pay taxes is a covenant which runs with the land, and binds those who acquire by deed or assignment the whole estate of the covenantor in the whole or some part of the land. If the whole of the unexpired leasehold estate is conveyed, then the party to whom it is conveyed is bound, whether the conveyance is in form an assignment of the remainder of the term, or is a sub-lease. The test to be applied is whether the lessee has parted with his whole interest in the leased premises.

In the case at bar, the interest which came to the defendant was conveyed by a lease of the premises containing all the agreements and covenants usually found in such an instrument. There is no reference in it to the original demise, and no indication of an intention on the part of Ostrom, the sub-lessor, to part with his whole interest in the leasehold estate, or to lose control of it as lessor. He provides that Johnson, the tenant, shall hold under him and pay rent to him and no one else. The rent reserved was larger in amount than that reserved in the original lease, and was payable at different times, and the lessee covenants to deliver up the premises to Ostrom, the lessor, at the end of the term. But what is more in point, the right is reserved to the lessor to enter and expel the lessee for nonpayment of rent, or breach of any of the covenants in the lease. It is clear that the parties to this lease intended to create the relation of landlord and tenant between themselves. And it is the duty of the court to give effect to this intention, unless controlled by some positive rule of law.

To constitute an assignment of a leasehold interest, the assignee must take precisely the same estate in the whole or in a part of the leased premises which his assignor had therein. He must not only take for the whole of the unexpired time, but he must take the whole estate, or, in other words, the whole term; for, in the language of Blackstone, "the word 'term' does not merely signify the time specified in the lease, but the estate also and interest that passes by that lease; and therefore the term may expire during the continuance of the time, as by surrender, forfeiture and the like." 2 Bl.Com. 144. The grant of an interest therefore which may possibly endure to the end of the term is not necessarily a grant of all the estate in the term. If by the terms of the conveyance, be it in the form of a lease or an assignment, new conditions with a right of entry, or new causes of forfeiture are created, then the tenant holds by different tenure, and a new leasehold interest arises, which cannot be treated as an assignment or a continuation to him of the original term.

Where an estate is conveyed to be held by the grantee upon a condition subsequent, there is left in the grantor a contingent reversionary interest. It was said in Austin v. Cambridgeport Parish, 21 Pick. 215, 223, that the grantor's contingent interest in such case was an estate which was transmissible by devise and passed under a residuary devise in the will of the grantor. It was declared to be a contingent possible estate, which, united with that of the tenants, "composed only the entire fee simple estate, as much so as in the ordinary case of an estate for life to A., remainder to B." In Brattle Square Church v. Grant, 3 Gray, 142, 147, it was said, that when such an estate is created "the entire interest does not pass out of the grantor by the same instrument or conveyance. All that remains, after the gift or grant takes effect, continues in the grantor, and goes to his heirs. This is the right of entry, which, from the nature of the grant, is reserved to the grantor and his heirs only, and which gives them the right to enter, as of their old estate, upon the breach of the condition." These considerations are equally applicable whether the estate subject to the condition subsequent is an estate in fee, or an estate for life or years. They apply where, by the terms of an instrument which purports to be an underlease, there is left in the lessor a contingent reversionary interest, to be availed of by an entry for breach of condition which restores the sub-lessor to his former interest in the premises. The sub-lessee under such an instrument takes an inferior and different estate from that which he would acquire by an assignment of the remainder of the original term, that is to say, an interest which may be terminated by forfeiture on new and independent grounds long before the expiration of the original term. If the smallest reversionary interest is retained, the tenant takes as sub-lessee, and not as assignee.

The law in this Commonwealth is settled by the cases of Patten v. Deshon, 1 Gray 325, and McNeil v. Kendall, 128 Mass. 245. In the first-named case, Walker, the lessee of Haywood, underlet a portion of the premises to Deshon for the remainder of his term, and then assigned all his interest in the original lease to Patten. It was held that, prior to the assignment to Patten, a substantial interest remained in Walker in all that part of the leased premises which had been underlet to Deshon, and which was the right to use and enjoy, for the remainder of the term, that part of the premises let to Deshon, upon a surrender or forfeiture of the sub-lease for nonpayment of rent; and that this interest passed to the plaintiff by Walker's assignment. In McNeil v. Kendall, it was said that the decision in Patten v. Deshon had never been questioned to the knowledge of the court, and had been cited with approval in many cases in our own reports, and laid down a just and equitable rule which had been the law of Massachusetts for more than twenty years.

Judgment for the defendant.

NOTES

1. Although the concept of horizontal privity has been widely adopted in this country, states differ in the precise tests they apply. The strictest—and least frequently applied—test, *tenurial privity*, requires that a tenurial relationship, such as landlord-tenant or reversioner and life tenant, exist, not only between the original covenantee and covenantor, A and B, but also between their successors, Y and Z. McIntosh v. Vail, 126 W.Va. 395, 28 S.E.2d 607 (1943). As a practical matter, this test restricts the enforcement of covenants to holders of future and present possessory interests in the same parcel. A second test, *substituted privity*, allows an easement to substitute for the tenurial relationship. This test is sometimes called "Massachusetts privity" after the state that first adopted it. Compare Hurd v. Curtis, 36 Mass. (19 Pick.) 459 (1837) with Morse v. Aldrich, 36 Mass. (19 Pick.) 449 (1837). Finally, the least demanding test, *instantaneous privity*, requires that, at the moment A and B make the covenant, some other, independent interest in land pass between them; the other interest can be a fee, a lease, an easement or, arguably, another covenant. See, for example, Carlson v. Libby, 137 Conn. 362, 77 A.2d 332 (1950).

Which of these three tests did Wheeler v. Schad apply, or misapply? How, if at all, could the parties have restructured their relationship on June 11, after the conveyance of the premises to Doscher and company, to meet the requirement of tenurial privity? Would a sham easement, giving each group of owners the right to go over the land of the other—say, to inspect the mill—have sufficed to create substituted privity? What kind of paper-shuffling might have satisfied the instantaneous privity requirement?

Consider how *Wheeler* would have been decided under Restatement of Property § 534 (1944):

> The successors in title to land respecting the use of which the owner has made a promise are not bound as promisors upon the promise unless
>
>> (a) the transaction of which the promise is a part includes a transfer of an interest either in the land benefited by or in the land burdened by the performance of the promise; or
>>
>> (b) the promise is made in the adjustment of the mutual relationships arising out of the existence of an easement held by one of the parties to the promise in the land of the other.

Note that subsections (a) and (b) are phrased in the alternative, and that (a) embodies the instantaneous privity rule while (b) embodies the substituted privity rule.

2. The horizontal privity requirement, commonly traced to Lord Kenyon's offhand dictum quoted in Wheeler v. Schad, has been widely criticized as lacking any substantial foundation in history or policy. What, then, explains the flowering of horizontal privity in the United States, and its warm embrace by the Restatement? One possibility is that because covenants gained a far wider ambit here than in England, American courts perceived horizontal privity as a necessary brake on more adventuresome applications. The Restatement's reporter on servitudes put the view succinctly: "The answer is that there is a rule of policy which can be expressed in the form of a rule of law that one man cannot make another man legally responsible as a promisor; that there is an exception to that rule in the case of promises respecting the use of land; that the exception has limits; that those limits can be stated; and that section [534] is an attempt to state one of them." Rundell, Judge Clark on the American Law Institute's Law of Real Covenants: A Comment, 53 Yale L.J. 312, 325 (1944).

Given the restrictions imposed by the intent, notice and vertical privity requirements, why is this added restraint necessary? How does the requirement separate those covenants that, as a matter of policy, should run, from those that should not? Is horizontal privity anything more than another way of stating the intent requirement—using the tenurial, easement or grantor-grantee relationship as evidence of the original parties' seriousness about their intent to bind successors? Could Wheeler v. Schad have been more easily disposed of on the ground that the parties did not intend to bind their successors?

One answer to these objections is that the costs of having a horizontal privity requirement are not that great. Compliance with the requirement—at least with substituted or instantaneous privity—can easily be achieved by the adept draftsman—which may explain why horizontal privity so rarely arises as an issue today. Also, cases in which the parties lack horizontal privity can frequently be resolved on the threshold ground that the intent requirement has not been met. Yet, cases directly addressing the horizontal privity requirement do arise from time to time and, when the requirement is not met, courts have not hesitated to refuse to enforce the covenant. See, for example, Johnson v. Myers, 226 Ga. 23, 172 S.E.2d 421 (1970).

3. What policies underlie the vertical privity requirement applied in Dunlap v. Bullard? The Restatement rests its endorsement of the requirement on the "feeling that the imposition of an obligation as a promisor, upon one who has not promised, by virtue of succession to another who has should be kept within relatively narrow even though formal limits. Hence the persistence of and the justification for the retention of the rule that promises respecting the use of land of the promisor run only with an estate or interest in the land held by the promisor or an interest of like duration." § 535, comment a.

What will A or B gain or lose if the burden of B's covenant is held to run in the absence of vertical privity? A, who originally had an action only against B, loses nothing since, even after the transfer, B remains liable on the promise; A will, however, gain an added defendant, Z. B loses nothing since she cannot unilaterally end her liability to A; but she may, at least, have recourse against her transferee, Z, whose breach precipitates B's liability to A.

Note also that vertical privity and horizontal privity are concurrent, not alternative, requirements for the burden of a covenant to run. Can vertical privity, like horizontal privity, be viewed as just another device for measuring the force of A's and B's intent to bind B's successor in interest? For example, if A and B enter into a twenty-year lease for an office building, obligating B to pay an annual rent, to perform necessary repairs on the premises and to reconstruct the building's facade, is it likely that they intended Z, a one-year subtenant of B, to perform all these obligations? If Z is instead an assignee, who succeeds to B's entire interest, is it more or less likely that they intended her to perform these obligations?

Merging vertical privity into the intent requirement would have two immediate advantages. First, in the example just given, it would allow some differentiation among the duties with which A seeks to charge the one-year subtenant; presumably A and B did not intend her to undertake capital repairs whose value would extend over the full twenty-year term, while they probably did intend that she pay the annual rent. Second, *A* and *B* can control the issue of intent by express language in the instrument creating the covenant. Thus, if they want to make the one-year subtenant liable for the cost of repairs, they can accomplish this by saying so in the lease. *Z* will doubtless take this heavy burden into account in determining how much she is willing to pay—or accept from—*B* in consideration for taking the sublease with all of its burdens.

4. Does vertical privity require that *Z* receive *B*'s entire interest, or does it require only that *B* part with her entire interest in Blackacre? Say, for example, *B* conveys the eastern half of Blackacre to *Z–1* and the western half to *Z–2*. Will either *Z–1* or *Z–2*, both, or neither, be bound? According to Restatement of Property § 536, "The successor to the estate or interest of the promisor in any part of the land respecting the use of which he has so made a promise that it is capable of running with the land becomes proportionally liable as a promisor upon the promise." On principle, how can the Restatement distinguish between spatial divisions, which do not destroy vertical privity, and temporal divisions, which do?

iii. Touch or Concern

NEPONSIT PROPERTY OWNERS' ASSOCIATION, INC. v. EMIGRANT INDUSTRIAL SAVINGS BANK

Court of Appeals of New York, 1938.
278 N.Y. 248, 15 N.E.2d 793.

LEHMAN, Judge.

The plaintiff, as assignee of Neponsit Realty Company, has brought this action to foreclose a lien upon land which the defendant owns. The lien, it is alleged, arises from a covenant, condition or charge contained in a deed of conveyance of the land from Neponsit Realty Company to a predecessor in title of the defendant. The defendant purchased the land at a judicial sale. The referee's deed to the defendant and every deed in the defendant's chain of title since the conveyance of the land by Neponsit Realty Company purports to convey the property subject to the covenant, condition or charge contained in the original deed. The answer of the defendant contains, in addition to denials of some of the allegations of the complaint, seven separate affirmative defenses and a counterclaim. The defendant moved for judgment on the pleadings, dismissing the complaint pursuant to rule 112 of the Rules of Civil Practice. The plaintiff moved to dismiss the counterclaim pursuant to rule 109, subdivision 6, and to strike out the affirmative defenses contained in the answer pursuant to rule 103, as well as pursuant to rule 109, subdivision 6, of the Rules of Civil Practice. The motion of the plaintiff was granted and the motion of the defendant denied. The Appellate Division unanimously affirmed the order of the Special Term and granted leave to appeal to this court upon certified questions. . . .

Upon this appeal the defendant contends that the land which it owns is not subject to any lien or charge which the plaintiff may enforce . . ..

It appears that in January, 1911, Neponsit Realty Company, as owner of a tract of land in Queens county, caused to be filed in the office of the clerk of the county a map of the land. The tract was developed for a strictly residential community, and Neponsit Realty Company conveyed lots in the tract to purchasers, describing such lots by reference to the filed map and to roads and streets shown thereon. In 1917, Neponsit Realty Company conveyed the land now owned by the defendant to Robert Oldner Deyer and his wife by deed which contained the covenant upon which the plaintiff's cause of action is based.

That covenant provides:

"And the party of the second part for the party of the second part and the heirs, successors and assigns of the party of the second part further covenants that the property conveyed by this deed shall be subject to an annual charge in such an amount as will be fixed by the party of the first part, its successors and assigns, not, however exceeding in any year the sum of four ($4.00) Dollars per lot 20 × 100 feet. The assigns of the party of the first part may include a Property Owners' Association which may hereafter be organized for the purposes referred to in this paragraph, and in case such association is organized the sums in this paragraph provided for shall be payable to such association. The party of the second part for the party of the second part and the heirs, successors and assigns of the party of the second part covenants that they will pay this charge to the party of the first part, its successors and assigns on the first day of May in each and every year, and further covenants that said charge shall on said date in each year become a lien on the land and shall continue to be such lien until fully paid. Such charge shall be payable to the party of the first part or its successors or assigns, and shall be devoted to the maintenance of the roads, paths, parks, beach, sewers and such other public purposes as shall from time to time be determined by the party of the first part, its successors or assigns. And the party of the second part by the acceptance of this deed hereby expressly vests in the party of the first part, its successors and assigns, the right and power to bring all actions against the owner of the premises hereby conveyed or any part thereof for the collection of such charge and to enforce the aforesaid lien therefor.

"These covenants shall run with the land and shall be construed as real covenants running with the land until January 31st, 1940, when they shall cease and determine."

Every subsequent deed of conveyance of the property in the defendant's chain of title, including the deed from the referee to the defendant, contained, as we have said, a provision that they were made subject to covenants and restrictions of former deeds of record.

There can be no doubt that Neponsit Realty Company intended that the covenant should run with the land and should be enforceable by a property owners' association against every owner of property in the residential tract which the realty company was then developing. The language of the covenant admits of no other construction. Regardless of the intention of the parties, a covenant will run with the land and will be enforceable against a subsequent purchaser of the land at the suit of one who claims the benefit of the covenant, only if the covenant complies with certain legal requirements. These requirements rest upon ancient rules and precedents. The age-old essentials of a real covenant, aside from the form of the covenant, may be summarily formulated as follows: (1) It must appear that grantor and grantee intended that the covenant should run with the land; (2) it must appear that the covenant is one "touching" or "concerning" the land with which it runs; (3) it must appear that there is "privity of estate" between the promisee or party claiming the benefit of the covenant and the right to enforce it, and the promisor or party who rests under the burden of the covenant. Clark on Covenants and Interests Running with Land, p. 74. Although the deeds of Neponsit Realty Company conveying lots in the tract it developed "contained a provision to the effect that the covenants ran with the land, such provision in the absence of the other legal requirements is insufficient to accomplish such a purpose." Morgan Lake Co. v. New York, N.H. & H.R.R. Co., 262 N.Y. 234, 238, 186 N.E. 685, 686. In his opinion in that case, Judge Crane posed but found it unnecessary to decide many of the questions which the court must consider in this case.

The covenant in this case is intended to create a charge or obligation to pay a fixed sum of money to be "devoted to the maintenance of the roads, paths, parks, beach, sewers and such other public purposes as shall from time to time be determined by the party of the first part [the grantor], its successors or assigns." It is an affirmative covenant to pay money for use in connection with, but not upon, the land which it is said is subject to the burden of the covenant. Does such a covenant "touch" or "concern" the land? These terms are not part of a statutory definition, a limitation placed by the State upon the power of the courts to enforce covenants *intended* to run with the land by the parties who entered into the covenants. Rather they are words used by courts in England in old cases to describe a limitation which the courts themselves created or to formulate a test which the courts have devised and which the courts voluntarily apply. In truth such a description or test so formulated is too vague to be of much assistance and judges and academic scholars alike have struggled, not with entire success, to formulate a test at once more satisfactory and more accurate. "It has been found impossible to state any absolute tests to determine what covenants touch and concern land and what do not. The question is one for the court to determine in the exercise of its best judgment upon the facts of each case." Clark, op.cit. p. 76.

Even though that be true, a determination by a court in one case upon particular facts will often serve to point the way to correct decision in other cases upon analogous facts. Such guideposts may not be disregarded. It has been often said that a covenant to pay a sum of money is a personal affirmative covenant which usually does not concern or touch the land. Such statements are based upon English decisions which hold in effect that only covenants, which compel the covenanter to submit to some *restrictions on the use* of his property, touch or concern the land, and that the burden of a covenant which requires the covenanter to do an affirmative act, even on his own land, for the benefit of the owner of a "dominant" estate, does not run with his land. Miller v. Clary, 210 N.Y. 127, 103 N.E. 1114, L.R.A.1918E, 222, Ann.Cas.1915B, 872. In that case the court pointed out that in many jurisdictions of this country the narrow English rule has been criticized and a more liberal and flexible rule has been substituted. In this State the courts have not gone so far. We have not abandoned the historic distinction drawn by the English courts. So this court has recently said: "Subject to a few exceptions not important at this time, there is now in this state a settled rule of law that a covenant to do an affirmative act, as distinguished from a covenant merely negative in effect, does not run with the land so as to charge the burden of performance on a subsequent grantee [citing cases]. This is so though the burden of such a covenant is laid upon the very parcel which is the subject-matter of the conveyance." Guaranty Trust Co. of New York v. New York & Queens County Ry. Co., 253 N.Y. 190, 204, 170 N.E. 887, 892, opinion by Cardozo, Ch. J.

Both in that case and in the case of Miller v. Clary, supra, the court pointed out that there were some exceptions or limitations in the application of the general rule. Some promises to pay money have been enforced, as covenants running with the land, against subsequent holders of the land who took with notice of the covenant. It may be difficult to classify these exceptions or to formulate a test of whether a particular covenant to pay money or to perform some other act falls within the general rule that ordinarily an affirmative covenant is a personal and not a real covenant, or falls outside the limitations placed upon the general rule. At least it must "touch" or "concern" the land in a substantial degree, and though it may be inexpedient and perhaps impossible to formulate a rigid test or definition which will be entirely satisfactory or which can be applied mechanically in all cases, we should at least be able to state the problem and find a reasonable method of approach to it. It has been suggested that a covenant which runs with the land must affect the legal relations—the advantages and the burdens—of the parties to the covenant, as owners of particular parcels of land and not merely as members of the community in general, such as taxpayers or owners of other land. Clark, op.cit. p. 76. Cf. Professor Bigelow's article on

The Contents of Covenants in Leases, 12 Mich.L.Rev. 639; 30 Law Quarterly Review, 319. That method of approach has the merit of realism. The test is based on the effect of the covenant rather than on technical distinctions. Does the covenant impose, on the one hand, a burden upon an interest in land, which on the other hand increases the value of a different interest in the same or related land?

Even though we accept that approach and test, it still remains true that whether a particular covenant is sufficiently connected with the use of land to run with the land, must be in many cases a question of degree. A promise to pay for something to be done in connection with the promisor's land does not differ essentially from a promise by the promisor to do the thing himself, and both promises constitute, in a substantial sense, a restriction upon the owner's right to use the land, and a burden upon the legal interest of the owner. On the other hand, a covenant to perform or pay for the performance of an affirmative act disconnected with the use of the land cannot ordinarily touch or concern the land in any substantial degree. Thus, unless we exalt technical form over substance, the distinction between covenants which run with land and covenants which are personal, must depend upon the effect of the covenant on the legal rights which otherwise would flow from ownership of land and which are connected with the land. The problem then is: Does the covenant in purpose and effect substantially alter these rights? . . .

Looking at the problem presented in this case from the same point of view and stressing the intent and substantial effect of the covenant rather than its form, it seems clear that the covenant may properly be said to touch and concern the land of the defendant and its burden should run with the land. True, it calls for payment of a sum of money to be expended for "public purposes" upon land other than the land conveyed by Neponsit Realty Company to plaintiff's predecessor in title. By that conveyance the grantee, however, obtained not only title to particular lots, but an easement or right of common enjoyment with other property owners in roads, beaches, public parks or spaces and improvements in the same tract. For full enjoyment in common by the defendant and other property owners of these easements or rights the roads and public places must be maintained. In order that the burden of maintaining public improvements should rest upon the land benefited by the improvements, the grantor exacted from the grantee of the land with its appurtenant easement or right of enjoyment a covenant that the burden of paying the cost should be inseparably attached to the land which enjoys the benefit. It is plain that any distinction or definition which would exclude such a covenant from the classification of covenants which "touch" or "concern" the land would be based on form and not on substance. . . .

We have considered the other contentions of the defendant and especially the defense that the alleged lien based upon the covenant set forth in the complaint constitutes an interest in land and is unenforceable under the provisions of sections 242 and 259 of the Real Property Law (Cons.Laws, ch. 50). We find the defense insufficient.

The order should be affirmed, with costs, and the certified questions answered in the affirmative.

CRANE, C.J., and O'BRIEN, LOUGHRAN, FINCH, and RIPPEY, JJ., concur.

NOTES

1. The origins of the touch or concern test are commonly traced to *dicta* in Spencer's Case, 5 Coke 16a, 77 Eng.Rep. 72 (Q.B.1583), that the burden of a covenant cannot be made to run if "the thing to be done be merely collateral to the land and doth not touch or concern the thing demised in any sort." Thus, for example, "if the lessee covenants for him and his assigns to build a house upon the land of the lessor which is no parcel of the demise, or to pay any collateral sum to the lessor, or to a stranger, it shall not bind the assignee, because it is merely collateral, and in no manner touches or concerns the thing that was demised, or that is assigned over . . . .." 5 Coke at 16b, 77 Eng.Rep. at 74.

The *Spencer* test, specifically formulated for landlord-tenant covenants, was eventually adapted in this country to apply to covenants made as part of a fee conveyance. In place of the requirement that the burden on the tenant's estate in Blackacre operate to benefit the landlord's reversionary estate in the same parcel, American courts imposed the requirement that the burden on *B*'s fee estate in Blackacre benefit *A*'s fee estate in an adjacent parcel, Whiteacre. Transformation of the English test was aided by the fact that *A* commonly obtained *B*'s covenant at the time he sold Blackacre to *B*, retaining Whiteacre for himself.

The next step in Americanizing the *Spencer* test was to enlarge the range of conduct that would be held to touch or concern. Spencer's Case, and the early American decisions following it, all involved covenants to perform some physical act on the servient estate—building and maintaining fences, walls, dams, bridges, drainage ditches—and it was widely assumed that physical conduct was essential for a covenant to touch or concern. Such a limitation would pose obvious problems for the enforcement of homeowner assessment covenants like the one in *Neponsit*. To bring these cases within the realm of enforceable covenants, Professor Harry Bigelow devised the "legal relations" test later cited and adopted in *Neponsit*. Bigelow, The Content of Covenants in Leases, 12 Mich.L.Rev. 639 (1914). Charles Clark put the test into somewhat plainer terms: "Where the parties, as laymen and not as lawyers, would naturally regard the covenant as intimately bound up with the land, aiding the promisee as landowner or hampering the promisor in similar capacity, the requirement should be held fulfilled." C. Clark, Real Covenants and Other Interests Which "Run With the Land," 99 (2d ed. 1947).

2. The Restatement incorporated some of the English and American developments and added a twist or two of its own. Section 537, entitled "Relation of Benefit and Burden," provides:

> The successors in title to land respecting the use of which the owner has made a promise can be bound as promisors only if
>
>> (a) the performance of the promise will benefit the promisee or other beneficiary of the promise in the physical use or enjoyment of the land possessed by him, or
>>
>> (b) the consummation of the transaction of which the promise is a part will operate to benefit and is for the benefit of the promisor in the physical use or enjoyment of land possessed by him,
>
> and the burden on the land of the promisor bears a reasonable relation to the benefit received by the person benefited.

If you find the wording opaque, you are in good company. An early, similarly worded draft had "been objected to as unintelligible, and the draft originally presented to the Council was sent back because no one could understand it." Clark, The American Law Institute's Law of Real Covenants, 52 Yale L.J. 699, 711 (1943).

Restatement section 537 clearly restores the old requirement that the covenant have demonstrable, physical effects: "it is not enough that the performance of the promise operates to benefit either the promisor or the beneficiary of the promise in the use of his land but it must operate to benefit him in the physical use of his land." Restatement § 537, comment f (1944). Subsection (b) of section 537 would appear to drop the requirement that the benefit must attach to an adjacent parcel for the burden to run. But, how many situations can you think of, outside the landlord-tenant context, in which the benefit will be in gross and the requirement respecting "physical use and enjoyment" will be met?

Would the covenant in *Neponsit* touch or concern under section 537(b)? Was the benefit there appurtenant or in gross? What policy justification is there for section 537's final requirement, that the burden bear a reasonable relation to the benefit?

3. New York's decisions on the touch or concern requirement have been sparse, inconsistent and unenlightening. It was more than twenty years after *Neponsit* before the Court of Appeals addressed the question again, this time in the context of a covenant made by the defendant's predecessor in title to furnish steam heat to buildings on plaintiff's land. In Nicholson v. 300 Broadway Realty Corp., 7 N.Y.2d 240, 196 N.Y.S.2d 945, 164 N.E.2d 832 (1959), the court held that the covenant met *Neponsit's* touch or concern test. It was almost another twenty years before the court next squarely addressed the issue. This time it held that the covenant—to accept, and to pay

thirty-five dollars per year for, well water provided by defendant's neighbor between 1 May and 1 October—did not run. Eagle Enterprises, Inc. v. Gross, 39 N.Y.2d 505, 384 N.Y.S.2d 717, 349 N.E.2d 816 (1976).

The court in *Eagle* rested its decision on the conclusion that the covenant "does not substantially affect the ownership interest of landowners in the Orchard Hill subdivision. The covenant provides for the supplying of water for only six months of the year; no claim has been advanced by appellant that the lands in the subdivision would be waterless without the water it supplies." According to the court, the record did "not demonstrate that other property owners in the subdivision would be deprived of water from appellant or that the price of water would become prohibitive for other property owners if respondent terminated appellant's service. Thus, the agreement for the seasonal supply of water does not seem to us to relate in any significant degree to the ownership rights of respondent and the other property owners in the subdivision of Orchard Hill." 39 N.Y.2d at 509, 384 N.Y.S.2d at 720, 349 N.E.2d at 819.

4. *Covenants Against Competition.* Do covenants against competition meet the touch or concern requirement? In a landmark case, Norcross v. James, 140 Mass. 188, 2 N.E. 946 (1885), the Massachusetts Supreme Court held that a grantor's covenant not to operate a competing quarry on his neighboring land did not touch or concern the land, and thus did not bind the grantor's successors. Writing for the court, Justice Holmes observed that the covenant did not "make the use or occupation" of plaintiff's alleged dominant estate "more convenient." "It does not in any way affect the use or occupation; it simply tends indirectly to increase its value, by excluding a competitor from the market for its products. If it be asked what is the difference in principle between an easement to have land unbuilt upon, such as was recognized in Brooks v. Reynolds, 106 Mass. 31, and an easement to have a quarry left unopened, the answer is, that, whether a difference of degree or of kind, the distinction is plain between a grant or covenant that looks to direct physical advantage in the occupation of the dominant estate, such as light and air, and one which only concerns it in the indirect way which we have mentioned." 140 Mass. at 192, 2 N.E. at 949.

After almost a century of following *Norcross*, but expressing growing discomfort with its limitations, the Massachusetts Supreme Court finally overruled it expressly and joined the mainstream of American decisions in Whitinsville Plaza, Inc. v. Kotseas, 378 Mass. 85, 390 N.E.2d 243 (1979). Enforcing a covenant not to compete with plaintiff's neighboring discount store, the court ruled that "reasonable covenants against competition *may* be considered to run with the land when they serve a purpose of facilitating orderly and harmonious development for commercial use." 390 N.E.2d at 250. In part the court rested its decision on the fact that "[w]ith respect to covenants in commercial leases, we have long held that reasonable anticompetitive covenants are enforceable by and against successors to the original parties." 390 N.E.2d at 249. What relevant differences, if any, are there between the leasehold and fee context?

Can you think of any good reason why the burden of anticompetitive covenants should not run? Does *Norcross* at least vindicate society's interests in free competition? Consider Professor Lawrence Berger's observation that if "the covenant is against the common law policy favoring competition, it ought to be invalid as between the original parties to the transaction, and not just unenforceable by subsequent parties." Berger, A Policy Analysis of Promises Respecting the Use of Land, 55 Minn.L.Rev. 167, 214 (1970).

5. *Liens*. Covenants to pay money are sometimes secured by a lien on the servient estate. The lien operates as a secured alternative to the personal liability of the landowner and his successors, and enables the covenant's beneficiary to proceed directly against the land, forcing its sale and application of the proceeds to satisfaction of the debt. Will a lien be implied if it is not expressly created in the covenant itself? Under one view, a construction "which imposes simultaneously a contractual liability upon the landowner and also a lien upon his land, should only result where the language of the covenant expressly provides that the monetary obligation under the covenant shall become a lien upon the land." 2 American Law of Property § 9.17 (1952). But, "Restatement, Property (1944), § 540, comment c, takes a contrary position by recognizing a lien by operation of law in any covenant, notwithstanding the absence of any express provision for a lien." *Id.* n. 7.

Enforcement of a lien against successors to the original covenantor presupposes that the burden of the covenant runs with the land; the lien is only a remedial alternative. A few courts have made a far more dramatic use of lien theory, holding that if the burden of a covenant does not run and the successor is not personally liable, the lien will run, nonetheless, subjecting the land to compliance with the obligation. Thus, for example, in Orchard Homes Ditch Co. v. Snavely, 117 Mont. 484, 159 P.2d 521 (1945), the court approved enforcement of plaintiff's lien upon defendant's property for unpaid irrigation charges. The court ruled that under Montana law "there can be no covenant running with the land when it is not contained in the grant of the real property to be charged," but that this "does not mean that there may not be a lien against the land," for "[b]y express stipulation of the parties, a covenant which of itself would not run with the land may be binding as a lien." 117 Mont. at 488–489, 159 P.2d at 523. Although there was no express agreement that the land be so burdened, the court found that there was nevertheless an implied understanding between the original parties that the conveyance of the water rights would create a lien against the lot to which the rights were appurtenant.

The Restatement gives *carte blanche* to the imposition of liens upon nonpromising parties. According to the Reporter, "I believe that it is much wiser social policy to let land bear the burden associated with benefits that it may receive than it is to impose, merely because he has succeeded to the ownership of land once owned by one who has made a promise, the personal liability of a promisor upon one who has never made a promise." Rundell, Judge Clark on the American Law Institute's Law of Real Covenants: A Comment, 53 Yale L.J. 312, 322 (1944).

To what extent can parties use the lien device to circumvent the requirements that must be met in order for the burden of a covenant to run? Intent that the lien be created and notice by the successor to be charged are certainly required. But horizontal privity, vertical privity and touch or concern do not apply. See Restatement of Property, § 540, comment h (1944). Can a lien effectively secure other than a promise to pay money? Say, for example, A airline company obtains B's promise to erect and maintain a billboard on Blackacre advertising the airline's flights. Can A and B, by including a liquidated damages clause in the agreement and creating a lien on the land to secure payment of the liquidated damages, effectively make the burden of the promise run to successors in interest of B?

6. One perceived value of the touch or concern requirement is that it prevents all but the most physically evident and geographically confined covenants from encumbering title over a period that may well outlast the covenant's utility. Requiring a landlord-tenant relationship or a benefit to a related piece of land will reduce the number of a covenant's possible beneficiaries and thus, presumably, reduce problems of marketability. At the same time, though, the touch or concern requirement reduces A's and B's land use choices, effectively barring them from making covenants that will put land to its most productive use.

Do the *Neponsit* and Restatement tests balance these competing interests by assuring that covenant arrangements will be privately terminated when the value to Whiteacre of enjoying the covenant's benefit falls below the value to Blackacre of being free of the burden? The fact that the necessary parties to the negotiation will all be adjacent landowners, rather than dispersed and multitudinous beneficiaries, may mean that transaction costs will be relatively low. Does the Restatement bolster this position by its requirement that "the burden on the land of the promisor bear a reasonable relation to the benefit received by the person benefited"? Although the formula has some surface similarity to nuisance law's gravity-utility formula, the functions of the two differ. While the role of nuisance law is to approximate the land use decisions private parties would have made absent transaction costs, the function of section 537 is to *unmake* private decisions. What is the practical difference between the two? Would the Restatement test be improved by adding the limitation

b. Who Gets the Benefit? Does the Benefit Run?

NEPONSIT PROPERTY OWNERS' ASSOCIATION, INC. v. EMIGRANT INDUSTRIAL SAVINGS BANK, 278 N.Y. 248, 260–262, 15 N.E.2d 793, 797–798 (1938). LEHMAN, J.: . . . Another difficulty remains. Though between the grantor and the grantee there was privity of estate, the covenant provides that its benefit shall run to the assigns of the grantor who "may include a Property Owners' Association which may hereafter be organized for the purposes referred to in this paragraph." The plaintiff has been organized to receive the sums payable by the property owners and to expend them for the benefit of such owners. Various definitions have been formulated of "privity of estate" in connection with covenants that run with the land, but none of such definitions seems to cover the relationship between the plaintiff and the defendant in this case. The plaintiff has not succeeded to the ownership of any property of the grantor. It does not appear that it ever had title to the streets or public places upon which charges which are payable to it must be expended. It does not appear that it owns any other property in the residential tract to which any easement or right of enjoyment in such property is appurtenant. It is created solely to act as the assignee of the benefit of the covenant, and it has no interest of its own in the enforcement of the covenant.

The arguments that under such circumstances the plaintiff has no right of action to enforce a covenant running with the land are all based upon a distinction between the corporate property owners' association and the property owners for whose benefit the association has been formed. If that distinction may be ignored, then the basis of the arguments is destroyed. How far privity of estate in technical form is necessary to enforce in equity a restrictive covenant upon the use of land, presents an interesting question. Enforcement of such covenants rests upon equitable principles (Tulk v. Moxhay, 2 Phillips, 774; Trustees of Columbia College v. Lynch, 70 N.Y. 440, 26 Am.Rep. 615; Korn v. Campbell, 192 N.Y. 490, 85 N.E. 687, 37 L.R.A.,N.S., 1, 127 Am.St.Rep. 925), and at times, at least, the violation "of the restrictive covenant may be restrained at the suit of one who owns property or for whose benefit the restriction was established, irrespective of whether there were privity either of estate or of contract between the parties, or whether an action at law were maintainable." Chesebro v. Moers, 233 N.Y. 75, 80, 134 N.E. 842, 843, 21 A.L.R. 1270. The covenant in this case does not fall exactly within any classification of "restrictive" covenants, which have been enforced in this State and no right to enforce even a restrictive covenant has been sustained in this State where the plaintiff did not own property which would benefit by such enforcement so that some of the elements of an equitable servitude are present. In some jurisdictions it has been held that no action may be maintained without such elements. But cf. VanSant v. Rose, 260 Ill. 401, 103 N.E. 194, 49 L.R.A.,N.S., 186. We do not attempt to decide now how far the rule of Trustees of Columbia College v. Lynch, supra, will be carried, or to formulate a definite rule as to when, or even whether, covenants in a deed will be enforced, upon equitable principles, against subsequent purchasers with notice, at the suit of a party without privity of contract or estate. There is no need to resort to such a rule if the courts may look behind the corporate form of the plaintiff.

The corporate plaintiff has been formed as a convenient instrument by which the property owners may advance their common interests. We do not ignore the corporate form when we recognize that the Neponsit Property Owners' Association, Inc., is acting as the agent or representative of the Neponsit property owners. As we have said in another case: when Neponsit Property Owners' Association, Inc., "was formed, the property owners were expected to, and have looked to that organization as the medium through which enjoyment of their common right might be preserved equally for all." Matter of City of New York, Public Beach, Borough of Queens, 269 N.Y. 64, 75, 199 N.E. 5, 9. Under the conditions thus presented we said: "It may be difficult, or even impossible, to classify into recognized categories the nature of the interest of the membership corporation and its members in the land. The corporate entity cannot be disregarded, nor can the separate interests of the members of the corporation" (page 73, 199 N.E. page 8). Only blind adherence to an ancient formula devised to meet entirely different conditions could constrain the court to hold that a corporation formed as a medium for the enjoyment of common rights of property owners owns no property which would benefit by enforcement of common rights and has no cause of action in equity to enforce the covenant upon which such common rights depend. Every reason which in other circumstances may justify the ancient formula may be urged in support of the conclusion that the formula should not be applied in this case. In substance if not in form the covenant is a restrictive covenant which touches and concerns the defendant's land, and in substance, if not in form, there is privity of estate between the plaintiff and the defendant.

MATTER OF TURNERS CROSSROAD DEVELOPMENT CO.

Supreme Court of Minnesota, 1979.
277 N.W.2d 364.

YETKA, Justice.

Appeal by McCarthy Enterprises from order of Hennepin County District Court of May 5, 1978, granting summary judgment to Turners Crossroad Development Co. and Klodt Companies, Inc., and directing deletion of certain restrictions from certificates of title for a tract of land, in a proceeding subsequent to the initial registration of land, and judgment entered June 7, 1978. Respondents have filed a notice of review pursuant to Rule 106, Rules of Civil Appellate Procedure. We affirm. . . .

On April 22, 1949, McCarthy's St. Louis Park Cafe, Inc. (hereinafter referred to as "McCarthy's") conveyed a tract of land located near the intersection of U.S. Highway No. 12 and Turners Crossroad in St. Louis Park to the Minneapolis Baseball and Athletic Association (hereinafter referred to as "Baseball"). This tract of land shall be referred to herein as Tract I. The warranty deed by which the tract was conveyed contained the following restrictive covenant:

"The grantee, its successors and assigns, shall not keep or permit to be kept on the demised premises . . . or on any buildings erected thereon, intoxicating liquors or foods for commercial sale other than as is usually incident to the operation of ball park athletic contests of all kinds, circuses and exhibitions, nor shall any on-or-off sale liquor establishment of any kind or description be operated, permitted or kept on said premises, nor shall any restaurant where food is served to the public be maintained or operated on said premises, or in any building erected thereon, provided however, nothing herein contained shall prohibit the use of said premises for the preparation, serving and sale of beer, food and refreshments of all kinds incident to and usually prepared, served and sold in connection with the operation or conduct of ball park athletic contests of all kinds, circuses and other exhibitions of any kind or description. The sale of all of the foregoing is hereby expressly permitted. The above covenant shall run with the land."

At the time of the conveyance to Baseball, McCarthy's owned a tract of land located directly north of Tract I, across Wayzata Boulevard, upon which it operated an on- and off-sale liquor establishment and a restaurant (Tract II). During the negotiations between Baseball and McCarthy's, Baseball's counsel suggested that the restrictive covenant "should only last during such time as McCarthy's owned that restaurant." However, the purpose of the covenant, according to McCarthy's counsel, was for "protection against anybody using the [Baseball] property for a purpose they did not want it for or want there"; accordingly, the suggestion made by Baseball's counsel did not survive the negotiations. At the time those negotiations were being conducted, Baseball intended to use Tract I for the construction and operation of an athletic stadium. Although Baseball obtained municipal authorization to build and operate such a stadium, it did not do so.

On April 15, 1968, appellant McCarthy Enterprises acquired all of the assets of McCarthy's. The purchase agreement specifically provided that appellant was acquiring "all contingent remainders, rights of reverter, and/or contract rights" which McCarthy's owned in Tract I. A quit claim deed was executed and delivered by McCarthy's to appellant on April 15, 1968, "for the express purpose of assigning to party of the second part all rights which party of the first part shall have in [Tract I], which rights to be so transferred shall include without limitation those rights in the nature of contractual covenants, contingent remainders, and rights of reverter."

On April 10, 1975, appellant and Eddie Webster's Inc. and Eddie Webster's Pub (hereinafter referred to collectively as "Webster's") entered into a property exchange agreement pursuant to which appellant agreed to convey Tract II to Webster's. The property exchange agreement specifically provided that Webster's "shall not obtain any right, title or interest in the benefits of" the restrictive covenant burdening Tract I. Thereafter, on September 5, 1975, appellant executed and delivered a warranty deed conveying Tract II to Webster's. That warranty deed contained the following limitation:

". . . subject to the reservation by the party of the first part [Appellant] of the rights reserved by the Grantor in that certain deed [conveying Tract I to Baseball], it being the intent of parties of the first part and second part hereto that *said rights shall not, in any event, be extinguished by the reservation herein provided for.* With respect to such reserved rights, party of the first part hereby affirms to second party the covenant set forth in Exhibit A annexed hereto which has heretofore been made by first party to second party and which is hereby incorporated herein. . . ." (Italics supplied.)

The covenant last referred to provided that appellant "shall not, for a period of 7 years from and after April 10, 1975, consent and agree to the use of the parcel of land [Tract I] . . . for a restaurant which would be competitive with that operated by Eddie Webster's, Inc. on the property described in the deed to which this Exhibit is attached and which would violate the restrictions contained in the aforesaid deed dated April 22, 1949."

On December 2, 1977, respondent Turners Crossroad Development Co. was issued a certificate of title to Tract I subject to the restrictive covenant. Thereafter, a portion of Tract I was conveyed to respondent Klodt Companies, Inc. Respondents allege that they now desire to utilize Tract I to construct restaurants and bars.

Respondent Turners Crossroad Development Co. commenced this action in Hennepin County District Court in January 1978 as a proceeding subsequent to the initial registration of land seeking an order pursuant to Minn.St. 508.71 directing the deletion of certain restrictions from the certificates of title for Tract I. Responses were filed by appellant McCarthy Enterprises and by Webster's. Respondent Klodt Companies, Inc., intervened.

On February 28, 1978, respondents moved for summary judgment. The motion was briefed extensively and orally argued at a special term of the district court on March 10, 1978. In its order of May 5, 1978, granting summary judgment to respondents, the trial court held that the restrictions are not enforceable because they have become nominal and of no actual and substantial benefit to any party and because they have been extinguished. With respect to the first of those grounds, the court apparently found there was no genuine issue of material fact that the benefit of the restrictive covenant ran with Tract II and that:

". . . There is a patent injustice in allowing McCarthy's to enforce a covenant not to sell liquor in a matter in which it retains no interest whatsoever. This Court has serious reservations about the wisdom of allowing provisions contained in a 1949 real estate transaction, made to facilitate the bringing of a major league baseball team to the Twin Cities, to prevent the development of a substantial piece of real estate in 1978."

With respect to the latter issue, the trial court found that appellant's reservation of rights in the restrictive covenant at the time it conveyed Tract II to Webster's extinguished the restrictions as a matter of law "the intent of the parties otherwise notwithstanding." . . .

1. The first issue raised is whether the restriction on the sale of liquor and food in the 1949 deed is a covenant that runs with the land. This court defined a covenant that runs with the land in Pelser v. Gingold, 214 Minn. 281, 285, 8 N.W.2d 36, 39 (1943):

". . . A covenant is said to run with the land when it touches or concerns the land granted or demised. Generally speaking, a covenant touches or concerns the land if it is such as to benefit the grantor or the lessor, or the grantee or lessee, as the case may be. As the term implies, the covenant must concern the occupation or enjoyment of the land granted or demised and the liability to perform it, and the right to take advantage of it must pass to the assignee. Conversely, if the covenant does not touch or concern the occupation or enjoyment of the land, it is the collateral and personal obligation of the grantor or lessor and does not run with the land. . . ."

The covenant must not only touch and concern the land; it must also be the intent of the covenanting parties that the covenant run with the land, that is, that their successors or assigns will be bound by the terms of the covenant.

The principal evidence of intent in the instant case is this sentence, at the end of the paragraph containing the restriction: "The above covenant shall run with the land." Although such a statement is not necessarily conclusive on the issue of intent, neither party to this appeal argues that this statement is not to be given effect. Appellant does argue, however, that only the burden of the covenant, not the benefit, is intended to run with the land. According to appellant's argument, the burden of the covenant runs with Tract I and is binding on all successors or assigns of Baseball (the grantee of the 1949 deed) but the benefit of the covenant does not run with Tract II, being instead personal to McCarthy's (grantor of the 1949 deed).

Appellant's position with respect to Tract I is inconsistent with the general policy against restraints on free alienation of property. This policy is discussed in Restatement, Property, § 543, comment *c*:

> "In order that the burden of a promise respecting the use of land of the promisor may run with that land, it is necessary that, by the performance of the promise, there will be a benefit realized by the beneficiary in the use of his land, or that, by the carrying out of the transaction of which the promise is a part, there will come to the promisor a benefit in the use of his land. Thus a promise that the promisor will not carry on a certain kind of business on his land will not run with that land unless the performance of the promise aids the beneficiary of it in the use by him of some land, and a promise by the promisor that he will make certain payments will not run with specific land owned by him unless the payments are to be made in return for benefits received by him in the use of that land . . . . The requirement of 'reciprocal benefit,' as applied to the running of the burden of promises respecting the use of land, is based upon a social policy adverse to the placing of undue restrictions upon the freedom of alienation of land. If the burden of a promise runs with land, the freedom of alienation of that land is to some extent restricted. The resulting restriction is permitted only when there is a countervailing benefit in the use of either the burdened land or of some other land . . . ."

The effect of this policy is illustrated by the treatment given by the Restatement to covenants of the type at issue here. Section 537 provides:

> "The successors in title to land respecting the use of which the owner has made a promise can be bound as promisors only if
>
> (a) the performance of the promise will benefit the promisee or other beneficiary of the promise in the physical use or enjoyment of the land possessed by him, or
>
> (b) the consummation of the transaction of which the promise is a part will operate to benefit and is for the benefit of the promisor in the physical use or enjoyment of land possessed by him,
>
> and the burden on the land of the promisor bears a reasonable relation to the benefit received by the person benefited."

In discussing "physical use or enjoyment," comment *f* states:

> "For a promise to run with the land of the promisor it is not enough that the performance of the promise operates to benefit either the promisor or the beneficiary of the promise in the use of his land but it must operate to benefit him in the physical use of his land. It must in some way make the use or enjoyment more satisfactory to his physical senses. It is not enough that the income from it is increased by virtue of it. Thus a promise that

land of the promisor will not be so used as to compete with a business carried on upon the land of the promisee does not so affect the land of the promisor that it can be made to run with it. Though the benefit to the promisee in being free from competition may be clear, the risk of social harm involved in a possible monopoly of the business uses of land in an extended area is sufficient to induce the refusal to extend the 'running of promises' to such cases."[3]

In contrast, section 543 provides:

"(1) The benefit of a promise can run with land only if it is a promise respecting the use of land of the beneficiary of the promise.

"(2) A promise is a promise respecting the use of land of the beneficiary of the promise if and only if the performance of the promise will

"(a) constitute an advantage in a physical sense to the beneficiary in the use of his land, or

"(b) decrease the commercial competition in his use of it, or

"(c) constitute a return to the beneficiary of the promise for a use of it by the promisor."

Comment *e* states:

"A promise is a promise respecting the use of land in such a sense as to enable the benefit of the promise to run with land though the performance of the promise affects the use of the land of the beneficiary of the promise in no way other than to decrease the commercial competition in the use of it as in the case of promises not to compete with a business use carried on upon the land . . . . The promise may be, on the part of the promisor, personal only in the sense that it is not a promise respecting the use of any land of the promisor, or it may be a promise that the competing use shall not be carried on upon neighboring premises owned by him. The fact that the promise is personal on the part of the promisor does not prevent the benefit of it from running . . . ."

Applying the reasoning of the Restatement to the present case, we cannot accept appellant's argument that the burden of the covenant runs with Tract I but the benefit of the covenant does not run with Tract II. It is clear from both the language of the restriction and the surrounding circumstances that, when created, the purpose of the restriction was to protect McCarthy's restaurant and liquor store from competition. Thus the covenant appears to fall within sec-

3. This comment is illustrated by the following example: "A, the owner of two vacant lots lying side by side, sells one to B who contemplates erecting and operating a drug store upon it. A agrees on behalf of himself and his assigns that no drug store will be operated upon the lot retained. A's promise does not so affect the land as to enable A's successor to be held liable as a promisor upon A's promise." Restatement, Property, § 537, Illustration 1.

tion 543(2)(b): where performance of a promise will decrease the commercial competition in the beneficiary's use of his land, that promise is "a promise respecting the use of land," and consequently, the benefit of that promise can run with the benefited land. The covenant is also covered by the statement in comment *f* to section 537 that a promise that the land of the promisor will not be used so as to compete with a business being conducted on the land of the promisee does not so "affect" the land of the promisor that it will run with that land.

2. Section 545 of the Restatement provides:

"The beneficiary of a promise respecting the use of land of the beneficiary, which promise is capable of running with the land, can, when conveying the land, prevent, by manifesting an intention to that effect, the promise from running with the land."

In the instant case, the promise in the 1949 deed is capable of running with the land. Appellant, when conveying Tract II to Webster's manifested the intention that the promise not run with the land by including the following provision in the deed to Webster's:

"Subject to all restrictions, reservations, easements, and encumbrances of record, if any, and subject to the reservation by the party of the first part of the rights reserved by the Grantor in that certain deed dated April 22, 1949, . . . it being the intent of parties of the first and second part hereto that said rights shall not, in any event, be extinguished by the reservation herein provided for. . . ."

Comment *b* to section 545 states that "[t]he effect of withholding the promise from the operation of a conveyance may be to extinguish liability on the promise." If in the original promise the beneficiary is given "the power to sever the promise from one piece of land and either attach it to another piece or turn it into a promise the benefit of which accrues to him personally," liability on the promise will not be extinguished. Absent such explicit authorization, however, the effect of severance will be to extinguish liability on the promise. Nothing in the promise at issue here authorizes appellant to sever the promise from the land. Thus, under the rule of section 545, the covenant was extinguished by appellant's attempted reservation of rights to the benefits of the covenant. Cf., Cadwalader v. Bailey, 17 R.I. 495, 502, 23 A. 20, 23 (1891) ("The easement, being appurtenant to the land, cannot exist alone.")

3. Because we have found that the covenant was extinguished, neither appellant nor Webster's may enforce it. Even if we had found that the benefit of the original promise was personal to appellant, appellant would not be able to enforce it because appellant no longer has any interest in the benefited land and because appellant can no longer benefit from the protection provided by the promise. The original covenant was clearly intended to benefit appellant's business interest in Tract II. Because that interest no longer exists, the

covenant is of no further value to and cannot be enforced by appellant. . . .

Affirmed.

SNOW v. VAN DAM

Supreme Court of Massachusetts, 1935.
291 Mass. 477, 197 N.E. 224.

LUMMUS, Justice.

This suit, although brought in Middlesex county, relates to land on the seashore at Brier Neck in Gloucester in Essex county, title to which, after the decision in Luce v. Parsons, 192 Mass. 8, 77 N.E. 1032, was registered on September 5, 1906, in the name of one Luce, from whom title soon passed to one Shackelford. The tract so registered was bounded northerly by a line through a pond not far northerly from a county road called Thatcher Road, which ran through the tract from west to east; easterly by land of other owners; southerly by the Atlantic Ocean, where there was a fine bathing beach; and westerly by Witham Road. The entrance to the tract was at the northwesterly corner, where is situated the lot now owned by the defendant Van Dam, which is the larger part of a triangular piece of land lying north of Thatcher Road and enclosed by Thatcher Road, Witham Road and another road.

The northerly part of the tract, including the lot of the defendant Van Dam, is low and marshy. When the tract was registered in 1906, this northerly part was deemed unsuitable for building, and worthless, and consequently was not divided into lots on the earlier plans. Thatcher Road is a public way on which electric cars used to run. There is no summer residence on the north side of that way, and only one bounding on that way on the south side.

From Thatcher Road, going south, there is a fairly sharp ascent to the top of a low hill, from which there is a gentle slope southward to the beach. This hill and slope were in 1906, and still are, well adapted to summer residences. In 1907 the whole tract, except the part north of Thatcher Road, was divided into building lots. By later plans some of the lots were further subdivided and the boundaries of others were changed. In all, about a hundred building lots were laid out. Each of the plaintiffs owns one of these building lots, either on the hill or on the southerly slope, on which he has built a summer residence.

Between July 8, 1907, and January 23, 1923, almost all the lots into which the part of the tract south of Thatcher Road was divided, including the lots of most of the plaintiffs, were sold at various times by the general owner of the tract to various persons. With negligible exceptions, the deeds contained uniform restrictions, of which the material one is that "only one dwelling house shall be erected or maintained thereon at any given time which building shall cost not less than $2500 and no outbuilding containing a privy shall be erected or maintained on said parcel without the consent in writing of the grantor or their [sic] heirs." The entire unsold remainder of the land south of Thatcher Road was conveyed, on June 15, 1923, by Shackelford, the general owner of the unsold parts of the tract, to J. Richard Clark, subject to similar restrictions.

The low and marshy land north of Thatcher Road was first divided, on a revised plan of 1919, into three parcels, called C, D and E. The revised plan covered the whole Brier Neck tract. On January 23, 1923, about five months before the deed to J. Richard Clark, already mentioned, said Shackelford conveyed said lots C, D and E to one Robert C. Clark, subject to the following restrictions: "Only one dwelling house may be maintained on each of said parcels of land at any given time, which dwelling house shall cost not less than Twenty-Five Hundred Dollars ($2500) unless plans and specifications for a dwelling house of less cost shall be approved in writing by the grantor of said parcels of land, and no outbuilding containing a privy shall be maintained on either of said parcels of land without the consent in writing of the grantor. . . ." Lot D is the lot of which the larger part is now owned by the defendant Van Dam, having been conveyed to him by Robert C. Clark on February 18, 1933, subject to the restrictions contained in the deed to him "in so far as the same may be now in force and applicable." This phrase did not purport to create any new restriction, and could have no such effect. The defendants have erected on lot D a large building to be used for the sale of ice cream and dairy products and the conducting of the business of a common victualler. The plaintiffs bring this suit for an injunction, claiming a violation of the restrictions. We think that the erection of a building to be used for business purposes was a violation of the language of the restriction. The zoning of the land for business in 1927 by the city of Gloucester could not operate to remove existing restrictions.

Prior to the conveyance from Shackelford to Robert C. Clark on January 23, 1923, there could not have been, under the law of this commonwealth, any enforceable restriction upon lot D. Sprague v. Kimball, 213 Mass. 380, 100 N.E. 622, Ann.Cas. 1914A, 431. If any now exists in favor of the lands of the plaintiffs, it must have been created by that deed.

A restriction, to be attached to land by way of benefit, must not only tend to benefit that land itself but must also be intended to be appurtenant to that land. If not intended to benefit an ascertainable dominant estate, the restriction will not burden the supposed servient estate, but will be a mere personal contract on both sides.

In the absence of express statement, an intention that a restriction upon one lot shall be appurtenant to a neighboring lot is sometimes inferred from the relation of the lots to each other. But in many cases there has been a scheme or plan for restricting the lots in a tract undergoing development to obtain substantial uniformity in building and use. The existence of such a building scheme has often been relied on to show an intention that the restrictions imposed upon the several lots shall be appurtenant to every other lot in the tract included in the scheme. In some cases the absence of such a scheme has made it impossible to show that the burden of the restriction was intended to be appurtenant to neighboring land. In the present case, unless the lots of the plaintiffs and the defendant Van Dam were included in one scheme of restrictions, there is nothing to show that the restrictions upon the lot of the defendant Van Dam were intended to be appurtenant to the lots of the plaintiffs.

What is meant by a "scheme" of this sort? In England, where the idea has been most fully developed, it is established that the area covered by the scheme and the restrictions imposed within that area must be apparent to the several purchasers when the sales begin. The purchasers must know the extent of their reciprocal rights and obligations, or, in other words, the "local law" imposed by the vendor upon a definite tract. Where such a scheme exists, it appears to be the law of England and some American jurisdictions that a grantee subject to restrictions acquires by implication an enforceable right to have the remaining land of the vendor, within the limits of the scheme, bound by similar restrictions. Traces of that idea can be found in our own reports. But it was settled in this commonwealth by Sprague v. Kimball, 213 Mass. 380, 100 N.E. 622, Ann.Cas. 1914A, 431, that the statute of frauds prevents the enforcement against the vendor, or any purchaser from him of a lot not expressly restricted, of any implied or oral agreement that the vendor's remaining land shall be bound by restrictions similar to those imposed upon lots conveyed. Only where, as in Kimball v. Commonwealth Avenue Street Railway, 173 Mass. 152, 53 N.E. 274 the vendor binds his remaining land by writing, can reciprocity of restriction between the vendor and the vendee be enforced.

Nevertheless, the existence of a "scheme" continues to be important in Massachusetts for the purpose of determining the land to which the restrictions are appurtenant. Sometimes the scheme has been established by preliminary statements of intention to restrict the tract, particularly in documents of a public nature. More often it is shown by the substantial uniformity of the restrictions upon the lots included in the tract. In some jurisdictions the logic of the English rule, that the extent and character of the scheme must be apparent when the sale of the lots begins, has led to rulings that the restrictions imposed in later deeds are not evidence of the existence or nature of the scheme. In the present case there is no evidence of a scheme except a list of conveyances of different lots from 1907 to 1923 with substantially uniform restrictions. Although the point has not been discussed by this court, the original papers show, more clearly than the reports, that subsequent deeds were relied on to show a scheme existing at the time of the earlier conveyances to the parties or their predecessors in title, in Hills v. Metzenroth, 173 Mass. 423, 53 N.E. 890; Bacon v. Sandberg, 179 Mass. 396, 60 N.E. 936; Stewart v. Finkelstone, 206 Mass. 28, 92 N.E. 37, 28 L.R.A.(N.S.) 634, 138 Am.St.Rep. 370; and Storey v. Brush, 256 Mass. 101, 152 N.E. 225. Apparently in Massachusetts a "scheme" has legal effect if definitely settled by the common vendor when the sale of lots begins, even though at that time evidence of such settlement is lacking and a series of subsequent conveyances is needed to supply it. In Bacon v. Sandberg, 179 Mass. 396, 398, 60 N.E. 936, 937, it was said, "the criterion in this class of cases is the intent of the grantor in imposing the restrictions."

Neither the restricting of every lot within the area covered, nor absolute identity of restrictions upon different lots, is essential to the existence of a scheme. But extensive omissions or variations tend to show that no scheme exists, and that the restrictions are only personal contracts.

The existence of a "scheme" is important in the law of restrictions for another purpose, namely, to enable the restrictions to be made appurtenant to a lot within the scheme which has been earlier conveyed by the common vendor. In the present case the lots of some of the plaintiffs were sold before, and the lots of others after, the conveyance from Shackelford to Robert C. Clark on January 23, 1923, which first imposed a restriction upon the lot now owned by the defendant Van Dam. The plaintiffs whose lots were sold before January 23, 1923, cannot claim succession to any rights of Shackelford or of land then retained by him. In general, an equitable easement or restriction cannot be created in favor of land owned by a stranger. Nevertheless an earlier purchaser in a land development has long been allowed to enforce against a later purchaser the restrictions imposed upon the latter by the deed to him in pursuance of a scheme of restrictions. . . .

The rationale of the rule allowing an earlier purchaser to enforce restrictions in a deed to a later one pursuant to a building scheme, is not easy to find. The simple explanation that the deed to the earlier purchaser, subject to restrictions, implied an enforceable agreement on the part of the vendor to restrict in like manner all the remaining land included in the scheme cannot be accepted in Massachusetts without conflict with Sprague v. Kimball, 213 Mass. 380, 100 N.E. 622, Ann.Cas. 1914A, 431. In Bristol v. Woodward, 251 N.Y. 275, 288, 167 N.E. 441, 446, Cardozo, C.J., said, "If we regard the restriction from the point of view of contract, there is trouble in understanding how the purchaser of lot A can gain a right to enforce the restriction against the later purchaser of lot B without an extraordinary extension of Lawrence v. Fox, 20 N.Y. 268. . . . Perhaps it is enough to say that the extension of the doctrine, even if illogical, has been made too often and too consistently to permit withdrawal or retreat."

It follows from what has been said, that if there was a scheme of restrictions, existing when the sale of lots began in 1907, which scheme included the lands of the plaintiffs and of the defendant Van Dam, and if the restrictions imposed upon the land of the defendant Van Dam in 1923 were imposed in pursuance of that scheme, then all the plaintiffs are entitled to relief, unless some special defense is shown. The burden is upon the plaintiffs to show the existence of such a scheme. In our opinion they have done so. Unquestionably there was a scheme which included all the land south of Thatcher Road. The real question is, whether in its origin it included the land north of that road, where is situated the lot of the defendant Van Dam. That lot lies at the gateway of the whole development. One must pass it to visit any part of Brier Neck. The use made of that lot tends strongly to fix the character of the entire tract. It is true, that the land north of Thatcher Road was not divided into lots until 1919, but it was shown on all the plans from the beginning. The failure to divide it sooner was apparently due to a belief that it could not be sold, not to an intent to reserve it for other than residential purposes. We think that the scheme from the beginning contemplated that no part of the Brier Neck tract should be used for commercial purposes. When the lot of the defendant Van Dam was restricted in 1923, the restriction was in pursuance of the original scheme and gave rights to earlier as well as to later purchasers.

The violation of some of the restrictions by some of the purchasers of lots in the tract, without action by these plaintiffs, does not affect their right to enforce the restrictions against the defendants. There has been no fundamental change in the character of Brier Neck, making inequitable the specific enforcement of the restrictions, within the rule of Jackson v. Stevenson, 156 Mass. 496, 31 N.E. 691, 32 Am.St.Rep. 476. Neither does the violation of some of the less important restrictions, but not of the restriction in question, by some of the plaintiffs deprive them, much less the other plaintiffs, of the right to relief in equity. The failure of the plaintiffs to object to a petty business carried on by the grantor of the defendant Van Dam does not bar them from objecting to the large project now undertaken.

G.L. (Ter.Ed.) c. 184, § 23, provides that "restrictions, unlimited as to time, . . . shall be limited to the term of thirty years after the date of the deed or other instrument . . . creating them. . . ." The defendants contend that the restrictions in question were created in 1907, and therefore will expire in 1937 under the statute. But it has already been shown that no restriction existed upon the lot of the defendant Van Dam until January 23, 1923, when the conveyance to his grantor was made. Although the deed was dated January 19, 1923, the registration, which was the operative act of conveyance (G.L. c. 185, § 57), took place on January 23, 1923. The latter date is the one from which the period of thirty years runs. The final decree is to be modified by striking out the word "permanently" in paragraphs 4 and 5, and by inserting a provision limiting the period of the injunction to the time prior to and including January 23, 1953. As thus modified, the final decree is affirmed, with costs.

Ordered accordingly.

NOTES

1. *Who Can Enforce the Benefit of a Covenant?* As a general rule, anyone whom the covenantee and covenantor, *A* and *B*, expressly or impliedly intended to receive the benefit can enforce it. In *Neponsit*, for example, the court honored the parties' expressed intent that the benefit be enforced by Neponsit Realty Company and its assigns. And in Snow v. Van Dam the court honored the parties' presumed intent that the benefit be enforceable by residents south of Thatcher Road.

Under the theory of Snow v. Van Dam, could individual homeowners in the *Neponsit* subdivision, or homeowners as a class, also have enforced the covenant?

2. *Can the Benefit of a Covenant Be Held in Gross?* In looking behind plaintiff's corporate form to find the interests of benefited neighbors, was the *Neponsit* court saying that the benefit of an affirmative covenant cannot be held in gross? Did *Turners Crossroad* hold that the benefit of a negative covenant cannot be held in gross?

Many courts—even some that enforce easements in gross—will not enforce the benefit of a covenant in gross. Is there any good reason for the rule? Does it make sense to distinguish for this purpose between affirmative covenants and negative covenants? When would *A*, not owning adjacent land, pay to obtain a negative covenant from *B*? *Cf.* Van Sant v. Rose, 260 Ill. 401, 407, 103 N.E. 194, 196 (1913), enforcing a building restriction against defendants, even though plaintiffs owned no neighboring land: "The right to enjoin the breach of restrictive covenants does not depend upon whether the covenantee will be damaged by the breach."

What economic or spiritual advantages might McCarthy's have derived from the Baseball covenant after selling its land to Webster's? Why did the court hold that McCarthy's attempted reservation extinguished the benefit? Would it not have been more consistent with the court's theory, and with the italicized language in Webster's warranty deed, to hold that the benefit was appurtenant, and enforceable by Webster's? According to a footnote, "The current owner of Tract II apparently has little interest in the benefit of the covenant. Webster's was unwilling to pay $100,000 for the restriction, although its president stated that the restriction was of 'substantial economic benefit' to it and that it did not intend the restriction to be extinguished." 277 N.W.2d at 371, n. 5. If the court had held that the benefit was appurtenant, would it have held that it ran with the land?

3. Covenant benefits were allowed to run long before covenant burdens. The early title covenant cases all involved the question whether the covenantee's successors could enforce the warranty against the covenantor, and Pakenham's Case later expanded the arena for running benefits to include covenants for personal services. See page 729 above. Perhaps influenced by this early solicitude, courts continue to be comparatively generous to beneficiaries, allowing benefits to run under circumstances in which the burden clearly would not.

For the benefit of a covenant to run, the covenantee's successor, Y, must be able to demonstrate that the original parties, A and B, intended that it run. There is, however, no requirement that Y have notice of the covenant since it is thought that windfall benefits bear none of the hazards of unexpected burdens. Horizontal privity, required for the burden to run, need not be shown for the benefit to run; the Nevada Supreme Court, which in Wheeler v. Schad, page 746, above, required horizontal privity on the burden side, has expressly omitted it for the benefit side. City of Reno v. Matley, 79 Nev. 49, 378 P.2d 256 (1963). Although Y must succeed to some interest of A for the benefit to run, the strict relationship of vertical privity required of burdens is not required. See, for example, St. Louis, Iron Mountain & Southern Railway v. O'Baugh, 49 Ark. 418, 5 S.W. 711 (1887). And, as indicated in the *Turner's Crossroad* comparison of Restatement sections 537 and 543, the touch and concern test is less stringent for benefits than for burdens.

Should the requirements for benefits to run be less rigorous than those for burdens? Do you agree with the Restatement's assertion that "the running of the burden of a promise tends to reduce the alienability of the land with which it runs while the opposite is true with respect to the running of the benefit"? Restatement of Property Ch. 46 Introductory Note (1944). Although looking at the benefited and burdened parcels, and their relative marketability separately might appear to support this view, can the questions in fact be separated? Every decision that enforces a benefit will presumably inhibit the marketability of the burdened estate. Does the Restatement's touch and concern test inextricably link the two parcels, in any event? As a practical matter, since the usual action to enforce a covenant will not be between A and B, or Y and B, but rather between Y and Z, will not the more rigorous set of requirements—here, the requirements for the burden to run—inevitably control the outcome of most cases?

What purpose is served by Restatement § 543's requirement that for the benefit of a covenant to run it must respect "the use of the land of the beneficiary of the promise." Does the restriction of running benefits to land-related uses, when taken together with the different standards for the benefit and burden of a covenant to run, produce undesirable anomalies? Say that A and B, neighboring lot owners, enter into reciprocal covenants, A agreeing not to sell shoes on Whiteacre, and B agreeing not to sell gloves on Blackacre. If A later sells Whiteacre to Y, it would appear that, although Y would not be burdened by A's covenant, he could, as successor to the benefit of B's promise, enforce B's promise against her.

c. ENFORCEMENT AT EQUITY: EQUITABLE SERVITUDES

SUN OIL CO. v. TRENT AUTO WASH, INC.
Supreme Court of Michigan, 1967.
379 Mich. 182, 150 N.W.2d 818.

ADAMS, J.

On September 28, 1962, Clara Williams gave a warranty deed to Sun Oil Company by which she conveyed to that company two lots. Contained in her deed is the following agreement:

> "Grantor agrees *that property* now owned by Grantor lying north of and adjacent to the within described premises *shall not be used* for or in connection with the operation of a gasoline service station or filling station for the sale of gasoline, motor fuel, petroleum products, automotive accessories or automotive services generally." (Emphasis added.)

On February 1, 1964, Clara Williams executed a land contract to defendant, Trent Auto Wash, Inc. It is admitted that the land contract covered "that property now owned by grantor lying north of and adjacent to" the lots Clara Williams conveyed to Sun Oil Company. The defendant also "admits that it had knowledge of the alleged covenant; that plaintiff's agents informed it that plaintiff would attempt to enforce said covenant, and that defendant intends to construct under ground storage tanks and above ground pumps," etc.

It is unnecessary to determine whether the above agreement is a covenant running with the land to afford plaintiff the relief it seeks. The agreement relates to the property purchased by Trent Auto Wash and it is equally clear that it was intended for the benefit of the adjacent property of Sun Oil Company. The agreement does not relate to any activities on the part of Clara Williams, but, rather, contemplates a restriction upon the use of property retained by her. Whatever she could not do, chancery may also enjoin those in privity with her and with notice of the restriction from doing.

The principle is stated by the Lord Chancellor in the case of Tulk v. Moxhay (1848), 2 Ph. 774 (41 Eng.Rep. 1143), affirming 11 Beav. 571 (50 Eng.Rep. 937):

> ". . . the question does not depend upon whether the covenant runs with the land . . . if there was a mere agreement and no covenant, this Court would enforce it against the party purchasing with notice of it; for if an equity is attached to the

property by the owner, no one purchasing with notice of that equity can stand in a different situation from the party from whom he purchased."

The principle of *Tulk* has been widely recognized and followed in numerous cases. In the case of Langenback v. Mays (1950), 207 Ga. 156, 60 S.E.2d 240, the defendants sold to plaintiffs a small tract of land on which several tourist cabins were located, and orally agreed not to use their remaining land for a tourist camp. The defendants constructed a tourist camp in violation of their contract and, when enjoined from operating it, executed an instrument purporting to be a lease to their daughter for the tourist camp. The daughter operated the business with actual knowledge of the injunction granted against her parents. The Supreme Court of Georgia's opinion states:

> "Equity will enforce a lawful restrictive agreement concerning land against a person who takes with notice of the contract. In such a case, the person violating the agreement, though not a party to it, is a privy in conscience with the maker."

In the case of Thodos v. Shirk (1956), 248 Iowa 172, 79 N.W.2d 733, plaintiff, owner of certain lots in a subdivision, brought an action in equity asking that defendants be enjoined from using their property as a trailer court in violation of the restrictive covenant in their deed which provided: "No building shall be placed or erected on said premises except for residence purposes, ..." The Court in discussing the doctrine of equitable servitudes said:

> "Since the doctrine of equitable servitudes rests upon the theory of a servitude imposed upon the land, enforceable against all subsequent purchasers of the land who are charged with notice actual or constructive, the requirement of the special words such as 'and assigns' is unnecessary in the deed. The sole test for the running of the burden in equity, is the intention of the parties to impose a servitude upon the land as distinguished from a personal promise of the present owner." . . .

The agreement between Clara Williams and Sun Oil Company is not so ambiguous as to be incapable of enforcement against those who have taken with notice of it. The commitment is that "that property . . . shall not be used for or in connection with the operation of a gasoline service station." There is nothing personal as to Mrs. Williams in this language. It clearly refers to the land. While the time of the commitment is not expressed, this is no insuperable obstacle. Courts are quite accustomed to making determinations of what is a reasonable time in terms of the presumed intent of the parties. Finally, if the agreement is not enforced by equity, it becomes completely vitiated. Obviously, plaintiff has no adequate remedy at law. If equity cannot grant relief, a covenantor need only convey the land to destroy today the covenant he made yesterday—or, as in Mrs. Williams' case, the covenant made by her a short 16 months before her conveyance to defendant.

Both the trial judge and the Court of Appeals disposed of this matter by holding that the covenant or agreement of the parties ran with the land, a determination I do not regard as necessary for disposition of this case. The chancellor also recognized the equitable doctrine as being applicable if the covenant did not run with the land. I would remand to him for such hearing as may be required to apply that doctrine. Determination of possible questions such as a change in circumstances relating to the lands in question may be necessary. Other aspects of the transaction not presently before us may bear upon the equities of the parties. This is a traditional equity action which does not lend itself to summary disposition. Upon the conclusion of a full hearing, the chancellor will be in a position to shape a proper decree.

I agree that the covenant does not violate C.L.1948, § 750.151 (Stat.Ann.1962 Rev. § 28.348).

I would remand with costs to abide final result.

KELLY, BLACK, and T.M. KAVANAGH, JJ., concurred with ADAMS, J.

O'HARA, J. (dissenting).

Two questions are presented by this appeal on our leave granted from the Court of Appeals. The first is whether the restrictive covenant here involved is personal and limited in its application to the grantor who executed it, or whether it is a covenant running with the land and binding upon subsequent purchasers. The second is what is the effect, if any, of the covenant upon a purchaser who takes with notice thereof. The relevant facts are as follows:

Appellant Sun Oil Company bought 3 lots in a desirable location in St. Clair Shores. It built and equipped a filling station upon them and leased out its operation. In the fractional plat there was a total of 9 lots. The 6 remaining after Sun's purchase were owned by a Clara Williams. They were adjacent to and north of the 3 Sun had previously purchased. Thereafter Sun Oil bought 2 of those lots as a protective measure against the erection of competitive filling stations upon any of the remaining 4. To this end it required that its grantor, Mrs. Williams, include in the warranty deed conveying the 2 lots the following reservation:

> "Grantor agrees that property now owned by grantor lying north of and adjacent to the within described premises shall not be used for or in connection with the operation of a gasoline service station or filling station for the sale of gasoline motor fuel."

It is stipulated that the remaining lots constitute "the property" which is the subject of this litigation.

Subsequent to this conveyance, appellee Trent purchased the 4 lots on land contract. Prior to the purchase, its attorney examined the reservation affecting the 4 lots and Trent was advised by counsel for Sun that Sun would seek to enforce it.

The case was tried in the circuit court on a stipulated record. No fact questions are involved. The trial judge found the restrictive covenant to be a covenant running with the land and hence binding upon the subsequent purchaser. The court added in its opinion:

"Even if this be considered under defendant's theory to be a personal covenant, defendant having admittedly taken title with knowledge of its existence, then equity will enforce its observance by enjoining defendant's violation of said covenant for defendant is 'privy in conscience with the maker of the restrictive agreement.'"

The Court of Appeals affirmed. Its rationale was that the restriction was not clear and unambiguous. Therefore, that case precedent holding that such restrictions cannot be extended beyond the plain meaning of the words used in them did not control. From this premise the court proceeded to a determination of "the nature of the subject matter, and the apparent purpose in making the agreement;" citing Moore v. Kimball, 291 Mich. 455, p. 461, 289 N.W. 213, p. 215. Thereupon, the court found that purpose "patently is the limitation of competition on this land." In expanding its opinion, our able intermediate Associates used the following language:

"We acknowledge that our decision is not in accord with the case of Lowe v. Wilson (1952), 194 Tenn. 267, 250 S.W.2d 366, or the authorities cited therein for we are not persuaded *that blind adherence to such a technical rule is required by or desirable* (in our view) *for the jurisprudence of Michigan.*" (Emphasis this Court's).

In its conclusionary paragraph the court adds:

"Finally we mention that our view is not in accord with that expressed in 5 Restatement of Property, § 537. We do not share the concern there expressed in the comment (f) on that section (p. 3221) anent the social harm involved."

We are compelled to disagree. First, we do not believe to hold with appellant that we adhere blindly to a technical rule. Rather, we believe we follow wise precedent efficacious as applied to transactions involving the transfer of and limitations upon the use of real property. We might well agree that the apparent purpose of appellee Sun in phrasing the restriction was to limit competition on the lots not owned by it and contiguous to those which it purchased from grantor Williams. Such unilateral intention on its part, however, in our view is not sufficient to establish that such was the intention of the grantor and binding upon subsequent grantees. If Sun intended the restriction to be a covenant running with the land, it was Sun's obligation to phrase the restriction or to insist upon phrasing that would create no ambiguity at the peril of having any ambiguity resolved in favor of the free use of land. To follow the Court of Appeals, we would do violence to the rule enunciated in Bastendorf v. Arndt, 290 Mich. 423, p. 426, 287 N.W. 579, p. 580, 124 A.L.R. 445:

> "Where restrictions are ambiguous, it is axiomatic that uncertainties are resolved in favor of the free use of property."

We agree with the Court of Appeals that the restrictions "might be read as an undertaking on the part of the covenantor that the property would *never* be used or it might be read as an undertaking that it would not be used so long as the grantor had title." (Emphasis added by the Court of Appeals.) To read "never" into the restriction here involved is to resolve the ambiguity against the free use of property and is to abrogate the salutary rule of *Bastendorf* to the exact contrary. We follow the established rule.

Next we consider the language of the learned Chancellor that even if the covenant be interpreted as a personal covenant, appellant having taken with notice equity will enforce its observance. We have no quarrel with the statement of principle. We believe, however, it contains an omission that would render its application inequitable rather than equitable. The omission is the answer to the question "notice of what?" It is stipulated that appellee had notice that a restriction had been included in the deed from Mrs. Williams to Sun and made applicable to the lots not conveyed which she retained. Even the plenary power of equity cannot decree the effect of notice to be greater than that which the thing noticed creates. A purchaser with notice of the restriction, as was appellee Trent, is as the Chancellor held "privy in conscience with the maker of [the] restrictive agreement." Equity would have no great problem in knowing what the "conscience" of Sun was. It wanted to keep filling stations off 4 lots that it did not buy that were contiguous to 2 lots it did buy, all owned by the same person. We cannot, however, span the wide gap from Sun's "conscience" to Mrs. Williams' "conscience" on the language of the deed. In examining the conveyance of the 2 lots from Mrs. Williams to Sun, counsel for Trent had a right to conclude that the restriction was personal to the grantor under well-settled law, and that when the lots passed to Trent the restriction no longer applied. Trent could well have been "privy in conscience" to Mrs. Williams and still be free to use the 4 lots it purchased as it chose. Having held the covenant personal and not binding on appellant Trent, we do not reach nor pass upon its contention that if it were valid, the intended use was not in fact violative of the language of the restriction.

Appellant Trent further urges that if the restriction does run with the land and thus is binding upon it, the limitation is in restraint of trade and violative of the applicable State statute. Strictly speaking, for decisional purpose in this Court, we need not pass upon it. However, because the Court of Appeals held the restriction binding on Trent, it had to pass upon this issue. It is important to the jurisprudence of our State and likelihood exists that the question will arise. For this reason we here approve the position of the Court of Appeals and for the reasons assigned. . . .

DETHMERS, C.J., and SOURIS, J., concurred with O'HARA, J.

NOTES

1. Tulk v. Moxhay, 2 Ph. 774, 41 Eng.Rep. 1143 (1848), cited in the *Sun Oil* majority opinion, is a landmark in property jurisprudence. In 1808, plaintiff, who owned a vacant parcel, Leicester Square Garden, as well as several neighboring houses in Leicester Square, conveyed the garden to Elms by a deed under which Elms covenanted "that Elms, his heirs and assigns should, and would from time to time, and at all times thereafter at his and their own costs and charges, keep and maintain the said piece of ground and square garden, and the iron railing around the same in its then form, and in sufficient and proper repair as a square garden and pleasure ground, in an open state, uncovered with any buildings, in neat and ornamental order." The garden passed by subsequent conveyances to defendant who purchased with notice of the 1808 covenant. When defendant indicated his intention to alter the garden, plaintiff, who continued to own several houses in the square, sought an injunction.

Plaintiff could not succeed on a negative easement theory for, as has already been seen, the common law would not expand the traditional categories of negative easements to include residential restrictions. See page 670, above. Because the burden of covenants had long been held not to run at law outside the landlord-tenant context, this theory was also unavailable. And, in Keppel v. Bailey, 2 My. & K. 517 (1834), Lord Brougham had ruled that equity would not aid one seeking to enforce a covenant whose burden did not run at law. It remained for Lord Brougham's successor as Chancellor, Lord Cottenham, to establish the rule in Tulk v. Moxhay that the burden of the covenant may run at equity, even if not at law.

Lord Cottenham took a tack quite different from Lord Brougham. "It is said that, the covenant being one which does not run with the land, this Court cannot enforce it; but the question is, not whether the covenant runs with the land, but whether a party shall be permitted to use the land in a manner inconsistent with the contract entered into by his vendor, and with notice of which he purchased. Of course, the price would be affected by the covenant, and nothing could be more inequitable than that the original purchaser should be able to sell the property the next day for a greater price, in consideration of the assignee being allowed to escape from the liability which he had himself undertaken." 2 Ph. at 778, 41 Eng.Rep. at 1144.

2. *Does the Burden Run?* For the burden of an equitable servitude to run, the original parties, A and B, must have intended that it run, and Z, the successor in interest to the servient estate, must have

had notice of the servitude at the time she acquired the parcel. Notice may be actual, inquiry or constructive. As indicated in *Sun Oil,* the requisite intent need not be evidenced by either the formulaic "heirs, successors, assigns" language, or by any other specific incantation; surrounding circumstances from which intent can be inferred will suffice. At what point should the policy favoring enforcement of customary expectations, apparently espoused by the majority, be outweighed by the policy favoring free use of property, espoused by the dissent?

Few, if any, courts today require horizontal or vertical privity for on equitable servitude's burden to run. The touch or concern requirement, though applicable, is only rarely explicated since the context in which these cases typically arise—one neighbor seeking to enforce a building or use restriction against another—is one in which the arrangement is physically accomplished on the servient estate and will affect the physical enjoyment of some related land. There is some indication, though, that equity's touch or concern standard is looser than the one applied at law. Strict adjacency is not required, and distant neighbors in a subdivision have been given injunctive relief.

See generally, Berger, A Policy Analysis of Promises Respecting the Use of Land, 55 Minn.L.Rev. 167, 184–187 (1970).

3. The English and American cases decided since Tulk v. Moxhay have mostly involved restrictive arrangements of a sort that, at law, would be labelled negative covenants. Is there an equitable counterpart to *affirmative* covenants, enabling a mandatory injunction against successors to the servient estate, absent proof of vertical and horizontal privity? At first, the English courts applied *Tulk* to enforce affirmative as well as negative obligations. See, for example, Cooke v. Chilcott, 3 Ch.D. 694 (1876), requiring a purchaser, with notice, to supply spring water to neighbors in accordance with his predecessor's agreement. But, five years later, the courts reversed their position by holding that the principle of *Tulk* could not be applied to enforce an affirmative obligation to build and maintain premises. Haywood v. Brunswick Building Society, 8 Q.B.D. 403 (1881). The concern, expressed by one of the judges, was that "[t]he covenant to repair can only be enforced by making the owner put his hand into his pocket, and there is nothing which would justify us in going that length." 8 Q.B.D. at 409.

American courts, which unlike their English counterparts have generally enforced covenant burdens at law, have also been open to enforcing the burden of affirmative obligations at equity. See, for example, Petersen v. Beekmere, Inc., 117 N.J.Super. 155, 283 A.2d 911 (1971) ("It would thus appear, by the weight of authority and logic, that the distinction between 'affirmative' and 'negative' covenants is an anachronism which all too often precludes an analysis of the covenant itself in order to determine whether it should be enforced, whether at law as a covenant running with the land or in equity as an equitable servitude enforceable against the original grantee and all successors having notice." 117 N.J.Super. 164, 283 A.2d 916.)

4. *Remedies.* The remedy at law for breach of an affirmative or negative covenant is damages. The remedy for breach of an equitable servitude is a prohibitory injunction in the case of negative undertakings, and a mandatory injunction in the case of affirmative undertakings. Equity will, however, exercise its "cleanup" jurisdiction and award damages when needed to make the beneficiary whole.

The threat of injunctive relief gives the beneficiary greater leverage at the bargaining table than damages. Is it topsy-turvy to give the stronger, injunctive remedy when the beneficiary has been able to demonstrate only that the requirements of intent, notice and touch or concern have been met, and to allow the weaker, damages remedy only when the beneficiary has been able to demonstrate horizontal and vertical privity in addition to intent, notice and touch and concern? Should courts withhold injunctive relief if it will inflict disproportionate harm on the holder of the servient estate? Could a court withhold injunctive relief, and award damages only, without also insisting that the common law requirements of horizontal and vertical privity be met?

C. INTERPRETING EASEMENTS, COVENANTS AND SERVITUDES

KELLY v. SCHMELZ

Court of Appeals of Missouri, 1969.
439 S.W.2d 211.

P.F. PALUMBO, Special Judge.

This is a suit brought by Melvin Kelly and Florence M. Jaris, owners of a parcel of land, seeking to enjoin defendants, Lee F. Schmelz and Katie Schmelz, his wife, from interfering with the installation of electric poles and wires thereon by the Union Electric Company on an easement held by plaintiffs over the land of defendants.

The trial court denied the petition and entered judgment for defendants. The plaintiffs have appealed.

The issues on appeal are whether injunction is the proper remedy and if so whether plaintiffs are entitled to the relief requested.

Plaintiffs are the owners of a parcel of land in Jefferson County, Missouri, consisting of 6.05 acres. The deed by which plaintiffs acquired the land describes the land and then further grants:

> "Also, an easement 18 feet wide from the Northwest corner of above described tract Northwardly to the county road."

The county road—called Bony Mill Road—is approximately 900 feet North of plaintiffs' land. The location of the easement is not in dispute. It runs Northwardly from the Northwest corner of plaintiffs' land to Bony Mill Road, a distance of 900 feet. The plaintiffs have been using the easement as a private roadway for ingress and egress. The center line of this private roadway is the center line of the easement. The easement runs through land owned by defendants. Defendants' land, approximately 50 acres on each side of the roadway, is used by them for growing crops. A drainage ditch runs along the West side of the roadway. The center line of the ditch is about 3 feet from the West wheel track of the roadway.

Plaintiffs' land is adjacent to defendants' land on the North. Situated on plaintiffs' land is a house consisting of one large room and a screened-in porch. Plaintiff, Melvin Kelly, testified that he intended to add two rooms and a bath to the house, install a deep well and then move permanently into the house. He further testified that there is no electricity on his land and that he needs electricity to run a pump for a well, a deep freeze and other appliances. He applied for service to Union Electric Company of Missouri which services this section of Jefferson County. The company at present has poles and electric lines on the poles on the South side of Bony Mill Road approximately 900 feet from plaintiffs' land.

Plaintiff, Melvin Kelly, testified that he and three men from Union Electric went to see defendants; that one of the Union Electric men requested permission to install the poles and that Mrs. Schmelz said that he, meaning Melvin Kelly, "would never get electric." After plaintiff explained to defendants that he needed the electric for a deepfreeze and water, defendants again told him that he "would never get electric."

Plaintiffs offered testimony that there would be no damage to the defendants by the placement of the poles and wires thereon since defendants did not cultivate the area between the drainage ditch and the roadway.

A supervisor for Union Electric Company testified that his company intended to place three poles on the easement between the drainage ditch and the roadway with the poles located 6 feet from the center line of the easement. He further testified that he and plaintiff, Melvin Kelly, talked to one of the defendants and asked if he could place the poles on the easement but that permission was refused and the following reasons given: that they "would have obstructed the fields; that Mrs. Schmelz had lived there without electricity." The supervisor stated that there was no other way to bring in electricity to plaintiffs.

On cross-examination by defendants the supervisor testified that Union Electric and Southwestern Bell Telephone Company have a working agreement whereby each uses the other's poles and that Southwestern Bell attempted to place poles on the right-of-way but was refused. On further cross-examination the supervisor identified Defendants' Exhibit B as being a request from Union Electric to

Southwestern Bell which bore the notation of Southwestern Bell "Right of way refused." "Attempted to place pole and Right of Way refused by Mrs. Schmelz." He was also asked by defendants whether they (Southwestern Bell) attempted to place the poles on the easement and he testified they did so attempt to place the poles.

Defendants' evidence consisted of the testimony of defendant Katie Schmelz and her daughter Laverne Buckmiller. Katie Schmelz testified that both sides of the private roadway leading to plaintiffs' place were used for crops; that she and her husband had no electricity when they moved into their place in 1947; that her husband used the private roadway for farm equipment when he harvests. Laverne Buckmiller identified the exhibits showing the roadway leading to plaintiffs' property. She further testified to the placement of stakes and that the location of the stakes represented where the poles were to be set and that the placement of the stakes indicated that the poles would be placed in the drainage ditch and not between the ditch and the roadway.

This is a proceeding in equity. The Appellate Court on review is required to review the evidence de novo and arrive at a result that should have been reached on evidence adduced with due deference accorded chancellor in his determination of factual questions.

That the plaintiffs own an easement and the location of the easement are not in dispute.

Injunction is a proper remedy for an interference with a right-of-way whenever injury complained of is irreparable, the interference is of a permanent and continuous character or the remedy at law by an action for damages will not afford adequate relief.

The easement herein while used as a roadway by plaintiffs contains no limitations as to its use. It is in the nature of a general easement. An independent research by us disclosed no Missouri cases where the grant of the easement was "General." However, where the grant is specifically for a "way or roadway," but without limitation, Missouri follows the rule as set out in 28 C.J.S. Easements § 87, pages 766–767: ". . . where a way is granted or reserved without limitation as to its use, it will not necessarily be confined to the purpose for which the land was used at the time the way was created, but may be used for any purpose to which the land accommodated by the way may naturally and reasonably be devoted. . . . The grantee is entitled to vary his mode of enjoying the same, and from time to time avail himself of modern inventions if by so doing he can more fully exercise and enjoy or carry out the object for which the way was granted. . . ."

The Supreme Court of Missouri in Stotzenberger v. Perkins, 332 Mo. 391, 58 S.W.2d 983, a case involving a dispute over a specific grant of a roadway easement, stated (l.c. 987): "As the owner of the dominant estate, the defendant has, under our interpretation of the deed, the right to put and maintain the roadway strip in a condition for passage thereon and the right to free passage on such portions or all of the way as he thinks proper or necessary to make repairs, *or for any purpose connected with the enjoyment of his estate . . . ."*

We were unable to find any Missouri cases dealing with the factual situation in the instant case. However, in the case of Davis v. Jefferson County Telephone Co., 82 W.Va. 357, 95 S.E. 1042, a West Virginia case, decided by the Supreme Court of Appeals, there was a specific grant of way and the owner of the dominant estate wanted to place telephone poles on the roadway. Davis filed action to require the Telephone Company to remove poles erected or to be erected along and over the right-of-way. The trial court granted him an injunction. The appellate court reversed and in so doing held: "Injunction will not lie against telephone company employed by owner of a right of way to restrain it from erecting poles and wires along and over such way to provide the owner thereof with private telephone service at his place of residence on the land to which such way is appurtenant."

In a more recent case, Fleming v. Napili, Kai, Ltd., 430 P.2d 316, the Supreme Court of the State of Hawaii, in a proceeding to enjoin owners of lots adjoining a road from excavating road and converting it into a ditch and to compel the owners to restore the road to the condition that existed prior to the excavation, the appellate court in reversing the trial court held: "Courts have held that a grant or reservation of an easement of right of way in general terms should be construed as creating a general right of way for all reasonable purposes." The court cited with approval the West Virginia Case of Davis v. Jefferson County Telephone Co.

In the case of New York Central R.R. Co. v. Yarian, 219 Ind. 477, 39 N.E.2d 604, the Supreme Court of Indiana, in construing a reservation to maintain a farm crossing over land conveyed in fee for railroad right of way, at page 607 held, "that the reservation of a farm crossing is broad enough to permit the bringing in of a conduit underground for the purpose of supplying electricity."

In the case of Dowgiel v. Reid, et al., 359 Pa. 448, 59 A.2d 115, the Supreme Court of Pennsylvania stated at page 121 that use of a private roadway for transmission of electricity from the power line on the main highway to a home ". . . is a reasonable and natural use of the private road for the purpose for which it was created, to-wit: to enable the owners and occupants of the premises to which the road is appurtenant to obtain something which is essential to the livableness of the home, to-wit: electricity the same obtainable only by the means above stated . . . ."

In the instant case the defendants offered no evidence that the placing of the poles and wires would result in any damage to them. The defendants in their brief admit that they refused to grant permission to Union Electric Company acting in behalf of plaintiffs and they do not challenge the appellants' statement of the law applicable to the issuance of injunctions. They contend, however, that there has been no showing of interference with the rights of plaintiffs. The refusal of defendants to permit Union Electric, acting for the owner of the easement, to place the poles on the easement and defendants' verbal act in stating that plaintiff would never get electric, effectively precluded the obtaining of electricity by plaintiffs and we think constituted an interference with plaintiffs' use of the easement. They are entitled to injunctive relief.

The defendants should be enjoined from interfering with the plaintiffs or their agents in the placing of the poles and wires thereon described in plaintiffs' petition on the above described easement. Judgment of the trial court is reversed and the cause is remanded with directions to enter judgment in accordance with the views herein expressed.

ANDERSON, P.J., and RUDDY, J., concur.

WOLFE, J., not participating.

JOLLIFF v. HARDIN CABLE TELEVISION CO.

Supreme Court of Ohio, 1971.
55 Ohio Op.2d 203, 26 Ohio St.2d 103, 269 N.E.2d 588.

Plaintiffs, Chester and Thelma Jolliff, Avanelle Frazer and Frank Bondi, filed an action in the Court of Common Pleas against defendants, Hardin Cable Television Company, appellant in case No. 70–351, and Ohio Power Company, appellant in case No. 70–357, for a mandatory injunction to compel Hardin Cable "to remove the supporting cable and co-axial television cable . . . attached to the poles running across their lands." They also asked "that a permanent restraining order be issued forbidding defendant Hardin Cable Television Company from entering upon said lands for the purpose of erecting or attaching any other type of cable or appurtenance to the poles owned by defendant Ohio Power Company and which are located on the plaintiffs' lands."

Plaintiffs also prayed "that defendant Ohio Power Company be permanently restrained from permitting defendant Hardin Cable Television Company or any other individual or company, to use their poles located on plaintiffs' lands for the purpose of attaching thereto support cable and co-axial television cable and appurtenances thereto."

Plaintiffs' predecessors in title had granted easements to Ohio Power in 1940. The pertinent language of one of the deeds (the other three deeds reading substantially the same) reads as follows:

". . . said party of the first part hereby grants, bargains, sells, conveys, and warrants to the party of the second part, its successors and assigns forever, a right of way and easement with the right, privilege and authority to said party of the second part, its successors, assigns, lessees, and tenants to construct, erect, operate and maintain a line of poles and wires for the purpose of transmitting electric or other power, *including telegraph* or telephone wires in, on, along, over, through or across the following described lands . . . ..

"Together with the right to said party of the second part, its successors and assigns, to place, erect, maintain, inspect, *add to the number of,* and relocate at will, poles, crossarms or fixtures, and string wires and cables, adding thereto from time to time, across, through or over the above described premises, to cut and, at its option, remove from said premises or the premises of the parties of the first part adjoining the same on either side, any trees, overhanging branches or other obstructions which may endanger the safety or interfere with the use of said poles or fixtures or wires attached thereto or any structure on said premises . . . .." (Emphasis added).

In the fourth conveyance in question, the word "company" was inserted between the words "including" and "telegraph" (italicized in the first paragraph quoted above), and the words "add to the number of" (italicized in the second paragraph quoted above) were deleted.

In 1965, Hardin Cable and Ohio Power entered into an agreement whereby Ohio Power granted permission to Hardin Cable to utilize Ohio Power's poles for the attachment of cables to transmit television signals to Hardin Cable's subscribers. After Hardin Cable, acting pursuant to its agreement with Ohio Power, attached lines across plaintiffs' property, the present action was instituted.

The Court of Common Pleas found that the "low use" of the easements constituted a "restrictive impediment to the enjoyment" of plaintiffs' land and decreed that the "cable be substantially raised" or "else removed."

Plaintiffs appealed to the Court of Appeals on questions of law and fact. That court found that plaintiffs were entitled to the injunctions prayed for in their petition and granted judgment for plaintiffs.

The causes are before this court pursuant to the allowance of defendants' motions to certify the record.

CORRIGAN, J. The determinative issue raised in these appeals is whether, under the easements granted to Ohio Power by plaintiffs' predecessors in title, Ohio Power can apportion its rights thereunder and permit Hardin Cable, as sublessee, to make use of the easements for the purpose of attaching its co-axial cable.

On that issue, the Court of Appeals expressed the view that the easements in question did not convey to Ohio Power "an exclusive right to use the servient tenement for electric or other power right of way purposes" and that "for Ohio Power to apportion its rights" would constitute "competition with the owners for the sale of easement rights, not contemplated by the deeds of easement." It concluded that "the assignment (or lease) . . . to Cable TV was not authorized," and that "the sharing of the rights of way and easements pursuant thereto constituted an unlawful surcharge on the servient tenements."

Although we are referred in the briefs to the rules of construction governing easements in gross, we are bound first to examine the deeds in question to ascertain whether the language employed therein is capable of an interpretation which will resolve the issue presented. As stated in Hinman v. Barnes (1946), 146 Ohio St. 497, 508, 32 O.O. 564, 569, " 'if the intention of the parties is apparent from an examination of the deed "from its four corners," it will be given effect regardless of technical rules of construction.' "

We therefore must study the deeds to see if the language used casts light on the question of the apportionability of the easements granted therein.

In the deeds, the grantors conveyed to Ohio Power ". . . . its successors and assigns forever, a right of way and easement with the right, privilege and authority to said party of the second part [Ohio Power], its successors, assigns, lessees, and tenants to construct, erect, operate and maintain a line of poles and wires for the purpose of transmitting electric or other power, including telegraph or telephone wires . . .."

The crucial words of the grants which are determinative of the intention of the grantors are "successors, assigns, lessees and tenants." (Emphasis added.) The words "lessees and tenants" indicate, particularly, that it was clearly intended by the parties to the grants that Ohio Power could lease some portion of its interests to third parties. Such language ("its . . . lessees" obviously means "its . . . sub-lessees," in the absence of any restrictive definition of "lessee" in the easements—and there is none) is open to no other interpretation.

In view of that clearly expressed intention, we find it unnecessary to employ rules of construction in interpreting the easements in question. We merely note the statement found in 5 Restatement of the Law, Property, 3053, Section 493b, that: ". . . Where it [easement in gross] is created by conveyance, apportionability depends upon the intention of the parties to the conveyance." That intention here, as expressed in the language of the easements, is that the easements are apportionable and we so hold.

We proceed now to determine whether the sub-lease granted by Ohio Power to Hardin Cable results in the imposition of an additional burden on the servient estates beyond the terms of the grants so as to constitute, as the Court of Appeals stated, an "unlawful surcharge on the servient tenements."

In Friedman Transfer & Construction Co. v. Youngstown (1964), 176 Ohio St. 209, 27 O.O.(2d) 91, this court held that a water pipeline installed by a city on a bridge, under an aerial easement granted to the state for construction of the bridge, "did not constitute an additional burden upon the abutting freeholder, such as to require the payment of additional compensation . . .."

Subsequently, in Ziegler v. Ohio Water Service Co. (1969), 18 Ohio St.(2d) 101, 47 O.O.(2d) 244, it was held that:

"The construction and maintenance underground of a water pipeline, for public purposes, in real property outside a municipal corporation which is subject to an easement for highway purposes, is not an added burden on such property for which compensation must be awarded."

Although both *Friedman* and *Ziegler* were concerned with highway easements, while here we are dealing with a sub-lease to a private company of certain easement rights of a public utility, the question whether the added use constitutes an additional burden on the property is the same.

It is noteworthy that, in both *Friedman* and *Ziegler*, the added uses, construction and maintenance of pipelines, were of an entirely different nature than the highway-purpose uses which were specified in the original grants.

The easements involved here were granted for "transmitting electric or other power, including telegraph and telephone wires." It is apparent that the attachment of a television co-axial cable, which is comprised of bound wires for transmitting high frequency electrical impulses, is a use similar to that granted in the easements to Ohio Power. In fact, such use constitutes no more of a burden than would the installation of telegraph and telephone wires. That burden was clearly contemplated at the time of the grants, as evidenced by the specific reference to telegraph and telephone wires therein.

In American Tel. and Tel. Co. v. McDonald, 273 Mass. 324, 173 N.E. 502, a telephone company, as grantee in an easement to erect and maintain telephone poles and wires, granted another telephone company the right to attach a telephone toll cable on its poles. In addressing itself to the question whether attachment of the toll cable constituted an additional burden, the court there said, at page 326:

"There is no additional burden imposed by the grantee. Nothing granted to the plaintiff enables it to do anything which the original grantee could not have done. The latter could have hung a toll cable of its own from the cross arms upon its poles. It could have put up guy wires or poles needed for the support of the poles carrying the cable, and such apparatus as was necessary to enable its wires so hung to transmit telephone and telegraph messages. The plaintiff has done no more . . .."

That reasoning, with which we agree, is equally applicable here, where Hardin Cable, in attaching its television cable to Ohio Power's poles, is doing no more than Ohio Power or a telegraph or telephone lessee could have done under the terms of the original grants. We therefore conclude that the attachment of the television cable involved herein does not impose an additional burden on plaintiffs' lands.

In respect to the argument that the insertion of the word "company" in one of the deeds of easement demonstrates that that grantor, Frazer, intended to limit use of the poles to Ohio Power, we are of the opinion that such addition to the terms of the deed does not overcome the clearly expressed language contained therein that the easement was granted to Ohio Power, "its successors, assigns, lessees, and tenants."

From the foregoing, we conclude that an easement granted to a power company, "its successors, assigns, lessees, and tenants to construct, erect, operate and maintain a line of poles and wires for the purpose of transmitting electric or other power, including telegraph or telephone wires," is, by its terms, apportionable and that the grantee of such easement may by sub-lease assign a portion of its interest in the easement to a television cable company. In such case, the attachment of the television cable constitutes a use similar to that granted in the easement and does not create an additional burden on the land of the original grantor.

The judgment of the Court of Appeals is reversed and, in each case, final judgment is rendered for the defendant.

Judgment reversed.

O'NEILL, C.J., SCHNEIDER, HERBERT, DUNCAN, STERN and LEACH, JJ., concur.

NOTES

1. Do you agree with the decision in Kelly v. Schmelz? To what extent did the court rest its decision on the presumed intent of the parties at the time they executed the "general easement"? To what extent *should* it have? If no general easement had been expressly granted, would the court in the circumstances have implied one, by reason of necessity, into an earlier severance of the two parcels? Since a general easement had been expressly granted, could the court have used the fact of necessity to imply a power line easement into the grant? If plaintiffs had resorted to self-help rather than litigation, and had placed the poles and lines across defendants' property without permission, would they have prevailed in a later trespass or nuisance action brought by Mr. and Mrs. Schmelz by defending on an improving trespasser theory? Compare Somerville v. Jacobs, page 60 above. Of what relevance is the court's observation that "defendants offer no evidence that the placing of the poles and wires would result in any damage to them"?

2. Two sometimes competing approaches dominate judicial interpretation of easements, covenants and servitudes: the "rule of rea-

sonableness," and the policy favoring free marketability of interests in land. The rule of reasonableness follows the method of contract interpretation generally. It asks what the original parties probably would have provided had they contemplated the present dispute and seeks to give the language creating the nonpossessory interest a meaning that is reasonable in the circumstances. The policy favoring free marketability, by contrast, disregards the parties' intent and asks what resolution of the dispute will lead to the more productive use of land; courts generally apply this policy to construe nonpossessory interests narrowly on the theory that they inhibit the most productive use of the servient estate.

The role of the two approaches, particularly the second, is not always clear. There is, for example, growing recognition that a nonpossessory interest's interference with the marketability of the servient estate may be significantly outweighed by the increased marketability of the dominant estate, and that, taking the two estates together, a liberal construction will enhance rather than impede marketability overall. This new attitude is particularly evident in the interpretation of subdivision covenants. See, for example, Highbaugh Enterprises, Inc. v. Deatrick & James Construction Co., 554 S.W.2d 878, 879 (Ky.App.1977) ("Kentucky has approached restrictive covenants from the viewpoint that they are to be regarded more as a protection to the property owner and the public rather than as a restriction on the use of property, and that the old-time doctrine of strict construction no longer applies").

3. *Apportionability.* Appurtenant easements are presumed to be apportionable and, absent an express indication to the contrary, can be enforced by a successor to any part of the dominant estate. Restatement of Property § 488, comment b (1944), offers one rationale: "The burden upon a servient tenement frequently will not be greatly increased by permitting an easement appurtenant to attach to each of the parts into which the dominant tenement may be subdivided. Though some increase in burden may result from the fact that the number of users is increased by the subdivision, the extent of the use is still measured by the needs of the land which constituted the original dominant tenement. Moreover, dominant tenements are ordinarily divisible and their division is so common that it is assumed that the possibility of their division is contemplated in their creation."

Do rules on the apportionability of appurtenant easements offer any principles for resolving disputes, such as the one in Jolliff v. Hardin Cable, involving the apportionability of easements in gross? Courts dealing with easements in gross generally distinguish between nonexclusive easements—to be enjoyed both by the beneficiary and the owner of the servient estate—and exclusive easements—to be enjoyed only by the beneficiary. Absent a clear indication to the contrary, exclusive benefits can be apportioned and nonexclusive benefits cannot, essentially for the reasons referred to in the second paragraph of Judge Corrigan's *Jolliff* opinion. Do you agree with *Jolliff* that use of the words, "lessees and tenants," reflects a clear intent to allow apportionment? "Lessees and tenants" of *what*—Ohio Power's right to string power and two-way communications lines across plaintiffs' lands, or to carve out and transfer some entirely new right?

Assuming apportionability, do you agree with *Jolliff* that Hardin's attachment of the television cables did not impose an additional burden on plaintiffs' land? Was the court correct to consider only the additional physical burden imposed by the cable, and not the economic loss represented by plaintiffs' consequent inability to negotiate for this new use of their land? Would your answer differ if plaintiffs had brought their action, not in the hope of obtaining a reasonable fee for the easement, but rather with the intent of stopping Hardin's operations altogether? Say, for example, Jolliffs' lawsuit was supported by television broadcasters anxious to thwart the growth of cable television.

4. *Locating Easements*. As a result of shifts in circumstance on the servient or dominant estate, the location of an easement that made sense one hundred years ago may make little sense today. In Davis v. Bruk, 411 A.2d 660 (Me.1980), the trial court decree relocated a right of way easement that had originally been located across defendant Bruk's land in 1896, on the ground that "the approved relocated route would not create an unreasonable burden upon the plaintiffs, and that would alleviate Bruk's problems with dust and traffic hazards posed by the use of the existing right of way."

The Maine Supreme Court reversed. "In the great majority of jurisdictions the rule is, that, once the location of an expressly deeded easement is established, whether by the language of the instrument creating the easement or by subsequent acts of the parties, fixing on the ground the location of a general grant of a right of way, the site location may not be changed thereafter by either the owner of the dominant estate or the owner of the servient estate, unless both parties consent to the relocation, excepting, however, where the document creating the easement also contains an express or implied grant or reservation of power to relocate." 411 A.2d at 664.

Recognizing "that a few courts have carved out an exception to the general rule," the court specifically rejected defendant's suggestion that the rule be modified in Maine to "permit unilateral relocation of easements where, as in the instant case, the following conditions exist: (1) the change of location by the owner of the servient estate is slight; (2) the servient owner will bear the expense of relocation; (3) the new right of way retains the same terminal points as the old way; and (4) the new way is as convenient as or more convenient, than the old way is to the dominant estate." In the court's opinion, "such an exception-rule would definitely introduce considerable uncertainty into land ownership, as well as upon the real estate market, and serve to proliferate litigation which the general rule as prevails in Maine has tended to prevent. Indeed, the owner of the dominant estate would be deprived of the present security of his property rights in the servient estate and could be subjected to harassment by the servient owner's attempts at relocation to serve his own conveniences." 411 A.2d at 665.

The supreme court did, however, affirm the trial court's decision denying plaintiffs' claim respecting a particular spring upon defendant's land that defendant had filled in. "The trial court found that, although the plaintiffs' deeds did grant them an easement to use a spring on the Bruk property, they did not specify any particular spring. The Court concluded that, unlike the easement of the right of way to the Town Road, the plaintiffs had failed to prove that the location of the right of way to a spring had ever been fixed . . . . Although one spring was filled in, other springs on the defendant Bruk's property remain accessible to the plaintiffs, from which one may be selected for the exercise of their right to take water from a spring on Bruk's property. There was no error in rejecting the plaintiffs' claim for compensatory damages for interference with their right of access to a spring." 411 A.2d at 666.

5. *Interpreting Easements by Necessity and Prescription.* Special rules have evolved for determining the scope of easements by necessity and prescription, for which there is no written instrument to express the parties' intent. Presumed intent, which forms the basis for implying easements, also forms the benchmark for determining their scope. For example, in Soltis v. Miller, 444 Pa. 357, 282 A.2d 369 (1971), the Pennsylvania Supreme Court agreed with the decision below that plaintiff's landlocked parcel enjoyed a right of way by necessity over defendant's adjoining parcel, but overturned the lower court's restriction of the right of way to the domestic and farming uses that had obtained at the time the two parcels were severed. In the court's view, the scope of the easement should have been measured by the original parties' forecast of the dominant estate's reasonable needs over time: "the preferable policy is to define the enjoyment of a way of necessity with a view to the reasonable and lawful uses of the land it benefits." 444 Pa. at 360, 282 A.2d at 371.

Prescriptive easements, because they originate not in the parties' expressed intent, but rather in the statute of limitations, must be measured by a different yardstick. Generally, the scope of a prescriptive easement will correspond to the inner boundaries of its use over the statutory period. Thus, if during the prescriptive period A commonly traversed a roadway over Blackacre in his car, but occasionally held family picnics during which dozens of cars crossed Blackacre, his prescriptive easement would probably be limited to use by the one car, since that was the only use of which Blackacre's owner, B, had notice over the full statutory period. Expanded use, for two or more cars, or for power lines and irrigation ditches, will ripen into prescriptive rights only when the statutory period, dated from commencement of the continuous, expanded use, has elapsed.

6. *Can a Covenant or Servitude Be Implied Into an Easement?* If A has the benefit of a right of way across B's parcel, Blackacre, it is generally held that, unless the instrument creating the easement expressly provides to the contrary, B and her successors have no implied duty to keep the right of way in good repair. However, A and his successors to the benefit have the right to go onto Blackacre for the purpose of making the repairs themselves. The rules do not change if the easement is in gross rather than appurtenant. Thus, if A holds the benefit of an easement to string utility lines across B's parcel, Blackacre, B and her successors will have no obligation to maintain the lines, but A and his successors will have the right to go onto Blackacre for the purpose of maintenance and repair.

Since the right to make repairs can impose a substantial burden on Blackacre, A and B are well advised to use care in negotiating and drafting their agreement on the subject. Consider, for example, the factors you would weigh, and the language you would employ, in negotiating and drafting an agreement giving A access for repairs to its sewer line that runs under B's soon-to-be-developed shopping center.

Do A and his successors, who at common law have the *right* to make repairs, also have the *duty* to make repairs? In the usual case, A's self-interest in the continuing use of the roadway, power lines or sewer pipes will provide sufficient incentive to maintain them adequately. But if A's interest wanes, and the use falls into disrepair, does B, whose parcel may consequently decline in value, have any recourse against A? Although it is commonly said that the benefit holder has the duty as well as the right of repair, the case authority is sparse. See 2 Am. Law of Property § 8.66 n. 4 (A. J. Casner ed. 1952); R. Powell, Real Property § 415 (1981). Even if A and B expressly address the issue in the instrument creating the easement, they must use special care if they wish the burden and benefit of this independent obligation to run to their successors since it is not an easement that is involved, but, rather, a covenant or servitude with its additional common law requirements for the burden and benefit to run. Note, too, that the holder of the easement's burden will typically be the holder of the covenant's benefit, and vice-versa. What is the servient estate of an affirmative covenant to repair an easement in gross?

D. TERMINATING EASEMENTS, COVENANTS AND SERVITUDES

WITT v. REAVIS

Supreme Court of Oregon, 1978.
284 Or. 503, 587 P.2d 1005.

BRYSON, Justice.

Plaintiffs Robert and Edna Witt brought this suit to establish an easement by prescription over an existing road on the property of defendants Gerald and Donna Reavis. Plaintiffs also sought to enjoin defendants from interfering with plaintiffs' use of the road and requiring defendants to keep the road in good repair. The trial court entered a decree in favor of defendants and made the following findings:

"1. An easement by prescription for the benefit of [plaintiffs' land] was created over [defendants' land] prior to 1966.

"2. That easement was extinguished by the unity of title which arose when the Sauers acquired both the tax lots in 1966.

"3. Severance of the estate did not occur until January 1, 1969, thus not permitting sufficient time for a new prescriptive easement to have been created.

"4. It is unnecessary for the Court to determine the scope, location and width of the easement that was extinguished by merger.

". . .."

Plaintiffs appeal and we review de novo.

Plaintiffs contend "[t]he Trial Court Erred in Finding That The Easement by Prescription was Extinguished by Unity of Title and Did Not Revive Upon Severance." Plaintiffs (Witt) and defendants (Reavis) own adjoining real property near Florence, Oregon, as shown by the following sketch (not to scale). The road on which the easement is claimed is some eight to ten feet wide.

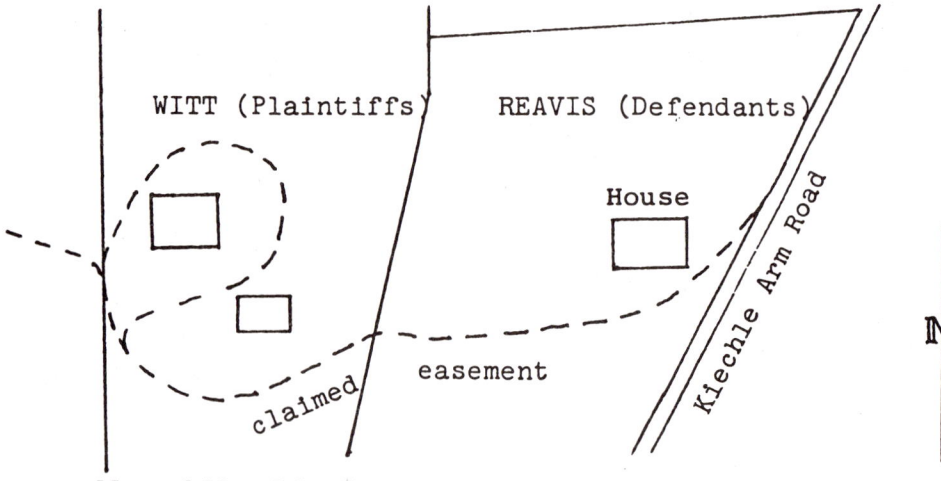

Mr. and Mrs. John Sauer were the common grantors to plaintiffs and defendants. The Sauers acquired the plaintiffs' property in 1956 and the defendants' property in 1959.[1] The Sauers lived on the plaintiffs' parcel from 1956 to 1960. They rented plaintiffs' parcel to

---

1. Pursuant to the testimony, there was a question about the validity of the deeds to the Sauers in 1956 and 1959 and, for this reason, the Sauers and their predecessors in title re-executed deeds to the property involved in favor of the Sauers in 1966. This accounts for the trial court's finding that "the Sauers acquired both the [parcels] in 1966."

others from 1960 until 1969. They also rented the defendants' parcel *at all times* from 1959 to 1969.

In January, 1969, the Sauers sold the defendants' parcel to defendants. In February, 1969, the Sauers sold the plaintiffs' parcel to Browne, plaintiffs' predecessor, who in turn sold to plaintiffs in 1975.

We agree with the trial court that plaintiffs' easement if any, was extinguished by merger. Therefore, we need not discuss the facts or the law as to whether an easement in favor of plaintiffs was established by adverse possession.

The principal issue in this case is whether plaintiffs' claimed easement by prescription was extinguished by unity of title in the Sauers.

The only reference to merger of easements following unity of title that we have found in Oregon is the following statement from Dressler et al. v. Isaacs et al., 217 Or. 586, 591, 343 P.2d 714 (1959):

> ". . . The union of the dominant and servient estates in [one person] would, of course, destroy the easement. 3 Tiffany, Real Property (3rd ed.), § 822, p. 377. . . ."

Tiffany, at 377, states:

> "An easement is ordinarily extinguished if one person acquires an estate in fee simple in possession in both the dominant and servient tenements. By reason of the perpetual right of possession of the tenement which was previously subject to the easement, such person and his heirs can make any use whatsoever thereof, and the inferior right of easement, its utility having thus disappeared, is swallowed up in the superior right of possession."

The rule in the Restatement, Property § 497 (1944), is not too clear but states:

> "An easement appurtenant is extinguished by unity of ownership of estates in the dominant and servient tenements to the extent to which the uses which could have been made prior to the unity by virtue of ownership of the estate in the dominant tenement can be made after unity by virtue of ownership of the estate in the servient tenement."

Where the fee owner of the dominant parcel acquires the fee subject to an estate for years in the servient parcel, the owner does *not* have a present possessory interest in the servient parcel. He has only a reversionary interest that will become possessory after termination of the estate for years. Therefore, the dominant owner's interest in the servient parcel does not give him the present right to use the easement. For the right to use the easement, he must rely on his rights as owner of the *dominant* parcel. Under these circumstances, the easement would not be extinguished by merger.

However, as in this case, if at any time the owner in fee of the dominant parcel acquires the fee in the servient parcel *not* subject to any other outstanding estate, the easement is then extinguished by merger. Merger would occur at the time the property was acquired or at the termination of the outstanding estates, if any, whenever the owner acquired the unrestricted fee.

From the evidence in the record, the Sauers did acquire simultaneous fee interests in the two parcels in 1966, when the deeds were executed conveying the servient parcel to Sauers. Those deeds to the Sauers do not provide for any outstanding estates. In light of these unrestricted deeds, the plaintiffs had the burden of producing evidence to show that the Sauers acquired the servient parcel subject to an existing estate for years. There is no evidence that they did; therefore, we conclude that the easement was extinguished by merger in 1966.

The effect of merger is usually held to be a complete destruction of the easement, but some states, notably Pennsylvania, have held that sometimes the easement is only suspended. Tiffany states both rules as follows:

"The rule is said to be that an easement is not merely suspended by the union of title, reviving when the tenements again become the subject of separate ownership, but any subsequent easement must arise from a new grant and is a new easement. It has been held, however, that an easement which would ordinarily be extinguished by the merger of the dominant and servient estates is said to be preserved or revived in cases where such is required by the estate and where, in the interest of honest owners, it should be preserved to effect a valid and legitimate purpose. The exception obtains, it is said, only where there is a strong equity and circumstances giving ground for the clear inference that the parties intended to preserve or revive the easement." 3 Tiffany, Law of Real Property 381, § 822 (1939). (Footnotes omitted.)

Plaintiffs would have us follow the Pennsylvania rule. However, it appears that the minority Pennsylvania rule has simply grafted the rules of implied easements onto those for extinguishment by merger.

We see nothing to be gained by adopting the Pennsylvania rule and, instead, follow the Restatement rule that an easement once extinguished is gone forever. Indeed, this is the rule established in the opinion by Justice O'Connell in Dressler et al. v. Isaacs et al., supra. Where merger is established, this rule will enable the parties to focus on the separate issue of whether a new easement was thereafter created by implication and will, we hope, avoid confusion as to the precise issues involved in such cases.

Plaintiffs argue that they are entitled to an easement by implication; however, their theory in their pleadings and at trial was that an easement had been created through adverse possession. They cannot argue this new theory on appeal. . . .

Assuming, in the case before us, that plaintiffs' predecessors once had an easement, they lost it through merger.

Plaintiffs finally argue that it would be inequitable to deny them the use of the easement. They quote the following from South Beach Lumber Corp. v. Swank, 210 Or. 383, 392–93, 311 P.2d 1018, 1023 (1957):

> " '. . . Mergers are not favored in equity. When a lesser and a higher estate meet and coincide in the same person they will be kept separate when equity and justice require it, unless there is an expressed intention to the contrary. . . .' " (Citing Katz v. Obenchain, 48 Or. 352, 85 P. 617 (1909).)

This quotation, however, is taken out of context. That rule applies to the case where a mortgagee of land later acquires the fee; the mortgage interest normally merges in the higher fee interest but not where such a merger would harm the mortgagee. We are not aware of any case, and none has been cited to us, that holds that a merger like the one in the case at bar is "not favored in equity."

The trouble with this final argument, and any argument based solely on general feelings of fairness, is that it affords no principled basis for decision. The common law has established the principle of merger and the principle of implied easements. To set aside the result in this case would confuse the rule of law for such cases in the future.

Affirmed.

HATCHER v. CHESNER

Supreme Court of Pennsylvania, 1966.
422 Pa. 138, 221 A.2d 305.

EAGEN, Justice.

This is an appeal from a final decree in equity enjoining the defendant from obstructing a right of way over his land.

The facts supported by the record and the chancellor's findings may be summarized as follows:

The plaintiff and the defendant are owners of bordering pieces of improved land. In 1894, the then common owner of both properties created by deed a perpetual ten foot right of way over the land, now owned by the defendant, for the benefit of the owners and occupiers of the land, now owned by the plaintiff.

The plaintiff acquired title to his land on March 22, 1961; the defendant title to his land on July 31, 1957. Both the deeds of the plaintiff and the defendant and, in fact, all deeds in the chain of title since 1894 have unequivocally stated that title was subject to the reservation and the right of way.

Both pieces of land front on the same street and extend back therefrom a distance of 140 feet. On defendant's land, along the line common to that of plaintiff's, there exists a continuous row of out buildings. At one point where the right of way should exist, there is a small frame shed or garage 18 feet long with double doors, approximately 9 feet in width, on both ends. On one end, these doors, when opened, extend out on plaintiff's land. For the right of way to be usable, the double doors on both ends of the garage would necessarily have to be opened and the right of way would then extend through the garage for a distance of 18 feet.

The right of way has not been used since at least 1932. Also, a tree has been permitted to grow on plaintiff's property for at least 35 years in such close proximity to the double doors of the garage, which open on his property, as to preclude their use. A board has also been nailed across both doors on plaintiff's side which completely bars their use.

The defendant contends here, as he did below, that under the facts the plaintiff has lost the right to use of the easement by non-use, abandonment and adverse possession.

Mere non-use, no matter how long extended, will not result in extinguishment of an easement created by deed.

The problems raised by the defenses of abandonment and adverse possession are so interrelated that they must be considered together.

The Restatement of Property, § 504 (1944), recognizes that an easement may be lost by abandonment. It states "an easement may be extinguished by an intentional relinquishment thereof indicated by conduct respecting the use authorized thereby." The comments to this section make it clear that failure to use the easement is a fact from which an inference of abandonment can be drawn and found to exist. A number of states adhere to this view. The theory behind these decisions apparently is that abandonment of an easement can be recognized because there is no void of ownership. The servient tenement merely succeeds to the interest which is abandoned. Such, of course, would not be the case if abandonment were recognized in a fee.

Pennsylvania, however, has always been reluctant to accept this theory. Instead, where an easement is created by deed, Pennsylvania has required not only intent to abandon by the dominant tenement, but adverse possession by the servient tenement as well. Thus the Pennsylvania courts look not only to the actions and intentions of the dominant tenement with which the Restatement limits its consideration, but also to the *intentions and actions* of the servient tenement as well. The rationale behind the Pennsylvania rule was stated in Lindeman v. Lindsey, 69 Pa. 93, 100 (1871), wherein this Court said: "A man ought not to be obliged unless he requires it, actually to use a right or privilege secured to him by deed, nor resort to legal proceedings unless his title is denied, and he is actually ousted, disseised, obstructed or prevented by some wrongdoer from an enjoyment of it when he requires and demands such enjoyment." It is clear from this and later cases that our courts equate ownership of an easement with ownership of a fee for these purposes. See, Weaver v. Getz, 16 Pa.Super. 418 (1901). Another factor in the view held by this state is the general dislike of forfeiture by our courts.

The court below, relying on the Pennsylvania rule of looking to both the intent of the dominant and servient tenement, admitted in evidence the deeds of conveyance in both parties' chain of title. It reasoned that these documents were relevant in the case of the defendant to show whether the hostility necessary to establish adverse possession had been displayed by the servient tenement; and, on the part of the dominant tenement, whether such indicated an intent to abandon. On both points, the lower court was correct.

The lower court decreed that the plaintiff had not lost the legal right to use the easement. While it found the evidence convincing, if not conclusive, as to an intent to abandon by the plaintiff and his predecessors in title, it based its final judgment on the conclusion that the necessary adverse possession on the part of the owner or owners of the servient tenement had not been established. This conclusion was dictated by language in the deeds in the defendant's chain of title, wherein the existence of the right to use the easement was continuously recognized and kept alive. In this the lower court was also correct.

However, we disagree with one crucial conclusion of the lower court wherein it stated, that the existence of the tree on plaintiff's land, as described before, and the board nailed across the garage doors had no effect on the outcome of the case. In this connection the lower court failed to recognize and apply one exception that exists in Pennsylvania to the rule of abandonment. It is this: If the owner of the easement by his own affirmative act renders use thereof impossible, or if he obstructs it in a manner that is inconsistent with its further enjoyment, the easement will be deemed to have been abandoned, even in the absence of adverse use on the part of the owner of the servient tenement.

In the instant case, the plaintiff, or his predecessors in title by whose actions in relation to the property he is bound, planted or permitted a tree to grow on the land now owned by the plaintiff which obstructed use of the easement to a material extent. Further, the same parties placed, or permitted to be placed, a bar across the doors of the garage serving as the only entrance to the easement right of way. These acts, in our opinion, were not mere inaction, but rather affirmative acts on the part of the plaintiff and his predecessors in title, which were sufficiently inconsistent with further use of the easement to constitute an abandonment thereof and to bring the issue squarely within the rule of Eagen v. Nagle, supra.

Decree reversed. Each side to pay own costs.

MORRIS v. NEASE

Supreme Court of West Virginia, 1977.
238 S.E.2d 844.

NEELY, Justice:

In this appeal from the Circuit Court of Cabell County Dr. William F. Nease, a chiropractor, challenges the enforcement against him of restrictive covenants affecting property he owns in Huntington. In 1972 Dr. Nease opened a chiropractic clinic at 2703 Third Avenue, and a number of his neighbors brought suit against him to have the clinic closed. They contended that Dr. Nease's clinic violated applicable restrictive covenants, and the Circuit Court agreed, issuing a permanent injunction that prohibits Dr. Nease from operating a chiropractic clinic at 2703 Third Avenue. We reverse.

The land owned by Dr. Nease, as well as that owned by the neighbors seeking to enforce the restrictive covenants, was originally developed by the Huntington Land Company in the early 1900s. At that time the following restrictions were imposed:

> [T]here shall be left an open space or courtyard bounding on Third Avenue of not less than forty feet in depth exclusive of porch in front of any building erected on said premises, which space shall extend the entire width of said premises; that there shall not be erected on said premises hereby conveyed more than one single dwelling, and any dwelling erected thereon shall not cost less than three thousand dollars; that there shall not be erected on said premises any building other than for dwelling or residence purposes, or purposes of like nature, and the necessary outbuildings pertaining thereto, nor shall any building erected thereon be used for other than dwelling or residence purposes, or purposes of like nature, and as such outbuildings pertaining thereto; that these covenants and agreements shall run with the land.

It was conceded that all parties to this action, including Dr. Nease, had record notice of these restrictions and took their property subject to the restrictions. Dr. Nease, accordingly, accepts the fact that he is bound by the restrictions to the extent they remain in force, but he argues that the restrictions have been effectively nullified through changes in the character of the neighborhood where his clinic is located. Alternatively, Dr. Nease has raised personal equitable defenses which would prevent the complainants from enforcing the restrictive covenants against him, in the event the Court finds that the covenants remain in force.

I

West Virginia recognizes the commonly accepted legal proposition that changes in a neighborhood's character can nullify restrictive covenants affecting neighborhood property. Technically, there is a distinction between changes which occur within the restricted neighborhood itself and changes in the surrounding, unrestricted area. The "problem of *change of conditions* arises where the complainant's and defendant's lots lie within a restricted subdivision, but the area surrounding the restricted subdivision has been so changed by the acts of third persons that the building scheme for the subdivision has been frustrated through no fault of the lot owners themselves." 2 American Law of Property 445–446 (A.J. Casner ed. 1952, emphasis added) [hereinafter cited as 2 American Law of Property]. When, however, the change in the neighborhood's character is a result of "violations within the subdivision itself, a problem of *abandonment* rather than change of conditions is involved." 2 American Law of Property 446 (emphasis added).

Some of the evidence in this case concerns the complainants' own violations of the restrictive covenants. This evidence properly goes to the question of abandonment, since the complainants' property clearly lies within the restricted area. Other evidence concerns non-residential uses of nearby property, some of which may lie within, and some outside, the restricted area. This evidence could show either abandonment or change of conditions, depending on the exact location of the property having the non-residential use. We will consider all the evidence relating to the changing character of the neighborhood here, and we will refrain from drawing technical distinctions between abandonment and change of conditions. Regardless of how it is characterized or labeled, the fundamental issue of this case is the viability of restrictive covenants in a changing neighborhood.

The evidence shows that a substantial amount of commercial property is located a short distance from Dr. Nease's clinic. Twenty-seventh Street, the nearest cross street to his Third Avenue clinic, has a maintenance company, a brokerage company, a repair shop, and a beauty shop, all within two blocks of Third Avenue. Another beauty shop is located on Twenty-eighth Street within half a block of Third Avenue. The 2800 block of Third Avenue itself has a service station, a laundry, and a church, while the 2600 block has an antique shop, a church, and a ball field.

These properties significantly change the original residential character of the neighborhood. It does not follow, however, that the entire neighborhood is perforce released from the burden of the restrictive covenants. On the contrary, every effort must be exerted to protect the unchanged portions of residential neighborhoods when businesses begin to encroach on the fringes. The obvious danger is that restrictions throughout an entire area can eventually be destroyed through succeeding block-by-block changes in the neighborhood's character:

> [A]s soon as the border lots are freed, the next tier of lots is put in the same position as that in which the border lots were originally. Thus by a step-by-step process the restrictions must be re-

laxed until the plan is totally defeated. [2 American Law of Property 446]

To guard against such an eventuality courts in a majority of jurisdictions have evolved the rule that "if the benefits of the original plan for a restricted subdivision can still be realized for the protection of interior lots, the restrictions should be enforced against the border lots, notwithstanding the fact that such lot owners are deprived of the most valuable use of their lots." 2 American Law of Property 447. West Virginia has adopted the essence of this salutary rule by holding that "changed conditions of the neighborhood will not be sufficient to defeat the right [to enforce restrictive covenants] unless the changes are 'so radical as practically to destroy the essential objects and purposes of the agreement.'" Wallace v. St. Clair, 147 W.Va. 377 at 399, 127 S.E.2d 742 at 757 (1962). Based on the evidence thus far discussed, we can say that the non-residential uses of property in the complainants' neighborhood have not destroyed the essential objects and purposes of the restrictive covenants and that the benefits of the original plan can still be realized for that portion of the neighborhood which retains its residential character. In this respect we note that protection against covenant violations can be afforded to an area as small as one block.

There are additional changes affecting the character of the neighborhood which remain to be considered. These changes have occurred in the block where the complainants reside and the chiropractic clinic is located. On a corner property at one end of the block is the Highlawn United Methodist Church. The evidence shows that the church building was constructed in compliance with neighborhood setback requirements, and with the permission of the property owners in the 2700 block of Third Avenue. The church blends well with the character of the neighborhood; nonetheless, it is a non-residential use. Another change in the neighborhood is the shift in the use of many properties from single-family occupancy to multi-family occupancy, apparently in violation of the applicable restrictive covenants. This change for the most part stems from the conversion into apartment units of garage-stable facilities formerly used by servants or guests. The evidence shows that a number of such apartment units existed in the 2700 block of Third Avenue, and that these units were in various stages of occupancy including unoccupied but available for rent, occupied by extended family members related to the main dwelling's owners, and occupied by unrelated tenants. In addition, at least one main house on the block was divided into two rental units. Despite these significant departures from the neighborhood plan of limiting the occupancy of each lot to single families, the 2700 block of Third Avenue has retained the residential character which was also an important and essential part of the original plan. Even the church, which represents the most drastic change in the block, complements the residential character of the area in a manner that business enterprises do not. Accordingly, we find that the changes in the neighborhood's character, both in the 2700 block of Third Avenue and in the nearby area, have not been so radical that the restrictive covenants involved here are nullified.

II

Having found Dr. Nease's arguments concerning the neighborhood's changing character to be unconvincing, we turn now to the personal equitable defenses he raised in this proceeding. The foremost among these defenses is acquiescence, which may be described as follows:

> The equitable defense of acquiescence arises where the complainant has acquiesced in the violation of the same type of restriction by third parties. Where the complainant has failed to enforce a similar equitable servitude against third parties, he has debarred himself from obtaining equitable relief against the defendant for subsequent violations of the same character. The reason for allowing this defense of acquiescence is the belief that the complainant, by his conduct in failing to seek enforcement against similar violations by third parties, has induced the defendant to assume that the restrictions are no longer in effect. Thus, acquiescence by the complainant to the violations of dissimilar restrictions cannot be a bar to enforcement where the restrictions are essentially different so that abandonment of one would not induce a reasonable person to assume that the other was also abandoned. Likewise, failure to sue for prior breaches by others where the breaches were noninjurious to the complainant cannot be treated as an acquiescence sufficient to bar equitable relief against a more serious and damaging violation. [2 American Law of Property 441–442, footnotes omitted]

This defense is recognized in West Virginia. In analyzing this defense, we must compare Dr. Nease's covenant violations with other violations in the same neighborhood in which the complainants have acquiesced. The violations outside the 2700 block of Third Avenue are too remote to be considered injurious to the complainants' interests. Accordingly, these violations do not provide the basis for the defense of acquiescence. Likewise, the apparent violations in the 2700 block itself, such as the rental of garage apartments and the construction of a church, are not so similar in character to Dr. Nease's clinic, or so injurious to the complainants, that they entitle Dr. Nease to raise the defense of acquiescence. There is one significant violation, however, which we find to be critical to Dr. Nease's defense of acquiescence, namely the use of Dr. Nease's property by his predecessor in title before Dr. Nease established his clinic.

The evidence shows that the property Dr. Nease purchased was divided into five rental units, four in the main structure and one in an outbuilding. There is a very fine line between residential and commercial use in this instance, and Dr. Nease could fairly have assumed that the neighborhood acquiesced in a commercial use of 2703 Third Avenue. This assumption was warranted, we believe, by the fact that in this particular neighborhood the operation of five rental units on one lot is essentially a commercial undertaking. Although the character of Dr. Nease's business differs from that of the preceding business at the same location, the similarities between the businesses are sufficient in our view to entitle Dr. Nease to raise the defense of acquiescence. Both businesses brought added traffic into the neighborhood and resulted in other minor disruptions which are out of the ordinary. Furthermore, it would appear that both businesses resulted in about the same injury to the complainants. In any case it does not seem that the clinic is a significantly more serious and damaging covenant violation than the five-unit rental property.

We can only judge the similarities between Dr. Nease's clinic and the preceding use of the same property on the basis of the record before us. The record indicates that Dr. Nease rehabilitated his property in such a manner that it harmonizes well with other dwellings on the block. In addition there was testimony that Dr. Nease did not conduct a high-volume practice. Furthermore, the discreet sign which identifies the clinic is placed on the building itself, rather than at the curb, where it would call more attention to the commercial character of the property. In short, Dr. Nease's commercial use of the property appears to be restrained and dignified, and we note that the complainants have acquiesced in only such a use. Should Dr. Nease significantly alter the character of his clinic, or should some other less restrained business move into the property, the complainants would have cause to reexamine the situation and take whatever action they deem appropriate to protect their interests.

We need not consider the other errors assigned by Dr. Nease because our decision with respect to the defense of acquiescence is dispositive of the case. Accordingly, for the foregoing reasons, the judgment of the Circuit Court of Cabell County is reversed.

Reversed.

NOTE

1. *Consensual Termination.* A nonpossessory interest may be terminated or modified at any time through a release executed by the owner of the benefit to the owner of the servient estate. The release must comply with the Statute of Frauds and with all other formalities required for the creation of the interest being terminated. If, as is commonly the case in subdivisions, there is more than one benefit holder, a release, to be effective, must be executed by all. Negotiations, relatively simple when only a single servient and dominant estate are involved, can become extraordinarily complex when the interests of all the homeowners in a subdivision—each owning a parcel that is both dominant and servient—must be accommodated. Al-

though most, or even all, may desire a complete release, negotiation costs and strategic behavior may very well block the transaction.

Parties drafting an easement, covenant or servitude sometimes anticipate the transaction costs that will surround efforts at termination and expressly provide shortcuts to termination in the instrument itself. The most obvious method, employed by the subdivider in *Neponsit*, p. 755, above, is to provide that the interest will expire after a specified period. Another method, sometimes employed in subdivisions, is to limit the duration of the covenants but provide that they will automatically be extended for successive periods unless a specified majority of homeowners in the subdivision votes to amend or rescind the covenants. Do you see any problems with such provisions? Compare Ridge Park Homeowners v. Pena, 88 N.M. 563, 544 P.2d 278 (1976) ("Absent a specific provision in the agreement stating otherwise, we hold that the requisite vote cannot change the applicability of [residential] restrictive covenants to a few of the lots; the change must apply to all lots." 88 N.M. at 565, 544 P.2d at 280).

2. If the parties who created the nonpossessory interest failed to express their full intent respecting the conditions under which the interest should end, courts will attempt to determine this intent from the instrument's language and surrounding circumstances. Do the rules of merger, abandonment, acquiescence and changed neighborhood conditions, applied in the principal cases, attempt to approximate the results the original parties would have dictated had they contemplated the events that later occurred on the servient and dominant estates? Or are these rules of law, followed on principle, without regard for the original parties' intent?

3. *Merger.* The doctrine of merger, considered in Witt v. Reavis, applies to easements in gross as well as to easements appurtenant, and to covenants and servitudes as well as to easements. Courts generally follow the doctrine's standard metaphor, that when one person takes fee title to both the dominant and servient estates, his ownership right to use the servient estate swallows up the lesser rights incident to the nonpossessory interest. When *Z*, who owns the servient estate, Blackacre, leases Blackacre to *Y*, who owns the dominant estate, Whiteacre, the nonpossessory interest will only be suspended during the period of unitary possession under the lease, and will revive when the lease term expires. And, if *Y* acquires only a portion of Blackacre in fee or under lease, the nonpossessory interest will be terminated or suspended only with respect to that portion.

To what extent do merger rules approximate the original parties' probable intent as to what should happen when Blackacre and Whiteacre are owned by a single person? Is it likely they intended that the interest be terminated, and not just suspended during the period of unitary ownership? Does the Pennsylvania rule, rejected in Witt v. Reavis, better approximate the original parties' probable intent? If at trial the plaintiffs had argued for an easement by implication, would they have prevailed? When will an easement terminated by merger not be revived by implication or necessity?

To what extent do merger rules seek to effectuate the intent of the successor parties, Y and Z, at the time of merger? If Y and Z addressed the issue, is it likely they would execute a release of their nonpossessory interests?

4. *Abandonment.* What rationale underlies (a) the general rule on abandonment; (b) the Pennsylvania rule on abandonment applied in Hatcher v. Chesner; (c) the exception to the Pennsylvania rule, also applied in *Hatcher*? What difference, if any, is there between the general rule and the Pennsylvania rule when it is taken together with its exception? Is there any connection between the Pennsylvania rule on abandonment and the Pennsylvania rule on merger, discussed in Witt v. Reavis, apart from the fact that both appear to reflect a special solicitude for easements? Is the general rule or the Pennsylvania rule better calculated to encourage the productive use of the servient estate and of the easement's benefit? Does the exception to the Pennsylvania rule add to, or detract from, its ability to encourage productive land use?

5. *Estoppel; Laches; Acquiescence.* Abandonment is not the only doctrine under which elapsed time will contribute to the termination of a nonpossessory interest. A benefit owner who stops using his nonpossessory interest may be barred by estoppel from later enforcing the interest against a servient owner who relied to her detriment on the benefit holder's representation that he did not intend to resume use. A benefit holder who delays filing suit against a servient owner who is violating the nonpossessory interest may be barred on the equitable ground of laches if the delay prejudiced the defendant. And, as noted in Morris v. Nease, a benefit owner who fails to proceed against some violators may, by his acquiescence in their conduct, later be barred from relief against another servient owner who has committed the same violation.

Should *Nease* have been decided on the ground of laches rather than acquiescence?

6. *Changed Conditions.* Is there any difference in underlying rationale between the doctrine of abandonment, which *Nease* said applies to changes within the subdivision, and the doctrine of changed neighborhood conditions, which *Nease* said applies to changes outside the subdivision? If so, was it proper for the court in deciding the case to "refrain from drawing technical distinctions between abandonment and change of conditions"? Was the court properly sensitive to the buffering role of border lots in a subdivision?

Courts divide on whether changed neighborhood conditions constitutes only an equitable defense—immunizing the servient owner from injunctive but not monetary relief—or constitutes a ground for terminating the interest entirely. Although the first view once predominated, the second is gaining increased support. One practical effect of the distinction is that, since an equitable defense will not terminate the restriction, the defense offers no basis for removing the restriction as a continuing cloud on title. However, by limiting the benefit holder to damages, the equitable defense should make it less costly for the servient owner to buy him off. See generally, Stoebuck, Running Covenants: An Analytical Primer, 52 Wash.L. Rev. 861, 882–885 (1977). Did *Nease* offer another, preferable alternative by allowing defendant to continue his practice, so long as it was "restrained and dignified"?

Does termination on the ground of changed conditions unfairly deprive the benefit holder Y of a property interest while conferring a windfall on Z, the owner of the servient estate? Is the older equitable approach, that would give Y damages, fairer? Can courts justify termination on this ground as simply effectuating the intent of the original parties, A and B, who, had they contemplated the change in neighborhood conditions, would have provided for termination of the interest? Is it preferable to disregard presumed intent and to rest these decisions on the assumption that when individuals acquire land they take into account not only the nature and limits of the applicable land use restrictions, but also the legal rules that will be applied in terminating these restrictions? Under this view, termination produces neither a wipe-out nor a windfall for benefit owner and servient owner since each can be expected to have taken the possibility of termination into account at the time he purchased his interest. Is this a plausible view of investment behavior?

7. *Misuse*. Will misuse terminate an easement? Clearly it will if the governing instrument so provides. But what if the original parties did not express their intentions on the point? The universally adopted rule is that misuse does not provide a basis for termination but only for an injunction requiring the beneficiary to conform his use to the terms of the easement.

Occasionally, however, if injunctive relief cannot effectively curtail the misuse, courts will terminate the easement. For example, in Crimmins v. Gould, 149 Cal.App.2d 383, 308 P.2d 786 (1st Dist.1957), defendants owned two adjoining parcels, only one of which, Parcel 1, had the benefit of a right of way easement over plaintiff's land. Defendant developed a residential subdivision on both Parcel 1 and 2, and subdivision residents from both parcels used the right of way appurtenant to Parcel 1, gaining access through roadway extensions from the easement built by defendant, dedicated by him to the public, accepted by the town, and used by the public. Plaintiff sued to have Parcel 1's easement terminated on the ground that its use by residents from Parcel 2 and by the public exceeded the terms of the easement.

The court found that, because the roadway extensions added by defendant had become public streets, their use could not be effectively controlled by an injunction that allowed only residents of Parcel 1 to use the easement. Thus, the court held that terminating the easement was the only just alternative. "The general rule is that misuse or excessive use is not sufficient for abandonment or forfeiture, but an injunction is the proper remedy. But where the burden of the servient estate is increased through changes in the dominant estate which increase the use and subject it to use of non-dominant property, a forfeiture will be justified if the unauthorized use may not be severed and prohibited." 149 Cal.App.2d at 391, 308 P.2d at 791.

The court rested its decision in part on West's Ann.Cal. Civil Code § 811(3) which provides that a servitude is extinguished by "the performance of any act upon either tenement, by the owner of the servitude, or with his assent, which is incompatible with its nature or exercise". It also relied on Lux v. Haggin, 69 Cal. 255, 10 P. 674 (1886), which "said the section was a statutory declaration of the well-settled rule 'that if the owner of a dominant estate do acts thereon which permanently prevent his enjoying an easement, the same is extinguished, or if he authorize the owner of the servient estate to do upon the same that which prevents the dominant estate from any longer enjoying the easement, the effect will be to extinguish it.'" 308 P.2d at 790.

8. *Statutory Approaches.* Several states have by statute augmented the common law methods for terminating nonpossessory interests. West's Ann. Civil Code § 811, relied on in part in Crimmins v. Gould, above, provides that a servitude is extinguished '(1.) By the vesting of the right to the servitude and the right to the servient tenement in the same person; (2.) By the destruction of the servient tenement; (3.) By the performance of any act upon either tenement, by the owner of the servitude, or with his assent, which is incompatible with its nature or exercise; or, (4.) When the servitude was acquired by enjoyment, by disuse thereof by the owner of the servitude for the period prescribed for acquiring title by enjoyment." In some states these interests are controlled by marketable title acts requiring that, to keep his interest alive, the interest owner must periodically record a notice of intent to preserve the interest.

Statutes in New York and Massachusetts authorize courts to extinguish obsolete restrictions. N.Y.—McKinney's Real Prop. Acts & Proc. Law § 1951 provides that no restriction on the use of land created by "covenant, promise or negative easement" shall be enforced "if, at the time the enforceability of the restriction is brought in question, it appears that the restriction is of no actual and substantial benefit to the persons seeking its enforcement or seeking a declaration or determination of its enforceability, either because the purpose of the restriction has already been accomplished or, by reason of changed conditions or other cause, its purpose is not capable of accomplishment, or for any other reason." Upon a finding of unenforceability, the court may extinguish the interest, "upon payment, to the person or persons who would otherwise be entitled to enforce it in the event of a breach at the time of the action, of such damages, if any, as such person or persons will sustain from the extinguishment of the restriction."

Mass.Gen. Laws Ann. c. 184, § 30, (1977; Supp.1983), starts from the same position as its New York counterpart, terminating restrictions that have no "actual and substantial benefit," but adds a presumption, with specified exceptions, against the existence of an "actual and substantial benefit," if "any part of the subject land lies within a city or town having a population greater than 100,000 persons." Further, no restriction determined to be of benefit shall be enforced, other than by an award of damages, if, among other alternatives, "changes in the character of the properties affected or their neighborhood, in available construction materials or techniques, in access, services or facilities, in applicable public controls of land use or construction, or in any other conditions or circumstances, reduce materially the need for the restriction or the likelihood of the restriction accomplishing its original purposes or render it obsolete or inequitable to enforce except by award of money damages," or "continuation of the restriction on the parcel against which enforcement is claimed or on parcels remaining in a common scheme with it or subject to like restrictions would impede reasonable use of land for purposes for which it is most suitable, and would tend to impair the growth of the neighborhood or municipality in a manner inconsistent with the public interest or to contribute to deterioration of properties or to result in decadent or substandard areas or blighted open areas." See also, Mass.Gen. Laws Ann. c. 184, §§ 23–29.

III. LANDLORD AND TENANT

A. THE LEASEHOLD ESTATE

FOWLER v. BOTT, 6 MASS. 62, 67 (1809), SEWALL, J.: By a motion in arrest of judgment, this question, arising upon the defendants' third plea, is to be decided by the Court, *viz.*—whether, after a destruction by fire of the buildings demised, the lessors, without rebuilding, can recover their rent.

The supposed hardship of the case has been urged upon the attention of the Court, as an argument for the defendants. The answer to this argument is, that a lease for years is a sale of the demised premises for the term; and, unless in the case of an express stipulation for the purpose, the lessor does not insure the premises against inevitable accidents, or any other deterioration. The rent is in effect the price, or purchase money, to be paid for the ownership of the premises during the term; and their destruction, or any depreciation of their value, happening without the fault of the lessor, is no abatement of his price, but entirely the loss of the purchaser.

ALBERT M. GREENFIELD & CO., INC. v. KOLEA

Supreme Court of Pennsylvania, 1977.
475 Pa. 351, 380 A.2d 758.

MANDERINO, Justice.

This is an appeal from an order of the Superior Court, affirming the judgment of the Court of Common Pleas of Delaware County. Appellee (lessor) had sued appellant (lessee) for breach of two lease agreements. The trial court awarded appellee $7,200.00. Appellant's motions for judgment n.o.v., arrest of judgment, and new trial were denied. The Superior Court affirmed the trial court *per curiam*. Appellant's petition for allowance of appeal was granted by us and this appeal followed. We reverse.

The appellee's claim in this case is based on two separate, but related, lease agreements. The first lease, executed on March 20, 1971, covered ". . . all that certain one story garage building and known as 5735–37 Wayne Avenue, extending to Keyser Street in the rear [Philadelphia] . . . to be used and occupied as storage of automobiles . . . ." This lease, executed for a term of two years beginning May 1, 1971, provided for an annual rental of $4,800.00. The second lease, covering adjoining property, was also executed on

March 20, 1971. The second lease covered " . . . all those certain lots or pieces of ground known as 5721–33 Wayne Avenue . . . to be used and occupied for the sale and storage of automobiles . . . ." The second lease, also executed for a two-year term beginning May 1, 1971, provided for an annual rental of $2,500.00. There was no building located on the real estate covered by the second lease. Neither lease contained a provision with respect to the tenant's obligations in the event of destruction of the building.

On May 1, 1972, after the appellant had occupied the premises for one year, fire completely destroyed the building covered by lease number one. The fire was labeled as accidental by the Fire Marshall's office. The day after the fire the remaining sections of the exterior walls were razed by the lessor, and barricades were placed around the perimeter of the premises covered by both leases. Appellant thereafter refused to pay rent under either of the leases.

The general rule has been stated that in the absence of a lease provision to the contrary, a tenant is not relieved from the obligation to pay rent despite the total destruction of the leased premises. Magaw v. Lambert, 3 Pa. 444 (1846); Hoy v. Holt, 91 Pa. 88 (1879).

The reason for the rule has been said to be that although a building may be an important element of consideration for the payment of rent, the interest in the soil remains to support the lease despite destruction of the building. It has also been said that since destruction of the building is usually by accident, it is only equitable to divide the loss; the lessor loses the property and the lessee loses the term.

Two exceptions designed to afford relief to the tenant from the harshness of the common law principle have been created. These exceptions reflect the influence of modern contract principles as applied in the landlord-tenant relationship.

The first exception provides that where only a portion of a building is leased, total destruction of the building relieves the tenant of the obligation to pay rent. This exception recognizes that in the leasing of a part of a building there is no implication that any estate in land is granted. This Court, in other words, has recognized that in a landlord-tenant relationship with respect to an apartment, the parties have *bargained for* a part of a building and not the land beneath.

The influence of contract principles of bargained for exchange is also apparent in the second exception to the general common law rule. The second exception is based on the doctrine of *impossibility of performance*, and is stated in Greenburg v. Sun Shipbuilding Co., 277 Pa. 312, 313, 121 A. 63, 64 (1923):

"Where a contract relates to the use and possession of specific property, the existence of which is necessary to the carrying out of the purpose in view, a condition is implied by law, as though written in the agreement that the impossibility of performance arising from the destruction of the property without fault of either party, shall end all contractual obligations relating to the thing destroyed."

As was said in West v. Peoples First Nat'l. Bank & Trust Co., 378 Pa. 275, 106 A.2d 427 (1954),

". . . where a contract relates to specific property the existence or maintenance of which is necessary to the carrying out of the purpose of the agreement, the condition is implied by law, just as though it were written into the agreement, that the impossibility of performance or the frustration of purpose arising from the destruction of the property or interference with its use, without the fault of either party, ends all contractual obligations relating to the property. Moreover, impossibility in that connection means not only strict impossibility but impracticability because of extreme and unreasonable difficulty, expense, or loss involved." (footnote omitted.)

The Rest. Contracts § 454, also applies the test of impracticability rather than strict impossibility:

". . . [I]mpossibility means not only strict impossibility but *impracticability* because of extreme and unreasonable difficulty, expense, injury, or loss involved." (Emphasis added.)

In the instant case, it is apparent that when the building was destroyed by fire it became impossible for the appellee to furnish the agreed consideration—". . . all that one story garage building . . ." Nothing in the first lease implies that any interest in the land itself was intended to be conveyed. It is also obvious that the purpose of the lease with respect to the appellant was thereby frustrated. As noted in the lease, the parties contemplated that appellant would use the building for the repair and sale of used motor vehicles. Without a building appellant could no longer carry on a used car business as contemplated by the parties at the time they entered into the lease agreement. It became extremely impracticable for the appellant to continue using the adjoining lot when his business office and repair stations were destroyed by the fire. Additionally, because of the dangerous condition created by the fire, the city required appellee to barricade the property covered by both leases, thus preventing appellant from entering the property.

In reaching our decision that the accidental destruction of the building by fire excused the parties from further performance of their obligations under the lease agreements, we are cognizant of the fact that we are allocating the risk to be assumed by the parties. Such an allocation of risk can be accomplished in one of two ways. First, the parties could specifically provide for risk assumption with respect to certain possible contingencies. In the absence of an express recognition and assumption by the parties, the court is left with the task of determining what the parties would have done had the issue arisen in the contract negotiations. In reaching such a decision a court must consider many factors. As stated in 6 Corbin on Contracts § 1325:

> "There is no rule of law by which the issue can be deductively determined; it depends upon the practices and customs of men in like cases, upon the prevailing mores of the time."

In reaching a decision involving the landlord-tenant relationship, too often courts have relied on outdated common law property principles and presumptions and have refused to consider the factors necessary for an equitable and just conclusion. In this case, for example, if we applied the general rule and ignored the realities of the situation, we would bind the appellant to paying rent for barren ground when both parties to the lease contemplated that the building would be used for the commercial enterprise of repair and sale of used motor vehicles.

The trial court's decision to bind the lessee to the lease was simply an application of an outdated common law presumption. That presumption developed in a society very different from ours today: one where the land was always more valuable than the buildings erected on it. Buildings are critical to the functioning of modern society. When the parties bargain for the use of a building, the soil beneath is generally of little consequence. Our laws should develop to reflect these changes. As stated in Javins v. First Nat'l. Realty Corp., 138 U.S.App.D.C. 369, 372, 428 F.2d 1071, 1074, *cert. denied*, 400 U.S. 925, 91 S.Ct. 186, 27 L.Ed.2d 185 (1970):

> "Courts have a duty to reappraise old doctrines in the light of the facts and values of contemporary life—particularly old common law doctrines which the courts themselves created and developed. As we have said before, '[T]he continued vitality of the common law . . . depends upon its ability to reflect contemporary values and ethics.'" (Footnote omitted.)

The presumption established in *Magaw* and *Hoy, supra,* no longer has relevance to today's landlord-tenant relationships. It is no longer reasonable to *assume* that in the absence of a lease provision to the contrary the lessee should bear the risk of loss in the event of total destruction of the building. Where the parties do not expressly provide for such a catastrophe, the court should analyze the facts and the lease agreement as any other contract would be analyzed. Following such an analysis, if it is evident to the court that the parties bargained for the existence of a building, and no provision is made as to who bears the risk of loss if the building is destroyed, the court should relieve the parties of their respective obligations when the building no longer exists.

Accordingly, we reverse the order of the Superior Court, and remand to the trial court with directions to grant the appellant's motion for judgment n.o.v.

JONES, former C.J., did not participate in the decision of this case.

ROBERTS, J., filed a concurring opinion.

NIX, J., filed a concurring opinion.

POMEROY, J., concurs in the result.

ROBERTS, Justice, concurring.

I join in the opinion of the majority because the rule established reaches the same result as the Restatement, Second, Property (Landlord and Tenant) Section 5.4 (Unsuitable Condition Arises After Entry—Remedies Available) which states:

> Except to the extent the parties to a lease validly agree otherwise, there is a breach of the landlord's obligation if, after the tenant's entry and without fault of the tenant, a change in the condition of the leased property . . . . caused suddenly by a nonmanmade force, makes the leased property unsuitable for the use contemplated by the parties and the landlord does not correct the situation within a reasonable time after being requested by the tenant to do so. For that breach, the tenant may:
>
> (1) terminate the lease . . . .

The unexpressed intent of the parties is thus irrelevant.

NIX, Justice, concurring.

Insofar as the majority opinion represents the adoption in this Commonwealth of Section 5.4 of the Restatement, Second, Property, I am in complete agreement. The common law rule that an accidental fire which totally destroys a building is no defense to the claim for rent for the premises, is clearly inappropriate in our present society.

As I view our holding today, it replaces a rule of law, which may have had validity in a predominantly agrarian society but is clearly outmoded today.

NOTES

1. Which decision is better, Fowler v. Bott or Greenfield v. Kolea? Representing a prospective lessor or lessee in a *Fowler* jurisdiction, what positions would you take in negotiating over allocation of risk of loss? What positions would you take in a *Greenfield* jurisdiction? A majority of states now follow the *Greenfield* rule on risk of accidental loss. See 2 R. Powell, The Law of Real Property ¶ 233 [4] (1982).

2. *Is a Lease a Conveyance or a Contract?* Many contemporary courts and commentators view the lease as having steadily evolved over time, from conveyance to contract. *Fowler* is thus taken as evidence of the old view that leases are conveyances of interests in land, and *Greenfield* as evidence of the modern view that leases are con-

tracts respecting the possession of land. In fact, the history of the real property lease is far more checkered than is commonly thought.

The earliest tenants were *villeins* who held neither by contract nor conveyance but rather at the will of their manorial lord. By the end of the fifteenth century, the villein's uncertain status had evolved into the far more secure estate of copyhold tenure. See pages 470 to 471 above. At the same time that villeinage was maturing into copyhold, a new class of agricultural laborers was beginning to work manorial lands under strictly contractual arrangements for terms of years or shorter periods. Although these termors originally had no tenure or interest in land, and hence none of the real property rights or remedies available to more secure freeholders like life tenants, their lot, too, eventually improved, as they received an increasing array of real actions to protect their tenancies. These developments culminated in 1499 when termors were given the action for ejectment, entitling them to recover their leased lands as against third-party trespassers.

The leasehold, which by the sixteenth century had evolved from contract to estate, continued its cyclical course. By the eighteenth and nineteenth centuries, courts in England and America were once again interpreting leases mainly according to contract principles. (It was the nineteenth-century emphasis on freedom of contract, and not sixteenth-century conveyance notions, that bound the tenant in *Fowler* to his promise to pay rent even though the premises had been destroyed.) By the early decades of the twentieth century the lease was once again being treated mainly as an estate rather than as a contract, and by the middle of the century, with decisions like *Greenfield*, the cycle began anew.

These cycles of contract and conveyance represent, at most, shifts in emphasis. At no time, including the present, has the lease been treated exclusively as a contract or as a conveyance. Rather, it has at all times been treated as a mix of the two. This suggests that the correct question to ask in any case is not whether the lease in suit is a conveyance or a contract but, rather, which characterization—contract or conveyance—will produce the better result?

For background on the changing nature of the lease over time, see generally, Glendon, The Transformation of American Landlord-Tenant Law, 23 B.C.L.Rev. 503 (1982); Weinberg, From Contract to Conveyance: The Law of Landlord and Tenant, 1800–1920, 1980 So.Ill. L.J. 29; McGovern, The Historical Conception of a Lease for Years, 23 UCLA L.Rev. 501 (1976). For a perceptive functional analysis of the choice between contract and conveyance, see Humbach, The Common-Law Conception of Leasing: Mitigation, Habitability, and Dependence of Covenants, 60 Wash.U.L.Q. 1213 (1983); Chase, The Property-Contract Theme in Landlord and Tenant Law: A Critical Commentary on Schoshinski's American Law of Landlord and Tenant, 13 Rutgers L.J. 189 (1982).

R. Schoshinski, American Law of Landlord and Tenant (1980) is an excellent one-volume treatise on landlord-tenant law generally.

3. Should contract rules or conveyance rules govern lease formation? If contract rules apply, a meeting of minds between landlord and tenant will suffice to create an enforceable lease. If, however, conveyance rules apply, all of real property law's conveyancing formalities—including delivery and the requirements imposed by the Statute of Frauds—must be met for the tenant to receive a leasehold interest.

In 219 Broadway Corp. v. Alexander's Inc., 46 N.Y.2d 506, 414 N.Y.S.2d 889, 387 N.E.2d 1205 (1979), the New York Court of Appeals ruled that conveyance rather than contract rules governed, and that because the lessor had not formally delivered the executed lease, no interest passed to the putative lessee. Recognizing that a "lease is often chameleonic in both character and function, its fundamental purpose remains to serve as a vehicle for the conveyance of an interest in real property. Until this end is achieved, any rights or obligations of the parties which may be embodied in the lease remain dormant. Thus, the threshold inquiry in this case becomes whether, under the facts alleged, the lease served to convey an estate in real property from the defendant to the plaintiff." 46 N.Y.2d at 511, 414 N.Y.S.2d at 891, 387 N.E.2d at 1207.

In the court's opinion, "the underlying justification for viewing delivery as fundamental to the conveyance of an interest in land is not grounded in the blind application of what some may consider archaic principles of property law. On the contrary, delivery serves a very practical end. It is a common practice in the contemporary business world for parties to draft and sign instruments of conveyance prior to the time at which they intend their contemplated transaction to become irrevocable. By requiring delivery, the law facilitates the true expectations of the parties by ensuring that the interest in the property is not conveyed until that moment when the parties so intend . . . . The due signature of the lease instrument is but one step in the process of conveying an interest in land. Delivery requires something more. There must be evidence of an unequivocal intent that the interest intended to be conveyed is, in fact, being conveyed. The mere signing of the instrument by parties not in the presence of each other, without more, does not evince such intent." 46 N.Y.2d at 511–512, 414 N.Y.S.2d at 892, 387 N.E.2d at 1208.

4. Courts and legislatures have in recent years begun to recognize the importance of yet another distinction to the law of leases: whether the lease is for residential or commercial purposes. One result of this development is that it may soon be impossible to generalize about landlord-tenant law as a body of rules that applies uniformly across all forms of tenancies. Rules developed in response to the special needs of residential tenancies may be entirely out of place in

the context of commercial tenancies. Cases decided in one context may have only limited authority in the other.

The organization of this chapter reflects this modern trend. The first part of the chapter considers those rules that continue to apply across the board to all landlord-tenant contexts. The second part considers rules that have evolved in the residential setting, specifically in the context of substandard housing. The third part considers commercial tenancies in the specific context of the shopping center.

1. CLASSIFICATION

There are four common law landlord-tenant estates: the term of years tenancy, the periodic tenancy, the tenancy at will and the tenancy at sufferance. Although these four share many attributes, they also possess important differences, principally in terms of duration and the nature of the conduct that will operate to terminate or extend the tenancy.

a. Types Of Tenancies

i. *Term of Years.* The term of years tenancy (also called an estate for years) has a *fixed duration*. As a consequence, the tenant's possessory right automatically terminates, and the landlord's right to retake possession automatically accrues, at the end of the fixed term. Thus, "*A* to *B* for three years, to commence June 1, 1984," is a term of years tenancy and, without more, *B*'s right to possess the premises will terminate, and *A*'s right will begin, at midnight on May 31, 1987. The fixed term need not be measured in years. Had *A* conveyed to *B* for one year, three months, two weeks or even one day, a term of years tenancy would have been created.

Would the language, "*A* to *B* for five years unless *B* earlier graduates from law school," create a term of years tenancy? Virtually all courts hold that it will, on the ground that there is an outside, fixed term to the tenancy. What of the language, "*A* to *B*, to commence June 1, 1984 and to terminate when *C* shall reach the age of 21?" Again, most courts will call this a term of years since its outside duration can be exactly computed at the moment *B* takes possession.

Term of years estates are subject to two constraints that ordinarily do not apply to the other landlord-tenant estates. One is the Statute of Frauds which in most states requires leases for more than one year to be written and signed by the party to be charged; the Statute also typically requires the lease to specify the parties, the premises, the duration of the lease and the rent to be paid. Second, statutes in many states impose a limit, commonly ninety-nine years, on the length of the lease term. See, for example, Nev.Rev.Stat. § 111.200 (1979) (25 years for agricultural or grazing leases, 99 years for other leases; "all leases hereafter made contrary to the provisions of this chapter shall be void as to any periods of time in excess of those enumerated.") What purpose or purposes do you suppose these statutes serve?

ii. *Periodic Tenancy.* Unlike the term of years, with its fixed duration, the periodic tenancy is *continuous*, renewing itself automatically at the end of each specified period, typically a month or a year, unless and until landlord or tenant terminates the tenancy by prior notice to the other. For example, A's lease "to B from year to year, commencing June 1, 1984," will give B a periodic tenancy—specifically a tenancy from year to year. If B, having neither given nor received notice to terminate, continues in possession on June 1, 1985, he will be entitled—and bound—to the lease terms for another year, and for each succeeding year, every June 1, without prior notice.

When must a landlord or tenant give notice to the other in order to terminate a periodic tenancy? At common law, the notice required to terminate a year-to-year tenancy had to be given no later than six months before the end of the period. Thus, if B is a year to year tenant for a term beginning June 1, 1984, he must, to have his tenancy terminate on May 31, 1985, give A notice of his intent to terminate no later than November 30, 1984; otherwise, he will be bound for another one-year term, beginning June 1, 1985 and ending May 31, 1986. Periodic tenancies shorter than one year require notice that corresponds with the period: three months' notice to terminate a tenancy from quarter-to-quarter, and one month's notice to terminate a month-to-month tenancy. Statutes in a number of states have altered the common law notice requirements. See, for example, Colo.Rev. Stat.1973, 13–40–107 (three months for year-to-year tenancy; one month for tenancies of six months or longer but less than one year; ten days for month-to-month tenancies; three days for week-to-week tenancies; one day for periods less than one week).

Although periodic tenancies can, as in the examples above, be created expressly, they are more commonly created by implication. If, for example, the parties fail to specify a fixed term, but apparently contemplate a continuing relationship, a periodic tenancy will be implied. Thus, the lease, "A to B at a monthly rental of $300.00," will create a month-to-month tenancy, and the lease, "A to B at an annual rental of $3,600," will create a year-to-year tenancy.

iii. *Tenancy at Will.* A tenancy at will has neither fixed duration nor periodicity and *can be terminated at any time* by landlord or tenant without prior notice to the other. (Statutes in some states have introduced a requirement of prior notice ranging from three days to three months.) The arrangement may be express—"A to B subject to termination at the will of A or B"—or it may be implied. If the lease read, "A to B at the will of A," most courts would imply a corresponding right to terminate in tenant B, and call it a tenancy at will. If, however, the lease read, "A to B at the will of B," most courts would not imply a corresponding right of termination in landlord A. See 1 American Law of Property § 3.30 (A.J. Casner, ed.

1952). If *B* is not a tenant at will in this last example, what is he? See Thompson v. Baxter, 107 Minn. 122, 119 N.W. 797 (1909) (language, *A* to *B* "for the full term of while he shall wish to live in Albert Lea," held to create a life estate in *B* "terminable only at his death or removal from Albert Lea").

Most often tenancies at will are entirely disconnected from the intent, express or implied, of the parties and represent instead a judicial or legislative patching over of the parties' failed effort at creating some other arrangement. Thus, if *B* enters Blackacre under a lease that violates the Statute of Frauds, he will be considered a tenant at will. See, for example, Mass.Gen.Laws Ann. c. 183, § 3 (1977) ("an estate or interest in land created without an instrument in writing signed by the grantor or by his attorney shall have the force and effect of an estate at will only").

iv. *Tenancy at Sufferance*. A tenancy at sufferance arises when *B*, who lawfully entered into possession of Blackacre, *wrongfully continues in possession* after his right to be there has ended. Thus, if *B* entered Blackacre under a valid lease, he will become a tenant at sufferance when he holds over after the lease expires and remains in possession without the landlord's consent. The status of a tenant at sufferance falls just short of trespass since, although the tenant is in possession without owner *A's* consent, his initial entry onto the land was lawful. As a result, *B's* possession is not sufficiently adverse to ripen into title by adverse possession.

In appropriate circumstances, the landlord may elect between evicting the holdover tenant and accepting him as a lawful tenant. When should the landlord have this election? How should the landlord manifest her election? If the landlord effectively elects to treat the holdover as a lawful tenant, what terms will govern the new tenancy? Consider the next principal case.

b. THE HOLDOVER TENANT

DONNELLY ADVERTISING CORP. v. FLACCOMIO

Supreme Court of Maryland, 1958.
216 Md. 113, 140 A.2d 165.

HORNEY, Judge.

This is an appeal by the Donnelly Advertising Corporation of Maryland (the tenant), from a judgment for $350 obtained by Annie Flaccomio (the landlord), in the Superior Court of Baltimore City (Mason, J., sitting without a jury). The judgment represents two months' rent which the trial court held was due under an "implied" lease which arose as a result of the tenant holding over after the expiration of a written lease which expired on March 20, 1956.

On November 16, 1955, the tenant acquired all of the property of the Morton Company, Inc. (the previous tenant), including the lease from the landlord to the previous tenant. The term of the original lease, which began on August 1, 1947, and ended on March 20, 1953, had been extended by written agreements for three successive terms of one year each, the last extension ending, as stated, on March 20, 1956. Each of the written agreements provided that the extended term would be on "the same terms and conditions of the original lease". The tenant was obliged to pay rent of $175 per month, plus ground rent of $60 per annum, water rent, and various taxes.

The property leased is a row house at 405 North Exeter Street in Baltimore City. It was particularly desirable as advertising space since it had acquired a side exposure towards Orleans Street after the condemnation by the City of the two adjacent houses to the south in connection with the construction of the Orleans Street Viaduct. The condemnation left alongside of the landlord's house a small lot of land owned by the City. When the original lease was executed the house was vacant and in an uninhabitable condition. At first the previous tenant used the building for the support of a signboard on the south wall facing Orleans Street and as space for another painted sign. It was also used for housing the electrical equipment for the sign and part of the equipment for the thermometer on the sign. A hole was cut through the wall of the house for that purpose. Later the previous tenant sank steel girders into the adjacent vacant lot of the City. Although some steel braces between the sign and the house remained until the tenant vacated, the billboard was thereafter supported in the main by these girders. While the previous tenant had the right under the lease to use the property for any purpose whatsoever, there is no evidence that any part of it was used for any purpose other than those mentioned above, except the first floor which was sublet to a neighboring manufacturer for the storage of equipment.

Since a decision of this case depends primarily on the interpretation of a series of letters between the parties, it is necessary to discuss and analyze such letters with particularity. On December 8, 1955, the tenant wrote to Murray McNabb, Esq., who was then the attorney for the landlord, stating that it had acquired the interest of the previous tenant in the property. Realizing that the then current extension expired on March 20, 1956, it said: "We will at that time arrange for an assignment of lease between the proper parties." On February 29, 1956, the tenant wrote to the landlord confirming a verbal offer made by it on February 23, 1956, to pay a rental reduced from $2,100 a year to $1,000 a year, but for a five-year term instead of a one-year term. On March 12, 1956, the attorney for the landlord replied to this offer: ". . . [the landlord] is not willing to rent her property for less than the amount it has been bringing for the past several years, as she said she could have put stores here but for this lease."

By March 20, 1956, the expiration date of the lease, nothing further had been done. Until this date, the tenant had offered to lease at a lower rental, but the landlord had flatly refused to accept the offer. On March 23, 1956, the third day after it had begun to hold over, the tenant wrote the following letter to the landlord:

"Due to the fact that the present lease has expired, and as you are aware, we are attempting to renegotiate a new lease with you.

"We will continue on the same rental basis from month to month until such time as we can come to some agreement as to the future.

"We reserve the right to vacate the property upon thirty (30) days' written notice at any time should we fail to be able to make satisfactory arrangements.

"Check for one month is enclosed."

On March 30, 1956, the tenant received the following letter from the landlord's attorney:

"Your lease has expired and I have authorized . . . [the landlord] to deposit the one check which pays for the current month, but . . . [the landlord] desires me to inform you that she is not willing for you to continue on a month to month basis, but she will rent year to year.

"Please arrange to sign a lease for a year or remove your property from the premises and restore the premises to its former condition prior to the lease."

Nothing further was heard from the tenant until April 16, 1956, when the landlord received a check for the rent from April 20, 1956 to May 20, 1956. In the letter accompanying the check the tenant stated that it would not continue to lease the property beyond May 20, 1956. Therein the tenant also stated that there had not been a renewal of the "previous agreement". On the same day, April 16, 1956, the landlord's attorney wrote to the tenant enclosing the bill for the ground rent which the tenant was obliged to pay under the original lease. The attorney added:

"I have heretofore notified you that . . . [the landlord] is not willing to rent this property from month to month but must be from year to year so that if you are not out of there immediately and have not moved your equipment we shall consider that you are taking it for another year under the same terms or I shall have to issue ejectment proceedings, whichever we find most advantageous to us.

"You must understand that . . . [the landlord] does not wish to lose any of her rights in the property by letting you stay there without a lease and it is my duty to protect her in this respect."

On April 20, 1956, the tenant replied to the attorney, stating that it would send $30 in payment of six months' ground rent to the owner of the reversion. On April 25, 1956, the attorney wrote to the tenant that:

> "Inasmuch as you have gone over two months since the termination of the lease, I believe that under the law you have automatically renewed the lease for another term of year to year."

The tenant countered on April 27, 1956, by stating that it would vacate on May 20, 1956, but once again, on May 2, 1956, the attorney for the landlord insisted that the lease had been "automatically renewed . . . for a period of a year on the same terms."

This suit was brought to recover the rent claimed to be due for the months beginning May 21, 1956, and June 21, 1956, respectively, on the theory that the tenant was holding over under an implied lease for one year beginning March 21, 1956, and ending March 20, 1957, since it remained on the premises after March 20, 1956, until May 15, 1956. The landlord further contended in the alternative that the tenant continued to occupy the premises after May 15, 1956, but the trial court rejected this contention as not being supported by the evidence, finding as a fact that the tenant had vacated on May 15, 1956. However, the trial court accepted the landlord's implied lease theory and awarded her a judgment for two months' rent and costs.

Estates from year to year are a class of estates at will, from which they originated. Such estates may endure for one or more years, and are now terminable in Baltimore City at the end of thirty days' notice expiring at that period of the year at which the tenancy commenced, or that period fixed by the parties for the tenancy to end. The tenancy is created by express agreement or by implication. A peculiar form of this tenancy occurs where a tenant for years holds over after the expiration of the term, and the landlord accepts rent accruing after such expiration. The *provisions and covenants* of the original lease, so far as they are consistent with a yearly holding, *continue*, and the parties are mutually bound by them. Venable, Real Property, p. 60. And see Hall v. Myers, 1876, 43 Md. 446, in which it was held that where property is rented for a term of years, at an annual rent, and the tenant remains in possession after the expiration of the original term of renting, paying rent therefor at the rate agreed upon when he took possession of the property, he is to be regarded as a tenant from year to year.

However, the general rule is that a tenant who has remained after the expiration of the term is not a tenant holding over, and thus liable for a full year's rent, if such tenant has remained *with the express or tacit consent* of the landlord while the parties negotiate for a new lease. But the mere existence of negotiations is not sufficient to relieve the tenant from liability if the landlord has not actually consented to the holding over. Of course, as stated, if the parties are actually negotiating for a new lease at the time the prior lease expired, and the tenant remains in possession pending such negotiations, with either the express or tacit consent of the landlord, the landlord would be estopped from thereafter treating the tenant as holding over for another term on the same conditions as before. But in order for negotiations to exist there must be two parties to consider the matter. If one of them is *not negotiating* when the term ends, then surely there has been a cessation of negotiations.

Stated otherwise, the landlord is entitled to treat the tenant *as a tenant holding over* for another term of one year unless the tenant has definitely established one of two circumstances: either (i) that the landlord *consented* to the tenant remaining in the premises on a month-to-month basis, or some other specified time, for a temporary period, or (ii) that the parties were *actually engaged in negotiations* as to a renewal of the lease when the previous term ended. We think it is clear that the tenant failed to prove either of the determining factors.

We are unable to hold, under any reasonable construction of the acts of the parties, including particularly the correspondence between them, that the landlord gave the tenant either express or implied consent to remain on the premises after the date of the expiration of the lease. Only three letters had passed between the parties prior to March 20, 1956: (i) the letter of December 8, 1955, in which the *tenant merely informed the landlord* of its purchase of the interest of the previous tenant; (ii) the letter of February 29, 1956, in which the *tenant confirmed an offer* to pay the landlord a lower rental for a new five-year lease; and (iii) the letter of March 12, 1956, in which the *landlord flatly rejected* the offer of the tenant by informing it that she did not wish to rent her property for less than she had been receiving. There was no suggestion or intimation in that letter that she was willing to either bargain or negotiate further. Nor is there anything in that letter that should have led the tenant to believe that the landlord was consenting to its remaining in the premises until a new lease could be negotiated or until the bargaining therefor had terminated either one way or another.

The tenant insists that the existence of "negotiations" led it to believe that it could hold over for that purpose. The weakness of this theory, which makes it untenable, is that it would permit a tenant, who blithely writes a letter to the landlord offering a lower rental for a renewal lease, to remain on the premises after the expiration date with impunity. Under such circumstances, even if the landlord rejected the offer, the tenant could successfully defend by asserting that it was not a tenant holding over, but was simply engaging in negotiations. In the case at bar, even if actual negotiations had been in progress before the expiration of the lease, such negotiations were obviously unsuccessful and were abandoned. Certainly the existence of abandoned negotiations would not justify a tenant remaining on the premises, and it would be unreasonable to permit the tenant to dictate to the landlord the terms under which it would continue to remain after it had held over for several days, and then claim that such tactics constituted negotiations still in progress. That is precisely what the tenant did in its letter of March 23, 1956.

The case of Tonkel v. Riteman, [163 Miss. 216] cited by the tenant, is cogent authority for the position taken by the landlord. In that case, during the month preceding the expiration of the lease, the tenant informed the agent of the landlord that he wanted a reduction in the rent or else he would hold the premises only from month to month. The agent made no agreement one way or the other, promising only to discuss the matter with the landlord. No further negotiations were held, and the tenant remained in possession after the expiration of the term. The language of the Court is particularly appropriate to the instant case:

> "It is immaterial that the tenant may have notified the landlord that he will not renew the lease, or that he will remain only for a lesser period than that of the original lease or that he will pay a lesser amount in rent, . . . unless the landlord thereupon consents that the holding over shall be upon new or different terms, or unless the equivalent of consent shall arise out of the fact that the tenant has remained in possession pending negotiations for a new lease. . . . And in order that the negotiations shall be fairly and justly the equivalent of, or a substitute for, consent, the negotiations . . . must be actual and substantial . . ., not mere suggestions or requests or demands therefor or tentative approaches thereto, but upon which there has been no actual or substantial entry and upon which there has been no commitment that the landlord will in fact enter. . . . Such negotiations must amount to more than a request for the consideration of new terms on the side of the tenant and the promise by the agent without any further commitment to refer the question to the landlord on the other, ... The conversation between the tenant and the agent in respect to a new lease had not brought the transaction into such a state of progress as that it may be considered as having attained to the dignity of negotiations." [163 Miss. 216, 141 So. 344.] . . .

Finally, we cannot hold that the trial court was clearly wrong in finding that the landlord had not committed herself to a month-to-month lease by reason of the letter of March 29, 1956, and the acceptance of a month's rent. We think there is no persuasive evidence that a *new* lease from month to month was substituted for the implied lease which arose as a result of the tenant holding over after the expiration of the *old* lease which expired on March 20, 1956. In all of the correspondence there is not the slightest indication that the landlord would consent to anything but a renewal of the old written lease from year to year or the execution of a new written lease embodying precisely the same terms and conditions as were in the old lease, and there is nothing in the record to refute this. The fact that the landlord wanted and kept insisting upon either a renewal of the old or the execution of a new written lease would not be fatal to her right to claim under the implied lease.

By operation of law, the tenant holding over became a trespasser, in the sense of being wrongfully in possession, or a tenant from year to year at the election of the landlord, regardless of the wishes of the tenant. But in this State it is doubtful that a landlord is required to make a prompt election. The substance of the rule as expressed in Tiffany, Real Property, Sec. 175, p. 281 (3d ed.1939), and other authorities, is to the effect that the landlord has the option to treat the tenant as *wrongfully* retaining possession or as *rightly* doing so. However, as we pointed out in the Fetting case, 160 Md. at page 53, 152 A. at page 435: "This rule does not seem to have been expressly adopted in this jurisdiction." The fact that the tenant sent a check for one month's rent after the crucial date, proposing that it be accepted as a tenant from month-to-month does not alter the situation. The landlord never agreed to the proposal, so there was no substitution of a new lease for the implied lease which arose by operation of law, nor was there any alteration in the terms and conditions of the then existing implied lease. While it is true that the landlord, in accepting the check, did not at that time expressly elect to treat the tenant as a tenant holding over, it is clear that she definitely declined the tenant's proposal. For this reason we think the acceptance of the check, which was in the exact amount the landlord was entitled to receive for a month's rent under the old lease and from a *tenant holding over* under the implied lease for another year, did not bar her recovery of subsequent installments. The landlord demanded that the tenant "sign a lease for a year or remove . . . [its] property from the premises." Subsequently, she threatened ejectment proceedings if the tenant did not vacate immediately, but at the same time she stated that she reserved the right to hold the tenant from year to year or to eject it, whichever was "most advantageous to her". Still later, she informed the tenant that it had "automatically renewed the lease for another term of year to year." We think the landlord was not barred from subsequently making the election to hold the tenant under the implied lease after her previous demand and ultimatum had been declined and ignored, and the tenant continued to remain in the premises. Moreover, we think it is a persuasive indication that the tenant must have had some doubt that it was not a tenant from month to month in that it paid one-half of the yearly ground rent when it became due.

Even if it is assumed that the acceptance by the landlord of a month's rent constituted tacit consent that the tenant could remain on the premises pending negotiations for a new written lease or a further extension of the old one, it is clear that such negotiations finally ceased on April 16, 1956, yet the tenant continued to remain on the premises until it saw fit to vacate.

Since we have decided that the tenant was *a tenant holding over* for the period of one year from March 21, 1956, to March 20, 1957, it is not necessary for us to decide in this case whether the tenant *completely* vacated the demised premises on May 15, 1956. In fact there is nothing more before us to decide. Apparently, the lower court did not pass directly upon the question of partial occupancy except to say that the tenant vacated on May 15, 1956.

The judgment of the lower court should be affirmed.

Judgment affirmed, the appellant to pay the costs.

BRUNE, C.J., and PRESCOTT, J., dissent.

PRESCOTT, Judge (dissenting).

I do not wish any one to think that I disagree with the principles of law as they are so clearly enunciated by Judge HORNEY in his brilliant majority opinion. It is the treatment of the facts and their effect that prevent my concurrence. These facts, as related in the majority opinion, seem clearly to demonstrate that the parties had begun, and were conducting, negotiations having as their object a renewal of the lease—both sides, legitimately, attempting to obtain advantageous terms. The appellant and its predecessors had leased the property since 1947; the original lease had been extended *three* successive terms by written agreements; the tenant wrote the appellee's attorney as early as December 8, 1955, concerning the lease; and verbal and written negotiations before March 20, 1956, the expiration date of the lease, followed. *Three days* after the expiration date, the tenant wrote to the landlord the first letter quoted in the majority opinion. In it, the tenant specifically stated the parties were negotiating for a new lease and offered to continue on the previous rental basis from month to month until such time as the negotiations were successful or broke down. A check for one month's rent was enclosed. Within a week, the landlord's attorney replied. The letter did not deny that negotiations were being conducted by the parties; nor did it make any claim that the tenant was holding over under a lease imposed by law for a year. On the contrary, it explicitly stated the check was *accepted* for the current month's rent and then went on to say, the landlord "desires me to inform you that she is not willing for you to *continue on a month to month basis*, but she will rent year to year." It is extremely difficult to comprehend how the tenant could "continue" on a month to month basis, if it never occupied that status, as the majority opinion holds. It was not until April 16, 1956, that any claim was made that the tenant was holding over under a new lease imposed by law. The tenant took the position, which seems proper especially when its letter so stated, that, upon the acceptance of its check for one month's rent, it became a tenant from month to month, and, in order to terminate this tenancy, it must give the landlord thirty days' notice, which it did. This made the expiration date May 20, 1956. The rent was paid in full until that time, and the tenant properly vacated the premises by that date. The above facts seem to make it clear the tenant was not only remaining in possession of the property with the tacit, but the express, consent of the landlord. She was anxious, as she had done before, to obtain a written lease for a year upon favorable terms. The dilapidated condition of the property rendered it particularly desirable for her to lease to some one in such a business as that conducted by the appellant. For these reasons, I think the appellant should have prevailed.

BRUNE, C.J., has authorized me to say he concurs in this opinion.

QUESTIONS

What were Donnelly's likely objectives between February 23, 1956, when it first proposed a new lease on different terms, and March 20, 1956, when the existing lease expired? What were Flaccomio's likely objectives during this period? Representing Donnelly, what steps would you have suggested it take in order to achieve these objectives without exposing itself to a new one-year lease commitment on the prevailing terms? For example, how might Donnelly have replied to the March 12 letter from Flaccomio's lawyer in order to keep at least the appearance of negotiations alive through March 20? Would a new offer—say $1,000 per year for a six-year term—have kept the negotiations alive? Would it have been too risky to write a letter saying, "We will stay on unless you seek to terminate the negotiations through an action for eviction"? What, if anything, could Flaccomio have done to dispel even the appearance that negotiations were continuing through this period?

What were Donnelly's likely objectives during the period between March 20, 1956, when its lease expired, and May 15, 1956, when it quit the premises? What were Flaccomio's likely objectives during this period? Representing Donnelly, what steps would you have suggested it take in order to achieve its objectives without exposing itself to a new one-year lease commitment? Courts in a handful of states will subject a holdover tenant to a new term on the theory that the tenant's continued possession constitutes an implied offer for a new term that the landlord may accept through action or inaction. Most states reject the implied contract theory and will impose a new term on the holdover as a matter of law. What could Donnelly have done that it did not do in order to avoid the effect of either rule? Note that Flaccomio at no time instituted eviction proceedings; that her lawyer's March 30 letter contained only a mild request ("Please arrange to sign a lease for a year or remove your property from the premises . . ."); and that her lawyer's April 16 letter only rattled the sword (". . . or I shall have to issue ejectment proceedings").

Would it be accurate to say that, at least through April 16, Donnelly was a tenant at sufferance and not, as the court concluded, a tenant for a new one-year term? Was it in Flaccomio's perceived best interest to treat Donnelly as a tenant at sufferance during this period? Recall that a new one-year term would bind Donnelly *and* Flaccomio. Might the landlord during this period have been trying to keep *her* options open by not committing herself to Donnelly for a new one-year term? Representing Flaccomio, what different steps, if any, would you have taken to achieve this object?

Representing Donnelly after May 15, 1956, and preparing for litigation, what arguments would you have made on its behalf? Is it plausible that Donnelly's post-March 20 tenancy at sufferance was quickly transformed by the parties' correspondence into a tenancy at will? "At common law the owner had the option of evicting the tenant at sufferance or of converting his occupancy into another form of tenancy. The same rule generally prevails today. The nature of the new tenancy may be at will, from month to month, from year to year, or it may be a renewal of the original term, depending on the circumstances. Ordinarily the owner's option is to renew for the length of the original period. While it is true that a tenant at sufferance can hardly be called a tenant at all, and that his holding is without right of any kind, yet if a landlord permits him to remain, and especially if he receives rent of him, he then becomes a tenant at will . . ." 3 G. Thompson, Commentaries on the Modern Law of Real Property 63–64 (1959).

2. TENANT RIGHTS AND REMEDIES

a. THE RIGHT TO POSSESSION

DIEFFENBACH v. McINTYRE

Supreme Court of Oklahoma, 1952.
208 Okl. 163, 254 P.2d 346.

BINGAMAN, Justice.

This action was brought by plaintiff Mildred E. McIntyre against the defendant Nevin J. Dieffenbach, seeking to recover rental paid, damages for repairs made upon a building leased by her from the defendant, and anticipated profits lost by her because of her removal from the building. The trial court submitted the cause to the jury as to the rental paid and cost of repairs, but refused to permit the introduction of evidence as to loss of anticipated profits. Defendant appeals from the judgment against him rendered on a verdict by the jury in favor of plaintiff, and plaintiff cross-appeals from the refusal of the court to permit her to introduce evidence as to loss of anticipated profits.

Undisputed facts are that plaintiff, prior to the time she leased the building from defendant, was operating a beauty parlor in one of the downtown buildings in Tulsa; that she was required to vacate the rooms used by her in said building on or before May 1, 1946, and that during the month of April she sought to find another place in which to conduct her beauty parlor. She got in touch with defendant, who was attorney in fact for his mother-in-law, who owned a building farther removed from the business section of Tulsa, and sought to lease a portion thereof from him for a term of years. The transaction finally resulted in her leasing the entire building, which consisted of four units of several rooms each, two upstairs and two downstairs. She installed her beauty parlor in one of the downstairs units, but upon failure to obtain the possession of the entire building removed therefrom to other quarters on or about the 1st of August, 1946.

Plaintiff testified that at or prior to the time she signed the lease on the building, which lease ran for a term of three years at a rental of $500 per month, she was assured by defendant that he had raised the rent on the other three units in the building from $50 to $150 per month, and had given thirty day notices requiring them to remove, and that they could not possibly remain there and pay the rental which he had fixed as the new rate on the property. Thereafter, she testified, he informed her that he could not give her possession until the 1st of June, and she made arrangements to stay in her old quarters for another month. On the 1st of June, when she was ready to move in, two of the units in the building were still occupied, and she hesitated to move in, but upon assurance from defendant to her attorney that he would obtain possession of the two occupied units on or before June 7th, she moved into the unit which she proposed to use as a beauty parlor. When the lease was signed she paid defendant one month's rent of $500, and she expended additional sums in fixing up the unit occupied by her. She testified that defendant failed to oust the tenants from the two units occupied by them, although one of them subsequently left, and that the occupant of the other unit offered her the regular $50 per month rental, but she refused to accept the same, telling them that arrangements for payments should be made with defendant. This unit was still occupied when she left the building and the tenants testified that they thereafter paid defendant the regular rental of $50 per month and were still occupying the unit and paying such rental at the time of the trial.

Plaintiff's attorney testified that when he found out the defendant could not deliver possession on the 1st of June, he talked to him with a view of revising the lease to include only a portion of the building, but that defendant assured him that he would have all of the tenants out by June 7th and that it would be all right for plaintiff to move in.

The defendant denied all these statements. Therefore the evidence being conflicting the question was properly submitted to the jury by the trial court and their verdict in favor of plaintiff was supported by competent evidence.

When plaintiff sought to introduce testimony as to the profits she made in her former location and the profits she made while in defendant's building, and the drop in her profits when she removed to another building, the trial court sustained defendant's objection thereto, and did not permit that testimony to go to the jury.

Defendant in his brief asserts that the major and paramount question for decision is whether as a matter of law the defendant, when he executed the lease of April 30th, transferred to the plaintiff the legal right to possession, and was under no further obligation, or whether he was obligated to go further and place the plaintiff in actual possession of the property on June 1st. In arguing this question he asserts that the lease transferred the legal right to possession to the plaintiff, which was all he was required to do; that the occupants holding over after the term of their rental periods had expired by reason of his notices to them were trespassers, or tenants at sufferance of plaintiff, and that he was not required to place the plaintiff in possession as against them. In support of this contention, which is argued in several sub-heads, he cites Brown v. International Land Co., 29 Okl. 341, 116 P. 799; Holden v. Tidwell, 37 Okl. 553, 133 P. 54, 49 L.R.A.,N.S., 369, and other similar cases. We do not agree with this contention. An examination of the cases cited in support thereof discloses that they are not applicable to the fact situation herein involved. In none of them was the question of the failure of the lessor to place the lessee in actual possession at the beginning of the term involved, but rather they involved trespassing committed upon the property subsequent to the taking of possession thereof by the lessee.

Defendant calls attention to the fact that the so-called American rule as to the placing of a lessee in possession required only that he be placed in legal possession, while the other or English rule holds that there is an implied covenant to place the lessee in actual possession, see, Hannan v. Dusch, 154 Va. 356, 153 S.E. 824, 70 A.L.R. 141, and asserts that the American rule is generally prevalent in the United States. This state, among numerous others, has followed the other or so-called English rule, and holds that the lessor is required to place the lessee in actual possession of the property. King v. Coombs, 36 Okl. 396, 122 P. 181; Flannagan v. Dickerson, 103 Okl. 206, 229 P. 552. In these cases we recognized and adhered to the rule holding that the lease contained an implied obligation to place the lessee in actual possession. In Hannan v. Dusch, supra, the court cited and discussed numerous cases which adhered to either one rule or the other, and in the note to that case a number of these cases are analyzed. The cases listed in the opinion, 154 Va. 356, 153 S.E. 824,

70 A.L.R. on page 142, show that a large majority of the states follow the so-called English rule adopted and followed by this court in the cases above cited, and in Stewart v. Murphy, 95 Kan. 421, 148 P. 609, it is stated that by the great weight of authority the covenant to put the lessee in possession at the beginning of the term is implied, citing numerous cases.

It follows that in the instant case the lessee was entitled to be put in possession of the entire building by the lessor on or before June 1, 1946, and the failure of the defendant to so place her in possession, or at least to place her in possession June 7, at which time he assured her attorney she would receive possession of the entire building, was a breach of the lease.

Defendant contends that the breach was only a partial breach since it did not interfere with the operation of the beauty parlor by plaintiff, but we think it was a complete breach, since it forced the plaintiff either to bring ouster proceedings against the tenants holding over, or to continue to pay $500 a month rent for a portion of the premises only.

Defendant further claims that the trial court erred in giving to the jury instructions Nos. 3 and 4. By instruction No. 3, the jury was told that if they found by a preponderance of the evidence that plaintiff entered into possession of two units of the leased premises on June 1st, with the promise and agreement on the part of defendant that if she would take possession of said units on that date he would place her in possession of the remaining units on June 7th or 8th, and he failed to do so, the defendant committed an actionable breach of the contract and their verdict should be for plaintiff. By instruction No. 4, they were told that if they found for the plaintiff, her damages should be for the sum of $500, the first month's rental, admittedly paid by her to the defendant on April 30th, and also such additional damages as would compensate her for moving into the building and remodeling the part which she used for the beauty parlor, not to exceed the sum of $574.95, claimed by plaintiff for such expenses. Plaintiff contends that the true measure of damages due a tenant on failure of the landlord to deliver possession is the difference between the rental agreed upon and the actual rental value of the property, together with special damages incurred by the lessee or tenant in preparing to occupy the premises, citing Anderson v. Hodges, 187 Okl. 43, 100 P.2d 853; Dills v. Calloway, 175 Okl. 395, 52 P.2d 707, and other similar cases. However, in these cases the tenants had paid no rental and had not moved into the property in reliance upon any representation of defendant that the defendant would place them in the undisturbed possession thereof. Defendant also asserts that the trial court erred in refusing to give the jury several requested instructions upon his theory of the case as heretofore outlined in this opinion. We have examined the instructions given and the requested instructions refused and hold that the trial court properly instructed the jury, and that it did not err in refusing to give the instructions requested by defendant.

Plaintiff in her cross-appeal contends that the court erred in refusing to permit her to present to the jury for its consideration the profits made by her while operating in her previous location, the profits made by her while located in defendant's building, and the loss of profits occasioned by her removal therefrom. We are unable to agree with this contention.

While it is true that we have in numerous cases held that the loss of profits in an established business is a proper element of damages, the business of plaintiff in her former uptown location could not be used, we think, to measure the damages sustained by her, because of her removal from the buildings of defendant. She occupied the building of defendant only two months, and that in our opinion was not a sufficient length of time to constitute her business there an established business. In 25 C.J.S., Damages, § 42b, p. 518, it is stated that in cases where the loss of anticipated profits is claimed as an element of damages, the business claimed to have been interrupted must be an established one, and it must be shown that it has been successfully conducted for such a length of time and has such a trade established that the profits therefrom are reasonably ascertainable. In our judgment the business of defendant, after her removal from her uptown location to defendant's building, had not been conducted for such length of time as to render it an established business, and the trial court properly refused to permit evidence of her claimed losses to go to the jury.

It follows that the judgment for plaintiff as rendered by the lower court must be and hereby is affirmed.

In her brief plaintiff calls attention to the fact that a supersedeas bond has been filed by defendant and asks for judgment on the supersedeas bond. Judgment is therefore rendered against Julia LeBus and Kay L. Dieffenbach, sureties on the supersedeas bond, for $1,152.92, with interest at the rate of six percentum from October 26, 1949, and for costs.

HALLEY, V.C.J., and WELCH, CORN, GIBSON, DAVISON, JOHNSON and O'NEAL, JJ., concur.

ADRIAN v. RABINOWITZ, 116 N.J.L. 586, 186 A. 29, 31 (1936), HEHER, J.: The English rule so-called, is on principle much the better one. It has the virtue, ordinarily, of effectuating the common intention of the parties—to give actual and exclusive possession of the premises to the lessee on the day fixed for the commencement of the term. This is what the lessee generally bargains for; and it is the thing the lessor undertakes to give. Such being the case, there is no warrant for placing upon the lessee, without express stipulation to that effect, the burden of ousting, at his own expense, the tenant wrongfully holding over, or the trespasser in possession of the premises without color of right at the commencement of the term; and thus to impose upon him who is not in possession of the evidence the burden of establishing the respective rights and duties of the lessor and the possessor of the lands inter se, as well as the consequences of the delay incident to the adjudication of the controversy, and the obligation to pay rent during that period. As was said by Baron Vaughan in Coe v. Clay, supra: "He who lets agrees to give possession, and not merely to give a chance of a law suit." This doctrine is grounded in reason and logic. The underlying theory is that the parties contemplated, as an essential term of their undertaking, without which the lease would not have been made, that the lessor should, at the beginning of the term, have the premises open to the entry and exclusive possession of the lessee. This is certainly the normal course of dealing, and, in the absence of stipulation to the contrary, is to be regarded as the parties' understanding of the lessor's covenant to deliver possession of the demised premises at the time prescribed for the commencement of the term.

HANNAN v. DUSCH, 154 Va. 356, 373, 153 S.E. 824, 830 (1930), PRENTIS, C.J.: Mr. Freeman supports the American rule with the calm cogency which should be convincing. He summarizes this conclusion thus: "The gist of the reason advanced in favor of the English rule is that under the American rule, in case the demised premises are in the possession of a person wrongfully holding over or of some trespasser at the beginning of the tenant's term, and the tenant is forced to resort to litigation to oust the one in such possession, all he obtains by his lease is a chance for a lawsuit. It is conceded that under the English rule it becomes the duty of the tenant to maintain his possession at his own expense after once being placed in possession. It is also conceded that if the premises are withheld by the landlord or someone holding a paramount title, that the tenant has a right of recovery against the landlord for a breach of his covenant of quiet possession. It must be conceded also that if the premises are withheld from the possession of the tenant by reason of the wrongful act of a trespasser or of some former tenant who wrongfully holds over, the tenant has a right to recover his damages from such person. In other words, the tenant is protected, no matter in what manner the possession is withheld from him. It is, of course, true that the tenant will suffer delay in obtaining possession if he is forced to sue for it, but so would the landlord under the same circumstances. It is not, we believe, customary for a person who contracts in respect to any subject to insure the other party against lawsuits. Indeed, both the landlord and tenant have a right to presume that a former tenant will vacate at the end of his term, and that no one will unlawfully prevent the new tenant from going into possession. To sue or be sued is a privilege or misfortune which may occur to anyone. We believe that the American, or New York rule as it is sometimes called, under which it is held that there is no implied covenant that the premises shall be open to entry by the tenant at the time fixed for the beginning of the term, but merely that the tenant shall have a right to the possession at that time is more in accord with substantial justice to both the landlord and tenant, and in accordance with the general course of business dealings in respect to insurance against the chances of a lawsuit in a court of justice."

There are some underlying fundamental considerations. Any written lease, for a specific term, signed by the lessor, and delivered, is like a deed signed, sealed, and delivered by the grantor. This lease for fifteen years is, and is required to be, by deed. It is a conveyance. During the term the tenant is substantially the owner of the property, having the right of possession, dominion, and control over it. Certainly, as a general rule, the lessee must protect himself against trespassers or other wrongdoers who disturb his possession. It is conceded by those who favor the English rule that, should the possession of the tenant be wrongfully disturbed the second day of the term, or after he has once taken possession, then there is no implied covenant on the part of his landlord to protect him from the torts of others. The English rule seems to have been applied only where the possession is disturbed on the first day, or, perhaps more fairly expressed, where the tenant is prevented from taking possession on the first day of his term; but what is the substantial difference between invading the lessee's right of possession on the first or a later day? To apply the English rule you must imply a covenant on the part of the landlord to protect the tenant from the tort of another, though he has entered into no such covenant. This seems to be a unique exception, an exception which stands alone in implying a contract of insurance on the part of the lessor to save his tenant from all the consequences of the flagrant wrong of another person. Such an obligation is so unusual and the prevention of such a tort so impossible as to make it certain, we think, that it should always rest upon an express contract.

NOTES

1. The Restatement (Second), of Property, Landlord and Tenant (1976), offers five rationales for its adoption of the so-called English rule that every lease contains an implied covenant that the landlord will give the tenant actual possession of the premises at the outset of the lease term:

> (1) The landlord knows, or should know, the status of the possession of the leased property better than the tenant in the period before the date the tenant is entitled to possession.

> (2) The landlord knows, or should know, better than the tenant whether a person in possession of the leased property before the date the tenant is entitled to possession is properly or improperly on the leased property.

(3) Before the date the tenant is entitled to possession of the leased property, the landlord is the only one of the two who can evict a person improperly in possession of the leased property.

(4) In the situation where the person in possession of the leased property is entitled to be there until the date the tenant is entitled to possession, the case of the possible holdover prior tenant, the landlord is the only one of the two who has an opportunity to get some assurance that the prior tenant will not hold over.

(5) The tenant will have received less than he bargained for if he must go forward with the lease and bear the cost of legal proceedings to clear the way for his entry on the leased property.

Section 6.2 comment a.

Do you agree? What counter-arguments can you muster in favor of the American rule? Do the Restatement's assumptions respecting the landlord's superior access to information correspond with the realities of all types of lease negotiations? Consider, for example, the relative positions of landlord and tenant under a fifty-year lease obligating tenant, a major department store chain, to build and occupy a store on the leased premises.

2. The covenant created by the English rule, and the more limited covenant created by the American rule, are *implied* covenants and can be overriden by the parties' express agreement. Does this suggest that the real question in these cases is not which rule—English or American—better allocates the risk that a third party will hold over, but, rather, which better allocates the burden, during lease negotiations, of proposing a lease provision that deals with the risk? Should the burden be made to differ depending on whether a residential or a commercial lease is involved?

3. According to one writer who has closely canvassed the field, a majority of states presently follow the English rule and imply a covenant that the landlord will give the tenant physical possession at the beginning of the lease term. Weissenberger, The Landlord's Duty to Deliver Possession: The Overlooked Reform, 46 U.Cin.L.Rev. 937 (1977). Support for the English rule is not, however, overwhelming. By Professor Weissenberger's count, at least eleven states follow the American rule, another eleven have not addressed the issue, and six "have remained neutral when faced with a holdover tenant situation." *Id.* at 938, n. 8. Indeed, some commentators even claim that the American rule is the majority position in the country. See, for example, J. Cribbet, Principles of the Law of Property 204 (2d ed.1975).

Does the modern emphasis on the contract aspect of leases have any implications for the further acceptance, or rejection, of the English rule?

4. Generally in English rule jurisdictions the tenant who has been denied possession may unilaterally rescind the lease—so long as he has given prior notice to the landlord and immediately vacates any

part of the premises possessed. In addition to any rental improperly paid, the rescinding tenant is entitled to recover loss of bargain damages (typically the difference between reserved rental and the cost of other comparable premises) and consequential damages (reasonable expenditures made by the tenant before the landlord's default, relocation expenses and, if the tenant is an established commercial enterprise, lost profits). If the tenant elects not to rescind, he can recover damages measured by the difference between the value of the lease without the default and with the default, and consequential damages including lost profits, the cost of substitute premises during the period of default and, in some states, the expense of proceedings to remove the tenant holding over.

The wronged tenant must choose his remedies carefully. The tenant who elects to rescind faces several risks: that a court will consider the landlord's default to be insufficiently material to justify rescission; that the court will find the tenant's notice to have been insufficiently timely or explicit; or that damages will fail to make the tenant whole since, in the usual short-term tenancy, the lease will have no value and other damages may be considered speculative or the result of the tenant's failure to mitigate. With the benefit of hindsight, do you think that the tenant in *Dieffenbach* took the best remedial route? What relief would the tenant have received, if, instead of rescinding, she had honored the lease and continued in possession of part of the premises?

5. Model and uniform state acts offer two approaches to the allocation of responsibility for the removal of holdover tenants. The Model Residential Landlord-Tenant Code, published by the American Bar Foundation in 1969, adopts the English rule for residential tenancies, requiring the landlord to "put the tenant into full possession," and also allows the tenant to proceed directly against the holdover. §§ 2–201, 2–202(3). The Uniform Residential Landlord-Tenant Act, approved by the National Conference of Commissioners on Uniform State Laws in 1972, and endorsed by the American Bar Association in 1974, takes a less forceful approach. Providing that, "at the commencement of the term a landlord shall deliver possession of the premises to the tenant in compliance with the rental agreement," section 2.103 leaves some doubt as to whether it adopts the English rule, the American rule, or neither. See generally, Report of the Subcomm. on the Model Landlord-Tenant Act of the Comm. on Leases, Proposed Uniform Residential Landlord and Tenant Act, 8 Real Prop., Prob. & Trust J. 104 (1973).

At least one state has adopted the Model Act and several others have adopted the Uniform Act. Still other states have taken distinctive approaches of their own. New York, which once followed the American rule, changed course in 1962. N.Y.—McKinney's Real Prop. Law § 223–a provides "In the absence of an express provision to the contrary, there shall be implied in every lease of real property a condition that the lessor will deliver possession at the beginning of the term. In the event of breach of such implied condition the lessee shall have the right to rescind the lease and to recover the consideration paid. Such right shall not be deemed inconsistent with any right of action he may have to recover damages."

b. The Right To Quiet Enjoyment

DYETT v. PENDLETON, 8 Cow. 727, 728–731 (1826): ["The plea is, that before any part of the rent claimed became due, the lessor entered upon his lessee, evicted him, and kept him out of possession during the residue of the term.

Upon the trial, the tenant offered to prove that about the month of February, 1820, to the 1st day of which month the rent had been paid, the lessor from time to time introduced and kept in the house of which the demised premises were a part, lewd women and men for the purpose of prostitution; that the lessee was disturbed by the noise, indecent and riotous conduct of the lessor and those he so introduced; that these practices rendered the house infamous, so that it was disreputable to be one of its inhabitants; and that in consequence, the lessee felt himself compelled to leave the premises, and did leave them about the 1st of March, 1820, after which he did not return."] f

SPENCER, Senator: It seems to be conceded that the only plea which could be interposed by the defendant below, to let in the defence which he offered, if any would answer that purpose, was, that the plaintiff had entered in and upon the demised premises, and ejected and put out the defendant. Such a plea was filed; and it is contended on the one side, that it must be literally proved, and an actual entry and expulsion established: while on the other side it is insisted, that a constructive entry and expulsion is sufficient, and that the facts which tended to prove it, should have been left to the jury. . . . The agreement set forth in the plea, contains a covenant that the defendant shall have "peaceable, quiet and indisputable possession" of the premises. This is, in its nature, a condition precedent to the payment of rent; and whether the possession was peaceable and quiet, was clearly a question of fact for the jury. Such conduct of the lessor as was offered to be proved in this case, went directly to that point; and without saying at present, whether it was or was not sufficient to establish a legal disturbance, it is enough that it tended to that end, and should have been received, subject to such advice as the judge might give to the jury.

The opinion of the supreme court proceeds upon the ground that there must be an actual physical eviction, to bar the plaintiffs; and in most of the cases cited, such eviction was proved; and all of them

---

f. Excerpted from the opinion of Senator Colden, 8 Cow. 738–739.

show that such is the form of the plea. But the forms of pleading given, and the cases cited, do not establish the principle on which the recovery of rent is refused, but merely furnish illustrations of that principle, and exemplifications of its application. The principle itself is deeper and more extensive than the cases. It is thus stated by Baron Gilbert, in his essay on rents, p. 145: "A rent is something given by way of retribution to the lessor, for the land demised by him to the tenant, and consequently the lessor's title to the rent is founded upon this: that the land demised, is enjoyed by the tenant during the term included in the contract; for the tenant can make no return for a thing he has not. If, therefore, the tenant be deprived of the thing letten, the obligation to pay the rent ceases, because such obligation has its force only from the consideration, which was the enjoyment of the thing demised." And from this principle, the inference is drawn, that the lessor is not entitled to recover rent in the following cases: 1st. If the lands demised be recovered by a third person, by a superior title, the tenant is discharged from the payment of rent after eviction by such recovery. 2d. If a part only of the lands be recovered by a third person, such eviction is a discharge only of so much of the rent as is in proportion to the value of the land evicted. 3d. If the lessor expel the tenant from the premises, the rent ceases. 4th. If the lessor expel the tenant from a part only of the premises, the tenant is discharged from the payment of the whole rent; and the reason for the rule why there shall be no apportionment of the rent in this case as well as in that of an eviction by a stranger, is, that it is the wrongful act of the lessor himself, "that no man may be encouraged to injure or disturb his tenant in his possession, whom, by the policy of the feudal law, he ought to protect and defend."

This distinction, which is as perfectly well settled as any to be found in our books, establishes the great principle that a tenant shall not be required to pay rent, even for the part of the premises which he retains, if he has been evicted from the other part by the landlord. As to the part retained, this is deemed such a disturbance, such an injury to its beneficial enjoyment, such a diminution of the consideration upon which the contract is founded, that the law refuses its aid to coerce the payment of any rent. Here, then, is a case where actual entry and physical eviction are not necessary to exonerate the tenant from the payment of rent; and if the principle be correct as applied to a part of the premises, why should not the same principle equally apply to the whole property demised, where there has been an obstruction to its beneficial enjoyment, and a diminution of the consideration of the contract, by the acts of the landlord, although those acts do not amount to a physical eviction? If physical eviction be not necessary in the one case, to discharge the rent of the part retained, why should it be essential in the other, to discharge the rent of the whole? If I have not deceived myself, the distinction referred to settles and recognizes the principle for which the plaintiff in error contends, that there may be a constructive eviction produced by the acts of the landlord.

BARASH v. PENNSYLVANIA TERMINAL REAL ESTATE CORP.

Court of Appeals of New York, 1970.
26 N.Y.2d 77, 308 N.Y.S.2d 649, 256 N.E.2d 707.

BREITEL, Judge.

Defendant landlord appeals from an affirmed order denying its motion to dismiss tenant's complaint for legal insufficiency. The allegations for this purpose are accepted as true.

The first cause of action, alleging a partial actual eviction, is to relieve tenant from payment of rent, and, notably, is not a claim for damages. The second is for reformation of the lease to conform to alleged prior oral agreements.

With respect to the first cause of action, the question is whether landlord's allegedly wrongful failure to supply a continuous flow of fresh air on evenings and weekends to offices leased by tenant constitutes a partial actual eviction relieving tenant from the payment of rent or, at most, a constructive eviction requiring the tenant to abandon the premises before he may be relieved of the duty to pay rent. Also at issue is whether grounds for reformation are pleaded by the second cause of action.

Plaintiff, a lawyer, alleges that on September 15, 1967, while the premises known as 2 Pennsylvania Plaza in New York City were being constructed, he entered into a written lease with defendant landlord for rental of office space to be used for the practice of law. Involved is a 29-story glass-enclosed, completely air-conditioned office building. Its windows are sealed and the supply and circulation of air inside the building is under the landlord's exclusive control.

Defendant landlord, through its authorized renting agents, had represented that the building would be open 24 hours a day, 7 days each week, to enable tenants and others to occupy the offices at all times. Prior to signing the lease, plaintiff inquired as to the manner in which air would be circulated "when the air-conditioning system was not in operation." He was informed, fraudulently he alleges, "that the offices in question would be constructed with a duct system, which would always provide a natural and continuous flow of air . . . [making] the offices . . . comfortable and usable at all evening hours and also on weekends, even when the air-conditioning and heating systems were not in operation." The tenant, on the basis of these representations, known by the landlord to be false, signed the lease.

The lease provides, in pertinent part: "As long as Tenant is not in default under any of the covenants of this lease Landlord shall furnish air cooling during the months of June, July, August and September on business days from 9 A.M. to 6 P.M. when in the judgment of the Landlord it may be required for the comfortable occupancy of the demised premises and at other times during business days and similar hours, ventilate the demised premises."

The lease also contains a general merger clause: "Landlord or Landlord's agents have made no representations or promises with respect to said building, the land upon which it is erected or the demised premises except as herein expressly set forth and no rights, easements or licenses are acquired by Tenant by implication or otherwise except as expressly set forth herein. The taking possession of the demised premises by Tenant shall be conclusive evidence, as against Tenant, that Tenant accepts the same, 'as is' and that said premises and the building of which the same form a part were in good and satisfactory condition at the time such possession was so taken."

Plaintiff tenant took possession on May 15, 1968 and that evening at 6:00 P.M. defendant "turned off all air" in the offices. By 7:00 P.M. the offices became "hot, stuffy, and unusable and uninhabitable". Upon protest the landlord refused to provide after hour ventilation unless paid for by the tenant at a rate of $25 per hour. The tenant refused to pay the reserved rent or the additional charge and brought the instant action. The landlord sought dispossession for the nonpayment. This was denied, but the tenant was directed to pay rent into court pending the outcome of the instant action.

The first cause of action, based on the unreformed lease, alleges a partial actual eviction. Even assuming that the leased premises became "hot, stuffy, and unusable and uninhabitable" so that no one was able to work or remain in the offices after 7:00 P.M., these allegations are insufficient, as a matter of law, to make out an actual eviction.

To be an eviction, constructive or actual, there must be a wrongful act by the landlord which deprives the tenant of the beneficial enjoyment or actual possession of the demised premises. Of course, the tenant must have been deprived of something to which he was entitled under or by virtue of the lease. A right to 24-hour ventilation cannot be established, in the absence of reformation of the lease, by alleging fraudulent representations concerning ventilation when the lease itself expressly limits ventilation rights.

But even if the lease were to be read to include the allegations concerning ventilation (the gravamen of the tenant's second cause of action in reformation), the facts alleged, and accepted as true, would still fall short of, and not constitute, an actual eviction.

An actual eviction occurs only when the landlord wrongfully ousts the tenant from physical possession of the leased premises. There must be a physical expulsion or exclusion. And where the tenant is ousted from a portion of the demised premises, the eviction is actual, even if only partial.

Thus, for example, where the landlord barred the tenant from entering the premises it has been held a partial actual eviction. Similarly, where the landlord changes the lock, or padlocks the door, there is an actual eviction.

On the other hand, constructive eviction exists where, although there has been no physical expulsion or exclusion of the tenant, the landlord's wrongful acts substantially and materially deprive the tenant of the beneficial use and enjoyment of the premises (City of New York v. Pike Realty Corp., 247 N.Y. 245, 160 N.E. 359). The tenant, however, must abandon possession in order to claim that there was a constructive eviction.

Thus, where the tenant remains in possession of the demised premises there can be no constructive eviction. It has been said to be inequitable for the tenant to claim substantial interference with the beneficial enjoyment of his property and remain in possession without payment of rent. In the case of actual eviction, even where the tenant is only partially evicted liability for all rent is suspended although the tenant remains in possession of the portion of the premises from which he was not evicted. In the leading case of Fifth Ave. Bldg. Co. v. Kernochan (221 N.Y. 370, 373, 117 N.E. 579, 580), the court stated: "We are dealing now with an eviction which is actual and not constructive. If such an eviction, though partial only, is the act of the landlord, it suspends the entire rent because the landlord is not permitted to apportion his own wrong."

This then presents the nub of the appeal. The tenant, who has not abandoned the premises, asserts that there has been an actual eviction, though partial only, thus permitting him to retain possession of the premises without liability for rent. To support this contention it is claimed that failure to supply fresh air constitutes actual eviction, if only, albeit, during the hours after 6:00 P.M. and on weekends.

There is no previous known reported case involving a like situation in a substantially sealed building. The resolution of this appeal turns therefore on the application of general principles to the novel complex of facts presented.

All that tenant suffered was a substantial diminution in the extent to which he could beneficially enjoy the premises. Although possibly more pronounced, tenant's situation is analogous to cases where there is a persistent offensive odor, harmful to health, arising from a noxious gas (Tallman v. Murphy, 120 N.Y. 345, 24 N.E. 716), an open sewer (Sully v. Schmitt, 147 N.Y. 248, 41 N.E. 514), or defective plumbing (Lathers v. Coates, 18 Misc. 231, 41 N.Y.S. 373 [App. Term]). The possible odor-producing causes are innumerable. In all such cases there has been held to be only a constructive eviction.

In the *Tallman* case (*supra*), which involved coal gas, the court stated: "In such a building as the one under consideration there is very much that remains under the charge and control of the landlord

. . . [I]f he persistently neglects them, and by reason of such neglect . . . his apartments are filled with gas or foul odors . . . and the apartments become unfit for occupancy, the tenant is deprived of the beneficial enjoyment thereof . . . and there is a constructive eviction" (*id.* 120 N.Y. at p. 352, 24 N.E. at p. 718).

Given these well-established rules, proper characterization of the instant failure to ventilate follows easily, assuming there be such duty under the lease as written, or as reformed to conform to the representations. The tenant has neither been expelled nor excluded from the premises, nor has the landlord seized a portion of the premises for his own use or that of another. He has, by his alleged wrongful failure to provide proper ventilation, substantially reduced the beneficial use of the premises.

As long as the tenant remains in possession it matters little whether he can remedy the situation by his independent action. Nor does it matter whether the proposed 24-hour use has become practically impossible. In City of New York v. Pike Realty Corp. (*supra*), the land was leased from the city for construction of a parking garage. The city, however, thereafter refused to give tenant a building permit. The court held this refusal "was at most a . . . constructive eviction" (*id.* 247 N.Y at p. 247, 160 N.E. at p. 360).

Tenant's reliance on Schulte Realty Co. v. Pulvino, 179 N.Y.S. 371 [App.Term, per Lehman, J.], which held that a tenant had suffered a partial actual eviction, is misplaced. The landlord, in that case, interfered with tenant's "easement" of light and air by allowing another to cover a large portion of an airshaft upon which tenant's windows opened. The court, relying on Adolphi v. Inglima, 130 N.Y.S. 130 [App.Term], held that the lease included a right to light and air from the shaftway, and that there was, therefore, a partial eviction. It was observed that there could be no constructive eviction because the premises had not been rendered untenantable. In the *Adolphi* case a landlord had sealed up a window on the tenant's premises, and it was said to justify a finding of a partial eviction. On the other hand, in Solomon v. Fantozzi, 43 Misc. 61, 86 N.Y.S. 754 [App.Term] the court held that blocking the ventilation of a water closet did not constitute a partial constructive eviction, let alone a partial actual eviction. The distinguishing feature of these cases, if indeed they be not anomalies, is that they deal with the destruction of an easement or appurtenance of light and air granted by the landlord. Here there is no claim to an appurtenant right to air external to the demised premises but rather the failure to provide an essential service within the demised premises, which failure traditionally constitutes a constructive eviction.

It would seem moreover, apart from or despite the cases last discussed, that interference with easements or appurtenances of light and air insofar as they diminish the tenant's beneficial enjoyment of the demised premises, constitutes a constructive and not an actual eviction. Thus in Two Rector St. Corp. v. Bein (226 App.Div. 73, 234

N.Y.S. 409) the substantial "diminution of light, air and view" constituted at most a constructive eviction requiring a surrender by the tenant.

Since the eviction, if any, is constructive and not actual, the tenant's failure to abandon the premises makes the first cause of action insufficient in law. The first cause of action, therefore, should have been dismissed.

Tenant, in his second cause of action for reformation, repeats all the allegations made in support of his first cause of action. He adds, however, that the lease as signed "does not reflect the actual and total agreement of/and between the parties, and the lease was incorrectly drawn regarding the defendant's representations and warranties as to the 'continuous flow of air' and 'usability of the said offices in the evenings and weekends'." He further alleges that these fraudulent representations induced the execution of the lease.

It is argued that because of the fraud of the landlord plus the unilateral mistake of the tenant, an agreement intended to be a part of the written lease was omitted. To be sure, this constitutes the classic case for reformation. The presence of the general merger clause does not bar the introduction of the parol evidence of fraudulent representations in actions to rescind a contract. So, too, a general merger clause does not bar an action to reform a contract, which by reason of fraud and mistake does not contain the agreement of the parties.

The rule of Fogelson v. Rackfay Constr. Co. (300 N.Y. 334, 340, 90 N.E.2d 881, 883) is inapplicable since in that case there was no allegation of fraud. Also, since the merger clause in this case is a general one, the limited exception in cases of specific merger clauses does not control.

However, the fatal defect in the second cause of action is tenant's failure to allege that there was a unilateral mistake on his part. All that is pleaded is that "the lease was incorrectly drawn". It does not appear from this ambiguous and conclusory allegation that the pleader is alleging unilateral mistake, an essential element in an action for reformation based on another's fraud. So critical a fact should be made express and clear if it indeed is present in the action. Therefore, this cause of action should be dismissed.

Although it is necessary to dismiss the complaint because neither cause of action is legally sufficient, plaintiff may wish to move for permission to replead. The record does not reveal that plaintiff sought leave to replead in the event that the motion to dismiss was granted. Consequently, plaintiff may not be granted leave to replead based on the present state of the record.

Accordingly, the order of the Appellate Division should be reversed, the question certified answered in the negative, with costs to abide the ultimate event, the complaint dismissed, but with leave to plaintiff tenant to apply at Special Term for leave to replead, if so advised.

FULD, Chief Judge (dissenting in part).

I agree with the court's opinion that a plaintiff, in order to state a sufficient cause of action for reformation, must allege fraud by the defendant and unilateral mistake on his own part. The plaintiff before us has, concededly, pleaded fraud and it seems to me that his allegation that "the lease was incorrectly drawn" is the equivalent of an assertion that he was under a mistake when he signed the lease. Our rules of pleading have never demanded the use of particular or magic words as long as the language employed conveys the requisite meaning. In the present case, only insistence on an excessive technicality can justify dismissal of the second cause of action. I would, therefore, affirm so much of the order appealed from as sustains that count.

BURKE, SCILEPPI, BERGAN, JASEN and GIBSON, JJ., concur with BREITEL, J.

FULD, C.J., dissents in part and votes to affirm so much of the order appealed from as sustains the second cause of action, in a memorandum.

Order reversed and the case remitted to Special Term for further proceedings in accordance with the opinion herein, with costs to abide the ultimate event. Question certified answered in the negative.

EAST HAVEN ASSOCIATES, INC. v. GURIAN

Civil Court of the City of New York, 1970.
64 Misc.2d 276, 313 N.Y.S.2d 927.

LEONARD H. SANDLER, Judge.

The most important of the several interesting issues presented by the proof in this case is whether or not the doctrine of constructive eviction is available to a residential tenant when a landlord is responsible for conditions that render part of the premises uninhabitable, and the tenant abandons that part but continues to reside in the rest of the premises. Put in another way, the question is whether New York Law should recognize the doctrine of partial constructive eviction as a counterpart to partial actual eviction precisely as it has recognized for over a century constructive eviction as a counterpart to actual eviction. See Dyett v. Pendleton, 8 Cow. 727 (Ct. of Errors, 1826).

After a careful review of the authorities, I have concluded that the concept of partial constructive eviction is sound in principle, is supported by compelling considerations of social policy and fairness, and is in no way precluded by controlling precedent.

On May 26, 1963, the defendant entered into a lease with the then owner of 301 East 69 Street, with respect to Apartment 18E under which the defendant agreed to pay rent for the apartment from Dec. 1, 1963 to November 30, 1966 in the amount of $425.00 per month. The apartment in question had a terrace.

In April, 1966, the plaintiff acquired the building. At the end of July, 1966, the defendant and his family vacated the apartment and refused to pay rent for the months of August, September, October and November, 1966, the remaining period of the lease. Accordingly, plaintiff sued for the total of the four months rent, for the reasonable value of legal services, and for specific items of damages allegedly caused by the defendants. As to the last, I find the proof wholly deficient and these claims are accordingly dismissed.

The defense to the suit for rent rests upon the claim that the defendant was constructively evicted from the apartment as a result of the misconduct and neglect of the landlord, which allegedly rendered the terrace uninhabitable.

In addition, the defendant sues for damages to his furniture caused by the landlord's neglect, but this claim clearly must fail since the proof established that the damage complained of occurred before the plaintiff acquired the building. Finally, the defendant seeks return of his security in the amount of $425.00.

The central factual issue turns on the condition of the terrace and the factors causing that condition.

I find that from early 1965 the central air conditioner emitted quite steadily a green fluid and a stream of water overflow that fell in significant quantities on the terrace. I further find that the incinerator spewed forth particles of ash that were deposited in substantial part upon the terrace. The result was to render the terrace effectively unusable for its intended purposes, and the defendant and his family promptly abandoned the terrace, although it had been a prime factor in inducing them to enter the lease.

Nevertheless, I am unable to conclude that the departure of the defendant and his family from the apartment at the end of July, 1966 constituted their constructive eviction from the entire premises. The evidence clearly discloses that the terrace had become unusable no later than the early spring of 1965, and quite possibly earlier. The law is clear that the abandonment must occur with reasonable promptness after the conditions justifying it have developed.

Unquestionably, this rule should be given a flexible interpretation in light of the practical difficulties these days in finding satisfactory apartments. Moreover, tenants have a right to rely on assurances that the landlord will correct the objectionable conditions.

Although the question is troublesome, I have concluded that a delay of at least 17 months in moving, without any significant proof of an early sustained effort to find other apartments, cannot be reconciled with the current requirements of law.

Turning to the issue of partial eviction, the proof quite plainly established that the terrace had been promptly abandoned once the condition complained of had developed. I am satisfied that conforming the pleadings to the proof to permit consideration of the issue of partial eviction would serve the interests of justice.

Although the matter is not clear, I am inclined to believe that the proof before me spelled out an actual partial eviction. It seems to me that the tangible and concrete physical character of the substances falling on the terrace provides a substantial basis for such a finding.

However, I do not rest my decision on that ground in view of the decision of the New York Court of Appeals in Barash v. Pennsylvania Terminal Real Estate Corporation, 26 N.Y.2d 77, 308 N.Y.S.2d 649, 256 N.E.2d 707 (1970). Although the facts of the Barash case do not preclude such a finding, the wording of the opinion plainly suggests a disposition to define actual eviction rather narrowly. I therefore turn to consider the status of partial constructive eviction under New York law.

In his authoritative treatise, Rasch flatly asserted that constructive eviction requires "surrender of the entire possession by the tenant." See Rasch, [Landlord and Tenant], Sec. 876.

None of the cases he cites, however, supports that sweeping assertion. These cases, with many others, repeat the general formula that constructive eviction requires abandonment of the premises. None of the cases I have examined squarely address the question here presented of the legal effect of abandonment of only that part of the premises rendered uninhabitable.

The doctrine of constructive eviction was developed by analogy to actual eviction on the basis of a very simple and obvious proposition. If a tenant is effectively forced out of leased premises as a result of misconduct by a landlord that substantially impairs enjoyment of the leased premises, the same legal consequences should follow as though the evicted were physically evicted.

In the eloquent landmark decision that firmly established constructive eviction in New York law, Dyett v. Pendleton, 8 Cow. 727 (Ct. of Err. 1826) the following was said at p. 734:

> "Suppose the landlord had established a hospital for the small pox, the plague, or the yellow fever, in the remaining part of the house; suppose he had made a deposit of gunpowder, under the tenant, or had introduced some offensive and pestilential materials of the most dangerous nature; can there be any hesitation in saying that if, by such means, he had driven the tenant from his habitation, he should not recover for the use of that house, of which, by his own wrong, he had deprived his tenant? It would need nothing but common sense and common justice to decide it."

Why should a different test be applied where the tenant, through comparable means, is effectively deprived of the use of part of his residence, and abandons that part? Ought not the same consequences to follow as would follow an "actual partial eviction"?

I am unable to see any basis in "common sense and common justice" for treating the two situations differently.

Support for this view appears in the careful phrasing of the first decision to establish the requirement of abandonment in constructive eviction cases: Edgerton v. Page, 20 N.Y. 281 (1859). The Court of Appeals squarely rested the requirement on the unfairness of suspending rent while the tenant continued to occupy the "entire premises."

> "I cannot see upon what principle the landlord should be absolutely barred from a recovery of rent when his wrongful acts stop short of depriving the tenant of the possession of *any part* of the premises. The true Rule from all the authorities is that while the tenant remains in possession of the *entire premises* demised, his obligation to pay rent continues." (at pp. 284, 285).

While some later opinions have been less carefully worded, I know of none that requires a different result.

While the view here expressed seems to me inherent in "common sense and common justice" that gave rise originally to the doctrine of constructive eviction, the result is independently compelled by considerations of fairness and justice in the light of present realities.

It cannot be seriously disputed that a major shortage in residential housing has prevailed in our metropolitan area for several decades. The clear effect has been to undermine so drastically the bargaining power of tenants in relation to landlords that grave questions as to the fairness and relevance of some traditional concepts of landlord-tenant law are presented.

The very idea of requiring families to abandon their homes before they can defend against actions for rent is a baffling one in an era in which decent housing is so hard to get, particularly for those who are poor and without resources. It makes no sense at all to say that if part of an apartment has been rendered uninhabitable, a family must move from the entire dwelling before it can seek justice and fair dealing.

Accordingly, I hold that when the defendant and his family ceased to use the terrace, a partial constructive eviction occurred with the same legal consequences as attends a partial "actual" eviction.

These consequences were comprehensively defined in Peerless Candy Co., Inc. v. Halbreich, 125 Misc. 889, 211 N.Y.S. 676, 213 N.Y.S. 49 (App. Term, 1925). It is clear that from the time of the partial eviction, the defendant had the right to stop paying rent. Accordingly, I find against the plaintiff on its action for rent and legal expenses, and for the defendant on his action to recover the security deposit of $425.00.

Judgment should be entered for the defendant for $425.00 with interest from Aug. 1, 1966.

NOTES

1. *The Right to Quiet Enjoyment and the Right to Possession Compared.* Like the covenant to deliver possession, the covenant for quiet enjoyment is aimed at securing the tenant's exclusive possession of the leased premises and will, unless expressly waived, be implied into all leases. The principal distinction between the two covenants is that the covenant to deliver possession is breached, if at all, at the very outset of the lease, before the tenant goes into possession, while the covenant for quiet enjoyment can be breached only after the tenant has entered into possession. Courts occasionally emphasize the similarities and downplay the distinctions between the two covenants. For example, several early decisions explained their adoption of the American rule, limiting the landlord's duty to deliver possession, by noting that since, under the covenant for quiet enjoyment, a landlord has no responsibility for third party interferences during the term, he should have no greater responsibility for third party interferences at the outset of the term. See, for example, Gardner v. Keteltas, 3 Hill 330 (N.Y.Sup.Ct.1842).

Should the two covenants be distinguished? Recall that the arguments in favor of the English rule on delivery of possession rest mainly on the fact that, at all times before the lease term commences, it is the landlord, not the tenant, who is best placed to deal with third-party intruders. See page 840 above. By contrast, the rule on quiet enjoyment appears to assume that, once the tenant becomes entitled to possession, it is the tenant and not the landlord who is best placed to deal with third-party intruders. Are there circumstances in which landlord liability for the acts of third parties—assumed by the English rule on the right to possession—might properly be introduced into the covenant for quiet enjoyment?

2. Dyett v. Pendleton is a landmark in the law of quiet enjoyment, holding that nonphysical as well as physical intrusions can breach the covenant. *Dyett* may also be a high water mark, too, in holding that psychic affronts, as well as more concrete interferences such as smoke, odor and loud noise, can breach the covenant. Was it accurate for Senator Spencer to say that Baron Gilbert's fourth rule—discharging the tenant from the whole rent if the lessor expels him from a part of the premises—is in fact "a case where actual entry and physical eviction are not necessary to exonerate the tenant from the payment of rent"? Would Spencer have allowed the tenant in *Dyett* to abate his rent if he had stayed on the premises rather than promptly vacated? After *Dyett*, what basis is there for distinguishing between actual and constructive eviction?

What justification is there for the rule followed in *Barash* that, where the eviction is constructive rather than actual, the tenant must promptly abandon in order to maintain the quiet enjoyment defense? Is it that the claim of substantial interference is inconsistent with the fact that the tenant is staying on and managing to make the best of a bad situation? Is the constructive eviction claim of a tenant who stays on any less plausible than the claim of a partially, actually evicted tenant whom Baron Gilbert would allow to stay on rent-free? One difference between *Barash* and Gilbert's fourth rule may be that *Barash* sought to prevent the tenant who stays on from reaping a windfall while Gilbert's fourth rule sought to deter landlords from inflicting a harm. Which is the preferable emphasis? Can *Dyett* and *Barash* be distinguished on the ground that *Dyett* involved residential premises while *Barash* involved commercial premises?

Did *Gurian* in fact hold "that when the defendant and his family ceased to use the terrace, a partial constructive eviction occurred with the same legal consequences as attends a partial 'actual' eviction"? If so, should the court not only have excused the tenants from paying rent from the time they moved out of the premises, at the end of July, 1966, but also, on the theory of Baron Gilbert's fourth rule, have awarded them all rents paid to the landlord from the time the partial eviction first occurred, seventeen months earlier, in 1965? (Note the court's observation that "It is clear that from the time of the partial eviction, the defendant had the right to stop paying rent.")

Was *Gurian* overly cautious in reading *Barash* to prohibit a finding of partial, actual eviction under the facts? Was it overly ambitious in striking out on the new tack of partial constructive eviction? One clue to the court's motives is its observation that "the very idea of requiring families to abandon their homes before they can defend against actions for rent is a baffling one in an era in which decent housing is so hard to get, particularly for those who are poor and without resources." The neighborhood of 301 East 69th Street in Manhattan is comparatively plush and its inhabitants hardly qualify as "poor and without resources." But at the time *Gurian* arose there was considerable ferment elsewhere in New York City over the plight of poor tenants in deteriorating rental housing, plagued not by leaking air conditioners but by faulty wiring, malfunctioning plumbing and peeling paint. It is entirely possible that Judge Sandler took *Gurian* as an opportunity to make new law aimed at resolving a social and economic problem that was far more compelling than the one raised by the immediate facts before him.

3. *What Constitutes Substantial Interference?* For the covenant of quiet enjoyment to be breached, the interference with the tenant's possession must be substantial. Although the substantiality requirement applies to all forms of claimed eviction—actual and constructive, partial and complete—and to all contexts—residential

and commercial—the specific measure of substantiality will differ depending on the setting in which the question is raised.

Constructive Eviction. In the setting of constructive eviction, the general test for substantiality is whether the tenant has been "deprived of the full use and enjoyment of the leased property for a material period of time." First Wisconsin Trust Co. v. L. Wiemann Co., 93 Wis.2d 258, 269, 286 N.W.2d 360, 365 (1980). In the residential context, this means landlord interferences such as noisy parties or noisome activities that seriously inhibit the premises' use as a dwelling. In the commercial context, it means landlord conduct, such as obstructing customer parking spaces, that injure the tenant's business. In both residential and commercial contexts the breach of a separate covenant imposing a specific duty on the landlord may also be held to result in constructive eviction. Compare Charles E. Burt, Inc. v. Seven Grand Corp., 340 Mass. 124, 163 N.E.2d 4 (1959) (breach of express covenant to furnish heat and other services constitutes constructive eviction) with Fitts v. Hanks, 209 Or. 1, 303 P.2d 220 (1956) (breach of covenant to supply tenant hop farmers with properly functioning irrigation equipment and hops-picking machines constitutes constructive eviction).

Actual Eviction. The early actual eviction cases rarely confronted the substantiality question directly. So long as the physical intrusion was more than *de minimus*, the tenant would prevail. In the much-cited Smith v. McEnany, 170 Mass. 26, 48 N.E. 781 (1897), the court ruled that an encroachment, estimated to be between nine inches and two feet wide, and thirty-four feet long, entitled tenant to a complete abatement; "this is partly due to the traditional doctrine that the rent issues out of the land, and that the whole rent is charged on every part of the land." The modern trend, at least in partial actual eviction cases, is to require the same proof of substantial interference as is required in constructive eviction cases. See, for example, Dussin Investment Co. v. Bloxham, 96 Cal.App.3d 308, 317, 157 Cal.Rptr. 646, 651 (1979) ("We are persuaded by our analysis of the California cases that a tenant is not relieved entirely of the obligation to pay rent by an actual, partial eviction unless the eviction is from a substantial portion of the premises and that in determining the question of substantiality, the court may and should consider the extent of the interference with the tenant's use and enjoyment of the property.").

4. *What Constitutes Landlord Conduct?* For an interference to breach the covenant of quiet enjoyment, it must not only be substantial, but must also be directly attributable to the landlord. If a third party, such as another tenant, causes the disturbance, the landlord is generally held not liable and the injured tenant must wage his cause directly against the third party, presumably on a nuisance ground. See, for example, Stewart v. Lawson, 199 Mich. 497, 500, 165 N.W. 716, 717 (1917) (plaintiff landlord not liable for noise of oth-

er tenants, notwithstanding provision in all leases prohibiting each tenant from becoming a nuisance to other tenants; "the most that can be said, if the testimony of defendant is to be believed, is that plaintiff suffered it to continue. This would not be sufficient to bind her, unless she gave some active support or encouragement to their wrongful acts.").

There is, however, a growing inclination among courts to hold landlords liable for the acts of third parties where the landlord had the right to control the offensive use. In Blackett v. Olanoff, 371 Mass. 714, 358 N.E.2d 817 (1977), the court upheld tenants' defense that they had been constructively evicted by noise coming from nearby premises which their landlords had leased to others for use as a cocktail lounge. Against the landlords' claim "that they are not responsible for the conduct of the proprietors, employees, and patrons of the lounge," the court observed that "landlords had a right to control the objectionable noise coming from the lounge," and concluded that, because "the disturbing condition was the natural and probable consequence of the landlords' permitting the lounge to operate where it did and because the landlords could control the actions at the lounge, they should not be entitled to collect rent for residential premises which were not reasonably habitable." 371 Mass. at 716–718, 358 N.E.2d at 819–820.

Would, and should, the result in *Blackett* have differed if the lounge lease had not specifically prohibited the tenant from making excessive noise? Is a landlord under a duty to require that such a clause be included in all her leases? Would the residential tenants have had a stronger or weaker case against the landlord if they could not demonstrate that the offending conduct constituted an actionable nuisance? As between landlord and tenant, who should bear the risk of loss arising from substantial interferences that fall outside the direct control of both—for example, when a city closes off one lane in the highway running past landlord's shopping center, substantially reducing the tenant's business.

5. *Eviction by Paramount Title.* Although, as a general rule, landlords are not responsible for the acts of third parties, they are liable for the acts of paramount title holders. Who are paramount title holders? One might be a bank which took a mortgage from the landlord before the tenant's lease began and now seeks to oust the tenant in order to give possession to the purchaser at a foreclosure sale. Another might be lessor *A* whose lessee *B* sublet the premises to sublessee *C*. When *A* removes *C* from the premises because *B* has failed to pay the rent due, *C* has been evicted by a paramount title holder and has an action against *B* for breach of the covenant of quiet enjoyment contained in their sublease. See Dupree v. Worthen Bank & Trust Co., 260 Ark. 673, 543 S.W.2d 465 (1976).

6. Restatement (Second) of Property § 6.1 (1976), provides that "there is a breach of the landlord's obligations if, during the period

the tenant is entitled to possession of the leased property, the landlord, or someone whose conduct is attributable to him, interferes with a permissible use of the leased property by the tenant." Section 6.1 departs from current common law in several respects. First, as recognized by the Reporter, the "emphasis in this section is on whether the interference with a permissible use is more than insignificant, whereas the cases generally use language that calls for the interference being substantial." Reporter's Note 1. Second, the Restatement adopts the *Blackett* approach to liability for the acts of third parties: "The conduct of a third person outside of the leased property that is performed on property in which the landlord has an interest, which conduct could be legally controlled by him, is attributable to the landlord for the purposes of applying the rule of this section." Comment d.

Section 6.1 departs even more substantially from existing law in its provision for remedies, allowing the tenant to terminate the lease and recover damages; to continue the lease and obtain equitable and legal relief including damages; to abate rent; to use the rent to eliminate the interference; or to withhold rent. Two other departures are the rejection of Baron Gilbert's fourth rule allowing total suspension of rent for partial eviction, and the rejection of the *Barash* requirement that the tenant promptly abandon the leased premises before claiming constructive eviction; in the Reporter's view, the abandonment requirement "has been widely criticized on the grounds that it makes the law completely unavailable to tenants who for one reason or another cannot move, e.g., indigent urban apartment dwellers in many cities, and available only at great risk to others, who must first deprive themselves of such benefit as they are deriving from the premises before getting a ruling on whether they were justified in doing so." Reporter's Note 6.

c. THE RIGHT TO SAFE PREMISES

KLINE v. 1500 MASSACHUSETTS AVENUE APARTMENT CORP.

United States Court of Appeals, District of Columbia Circuit, 1970.
439 F.2d 477.

WILKEY, Circuit Judge:

The appellee apartment corporation states that there is "only one issue presented for review * * * whether a duty should be placed on a landlord to take steps to protect tenants from foreseeable criminal acts committed by third parties". The District Court as a matter of law held that there is no such duty. We find that there is, and that in the circumstances here the applicable standard of care was breached. We therefore reverse and remand to the District Court for the determination of damages for the appellant.

I

The appellant, Sarah B. Kline, sustained serious injuries when she was criminally assaulted and robbed at approximately 10:15 in the evening by an intruder in the common hallway of an apartment house at 1500 Massachusetts Avenue. This facility, into which the appellant Kline moved in October 1959, is a large apartment building with approximately 585 individual apartment units. It has a main entrance on Massachusetts Avenue, with side entrances on both 15th and 16th Streets. At the time the appellant first signed a lease a doorman was on duty at the main entrance twenty-four hours a day, and at least one employee at all times manned a desk in the lobby from which all persons using the elevators could be observed. The 15th Street door adjoined the entrance to a parking garage used by both the tenants and the public. Two garage attendants were stationed at this dual entranceway; the duties of each being arranged so that one of them always was in position to observe those entering either the apartment building or the garage. The 16th Street entrance was unattended during the day but was locked after 9:00 P.M.

By mid-1966, however, the main entrance had no doorman, the desk in the lobby was left unattended much of the time, the 15th Street entrance was generally unguarded due to a decrease in garage personnel, and the 16th Street entrance was often left unlocked all night. The entrances were allowed to be thus unguarded in the face of an increasing number of assaults, larcenies, and robberies being perpetrated against the tenants in and from the common hallways of the apartment building. These facts were undisputed, and were supported by a detailed chronological listing of offenses admitted into evidence. The landlord had notice of these crimes and had in fact been urged by appellant Kline herself prior to the events leading to the instant appeal to take steps to secure the building.

Shortly after 10:00 P.M. on November 17, 1966, Miss Kline was assaulted and robbed just outside her apartment on the first floor above the street level of this 585 unit apartment building. This occurred only two months after Leona Sullivan, another female tenant, had been similarly attacked in the same commonway.

II

At the outset we note that of the crimes of violence, robbery, and assault which had been occurring with mounting frequency on the premises at 1500 Massachusetts Avenue, the assaults on Miss Kline and Miss Sullivan took place in the hallways of the building, which were under the exclusive control of the appellee landlord. Even in those crimes of robbery or assault committed in individual apartments, the intruders of necessity had to gain entrance through the common entry and passageways. These premises fronted on three heavily traveled streets, and had multiple entrances. The risk to be guarded against therefore was the risk of unauthorized entrance into the apartment house by intruders bent upon some crime of violence or theft.

While the apartment lessees themselves could take some steps to guard against this risk by installing extra heavy locks and other security devices on the doors and windows of their respective apartments, yet this risk in the greater part could only be guarded against by the landlord. No individual tenant had it within his power to take measures to guard the garage entranceways, to provide scrutiny at the main entrance of the building, to patrol the common hallways and elevators, to set up any kind of a security alarm system in the building, to provide additional locking devices on the main doors, to provide a system of announcement for authorized visitors only, to close the garage doors at appropriate hours, and to see that the entrance was manned at all times.

The risk of criminal assault and robbery on a tenant in the common hallways of the building was thus entirely predictable; that same risk had been occurring with increasing frequency over a period of several months immediately prior to the incident giving rise to this case; it was a risk whose prevention or minimization was almost entirely within the power of the landlord; and the risk materialized in the assault and robbery of appellant on November 17, 1966.

III

In this jurisdiction, certain duties have been assigned to the landlord because of his *control* of common hallways, lobbies, stairwells, etc., used by all tenants in multiple dwelling units. This Court in Levine v. Katz, 132 U.S.App.D.C. 173, 174, 407 F.2d 303, 304 (1968), pointed out that:

> It has long been well settled in this jurisdiction that, where a landlord leases separate portions of property and reserves under his own control the halls, stairs, or other parts of the property for use in common by all tenants, he has a duty to all those on the premises of legal right to use ordinary care and diligence to maintain the retained parts in a reasonably safe condition.

While Levine v. Katz dealt with a physical defect in the building leading to plaintiff's injury, the rationale as applied to predictable criminal acts by third parties is the same.[5] The duty is the landlord's because by his control of the areas of common use and common danger he is the only party who has the *power* to make the necessary repairs or to provide the necessary protection.

As a general rule, a private person does not have a duty to protect another from a criminal attack by a third person. We recognize that this rule has sometimes in the past been applied in landlord-tenant

---

5. Kendall v. Gore Properties, 98 U.S. App.D.C. 378, 236 F.2d 673 (1956).

law, even by this court. Among the reasons for the application of this rule to landlords are: judicial reluctance to tamper with the traditional common law concept of the landlord-tenant relationship; the notion that the act of a third person in committing an intentional tort or crime is a superseding cause of the harm to another resulting therefrom; the oftentimes difficult problem of determining foreseeability of criminal acts; the vagueness of the standard which the landlord must meet; the economic consequences of the imposition of the duty; and conflict with the public policy allocating the duty of protecting citizens from criminal acts to the government rather than the private sector.

But the rationale of this very broad general rule falters when it is applied to the conditions of modern day urban apartment living, particularly in the circumstances of this case. The rationale of the general rule exonerating a third party from any duty to protect another from a criminal attack has no applicability to the landlord-tenant relationship in multiple dwelling houses. The landlord is no insurer of his tenants' safety, but he certainly is no bystander. And where, as here, the landlord has notice of repeated criminal assaults and robberies, has notice that these crimes occurred in the portion of the premises exclusively within his control, has every reason to expect like crimes to happen again, and has the exclusive power to take preventive action, it does not seem unfair to place upon the landlord a duty to take those steps which are within his power to minimize the predictable risk to his tenants.

This court has recently had occasion to review landlord-tenant law as applied to multiple family urban dwellings. In Javins v. First National Realty Corporation, the traditional analysis of a lease as being a conveyance of an interest in land—with all the medieval connotations this often brings—was reappraised, and found lacking in several respects. This court noted that the value of the lease to the modern apartment dweller is that it gives him "a well known package of goods and services—a package which includes not merely walls and ceilings, but also adequate heat, light and ventilation, serviceable plumbing facilities, *secure windows and doors*, proper sanitation, and proper maintenance." [8] It does not give him the land itself, and to the tenant as a practical matter this is supremely unimportant. Speaking for the court, Judge Wright then went on to state, "In our judgment the trend toward treating leases as contracts is wise and well considered. Our holding in this case reflects a belief that leases of urban dwelling units should be interpreted and construed like any other contract." [9]

Treating the modern day urban lease as a contract, this court in *Javins, supra,* recognized, among other things, that repair of the leased premises in a multiple dwelling unit may require access to

---

8. 138 U.S.App.D.C. at 372, 428 F.2d at 1074, (emphasis added).

9. *Id.* 138 U.S.App.D.C. at 373, 428 F.2d at 1075.

equipment in areas in the control of the landlord, and skills which no urban tenant possesses. Accordingly, this court delineated the landlord's duty to repair as including continued maintenance of the rented apartment throughout the term of the lease, rightfully placing the duty to maintain the premises upon the party to the lease contract having the capacity to do so, based upon an implied warranty of habitability.

In the case at bar we place the duty of taking protective measures guarding the entire premises and the areas peculiarly under the landlord's control against the perpetration of criminal acts upon the landlord, the party to the lease contract who has the effective capacity to perform these necessary acts.

As a footnote to *Javins, supra,* Judge Wright, in clearing away some of the legal underbrush from medieval common law obscuring the modern landlord-tenant relationship, referred to an innkeeper's liability in comparison with that of the landlord to his tenant. "Even the old common law courts responded with a different rule for a landlord-tenant relationship which did not conform to the model of the usual agrarian lease. Much more substantial obligations were placed upon the keepers of inns (the only multiple dwelling houses known to the common law)."

Specifically, innkeepers have been held liable for assaults which have been committed upon their guests by third parties, if they have breached a duty which is imposed by reason of the innkeeper-guest relationship. By this duty, the innkeeper is generally bound to exercise reasonable care to protect the guest from abuse or molestation from third parties, be they innkeeper's employees, fellow guests, or intruders, if the attack could, or in the exercise of reasonable care, should have been anticipated.

Liability in the innkeeper-guest relationship is based as a matter of law either upon the innkeeper's supervision, care, or control of the premises, or by reason of a contract which some courts have implied from the entrustment by the guest of his personal comfort and safety to the innkeeper. In the latter analysis, the contract is held to give the guest the right to expect a standard of treatment at the hands of the innkeeper which includes an obligation on the part of the latter to exercise reasonable care in protecting the guest.

Other relationships in which similar duties have been imposed include landowner-invitee, businessman-patron, employer-employee, school district-pupil, hospital-patient, and carrier-passenger. In all, the theory of liability is essentially the same: that since the ability of one of the parties to provide for his own protection has been limited in some way by his submission to the control of the other, a duty should be imposed upon the one possessing control (and thus the power to act) to take reasonable precautions to protect the other one from assaults by third parties which, at least, could reasonably have been anticipated. However, there is no liability normally imposed upon the one having the power to act if the violence is sudden and unexpected provided that the source of the violence is not an employee of the one in control. . . .

In the instant case, the landlord had notice, both actual and constructive, that the tenants were being subjected to crimes against their persons and their property in and from the common hallways. For the period just prior to the time of the assault upon appellant Kline the record contains unrefuted evidence that the apartment building was undergoing a rising wave of crime. Under these conditions, we can only conclude that the landlord here "was aware of conditions which created a likelihood" (actually, almost a certainty) that further criminal attacks upon tenants would occur.

Upon consideration of all pertinent factors, we find that there is a duty of protection owed by the landlord to the tenant in an urban multiple unit apartment dwelling.

Summarizing our analysis, we find that this duty of protection arises, first of all, from the logic of the situation itself. If we were answering without the benefit of any prior precedent the issue as posed by the appellee landlord here, "whether a duty should be placed on a landlord to take steps to protect tenants from foreseeable criminal acts committed by third parties," we should have no hesitancy in answering it affirmatively, at least on the basis of the facts of this case.

As between tenant and landlord, the landlord is the only one in the position to take the necessary acts of protection required. He is not an insurer, but he is obligated to minimize the risk to his tenants. Not only as between landlord and tenant is the landlord best equipped to guard against the predictable risk of intruders, but even as between landlord and the police power of government, the landlord is in the best position to take the necessary protective measures. Municipal police cannot patrol the entryways and the hallways, the garages and the basements of private multiple unit apartment dwellings. They are neither equipped, manned, nor empowered to do so. In the area of the predictable risk which materialized in this case, only the landlord could have taken measures which might have prevented the injuries suffered by appellant.

We note that in the fight against crime the police are not expected to do it all; every segment of society has obligations to aid in law enforcement and to minimize the opportunities for crime. The average citizen is ceaselessly warned to remove keys from automobiles and, in this jurisdiction, may be liable in tort for any injury caused in the operation of his car by a thief if he fails to do so, notwithstanding the intervening criminal act of the thief, a third party. In addition, auto manufacturers are persuaded to install special locking devices and buzzer alarms, and real estate developers, residential communities, and industrial areas are asked to install especially bright lights to deter the criminally inclined. It is only just that the obligations of landlords in their sphere be acknowledged and enforced.

Secondly, on the rationale of this court in Levine v. Katz, Kendall v. Gore Properties, and Javins v. First National Realty Corporation, *supra*, there is implied in the contract between landlord and tenant an obligation on the landlord to provide those protective measures which are within his reasonable capacity. Here the protective measures which were in effect in October 1959 when appellant first signed a lease were drastically reduced. She continued after the expiration of the first term of the lease on a month to month tenancy. As this court pointed out in *Javins, supra*, "Since the lessees continued to pay the same rent, they were entitled to expect that the landlord would continue to keep the premises in their beginning condition during the lease term. It is precisely such expectations that the law now recognizes as deserving of formal, legal protection."

Thirdly, if we reach back to seek the precedents of common law, on the question of whether there exists or does not exist a duty on the owner of the premises to provide protection against criminal acts by third parties, the most analogous relationship to that of the modern day urban apartment house dweller is not that of a landlord and tenant, but that of innkeeper and guest. We can also consider other relationships, cited above, in which an analogous duty has been found to exist.

IV

We now turn to the standard of care which should be applied in judging if the landlord has fulfilled his duty of protection to the tenant. Although in many cases the language speaks as if the standard of care itself varies, in the last analysis the standard of care is the same—reasonable care in all the circumstances. . . .

We therefore hold in this case that the applicable standard of care in providing protection for the tenant is that standard which this landlord himself was employing in October 1959 when the appellant became a resident on the premises at 1500 Massachusetts Avenue. The tenant was led to expect that she could rely upon this degree of protection. While we do not say that the precise measures for security which were then in vogue should have been kept up (e.g., the number of people at the main entrances might have been reduced if a tenant-controlled intercom-automatic latch system had been installed in the common entryways), we do hold that the same relative degree of security should have been maintained.

The appellant tenant was entitled to performance by the landlord measured by this standard of protection whether the landlord's obligation be viewed as grounded in contract or in tort. As we have pointed out, this standard of protection was implied as an obligation of the lease contract from the beginning. Likewise, on a tort basis, this standard of protection may be taken as that commonly provided in apartments of this character and type in this community, and this is a reasonable standard of care on which to judge the conduct of the landlord here.

V

Given this duty of protection, and the standard of care as defined, it is clear that the appellee landlord breached its duty toward the appellant tenant here. The risk of criminal assault and robbery on any tenant was clearly predictable, a risk of which the appellee landlord had specific notice, a risk which became reality with increasing frequency, and this risk materialized on the very premises peculiarly under the control, and therefore the protection, of the landlord to the injury of the appellant tenant. The question then for the District Court becomes one of damages only. To us the liability is clear.

Having said this, it would be well to state what is *not* said by this decision. We do not hold that the landlord is by any means an insurer of the safety of his tenants. His duty is to take those measures of protection which are within his power and capacity to take, and which can reasonably be expected to mitigate the risk of intruders assaulting and robbing tenants. The landlord is not expected to provide protection commonly owed by a municipal police department; but as illustrated in this case, he is obligated to protect those parts of his premises which are not usually subject to periodic patrol and inspection by the municipal police. We do not say that every multiple unit apartment house in the District of Columbia should have those same measures of protection which 1500 Massachusetts Avenue enjoyed in 1959, nor do we say that 1500 Massachusetts Avenue should have precisely those same measures in effect at the present time. Alternative and more up-to-date methods may be equally or even more effective.

Granted, the discharge of this duty of protection by landlords will cause, in many instances, the expenditure of large sums for additional equipment and services, and granted, the cost will be ultimately passed on to the tenant in the form of increased rents. This prospect, in itself, however, is no deterrent to our acknowledging and giving force to the duty, since without protection the tenant already pays in losses from theft, physical assault and increased insurance premiums.

The landlord is entirely justified in passing on the cost of increased protective measures to his tenants, but the rationale of compelling the landlord to do it in the first place is that he is the only one who is in a position to take the necessary protective measures for overall protection of the premises, which he owns in whole and rents in part to individual tenants.

Reversed and remanded to the District Court for the determination of damages.

[Judge MacKINNON'S dissenting opinion is summarized in note 4.]

NOTES

1. As a general rule, a landlord is not liable in tort for injuries caused by defects in the leased premises. The rule rests on the premise that a lease is predominantly a conveyance of an interest in land and that it is the conveyee, in possession of the land, who is best placed to control the condition of the premises. Does the modern emphasis on the contract aspect of leases argue for a change in the general rule? Should the rule differ depending on whether a residential or commercial setting is involved?

The general rule of landlord tort immunity has been riddled with exceptions almost from the start. The landlord has traditionally been held liable for defects in common areas such as hallways and entrances over which she, rather than the tenant, is presumed to have control. The landlord is also liable for hidden defects of which she is aware, and for negligence in performing repairs voluntarily undertaken. Some states hold the landlord to tort liability for breaching an express agreement to repair. See W. Prosser, Handbook of the Law of Torts 399–412 (4th ed. 1971). See generally, Love, Landlord's Liability for Defective Premises: Caveat Lessee, Negligence, or Strict Liability? 1975 Wis.L.Rev. 19; Browder, The Taming of a Duty—The Tort Liability of Landlords, 81 Mich.L.Rev. 99 (1982).

2. The New Hampshire Supreme Court has taken the lead in replacing landlord tort immunity with general liability for negligence. In Sargent v. Ross, 113 N.H. 388, 308 A.2d 528 (1973), the court upheld a jury verdict for plaintiff administratrix, whose four-year old daughter had fallen to her death from an outdoor stairway in defendant landlord's building. The apparent cause of the fall was that the stairs, installed by defendant about eight years before the accident, "were dangerously steep, and that the railing was insufficient to prevent the child from falling over the side." 113 N.H. 390, 308 A.2d 530.

Recognizing that it could stretch the existing common law exceptions respecting common areas and negligent repair to cover the claim before it, the court chose instead to overturn the general rule of nonliability. In the court's view, the result flowed "naturally and inexorably" from its decision in Kline v. Burns, 111 N.H. 87, 276 A.2d 248 (1971), which had "modernized the landlord-tenant contractual relationship by holding that there is an implied warranty of habitability in an apartment lease transaction . . . . In so doing, we discarded the very legal foundation and justification for the landlord's immunity in tort for injuries to the tenant or third persons." The court took care, however, not to discard the common law exceptions entirely: "The questions of control, hidden defects and common or public use, which formerly had to be established as a prerequisite to even considering the negligence of a landlord, will now be relevant only inasmuch as they bear on the basic tort issues such as the foreseeability and unreasonableness of the particular risk of harm" 113 N.H. 396–398, 308 A.2d 533–534.

3. *Strict Liability.* Should landlords be subject to strict liability for injuries occurring on their premises? Although courts have generally answered in the negative, consider whether the parallels to products liability law argue for an affirmative answer: "One of the reasons commonly given for imposing strict liability is that the products liability defendant has superior knowledge of the product and is in a superior position to discover its defects, while the consumer is encouraged to rely on the defendant's skill, reputation, and express or implied representations of safety. Certainly a landlord who has a duty to maintain the premises in a habitable condition is in a superior position to know of or discover latent defects . . . . A second reason for imposing strict liability is that the defendant is in a better position to bear and distribute the risk of loss. Only landlords in the business of leasing can be held strictly liable. Such landlord is normally in a position to spread the risk of loss by purchasing liability insurance (or by acting as a self-insurer) and passing the cost on to his tenants . . . . A final reason for imposing strict liability is to eliminate the barrier of having to prove negligence . . . . When the landlord fails to discover or repair a defective condition created by a third person, the plaintiff is in a position analogous to that of a consumer in an action against a retailer. It may be impossible for the plaintiff to prove that the landlord knew or should have known of the defective condition." Love, Landlord's Liability for Defective Premises: Caveat Lessee, Negligence, or Strict Liability? 1975 Wis. L.Rev. 19, 134–136.

4. Does Kline v. 1500 Massachusetts Avenue stake out new ground for landlord tort liability, or is it only an application of the traditional rule that makes landlords liable for injuries suffered in common areas? Would the court have reached the same result if plaintiff had been attacked inside her apartment rather than in an outside hallway? If plaintiff's attacker had entered through a window in her apartment? If plaintiff was injured not by an attacker but by a ceiling collapsing into her apartment?

Did *Kline* efficiently allocate liability for attacks by intruders? As between landlord and tenant, who is better placed to undertake security measures? To obtain liability insurance? Does the answer depend upon the landlord's ability to pass increased security and insurance costs on to her tenants? Are security and insurance costs likely to be highest in those very areas—crime-ridden ghettos—where tenants are least able to afford rent increases?

Was *Kline* correct to identify the relevant standard of care as the level that obtained when plaintiff first signed a lease? Note that, according to the facts stated, the original tenancy had expired and was succeeded by a month-to-month tenancy. Would it have been more appropriate to alter the applicable standard to the level that obtained at the beginning of each month, when the terms of the landlord-tenant relationship were renewed? In apartment buildings the size of 1500 Massachusetts Avenue, some tenancies will usually have begun many years earlier, while others will have started only recently. If conditions are deteriorating, should recent tenants become the beneficiaries of a standard that obtained when the earliest tenant first arrived?

Should the applicable tort standard vary with the nature of the building and the neighborhood in which it is situated? Judge MacKinnon, dissenting, was disturbed by the fact that "1500 Massachusetts Avenue is *not* a luxury type apartment, but instead is a *combination office building and apartment building* with some commercial and professional offices interspersed with apartments located on the ground and second floor of the building (where subject offense occurred) . . . . Obviously since a number of business offices occupied the lower floors, the fortress type security precautions the panel opinion finds to be required would be wholly out of the question because such offices require free public access. The degree of protection appellant seeks could only be afforded by the equivalent of policemen patrolling the corridors which even if it were practical for the upper apartment areas would be impractical for the floors housing business offices where this assault occurred." (Emphasis in original) 439 F.2d at 489–490.

See generally, Selvin, Landlord Tort Liability for Criminal Attacks on Tenants: Developments Since Kline, 9 Real Estate L.J. 311 (1981); Smith, The Landlord's Duty to Defend His Tenants Against Crime on the Premises, 4 Whittier L.Rev. 587 (1982).

d. THE RIGHT TO ASSIGN AND SUBLET

FUNK v. FUNK

Supreme Court of Idaho, 1981.
102 Idaho 521, 633 P.2d 586.

SHEPARD, Justice.

This is an appeal from a summary judgment which denied the relief sought by plaintiff-lessors, *i.e.*, the termination of a farm lease. We affirm.

The principal question presented is the ability of a lessee to sublease without the consent of the lessor when the lease allows subletting conditioned on the lessor's consent and the lessor arbitrarily and capriciously withholds such consent.

In November of 1969, plaintiff-appellants Ewald and Pearl Funk [hereinafter lessors] leased certain farm land to Melvin and Diane

Funk [hereinafter lessees] for a ten year period commencing January 1, 1970 and ending December 31, 1979. Semi-annual rental payments were required on or before March 1 and December 1 of each year. The written lease provided in pertinent part: "(e) That the Lessee shall have the right and privilege of sub-leasing or assigning this instrument provided that the consent of the Lessor is first obtained."

During early 1978 the lessees were desirous of subleasing the property for the 1978 crop year. In January, the then attorney for the lessees wrote a letter expressing the lessees' desire to sublet the property and indicated that the lessees would make both 1978 lease payments on March 1 to ensure that the entire 1978 rent was paid in advance. They also promised to supervise the subtenant's operations to assure that the land was farmed in a good and husbandry-like manner and that proper weed control was practiced. They also offered to provide any additional information concerning the sub-tenant that might be requested by the lessors.

In February, lessors responded ". . . that we cannot allow a sublease of any type" and declared ". . . that we do not intend to allow a sublease of this property." In response to further correspondence from lessees' attorney, the lessors in February expressed their belief that the rental fee was below the fair rental value and again emphasized their refusal to allow a sublease, stating: ". . . we do not now or in the future wish to honor any subleasing of this property. We already have more information concerning the proposed sublessees than you can possibly assemble." Thereafter, an additional letter was written on behalf of lessors indicating that a sublease would be allowed if the lessees would assign one-half of the sublease proceeds to the lessors, if the lessees would pay the 1978 property taxes and if the lessees would agree to terminate the underlying lease on December 31, 1978. Thereafter, the lessees indicated they would farm the property themselves and would not sublease it.

Lessees did, however, sublet at least a portion of the premises for the 1978 crop year. When lessors learned of that sublease in September of 1978 they served notice of termination of the lease agreement. When lessees refused to quit the premises, this action was commenced. In March, 1979, summary judgment was entered in favor of the lessees declaring the lease agreement to be in full force and effect. The lessees continued to farm the property through the final year of the lease, 1979, and lessors accepted semi-annual rental payments in March and December of both 1978 and 1979. . . .

We now turn to the principal question presented here, *i.e.*, whether a lessor has an absolute right to withhold consent to a proposed sublease when the underlying lease grants to the lessee a right of assigning or subleasing upon the consent of a lessor.

A tenant holding under a lease for a definite period may sublet the premises in whole or in part in the absence of restrictions placed thereon by the parties or by statute. Homa-Goff Interiors, Inc. v.

Cowden, 350 So.2d 1035 (Ala.1977); 49 Am.Jur.2d, Landlord and Tenant, § 481 (1970). That common law right is limited to the extent that a lessee may not sublet premises to be used in a manner which is injurious to the property or inconsistent with the terms of the original lease.

In the case at bar the lessees' right to assign or sublet existed by virtue of the parties' written agreement, as well as by virtue of common law, but was also subject to a contractual restriction. The effect of such contractual restrictions on a right to assign or sublet has not been previously presented to this Court. In Enders v. Wesley W. Hubbard & Sons, Inc., 95 Idaho 590, 513 P.2d 992 (1973), a lease of grazing land was forfeited under a lease provision prohibiting assignment or subletting without the consent of the lessor. However, the sublease issue there was whether the actions of the lessee constituted a sublease or merely a granting of a license. In *Enders* the question of whether the consent of a lessor could be unreasonably withheld was not presented nor discussed.

The appellant-lessors correctly argue that the traditional majority position is that unless the lease provides that the lessors' consent shall not be unreasonably withheld, a provision against assignment or subletting without the lessors' consent authorizes the lessor to arbitrarily withhold consent for any reason or for no reason.

We find, however, an increasing number of jurisdictions departing from that traditional position and an increasing volume of authority that the consent of a lessor may not be *unreasonably* withheld. As stated in *Homa-Goff, supra,* "[the majority] rule, however, has been under steady attack in several states in the past twenty years; and this for the reason that, in recent times, the necessity of reasonable alienation of commercial building space has become paramount in our ever-increasing urban society." *Id.* at 1037.

We deem the principal enunciated in the minority position to be based on more solid policy rationale than is the traditional orthodox majority's position. A landlord may and should be concerned about the personal qualities of a proposed subtenant. A landlord should be able to reject a proposed subtenant when such rejection reflects a concern for the legitimate interest of the landlord, such as assurances of rent receipt, proper care of the property and in many cases the use of the property by the subtenant in a manner reasonably consistent with the usage of the original lessee. Such concerns by the landlord should result in the upholding of a withholding of consent by a landlord. However, no desirable public policy is served by upholding a landlord's arbitrary refusal of consent merely because of whim or caprice or where, as here, it is apparent that the refusal to consent was withheld for purely financial reasons and that the landlord wanted the lessees to enter into an entirely new lease agreement with substantial increased financial benefits to the landlord. If the lessor is allowed to arbitrarily refuse consent to a sublease for what is in effect no reason at all, such would virtually nullify the right of a lessee to sublet. The imposition of a reasonableness standard also gives greater credence to the doctrine that restraints on alienation of leased property are looked upon with disfavor and are strictly construed against the lessor.

The burden of proving that the landlord's conduct is unreasonable rests upon the party challenging that conduct. A standard of reasonableness has been applied in cases which have *implied* a reasonable standard as well as those cases in which the lease contained express language that consent could not be unreasonably withheld. "Arbitrary considerations of personal taste, sensibility, or convenience do not constitute the criteria of landlord's duty under an agreement such as this . . . the standard is the action of a reasonable man in the landlord's position." Chanslor-Western, 266 N.E.2d at 407, quoting Broad & Branford Place Corp. v. J.J. Hockenjos Co., 132 N.J.Law 229, 39 A.2d 80, 82 (1944).

In the instant case, the proper standard by which to review the lessors' refusal to consent to the proposed sublease is one of a reasonable person in the position of a landlord owning and leasing commercial farm land. Criteria to be utilized in application of that standard would include, but would not necessarily be limited to, assurances of proper farming practices and financial responsibility. In the instant case the record discloses no contentions by the landlord of the absence of these or any other criteria and hence we hold that the arbitrary refusal of the appellant-lessors in the instant case to grant their consent to the sublease was unreasonable.

We have considered appellants' remaining assignments of error and find them to be without merit.

Judgment is affirmed. Costs to respondents.

McFADDEN, BISTLINE and DONALDSON, JJ., concur.

BAKES, Chief Justice, dissenting:

I must dissent from the majority's decision to rewrite the lease provision in question. The lessee's right to assign or sublease the premises was unambiguous and unconditional in its requirement that the lessor consent. For the members of this Court to inject a new requirement that "the consent of the lessor may not be unreasonably withheld" is in effect to say that this Court may at any time disregard the intentions of the parties as expressed in their unambiguous agreement and rewrite the contract because a majority of this Court is of the opinion that it should be altered. The action of the majority constitutes not only a severe encroachment upon the right of persons to freely contract and to maintain control over their own property, but is also a serious intrusion into the province of the legislature.

In support of its action, the majority adopts a minority rule which it implies is the trend of the future. However, the majority's own citations manifest no such trend. Clearly, in the last year jurisdictions have split on the issue. *Compare* B & R Oil Co., Inc. v. Ray's Mobile Homes, Inc., 422 A.2d 1267 (Vt.1980) (permitting arbitrary refusal of consent) *with* Warmack v. Merchants Nat. Bank of Fort Smith, 612 S.W.2d 733 (Ark.1981) (prohibiting unreasonable withholding of consent). The majority cites only three states which have adopted the majority rule. However, there are at least five other recent cases not cited by the majority which in some manner either recognize the continuing validity of, or apply, the majority rule. Carleno v. Vollmert Tire Co., 36 Colo.App. 446, 540 P.2d 1149, 1151 (1975); Robinson v. Weitz, 171 Conn. 545, 370 A.2d 1066, 1068 (1976); Kruger v. Page Management Co., 105 Misc.2d 14, 432 N.Y.S.2d 295, 300 (1980) (recognizing rule absent applicability of statute governing residential leases); Herlou Card Shop, Inc. v. Prudential Ins. Co. of America, 73 A.D.2d 562, 422 N.Y.S.2d 708 (1979). *See also* Dutch Inns of America, Inc. v. United Virginia Leasing Corp., 134 Ga.App. 525, 215 S.E.2d 290, 291 (1975); Moritz v. S & H Shopping Centers, 197 Neb. 206, 247 N.W.2d 454, 456 (1976) (both cases applying the rule that lessee has no authority to assign the lease without consent of the lessor, but not addressing issue of unreasonable withholding of consent). Including the majority's citation to Food Pantry v. Waikiki Business Plaza, Inc., 58 Hawaii 606, 575 P.2d 869 (1978), it appears that even in recent years the majority rule of allowing freedom in contracting continues to far outdistance the minority view.

More important than numbers, however, are the reasons behind the rules. The majority opinion states that "the minority position [is] based on more solid policy rationale than is the traditional orthodox majority's position," and that "no desirable public policy is served by upholding a landlord's arbitrary refusal to consent." I disagree. Upholding contracts and deeds voluntarily entered into between two parties is certainly a "desirable public policy." We said so unanimously in Mollendorf v. Derry, 95 Idaho 1, 501 P.2d 199 (1972). "The policy of the law is not to defeat a grantor's intent." 95 Idaho at 3, 501 P.2d 199.

The rationale behind the majority rule is supported by several basic concepts of property law.

> "The reasons expressed in support of this rule are that, since the lessor has exercised a personal choice in the selection of a tenant for a definite term and has expressly provided that no substitute shall be acceptable without his written consent, no obligation rests upon him to look to anyone but the lessee for his rent . . . ; that a lease is a conveyance of an interest in real property and, when a lessor has delivered the premises to his lessee, the latter is bound to him by privity of estate as well as by privity of contract . . . ; that a lessor's right to reenter the premises upon lessee's default or abandonment thereof is at the lessor's option and not the lessee's . . . ; and that a lessee's unilateral action in abandoning leased premises, *unless accepted by his lessor*, does not

terminate the lease or forfeit the estate conveyed thereby, nor the lessee's right to use and possess the leased premises and, by the same token, his obligation to pay the rent due therefor." Gruman v. Investors Diversified Services, 247 Minn. 502, 78 N.W.2d 377, 380 (1956) (citations omitted, emphasis in original).

The reasons given in the *Gruman* case are supported by the fundamental principle that the owner of property may transfer as much or as little control over his property as he sees fit. Freedom of ownership and control over one's own property forms the very basis of our social system. If that is to change, the proper forum for such changes is the legislature and not this Court.

The unsettling nature of the majority opinion is magnified when one realizes that the effect of the decision is to potentially subject every denial of consent to litigation and approval by a judge. Rather than the lessor being sure of his right to control his property by retaining an unrestricted right to deny consent to assign or sublease, by its decision today this Court has destroyed that right and vested in the courts the power to determine what the lessor *should have intended* and award control of the property based upon that determination. Certainly, as evidenced by this case, the parties will rarely agree on what is reasonable under particular circumstances. Is there any assurance that judges will be unified in their opinions on what is reasonable? The only assurance to be gained by the rule adopted by the majority today is that the parties' attempt to write their lease to avoid litigation will be frustrated. Had the parties wished or bargained to place a question mark on the lessor's right to withhold consent, they would have provided in the agreement that consent would not be arbitrarily or unreasonably withheld. This Court should not foist that uncertainty off on them.

It is not clear from the majority opinion whether lessors in the future will have the right to contract for "an absolute right to withhold consent." The Restatement (Second) of Property, § 15.2, and Warmack v. Merchants Nat. Bank of Fort Smith, *supra*, the most recent case cited by the majority in support of its position, both so provide when they state: "The landlord's consent to an alienation by the tenant cannot be withheld unreasonably, unless a freely negotiated provision in the lease gives the landlord an absolute right to withhold consent." The broad language of the majority opinion suggests that even that provision would violate its "public policy." The Court's decision today will no doubt disrupt, dislocate and confuse thousands of existing contractual leasehold relationships which have provisions limiting the right to assign the lessee's interest.

When a court injects a new requirement that "the consent of the lessor may not be unreasonably withheld," as the majority has done in this case, it not only constitutes an interference with the right of persons to freely contract, but also interferes with the traditional rules for conveyancing real property. If, as the majority holds, it is against public policy for a lessor to provide in his lease that the lessee cannot assign his interest without the lessor's consent which may be denied for any reasons the lessor may give, including those which the majority concludes are arbitrary, the effect of such a rule is to modify the nature of the estate conveyed by the lessor. One wonders what the majority of this Court will do when faced with the conveyance of a fee conditional, the condition being an event which the majority might conclude is arbitrary or unreasonable. As an example, it is not uncommon for a benefactor to convey real property to a city in fee conditional, the condition being that the property be used perpetually for a park to be named after the benefactor, *e.g.*, In re Hart's Estate, 151 Cal.App. 271, 311 P.2d 605 (1957), and in the event that any part of the park is not used for that purpose then the property reverts to the heirs of the benefactor. If this Court, as it has done today, can modify the conditions of a grant of a lease, then it is only a short step to stating that it can also modify the terms of a grant of a fee conditional estate. The decision of the Court today will have a tremendously unsettling effect not only upon the conveyancing of real property but also upon the execution of contracts in this state. . . .

I would vote to carry out the contract as the parties negotiated it, and not as the majority of this Court thinks they should have negotiated it.

NOTES

1. Like other interests in land, a tenant's leasehold interest is freely alienable. But, unlike most other real property interests, and notwithstanding real property law's general preference for free alienability, leaseholds can be subjected to absolute restraints on alienation. Courts will, however, interpret these restraints stringently. A lease provision that only prohibits assignments will generally be held to permit subletting, and a prohibition against subletting will be held to permit assignments. The Rule in Dumpor's Case, 4 Coke 119b, 76 Eng.Rep. 1110 (K.B.1603), holds that if, under a lease prohibiting assignment without the landlord's consent, the landlord once gives her consent to an assignment, she is thereafter disabled from prohibiting subsequent assignments. Although the rule was abolished by statute in England, Law of Property Amendment Act, 22 & 23 Vict. c. 35 § 1 (1859), it still has some force in this country. See generally, 1 American Law of Property § 3.58 (A.J. Casner, ed. 1952).

2. Did *Funk* hold that, at the time they signed the lease, landlord and tenant *intended* to require the landlord to behave reasonably in rejecting proposed sublessees? Or did it hold that because the parties *should* have had this intent, the court would ascribe it to them? Can Idaho landlords avoid the *Funk* rule by simply insisting on language to the effect that "landlord may withhold consent in its sole and absolute discretion, for any reason or for no reason at all"? As a

lawyer in Idaho after *Funk*, would you give your landlord client an unqualified opinion that this language would allow absolute discretion in deciding whether to accept or reject a proposed assignment or sublease? (Reread Chief Justice Bakes' dissent carefully before answering.)

When is a landlord likely to behave unreasonably in withholding consent to an assignment or sublease? In *Funk*, the landlord was apparently trying to use the consent privilege as a lever to negotiate more favorable rent terms. Would the *Funk* majority enforce a lease provision that expressly gave the landlord the right to increase the rent periodically? Was the court simply saying that parties, though free to agree on any terms they wish, must be careful to draft them in specific rather than general terms?

Although some states have, like Idaho, implied the reasonableness standard by judicial decision, others have accomplished essentially the same result by statute. See for example, Alaska Stat. 34.03.060 (1975); 25 Del.Code § 5512 (1975).

3. *The Reasonableness Standard.* What grounds will entitle a landlord who is under an implied or expressed obligation of reasonable behavior to reject a proposed assignee or sublessee? Courts will generally apply an objective standard, upholding refusals if the proposed transferee's questionable reputation, his intended use of the leased premises or, most commonly, his financial irresponsibility, are likely to depress the value of the premises. Even in these circumstances, the original tenant can make the landlord's rejection appear unreasonable by offering to guarantee his proposed transferee's performance.

Courts applying an objective standard will question landlord motives founded on personal taste or an effort to obtain a collateral economic advantage. For example, lessor's affiliation with a religion opposed to birth control was held not to justify its refusal of a sublease to the Planned Parenthood Federation of America. American Book Co. v. Yeshiva University Development Foundation, Inc., 59 Misc.2d 31, 33, 297 N.Y.S.2d 156, 159–160 (Sup.Ct.1969) ("By 'objective' are meant those standards which are readily measurable criteria of a proposed subtenant's or assignee's acceptability, from the point of view of *any* landlord . . .."). And in Krieger v. Helmsley-Spear, Inc., 62 N.J. 423, 302 A.2d 129 (1973), the New Jersey Supreme Court held that the landlord could not reject an office sublease on the ground that the proposed sublessee was a tenant in another of the landlord's buildings whose lease there was about to expire and who was in the midst of negotiating a new term. ("The clause [that lessor shall not unreasonably withhold consent] is for the protection of the landlord in its ownership and operation of the particular property—not for its general economic protection. Otherwise the landlord could refuse consent if it had vacancies in its other building.")

Should the reasonableness standard differ depending on whether the proposed transfer occurs in a residential or a commercial context? On whether the landlord's duty to act reasonably is imposed by the express terms of the lease or is imposed by judicial implication? Who should bear the burden of proof on the question of reasonableness? *Funk* appears to make the tenant bear the burden of proving that the landlord's refusal is unreasonable. Yet, the court concluded its decision against the landlord with the observation that "the record discloses no contention by the landlord of the absence of these or any other [reasonable] criteria . . . ." Was the court in effect saying that it is the landlord who bears the burden of proving the reasonableness of her conduct? Who—tenant or landlord—is better placed to bear the burden in these cases? Note that, particularly on questions of intent and motive, placing the burden of proof on one party is often a gentle way of saying that party will lose the case.

See generally, Levin, Withholding Consent to Assignment: The Changing Rights of the Commercial Landlord, 30 DePaul L.Rev. 109 (1980); Todres & Lerner, Assignment and Subletting of Leased Premises: The Unreasonable Withholding of Consent, 5 Fordham Urban L.J. 195 (1977).

4. *Assignment or Sublease?* In weighing the reasonableness of a landlord's refusal, should it matter whether the consent sought is for an assignment or for a sublease? An original tenant, B, is bound to his landlord, A, both by privity of contract (created by the lease covenants) and by privity of estate (created by transfer of the leasehold estate). When the tenant *assigns* the lease, he transfers his entire estate and thus is no longer in privity of estate with the landlord, but continues to be in privity of contract, and remains personally liable on his leasehold obligations throughout the lease term. The assignee, C, though not in privity of contract with the landlord, is in privity of estate, and is thus bound to perform all leasehold covenants, such as for rent and repairs, whose burdens run with the land. The assignee's privity of estate, and hence his obligations to the landlord, will end in the event that he transfers to yet another assignee.

When the original tenant, B, *subleases*, he transfers less than his entire estate—for example, six months out of a two year term—and thus continues to be both in privity of contract and privity of estate with his landlord, A. The sublessee, C, is neither in privity of contract nor privity of estate with the landlord, with the result that landlord A can enforce none of the covenants against sublessee C and the sublessee can enforce none of the landlord's covenants against her. But sublessee C is in privity of contract *and* of estate with B who, effectively, has become C's landlord, retaining a reversionary interest, entitling B to retake the premises at the end of C's six-month term.

Does this pattern of liability, and specifically the fact that the original tenant will always be liable on his original leasehold promises, suggest that courts are mistaken to focus on the proposed transferee's financial responsibility as an index of the landlord's reasonableness in rejecting him? At the least, does this pattern of liability suggest that courts are mistaken to treat the original tenant's offer to guarantee his transferee's performance as an added factor weighing against the reasonableness of the landlord's rejection?

3. LANDLORD RIGHTS AND REMEDIES

Just as a well-drafted lease will spell out the landlord's agreed-upon obligations to the tenant, it will also detail the tenant's obligations to the landlord. Also, absent controlling language in the lease, the tenant, like the landlord, will be subject to a handful of implied obligations. The tenant's principal implied obligation is to return the premises to the landlord at the end of the term in substantially the condition they were in at the beginning of the term. Unless the lease provides otherwise, the tenant cannot commit acts, such as tearing out walls or doors, that will substantially impair the value of the premises (*affirmative waste*) or acts, such as adding a second story to a one-story house, that, though they will not impair the premises' value, will substantially alter their identity (*ameliorative waste*).

In addition to his obligations respecting affirmative and ameliorative waste, the tenant is under an implied obligation not to commit *permissive waste* by allowing the premises to fall into disrepair. Some modern courts and legislatures have dramatically shifted the obligation to keep residential premises in good repair from tenant to landlord. 1 American Law of Property, § 3.78 (A.J. Casner, ed. 1952) offers the rationale for the shift: "The rule that the tenant must make repairs was probably fair when applied in an agrarian economy where the materials for repair were simple and at hand, and the tenant capable of making them himself. At least as concerns the actual making of repairs, the rule seems archaic and completely out of harmony with the facts when applied in a complicated society to urban dwellings occupied by persons on salary or weekly wage . . . . It would seem that the lessor is in the better position, from the viewpoint of economic situation and interest, to make repairs, and that the tenant ought to have no duty in the absence of a specific covenant." Do you agree?

While the evolution from an agrarian to an urban economy may justify the reallocation of some responsibilities from tenant to landlord, it may also require the reallocation of other responsibilities in the opposite direction. For example, it was entirely consistent with an agrarian setting that the landlord should have no rights against the tenant's use of the premises in a noisy, noisome or other offensive manner; these rights were more efficiently given to neighbors on a nuisance theory. Should the landlord be given these rights in an urban society? Should the answer turn on whether the jurisdiction follows the rule of Blackett v. Olanoff, page 857, holding the landlord liable to neighboring tenants for the offensive activities of another tenant?

Although modern leases are usually quite explicit in prescribing the tenant's obligations, they are often surprisingly bare when it comes to the equally important question of the remedies available to the landlord in the event the tenant breaches any of these obligations. If the tenant breaches, but refuses to leave the premises, can the landlord employ self help to remove him? Which obligations, if breached, will entitle the landlord to evict the tenant and which will entitle him only to specific performance or damages? What are the landlord's remedies when a breaching tenant abandons the premises? Can the landlord hold the tenant for the entire reserved rental for the remainder of the lease term, or can she only obtain damages for her loss of bargain? These questions are considered in the following materials.

a. Tenant Breaches And Refuses To Leave

BERG v. WILEY

Supreme Court of Minnesota, 1978.
264 N.W.2d 145.

ROGOSHESKE, Justice.

Defendant landlord, Wiley Enterprises, Inc., and defendant Rodney A. Wiley (hereafter collectively referred to as Wiley) appeal from a judgment upon a jury verdict awarding plaintiff tenant, A Family Affair Restaurant, Inc., damages for wrongful eviction from its leased premises. The issues for review are whether the evidence was sufficient to support the jury's finding that the tenant did not abandon or surrender the premises and whether the trial court erred in finding Wiley's reentry forcible and wrongful as a matter of law. We hold that the jury's verdict is supported by sufficient evidence and that the trial court's determination of unlawful entry was correct as matter of law, and affirm the judgment.

On November 11, 1970, Wiley, as lessor and tenant's predecessor in interest as lessee, executed a written lease agreement letting land and a building in Osseo, Minnesota, for use as a restaurant. The lease provided a 5-year term beginning December 1, 1970, and specified that the tenant agreed to bear all costs of repairs and remodeling, to "make no changes in the building structure" without prior written authorization from Wiley, and to "operate the restaurant in a lawful and prudent manner." Wiley also reserved the right "at [his] option [to] retake possession" of the premises "[s]hould the Lessee fail to meet the conditions of this Lease."[1] In early 1971, plaintiff

---

1. The provisions of the lease pertinent to this case provide: "Item #5 The Lessee will make no changes to the building structure without first receiving written authorization from the Lessor. The Lessor will promptly reply in writing to

Kathleen Berg took assignment of the lease from the prior lessee, and on May 1, 1971, she opened "A Family Affair Restaurant" on the premises. In January 1973, Berg incorporated the restaurant and assigned her interest in the lease to "A Family Affair Restaurant, Inc." As sole shareholder of the corporation, she alone continued to act for the tenant.

The present dispute has arisen out of Wiley's objection to Berg's continued remodeling of the restaurant without procuring written permission and her consequent operation of the restaurant in a state of disrepair with alleged health code violations. Strained relations between the parties came to a head in June and July 1973. In a letter dated June 29, 1973, Wiley's attorney charged Berg with having breached lease items 5 and 6 by making changes in the building structure without written authorization and by operating an unclean kitchen in violation of health regulations. The letter demanded that a list of eight remodeling items be completed within 2 weeks from the date of the letter, by Friday, July 13, 1973, or Wiley would retake possession of the premises under lease item 7. Also, a June 13 inspection of the restaurant by the Minnesota Department of Health had produced an order that certain listed changes be completed within specified time limits in order to comply with the health code. The major items on the inspector's list, similar to those listed by Wiley's attorney, were to be completed by July 15, 1973.

During the 2-week deadline set by both Wiley and the health department, Berg continued to operate the restaurant without closing to complete the required items of remodeling. The evidence is in dispute as to whether she intended to permanently close the restaurant and vacate the premises at the end of the 2 weeks or simply close for about 1 month in order to remodel to comply with the health code. At the close of business on Friday, July 13, 1973, the last day of the 2-week period, Berg dismissed her employees, closed the restaurant, and placed a sign in the window saying "Closed for Remodeling." Earlier that day, Berg testified, Wiley came to the premises in her absence and attempted to change the locks. When she returned and asserted her right to continue in possession, he complied with her request to leave the locks unchanged. Berg also testified that at about 9:30 p.m. that evening, while she and four of her friends were in the restaurant, she observed Wiley hanging from the awning peering into the window. Shortly thereafter, she heard Wiley pounding on the back door demanding admittance. Berg called the county sheriff to come and preserve order. Wiley testified that he observed Berg and

each request and will cooperate with the Lessee on any reasonable request.

"Item #6 The Lessee agrees to operate the restaurant in a lawful and prudent manner during the lease period.

"Item #7 Should the Lessee fail to meet the conditions of this Lease the Les-

sor may at their option retake possession of said premises. In any such event such act will not relieve Lessee from liability for payment the rental herein provided or from the conditions or obligations of this lease."

a group of her friends in the restaurant removing paneling from a wall. Allegedly fearing destruction of his property, Wiley called the city police, who, with the sheriff, mediated an agreement between the parties to preserve the status quo until each could consult with legal counsel on Monday, July 16, 1973.

Wiley testified that his then attorney advised him to take possession of the premises and lock the tenant out. Accompanied by a police officer and a locksmith, Wiley entered the premises in Berg's absence and without her knowledge on Monday, July 16, 1973, and changed the locks. Later in the day, Berg found herself locked out. The lease term was not due to expire until December 1, 1975. The premises were re-let to another tenant on or about August 1, 1973. Berg brought this damage action against Wiley and three other named defendants, including the new tenant, on July 27, 1973. A second amended complaint sought damages for lost profits, damage to chattels, intentional infliction of emotional distress, and other tort damages based upon claims in wrongful eviction, contract, and tort. Wiley answered with an affirmative defense of abandonment and surrender and counterclaimed for damage to the premises and indemnification on mechanics lien liability incurred because of Berg's remodeling. At the close of Berg's case, all defendants other than Rodney A. Wiley and Wiley Enterprises, Inc., were dismissed from the action. Only Berg's action for wrongful eviction and intentional infliction of emotional distress and Wiley's affirmative defense of abandonment and his counterclaim for damage to the premises were submitted by special verdict to the jury. With respect to the wrongful eviction claim, the trial court found as a matter of law that Wiley did in fact lock the tenant out, and that the lockout was wrongful.

The jury, by answers to the questions submitted, found no liability on Berg's claim for intentional infliction of emotional distress and no liability on Wiley's counterclaim for damages to the premises, but awarded Berg $31,000 for lost profits and $3,540 for loss of chattels resulting from the wrongful lockout. The jury also specifically found that Berg neither abandoned nor surrendered the premises. The trial court granted Wiley's post-trial motion for an order decreeing that Berg indemnify Wiley for any mechanics lien liability incurred due to Berg's remodeling by way of set-off from Berg's judgment and ordered the judgment accordingly amended.

On this appeal, Wiley seeks an outright reversal of the damages award for wrongful eviction, claiming insufficient evidence to support the jury's finding of no abandonment or surrender and claiming error in the trial court's finding of wrongful eviction as a matter of law.

The first issue before us concerns the sufficiency of evidence to support the jury's finding that Berg had not abandoned or surrendered the leasehold before being locked out by Wiley. Viewing the evidence to support the jury's special verdict in the light most favorable to Berg, as we must, we hold it amply supports the jury's finding of no abandonment or surrender of the premises. While the evidence bearing upon Berg's intent was strongly contradictory, the jury could reasonably have concluded, based on Berg's testimony and supporting circumstantial evidence, that she intended to retain possession, closing temporarily to remodel. Thus, the lockout cannot be excused on ground that Berg abandoned or surrendered the leasehold.

The second and more difficult issue is whether Wiley's self-help repossession of the premises by locking out Berg was correctly held wrongful as a matter of law.

Minnesota has historically followed the common-law rule that a landlord may rightfully use self-help to retake leased premises from a tenant in possession without incurring liability for wrongful eviction provided two conditions are met: (1) The landlord is legally entitled to possession, such as where a tenant holds over after the lease term or where a tenant breaches a lease containing a reentry clause; and (2) the landlord's means of reentry are peaceable. Under the common-law rule, a tenant who is evicted by his landlord may recover damages for wrongful eviction where the landlord either had no right to possession or where the means used to remove the tenant were forcible, or both. See, e.g., Poppen v. Wadleigh, 235 Minn. 400, 51 N.W.2d 75 (1952); Sweeney v. Meyers, 199 Minn. 21, 270 N.W. 906 (1937); Lobdell v. Keene, 85 Minn. 90, 88 N.W. 426 (1901). See, also, Minn. St. 566.01 (statutory cause of action where entry is not "allowed by law" or, if allowed, is not made "in a peaceable manner").

Wiley contends that Berg had breached the provisions of the lease, thereby entitling Wiley, under the terms of the lease, to retake possession, and that his repossession by changing the locks in Berg's absence was accomplished in a peaceful manner. In a memorandum accompanying the post-trial order, the trial court stated two grounds for finding the lockout wrongful as a matter of law: (1) It was not accomplished in a peaceable manner and therefore could not be justified under the common-law rule, and (2) any self-help reentry against a tenant in possession is wrongful under the growing modern doctrine that a landlord must always resort to the judicial process to enforce his statutory remedy against a tenant wrongfully in possession. Whether Berg had in fact breached the lease and whether Wiley was hence entitled to possession was not judicially determined. That issue became irrelevant upon the trial court's finding that Wiley's reentry was forcible as a matter of law because even if Berg had breached the lease, this could not excuse Wiley's nonpeaceable reentry. The finding that Wiley's reentry was forcible as a matter of law provided a sufficient ground for damages, and the issue of breach was not submitted to the jury.

In each of our previous cases upholding an award of damages for wrongful eviction, the landlord had in fact been found to have no legal right to possession. In applying the common-law rule, we have not before had occasion to decide what means of self-help used to dispossess a tenant in his absence will constitute a nonpeaceable entry, giving a right to damages without regard to who holds the legal right to possession. Wiley argues that only actual or threatened violence used against a tenant should give rise to damages where the landlord had the right to possession. We cannot agree.

It has long been the policy of our law to discourage landlords from taking the law into their own hands, and our decisions and statutory law have looked with disfavor upon any use of self-help to dispossess a tenant in circumstances which are likely to result in breaches of the peace. We gave early recognition to this policy in Lobdell v. Keene, 85 Minn. 90, 101, 88 N.W. 426, 430 (1901), where we said:

> "The object and purpose of the legislature in the enactment of the forcible entry and unlawful detainer statute was to prevent those claiming a right of entry or possession of lands from redressing their own wrongs by entering into possession in a violent and forcible manner. All such acts tend to a breach of the peace, and encourage high-handed oppression. The law does not permit the owner of land, be his title ever so good, to be the judge of his own rights with respect to a possession adversely held, but puts him to his remedy under the statutes."

To facilitate a resort to judicial process, the legislature has provided a summary procedure in Minn.St. 566.02 to 566.17 whereby a landlord may recover possession of leased premises upon proper notice and showing in court in as little as 3 to 10 days. As we recognized in Mutual Trust Life Life Ins. Co. v. Berg, 187 Minn. 503, 505, 246 N.W. 9, 10 (1932), "[t]he forcible entry and unlawful detainer statutes were intended to prevent parties from taking the law into their own hands when going into possession of lands and tenements . . . ." To further discourage self-help, our legislature has provided treble damages for forcible evictions, §§ 557.08 and 557.09, and has provided additional criminal penalties for intentional and unlawful exclusion of a tenant. § 504.25. In Sweeney v. Meyers, *supra*, we allowed a business tenant not only damages for lost profits but also punitive damages against a landlord who, like Wiley, entered in the tenant's absence and locked the tenant out.

In the present case, as in Sweeney, the tenant was in possession, claiming a right to continue in possession adverse to the landlord's claim of breach of the lease, and had neither abandoned nor surrendered the premises. Wiley, well aware that Berg was asserting her right to possession, retook possession in her absence by picking the locks and locking her out. The record shows a history of vigorous dispute and keen animosity between the parties. Upon this record, we can only conclude that the singular reason why actual violence did not erupt at the moment of Wiley's changing of the locks was Berg's absence and her subsequent self-restraint and resort to judicial process. Upon these facts, we cannot find Wiley's means of reentry peaceable under the common-law rule. Our long-standing policy to discourage self-help which tends to cause a breach of the peace compels us to disapprove the means used to dispossess Berg. To approve this lockout, as urged by Wiley, merely because in Berg's absence no actual violence erupted while the locks were being changed, would be to encourage all future tenants, in order to protect their possession, to be vigilant and thereby set the stage for the very kind of public disturbance which it must be our policy to discourage.

Consistent with our conclusion that we cannot find Wiley's means of reentry peaceable under the common-law rule is Gulf Oil Corp. v. Smithey, 426 S.W.2d 262 (Tex.Civ.App.1968). In that case the Texas court, without departing from the common-law rule, held that a landlord's reentry in the tenant's absence by picking the locks and locking the tenant out, although accomplished without actual violence, was forcible as a matter of law. The Texas courts, by continuing to embrace the common-law rule, have apparently left open the possibility that self-help may be available in that state to dispossess a tenant in some undefined circumstances which may be found peaceable.

We recognize that the growing modern trend departs completely from the common-law rule to hold that self-help is never available to dispossess a tenant who is in possession and has not abandoned or voluntarily surrendered the premises. This growing rule is founded on the recognition that the potential for violent breach of peace inheres in any situation where a landlord attempts by his own means to remove a tenant who is claiming possession adversely to the landlord. Courts adopting the rule reason that there is no cause to sanction such potentially disruptive self-help where adequate and speedy means are provided for removing a tenant peacefully through judicial process. At least 16 states [6] have adopted this modern rule, holding that judicial proceedings, including the summary procedures provided in those states' unlawful detainer statutes, are the exclusive remedy by which a landlord may remove a tenant claiming possession. While we would be compelled to disapprove the lockout of Berg in her absence under the common-law rule as stated, we approve the trial court's reasoning and adopt as preferable the modern view represented by the cited cases. To make clear our departure from the common-law rule for the benefit of future landlords and tenants, we hold that, subsequent to our decision in this case, the only lawful means to dispossess a tenant who has not abandoned nor voluntarily surrendered but who claims possession adversely to a landlord's claim of breach of a written lease is by resort to judicial process. We find that Minn.St. 566.02 to 566.17 provide the landlord with an adequate remedy for regaining possession in every such case.[8] Where speedier

6. Annotation, 6 A.L.R.3d 177, 186, Supp. 13, shows this modern rule to have been adopted in California, Connecticut, Delaware, Florida, Georgia, Illinois, Indiana, Louisiana, Nebraska, North Carolina, Ohio, Tennessee, Texas, Utah, Vermont, and Washington.

8. Under §§ 566.05 and 566.06, a landlord may regain possession in default

action than provided in §§ 566.02 to 566.17 seems necessary because of threatened destruction of the property or other exigent circumstances, a temporary restraining order under Rule 65, Rules of Civil Procedure, and law enforcement protection are available to the landlord. Considered together, these statutory and judicial remedies provide a complete answer to the landlord. In our modern society, with the availability of prompt and sufficient legal remedies as described, there is no place and no need for self-help against a tenant in claimed lawful possession of leased premises.

Applying our holding to the facts of this case, we conclude, as did the trial court, that because Wiley failed to resort to judicial remedies against Berg's holding possession adversely to Wiley's claim of breach of the lease, his lockout of Berg was wrongful as a matter of law. The rule we adopt in this decision is fairly applied against Wiley, for it is clear that, applying the older common-law rule to the facts and circumstances peculiar to this case, we would be compelled to find the lockout nonpeaceable for the reasons previously stated. The jury found that the lockout caused Berg damage and, as between Berg and Wiley, equity dictates that Wiley, who himself performed the act causing the damage, must bear the loss.

Affirmed.

OTIS, J., took no part in the consideration or decision of this case.

MORRIS v. AUSTRAW

Supreme Court of North Carolina, 1967.
269 N.C. 218, 152 S.E.2d 155.

PARKER, Chief Justice.

Defendants assign as errors each of Judge Martin's two conclusions of law, each of the three matters adjudged and decreed in the judgment, and the entry of the judgment.

The written lease between the parties referred to in the first paragraph of the stipulated and agreed facts is set forth in fourteen

proceedings against a tenant personally served with process in as little as 3 to 10 days. Default judgment against a tenant not present and served by posting may be procured in a week to 10 days. §§ 566.05 and 566.06. Trial is by the court unless either party demands a jury trial. § 566.07. Proceedings are stayed on appeal except as against a holdover tenant. § 566.12. Upon execution of a writ of restitution, the tenant is allowed 24 hours to vacate the property.

We are mindful that by § 566.04 the summary remedy of § 566.02 to 566.17 is made unavailable against any tenant having been "in quiet possession for three years next before the filing of the complaint . . . ." This reflects an appropriate policy choice by the legislature to require full litigation of the right to possession in a common-law ejectment action before judicially ousting a tenant of such long tenure. Our holding, disallowing self-help in such cases as well, is consistent with the legislative policy protecting the long-term tenant. The availability of temporary restraining orders, temporary injunctions against waste, and eventual damages for unlawful detainer or unpaid rent provides an adequate compensating remedy to the landlord for any delay in obtaining possession during judicial proceedings.

pages in the record. The basis and scope of summary ejectment in actions between the landlord and tenant are established by G.S. § 42–26. Defendants' brief states that the first question involved is: "Did Richard F. Austraw's violation of 21 USC 331 and 333 constitute a forfeiture of all appellant tenants' rights under the terms and conditions of their lease with appellee landlords?" Plaintiffs' brief states likewise. It seems clear from the stipulated and agreed facts and the first identical question stated in the briefs of the parties that the only section of G.S. § 42–26 which could possibly fit the facts stipulated and agreed to is subsection (2), which provides: "When the tenant . . . has done or omitted any act by which, according to the stipulations of the lease, his estate has ceased."

Paragraph 1(a) of the lease between the plaintiffs as landlord and the defendants as tenants provides, *inter alia*: "Tenant shall not use or permit the use of any portion of said premises for any unlawful purpose or purposes." The lease or contract of rental disclosed in the record before us contains no provision automatically terminating the estate for breach of provisions of the lease that "tenant shall not use or permit the use of any portion of said premises for any unlawful purpose or purposes," nor does such contract or lease reserve the right of re-entry for breach of the quoted provisions of the lease. Appellees in their brief contend:

"Section 16(b) of the lease clearly contemplates in unmistakable language that suit might be brought by the Landlord for possession of the premises in the event of the breach of *any covenant* that may be set forth in the lease. The language of the lease is as follows: 'In case Landlord should bring suit for the possession of the premises, for the recovery of any sum due hereunder, *or because of the breach of any covenant herein.*' This clearly indicates that it was the intention of the parties that the landlord might bring suit for possession of the premises if any covenant or promise in the contract was broken."

Paragraph 16(b) of the lease reads as follows:

"In case Landlord should bring suit for the possession of the premises, for the recovery of any sum due hereunder, or because of the breach of any covenant herein, or for any other relief against Tenant, declaratory or otherwise, or should Tenant bring any action for any relief against Landlord, declaratory or otherwise, arising out of this lease, and Landlord should prevail in any such suit, Tenant shall pay Landlord a reasonable attorney's fee which shall be deemed to have accrued on the commencement of such action and shall be enforceable whether or not such action is prosecuted to judgment."

Except in cases where G.S. § 42–3 writes into a contract of a lease of lands, when the lease is silent thereon, a forfeiture of the terms of the lease upon failure of the lessee to pay the rent within ten days after a demand is made by the lessor or his agent for all past due rent, with right of the lessor to enter and dispossess the lessee, Ryan v. Reynolds, 190 N.C. 563, 130 S.E. 156, a breach of the conditions of a lease between a landlord and tenant cannot be made the basis of summary ejectment unless the lease itself provides for termination on such breach or reserves the right of re-entry for such breach.

This is said in 32 Am.Jur., Landlord and Tenant, § 848:

> "Generally, unless there is an express stipulation for a forfeiture, the breach of a covenant in a lease does not work a forfeiture of the term. Moreover, the settled principle of both law and equity that contractual provisions for forfeitures are looked upon with disfavor applies with full force to stipulations for forfeitures found in leases; such stipulations are not looked upon with favor by the court, but on the contrary are strictly construed against the party seeking to invoke them. As has been said, the right to declare a forfeiture of a lease must be distinctly reserved; the proof of the happening of the event on which the right is to be exercised must be clear; the party entitled to do so must exercise his right promptly; and the result of enforcing the forfeiture must not be unconscionable."

We do not agree with appellees' contention that the provisions of paragraph 16(b) of the lease automatically terminate the tenants' estate for breach of the provisions of the lease that "tenant shall not use or permit the use of any portion of said premises for any unlawful purpose or purposes," and that such provisions of paragraph 16(b) of the lease reserve the right of re-entry to plaintiffs. Appellants' assignments of error to Judge Martin's two conclusions of law are good and are sustained.

The second and last question presented in the brief of each party is: "Are appellee landlords entitled, under the terms and conditions of the lease in question, to the present possession of the premises described in such lease?" Considering the stipulated and agreed facts and what has been said above, the answer to the question is, No.

The remedy by summary proceedings in ejectment is restricted to those cases expressly provided by G.S. § 42–26. The proceeding should be dismissed as in case of nonsuit.

The judgment below is

Reversed.

NOTES

1. As a general rule, unless the lease or an applicable statute provides otherwise, the tenant's breach of his lease obligations will not entitle the landlord to terminate the lease and retake possession. The landlord's only recourse is an action for damages or, possibly,

specific performance or injunctive relief. The rule rests on the traditional view that a lease is a conveyance of an interest in land rather than a bilateral contract containing mutually dependent covenants. See, for example, State v. Brown, 203 Minn. 505, 282 N.W. 136, 137 (1938) ("The reason for the common law rule was logical. The tenant was regarded as the purchaser of an estate. He was obligated to pay rent as much as if he had bought a suit of clothes or a horse to be paid for by instalments. Clearly the tailor could not repossess the suit upon default unless the right were reserved. Likewise the landlord cannot retake possession of the premises when the tenant defaults unless he reserves the right.").

The only reason the common law rule has endured so long is that modern leases and statutes have emptied it of consequence. Landlords and tenants, and the lease forms they employ, will usually be sufficiently farsighted to provide expressly that the tenant's default on any one or more specified covenants will terminate the lease either automatically or at the landlord's election. Further, statutes in more than forty states allow the landlord to summarily evict a tenant who fails to pay rent, even though the lease contains no express provision for forfeiture. Statutes in several states also allow the landlord to terminate for such other tenant breaches as waste, illegal use, or failure to obtain the landlord's required consent to assignment or subletting.

Despite these substantial contractual and statutory inroads, the common law rule continues to possess considerable force in one important area: the interpretation of leases. As indicated by Morris v. Austraw, if there is any question whether the lease makes forfeiture a consequence of breach, the doubt will be resolved against forfeiture.

2. *Summary Proceedings.* Summary judicial proceedings, available in every state, give landlords a comparatively expeditious means for regaining possession of the leased premises when their tenants fail to pay rent, commit some other specified breach, or hold over after expiration of their term. These statutes, variously labelled "forcible entry and detainer," "unlawful detainer," "summary proceedings," or "summary ejectment," were first enacted in the latter part of the nineteenth century in an effort to resolve the perennial conflict between landlords and tenants over eviction procedures. Landlords, frustrated by the lengthy and tortuous common law ejectment proceeding, typically used self-help to regain their premises. Tenants opposed self-help because of its potential for abuse. By giving landlords a simpler and safer procedural alternative, the new statutes reduced landlord incentives to pursue self-help evictions.

Although summary procedures vary from state to state, most follow the same general pattern. Ohio's Forcible Entry and Detainer Statute, Ohio Rev.Code Ch. 1923 (1981 Supp.), is typical. The statute gives landlords a summary action against tenants holding over after their term, tenants who have breached leasehold obligations, and tenants whose breach of applicable statutory obligations materially "affects health and safety." § 1923.02. The landlord must give the tenant three days' notice before filing the action, § 1923.04, and after notice has been given, and before the summons issues, must file a complaint describing the premises and the nature of the unlawful detainer, § 1923.05. The summons, stating the cause of complaint and the time and place for trial, must be served no less than five days before the date set for trial, § 1923.06.[g]

Summary proceedings will not always be that summary. As the tenant's obligation to perform his duties under the lease has increasingly come to depend on the landlord's performance of her duties, the tenant's possible defenses have increased, as well. Summary proceeding statutes in many states require that these defenses be tried before an order of eviction can issue. See Ohio Rev.Code § 1923.061. Continuances and appeals are other possible sources of delay. See §§ 1923.08, 1923.12. Nor will resolution of all defenses, continuances and appeals in the landlord's favor necessarily result in immediate repossession: "Within ten days after receiving the writ of execution described in § 1923.13 of the Revised Code, the sheriff, bailiff, or constable shall execute it by restoring the plaintiff to the possession of the premises, and shall levy and collect the costs and make return, as upon other executions." § 1912.14.

For an analysis of summary proceeding statutes across the country, see 1 & 2 Restatement (Second) of Property, Landlord and Tenant, Statutory Notes to sections 12.1, 14.1 (1976).

3. Do you agree with the rule adopted in Berg v. Wiley? Who is better placed to bear the loss occasioned by the delays of judicial process—the tenant, removed by self-help, who may be wrongly deprived of his shelter or place of business before he can get possession back, or the landlord who, while awaiting trial of her summary proceeding, may see her investment further threatened by the acts of a breaching tenant? Should the answer depend upon whether the lease is for residential or commercial purposes? On whether one party is willing to

---

g. The Ohio statute offers two innovations aimed at protecting the oppressed tenant. Section 1923.04 requires that every "notice given under this section by a landlord to recover residential premises shall contain the following language printed or written in a conspicuous manner: 'You are being asked to leave the premises. If you do not leave, an eviction action may be initiated against you. If you are in doubt regarding your legal rights and obligations as a tenant, it is recommended that you seek legal assistance.'" Section 1923.06(B) provides that "Every summons issued under this section to recover residential premises shall contain the following language printed in a conspicuous manner: 'A complaint to evict you has been filed with this court. No person shall be evicted unless his right to possession has ended and no person shall be evicted in retaliation for the exercise of his lawful rights. If you are depositing rent with the clerk of this court you shall continue to deposit such rent until the time of the court hearing. The failure to continue to deposit such rent may result in your eviction. You may request a trial by jury. You have the right to seek legal assistance. If you cannot afford a lawyer, you may contact your local legal aid or legal service office. If none is available, you may contact your local bar association.'"

indemnify the other for losses wrongfully suffered as a result of delay in the determination of rights?

Does *Berg* say that a tenant who believes he has been wrongfully evicted by self-help cannot himself use self-help to regain possession? That he cannot use summary proceedings? Berg and Wiley had been before the Minnesota Supreme Court three years earlier on the same facts. Two months after filing its damage action for wrongful eviction, plaintiff Berg brought an action against Wiley for possession under Minnesota's unlawful detainer statute. Reversing the lower court's judgment awarding possession to the plaintiff, the Minnesota Supreme Court held that the state's unlawful detainer statute did not give a tenant an action against his landlord: "Plaintiff's proper remedy here was an ejectment action in district court, where it could not only have claimed repossession but where any and all necessary legal and equitable remedies were available to it, and where the right to possession and damages could be resolved in one action." Berg v. Wiley, 303 Minn. 247, 251, 226 N.W.2d 904, 907 (1975).

4. Despite its natural appeal, stemming from modern notions of due process, fairness and civility, *Berg* still represents the minority position in this country. Most states at least nominally allow landlords to elect self-help repossession accompanied by varying degrees of force. Within this majority, a handful of states continue to follow the English common law rule entitling the landlord to employ any reasonable and necessary force to retake possession. See, for example, Shorter v. Shelton, 183 Va. 819, 825, 33 S.E.2d 643, 646 (1945). ("At common law a landlord, entitled to possession of the leased premises which were being wrongfully withheld from him, had the right to make re-entry by such reasonable force as was necessary, short of that which threatened death or serious bodily harm, to regain possession.") Although the landlord will not be liable to the tenant in damages, she may be subject to criminal sanction under the state's applicable Forcible Entry and Detainer Statute if her entry was too forceful.

Most states following the majority position allow the landlord to employ self-help so long as she does so peaceably. Judicial use of the concept, "peaceable," ranges from literal applications, permitting the landlord to take steps that are neither injurious to the tenant nor a breach of the public peace, to applications so narrow and rigorous that they effectively bar any resort to self-help—for example, prohibiting such comparatively inoffensive measures as entry through an open window or by use of a passkey. R. Schoshinski, American Law of Landlord and Tenant 404–405 (1980).

Faced with the difficulty in any case of determining whether their acts will qualify as a "peaceable entry," how many landlords will risk the substantial damages that may attend a retaking of possession by self-help? Does this pervasive uncertainty and ambiguity respecting the boundaries of legitimate self-help suggest that, as a practical matter, few landlords will employ self-help, and that *Berg's* minority rule may actually, if not nominally, be the overwhelming rule of conduct today?

5. Did *Berg* intend that its rule prohibiting landlord self-help be waivable by the parties? Should it have? Although some courts have held that a lease provision expressly permitting the landlord to pursue reasonable self-help measures will supersede an applicable common law rule imposing a stricter standard, or outlawing self-help entirely, a small but growing number of jurisdictions hold these provisions void as against public policy. See, for example, Jordan v. Talbot, 55 Cal.2d 597, 12 Cal.Rptr. 488, 361 P.2d 20 (1961).

6. *Distress; Statutory Lien.* The landlord concerned that her defaulting, and possibly impecunious, tenant will be unable to satisfy a judgment for rental owed, may have one or two additional remedies in her arsenal: the common law remedy of distress (sometimes called the right of distraint), entitling her to seize personal property found on the premises as security for the rent, and a statutory lien on all personal property on the leased premises.

At early common law, the right of distress entitled the landlord to seize any chattels found on the leased premises belonging to the tenant, or even to a third party, and to hold them as security for rent. The statute, 2 Wm. & Mary, c. 5 (1689) gave the landlord the additional right to sell the chattels. Distress with power of sale was widely imported into the American states and, although later abolished in some, is still available in others with a variety of statutory modifications. For example, New Jersey and some other states generally allow distraint, but exempt residential leases. N.J.Stat.Ann. 2A:33–1 (West 1982 Supp.). The most pervasive statutory modification has been to eliminate or closely confine the landlord's ability to distrain through self-help rather than judicial process, and to surround the process with a number of procedural safeguards for the tenant.

Most states have, as an alternative or complement to distress, given landlords a statutory lien on their tenants' chattels, securing the tenants' obligation to pay rent. Unlike distress, which gives the landlord an interest in the chattels only upon the tenant's default, statutory liens typically attach at the beginning of the term; the landlord's right to enforce the lien does not, however, generally arise until the tenant defaults on the rental obligation.

7. *Constitutional Constraints.* In giving landlords speedy and effective relief against defaulting tenants, states that permit self-help repossession and such summary judicial remedies as distraint, statutory lien and unlawful detainer proceedings, may violate the tenant's interest, under the fourteenth amendment to the United States Constitution, in not being deprived of property without due process of law. Ironically, it is the least proceduralized seizures that are most completely immune from constitutional attack. If the landlord takes possession of the premises or the tenant's personal property without

resorting to the state's judicial machinery, it is likely that state action, required for the fourteenth amendment to apply, will be found missing. Although the law is by no means clear on the extent of state involvement required to constitute "state action," the Supreme Court's position has generally been to allow self-help. See, for example, Flagg Brothers, Inc. v. Brooks, 436 U.S. 149, 98 S.Ct. 1729, 56 L.Ed.2d 185 (1978) (upholding the enforcement, through private sale, of a warehouseman's lien under U.C.C. § 7–210).

Ex parte proceedings, in which the landlord invokes the judicial process, have been more susceptible to constitutional attack. Two Supreme Court decisions, Sniadach v. Family Finance Corp., 395 U.S. 337, 89 S.Ct. 1820, 23 L.Ed.2d 349 (1969) and Fuentes v. Shevin, 407 U.S. 67, 92 S.Ct. 1983, 32 L.Ed.2d 556 (1972), invalidating creditor remedies aimed at seizing a debtor's property without prior notice and hearing, spurred state and lower federal courts to invalidate state procedures allowing landlords to seize their tenants' property without prior notice or hearing. See, for example, Hall v. Garson, 468 F.2d 845 (5th Cir. 1972). However, the Supreme Court's subsequent decision in Mitchell v. W.T. Grant Co., 416 U.S. 600, 94 S.Ct. 1895, 40 L.Ed.2d 406 (1974), has brought the *Fuentes-Shevin* line of decisions into question, and the implications for landlord remedies are by no means clear. See also, North Georgia Finishing, Inc. v. Di-Chem, Inc., 419 U.S. 601, 95 S.Ct. 719, 42 L.Ed.2d 751 (1975).

Inter partes proceedings have also come under constitutional attack. In Greene v. Lindsey, 456 U.S. 444, 102 S.Ct. 1874, 72 L.Ed.2d 249 (1982), the Supreme Court invalidated a Kentucky statute allowing service of process in a summary proceeding under the state's Forcible Entry and Detainer Act to be made by posting a summons on the tenant's apartment door. Noting that the "question presented is whether this statute, as applied to tenants in a public housing project, fails to afford those tenants the notice of proceedings initiated against them required by the Due Process Clause of the Fourteenth Amendment," the Court concluded that "in this case, appellees have been deprived of a significant interest in property: indeed, of the right to continued residence in their homes. In light of this deprivation, it will not suffice to recite that because the action is *in rem*, it is only necessary to serve notice 'upon the thing itself.'" 102 S.Ct. at 1879.

Justice O'Connor, joined by the Chief Justice and Justice Rehnquist, entered a sharp dissent. In her view, the Court "holds that notice via the mails is so far superior to posted notice that the difference is of constitutional dimension. How the Court reaches this judgment remains a mystery, especially since the Court is unable, on the present record, to evaluate the risks that notice mailed to public housing projects might fail due to loss, misdelivery, lengthy delay, or theft. Furthermore, the advantages of the mails over posting, if any, are far from obvious. It is no secret, after all, that unattended mailboxes are subject to plunder by thieves. Moreover, unlike the use of the mails, posting notice at least gives assurance that the notice has gotten as far as the tenant's door."

b. Tenant Breaches and Leaves

SAGAMORE CORP. v. WILLCUTT

Supreme Court of Connecticut, 1935.
120 Conn. 315, 180 A. 464.

BANKS, Judge.

The complaint alleged that on October 1, 1934, the plaintiff leased to the defendant for the term of one year from that date certain premises for the annual rental of $480 payable at the rate of $40 a month on the first day of each month in advance, that the defendant occupied the premises until February 1, 1935, on which day he moved out and thereafter notified the plaintiff that he would no longer comply with the terms of the lease and would pay no further rent, and that as a result of the defendant's breach of the lease the plaintiff has suffered as damages the difference between the rental specified in the lease and the reasonable rental value of the premises for the remainder of the term. The defendant's demurrer to the complaint, stated in four paragraphs, makes a single claim; that the breach of a covenant to pay rent creates no debt until the time stipulated for payment arrives, that the defendant owes the plaintiff no duty except to pay the rent on the first of each month during the remainder of the term, and consequently the plaintiff is not entitled, in an action brought before the expiration of the term of the lease, to recover damages for the defendant's anticipatory breach of his covenant to pay rent.

The lessee has abandoned the leased premises and refused to pay any further rent. The lessor in such a situation has two courses of action open to him. He may accept the surrender of the premises, thereby terminating the lease and effecting a rescission of the contract, or he may refuse to accept the surrender. In the latter case he may let the property lie idle and collect the balance of the rent due under the lease, or he may take possession of the property and lease it to others, in which case he may recover from the original lessee the balance of the rent due under his lease less the rent received from the new lessee. Whether the taking possession of the premises constitutes a rescission of the contract depends upon his intent. The action in that case is one to recover the rent which the lessee has covenanted to pay, and of course cannot be maintained until such rent becomes due and payable under the terms of the lease. By bringing this action for damages for breach of contract, the plaintiff has manifested its intention to accept the surrender of the premises, and has acquiesced in the termination of the lease and the rescission of the contract. Its action is one for damages for the breach by the defendant of his covenant to pay rent.

The arguments and briefs of counsel appear to have proceeded largely upon the assumption that the breach arose out of the repudiation by the defendant of his obligation to pay rent which would accrue in the future and therefore constituted an anticipatory breach, or, more accurately, a breach by anticipatory repudiation of his contract. A positive statement to the promisee that the promisor will not perform his contract constitutes an anticipatory repudiation which is a total breach of contract, except in cases of a contract originally unilateral and not conditional on some future performance by the promisee and of a contract originally bilateral that has become unilateral and similarly unconditional by full performance by one party. Where the contract was originally unilateral or has become so by the performance of one party, no breach can arise before the time fixed in the contract for some performance. There must be some dependency of performance in order to make anticipatory breach possible. A lease is primarily a conveyance of an interest in land and its execution by the lessor may be said to constitute performance on his part, making the instrument, when considered as a contract, a unilateral agreement with no dependency of performance which would make an anticipatory breach possible. This, we take it, is the basis of the distinction which the defendant claims to exist between a covenant to pay rent in a lease of real estate and an ordinary executory contract.

But the plaintiff is not obliged to rely solely upon the rules controlling a right to recover for an anticipatory breach arising out of the defendant's repudiation of his obligation to pay rent to accrue in the future. The complaint alleges that the rent was payable on the first day of each month in advance, that the defendant moved out on the first day of February, 1935, and thereafter notified the plaintiff that he would pay no further rent. This can only be construed as an allegation of a refusal to pay the rent which had fallen due on that date as well as that to accrue in the future. This constituted a present breach of his covenant to pay rent when due. Granting the defendant's contention that a covenant to pay rent creates no debt until the time stipulated for payment arrives, that time had arrived, so far as the rent due February 1st was concerned, and his failure to pay that rent constituted a breach of the covenants of his lease. The question remains whether this was a total or only a partial breach. If the former, the plaintiff would be entitled to maintain this action to recover the damages alleged in its complaint; if the latter it would be limited to those resulting from the refusal to pay the rent due on February 1st. Considering a lease as a unilateral contract, or a bilateral contract that has been wholly performed by the lessor, the covenant to pay rent at certain fixed periods is a contract for the payment of money in installments, and the failure to pay any installment of rent as it falls due would constitute a partial breach of the lessee's contract. But when such a partial breach is accompanied or followed by a repudiation of the entire contract, the promisee may treat it as a total breach. Defendant's failure to pay the rent due on February 1st, considered alone, constituted a breach only of his agreement to pay that particular installment of rent. His subsequent statement to the plaintiff that he would no longer comply with the terms of the lease and would pay no further rent was a repudiation of his entire contract. The breach thereupon became a total one justifying an immediate action by the plaintiff to recover the damages which would naturally follow from such a breach.

. . .

There is no error.

In this opinion, the other Judges concurred.

SOMMER v. KRIDEL

Supreme Court of New Jersey, 1977.
74 N.J. 446, 378 A.2d 767.

PASHMAN, J.

We granted certification in these cases to consider whether a landlord seeking damages from a defaulting tenant is under a duty to mitigate damages by making reasonable efforts to re-let an apartment wrongfully vacated by the tenant. Separate parts of the Appellate Division held that, in accordance with their respective leases, the landlords in both cases could recover rents due under the leases regardless of whether they had attempted to re-let the vacated apartments. Although they were of different minds as to the fairness of this result, both parts agreed that it was dictated by Joyce v. Bauman, 113 N.J.L. 438, 174 A. 693 (E. & A. 1934), a decision by the former Court of Errors and Appeals. We now reverse and hold that a landlord does have an obligation to make a reasonable effort to mitigate damages in such a situation. We therefore overrule Joyce v. Bauman to the extent that it is inconsistent with our decision today.

I

A.

Sommer v. Kridel

This case was tried on stipulated facts. On March 10, 1972 the defendant, James Kridel, entered into a lease with the plaintiff, Abraham Sommer, owner of the "Pierre Apartments" in Hackensack, to rent apartment 6–L in that building.[1] The term of the lease was from

---

1. Among other provisions, the lease prohibited the tenant from assigning or transferring the lease without the consent of the landlord. If the tenant defaulted, the lease gave the landlord the

May 1, 1972 until April 30, 1974, with a rent concession for the first six weeks, so that the first month's rent was not due until June 15, 1972.

One week after signing the agreement, Kridel paid Sommer $690. Half of that sum was used to satisfy the first month's rent. The remainder was paid under the lease provision requiring a security deposit of $345. Although defendant had expected to begin occupancy around May 1, his plans were changed. He wrote to Sommer on May 19, 1972, explaining

> I was to be married on June 3, 1972. Unhappily the engagement was broken and the wedding plans cancelled. Both parents were to assume responsibility for the rent after our marriage. I was discharged from the U.S. Army in October 1971 and am now a student. I have no funds of my own, and am supported by my stepfather.
>
> In view of the above, I cannot take possession of the apartment and am surrendering all rights to it. Never having received a key, I cannot return same to you.
>
> I beg your understanding and compassion in releasing me from the lease, and will of course, in consideration thereof, forfeit the 2 month's rent already paid.
>
> Please notify me at your earliest convenience.

Plaintiff did not answer the letter.

Subsequently, a third party went to the apartment house and inquired about renting apartment 6–L. Although the parties agreed that she was ready, willing and able to rent the apartment, the person in charge told her that the apartment was not being shown since it was already rented to Kridel. In fact, the landlord did not re-enter the apartment or exhibit it to anyone until August 1, 1973. At that time it was rented to a new tenant for a term beginning on September 1, 1973. The new rental was for $345 per month with a six week concession similar to that granted Kridel.

Prior to re-letting the new premises, plaintiff sued Kridel in August 1972, demanding $7,590, the total amount due for the full two-year term of the lease. Following a mistrial, plaintiff filed an amended complaint asking for $5,865, the amount due between May 1, 1972 and September 1, 1973. The amended complaint included no reduction in the claim to reflect the six week concession provided for in the lease or the $690 payment made to plaintiff after signing the agreement. Defendant filed an amended answer to the complaint, alleging that plaintiff breached the contract, failed to mitigate damages and accepted defendant's surrender of the premises. He also counterclaimed to demand repayment of the $345 paid as a security deposit.

option of re-entering or re-letting, but stipulated that failure to re-let or to recover the full rental would not discharge the tenant's liability for rent.

The trial judge ruled in favor of defendant. Despite his conclusion that the lease had been drawn to reflect "the 'settled law' of this state," he found that "justice and fair dealing" imposed upon the landlord the duty to attempt to re-let the premises and thereby mitigate damages. He also held that plaintiff's failure to make any response to defendant's unequivocal offer of surrender was tantamount to an acceptance, thereby terminating the tenancy and any obligation to pay rent. As a result, he dismissed both the complaint and the counterclaim. The Appellate Division reversed in a *per curiam* opinion, 153 N.J.Super. 1 (1976), and we granted certification.

B.

Riverview Realty Co. v. Perosio

This controversy arose in a similar manner. On December 27, 1972, Carlos Perosio entered into a written lease with plaintiff Riverview Realty Co. The agreement covered the rental of apartment 5–G in a building owned by the realty company at 2175 Hudson Terrace in Fort Lee. As in the companion case, the lease prohibited the tenant from subletting or assigning the apartment without the consent of the landlord. It was to run for a two-year term, from February 1, 1973 until January 31, 1975, and provided for a monthly rental of $450. The defendant took possession of the apartment and occupied it until February 1974. At that time he vacated the premises, after having paid the rent through January 31, 1974.

The landlord filed a complaint on October 31, 1974, demanding $4,500 in payment for the monthly rental from February 1, 1974 through October 31, 1974. Defendant answered the complaint by alleging that there had been a valid surrender of the premises and that plaintiff failed to mitigate damages. The trial court granted the landlord's motion for summary judgment against the defendant, fixing the damages at $4,050 plus $182.25 interest.[2]

The Appellate Division affirmed the trial court, holding that it was bound by prior precedents, including Joyce v. Bauman, *supra*, 138 N.J.Super. 270, 350 A.2d 517 (App.Div.1976). Nevertheless, it freely criticized the rule which it found itself obliged to follow:

> There appears to be no reason in equity or justice to perpetuate such an unrealistic and uneconomic rule of law which encourages an owner to let valuable rented space lie fallow because he is assured of full recovery from a defaulting tenant. Since courts in New Jersey and elsewhere have abandoned ancient real property concepts and applied ordinary contract principles in other conflicts between landlord and tenant there is no sound reason for a contin-

---

2. The trial court noted that damages had been erroneously calculated in the complaint to reflect ten months rent. As to the interest awarded to plaintiff, the parties have not raised this issue before this Court. Since we hold that the landlord had a duty to attempt to mitigate damages, we need not reach this question.

uation of a special real property rule to the issue of mitigation. . . . [138 N.J.Super. at 273–74, 350 A.2d at 519; citations omitted]

We granted certification.

II

As the lower courts in both appeals found, the weight of authority in this State supports the rule that a landlord is under no duty to mitigate damages caused by a defaulting tenant. This rule has been followed in a majority of states, and has been tentatively adopted in the American Law Institute's Restatement of Property. Restatement (Second) of Property, § 11.1(3) (Tent. Draft No. 3, 1975).

Nevertheless, while there is still a split of authority over this question, the trend among recent cases appears to be in favor of a mitigation requirement.

The majority rule is based on principles of property law which equate a lease with a transfer of a property interest in the owner's estate. Under this rationale the lease conveys to a tenant an interest in the property which forecloses any control by the landlord; thus, it would be anomalous to require the landlord to concern himself with the tenant's abandonment of his own property.

For instance, in Muller v. Beck, [94 N.J.L. 311, 110 A. 831 (1920)], where essentially the same issue was posed, the court clearly treated the lease as governed by property, as opposed to contract, precepts.[3] The court there observed that the "tenant had an estate for years, but it was an estate qualified by this right of the landlord to prevent its transfer," 94 N.J.L. at 313, 110 A. at 832, and that "the tenant has an estate with which the landlord may not interfere." Id. at 314, 110 A. at 832. Similarly, in Heckel v. Griese, [12 N.J.Misc. 211, 171 A. 148 (1934)], the court noted the absolute nature of the tenant's interest in the property while the lease was in effect, stating that "when the tenant vacated, . . . no one, in the circumstances, had any right to interfere with the defendant's possession of the premises." 12 N.J.Misc. at 213, 171 A. 148, 149. Other cases simply cite the rule announced in Muller v. Beck, *supra*, without discussing the underlying rationale.

Yet the distinction between a lease for ordinary residential purposes and an ordinary contract can no longer be considered viable. As Professor Powell observed, evolving "social factors have exerted increasing influence on the law of estates for years." 2 *Powell on*

---

3. It is well settled that a party claiming damages for a breach of contract has a duty to mitigate his loss.

Real Property (1977 ed.), § 221[1] at 180–81. The result has been that

> [t]he complexities of city life, and the proliferated problems of modern society in general, have created new problems for lessors and lessees and these have been commonly handled by specific clauses in leases. This growth in the number and detail of specific lease covenants has reintroduced into the law of estates for years a predominantly contractual ingredient. [*Id.* at 181]

Thus in 6 *Williston on Contracts* (3 ed. 1962), § 890A at 592, it is stated:

There is a clearly discernible tendency on the part of courts to cast aside technicalities in the interpretation of leases and to concentrate their attention, as in the case of other contracts, on the intention of the parties, ...

This Court has taken the lead in requiring that landlords provide housing services to tenants in accordance with implied duties which are hardly consistent with the property notions expressed in Muller v. Beck, *supra*, and Heckel v. Griese, *supra*. *See* Braitman v. Overlook Terrace Corp., 68 N.J. 368, 346 A.2d 76 (1975) (liability for failure to repair defective apartment door lock); Berzito v. Gambino, 63 N.J. 460, 308 A.2d 17 (1973) (construing implied warranty of habitability and covenant to pay rent as mutually dependent); Marini v. Ireland, 56 N.J. 130, 265 A.2d 526 (1970) (implied covenant to repair); Reste Realty Corp. v. Cooper, 53 N.J. 444, 251 A.2d 268 (1969) (implied warranty of fitness of premises for leased purpose). In fact, in Reste Realty Corp. v. Cooper, *supra*, we specifically noted that the rule which we announced there did not comport with the historical notion of a lease as an estate for years. 53 N.J. at 451–52, 251 A.2d 268. And in Marini v. Ireland, *supra*, we found that the "guidelines employed to construe contracts have been modernly applied to the construction of leases." 56 N.J. at 141, 265 A.2d at 532.

Application of the contract rule requiring mitigation of damages to a residential lease may be justified as a matter of basic fairness. Professor McCormick first commented upon the inequity under the majority rule when he predicted in 1925 that eventually

> the logic, inescapable according to the standards of a 'jurisprudence of conceptions' which permits the landlord to stand idly by the vacant, abandoned premises and treat them as the property of the tenant and recover full rent, will yield to the more realistic notions of social advantage which in other fields of the law have forbidden a recovery for damages which the plaintiff by reasonable efforts could have avoided. [McCormick, "The Rights of the Landlord Upon Abandonment of the Premises by the Tenant," 23 Mich.L.Rev. 211, 221–22 (1925)]

Various courts have adopted this position.

The pre-existing rule cannot be predicated upon the possibility that a landlord may lose the opportunity to rent another empty apartment because he must first rent the apartment vacated by the defaulting tenant. Even where the breach occurs in a multi-dwelling building, each apartment may have unique qualities which make it attractive to certain individuals. Significantly, in Sommer v. Kridel, there was a specific request to rent the apartment vacated by the defendant; there is no reason to believe that absent this vacancy the landlord could have succeeded in renting a different apartment to this individual.

We therefore hold that antiquated real property concepts which served as the basis for the pre-existing rule, shall no longer be controlling where there is a claim for damages under a residential lease. Such claims must be governed by more modern notions of fairness and equity. A landlord has a duty to mitigate damages where he seeks to recover rents due from a defaulting tenant.

If the landlord has other vacant apartments besides the one which the tenant has abandoned, the landlord's duty to mitigate consists of making reasonable efforts to re-let the apartment. In such cases he must treat the apartment in question as if it was one of his vacant stock.

As part of his cause of action, the landlord shall be required to carry the burden of proving that he used reasonable diligence in attempting to re-let the premises. We note that there has been a divergence of opinion concerning the allocation of the burden of proof on this issue. While generally in contract actions the breaching party has the burden of proving that damages are capable of mitigation, here the landlord will be in a better position to demonstrate whether he exercised reasonable diligence in attempting to re-let the premises.

III

The Sommer v. Kridel case presents a classic example of the unfairness which occurs when a landlord has no responsibility to minimize damages. Sommer waited 15 months and allowed $4658.50 in damages to accrue before attempting to re-let the apartment. Despite the availability of a tenant who was ready, willing and able to rent the apartment, the landlord needlessly increased the damages by turning her away. While a tenant will not necessarily be excused from his obligations under a lease simply by finding another person who is willing to rent the vacated premises, here there has been no showing that the new tenant would not have been suitable. We therefore find that plaintiff could have avoided the damages which eventually accrued, and that the defendant was relieved of his duty to continue paying rent. Ordinarily we would require the tenant to bear the cost of any reasonable expenses incurred by a landlord in attempting to re-let the premises, but no such expenses were incurred in this case.

In Riverview Realty Co. v. Perosio, no factual determination was made regarding the landlord's efforts to mitigate damages, and defendant contends that plaintiff never answered his interrogatories. Consequently, the judgment is reversed and the case remanded for a new trial. Upon remand and after discovery has been completed, R. 4:17 *et seq.*, the trial court shall determine whether plaintiff attempted to mitigate damages with reasonable diligence, and if so, the extent of damages remaining and assessable to the tenant. As we have held above, the burden of proving that reasonable diligence was used to re-let the premises shall be upon the plaintiff.

In assessing whether the landlord has satisfactorily carried his burden, the trial court shall consider, among other factors, whether the landlord, either personally or through an agency, offered or showed the apartment to any prospective tenants, or advertised it in local newspapers. Additionally, the tenant may attempt to rebut such evidence by showing that he proffered suitable tenants who were rejected. However, there is no standard formula for measuring whether the landlord has utilized satisfactory efforts in attempting to mitigate damages, and each case must be judged upon its own facts. Compare Hershorin v. La Vista, Inc., 110 Ga.App. 435, 138 S.E.2d 703 (App.1964) ("reasonable effort" of landlord by showing the apartment to all prospective tenants); Carpenter v. Wisniewski, 139 Ind.App. 325, 215 N.E.2d 882 (App.1966) (duty satisfied where landlord advertised the premises through a newspaper, placed a sign in the window, and employed a realtor); Re Garment Center Capitol, Inc., 93 F.2d 667, 115 A.L.R. 202 (2 Cir. 1938) (landlord's duty not breached where higher rental was asked since it was known that this was merely a basis for negotiations); Foggia v. Dix, 265 Or. 315, 509 P.2d 412, 414 (1973) (in mitigating damages, landlord need not accept less than fair market value or "substantially alter his obligations as established in the pre-existing lease"); with Anderson v. Andy Darling Pontiac, Inc., 257 Wis. 371, 43 N.W.2d 362 (1950) (reasonable diligence not established where newspaper advertisement placed in one issue of local paper by a broker); Scheinfeld v. Muntz T.V., Inc., 67 Ill.App.2d 8, 214 N.E.2d 506 (Ill.App.1966) (duty breached where landlord refused to accept suitable subtenant); Consolidated Sun Ray, Inc. v. Oppenstein, 335 F.2d 801, 811 (8 Cir. 1964) (dictum) (demand for rent which is "far greater than the provisions of the lease called for" negates landlord's assertion that he acted in good faith in seeking a new tenant).

IV

The judgment in Sommer v. Kridel is reversed. In Riverview Realty Co. v. Perosio, the judgment is reversed and the case is remanded to the trial court for proceedings in accordance with this opinion.

For reversal in *Sommer* and reversal and remandment in *Riverview Realty Co.*: Chief Justice HUGHES, Justices MOUNTAIN,

NOTES

1. *Damages.* The landlord who accepts her tenant's surrender and pursues a damage theory, as in Sagamore v. Willcutt, is generally entitled to recover the difference between the rent reserved in the lease and the reasonable rental value of the premises—what a willing tenant would pay a willing landlord for the remainder of the term. Thus in *Willcutt*, where the tenant had promised to pay $480 annual rent in monthly installments of $40 each, and abandoned the premises with eight months remaining on the lease, if the reasonable rental value was $30 per month, plaintiff would have been entitled to damages of $10 per month [$40–$30] or a total of $80.00 damages for the remaining eight months.

Under what circumstances is reasonable rental value likely to differ from reserved rental? Is it more likely to differ in a short term or a long term lease? Is it fair to the defaulting tenant, or to the landlord, to measure reasonable rental by the value of the premises for the remainder of the term (eight months) rather than for a period equal to the entire term (one year)? As a practical matter, if the landlord promptly relets the premises to another tenant in an arms-length transaction, what figure will a court likely employ as the measure of reasonable rental value?

The general rule on damages is subject to two qualifications. First, if damages are awarded before the end of the term—say, on April 1, two months after the breach and six months before the end of the lease—an award of $60 for the period remaining ($10 damages per month × 6 months) will overcompensate the landlord by giving her presently a sum that, had the tenant not breached, she would only have received in future monthly installments of $10 each. Recognizing the time value of money, a court will discount awards based on future rents to present value so that, in the example just given, the landlord would receive not $60, but rather the present value of the right to receive $10 per month for the next six months. (For a refresher on the technique of discounting to present value, see pages 527 to 528 above.) The time value of money also means that awarding the landlord $20 on April 1 for the two months that have already elapsed will undercompensate her; a court would thus award the landlord interest on each $10 installment to compensate her for her lost use of money during the two-month period.

The second qualification to the general damages measure is that the landlord will be allowed to receive the entire amount of rentals lost over a reasonable period, and reasonable costs incurred in connection with reletting the premises. Thus, if Sagamore had been unable to find a new tenant to take possession until March 1, 1935, it would have been entitled to collect $40—the entire rent lost in February—rather than just the $10 loss of bargain, together with any brokerage or advertising expenses incurred in the course of reletting. See generally, R. Schoshinski, American Law of Landlord and Tenant 684–689 (1980).

2. *Reletting on Tenant's Account.* As an alternative to damages, the landlord may refuse to accept the tenant's surrender and, after notice to the tenant, relet the premises on the tenant's account—"in which case," as *Sagamore* notes, she "may recover from the original lessee the balance of the rent due under this lease less the rent received from the new lessee." Thus, if Sagamore had immediately relet the premises on February 1, for an eight-month term at $25 per month, it would have been entitled to receive $120 from Willcutt (eight months × $15 [$40–$25] per month), discounted to present value.

As its name suggests, the tenant's account theory rests on a conveyance view of leases: the premises belong to the tenant for the entire leasehold term and, in reletting them, the landlord is effectively acting as the tenant's agent. Under conveyance theory, if Sagamore had relet the premises for eight months at $50, rather than $25, per month, would Willcutt have been entitled to recover the $80 overage [($50–$40) × 8]? See Whitcomb v. Brant, 90 N.J.L. 245, 100 A. 175 (1917) (No). Why do you suppose the question arises so infrequently?

If *T*, to whom Sagamore relet the premises, defaulted and abandoned before the end of the eight-month term, would Willcutt be liable for the full reserved rental of $40 per month until Sagamore relet the premises again or the lease expired? If Sagamore relet to *T* for a one-year term, rather than for the eight months remaining on the Willcutt lease, would this have instantly relieved Willcutt of all liability? See United States National Bank of Oregon v. Homeland, Inc., 291 Or. 374, 631 P.2d 761 (1981).

3. *Is There a Landlord Duty to Mitigate?* Although it is probably still the majority rule that a landlord whose tenant has abandoned the premises is under no duty to mitigate damages, the position is not nearly as solid today as it was a half-century ago when *Sagamore* observed that the landlord "may let the property lie idle and collect the balance of the rent due under the lease."

According to one recent survey, "only twenty-five jurisdictions refuse to impose a duty to mitigate damages on landlords of residential tenancies when the tenant has abandoned. In seven states there are either no cases or the authority is divided. Twenty states have either judicially or legislatively imposed a duty upon the residential landlord to minimize the losses." With respect to commercial leases, "thirty-two jurisdictions still cling to the doctrine that the landlord need do nothing on the tenant's abandonment . . . . In ten states there are either no reported cases or the authority is divided on the question of mitigation. Ten other states have imposed a duty to minimize losses on landlords of commercial tenancies." The author concludes that the "trend in recent years has been to impose a mitigation duty on landlords, especially on those who let residential property, and there appears to be little reason to doubt that the trend is gaining momentum." Weissenberger, The Landlord's Duty to Mitigate Damages on the Tenant's Abandonment: A Survey of Old Law and New Trends, 53 Temple L.Q. 1, 7–10, (1980).

Should there be a landlord duty to mitigate? Do you find the reasons advanced in *Sommer* persuasive? Consider the opposing view, taken by the Restatement (Second) of Property, Landlord and Tenant, which imposes no duty to mitigate: "Abandonment of property is an invitation to vandalism, and the law should not encourage such conduct by putting a duty of mitigation of damages on the landlord." Section 12.1, Comment (i). Does a duty to mitigate encourage the productive use of property by giving the landlord an incentive to find a new tenant who can make at least some beneficial use of the premises? By allowing the landlord to let the premises lie idle, at no cost to her, but at substantial cost to the tenant, what kinds of settlements between landlords and tenants is the Restatement position likely to encourage?

4. When a duty to mitigate is imposed, what must the landlord do to discharge it? Reasonableness seems to be the watchword: the landlord must, to be excused, make a reasonable effort to advertise and show the premises for reletting, and must offer the reletting at a reasonable rent. As between landlord and tenant, who should bear the all-important burden of proof on the question whether the landlord acted reasonably? Compare MAR–SON, Inc. v. Terwaho Enterprises, Inc., 259 N.W.2d 289 (N.D.1977) (tenant must prove that landlord acted unreasonably) with Vawter v. McKissick, 159 N.W.2d 538 (Iowa 1968) (landlord must prove she acted reasonably). What position does Sommer v. Kridel take on the issue?

5. What, if anything, does *Sommer* enable a landlord to recover from an abandoning tenant? If the landlord acts promptly and reasonably to mitigate damages, *Sommer* would presumably give her the difference between the abandoning tenant's reserved rental and any amounts realized by the landlord from her efforts to mitigate. But what if the landlord elects not to mitigate? Does *Sommer* say that she will be entitled to recover nothing at all, or that she will be entitled to recover the difference between reserved rental and the amount she would have realized had she mitigated? Does *Sommer* say that there is a *legal duty* to mitigate, enforceable by specific performance? Or does it say only that the landlord has an *incentive* to mitigate since, if she fails to mitigate and lets the premises lie idle, the most that she can recover is the difference between reserved rental and fair rental value?

Was *Sommer* correct to impose a duty to mitigate on a landlord who, at the time the defaulting tenant abandoned, had several equivalent units vacant? Would it have been appropriate to require the landlord to lease the abandoned unit first, to a new tenant who might otherwise have taken one of the vacant units from the already existing stock? Would treating the apartment in question "as if it was one of his vacant stock" entitle the landlord to place the vacated unit last in his inventory, renting it only when the others were filled?

6. Is there any connection between a landlord's duty to mitigate damages and her duty not unreasonably to withhold consent to an assignment or sublease? It is not unusual for a tenant who wishes to leave the premises before the expiration of his term to present the landlord with a proposed assignee for the remainder of the term. If the landlord withholds consent to the assignment, the tenant will often leave anyway and, in a later action by the landlord to recover rent, will defend that the landlord failed to mitigate damages, as evidenced by her refusal to accept the proposed assignee. See, for example, Gruman v. Investors Diversified Services Inc., 247 Minn. 502, 78 N.W.2d 377 (1956).

The two duties possess at least surface differences. The minority rule prohibiting landlords from unreasonably withholding their consent to assignments and subleases is effectively a rule of contract interpretation and illegality, modifying lease provisions that give landlords this power. The minority rule on mitigation is effectively a rule respecting remedies, and rests on the view that, for remedial purposes, a lease is to be treated as a contract rather than as a conveyance. But do the two doctrines share deeper roots in notions of good faith, reasonableness and efficient land use? See, for example, Marmont v. Axe, 135 Kan. 368, 369, 10 P.2d 826, 827 (1932) ("Admitting the [landlords'] contention that there was no agreement on their part to accept the [proposed assignee] for a tenant, what was [the landlords'] duty? Clearly it was to do everything they reasonably could to lessen the injury they were about to suffer on account of losing [the tenant].").

Is it inconsistent for a jurisdiction to follow one rule but not the other? Suppose the reason the original tenant wished to assign was that the reserved rental was below current market value and the proposed assignee had agreed to pay him a premium for the right to take over the lease. Does the landlord's refusal to accept the proposed assignee necessarily imply that she will not mitigate if and when the original tenant abandons?

7. How much freedom does a landlord enjoy in seeking to mitigate damages? United States National Bank of Oregon v. Homeland, Inc., 291 Or. 374, 631 P.2d 761 (1981), raised the question, "When a leasehold tenant of commercial premises abandons the premises prior to the expiration of the lease, and the lessor relets the premises for a term extending beyond the expiration of the original

lease and at a higher rent, does such reletting constitute a termination of the lease, as a matter of law, thus freeing the tenant from any claim for damages accruing subsequent to the reletting?" 291 Or. at 375, 631 P.2d at 762. The question was important to the lessor, for the tenant to whom it relet had also defaulted and abandoned the premises before the end of the original term.

Resolving the issue in the negative, and holding for the landlord, the Oregon Supreme Court had "no hesitancy in concluding that attempting to relet for a longer or shorter term does not, of itself, bar the lessor's claim for damages as a matter of law, for to insist that the lessor relet only for the unexpired term of the lease might well inhibit marketability of the premises, particularly when a short term remained on the original lease. A new tenant might prefer or demand a shorter term or a longer term, depending on need." And, although "reletting or attempting to relet at the higher rent poses a more challenging inquiry, we also conclude that reletting or attempting to relet at the higher rate does not, as a matter of law, bar the landlord's claim for damages. Although any increase in rent may have a theoretical effect in limiting marketability, a lessor's duty to mitigate damages does not compel the reletting at less than the then fair rental value." 291 Or. at 379, 631 P.2d at 766.

8. *Landlord Strategy: Measure of Recovery.* Although the available common law remedies are all aimed at making the landlord whole, each may in fact leave her more or less than whole depending on the circumstances. Which remedy would you propose to a landlord client faced with an abandoning tenant in each of the following two recurrent circumstances:

(a) The premises were originally let for $40 per month, the fair market value after breach is $35 per month, and the most the landlord can find someone (her brother-in-law) to pay for them is $25. When will the amount to be paid by a new tenant *ever* differ from fair market value? Note that if the landlord relets on the tenant's account, and if the rental obtained from the new tenant was not arrived at in good faith, the landlord will recover only the difference between the reserved rental and the reasonable rental value of the premises.

(b) The fair rental value—say, $50 per month—*exceeds* the reserved rental? When will a tenant ever abandon or not assign or sublet in these circumstances?

Will it ever be in the landlord's interest to let the premises lie idle? Note that this remedy will give her no more than the reserved rental and, possibly, much less, if the abandoning tenant is either without resources or manages to convince a court that the duty of mitigation should be imposed.

9. *Landlord Strategy: Surrender.* Having chosen a remedy, the landlord must be careful to conform her conduct to her choice. The most troublesome issue is whether the circumstances indicate

that the premises have been surrendered, ending the landlord-tenant relationship. Surrender requires a meeting of minds between landlord and tenant and may occur when the two execute an instrument, complying with the Statute of Frauds, embodying their agreement to terminate the tenancy. More commonly, surrender occurs when the tenant performs some act, typically abandonment, indicating an offer to surrender, and landlord performs some act, typically retaking the premises, indicating an acceptance of that offer. Other acts inconsistent with a continued tenancy, such as accepting back the keys, changing the locks, altering the premises or reletting them for a longer term or higher rent may also be treated as evidence of an accepted surrender.

What steps should a landlord take if she wishes to proceed on a tenant's account theory and does not want her retaking of the premises to be later construed as an acceptance of surrender? One commentator suggests the difficulties landlords face in determining appropriate behavior: "The question whether, upon the tenant's abandonment of the premises, the landlord may lease them to another without thereby causing a surrender of the lease, and consequent termination of the tenant's liability for rent, is one of great practical interest, upon which the authorities are not in accord. There are a number of decisions to the effect that the landlord may so 'relet' to another and still hold the former tenant. By others it is regarded as necessary, in order that such reletting shall not effect a surrender, that the landlord, before making the new lease, inform the tenant that he is about to do so on the latter's account, that is, that the purpose is to reduce, but not necessarily to extinguish, the latter's liability for rent. By still another line of decisions it is adjudged that the reletting will terminate the liabilities under the previous lease, without any suggestion being made that a notice to the previous tenant would prevent this result." 2 H. Tiffany, The Law of Landlord and Tenant 1338–1339 (1910).

Some states offer statutory guides to landlord conduct. Wis.Stat. Ann. 704.29(4) (West 1981) spells out several "acts privileged in mitigation of rent or damages" which "do not constitute an acceptance of surrender," among them: "(a) entry, with or without notice, for the purpose of inspecting, preserving, repairing, remodeling and showing the premises; (b) rerenting the premises or a part thereof, with or without notice, with rent applied against the damages caused by the original tenant and in reduction of rent accruing under the original lease; (c) use of premises by the landlord until such time as rerenting at a reasonable rent is practical, not to exceed one year, if landlord gives prompt written notice to the tenant that the landlord is using the premises pursuant to this section and that he will credit the tenant with the reasonable value of the use of the premises to the landlord for such period; (d) any other act which is reasonably subject to interpretation as being in mitigation of rent or damages and which does not unequivocally demonstrate an intent to release the defaulting tenant." See generally, First Wisconsin Trust Co. v. L. Wiemann Co., 93 Wis.2d 258, 286 N.W.2d 360 (1980).

How would you draft a lease provision that will, on breach, protect a reletting landlord against a subsequent finding of an accepted surrender?

10. *Security Deposits*. However effective the elaborate edifice of landlord remedies may be in the context of commercial leaseholds, it is only rarely employed in short-term residential tenancies. It is the unusual residential landlord who thinks she can be made whole by letting the premises lie idle or by reletting them immediately and going after her departing tenant for the balance due. The costs of litigation are just too high, departing tenants too hard to find, and their pockets too often empty for the effort to be worthwhile. Rather, landlords will typically relet as quickly as possible, pocketing the one or two months' security deposit that they may have been sufficiently farsighted to obtain from their tenants at the outset of the term.

Security deposits are intended to secure tenant performance of lease obligations. Thus, at the end of the term, the tenant is to receive the deposit back, less any amounts required to compensate the landlord for losses incurred as a consequence of the tenant's breach. In the best of all possible worlds for landlords, the deposit could be as large as the landlord could convince the tenant to pay; the landlord could delay as long as she wished in returning the deposit at the end of the term and would be under no obligation to itemize or document her deductions for damage; and the fund would be hers to use throughout the leasehold term—an interest-free loan, with no strings on the landlord's power to invest it as she wished or to commingle it with her other funds. In short, the security deposit would have all of the self-help advantages, but none of the disadvantages, of distraint.

Although some elements of this landlord never-never land still exist in various places, common law developments and statutes enacted in more than half the states have substantially curbed landlord prerogative. Most of these statutes apply only to residential leases. Ariz.Rev.Stat. § 33–1321 (1974), to take one example, provides that the security deposit may not exceed one and one half months' rent and that the landlord must return the deposit, less accrued rent and itemized damages if any, within fourteen days after the lease terminates; noncompliance will entitle the tenant to recover the deposit together with damages equal to twice the amount wrongfully withheld.

Can a landlord escape these curbs by characterizing the tenant's front money as something other than a security deposit? As a general rule she can, although courts will resolve any doubt about the nature of the fund in favor of calling it a security deposit. A *bonus* paid by the tenant at the outset of the term as consideration for the landlord's entering into the lease belongs to the landlord free and clear, without any obligation to account or refund to the tenant. *Pre-*

paid rent, typically for the last month of the term also belongs exclusively to the landlord, although, of course, the tenant may occupy the premises for the prepaid period without further rental payments. *Liquidated damages* entitle the landlord to retain a fixed, prepaid sum if the tenant breaches and a court accepts the sum as reasonable and finds that under the circumstances it would have been difficult to calculate actual damages.

See generally, Kalish, Residential Tenant Security Deposits: A Legislative Proposal, 1974 U.Ill.L.F. 569; Note, Security Deposits in Residential Leases, 8 Val.U.L.Rev. 63 (1973).

B. RESIDENTIAL LEASES: THE PROBLEM OF SUBSTANDARD HOUSING

HEARINGS BEFORE SUBCOMM. ON BUSINESS AND COMMERCE OF SEN. COMM. ON THE DISTRICT OF COLUMBIA ON S. 2331, S. 3549, S. 3558

89th Cong. 2d Sess. 128–138 (1966).

SAMPLE DISTRICT OF COLUMBIA RENTAL AGREEMENT

THIS MONTHLY RENTAL AGREEMENT, made in duplicate original, this _____ day of _____ 19__ by and between _____ a corporation, hereinafter called Landlord, party of the first part, and _____, hereinafter called Tenant, party of the second part.

WITNESSETH: That the Landlord does hereby let unto the Tenant the premises known as No. _____, located in the District of Columbia, the same being a _____, by the month, commencing on the _____ day of _____ 19__, and for the monthly rental of _____ Dollars, payable in advance at the office of the Landlord, 829 13th ST., N. W. Washington, D.C., that is to say, on the _____ day of each ensuing month, in advance.

AND THE TENANT, does hereby agree as follows:

1. That he will, and does hereby take and hold said premises as Tenant by the month, subject to the delivery of possession by any present occupant, and agrees that the representations made on the signed application attached hereto, or material representation, and are made part of this agreement.

2. That he will pay said rent, at the time specified, without deduction or demand.

3. THAT HE WILL PAY ALL GAS AND ELECTRIC BILLS, AND OTHER CHARGES PROVIDED FOR HEREIN, AS THE SAME BECOMES DUE AND HE WILL MAKE THE NECESSARY DEPOSIT REQUIRED BY THE UTILITY COMPANY.

4. That he will not use, nor permit the premises or any part thereof to be used for any unlawful or disorderly purpose, nor will he permit any nuisance to be kept, conducted or permitted on or about said premises, and he will not permit any waste to be committed to said premises.

5. That he will use said premises for a private residence for himself and his immediate family, and he will not rent rooms to roomers, guests or other persons, nor will he part with possession of said premises, nor will he permit more than _____ persons to occupy said premises.

6. That he will comply with all health regulations or other Municipal regulations of the District of Columbia at his own cost and expense, and he will permit the Landlord, or any of the agents, servants or employees or contractors of the Landlord, or any inspector or official of the District of Columbia to make inspection of said premises at reasonable hours.

7. That he will not transfer or assign this agreement, nor let nor sub-let the premises in whole or in part, without the written consent of the Landlord, first had and obtained.

8. That he will keep the said premises, including any garages, if the same are rented under this agreement, or out-houses, in good order and condition, and in sanitary condition, and surrender the same at the expiration of this term in the same good order in which they are received, usual wear and tear and damage by fire, storm and the public enemy only excepted.

9. That he will keep the side-walks immediately in front of the said premises free from obstructions of all nature, properly sweep, and will remove snow and ice therefrom, unless he shall occupy an apartment in an apartment building.

10. That he will promptly give the Landlord notice of all damage or fire that may be caused to said premises and will permit the Landlord, or any of his agents, servants or employees or contractors, to make repairs thereon, which the Landlord considers necessary or desirable.

11. That he will not make any alterations or additions to the structure, equipment or fixtures of said premises without the written consent of the Landlord, first had and obtained.

12. That he will not do anything which would increase the rate of fire insurance upon the building.

13. All personal property in said premises shall be, and remain at his sole risk, and the Landlord shall not be liable for any damage to, or loss of such personal property arising from any acts of negligence of any other persons, nor from the leakings of the roof, or from the bursting, leaking or over-flowing of water, sewer or steam pipes, or from any heating or plumbing fixtures, or from electric wires or fixtures, or from any other cause whatsoever, nor shall the Landlord be

liable for any injury to the person of the Tenant or other persons in and about the said premises, including the family of the Tenant, and the Tenant expressly agreeing to save the Landlord harmless in all such cases.

14. That he will make repairs to any damages to the heating plant, pipes, radiators or plumbing fixtures caused by freezing, and repair or replace any other damage caused by freezing, and repair or replace any other damage caused to the premises by his negligence or the negligence of his servants, members of his family or other persons who may visit him, or any damages to the fixtures therein caused by improper use, or caused by failing to give them proper service.

15. That he will permit the Landlord to post a "For Rent" sign on said premises and show the same at reasonable hours to prospective Tenants in the event that he shall be given a notice to quit said premises by the Landlord.

16. That he will use said premises in a normal manner, and he will not permit noisy, boisterous or other conduct which shall be offensive to any other occupant of the building, and that he will conform to the rules and regulations now made, or hereafter made, by the Landlord for the Management of the building, its corridors, porches, lobbies, drives, grounds and other appurtenances, and of the delivery of goods, merchandise and other things by trades people and other persons.

17. THAT HE WILL NOT PERMIT, OR PERMIT TO BE KEPT, ANY LIVE ANIMALS OF ANY KIND, INCLUDING, BUT NOT LIMITED THERETO, OF BIRDS, DOGS, CATS, WITHOUT THE WRITTEN CONSENT OF THE LANDLORD, FIRST HAD AND OBTAINED.

18. PROVIDED ALWAYS, That if the Tenant shall fail to pay said rent, in advance, as aforesaid, although there should have been no legal or formal demand made, or break or violate any of the within covenants, conditions or agreements, then, and in any of said events, this agreement and all things herein contained shall, at the option of the Landlord, cease and determine, and shall operate as a Notice to Quit, the Thirty (30) days' written notice to quit being hereby expressly waived, and the Landlord may proceed to recover possession of said premises under and by virtue of the provisions of the Code of Laws for the District of Columbia, or by such legal process as may be, at the time, in operation and in force, in like cases relating to proceedings between Landlords and Tenants.

19. IT IS EXPRESSLY AGREED, THAT IN THE EVENT THAT A SEVEN (7) DAYS' SUMMONS IS ISSUED, AS AFORESAID, AND THE RENT IS SUBSEQUENTLY PAID, THE TENANT EXPRESSLY PROMISES AND AGREES TO PAY ALL COSTS, EXPENDED BY THE LANDLORD, INCLUDING COURT COSTS, NOTARY FEES, ATTORNEY'S FEES, AND COST OF WRIT OF RES-

TITUTION, SAID ATTORNEY'S FEE BEING $1.00. WHICH SUM SHALL BE DUE AND PAYABLE FROM THE TENANT BEFORE THE RENT DUE MAY BE PAID OR THE LANDLORD REQUIRED TO ACCEPT THE SAME AND UNLESS PAID, THE LANDLORD MAY, AT ITS OPTION, LAWFULLY REFUSE PAYMENT OF THE RENT, OR THE LANDLORD, MAY, AT ITS OPTION, DEDUCT SUCH ITEMS OF COST, AFORESAID, FROM SUCH SUMS PAID BY THE TENANT FIRST, AND APPLY THE BALANCE OF THE PAYMENT TO THE OVER-DUE RENT.

20. If proceedings shall, at any time, be commenced for the recovery of possession, as aforesaid, and a compromise or settlement shall be effected, either before or after judgment, whereby the Tenant shall be permitted to retain possession of said premises, then, such proceedings shall not constitute a waiver of any condition or agreement contained herein, or of any subsequent breach thereof, or of this agreement.

21. IT IS FURTHER UNDERSTOOD AND AGREED, That in the event the Tenant is adjudged a bankrupt, or makes an assignment for the benefit of his creditors, then, this agreement shall, at the option of the Landlord, immediately cease and determine, and said premises shall be surrendered to the Landlord, who hereby reserves the right, in either of said events to forthwith re-enter and repossess said premises.

22. IN THE EVENT THAT THE TENANT DESIRES TO GIVE UP SAID PREMISES, HE SHALL GIVE TO THE LANDLORD AT LEAST THIRTY (30) DAYS' WRITTEN NOTICE OF ANY INTENTION TO MOVE FROM SAID PREMISES, SAID NOTICE TO BE GIVEN ON OR PRIOR TO THE RENT DUE, AND SHALL BE ENTITLED TO LIKE NOTICE FROM THE LANDLORD, IN THE EVENT THE LANDLORD DESIRES POSSESSION OF SAID PREMISES, PROVIDED, HOWEVER, THAT THE TENANT, BY THE MONTH SHALL NOT BE ENTITLED TO ANY NOTICE IN THE EVENT SAID RENT IS NOT PAID, IN ADVANCE, WITHOUT DEMAND, OR IN THE EVENT OF THE BREACH OF THE AFORESAID COVENANTS, THE USUAL THIRTY (30) DAYS' WRITTEN NOTICE BEING HEREBY EXPRESSLY WAIVED IN SUCH EVENT.

23. IT IS EXPRESSLY UNDERSTOOD AND AGREED, THAT IF ELECTRICITY IS FURNISHED BY THE LANDLORD, THE SAME SHALL BE USED BY THE TENANT FOR LIGHTING, RADIO & TELEVISION ONLY, AND NO ELECTRIC HEATERS OR OTHER APPLIANCES OF ANY KIND SHALL BE USED BY THE TENANT, WITHOUT WRITTEN CONSENT OF THE LANDLORD. IT IS AGREED THAT THE TENANT WILL NOT INSTALL ANY AIR CONDITIONING EQUIPMENT IN SAID APARTMENT WITHOUT WRITTEN CONSENT OF THE LANDLORD, AND IN THE EVENT SUCH CONSENT IS GRANTED, THE TENANT SHALL

PAY AN INCREASE IN RENT BY THE SUM OF _____ PER MONTH PER AIR CONDITIONER FOR THE MONTHS BEGINNING MAY THRU SEPTEMBER.

24. IT IS FURTHER UNDERSTOOD AND AGREED, That in the event the Landlord sets apart, in the building, a laundry or storage room for the convenience of Tenants, Tenants may, at their own risk, and without cost, use the said laundry and storage facilities, if such is available; that such laundry or storage ingress or egress thereto and therefrom is for the convenience of the respective Tenants and is not operated or controlled by the Landlord; that employees of the Landlord are prohibited from, in any way, accepting any property of the Tenant as bailee or otherwise, or for safe keeping. And in the event that any such employee of the Landlord shall accept any property of the Tenant, in such event, the said employee shall thereupon become the agent of the Tenant which shall also apply to services rendered in moving and handling of articles in and for such laundry or storage room; the Tenant assumes all risk of loss and damage to said articles or things while in transit to and from said storage or laundry room.

25. IT IS FURTHER UNDERSTOOD AND AGREED, That if the Landlord furnishes heat for the entire building, the Landlord shall have no liability to the Tenant, due to any discontinuance of heat, hot water, for such services furnished, or for the discontinuance of any other services caused by accident, breakage, strikes, or for any other reason. And the Landlord shall not be liable for loss or damage to the property of the Tenant caused by moths, termites or other vermin, or by rain, water or steam that may leak into or flow from any part of said building or from any adjacent building or through any defects in the roof or plumbing or any other source.

IT IS FURTHER UNDERSTOOD AND AGREED, That the Tenant agrees to provide necessary trash and garbage receptacles for their own use, and not to mix the same and dispose of said trash and garbage, as required by law.

IT IS FURTHER UNDERSTOOD AND AGREED, That no waiver by the Landlord of any breach of any provision hereof shall operate as a waiver of the provision, itself, or any subsequent breach thereof. And the acceptance of rent by the Landlord with, or with the knowledge of such breach, shall, in no way, have any effect thereon and shall not operate as a waiver of the breach; in the event of any case filed in Court, the Tenant waives trial by jury. It being agreed that in the event that the Tenant shall depart this life hereafter and the Landlord shall desire to proceed to obtain possession, although there shall not be any administration of the estate of the Tenant, it is expressly understood and agreed that the Landlord may proceed by naming the Tenant to obtain possession, as in rem.

IN TESTIMONY WHEREOF, the parties have hereunto affixed their hands and their seals the day and year hereinabove first written,

I acknowledge receipt of a copy of the within agreement.

WILLIAM J. DAVIS, INC.,

_____(SEAL)
Tenant

By _____ (SEAL)
Authorized signature

_____(SEAL)
Tenant

NOTES

1. Would you, as tenant, sign the "Sample District of Columbia Rental Agreement" reprinted above? Would you be comfortable with your rights and liabilities under the lease? Are you certain that you know what those rights and liabilities are? For example, does the landlord have the obligation to put the tenant in possession at the commencement of the term? Under Paragraph 1, to what extent will a holdover tenant's refusal to vacate the premises relieve the new tenant of liability under the lease? Can you make any sense out of the tenant's agreement in Paragraph 1 "that the representations made on the signed application attached hereto, or material representation, and are made part of this agreement?"

Under Paragraph 4, is the tenant liable for permissive as well as affirmative waste? What is the content of tenant's agreement in Paragraph 5 not to "part with possession of said premises"? Does this do anything more than duplicate Paragraph 7's restrictions on assignment or subletting? Reread Paragraph 7 closely. Impelled by the policy favoring free alienability, might a court hold that Paragraph 7 does not prohibit the tenant's assignment of the right to possession? Does it make any sense to have a restriction on assignment or subletting in a month-to-month lease? In a lease in which the tenant's responsibilities respecting waste and other conduct are so closely circumscribed?

What opportunities do Paragraphs 16, 17 and 18 give the landlord for harassing and evicting a tenant for any reason or for no reason at all? Must the "rules and regulations" to which the tenant is required to "conform" be in writing and shown to the tenant? Does it matter, anyway, since the tenant is binding himself not only to existing rules but also to rules "hereafter made"? Are *all* of the "within covenants, conditions or agreements" likely to be so material to the lease that their violation will constitute grounds for termination? Although these restrictions might not appear overly cumbersome in a lease that tenant or landlord can terminate on thirty days' notice, would you allow your client to sign a one- or two-year lease containing the same restrictions?

Are the tenant's waivers of landlord tort liability in Paragraphs 13 and 25, and of the right to trial by jury in Paragraph 25, enforceable? A study of form residential leases in the New York metropolitan area disclosed that, although state legislation made such clauses wholly unenforceable, form leases there continued to include them. Bentley, An Alternative Residential Lease, 74 Colum.L.Rev. 836 (1974). What practical effect do these unenforceable clauses have in landlord dealings with tenants? What are the ethical obligations, if any, of a lawyer who finds such unenforceable clauses in the course of reviewing his or her client-landlord's form lease? See generally, Note, Preventing the Use of Unenforceable Provisions in Residential Leases, 64 Cornell L.Rev. 522 (1979).

Does the Sample Lease Agreement contain a single obligation undertaken by the landlord? Does it contain any landlord obligations that would not be required anyway, such as the obligation to give thirty days' notice to terminate a month-to-month tenancy? Will a covenant of quiet enjoyment be implied into this lease? If so, what does the landlord gain by not expressly including it?

For an analysis of standard form apartment leases used in sixteen cities across the United States, and a call for statutory reform aimed at requiring leases to disclose the full range of landlord and tenant rights against each other, see Berger, Hard Leases Make Bad Law, 74 Colum.L.Rev. 791 (1974).

2. Do tenants negotiate form leases? Do they even read them? A survey of one hundred tenants in three large apartment complexes in Ann Arbor, Michigan revealed that:

> . . . about half of a highly educated sample population never, in any meaningful sense, read the leases presented to them for signature, primarily because of a combined sense of powerlessness and frustration with the forbidding jungle of legal expertise. As a result, a large number of tenants were unaware of the existence of numerous important printed terms in their leases. Second, while about seventy per cent of the tenants thought most of their lease terms were "fairly easy to understand," at best only fifty per cent were able to answer simple problems posed about typical lease terms. Third, many tenants felt that a number of typical lease terms were either "somewhat unfair" or "grossly unfair." Fourth, and perhaps most important, the standard-form lease does not appear to be a negotiated document. While a few of the hardy souls who have swum against the current have achieved a modicum of success, it may well be that the lessor's iron gage will be exchanged for a velvet glove only so long as venturesome individuals remain a small minority. Furthermore, even these individuals have bargained with regard to one or two

fine-print terms at most. The single overwhelming fact is that the sample tenants were on the whole acutely conscious of their weak bargaining position.

Mueller, Residential Tenants and Their Leases: An Empirical Study, 69 Mich.L.Rev. 247, 276–277 (1970). These results probably overstate the comprehension and negotiability of residential leases among the public generally, for Mueller's respondents were unusually well-educated and informed. His sample consisted primarily of professionals (37%) and university students (33%); only one respondent had not completed high school, and 60% had obtained some graduate education.

3. Form leases save money for landlords and tenants alike by reducing drafting, negotiation, and other transaction costs. In terms of the cost and quality of housing that consumers get, does it really matter whether tenants read, or are able to negotiate, their leases? If landlords in a community compete for tenants, each will presumably seek to outdo the other in making its lease terms most attractive and in highlighting its most attractive terms. If the most important term to tenants is price, each landlord will presumably seek to underbid the other. If other terms—such as the duty to deliver possession or to provide heat and hot water—matter more to at least some tenants, landlords can be expected to compete by offering form leases embodying and highlighting their best offer on these terms, too—albeit at presumably higher rents than they could charge without these terms. Are there too many "ifs" in this paragraph to justify the operation of a marketplace unencumbered by government regulation?

4. The Uniform Residential Landlord and Tenant Act is doubtless the single most significant statutory development in the evolution of tenants' rights respecting the conditions under which they live. Based on the Model Residential Landlord and Tenant Code, which had been drafted and published under the auspices of the American Bar Foundation in 1969, the Act was promulgated by the National Conference of Commissioners on Uniform State Laws in 1972, and endorsed by the American Bar Association in February, 1974. Since 1972, at least sixteen states have enacted legislation incorporating substantial elements of the Act.

Taking as its central purposes, "to simplify, clarify, modernize, and revise the law governing the rental of dwelling units and the rights and obligations of landlords and tenants," and "to encourage landlords and tenants to maintain and improve the quality of housing," § 1.102(b)(1), (2), the Uniform Act incorporates, consolidates and rationalizes many of the common law and statutory reforms—considered in the pages that follow—that had evolved over the preceding decade.

On the origins, purposes and effects of URLTA generally, see Note, The Uniform Residential Landlord and Tenant Act: Facilitation of or Impediment to Reform Favorable to the Tenant? 15 Wm. &

Mary L.Rev. 845 (1974); Note, The Uniform Residential Landlord and Tenant Act: Reconciling Landlord-Tenant Law with Modern Realities, 6 Ind.L.Rev. 741 (1973); Blumberg & Robbins, Beyond URLTA: A Program for Achieving Real Tenant Goals, 11 Harv.C.R.–C.L.L.Rev. 1 (1976).

For criticisms, and proposals for amendment, of URLTA, see Strum, The Uniform Residential Landlord and Tenant Act: Some Suggestions for Improvement, 9 Real Prop.Prob. & Tr.J. 402 (1974); Clocksin, Consumer Problems in the Landlord-Tenant Relationship, 9 Real Prop.Prob. & Tr.J. 572 (1974).

5. The actual effects of legislation modelled after URLTA were observed in two cities—Portland, Oregon and Cleveland, Ohio—and the results were reported in Brakel, URLTA in Operation: The Oregon Experience, 1980 A.B.F. Research J. 565, and McIntyre, URLTA in Operation: The Ohio Experience, 1980 A.B.F. Research J. 587. An abstract introducing the two articles offers a sharp reminder of law's limits in effecting fundamental social and economic change. The authors' conclusion, "is that the legislation has been only marginally effective, benefiting primarily middle-income tenants in the suburbs or in the cities' better neighborhoods, while largely failing in the aim of helping the inner-city poor and upgrading the quality of slum housing. The general lesson is an old one: law reform attempts at rearranging basic socio-legal relationships often fail to achieve their intended effects, particularly when their effectuation is left to the initiative or ingenuity of those individual private parties who are least likely to possess or display these traits." 1980 A.B.F. Research J. 559.

6. As you read the following materials on the problem of substandard housing, you may find it useful, first, to try to form a clear idea of precisely what the problem is. Having characterized the problem, you might next consider the effects that different law reform vehicles—housing codes, common law doctrine, legislation—will have on the problem's resolution. Are these reforms, however well-intentioned, likely to improve the quality of housing significantly or even slightly? Are they likely to have no effect at all? Are they likely to lead to further declines in the quality and quantity of housing? Over the short run? Over the long run? What alternative reforms might be more effective? Equitable? Efficient? Assuming that some effective, equitable and efficient techniques can be found for upgrading the quality of housing, what does society gain, and what does it lose, by affirmatively restricting the quality of housing in which individuals can live?

1. THE MARKET FOR SUBSTANDARD HOUSING

J. LEVI, P. HABLUTZEL, L. ROSENBERG, J. WHITE, MODEL RESIDENTIAL LANDLORD–TENANT CODE 6–10 (1969)

1. Industrial Specialization Means Tenant Incompetence

The industrial revolution, aside from its purely economic effects, has influenced the landlord and tenant relationship significantly in two ways. First, the specialization required of workers on an assembly line means that the "rugged individualist" of American rural folklore is no more. The farmer is perforce a jack of all trades, but the urban worker at virtually any level needs but a single skill. Secondly, the increasing complexity of even simple dwelling facilities requires greater sophistication to properly maintain them or repair them. Thus, while the farmer of old could legitimately be asked to assume responsibility for extensive repairs and maintenance of his dwelling, the urban dweller, often as a matter of law, cannot.

The urban dweller cannot work on his own electrical system beyond replacing fuses and light bulbs; he cannot repair his own furnace; he can hardly work on his own plumbing. Specialists are needed for these functions.

2. Urbanization Means Multiple Dwellings

An industrial society, which requires a concentrated labor force, seems necessarily to imply the existence of multiple dwellings. It is significant that the only numerous multiple dwellings known to common law—inns, and later rooming houses—were governed by a law quite unlike that relating to leases. The proprietor of an inn assumed many more responsibilities in relation to his guest than a landlord does to a tenant, and at the same time the guest was more accountable to the proprietor for *his* actions. The modern apartment dweller more closely resembles the guest in an inn than he resembles an agrarian tenant, but the law has not generally recognized the similarity. In particular, the incompetence of the apartment dweller to make meaningful repairs is exacerbated by the difficulty of obtaining access to parts of the building under the landlord's control, and the necessity of obtaining the consent, if not the assistance, of fellow tenants.

3. Urbanization Means Externalities

A further consequence of urbanization is the increase of economic externalities. As used in economics, externalities are simply the cost or benefit imposed on or derived by persons not otherwise affected by private or public decision-making. In an ideal economic world, externalities are minimal, and decision-makers can give proper consideration to all costs and benefits created by their decision. Externalities increase in an urban situation as land is more densely settled, so that the decisions of a private developer increasingly affect his neighbor.

Externalities show up in their worst form in the urban situation in relation to deteriorating structures. If A owns an apartment building in a fairly nice neighborhood and lets it run down appreciably, he imposes a cost thereby on neighboring owners, who can no longer attract the same quality of tenants. As rents decrease, they, too, are no longer motivated to exert much energy on behalf of their property. As a result of one man's dereliction, a loss in economic worth has been suffered by an entire neighborhood.

The private market provides an excellent theoretical solution which is unworkable in practice. The neighboring apartment owners *could* buy out the offending property and maintain it themselves, or perhaps even negotiate an agreement whereby A promises to keep his building up. In real life, information costs and money costs prevent efficient solutions.

Private means of reducing externalities by contract become increasingly expensive where the number of people involved increases. Thus, for the maximization of public good, it becomes more and more necessary to make an agency of the collective will—the state—a party to private agreements. Common law reacted to this need with the unfortunately clumsy and limited law of nuisance. While there is a strong legitimate public policy to allow landlord and tenant to bargain freely regarding the condition of leased premises, other public interests are not reflected in the bargaining process, such as the effective integration of the lower-class tenant into the majority culture.

II. EXISTING LAW AS A CONTRIBUTING FACTOR IN SLUMS

1. The Irrelevance of Evil Slumlords

Are Slum Tenants Actually Oppressed? Available published figures are inconclusive, but isolated findings indicate that the return on slum property can be very good indeed. One critic has stated that a thirty percent return is not unusual. Slum property is sometimes recommended for those with nerve and capital to invest as a "smart" but tough investment. It is probably true that for every grasping slumlord, there are slum property-owners in great number who were locked into their unprofitable position by accident or without their control, and are unable to sell or improve the property in the existing market.

While landlords are locked into an unprofitable ownership in many cases, it is perhaps even more common that the tenant is locked into a position of frustration, indignation, and outright squalor. Even the non-slum urban dweller is usually surprised to learn that the landlord need not do anything for his property. The frustrated expectations of urban dwellers constitute, in economic terms, an externality which is not easily assessable in money terms.

Present Law and Market Operation Create Slums. The low-income tenant already spends the major portion of his income for housing, and can spend little, if any more, regardless of how much the property is improved. The landlord of bad property is therefore faced with the cost (amortization) of a potential improvement, together with potentially higher taxes which result from upgrading his property, compared with no significant increase in rental income. No landlord seeking a reasonable return from his property can make such an investment, however good his social conscience. A possible high-gain investment in slum property is an illegal conversion to create more units—which in turn facilitates the decline of the property "improved."

2. Specialized Incompetence

As discussed above, the typical urban dweller cannot, as a matter of fact and law, make any meaningful improvements in his dwelling unit. Particular specialists—plumbers, electricians, tuck-pointers, furnace repairmen—must be bought on the private market where the cost of information must be added to the cost of the service itself. The cost of information is the cost imposed on a market searcher to discover the "best deal." A property system like the existing one—which usually imposes this cost on the one-time user of the project, the tenant—is less efficient than a hypothetical system which imposes this cost on a multiple user of such services, the landlord. Even if the information cost is passed on to the tenants in higher rent (which it will be), the net average cost to a single tenant will be lower, simply because the landlord can achieve economies of scale unavailable to individual tenants.

3. Tenant Insecurity

Because of the shortage of housing in relation to available tenants, landlords are able to choose tenants economically on irrational grounds. Invidious discrimination is thus feasible. In particular, the landlord is able to select tenants who do not demand fit housing. The landlord can thus profitably err on the side of allowing his property to decline, whether this is in fact in his best long-run interest or not. Existing law further allows the landlord to discriminate in favor of tenants who give him the least trouble—those who do not organize tenant unions, or complain to code enforcement officials, or complain to him about stopped-up toilets. A landlord can effectively stifle legitimate desires and free speech without threatening his own profit.

Even where security of tenure is commonly higher, where residential printed lease forms are typical, the bargaining position of the landlord results in imaginatively oppressive lease forms, in which the tenant perforce agrees that any breach—such as carrying groceries up the front stairs, taking a vacation for longer than 10 days, or keeping a parakeet—will entitle the landlord to terminate the lease.

The result is that even tenants who perform in good faith cannot be certain of their duration of tenancy. Deterioration of housing is accelerated when tenants hesitate to make repairs themselves because they may not be in the dwelling unit long enough to enjoy the fruits of their labors.

HEARINGS BEFORE THE SUBCOMM. ON BUSINESS AND COMMERCE OF THE SEN. COMM. ON THE DISTRICT OF COLUMBIA ON S. 2311, S. 3549, S. 3558

89th Cong.2d Sess., 165, 167–169, 185–186, 192–193 (1966).

BACKGROUND MEMORANDUM ON SLUM HOUSING AND LANDLORD–TENANT RELATIONS IN THE DISTRICT OF COLUMBIA

Census data shows that there were 3,870 dilapidated units and 23,143 deteriorating units in the District of Columbia in 1960.

An additional 16,909 housing units lacked some or all plumbing facilities. (U.S. Censuses of Population and Housing: 1960—Census Tracts—Washington D.C.—Md., Va. 145 (1960)).

Using Census data, National Capital Housing Authority concluded that 61,300 housing units in D.C. were either structurally substandard, overcrowded or lacked facilities.

91,900 renter households, amounting to 36.5 percent of the city's total households, could not afford sound uncrowded housing on the private market by paying 25 percent or less of gross annual household income for rent. Translated into population, these figures mean that 269,200 persons, amounting to 37.3 percent of the District's total household population were deprived of sound uncrowded housing at rentals reasonable in comparison with income.

20,900 renter households earned more than the maximum allowable for entrance to public housing but less than required to obtain sound uncrowded housing on the private market.

UPO interviewed tenants in six low income areas of Washington during summer 1965. (12,000 units) : 12% of units surveyed reported hand rails missing; 41% reported cracking plaster—35% falling plaster; 33% reported broken window panes; 35% rotting woodwork; 33% holes in walls; 31% reported plumbing leaks.

This situation persists a decade after promulgation of the District of Columbia Housing Regulations which were designed to alleviate these conditions. At the time of their enactment it was anticipated that the Housing Regulations, extensively realigning duties and responsibilities of landlord and tenant, would effectively ameliorate slum housing conditions.

STATEMENT OF NATHAN HABIB, WASHINGTON HOMEOWNERS & PROPERTY OWNERS ASSOCIATION

Mr. HABIB. I am executive vice president of the Washington Homeowners & Property Owners Association. I represent people who own homes, rent homes, live in the District and in these surrounding areas.

Washington Homeowners & Property Owners Association would like to thank Senator Tydings, Senator Dominick, and members of the Senate District Committee for giving the courtesy of allowing me to comment and review the salient provisions of S. 3549 and S. 2331 as it affects District of Columbia property owners. We believe that this legislation would not accomplish its objectives because it has put the major responsibility for the housing of the poor on the property owner with little regard for the tenants whose lack of interest, performance, and respect for the District of Columbia codes on housing and sanitation is so obvious. . . .

There are basic differences between Washington and other areas. Every District of Columbia property owner has due regard for the Department of Licenses and Inspections for if he does not he will be summoned to court quickly. The housing laws of the District of Columbia depend on the quality of enforcement through the number of men budgeted for inspection. If you require tighter enforcement, then you need more men; but if you get too tight, no one can keep up with the demands and you will have to dispose of rental properties.

Washington at 1.7 has the lowest vacancy ratio in the United States.

With regard to the profits in rental housing, any contact with the Internal Revenue records for District of Columbia would eliminate this solution. With taxes increasing in the District of Columbia by use of increased appraised values on improvements and low income areas; increased taxes on land values on select areas; increased maintenance and repair costs; greater emphasis on quality by inspectors for painting, plastering, carpentry, masonry, et cetera; cost of labor doubling so that one inspection of code survey eliminates your profit on rental housing for the whole year; in addition the actions of the tenants who skip in the night plus freezes in the cold of winter, vandalism, stopped up sinks, broken windows, missing door knobs, missing balustrades, doors off hinges and piles of trash and filth all turning to reduce profits to less than 6 percent of investment. If there is any way to make money in low income rentals by one who has many years of experience, willing to work 7 days a week all hours of the day and night, must have the patience of a saint, skill in collecting rents, making repairs, handling tenants, community organizations and be willing to comply with the demands of inspection organizations of the District of Columbia government, and satisfy these demands—

Senator KENNEDY. What do you receive, what is your income then each year?

Mr. HABIB. In the neighborhood of $220,000.

Senator KENNEDY. Well, you are doing reasonably well.

Mr. HABIB. No; I am not, sir.

Senator KENNEDY. $220,000?

Mr. HABIB. When you look at some of the maintenance bills and the repairs and the water bills and the architect and gas bills, these would compare very favorably with your bills in maintaining a big property which you live in.

Senator KENNEDY. What are your expenses then of the $220,000?

Mr. HABIB. Over 30 percent.

Senator KENNEDY. Thirty percent of what?

Mr. HABIB. Of the gross.

Senator KENNEDY. What is your investment here?

Mr. HABIB. My investment is over $1.7 million.

Senator KENNEDY. Then you are grossing $220,000?

Mr. HABIB. That is my gross. Then we take off 6 percent interest, all the water, electric, gas bills to the dwelling and we get into a loss position.

Senator KENNEDY. In your tax return last year you had a loss?

Mr. HABIB. Yes, sir.

Senator KENNEDY. You got a loss in your tax returns; you reported a loss in your tax returns last year?

Mr. HABIB. Yes, sir. . . .

Senator TYDINGS. Now I gather from your testimony the 1.9 percent housing vacancy in the District of Columbia and the fact that you consider Washington to have a better housing court, better housing provisions, better housing situation, that Washington is really in excellent condition compared with the other cities of the country. Is that right?

Mr. HABIB. With regard to the availability of an instrument that can be responsible under law and due process of law it ranks first in the United States in terms of the large cities. Any city that has a population of 700,000 or better, yes, without any equivocation.

Senator TYDINGS. And, of course, when you have a 1.9 vacancy rate that means that anybody who owns property does far better, say, than if he owned property in Cleveland, Baltimore, New York, where you have a 7 percent?

Mr. HABIB. Not only do they do better, but I would like to remind the Senator that the foundation of democracy and the capitalist system is based on the true work of supply and demand. In the marketplace where you have a tremendous demand you have the key and optimum situation for an industry running on a maximum efficiency and for enforcement if you have laws, and you do have laws.

Senator TYDINGS. Would you say that Washington would be the most advantageous city to own housing property in the country?

Mr. HABIB. No; it is no longer the most advantageous city because in the 2d, 9th, 10th, and 13th precincts we are going through a social revolution. We are going through a situation where we have a tremendous maintenance and repair cost, we have conservation programs, we have community organizations, tenants, not working as a coordinated team with the District of Columbia and the landlords and the people in the community but rather in competition.

Senator TYDINGS. Is it a true fact that if you acquire real estate, multifamily dwellings, rental dwellings from Washington you can initially pay off the purchase price sooner than in most other cities in the country in the like-type of housing?

Mr. HABIB. No; because in the District of Columbia you have a situation where you have annual inspection. Each year, for example, if you put in for a license in 1965 you could have your 1965 license in December of that year. When 1966 comes you get another inspection.

Senator TYDINGS. I thought you said the District had the best system of housing inspection.

Mr. HABIB. All of this housing inspection with the low-income families and the regularity of the inspection calls for costs and this increases your cost to the point where you cannot get a high return whereas in Maryland and Virginia there are no such regular inspections.

As a result you have a situation where people are making investments in these multidwelling units and getting a higher return and the key question is the vacancy factor in the metropolitan area. The intelligent investor is going into the suburbs of Maryland and Virginia and paying a little bit more but he is getting a better return due to the fact that his maintenance and repair costs are not comparable, they are much higher in the District of Columbia with regard to multidwellings. There is very little financing available for multidwellings in those units. One of the things that you may not realize is that the people in the District of Columbia who own property do not put out 100-percent cash, they buy their property if there is financing, and if the climate is bad and there is no financing there are very few people who can put out $4,000 to $8,000 to buy a multidwelling unit and exist; they just don't have it.

Senator TYDINGS. You indicated you owned some 300 units in the District of Columbia.

Mr. HABIB. That is correct.

Senator TYDINGS. How many units did you purchase before 1960?

Mr. HABIB. A hundred.

Senator TYDINGS. What would be approximately the average number of years—2 years, 3 years, 4 years—that you pay off the purchase price of that property?

Mr. HABIB. I never paid off the purchase price; I am still paying on it.

Senator TYDINGS. Your gross rentals on that property, how many years before they would total the purchase price?

Mr. HABIB. Senator, the gross rentals on the property—

Senator TYDINGS. The next question I am going to ask you would be your net rental.

Mr. HABIB. The gross rentals on the property, the maximum rents that we get for an efficiency—

Senator TYDINGS. I am talking about the properties you acquired prior to 1960, the 100 properties. I am trying to find out what was the average period of time you held the property before they paid for themselves. Just roughly. Two years? Below or above?

Mr. HABIB. It is 5 and 6 years for property before 1960, 6 to 10 years for property after 1960.

NOTE

Legal rules on habitability cannot be assessed in a vacuum. Facts and theory are needed to delineate the contexts in which these rules are applied. Unfortunately, the available facts and theory fall far short of the detail needed for a complete understanding of the effect of legal rules on rental housing markets. For example, it is one thing for the Levi excerpt, above, to theorize about the "information costs and money costs" that in real life "prevent efficient solutions," and quite another to explain why urban landlords have not entered into arrangements like those employed by neighbors in residential subdivisions aimed at stabilizing property values and maintaining efficient uses over large areas. And, it is one thing for a landlord to perplex a United States Senator with the assertion that he reported "a loss" in last year's tax return, and quite another to analyze that loss, identifying the extent to which it represents a loss actually incurred and the extent to which it represents only a paper loss—and a tax benefit—created by the Internal Revenue Code's generous allowance for depreciation deductions.

A small handful of empirical studies provide probably the best available information on rental housing markets. Although these studies are limited by methodological flaws, they do enable some fairly confident generalization. Indeed, given the disparity in their methodologies and locale, the most striking feature of these studies is their unanimity in rejecting the prevalent stereotype of substandard housing: that it is the product of wealthy, monopolistic landlords who, in their zeal to reap huge profits from desperately substandard premises, will steadfastly refuse to bring their buildings up to standard.

Who Are the Slumlords? George Sternlieb's study of Newark, New Jersey's slum housing in the 1960's, revealed that ownership was scattered among a large number of small landlords rather than among a small number of large ones: 42.8% of the properties in Sternlieb's 385-parcel sample were owned by individuals who owned no other houses; 21.6% by individuals who owned only one or two other properties; 10.9% by those owning three to six other properties; 7.8% by those owning seven to twelve other properties, and 15.8% by those owning more than twelve. G. Sternlieb, The Tenement Landlord 122–123 (1966). A 1973 RAND study of housing in Brown County, Wisconsin, revealed that "nearly all rental real estate in the county" is "owned and managed as a sideline by nonprofessional investors. The typical landlord is the owner of a small multiunit property on which he lives, caring for the property after work or on weekends. Only thirteen landlords own more than ten properties, and only large apartment buildings, mobile home parks, and a few rooming houses seem to be professionally developed and managed." RAND, Second Annual Report of the Housing Assistance Supply Experiments 63 (May 1976).

What Do These Slumlords Earn on Their Investments? At the high end, a study of 123 parcels in Milwaukee indicated an average 19.8% rate of return on equity. (In arriving at this figure, the study apparently did not count as a cost the owners' unpaid efforts at managing and maintaining their properties.) Sporn, Empirical Studies in the Economics of Slum Ownership, 36 Land Econ. 333, 336 (1960). Sternlieb's Newark study found that landlords' average return on investment was "in the neighborhood of 10 to 12 percent." G. Sternlieb, The Tenement Landlord 88 (1966). An earlier study of New York City's West Side Urban Renewal Area estimated a 10% rate of return. C. Rapkin, The Real Estate Market in an Urban Renewal Area 81–82 (1959). And RAND's Brown County study showed an average 2.4% net rate of return on capital. RAND, Second Annual Report of the Housing Assistance Supply Experiment 78 (May 1976). All of these figures should be taken with a grain of salt. None, apparently, accounted for the real changes in income represented by capital gains and losses, or for the tax benefits yielded by use of the depreciation deduction available under the Internal Revenue Code.

How Substandard Is Slum Housing? After reviewing several studies, one writer concluded that "there seems to be general agreement that the quality of American housing has steadily improved since the Depression years of the 1930's when President Franklin D. Roosevelt spoke of a third of the population being ill-housed. Traditionally, a dwelling was considered inadequate if it was in need of major repairs or if it lacked complete plumbing. Under these standards of physical condition and sanitation, nearly a quarter of all occupied units in 1960 were still substandard, with the highest incidence of problems occurring in rural areas. By 1970, however, only 11 percent of households, most of them in rural areas, still lived in physically inadequate housing even though the concept of housing adequacy had become steadily more demanding . . . . In 1980, a study by the United States Department of Housing and Urban Development found that only 5.3 million households (4.4 percent) were then living in physically inadequate conditions as judged by current standards. According to every available measure of quality, the housing stock steadily improved from 1970 to 1977. Nevertheless, certain geographical areas have not followed the national trend. According to the 1981 Interim Report of the President's Commission on Housing:

> They [inadequate units] are found disproportionately in rural areas in the South and in older, larger cities. New York City and the nearby New Jersey cities of Newark, Paterson, and Jersey City showed a particularly high concentration (almost 19 percent), double the average of other large cities. New York City alone accounted for more than 29 percent of all deficient housing in large cities identified in the 1977 Annual Housing Survey and for 9 percent of all deficient housing in the country. Miami and Washington, D.C. both had more than a 16 percent incidence of inadequate units.

Although substandard housing has been reduced nationwide, it clearly remains a severe hardship for many persons." Glendon, The Transformation of American Landlord-Tenant Law, 23 B.C.L.Rev. 503, 564–565 (1982).

Will Tenants Pay for More Quality? "Housing deprivation is changing from a problem of physically inadequate shelter to a problem of excessive cost. The number of households living in physically inadequate units has declined sharply since 1960. However, the number of those paying an unreasonably high percentage of their incomes for rent has increased rapidly." B. Frieden & A. Solomon, The Nation's Housing: 1975 to 1985, 87 (1977). The President's Commission on Housing reported that, of the 10.5 million poorest households in the country, two million dwelt in substandard housing and that almost 6.5 million spent more than 30% of their income on rent. Report of the President's Commission on Housing 11–12 (1982). Absent subsidy, the implications for housing quality are clear: tenants, already strapped by the expense of survival cannot be expected to shift expenditures from other necessities, such as food and clothing, to improvements in the quality of shelter.

2. EFFORTS TO REGULATE QUALITY

a. Administrative Enforcement

ABBOTT, HOUSING POLICY, HOUSING CODES AND TENANT REMEDIES: AN INTEGRATION
56 B.U.L.Rev. 1, 41–44, 49–51 (1976).

The earliest antecedent of modern housing codes may have been a colonial ordinance designed to create fireproof zones in New York City by requiring houses to be constructed of stone or brick and roofed with tile or slate. The ordinance presumably included any structure in the fireproof zone and not specifically residences. Its subject matter would be found today in a building or zoning code. The earliest example of a housing law as such is the New York tenement house law of 1867. This law only applied to lodging houses and to multi-unit dwellings housing three or more families within the building or two or more families on the same floor. The nineteen sections of the act mandated, among other things, that tenements be equipped with ventilators, fire escapes, "good and sufficient water closets or privies," refuse containers, watertight roofs and adequate chimneys. The law also regulated ceiling height and window area in tenement houses erected after its passage.

The enactment of the tenement house law by New York was apparently prompted by two reasons: the concentration of the immigrant poor of New York City in abysmal living conditions and the fear that such conditions contributed to recurrent cholera epidemics that carried poor and rich alike to an early grave. The public health purpose of the statute was clear by the designation of the Metropolitan Board of Health, created in the previous year, as the enforcement agency. In 1868, Massachusetts enacted a statute for Boston that was patterned after the 1867 New York law. In 1901, New York enacted a new tenement house law, expanding the sections on minimum standards from nineteen to more than 100. A system of building permits and tenement house registration supplemented administrative action by the Board of Health to vacate or condemn noncomplying structures. By 1920, some twelve states and forty municipalities had some form of housing law. Most of these housing laws applied only to multi-unit dwellings, and many of the state laws applied only to the larger cities within the state.

The evil perceived in enacting these laws remained the same: the effect of dilapidated and crowded tenements on the immigrant urban poor and, through contagion, on the rest of society. Lawrence Veiller, an early housing reformer, expounded the public health philosophy of tenement laws:

> Housing evils as we know them today are to be found in dangerous and disease-breeding privy vaults, in lack of water supply, in dark rooms, in filthy and foul alleys, in damp cellars, in basement living rooms, in conditions of filth, in inadequate methods of disposal of waste, in fly-born disease, in cramped and crowded quarters, in promiscuity, in lack of privacy, in buildings of undue height, in inadequate fire protection, in the crowding of buildings too close together, in the too intensive use of land.[241]

To Veiller the solution was legislative prohibition, "the most effective remedy."

> The only way that we know of by which such conditions can be ended is through the enactment of laws which will compel the removal of these evils and the substitution of right conditions.[242]

The transition from center city tenement house regulation to statewide regulation of all dwelling units was largely prompted by the federal government. By 1949, the effect of little new construction during the Depression and World War II had created considerable obsolescence in the center city housing stock. Most of the available land within cities had been developed. The middle class exodus to the suburbs gathered momentum as the insurance benefits provided by the Veterans Administration and the Federal Housing Administration brought mortgage financing of new home purchases within the financial reach of an upwardly mobile urban middle and lower-middle class. The migration to the cities of lower income blacks and whites from rural America, increasing during the war years, continued unabated. Faced with evidence of urban stagnation, Congress enacted the Housing Act of 1949 [244] to provide federal grants and loans for slum clearance and urban redevelopment. Under the Act, the program administrator, in deciding whether to extend aid to a particular city, was to consider if the local government had undertaken

> positive programs . . . for preventing the *spread or recurrence* . . . of slums and blighted areas through the adoption, improvement and modernization of local codes and regulations relating to land use and adequate standards of health, sanitation, and safety for dwelling accommodations.[245]

Implicit in this legislative direction to the program administrator was the belief that a housing code, properly drafted and effectively enforced, would be a significant weapon in the fight against spreading "blight"—the phenomenon of undermaintenance and obsolescence ac-

241. L. Veiller, A Model Housing Law 5 (rev. ed. 1920).

242. *Id.*

244. Housing Act of 1949, ch. 338, §§ 101–10, 63 Stat. 413, *as amended,* 42 U.S.C. §§ 1450–90 (1970).

245. *Id.* § 101(a), 63 Stat. 414, *as amended,* 42 U.S.C. § 1451(a) (1970) (emphasis added).

companied by deteriorating public services that planners in the 1950s likened to a plant disease. The Housing Act of 1954 [246] changed the concept from urban *redevelopment* to urban *renewal.* The change signaled the belated recognition that conserving and upgrading existing structures and neighborhoods might, in some cases, be preferable to bulldozing away whole sections of cities. As a prerequisite both for urban renewal funding and for federal housing subsidies, each city needed a federally approved "workable program for community improvement." [247] The 1954 statute authorized housing codes as elements of a "workable program." Administratively, housing codes were made a requirement for workable program approval. This administrative requirement was incorporated into the urban renewal statute in 1964.[248] As a justification for requiring housing codes, the associate general counsel for the Housing and Home Finance Agency—the agency that administered the urban renewal program—stated:

> Slums and blight are brought about by owners of property who are unable or unwilling to maintain or improve their property at decent levels, by unconscionable, profiteering landlords squeezing bootleg profits out of wretched housing, and occasionally by tenants who are indifferent to their squalid environments. But . . . the ultimate causation factor is the local government itself [that fails] to enforce effectively . . . adequate police power measures to control bad housing, improper environments and overcrowding.[250]

As a result of the federal housing code requirement conditioning urban renewal and housing subsidies, the adoption and revision of codes proceeded rapidly. The Housing and Home Finance Agency reported that in 1956 only about fifty-six communities had housing codes. By 1968, the National Commission on Urban Problems counted 4,904 communities with housing codes, not including statewide codes. Although this 1968 figure represented only about twenty-five percent of the nation's urban communities—communities either within a standard metropolitan statistical area (SMSA) or without but with over 1,000 population—some eighty-five percent of the cities with over 50,000 population and about fifty percent of the cities with between 5,000 and 50,000 population had housing codes. No tabulation has been made since 1968, but presumably the trend has

246. Housing Act of 1954, ch. 649, § 303, 68 Stat. 623, *as amended,* 42 U.S.C. § 1451(c) (1970).

247. The requirement of an approved workable program for receipt of federal subsidies under the public housing program, Housing Act of 1956, ch. 1029, § 401, 70 Stat. 1103, or the section 221(d)(3) program, Housing Act of 1961, Pub.L. No. 87–70, § 101(b), 75 Stat. 153, was eliminated in 1969. Housing and Urban Development Act of 1969 § 217(a), 42 U.S.C. § 1451(c) (1970).

248. Housing Act of 1964, § 301(a), Pub.L. No. 88–560, 78 Stat. 785, *as amended,* 42 U.S.C. § 1451(c) (1970).

250. Guandolo, Housing Codes in Urban Renewal, 25 George Washington L.Rev. 1, 3 (1956).

continued. In addition, at least six states have statewide codes.[255]
. . .

C. *The Problem of Effective Code Enforcement*

Whatever the efficiency of their standards, housing codes cannot achieve their purposes unless they are enforced. Although much discussion has been devoted to the problem of ineffective enforcement, surprisingly little attention has been paid to the meaning of "effective" enforcement. One possible measure would be the elimination of substandard housing. By this measure few communities would approach effective enforcement. An economist might refine the concept from effective to "cost-effective" code enforcement—enforcement up to the point at which an additional unit of enforcement costs the community more than it will return in additional benefit. Most commentators agree that effective code enforcement at least means a higher level of code compliance than is now evident in communities that have enacted codes.

Two questions bear upon the problem of effective code enforcement: (1) How to enforce a code—what remedies for noncompliance administered by which institutions will best enforce it? (2) Where to enforce a code—in all neighborhoods, the worst neighborhoods, or neighborhoods where property values and maintenance are declining?

1. Administrative Enforcement of Housing Codes

Initially, code enforcement remedies were administratively enforced. Early tenement house laws empowered the board of health to order premises vacated that were not in code compliance once the owner had been notified of the violation and had failed to repair within a reasonable time. Vacated structures were then ordered demolished if they had not been repaired within six months. If the owner failed to comply, the municipality was usually authorized to board up the building and eventually demolish it. The costs in doing so became a lien against the property.

The order to vacate, followed by demolition, is a drastic remedy; it removes dwelling units from the housing stock, temporarily or permanently, and leaves the tenants homeless. Unless the community has standard relocation housing into which the displaced families can move, their eviction may be politically unpopular and futile in improving their housing conditions. They will be forced to absorb the costs, psychological and monetary, of moving and may end up in equally substandard housing. Thus, to be effective, the remedy needs a very high vacancy rate—estimated at over twenty-five percent—in standard housing to avoid these harsh consequences. For example, va-

---

255. Cal. Health & Safety Code § 17910 *et seq.* (West Supp. 1975); Iowa Code Ann. § 413.1 *et seq.* (Supp. 1975–1976); Mich.Stat.Ann. § 5.2771 *et seq.* (1969); Minn.Stat.Ann. § 460.01 *et seq.* (1963); Wis.Stat.Ann. § 704.01 *et seq.* (Spec. Pamphlet 1975); Mass. Dep't of Public Health, State Sanitary Code art. II (1969).

cate orders were used effectively in New York City in the early 1900s and again in the 1930s when such high vacancy rates existed in the housing market. But such high vacancy rates are unlikely to obtain today.

As a code enforcement remedy, a vacate order can play into the hands of a recalcitrant landlord who wishes to rid himself of troublesome tenants without resort to the eviction process. By allowing his building to become seriously substandard, the landlord can trigger an order to vacate that would then allow him to remodel or tear down the vacant structure. Yet the vacate order can be a powerful sanction because it cuts off entirely the landlord's rent revenues. However, it must be a credible threat to effect code compliance; at present, because of housing market conditions, it seldom is.

The other traditional administrative remedy is criminal prosecution leading to fine or imprisonment. Under most codes, the continued existence of housing code violations is a misdemeanor. Each additional day the condition persists often constitutes a separate violation. However, criminal prosecution poses many problems. One major hurdle is obtaining personal jurisdiction over the owner. In the ownership of low income urban apartments, corporations whose officers and places of business cannot be located, agents who cannot locate or identify their principals, and titles that are frequently transferred are not uncommon. Determining and finding responsible parties is difficult. Some jurisdictions require registration of owners and the authorization of service of process on a natural person living within the jurisdiction. But the jurisdictional problem can still recur in prosecuting owners of unregistered buildings.

Another difficulty with this remedy is the delay in criminal court calendars compounded by delay in building inspections. Once the owner is brought within the jurisdiction of the court and tried, sentencing can create still another problem. Judges traditionally have taken the view that housing code violations are not serious offenses, apparently because the failure to correct the condition alone constitutes the offense and financial incapacity or a good faith attempt is no defense. Judges, therefore, grant continuances to encourage eventual compliance and mete out small fines when compliance is not forthcoming. Teitz and Rosenthal summarized their survey of criminal prosecutions for housing violations in New York City as follows:

> Criminal Court prosecution is slow and its impact is negligible. In 1968–69, the average time between placement of a violation and first court appearance was over 18 months. For those cases adjudicated in 1969, the average fine imposed by the Court was $12.62, or $1 to $3 per violation. Criminal prosecutions have little effect on violation removal. Of 329 cases studied in 1968–69, only 53 percent of the violations brought to court had been removed one

year later; more than half of these had been removed before the case reached the Criminal Court.[284]

The modest sanctions and the long delays readily explain why landlords may submit to prosecution and pay the fine as a cost of doing business rather than make costly repairs.

HEARINGS BEFORE SUBCOMM. ON BUSINESS AND COMMERCE OF SEN. COMM. ON THE DISTRICT OF COLUMBIA ON S. 2331, S. 3549, S. 3558

89th Cong., 2d Sess. 193–195 (1966).

The [District of Columbia] Housing Regulations apply "to every premises or part thereof, occupied, used, or held out for use as a place of abode for human beings," (D.C. Housing Regulations § 2102 (1965) and lay down minimum standards of repair and sanitation. As to leased premises, Section 2304 of the Regulations prohibits the rent or offering to rent any habitation "unless such habitation and its furnishings are in a clean, safe and sanitary condition, in repair and free from rodents or vermin." After the premises are rented, the tenant is responsible for maintaining sanitary conditions in the premises under his exclusive control, the landlord being responsible for the sanitation of all other areas. (D.C. Housing Regulations § 2601 (1965)). The Regulations impose on the lessor the duty to provide heat and other utilities and to maintain ventilation equipment when such facilities are under his control. (D.C. Housing Regulations §§ 2401–10 (1965)). It is the further responsibility of the owner or licensee of the premises to provide and maintain plumbing facilities, hot water equipment, lighting in common areas, electrical outlets and certain kitchen facilities. (D.C. Housing Regulations §§ 2401–10 (1965)).

Sections 2501–2515 of the Regulations set out minimum standards of general maintenance and repair required of all habitations but are silent as to where the responsibility lies for compliance with these standards when premises are rented. The courts, however, have held that the responsibility for compliance with Sections 2501–2515 lies with the owner-lessor (National Bank v. Dixon, 112 U.S.App.D.C. 183, 301 F.2d 507 (1961); Whetzel v. Jess Fisher Management Co., 108 U.S.App.D.C. 385, 282 F.2d 943 (1969)).

B. ADMINISTRATION AND ENFORCEMENT OF THE HOUSING REGULATIONS

The agency primarily charged with enforcement of Housing Regulations is the Housing Division of the Department of Licenses and Inspections. Violations of the Housing Regulations are detected by inspections conducted by this Department.

---

284. M. Teitz & S. Rosenthal, Housing Code Enforcement in New York City xi (1971).

Licenses and Inspections Housing Inspectors: There are 77 including 3 field supervisors. There are also 6 regular supervisors. They are requesting funds for 30 more.

Inspections are made approximately every two years, but if complaints are received from the public an immediate inspection is made, usually within twenty-four hours. (There were 10,784 complaints in fiscal 1964. Annual Report—Fiscal Year 1964, Department of Licenses and Inspections, Housing Division.) Inspections are made of exteriors on a continuing basis by inspectors assigned to particular areas for this purpose. Often exterior inspection will lead to detection of interior violations. Inspections are made, also, upon referrals from other agencies. In 1965, these referrals totaled 2381.

When violations are detected the normal procedure is to issue a notice of violation and order to correct. In 1965 the Housing Division processed 154,959 violations. Basically, the violations appear to deal mainly with rodents, vermin, trash and garbage disposal and structural defects. This order gives the responsible party (the owner, the manager, or the licensee of the property) a reasonable time in which to correct defects set out in the notice. What constitutes a reasonable time depends upon the nature and extent of the particular violation, and seems to rest with the discretion of the individual inspector issuing the notice. The usual period for compliance is thirty days. Extensions up to sixty days are granted by supervisory personnel when the party responsible for the violation shows good cause why he cannot comply with the time originally allowed. Usually extensions are granted when the owner must vacate the premises in order to correct the violations, or when a good faith attempt to comply has been made, but due to labor or material shortage or financial conditions, the work cannot be completed within the time initially allotted.

The Housing Division of Licenses and Inspections reports that of its 154,595 cases in 1965, 145,069 were corrected by notices: 5592 were dismissed as constituting no violation; and only 4328 were referred to the Corporation Counsel. Furthermore, they report that 55% of their cases are closed within 30 days of notice served and an additional 35% within 90 days of notice served.

The Housing Regulations provide for the granting of a variance, in effect an excusal from correcting a violation, in the case of excessive structural or mechanical difficulty or impracticability. (D.C. Housing Regulations § 2702 (1965).) The request for a variance must be filed within the period for compliance specified in the notice, or within thirty days from the time of service of the notice, whichever is earlier. The decision to grant or deny a variance is made by the Director of Licenses and Inspections or the Board of Appeals and Review (an administrative appeals board), if the matter is either referred to it by the Director, or if an adverse decision by the Director is appealed in accordance with procedures set out in Section 2703 of the Regulations.

Upon failure to comply with the order of the Department of Licenses and Inspections or with the decision of the Board of Appeals, the case is referred to the Corporation Counsel. The Corporation Counsel will issue a summons to the responsible party to appear for a "compliance hearing" at the Corporation Counsel's office. The return date is generally fourteen days after issuance of the summons. The hearing consists of an informal appearance before a representative of the Enforcement Branch of the Department of Licenses and Inspections and an Assistant Corporation Counsel. If the offending party indicates that the violations have been corrected, an immediate reinspection of the premises is made either by the agency which initially issued the violation notice or by an inspector in the Enforcement Branch. If the violations have been corrected, the case will be dismissed by the Corporation Counsel. If it is found that the violation persists, the recalcitrant landowner is often given another extension of time in which to comply. Upon compliance the case is dropped.

If an extension is not given, or upon expiration of the continuance, Corporation Counsel will proceed to prosecution of the responsible party by ordering a warrant of arrest to be issued. The defendant is required to post collateral as security for his later appearance in court. The amount of collateral required is determined from a schedule fixed by the Court of General Sessions depending upon the violation. Time within which the warrant is returnable varies from case to case, depending in part on the status of the court docket. The premises are reinspected before the return date. If the violations have been corrected, a representative of the Corporation Counsel so informs the judge. At this point, if the defendant pleads guilty a suspended sentence (no fine) is often imposed upon the recommendation of the Assistant Corporation Counsel. If the defendant has not corrected the violations by the time of his appearance and has a tenable excuse for not doing so, he may plead guilty and obtain a continuance of sentence. Usually the continuance is granted on the consent of the Corporation Counsel. Then, if the violations are corrected before the adjourned date, a suspended sentence is ordinarily imposed. A great majority of the cases which reach the Court are disposed of without trial.

In fiscal year 1964 only 115 cases reached the General Sessions Court, as compared to the 7,440 cases referred to the Corporation Counsel's office. (Workable Program 1963–1964, report on the District of Columbia Office of Urban Renewal submitted by the District Commissioners to the HHFA, July 21, 1964, p. 7E.)

For a violation of the Housing Code, the maximum punishment is $300 fine or ten days in jail or both. (D.C. Housing Regulations § 2104 (1965).) Every day in which the defendant continues in violation constitutes a separate offense.

A person is not in violation until after expiration of the time fixed for compliance in the notice of violation. In the past few jail sentences have been imposed for housing violations.

C. TENANT RESPONSIBILITY

Some cities, like Chicago and New York, avoid prosecuting tenants, relying instead on the general maintenance provisions of the code to hold landlords liable. Tenant prosecutions are unpopular with politically vocal minority groups. In addition, problems of proof and high tenant mobility in blighted areas make prosecution complicated and expensive. Furthermore, criminal sanctions may be ineffective to deter tenant violations that stem from ignorance or urban life, malicious attitudes toward landlords, or general frustration. Nonetheless, a city actively enforcing its code would seem morally obligated to prosecute violating tenants as well as landlords. Failure to deter tenant violation impedes effective enforcement by placing on the owner the burden of excessive maintenance costs and by fostering landlord resentment of the enforcement program. But because immediate correction of existing violations is necessary, landlords will probably remain the focus of enforcement. By prosecuting a tenant for causing a violation and the landlord for permitting the condition to persist a city could, perhaps, deter future tenant violations while assuring correction of existing defects. . . .

SUMMARY ENFORCEMENT PROCEDURE

The enforcement procedure currently followed sometimes leads to the ultimate punishment of the offender but does not provide an effective means of prompt abatement of the condition resulting from the violation. Following the present procedure for processing violations, a conservative estimate of the time lapse between detection of a violation and final disposition of the case by Court, the violator availing himself of all appeals and extensions within the Housing Division, at the Corporation Counsel stage and at trial, would be six to seven months. Thus, many violators procrastinate for many months before making any effort to comply, secure in the knowledge that they will not be penalized for their delay and that most probably any fine imposed for the initial violation will be suspended upon eventual compliance.

The time-consuming procedures within the Corporation Counsel's Office, such as summons to appear at compliance hearing, the hearing itself, further extensions, reinspections, and eventual issuance of an arrest warrant, would thus be eliminated. Increasing the amount of collateral would undoubtedly prompt more serious efforts to comply within the time initially allotted in order to avoid the depositing of substantial collateral.

QUESTIONS

A newspaper article published shortly before the hearings excerpted above highlighted several problems with housing code enforcement in the District of Columbia. One problem that both landlords and tenants complained about was "the lack of a clear standard for enforcement. The landlords say different inspectors use different criteria for spotting violations and the tenants complain that the lack of quality control permits landlords to use cheap materials in repairs." But, according to the article, "mostly it is the long delays and the constant threat of retaliatory evictions that frustrate these dwellers seeking to get repairs in their homes." "Compliance on Repairs is Often Delayed," Washington Star, July 20, 1965.

The article also notes "the suspicion by tenants that inspectors can be bought off by landlords." "One real estate man said that years ago, owners and agents always provided the inspectors with generous Christmas gifts. 'We all used to do it,' he said, 'but then one time an inspector came by to get his gift, and I saw his car was packed full of whiskey so I cut it out.' The agent said he now occasionally will ask an inspector to come by one of his properties to advise him about repairs that will be necessary to meet the code. 'I usually give them $5 or $10 for the favor,' he said, 'but I've only done this a couple of dozen times in the past 25 years.'" The article reported the fear of District Commissioner Walter N. Tobriner, "that with strict enforcement and lower profits the landlord either evicts the tenants, rehabilitates the property and rents to high income groups, or evicts the tenants, razes the building and converts the land to some other use.' 'There is a dilemma,' Tobriner said. 'Tough enforcement could have the unintended effect of reducing the housing supply rather than improving housing conditions.'"

On housing codes and their enforcement see generally, Gribetz & Grad, Housing Code Enforcement: Sanctions and Remedies, 66 Colum.L.Rev. 1254 (1966); Note, Enforcement of Municipal Housing Codes, 78 Harv.L.Rev. 801 (1965); Note, Building Codes, Housing Codes and the Conservation of Chicago's Housing Supply, 31 U.Chi.L. Rev. 180 (1963).

b. Common Law Doctrine

SCHOSHINSKI, REMEDIES OF THE INDIGENT TENANT: PROPOSAL FOR CHANGE, 54 Geo.L.J. 519, 520–521 (1966): The following are common problems of the indigent tenant which sorely need the aid of legal counsel in their solution:

(1) Because of the current shortage of urban housing and his poor economic position, the indigent tenant is often forced to accept premises at the commencement of a tenancy in an "as is" condition falling

short of habitability. Can the landlord be compelled to deliver possession of premises in a habitable state?

(2) The housing shortage also curtails the indigent tenant's freedom to move when his premises become uninhabitable due to landlord neglect during the tenancy. Must the tenant continue to pay rent while the premises are uninhabitable?

(3) When a tenant attempts to better his housing condition by withholding rent or by taking affirmative action in the courts or by seeking compliance with housing regulations, he is often subjected to retaliatory rent increase or eviction. Can these landlord reprisals be effectively restrained?

(4) Because of his lack of bargaining power, the indigent tenant is forced to accept many onerous terms in his lease. Is the indigent tenant bound by these terms?

i. Contract

(A) Illegality

BROWN v. SOUTHALL REALTY CO.
District of Columbia Court of Appeals, 1968.
237 A.2d 834.

QUINN, Judge.

This appeal arises out of an action for possession brought by appellee-landlord, against appellant-tenant, Mrs. Brown, for nonpayment of rent. The parties stipulated, at the time of trial, that the rent was in arrears in the amount of $230.00. Mrs. Brown contended, however, that no rent was due under the lease because it was an illegal contract. The court held to the contrary and awarded appellee possession for nonpayment of rent.

Although counsel for appellant stated at oral argument before this court that Mrs. Brown had moved from the premises and did not wish to be returned to possession, she asserts that this court should hear this appeal because the judgment of the court below would render certain facts res judicata in any subsequent suit for rent.[1] In Bess v. David, supra, a suit by a landlord against a tenant for recovery of rent owed, defendant contended that he did not owe rent because he was not a tenant during the time alleged. The defendant was, however, denied that defense, this court stating on appeal that ". . . we think *any* question of appellant's tenancy is foreclosed

---

1. Edwards v. Habib, D.C.App., 227 A.2d 388 (1967); Bess v. David, D.C.Mun. App., 140 A.2d 316 (1958); David v. Nemerofsky, D.C.Mun.App., 41 A.2d 838 (1945).

by the judgment in the previous *possessory* action." (Emphasis supplied.) 140 A.2d 317.

Thus, because the validity of the lease and the determination that rent is owing will be irrevocably established in this case if the judgment of the trial court is allowed to stand, we feel that this appeal is timely made.

Although appellant notes a number of errors, we consider the allegation that the trial court erred in failing to declare the lease agreement void as an illegal contract both meritorious and completely dispositive, and for this reason we reverse.

The evidence developed at the trial revealed that prior to the signing of the lease agreement, appellee was on notice that certain Housing Code violations existed on the premises in question. An inspector for the District of Columbia Housing Division of the Department of Licenses and Inspections testified that the violations, an obstructed commode, a broken railing and insufficient ceiling height in the basement, existed at least some months prior to the lease agreement and had not been abated at the time of trial. He also stated that the basement violations prohibited the use of the entire basement as a dwelling place. Counsel for appellant at the trial below elicited an admission from the appellee that "he told the defendant after the lease had been signed that the back room of the basement was habitable despite the Housing Code Violations." In addition, a Mr. Sinkler Penn, the owner of the premises in question, was called as an adverse witness by the defense. He testified that "he had submitted a sworn statement to the Housing Division on December 8, 1964 to the effect that the basement was unoccupied at that time and would continue to be kept vacant until the violations were corrected."

This evidence having been established and uncontroverted, appellant contends that the lease should have been declared unenforceable because it was entered into in contravention to the District of Columbia Housing Regulations, and knowingly so.

Section 2304 of the District of Columbia Housing Regulations reads as follows:

> No persons shall rent or offer to rent any habitation, or the furnishings thereof, unless such habitation and its furnishings are in a clean, safe and sanitary condition, in repair, and free from rodents or vermin.

Section 2501 of these same Regulations, states:

> Every premises accommodating one or more habitations shall be maintained and kept in repair so as to provide decent living accommodations for the occupants. This part of the Code contemplates more than mere basic repairs and maintenance to keep out the elements; its purpose is to include repairs and maintenance designed to make a premises or neighborhood healthy and safe.

It appears that the violations known by appellee to be existing on the leasehold at the time of the signing of the lease agreement were of a nature to make the "habitation" unsafe and unsanitary. Neither had the premises been maintained or repaired to the degree contemplated by the regulations, i.e., "designed to make a premises . . . healthy and safe." The lease contract was, therefore, entered into in violation of the Housing Regulations requiring that they be safe and sanitary and that they be properly maintained.

In the case of Hartman v. Lubar, 77 U.S.App.D.C. 95, 96, 133 F.2d 44, 45 (1942), cert. denied, 319 U.S. 767, 63 S.Ct. 1329, 87 L.Ed. 1716 (1943), the court stated that, "[t]he general rule is that an illegal contract, made in violation of the statutory prohibition designed for police or regulatory purposes, is void and confers no right upon the wrongdoer." The court in Lloyd v. Johnson, 45 App.D.C. 322, 327 (1916), indicated:

> To this general rule, however, the courts have found exceptions. For the exception, resort must be had to the intent of the legislature, as well as the subject matter of the legislation. The test for the application of the exception is pointed out in Pangborn v. Westlake, 36 Iowa 546, 549, and approved in Miller v. Ammon, 145 U.S. 421, 426, 36 L.Ed. 759, 762, 12 Sup.Ct.Rep. 884, as follows: "We are, therefore, brought to the true test, which is, that while, as a general rule, a penalty implies a prohibition, yet the courts will always look to the subject matter of it, the wrong or evil which it seeks to remedy or prevent, and the purpose sought to be accomplished in its enactment; and if, from all these, it is manifest that it was not intended to imply a prohibition or to render the prohibited act void, the court will so hold and construe the statute accordingly."

Applying this general rule to the Housing Regulations, it may be stated initially that they do provide for penalties for violations. A reading of Sections 2304 and 2501 infers that the Commissioners of the District of Columbia, in promulgating these Housing Regulations, were endeavoring to regulate the rental of housing in the District and to insure for the prospective tenants that these rental units would be "habitable" and maintained as such. The public policy considerations are adequately stated in Section 2101 of the District of Columbia Housing Regulations, entitled "Purpose of Regulations." To uphold the validity of this lease agreement, in light of the defects known to be existing on the leasehold prior to the agreement (i.e., obstructed commode, broken railing, and insufficient ceiling height in the basement) would be to flout the evident purposes for which Sections 2304 and 2501 were enacted. The more reasonable view is, therefore, that where such conditions exist on a leasehold prior to an agreement to lease, the letting of such premises constitutes a violation of Sections 2304 and 2501 of the Housing Regulations, and that these Sections do indeed "imply a prohibition" so as "to render the prohibited act void."

Neither does there exist any reason to treat a lease agreement differently from any other contract in this regard.

Thus, for this reason and those stated above, we reverse.

Reversed.

DIAMOND HOUSING CORP. v. ROBINSON, 257 A.2d 492, 495 (D.C.Ct.Apps.1969), HOOD, C.J.: In view of the fact that our opinion in Brown v. Southall Realty Co., has caused some confusion regarding the proper procedure for a landlord to regain possession when the lease has been held illegal and unenforceable, we add the following. When it is established that a lease is void and unenforceable under the Brown v. Southall ruling, the tenant becomes a tenant at sufferance and the tenancy, like any other tenancy at sufferance, may be terminated on thirty days' notice. The Housing Regulations do not compel an owner of housing property to rent his property. Where, as here, it has been determined that the property when rented was not habitable, that is, not safe and sanitary, and should not have been rented, and if the landlord is unwilling or unable to put the property in a habitable condition, he may and should promptly terminate the tenancy and withdraw the property from the rental market, because the Regulations forbid both the rental and the occupancy of such premises.

QUESTIONS

Is Brown v. Southall likely to encourage tenants to demand, and landlords to make, the repairs needed to upgrade substandard premises? Will tenants under illegal leases be likely to complain if, as Diamond v. Robinson holds, their tenancies can be terminated on thirty days' notice? A later decision, William J. Davis, Inc. v. Slade, 271 A.2d 412 (D.C.App.1970), held that although the tenant can recover any rent paid under the illegal lease, the landlord can set off against this sum the premises' reasonable rental value. Will landlords be likely to make needed repairs if they know that they can recover the leased premises' reasonable rental value from these statutory tenants at sufferance? When will reasonable rental value—the fair market value of the premises in substandard condition—ever be less than the reserved rental—the rent the tenant agreed to pay for the premises in their substandard condition?

The illegality defense innovated in Brown v. Southall has won few adherents outside the District of Columbia, doubtless because of its intrinsic limitations and the comparative attractiveness of an alternative contract theory—the implied warranty of habitability.

(B) Implied Warranty of Habitability

JAVINS v. FIRST NATIONAL REALTY CORP.

United States Court of Appeals, District of Columbia Circuit, 1970.
428 F.2d 1071.

J. SKELLY WRIGHT, Circuit Judge:

These cases present the question whether housing code violations which arise during the term of a lease have any effect upon the tenant's obligation to pay rent. The Landlord and Tenant Branch of the District of Columbia Court of General Sessions ruled proof of such violations inadmissible when proffered as a defense to an eviction action for nonpayment of rent. The District of Columbia Court of Appeals upheld this ruling. Saunders v. First National Realty Corp., 245 A.2d 836 (1968).

Because of the importance of the question presented, we granted appellants' petitions for leave to appeal. We now reverse and hold that a warranty of habitability, measured by the standards set out in the Housing Regulations for the District of Columbia, is implied by operation of law into leases of urban dwelling units covered by those Regulations and that breach of this warranty gives rise to the usual remedies for breach of contract.

I

The facts revealed by the record are simple. By separate written leases, each of the appellants rented an apartment in a three-building apartment complex in Northwest Washington known as Clifton Terrace. The landlord, First National Realty Corporation, filed separate actions in the Landlord and Tenant Branch of the Court of General Sessions on April 8, 1966, seeking possession on the ground that each of the appellants had defaulted in the payment of rent due for the month of April. The tenants, appellants here, admitted that they had not paid the landlord any rent for April. However, they alleged numerous violations of the Housing Regulations as "an equitable defense or [a] claim by way of recoupment or set-off in an amount equal to the rent claim," as provided in the rules of the Court of General Sessions.[3] They offered to prove

"[t]hat there are approximately 1500 violations of the Housing Regulations of the District of Columbia in the building at Clifton

---

3. Rule 4(c) of the Landlord and Tenant Branch of the Court of General Sessions provides:

"In suits in this branch for recovery of possession of property in which the basis of recovery of possession is nonpayment of rent, tenants may set up an equitable defense or claim by way of recoupment or set-off in an amount equal to the rent claim. No counterclaim may be filed unless plaintiff asks for money judgment for rent. The exclusion of prosecution of any claims in this branch shall be without prejudice to the prosecution of any claims in other branches of the court."

Terrace, where Defendant resides some affecting the premises of this Defendant directly, others indirectly, and all tending to establish a course of conduct of violation of the Housing Regulations to the damage of Defendants . . . ."

Settled Statement of Proceedings and Evidence, p. 2 (1966). Appellants conceded at trial, however, that this offer of proof reached only violations which had arisen since the term of the lease had commenced. The Court of General Sessions refused appellants' offer of proof and entered judgment for the landlord. The District of Columbia Court of Appeals affirmed, rejecting the argument made by appellants that the landlord was under a contractual duty to maintain the premises in compliance with the Housing Regulations.

II

Since, in traditional analysis, a lease was the conveyance of an interest in land, courts have usually utilized the special rules governing real property transactions to resolve controversies involving leases. However, as the Supreme Court has noted in another context, "the body of private property law . . ., more than almost any other branch of law, has been shaped by distinctions whose validity is largely historical." [6] Courts have a duty to reappraise old doctrines in the light of the facts and values of contemporary life—particularly old common law doctrines which the courts themselves created and developed. As we have said before, "[T]he continued vitality of the common law . . . depends upon its ability to reflect contemporary community values and ethics." [8]

The assumption of landlord-tenant law, derived from feudal property law, that a lease primarily conveyed to the tenant an interest in land may have been reasonable in a rural, agrarian society; it may continue to be reasonable in some leases involving farming or commercial land. In these cases, the value of the lease to the tenant is the land itself. But in the case of the modern apartment dweller, the value of the lease is that it gives him a place to live. The city dweller who seeks to lease an apartment on the third floor of a tenement has little interest in the land 30 or 40 feet below, or even in the bare right to possession within the four walls of his apartment. When American city dwellers, both rich and poor, seek "shelter" today, they seek a well known package of goods and services [9]—a package which in-

Appellants have sought only to defeat the landlord's action; they have not as yet claimed any money damages for the landlord's alleged breach of contract. Under Rule 4(c) *supra*, they may not counterclaim for money damages if the landlord seeks only possession and no money judgment, as it has done here. . . .

6. Jones v. United States, 362 U.S. 257, 266, 80 S.Ct. 725, 733, 4 L.Ed.2d 697 (1960).

8. Whetzel v. Jess Fisher Management Co., 108 U.S.App.D.C. 385, 388, 282 F.2d 943, 946 (1960).

9. *See, e.g.,* National Commission on Urban Problems, Building the American City 9 (1968). The extensive standards set out in the Housing Regulations pro-

cludes not merely walls and ceilings, but also adequate heat, light and ventilation, serviceable plumbing facilities, secure windows and doors, proper sanitation, and proper maintenance.

Professor Powell summarizes the present state of the law:

" . . . The complexities of city life, and the proliferated problems of modern society in general, have created new problems for lessors and lessees and these have been commonly handled by specific clauses inserted in leases. This growth in the number and detail of specific lease covenants has reintroduced into the law of estates for years a predominantly contractual ingredient. In practice, the law today concerning estates for years consists chiefly of rules determining the construction and effect of lease covenants. . . ." [10]

Ironically, however, the rules governing the construction and interpretation of "predominantly contractual" obligations in leases have too often remained rooted in old property law.

Some courts have realized that certain of the old rules of property law governing leases are inappropriate for today's transactions. In order to reach results more in accord with the legitimate expectations of the parties and the standards of the community, courts have been gradually introducing more modern precepts of contract law in interpreting leases. Proceeding piecemeal has, however, led to confusion where "decisions are frequently conflicting, not because of a healthy disagreement on social policy, but because of the lingering impact of rules whose policies are long since dead." [12]

In our judgment the trend toward treating leases as contracts is wise and well considered. Our holding in this case reflects a belief that leases of urban dwelling units should be interpreted and construed like any other contract.

III

Modern contract law has recognized that the buyer of goods and services in an industrialized society must rely upon the skill and honesty of the supplier to assure that goods and services purchased are of adequate quality. In interpreting most contracts, courts have sought to protect the legitimate expectations of the buyer and have steadily widened the seller's responsibility for the quality of goods and services through implied warranties of fitness and merchantability. Thus without any special agreement a merchant will be held to warrant that his goods are fit for the ordinary purposes for which

---

vide a good guide to community expectations.

10. 2 R. Powell, Real Property ¶ 221[1] at 179 (1967).

12. Kessler, The Protection of the Consumer Under Modern Sales Law, 74 Yale L.J. 262, 263 (1964).

such goods are used and that they are at least of reasonably average quality. Moreover, if the supplier has been notified that goods are required for a specific purpose, he will be held to warrant that any goods sold are fit for that purpose. These implied warranties have become widely accepted and well established features of the common law, supported by the overwhelming body of case law. Today most states as well as the District of Columbia have codified and enacted these warranties into statute, as to the sale of goods, in the Uniform Commercial Code.

Implied warranties of quality have not been limited to cases involving sales. The consumer renting a chattel, paying for services, or buying a combination of goods and services must rely upon the skill and honesty of the supplier to at least the same extent as a purchaser of goods. Courts have not hesitated to find implied warranties of fitness and merchantability in such situations. In most areas products liability law has moved far beyond "mere" implied warranties running between two parties in privity with each other.

The rigid doctrines of real property law have tended to inhibit the application of implied warranties to transactions involving real estate. Now, however, courts have begun to hold sellers and developers of real property responsible for the quality of their product. For example, builders of new homes have recently been held liable to purchasers for improper construction on the ground that the builders had breached an implied warranty of fitness. In other cases courts have held builders of new homes liable for breach of an implied warranty that all local building regulations had been complied with. And following the developments in other areas, very recent decisions and commentary suggest the possible extension of liability to parties other than the immediate seller for improper construction of residential real estate.

Despite this trend in the sale of real estate, many courts have been unwilling to imply warranties of quality, specifically a warranty of habitability, into leases of apartments. Recent decisions have offered no convincing explanation for their refusal; rather they have relied without discussion upon the old common law rule that the lessor is not obligated to repair unless he covenants to do so in the written lease contract. However, the Supreme Courts of at least two states, in recent and well reasoned opinions, have held landlords to implied warranties of quality in housing leases. Lemle v. Breeden, S.Ct.Hawaii, 462 P.2d 470 (1969); Reste Realty Corp. v. Cooper, 53 N.J. 444, 251 A.2d 268 (1969). *See also* Pines v. Perssion, 14 Wis.2d 590, 111 N.W.2d 409 (1961). In our judgment, the old no-repair rule cannot coexist with the obligations imposed on the landlord by a typical modern housing code, and must be abandoned in favor of an implied warranty of habitability. In the District of Columbia, the standards of this warranty are set out in the Housing Regulations.

IV

A. In our judgment the common law itself must recognize the landlord's obligation to keep his premises in a habitable condition. This conclusion is compelled by three separate considerations. First, we believe that the old rule was based on certain factual assumptions which are no longer true; on its own terms, it can no longer be justified. Second, we believe that the consumer protection cases discussed above require that the old rule be abandoned in order to bring residential landlord-tenant law into harmony with the principles on which those cases rest. Third, we think that the nature of today's urban housing market also dictates abandonment of the old rule.

The common law rule absolving the lessor of all obligation to repair originated in the early Middle Ages. Such a rule was perhaps well suited to an agrarian economy; the land was more important than whatever small living structure was included in the leasehold, and the tenant farmer was fully capable of making repairs himself. These historical facts were the basis on which the common law constructed its rule; they also provided the necessary prerequisites for its application.

Court decisions in the late 1800's began to recognize that the factual assumptions of the common law were no longer accurate in some cases. For example, the common law, since it assumed that the land was the most important part of the leasehold, required a tenant to pay rent even if any building on the land was destroyed. Faced with such a rule and the ludicrous results it produced, in 1863 the New York Court of Appeals declined to hold that an upper story tenant was obliged to continue paying rent after his apartment building burned down.[35] The court simply pointed out that the urban tenant had no interest in the land, only in the attached building.

Another line of cases created an exception to the no-repair rule for short term leases of furnished dwellings. The Massachusetts Supreme Judicial Court, a court not known for its willingness to depart from the common law, supported this exception, pointing out:

" . . . [A] different rule should apply to one who hires a furnished room, or a furnished house, for a few days, or a few weeks or months. Its fitness for immediate use of a particular kind, as indicated by its appointments, is a far more important element entering into the contract than when there is a mere lease of real estate. One who lets for a short term a house provided with all furnishings and appointments for immediate residence may be supposed to contract in reference to a well-understood purpose of the hirer to use it as a habitation. . . . It would be unreasonable to hold, under such circumstances, that the landlord does not

---

35. Graves v. Berdan, 26 N.Y. 498 (1863).

impliedly agree that what he is letting is a house suitable for occupation in its condition at the time. . . . "[37]

These as well as other similar cases demonstrate that some courts began some time ago to question the common law's assumptions that the land was the most important feature of a leasehold and that the tenant could feasibly make any necessary repairs himself. Where those assumptions no longer reflect contemporary housing patterns, the courts have created exceptions to the general rule that landlords have no duty to keep their premises in repair.

It is overdue for courts to admit that these assumptions are no longer true with regard to all urban housing. Today's urban tenants, the vast majority of whom live in multiple dwelling houses, are interested, not in the land, but solely in "a house suitable for occupation." Furthermore, today's city dweller usually has a single, specialized skill unrelated to maintenance work; he is unable to make repairs like the "jack-of-all-trades" farmer who was the common law's model of the lessee. Further, unlike his agrarian predecessor who often remained on one piece of land for his entire life, urban tenants today are more mobile than ever before. A tenant's tenure in a specific apartment will often not be sufficient to justify efforts at repairs. In addition, the increasing complexity of today's dwellings renders them much more difficult to repair than the structures of earlier times. In a multiple dwelling repair may require access to equipment and areas in the control of the landlord. Low and middle income tenants, even if they were interested in making repairs, would be unable to obtain any financing for major repairs since they have no long-term interest in the property.

Our approach to the common law of landlord and tenant ought to be aided by principles derived from the consumer protection cases referred to above. In a lease contract, a tenant seeks to purchase from his landlord shelter for a specified period of time. The landlord sells housing as a commercial businessman and has much greater opportunity, incentive and capacity to inspect and maintain the condition of his building. Moreover, the tenant must rely upon the skill and *bona fides* of his landlord at least as much as a car buyer must rely upon the car manufacturer. In dealing with major problems, such as heating, plumbing, electrical or structural defects, the tenant's position corresponds precisely with "the ordinary consumer who cannot be expected to have the knowledge or capacity or even the opportunity to make adequate inspection of mechanical instrumentalities, like automobiles, and to decide for himself whether they are reasonably fit for the designed purpose." Henningsen v. Bloomfield Motors, Inc., 32 N.J. 358, 375, 161 A.2d 69, 78 (1960).

Since a lease contract specifies a particular period of time during which the tenant has a right to use his apartment for shelter, he may

---

37. Ingalls v. Hobbs, 156 Mass. 348, 31 N.E. 286 (1892).

legitimately expect that the apartment will be fit for habitation for the time period for which it is rented. We point out that in the present cases there is no allegation that appellants' apartments were in poor condition or in violation of the housing code at the commencement of the leases. Since the lessees continue to pay the same rent, they were entitled to expect that the landlord would continue to keep the premises in their beginning condition during the lease term. It is precisely such expectations that the law now recognizes as deserving of formal, legal protection.

Even beyond the rationale of traditional products liability law, the relationship of landlord and tenant suggests further compelling reasons for the law's protection of the tenants' legitimate expectations of quality. The inequality in bargaining power between landlord and tenant has been well documented. Tenants have very little leverage to enforce demands for better housing. Various impediments to competition in the rental housing market, such as racial and class discrimination and standardized form leases, mean that landlords place tenants in a take it or leave it situation. The increasingly severe shortage of adequate housing further increases the landlord's bargaining power and escalates the need for maintaining and improving the existing stock. Finally, the findings by various studies of the social impact of bad housing has led to the realization that poor housing is detrimental to the whole society, not merely to the unlucky ones who must suffer the daily indignity of living in a slum.

Thus we are led by our inspection of the relevant legal principles and precedents to the conclusion that the old common law rule imposing an obligation upon the lessee to repair during the lease term was really never intended to apply to residential urban leaseholds. Contract principles established in other areas of the law provide a more rational framework for the apportionment of landlord-tenant responsibilities; they strongly suggest that a warranty of habitability be implied into all contracts for urban dwellings.

B. We believe, in any event, that the District's housing code requires that a warranty of habitability be implied in the leases of all housing that it covers. The housing code—formally designated the Housing Regulations of the District of Columbia—was established and authorized by the Commissioners of the District of Columbia on August 11, 1955. Since that time, the code has been updated by numerous orders of the Commissioners. The 75 pages of the Regulations provide a comprehensive regulatory scheme setting forth in some detail: (a) the standards which housing in the District of Columbia must meet; (b) which party, the lessor or the lessee, must meet each standard; and (c) a system of inspections, notifications and criminal penalties. The Regulations themselves are silent on the question of private remedies.

Two previous decisions of this court, however, have held that the Housing Regulations create legal rights and duties enforceable in tort by private parties. In Whetzel v. Jess Fisher Management Co., 108 U.S.App.D.C. 385, 282 F.2d 943 (1960), we followed the leading case of Altz v. Lieberson, 233 N.Y. 16, 134 N.E. 703 (1922), in holding (1) that the housing code altered the common law rule and imposed a duty to repair upon the landlord and (2) that a right of action accrued to a tenant injured by the landlord's breach of this duty. As Judge Cardozo wrote in *Lieberson:*

> ". . . We may be sure that the framers of this statute, when regulating tenement life, had uppermost in thought the care of those who are unable to care for themselves. The Legislature must have known that unless repairs in the rooms of the poor were made by the landlord, they would not be made by any one. The duty imposed became commensurate with the need. The right to seek redress is not limited to the city or its officers. The right extends to all whom there was a purpose to protect. . . ."

134 N.E. at 704. Recently, in Kanelos v. Kettler, 132 U.S.App.D.C. 133, 135, 406 F.2d 951, 953 (1968), we reaffirmed our position in *Whetzel,* holding that "the Housing Regulations did impose maintenance obligations upon appellee [landlord] which he was not free to ignore."

The District of Columbia Court of Appeals gave further effect to the Housing Regulations in Brown v. Southall Realty Co., 237 A.2d 834 (1968). There the landlord knew at the time the lease was signed that housing code violations existed which rendered the apartment "unsafe and unsanitary." Viewing the lease as a contract, the District of Columbia Court of Appeals held that the premises were let in violation of Sections 2304 and 2501 of the Regulations and that the lease, therefore, was void as an illegal contract. In the light of *Brown,* it is clear not only that the housing code creates privately enforceable duties as held in *Whetzel,* but that the basic validity of every housing contract depends upon substantial compliance with the housing code at the beginning of the lease term. The *Brown* court relied particularly upon Section 2501 of the Regulations which provides:

> "Every premises accommodating one or more habitations shall be maintained and kept in repair so as to provide decent living accommodations for the occupants. This part of this Code contemplates more than mere basic repairs and maintenance to keep out the elements; its purpose is to include repairs and maintenance designed to make a premises or neighborhood healthy and safe."

By its terms, this section applies to maintenance and repair during the lease term. Under the *Brown* holding, serious failure to comply with this section before the lease term begins renders the contract void. We think it untenable to find that this section has no effect on the contract after it has been signed. To the contrary, by signing the lease the landlord has undertaken a continuing obligation to the tenant to maintain the premises in accordance with all applicable law.

This principle of implied warranty is well established. Courts often imply relevant law into contracts to provide a remedy for any damage caused by one party's illegal conduct. In a case closely analogous to the present one, the Illinois Supreme Court held that a builder who constructed a house in violation of the Chicago building code had breached his contract with the buyer:

> ". . . [T]he law existing at the time and place of the making of the contract is deemed a part of the contract, as though expressly referred to or incorporated in it. . . .
>
> "The rationale for this rule is that the parties to the contract would have expressed that which the law implies 'had they not supposed that it was unnecessary to speak of it because the law provided for it.' . . . Consequently, the courts, in construing the existing law as part of the express contract, are not reading into the contract provisions different from those expressed and intended by the parties, as defendants contend, but are merely construing the contract in accordance with the intent of the parties."[56]

We follow the Illinois court in holding that the housing code must be read into housing contracts—a holding also required by the purposes and the structure of the code itself. The duties imposed by the Housing Regulations may not be waived or shifted by agreement if the Regulations specifically place the duty upon the lessor.[58] Criminal penalties are provided if these duties are ignored. This regulatory structure was established by the Commissioners because, in their judgment, the grave conditions in the housing market required serious action. Yet official enforcement of the housing code has been far from uniformly effective. Innumerable studies have documented

---

56. Schiro v. W.E. Gould & Co., *supra* Note 23, 18 Ill.2d at 544, 165 N.E.2d at 290. As a general proposition, it is undoubtedly true that parties to a contract intend that applicable law will be complied with by both sides. We recognize, however, that reading statutory provisions into private contracts may have little factual support in the intentions of the particular parties now before us. But, for reasons of public policy, warranties are often implied into contracts by operation of law in order to meet generally prevailing standards of honesty and fair dealing. When the public policy has been enacted into law like the housing code, that policy will usually have deep roots in the expectations and intentions of most people.

58. Any private agreement to shift the duties would be illegal and unenforceable. The precedents dealing with industrial safety statutes are directly in point:

> ". . . [T]he only question remaining is whether the courts will enforce or recognize as against a servant an agreement express or implied on his part to waive the performance of a statutory duty of the master imposed for the protection of the servant, and in the interest of the public, and enforceable by criminal prosecution. We do not think they will. To do so would be to nullify the object of the statute. . . ."

Narramore v. Cleveland, C., C. & St. L. Ry. Co., 6 Cir., 96 F. 298, 302 (1899). See W. Prosser, Torts § 67 at 468–469 (3d ed. 1964) and cases cited therein.

the desperate condition of rental housing in the District of Columbia and in the nation. In view of these circumstances, we think the conclusion reached by the Supreme Court of Wisconsin as to the effect of a housing code on the old common law rule cannot be avoided:

> ". . . [T]he legislature has made a policy judgment—that it is socially (and politically) desirable to impose these duties on a property owner—which has rendered the old common law rule obsolete. To follow the old rule of no implied warranty of habitability in leases would, in our opinion, be inconsistent with the current legislative policy concerning housing standards. . . ."[60]

We therefore hold that the Housing Regulations imply a warranty of habitability, measured by the standards which they set out, into leases of all housing that they cover.

V

In the present cases, the landlord sued for possession for nonpayment of rent. Under contract principles,[61] however, the tenant's obligation to pay rent is dependent upon the landlord's performance of his obligations, including his warranty to maintain the premises in habitable condition. In order to determine whether any rent is owed to the landlord, the tenants must be given an opportunity to prove the housing code violations alleged as breach of the landlord's warranty.[62]

At trial, the finder of fact must make two findings: (1) whether the alleged violations[63] existed during the period for which past due rent is claimed, and (2) what portion, if any or all, of the tenant's obligation to pay rent was suspended by the landlord's breach. If no part of the tenant's rental obligation is found to have been suspended, then a judgment for possession may issue forthwith. On the other hand, if the jury determines that the entire rental obligation has been extinguished by the landlord's total breach, then the action for possession on the ground of nonpayment must fail.[64]

---

60. Pines v. Perssion, 14 Wis.2d 590, 596, 111 N.W.2d 409, 412–413 (1961).

61. In extending all contract remedies for breach to the parties to a lease, we include an action for specific performance of the landlord's implied warranty of habitability.

62. To be relevant, of course, the violations must affect the tenant's apartment or common areas which the tenant uses. Moreover, the contract principle that no one may benefit from his own wrong will allow the landlord to defend by proving the damage was caused by the tenant's wrongful action. However, violations resulting from inadequate repairs or materials which disintegrate under normal use would not be assignable to the tenant. Also we agree with the District of Columbia Court of Appeals that the tenant's private rights do not depend on official inspection or official finding of violation by the city government. Diamond Housing Corp. v. Robinson, 257 A.2d 492, 494 (1969).

63. The jury should be instructed that one or two minor violations standing alone which do not affect habitability are *de minimis* and would not entitle the tenant to a reduction in rent.

64. As soon as the landlord made the necessary repairs rent would again become due. Our holding, of course, affects only eviction for nonpayment of rent. The landlord is free to seek evic-

The jury may find that part of the tenant's rental obligation has been suspended but that part of the unpaid back rent is indeed owed to the landlord. In these circumstances, no judgment for possession should issue if the tenant agrees to pay the partial rent found to be due. If the tenant refuses to pay the partial amount, a judgment for possession may then be entered.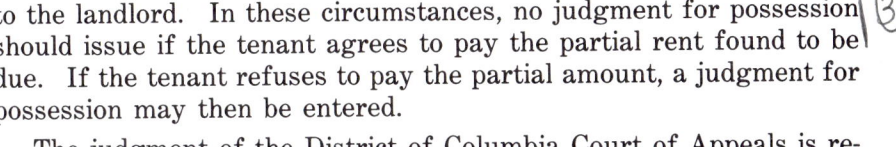

The judgment of the District of Columbia Court of Appeals is reversed and the cases are remanded for further proceedings consistent with this opinion.[67]

So ordered.

Circuit Judge ROBB concurs in the result and in Parts IV–B and V of the opinion.

NOTES

1. Is *Javins'* warranty of habitability likely to encourage tenants to demand, and landlords to make, the repairs needed to upgrade substandard premises? Are tenants occupying substandard premises under month-to-month leases likely to complain if they know that their tenancies can be terminated on thirty days' notice? Will landlords be likely to make needed repairs if they know that, by employing month-to-month tenancies, they can quickly replace complaining tenants with more docile ones? Under *Javins*, not all dilapidations will be held to violate the covenant of habitability, and even those that do will not invariably entitle the tenant to withhold his entire rent. What risk does a tenant face in guessing wrong about the degree of dilapidation required to violate the covenant and about the proportion of rent that he can legally withhold?

Javins' frequent rhetorical bows in the direction of contract law may make the opinion look like just another example of landlord-tenant law's modern emphasis on the contract aspect of leases. Is the

---

tion at the termination of the lease or on any other legal ground.

67. Appellants in the present cases offered to pay rent into the registry of the court during the present action. We think this is an excellent protective procedure. If the tenant defends against an action for possession on the basis of breach of the landlord's warranty of habitability, the trial court may require the tenant to make future rent payments into the registry of the court as they become due; such a procedure would be appropriate only while the tenant remains in possession. The escrowed money will, however, represent rent for the period between the time the landlord files suit and the time the case comes to trial. In the normal course of litigation, the only factual question at trial would be the condition of the apartment during the time the landlord alleged rent was due and not paid.

As a general rule, the escrowed money should be apportioned between the landlord and the tenant after trial on the basis of the finding of rent actually due for the period at issue in the suit. To issue fair apportionment, however, we think either party should be permitted to amend its complaint or answer at any time before trial, to allege a change in the condition of the apartment. In this event, the finder of fact should make a separate finding as to the condition of the apartment at the time at which the amendment was filed. This new finding will have no effect upon the original action; it will only affect the distribution of the escrowed rent paid after the filing of the amendment.

appearance deceiving? Was it contract theory or some other rationale that made the local housing code the appropriate source for the habitability standard? That led the court to hold that the warranty was nonwaivable? That led to the measure of damages that the court employed? (What *was* the measure of damages employed?) Why did the court sidestep two other contract remedies—rescission and specific performance?

On *Javins* and the warranty of habitability generally, see Abbott, Housing Policy, Housing Codes and Tenant Remedies: An Integration, 56 B.U.L.Rev. 1 (1976); Cunningham, The New Implied and Statutory Warranties of Habitability in Residential Leases: From Contract to Status, 16 Urb.L.Ann. 3 (1979); and Glendon, The Transformation of American Landlord-Tenant Law, 23 B.C.L.Rev. 503 (1982).

2. *Habitability and Quiet Enjoyment Compared*. Which will better serve the interests of tenants living in substandard housing—the warranty of habitability endorsed in *Javins*, or the covenant of quiet enjoyment? Why do you suppose courts, determined to protect tenants from substandard premises, have chosen to adopt the warranty of habitability rather than to enlarge the well-worn covenant of quiet enjoyment?

Doubtless, one reason courts have ignored quiet enjoyment theory is that its traditional requirements might appear to block tenant relief in most cases. Unlike the warranty of habitability, the traditional quiet enjoyment rules require the tenant to show that he did not waive the covenant, that he promptly vacated the premises, and that the landlord actively participated in the interference. Yet, even at the time the habitability decisions were being rendered, these quiet enjoyment requirements were being loosened. For example, East Haven Associates v. Gurian, page 850, dropped the requirement that the tenant promptly vacate the premises, and Blackett v. Olanoff, page 857, held landlords liable for acts of omission as well as commission.

New York, which had since Dyett v. Pendleton, page 843, provided such fertile ground for quiet enjoyment, definitively turned to the warranty of habitability in 1975. Real Prop. Law § 235–b. See generally, Note, New York's Search for an Effective Implied Warranty of Habitability in Residential Leases, 43 Albany L.Rev. 661 (1978–1979).

3. *Is Slumlordism a Tort?* Does tort law offer an effective alternative to the implied warranty of habitability? How does Kline v. 1500 Massachusetts Ave. Apartment Corp., page 858, above, fit into the District of Columbia's habitability jurisprudence? Should substandard conditions, without more, expose a landlord to tort liability for physical discomfort or emotional harm? See Simon v. Solomon, 385 Mass. 91, 431 N.E.2d 556 (1982). See generally, Sax & Hiestand, Slumlordism as a Tort, 65 Mich.L.Rev. 869, 875 (1967). See also Blum & Dunham, Slumlordism as a Tort—A Dissenting View, 66

Mich.L.Rev. 451 (1968); Sax, Slumlordism as a Tort—A Brief Response, 66 Mich.L.Rev. 465 (1968).

4. Few common law rules have been reversed so quickly or definitively as the rule on landlord duties respecting habitability. The American Law of Property, published in 1952, stated flatly: "There is no implied covenant or warranty that at the time the term commences the premises are in a tenantable condition or that they are adapted to the purpose for which leased . . . . The reason assigned for this rule is that the tenant is a purchaser of an estate in land, subject to the doctrine of *caveat emptor*. He may inspect the premises and determine for himself their suitability or he may secure an express warranty." 1 American Law of Property § 3.45 (A. J. Casner, ed. 1952). The 1977 Supplement rewrote section 3.45 completely: "Beginning in 1968, the courts, with very little dissent, did an abrupt aboutface, as to one type of lease: In more than a dozen jurisdictions they have stated, sometimes going out of their way to do so, that there is an implied covenant or warranty of habitability in leases of residential property."

By recent count, the implied warranty of habitability exists in some form in at least forty-one states and the District of Columbia. See Glendon, The Transformation of American Landlord-Tenant Law, 23 B.C.L.Rev. 503, 523–524 (1982). Although some states initially crafted the warranty out of their common law, most have since enacted statutes, ranging from specifically-focussed habitability and repair statutes to comprehensive landlord-tenant codes. The Uniform Residential Landlord and Tenant Act has been the single most powerful influence on state legislation, obligating landlords to "comply with the requirements of applicable building and housing codes materially affecting health and safety;" to "do whatever is necessary to put and keep the premises in a fit and habitable condition;" to keep all common areas and utilities clean, safe, and operative; to provide for garbage and other waste removal; and, under specified conditions, to "supply running water and reasonable amounts of hot water and heat." Uniform Residential Landlord and Tenant Act § 2.104 (1972). URLTA sections 4.101 to 4.107 give the tenant a wide array of remedies for landlord breach, including rescission, self-help repair, and damages.

5. *The Habitability Standard.* Some states follow *Javins* and hold residential landlords to the habitability standard imposed by the local housing code. Other states have developed *ad hoc* standards of health and safety. In practice, the two standards tend to merge. Courts following the *ad hoc* approach often look to the local housing code for evidence of a reasonable standard. See Boston Housing Authority v. Hemingway, 363 Mass. 184, 293 N.E.2d 831 (1973). And courts following *Javins* generally hold that only those code violations that substantially threaten health and safety will be actionable, and that substantial violations falling outside the code will also breach the

warranty. See generally, Abbott, Housing Policy, Housing Codes and Tenant Remedies: An Integration 56 B.U.L.Rev. 1, 17–20 (1976).

At what point does a particular habitability standard become operative? *Javins* held that the housing code in force at the outset of the lease established the governing standard and that only subsequent dilapidations during the leasehold term would violate the warranty. This rule, easy to apply in the case of one- or two-family dwellings, poses considerable difficulty in the context of multiple dwellings in which different tenants will typically have begun their tenancies at different times and, most likely, under different housing code standards. Is the practical effect of the *Javins* rule that the landlord will be forced to keep the entire premises at the level set by the most stringent of several applicable standards? Tenants will commonly occupy slum dwellings under month-to-month periodic tenancies. Does this mean that a new habitability standard will apply at the beginning of each month, or that the standard that applies at the beginning of the tenancy will continue to apply so long as the tenant continues in possession?

6. How promptly must the landlord act to avoid breaching the warranty of habitability? In Berman & Sons, Inc. v. Jefferson, 379 Mass. 196, 396 N.E.2d 981 (1979), the Massachusetts Supreme Court held that the covenant is breached from the moment the landlord receives notice of the substandard condition, even though she then promptly moves to correct it. "The landlord may be correct in characterizing itself as an innocent party, and we are cognizant of the economic burdens that a landlord typically bears. Nevertheless, we note that the landlord's liability without fault is merely an economic burden; the tenant living in an uninhabitable building suffers a loss of shelter, a necessity." 396 N.E.2d at 984–985. Under this standard, should the landlord be liable for conditions caused by a strike of maintenance and janitorial employees? See Park West Management Corp. v. Mitchell, 47 N.Y.2d 316, 418 N.Y.S.2d 310, 391 N.E.2d 1288 (1979), cert. denied, 444 U.S. 992, 100 S.Ct. 523, 62 L.Ed.2d 421 (Yes).

7. *Remedies.* Courts and legislatures have employed the contract metaphor not only in implying the warranty of habitability but also in prescribing remedies for its breach. In addition to rescission, injunctive relief and specific performance, the tenant may recover consequential and loss of bargain damages either in an affirmative action or by way of setoff in the landlord's action for rent. Of these remedies, damages have proved the hardest to administer, with the major appellate decisions, like *Javins*, sketching only the barest outlines and offering few guidelines to trial courts faced with the difficult task of applying the damage remedy to the concrete facts of a particular case.

In Cazares v. Ortiz, 109 Cal.App.3d Supp. 23, 168 Cal.Rptr. 108 (1980), one lower California court sought to fill in the outlines sketched by the California Supreme Court's leading habitability decision,

Green v. Superior Court, 10 Cal.3d 616, 111 Cal.Rptr. 704, 517 P.2d 1168 (1974). The court began by identifying the four principal methods used across the country to compute the tenant's damages for breach of the implied warranty of habitability:[h] 1. The difference between the premises' market rental value as impliedly warranted and market rental values "as is"; 2. Taking the reserved rental to reflect the value of the premises as impliedly warranted, reducing this amount by a fraction that will account for the reduced habitability of the premises; 3. The difference between the reserved rental and the rental value of the premises "as is"; and 4. "Just give the tenant a recovery for his 'discomfort and annoyance.'"

The court rejected the first, third and fourth approaches. The problem with the first approach was that "*market* rental value can properly be testified to only by experts who qualify by experience and the performance of market studies. In the usual small case like the present no one can afford to hire the experts." 109 Cal.App.3d Supp. at 28, 168 Cal.Rptr. at 110. The third approach, borrowed unwittingly from personal property warranty cases, ignored "the public policy behind the adoption of the doctrine of implied warranty of habitability of residences. That purpose is to force the rehabilitation of substantially defective slum dwellings so that the poor may live decently. This third suggested method would only further this policy if the landlord was a 'rent gouger.' If he charged low rents because of the poor quality of his premises, the agreed rent and the market rent for the 'as is' premises would differ little, if at all. A tenant living in a pigsty would recover nothing because he was paying pigsty rents. This is probably good contract law, but it is poor implied warranty of habitability law." 109 Cal.App.3d Supp. at 31, 168 Cal.Rptr. at 111, 112. Finally, the court rejected the fourth approach: "A measure of damages which *bears no relation to the value of the lease contract to either party* . . . and which is so open-ended, will either drive landlords out of business (and thus dry up rental housing) or drive their insurance rates sky high (to be taken out of the hides of tenants)." 109 Cal.App.3d Supp. at 31, 168 Cal.Rptr. at 112.

Conceding that all the methods considered were "lamentable," the court concluded that the second—the method most widely employed across the country—"is the least of the evils, and the one selected by this court as (1) most likely to achieve the goals desired by the Supreme Court in creating the implied warranty of habitability (residential), as (2) least likely to cause the shift of landlords' capital to the Zurich gold market, and (3) as manageable by trial courts." 109 Cal.App.3d Supp. 33, 168 Cal.Rptr. 113.

Do you agree? The *Cazares* court recognized that the second method "does have a substantial possibility of injustice to the land-

---

[h]. The court also discussed a fifth method, proposed by the Restatement of Property, Second, that has apparently not been adopted in any state. The Restatement approach is considered in note 10, below.

lord in one situation, to wit: where he has by reason of premise defects set a low rent (by negotiation with a knowledgeable tenant or not) for the premises and later is faced with a bludgeon of even lower rents through a claim of a breach of the implied warranty of habitability. Thus, there is justice in forcing a landlord to disgorge $50 per month for premises that rented for $150 but were only worth $90 to $110. There is, however, a visceral queasiness in nailing a landlord who has rented the place for $90 because of the defects (perhaps after a discussion of the defects with the tenant), being forced to reimburse the tenant $30 a month because a court finds that the premises are 30 percent less habitable than a similar place in good condition. This, however, would be a result of the mandatory nature of the implied warranty of habitability and the policy of forcing the rehabilitation of markedly substandard dwellings." 109 Cal.App.3d Supp. at 33, 168 Cal.Rptr. at 108.

Is this second method too easily circumvented to be effective? What simple step might a landlord take to avoid any loss under this method without making repairs?

8. *Remedies: Self-Help.* Standard contract remedies have little attraction for the typical tenant of substandard housing. A judicial award of damages or specific performance will rarely repay the time and expense of litigation. Rescission, though speedy and cheap, will leave the tenant out on the street, usually with no better housing available at a price he can afford. The tenant's real desire is for a quick and inexpensive remedy that will entitle him to stay on the premises at a reduced rent, or no rent, until needed repairs are made. Courts and legislatures have obliged tenants with three self-help remedies.

Abatement. This self-help remedy, endorsed in *Javins* and in most other contemporary habitability decisions, is a corollary of the damages remedy for breach of warranty, allowing the tenant to continue occupying the premises while setting off the damages incurred against the monthly rent due. Thus, in a jurisdiction adopting the *Cazares* measure of damages, note 7, above, the tenant would be allowed to reduce his monthly rental payments by a fraction that corresponds to the premises' reduced habitability.

Repair and Deduct. If the dilapidations are reparable, and are located in or around the complaining tenant's apartment, many states allow the tenant, after notice to the landlord, to apply part or all of the rent due toward the expense of repair. In some places, the repair and deduct remedy was a judicial innovation. See, for example, Marini v. Ireland, 56 N.J. 130, 265 A. 2d 526 (1970). Other states have authorized the remedy by statute. See, for example, West's Ann.Cal.Civ.Code § 1942 (within a reasonable time—presumptively 30 or more days after giving landlord notice of the defective condition—tenant may repair and deduct up to one month's rent; tenant may not resort to this remedy more than twice in any twelve-month period).

Escrow and Receivership. Escrow statutes, in force in several states, permit tenants in substandard dwellings to withhold rental payments owed to their landlord only on the condition that they deposit them into an escrow established by a court or some other designated agency. See, for example, Mass.Gen.Laws.Ann. c. 111, § 127F (West Supp. 1982). In some places, the rents deposited will be directly applied to repairing the premises. Elsewhere, the escrowed rents will be given to the landlord once she has repaired the defects. A few states have further systematized rent deposit procedures by providing for the appointment of a receiver to collect rents and oversee their expenditure toward upgrading the premises. See generally, Rosen, Receivership: A Useful Tool for Helping to Meet the Needs of Low Income People, 3 Harv.C.R.-C.L.L.Rev. 311 (1968).

9. *Can the Habitability Covenant Be Waived?* Several states take the *Javins* position that the warranty of habitability is implied by law and cannot be waived by the parties. Foisy v. Wyman, 83 Wn. 2d 22, 515 P.2d 160 (1973), took this position to its extreme, allowing a tenant who occupied a single family home under a six-month lease, with an option to buy, to assert breach of warranty even though he and the landlord had expressly negotiated a reduced rental to account for substantial defects in the premises. The Washington Supreme Court rested its decision on the ground that "this type of bargaining by the landlord with the tenant is contrary to public policy and the purpose of the doctrine of implied warranty of habitability. A disadvantaged tenant should not be placed in a position of agreeing to live in uninhabitable premises." 83 Wn.2d at 28, 515 P.2d at 164.

Many states permit limited waivers. Minnesota, for example, allows landlords to shift the duty to perform specified repairs or maintenance to their tenants, but only if the agreement is supported by adequate consideration and set forth in a conspicuous writing. No such agreement, however, may waive the requirement that the landlord maintain the common areas, keep the premises in reasonable repair and in compliance with applicable health and safety laws. Minn.Stat.Ann. § 504.18 subd. 2 (West Supp. 1982).

10. The Restatement (Second) Property, Landlord and Tenant (1976), consolidates and enlarges several of the main common law and statutory themes in habitability law. Sections 5.1, 5.4 and 5.5 imply the covenant and set its standard. Section 5.1 provides: "Except to the extent the parties to a lease validly agree otherwise, there is a breach of the landlord's obligations if the parties contemplate that the leased property will be used for residential purposes and on the date the lease is made and continuously thereafter until the date the tenant is entitled to possession, the leased property, without fault of the tenant, is not suitable for residential use."

The Restatement gives five remedies for breach: rescission, damages, abatement, repair and deduct, and rent withholding. Abatement, probably the most innovative remedy, calls for the reserved rental to be abated as follows: "If the tenant is entitled to an abatement of the rent, the rent is abated to the amount of that proportion of the rent which the fair rental value after the event giving the right to abate bears to the fair rental value before the event. Abatement is allowed until the default is eliminated or the lease terminates, whichever first occurs." Restatement (Second) of Property, Landlord and Tenant § 11.1 (1976).

In the course of the American Law Institute's discussion of the abatement provision, a question was asked from the floor: "If the fair rental value of the premises in 'suitable' condition (that is, in substantial compliance with the housing code) would be $100 a month, and if at the beginning of the tenancy the fair rental value of the premises in their existing, dilapidated condition is $20 a month, and if the contract rent is $30 a month, is the tenant entitled to reduce his rent by the amount of $24 a month to the sum of $6 a month?" The answer from the Reporter: "Yes." Meyers, The Covenant of Habitability and the American Law Institute, 27 Stan.L.Rev. 879, 883 (1975). The Meyers article offers a stinging critique of the Restatement provisions generally.

11. *Does the Warranty of Habitability Work?* Two field studies conducted in the wake of Green v. Superior Court, 10 Cal.3d 616, 111 Cal.Rptr. 704, 517 P.2d 1168 (1974), the California Supreme Court's landmark decision implying a warranty of habitability into all residential leases, produced a mixed answer. Although both studies indicate that *Green* was effective in tilting the balance of power away from landlords and toward tenants, neither study drew more definitive conclusions respecting *Green's* effect on the inclination of landlords to repair, abandon, evict or raise rents.

The first study, by two law students, was based on an exhaustive search of the docket records of the San Francisco courts in which unlawful detainer actions are commonly brought, and on interviews with judges, representatives of local tenant organizations and with landlord and tenant attorneys. Although the study concluded that *Green's* warranty was "not being extensively used"—"few low income tenants receive the legal advice necessary to make use of this innovation in landlord-tenant law"—it did find that "if the implied warranty of habitability is intended to shift some bargaining power from landlords to tenants in litigation, the rule has had some success. Thus, as of the time of this study, the primary effect of *Green* probably has not been to improve housing quality, but rather to give tenants more favorable results in landlord-tenant litigation." Note, the Great *Green* Hope: The Implied Warranty of Habitability in Practice, 28 Stan.L.Rev. 729, 776 (1976).

The second study, Heskin, The Warranty of Habitability Debate: A California Case Study, 66 Calif.L.Rev. 37, 55 (1978), was conducted in a low-income area of Southern California, and found that the "court docket, employed as an indicator in the San Francisco study, was an inadequate indicator of *Green* activity in the study area, because a substantial portion of warranty use did not involve the courts." The Heskin study focused instead on the files of local legal services lawyers: "It is believed that legal services attorneys are the primary medium connecting the warranty with the tenant, and that like other lawyers, they do much of their work out-of-court." *Id.* at 40.

The study found that the post-*Green* situation was neither as disastrous as its opponents had predicted, nor as constructive as its proponents had hoped: "The opponents of *Green* point to eastern slums with deteriorated tenements, fleeing investors and massive abandonment, arguing that anything, including the warranty, that places additional pressures on the landlords can only drive California toward the eastern situation. Proponents argue instead that *Green* will slow that decline. The proponents argue that the nature of the housing market in low-income areas necessitates legal intervention, and that there is money which can be diverted to repair of the property. All parties seem to assume that *Green* addresses a pervasive problem of California's low-income housing stock." *Id.* at 43.

The Heskin study "disclosed six factors limiting the enforcement of the warranty. The first among these was the perceived hostility of the local branch of the municipal court. Second, the lawyers responded to their perception of the court's attitude with a conservative interpretation and application of the law. Third, the lawyers were overworked and not fully prepared to exploit the case's potential. Fourth, the language of the *Green* decision is ambiguous, making it difficult for lawyers to explain the law to their clients and to enforce it according to their clients' desires. Fifth, the clients had a variety of problems that limited their ability to engage in and sustain litigation. Last, the tenant unions, which the proponents expected to expand the use of *Green*, did not materialize." *Id.* at 59.

ii. Remedial Strategies

ROBINSON v. DIAMOND HOUSING CORP.
United States Court of Appeals, District of Columbia Circuit, 1972.
463 F.2d 853.

J. SKELLY WRIGHT, Circuit Judge:

In Edwards v. Habib, 130 U.S.App.D.C. 126, 397 F.2d 687 (1968), cert. denied, 393 U.S. 1016, 89 S.Ct. 618, 21 L.Ed.2d 560 (1969), this court held that a tenant may assert the retaliatory motivation of his landlord as a defense to an otherwise proper eviction. In Brown v. Southall Realty Co., D.C.App., 237 A.2d 834 (1968), the District of Columbia Court of Appeals held that a lease purporting to convey property burdened with substantial housing code violations was illegal and void and that hence the landlord was not entitled to gain possession for rent due under the invalid lease. The case before us involves the intersection of these two principles. Specifically, it raises the question whether a landlord who has been frustrated in his effort to evict a tenant for nonpayment of rent by successful assertion of a *Southall Realty* defense may automatically accomplish the same goal by serving a 30-day notice to quit.

Appellant argues that she should be permitted to show that her landlord, Diamond Housing, was motivated by a retaliatory intent when it served the notice to quit. Diamond Housing contends that a retaliatory eviction defense has no place in a situation where, as here, the landlord is unable or unwilling to make the repairs on the premises that would entitle it to rent under *Southall Realty* and alleges an intent to take the property off the housing market. When the District of Columbia Court of General Sessions granted summary judgment to appellee, appellant renewed her arguments in the District of Columbia Court of Appeals. That court affirmed, holding:

> ". . . [T]he retaliatory defense of Edwards v. Habib . . . is not available to a tenant in a case such as this where she was successful in a prior Landlord and Tenant action and is being evicted after the expiration of a thirty-day notice because the landlord wishes to withdraw the property from the rental market. The *Edwards* case involved a situation where the landlord attempted to evict the tenant because of her complaints to the housing authorities and it should be, we think, limited to its facts."

Robinson v. Diamond Housing Corp., D.C.App., 267 A.2d 833, 835 (1970).

We can find nothing about the *Edwards* principle which necessitates such a drastic limitation on its applicability. Indeed the prohibition against retaliatory evictions generally, without limitation to the facts of *Edwards*, and in terms applicable to *Southall Realty* rights,[1] has become part of the housing code of the District of Columbia. We see no reason why the rights protected in *Southall Realty* and

---

1. Housing Regulations of the District of Columbia (hereinafter cited as "Regulations") § 2910 provides:

"No action to recover possession of a habitations [sic] may be brought against a tenant, nor shall an owner otherwise cause a tenant to quit a habitation involuntarily—. . . in retaliation against a tenant's:

. . .

"(c) good faith assertion of rights under these Regulations, including rights under Sections 2901 or 2902."

Section 2902.1(a) states:

"Any letting of a habitation which, at the inception of the tenancy, is unsafe or unsanitary by reason of violations of these Regulations with respect to the particular habitation let or the common space of the premises, whether or not such violations are subject of a notice issued pursuant to these Regulations, of which the owner has knowledge or reasonably should have knowledge, shall render void the lease or rental agreement for such habitation."

It should be obvious from the plain language of § 2910 of the Regulations that the prohibition against retaliatory evictions applies whether the landlord's retaliation results from the tenant's complaints to the housing authorities or, as here, the tenant's successful assertion of a *Southall Realty* defense.

Javins should be rendered nugatory by a restrictive reading of *Edwards* or by a judicial failure to respect the legislative will. We are therefore of the view that appellant should have been given the opportunity to prove the facts necessary to make out an *Edwards* defense and that the trial judge erred in aborting this opportunity by prematurely granting summary judgment. It follows that the decision of the District of Columbia Court of Appeals must be reversed.[i]

. . .

II

A panel of this court recently had occasion to observe that there is an "apparently rising incidence of possessory actions based on notices to quit following closely on the heels of possessory actions based on nonpayment of rent." Cooks v. Fowler, 141 U.S.App.D.C. 236, 240, 437 F.2d 669, 673 (1971). This trend is disturbing because, if judicially encouraged, it would vitiate tenants' rights recognized in *Southall Realty* and *Javins* and now protected by statute in the District of Columbia. As one commentator has observed:

> "In large measure, the scope and effectiveness of tenant remedies for substandard housing will be determined by the degree of protection given tenants against retaliatory actions by landlords. If a landlord is free to evict or otherwise harass a tenant who exercises his right to secure better housing conditions, few tenants will use the remedies for fear of being put out on the street. . . ."

Daniels, Judicial and Legislative Remedies for Substandard Housing: Landlord-Tenant Law Reform in the District of Columbia, 59 Geo.L.J. 909, 943 (1971). The *Javins* and *Southall Realty* decisions—as well as the District of Columbia regulations patterned after them—were based on the express premise that private remedies for housing code violations would increase the stock of livable low-cost housing in the District. If exercise of those remedies leads instead to eviction of tenants and abandonment of what little low-cost housing remains in the District, the great goal of "a decent home and a suitable living environment for every American family," Section 1 of the Housing Act of 1937, 50 Stat. 888, as amended by the Housing Act of 1949, 63 Stat. 413, will be frustrated.

Of course, if the housing market is structured in such a way that it is impossible for landlords to absorb the cost of bringing their units into compliance with the housing code, there may be nothing a court can do to prevent vigorous code enforcement from driving low-cost

---

i. "If lawsuits were won by perseverance alone, Diamond Housing could hardly lose this suit. Appellee has been attempting to evict Mrs. Robinson for over three and a half years. It has proceeded under no fewer than three legal theories and has remained undaunted through an adverse jury verdict, a dismissal of its action by the Court of General Sessions, an adverse decision by the District of Columbia Court of Appeals, and action by the District of Columbia City Council which seemingly cut the heart out of its case." 463 F.2d 857–858.

housing off the market. But the most recent scholarship on the subject indicates this danger is largely imagined. In fact, it appears that vigorous code enforcement plays little or no role in the decrease in low-cost housing stock. When code enforcement is seriously pursued, market forces generally prevent landlords from passing on their increased costs through rent increases. *See generally* Ackerman, Regulating Slum Housing Markets on Behalf of the Poor: Of Housing Codes, Housing Subsidies and Income Redistribution Policy, 80 Yale L.J. 1093 (1971). The danger stems not from the possibility that landlords might take low-cost units off the market altogether, but rather from the possibility that they will do so selectively in order to "make an example" of a troublesome tenant who has the temerity to assert his legal rights in court. We can be fairly confident that most landlords will find ownership of property sufficiently profitable—even with vigorous code enforcement—to remain in business. But it is undoubtedly true that the same landlords would be able to make a greater profit if the housing code were enforced laxly or not at all. There is thus a real danger that landlords may find it in their interest to sacrifice the profits derived from operation of a few units in order to intimidate the rest of their tenants.

Fortunately, this is a danger with which the law is better equipped to deal. While the judiciary may be powerless to control landlords who no longer wish to remain landlords, it can prevent landlords from conducting their business in a way that chills the legally protected rights of tenants. . . .

Although the broad principles which underlie *Edwards* would seem squarely applicable, it is possible that something special about this fact pattern would make it unwise or impermissible to utilize *Edwards* here. Diamond Housing takes the position that this case is, in fact, special and that the special circumstances surrounding it make an application of *Edwards* unjust. Diamond's argument begins with the premise—apparently shared by the District of Columbia Court of Appeals—that *Edwards* should be narrowly "limited to its facts." Since *Edwards* involved reporting of code violations to city officials while this case involves setting up those violations as a defense to an action for eviction, it is contended that *Edwards* does not compel reversal here. Moreover, Diamond argues that, even if *Edwards* is more broadly read, it still should not be applied to a case such as this where the landlord is prevented from collecting rent by *Southall Realty*, refuses to repair the premises, and wishes to take the housing off the market altogether. Closely allied to this contention is the further argument that Mrs. Robinson is precluded from remaining in possession by Section 2301 of the Housing Regulations which makes it illegal to occupy premises which are in violation of the Regulations. Finally, Diamond argues that in any event this case is now moot since Mrs. Robinson has voluntarily surrendered possession and Diamond has chosen to forego any claim it might have to back rent.

We have carefully examined each of these arguments and have concluded that none of them sufficiently distinguishes this case from *Edwards* or precludes application of the District of Columbia law against retaliatory evictions. If we resolve all reasonable doubts in favor of appellant—as we must when reviewing a summary judgment—it becomes plain that a jury might find Diamond Housing to be using the eviction machinery to punish Mrs. Robinson for exercising her legal rights. *Edwards* squarely holds that the state's judicial processes may not be so used, and nothing which has transpired since *Edwards* was decided has caused us to change our view. Indeed, if anything, the creation by the District of Columbia City Council of new private remedies for code violations since *Edwards* reinforces our belief in the necessity for a broad retaliatory eviction defense. If the housing code were effectuated solely by a system of comprehensive public enforcement, the situation might perhaps be different. But by legislating a system of private remedies conforming to the *Javins* and *Southall Realty* decisions, the City Council has made plain that the code is to be enforced in large part through the actions of private tenants. Having put at least some of its eggs in the private enforcement basket, the legislature should not at the same time be taken as having authorized use of legal processes by those who seek to frustrate private enforcement. The right to a decent home is far too vital for us to assume that government has taken away with one hand what it purports to grant with the other. . . .

It must nonetheless be conceded that implementing the legislative will in this fact situation leads to some difficulties and ambiguities. For example, Diamond Housing argues that permitting a retaliatory eviction defense here may mean that it will never be able to recover possession of its property. Nonreceipt of rent is a continuing injury, Diamond argues, and it will always want to remove the tenant so as to remove the source of injury. Yet ironically, so long as it is motivated by this goal, the *Edwards* defense will prevent achievement of it. Thus Diamond fears that its shotgun marriage to Mrs. Robinson may last till death do them part.

Moreover, Diamond points out, it is not trying to evict Mrs. Robinson so that it may rent the premises to someone else. It does not want a quickie divorce in order to permit a hasty remarriage. Rather, if freed from Mrs. Robinson, Diamond promises to beat a strategic retreat to a monastery where it will go and sin no more. Thus Diamond says that it intends to take the unit off the market altogether when Mrs. Robinson leaves—the very thing which this court has suggested a landlord do when he is unwilling or unable to repair the premises. There is nothing in the Housing Regulations which prevents it from going out of business, Diamond argues. Whatever limitations the law imposes on how it chooses its tenants, Diamond claims an absolute right to choose not to have any tenants.

In order to clarify these and other ambiguities inherent in the *Edwards* defense, attorneys for Mrs. Robinson have suggested that we formulate comprehensive guidelines for the circumstances under which a landlord may evict his tenants when the premises contain unremedied housing code violations. We respectfully decline this invitation. . . .

But while we are unwilling to write comprehensive guidelines for application of the *Edwards* defense, we do feel it may be useful to clarify some of the confusion which has evidently surrounded it. These clarifications should, in turn, be incorporated into appropriate instructions which the trial judge should give to the jury when it considers the underlying factual question. First, then, it should be noted that the *Edwards* defense deals with the landlord's subjective state of mind—that is, with his motive. If the landlord's actions are motivated by a desire to punish the tenant for exercising his rights or to chill the exercise of similar rights by other tenants, then they are impermissible.

It is commonplace, however, that a jury can judge a landlord's state of mind only by examining its objective manifestations. Thus when the landlord's conduct is "inherently destructive" of tenants' rights, or unavoidably chills their exercise, the jury may, under well recognized principles, presume that the landlord intended this result. An unexplained eviction following successful assertion of a *Javins* or *Southall Realty* defense falls within this inherently destructive category and hence gives rise to the presumption. Once the presumption is established, it is then up to the landlord to rebut it by demonstrating that he is motivated by some legitimate business purpose rather than by the illicit motive which would otherwise be presumed. We wish to emphasize, however, that the landlord's desire to remove a tenant who is not paying rent is not such a legitimate purpose. *Southall Realty* and the housing code guarantee the right of a tenant to remain in possession without paying rent when the premises are burdened with substantial housing code violations making them unsafe and unsanitary. The landlord of such premises who evicts his tenant because he will not pay rent is in effect evicting him for asserting his legal right to refuse to pay rent. This, of course, is the very sort of reason which, according to *Edwards* and the housing code, will not support an eviction.

Thus Diamond Housing is correct when it asserts it will never be able to evict Mrs. Robinson so long as it is motivated by a desire to rid itself of a tenant who is not paying rent. But it does not follow that Diamond will be burdened by its unwanted tenant forever. If Diamond comes forward with a legitimate business justification—other than the mere desire to get rid of a tenant exercising *Southall Realty* rights—it may be able to convince a jury that it is motivated by this proper concern. For example, if Diamond brought the premises up to housing code standards so that rent was again due and then evicted the tenant for some unrelated, lawful reason, the eviction would be permissible. Similarly, if Diamond were to make a convincing showing that it was for some reason impossible or unfeasible to make repairs, it would have a legitimate reason for evicting the tenant and taking the unit off the market.

It does not follow, however, that mere desire to take the unit off the market is by itself a legitimate business reason which will justify an eviction. Expression of such a desire begs the further question of why the landlord wishes to remove the unit. If he wishes to remove the unit for some sound business reason, then of course he is free to do so. But such a removal, following a tenant's *Southall Realty* defense, is as inherently destructive of tenants' rights as an ordinary eviction. Therefore, a landlord who fails to come forward with a substantial business reason for removing a unit from the market—such as, for example, his financial inability to make the necessary repairs—may be presumed to have done so for an illicit reason. . . .

It should be plain from the above discussion that the landlord's assertion that he wishes to remove the property from the market, even when coupled with the assertion that he is unwilling to remedy housing code violations, is legally insufficient to justify summary judgment over a *Southall Realty* defense. Indeed, the offer to take the unit off the market is totally irrelevant to the issue of motive unless it is accompanied by the further declaration that the landlord is unable to correct housing code violations which preclude his receipt of rent. But while inability to repair *is* a legitimate business reason which would justify removing the unit from the market, even this allegation is not sufficient to justify summary judgment. . . .

Thus the landlord's mere allegation that he is removing the unit from the market because he cannot afford to make repairs does not mean that the jury will find that he is *in fact* unable to make the necessary repairs. Moreover, even if the jury makes such a finding, it still does not follow that judgment for the landlord is compelled. We must remember that we are dealing with a question of subjective motive, and that objective factors are relevant only as indicia of motive. Thus the mere existence of a legitimate reason for the landlord's actions will not help him if the jury finds that he was in fact motivated by some illegitimate reason. In cases of mixed motives, the jury will have the difficult task of weighing one against the other and determining which was the causative factor.

None of this is to say that the landlord may not go out of business entirely if he wishes to do so or that the jury is authorized to inspect his motives if he chooses to commit economic hara-kiri. There would be severe constitutional problems with a rule of law which required an entrepreneur to remain in business against his will. But in a closely analogous area, the Supreme Court has distinguished sharply between a businessman's absolute right to go out of business altogether and his more limited right to discontinue part of his enterprise so as to benefit the rest of it.

"The closing of an entire business, even though discriminatory, ends the employer-employee relationship; the force of such a closing is entirely spent as to that business when termination of the enterprise takes place. On the other hand, a discriminatory partial closing may have repercussions on what remains of the business, affording employer leverage for discouraging the free exercise of § 7 rights among the remaining employees . . . ."

Textile Workers Union v. Darlington Manufacturing Co., 380 U.S. at 274–275, 85 S.Ct. at 1002. Thus we hold that the landlord's right to discontinue rental of all his units in no way justifies a partial closing designed to intimidate the remaining tenants. . . .

III

We do not pretend that allowing Mrs. Robinson to assert an *Edwards* defense will solve the housing crisis in the District of Columbia. That crisis is the product of a constellation of social and economic forces over which no court—and indeed perhaps no legislature—can exercise full control. But while the judicial process is not a *deus ex machina* which can magically solve problems where the legislature and the executive have failed, neither is it a mere game of wits to be played without regard for the well-being of the helpless spectators. We cannot expect judges to solve the housing dilemma, but at least they should avoid affirmative action which makes it worse. The District's legislative body has formulated a comprehensive plan, including criminal sanctions, public inspections, subsidies and rent withholding, to tackle our housing difficulties. In the end, that plan may not work. But if it fails, at least the failure should be caused by inherent weaknesses rather than by judicial subversion.

Thus all we hold today is that when the legislature creates a broad based scheme for dealing with a problem in the public interest, courts should not permit private, selfishly motivated litigants to undermine it. This result is required by the clear wording of the applicable statute, by the dictates of legislatively declared social policy, and, in the final analysis, by respect for the separation of powers and the rule of law.

Reversed and remanded with instructions.

ROBB, Circuit Judge (dissenting):

. . . I cannot accept the proposition espoused by the majority that when a landlord states under oath and without contradiction that he wishes to remove a housing unit from the market it will be presumed that his reasons are "illicit", unless he is able to prove to the satisfaction of a jury that he is financially unable to make necessary repairs or has some other "substantial business reason" for removing the unit from the market. I find no warrant in law for any such presumption or requirement of proof.

The theory of the majority seems to be that if not an outlaw a landlord is at least a public utility, subject to regulation by the court in conformity with its concept of public convenience and necessity. I reject that notion, which in practical application will commit to the discretion of a jury the management of a landlord's business and property.

The majority suggests that its decision will promote the development of more and better low-cost housing. This reasoning passes my understanding. In my judgment the majority's Draconian treatment of landlords will inevitably discourage investment in housing for rental purposes.

I dissent. I would affirm the judgment of the District of Columbia Court of Appeals.

HEARINGS BEFORE THE SUBCOMM. ON BUSINESS AND COMMERCE OF THE SEN. COMM. ON THE DISTRICT OF COLUMBIA ON S. 2311, S. 3549, S. 3558

89th Congress, 2d Session, 181–182 (1966).

Senator KENNEDY. Mr. Chairman, could I ask a question?

There seems to be a direct conflict between what the witness says and the statement that the chairman made.

Is it that you never tried to evict Mrs. Edwards and what the chairman said is entirely untrue?

Mr. HABIB. No; I didn't say that. I said that I did not evict her for complaining to the Housing Division. I have not evicted her, she is still a tenant in the house and the court has upheld my position.

Senator KENNEDY. Let me just ask here: Did you try to evict her?

Mr. HABIB. I tried to evict Mrs. Edwards for being a tenant who did not pay her rent on time and who threatened me for filing a landlord and tenant suit to collect my rent.

Senator KENNEDY. Why was she not evicted then?

Mr. HABIB. Because of objections raised without any proof being established—

Senator KENNEDY. By whom?

Mr. HABIB. By the Neighborhood Legal Service, and this issue is still a matter of court.

Senator KENNEDY. What did they do then? They stopped it themselves?

Mr. HABIB. You can stop any eviction by filing an appeal.

Senator KENNEDY. And they filed an appeal with whom?

Mr. HABIB. First we came up in court.

Senator KENNEDY. What happened then?

Mr. HABIB. We got a judgment on our 30-day notice to move and the lawyer for the case went before Judge Green on a motion which said that he did not appear on the day that the case was scheduled because he had made an oversight and he did not feel that because of his incompetence that Mrs. Edwards should be denied her day in court. At that point Judge Green also raised a constitutional question of eviction under the civil rights bills. Judge Green then took it under advisement and prepared a paper which stated his famous position that the case should be referred back to the court, the judgment vacated, and that the question of retaliatory eviction should not be condoned by the courts, that he would not participate in any eviction.

When the landlord ended up in court and Judge Malloy heard the case he threw out the retaliatory eviction and stated that I had every right to evict Mrs. Edwards on the grounds that she was a monthly tenant and that a 30-day notice had been given. That decision was appealed.

After it went through the court of appeals, after it went through Judge Corcoran who also threw it out and cautioned the court about opening up a "Pandora's box" and flooding the landlord and tenant court and then we are now in the District of Columbia Court of Appeals. It is over 10 months now and we are still on first base. We have been upheld in our right to make the eviction under the 30-day notice but we are still going through the courts.

Senator KENNEDY. What has Judge Wright held on this matter?

Mr. HABIB. Judge Wright held that she had the right to be heard on the question if she would appeal to the District of Columbia Court of Appeals. This case has been appealed to the District of Columbia Court of Appeals and no action has been forthcoming.

Senator KENNEDY. Therefore, the question on the merits of this, it is not correct to say it has been dismissed on the merits, the question of merits is up before the court at the present time?

Mr. HABIB. With all due respect, sir, the case was dismissed by the landlord and tenant court. Even murderers who murder people can go up to the Supreme Court and take 10 years to get there. Anyone can appeal who is a tenant if he has a lawyer, and there are plenty of lawyers who will represent tenants at no charge but there are no lawyers who represent landlords at no charge. We spent over 1,000 hours of legal time in this case and we still get an income from the property paid by the tenant under the District of Columbia court under Judge Wright's stipulation and that was a divided opinion of 2 to 1. If you read the case I think you will find that in Judge Wright's ruling and Judge Corcoran and Judge Malloy that there is quite a difference of opinion and this is a cause celebre which will be a very far-reaching decision.

NOTES

1. Edwards v. Habib, discussed in *Robinson*, was the first American decision to definitively adopt the retaliatory eviction defense. Since *Edwards*, courts and legislatures in over half the states have employed the defense to quash improperly motivated refusals to renew, and substantial increases in rent or decreases in services, as well as outright evictions. See R. Schoshinski, American Law of Landlord and Tenant 717–748 (1980). The defense has found its way into the Restatement (Second) of Property, Landlord and Tenant §§ 14.8, 14.9 (1976), and into the Uniform Residential Landlord and Tenant Act § 5.01.

2. Is *Robinson's* retaliatory eviction defense likely to encourage tenants to demand, and landlords to make, the repairs needed to upgrade substandard premises? How long can a tenant stay on after succeeding in a *Robinson* defense? Edwards v. Habib was careful to reject the proposition that "if the tenant can prove a retaliatory purpose she is entitled to remain in possession in perpetuity." According to *Edwards* once the landlord's illegal purpose is "dissipated," the landlord can "evict his tenants or raise their rents for economic or other legitimate reasons, or even for no reason at all." 397 F.2d at 702. As a tenant, what might you do to assure that before one apparently illegal motive dissipates, another arises? Does *Robinson* provide landlords with any safeguards against such tactics? Does *Robinson* offer any guidelines for determining whether the *tenant* is motivated by good faith or bad?

Is the *Robinson* defense as closely connected to the *Southall-Javins* contract rationale as the court claimed? Did *Southall* in fact "guarantee the right of a tenant to remain in possession without paying rent when the premises are burdened with substantial housing code violations making them unsafe and unsanitary"? If an innkeeper refused to put up with a guest who complained about conditions in the hotel, would the common law rules adverted to in *Javins*—or would *Javins* itself—require the innkeeper to accommodate the guest indefinitely?

Can *Robinson* be reconciled with Kline v. 1500 Massachusetts Avenue, page 858? Will a landlord with tainted, retaliatory motives be exposed to tort liability for injuries suffered by striking tenants? If so, would *Robinson* include the cost of landlord liability insurance in determining whether it was "impossible or unfeasible to make repairs," thus constituting a "legitimate reason for evicting the tenant and taking the unit off the market"?

3. *Proof of Motive.* Landlords will commonly have good reasons as well as bad to evict their tenants. Should a landlord prevail if she can prove that reprisal was only one of the motives behind an attempted eviction? At least one state requires tenants to prove that retaliation was the landlord's sole motive. See Dickhut v. Norton, 45

Wis.2d 389, 173 N.W.2d 297 (1970). Other states are less demanding. See, for example, Minn.Stat.Ann. § 566.03 (West Supp.1983) ("termination was intended in whole or part as a penalty"). What position does *Robinson* take on the question?

As a practical matter, the crux of the retaliatory eviction defense is whether landlord or tenant bears the burden of proof. To require the tenant to come forward with proof that the landlord harbored a retaliatory motive effectively means that tenants will rarely prevail, for the facts to be proved are almost always exclusively within the landlord's control. Yet, to require the landlord to prove that she did *not* have a retaliatory motive carries all the hazards of proving a negative proposition, particularly in jurisdictions that do not allow evidence of concurrent good motives to defeat the retaliatory eviction defense. Where should the burden be placed? Where does *Robinson* place it?

Some states alter the burden of proof to accommodate probable shifts in the parties' motives. For example, states following Uniform Residential Landlord and Tenant Act § 5–101(b) provide that "In an action by or against the tenant, evidence of a complaint within [1] year before the alleged act of retaliation creates a presumption that the landlord's conduct was in retaliation. The presumption does not arise if the tenant made the complaint after notice of a proposed rent increase or diminution of services. 'Presumption' means that the trier of fact must find the existence of the fact presumed unless and until evidence is introduced which would support a finding of its nonexistence."

4. Should the retaliatory eviction defense be confined to situations in which the landlord's reprisal is specifically directed against the tenant's effort to improve housing quality? In Barela v. Superior Court, 30 Cal.3d 244, 178 Cal.Rptr. 618, 636 P.2d 582 (1981), the California Supreme Court reviewed an unlawful detainer action against a tenant who, after four years of uneventful tenancy, saw her rent jump from $200 to $650 per month seven days after she complained to the police that her landlord had sexually molested her nine-year old daughter. Rejecting the argument that landlords are only prohibited from retaliating against housing complaints, the court held that a tenant may "raise as an affirmative defense the claim that a landlord seeks to evict in retaliation for the tenant's complaint to the police that the landlord has committed a crime." 30 Cal.3d at 247, 178 Cal. Rptr. 618, 636 P.2d 582.

The court, in an opinion by Chief Justice Bird, rested its decision on the policies behind the applicable statute, Cal.Civil Code § 1942.5, and the common law—California's "two parallel and independent sources for the doctrine of retaliatory eviction." As to the first, the court noted that section 1942.5(c) "provides that it is unlawful for a lessor to increase rent, decrease services, cause a lessee to quit involuntarily, bring an action to recover possession, or threaten to do any of such acts, *for the purpose of retaliating against the lessee because he or she has . . . lawfully and peaceably exercised any rights under the law.* (Emphasis added)." "Thus," the court concluded, "every citizen has a right protected by state law to report criminal violations to the police. Since petitioner merely engaged in a peaceful and lawful exercise of this basic right when she reported her landlord's crime to the police, her eviction violated the statutory prohibition against evictions in retaliation for the exercise of any rights under the law." 30 Cal.3d at 251–252, 178 Cal.Rptr. at 622–623, 636 P.2d at 586–587.

In the court's view, an analysis of the common law defense of retaliatory eviction led to a similar conclusion. "To hold otherwise," the court concluded, "would be to create a special class of criminals—those who also happen to be landlords—with a legally sanctioned means of punishing the victims or witnesses of their crime." 30 Cal. 3d at 253, 178 Cal.Rptr. at 623, 636 P.2d at 587.

5. *Habitability, Retaliatory Eviction and Summary Proceedings.* The new tenant rights and remedies announced in *Javins* and *Robinson* inevitably ran head-on into the summary eviction procedures then available to landlords in all states. Aimed at giving landlords speedy repossession against defaulting tenants, the original summary eviction statutes limited triable issues to the landlord's claim that the lease had expired or that the tenant had failed to pay rent or had otherwise violated the lease terms. Affirmative defenses or counterclaims would not be entertained and could be pursued only in a separate action. Yet, to deprive the tenant of possession and consign him to a separate action for damages would effectively deprive rent abatement and the retaliatory eviction defense of any force. Which goal should have prevailed in the circumstances—efficiency for landlords or equity for tenants?

In Lindsey v. Normet, 405 U.S. 56, 92 S.Ct. 862, 31 L.Ed.2d 36 (1972), the Supreme Court ruled in favor of efficiency and against a tenant claim that Oregon's Forcible Entry and Detainer Statute, which limited triable issues to the question of default and precluded defenses based on the landlord's failure to maintain the premises, violated the Due Process and Equal Protection Clauses of the Fourteenth Amendment. As to due process, the Court recognized that the tenant "is barred from raising claims in the FED action that the landlord has failed to maintain the premises, but the landlord is also barred from claiming back rent or asserting other claims against the tenant. The tenant is not foreclosed from instituting his own action against the landlord and litigating his right to damages or other relief in that action." 405 U.S. at 65–66, 92 S.Ct. at 869–870. Specifically, the Court asserted that the "Constitution has not federalized the substantive law of landlord-tenant relations, however, and we see nothing to forbid Oregon from treating the undertakings of the tenant and those of the landlord as independent rather than dependent covenants." 405 U.S. at 68, 92 S.Ct. at 871.

Noting that the tenant's equal protection claim "depends on whether the State may validly single out possessory disputes between landlord and tenant for especially prompt judicial settlement," the Court concluded that there are "unique factual and legal characteristics of the landlord-tenant relationship that justify special statutory treatment inapplicable to other litigants. The tenant is, by definition, in possession of the property of the landlord; unless a judicially supervised mechanism is provided for what would otherwise be swift repossession by the landlord himself, the tenant would be able to deny the landlord the rights of income incident to ownership by refusing to pay rent and by preventing sale or rental to someone else. Many expenses of the landlord continue to accrue whether a tenant pays his rent or not. Speedy adjudication is desirable to prevent subjecting the landlord to undeserved economic loss and the tenant to unmerited harassment and dispossession when his lease or rental agreement gives him the right to peaceful and undisturbed possession of the property." 405 U.S. at 71, 72–73, 92 S.Ct. at 873–874.

To the tenant's argument that the "need for decent shelter" and the " 'right to retain peaceful possession of one's home' are fundamental interests which are particularly important to the poor and which may be trenched upon only after the State demonstrates some superior interest," the Court responded that "the Constitution does not provide judicial remedies for every social and economic ill. We are unable to perceive in that document any constitutional guarantee of access to dwellings of a particular quality, or any recognition of the right of a tenant to occupy the real property of his landlord beyond the term of his lease without the payment of rent or otherwise contrary to the terms of the relevant agreement . . . . Nor should we forget that the Constitution expressly protects against confiscation of private property or the income therefrom." 405 U.S. at 73–74, 92 S.Ct. at 874.

Lindsey's holding that states are not constitutionally compelled to give tenants an opportunity to raise habitability defenses in summary proceedings obviously leaves states free to give this opportunity if they wish. Most states that have adopted the implied warranty of habitability have correspondingly enlarged the defenses that tenants can raise in summary proceedings. Indeed, Oregon took this route less than a year after *Lindsey* was decided. See Robbins, The New Oregon Landlord-Tenant Act and the Uniform Residential Landlord and Tenant Act—A Comparison, 7 Clearinghouse Rev. 327 (1973). Are states entirely free to act in this area, or does *Lindsey* suggest some limits in its reminder "that the Constitution expressly protects against confiscation of private property or the income therefrom"? What property? Whose property?

6. Politics and bureaucratic behavior may constrain evictions more effectively than legal rules. According to a District of Columbia Auditor's report, only 2,751, or roughly 12 per cent, of the 24,000 evictions ordered by the District of Columbia Superior Court during the preceding year were carried out. (Some of the 4,800 scheduled evictions were cancelled after the tenants paid their back rent or agreed to move out.) According to the report, larger numbers of evictions were not enforced because the marshal's office gave these duties a low priority. Pianin, Few Evictions Enforced Here, Auditor Says, Washington Post, A1, A16, Sept. 29, 1983.

3. REGULATION OF PRICE AND ACCESS

BLUMBERG, ROBBINS & BAAR, THE EMERGENCE OF SECOND GENERATION RENT CONTROLS
8 Clearinghouse Review 240–245 (1974).

1. INTRODUCTION

One of the most oppressive and recurring problems facing tenants today, excluding deteriorated housing conditions, is exorbitant and continuing general rent increases. Legal Services attorneys representing tenants have available numerous judicial approaches to virtually every landlord-tenant problem except general increases of rent in private housing. American courts will not invalidate a rent increase simply on the ground that it is excessive, except in cases where retaliatory motive was proven or rent controls were in effect. Therefore, tenant protection in this area must be achieved by the legislative process, specifically by rent control.

In the wake of the national economic crisis that grew out of the spiraling inflation of the late 1960's, legislators and citizen groups began to look to the invocation of rent controls as a means of protecting tenants from unwarranted rent increases.[2] In 1971 President Nixon invoked the standby powers of the Economic Stabilization Act of 1970 in the form of a 90-day absolute freeze on all prices, wages and rents. This freeze was replaced by Phase II stabilization which was a milder form of wage, price and rent controls. On January 10, 1973, Phase II was replaced by the voluntary restraint system of Phase III which in practice became federal decontrol under Phase IV. This economic crisis has led to significant rent control activity at the state and local level throughout the nation. It is this recent upsurge which we characterize as the movement toward "Second Generation Rent Control."

2. There was national rental control during World War II. In the post war period rent control was retained only in New York City and Washington, D.C. See, Willis, A Short History of Rent Control Laws, 36 CORNELL LAW Q. 54 (1950) and Comment, Residential Rent Control in New York City, 3 COLUM.J. OF LAW AND SOCIAL PROBLEMS 30 (1967) for a detailed history of rent control up to World War II.

Second Generation rent controls are peacetime regulation of rents which have been enacted in communities with low vacancy rates and a spiraling rent inflation rate. Unlike World War II and Phase I rent controls these controls are not absolute rent freezes. Indeed they allow for restricted rent increases. Landlords are protected by tax and capital improvement pass-throughs and very often by "across the board" cost of living increases. Alternatively, landlords are guaranteed a "fair return on investment" in some of the Acts. Second Generation rent controls are an attempt to equalize and balance rents in the private housing market which undeniably places tenants in an inferior bargaining position with landlords over rents and the condition of the premises. It is the goal of this article to describe the development, content, pitfalls, legal challenges and progress of Second Generation rent controls as they presently exist in the United States. Analysis of available alternatives is provided, but value judgments concerning these alternatives are kept to a minimum. Readers of this article should be aware that many economists believe that rent controls will not provide the intended benefits to tenants, particularly low income tenants. The article neither defends nor advocates implementation of rent controls, but rather recognizes the growing national trend toward proposal and/or enactment by many tenant organizations. In recognition of this trend the article seeks to provide Legal Services attorneys with basic rent control information to aid them in the representation of their clients.

II. RECENT DEVELOPMENTS

Massachusetts was the first state to adopt Second Generation rent control by enacting legislation enabling municipalities to pass local rent controls in 1970. Subsequently, Boston, Cambridge, Somerville, Brookline and Lynn passed local rent control ordinances. Maine enacted an adaptation of the Massachusetts state enabling act in 1973. Alaska enacted a state enabling act in 1974.

In New Jersey over eighty municipalities responded to pressure from the state-wide tenants organization (N.J.T.O.) and enacted local rent control ordinances. Approximately seventy-five of these ordinances were adopted after the New Jersey Supreme Court upheld the municipality's power to enact local rent controls in the case of Inganamort v. Borough of Fort Lee.[11] Maryland has enacted a state-wide rent control statute, which has been supplemented by stronger county ordinances. In November, 1973, Congress enacted a law authorizing the District of Columbia to adopt local rent control. The Connecticut state legislature has passed a statute authorizing the creation of limited jurisdiction Rent Review Boards.

11. 62 N.J. 521, 303 A.2d 298 (1973).

Miami Beach, Florida passed a local rent control ordinance in 1969, which was struck down by the Florida Supreme Court in 1972. In 1973 Miami Beach enacted a new rent control ordinance which is presently pending before the State Supreme Court. Berkeley, California tenants placed a rent control measure on the ballot in 1972 by use of California's initiative process. The ordinance was invalidated by the county trial court and is presently on appeal. Rent control measures have also been introduced in the Hawaii state legislature and in Madison, Wisconsin. Several other jurisdictions have considered rent control proposals during the past year.

As long as rents continue to rise at a high inflationary rate tenants around the country in all likelihood will continue to support and propose rent control as the only viable interim protection available to curb rising rent. Second Generation control has already established a significant foothold in the East and interest is spreading across the country.

There are probably as many varying approaches to rent control as there are cities and states considering enactment. It will therefore be valuable to analyze basic components and alternatives available in the construction of a rent control ordinance. Emphasis will be placed upon those elements which are especially indicative of Second Generation rent control legislation.

III. DRAFTING RENT CONTROL LEGISLATION

A. Generic Types

There are three generic types of rent control legislation: (1) *Local Ordinance* where the municipality or county enacts rent controls pursuant to home rule authority, or its local police powers without benefit of any state action. This is usually accomplished by local city council action as in New Jersey and Miami Beach, Florida. Municipal rent control can also be enacted by use of the initiative process where available. (2) *State Rent Control Statute* where a state enacts a rent control scheme mandatorily applicable to every residential rental unit in that state. (3) *State Enabling Legislation* where local governments are specifically empowered by state statute to enact rent control legislation without the danger of state preemption.

The states which so far have adopted state-wide rent control laws have chosen not to adopt a pure form of either mandatory state rent controls or state enabling legislation. Instead, they have formulated hybrids drawn from the two alternatives. For example, Maryland has enacted a state statute which mandates a state-wide rent control law but also allows all counties and the City of Baltimore to "supersede" the state law with their own legislation.

For tenants the most important consideration is not the gender of a rent control law, but rather the scope of its content, coverage and protective nature. The direct and immediate effects upon present rent levels and potential rent increases are also crucial tenant considerations.

An analysis of the actual contents of existing Second Generation rent control laws, with the goal of suggesting factors that should be considered, follows.

B. Contents of Rent Control Legislation

(1) Declaration of Emergency

Virtually every recent rent control measure proposed or enacted in the United States contains a preamble which recites in "boiler plate" terms the existence of a "housing emergency." This emergency is linked either to a declining vacancy rate or to increasing rent costs, or both. The conception that rent regulations require an emergency as a prerequisite to use of police power stems from the early twentieth century concept of "economic due process" as applied by the United States Supreme Court in Block v. Hirsh [25] (Washington, D.C. rent control circa World War I) and Marcus Brown Holding Company v. Feldman [26] (New York rent control circa World War I). The Supreme Court retreated from the doctrine of "economic due process" in Nebbia v. New York.[27] Nonetheless, the emergency doctrine appears to have outlived the cases from which it was spawned, and to date the courts have consistently held that emergency is a necessary prerequisite to rent regulation. In fact many courts have treated the existence of an emergency as an important factual matter supporting the need for rent controls. Most courts, however, have given great deference to the legislative finding of emergency, no matter how *pro forma* it appears. Since emergency is generally the basis for governmental consideration of rent controls it is advisable at this point in time to include a declaration of emergency in all rent control legislation.

(2) Exemptions

Rent control legislation need not cover every rental unit on the market; however, a considered decision must be made as to which units will be covered and which will be exempted. Typically New Jersey ordinances exempt dwellings with four units or less. Exemptions of this nature can exclude a substantial percentage of all rental units. For example, 53 per cent of all rental units in New Jersey are in dwellings with four units or less.

The Massachusetts enabling act exempts two and three family owner-occupied units while Maryland covers all premises with four or more units. Many New Jersey cities have excluded "luxury" housing

---

25. 256 U.S. 135 (1921).
26. 256 U.S. 1970 (1921).
27. 291 U.S. 502 (1934).

and the Massachusetts Act allows cities to exclude up to 25 per cent of its highest rent units.

Second Generation rent control laws exclude new construction and newly offered units from control to avoid discouraging housing production by scaring off investors, developers and/or lending institutions. Massachusetts has accomplished this goal by giving a blanket exemption to all housing built after January 1, 1969. New Jersey municipalities have exempted all newly constructed units for the first setting of rents upon the first offering of the unit on the market. Subsequently, all such units come under the provisions of municipal rent control.

The question has arisen concerning FHA housing (usually Sections 221(d)(3) and 236) and federal preemptions. The United States District Court of New Jersey has held in Helmsley v. Borough of Fort Lee [39] that FHA housing is not exempt from local rent controls by virtue of its federally insured mortgage. Moreover, the court held that federal preemption does not apply because federal control of FHA housing is minimal in the area of rent controls and because the legislature did not intend to control rents. The Boston Housing Court has already decided the issue along the same lines as *Helmsley*. However, similar cases are now pending in federal court in Massachusetts. Maryland excludes all residential units which are federally financed *and* where rents are determined as a percentage of the tenants' income.

Drafters of rent control legislation should consult the *1970 U.S. Census*, "Housing Characteristics for States, Cities and Counties, Part 1, U.S. Summary" before making final decisions concerning exemptions from coverage. The criteria to be considered include: how many units will be excluded, what kind of units will be excluded, who lives in these units (low or moderate income people), and what other forms of control already cover these units. Local planners and economists also should be consulted. In this way a predetermination can be made concerning the direct effect of a given exclusion.

(3) Roll Backs

There is invariably a time lag between the proposal of a rent control system and its final enactment or effective date. During this time lag, landlords in anticipation of future rent controls may raise rents either to avoid control or to create a higher base rent to which the control scheme will apply. To avoid such rent increases many rent control laws include a roll back provision which selects a date prior to proposal of the rent control law as the base period for determining the rent level of a given unit. This base period level is then used in the rent control formula to determine rent increases or decreases.

---

39. 362 F.Supp. 581 (1973).

(4) Setting Rent Levels

There are three primary ways that rent levels can be set in a rent control scheme: a formula which regulates the landlords' return on investment (limits profits); a specified base period rent with annual percentage increases and allowable pass-throughs; and a limitation on the amount of rent a tenant has to pay based on that tenant's ability to pay. While the third approach is currently the law nationally for setting rents in public housing, it has neither been proposed nor applied in private housing.

Massachusetts and Maine currently have rent controls which restrict the landlord's return on investment by use of a rent formula. Both states have chosen the "fair net operating income" method, which takes into account increases or decreases in property taxes, unavoidable increases or any decreases in operating expenses, capital improvements, increases or decreases in living space or services, substantial deterioration, and the failure to perform ordinary repairs.

The fair net operating income formula is administered by a local Rent Board. Starting with a base year from which fair profit levels are determined, the Board then takes the objective factual data (taxes, operating expenses, and capital improvements) and combines them with a subjective judgment based upon the condition of the building (deterioration and maintenance) in order to make a determination as to whether a specific request for rent increase or decrease should be granted. The Board is of course required to adopt rules and regulations which are to be applied uniformly and reasonably to all questions of rent increase or decrease. Since all rents are initially frozen at their current level when the act takes effect, no rent increase is valid without prior Board approval. In this manner the tenant is not responsible for policing enforcement of the law.

Maryland and New Jersey have chosen a system which employs a base rental period with allowable annual percentage increases and pass-throughs. The percentage increase can be determined in two general ways and must be specifically set in the statute or ordinance upon adoption. The first method, used principally in New Jersey, ties the annual increase to fluctuations in the Cost of Living Index (CLI) and Consumer Price Index (CPI). A number of New Jersey cities have allowed the full cost of living increase to be translated into the local annual rent increase. However, because of recent unprecedented raises in CLI a number of New Jersey cities have set an upper limit or ceiling on the annual allowable percentage increase. The state of Maryland along with a number of New Jersey cities which became dissatisfied with the CPI approach, have adopted the second alternative which is a simple statutorily fixed annual percentage increase. This approach limits rent increases to an annual maximum not to exceed a fixed percentage, but also allows for specified pass-throughs and/or hardship exemptions. The pass-throughs allowed for tax increases or capital improvements for example, are in addition to the annual percentage increase.

The entire concept of pass-throughs creates a difficult problem because by definition such pass-throughs escape rent control. In the area of tax pass-throughs important issues to be considered are: should taxes be apportioned by rent paid, square feet occupied, or rooms rented; should landlords pay taxes for common areas over which control is retained; should tenants benefit from successful tax appeals and/or tax reductions; should the tax pass-through be effective at the time the tax is levied or at the time it is actually paid; and finally should tenants have to pay or assume the entire tax burden of the landlord, and if so, should they not be given a rent reduction in proportion to the landlord's actual tax benefit?

Capital improvement pass-throughs may present an even greater problem to tenants than tax pass-throughs because tenants may be called upon to assume the full cost of landlord repairs of code violations which the landlord may have been otherwise legally obligated to maintain. Furthermore, such pass-throughs may in effect violate existing tenant protections against retaliatory rent increases for the reporting of code violations. In response to this threat several rent control schemes limit the concept of capital improvement pass-throughs by conditioning such a pass-through on a subjective judgment of the good faith maintenance of the premises by the landlord. Other schemes limit capital improvement pass-throughs to those improvements which can be characterized as major and in no case exceed a fifteen per cent increase in rent. In this way the cost of repair of most housing code violations reported by the tenant, but not caused by the tenant, cannot be passed through.

In comparing the return on investment formula with the annual percentage increase system it is apparent that neither approach is inherently more strict in controlling rents. The strictness of each depends upon the level at which the allowable return on investment or the permitted annual increase is set. Moreover, the subjective elements of each play a significant role in determining the stringency of the rent control system.

The desirability of either a return on investment formula or annual percentage increase system of rent controls depends primarily on the condition of existing housing and rent levels within the state or municipality. Where the housing stock is in relatively sound condition and rents are generally equalized and not excessive, the annual percentage increase approach can provide an effective and equitable rent control system which will furnish a hedge against inflation and future rent gouging. It should be noted however, that under this system of rent controls the burden of reporting violations is usually upon the tenant. If the tenant is supplied with adequate information concerning allowable rent increases then self enforcement of the simple percentage system is feasible.

Conversely, where the housing stock suffers from significant deterioration or where rents are excessive or in great disparity, a return on investment formula which relates housing condition to rent level is uniquely applicable. Because the return on investment formula operates on an individual case by case basis it allows rent control authorities to take into account situations where the landlord has disinvested by failing to properly maintain the property, but continues to increase rent. Moreover, where there is a wide divergence in rents for similar units the annual percentage increase system will in effect penalize landlords who have kept their rents low, while allowing landlords with high rental levels to retain their increases. The return on investment formula can equalize these rents by denying rent increases, decreasing excessive rents, or allowing moderate increases on existing low rents. In areas where rents are uniformly exorbitant a return on investment formula might allow a resetting of rents to reasonable levels.

HUDSON VIEW PROPERTIES v. WEISS

Supreme Court of New York, Appellate Term, First Department, 1981.
109 Misc.2d 589, 442 N.Y.S.2d 367.

PER CURIAM:

Order entered July 28, 1980, 106 Misc.2d 251, 431 N.Y.S.2d 632 is reversed with $10 costs; the tenant's motion to dismiss the petition (CPLR 3211[a][7]) is denied.

The record before us is sparse and its principal elements are easily recounted. Landlord served a notice to cure, dated January 24, 1980, upon Julia Weiss "and all other occupants" of the apartment here at issue. That notice to cure stated, ". . . you are violating a substantial obligation of your tenancy . . ., viz., you are allowing a person who is not a tenant to reside in and occupy the premises." The January 24, 1980 notice afforded tenant 10 days to cure the alleged violation. On February 5, 1980, landlord served upon the tenant a thirty day notice of termination, which purported to terminate the subject tenancy on March 17, 1980, on the ground that the violation set forth in the January 24, 1980 notice had not been cured. The instant holdover proceeding was commenced after the tenant failed to surrender the premises as demanded in the February 5, 1980 notice of termination. The petition indicates that the premises are subject to rent control.

Tenant Weiss moved to dismiss the petition for failure to state a cause of action. In support of that motion Ms. Weiss submitted an affidavit, dated April 21, 1980, in which she states, upon information and belief, that the unauthorized occupant referred to by the landlord is one Jack A. Wertheimer ". . . who lives in my apartment, who did not sign the lease, and to whom I am not related by blood or marriage." Ms. Weiss goes on to allege in her affidavit in support of the motion to dismiss, again upon information and belief, that

". . . the landlord through his attorney has stated that if I marry Mr. Wertheimer, he will withdraw his claim that I have violated the lease and will not seek to evict me. If I remain single, this action will continue. I am moving to dismiss on the grounds that these actions violate the State Human Rights Law [Executive Law] § 296(5)(a) and the City Human Rights Law § B1–7.0(5a) which prohibit discrimination in housing on the basis of marital status."

Finally Ms. Weiss notes in her affidavit of April 21, 1980 that she does not believe that the nature of her relationship with Mr. Wertheimer is relevant to her motion. She states, however, that the Court has inquired into that issue, and she goes on to note that Mr. Wertheimer and I have a "close and loving relationship."

In an affidavit submitted on behalf of the landlord by the managing agent for the subject premises, in opposition to tenant's motion to dismiss the petition, it is stated that Ms. Weiss moved into the apartment at issue on or about February 1, 1967 pursuant to a written lease between the then landlord and her husband, Lawrence Weiss. Ms. Weiss was never a signatory to that lease. Mr. Weiss subsequently vacated the premises, but it is unknown whether Mr. Weiss and Ms. Weiss are legally separated or divorced (whether Ms. Weiss or Mr. Wertheimer are single or married is not revealed in the record; what is clear is that they are not married to one another). Thereafter and shortly before the commencement of this proceeding an "unauthorized occupant", identified in the caption as "John Doe" (i.e. Mr. Wertheimer) moved into the apartment.

Landlord, through its managing agent's affidavit in opposition to tenant's motion to dismiss the petition, professes no concern as to the nature of the relationship between the unauthorized occupant of the apartment and Ms. Weiss, other than that he is not a member of the immediate family of the tenant. Landlord notes, however, that were he (the unauthorized occupant) a member of the tenant's immediate family, there would be no basis for the proceeding.

Although the lease underlying Ms. Weiss' tenancy has not been included in the record on appeal, the lease, as quoted in the opinion of the Court below, contains a restrictive covenant that ". . . the demised premises and any part thereof shall be occupied only by tenant and members of the immediate family of tenant. . . ." The occupancy of Ms. Weiss—she not having been a party to the original lease—was sanctioned by virtue of her status as a member of the original tenant's immediate family. The New York State Attorney General intervened in this proceeding and, in both the Court below and on this appeal, has joined with the tenant in arguing that the petition fails to state a cause of action (citing State Human Rights Law [Executive Law] § 296[5][a]).

Section 296(5)(a) of the State Human Rights Law [Executive Law] provides that:

> It shall be an unlawful discriminatory practice for the owner . . . or managing agent of, or other person having the right to sell, rent, or lease a housing accommodation . . . or any agent or employee thereof:
>
> (1) To refuse to sell, rent, lease or otherwise deny to or withhold from any person or group of persons such a housing accommodation because of the . . . marital status of such person or persons [L.1975 ch. 803, eff. on the 60th day after August 9, 1975].

§ 296(5)(a)(2) contains an identical provision prohibiting discrimination "in the terms, conditions, or privileges of the sale, rental or lease of any such housing accommodation or in the furnishing of facilities or services in connection therewith."

§ B1–7.0(5a) of the Law on Human Rights of the City of New York is identical to State Human Rights Law [Executive Law] § 296(5)(a) and § B1–7.05(a)(2) is identical to § 296(5)(a)(2).

A motion to dismiss for failure to state a cause of action may lie if the pleading is defective on its face, or, even if the claim is perfectly pleaded, if, upon affidavits and other permissible proof, the movant is able to go behind the pleading and establish that it lacks merit (Siegel, New York Practice, Section 265; Kelly v. Bank of Buffalo, 32 A.D.2d 875, 302 N.Y.S.2d 60). "[I]n order to succeed on such a motion, the defendant must convince the court that nothing the plaintiff might reasonably be expected to prove would help him; that the plaintiff simply does not have a claim" (Siegel, New York Practice, Section 265).

The pleading at issue is not defective upon its face. Landlord seeks to enforce a restrictive covenant contained in the lease executed at the inception of the subject tenancy. In the case of a statutory tenancy—such as that of the tenant Weiss—". . . with the exceptions of the duration of the term, and the amount of rent payable, the rule established by the weight of authority is that insofar as the provisions of a lease which has expired are not in conflict with the then prevailing emergency rent statutes, and are not confined to the period of the expired lease, they are projected into the statutory tenancy, and will continue in effect during the term of the statutory tenancy." (Rasch, New York Landlord and Tenant, 2d Ed., Section 286).

The law favors free and unrestricted use of property, and all doubts and ambiguities in a lease will be resolved in favor of the natural right to free use and enjoyment of premises against restrictions. A landlord, however, does have the right to limit a tenant's use of the premises and where covenants restricting the use of property are reasonable and not contrary to public policy, they will be enforced by the courts. Indeed, it has long been held that parties to a lease may, by express provision therein, restrict the uses to which the lessee may put the demised premises and lease provisions restricting the use of premises to "tenant and members of tenant's immediate family"—the very provision here sought to be enforced by the landlord—have consistently been sustained. Tenant alludes to no judicial or statutory authority which expressly proscribes or declares it to be against public policy for landlord to limit the use of demised premises to the tenant or tenants and members of his or their immediate family.

Believing as we do that the pleading is sufficient on its face, the record must be examined to determine whether the tenant has offered evidence sufficient to establish that the landlord does not have a cause of action. Tenant sought to establish upon her motion to dismiss the petition, and the Court below concluded, that the attempt of the landlord to enforce the restriction in the lease limiting the use of the premises to tenant and members of the tenant's immediate family constituted unlawful discrimination against the tenant upon the basis of her "marital status".

We are cognizant that § 300 of the State Human Rights Law [Executive Law] provides that "the provisions of this article [including of course § 296(5)(a)] shall be construed liberally for the accomplishment of the purposes thereof" and that § B1–11.0 of the City Law on Human Rights similarly so provides. There is nonetheless little in this sparse record to suggest that the landlord, in seeking to enforce the restrictive covenant in the lease limiting occupancy to the tenant and members of tenant's immediate family, had any interest in the marital status of the tenant Weiss or the occupant Wertheimer, other than that Wertheimer was not a member of Weiss' immediate family. An interest in ascertaining whether an occupant qualifies for occupancy of a demised premises, under a lease provision authorizing occupancy by tenant and members of tenant's immediate family (i.e., whether the occupant is a spouse, son, parent or other relation within the scope of "immediate family") does not ipso facto connote discrimination on the basis of "marital status"; thus we are not persuaded by this sparse record that there has been a showing of discrimination by the landlord against the tenant upon the basis of her "marital status". While clearly no cause of action lies under a restrictive covenant in a lease limiting occupancy to the tenant and members of tenant's immediate family, where the tenant has married a newly arrived occupant, it does not follow that a landlord is automatically precluded by § 296(5)(a) from enforcing such a restrictive covenant where the tenant and the new occupant are, for whatever reason, unmarried. In summary, landlord's cause of action predicated upon the covenant in the specified lease restricting occupancy of the subject premises to the tenant and members of tenant's immediate family does not appear to us to constitute discrimination per se on the basis of tenant's "marital status." In concluding that tenant failed to demonstrate that she is entitled to a dismissal of landlord's petition pursuant to CPLR 3211(a)(7), we do not, however, foreclose the tenant from offering proof at the time of trial that she is entitled to prevail in this proceeding because the landlord in maintaining this proceeding is indeed unlawfully discriminating against her on the basis of her "marital status". Contrary to the argument made by the landlord, the proscriptions set forth in State Human Rights Law [Executive Law] § 296(5)(a) do not only apply to circumstances existing at the inception of a landlord-tenant relationship. A landlord's conduct during the course of a tenancy may be shown to violate the provisions of § 296(5)(a).

TIERNEY and RICCOBONO, JJ., concur.

ASCH, J., dissents in the following memorandum.

ASCH, Justice, dissenting.

In my opinion, this court should affirm Judge Wilk's dismissal and hold that, under the peculiar facts of this case, to oust Ms. Weiss would be violative of Human Rights Law § 296.

Preliminarily, landlord argues that § 296 has no application to a situation where the marital status of the apartment occupants changes *after* the rental term has begun. Although this position is not entirely untenable, I would hold to the contrary. Adopting landlord's construction would, in my view, be to hew to an overly technical reading of the Human Rights Law. Section 300 of that statute mandates that HRL is to be liberally construed. Therefore, I would opt for an interpretation which would encompass a case where the marital status discrimination occurs after the initial leasing.

Furthermore, the very language of § 296 speaks of a refusal to "sell, rent, lease *or otherwise* to deny to . . . any person . . . because of . . . marital status." (Emphasis added.) These statutory phrases, read in the light of the command that the HRL be liberally construed mean, to my mind, that in a case like the one presented here, where discrimination takes place after the initial leasing the proscriptions of § 296 are fully operative.

Moreover, to adopt landlord's construction of § 296 would leave a gaping and illogical lacuna in the HRL. If (as its sparse legislative history indicates), the purpose of § 296 was to provide unmarried couples an unimpeded opportunity to obtain housing, it would stand to reason that the legislature would have wanted the protections of that section to remain in force even after the commencement of the lease. Consequently, an attempt to oust a tenant because of a change in the marital status of the partners occupying her apartment should be judged in the same light as would be a threshold refusal to rent.

I find unpersuasive the remonstrances by landlord that the lower court's decision has the effect of nullifying a landlord's right to pass upon and approve those who are to occupy his premises. Certainly, the existing lease clause restricting occupancy to close family members, impinges to a large degree on a landlord's veto over those who are to share in the premises. A close family member may be just as objectionable as an unrelated party deciding to share house with an unmarried mate. But, as the Court noted below, all things being equal, discrimination on the basis of marital status is precisely what HRL § 296 proscribes. In short, that the objectionable occupant is unrelated by marriage to tenant may not, consistent with the Human Rights Law be used as a predicate for ouster.

Landlord's final challenge to the dismissal of its petition focuses on the rent controlled status of the premises in dispute. It was never the intent of the legislature, argues landlord to extend the benefits of those laws to lovers. To the contrary, contends landlord, the statutory structure reveals a clear bias in favor of bestowing rent advantages on the families and spouses of rent control tenants. Prime reliance is placed by landlord on § 56 of New York City Rent and Eviction Regulations which states that where a tenant no longer occupies his apartment, a certificate of eviction may issue, except when the remaining occupant is either the surviving spouse or some other member of the deceased tenant's family. Case law also betrays a pro-tenant bias. (See Herzog v. Joy, 74 A.D.2d 372, 428 N.Y.S.2d 1 [1st Dept.1980] [where tenant of rent controlled unit vacates apartment family members and spouses are entitled to continue reaping benefits of rent control laws]).

While these regulations do show a pro-family bias, they have no role to play under the facts of this case. Tenant Weiss has neither died nor vacated unit 15H. The Human Rights Law permits Wertheimer to occupy the apartment. Hence, he falls within the broad definition of tenant spelled out in § Y51–3.0m of New York City's Rent and Rehabilitation Law and is entitled to continue residing in the apartment. Whether, if Ms. Weiss left the apartment, Wertheimer could maintain his possession is a knotty question which need not be addressed here. For purposes of this case, it is sufficient to note that under § 296 of the HRL, Ms. Weiss and Wertheimer are completely within their rights in staying in apartment 15H.

As a postscript, it should be noted that the grounds for the dissent are fairly narrow. Concededly, the occupants of the apartment "maintain a close and loving relationship." Yet, it is indisputable that the landlord required a formal marriage as the essential condition for continuing the tenancy. The marriage certificate does not always supply a litmus test for love. Further, under the Human Rights Law, it cannot serve as the key which opens the door to the tenancy of an apartment.

The landlord still has ample discretion to select and reject tenants provided that he does not use categories interdicted under the law, such as marital status, in screening their suitability.

I would affirm the lower court's dismissal of the petition.

HUDSON VIEW PROPERTIES v. WEISS

Supreme Court of New York, Appellate Division, First Department, 1982.
86 A.D.2d 803, 448 N.Y.S.2d 649.

Order, Appellate Term, Supreme Court, First Department, entered on July 17, 1981, 109 Misc.2d 589, 442 N.Y.S.2d 367, unanimously reversed, on the law, without costs and without disbursements, for the reasons stated by Asch, J., dissenting at Appellate Term and Wilk, J., at Civil Court and the motion to dismiss the petition of petitioner-respondent granted. [Ross, J., concurs in the result only.]

SANDLER, J.P., and ROSS, CARRO and SILVERMAN, JJ., concur.

HUDSON VIEW PROPERTIES v. WEISS

Court of Appeals of New York, 1983.
59 N.Y.2d 733, 463 N.Y.S.2d 428, 450 N.E.2d 234.

MEMORANDUM.

The order of the Appellate Division should be reversed, 86 A.D.2d 803, 448 N.Y.S.2d 649, with costs, the landlord's petition reinstated and the case remitted to Civil Court, City of New York, for further proceedings.

Petitioner landlord, in this holdover proceeding, seeks to evict respondent tenant from a rent-controlled apartment on the ground that tenant violated a substantial obligation of her tenancy by allowing a person not a tenant and not part of her "immediate family" to occupy the apartment with her.

Tenant contends that the landlord in seeking to enforce the restrictive covenant in the lease limiting occupancy to the tenant and members of tenant's immediate family discriminates against her on the basis of marital status in violation of the State Human Rights Law (Executive Law, § 296, subd. 5, par. [a]) and the New York City Human Rights Law (Administrative Code of City of New York, § B1-7.0, subd. 5, par. [a]).

We have recently addressed an analogous question: whether an employer's antinepotism rule which forbids an employee from working under the supervision of a relative (including a spouse) violates section 296 of the Executive Law by discriminating on the basis of marital status. (Matter of Manhattan Pizza Hut v. New York State

Human Rights Appeal Bd., 51 N.Y.2d 506, 434 N.Y.S.2d 961, 415 N.E.2d 950.) In that case, we held there was no statutory violation inasmuch as the disqualification of the employee under the company policy was not for being married (i.e., on the basis of her marital status), but for being married to her supervisor (i.e., on the basis of her relationship vis-à-vis a particular individual).

In this case, the issue arises not because the tenant is unmarried, but because the lease restricts occupancy of her apartment, as are all apartments in the building, to the tenant and the tenant's immediate family. Tenant admits that an individual not part of her immediate family currently occupies the apartment as his primary residence. Whether or not he could by marriage or otherwise become a part of her immediate family is not an issue. The landlord reserved the right by virtue of the covenant in the lease to restrict the occupants and the tenant agreed to this restriction. Were the additional tenant a female unrelated to the tenant, the lease would be violated without reference to marriage. The fact that the additional tenant here involved is a man with whom the tenant has a loving relationship is simply irrelevant. The applicability of that restriction does not depend on her marital status.

Thus, we conclude that the landlord in this holdover proceeding has not discriminated against the tenant in violation of the State or City Human Rights Law.

COOKE, C.J., and JASEN, JONES, WACHTLER, MEYER and SIMONS, JJ., concur in memorandum.

FUCHSBERG, J., taking no part.

Order reversed, etc.

NOTES

1. Rent control is not a twentieth-century American innovation. Dating back at least to medieval Europe, rent control at one time or another has been employed in more than one hundred countries. See Willis, A Short History of Rent Control Laws, 36 Cornell L.Q. 54 (1950). Yet, modern housing codes and abatement remedies do give rent control a sometimes poignant twist: required to repair substandard premises, and barred from raising rents to cover the costs of repair, landlords may be faced with no choice but to abandon their buildings—to the injury of landlord and tenant alike.

What are the arguments in favor of rent control? One is that the structure of the rental housing market and the continued scarcity of rental housing puts landlords in a superior bargaining position, effectively disabling tenants from negotiating on price. Controlled rents, it is thought, will approximate the price that landlord and tenant would have agreed upon had they been able to bargain freely. A connected argument is that housing, like water and electricity, is a necessity of life and, like these necessities, should be treated as a public utility, regulated in all respects including price.

Opponents of rent control argue that there is nothing in the structure of rental housing markets to give landlords the ability to set price substantially over cost. Under this view, housing scarcity is the result of—and not the justification for—rent and quality controls; if investors were promised unregulated returns they would quickly build additional housing. Opponents note that the prices of other necessities, such as food and clothing, are not controlled, and that public utilities are regulated not because they provide necessities but because efficiency dictates that they be given a monopoly position in the areas they serve. Because there are no equivalent monopolies in the housing market, there is no need to prohibit monopoly pricing. Opponents also argue that price regulation will in fact harm tenants over the long run. Guaranteed a minimum rental, landlords will have little incentive to invest in cost-cutting innovations and tenants will occupy more space than they really need, thus excluding others from needed housing.

There is a large, and largely inconclusive, theoretical and empirical literature on the positions for and against rent control. Essays in favor of rent control are collected in J. Gilderbloom, Rent Control: A Sourcebook (1981). Essays opposed are collected in Rent Control: Myths and Realities (W. Block & E. Olsen, eds. 1981). Both books have extensive bibliographies. For an overview of the issue, see U.S. President's Commission on Housing, Report of the President's Commission on Housing 91 *et seq.* (1982). The history of rent control is chronicled in M. Lett, Rent Control ch. 1 (1976).

2. *Condominium Conversions.* In some markets, landlords facing rent and quality controls do have an alternative to abandonment or repair: converting their buildings to condominiums and selling the individual units outright. (The condominium concept is considered in detail at pages 1044 to 1073 below.) Thanks in large part to the tax, finance and investment advantages of fee ownership, condominium unit buyers in the aggregate are willing to pay far more for a building than the landlord could possibly obtain from an investor planning to hold the property for rental purposes. Thus it is no surprise that many landlords in the District of Columbia opted for condominium conversion after rent control was introduced there. See Meyer, "The Condo Craze," Washington Post, Jan. 20, 1974, Potomac at 13.

Many of those who lobbied for rent controls have also lobbied for limits on condominium conversions. The legislative response has taken a variety of forms. The most common legislative action is a moratorium on conversion for a month, a year or even longer, purportedly to allow the municipality to study the issue. Longer range programs have required the condominium converter to give three years' removal notice to tenants and to aid displaced tenants in finding new housing; to give tenants a right of first refusal to purchase their apartments; or to obtain purchase commitments from a specified number of tenants. Other jurisdictions have limited the total number of conversions that may occur in any year or prohibited any conversions at all if the rental vacancy rate falls below a specified figure. See generally, Comment, The Regulation of Rental Apartment Conversions, 8 Fordham Urb.L.J. 507 (1979–1980).

For a comprehensive overview of condominium conversions, and conversion regulation, see, U.S. Dep't of Housing & Urban Development, The Conversion of Rental Housing to Condominiums and Cooperatives (1980).

3. *Housing Discrimination.* Price and quality are only two of the points at which government regulation has curbed landlord prerogatives. The Civil Rights movement of the 1960's produced legislation and decisions substantially curtailing the landlord's freedom to discriminate in choice of tenants. Title VIII of the 1968 Civil Rights Act, 42 U.S.C.A. §§ 3601 *et seq.,* outlawed discrimination in the sale or rental of residential real estate on the grounds of race, color, religion, or national origin. The Act was amended in 1974 to prohibit sex-based discrimination. Further, the Supreme Court's 1968 decision in Jones v. Alfred H. Mayer Co., 392 U.S. 409, 413, 88 S.Ct. 2186, 2188, 20 L.Ed.2d 1189 (1968), interpreted the moribund Civil Rights Act of 1866 to bar "*all* racial discrimination, private as well as public, in the sale or rental of property . . .." Although the two acts overlap, they also differ in important respects. The 1866 Act prohibits only racial discrimination and, unlike the 1968 Act, allows no exceptions such as Title VIII's exemption for owner-occupied housing. 42 U.S.C.A. § 3603 (1976).

A substantial majority of states have enacted fair housing statutes and the number continues to grow. Virtually all of these states prohibit discrimination on the basis of race, color, religion, sex or national origin. Several have also specifically proscribed discrimination on other bases, such as that the tenant has minor children, is over or under a certain age or has a physical handicap. See generally, R. Schoshinski, American Law of Landlord and Tenant §§ 11:9–11:12 (1980). Which opinion in *Hudson View Properties* do you think best applied New York's prohibitions against discrimination on the basis of marital status?

4. Have anti-discrimination rules, when taken together with price and quality controls and the retaliatory eviction defense, effectively converted private residential landlords into public utilities? What protections and incentives do public utilities enjoy that private landlords do not? What difference is there between highly regulated ownership by private landlords and unregulated ownership by gov-

ernment landlords? See generally, Berger, The New Residential Tenancy Law—Are Landlords Public Utilities? 60 Neb.L.Rev. 707 (1981).

4. ALTERNATIVES TO REGULATION

CONGRESSIONAL BUDGET OFFICE, FEDERAL HOUSING POLICY: CURRENT PROGRAMS AND RECURRING ISSUES

23–37 (1978).

HOUSING ASSISTANCE PROGRAMS

The Department of Housing and Urban Development (HUD) administers several programs designed to reduce the housing costs of lower-income persons and to provide them with physically standard housing. The principal federal housing assistance programs are: (1) low-rent public housing, (2) Section 8 new construction/substantial rehabilitation, (3) Section 8 existing housing, (4) Section 235 homeownership assistance, (5) Section 236 rental assistance and (6) rent supplements. For thirty years following its authorization in 1937, the public housing program served as the federal government's primary housing assistance mechanism. The Section 235, Section 236, and rent supplement programs were authorized during the late 1960s and were the most heavily utilized programs for several years thereafter. In 1973, activity under all of these programs was halted under a national moratorium imposed by the Nixon Administration. Housing assistance activity resumed with the passage of the 1974 Housing and Community Development Act, which authorized the Section 8 programs. Since then, Section 8, public housing, and a revised Section 235 program have been the most heavily used housing assistance devices. During fiscal year 1978, federal outlays for assisted housing are expected to total about $4 billion. Table 11 describes the status of the assistance programs as of 1977.

TABLE 10. PRIMARY AND SECONDARY OBJECTIVES OF CURRENT FEDERAL HOUSING PROGRAMS AND HOUSING-RELATED ACTIVITIES [a]

Federal Housing Programs and Activities	Providing Adequate and Affordable Housing	Increasing or Stabilizing Residential Construction Activity	Expanding Access to Mortgage Credit	Encouraging Homeownership	Ensuring Equal Housing Opportunity	Providing Housing for Special Users	Encouraging Community Development and Neighborhood Preservation and Revitalization
Housing Assistance Programs							
Low-rent public housing	XX	XX			X	X	X
Section 8 new construction/substantial rehabilitation	XX	XX			X	X	X
Section 8 existing housing	XX				XX		X
Section 235 homeownership assistance	XX	XX	XX	XX	X		
Section 236 rental assistance and rent supplements	XX	XX				X	
Section 202 elderly/handicapped housing	XX	XX	X			XX	
Community Development Programs							
Community development block grants	X						XX
Urban development action grants							XX
Section 312 rehabilitation loans	XX	X	X				XX
Urban homesteading	X			XX			XX
Mortgage Credit Activities							
FmHA direct loans	XX	XX	XX	XX			
VA direct loans		X	XX	XX			
FHA insured loans		X	XX	XX			
VA insured loans		X	XX	XX			
FNMA, GNMA, FHLB and FHLMC secondary mortgage market activities		XX	XX	XX			
Tax Expenditures							
Deduction of mortgage interest and property tax payments		X		XX			
Deferrals and exclusions of capital gains on sales of homes		X		XX			
Favorable depreciation for rental housing	X	XX					
Favorable treatment of construction-period development costs	X	XX					
Preferential treatment of real estate tax shelter	X	XX					
Tax benefits for financial institutions	X	XX	X				
Housing and Credit-Market Regulations							
Prohibitions against discrimination in sale/rental of housing and mortgage lending			XX		XX		
Regulation of financial institutions and mortgage credit markets		XX	XX	XX			

Note: XX = Primary Objectives

X = Secondary Objectives

[a] The classification scheme presented here is based on similar typologies developed by several housing analysts. It is meant to depict the key relationships between programs and policy objectives; it is not intended to be exhaustive of possible program effects.

TABLE 11. APPROXIMATE NUMBER OF ASSISTED HOUSING UNITS OCCUPIED AND IN PROCESS, BY PROGRAM, 1977 [a]

Number of Housing Units	All Programs	Public Housing	Section 8 New Construction/ Substantial Rehabilitation	Section 8 Existing Housing	Section 235 Original Program [b]	Section 235 Revised Program [c]	Section 236 and Rent Supplements
Currently Occupied	2,448,300	1,147,700	30,000	327,800	287,300	7,500	648,000
In Processing Pipeline							
Available for occupancy but not occupied	188,400	29,400	12,900	146,100	—	—	—
Under construction	188,400	62,700	117,800	—	—	6,300	1,600
With initial commitments; construction not yet begun, subsidy contracts not yet executed	357,200	85,100	205,000	57,800	—	9,300	—
Without initial commitments	425,900	66,400	177,600	152,500	—	29,400	—
Subtotal	1,159,900	243,600	513,300	356,400	—	45,000	1,600
Total	3,608,200	1,391,300	543,300	684,200	287,300	52,500	649,600

SOURCE: HUD Budget Office.

[a] Data for Section 8 and the revised Section 235 program are as of December 31, 1977. Data for public housing, the original Section 235 program, Section 236, and Rent Supplements are as of September 30, 1977.

[b] Suspended in 1973.

[c] Initiated in 1975.

Although all assisted housing programs serve limited-income persons, each program assists a somewhat different group of families and individuals. Section 8, public housing, and rent supplements serve the poorest households, those with an average annual income between $3,500 and $4,500; Section 236 serves somewhat higher-income persons; the Section 235 program serves the highest-income persons among those receiving housing assistance (See Table 12).

Low-Rent Public Housing

The low-rent public housing program funds the construction or the purchase and rehabilitation costs (including financing expenses), and a portion of the operating expenses, of rental projects that are owned and managed by state or local government agencies and made available to lower-income tenants at reduced charges. Public housing is generally limited to low- and moderate-income families and to elderly, handicapped, or displaced individuals. Tenant rental and utility charges are limited to a total of not more than 25 percent of adjusted family income. As of the end of fiscal year 1977, nearly 1.2 million public housing units were available for occupancy, with more than 40 percent designated for elderly or handicapped persons.

In addition to being designed as a mechanism for providing lower-income persons with physically standard low-cost housing, public housing is also viewed as a means of increasing housing production. Nevertheless, during the last 20 years, public housing construction and rehabilitation starts have averaged only about 36,000 units annually and that figure has exceeded 50,000 only four times during that period. Further, there is no way of determining the extent to which public housing construction may be merely substituting for private development. By building units specifically designed for the elderly or handicapped or for large families, public housing may, however, serve special housing needs inadequately met by the private market.

TABLE 12. SELECTED CHARACTERISTICS OF RECIPIENT HOUSEHOLDS IN CURRENT MAJOR HOUSING ASSISTANCE PROGRAMS, 1977 [a]

Household Characteristics	Section 8 New Const'n/ Substantial Rehab.	Section 8 Existing Housing	Public Housing	Section 235 Original Program	Section 235 Revised Program	Section 236	Rent Supplements
Average Family Income [b]	$4,376	$3,506	$3,691	$8,085	$11,532	$6,285	$3,544
Annual Family Income (as a percent of all households)							
Below $3,000	27.7	37.3	35.4	NA	NA	NA	NA
$3,000 to $4,999	39.0	38.6	32.6	NA	NA	NA	NA
$5,000 to $6,999	21.6	16.0	15.4	NA	NA	NA	NA
$7,000 to $9,999	10.0	7.1	9.6	NA	NA	NA	NA
Above $10,000	1.7	1.0	6.9	NA	NA	NA	NA
Percent of All Households with Some Welfare Income	16.2	26.7	42.6	NA	NA	NA	NA
Percent with Minority Head	27.7	29.8	62.9	NA	23.0	NA	NA
Percent with Elderly Head	42.9	33.4	35.8	NA	2.1	26.0	31.0
Percent with Handicapped Member	2.0	2.3	1.2	NA	NA	NA	NA
Household Size (as percent of all households)							
Single person	43.1	36.0	33.3	NA	NA	NA	NA
2–4 persons	50.9	53.3	45.2	NA	NA	NA	NA
5–6 persons	5.4	8.4	14.6	NA	NA	NA	NA
7 or more persons	0.6	2.3	6.9	NA	NA	NA	NA

SOURCE: HUD Office of the Budget.
[a] Data for Section 8 are as of June 1977; data for public housing, the original Section 235 program, Section 236, and rent supplements are as of September 1977; data for the revised Section 235 program are as of December 1977.
[b] Figure reported is the mean family income for the original Section 235 program, Section 236, and rent supplements. Median family income is reported for Section 8, public housing, and the revised Section 235 program.

During the years of large-scale urban redevelopment, in the 1950s and 1960s, public housing was viewed as a tool for dealing with displaced households and encouraging the creation of heterogeneous neighborhoods in redeveloped areas. The program has been used more recently as a means of expanding the housing opportunities of lower-income families and minorities in areas previously closed to them. The overall record of the public housing program in promoting either redevelopment or residential integration has, however, not been good; in fact, some critics have argued that public housing has actually contributed to segregation and urban decay by accelerating the flight of whites and higher-income families from racially mixed and declining areas.

Section 8 New Construction/Substantial Rehabilitation

The Section 8 new construction/substantial rehabilitation programs provide assistance on behalf of lower-income households occupying newly built or significantly rehabilitated units that meet certain criteria as to cost, physical adequacy, and location. Under these programs, public agencies or private sponsors develop housing projects in which a portion of the units are made available to low- and moderate-income renters at reduced costs. The difference between the HUD-established allowable rent for each unit and the household contribution—limited to 15–25 percent of family income—is made up by regular payments from HUD to the project owner/manager. Assistance contracts between HUD and project sponsors cover five-year periods and are renewable at the owner's discretion for 20 to 40 years, depending on the type of sponsor and the kind of financing used. Income limits for Section 8 assistance recipients are set at approximately 80 percent of the area median. Only about 30,000 new construction/substantial rehabilitation units were occupied as of December 1977, but more than 500,000 units were in the processing pipeline.

The brief time these programs have been underway precludes firm conclusions concerning their effects. Although they are intended to encourage the production of additional housing by guaranteeing an income stream to potential developers, interest among private developers has not been strong during the initial implementation period. Further, concerns have been raised that the interest the developers have shown may merely reflect a desire to have a federal guarantee of rental income for units that will be made available to lower-income persons only if unassisted tenants cannot be found.

The effect of the Section 8 new construction and substantial rehabilitation programs on racial and economic integration will depend largely on the location of Section 8 projects and the ability of project managers to maintain a demographic mix among tenants. Anecdotal evidence suggests that the new construction program may be somewhat more successful in locating projects in desirable neighborhoods than earlier subsidy programs have been. The designation of nearly all Section 8 new construction/substantial rehabilitation projects as 100-percent subsidized suggests, however, that the program may be less successful in maintaining economically mixed projects than had been expected. The substantial rehabilitation program may be especially useful in promoting neighborhood revitalization; it may also encourage economic integration if the projects enable lower-income persons to remain in previously depressed areas undergoing housing cost increases.

Section 8 Existing Housing

The existing housing component of the Section 8 program provides assistance on behalf of lower-income households occupying physically adequate, moderate-cost rental housing of their own choosing in the private market. Public housing agencies under contract to HUD subsidize the housing costs of lower-income families by paying their landlords the difference between the tenants' rental fee and the tenants' contribution of 15 to 25 percent of their monthly income. All housing units must meet standards of physical adequacy, must be located within the jurisdiction served by the local agency, and must rent for an amount equal to or less than a HUD-established maximum. Beyond these restrictions, assisted households are free to select the location and type of housing, so long as the landlord is willing to enter into a lease with the tenant and a participation agreement with the administering agency. The reliance on the initiative of the household and the latter's freedom to choose from among existing rental units in the private market distinguish this program from all other federal housing assistance efforts. After some initial delays, implementation of this program has been quite smooth and much more rapid than has been the case with the new construction and substantial rehabilitation programs. As of December 1977, more than 300,000 households were receiving assistance under the Section 8 existing housing program.

The most obvious effect of the Section 8 existing housing program has been on recipients' housing costs. Of households receiving assistance in October 1976, the average share of their income going towards housing before joining the program was in excess of 40 percent; after enrollment, that figure dropped to between 20 and 25 percent. The effect of the program on recipients' housing conditions has been less striking. About half of all households receiving assistance remained in their original units, only a minority of which had to be upgraded in order to enter the program. But studies of similar programs indicate that, in the absence of a requirement that households live in physically adequate units, many families living in standard housing would either move to substandard housing or allow their units to deteriorate.

There is no evidence that the demand generated by an existing housing program is sufficient to induce the construction of new units. On the other hand, this type of program does not appear to inflate housing costs—a commonly expressed fear—even when assisted households constitute a substantially greater proportion of a local market than is now the case with Section 8 households.

One of the arguments in support of this kind of program is that it can both promote racial and economic deconcentration and revitalize neighborhoods. Available evidence indicates that although it does not induce mobility, when minority-headed households receiving this type of assistance do move, they are indeed more likely to relocate in areas of lower concentrations of minority households. Its effects on neighborhood revitalization, on the other hand, appear to be minimal.

Section 235 Homeownership Assistance

The Section 235 program provides mortgage assistance to lower-income households purchasing new or substantially-rehabilitated homes. Families with an income of up to 95 percent of the area median may buy modest homes at a reduced rate of interest on the mortgage, with HUD making up the difference between the family's payment and the amount due the mortgagee.

The Section 235 program was first authorized in 1968 and was suspended in 1973 as part of the national moratorium on housing assistance programs. Because program rules permitted minimal down-payments and effective interest rates as low as 1 percent many families unable to handle the financial burden became homeowners under this program. In addition, many only marginally adequate or completely inadequate units were certified as eligible for the program. As a result, more than 15 percent of all the homes purchased under the original Section 235 program have already been acquired by HUD, often in barely salvageable condition. Section 235 was reinstated in 1975, with the minimum effective rate of interest to the buyer raised to 4 percent and the minimum downpayment set at 3 to 5 percent of the purchase price. The tighter restrictions, designed to reduce the problem of defaults, have limited program activity: in the two years since the reinstatement of the program, subsidy commitments were made for only about 23,000 homes.

The principal effects of the Section 235 program have been on the level of residential construction and the incidence of homeownership among lower-income households. During the years in which the original Section 235 program was active, units built under the program represented as much as 6 percent of the annual number of single-family housing starts.

Section 236 Rental Assistance and Rent Supplements

The Section 236 program, authorized in 1968, provides mortgage interest subsidies to developers of rental projects in which a portion of the housing units are made available to lower-income persons at reduced rates. The interest subsidy alone is sufficient to reduce tenant rental payments to an average of about 30 percent of family income. Additional subsidies are provided on behalf of the occupants of some of the units through rent supplement payments, Section 8 assistance, or "deep subsidy" payments specifically authorized for use in conjunction with Section 236. This piggybacking of those subsidies, which are paid to the project owner, permits tenants' rents for some units to be reduced to 25 percent of their income without jeopardizing the financial viability of the projects. Despite these multiple subsidies, Section 236 has been plagued by the defaults that characterized the original Section 235 program. More than 14 percent of the approximately 4,000 Section 236 mortgages written through 1976 had been assigned to HUD by the mortgagee or foreclosed by the end of that year. A small number of new subsidy commitments are still being made under the program, utilizing spending authority released by the Congress before the 1973 housing moratorium.

The rent supplement program was authorized in 1965 to provide payments to the owners of private rental housing on behalf of lower-income tenants, but it has been used primarily to reduce rental charges in Section 236 and other mortgage subsidy projects. As of the end of fiscal year 1977, there were active rent supplement commitments for approximately 180,000 units.

Section 202 Housing for the Elderly and Handicapped

The Section 202 program provides direct federal loans to nonprofit organizations developing rental housing for the elderly and the handicapped. Under the original Section 202 program authorized in 1959, loans were written at a 3 percent rate of interest and the program primarily benefited persons with incomes too high to qualify for public housing. The program in that form was suspended in 1970, but it was reinstituted in 1974 with the interest charge raised to slightly above the yield on all outstanding Treasury obligations—an interest rate more nearly approximating that of conventional financing. Projects developed under the revised Section 202 program also carry a Section 8 subsidy, which enables the rents of lower-income families and individuals to be reduced to a maximum of 25 percent of their income. To date, the Section 202 program has been used primarily to build housing for the elderly. In recent years, an interest in developing a portion of all Section 202 projects for the exclusive use of the handicapped has been expressed. Through the end of fiscal year 1977, subsidy commitments under the revised Section 202/8 program had been made for about 55,000 units.

HOUSING–RELATED COMMUNITY DEVELOPMENT PROGRAMS

Several community development programs provide housing benefits to a wider range of income groups than are eligible for housing assistance programs. The principal housing-related community development programs are: (1) community development block grants, (2) urban development action grants, (3) Section 312 rehabilitation loans, and (4) urban homesteading.

The Community Development Block Grants (CDBG)

The CDBG program, authorized in 1974, provides grants to state and local governments to fund projects designed to promote viable urban communities. Most CDBG funds are allocated by means of needs-based formulae among cities within metropolitan areas with populations of 50,000 or more and urban counties with populations of 200,000 or more. Beginning in fiscal year 1978, two formulae are used to distribute these entitlement grants. Both consider the number of persons in the jurisdiction with incomes below the poverty line. One of the formulae also takes into account total population and the number of overcrowded housing units within the jurisdiction; the other formula considers lag in population growth relative to the national rate and the number of pre-1940 housing units. Communities that receive entitlement grants must also submit housing assistance plans that estimate the extent and nature of housing needs among low- and moderate-income persons residing or expected to reside in the jurisdiction and indicate how federal housing assistance will be used to address those needs. Communities that fail to provide lower-income housing assistance may forfeit their eligibility for the community development funds.

During fiscal year 1978, $3.6 billion are available for community development block grants; that sum is expected to fund approximately 3,200 grants, including as many as 637 grants to entitlement jurisdictions. About 26 percent of the funds to be expended in grants to entitlements cities during fiscal year 1977 are expected to be used for projects involving housing rehabilitation, building code enforcement, or relocation assistance for displaced persons.

Urban Development Action Grants (UDAG)

The UDAG program was authorized in 1977 as an adjunct to block grants, and the program is being implemented for the first time in fiscal year 1978. UDAG funds are available only to distressed cities and they are to be used to support projects involving private investment as well as public funds. Current criteria for determining urban distress include: the proportion of the housing stock constructed before 1940, net increase in per capita income from 1969 to 1974, population growth between 1960 and 1975 relative to the national rate, the level of unemployment, the rate of growth in employment, the percent of the population below the poverty level, and unique local factors. More than 300 localities are eligible for UDAG funding under those criteria—a number that has been criticized by some as being too high and by others as too low.

During fiscal year 1978, $400 million are available for urban development action grants. Through April 1978, 50 projects, involving $150 million in federal funding, had been approved. The majority of the UDAG funds approved thus far are earmarked for commercial redevelopment. Subsequent grants are expected to focus somewhat more heavily on neighborhood-based projects.

Section 312 Rehabilitation Loans

The Section 312 loan program, authorized in 1964, provides direct financing for the rehabilitation of privately owned residential and commercial buildings in designated urban renewal, neighborhood-development, and code-enforcement areas. Loans bear a 3-percent interest rate, with a maximum repayment period of 20 years. Most of the approximately 58,000 Section 312 loans made through the end of fiscal year 1977 financed the rehabilitation of owner-occupied housing. The Section 312 program provides benefits to people with higher incomes than those who receive direct federal housing assistance. Less than 4 percent of the Section 312 funds lent to owner-occupants during 1977 went to families with an annual income below $4,000; nearly one-third of the funds went to families with an income of more than $15,000.

Despite low levels of activity in the past, there has been considerable interest recently in expanding this program. For fiscal year 1978,

$80 million is expected to finance 6,800 loans. The Administration's urban policy proposals, announced in March 1978, include a significant increase in funding for the Section 312 program.

Urban Homesteading

A small-scale urban homesteading demonstration program, under which federally held single-family properties are deeded to localities and sold by them at nominal cost to persons willing to rehabilitate and occupy them, has been operating since 1976. This program is intended to encourage residential reinvestment in distressed areas and to stimulate economic integration and neighborhood revitalization. In fiscal year 1978, 2,500 homes are to be conveyed to local governments for disposition under the program, at a cost to the Federal Housing Administration fund of $15 million. The HUD budget submission for fiscal year 1979 includes a proposal to make urban homesteading an ongoing program.

FRIEDEN, HOUSING ALLOWANCES: AN EXPERIMENT THAT WORKED

59 The Public Interest 15–22; 25–27; 32; 35
(Spring 1980).

One of the biggest social experiments ever undertaken, the Department of Housing and Urban Development's experimental housing allowance program began with great fanfare in 1973 and is ending quietly in 1979–1980. It has involved more than 25,000 families in 12 metropolitan areas, at a cost that is expected to add up to $160 million. As is true of most ambitious programs, it owes its origin to the convergence of several different lines of thought on how government should cope with a problem. The problem in this case was how to improve housing conditions for low-income people. Two key ideas prompted the experiment. One was that the best way to help families who needed better housing was to give them money that they could use on their own, instead of building subsidized housing for them. The other was that the best way to learn how a new approach would work in practice was to conduct a large-scale social experiment, following a systematic design and using control groups to check the validity of the results.

Six years later, the data coming off the computers do not provide clear-cut answers to all the questions that were investigated, since the realities of human behavior turned out to be more complicated than the designers of the experiment had assumed. But the experiment produced unexpected results that challenge the traditional conception of low-income housing problems and reveal a sharp conflict between the priorities of federal officials and those of poor families.

Troubled subsidy programs

The underlying cause of the housing allowance experiment was widespread disillusionment with the conventional approach to subsidizing housing for the poor. Ever since the mid-1930's, housing reformers and their political allies had favored a construction strategy. This meant using federal subsidies to build new housing which was then made available to poor people at below-market rents. A series of housing acts from 1937 through the mid-1960's had established first low-rent public housing and then several variations of it, all following essentially the same approach. Yet the flooding tide of housing legislation produced only a trickle of housing. The main problem with this strategy (as has also been said of Christianity) was not that it had been tried and found wanting, but that it had never been tried—at least not on a scale large enough to put it to a real test. Then, in the special political climate of the late 1960's Congress enacted the landmark Housing Act of 1968, interpreted by many as a memorial to Martin Luther King. This act set up two important construction programs backed by the usual federal subsidies. One (known as Section 236) offered rental housing, and the other (Section 235) offered home-ownership opportunities for low- and moderate-income families. Both were designed to attract developers and investors in the hope that private sector involvement would generate a high volume of construction commensurate with the country's needs. The 1968 act, in fact, set a target of 2.6 million subsidized housing units to be built within 10 years.

Beginning in 1969, HUD Secretary George Romney gave top priority to putting the new programs into operation and meeting the ambitious targets of the 1968 act. Between 1969 and 1972, the federal government sponsored more subsidized construction than in the preceding 35 years combined. Yet as the HUD programs, together with their rural counterparts in the Farmers Home Administration, grew to a volume of 400,000 starts per year, both their financial and political costs became troublesome. The new housing required annual federal contributions to help the residents pay the rent or the cost of home ownership. By the early 1970's, yearly outlays began to approach 2 billion dollars. Although this figure was no more than one-fifth of the total cost of federal tax benefits given to middle-income homeowners, it was a natural target for a conservative administration looking for places to cut the federal budget. In addition, poor administration of these programs led to widespread corruption within the Federal Housing Administration that escaped full notoriety only because Watergate created a bigger scandal. President Nixon's annual report on national housing goals for 1972 complained about the rapid growth of future housing subsidy commitments, then estimated at some $12 billion merely to cover housing already approved. These programs were expensive, and getting more so. Worse still, the

President's report also noted that the programs were failing to reach the lowest-income families.

Housing experts sponsored by the House of Representatives Subcommittee on Housing were also finding serious faults with these large-scale programs. A group of researchers at M.I.T. estimated that from one-fifth to one-half the total federal subsidy was not reaching the residents of the new housing, but went for federal and local administrative expenses and for tax benefits to investors. The same study found that subsidy arrangements were regressive, with greater assistance going to families at the upper end of the eligibility range than to low-income families at the bottom. The programs were serving mainly families above the poverty level in lower-middle-income brackets. Further, the families themselves had little freedom of choice in deciding where to live. To get federal housing assistance, they had to move to a designated development whose sponsor had been selected by the local FHA field office. As a result, the allocation of subsidized housing to communities across the country did not correspond as much to the needs of low-income residents as it did to the energy, activity, and political muscle of local sponsors.

An underlying reason for these problems was that the programs were designed to achieve two different purposes that were partially in conflict with each other. One purpose was to encourage new construction; the second to give financial help to families who could not afford good housing on their own. The construction objective overrode the housing assistance purpose at many critical points. The high cost and the generous payments to middlemen were part of the construction strategy. So, too, was the reliance on local sponsors to make key decisions about where to locate projects and whom to admit. Ceilings on the subsidy per family made it hard to bring the cost down low enough for the very poor, and therefore tipped the balance of effort toward families who were better off.

The logic of this critique of production subsidies led toward the conclusion that direct cash payments to low-income families might well be a more effective form of housing assistance. Direct payments to the poor would bypass the project sponsors and other middlemen who were draining off so large a share of the federal housing dollar. Families with cash in hand would be able to make their own decisions about where to live, instead of being limited to designated projects or locations. Rather than having to use their money for costly new housing, they could shop around to find less expensive existing homes. Eligible families would not have to be excluded because they happened to live in communities where developers were not making use of federal housing programs. In addition, direct cash payments could be scaled according to a family's income, rather than following the complicated and regressive formulas that resulted from an attempt to stimulate new construction.

Other analyses presented to the House Subcommittee on Housing pointed in the same general direction. The New York City Rand Institute had made some startling discoveries in its detailed analyses of the New York City housing market during the 1960's. From year to year, a large volume of sound housing was deteriorating in quality and more than 30,000 units per year were being taken off the market through demolition, conversion to non-residential use, or outright abandonment. Between 1965 and 1968, housing losses were greater than new construction by a substantial margin. The main reason for this rising volume of deterioration and abandonment was that a large number of the city's low-income families were unable to pay enough rent to cover the rising costs of operating and maintaining rental property. Landlords who were unable to earn a competitive return were cutting back on maintenance, and, in time, walking away from their buildings.

Ira S. Lowry of the Rand Institute staff concluded from the Rand studies that the most effective way to meet the housing needs of low-income families in New York City was to raise the level of maintenance in existing buildings while they were still in good condition. He estimated that a rent increase of from $400 to $700 per year was needed to support moderate renovation and good maintenance in typical older apartments. Even these small increases, however, were beyond the means of low-income families. Lowry accordingly proposed a housing allowance plan that would make available rent certificates at an average cost of little more than $600 per family.

Proposals for a housing allowance program were timely not only because of disappointments with the prevailing approach to low-income housing, but also because the housing allowance idea had already caught the attention of top policy makers. President Johnson's Committee on Urban Housing (the Kaiser Committee) in its 1968 report had argued the case for housing allowances. The Committee was concerned, however, that a massive housing allowance system could lead to inflation in the general cost of housing and also doubted whether housing allowances would work effectively without parallel measures to counter racial discrimination and provide effective consumer education. It proposed an experimental program to find out. One reason for caution was that the public welfare program, which provided families with cash income intended to cover housing costs as well as other expenses, had many of the characteristics of a housing allowance program. Yet a national survey showed that welfare families had severely inadequate housing, a majority of them living in either substandard or overcrowded conditions. The low level of welfare support did not fully explain this situation. Other families in the same income brackets lived in better housing than those on welfare. It was possible, therefore, that money given to poor families through transfer payments might not open up the same access to housing markets that most people already enjoyed.

Limited trials of the housing allowance idea began in 1970 under the auspices of federally funded Model Cities programs in Kansas City, Missouri and Wilmington, Delaware. The Department of Housing and Urban Development began preliminary studies and designs for a systematic national experiment in 1970 and 1971, and then organized its Experimental Housing Allowance Program.

In January 1973, the Nixon Administration suspended almost all existing federal housing subsidies for the poor and announced its intention to search for more effective programs. The housing allowance experiment, then getting under way in 12 selected cities, took on special importance as part of that search. Meanwhile, Congress enacted a new subsidy program, known as Section 8, to replace those that had been suspended. The new program was a hybrid, based on a flexible financing arrangement that could be used either to promote new construction or, in the manner of a housing allowance, to help people pay for existing houses that met program standards.

Debating housing strategies

While the housing allowance experiments were enrolling families and collecting data, but long before any results were available, policy analysts were carrying on a lively debate over the merits of housing allowances. One school of thought held that housing markets were so restricted and defective that making more money available would still not enable poor people to find decent housing. Others believed that housing markets would respond to a moderate boost in rent levels by increasing the supply of decent, well-maintained housing.

Among the skeptics was Chester Hartman, a long-time critic of federal housing programs, who contended in an article with Dennis Keating that "the shortcomings of the past programs inhere in the nature of the housing market itself." The key assumptions were that little housing is available for the poor, markets are non-competitive, and landlords are dominant. In Hartman's view, the housing allowance approach "pays insufficient attention to the vast shortage of decent, moderate-rent housing in most urban and suburban areas, particularly for groups the market now serves poorly, such as large families." Because of this shortage, he contended, "few doubt that the introduction of housing allowances into a static supply of housing will lead to rent inflation (on a short-term basis at least), not only for recipients, but also for other low- and moderate-income households competing for the same units."

In contrast to this view of a captive market, a series of empirical studies in the 1960's found that landlords were in a precarious position themselves, caught between increasing operating costs and limited rental income. George Sternlieb's study of Newark (*The Tenement Landlord*) and Michael Stegman's study of Baltimore (*Housing Investment in the Inner City*) went a long way toward revising the stereotyped image of the powerful slum landlord who reaped great profits by milking his properties and plundering his tenants. As Stegman described the situation, "Many inner-city landlords are today as victimized as are those to whom they provide inadequate shelter."

Although a casual look at inner-city rent levels might indeed suggest that landlords were succeeding in charging exorbitant and discriminatory rents while giving little service, Stegman found the reality to be different. Inner-city landlords were incurring high operating costs as a result of such factors as non-payment of rent, high vacancy rates, and vandalism to their property. These costs were much higher than in middle-income areas and helped to explain why prevailing rent levels were neither profitable to most landlords nor adequate to provide good maintenance:

> Over 10 percent of cash inflow—an amount equal to about 80 percent of net income—is dissipated on expenditures that do not contribute directly to maintaining or improving resultant flows of housing services. This is why apparently high rents with respect to housing quality can result in little or no profit to the investor. In part, this also explains why housing quality in the inner-city is inferior to that obtainable elsewhere in the city at comparable or only slightly higher rents.

The shortfall between rent collections and maintenance demands suggested that lack of rent money was one of the most important reasons why inner-city housing markets were failing to meet the needs of the poor. Stegman's careful analysis of Baltimore led to conclusions remarkably similar to those of the New York City Rand Institute. Although Stegman himself did not endorse a housing allowance strategy, his findings gave strong support to the view that inner-city housing markets were not locked under the control of powerful slumlords and that public-policy initiatives could indeed create more effective incentives for responsible property management.

In designing the rent allowance experiment, the Department of Housing and Urban Development was concerned with specific questions about how poor families would make use of their housing allowances, how local housing markets would respond to the increased demand generated by direct cash payments, and how different administrative arrangements would influence the results. Accordingly, the program was divided into three parts—a demand experiment, a supply experiment, and an administrative-agency experiment.

In the demand experiment (conducted in Pittsburgh and Phoenix), the research focused on the extent to which eligible families took part in the experiment, changes in housing expenditures for participating families, the choices people made with respect to the quality and location of their housing, and their satisfaction with these choices.

The supply experiment (in Green Bay, Wisconsin and South Bend, Indiana) was designed to test how a large-scale infusion of housing allowance dollars in a single housing market would affect the cost and quality of housing, the behavior of landlords and realtors, and patterns of residential mobility. The supply experiment offered open enrollment to homeowners as well as renters whose incomes were within the established ceilings, and set no limit on the number of families that would be permitted to enroll. (Other parts of the experiment were open to renters only, and the number of participants was limited in advance.)

The administrative-agency experiment selected eight different agencies to carry out housing allowance programs—local housing authorities in Salem, Oregon and Tulsa, Oklahoma; metropolitan government agencies in Jacksonville, Florida and San Bernardino County, California; state community-development agencies in Peoria, Illinois and Springfield, Massachusetts; and the state welfare departments in Durham, North Carolina and Bismarck, North Dakota. In these communities, research focused on the administrative performance of such functions as screening and enrolling applicants, certifying eligibility, providing counseling, and making household inspections.

In all areas, however, the basic requirements were the same. The program was open to families of two or more people and to single individuals who were elderly or handicapped. To receive a housing allowance, a family had to have an income below a ceiling that took into account the local cost of adequate housing and the size of the household. For a family of four, the upper income limit was generally below $7,000. Allowance payments in most cases were set to equal the difference between the estimated cost of adequate housing and one-fourth of the family's income; payments averaged $75 per month. Families in the program were free to spend more or less than the estimated amount for rent, but they had to live in or move to housing that met minimum quality standards set for each part of the experiment. The last requirement was relaxed only for two experimental groups in Pittsburgh and Phoenix that could receive the allowance without meeting any standards of housing quality. Despite the different purposes of the three parts of the experiment, it is possible to consider the twelve demonstration areas as a source of general information on policy issues that cut across the individual experiments. . . .

Did the program improve housing quality?

A central purpose of the experiment was to find out whether housing allowances would bring about improvement in the quality of the housing supply. Although a high proportion of participating families lived in housing that met the program's quality standards from the beginning, a majority did not and either had to make repairs or had to move in order to qualify. In the eight cities of the administrative experiment, an average of 57 percent of recipients either moved or upgraded their prior housing; in Pittsburgh and Phoenix, 61 percent either moved or upgraded, and in Green Bay and South Bend, 48 percent either moved or upgraded.

The housing standards that families had to meet varied somewhat in different parts of the experiment, but they were generally in line with local housing codes, model codes recommended by building code administrators, and standards developed by public health organizations.

In order to meet these standards, most families in the program did improve the quality of their housing, either by moving or by repairing their current residences. The substantial minority who upgraded without moving did so mainly by making minor repairs at low costs. Typical repairs involved fixing windows or installing handrails on stairs; some work was also done on structural components, plumbing, and heating systems. In Green Bay and South Bend, landlords and tenants split the work about evenly, using professional contractors for only about 10 percent of repairs. Three out of four below-standard dwellings that were brought up to an acceptable level involved cash costs of less than $25 in Green Bay and less than $30 in South Bend.

In Pittsburgh and Phoenix, tenants and landlords also divided the work of bringing failed units up to standard. Residents typically painted and papered the inside, while landlords did the bulk of the work on plumbing and heating equipment and general repairs. The mean cash cost of the improvement was $92. A control group of families in these cities who did not get housing allowances reported almost the same outlays for repairs, however, and about four-fifths of those in both the experimental and control groups reported that their landlords also made improvements. The main difference was in the kinds of repairs. Families getting housing allowances were more likely to have their houses brought up to "standard" condition as required by the program.

Very few families managed to use their housing allowance payments to switch from rental housing to home ownership. In Green Bay and South Bend, about 300 families who enrolled as renters bought homes while they were in the program; these were less than 3 percent of the renters enrolled. Yet in these cities almost half of the participants in the experiment were already homeowners. Many of these had undoubtedly bought their homes at times in the past when their incomes were higher. But however feasible ownership may be for low-income families, it is clear that housing allowance payments did not raise incomes or assets enough to enable families to improve their housing by becoming homeowners.

A survey of how participating families in Pittsburgh and Phoenix felt about their housing shows that they valued the quality improvements resulting from the program, but it also reveals a deep-seated reluctance to move in order to get quality improvements. Of the families who failed to meet housing standards at the beginning, the most satisfied of all were those who later met them by improving the places where they already lived: 70 percent of these families were "very satisfied" with their housing. But the second most satisfied group were the families who stayed where they were and failed to meet the standards for receiving housing allowances: 45 percent of these were "very satisfied," compared to 30 percent of those who moved and passed and 19 percent of those who moved and failed. The families in the program were strongly attached to their homes. They were pleased if they could make them better at small cost, but giving them up for higher physical standards somewhere else yielded little satisfaction.

For those who could not easily meet the standards where they were, the program required a move that was often unwelcome and unsatisfying. The program's objective of bringing everyone into housing of standard quality was out of touch with the preferences and priorities of many of the families who took part. . . .

Before the housing allowance experiment, conventional wisdom held that increases in the income of poor families would lead to nearly proportional increases in their housing expenditures—that a 10 percent increase in income would generate a 10 percent increase in rent payments. A recent Rand Corporation study, based on surveys of a sample of all households in Green Bay and South Bend, estimates the income elasticity of housing demand at only .19 for renters and .45 for homeowners. In these communities, a 10 percent increase in income for renters would lead to only a 1.9 percent increase in rent payments. Elasticities estimated for other cities in the housing allowance program were also low.

An implication is that if families who receive housing allowances are free to decide how much of their payment to spend for housing, they will not increase their rent outlays very much above the prior level. But if rent payments do not increase, giving cash to the poor is not likely to prompt landlords to spend much money for property improvements or better maintenance, as Lowry had anticipated when he proposed housing allowances as a solution to New York City's problems of deterioration and abandonment. Letting consumers make their own decisions regarding how much to spend for rent works against the goal of improving the quality of housing.

The housing allowance program was truly exceptional in allowing families to set their own priorities between spending on housing or spending on other items. Most housing programs sponsor construction to a predetermined standard and require the families involved to use most of their subsidy to pay for a level of housing quality chosen by an administrator. In the case of housing allowances, federal officials expected the typical family to move to better accommodations and to spend most of its subsidy for higher rent. The reality was that most families stayed put, made minor repairs if they were required to meet program standards, got marginally adequate housing if they did not have it to begin with, and used most of the payment to free their own funds for non-housing expenses. As a result, the program had only limited impact on the quality of the housing supply and on mobility; but these were unavoidable consequences of respecting the wishes of families in the program. . . .

The poor do not give housing *quality* the high priority that program administrators do. In the long history of housing reform in the United States, this is the first time the beneficiaries of a program have been able to make their views known on how the money should be spent. The views of the reformers have always dominated; in fact, we know almost nothing about whether earlier generations of slum-dwellers would rather have had the cash than either model tenements or public housing projects. But the poor of this generation, at least, have spoken clearly through the housing allowance experiment. Their main problem, as they see it, is cost, not quality. Interestingly, a household survey commissioned by HUD just before the housing allowance experiment began also suggested that housing quality was not a serious problem for the urban poor. In three cities surveyed in 1972, fully 84 percent of the households with incomes below $5,000 rated their housing units as "excellent" or "satisfactory." The housing allowance experience confirms and amplifies this finding. The poor still have serious housing problems, but they are not the ones most public programs address.

NOTES

1. What justifications are there for government's adoption of quality standards in the form of housing codes, and for its attempted implementation of these standards through code enforcement, covenants of habitability and subsidy programs? How can these justifications be reconciled with the fact, reflected in the Frieden excerpt, above, that some tenants will forego standard quality housing in order to enjoy more or better goods, services and amenities, such as food, medical care and proximity to friends and family?

Can government's adoption of quality standards be justified in neighborhoods of predominantly high quality housing on the ground that one substandard building will injure other buildings in the area? Can it be justified in neighborhoods of predominantly low quality housing on the ground that, without uniform standards, any single owner will be deterred from upgrading her building by the fact that the cost of bringing her building up to code will likely exceed any resulting increase in the building's value?

Is the real question not, *whether* we should have housing quality standards but, rather, what *level* of quality these standards should impose and what method or combination of methods is likely to achieve that level most efficiently and equitably? If housing codes are effectively enforced, landlords will either make the necessary repairs, passing the costs on to their tenants to the extent that the market allows, or will not make the repairs and eventually abandon their buildings. Does the first possibility suggest that code enforcement may be inequitable to landlords and their tenants? Does the second possibility suggest that code enforcement, either directly through housing officials or indirectly through tenant reliance on the covenant of habitability, may be an inefficient method for bringing premises up to code?

Do government subsidies offer a better approach? If so, should the subsidy take the form of public housing, owned and operated by the government? (How sensitive is government likely to be to consumer needs? How cost-conscious is it likely to be in building and operating public housing?) Or should the subsidy be paid to apartment developers and owners? (If so, should the subsidy take the form of cash or income tax deductions? What conditions should be placed on the developer's or owner's entitlement to the cash or tax subsidy?) Or is it better to give the subsidy directly to housing consumers? (If so, should any conditions be placed on their entitlement and on the quality of the premises toward which they can apply the subsidy? Should the subsidy take the form of cash, which the recipient can spend at will, or a voucher, which can be spent only on housing?)

In the last analysis, the appropriate level of housing standards and methods for their enforcement turn as much on moral aspirations and practical politics as on arid cost-benefit analyses. Some advocates defend housing code standards on the single ground that they reflect society's belief that it is intolerable for anyone to live in squalor. As a practical, political matter, will that same "society" vote the funds needed to upgrade substandard premises? Consider the observation that "[t]o deal with the problem of substandard housing by legal sanction has the additional attraction of enabling, or seeming to enable, a principal manifestation of poverty to be eliminated without any public expenditure." R. Posner, Economic Analysis of Law 356 (2d ed. 1977).

2. Housing experiments across the country have tested the theory that the key to upgrading and maintaining substandard premises is converting them from low income rental to low income ownership. The pride, and potential profit, of ownership will, it is thought, offer occupants the incentive needed to invest their own time and labor in improving and maintaining their homes.

One such experimental program in the District of Columbia involves equity sharing between the low income occupant—who puts up 10% of the down payment, gets 10% of the ownership, and pays all debt service and real property taxes—and an outside investor—who puts up 90% of the down payment, gets a 90% ownership interest, and 90% of the federal income tax benefits represented by the deductions for depreciation of the property. At the end of six years, the occupant can buy out the investor at a predetermined price. The result?

One family, with a combined annual income of about $17,000, will make monthly payments of about $425, less than the $450 monthly rent paid for a substandard rental home in the Columbia Heights section of Northwest Washington. Mariano, "Nonprofit Group Helps Create New Homeowners," Washington Post, January 1, 1983, C8.

3. The theoretical effects and comparative advantages of different forms of government regulation of housing quality are considered in Markovits, The Distributive Impact, Allocative Efficiency, and Overall Desirability of Ideal Housing Codes: Some Theoretical Clarifications, 89 Harv.L.Rev. 1815 (1976); Ackerman, Regulating Slum Housing Markets on Behalf of the Poor: Of Housing Codes, Housing Subsidies and Income Redistribution Policy, 80 Yale L.J. 1093 (1971); Komesar, Return to Slumville: A Critique of the Ackerman Analysis of Housing Code Enforcement and the Poor, 82 Yale L.J. 1175 (1973); Ackerman, More on Slum Housing and Redistribution Policy: A Reply to Professor Komesar, 82 Yale L.J. 1194 (1973).

There is also a growing empirical literature. See, for example, Hirsch, Hirsch & Margolis, Regression Analysis of the Effects of Habitability Laws Upon Rent: An Empirical Observation on the Ackerman-Komesar Debate, 63 Calif.L.Rev. 1098 (1975).

For an historical overview, see L. Friedman, Government and Slum Housing: A Century of Frustration (1968); J. Weicher, Housing: Federal Policies and Programs 31–91 (1980).

C. COMMERCIAL LEASES: THE SHOPPING CENTER

Leases are used in a wide variety of commercial settings, in a wide variety of ways. The intricacies of commercial lease practice are particularly evident in the contemporary shopping center. The shopping center's landlord may be a developer, limited partnership, lending institution or even a major retailer. Tenants will divide into a small number of large *anchor tenants* and a large number of small *satellite tenants.* Anchor tenants are so called because they provide the center's ballast, drawing customers into the center from the surrounding communities. The satellite tenants, clustered around the anchor or anchors, will largely draw their business from customers attracted to the center by the anchor tenant.

Shopping centers are usually classified in terms of the nature of their anchor tenant or tenants, and the size of the community that they serve. In a *neighborhood center*, designed primarily to serve the daily needs of the immediately surrounding neighborhood, the anchor tenant is usually a supermarket, and the satellites may be drug stores, dry cleaners, haircutters, and shoe repair shops. *Community centers* typically have a junior department store or variety store as an anchor in addition to a supermarket; satellites may include a clothing store, hardware store or appliance store in addition to convenience stores. *Regional* and *super-regional* centers have one or more full-line department stores as anchor tenants, and fifty, one hundred, or even more satellite tenants offering a full range of retail merchandise and services.

Because of their central role, the anchor tenant or tenants will have a substantial voice in determining the shopping center's physical layout and tenant mix. Others will have a voice too. The shopping center developer, who has an entrepreneurial stake in the enterprise, will contribute her expertise. The institutional lender, which provides the bulk of the financing that the developer needs to build the shopping center, will typically insist that the anchor and satellite tenants, and the terms of their leases, meet its approval. And satellite tenants, attracted to the center by the drawing power of a vital and established anchor, will try to condition their own lease performance on the anchor's continued presence. In a word, the shopping center rests on a complex economic structure and depends for its continued success on the deft coordination of lease clauses tying anchors, satellites, the developer and the developer's lender into the life of the center.

1. THE RETAIL LEASE

LEASE OF STORE—PERCENTAGE RENT

Cal.Forms § 22:94 (1975).

By this instrument, _____, of _____ [*address*], as lessor, leases to _____, of _____ [*address*], as lessee, the premises known as _____ [*description*], such premises to be used and occupied by lessee as a retail store for selling _____ and for no other purpose, for the term of _____ years commencing on _____, 19__, and ending on _____, 19__, for the rental and on the terms and conditions that follow.

    1. Lessee covenants and agrees to pay as rent for the premises, _____ Dollars ($_____) per year in equal monthly instalments of _____ Dollars ($_____), and in addition thereto such sums as may accrue by virtue of the percentage payable on gross sales as hereinafter more particularly provided. All such sums, unless otherwise provided, are due and payable in advance on the first day of each calendar month during the term of this lease at the office of lessor at _____ [*address*], or such other place as lessor may designate in writing.

    2. Lessee further covenants and agrees to pay to lessor as additional rent for the demised premises, over and above the minimum rent of _____ Dollars ($_____) per year, a sum equal to _____ per cent (\_\_%) on the amount of the gross sales in excess of _____ Dollars ($_____) made in, on or from the premises for each annual period of the lease. The method and manner of lessee's payment to lessor of such additional rent shall be based on gross sales as follows:

For each monthly period during the term of this lease, lessee shall pay to lessor as such additional rent on or before the _____ day of the next succeeding month, a sum determined by deducting _____ Dollars ($_____), being the amount of the minimum monthly rent payable hereunder for such month, from an amount equal to _____ per cent (\_\_%) on all gross sales made in, on, or from the leased premises during such preceding month. In the event the aggregate payments made as additional rent under the provisions of this paragraph for and during any yearly or annual term of this lease shall, together with the regular monthly instalments of minimum monthly rent, total an amount in excess of a sum equal to _____ per cent (\_\_%) of the total gross business done in, on or from the premises during such annual or yearly period, then lessor shall refund and pay to lessee the amount of such excess when and as the same shall be ascertained at the expiration of such yearly period. In no event, however, shall the rent stipulated to be paid by lessee to lessor under the provisions hereof be less than _____ Dollars ($_____) for any such yearly or annual period.

3. The term "gross sales" as herein used includes the sales price of all merchandise of every sort whatsoever sold, and the charges for all services performed for which charge is made by lessee or by other person, persons or corporation selling merchandise or performing service of any sort in, on, or from the premises, and shall include merchandise sold or services performed either for cash or for credit, regardless of collections in the case of the latter, but shall exclude merchandise so purchased that is returned by the purchaser and accepted by lessee, and all allowances made by lessee to its customers.

4. Lessee further covenants, and it is a condition of this lease, that lessee will keep separate and accurate records of the gross sales covering all business done or transacted in, on, or from the premises, and that lessee will give to lessor the right at any and all reasonable times to inspect such records. Lessor shall be given access at any and all reasonable times to any other books or records that may be necessary to enable it to make a full and proper audit of the gross income of all business done in, on or from the premises.

On or before the _____ day of each month during the term of this lease, commencing with the second month thereof, lessee shall deliver to lessor a correct statement of the gross sales of all business done in, on, or from the premises during the next preceding month as shown by lessee's records. In addition to such monthly statements, lessee shall, on the _____ day of _____ in each year during the term of this lease, and on expiration of the lease, render to lessor a certified public accountant's statement showing the total gross sales of all business done in, on, or from the premises for the year ending the _____ day of _____, or for such fractional part of a yearly period as occurs at the beginning and expiration of this lease.

If lessor is not satisfied with any monthly, annual, or other statement so submitted, then lessor shall give notice to lessee of such dissatisfaction within _____ days after receipt by lessor of the statement complained of. Unless within _____ days after lessee's receipt of such notice of dissatisfaction, lessee shall satisfy lessor with respect to such statement thus complained of, then lessor shall have the privilege of having an audit made of the account books and records pertaining to the business of lessee. Such audit shall be made by certified public accountants in good standing to be selected by lessor, which accountants shall work in conjunction with like accountants selected by lessee. The expense of such audit shall be borne jointly by lessor and lessee, and lessee shall render all possible assistance to such accountants and shall give them access to all books of accounts and other records that may be necessary to enable such accountants to make a full and complete audit of all gross income of all business done in, on or from the premises.

5. Lessee agrees to put in a new store front in the leased premises, such new front, however, and the installation thereof to be in all respects subject to the approval of lessor. Lessee shall submit plans and specifications therefor to lessor, and secure lessor's approval thereto, before any work is commenced.

6. It is a condition of this lease that lessee shall not assign this lease; let or sublet the premises or any part thereof; _____ [sell or permit to be sold liquors, whether spiritous, vinous or fermented, on the premises]; or use the same or permit the same to be used for any other purpose than as above specified. It is also a condition of this lease that lessee shall not make any alterations in or to the premises without written consent of lessor first being obtained and that all additions, fixtures (except movable trade fixtures not attached to the realty), improvements and repairs shall be made and paid for by lessee, and shall thereafter be the property of lessor. Any personal property in the leased premises shall be at risk of lessee only, and lessor shall not be liable for any damages to the personal property, to the premises, or to lessee, arising from bursting or leaking of water or steam pipes or from any acts of neglect of co-tenants or other occupants of the building, or any other persons. The rules and regulations in regard to the building, which are attached hereto and hereby made a part of this lease, shall, during the continuance of this agreement, be in all things observed and performed by lessee, and lessee's agents and employees. Lessee agrees to pay for all unnecessary damage done to the rooms or building, and for all unnecessary waste of water.

Lessee shall be responsible for all breakage or injury to plate glass in the premises during the term hereof, and shall carry insurance to cover such breakage or injury.

It shall be the duty of lessee to take care of and keep clean the sidewalk in front of the premises and to comply with all laws, ordinances and regulations of the public authorities with respect to care of the sidewalk. Lessee shall indemnify lessor from all loss, damage or claim arising out of lessee's failure in this regard.

7. The premises having been leased for the purpose of lessee's conducting a retail store for selling _____ and for no other purpose, it is understood to be a condition of this lease that the premises be used for no other purpose and that no other merchandise be sold therein, unless the written consent of lessor thereto is first obtained. Lessee covenants and agrees to conduct and operate such store and the business thereof as a high grade establishment and in a first-class manner at all times.

8. Lessor shall furnish lessee with _____ [water and heat, but not light, free of charge, and lessor agrees to furnish lessee with whatever electric power lessee may use on the premises, for which lessee shall pay lessor _____ cents (__¢) per kilowatt hour.] The payment to be made by lessee to lessor for _____ [electric power] shall be in addition to the rent hereinabove provided for, and shall be made immediately on presentation of bills therefor by lessor. Any default on the part of lessee in the payment of such bills shall be deemed and treated in all respects in a similar manner as a default in rent, with all rights and remedies to lessor in connection therewith that are herein provided in case of a default in rent.

It is mutually understood and agreed that any default on the part of lessor to furnish heat, water, light, elevator service, or electric power, by reason of accidents to machinery or equipment, strikes, fire or other causes beyond the control of lessor shall not entitle lessee to claim any damages or rebate of rent on account of such default. It is hereby further agreed that if, during the continuance of this lease, the premises shall be so injured by fire as to be rendered untenantable, the damage, insofar as the same pertains to the building itself, other than to lessee's fixtures, shall be repaired by lessor at its own expense as speedily as possible; however, if the damage is so extensive as to be impracticable of repair within _____ days, it shall be optional with either party hereto to cancel this lease, and in case of any such cancellation the rent shall be paid to the day of such fire.

9. It is mutually agreed that in the event of default in the punctual payment of the rent or any part thereof, or in the observance or performance of any of the conditions or agreements, lessor may, on _____ days' written notice, terminate the lease, re-enter the premises, and remove all persons and property therefrom. It is also agreed that lessee shall pay all costs, expenses, court costs, and attorney's fees incurred by lessor in making collection of the rent or in enforcing any of the provisions of this lease. If this lease is terminated before its expiration by reason of lessee's default, or if lessee abandons or vacates the premises before the termination of this lease, the same may be re-let by lessor for such rent and on such terms as lessor may see fit; if the full rental hereinbefore named is

not realized through such reletting, lessee agrees to pay all deficiency, and any expenses incurred by such re-letting. It is agreed by both parties hereto that if lessee makes an assignment under any insolvency act, or in the event bankruptcy proceedings are brought against lessee, or a voluntary petition in bankruptcy is filed by him, or in the event of any proceedings in law or equity to subject the interest of lessee in this lease, then this lease shall not pass, except by written consent of lessor, and in such event lessor may, at its option, terminate this lease.

10. It is understood and agreed that lessor shall not take advantage of any covenant or condition for the forfeiture or termination of the lease until after _____ [3] days from the mailing of notice by registered mail directed to lessee at its principal office at _____ [*address*], or such other place as lessee may hereafter designate, during which period lessee shall have the right to pay any arrearage of rent or rectify any breach of covenant.

11. The words "lessor" and "lessee" as used herein, include, apply to, bind and benefit the heirs, legal representatives, successors and assigns of the named lessor and lessee.

All rights and remedies of lessor under this lease or this instrument shall be cumulative, and none shall be exclusive of any rights or remedies allowed by law.

Executed in duplicate at _____ on _____, 19__.

[*Signatures*]

[*Acknowledgments*]

QUESTIONS

In what ways does the sample form of retail lease, above, differ from the form of residential lease at page 908? The sample represents the kind of lease a satellite tenant might be expected to sign. What differences would you expect to find in an anchor tenant's lease?

Does the first, unnumbered paragraph of the sample lease create a negative covenant, prohibiting the tenant from putting the premises to other than the specified use, or an affirmative covenant, requiring the tenant affirmatively to make the specified use? Can the clause be construed as a condition rather than a covenant? As merely precatory? What are the landlord's remedies for tenant breach of the clause? For breach of other obligations undertaken in the lease?

Shopping center leases frequently employ percentage rental provisions, like those in Paragraphs 2–4, as a vehicle for sharing the risks and rewards of the tenant's business and of the shopping center as a whole. Representing landlord or tenant in the lease negotiations, what changes might you want to make in the language of Paragraphs 2–4? Will your answer depend on the nature of the tenant's business—a high mark-up, low-volume gift store, say, rather than a low mark-up, high-volume supermarket? Representing the tenant, what reasonable changes would you propose in the provisions respecting the landlord's right to examine your client's books?

2. TENANT'S DUTIES

KROGER CO. v. CHEMICAL SECURITIES CO.

Supreme Court of Tennessee, 1975.
526 S.W.2d 468.

BROCK, Justice.

This case involves the construction of a shopping center lease to ascertain whether it contains an implied covenant by the tenant to occupy and operate a supermarket on the premises and an implied prohibition against subleasing to a nongrocery enterprise and without permission.

The Madison Square Shopping Center in Madison, Davidson County, Tennessee, was opened to the public in 1956. Located on thirty acres of land, the shopping center is comprised of seven buildings and a parking lot for 2500 vehicles. Forty-six independent businesses occupy the 343,000 square feet enclosed in the buildings.

The Kroger Company was among the original tenants of the shopping center; it entered a lease on January 1, 1956, with Madison Square Shopping Center, Inc., for an area at the end of the largest building and opened a supermarket. The leases of several other original tenants required the landlord to acquire a minimum ten year lease for a Kroger supermarket.

In 1962 Kroger threatened to close the grocery store and move out of the shopping center to larger accommodations; whereupon the landlord agreed to expend $100,000.00 for improvements requested by the tenant. The money was spent to remodel and enlarge the Kroger store by 50%.

At that time Mr. John Dyson, real estate manager for Kroger in Nashville, and Mr. W. H. Criswell, the agent for the shopping center, negotiated a new lease. According to Mr. Dyson, Mr. Criswell was known as the dean of real estate men and the leading shopping center negotiator in Nashville at the time. "He had the reputation of being an extremely tough negotiator."

The new lease was signed on June 5, 1962. The rental under this lease is $2,812.50 per month plus one percent of the tenant's annual sales in excess of $3,375,000.00. The base rental is high and has comprised the entire rental under this lease because Kroger's sales never achieved the sum necessary for an override payment. The term of the lease is ten years, and the tenant has the option to make three renewals of five years each. Due to a subsequent lease modification the ten year term commenced on November 1, 1963, and expired on October 31, 1973. The only express proscriptions in the lease on the tenant's use of the premises are that he not use them in an unlawful manner and that he not use them for a drugstore without written approval of the landlord. The landlord promised not to lease any premises for the sale of groceries within 1000 feet of the Kroger store, except one small corner store previously occupied by A & P Grocery. The lease states that its provisions shall bind and benefit the parties and their heirs, executors, administrators, successors and assigns. There is no clause in the lease concerning the right of the tenant to assign or sublet, but clause 26h provides that if the tenant voluntarily vacates the premises and they remain vacant for one year, the landlord has the right to cancel the lease and re-enter the premises.

On July 1, 1965, Chemical Securities Company, the plaintiff in this case, purchased all the real estate, store leases, and other assets of Madison Square Shopping Center, Inc., and the latter corporation was dissolved.

On July 16, 1973, shortly before the conclusion of the ten year term, Kroger entered into a sublease with Genesco, Inc., for the store, and on September 29 vacated the premises. According to Kroger the primary reason for the move was the declining sales at the supermarket. The subtenant assumed all of Kroger's obligations under the prime lease; the term of the sublease is equal to the three remaining extension periods of fifteen years and the subtenant's rental of $2,812.50 per month, to be paid to Kroger, is the same as the base rental under the prime lease. Genesco agreed not to assign or sublease the property without the consent of Kroger. The subtenant's use of the premises is limited to the sale of shoes, clothing and general merchandise, and he agreed not to use the premises in any manner which would compete with Kroger's business. The record reveals that Kroger operates another supermarket in Rivergate Shopping Center several miles away. The record also discloses that Winn-Dixie Louisville, Inc., has indicated to Chemical Securities Company that it is interested in leasing the Kroger store and opening a supermarket.

On September 19, 1973, the landlord filed a complaint in Chancery Court against the tenant and the subtenant claiming that Kroger's sublease of the property to Genesco for use as a commissary was inconsistent with the terms of the prime lease and a breach of the tenant's implied warranty to occupy the premises. The complaint requested a temporary injunction enjoining the transfer of the premises to Genesco during the pendency of the action, and that the sublease be annulled. The complainant further prayed that the prime lease be terminated or that the tenant be permanently enjoined from subleasing its premises to a nonretail grocery store and without prior approval of the landlord.

The Chancellor granted the temporary injunction and after a full hearing of the cause he found the prime lease vague and uncertain and admitted extrinsic evidence as to its meaning. He was particularly impressed by evidence of the cooperative nature of a shopping center operation and evidence of the essential role of a large grocery store in the economic success of the Madison Square Shopping Center. In his view Kroger could have vacated the premises without any further obligations but chose instead to sublease the premises at no profit to a nongrocery enterprise in order to lessen competition with its Rivergate Store. The Chancellor concluded that the intention of the parties to the prime lease was for the tenant to occupy and operate a grocery store on the demised premises and not to sublet. He ordered that the sublease be declared void and the prime lease terminated.

The Court of Appeals affirmed, finding the lease to be vague with respect to subletting. It concluded from evidence of the surrounding circumstances that if the subject of subletting by Kroger to a nongrocery operation had been mentioned the lessor would have insisted upon a covenant against subleasing without its permission and Kroger would have agreed. It also concluded that Kroger was guilty of bad faith in prohibiting its subtenant from going into the retail grocery business and that such bad faith warranted forfeiture of the prime lease as well as annulment of the sublease.

Whereupon, Kroger and Genesco petitioned this Court for a writ of certiorari which was granted. . . .

The primary issue to be resolved in this case is whether the Court of Appeals erred in construing the lease to contain an implied covenant of continuous occupancy and operation of a grocery business and an implied prohibition against subleasing without permission.

> "It may be stated generally that implied covenants are not favored in the law; and courts will declare the same to exist only when there is a satisfactory basis in the express contract of the parties which makes it necessary to imply certain duties and obligations in order to effect the purposes of the parties to the contract made. Furthermore, implied covenants can be justified only upon the ground of legal necessity arising from the terms of the contract, or the substance thereof, and the circumstances attending its execution; and the implication from the words must be such as will clearly authorize the inference of an imputation in law of the creation of a covenant." Cousins Investment Co. v. Hastings Clothing Co., 45 Cal.App.2d 141, 113 P.2d 878, 879 (1941).

This Court has applied this rule to implied covenants in leases. In Central Drug Store v. Adams, 184 Tenn. 541, 201 S.W.2d 682 (1947), the Court held that covenants restricting the use of leased property should be strictly construed according to their express terms and not expanded by implication.

The courts have no rightful authority to make contracts for litigants. With regard to subletting and assignment in particular, this Court has long held that a lessee may freely transfer the demised premises without the lessor's consent, absent a covenant in the lease restricting the right of assignment. Also, the general rule is that covenants against subletting are strictly construed against the lessor.

From these cases we have concluded that the landlord, Chemical Securities Company, bears a heavy burden in proving that the lease contains an implied covenant of continuous occupancy and operation of a grocery and an implied limitation on subleasing. Such implied covenants must arise from the terms of the lease itself.

One clause which might, arguably, support such covenants is the percentage rental clause. However, the Court of Appeals did not rely on this provision in reaching its conclusion, and considering the substantial sum set as the base rental and the small and speculative nature of the override, we likewise do not find that clause determinative.

It is also suggested that the implied covenants emanate from the landlord's promise not to lease any other premises in the shopping center, except the former A & P store, to any business for the sale of groceries. The Court of Appeals relied on this express covenant and the shopping center context and circumstances surrounding the execution of the lease as the source of the implied covenants.

However, in our opinion this restriction on competition written into the lease is not broad enough to give birth to implied covenants of continuous occupancy and operation of a grocery business and a prohibition against subleasing to a nongrocery and without the lessor's permission.

The absence of language in this lease on which to base such covenants distinguishes this case from two New Jersey shopping center cases cited by the landlord, Ingannamorte v. Kings Super Market, Inc., 55 N.J. 223, 260 A.2d 841 (1970) and Dover Shopping Center, Incorporated v. Cushman's Son's, Inc., 63 N.J.Super. 384, 164 A.2d 785 (1960). In *Dover Shopping Center, Inc.*, the tenant covenanted "beginning as soon after the commencement of the term as is reasonably possible and continuing during the full remaining term of this lease, to operate its business in the demised premises; to keep its store open daily for the regular conduct of its business therein during the same hours at least as are customarily employed by other similar stores in the neighborhood of the demised premises . . . ." Id. at 787. In *Ingannamorte*, the lease provided that the leased store was "to be used and occupied only for a supermarket . . . ." Id. at 841. The tenants in both cases had closed their stores and left the premises vacant although they continued to pay rent. In *Ingannamorte* the court concluded that an implied covenant of continuous use flowed from the express language of the lease taken in the shopping center context where tenants form interdependent economic units; it ordered the tenant to resume business or give up possession of the premises. In *Dover Shopping Center, Inc.* the court also found a covenant of continuous use and ordered the tenant to reopen his store.

The landlord also cites Slidell Investment Company, Inc. v. City Product Corporation, 202 So.2d 323 (La.App.1967), to support its propositions, and that case was heavily relied upon by the Court of Appeals. In *Slidell* the landlord "instituted a suit against a tenant who maintained a variety store in his shopping center for rental payments owing. The lease provided that the premises were to be used "for the sale, storage or display of goods, wares and merchandise" (Id. at 324) and that no other tenant of the center could operate a variety store. The tenant was obligated to pay a base rental and a percentage of his annual sales. In the year prior to the closing of the tenant's store the percentage override constituted nearly 50% of the rent. The tenant operated a very successful variety store on the premises for several years, but when a new shopping center opened across the street he decided to lease a store in that center, with exclusive rights as a variety store, and use the old store as a warehouse. The tenant subsequently vacated the old premises and sublet them, thereafter tendering to the landlord only the basic rental. The tenant prohibited the subtenant from using the premises as a variety store thus eliminating competition in both centers with his variety store. The court held the tenant liable to the landlord for the basic rental and override payments for the term of the lease on the theory that the lease contained an implied continuous operation clause. The court noted, however, that if the tenant's store had been a financial failure through no fault of his own before he moved out, that he would not have been obligated to continue operations. In our opinion the *Slidell* case is clearly distinguishable from the one at hand. *Slidell* was a suit for rent and was based on a lease where the percentage override was very substantial.

Unlike the leases in the cases above, we find no terms in this lease which justify the finding of the implied covenants. In fact the lease reveals that the parties considered departure from the premises by Kroger before the term expired to be a clear possibility. Clause 26h gives the landlord the right to cancel the lease and re-enter the premises if the tenant vacates them *and* they remain vacant for a year. In our opinion this clause recognizes Kroger's right to vacate the premises and the right to sublease them provided Kroger does so within one year of vacating.

The Court of Appeals found that the leases of four other major tenants of the center required the landlord to maintain a grocery store in the center. The petitioners assign error to this particular finding of fact and we sustain their assignment. The other leases merely provided that the landlord acquire a minimum ten year lease with Kroger; such a lease was obtained and it expired long before the sublease to Genesco.

The negotiators of this lease were very sophisticated and knowledgeable. In our opinion if they had intended the lease to contain a covenant of continuous occupancy and operation of a grocery business and a prohibition against subleasing for a nongrocery use, and without permission, they would have made an express statement in the lease. Evidence of the lease negotiations presented at trial indicates that these provisions were purposely excluded. Mr. Dyson recounted those negotiations:

> "Q. Do you recall whether the attention—your attention and the attention of Mr. Criswell—was drawn to the possibility of Kroger's vacating these premises?
>
> "A. Yes, sir, it was because one of the clauses in the lease—and Mr. Criswell made a point of this that if The Kroger Company ceased to operate that the owners wanted the right to cancel the lease if the premises were vacant, I believe for as much as a year. I'd like to review that. That is correct. Under paragraph 26-h of the lease.
>
> "Q. Your reference is to paragraph 26-h—was that the result of the concern over Kroger's vacating the premises? Was that provision put in there because of that?
>
> "A. Yes, Mr. Criswell said it did not do any shopping center any good to have a vacancy, somebody not occupying space within a center.
>
> . . .
>
> "Q. What was your practice at that time insofar as putting a restriction in a lease that would deny you the right to sublease?
>
> "A. To my knowledge I don't recall one ever being in any lease.
>
> "Q. How did you as a real estate manager of this division—what importance did you place upon your right to sublease this store if it became uneconomical?
>
> "A. I placed quite a bit of importance on it because we sublease quite a few stores in any tenure with The Kroger Company in Atlanta and in Nashville.
>
> "Q. Now with all due respect, Mr. Dyson, the lease also does not make any specific mention of any agreement on Kroger's part to continuously occupy the premises as a grocery store. Are you aware of that?
>
> "A. Yes, sir, I am, and that was one of the sanctimonious things, I guess, in the trade. They never put a restriction in a lease that they guaranteed to operate a facility.
>
> "Q. You say 'they'?
>
> "A. The Kroger Company. I don't believe that it would have been approved.

"Q. In your experience at that time being the real estate negotiator for Kroger in this vicinity, was that the case in your other leases here?

"A. Yes, sir.

"Q. Was that an important or unimportant factor to you—

"A. It's—

"Q. —that you did not have the obligation to continuously occupy?

"A. Very important factor if you wanted to make a deal."

It is our conclusion that the record does not support a finding that the parties impliedly agreed upon the covenants as asserted by the respondent. Therefore, we reverse the decree of the Court of Appeals and render judgment in favor of the defendants, Kroger and Genesco. All costs of this appeal are taxed against the plaintiff, Chemical Securities Company.

FONES, C.J., and COOPER, HENRY and HARBISON, JJ., concur.

FAIRLAWN PLAZA DEVELOPMENT, INC. v. FLEMING CO., INC.

Supreme Court of Kansas, 1972.
210 Kan. 459, 502 P.2d 663.

KAUL, Justice.

This is an action for a declaratory judgment to construe the terms of a shopping center "Build and Lease Agreement." The lease provides for payment of rents based on a percentage of gross sales of the lessee's supermarket if the percentage amounts to a sum greater than the minimum fixed cash rent agreed upon.

Defendant's sublessee operates a bakery on the premises. The question in the case is whether the portion of the baked goods sold or transferred to affiliated stores of the sublessee are to be included in the term "gross sale" as defined in the lease.

Plaintiff-lessor appeals from a summary judgment rendered for defendant-lessee.

Both parties filed motions for summary judgment, at which time the trial court had before it the pleadings, affidavits and exhibits from which the facts are gleaned.

The build and lease agreement was executed on September 20, 1960. It declared that:

". . . [T]he LESSOR desires to construct a building and surrounding area as a part of the FAIRLAWN PLAZA SHOPPING CENTER, said building to be located as approved by the parties hereto . . . and the LESSEE desires to lease said building and surrounding area for the operation of a retail food supermarket."

Section 2 of the lease agreement reads:

> "The LESSOR agrees to cause construction of a building containing approximately 18,561 square feet, together with a parking area and a service area (said building, parking area and service area herein together called the premises), all to be carried on in accordance with the *attached plans and specifications.*
>
> "This lease shall not become effective until both parties have *approved the plans and specifications* and have initialed and attached hereto a copy thereof. The LESSOR agrees that at the option of the LESSEE this lease shall become null and void if construction of the premises is not begun on or before December 1, 1960, and if thereafter construction is not completed with all reasonable diligence." (Emphasis supplied.)

The agreement further provides for a lease term of fifteen years with an option granted to lessee to extend the lease for three additional periods of five years.

Provisions concerning the amount of rent and the payment thereof appear in Section 5 of the lease agreement. In substance it was agreed that lessee should pay an annual rent of $26,727.84 in monthly payments of $2,227.32, or one and one-quarter percent of all gross sales, as defined, in any one calendar month, whichever is greater. This section of the lease was amended by a supplement to the lease executed on July 12, 1965. The supplement provides for an annual fixed rent of $15,000.00, instead of $26,727.84, until lessor had completed construction of an additional 80,000 square feet of building area in the shopping center. After completion of the additional construction the rent provisions originally agreed upon were to become effective.

The portion of the lease agreement which gives rise to the dispute between the parties is the definition of "gross sales" which appears in Section 5 as follows:

> "The term 'gross sales' as used herein shall include all sales of merchandise from, through, or out of the leased premises, including performance of any service for any customer or patron for compensation by the LESSEE, or by any salesman, saleswoman, or employee, and shall include all sales by every portion and department thereof, and sales by any sublessee, concessionaire, or licensee in said premises for cash or on a charge basis, paid or unpaid, collected or uncollected, and including all business in which orders come by mail, telephone or telegraph, and all business where goods are delivered directly by the supplier to the purchaser (whether or not actually handled by the LESSEE), less credit for returned merchandise, merchandise trade-ins, and credits of a similar nature; and 'gross sales' shall not include sales tax. *Transfers of merchandise between stores of sub-lessees are not Gross Sales.*" (Emphasis supplied.)

The remainder of the lease agreement deals with insurance responsibility, additions, alterations, damage to the premises, and other matters not pertinent to the dispute in litigation.

Plaintiff-lessor, as agreed, proceeded to construct the building according to plans and specifications attached. The building encompassed a total of 18,561 square feet of which 2,214 square feet was devoted to a bakery operation.

Three days after the execution of the "Build and Lease Agreement," on September 23, 1960, the defendant subleased the premises to Ernest R. Dibble; Paul L. Dibble and John W. Dibble. On April 3, 1968, the original sublessees assigned all of their interests as sublessees to Dibble's Fairlawn, Inc. John W. Dibble is the sole owner of all of the outstanding capital stock of Dibble's Fairlawn, Inc. Since the commencement of the terms of the lease between plaintiff and defendant, the sublessee has operated a retail grocery supermarket on the premises and during such time there were three other Dibble stores which were at all times, following the commencement of the lease term, affiliates and operated in conjunction with the store operated by the sublessee.

Since the commencement of the lease term the sublessee has operated a bakery on the premises in question, and part of the products of the bakery has been delivered to the three affiliated stores and sold at retail therein.

After the lease agreement had been in effect for about six years, plaintiff says it discovered that defendant had not included in gross sales the bakery products delivered to the three affiliated stores. Defendant took the position that the furnishing of bakery goods from the Dibble's Fairlawn Plaza store to the other Dibble stores did not fall within "gross sales" as used and defined in the "Build and Lease Agreement." Whereupon plaintiff filed this declaratory judgment action praying:

". . . that the Court interpret and construe the Build and Lease Agreement and the Supplement thereto . . .."

The trial court held that the bakery operation was excluded under the lease provisions defining "gross sales" because it is a transfer of merchandise between the stores of the sublessee.

On appeal both parties take the position that there are no ambiguities in the lease if the language used therein is given its ordinary meaning. Nevertheless, both parties supply us with citations of the various rules of construction which would be applicable if we were to find ambiguity in our examination of the lease on appeal.

Testing the lease provisions in question, by giving the language used its ordinary meaning, we do not believe the words used can genuinely be understood to have two different meanings. Thus, under familiar applicable rules, ambiguity does not exist. It follows that the meaning of the provisions in question must be determined by the contents of the lease agreement alone, and words cannot be written into it which import an intent wholly unexpressed when it was executed.

In its first and principal point of error on appeal, plaintiff contends the summary judgment of the trial court was erroneous because the bakery goods produced and processed in the leased facility and sold to other Dibble stores constituted wholesale sales subject to the rental based on percentage of gross sales and were not transfers of merchandise. Plaintiff argues that the furnishing of bakery products to the other Dibble stores constituted a sale of merchandise from or out of the leased premises or the performance of a service for compensation.

Defendant, lessee, on the other hand, argues that an examination of the language used in Section 5 reveals that the parties contemplated that gross sales were to include sales for profit to customers or patrons, or sales arranged by the retailer for its profit and delivered directly by a supplier to an ultimate purchaser. Defendant contends that a sale or transfer to an affiliate store cannot be considered a sale for profit to a customer, patron, or purchaser within the context of the term "gross sales" as defined, and, further, that the last sentence of Section 5, "Transfers of merchandise between stores of sub-lessees are not Gross Sales," clinches this interpretation of Section 5.

We are constrained to agree with the interpretation adopted by defendant and the trial court. We believe the parties, by the language used, contemplated sales to customers or patrons as distinguished from sales or transfers to affiliate stores, and it is of no moment whether the transfer of the baked goods in question be considered a sale or a transfer to the affiliate.

In support of its motion for summary judgment, plaintiff attached the affidavit of Chas. A. Bennett, president and managing officer of plaintiff. In his affidavit Mr. Bennett states:

> ". . . [H]e has been informed and therefore believes that the sale of 'bakery goods' processed by Dibble's Fairlawn, Inc., and sold to other 'Dibble' retail supermarkets were sold to such other outlets at the retail price less twenty-five (25%) per cent."

When a motion for summary judgment is submitted to the court for consideration, the movant's adversary is entitled to the benefit of all reasonable inferences that may be drawn from the facts under consideration. So, because of Mr. Bennett's affidavit, we shall treat the bakery transaction between the sublessee and affiliate stores as a sale, which, we assume, was the treatment given by the trial court.

For purposes of summary judgment, defendant concedes the Bennett statement stands admitted and that the transaction must be considered a sale, but contends this makes no difference because "transfer of merchandise" includes "sales of merchandise."

Despite an unchallenged statement of the trial court that the parties agreed, when the motions for summary judgment were submitted, that there was no factual dispute plaintiff now argues that since Mr. Bennett termed the transaction between stores of sublessee a "sale" rather than a "transfer," a dispute of fact exists. We cannot agree. In common usage of the terms "sale" is included in the broader term "transfer." A pertinent statement, in this regard, appears in 77 C.J.S. Sales § 2, p. 583:

"While in its broadest sense, the term 'sale' comprehends any transfer of personal property from one person to another for a valuable consideration, the words 'sale' and 'transfer' are not synonymous. The word 'transfer' is more comprehensive than the word 'sale,' and may involve a mode of disposing and parting with property other than by sale. . . ."

In Volume 3 Words & Phrases (Fourth Series), Sales, p. 429 this appears:

"A 'sale' is ordinarily understood to mean a transfer of property for money. Mifflin v. Shiki, 293 P. 1, 3, 77 Utah 190."

In Webster's Third New International Dictionary (unabridged) at page 2003, sale is defined:

". . . the act of selling: a contract transferring the absolute or general ownership of property from one person or corporate body to another for a price. . . ."

While transfer is defined:

". . . the conveyance of right, title, or interest in either real or personal property from one person to another by sale, gift, or other process . . . ." (p. 2427.)

The broad denotation of the word "transfer" is noted both by case law and statute in this state. The meaning of the words "assignment" and "transfer" were considered in Elwood v. Soldiers' Compensation Board, 117 Kan. 753, 232 P. 1049, wherein the word assignment was said to have a comprehensive meaning—the opinion continues:

". . . The word 'transfer' has a still wider meaning. It includes all translations [transactions] whereby property of one person becomes the property of another, whether by descent or purchase, and a will is the common assurance of a transfer which becomes effective at death of the testator . . . ." (p. 754, 232 P. p. 1049.)

We find no general statutory definition of the word "transfer." However, with respect to taxation of legacies, successions and estates, K.S.A. 79-1528(2) reads:

"The word 'transfer' shall be taken to include the passing of property or any interest therein in possession or enjoyment, present or future, by inheritance, descent, devise, succession, bequest, grant, deed, bargain, sale, gift or appointment in the manner herein prescribed."

Obviously, in common usage the word "transfer" includes "sale"—while transfer includes conveyance of property other than by sale, there is no circumstance wherein a sale would not be a transfer. It appears the broad terms "transfer" and "merchandise" were used to express the intent of the parties to exclude from gross sales any transfer of any merchandise between stores whether it be by trade, exchange, sale or however. An express covenant in a lease on a given subject matter excludes the possibility of an implied covenant of a different or conflicting nature. If the parties intended to give the word "transfer" other than its ordinary meaning it would have been a simple matter to do so in the lease agreement. We cannot make an agreement for the parties which they did not make for themselves. When language used is clear and unambiguous, the intention of the parties and the meaning of a contract are to be deduced from the content of the instrument alone.

Plaintiff argues that, under the trial court's interpretation of the lease, the defendant and its sublessee could change the entire operation from one of a retail supermarket to a wholesale bakery for its other stores and thus escape the percentage rents based on gross sales from the premises. Plaintiff is fully protected from any such happening. The instrument in question here is more than just a lease. It is a build and lease agreement for the declared purpose of constructing a building for use as a retail food supermarket in accordance with attached plans and specifications, which included 2,214 square feet of bakery space. Any attempt by a lessee or sublessee to convert the premises for a use other than a retail food supermarket, or to enlarge the bakery operation beyond that contemplated by the plans and specifications, would present a far different question than the one before us. Obviously, the parties contemplated the operation of a retail food supermarket with a bakery operation included. The lessor is adequately protected against any significant alteration of use from that contemplated in the agreement and attached plans and specifications.

From the language used by the parties here, we see no reason to distinguish baked goods from any other merchandise which might be packaged or processed, or otherwise changed from its original state into a different form and then transferred or sold to other stores of the lessee or of its sublessee. . . .

We conclude the trial court correctly interpreted the plain language of the provision of the lease agreement in question and did not abuse its discretion in denying post judgment relief to plaintiff.

The judgment is affirmed.

SCHROEDER, Justice (dissenting).

In my opinion the "Build and Lease Agreement" should be construed to require the payment of rents based on a percentage of gross sales of the lessee's supermarket, including the portion of baked goods sold or transferred to affiliated stores of the sub-lessee.

In construing the agreement in question the entire instrument must be interpreted as a whole from its four corners. When this is done the controversy can be resolved by determining the intention of the parties without resort to extrinsic evidence.

It seems to me the court has given insufficient consideration and weight to the *use clause* in the agreement. It provides that the building and surrounding area were leased "for operation of a *retail* food supermarket." (Emphasis added).

On the record here presented it must be conceded the sale of that portion of the bakery products here in question was sold at *wholesale* to affiliated stores of the sub-lessee. Whether it be denominated a "sale" or "transfer" as stated in the court's opinion is immaterial.

The foregoing must be reconciled with the facts giving rise to the controversy: (1) The bakery operation is one in which 2,214 square feet of floor space was provided by the lessor for a bakery in the "Build and Lease Agreement"; (2) The sub-lessee conducts baking operations for a period of twenty-four (24) hours per day, employing numerous persons, whose *services* together with raw eggs, milk, flour, sugar and other products are assembled, mixed and baked into finished bakery products "and packaged for ultimate sale at *retail*" (Emphasis added) (quote taken from the Affidavit of John W. Dibble); and (3) None of the bakery products are "transferred" in the original form in which they entered Dibble's Fairlawn Store.

The term "gross sales" in the lease is defined to cover sales of merchandise, *including any service by employees of the lessee and* "*shall include all sales by every portion and department thereof,* . . ." (Emphasis added).

Based on the foregoing an interpretation of the entire "Build and Lease Agreement" indicates the parties did not contemplate a *wholesale* operation on the premises for which no rents were payable to the lessor. The operation contemplated by the parties was clearly stated in the first section of the written agreement to be a *retail* food supermarket.

On the foregoing interpretation of the agreement between the parties rent was payable based on a percentage of gross sales of the lessee's supermarket, including the portion of baked goods sold to affiliated stores of the sub-lessee at a wholesale price.

It is respectfully submitted the judgment of the lower court should be reversed.

FATZER, C.J., joins in the foregoing dissent.

NOTES

1. *Tenant's Freedom to Assign and Sublet.* Real property law's general preference for free alienability explains the rule that, absent an express lease restriction, a tenant is free to assign or sublet his interest. Does *Kroger* support or undermine this general preference? Would it have been better for the court to hold that Kroger was free to sublet, but only on terms that did not limit the subtenant's right to further sublet or assign? Does freedom to assign or sublet necessarily imply freedom to impose any conditions, reasonable or unreasonable, on subsequent transfers? Would it have been better for the *Kroger* court to imply a covenant against assignments and subleases *and* a condition that the landlord not unreasonably withhold its consent to any proposed assignment or sublease? Under the circumstances, would it have been unreasonable for the landlord to withhold its consent to the Genesco sublease?

Would, and should, the *Kroger* court have reached a different result if other leases in the shopping center had been expressly conditioned upon the presence of a full-line supermarket in the center? Would, and should, the court have reached a different result if the action against Kroger and Genesco had been brought not by the landlord but by one or more of the other tenants?

2. *Percentage Rentals and the Right to Assign or Sublet.* Would and should the *Kroger* court have reached a different result if Kroger had assigned rather than sublet to Genesco? If Kroger's lease had called for a substantially lower base rental and a substantially higher override? ("One clause which might arguably support such covenants [of continuous occupancy and operation and against subleasing] is the percentage rental clause. However, the Court of Appeals did not rely on this provision in reaching its conclusion, and considering the substantial sums set as the base rental and the small and speculative nature of the override, we likewise do not find that clause determinative.")

Compare Brown v. Safeway Stores, Inc., 94 Wn.2d 359, 617 P.2d 704 (1980). Tenant Safeway's lease in plaintiff's shopping center required it to pay a rental of $4,278 per month or 1.5% of monthly gross sales, whichever was greater. Safeway began operations in 1969 and by 1973, and continuing through 1976, its business in the center had grown to a point at which the percentage rent became payable. In 1977 Safeway moved its operations from plaintiff's center to a substantially larger space in a shopping center a half-mile away. Relying on a clause in its lease allowing it to assign or sublet freely and, in the event of assignment, making it "liable as surety to lessor for full performance of lessee's obligation," Safeway sublet the premises to Uwajimaya, an Asian import and grocery business. Safeway continued to pay landlord the fixed minimum rent required by the lease.

Claiming that Safeway breached its lease by subleasing to Uwajimaya, the landlord argued that "the presence of the percentage rental provision in the Lease required Safeway to sublease only to a tenant capable of generating comparable gross sales and customer traffic." 94 Wn.2d at 370, 617 P.2d at 710. The Washington Supreme Court disagreed. "With regard to the percentage rental provision in the Lease, appellant relies on case authority interpreting such provisions to require the lessor to occupy and use the rental property and to employ reasonable diligence to operate the business in a manner productive of profits and receipts." Yet, these cases, in which implication of a special covenant "principally depends on whether the parties regarded the amount of the stipulated minimum rental as an adequate reflection of the full rental value of the premises, or whether they contemplated the full value would be realized only through the percentage provision," were "inapposite to the case at hand. First, our review of the record indicates there is sufficient evidence that the amount of the stipulated minimum rental was based upon a reasonable return to the appellant on its investment. Second, the decisions relied upon by appellant are inapplicable to a situation where, as here, the issue is the right to assign or sublease, and the lease itself provides for the unconditional right to sublease." 94 Wn.2d at 371–372, 617 P.2d at 711.

3. *Use Clauses.* Use clauses in shopping center leases take two forms. *Permitted use* clauses specify the use to which the leased premises are to be put—as a supermarket, say, or a bakery. *Exclusive use* clauses assure the tenant that his will be the only store in the center devoted to the specified use. The two clauses are closely connected. Indeed, the tenant whose landlord proposes a closely confined range of permitted uses can plausibly counter by asking that he be given the exclusive right to make those uses in the shopping center. Exclusive use clauses are considered in more detail at page 1041, below.

Permitted use clauses are often the object of intense negotiation. The landlord will want to specify the permitted use narrowly so that she can honor exclusive use clauses that may appear in other tenants' leases, and generally control the overall mix of goods and services in the shopping center. The tenant, by contrast, wants a broadly-worded use clause that will enable him to expand into new product or service lines, and drop old ones, to meet changing consumer tastes. A broad use clause will also, obviously, increase the range of businesses to which the tenant can assign or sublet the premises. Can a landlord effectively control permitted uses through careful administration of a clause requiring her reasonable consent to assignments or subleases?

Do use clauses impose only negative obligations—not to use the leased premises for other than the specified purposes—or do they also impose an affirmative obligation, requiring the tenant to occupy and use the premises for the specified purpose? Was the landlord in *Kroger* arguing that the tenant had such an affirmative obligation? Should the question whether the use clause imposes an affirmative as well as a negative obligation turn on the extent to which the landlord was expecting to receive percentage rental payments as well as basic, minimum rental payments? On whether the tenant is an anchor tenant—on whose continued operation the entire center depends—or a relatively less important satellite tenant? If a use clause is held to impose an affirmative obligation, how will that obligation be enforced against the tenant? Against an assignee from the tenant? A sublessee?

4. *Radius Clauses.* Would Chemical Securities have had an action if Kroger had remained in its shopping center, paying the minimum rental but directing its advertising and promotional expenditures at its store in the Rivergate Shopping Center, several miles away from plaintiff's Madison Square Center? Would your answer differ if Kroger's base rent was lower, and its override higher, than they were under the facts of the case? Would your answer depend upon the extent to which the Rivergate store competed with the Madison Square store? Upon whether Kroger had diverted trade to the Rivergate store with the specific intention of reducing sales, and consequently override payments, from the Madison Square store?

In Kauder, Klotz & Venitt v. Rose's Stores, Inc., 359 F.Supp. 1280 (E.D.N.C.1973), plaintiff, lessor of defendant tenant's Store #59, claimed that tenant breached its lease by opening a competing operation, Store #200, approximately 1.9 miles from Store #59. Specifically, plaintiff contended that "the opening of Store #200 in the immediate vicinity of the demised premises diverted business from the demised premises and thereby substantially diminished sales and income at the demised premises, resulting in a drop in plaintiff's rental income based on gross sales." *Id.* at 1281. This, plaintiff argued, violated a provision in tenant's lease that "tenant shall diligently and continuously operate and conduct its retail business throughout the entire term and shall use all proper and reasonable efforts consistent with good business practice to the end that the gross sales of such business shall throughout the entire term be as large as possible." *Id.* at 1282.

The court disagreed. First, "Rose's did not open Store #200 in the 'immediate vicinity' of Store #59. Store #200 is 1.9 miles from Store #59 and is in a suburban shopping center as opposed to Store #59's downtown location." Second, "in most cases which arise under similar circumstances the defendant has vacated the demised premises, changed the nature of the business, transferred operations to another location, or diverted his business. All of this is done in an attempt to diminish the rent paid the lessor on a percentage basis." By contrast, "Rose's is continuing to operate Store #59, has not changed the nature of the business, and is still paying a percentage on gross sales over $300,000 per year. The fact that some operations may have been transferred to Store #200 and that business may have been diverted from Store #59 does not appear to be the result of an attempt to diminish the rent payable to the plaintiffs on a percentage basis." 359 F.Supp. 1282–1283.

Shopping center landlords frequently seek to resolve these problems in advance by insisting on a radius clause under which the tenant agrees not to operate any other store within a specified radius, typically two to five miles, from the shopping center. Should the radius differ with the nature of the tenant's business? How should the clause be drafted to include not only the tenant, but also affiliates, subsidiaries, a parent corporation, stockholders and partners, and other stores owned by the same tenant, but operated under a different name and offering a different or similar class or line of goods?

5. How would the *Fairlawn* court have applied Paragraph 3 of the sample retail lease, page 1011 above, to the facts before it? Representing the landlord, how would you have redrafted the lease definition of "gross sales"? Representing the tenant? Under the lease in *Fairlawn*, would the tenant have been free to convert the bakery into a warehouse, thus entirely escaping liability for a percentage of gross sales?

3. LANDLORD'S DUTIES

POLLOCK v. MORELLI

Superior Court of Pennsylvania, 1976.
245 Pa.Super. 388, 369 A.2d 458.

JACOBS, Judge:

This appeal arises from the adjudication of the chancellor that the implied covenant of quiet enjoyment in the appellants' lease was not breached by their lessor, Thomas Morelli, and the consequent failure of the chancellor to find damages in the form of relocation expenses and lost profits of appellants' business.

In January and early February 1971, appellant Eugene Pollock purchased a dry cleaning business situated in Great Valley Shopping Center. In the process of acquiring the business, Mr. Pollock entered into a seven and one half year lease, with appellee as lessor, for the premises in which the dry cleaning establishment was located. At that time the shopping center was composed of two rectangular blocks of stores which met at their inside corners to form, roughly, an L shape, leaving a large open area for parking in the inside angle of the L and a small square of parking in the corner where the two blocks joined. Appellants' store was in this corner immediately adjacent to the small parking area, recessed from the sidewalk fronting all the other shops in such a way as to permit access directly from both parking areas, some spaces of which were as close as 20 feet from the door. Appellants' show windows and overhead sign were easily visible to potential customers using the shopping center. Conveniently for shoppers, the dry cleaning store was next door to a large supermarket.

In November of 1971, without prior notice to appellant, construction began for what appellee termed a "mini mall" which was to enclose and surround appellants' establishment. Individual appellant, Eugene Pollock, immediately protested this development and continued to object directly to appellee. However, the construction continued and at its conclusion, appellants were no longer occupying an outside store with visible display windows next to a parking lot. Instead they now have a six and one half year lease for one of eleven shops in a mall which extends over what had formerly been the small parking area. A store is located directly in front of the cleaning establishment and access is now gained by entering a set of double doors into the mall and proceeding down a hallway. The display windows are only visible from inside the mall and can be completely viewed only when a customer has passed through the double doors, traveled the full length of the hallway and turned the corner. The sign once directly over the store is now outside the mall over the discount center which is the store directly in front of appellants'. The nearest parking spaces in the remaining parking area are now 100 feet away.

Appellants brought a complaint in equity seeking an injunction compelling appellee to relocate appellants' cleaning business to a situation comparable to that previously enjoyed by them. As an alternative form of relief, they sought an injunction ordering the appellee to demolish the store in front of appellants' shop or to lease that store to appellants. The final prayer was for an award of damages and such further relief as is required. Due to an agreement between the parties by the terms of which appellants vacated the premises and were released from their obligations under the lease, we will limit our consideration to the issues of liability and damages.

In every lease of real property there will be implied a covenant of quiet enjoyment. The covenant is between the landlord and his tenant and it is breached when a tenant's possession is impaired by acts of the lessor or those acting under him, or of the holder of a better title. "[T]here is an implied covenant for the quiet enjoyment of the demised premises, and it is settled in this State that any wrongful act of the landlord which results in an interference of the tenant's possession, in whole or in part, is an eviction for which the landlord is liable in damages to the tenant." Kelly v. Miller, 249 Pa. 314, 316–17, 94 A. 1055, 1056 (1915). Recovery for breach of this covenant has been allowed in Pennsylvania where a landlord has evicted the tenant by locking up the leased premises and denying the tenant access, and where the landlord so substantially altered some essential features of the premises as to render the property unsuitable for the purpose for which it was leased. In Kelly v. Miller, supra, the landlord sealed off doors by which the building leased by the tenant to be used as a theater was connected to the adjoining building, which was used for theater related purposes such as dressing rooms, storage and offices. Closing off the connecting apertures was found to detract from the demise to the tenant and violate the covenant of quiet enjoyment implied in the lease. "[The openings] were part of the demised premises at the date of the lease, and any change in them to the detriment of the tenant was a violation of the tenant's implied covenant for the quiet enjoyment of the property." Kelly v. Miller, supra at 317, 94 A. at 1056.

Appellants point to the construction of the mini mall as a substantial alteration of the leased premises, detrimental to the business which the parties understood would be conducted thereon, and contend that this action by the landlord breached the covenant of quiet enjoyment. It is pointed out that when the store was leased for a dry cleaning establishment it was an outside store with a prominent display window and easily accessible parking for customers. All these features made the property desirable for the location of a dry cleaning enterprise. The store was visible to potential customers using the supermarket and the rest of the shopping center, the working cleaning plant could be observed through the window, and advertisements could be displayed. Customers carrying clothes to and from the establishment would find the adjacent parking lot convenient. Each of these valuable features were lost upon construction of the mini mall. The once open, visible and accessible store is now surrounded, enclosed and cut off, without prior knowledge or consent on the part of the tenant, as effectively as if appellants were suddenly moved to an entirely different location. Furthermore, the construction itself with its attendant obstruction and confusion is indicated by appellants as a disruption of their business.

The alteration of the premises in question is analogous to that in Kelly v. Miller, supra. In both situations the utility of the property leased is substantially decreased due to the basic structural changes wrought by the landlord. Just as in *Kelly*, where the feature that made the property desirable, the connecting doors, was eliminated, in the present case the attractive features of the demised premises were eliminated by the acts of the landlord. These acts substantially interfered with the tenant's anticipated use of the premises and represent a breach of the covenant of quiet enjoyment.

The use of windows and pathways granting access to the leased structure, as well as a visible location, has been found in other jurisdictions to be protected by the covenant for quiet enjoyment. Thus in Owsley v. Hamner, 36 Cal.2d 710, 227 P.2d 263 (1951) it was held that where tenants leased a store which enjoyed an adjacent patio with display windows and passageways connecting the patio with the store and two streets, an attempt by the landlord to close the passages and eliminate the patio would be detrimental to the tenants' business and so substantially impair the leased premises as to violate the covenant of quiet enjoyment. The covenant of quiet enjoyment was found to be breached and the tenant evicted from a portion of the leased premises again in James v. Haley, 212 Cal. 142, 297 P. 920 (1931). The tenant in that case constructed a real estate office on the leased property, but during the term of his lease the landlord caused two buildings and a high fence to be constructed within inches of the tenant's building, blocking the public's view of the building and occupying portions of the premises previously used by the tenant for advertising. In Leventhal v. Straus, 197 Misc. 798, 95 N.Y.S.2d 883 (1950) it was held that the covenant was breached when the landlord constructed a porch over the one window in the tenant's apartment in such a way as to cut out the natural light and reduce the circulation of fresh air to the interior, the court noting that the tenant's right to beneficial enjoyment extended to some extent beyond the interior of the apartment including certain rights of access, light and ventilation with which the landlord could not interfere. The Supreme Court of Massachusetts in Winchester v. O'Brien, 266 Mass. 33, 164 N.E. 807 (1929) found for the tenant on the basis of similar reasoning stating that a substantial and continued interference with the tenant's dentistry practice occurred when the noise, dirt and obstruction of prolonged construction embarked upon by the landlord, plus sporadic interruptions of utilities incident thereto, impaired the character and value of the leased premises.

In view of the decisions of the court of this Commonwealth and other jurisdictions which recognize a tenant's right to the use of the leased property without disruption by the landlord, it is clear that a remedy exists in favor of the appellant-tenants in the present case due to the landlord's activity in making structural changes detrimental to the tenant without obtaining his consent. Because the parties have already come to an agreement releasing the tenants from their rights and obligations under the lease, the equitable remedy of injunction is no longer appropriate. However, appellants can be awarded damages. In cases of breach of the covenant of quiet enjoyment, or where the tenant is deprived of the beneficial enjoyment of the premises, it has been held that damages can be awarded for losses which can be proved. "The general rule laid down in the cases cited is, that the lessee may recover . . . for all losses which he can prove he has actually sustained, or which he will necessarily sustain, under the circumstances, as a result of the unlawful eviction. The measure of damages has been liberally extended to include even well established profits of the business . . . .." Minnich v. Kauffman, 108 A. at 598.

Damages for alleged lost profits however, cannot be awarded where they are merely speculative. Evidence must be introduced which forms a sufficient basis for estimating with reasonable certainty the amount of the lost anticipated profits. Whereas recovery for the lost profits of an established business are considered ascertainable to a reasonable degree of certainty, when a business is new and untried, courts have declared the measure of anticipated profits too speculative to provide a basis for an award of damages.

In the present case, appellants' dry cleaning business was only in operation for nine months before the landlord commenced construction of the mall. Appellant sought to show a reduction of profits by introducing an accountant who testified that the store's profits did not increase according to his projections. The estimation of the anticipated increase was of necessity based only on the nine months of operation preceding the construction which allegedly marked the beginning of the decline of the business. The lower court found, and we agree, that the basis for the accountant's projections and estimation of increasing profits is not established in the record. No foundation is laid for the assumption that the business would increase annually or that it would increase at the percentage the accountant estimated from the first few months of operation. Consequently we cannot permit a recovery for lost profits.

However, our holding that the anticipated profits were too speculative to support an award of damages does not defeat appellant's claim for damages. There was evidence in the record relating to the cost of moving appellants' enterprise to a suitable location. Appellant would be entitled to recover such an expense from the landlord whose actions compelled the relocation of the business, and the difficulties of proof involved in establishing such uncertain matters as future profits are not present. Because the lower court neglected to consider this element of damages in its adjudication, the case must be remanded to determine appellants' moving expenses, if any, and enter the same in judgment for the appellants.

Decree reversed and case remanded for proceedings consistent with this opinion.

[The concurring and dissenting opinion of SPAETH, J. is omitted.]

TEODORI v. WERNER

Supreme Court of Pennsylvania, 1980.
490 Pa. 58, 415 A.2d 31.

ROBERTS, Justice.

Tenant William Werner (appellant) seeks to open both a confessed money judgment and a confessed judgment of possession entered in favor of landlords Carlo and Mildred Teodori (appellees). Primarily at issue on this appeal is whether landlords' breach of the lease's "non-competition" clause provides tenant a defense to the landlord's actions for sums due and in ejectment. We are persuaded by our established case law, e.g., McDanel v. Mack Realty Co., 315 Pa. 174, 172 A. 97 (1934), and modern authority, e.g., Restatement (Second) of

Property, Landlord and Tenant (1977), that tenant has a valid defense.

I

Tenant leases a 1500 square foot retail storeroom in Donaldson's Crossroads Shopping Center where he operates his own retail jewelry business and gift shop. The parties' most recent written lease agreement, executed in June of 1973, provides for a five-year term of occupancy beginning August 1, 1973 and ending July 31, 1978. In the parties' "non-competition" clause, landlords agree not to "lease or operate as owner any space in the shopping center or any extension thereof primarily as a jewelry or gift shop."

In addition to a monthly base payment of $437.50, tenant annually is to pay to landlords five percent of the gross proceeds from jewelry sales and ten percent from gifts. Tenant also is to pay ten cents per square foot annually for maintenance of outside areas as well as increases in taxes owed by landlords and all charges for gas, water, sewer use, steam, electricity, light, heat or power, and telephone. Tenant is to render an annual "certified statement" showing the total gross proceeds of all business done upon the premises during the preceding year. Tenant also agrees, "on every default of payment of rent," or "on any and every breach of covenant or agreement," to "empower any attorney of any court of record" to appear for tenant and confess judgment against him. By the terms of the instrument this power of confession extends to an action for the sum due and/or an action in ejectment.

On September 2, 1977, eleven months before expiration of the stated term of the lease, landlords instituted a proceeding against tenant for entry of judgments by confession, seeking both a "specific amount due" and ejectment. Landlords based their request for both judgments on averments that tenant owed them monthly base payments, maintenance charges and utilities, and increased taxes. Landlords additionally claimed that tenant failed to provide landlords with a timely certified statement of gross proceeds and failed to pay the percentage of proceeds owing. Acting pursuant to the warrant of attorney contained in the lease agreement, counsel appeared for tenant and confessed judgment in landlords' favor in the amount of $7,056.29. Counsel also confessed judgment of possession. The prothonotary entered judgments the same day.

On September 15, 1977, less than two weeks after entry of the confessed judgments, tenant petitioned the Court of Common Pleas of Washington County to open both of the confessed judgments. As a defense, tenant alleged that landlords violated the parties' non-competition clause by leasing shopping center space to "Pennsylvania Wholesalers" for operation of a competing jewelry and gift shop business. Tenant also alleged that he did provide a certified statement of gross receipts and did pay the appropriate percentage.

The same day the chancellor issued a rule on appellees to show cause why the confessed judgments should not be opened, "all proceedings to stay meanwhile." In landlords' answer, they claimed that as to the alleged breach of the non-competition clause tenant "has no legal ground to stop paying rent in the present case." As to the certified statement clause, landlord alleged that "regardless of the statement of the defendant, he did not file a certified statement and a simple showing of evidence will prove this."

Landlords did not, however, seek a rule on tenant either to take depositions on the disputed factual issue concerning compliance with the certified statement clause or to order the case for argument. Instead, at the time they filed their answer, landlords requested the chancellor to set the matter for hearing. The chancellor granted landlords' request and scheduled a hearing. Landlords then filed an amended answer, setting forth the same claims contained in their original answer.

The matter then proceeded to argument, as requested by landlords. After argument, the chancellor dismissed tenant's petition to open. Executions were stayed when tenant filed a bond of $7300. On tenant's appeal, the Superior Court affirmed. This Court granted allowance of appeal.

II

At the outset we agree with tenant that landlords have admitted the factual allegations of tenant's petition to open. . . .

Because we accept as true tenant's factual allegations, the confessed judgments cannot stand on landlords' claim that tenant failed to comply with the parties' certified statements clause. Rather, the judgments can stand only if landlords are correct in their claim that, regardless of their compliance with the parties' non-competition clause, tenants owe an independent, continuing obligation throughout the term fully to pay them the stated rents. We agree, however, with tenant that landlords' view of tenant's obligation must be rejected.

Landlords' theory is unsupportable. It is true that "[a]t old common law the promises made by a landlord in a lease were independent obligations, so that the failure of the landlord to perform them did not give the tenant any right to disregard his obligations under the lease." Restatement (Second) of Property, Landlord and Tenant, supra, Introductory Note to Chapter 7. It is now clear, however, that this view of landlord-tenant relations, incorrectly resting more on notions of property law than on principles of contracts, has no place in modern jurisprudence. As long ago as 1934 this Court in McDanel v. Mack Realty Co., supra, recognized the error of the independence-of-obligations approach as applied to a commercial lease transaction. At issue in *McDanel* was the scope of the commercial tenant's remedies where the commercial landlord defaulted on its covenant to heat the leased premises. In addition to the options of (1) performing "at his own expense" and deducting this cost from the rent due or (2) surrendering the premises "to relieve himself from any further payment of rent," the tenant

> "(3) . . . can retain possession of the premises and deduct from the rent the difference between the rental value of the premises as it would have been if the lease had been fully complied with by the landlord and the rental value in the condition it actually was."

McDanel, 315 Pa. at 178, 172 A. at 98. And "[t]he emerging judicial sentiment in regard to the landlord's obligation to provide leased property that meets health and safety standards repudiates the independence-of-obligations approach in leases in that area. . . ." Restatement (Second) of Property, Landlord and Tenant, supra. So too the independence-of-obligations approach must be rejected where the landlord's promise to perform "is a significant inducement to the making of the lease by the tenant." Restatement (Second) of Property, Landlord and Tenant, supra. It is obvious that a landlord's non-competition promise is critical to a commercial lease agreement like the one here. "The mere presence in a lease of a noncompetition promise by the landlord justifies the conclusion that it is essential that the promise be observed if the tenant is to conduct his business on the leased property profitably." Id. at § 7.2 Comment b, p. 254. It therefore must be concluded that absent a contrary agreement between the parties a tenant's obligations are not independent of a landlord's promise under a non-competition clause.

Here, in withholding the full prescribed payments, tenant acted well within his rights. Section 7.2 of the Restatement provides:

> "Except to the extent the parties to a lease validly agree otherwise, the failure of the landlord to perform a promise contained in the lease that he, or someone holding under him, will not use other property in a manner that will compete with a business of the tenant, or of someone holding under the tenant, on the leased property, makes the landlord in default under the lease, if he does not cease, or cause to cease, the competing business within a reasonable time after being requested by the tenant to do so. For that default, the tenant may
>
> . . .
>
> (2) continue the lease and, if the landlord's promise is valid, obtain appropriate equitable and legal relief including the various remedies prescribed in § 7.1(2)."

These parties have not agreed otherwise. There is no dispute that tenant seasonably requested landlords to cease their violation. Nor is there any dispute that landlords' promise is valid.[5] The "various

---

5. Indeed, this promise, reasonable both in duration and scope, can serve a proper function. As Commentary to the Restatement points out,

remedies prescribed" include under section 11.1 abatement of rent. Both judgments therefore must be opened to permit tenant an opportunity to establish his defense.

III

Tenant also claims that the confessed money judgment of $7,055.29 must not only be opened but must also be stricken off, in its entirety. According to tenant, the money judgment improperly includes $4,812.50 in future rents for the remainder of the stated term of occupancy even though landlords, by way of their confessed action in ejectment, simultaneously obtained judgment of immediate possession. We see no reason, however, to strike the money judgment in its entirety on this ground alone. In their answer to tenant's petition to strike off, "[landlords] . . . go on record as dropping the request for future rental payments and charges after the date of eviction of the defendants from the premises."

On remand, the money judgment should be modified accordingly.

Order of the Superior Court reversed and case remanded for proceedings consistent with this opinion.

NOTES

1. Is Pollock v. Morelli consistent with the rules respecting the covenant of quiet enjoyment explored at pages 843 to 858, above? Was the court saying that the landlord committed an *actual eviction*? If so, what conduct constituted the requisite substantial interference with the tenant's premises? Or was the court saying that the landlord's conduct constituted a *partial actual eviction*? If so, did the court apply the correct remedy? Or was the court saying that the landlord's conduct constituted a *constructive eviction*? If so, why did the tenant's apparent failure to leave the premises during the construction period not constitute waiver?

Would the *Pollock* court have reached the same result if the landlord's expansion of the shopping center had affected the tenant only by increasing competition for parking spaces outside its store? See Northern Terminals, Inc. v. Smith Grocery & Variety, Inc., 138 Vt. 389, 418 A.2d 22 (1980) (covenant for quiet enjoyment breached). If an anchor tenant had moved out of the shopping center before its lease expired? If a competing tenant moved into the shopping center? In each of these situations, what would constitute the af-

"the use of a landlord's noncompetition promises is particularly significant in connection with the development of a shopping center designed to provide complete shopping services within a specific area. Using the space in the area for several businesses of the same type cuts down on the space available to provide different types of businesses, and makes it less likely that the shopping center complex will be able to attract the quality of businesses that may be essential to its financial success." . . .

firmative landlord conduct required for the covenant of quiet enjoyment to be breached?

Representing tenant or landlord, how would you have drafted the lease in Pollock v. Morelli to avoid the problems that arose there?

2. *Exclusive Use Clauses.* Do you agree with the result in Teodori v. Werner? Was there sufficient evidence before the court to support a decision that the landlords' "non-competition" obligation was in fact so vital that it affected the tenant's obligation to pay rent? Are commercial tenants better placed than residential tenants to resist onerous lease terms? To insist on an express provision that their obligation to pay rent will continue only so long as the landlord is not in default of specified obligations?

Would *Teodori* have excused the tenant from performance if one of the anchor tenants had moved out? If a competitor had moved into a new shopping center next door? If the new shopping center next door was owned by the same landlords as the old? Compare The Great Atlantic & Pacific Tea Co., Inc. v. Bailey, 421 Pa. 540, 220 A.2d 1 (1966) (noncompetition clause in supermarket's shopping center lease did not prevent lessors from leasing space to other food markets in after-acquired parcel adjacent to the shopping center).

Noncompetition clauses—more commonly called "exclusive use" clauses—are employed less frequently today than formerly. One reason is that, with the move to large regional and super-regional shopping centers, it has become virtually impossible to give exclusives to each of fifty, one hundred, or even more tenants. Another reason is that marketing studies show that, even in small centers, consumers are drawn to sites in which several satellite shops, as well as anchor tenants, offer competing goods. Finally, the Federal Trade Commission and the courts have applied antitrust law to curtail the use of exclusive use clauses because of their anticompetitive effects. See generally, P. Goldstein, Real Estate Transactions: Cases and Materials on Land Transfer, Development, and Finance 803–805 (1980).

3. Although Teodori v. Werner appears to represent a trend, courts and legislatures have generally been slower to imply interdependent covenants into commercial leases than into residential leases. For example, in Interstate Restaurants, Inc. v. Halsa Corp., 309 A.2d 108 (D.C.App.1973), the District of Columbia Court of Appeals held that a breaching restaurant lessee could not defend an action for possession on the ground that plaintiff lessor had also breached its obligations under the lease. Recognizing that "unless a contrary intention is expressed, the covenants in a lease are independent," and that "[w]here covenants are independent, nonperformance by one party does not excuse the other party from the need to satisfy his obligations," 309 A.2d at 110, the court rejected lessee's contention that the court's contemporaneous decision in Javins v. First National Realty Corp., page 941, above, had changed the previously established rule. "It is one thing for a court to enforce in urban rental housing an

implied warranty of habitability in accordance with Housing Regulations but quite another to intrude into established business practices in the hotel-restaurant commerce, as delineated in a negotiated lease. This case is quite removed from the urban housing setting of *Javins*." 309 A.2d at 111.

Courts have, however, applied contract doctrines of impossibility, impracticability and frustration to excuse commercial tenants from performing leases whose purpose has been completely thwarted by events outside the control of both landlord and tenant. Thus, in Industrial Development & Land Co. v. Goldschmidt, 56 Cal.App. 507, 206 P. 134 (1922), the court held that the national enactment of Prohibition excused a tenant from performing a lease which provided that the premises could only be used as a winery or liquor business. The strength of the impossibility or frustration defense will often turn on the narrowness of the permitted use clause. Compare Grace v. Croninger, 12 Cal.App.2d 603, 55 P.2d 940 (1936), in which the use clause allowed not only a saloon, but also a cigar store and shoe shine stand. The court refused to terminate the lease after the Wartime Prohibition Act was passed, holding that the other two uses were still possible.

See generally, Greenfield & Margolies, An Implied Warranty of Fitness in Nonresidential Leases, 45 Albany L.Rev. 855 (1981).

4. *Tort Liability.* Landlords and tenants have long been held liable to invitees and business visitors injured on their premises as a result of their negligence. See W. Prosser, Handbook of the Law of Torts 385–398, 403–405 (4th ed. 1971). Although they have historically not been liable for injuries caused by the criminal acts of third parties, this immunity is breaking down in the context of shopping centers just as it is in the context of multiple family dwellings.

In Butler v. Acme Markets, Inc., 89 N.J. 270, 445 A.2d 1141 (1982), plaintiff had been criminally attacked in the parking lot outside defendant's supermarket in which she had been shopping; the New Jersey Supreme Court upheld her claim that defendant "had been negligent in failing to warn and in failing to provide a safe place in which to shop and park." 89 N.J. at 274, 445 A.2d at 1142. The court rested its decision on the propositions that "[t]he proprietor of premises to which the public is invited for business purposes of the proprietor owes a duty of reasonable care to those who enter the premises upon that invitation to provide a reasonably safe place to do that which is within the scope of the invitation," and that "[i]f the reasonably prudent person would foresee danger resulting from another's voluntary criminal acts, the fact that another's actions are beyond defendant's control does not preclude liability." 89 N.J. at 275–276, 445 A.2d at 1143. The court acknowledged, however, "that not all courts or commentators agree that such a duty should be imposed." 89 N.J. at 281, 445 A.2d at 1146.

In response to the defendant's claim that police and security work was too specialized to be undertaken by defendants, the court pointed out that "the store was in fact furnishing security through the services of the community's trained police officers in their off-duty status. Their skills and training had been previously provided by government. In addition, trained private security services have now become widespread." Addressing the claim that it would be unfair to impose the cost of security on the supermarket, the court noted that "in the modern context of merchandising, our placement of these costs is consistent with the principles of the common law. Just as it is deemed fair for the owners and therefore indirectly the tenants of an apartment building, or the operators and patrons of a parking lot, to bear the costs of avoiding negligence, it is fair that the costs of negligent failure to protect against crime be similarly borne by the operators and indirectly patrons of such shopping facilities." 89 N.J. at 278–279, 445 A.2d at 1145.

What other public responsibilities does a shopping center owner impliedly undertake as a consequence of the scale and importance of its enterprise? See PruneYard Shopping Center v. Robins, page 70, above.

IV. BUILDING ON THE BASICS: THE CONDOMINIUM

Condominiums combine the economic attractions of home ownership with the social attractions of apartment living. They enable occupants to acquire an equity stake, with related tax and finance advantages, in dwellings such as high-rise apartments that were traditionally available only as short-term rentals. They also liberate occupants from the homeowner's usual upkeep responsibilities and, at the same time, give them a degree of control over their environment—through the power to hire and fire building managers—that tenants probably never know. Like so many other contemporary land use arrangements, condominiums exemplify the business lawyer's ability to accommodate social and economic change by crafting new legal institutions out of traditional common law materials—estates, tenancies in common, easements, covenants and servitudes.

Each occupant in a condominium owns his unit in fee simple absolute. He will receive a deed that describes his fee as a cube of space bounded by the unit's interior walls, and that also gives him an undivided fractional interest, as a tenant in common with all the other unit owners, in the project's common areas—exterior walls, roof, land, hallways, and common facilities such as laundry rooms, tennis courts and swimming pools. Because he has fee title, the unit owner can finance his purchase by giving a mortgage on the unit to secure a purchase money loan. In addition to his responsibility for the debt service (mortgage interest and principal) and real property taxes on his own unit, the owner must also pay a periodic maintenance fee to the condominium association to support its upkeep of the common areas.

Condominium ownership can be contrasted with another form of shared ownership—the cooperative. In a cooperative, title to the entire project—all of the individual units and all of the common areas—is vested in a single, non-profit cooperative corporation. Unlike the condominium owner, who receives a deed conveying fee title to his unit and an undivided interest in the common areas, each cooperator receives two instruments: a perpetually renewable proprietary lease to her unit, between herself as tenant and the cooperative corporation as landlord, and shares of stock in the cooperative corporation. A single mortgage will encumber the entire project and the cooperative corporation, as mortgagor, will pay the entire debt service as well as all real property taxes. The corporation will meet these and any other obligations from monthly rentals collected from the cooperator-tenants. The cooperator who fails to pay rent or to comply with her other leasehold responsibilities faces both summary eviction from the unit and the loss of her stock.

Because the condominium occupant is a fee owner and the cooperator is a tenant, they are sometimes treated differently for purposes of federal income taxation and real estate finance. While condominium owners have always enjoyed the homeowner's income tax deductions for mortgage interest, real property taxes and casualty losses, cooperators have only gradually, and partially, achieved tax parity with homeowners. See 26 U.S.C.A. § 216 (1976). The fact that cooperatives are financed through a single, blanket mortgage while condominiums are financed through individual mortgages on each unit, means that cooperators are far more financially interdependent than condominium owners. If one cooperator fails to pay rent, the other cooperators must chip in to cover her share of debt service on the blanket mortgage as well as her share of real property taxes and maintenance expenses. In good times, the burden will only be temporary, for the defaulting tenant will be evicted and a new tenant will quickly be found to pick up the vacant unit's share of expenses. In bad times, the results can be disastrous. Unable to find a new tenant, and unable to share the expense of the vacant unit indefinitely, the remaining tenants may begin to default, one after another, until the whole house of cards tumbles. Not surprisingly, the cooperative form of ownership has steadily lost its appeal, even in New York City where it was once almost the exclusive form of communal ownership.

Cooperators' rights and duties will be set out in the corporate charter, bylaws and proprietary lease. In a condominium, the governing document is the declaration, an instrument that, in form and content, is much like the Covenants, Conditions and Restrictions employed in residential subdivisions. In addition to providing a legal description of the project and of the individual units and common areas, the declaration will establish guidelines for the condominium's bylaws. The bylaws, in turn, will outline the procedures to be followed by the management association—the decision-making body of unit owners—in selecting a board of managers to supervise the condominium's ongoing activities, in authorizing expenditures for maintenance and reconstruction of common areas and facilities, and in adopting house rules governing day-to-day life in the condominium.

For background on cooperatives and condominiums generally, see P. Rohan & M. Reskin, Cooperative Housing Law and Practice (1983); P. Rohan & M. Reskin, Condominium Law and Practice (1983). See also, Symposium on the Law of Condominiums, 48 St. John's L.Rev. 677 (1974); D. Clurman & E. Hebard, Condominiums and Cooperatives (1970); A. Ferrer & K. Stecher, Law of Condominiums (1967).

NOTES

1. Although the condominium concept can be traced back at least to medieval times, it did not become popular in the United States until 1961, when Congress amended the National Housing Act to authorize the Federal Housing Administration to insure mortgages on condo-

miniums in states that had statutorily authorized this form of ownership. (Considerable doubt existed whether, without such enabling legislation, an ownership unit described only as a cube dangling in space could be legally conveyed and mortgaged in fee simple.) A model statute promulgated by the FHA the following year was quickly adopted or adapted across the country and, by 1969, every state had enacted a condominium statute. The FHA prototype can be found in FHA, Dept. of Housing & Urban Development, Model Statute for Creation of Apartment Ownership, Form # 3285 (1962). Citations to the state statutes are collected at Appendix B–1 to P. Rohan & M. Reskin, 1A Condominium Law and Practice (1983).

2. *Condominium Statutes.* State condominium statutes prescribe the ground rules for condominium organization and management. They specify the instruments, such as declaration, bylaws and house rules needed to create the condominium and to govern the unit owners, the structure, jurisdiction and powers of the management association and its board of managers, and the voting requirements for changing the governing instruments or institutions. The statutes also impose several substantive rules. For example, because of the central importance of the common areas, in which all unit owners have an undivided interest, most statutes provide that they cannot be partitioned.

Condominium statutes differ from state to state, sometimes in important ways. One source of difference is the states' varying responses to the expressed interests of condominium developers and consumers. Developers had objected to the first generation of condominium statutes, modelled on the FHA prototype, on the ground that they had been framed with high-rise apartment buildings in mind and thus ignored problems posed by low-rise lateral developments and by the frequent need to develop condominiums in stages rather than all at once. Consumers had objected that the early statutes did not control such prevalent developer abuses as obtaining overly generous management contracts from captive management associations.

The second generation of condominium statutes, typified by the National Conference of Commissioners' 1977 Uniform Condominium Act, responded by introducing the concept of the "flexible condominium," enabling developers to phase their projects. These statutes also strictly regulated management contracts entered into between the developer and the condominium owners association in the project's early stages and gave consumers a "cooling-off period," allowing rescission after execution of the sales contract, and quality warranties respecting the individual units and common areas. See generally §§ 1–103(13), 2–111; Art. 4. The Uniform Act was extensively amended in 1980.

For background on the two generations of condominium legislation, see Schreiber, The Lateral Housing Development: Condominium or Home Owners Association? 117 Pa.L.Rev. 1104 (1969); Rohan,

The "Model Condominium Code"—A Blueprint for Modernizing Condominium Legislation, 78 Colum.L.Rev. 587 (1978); Note, Recent Innovations in State Condominium Legislation, 48 St. John's L.Rev. 994 (1974); Thomas, The New Uniform Condominium Act, 64 A.B.A.J. 1370 (1978).

3. *Timesharing.* Condominium ownership can be divided in time as well as space, giving each of several owners the exclusive right to possess a single unit for a predetermined week or month every year. Timesharing projects blossomed across the country in the early 1980's, enabling individuals to purchase the right to possess a single unit in a resort townhouse, hotel, motel, campground, or even in a yacht, for increments of one week each year in perpetuity. Under one commonly used technique, called *time span ownership,* each participant holds an undivided fee simple interest in the unit as a tenant in common with as many as fifty-one cotenants; a separate agreement between the cotenants will identify the specific week or weeks during the year when each cotenant is entitled to occupy the unit.

Another form of timesharing is the *interval estate,* defined by the Uniform Condominium Act § 4–103 (1978) as a

> combination of (i) an estate for years in a unit, during the term of which title to the unit rotates among the time-share owners thereof, vesting in each of them in turn for periods established by a fixed recorded schedule, with the series thus established recurring regularly until the term expires, coupled with (ii) a vested undivided fee simple interest in the remainder in that unit, the magnitude of that interest having been established by the declaration or by the deed creating the interval estate.

A more direct approach is simply to convey a "fee" estate for a specified week or weeks each year in perpetuity. Other timesharing programs employ contracts, rather than real property interests, to give the purchaser a right to periodic use of the real property. See generally, Comment, Time-Share Condominiums: Property's Fourth Dimension, 32 Me.L.Rev. 181 (1980); Comment, Legal Challenges to Time Sharing Ownership, 45 Mo.L.Rev. 423 (1980).

States moved quickly to regulate timesharing projects. See, for example, Block, Regulation of Timesharing, 60 U. Detroit J. Urban L. 23 (1982).

A. MANAGEMENT AND CONTROL

BARCLAY v. DeVEAU

Supreme Court of Massachusetts, 1981.
384 Mass. 676, 429 N.E.2d 323.

LIACOS, Justice.

At issue in this appeal is whether a provision contained in the declaration of a condominium trust that permits the condominium developer to appoint two of the three members of the board of trustees, even though the developer owns only a small percentage of the condominium units, is invalid under G.L. c. 183A, § 10(a). The statute provides: "Each unit owner shall have the same percentage interest in the corporation, trust or unincorporated association provided for in the master deed for the management and regulation of the condominium as his proportionate interest in the common areas and facilities. Such interest shall not be separated from ownership in the unit to which it appertains and shall be deemed conveyed or encumbered with the unit even though such interest is not expressly mentioned or described in the conveyance or other instrument." G.L. c. 183A, § 10(a), inserted by St.1963, c. 493, § 1.

In apparent conflict with the statute is § 3.1.3 of the condominium trust which provides that "[u]ntil [the developer] owns less than 12 units, there shall not be more than three Trustees and it shall be entitled to designate two such Trustees."

The plaintiff, trustee of the Vendome Development Trust (development trust), filed a complaint in the Superior Court seeking to enjoin the defendants, who had been selected by the unit owners to replace the plaintiff's appointees, from exercising any power as trustees. The judge entered judgment for the plaintiff. On appeal, the Appeals Court, with one judge dissenting, reversed. We granted the plaintiff's application for further appellate review.

The facts are as follows. In 1975 the Franchi Development Trust, of which Pasquale Franchi is the sole beneficiary, established the Vendome Condominium Trust (condominium trust). The Vendome is Boston's first mixed commercial and residential condominium. After the Franchi Development Trust defaulted on a construction loan with its mortgagee, the Commonwealth Capital Investment Corporation (CCIC), the name of the trust was changed to Vendome Development Trust, the former trustee resigned, and CCIC appointed the plaintiff as trustee to manage the condominium and market the unsold condominium units. The plaintiff, as trustee of the development trust, appointed two trustees to the condominium trust pursuant to § 3.1.3 of the condominium trust.

In late 1977 the trustees of the condominium trust approved a 38% increase in common area charges.[4] At this time all but one of the 110 residential units had been sold. The developer, however, owned twenty-three of the commercial units, twenty of which were under long or short term leases, most with options to purchase. At a special meeting called by the unit owners on May 23, 1978, the unit owners voted, by approximately a 60% majority, to remove the two appointed trustees, expand the board to seven, and appoint as new

---

4. The increase in costs of operating the public areas and common facilities of the building, shared among all unit owners, was caused by increases in insurance premiums, maintenance, repair costs, and payroll. The management fee of $2,000 a month did not increase. The defendants do not contend that the trustees misrepresented the operating costs or otherwise acted fraudulently in this matter.

trustees the five persons who are the defendants in this case.[6] The unit owners purported to act under § 3.3 of the condominium trust, which grants the unit owners the power to remove a trustee by a vote of the owners of 51% of the beneficial interest. By the terms of § 3.3, however, this right is subordinate to the right of the development trust under § 3.1.3 to retain the trustees of its choice until fewer than twelve units remain unsold.[7]

The defendants, newly elected as trustees, claim that §§ 3.1.3 and 3.3 of the trust violate G.L. c. 183A, § 10.[8] The defendants argue that § 10(a) requires that a unit owner's percentage ownership interest in the association of unit owners, set up for the management and regulation of the condominium, be the same as his proportionate interest in the common areas and facilities. Although we agree that the unit owners have a proportionate interest in the association, we find nothing in the statute which prohibits the unit owners from entering into valid agreements for management and control of the condominium. The fact that the unit owners are entitled to a certain percentage interest in the association does not necessarily mean that the owners must have the same proportionate interest in management.

General Laws c. 183A, § 10(a), states that "[e]ach unit owner shall have the same percentage interest in the . . . trust . . . provided for in the master deed for the management and regulation of the condominium as his proportionate interest in the common areas and facilities." The defendants contend that this "interest" must include power to appoint and remove the trustees of the condominium trust and cannot be diluted through a developer control clause such as § 3.1.3. The plaintiff argues that a proportionate interest in the unit owners' association may be a beneficial one that includes, for example, rights in event of casualty losses and the right to make and the obligation to pay for capital improvements without including proportionate management rights.

1. *Legislative history of G.L. c. 183A.* We are mindful of the often-stated principle of statutory construction requiring us first to turn to the statutory language where it is plain and unambiguous for insight into the legislative purpose. But where the language of a provision is unclear, we may look to outside sources for assistance in determining the correct construction of the statute. The crucial language of G.L. c. 183A, § 10(a), is not free of ambiguity. To ascertain

6. The third member of the existing board, previously elected by the unit owners, was to remain in office. The seventh position on the new board was to be filled by the development trust.

7. Under the terms of the condominium trust, the trustees may amend the trust with the consent of the holders of 75% of the beneficial interest.

8. Section 2.1 of the condominium trust states that "this trust [is] the organization of the Unit Owners established pursuant to the provisions of section 10 of said Chapter 183A for the purposes therein set forth." The master deed and the confirmatory master deed of the Vendome Condominium recite that the condominium is governed by and subject to G.L. c. 183A. See G.L. c. 183A, § 2.

what the Legislature intended when it provided in G.L. c. 183A, § 10(*a*), that unit owners have a proportionate "interest" in the trust set up for the management of the condominium, we turn to the legislative history.

The legislative history of G.L. c. 183A indicates that the Legislature was aware of precisely this issue when it enacted the statute, i.e., whether and by what means the unit owners would be able to control the management association. What is now G.L. c. 183A was first reflected in 1963 House Doc. No. 1708. Under §§ 2(*d*), 18 & 19 of House 1708, the condominium would be administered by an unincorporated association whose by-laws were to be recorded as part of the declaration. This bill went further to structure that association and particularly referred to voting. Section 2(*k*) defined a majority for voting purposes as those "apartment owners with fifty-one per cent or more of the votes in accordance with the percentages assigned in the declaration to the apartments for voting purposes." Section 19 of House 1708 required that the by-laws provide for election of a board of directors for staggered terms from "among the apartment owners."

It was 1963 House Doc. No. 3324 that ultimately became G.L. c. 183A. Although retaining the concept of percentage interests expressed in House 1708 as the vehicle for shared ownership in the condominium, the provisions of House 1708 dealing with voting rights and the specific structure of the owners' organization were deleted and § 10(*a*) was substituted. Use of a corporate or trust form for the owners association was approved, rather than the unincorporated form found in House 1708. The Legislature refrained from including any specific language as to voting rights in § 10(*a*), which outlines the unit owners' powers of management, but retained certain limitations on majority rule by unit owners as set forth in House 1708. The Legislature apparently intended to leave the matter of who shall control the management of the common areas and facilities of the condominium to discretionary agreement among the unit owners and the developer. To infer that "interest" means "voting interest" would be to impose a structure in the association that the Legislature did not intend to require.

2. *Validity of § 3.1.3.* Although arguably the concept of a condominium was not unknown to the common law, condominium as a form of real estate ownership did not flourish until statutory authorization. The apparent purpose of c. 183A "was to clarify the legal status of the condominium in light of its peculiar characteristics." Grace v. Brookline, 379 Mass. 48, ___, 399 N.E.2d 1038 (1979). Statutes like c. 183A which imprint the condominium with legislative authorization are essentially enabling statutes. This statute provides planning flexibility to developers and unit owners. Unless expressly prohibited by clear legislative mandate, unit owners and developers may validly contract as to the details of management.

Absent overreaching or fraud by a developer, we find no strong public policy against interpreting c. 183A, § 10(a), to permit the developer and unit owners to agree on the details of administration and management of the condominium unit. Public policy actually favors this interpretation. Expert testimony at trial established that developer control clauses similar to § 3.1.3 of the condominium trust are common in Massachusetts. The developer and its mortgagee risk a great deal undertaking a condominium and, to protect their large investment, may need to maintain control of the project for a specific period of time. See Uniform Condominium Act (1977), 7 Uniform Laws Annot., § 3–103, Comment 3 (Master ed. 1978) (recognizing practical necessity of developer control during development phase of condominium project); 1 A. Ferrer & K. Stecher, Law of Condominium § 473, at 314 (1967) (developer desires effective role in project management if unsold units remain). Cf. D. Clurman & E. Hebard, Condominiums and Cooperatives 52 (1970) (unit mortgagees ordinarily impose controls on major management decisions by condominium boards).

The condominium trust in this case contains no express time limit on the developer's control. Under the express terms of the condominium trust the developer may retain control of the unit owners' association as long as twelve units are unsold. The defendants filed requests for rulings of law, one of which stated: "Because no time unit [sic] is placed on the power granted to the Vendome Development Trust by Article III, Section 3.1.3, the power, even if valid, will only be enforced for a reasonable period of time." The trial judge allowed this request, and the plaintiff concedes that a limitation of a reasonable period of time is properly placed on such a clause. Consequently, we need not determine whether such a limitation of time is necessarily implicit or will be imposed as a matter of policy on such provisions.

It is arguable, however, that an agreement designed to protect the developers' interests during the development and marketing phase of a condominium implicitly contains limitations of time on such a phase. "What is a reasonable time is a question of law, to be determined in reference to the nature of the contract and the probable intention of the parties as indicated by it." Warren v. Ball, 341 Mass. 350, 353, 170 N.E.2d 341 (1960), quoting from Campbell v. Whoriskey, 170 Mass. 63, 67, 48 N.E. 1070 (1898). A reasonable period of time is the period necessary to carry out the supposed intention of the parties, i.e., protect the developer while it is at risk. Such a view would be consistent with the basic concept of condominium, i.e., that unit owners will be afforded a proportionate voice in the management of the common areas and facilities.

We note that the judge treated the "marketing phase" of a condominium project as a reasonable period of time in which the developer may maintain control of the unit owners' association. The marketing phase of the condominium is that time during which the developer actively engages in selling the condominium units.[16] Notwithstanding this good faith effort, however, a point in time may be reached where, despite the presence of unsold units, the developer must relinquish control.[17]

The record before us does not clearly indicate what criteria the judge considered in determining that the Vendome Condominium was still in the marketing phase, nor does it reveal whether he considered the question of reasonable time apart from marketing efforts. In the amended findings and judgment, the judge stated that "[t]he primary aim of the Vendome Development Trust under Franchi's and the mortgage[e]'s direction, has been to sell the units and since twenty-three (23) commercial units were unsold, the Vendome Condominium was still in the marketing phase." As stated earlier, however, the inquiry is not whether a particular number of units remain unsold, but whether the developer is actively engaged in a bona fide effort to sell the units, and whether, in any event, the circumstances, considered as a whole, require a conclusion that control must pass to the unit owners.

3. *Conclusion.* We set aside the judgment and remand the case to the Superior Court for further proceedings consistent with this opinion.

So ordered.

---

16. Indicia of the "marketing phase" may include incomplete construction, retention of real estate brokers, advertisement in trade journals and local newspapers, and maintenance of a sales office. This list is neither exhaustive nor exclusive.

17. Although the Legislature has not adopted those portions of the Uniform Condominium Act dealing with developer control of a condominium association, § 3-103(d)-(e) of the Act may present useful guidelines to a trial judge in determining the reasonableness of developer control in terms of time, percentage interest owned, and marketing efforts. The relevant portions are as follows: "(d) Subject to subsection (e), the declaration may provide for a period of declarant control of the association, during which period a declarant, or persons designated by him, may appoint and remove the officers and members of the executive board. Regardless of the period provided in the declaration, a period of declarant control terminates no later than the earlier of: (i) [60] days after conveyance of [75] percent of the units which may be created to unit owners other than a declarant; (ii) [2] years after all declarants have ceased to offer units for sale in the ordinary course of business; or (iii) [2] years after any development right to add new units was last exercised. A declarant may voluntarily surrender the right to appoint and remove officers and members of the executive board before termination of that period, but in that event he may require, for the duration of the period of declarant control, that specified actions of the association or executive board, as described in a recorded instrument executed by the declarant, be approved by the declarant before they become effective.

"(e) Not later than [60] days after conveyance of [25] percent of the units which may be created to unit owners other than a declarant, at least one member and not less than [25] percent of the members of the executive board must be elected by unit owners other than the declarant. Not later than [60] days after conveyance of [50] percent of the units which may be created to unit owners other than the declarant, not less than [33^1/$_3$] percent of the members of the executive board must be elected by unit owners other than the declarant." Uniform Condominium Act (1980), 7 Uniform Laws Annot., § 3-103(d)-(e) (Master ed. supp. 1981).

B. RESTRAINTS ON ALIENATION

BREENE v. PLAZA TOWER ASSOCIATION
Supreme Court of North Dakota, 1981.
310 N.W.2d 730.

SAND, Justice.

This is an appeal by the defendant, Plaza Tower Association [hereinafter referred to as Association] from a summary judgment granted in favor of the plaintiffs, Janet Lucas Breene and A. William Lucas [hereinafter referred to as Breene], in which certain amendments to the by-laws of Plaza Tower were declared not legally binding upon Breene, and further, that any amendments that may be made to the declaration of restrictions of Plaza Tower would have only a prospective effect.

On 10 May 1974 Breene purchased unit 4D in the Plaza Tower condominium in the city of Bismarck, North Dakota. The association is a corporation organized under the North Dakota condominium statutes (Ch. 47–04.1, North Dakota Century Code) for the purpose of serving as managing and governing body for the condominium. When Breene purchased the interest in the condominium, there was no restriction relating to the sale or lease of the unit other than a provision giving the association the right of first refusal to purchase or lease the unit. The first-refusal option was in the association's bylaws by reference and specifically in the declaration of the condominium. At the time Breene purchased the unit, the declaration contained a provision which provided that the declaration could be amended at any regular or special meeting of the association by a vote of three-fourths of the members of the association.[1]

On 14 May 1979 the association passed and adopted an amendment to its bylaws. The amended bylaw in substance provided that all units of the condominium were to be occupied by the unit owner

---

1. This provision provides as follows:

"This Declaration may be amended at any regular or special meeting of the Association called or convened in accordance with the By-laws by the affirmative vote of the voting members casting not less than three-fourths (³/₄ths) of the total vote of the members of the Association. Each amendment shall be certified by the president and secretary of the Association as having been duly adopted and shall be effective when recorded in the office of the Register of Deeds of Burleigh County, North Dakota. No such amendment shall change any condominium parcel or a condominium unit's proportionate share of the common cost and expenses, nor the voting rights appurtenant to any unit unless all record owners thereof and all record owners of mortgages or other liens which have been voluntarily placed on a unit shall join in the execution of the amendment. No amendment shall be effective which shall impair or prejudice the rights or priorities of any mortgages or change the provisions of this Declaration with respect to mortgages without the written approval of the mortgagees of record."

and that the leasing of a unit to a non-owner was prohibited except in the following situations:

"a. An owner may enter a short term lease not to exceed four months provided the owner shall occupy the unit during the remainder of the calendar year within which the four month lease is granted.

"b. Leases which are in existence at the time this article is adopted shall not be impaired, but shall be permitted to continue during the designated lease term. Leases existing at the time of adoption of this article shall not be renewed or extended except to the extent that said renewal or extension would be in compliance with paragraph (a) above. Any month to month lease in existence at the time this article is adopted shall be terminated within three months of the adoption of this article.

"c. *Hardship Clause.* In the event that an owner, due to medical or health reasons or other justifiable cause constituting a hardship, shall be unable to occupy his unit for a period in excess of four months and based on said hardship desires to lease said unit, the owner shall make application to the Board of Directors which may, by majority vote and subsequent to a review of the application, grant to the owner an exception to the general leasing policy.

"d. This article shall not affect any unit which has been leased to the same tenant(s) by an owner in excess of three years, except that upon termination of any such tenancy in effect upon the date of adoption of this article all of the provisions of this article shall apply."

The amendment to the bylaws was not recorded in the office of the register of deeds of Burleigh County, pursuant to NDCC § 47–04.1–07.

By a letter dated 7 Nov. 1980, Breene requested permission from the president of the Association (Albert Hartl) to rent the condominium unit to another party. However, the request was denied and Breene commenced the present action to declare the Association's bylaws invalid as applied to unit 4D and to enjoin the Association from enforcing its bylaws against Breene.

Breene subsequently brought a motion for summary judgment and a hearing on that motion was held on 2 Feb. 1981. The district court granted Breene's motion in a memorandum opinion dated 3 Feb. 1981 and a judgment was entered on 9 Feb. 1981. A notice of appeal to this Court was filed on 11 Mar. 1981.

On 9 Feb. 1981, the same day the summary judgment was entered, the Association adopted two amendments to the declaration which placed restrictions on the right to lease which were similar to those contained in the bylaws adopted on 14 May 1979. The amendments to the declaration were recorded with the register of deeds of Burleigh County on 11 Feb. 1981.

The district court's memorandum opinion indicates that the subject matter before the court was tacitly heard and decided as if the amendment to the declaration had been adopted and recorded with the register of deeds' office.[2] Further, the judgment provided, in pertinent part, as follows:

"3.

"That any amendment to the declaration of restrictions of Plaza Tower Association which may be made or may become effective shall have prospective effect only, and shall not have any retroactive effect, and shall have no effect on owners of condominium units at the time such an amendment to the declaration should become effective."

Plaza Tower raised the following issue for our review:

Whether or not an amendment to the Declaration of a Condominium, restricting the use of an individual unit, may be applied retroactively to persons who had purchased a unit prior to promulgation of the amendments?

Breene asserts that this question was not a part of the declaratory judgment action and not part of the motion for summary judgment and, therefore, is not properly before this Court on appeal.

The judgment contains language giving only prospective effect to any amendment to the declaration of restrictions. Furthermore, the memorandum opinion contains similar language which reflects that the matter was tacitly heard and decided. Based on this, it is apparent that the district court judge considered the pending amendment to the declaration and tailored his ruling to deal with the amendment. Because of this we believe the issue concerning the amendment to the declaration is properly before this Court. . . .

Although it is inherent in the condominium concept that each unit owner must give up a certain degree of freedom of choice he might otherwise enjoy in separate, privately owned property, the condominium concept must operate within the applicable statutes as well as the constitutions.

The statutory provisions relating to condominiums requires that the declaration of condominium, the restrictions, and the bylaws must be recorded in the office of the register of deeds in the county where the property is located. These statutory provisions contemplate a method to put prospective purchasers and owners on notice as to the restrictions and bylaws which affect their interest in the property. A prospective purchaser's decision to buy a particular unit in a condominium may be based upon the recorded restrictions which encumber

---

2. The sequence of events, however, establishes that the amendment to the declaration was not adopted until after the judgment was entered. The judgment, and the record does not otherwise suggest how the amendment to the declaration was raised.

that unit. In order to exercise the decision to purchase a unit, the prospective buyer must be aware of restrictions on the use of the unit.

Of particular importance to the issue presented in this appeal is NDCC § 47–04.1–04, which deals with the requirements of a declaration of restrictions and provides, in part, as follows:

> "The owner of a project shall, *prior to the conveyance of any condominiums therein,* record a declaration of restrictions relating to such project which restrictions shall be enforceable equitable servitudes where reasonable, and shall inure to and bind all owners of condominiums in the project." [Emphasis added.]

This language contemplates that notice of restrictions through the recording procedures must be given to prospective buyers prior to the conveyance of any condominium unit. Although the statute provides that the restrictions shall be enforceable equitable servitudes, the statute also provides that a prerequisite to the enforceability is that the restriction be recorded prior to the conveyance of any condominium unit. A necessary corollary of this is that a restriction adopted after the purchase of a condominium unit would not be enforceable against the purchaser except through the purchaser's acquiescence.

We are cognizant that the benefits of statutory provisions may be waived. However, waiver requires knowledge of the rights intended to be waived and a voluntary and intentional relinquishment of those known rights. In this instance there is no indication and the issue was not raised that Breene waived the statutory rights contained in NDCC § 47–04.1–04. It is true, however, that the declaration provides that it may be amended, see footnote 1, and such a provision for an amendment may be broadly construed as a waiver of the rights contained in NDCC § 47–04.1–04. However, knowledge of the provisions for amendment does not, without more, constitute the degree of knowledge necessary to establish a voluntary and intentional relinquishment of the statutory right to notice of a restriction prior to the purchase of a condominium unit.

The Association cited several cases which they assert support their position and provide authority for imposing leasing restrictions retroactively by adopting an amendment to the declaration. We believe these cases are distinguishable.

Le Febvre v. Osterndorf, 87 Wis.2d 525, 275 N.W.2d 154 (Wis.App. 1979), involved a bylaw of a condominium which forbade the rental of condominium units. However, the particular bylaw was in effect when the buyer purchased his condominium unit and was not adopted, as in the instant case, after the buyer purchased his condominium unit.

Both Seagate Condominium Association, Inc. v. Duffy, 330 So.2d 484 (Fla.App.1976) and Ritchey v. Villa Nueva Condominium Association, 81 Cal.App.3d 688, 146 Cal.Rptr. 695, 100 A.L.R.3d 231 (1978) involved amendments to impose leasing restrictions which were adopted after the condominium unit was purchased. However, neither of these cases were decided in jurisdictions with a statutory provision such as NDCC § 47–04.1–04.

Although the California statute is somewhat similar, that statute goes on to provide for amendments to restrictions and that those amendments "shall be binding upon every owner and every condominium subject thereto whether the burdens thereon are increased or decreased thereby, and whether the owner of each and every condominium consents thereto or not." Cal.Civ.Code § 1355(c) (West).

The Florida statutes provide that the declaration "may include such covenants and restrictions concerning the use, occupancy and transfer of units as permitted by law." Fla.Stat. § 711.08(2). Additionally, "an amendment of a declaration shall become effective when recorded according to law." Fla.Stat. § 711.10(1).

These statutory provisions in essence permit amendments to the declaration of restrictions after a condominium is purchased and are not contained in the North Dakota statutes.

We have no doubt that amendments to the bylaws could be adopted which would be enforceable against those currently owning a condominium unit. However, these bylaws, pursuant to NDCC § 47–04.1–07, would have to relate to "maintenance of common elements, limited elements where applicable, assessment of expenses, payment of losses, division of profits, disposition of hazard insurance proceeds and similar matters." The action in the instant case is not within the scope of the subject matter of a bylaw and is, instead, governed by the provisions of NDCC § 47–04.1–04 relating to restrictions.

If the contentions of the Association are that the amendments are retroactive and apply to current owners, then the statutory provisions in NDCC § 47–04.1–04 requiring the recording of restrictions prior to any conveyance would in effect be treated as a nullity. This we cannot justifiably do. We are aware that NDCC Ch. 47–04.1 does not define "restrictions." In the absence of a definition, we believe "restrictions" within the context of Ch. 47–04.1 refers to restrictive covenants. However, it may be beneficial for the Legislature to enact a definition of "restrictions" indicating either what is embraced or excluded in the term.

Because the effect of the Association's amendment of the declaration of restrictions does not involve a genuine issue of material fact and the court construed and applied the applicable law correctly, we conclude that the district court properly entered summary judgment in favor of Breene, and accordingly the judgment is affirmed.

ERICKSTAD, C.J., and PAULSON, PEDERSON and VANDE WALLE, JJ., concur.

NOTE

One of the more publicized attributes of condominiums and cooperatives is the owner's reputed ability to control his environment, not only by voting on improvements, maintenance and repair, but also by prohibiting the resale or rental of units to people he would prefer not to have as neighbors. Newspapers periodically report the refusal by a condominium or cooperative board to allow resale to a celebrity whose lifestyle or entourage might prove disruptive. Former President Richard Nixon was rejected, first by a Manhattan cooperative board, and then by a condominium board, before giving up on his hopes for communal living and purchasing a townhouse on the City's Upper East Side. New York Times, October 5, 1979, B1; B3.

A board's rejection, or potential rejection, of a proposed purchaser may encounter one or more legal objections. If the board's refusal discriminates on a ground such as race or religion, it may violate the applicable Fair Housing Act. See Robinson v. 12 Lofts Realty, Inc., 610 F.2d 1032 (2d Cir.1979). Rights of first refusal, if not properly limited in time, may violate the Rule Against Perpetuities. See pages 575 to 587, above.

The common law rule against restraints on alienation, which is doubtless the major obstacle to enforcing these restrictions, treats cooperative and condominium restrictions differently. Courts have generally been more willing to accept restraints on the sale of a cooperator's stock and proprietary lease than to accept restraints on the sale of a condominium owner's fee interest. In part the difference in attitude stems from the technical distinction between leaseholds, which can lawfully be subjected to restraints on alienation, and fee estates, which cannot. And in part the difference stems from judicial recognition that, because cooperators are financially more interdependent than condominium owners, they have more legitimate reasons to screen prospective members who will, once accepted, share their communal mortgage and real estate tax burdens. See, for example, Weisner v. 791 Park Avenue Corp., 6 N.Y.2d 426, 434, 190 N.Y.S.2d 70, 74, 160 N.E.2d 720, 724 (1959) ("there is no reason why the owners of the co-operative apartment house could not decide for themselves with whom they wish to share their elevators, their common halls and facilities, their stockholders' meetings, their management problems and responsibilities and their homes").

Courts have also been more disposed, whether in the cooperative or condominium setting, to honor rights of first refusal—under which the Board may within a prescribed period match any offer received by a unit owner—than to honor outright prohibitions on resale without Board approval. The right of first refusal, also called a "preemptive option," can either be at a fixed, predetermined price, or at a price that matches the best *bona fide* offer received by the unit seller; the latter type is usually considered less offensive than the former. See Browder, Restraints on the Alienation of Condominium Units (The Right of First Refusal), 1970 U.Ill.L. Forum 231, 240–243.

The right of first refusal prescribed in the *Breene* declaration and bylaws would presumably pass muster as a reasonable restraint on alienation. Could the virtually absolute restriction on leases in excess of four months have been attacked as an unlawful restraint on alienation? Was the lower court correct to assume that, by giving the declaration amendments "prospective effect only," the amendments would not affect individuals who owned condominium units at the time the amendment was passed? Although the decision allowed Breene to freely lease his unit, it would appear that anyone who later purchased Breene's unit would not have this freedom. Would such a prospective purchaser take this restriction into account in deciding whether to purchase Breene's unit and, if so, how much to pay for it?

C. RESTRICTIONS ON OCCUPANCY AND USE

O'CONNOR v. VILLAGE GREEN OWNERS ASSOCIATION

Supreme Court of California, 1983.
33 Cal.3d 790, 191 Cal.Rptr. 320, 662 P.2d 427.

KAUS, Justice.

These consolidated appeals involve the validity and enforceability of an age restriction in the covenants, conditions and restrictions (CC & Rs) of a condominium development which limits residency to persons over the age of 18. In Marina Point, Ltd. v. Wolfson (1982) 30 Cal.3d 721, 180 Cal.Rptr. 496, 640 P.2d 115, we recently condemned such an age restriction in an apartment complex as violative of the Unruh Civil Rights Act (Civ.Code, § 51). We conclude that the age restriction in the CC & Rs of a condominium development also violates the act.

The Village Green is a housing complex of 629 units in the Baldwin Hills area of Los Angeles. It was built in 1942 and was operated as an apartment complex until 1973 when it was converted to a condominium development. As part of the condominium conversion the developer drafted and recorded a declaration of CC & Rs which run with the property and which contain a prohibition against residency by anyone under the age of 18. The CC & Rs also establish the Village Green Owners Association (association) and authorize it to enforce the regulations set forth therein. The association is a nonprofit organization whose membership consists of all owners of units at Village Green.

John and Denise O'Connor bought a two-bedroom unit in Village Green in 1975. On July 4, 1979, their son Gavin was born. Shortly thereafter, the association gave them written notice that the presence of their son Gavin in the unit constituted a violation of the CC & Rs and directed them to discontinue having Gavin live there.

After making unsuccessful attempts to find other suitable housing, the O'Connors filed a complaint against the association seeking to have the age restriction declared invalid and to enjoin its enforcement. The first amended complaint alleged, inter alia, that the age restriction violated the Unruh Civil Rights Act (Civ.Code, § 51).[2] The association filed a general demurrer which the trial court sustained without leave to amend. The action was dismissed and the O'Connors appealed.

After the O'Connors' notice of appeal was filed, the association filed an action to enjoin the O'Connors from residing in the condominium with their son. The trial court granted a preliminary injunction but stayed its enforcement for 90 days to allow the O'Connors to find other housing. The O'Connors filed a notice of appeal. Since the preliminary injunction was mandatory, the filing of the notice of appeal stayed its effect. This opinion disposes of both appeals.

In Marina Point, Ltd. v. Wolfson, *supra*, 30 Cal.3d 721, 180 Cal. Rptr. 496, 640 P.2d 115, we considered the question of whether the Unruh Civil Rights Act (the act) prohibited an apartment owner's discrimination against children. We reviewed the history of the act—Civil Code section 51—and noted that it had emanated from earlier "public accommodation" legislation and had extended the reach of such statutes from common carriers and places of accommodation to cover "all business establishments of every kind whatsoever."[3] Relying on our interpretation of the act in In re Cox (1970) 3 Cal.3d 205, 90 Cal.Rptr. 24, 474 P.2d 992, we held that the act barred all types of arbitrary discrimination. The act's reference to particular bases of discrimination—"sex, color, race, religion, ancestry or national origin"—was illustrative rather than restrictive.

We noted, however, that although the act prohibits a business establishment from engaging in any form of arbitrary discrimination, it does not absolutely prohibit such an establishment from excluding a customer in all circumstances. " 'Clearly, an entrepreneur need not tolerate customers who damage property, injure others or otherwise disrupt his business. A business establishment may, of course, promulgate reasonable deportment regulations that are rationally related to the services performed and the facilities provided.' " (Marina Point, Ltd. v. Wolfson, *supra*, 30 Cal.3d at p. 737, 180 Cal.Rptr. 496,

2. The complaint also alleged that the age restriction violated: (1) the Los Angeles City Ordinance which prohibits discrimination in rental housing on the basis of age, parenthood, or pregnancy; (2) the Fourteenth Amendment of the United States Constitution and article I, section 1, of the California Constitution; and (3) the California Fair Housing Law (Health & Saf.Code, § 35700 et seq.).

3. Unless otherwise noted, all section references hereafter are to the Civil Code.

Section 51 provides in relevant part: "This section shall be known, and may be cited, as the Unruh Civil Rights Act. All persons within the jurisdiction of this state are free and equal, and no matter what their sex, race, color, religion, ancestry, or national origin are entitled to the full and equal accommodations, advantages, facilities, privileges, or services in all business establishments of every kind whatsoever."

640 P.2d 115; quoting from In re Cox, *supra,* 3 Cal.3d at p. 217, 90 Cal.Rptr. 24, 474 P.2d 992.) We rejected, however, the landlord's contention in *Marina Point* that the exclusion of children was such a reasonable restriction. It was not a sufficient justification to state that children are "rowdier, noisier, more mischievous and more boisterous than adults." (30 Cal.3d at p. 737, 180 Cal.Rptr. 496, 640 P.2d 115.) Exclusion of persons based on a generalization about the class to which they belong is not permissible. Nor could exclusion of children from an ordinary apartment complex be justified on the basis that the presence of children does not accord with the nature of the business enterprise and of the facilities provided—as might be said of bars, adult book stores and senior citizens homes.

In sum, we held in *Marina Point* that the landlord's blanket exclusion of children from residency was prohibited by the act. It could not be justified by any claim about generalized characteristics of children or the nature of the apartment complex. Indeed, the claim that the facilities were incompatible with the presence of children was belied by the fact that children formerly had been permitted to reside in the complex.

In *Marina Point* there was no question that the apartment complex was a "business establishment" within the meaning of the act. The determinative question in that case was whether the act encompassed discrimination against children. Since that question was answered in *Marina Point,* the only question to be decided in the present case is whether the discriminatory policy against children is being invoked by a "business establishment" within the meaning of the act.

The act protects all persons from arbitrary discrimination in "accommodations, advantages, facilities, privileges or services in all business establishments of every kind whatsoever." We discussed the scope of that language in Burks v. Poppy Construction Co. (1962) 57 Cal.2d 463, 468–469, 20 Cal.Rptr. 609, 370 P.2d 313: "The Legislature used the words 'all' and 'of every kind whatsoever' in referring to business establishments covered by the Unruh Act (Civ.Code, § 51), and the inclusion of these words without any exception and without specification of particular kinds of enterprises, leaves no doubt that the term 'business establishments' was used in the broadest sense reasonably possible. The word 'business' embraces everything about which one can be employed, and it is often synonymous with 'calling, occupation, or trade, engaged in for the purpose of making a livelihood or gain.' The word 'establishment,' as broadly defined, includes not only a fixed location, such as the 'place where one is permanently fixed for residence or business,' but also a permanent 'commercial force or organization' or 'a permanent settled position as in life or business.' "

In *Burks,* we found it clear that a real estate developer who built and sold tract houses operated a "business establishment" within the meaning of the act.[4] We noted that the original version of the bill presented to the Legislature specifically referred to the right "to purchase real property" and to other rights, such as the obtaining of "professional" services, in addition to "business establishments." The final version, however, eliminated all specific references and added to the term "business establishments" the words "of every kind whatsoever." We concluded in *Burks* that the deletion of the specific reference to the purchase of real property could be explained on the ground that the Legislature deemed specific references no longer necessary in light of the broad language of the act as finally passed.

The O'Connors and amici urge us to apply the same reasoning to hold that the Village Green Owners Association is also a business establishment within the meaning of that term in the act. They note that among the specific references in the original version of the bill were "private or public groups, organizations, associations, business establishments, schools, and public facilities."[5] The broadened scope of business establishments in the final version of the bill, in our view, is indicative of an intent by the Legislature to include therein all formerly specified private and public groups or organizations that may reasonably be found to constitute "business establishments of every type whatsoever." Although our cases so far have all dealt with profit-making entities, we see no reason to insist that profit-seeking be a *sine qua non* for coverage under the act. Nothing in the language or history of its enactment calls for excluding an organization from its scope simply because it is nonprofit. Indeed, hospitals are often nonprofit organizations, and they are clearly business establishments to the extent that they employ a vast array of persons, care for an extensive physical plant and charge substantial fees to those who use the facilities. The Village Green Owners Association has sufficient businesslike attributes to fall within the scope of the act's reference to "business establishments of every kind whatsoever." Contrary to the association's attempt to characterize itself as but an organization that "mows lawns" for owners, the association in reality has a far broader and more businesslike purpose. The association, through a board of directors, is charged with employing a professional property management firm, with obtaining insurance for the bene-

---

4. The developer who established the Village Green CC & Rs, of course, would similarly be subject to the act. Thus the age restriction in this case, which was established by the developer, is invalid. This does not end our inquiry, however, since, as the association points out, it could simply cancel that age restriction and adopt one of its own. We therefore must also determine whether the association itself is a "business establishment" within the meaning of the act.

5. As introduced, the bill read in part: "All citizens within the jurisdiction of this State, no matter what their race, color, religion, ancestry, or national origin, are entitled to the full and equal admittance, accommodations, advantages, facilities, membership, and privileges in, or accorded by, all public or private groups, organizations, associations, business establishments, schools, and public facilities; to purchase real property; and to obtain the services of any professional person, group or associations."

fit of all owners and with maintaining and repairing all common areas and facilities of the 629-unit project. It is also charged with establishing and collecting assessments from all owners to pay for its undertakings and with adopting and enforcing rules and regulations for the common good. In brief, the association performs all the customary business functions which in the traditional landlord-tenant relationship rest on the landlord's shoulders. A theme running throughout the description of the association's powers and duties is that its overall function is to protect and enhance the project's economic value. Consistent with the Legislature's intent to use the term "business establishments" in the broadest sense reasonably possible, we conclude that the Village Green Owners Association is a business establishment within the meaning of the act.

Anticipating that it might be found to be a business establishment for purposes of applicability of the act, the association attempts to distinguish its discriminatory policy from that in *Marina Point* on the ground that it has fewer effective remedies for abating a nuisance caused by a child. Although a landlord does have the summary remedy of unlawful detainer proceedings for dealing with a disruptive child, we are not persuaded that the association is so powerless to remedy any problems arising from particular conduct that it must be permitted to maintain a discriminatory policy based on generalized traits. The association could adopt deportment regulations and rely on its normal procedures to enforce them. No reason appears why that would be any less effective than other use and conduct regulations the association may have. Moreover, we note that the restrictive covenant against children is already invalid under *Marina Point* as to units held as income property and rented out by their owners. The association therefore is already faced with the burden of planning for the presence of children.

The judgments in both actions are reversed.

BIRD, C.J., and REYNOSO and STERN, JJ., concur.

BROUSSARD, Justice, concurring.

I fully concur in the majority opinion. I would also rest our holding, however, on Civil Code section 53 as well as on Civil Code section 51.

Section 51 prohibits discrimination by a "business establishment" on grounds of "sex, race, color, religion, ancestry, or national origin . . . ." Section 53 deals more specifically with the problem of discriminatory restrictions on the use of real property. It provides in part: "(a) Every provision in a written instrument relating to real property which purports to forbid or restrict the conveyance, encumbrance, leasing, or mortgaging of such real property to any person of a specified sex, race, color, religion, ancestry, or national origin, is void and every restriction or prohibition as to the use or occupation of real property because of the user's or occupier's sex, race, color, religion, ancestry, or national origin is void. (b) Every restriction or prohibition, whether by way of covenant, condition upon use or occupation, or upon transfer of title to real property, which restriction or prohibition directly or indirectly limits the acquisition, use or occupation of such property because of the acquirer's, user's, or occupier's sex, race, color, religion, ancestry, or national origin is void. . . . ." Thus, *section 53 nullifies the arbitrarily discriminatory restriction itself.* Since the restriction is void, no party to it may enforce it, regardless of whether that party constitutes a "business establishment" under section 51.

Section 53 includes the same critical phrase as section 51: "sex, race, color, religion, ancestry, or national origin." In In re Cox (1970) 3 Cal.3d 205, 216, 90 Cal.Rptr. 24, 474 P.2d 992, we interpreted this phrase as used in section 51 as being "illustrative rather than restrictive . . . ."

. . . Section 51, originally enacted in 1905 (Stats.1905, ch. 413, § 1, p. 553) had been substantially amended to resemble more closely its current form in 1959 (Stats.1959, ch. 1866, § 1, p. 4424). Two years later, section 53 was enacted (Stats.1961, ch. 1877, § 1, pp. 3976–3977) and placed in close proximity to section 51 in part 2 of the Civil Code, entitled "Personal Rights." Section 53 contained the same critical phrase embodied in section 51 at that time. The critical phrase in section 53 has been amended only once since its enactment, and in the same 1974 legislation which amended the same clause in section 51. (Stats.1974, ch. 1193, § 1, p. 2568.)

These legislative actions clearly indicate that the Legislature has intended the critical phrase of section 53 to receive the same illustrative reading as is given to the identical phrase of section 51. Such an illustrative reading must similarly prohibit the *arbitrary discrimination* against families with children found to violate section 51 in *Wolfson.*[2] . . .

MOSK, Justice, dissenting.

I dissent.

Once again, a majority of this court undertake to legislate in a field—age preference—in which the Legislature has deliberately and repeatedly refused to act over the past six or more years. Having recently devised a new edict that there can be no age barriers in the business of rentals (Marina Point, Ltd. v. Wolfson (1982) 30 Cal.3d 721, 180 Cal.Rptr. 496, 640 P.2d 115), the majority now extend that rule by holding that a nonprofit association of condominium apartment owners is a "business" and therefore subject to the same prohibition against discrimination that is imposed on true business establishments.

2. Thus, as in *Wolfson,* restricting occupancy in a particular neighborhood to the elderly to create a senior environment may prove to be rationally related to a legitimate purpose, and *not* constitute arbitrary discrimination under section 53.

The majority are in error on both issues involved in this case. First, age preference has consistently been recognized as valid rather than invidious discrimination, both by the federal government and by the Legislature of California. Second, an association of homeowners—whether their homes are separate premises, or part of one structure as in a condominium apartment—cannot by any stretch of judicial imagination be held to be a business.

On the first point it bears emphasis that the United States Congress has adopted a number of programs to provide housing exclusively for those over 62. If an age restriction is valid at age 62, why cannot an age restriction be placed at age 18? Age preference is age preference, regardless of the precise chronological point at which it is placed.

Meanwhile our state Legislature, with knowledge that age preferences have been established in a number of housing developments, and that each was upheld whenever challenged in court, not only failed to add age to the other categories in Civil Code sections 51 and 53 which prohibit discrimination, but emphatically refused to do so whenever age was proposed as an addition to those sections. I fail to understand how my colleagues can arrogate to themselves the right to legislate in an area in which the Legislature has deliberately refused to do so.

Not only has the Legislature declined to outlaw age preferences, as recently as 1976 it placed its approval once again on Civil Code section 1355 which specifically directs, in the case of condominiums, that restrictions be recorded and they "shall be enforceable equitable servitudes where reasonable, and shall inure to and bind all owners of condominiums in the project. Such servitudes, unless otherwise provided, may be enforced by any owner of a condominium . . . ." The Legislature put only one limitation on the nature of restrictions that may be enforceable: they may not violate Civil Code section 711, which prohibits restraints on alienation. Indeed, the Legislature has preempted the entire field of condominium regulation in Civil Code section 1350 et seq., by adopting a uniform, comprehensive and pervasive means of creating condominium projects and defining the rights and obligations of owners of such projects.

On the second issue, the majority rely on *Marina Point, supra,* in which a divided court attempted to justify prohibiting age preference in the business of rental housing. In purporting to distinguish—and to permit—*some* age preferences, the majority's reasoning in that case seemed to depend on the "particular appurtenances and exceptional arrangements" (30 Cal.3d at p. 742, 180 Cal.Rptr. 496, 640 P.2d 115) for those housing units which are reserved for the elderly. Apparently my colleagues were primarily contemplating the archetypical homes for the aged and infirm—the "old folks' home." But their limited exception for the aged overlooked the numerous housing developments for those not elderly, but merely over 45, or over 55, or "senior citizens"—middle-aged or older persons who, in the words of Justice Richardson, dissenting in *Marina Point,* "having worked long and hard, having raised their own children, having paid both their taxes and their dues to society retain a right to spend their remaining years in a relatively quiet, peaceful and tranquil environment of their own choice" (*id.,* 30 p. 745).

Despite my misgivings in *Marina Point,* and those of Justice Richardson, I accept its result under compulsion. But *Marina Point* involved a business, a *rental business.* It did not affect the rights of individual owners in a condominium, bound together in a voluntary association operating for no profit, for no business purpose, solely for protection of the owner-members. Village Green owns no property; the transformation of such a loosely knit protective association into a "business" is stretching the concept of an entrepreneurial venture beyond all reason.

The Unruh Act (Civ.Code, § 51) provides, in relevant part: "All persons within the jurisdiction of this state are free and equal, and no matter what their sex, race, color, religion, ancestry, or national origin are entitled to the full and equal accommodations, advantages, facilities, privileges, or services in all *business establishments* of every kind whatsoever." (Italics added.)

Although the term "business establishments" is not defined in the foregoing code section, Chief Justice Gibson writing for a unanimous court in Burks v. Poppy Construction Co. (1962) 57 Cal.2d 463, 468, 20 Cal.Rptr. 609, 370 P.2d 313, defined the word "business" as: "[E]verything about which one can be *employed* and it is often synonymous with 'calling, occupation, or trade, *engaged in for the purpose of making a livelihood or gain.*'" (Italics added.) Again in Alcorn v. Anbro Engineering, Inc. (1970) 2 Cal.3d 493, 500, 86 Cal. Rptr. 88, 468 P.2d 216, this court, in discussing the 1959 amendments to section 51, stated in a unanimous opinion, "there is no indication that the Legislature intended to broaden the scope of section 51 to include discrimination other than those made by a 'business establishment' in the course of *furnishing goods, services or facilities to its clients, patrons or customers."* (Italics added.) The foregoing clearly demonstrate that the term "business establishments," as used in the Civil Code, is intended to apply only to commercial enterprises which serve customers, clients or patrons, and not to organizations which are in no way commercial or profit-seeking, such as a homeowners association.

Marina Point is not inconsistent with the foregoing. The majority opinion therein used the terms "business enterprise," "business establishment," or "entrepreneur" in referring to Civil Code section 51 on no less than 22 separate occasions, including the following quotes which clearly reveal the inapplicability of the section to a homeowners association: "As our prior decisions teach, the Unruh Act preserved the traditional broad authority of *owners and proprietors* of business establishments to adopt reasonable rules regulating the conduct of *patrons or tenants* . . . ." (30 Cal.3d at p. 725, 180 Cal. Rptr. 496, 640 P.2d 115, italics added.) "As we stated in *Cox:* 'In holding that the Civil Rights Act forbids a business establishment *generally open to the public* from arbitrarily excluding a prospective *customer,* we do not imply that the establishment may never insist that a *patron* leave the premises. Clearly, an *entrepreneur* need not tolerate *customers* who damage property, injure others or otherwise disrupt *his business.*'" (*Id.,* p. 737, 180 Cal.Rptr. 496, 640 P.2d 115, italics added.) "As these examples demonstrate, the exclusion of individuals from places of *public accommodation* or other business enterprises covered by the Unruh Act on the basis of class or group affiliation basically conflicts with the individual nature of the right afforded by the act of access to such enterprises . . . .. As our decisions in Cox, Orloff [v. Los Angeles Turf Club, 36 Cal.2d 734, 227 P.2d 449] and Stouman [v. Reilly, 37 Cal.2d 713, 234 P.2d 969], teach, although *entrepreneurs* unquestionably possess broad authority to protect their *enterprises* from improper and disruptive behavior, under the Unruh Act *entrepreneurs* must generally exercise this legitimate interest directly by excluding those persons who are in fact disruptive. *Entrepreneurs* cannot pursue a broad status-based exclusionary policy that operates to deprive innocent individuals of the services of the *business enterprise* to which section 51 grants 'all persons' access." (*Id.,* p. 740, 180 Cal.Rptr. 496, 640 P.2d 115, italics added.)

A homeowners association, the principal function of which is to perform or arrange for the services an owner of a single family dwelling would normally perform or arrange—such as mowing lawns, fixing defective plumbing, repairing roofs, cutting trees and watering gardens—does not come within the definition of the term "business establishment" as it is used throughout the decision in *Marina Point.* The association has no patrons, tenants or customers, only dues-paying members; it is in no way entrepreneurial in nature; and it is not open for public patronage. To consider the association a "business enterprise" under the Unruh Act would require the ludicrous holding that the owner-resident of a single family dwelling is engaged in a "business enterprise" when he or she hires a gardener or a plumber.

Again in Gay Law Students Ass'n v. Pacific Tel. & Tel. Co. (1979) 24 Cal.3d 458, 490, 156 Cal.Rptr. 14, 595 P.2d 592, this court emphasized that the Unruh Act represented a codification of the common law barring discrimination "*by public accommodations in the provision of services*" (italics added) and that other statutes on this subject "are in no sense declaratory of preexisting common law doctrine but rather include areas and subject matters of legislative innovation, creating new limitations." It followed that the statutory provisions were to be strictly construed, not merely deemed illustrative. There the court was concerned with employment practices, which would seem to be at least a first cousin to housing practices. . . .

The result in this case is disastrous for the many well-conceived, constructively operated developments in this state limited to persons over a prescribed age. They may not be a major factor in other jurisdictions, but they are particularly significant in California, which has the enticing environment and equable climate to attract many persons of middle and older age. These men and women, many of them having earned their right to retirement in other parts of the country, now make a major contribution to the economy of our state. Their comfort and peace of mind should not be deemed expendable on the altar of judicial creativity.

I would affirm the judgment.

RICHARDSON, J., concurs.

HIDDEN HARBOUR ESTATES, INC. v. BASSO

Court of Appeals of Florida, 1981.
393 So.2d 637.

MOORE, Judge.

Plaintiff, Hidden Harbour Estates, appeals from a final judgment denying its request for injunctive relief. Hidden Harbour had sought to enjoin the appellees from maintaining a shallow water well on their property. We affirm.

Hidden Harbour Estates is a condominium development containing mobile homes situated on lots owned by the individual residents. In 1975, Hidden Harbour's Board of Directors became aware of an increase in the salinity of the two deep well systems which supplied the water for the common usage of the unit owners. In May, 1975, the Board adopted a regulation that restricted lawn watering to one day per week while a member of the Board of Directors, Charles Burtoft, conducted a study of the water-salinity problem. Later in 1975, when the salinity of the well water decreased, the restriction was relaxed.

In November, 1975, the Bassos, who were owners of one of the mobile home units, applied to the Board of Directors for permission to drill a shallow well on their property. Such permission was allegedly required under the use restrictions in Article 13 of the Declaration of Condominium, which stated:

13.1. The use of the condominium will be in accordance with the following provisions, as long as the condominium exists:

a. . . . No temporary or permanent improvements or alterations may be made to any lot, and no lot owner may change the appearance of any portion of the exterior of his mobile home or apartment without the written approval of the Board of Directors of the Association.

A decision on the Bassos' request was not made until March, 1976, at which time it was denied, despite the fact that Burtoft had informed the Board that a shallow well would not affect the condominium water supply. The Board had three basic reasons, not articulated until the trial of this cause, for denying the Bassos' request:

(1) The threat of increased salinity;

(2) Staining of sidewalks and other common areas of the condominium;

(3) The proliferation of more wells by other unit owners.

The Bassos nonetheless drilled a well in early January, 1977. On January 31, 1977, Hidden Harbour brought an action for injunctive relief, alleging that the Bassos were in violation of the use restrictions of the Declaration of Condominium by drilling an unauthorized well. This action resulted in the judgment now appealed.

Before addressing ourselves to the merits of the trial court's decision, we will summarize the law in regard to the enforcement of use restrictions against condominium unit owners. As we opined in Sterling Village Condominium, Inc. v. Breitenbach, 251 So.2d 685 (Fla. 4th DCA 1971):

> Daily in this state thousands of citizens are investing millions of dollars in condominium property. Chapter 711, F.S.A., 1967, the Florida Condominium Act, and the Articles or Declarations of Condominiums provided for thereunder ought to be construed strictly to assure these investors that what the buyer sees the buyer gets. Every man may justly consider his home his castle and himself as the king thereof; nonetheless his sovereign fiat to use his property as he pleases must yield, at least in degree, where ownership is in common or cooperation with others. The benefits of condominium living and ownership demand no less. The individual ought not be permitted to disrupt the integrity of the common scheme through his desire for change, however laudable that change might be. Id. at 688.

Breitenbach involved an attempt by a unit owner to replace a screen enclosure with glass jalousies, even though the declaration of condominium prohibited "material alterations" or "substantial additions" to the common elements of the condominium. The screened enclosures were within the areas defined as common elements. Thus, even though Breitenbach's attempt to replace the screen enclosure was certainly a reasonable one and would have doubtlessly improved their unit, we were impelled to uphold the use restrictions in order to vindicate the condominium association's interest in maintaining a uniform exterior. A similar result occured in Pepe v. Whispering Sands Condominium Association, 351 So.2d 755 (Fla. 2nd DCA 1977), wherein the Court expressed the view that the restrictions in the declaration of condominium were of paramount importance in defining the rights and obligations of unit owners. The Court stated:

> A declaration of a condominium is more than a mere contract spelling out mutual rights and obligations of the parties thereto—

it assumes some of the attributes of a covenant running with the land, circumscribing the extent and limits of the enjoyment and use of real property. Stated otherwise, it spells out the true extent of the purchased, and thus granted, use interest therein. Absent consent, or an amendment of the declaration of condominium as may be provided for in such declaration, or as may be provided by statute in the absence of such a provision, this enjoyment and use cannot be impaired or diminished. Id. at 757–758.

Hidden Harbour Estates, Inc. v. Norman, 309 So.2d 180 (Fla. 4th DCA 1975) presented the question of whether a condominium association, through the exercise of its rule making powers, could prohibit the consumption of alcoholic beverages in the common areas of the condominium. In that case, we stated the "rule of reasonableness" to be the touchstone by which the validity of a condominium association's actions should be measured.

> Certainly, the association is not at liberty to adopt arbitrary or capricious rules bearing no relationship to the health, happiness and enjoyment of life of the various unit owners. On the contrary, we believe the test is reasonableness. If a rule is reasonable the association can adopt it; if not, it cannot. It is not necessary that conduct be so offensive as to constitute a nuisance in order to justify regulation thereof. Of course, this means that each case must be considered upon the peculiar facts and circumstances thereto appertaining. Id. at 182.

We found that the restriction on consumption of alcoholic beverages was reasonable because it was designed to "promote the health, happiness, and peace of mind of the majority of the unit owners." Id. at 182.

There are essentially two categories of cases in which a condominium association attempts to enforce rules of restrictive uses. The first category is that dealing with the validity of restrictions found in the declaration of condominium itself. The second category of cases involves the validity of rules promulgated by the association's board of directors or the refusal of the board of directors to allow a particular use when the board is invested with the power to grant or deny a particular use.

In the first category, the restrictions are clothed with a very strong presumption of validity which arises from the fact that each individual unit owner purchases his unit knowing of and accepting the restrictions to be imposed. Such restrictions are very much in the nature of covenants running with the land and they will not be invalidated absent a showing that they are wholly arbitrary in their application, in violation of public policy, or that they abrogate some fundamental constitutional right. Thus, although case law has applied the word "reasonable" to determine whether such restrictions are valid, this is not the appropriate test, and to the extent that our decisions have been interpreted otherwise, we disagree. Indeed, a use restriction *in a declaration of condominium* may have a certain degree of unreasonableness to it, and yet withstand attack in the courts. If it were otherwise, a unit owner could not rely on the restrictions found in the declaration of condominium, since such restrictions would be in a potential condition of continuous flux.

The rule to be applied in the second category of cases, however, is different. In those cases where a use restriction is not mandated by the declaration of condominium per se, but is instead created by the board of directors of the condominium association, the rule of reasonableness comes into vogue. The requirement of "reasonableness" in these instances is designed to somewhat fetter the discretion of the board of directors. By imposing such a standard, the board is required to enact rules and make decisions that are reasonably related to the promotion of the health, happiness and peace of mind of the unit owners. In cases like the present one where the decision to allow a particular use is within the discretion of the board, the board must allow the use unless the use is demonstrably antagonistic to the legitimate objectives of the condominium association, i.e., the health, happiness and peace of mind of the individual unit owners.

In the instant case, Hidden Harbour has articulated three basic reasons for denying the Bassos' request for permission to drill a well. First, the Board felt that such a well would increase the level of salinity in the deeper wells owned by the Hidden Harbour Condominium Association. Secondly, the Board believed the water pumped from the Bassos' well would impose a threat of staining the sidewalks and other common areas of the condominium association. Thirdly, the Board felt that if the Bassos were allowed to drill a well, then there would be a proliferation of other wells.

These reasons for denial were in the best interest of all of the unit owners, since they were legitimate objectives which would have promoted the aesthetic appeal of the condominium development. However, in order for the Board to justify its denial of the Bassos' application to drill a well, it was necessary that the Board be able to demonstrate that its denial was reasonably related to the fulfillment of the desired and laudable objectives mentioned above. This the Board failed to do. The evidence at trial indicated that the Bassos' well had no effect on the increased salinity of the wells owned by Hidden Harbour. In fact, this was known by one of the members of the Board of Directors at the time that the Bassos applied for permission to drill a well. No discoloration of commonly owned property had occurred at the time of trial, even though the Bassos frequently used the "illicit" well for more than a year and a half. Finally, there was not a shred of evidence to support a finding that the Bassos' well precipitated a proliferation of other wells in Hidden Harbour or that a proliferation of wells would be detrimental. Simply stated, Hidden Harbour failed to demonstrate a reasonable relationship between its denial of the Bassos' application and the objectives which the denial sought to achieve.

We also note that a trial court has wide discretion in denying or granting an injunction, and an appellate court will not interfere where no abuse of discretion has been made to appear.

We do not hold that, as a matter of law, Hidden Harbour was not entitled to injunctive relief in a situation similar to the one presently before this court. We merely hold that under the facts of this case, as demonstrated by the evidence at trial, such relief would not have been proper.

Accordingly, the judgment of the trial court is affirmed.

DOWNEY, J., concurs.

LETTS, C.J., concurs specially with opinion.

LETTS, Chief Judge, concurring specially.

I concur with the majority opinion with the additional comment that the Board's fear of a proliferation of wells, if a single one is allowed, would be justifiable as a matter of common sense. However, this comment in no way affects the failure to demonstrate any likelihood of increased salinity or staining.

Further, it goes without saying that if and when increased salinity or staining can be demonstrated, the Board will have the opportunity to return to court. Obviously on any such occasion, proliferation of wells will compound the adverse effect on the condominium property.

NOTE

The buyer who chooses the ease and efficiency of condominium ownership over the rigors and responsibilities of more traditional homeownership, must also give up some privacy and freedom in return. Living in a close-knit community means putting up with neighbors' often discrepant tastes in music, guests, pets and lifestyle. House rules will control some of this conduct but will also, necessarily, prevent the buyer from indulging her own full range of tastes. The fact that the line between permitted and proscribed conduct is set by a majority vote of unit owners, rather than by the impersonal decision of a landlord, is small solace to the owner who finds herself outlobbied and outvoted by her more aggressive or manipulative neighbors.

These perennial frustrations of communal life are doubtless aggravated by the fact that the ties that bind condominium owners are economic as well as social and political. All condominium owners are required to pay a periodic assessment for maintenance, repairs and improvements. When the assessment is for existing common areas and facilities, the gripes will be relatively few. Objections will, however, be far more frequent and substantial when the Board levies an assessment for construction of an improvement, such as a tennis court or swimming pool, that some members will never use, or refuses to levy an assessment to repair casualty damage that offends the handful of residents who live near the damaged area, but not residents in other parts of the project. See generally, Note, Living in a Condominium: Individual Needs Versus Community Interests, 46 Cin.L.Rev. 523 (1977).

Condominiums are in effect small, private communities and are governed and taxed—through assessments—much like more traditional communities such as villages and cities. Indeed, some of the obvious differences between these private communities and their public counterparts may be more apparent than real. Although the homeowners' grant of regulatory authority to their Association might seem to be more overtly premeditated and consensual than the social compact binding a polity, the two tend to approximate each other over time as homebuyers' decisions to move into one condominium or another begin to resemble homebuyers' decisions to move into one municipality or another. And, although the condominium community will typically be smaller than the political community, and the levers of power more evident and accessible, these are probably differences of degree rather than kind.

These similarities raise the obvious question whether rulemaking by condominium boards should, like land use decisions made by agencies of local government, be subjected to judicial review. Many courts have answered in the affirmative, and have tested board decisions against the same standards they apply to local governments' exercise of the police power: Is the rule reasonably related to its stated purposes? Are the stated purposes related to the community's health, safety, welfare and morals? Was the rule's enactment procedurally correct? Does it interfere with a vested right or expectation?

See generally, Ellickson, Cities and Homeowner Associations, 130 U.Pa.L.Rev. 1519 (1982); Reichman, Residential Private Governments: An Introductory Survey, 43 U.Chi.L.Rev. 253 (1976); Note, Judicial Review of Condominium Rulemaking, 94 Harv.L.Rev. 647 (1981).

Part Three

PUBLIC CONTROL OF OWNERSHIP AND USE

Historically, when landowners in the United States sought to impose order on their environment they relied on private easement and covenant arrangements with their neighbors and on the judicial enforcement of nuisance rules. Before 1916, when New York City enacted the country's first comprehensive zoning ordinance, regulating the location of office buildings, apartment houses and retail uses, municipalities generally confined their land use control efforts to excluding noxious industries from residential districts, setting maximum building heights and specifying safe building materials.

The development of public land use planning in the United States closely parallels the development of public land use controls. Throughout the nineteenth century, cities had engaged in a rough-hewn sort of planning by laying out the grids for prospective streets and avenues, effectively "drawing up a giant chessboard on which the forces of the market would build the future city." U.S. National Commission on Urban Problems, Building the American City 200 (1968). Then, in the 1890's, the so-called "City Beautiful" movement, sparked by the 1893 Chicago World's Fair, gave planners a grander object: to incorporate parks, plazas, boulevards and other such amenities into city life. Although the City Beautiful movement succeeded in crystallizing an ideal vision of the city, it ultimately had far less impact on urban design than the "City Practical" movement that followed it, focusing planners' efforts on good engineering principles and the efficient allocation of uses within a city.

The evolution toward comprehensive public land use controls and public land use planning, though steady, has not been uniform. For example, Houston, Texas has conscientiously resisted the adoption of a zoning ordinance and relies instead on private restrictive covenants; the City does, however, have subdivision controls, a building code and a planning department. Occasionally, voters will try to cast off land use controls altogether. In November, 1982, the voters of Tehama County, California, narrowly approved an initiative measure, the "Landowner's Bill of Rights," designed to repeal virtually all land use controls then operative in the county, as well as to prohibit the county legislature from enacting new ones. (Opponents of the measure argued that the "number of governmental departments, subdivisions, bureaus, public agencies, civil codes, and court decisions regulating land usage in behalf of public health and safety is so vast that no piece of legislation—on any level of government—designed to eradicate their control in one fell swoop could accomplish its goal."

Sample Ballot, General Election, Nov. 2, 1982, County of Tehama 52–14.) And a new wave of land use scholars has begun to ask whether market forces and private arrangements may, at least in some areas, produce better results than centralized planning and control. See, for example, Ellickson, Alternatives to Zoning: Covenants, Nuisance Rules, and Fines as Land Use Controls, 40 U.Chi.L.Rev. 681 (1973); B. Siegan, Land Use Without Zoning (1972).

Several of the themes and issues already considered in this book's discussion of private land use arrangements recur in the context of public land use controls. Nuisance law's strictly economic balance of utility and gravity of harm gains an added, political element when voters and public officials weigh the benefits and costs of adopting a land use measure. The problem of providing quality housing at a price that low income residents can afford has doubtless been aggravated by the efforts of suburbs to exclude low-income residential land uses from their borders.

Yet, the emphases differ. Because the public control of land use necessarily implicates state action, it unavoidably raises the question whether that action is properly grounded in the state's police power. And, because it is the use of land that is being regulated, the question often arises whether a measure, even if properly grounded in the police power, takes private property without the "just compensation" required by the Fifth Amendment to the United States Constitution, as applied to the states under the Fourteenth Amendment. Furthermore, even if there is an admitted, compensated taking, the questions arise whether it was animated by the constitutionally requisite "public purpose," and whether the compensation paid was "just."

Second, because control of land use is really control of individual behavior, civil liberties may be affected. Does the regulation of building design in order to preserve a homogenous neighborhood infringe on free speech interests protected by the First Amendment? And what of the interests of individuals—students, racial minorities, the poor—whom a municipality consciously excludes from its boundaries? Zoning has a long history of exclusion, beginning with efforts by California municipalities to exclude Chinese immigrants. And, as Richard Babcock has bluntly observed, zoning has, since the 1920's, "provided the device for protecting the homogenous, single-family suburb from the city." R. Babcock, The Zoning Game 3 (1966).

Finally, because political forces and bureaucratic structures dominate public land use controls, the decisions produced are not always amenable to the kind of neat doctrinal analysis that works so well in cases involving private land use arrangements. The play of bureaucratic and political forces also means that "law in the books" is far less important than "law in action"—law as it is shaped by the day-to-day dealings of public officials and private citizens. Recognizing this, I have, at pages 1213 to 1272, included a case study of a zoning variance proceeding from start to finish, in an attempt to give some flavor of the political and administrative realities that pervade this area.

For purposes of general reference, the standard treatises are: R. Anderson, American Law of Zoning (2d ed. 1976); A. Rathkopf & D. Rathkopf, The Law of Zoning and Planning (4th ed. 1983); and N. Williams, American Planning Law (1974). D. Hagman, Urban Planning and Land Development Control Law (1971) is a useful hornbook; R. Ellickson & A.D. Tarlock, Land-Use Controls (1981), is a fine casebook; and J. Delafons, Land-Use Controls in the United States (2d ed. 1969) provides an excellent overview of law and practice. For a lively and immensely readable tour through the history of zoning in the United States, see S. Toll, Zoned American (1969).

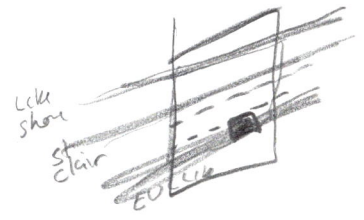

I. THE SOURCES AND LIMITS OF STATE POWER

A. "HEALTH, SAFETY, WELFARE AND MORALS"

VILLAGE OF EUCLID v. AMBLER REALTY CO.
Supreme Court of the United States, 1926.
272 U.S. 365, 47 S.Ct. 114, 71 L.Ed. 303.

Mr. Justice SUTHERLAND delivered the opinion of the Court.

The village of Euclid is an Ohio municipal corporation. It adjoins and practically is a suburb of the city of Cleveland. Its estimated population is between 5,000 and 10,000, and its area from 12 to 14 square miles, the greater part of which is farm lands or unimproved acreage. It lies, roughly, in the form of a parallelogram measuring approximately 3½ miles each way. East and west it is traversed by three principal highways: Euclid avenue, through the southerly border, St. Clair avenue, through the central portion, and Lake Shore boulevard, through the northerly border, in close proximity to the shore of Lake Erie. The Nickel Plate Railroad lies from 1,500 to 1,800 feet north of Euclid avenue, and the Lake Shore Railroad 1,600 feet farther to the north. The three highways and the two railroads are substantially parallel.

Appellee is the owner of a tract of land containing 68 acres, situated in the westerly end of the village, abutting on Euclid avenue to the south and the Nickel Plate Railroad to the north. Adjoining this tract, both on the east and on the west, there have been laid out restricted residential plats upon which residences have been erected.

On November 13, 1922, an ordinance was adopted by the village council, establishing a comprehensive zoning plan for regulating and restricting the location of trades, industries, apartment houses, two-family houses, single family houses, etc., the lot area to be built upon, the size and height of buildings, etc.

The entire area of the village is divided by the ordinance into six classes of use districts, denominated U–1 to U–6, inclusive; three classes of height districts, denominated H–1 to H–3, inclusive; and four classes of area districts, denominated A–1 to A–4, inclusive. The use districts are classified in respect of the buildings which may be erected within their respective limits, as follows: U–1 is restricted to single family dwellings, public parks, water towers and reservoirs, suburban and interurban electric railway passenger stations and rights of way, and farming, noncommercial greenhouse nurseries, and truck gardening; U–2 is extended to include two-family dwellings; U–3 is further extended to include apartment houses, hotels, churches, schools, public libraries, museums, private clubs, community center buildings, hospitals, sanitariums, public playgrounds, and recreation buildings, and a city hall and courthouse; U–4 is further extended to include banks, offices, studios, telephone exchanges, fire and police stations, restaurants, theaters and moving picture shows, retail stores and shops, sales offices, sample rooms, wholesale stores for hardware, drugs, and groceries, stations for gasoline and oil (not exceeding 1,000 gallons storage) and for ice delivery, skating rinks and dance halls, electric substations, job and newspaper printing, public garages for motor vehicles, stables and wagon sheds (not exceeding five horses, wagons or motor trucks), and distributing stations for central store and commercial enterprises; U–5 is further extended to include billboards and advertising signs (if permitted), warehouses, ice and ice cream manufacturing and cold storage plants, bottling works, milk bottling and central distribution stations, laundries, carpet cleaning, dry cleaning, and dyeing establishments, blacksmith, horseshoeing, wagon and motor vehicle repair shops, freight stations, street car barns, stables and wagon sheds (for more than five horses, wagons or motor trucks), and wholesale produce markets and salesrooms; U–6 is further extended to include plants for sewage disposal and for producing gas, garbage and refuse incineration, scrap iron, junk, scrap paper, and rag storage, aviation fields, cemeteries, crematories, penal and correctional institutions, insane and feeble-minded institutions, storage of oil and gasoline (not to exceed 25,000 gallons), and manufacturing and industrial operations of any kind other than, and any public utility not included in, a class U–1, U–2, U–3, U–4, or U–5 use. There is a seventh class of uses which is prohibited altogether.

Class U–1 is the only district in which buildings are restricted to those enumerated. In the other classes the uses are cumulative—that is to say, uses in class U–2 include those enumerated in the preceding class U–1; class U–3 includes uses enumerated in the preceding classes, U–2 and U–1; and so on. In addition to the enumerated uses, the ordinance provides for accessory uses; that is, for uses customarily incident to the principal use, such as private garages. Many regulations are provided in respect of such accessory uses.

The height districts are classified as follows: In class H–1, buildings are limited to a height of 2½ stories, or 35 feet; in class H–2, to 4 stories, or 50 feet; in class H–3, to 80 feet. To all of these, certain exceptions are made, as in the case of church spires, water tanks, etc.

The classification of area districts is: In A–1 districts, dwellings or apartment houses to accommodate more than one family must have at least 5,000 square feet for interior lots and at least 4,000 square feet for corner lots; in A–2 districts, the area must be at least

2,500 square feet for interior lots, and 2,000 square feet for corner lots; in A–3 districts, the limits are 1,250 and 1,000 square feet, respectively; in A–4 districts, the limits are 900 and 700 square feet, respectively. The ordinance contains, in great variety and detail, provisions in respect of width of lots, front, side, and rear yards, and other matters, including restrictions and regulations as to the use of billboards, signboards, and advertising signs.

A single family dwelling consists of a basement and not less than three rooms and a bathroom. A two-family dwelling consists of a basement and not less than four living rooms and a bathroom for each family, and is further described as a detached dwelling for the occupation of two families, one having its principal living rooms on the first floor and the other on the second floor.

Appellee's tract of land comes under U–2, U–3 and U–6. The first strip of 620 feet immediately north of Euclid avenue falls in class U–2, the next 130 feet to the north, in U–3, and the remainder in U–6. The uses of the first 620 feet, therefore, do not include apartment houses, hotels, churches, schools, or other public and semipublic buildings, or other uses enumerated in respect of U–3 to U–6, inclusive. The uses of the next 130 feet include all of these, but exclude industries, theaters, banks, shops, and the various other uses set forth in respect of U–4 to U–6, inclusive.

Annexed to the ordinance, and made a part of it, is a zone map, showing the location and limits of the various use, height, and area districts, from which it appears that the three classes overlap one another; that is to say, for example, both U–5 and U–6 use districts are in A–4 area districts, but the former is in H–2 and the latter in H–3 height districts. The plan is a complicated one, and can be better understood by an inspection of the map, though it does not seem necessary to reproduce it for present purposes.

The lands lying between the two railroads for the entire length of the village area and extending some distance on either side to the north and south, having an average width of about 1,600 feet, are left open, with slight exceptions, for industrial and all other uses. This includes the larger part of appellee's tract. Approximately one-sixth of the area of the entire village is included in U–5 and U–6 use districts. That part of the village lying south of Euclid avenue is principally in U–1 districts. The lands lying north of Euclid avenue and bordering on the long strip just described are included in U–1, U–2, U–3, and U–4 districts, principally in U–2.

The enforcement of the ordinance is intrusted to the inspector of buildings, under rules and regulations of the board of zoning appeals. Meetings of the board are public, and minutes of its proceedings are kept. It is authorized to adopt rules and regulations to carry into effect provisions of the ordinance. Decisions of the inspector of buildings may be appealed to the board by any person claiming to be adversely affected by any such decision. The board is given power in

1080   PUBLIC CONTROL OF OWNERSHIP AND USE   Pt. 3

specific cases of practical difficulty or unnecessary hardship to interpret the ordinance in harmony with its general purpose and intent, so that the public health, safety and general welfare may be secure and substantial justice done. Penalties are prescribed for violations, and it is provided that the various provisions are to be regarded as independent and the holding of any provision to be unconstitutional, void or ineffective shall not affect any of the others.

The ordinance is assailed on the grounds that it is in derogation of section 1 of the Fourteenth Amendment to the federal Constitution in that it deprives appellee of liberty and property without due process of law and denies it the equal protection of the law, and that it offends against certain provisions of the Constitution of the state of Ohio. The prayer of the bill is for an injunction restraining the enforcement of the ordinance and all attempts to impose or maintain as to appellee's property any of the restrictions, limitations or conditions. The court below held the ordinance to be unconstitutional and void, and enjoined its enforcement.

Before proceeding to a consideration of the case, it is necessary to determine the scope of the inquiry. The bill alleges that the tract of land in question is vacant and has been held for years for the purpose of selling and developing it for industrial uses, for which it is especially adapted, being immediately in the path of progressive industrial development; that for such uses it has a market value of about $10,000 per acre, but if the use be limited to residential purposes the market value is not in excess of $2,500 per acre; that the first 200 feet of the parcel back from Euclid avenue, if unrestricted in respect of use, has a value of $150 per front foot, but if limited to residential uses, and ordinary mercantile business be excluded therefrom, its value is not in excess of $50 per front foot.

It is specifically averred that the ordinance attempts to restrict and control the lawful uses of appellee's land, so as to confiscate and destroy a great part of its value; that it is being enforced in accordance with its terms; that prospective buyers of land for industrial, commercial, and residential uses in the metropolitan district of Cleveland are deterred from buying any part of this land because of the existence of the ordinance and the necessity thereby entailed of conducting burdensome and expensive litigation in order to vindicate the right to use the land for lawful and legitimate purposes; that the ordinance constitutes a cloud upon the land, reduces and destroys its value, and has the effect of diverting the normal industrial, commercial, and residential development thereof to other and less favorable locations.

The record goes no farther than to show, as the lower court found, that the normal and reasonably to be expected use and development of that part of appellee's land adjoining Euclid avenue is for general trade and commercial purposes, particularly retail stores and like establishments, and that the normal and reasonably to be expected use and development of the residue of the land is for industrial and trade purposes. Whatever injury is inflicted by the mere existence and threatened enforcement of the ordinance is due to restrictions in respect of these and similar uses, to which perhaps should be added—if not included in the foregoing—restrictions in respect of apartment houses. Specifically there is nothing in the record to suggest that any damage results from the presence in the ordinance of those restrictions relating to churches, schools, libraries, and other public and semipublic buildings. It is neither alleged nor proved that there is or may be a demand for any part of appellee's land for any of the last-named uses, and we cannot assume the existence of facts which would justify an injunction upon this record in respect to this class of restrictions. For present purposes the provisions of the ordinance in respect of these uses may therefore be put aside as unnecessary to be considered. It is also unnecessary to consider the effect of the restrictions in respect of U-1 districts, since none of appellee's land falls within that class.

We proceed, then, to a consideration of those provisions of the ordinance to which the case as it is made relates, first disposing of a preliminary matter.

A motion was made in the court below to dismiss the bill on the ground that, because complainant (appellee) had made no effort to obtain a building permit or apply to the zoning board of appeals for relief, as it might have done under the terms of the ordinance, the suit was premature. The motion was properly overruled, the effect of the allegations of the bill is that the ordinance of its own force operates greatly to reduce the value of appellee's lands and destroy their marketability for industrial, commercial and residential uses, and the attack is directed, not against any specific provision or provisions, but against the ordinance as an entirety. Assuming the premises, the existence and maintenance of the ordinance in effect constitutes a present invasion of appellee's property rights and a threat to continue it. Under these circumstances, the equitable jurisdiction is clear.

It is not necessary to set forth the provisions of the Ohio Constitution which are thought to be infringed. The question is the same under both Constitutions, namely, as stated by appellee: Is the ordinance invalid, in that it violates the constitutional protection "to the right of property in the appellee by attempted regulations under the guise of the police power, which are unreasonable and confiscatory"?

Building zone laws are of modern origin. They began in this country about 25 years ago. Until recent years, urban life was comparatively simple; but, with the great increase and concentration of population, problems have developed, and constantly are developing, which require, and will continue to require, additional restrictions in respect of the use and occupation of private lands in urban communities. Regulations, the wisdom, necessity, and validity of which, as applied to existing conditions, are so apparent that they are now uniformly sustained, a century ago, or even half a century ago, probably would have been rejected as arbitrary and oppressive. Such regulations are sustained, under the complex conditions of our day, for reasons analogous to those which justify traffic regulations, which, before the advent of automobiles and rapid transit street railways, would have been condemned as fatally arbitrary and unreasonable. And in this there is no inconsistency, for, while the meaning of constitutional guaranties never varies, the scope of their application must expand or contract to meet the new and different conditions which are constantly coming within the field of their operation. In a changing world it is impossible that it should be otherwise. But although a degree of elasticity is thus imparted, not to the *meaning*, but to the *application* of constitutional principles, statutes and ordinances, which, after giving due weight to the new conditions, are found clearly not to conform to the Constitution, of course, must fall.

The ordinance now under review, and all similar laws and regulations, must find their justification in some aspect of the police power, asserted for the public welfare. The line which in this field separates the legitimate from the illegitimate assumption of power is not capable of precise delimitation. It varies with circumstances and conditions. A regulatory zoning ordinance, which would be clearly valid as applied to the great cities, might be clearly invalid as applied to rural communities. In solving doubts, the maxim "sic utere tuo ut alienum non laedas," which lies at the foundation of so much of the common law of nuisances, ordinarily will furnish a fairly helpful clew. And the law of nuisances, likewise, may be consulted, not for the purpose of controlling, but for the helpful aid of its analogies in the process of ascertaining the scope of, the power. Thus the question whether the power exists to forbid the erection of a building of a particular kind or for a particular use, like the question whether a particular thing is a nuisance, is to be determined, not by an abstract consideration of the building or of the thing considered apart, but by considering it in connection with the circumstances and the locality. A nuisance may be merely a right thing in the wrong place, like a pig in the parlor instead of the barnyard. If the validity of the legislative classification for zoning purposes be fairly debatable, the legislative judgment must be allowed to control.

There is no serious difference of opinion in respect of the validity of laws and regulations fixing the height of buildings within reasonable limits, the character of materials and methods of construction, and the adjoining area which must be left open, in order to minimize the danger of fire or collapse, the evils of overcrowding and the like, and excluding from residential sections offensive trades, industries and structures likely to create nuisances.

Here, however, the exclusion is in general terms of all industrial establishments, and it may thereby happen that not only offensive or dangerous industries will be excluded, but those which are neither offensive nor dangerous will share the same fate. But this is no more than happens in respect of many practice-forbidding laws which this court has upheld, although drawn in general terms so as to include individual cases that may turn out to be innocuous in themselves. The inclusion of a reasonable margin, to insure effective enforcement, will not put upon a law, otherwise valid, the stamp of invalidity. Such laws may also find their justification in the fact that, in some fields, the bad fades into the good by such insensible degrees that the two are not capable of being readily distinguished and separated in terms of legislation. In the light of these considerations, we are not prepared to say that the end in view was not sufficient to justify the general rule of the ordinance, although some industries of an innocent character might fall within the proscribed class. It cannot be said that the ordinance in this respect "passes the bounds of reason and assumes the character of a merely arbitrary fiat." Purity Extract Co. v. Lynch, 226 U.S. 192, 204, 33 S.Ct. 44, 47 (57 L.Ed. 184). Moreover, the restrictive provisions of the ordinance in this particular may be sustained upon the principles applicable to the broader exclusion from residential districts of all business and trade structures, presently to be discussed.

It is said that the village of Euclid is a mere suburb of the city of Cleveland; that the industrial development of that city has now reached and in some degree extended into the village, and in the obvious course of things will soon absorb the entire area for industrial enterprises; that the effect of the ordinance is to divert this natural development elsewhere, with the consequent loss of increased values to the owners of the lands within the village borders. But the village, though physically a suburb of Cleveland, is politically a separate municipality, with powers of its own and authority to govern itself as it sees fit, within the limits of the organic law of its creation and the state and federal Constitutions. Its governing authorities, presumably representing a majority of its inhabitants and voicing their will, have determined, not that industrial development shall cease at its boundaries, but that the course of such development shall proceed within definitely fixed lines. If it be a proper exercise of the police power to relegate industrial establishments to localities separated from residential sections, it is not easy to find a sufficient reason for denying the power because the effect of its exercise is to divert an industrial flow from the course which it would follow, to the injury of the residential public, if left alone, to another course where such injury will be obviated. It is not meant by this, however, to exclude the possibility of cases where the general public interest would so far outweigh the interest of the municipality that the municipality would not be allowed to stand in the way.

We find no difficulty in sustaining restrictions of the kind thus far reviewed. The serious question in the case arises over the provisions of the ordinance excluding from residential districts apartment houses, business houses, retail stores and shops, and other like establishments. This question involves the validity of what is really the crux of the more recent zoning legislation, namely, the creation and maintenance of residential districts, from which business and trade of every sort, including hotels and apartment houses, are excluded. Upon that question this court has not thus far spoken. The decisions of the state courts are numerous and conflicting; but those which broadly sustain the power greatly outnumber those which deny it altogether or narrowly limit it, and it is very apparent that there is a constantly increasing tendency in the direction of the broader view. . . .

The matter of zoning has received much attention at the hands of commissions and experts, and the results of their investigations have been set forth in comprehensive reports. These reports, which bear every evidence of painstaking consideration, concur in the view that the segregation of residential, business and industrial buildings will make it easier to provide fire apparatus suitable for the character and intensity of the development in each section; that it will increase the safety and security of home life, greatly tend to prevent street accidents, especially to children, by reducing the traffic and resulting confusion in residential sections, decrease noise and other conditions which produce or intensify nervous disorders, preserve a more favorable environment in which to rear children, etc. With particular reference to apartment houses, it is pointed out that the development of detached house sections is greatly retarded by the coming of apartment houses, which has sometimes resulted in destroying the entire section for private house purposes; that in such sections very often the apartment house is a mere parasite, constructed in order to take advantage of the open spaces and attractive surroundings created by the residential character of the district. Moreover, the coming of one apartment house is followed by others, interfering by their height and bulk with the free circulation of air and monopolizing the rays of the sun which otherwise would fall upon the smaller homes, and bringing, as their necessary accompaniments, the disturbing noises incident to increased traffic and business, and the occupation, by means of moving and parked automobiles, of larger portions of the streets, thus detracting from their safety and depriving children of the privilege of quiet and open spaces for play, enjoyed by those in more favored localities—until, finally, the residential character of the neighborhood and its desirability as a place of detached residences are utterly destroyed. Under these circumstances, apartment houses, which in a different environment would be not only entirely unobjectionable but highly desirable, come very near to being nuisances.

If these reasons, thus summarized, do not demonstrate the wisdom or sound policy in all respects of those restrictions which we have indicated as pertinent to the inquiry, at least, the reasons are sufficiently cogent to preclude us from saying, as it must be said before the ordinance can be declared unconstitutional, that such provisions are clearly arbitrary and unreasonable, having no substantial relation to the public health, safety, morals, or general welfare. . . .

test

. . . What would be the effect of a restraint imposed by one or more or the innumerable provisions of the ordinance, considered apart, upon the value or marketability of the lands, is neither disclosed by the bill nor by the evidence, and we are afforded no basis, apart from mere speculation, upon which to rest a conclusion that it or they would have any appreciable effect upon those matters. Under these circumstances, therefore, it is enough for us to determine, as we do, that the ordinance in its general scope and dominant features, so far as its provisions are here involved, is a valid exercise of authority, leaving other provisions to be dealt with as cases arise directly involving them.

And this is in accordance with the traditional policy of this court. In the realm of constitutional law, especially, this court has perceived the embarrassment which is likely to result from an attempt to formulate rules or decide questions beyond the necessities of the immediate issue. It has preferred to follow the method of a gradual approach to the general by a systematically guarded application and extension of constitutional principles to particular cases as they arise, rather than by out of hand attempts to establish general rules to which future cases must be fitted. This process applies with peculiar force to the solution of questions arising under the due process clause of the Constitution as applied to the exercise of the flexible powers of police, with which we are here concerned.

Decree reversed.

NECTOW v. CITY OF CAMBRIDGE

Supreme Court of the United States, 1928.
277 U.S. 183, 48 S.Ct. 447, 72 L.Ed.2d 842.

Mr. Justice SUTHERLAND delivered the opinion of the Court.

A zoning ordinance of the city of Cambridge divides the city into three kinds of districts, residential, business, and unrestricted. Each of these districts is subclassified in respect of the kind of buildings which may be erected. The ordinance is an elaborate one, and of the same general character as that considered by this court in Euclid v. Ambler Co., 272 U.S. 365, 47 S.Ct. 114, 71 L.Ed. 303. In its general scope it is conceded to be constitutional within that decision. The land of plaintiff in error was put in district R–3, in which are permitted only dwellings, hotels, clubs, churches, schools, philanthropic institutions, greenhouses and gardening, with customary incidental accessories. The attack upon the ordinance is that, as specifically applied to plaintiff in error, it deprived him of his property without due process of law in contravention of the Fourteenth Amendment.

The suit was for a mandatory injunction directing the city and its inspector of buildings to pass upon an application of the plaintiff in error for a permit to erect any lawful buildings upon a tract of land without regard to the provisions of the ordinance including such tract within a residential district. The case was referred to a master to make and report findings of fact. After a view of the premises and the surrounding territory, and a hearing, the master made and reported his findings. The case came on to be heard by a justice of the court, who, after confirming the master's report, reported the case for the determination of the full court. Upon consideration, that court sustained the ordinance as applied to plaintiff in error, and dismissed the bill.

A condensed statement of facts, taken from the master's report, is all that is necessary. When the zoning ordinance was enacted, plaintiff in error was and still is the owner of a tract of land containing 140,000 square feet, of which the locus here in question is a part. The locus contains about 29,000 square feet, with a frontage on Brookline street, lying west, of 304.75 feet, on Henry street, lying north, of 100 feet, on the other land of the plaintiff in error, lying east, of 264 feet, and on land of the Ford Motor Company, lying southerly, of 75 feet. The territory lying east and south is unrestricted. The lands beyond Henry street to the north and beyond Brookline street to the west are within a restricted residential district. The effect of the zoning is to separate from the west end of plaintiff in error's tract a strip 100 feet in width. The Ford Motor Company has a large auto assembling factory south of the locus; and a soap factory and the tracks of the Boston & Albany Railroad lie near. Opposite the locus, on Brookline street, and included in the same district, there are some residences; and opposite the locus, on Henry street, and in the same district, are other residences. The locus is now vacant, although it was once occupied by a mansion house. Before the passage of the ordinance in question, plaintiff in error had outstanding a contract for the sale of the greater part of his entire tract of land for the sum of $63,000. Because of the zoning restrictions, the purchaser refused to comply with the contract. Under the ordinance, business and industry of all sorts are excluded from the locus, while the remainder of the tract is unrestricted. It further appears that provision has been made for widening Brookline street, the effect of which, if carried out, will be to reduce the depth of the locus to 65 feet. After a statement at length of further facts, the master finds:

"That no practical use can be made of the land in question for residential purposes, because among other reasons herein related, there would not be adequate return on the amount of any investment for the development of the property."

The last finding of the master is:

"I am satisfied that the districting of the plaintiff's land in a residence district would not promote the health, safety, convenience, and general welfare of the inhabitants of that part of the defendant city, taking into account the natural development thereof and the character of the district and the resulting benefit to accrue to the whole city and I so find."

It is made pretty clear that because of the industrial and railroad purposes to which the immediately adjoining lands to the south and east have been devoted and for which they are zoned, the locus is of comparatively little value for the limited uses permitted by the ordinance.

We quite agree with the opinion expressed below that a court should not set aside the determination of public officers in such a matter unless it is clear that their action "has no foundation in reason and is a mere arbitrary or irrational exercise of power having no substantial relation to the public health, the public morals, the public safety or the public welfare in its proper sense." Euclid v. Ambler Co., supra, p. 395 (47 S.Ct. 121).

An inspection of a plat of the city upon which the zoning districts are outlined, taken in connection with the master's findings, shows with reasonable certainty that the inclusion of the locus in question is not indispensable to the general plan. The boundary line of the residential district before reaching the locus runs for some distance along the streets, and to exclude the locus from the residential district requires only that such line shall be continued 100 feet further along Henry street and thence south along Brookline street. There does not appear to be any reason why this should not be done. Nevertheless, if that were all, we should not be warranted in substituting our judgment for that of the zoning authorities primarily charged with the duty and responsibility of determining the question. But that is not all. The governmental power to interfere by zoning regulations with the general rights of the land owner by restricting the character of his use, is not unlimited, and, other questions aside, such restriction cannot be imposed if it does not bear a substantial relation to the public health, safety, morals, or general welfare. Here, the express finding of the master, already quoted, confirmed by the court below, is that the health, safety, convenience, and general welfare of the inhabitants of the part of the city affected will not be promoted by the disposition made by the ordinance of the locus in question. This finding of the master, after a hearing and an inspection of the entire area affected, supported, as we think it is, by other findings of fact, is determinative of the case. That the invasion of the property of plaintiff in error was serious and highly injurious is clearly established; and, since a necessary basis for the support of that invasion is wanting, the action of the zoning authorities comes within the ban of the Fourteenth Amendment and cannot be sustained.

Judgment reversed.

VILLAGE OF BELLE TERRE v. BORAAS

Supreme Court of the United States, 1974.
416 U.S. 1, 94 S.Ct. 1536, 39 L.Ed.2d 797.

Mr. Justice DOUGLAS delivered the opinion of the Court.

Belle Terre is a village on Long Island's north shore of about 220 homes inhabited by 700 people. Its total land area is less than one square mile. It has restricted land use to one-family dwellings excluding lodging houses, boarding houses, fraternity houses, or multiple-dwelling houses. The word "family" as used in the ordinance means, "[o]ne or more persons related by blood, adoption, or marriage, living and cooking together as a single housekeeping unit, exclusive of household servants. A number of persons but not exceeding two (2) living and cooking together as a single housekeeping unit though not related by blood, adoption, or marriage shall be deemed to constitute a family."

Appellees, the Dickmans, are owners of a house in the village and leased it in December 1971 for a term of 18 months to Michael Truman. Later Bruce Boraas became a colessee. Then Anne Parish moved into the house along with three others. These six are students at nearby State University at Stony Brook and none is related to the other by blood, adoption, or marriage. When the village served the Dickmans with an "Order to Remedy Violations" of the ordinance, the owners plus three tenants thereupon brought this action under 42 U.S.C. § 1983 for an injunction and a judgment declaring the ordinance unconstitutional. The District Court held the ordinance constitutional, and the Court of Appeals reversed, one judge dissenting. The case is here by appeal, and we noted probable jurisdiction.

. . . The present ordinance is challenged on several grounds: that it interferes with a person's right to travel; that it interferes with the right to migrate to and settle within a State; that it bars people who are uncongenial to the present residents; that it expresses the social preferences of the residents for groups that will be congenial to them; that social homogeneity is not a legitimate interest of government; that the restriction of those whom the neighbors do not like trenches on the newcomers' rights of privacy; that it is of no rightful concern to villagers whether the residents are married or unmarried; that the ordinance is antithetical to the Nation's experience, ideology, and self-perception as an open, egalitarian, and integrated society.

. . . We deal with economic and social legislation where legislatures have historically drawn lines which we respect against the charge of violation of the Equal Protection Clause if the law be " 'reasonable, not arbitrary' " (quoting F.S. Royster Guano Co. v. Virginia, 253 U.S. 412, 415, 40 S.Ct. 560, 561, 64 L.Ed. 989) and bears "a rational relationship to a [permissible] state objective." Reed v. Reed, 404 U.S. 71, 76, 92 S.Ct. 251, 254, 30 L.Ed.2d 225.

It is said, however, that if two unmarried people can constitute a "family," there is no reason why three or four may not. But every line drawn by a legislature leaves some out that might well have been included. That exercise of discretion, however, is a legislative, not a judicial, function.

It is said that the Belle Terre ordinance reeks with an animosity to unmarried couples who live together. There is no evidence to support it; and the provision of the ordinance bringing within the definition of a "family" two unmarried people belies the charge.

The ordinance places no ban on other forms of association, for a "family" may, so far as the ordinance is concerned, entertain whomever it likes.

The regimes of boarding houses, fraternity houses, and the like present urban problems. More people occupy a given space; more cars rather continuously pass by; more cars are parked; noise travels with crowds.

A quiet place where yards are wide, people few, and motor vehicles restricted are legitimate guidelines in a land-use project addressed to family needs. This goal is a permissible one within Berman v. Parker, *supra* [348 U.S. 26, 75 S.Ct. 98, 99 L.Ed. 27 (1954)]. The police power is not confined to elimination of filth, stench, and unhealthy places. It is ample to lay out zones where family values, youth values, and the blessings of quiet seclusion and clean air make the area a sanctuary for people. . . .

Reversed.

[The opinion of BRENNAN, J., dissenting, is omitted.]

Mr. Justice MARSHALL, dissenting.

This case draws into question the constitutionality of a zoning ordinance of the incorporated village of Belle Terre, New York, which prohibits groups of more than two unrelated persons, as distinguished from groups consisting of any number of persons related by blood, adoption, or marriage, from occupying a residence within the confines of the township. Lessor-appellees, the two owners of a Belle Terre residence, and three unrelated student tenants challenged the ordinance on the ground that it establishes a classification between households of related and unrelated individuals, which deprives them of equal protection of the laws. In my view, the disputed classification burdens the students' fundamental rights of association and privacy guaranteed by the First and Fourteenth Amendments. Because the application of strict equal protection scrutiny is therefore required, I am at odds with my Brethren's conclusion that the ordinance may be sustained on a showing that it bears a rational relationship to the accomplishment of legitimate governmental objectives.

I am in full agreement with the majority that zoning is a complex and important function of the State. It may indeed be the most essential function performed by local government, for it is one of the primary means by which we protect that sometimes difficult to define concept of quality of life. I therefore continue to adhere to the principle of Village of Euclid v. Ambler Realty Co., 272 U.S. 365, 47 S.Ct. 114, 71 L.Ed. 303 (1926), that deference should be given to governmental judgments concerning proper land-use allocation. That deference is a principle which has served this Court well and which is necessary for the continued development of effective zoning and land-use control mechanisms. Had the owners alone brought this suit alleging that the restrictive ordinance deprived them of their property or was an irrational legislative classification, I would agree that the ordinance would have to be sustained. Our role is not and should not be to sit as a zoning board of appeals.

I would also agree with the majority that local zoning authorities may properly act in furtherance of the objectives asserted to be served by the ordinance at issue here: restricting uncontrolled growth, solving traffic problems, keeping rental costs at a reasonable level, and making the community attractive to families. The police power which provides the justification for zoning is not narrowly confined. And, it is appropriate that we afford zoning authorities considerable latitude in choosing the means by which to implement such purposes. But deference does not mean abdication. This Court has an obligation to ensure that zoning ordinances, even when adopted in furtherance of such legitimate aims, do not infringe upon fundamental constitutional rights.

When separate but equal was still accepted constitutional dogma, this Court struck down a racially restrictive zoning ordinance. I am sure the Court would not be hesitant to invalidate that ordinance today. The lower federal courts have considered procedural aspects of zoning, and acted to insure that land-use controls are not used as means of confining minorities and the poor to the ghettos of our central cities. These are limited but necessary intrusions on the discretion of zoning authorities. By the same token, I think it clear that the First Amendment provides some limitation on zoning laws. It is inconceivable to me that we would allow the exercise of the zoning power to burden First Amendment freedoms, as by ordinances that restrict occupancy to individuals adhering to particular religious, political, or scientific beliefs. Zoning officials properly concern themselves with the uses of land—with, for example, the number and kind of dwellings to be constructed in a certain neighborhood or the number of persons who can reside in those dwellings. But zoning authorities cannot validly consider who those persons are, what they believe, or how they choose to live, whether they are Negro or white,

Catholic or Jew, Republican or Democrat, married or unmarried. . . .

I respectfully dissent.

NOTES

1. What vision of the public's "health, safety, welfare and morals" lay behind the Village of Euclid's enactment of an ordinance "fixing the height of buildings within reasonable limits, the character of materials and methods of construction, and the adjoining area which must be left open, in order to minimize the danger of fire or collapse, the evils of overcrowding and the like, and excluding from residential sections offensive trades, industries and structures likely to create nuisances"? What vision lay behind the Village's adoption of an ordinance "excluding from residential districts apartment houses, business houses, retail stores and shops, and other like establishments"? Behind the Village of Belle Terre's enactment of an ordinance restricting land use to one-family dwellings?

Early land use regulations excluding noxious industries from residential districts, setting maximum building heights and specifying safe building materials were generally upheld on the basis of the state's traditional power to regulate nuisances. See, for example, Hadacheck v. Sebastian, 239 U.S. 394, 36 S.Ct. 143, 60 L.Ed. 348 (1915) (upholding city ordinance that prohibited brick manufacturing in a residential district in order to protect residents from noxious fumes).

What is the police power basis for the second generation of zoning regulations, excluding such comparatively innocuous uses, as apartments and retail stores, from residential districts? State courts before *Euclid* divided on the legality of these regulations. Compare City of Aurora v. Burns, 319 Ill. 84, 92, 149 N.E. 784, 787 (1925) (upholding ordinance excluding business uses from residential districts: "The police power may be exercised not only in the interest of the public health, morals and safety, but also for the promotion of the general welfare") with Spann v. City of Dallas, 111 Tex. 350, 355, 235 S.W. 513, 514–515 (1921) (invalidating similar ordinance: "The substantial value of property lies in its use. If the right of use be denied, the value of the property is annihilated and ownership is rendered a barren right").

Was the Court saying, in both *Euclid* and *Belle Terre*, that because the ordinance before it sought to regulate the use of private lands, rather than behavior unrelated to private land, the measure was entitled to a relaxed standard of constitutional scrutiny? Would the Court have upheld a Belle Terre ordinance that prohibited automobiles occupied by more than one "family" from traveling on public streets in the Village?

Whose health, safety, welfare and morals were the Villages of Euclid and Belle Terre purporting to protect? In what ways, if any, were homeowners, renters, merchants and land speculators in Belle Terre Village advantaged or disadvantaged by the Village ordinance? What effects, if any, did the Belle Terre ordinance have on individuals living outside the Village but interested in moving there? Is *Belle Terre* the case contemplated by *Euclid* "where the general public interest would so far outweigh the interest of the municipality that the municipality would not be allowed to stand in the way"?

2. Euclid v. Ambler is, by any measure, a landmark—probably *the* landmark—in American land use control law. Decided at a time when Supreme Court decisions had substantially curbed state regulatory power, and when land use reformers were increasingly pressing municipalities to exercise that power, the case continues to be widely cited. Even federal District Judge Westenhaver, who heard the case and rendered the initial decision against the Village, sensed the ultimate importance of the dispute before him. "This case," he began his opinion, "is obviously destined to go higher." Ambler Realty Co. v. Village of Euclid, 297 F. 307, 308 (N.D.Ohio 1924).

One paradox of *Euclid* is that this sweeping paean to the supremacy of state regulation over private property was written by that most ardent conservative, George Sutherland. The mystery is deepened by the fact that, after the initial oral argument, the Court had apparently voted 5–4 *against* the ordinance, with Justice Sutherland writing the majority opinion. What explains Sutherland's change of heart? According to Justice Stone's law clerk, "talks with his dissenting brethren (principally Stone, I believe) shook his convictions and led him to request a reargument, after which he changed his mind and the ordinance was upheld."[j] Robert Walker has speculated that it was a request for reargument, and an *amicus* brief, filed by Alfred Bettman on behalf of the National Conference on City Planning, that may have made the difference.[k] Sutherland's biographer suggests that it was scholarly reflection that led the Justice to conclude that the ordinance would produce "not the deprivation of property, but its enhancement. A distinction observed by Cooley long before was therefore pertinent. It pointed out 'the line between what would be a clear invasion of right on the one hand, and regulation not lessening the value of the right' on the other. On this basis the common law had allowed the abatement of nuisances, and the forbidden industrial plants would approximate nuisances in a residential area such as Euclid. The result of the statute, then, was beneficial to property, and grounded as it was on the ultimate fact of overcrowding, it could not be set aside."[l]

[j] McCormack, A Law Clerk's Recollections, 46 Colum.L.Rev. 710, 712 (1946).

[k] R. Walker, The Planning Function in Urban Government 77–78 (2d ed.1950).

[l] J. Paschal, Mr. Justice Sutherland 127 (1951).

3. How far will the Supreme Court let a municipality go in regulating the relationship, as well as the number, of individuals living in a single unit? In Moore v. City of East Cleveland, 431 U.S. 494, 97 S.Ct. 1932, 52 L.Ed.2d 531 (1977), the Court, in a 5–4 decision, drew the line at true families and overturned appellant's state court conviction, under which she had been sentenced to five days in jail and a $25 fine for living together with her son and two grandsons. Specifically, the Court struck down an East Cleveland ordinance that, unlike the *Belle Terre* ordinance, defined "family" in a way that excluded some related individuals. (The problem under the ordinance was that the two grandsons were cousins, not brothers.)

Announcing the judgment of the Court, and writing an opinion in which Justices Brennan, Marshall and Blackmun joined, Justice Powell contended that "one overriding factor sets this case apart from *Belle Terre*. The ordinance there affected only *unrelated* individuals. It expressly allowed all who were related by 'blood, adoption, or marriage' to live together, and in sustaining the ordinance we were careful to note that it promoted 'family needs' and 'family values.' East Cleveland, in contrast, has chosen to regulate the occupancy of its housing by slicing deeply into the family itself . . . . When a city undertakes such intrusive regulation of the family, neither *Belle Terre* nor *Euclid* governs; the usual judicial deference to the legislature is inappropriate. This Court has long recognized that freedom of personal choice in matters of marriage and family life is one of the liberties protected by the Due Process Clause of the Fourteenth Amendment." 431 U.S. at 499, 97 S.Ct. at 1935.

Justice Stevens concurred. Chief Justice Burger dissented on the ground that appellant had failed to exhaust her administrative remedies by seeking a variance from the ordinance. Justice Stewart, joined by Justice Rehnquist, dissented on the ground that *Belle Terre* was dispositive: "To suggest that the biological fact of common ancestry necessarily gives related persons constitutional rights of association superior to those of unrelated persons is to misunderstand the nature of the associational freedoms that the Constitution has been understood to protect." 431 U.S. at 535, 97 S.Ct. at 1953. Justice White dissented with the observation that "the Court should be extremely reluctant to breathe still further substantive content into the Due Process Clause so as to strike down legislation adopted by a State or city to promote its welfare. Whenever the Judiciary does so, it unavoidably pre-empts for itself another part of the governance of the country without express constitutional authority." 431 U.S. 544, 97 S.Ct. at 1958.

4. Both before and after *Belle Terre*, state courts have applied their state constitutions to invalidate zoning ordinances that restrict the number of unrelated individuals that can constitute a "family" for purposes of single-family residential districts. See, for example, State v. Baker, 81 N.J. 99, 114, 405 A.2d 368, 375 (1979) ("Given the

availability of less restrictive alternatives, such regulations are insufficiently related to the perceived social ills which they were intended to ameliorate").

These state court decisions have generally accepted the legitimacy of promoting "family values" and a "family style of living" through the maintenance of low density residential areas, and have disagreed only with the proposition that consanguinity is necessary to attain these goals. In the view of the California Supreme Court, "'residential character' can be and is preserved by restrictions on transient and institutional uses (hotels, motels, boarding houses, clubs, etc.). Population density can be regulated by reference to floor space and facilities. Noise and morality can be dealt with by enforcement of police power ordinances and criminal statutes. Traffic and parking can be handled by limitations on the number of cars (applied evenly to all households) and by off-street parking requirements. *In general, zoning ordinances are much less suspect when they focus on the use than when they command inquiry into who are the users.*" City of Santa Barbara v. Adamson, 27 Cal.3d 123, 133, 164 Cal.Rptr. 539, 545, 610 P.2d 436, 441–442 (1980).

See generally, Note, Single-Family Zoning: Ramifications of State Court Rejection of *Belle Terre* on Use and Density Control, 32 Hastings L.J. 1687 (1981).

B. "TAKINGS"

PENNSYLVANIA COAL CO. v. MAHON
Supreme Court of the United States, 1922.
260 U.S. 393, 43 S.Ct. 158, 67 L.Ed. 322.

Mr. Justice HOLMES delivered the opinion of the Court.

This is a bill in equity brought by the defendants in error to prevent the Pennsylvania Coal Company from mining under their property in such way as to remove the supports and cause a subsidence of the surface and of their house. The bill sets out a deed executed by the Coal Company in 1878, under which the plaintiffs claim. The deed conveys the surface but in express terms reserves the right to remove all the coal under the same and the grantee takes the premises with the risk and waives all claim for damages that may arise from mining out the coal. But the plaintiffs say that whatever may have been the Coal Company's rights, they were taken away by an Act of Pennsylvania, approved May 27, 1921 (P.L. 1198), commonly known there as the Kohler Act. The Court of Common Pleas found that if not restrained the defendant would cause the damage to prevent which the bill was brought but denied an injunction, holding that the statute if applied to this case would be unconstitutional. On appeal the Supreme Court of the State agreed that the defendant had contract and property rights protected by the Constitution of the

United States, but held that the statute was a legitimate exercise of the police power and directed a decree for the plaintiffs. A writ of error was granted bringing the case to this Court.

The statute forbids the mining of anthracite coal in such way as to cause the subsidence of, among other things, any structure used as a human habitation, with certain exceptions, including among them land where the surface is owned by the owner of the underlying coal and is distant more than one hundred and fifty feet from any improved property belonging to any other person. As applied to this case the statute is admitted to destroy previously existing rights of property and contract. The question is whether the police power can be stretched so far.

Government hardly could go on if to some extent values incident to property could not be diminished without paying for every such change in the general law. As long recognized some values are enjoyed under an implied limitation and must yield to the police power. But obviously the implied limitation must have its limits or the contract and due process clauses are gone. One fact for consideration in determining such limits is the extent of the diminution. When it reaches a certain magnitude, in most if not in all cases there must be an exercise of eminent domain and compensation to sustain the act. So the question depends upon the particular facts. The greatest weight is given to the judgment of the legislature but it always is open to interested parties to contend that the legislature has gone beyond its constitutional power.

This is the case of a single private house. No doubt there is a public interest even in this, as there is in every purchase and sale and in all that happens within the commonwealth. Some existing rights may be modified even in such a case. But usually in ordinary private affairs the public interest does not warrant much of this kind of interference. A source of damage to such a house is not a public nuisance even if similar damage is inflicted on others in different places. The damage is not common or public. The extent of the public interest is shown by the statute to be limited, since the statute ordinarily does not apply to land when the surface is owned by the owner of the coal. Furthermore, it is not justified as a protection of personal safety. That could be provided for by notice. Indeed the very foundation of this bill is that the defendant gave timely notice of its intent to mine under the house. On the other hand the extent of the taking is great. It purports to abolish what is recognized in Pennsylvania as an estate in land—a very valuable estate—and what is declared by the Court below to be a contract hitherto binding the plaintiffs. If we were called upon to deal with the plaintiffs' position alone we should think it clear that the statute does not disclose a public interest sufficient to warrant so extensive a destruction of the defendant's constitutionally protected rights.

But the case has been treated as one in which the general validity of the act should be discussed. The Attorney General of the State, the City of Scranton and the representatives of other extensive interests were allowed to take part in the argument below and have submitted their contentions here. It seems, therefore, to be our duty to go farther in the statement of our opinion, in order that it may be known at once, and that further suits should not be brought in vain.

It is our opinion that the act cannot be sustained as an exercise of the police power, so far as it affects the mining of coal under streets or cities in places where the right to mine such coal has been reserved. As said in a Pennsylvania case, "For practical purposes, the right to coal consists in the right to mine it." Commonwealth v. Clearview Coal Co., 256 Pa. 328, 331, 100 Atl. 820, L.R.A.1917E, 672. What makes the right to mine coal valuable is that it can be exercised with profit. To make it commercially impracticable to mine certain coal has very nearly the same effect for constitutional purposes as appropriating or destroying it. This we think that we are warranted in assuming that the statute does.

It is true that in Plymouth Coal Co. v. Pennsylvania, 232 U.S. 531, 34 Sup.Ct. 359, 58 L.Ed. 713, it was held competent for the legislature to require a pillar of coal to be left along the line of adjoining property, that with the pillar on the other side of the line would be a barrier sufficient for the safety of the employees of either mine in case the other should be abandoned and allowed to fill with water. But that was a requirement for the safety of employees invited into the mine, and secured an average reciprocity of advantage that has been recognized as a justification of various laws.

The rights of the public in a street purchased or laid out by eminent domain are those that it has paid for. If in any case its representatives have been so short sighted as to acquire only surface rights without the right of support we see no more authority for supplying the latter without compensation than there was for taking the right of way in the first place and refusing to pay for it because the public wanted it very much. The protection of private property in the Fifth Amendment presupposes that it is wanted for public use, but provides that it shall not be taken for such use without compensation. A similar assumption is made in the decisions upon the Fourteenth Amendment. When this seemingly absolute protection is found to be qualified by the police power, the natural tendency of human nature is to extend the qualification more and more until at last private property disappears. But that cannot be accomplished in this way under the Constitution of the United States.

The general rule at least is that while property may be regulated to a certain extent, if regulation goes too far it will be recognized as a taking. It may be doubted how far exceptional cases, like the blowing up of a house to stop a conflagration, go—and if they go beyond the general rule, whether they do not stand as much upon tradition as

Pt. 3   THE SOURCES AND LIMITS OF STATE POWER   1097

upon principle. In general it is not plain that a man's misfortunes or necessities will justify his shifting the damages to his neighbor's shoulders. We are in danger of forgetting that a strong public desire to improve the public condition is not enough to warrant achieving the desire by a shorter cut than the constitutional way of paying for the change. As we already have said this is a question of degree— and therefore cannot be disposed of by general propositions. But we regard this as going beyond any of the cases decided by this Court. The late decisions upon laws dealing with the congestion of Washington and New York, caused by the war, dealt with laws intended to meet a temporary emergency and providing for compensation determined to be reasonable by an impartial board. They went to the verge of the law but fell far short of the present act.

We assume, of course, that the statute was passed upon the conviction that an exigency existed that would warrant it, and we assume that an exigency exists that would warrant the exercise of eminent domain. But the question at bottom is upon whom the loss of the changes desired should fall. So far as private persons or communities have seen fit to take the risk of acquiring only surface rights, we cannot see that the fact that their risk has become a danger warrants the giving to them greater rights than they bought.

Decree reversed.

Mr. Justice BRANDEIS dissenting.

The Kohler Act prohibits, under certain conditions, the mining of anthracite coal within the limits of a city in such a manner or to such an extent "as to cause the . . . subsidence of . . . any dwelling or other structure used as a human habitation, or any factory, store, or other industrial or mercantile establishment in which human labor is employed." Coal in place is land, and the right of the owner to use his land is not absolute. He may not so use it as to create a public nuisance, and uses, once harmless, may, owing to changed conditions, seriously threaten the public welfare. Whenever they do, the Legislature has power to prohibit such uses without paying compensation; and the power to prohibit extends alike to the manner, the character and the purpose of the use. Are we justified in declaring that the Legislature of Pennsylvania has, in restricting the right to mine anthracite, exercised this power so arbitrarily as to violate the Fourteenth Amendment?

Every restriction upon the use of property imposed in the exercise of the police power deprives the owner of some right theretofore enjoyed, and is, in that sense, an abridgment by the state of rights in property without making compensation. But restriction imposed to protect the public health, safety or morals from dangers threatened is not a taking. The restriction here in question is merely the prohibition of a noxious use. The property so restricted remains in the possession of its owner. The state does not appropriate it or make any use of it. The state merely prevents the owner from making a use which interferes with paramount rights of the public. Whenever the use prohibited ceases to be noxious—as it may because of further change in local or social conditions—the restriction will have to be removed and the owner will again be free to enjoy his property as heretofore.

The restriction upon the use of this property cannot, of course, be lawfully imposed, unless its purpose is to protect the public. But the purpose of a restriction does not cease to be public, because incidentally some private persons may thereby receive gratuitously valuable special benefits. Thus, owners of low buildings may obtain, through statutory restrictions upon the height of neighboring structures, benefits equivalent to an easement of light and air. Furthermore, a restriction, though imposed for a public purpose, will not be lawful, unless the restriction is an appropriate means to the public end. But to keep coal in place is surely an appropriate means of preventing subsidence of the surface; and ordinarily it is the only available means. Restriction upon use does not become inappropriate as a means, merely because it deprives the owner of the only use to which the property can then be profitably put. The liquor and the oleomargarine cases settled that. Mugler v. Kansas, 123 U.S. 623, 668, 669, 8 Sup.Ct. 273, 31 L.Ed. 205; Powell v. Pennsylvania, 127 U.S. 678, 682, 8 Sup.Ct. 992, 1257, 32 L.Ed. 253. Nor is a restriction imposed through exercise of the police power inappropriate as a means, merely because the same end might be effected through exercise of the power of eminent domain, or otherwise at public expense. Every restriction upon the height of buildings might be secured through acquiring by eminent domain the right of each owner to build above the limiting height; but it is settled that the state need not resort to that power. If by mining anthracite coal the owner would necessarily unloose poisonous gases, I suppose no one would doubt the power of the state to prevent the mining, without buying his coal fields. And why may not the state, likewise, without paying compensation, prohibit one from digging so deep or excavating so near the surface, as to expose the community to like dangers? In the latter case, as in the former, carrying on the business would be a public nuisance.

It is said that one fact for consideration in determining whether the limits of the police power have been exceeded is the extent of the resulting diminution in value, and that here the restriction destroys existing rights of property and contract. But values are relative. If we are to consider the value of the coal kept in place by the restriction, we should compare it with the value of all other parts of the land. That is, with the value not of the coal alone, but with the value of the whole property. The rights of an owner as against the public are not increased by dividing the interests in his property into surface and subsoil. The sum of the rights in the parts can not be greater than the rights in the whole. The estate of an owner in land is grandiloquently described as extending ab orco usque ad coelum. But I suppose no one would contend that by selling his interest above 100 feet from the surface he could prevent the state from limiting, by the police power, the height of structures in a city. And why should a sale of underground rights bar the state's power? For aught that appears the value of the coal kept in place by the restriction may be negligible as compared with the value of the whole property, or even as compared with that part of it which is represented by the coal remaining in place and which may be extracted despite the statute. Ordinarily a police regulation, general in operation, will not be held void as to a particular property, although proof is offered that owing to conditions peculiar to it the restriction could not reasonably be applied. But even if the particular facts are to govern, the statute should, in my opinion be upheld in this case. For the defendant has failed to adduce any evidence from which it appears that to restrict its mining operations was an unreasonable exercise of the police power. Where the surface and the coal belong to the same person, self-interest would ordinarily prevent mining to such an extent as to cause a subsidence. It was, doubtless, for this reason that the Legislature, estimating the degrees of danger, deemed statutory restriction unnecessary for the public safety under such conditions. . . .

This case involves only mining which causes subsidence of a dwelling house. But the Kohler Act contains provisions in addition to that quoted above; and as to these, also, an opinion is expressed. These provisions deal with mining under cities to such an extent as to cause subsidence of—

(a) Any public building or any structure customarily used by the public as a place of resort, assemblage, or amusement, including, but not limited to, churches, schools, hospitals, theaters, hotels, and railroad stations.

(b) Any street, road, bridge, or other public passageway, dedicated to public use or habitually used by the public.

(c) Any track, roadbed, right of way, pipe, conduit, wire, or other facility, used in the service of the public by any municipal corporation or public service company as defined by the Public Service Law.

A prohibition of mining which causes subsidence of such structures and facilities is obviously enacted for a public purpose; and it seems, likewise, clear that mere notice of intention to mine would not in this connection secure the public safety. Yet it is said that these provisions of the act cannot be sustained as an exercise of the police power where the right to mine such coal has been reserved. The conclusion seems to rest upon the assumption that in order to justify such exercise of the police power there must be "an average reciprocity of advantage" as between the owner of the property restricted and the rest of the community; and that here such reciprocity is absent. Reciprocity of advantage is an important consideration, and may even be an essential, where the state's power is exercised for the purpose of conferring benefits upon the property of a neighborhood, as in drainage projects, or upon adjoining owners, as by party wall provisions. But where the police power is exercised, not to confer benefits upon property owners but to protect the public from detriment and danger, there is in my opinion, no room for considering reciprocity of advantage. There was no reciprocal advantage to the owner prohibited from using his oil tanks in 248 U.S. 498, 39 Sup.Ct. 172, 63 L.Ed. 381; his brickyard, in 239 U.S. 394, 36 Sup.Ct. 143, 60 L.Ed. 348, Ann.Cas.1917B, 927; his livery stable, in 237 U.S. 171, 35 Sup.Ct. 511, 59 L.Ed. 900; his billiard hall, in 225 U.S. 623, 32 Sup.Ct. 697, 56 L.Ed. 1229, 41 L.R.A. (N.S.) 153; his oleomargarine factory, in 127 U.S. 678, 8 Sup.Ct. 992, 1257, 32 L.Ed. 253; his brewery, in 123 U.S. 623, 8 Sup.Ct. 273, 31 L.Ed. 205; unless it be the advantage of living and doing business in a civilized community. That reciprocal advantage is given by the act to the coal operators.

PENN CENTRAL TRANSPORTATION CO. v. NEW YORK CITY

Supreme Court of the United States, 1978.
438 U.S. 104, 98 S.Ct. 2646, 57 L.Ed.2d 631.

Mr. Justice BRENNAN delivered the opinion of the Court.

The question presented is whether a city may, as part of a comprehensive program to preserve historic landmarks and historic districts, place restrictions on the development of individual historic landmarks—in addition to those imposed by applicable zoning ordinances—without effecting a "taking" requiring the payment of "just compensation." Specifically, we must decide whether the application of New York City's Landmarks Preservation Law to the parcel of land occupied by Grand Central Terminal has "taken" its owners' property in violation of the Fifth and Fourteenth Amendments.

I

[In 1965, New York City, seeking to foster "civic pride in the beauty and noble accomplishments of the past," to enhance "the city's attractions to tourists and visitors," and to stimulate business and industry, enacted a Landmarks Preservation Law.[m] The Law vested primary administrative responsibility in the Landmarks Preservation Commission, empowering the Commission to identify parcels and areas having "a special character or a special historical or aesthetic interest or value as part of the development, heritage or cultural characteristics of the city, state or nation," and, after applying prescribed criteria, to designate a building as a "landmark" or an area as an "historic district." A landowner whose building was designated

---

m. This summary is drawn from the Court's opinion, 438 U.S. at 107–122, 98 S.Ct. at 2650–2658.

as a landmark was required to keep the building's exterior in "good repair" and to obtain Commission approval before altering it.ⁿ

[Although they were thus restricted in their development opportunities, landmark owners did receive some compensating economic benefits that were unavailable to other landowners in the City. The City allowed a landowner who had not developed his property to the full extent permitted by the zoning ordinance to transfer these unused development rights—called "Transferable Development Rights"—to contiguous parcels on the same block, enabling these parcels, as a consequence, to be developed beyond the applicable zoning restriction. In 1968 the City increased the value of these transferable development rights by allowing landowners to transfer to noncontiguous parcels; a 1969 amendment loosened the transferability restrictions still further.

[On August 2, 1967, the Landmarks Preservation Commission designated Grand Central Terminal as a landmark. The Terminal, one of the City's "most famous buildings," and "a magnificent example of the French beaux-arts style," was owned by the Penn Central Transportation Company and its affiliates. Sometime after the designation, Penn Central applied to the Commission for permission to place an office building atop the terminal. One plan submitted by Penn Central involved the construction of a 55-story office building, to rest on the roof of the Terminal above the existing facade. A second plan was to demolish a portion of the Terminal and its facade and to erect a 53-story office building. Both plans complied with all applicable zoning requirements. The Commission denied the application:

> [We have] no fixed rule against making additions to designated buildings—it all depends on how they are done . . . . But to balance a 55-story office tower above a flamboyant Beaux-Arts facade seems nothing more than an aesthetic joke. Quite simply, the tower would overwhelm the Terminal by its sheer mass. The 'addition' would be four times as high as the existing structure and would reduce the Landmark itself to the status of a curiosity.

Penn Central filed an action in state court and obtained injunctive and declaratory relief against the Law's enforcement on the ground that it took its property without just compensation in violation of the Fifth and Fourteenth Amendments, and deprived it of its property without due process of law, in violation of the Fourteenth Amendment. The Appellate Division reversed, and the New York Court of Appeals af-

---

n. Three procedures were available for obtaining administrative approval of a proposed alteration. First, the owner could apply to the Commission for a "certificate of no effect on protected architectural features," approving the alteration on the ground that it would not change any protected architectural feature. Second, the owner could apply for a certificate of "appropriateness," which would be granted if the Commission found that the proposed construction would not interfere with the landmark's perpetuation. Third, the owner could seek a certificate of appropriateness on the ground of "insufficient return."

firmed the reversal. Penn Central filed a notice of appeal in the United States Supreme Court, which noted probable jurisdiction.]

II

The issues presented by appellants are (1) whether the restrictions imposed by New York City's law upon appellants' exploitation of the Terminal site effect a "taking" of appellants' property for a public use within the meaning of the Fifth Amendment, which of course is made applicable to the States through the Fourteenth Amendment, and, (2), if so, whether the transferable development rights afforded appellants constitute "just compensation" within the meaning of the Fifth Amendment. We need only address the question whether a "taking" has occurred.

A

Before considering appellants' specific contentions, it will be useful to review the factors that have shaped the jurisprudence of the Fifth Amendment injunction "nor shall private property be taken for public use, without just compensation." The question of what constitutes a "taking" for purposes of the Fifth Amendment has proved to be a problem of considerable difficulty. While this Court has recognized that the "Fifth Amendment's guarantee . . . [is] designed to bar Government from forcing some people alone to bear public burdens which, in all fairness and justice, should be borne by the public as a whole," Armstrong v. United States, 364 U.S. 40, 49, 80 S.Ct. 1563, 1569, 4 L.Ed.2d 1554 (1960), this Court, quite simply, has been unable to develop any "set formula" for determining when "justice and fairness" require that economic injuries caused by public action be compensated by the government, rather than remain disproportionately concentrated on a few persons. Indeed, we have frequently observed that whether a particular restriction will be rendered invalid by the government's failure to pay for any losses proximately caused by it depends largely "upon the particular circumstances [in that] case." United States v. Central Eureka Mining Co., 357 U.S. 155, 168, 78 S.Ct. 1097, 1104, 2 L.Ed.2d 1228 (1958).

In engaging in these essentially ad hoc, factual inquiries, the Court's decisions have identified several factors that have particular significance. The economic impact of the regulation on the claimant and, particularly, the extent to which the regulation has interfered with distinct investment-backed expectations are, of course, relevant considerations. So, too, is the character of the governmental action. A "taking" may more readily be found when the interference with property can be characterized as a physical invasion by government, than when interference arises from some public program adjusting the benefits and burdens of economic life to promote the common good.

"Government hardly could go on if to some extent values incident to property could not be diminished without paying for every such change in the general law," Pennsylvania Coal Co. v. Mahon, 260 U.S. 393, 413, 43 S.Ct. 158, 159, 67 L.Ed. 322 (1922), and this Court has accordingly recognized, in a wide variety of contexts, that government may execute laws or programs that adversely affect recognized economic values. Exercises of the taxing power are one obvious example. A second are the decisions in which this Court has dismissed "taking" challenges on the ground that, while the challenged government action caused economic harm, it did not interfere with interests that were sufficiently bound up with the reasonable expectations of the claimant to constitute "property" for Fifth Amendment purposes. See, e.g., United States v. Willow River Power Co., 324 U.S. 499, 65 S.Ct. 761, 89 L.Ed. 1101 (1945) (interest in high-water level of river for runoff for tailwaters to maintain power head is not property); United States v. Chandler-Dunbar Water Power Co., 229 U.S. 53, 33 S.Ct. 667, 57 L.Ed. 1063 (1913) (no property interest can exist in navigable waters).

More importantly for the present case, in instances in which a state tribunal reasonably concluded that "the health, safety, morals, or general welfare" would be promoted by prohibiting particular contemplated uses of land, this Court has upheld land-use regulations that destroyed or adversely affected recognized real property interests. Zoning laws are, of course, the classic example, see Euclid v. Ambler Realty Co., 272 U.S. 365, 47 S.Ct. 114, 71 L.Ed. 303 (1926) (prohibition of industrial use); Gorieb v. Fox, 274 U.S. 603, 608, 47 S.Ct. 675, 677, 71 L.Ed. 1228 (1927) (requirement that portions of parcels be left unbuilt); Welch v. Swasey, 214 U.S. 91, 29 S.Ct. 567, 53 L.Ed. 923 (1909) (height restriction), which have been viewed as permissible governmental action even when prohibiting the most beneficial use of the property.

Zoning laws generally do not affect existing uses of real property, but "taking" challenges have also been held to be without merit in a wide variety of situations when the challenged governmental actions prohibited a beneficial use to which individual parcels had previously been devoted and thus caused substantial individualized harm. Miller v. Schoene, 276 U.S. 272, 48 S.Ct. 246, 72 L.Ed. 568 (1928), is illustrative. In that case, a state entomologist, acting pursuant to a state statute, ordered the claimants to cut down a large number of ornamental red cedar trees because they produced cedar rust fatal to apple trees cultivated nearby. Although the statute provided for recovery of any expense incurred in removing the cedars, and permitted claimants to use the felled trees, it did not provide compensation for the value of the standing trees or for the resulting decrease in market value of the properties as a whole. A unanimous Court held that this latter omission did not render the statute invalid. The Court held that the State might properly make "a choice between the preservation of one class of property and that of the other" and since the apple industry was important in the State involved, concluded that the State had not exceeded "its constitutional powers by deciding upon the destruction of one class of property [without compensation] in order to save another which, in the judgment of the legislature, is of greater value to the public." *Id.*, at 279, 48 S.Ct., at 247. . . .

Finally, government actions that may be characterized as acquisitions of resources to permit or facilitate uniquely public functions have often been held to constitute "takings." United States v. Causby, 328 U.S. 256, 66 S.Ct. 1062, 90 L.Ed. 1206 (1946), is illustrative. In holding that direct overflights above the claimant's land, that destroyed the present use of the land as a chicken farm, constituted a "taking," *Causby* emphasized that Government had not "merely destroyed property [but was] using a part of it for the flight of its planes." *Id.*, 328 U.S., at 262–263, n. 7, 66 S.Ct., at 1066. See also Griggs v. Allegheny County, 369 U.S. 84, 82 S.Ct. 531, 7 L.Ed.2d 585 (1962) (overflights held a taking); Portsmouth Co. v. United States, 260 U.S. 327, 43 S.Ct. 135, 67 L.Ed. 287 (1922) (United States military installations' repeated firing of guns over claimant's land is a taking); United States v. Cress, 243 U.S. 316, 37 S.Ct. 380, 61 L.Ed. 746 (1917) (repeated floodings of land caused by water project is a taking); but see YMCA v. United States, 395 U.S. 85, 89 S.Ct. 1511, 23 L.Ed.2d 117 (1969) (damage caused to building when federal officers who were seeking to protect building were attacked by rioters held not a taking).

B

In contending that the New York City law has "taken" their property in violation of the Fifth and Fourteenth Amendments, appellants make a series of arguments, which, while tailored to the facts of this case, essentially urge that any substantial restriction imposed pursuant to a landmark law must be accompanied by just compensation if it is to be constitutional. . . .

They first observe that the airspace above the Terminal is a valuable property interest, citing United States v. Causby, *supra*. They urge that the Landmarks Law has deprived them of any gainful use of their "air rights" above the Terminal and that, irrespective of the value of the remainder of their parcel, the city has "taken" their right to this superadjacent airspace, thus entitling them to "just compensation" measured by the fair market value of these air rights.

Apart from our own disagreement with appellants' characterization of the effect of the New York City law, the submission that appellants may establish a "taking" simply by showing that they have been denied the ability to exploit a property interest that they heretofore had believed was available for development is quite simply untenable. Were this the rule, this Court would have erred not only in upholding laws restricting the development of air rights, but also in approving those prohibiting both the subjacent, and the lateral, development of particular parcels. "Taking" jurisprudence does not divide a single parcel into discrete segments and attempt to determine whether rights in a particular segment have been entirely abrogated. In deciding whether a particular governmental action has effected a taking, this Court focuses rather both on the character of the action and on the nature and extent of the interference with rights in the parcel as a whole—here, the city tax block designated as the "landmark site."

Secondly, appellants, focusing on the character and impact of the New York City law, argue that it effects a "taking" because its operation has significantly diminished the value of the Terminal site. Appellants concede that the decisions sustaining other land-use regulations, which, like the New York City law, are reasonably related to the promotion of the general welfare, uniformly reject the proposition that diminution in property value, standing alone, can establish a "taking," see Euclid v. Ambler Realty Co., 272 U.S. 365, 47 S.Ct. 114, 71 L.Ed. 303 (1926) (75% diminution in value caused by zoning law); Hadacheck v. Sebastian, 239 U.S. 394, 36 S.Ct. 143, 60 L.Ed. 348 (1915) ($87\frac{1}{2}$% diminution in value); and that the "taking" issue in these contexts is resolved by focusing on the uses the regulations permit. Appellants, moreover, also do not dispute that a showing of diminution in property value would not establish a taking if the restriction had been imposed as a result of historic-district legislation, but appellants argue that New York City's regulation of individual landmarks is fundamentally different from zoning or from historic-district legislation because the controls imposed by New York City's law apply only to individuals who own selected properties.

Stated baldly, appellants' position appears to be that the only means of ensuring that selected owners are not singled out to endure financial hardship for no reason is to hold that any restriction imposed on individual landmarks pursuant to the New York City scheme is a "taking" requiring the payment of "just compensation." Agreement with this argument would, of course, invalidate not just New York City's law, but all comparable landmark legislation in the Nation. We find no merit in it. . . .

Appellants' final broad-based attack would have us treat the law as an instance, like that in United States v. Causby, in which government, acting in an enterprise capacity, has appropriated part of their property for some strictly governmental purpose. Apart from the fact that *Causby* was a case of invasion of airspace that destroyed the use of the farm beneath, and this New York City law has in nowise impaired the present use of the Terminal, the Landmarks Law neither exploits appellants' parcel for city purposes nor facilitates nor arises from any entrepreneurial operations of the city. The situation is not remotely like that in *Causby* where the airspace above the property was in the flight pattern for military aircraft. The Landmarks Law's effect is simply to prohibit appellants or anyone else from occupying portions of the airspace above the Terminal, while permitting appellants to use the remainder of the parcel in a gainful fashion. This is no more an appropriation of property by government for its own uses than is a zoning law prohibiting, for "aesthetic" reasons, two or more adult theaters within a specified area, see Young v. American Mini Theatres, Inc., 427 U.S. 50, 96 S.Ct. 2440, 49 L.Ed.2d 310 (1976), or a safety regulation prohibiting excavations below a certain level.

C

Rejection of appellants' broad arguments is not, however, the end of our inquiry, for all we thus far have established is that the New York City law is not rendered invalid by its failure to provide "just compensation" whenever a landmark owner is restricted in the exploitation of property interests, such as air rights, to a greater extent than provided for under applicable zoning laws. We now must consider whether the interference with appellants' property is of such a magnitude that "there must be an exercise of eminent domain and compensation to sustain [it]." Pennsylvania Coal Co. v. Mahon, 260 U.S., at 413, 43 S.Ct., at 159. That inquiry may be narrowed to the question of the severity of the impact of the law on appellants' parcel, and its resolution in turn requires a careful assessment of the impact of the regulation on the Terminal site.

Unlike the governmental acts in *Goldblatt, Miller, Causby, Griggs,* and *Hadacheck*, the New York City law does not interfere in any way with the present uses of the Terminal. Its designation as a landmark not only permits but contemplates that appellants may continue to use the property precisely as it has been used for the past 65 years: as a railroad terminal containing office space and concessions. So the law does not interfere with what must be regarded as Penn Central's primary expectation concerning the use of the parcel. More importantly, on this record, we must regard the New York City law as permitting Penn Central not only to profit from the Terminal but also to obtain a "reasonable return" on its investment.

Appellants, moreover, exaggerate the effect of the law on their ability to make use of the air rights above the Terminal in two respects. First, it simply cannot be maintained, on this record, that appellants have been prohibited from occupying *any* portion of the airspace above the Terminal. While the Commission's actions in denying applications to construct an office building in excess of 50 stories above the Terminal may indicate that it will refuse to issue a certificate of appropriateness for any comparably sized structure, nothing the Commission has said or done suggests an intention to prohibit *any* construction above the Terminal. The Commission's report emphasized that whether any construction would be allowed depended upon whether the proposed addition "would harmonize in scale, material and character with [the Terminal]." Record 2251.

Since appellants have not sought approval for the construction of a smaller structure, we do not know that appellants will be denied any use of any portion of the airspace above the Terminal.

Second, to the extent appellants have been denied the right to build above the Terminal, it is not literally accurate to say that they have been denied *all* use of even those pre-existing air rights. Their ability to use these rights has not been abrogated; they are made transferable to at least eight parcels in the vicinity of the Terminal, one or two of which have been found suitable for the construction of new office buildings. Although appellants and others have argued that New York City's transferable development-rights program is far from ideal, the New York courts here supportably found that, at least in the case of the Terminal, the rights afforded are valuable. While these rights may well not have constituted "just compensation" if a "taking" had occurred, the rights nevertheless undoubtedly mitigate whatever financial burdens the law has imposed on appellants and, for that reason, are to be taken into account in considering the impact of regulation.

On this record, we conclude that the application of New York City's Landmarks Law has not effected a "taking" of appellants' property. The restrictions imposed are substantially related to the promotion of the general welfare and not only permit reasonable beneficial use of the landmark site but also afford appellants opportunities further to enhance not only the Terminal site proper but also other properties.

Affirmed.

[The opinion of REHNQUIST, J., dissenting, is omitted.]

NOTES

1. Was the Kohler Act, reviewed in *Pennsylvania Coal*, good legislation? Public land use regulation is often justified on the ground that it produces efficient results by approximating the private arrangements that landowners themselves would have made had transaction costs not prevented them from getting together. Was the Kohler Act passed to overcome transaction cost problems? Had not the Coal Company and Mahon already consummated their desired transaction, splitting the surface and subsurface rights to the land between themselves? How difficult would it have been for them, and for others similarly situated, to undo their transaction?

Was *Penn Central* correctly decided? Transaction costs there undoubtedly disabled City residents from organizing in order to reach a private agreement under which they would pay Penn Central to agree not to develop the Terminal. Although transaction costs may thus have justified the City's action in controlling the Terminal's development, does it also justify the City's refusal to compensate Penn Central for its consequent loss? Justice Rehnquist, dissenting, thought that the central issue in the case was "whether the cost associated with the City of New York's desire to preserve a limited number of 'landmarks' within its borders must be borne by all of its taxpayers or whether it can instead be imposed entirely on the owners of the individual properties." 438 U.S. at 139, 98 S.Ct. at 2666. Is *Penn Central* a situation like the one that prompted Justice Holmes' remark that "government hardly could go on if to some extent values incident to property could not be diminished without paying for every such change in the general law"? Note that although the beneficiaries of the Landmarks Preservation Law, and the extent of their benefit, were difficult, if not impossible, to identify, the victim—Penn Central—and the extent of its injury were relatively easy to identify.

2. As should be evident from *Pennsylvania Coal* and *Penn Central*, the United States Supreme Court has found no bright or principled line to separate legal regulations from illegal takings. The problem stems from the fact that the Constitution nowhere defines the term "taken," and is compounded by the fact that "property" is itself a highly malleable concept. Although courts and commentators have proposed several litmus tests for determining whether a taking has occurred, it is impossible to predict with confidence which test will be applied to a particular situation, much less the result that application of the test will produce. Yet the tests do at least help to focus the relevant issues. Among the more prominent are:

a. *Physical Invasion.* The takings clause clearly requires government to pay when it physically appropriates land for some public use such as a public park or highway. Early cases interpreted this rule to impose an absolute threshold for compensable takings, and excused governmental actions if they did not physically deprive the owner of some or all of his land. Thus, while a taking would be found if a public dam flooded plaintiff's land, it would not be found if a municipal construction project only interfered with plaintiff's access to his land. Compare Pumpelly v. Green Bay Co., 80 U.S. (13 Wall.) 166, 181, 20 L.Ed. 557 (1872) ("where real estate is actually invaded by superinduced additions of water, earth, sand or other materials, or by having any artificial structure placed on it, so as to effectually destroy or impair its usefulness, it is a taking . . . ") with Northern Transportation Co. v. City of Chicago, 99 U.S. 635, 642, 25 L.Ed. 336 (1879) ("No entry was made upon the plaintiff's lot. All that was done was to render for a time its use more inconvenient").

The physical invasion test has two major flaws. First, it is not predictive. Courts will often find a taking absent a physical invasion, Pennsylvania Coal Co. v. Mahon, above, and will sometimes find that a physical invasion is not a taking, Solly v. Toledo, 7 Ohio St.2d 16, 218 N.E.2d 463 (1966) (city may destroy houses constituting public nuisance). But see, Loretto v. Teleprompter Manhattan CATV Corp., note 3, below. Second, the test's "practical usefulness is limited by its anachronistic reliance on precommercial conceptions of property, ones which stressed title and dominion while tending to ignore the less tangible prerogatives of ownership such as use and enjoyment"; as a result, the test "treats two parties, both of whom may have lost the same amount of value, differently merely because the government 'touched' the land of the one but not the other. By compensating only the former property holder, the test ignores the fact that both intrusions leave their victim in the same aggrieved position." Developments in the Law—Zoning, 91 Harv.L.Rev. 1427, 1468–69 (1978).

b. *Noxious Use.* The noxious use test developed side-by-side with the physical invasion test and focused on the nature of the owner's land use rather than on the extent of the government's invasion. If the owner's use was noxious to her neighbors—a brick factory, say, or a slaughterhouse in a residential area—it could be regulated even though the regulation deprived the land of virtually all value. Goldblatt v. Town of Hempstead, 369 U.S. 590, 82 S.Ct. 987, 8 L.Ed.2d 130 (1962). The regulation would fail, however, if the proscribed conduct was essentially benign, such as altering the facade of an historical landmark.

One problem with the noxious use test is that states enjoy great latitude in determining what activities are noxious. It is purely legislative fiat that tells us that a tattoo parlor is offensive to neighboring residents and not the residences that are offensive to the parlor. Another problem is distinguishing between the noxious and innocuous aspects of a single use. Should an ordinance forbidding billboards within 100 yards of public highways be upheld as regulating an unsightly use of land that dangerously distracts motorists? Or should it be invalidated on the ground that billboards in fact promote safety by keeping drivers alert and giving motorcycle police a place to hide in order to trap speeders?

c. *Diminution in Value.* This test, first crystallized in Pennsylvania Coal v. Mahon, asks whether the challenged regulation cuts so deeply into the value of the claimant's property that it should be invalidated. (By making it "commercially impracticable to mine certain coal," the Pennsylvania statute had "very nearly the same effect for constitutional purposes as appropriating or destroying it.") The test has obvious roots in the physical invasion test, but substitutes the more sophisticated notion of economic detriment for the rudimentary concept of physical deprivation. As a result, it replaces a bright line (Has there been a physical appropriation?) with a far more sensitive and flexible inquiry (Has value been diminished too far?).

Although the diminution in value test has obvious advantages over both the physical invasion and noxious use tests, it also has problems of its own. To say that the test is sensitive and flexible is also to say that it is uncertain: "Ordinances which variously diminished property values from $1,500,000 to $275,000, $450,000 to $50,000, and $65,000 to $5000 have all been upheld. Ordinances which reduced property values from about $48,750 to about $11,250 and from $350,000 to $100,000 have been struck down." Developments in the Law—Zoning, 91 Harv.L.Rev. 1427, 1480. The test also leaves open whether diminution is to be measured by the amount of value lost, as in the examples just given, or by the amount of value remaining—whether, that is, claimant could after the regulation still earn a reasonable return on his investment.

d. *Balancing.* Justice Holmes' reference in *Pennsylvania Coal* to "average reciprocity of advantage" planted the seed for a test that balances a regulation's public benefits against its private costs. Employing the same sort of cost-benefit calculus as is used in nuisance cases, the test will uphold a regulation if it is efficient—if the public benefits derived from the regulation outweigh its costs to the regulated landowner. See, for example, State Department of Ecology v. Pacesetter Construction Co., Inc., 89 Wn.2d 203, 571 P.2d 196 (1977). See generally, Comment, Balancing Private Loss Against Public Gain to Test for a Violation of Due Process or a Taking Without Just Compensation, 54 Wash.L.Rev. 315 (1979).

The balancing test obviously suffers from the same problems of uncertainty as does the diminution in value test. Further, it is incomplete, for efficiency is not the only value to be served in a system that requires *just* compensation. Fairness plays a role, too. If efficiency were the sole criterion, government would be excused from compensating for physical appropriations of land for public uses such as parks, roads, schools and police stations, any time the public benefit derived from these uses outweighed their private costs.

e. *Utility and Fairness.* In an important article published in 1967, Professor Frank Michelman formulated a test that incorporated and refined the efficiency calculus of the balancing test. The test employs three concepts: "efficiency gains" (the excess of a measure's benefits over the losses it inflicts); "demoralization costs" (the total dollar value of (i) the discomfort to the regulated owner and her "sympathizers" for not being paid and (ii) the diminished productivity—"reflecting either impaired incentives or social unrest"—resulting from (i)); and "settlement costs" (the dollar cost of the "time, effort and resources" required to compensate affected parties in order to avoid all demoralization costs). The test holds that government should not undertake a regulation if the measure either would yield no efficiency gains, or if both demoralization costs and settlement costs would exceed efficiency gains. If the measure passes this first hurdle, then *compensation* must be made only if demoralization costs exceed settlement costs.

To this efficiency calculus, Michelman posed a fairness alternative, arguing that the denial of compensation "is not unfair as long as the disappointed claimant ought to be able to appreciate how such decisions might fit into a consistent practice which holds forth a lesser long-run risk to people like him than would any consistent practice which is naturally suggested by the opposite decision." Michelman, Property, Utility and Fairness: Comments on the Ethical Foundations of "Just Compensation" Law, 80 Harv.L.Rev. 1165, 1223 (1967).

The main problem with Michelman's approach is that it relies so heavily on the quantification of factors that courts and regulators are ill-equipped to measure. How, for example, are demoralization costs to be computed? And *whose* demoralization is to be taken into account? How are perceptions of fairness to be measured?

f. For other views on the takings issue, see B. Ackerman, Private Property and the Constitution (1977); Berger, A Policy Analysis of the Taking Problem, 49 N.Y.U.L.Rev. 165 (1974); Costonis, "Fair" Compensation and the Accommodation Power: Antidotes for the Taking Impasse in Land Use Controversies, 75 Colum.L.Rev. 1021 (1975); Sax, Takings, Private Property and Public Rights, 81 Yale L.J. 149 (1976); Sax, Takings and the Police Power, 74 Yale L.J. 36 (1964); Note, Reexamining the Supreme Court's View of the Taking Clause, 58 Tex.L.Rev. 1447 (1980).

3. The Supreme Court breathed new life into the physical invasion test in Loretto v. Teleprompter Manhattan CATV Corp., 458 U.S. 419, 102 S.Ct. 3164, 73 L.Ed.2d 868 (1982), holding that a New York statute permitting cable television companies to install cables and related equipment in apartment buildings, over the objections of the building's owner, constituted a taking: "We conclude that a permanent physical occupation authorized by government is a taking without regard to the public interests that it may serve." 102 S.Ct. at 3171. Writing for the majority, Justice Marshall rested his opinion on the view that permanent physical occupations are "perhaps the most serious form of invasion of an owner's property interest"—"the government does not simply take a single 'strand' from the 'bundle' of property rights: it chops through the bundle, taking a slice of every strand." 102 S.Ct. at 3176. Marshall distinguished PruneYard Shopping Center v. Robins, page 70, above, on the ground that it involved only a "temporary physical invasion." 102 S.Ct. at 3175.

Justice Blackmun, joined by Justices Brennan and White, dissented. Calling the decision "curiously anachronistic," and observing that "the nineteenth-century precedents relied on by the Court lack any vitality outside the agrarian context in which they were decided," Blackmun argued that "history teaches that takings claims are properly evaluated under a multifactor balancing test." Specifically, "because the extent to which the government may injure private interests now depends so little on whether or not it has authorized a 'physical contact,' the Court has avoided *per se* takings rules resting on outmoded distinctions between physical and non-physical intrusions." 102 S.Ct. at 3182.

How would *Loretto* have been decided under a balancing test? Under a diminution in value test? (Before the statute was enacted, Teleprompter customarily paid each landlord 5% of the gross revenues that the cable company received from that landlord's tenants. Pursuant to the statute, the State Commission on Cable Television ruled that the landlord was entitled to no more than a one-time, $1.00 payment from the cable company.) How would *Loretto* have been decided under Professor Michelman's utility and fairness measures? Should there be a *de minimis* requirement in the physical invasion test? Although there was some dispute over the total space taken up by Teleprompter's equipment, apparently everyone conceded that it occupied no more than slightly over 1.5 cubic feet of plaintiff's building.

What are *Loretto's* implications for the power of state courts and legislatures to require that landlords provide specific facilities and services to their tenants? "For example," Justice Blackmun noted, "New York landlords are required by law to provide and pay for mailboxes that occupy more than five times the volume that Teleprompter's cable occupies on appellant's building. If the State constitutionally can insist that appellant make this sacrifice so that her tenants may receive mail, it is hard to understand why the State may not require her to surrender less space, *filled at another's expense*, so that those same tenants can receive television signals." 102 S.Ct. at 3185. To this, Justice Marshall responded, "we do not agree with appellees that application of the physical occupation rule will have dire consequences for the government's power to adjust landlord-tenant relationships. This Court has consistently affirmed that States have broad power to regulate housing conditions in general and the landlord-tenant relationship in particular without paying compensation for all economic injuries that such regulation entails." 102 S.Ct. at 3178.

4. *Invasion of Air Space.* At common law, *cujus est solum, ejus est usque ad coelum* ("whose is the soil, his it is up to the sky"). The notion that real property rights extend to the heavens has necessarily been constrained by the practicalities of modern air travel. In United States v. Causby, 328 U.S. 256, 66 S.Ct. 1062, 90 L.Ed. 1206 (1946), the Supreme Court held that Causby, a chicken farmer whose land lay directly beneath the flight path used by military aircraft from a neighboring airport, was entitled to recover against the government for the diminution in value of his residence and poultry business. Recognizing that federal aviation statutes placed air space above specified heights in the "public domain," and that "flights over private land are not a taking, unless they are so low and so frequent as to be a direct and immediate interference with the enjoyment and use of the land," the Court concluded that a taking had occurred here because the frequent, low-level flights were the "direct and immediate" cause of the property's diminution in value.

Courts divide on whether flights must pass directly over the claimant's land in order for there to be a taking. The federal position, reflected in Batten v. United States, 306 F.2d 580 (10th Cir.1962), *cert. denied* 371 U.S. 955, 83 S.Ct. 506 (1963), is that they must. The question there was "whether a taking of property, compensable under the Fifth Amendment, occurs when there is no physical invasion of the affected property but the operation and maintenance of military jet aircraft on an Air Force Base of the United States produce noise, vibration and smoke which interfere with the use and enjoyment of the property." 306 F.2d at 581. The court concluded that this amounted to consequential damages, and not a taking. "The damages are no more than a consequence of the operation of the Base . . . they may be compensated by legislative authority, not by force of the Constitution alone." 306 F.2d at 585.

Although some states follow the federal view, others require government to compensate for damages caused by flights over neighboring lands. See, for example, Martin v. Port of Seattle, 64 Wn.2d 309, 316, 391 P.2d 540, 545 (1964), *cert. denied* 379 U.S. 989, 85 S.Ct. 701, 13 L.Ed.2d 610 (1965) (recovery should not be made to depend on "anything as irrelevant as whether the wing tip of the aircraft passes through some fraction of an inch of the airspace directly above the plaintiff's land"). Although *Martin's* more expansive view of compensable injury may stem from the fact that the Washington constitution requires compensation for "damaging" as well as for "taking" property, it seems likely that the court would have reached the same result under a strict "taking" analysis.

For a superb study of the aircraft noise problem generally, see Baxter & Altree, Legal Aspects of Airport Noise, 15 J.L. & Econ. 1 (1972).

5. *Inverse Condemnation.* The landowner who prevails in her claim that governmental action "takes" her property will commonly obtain injunctive relief. Alternatively the court may award the landowner compensation for the value taken under the theory of inverse condemnation. As its name implies, inverse condemnation is just the opposite of direct condemnation under the eminent domain power: rather than the government bringing an action against the landowner for a forced sale, the landowner initiates an action against the government for a forced purchase.

As a general rule, the inverse condemnation remedy has been confined to situations in which government has physically invaded the claimant's land, as in *Causby* and *Martin*, note 4 above. There is, however, a current move toward extending inverse condemnation to regulatory as well as physically invasive takings. In Knight v. City of Billings, 642 P.2d 141 (Mont.1982), the City was held liable in inverse condemnation to landowners whose residentially-zoned property had been made unsuitable for residential use by the widening of an adjacent street and the installation of high intensity street lamps.

Lower California courts have come even closer to remedying purely regulatory exercises with cash awards. For example, in Eldridge v. City of Palo Alto, 57 Cal.App.3d 613, 129 Cal.Rptr. 575 (1976), the court held that inverse condemnation damages could be awarded to remedy the effects of an overly restrictive zoning ordinance. The California Supreme Court later expressly disapproved the remedy in Agins v. City of Tiburon, 24 Cal.3d 266, 276–277, 157 Cal.Rptr. 372, 378, 598 P.2d 25, 31 (1979) ("In combination, the need for preserving a degree of freedom in the land use planning function, and the inhibiting financial force which inheres in the inverse condemnation remedy, persuade us that on balance mandamus or declaratory relief rather than inverse condemnation is the appropriate relief under the circumstances").

The United States Supreme Court has twice ducked the issue whether inverse condemnation can result from regulatory takings. When *Agins* came before it on appeal, the Court decided that the ordinance in question was constitutional, and thus found it unnecessary to reach the question of remedy. 447 U.S. 255, 100 S.Ct. 2138, 65 L.Ed.2d 106 (1980). The issue arose again the following term in San Diego Gas & Electric Co. v. City of San Diego, 450 U.S. 621, 101 S.Ct. 1287, 67 L.Ed.2d 551 (1981). This time the Court dismissed the appeal for want of a final judgment. However, Justice Rehnquist's concurring opinion, and a dissenting opinion joined in by Justices Brennan, Stewart, Marshall and Powell, suggest that at least five members of the Court favored the inverse condemnation remedy: "Police power regulations such as zoning ordinances and other land-use restrictions can destroy the use and enjoyment of property in order to promote the public good just as effectively as formal condemnation or physical invasion of property. From the property owner's point of view, it may matter little whether his land is condemned or flooded, or whether it is restricted by regulation to use in its natural state, if the effect in both cases is to deprive him of all beneficial use of it." 450 U.S. at 652, 101 S.Ct. at 1304.

See generally, Kmiec, Regulatory Takings: The Supreme Court Runs Out of Gas in *San Diego*, 57 Indiana L.J. 45 (1982).

6. *Incentive Zoning and TDRs.* Under incentive zoning a municipality first establishes height and bulk restrictions for a district and then agrees to relax the restrictions' application to a specific parcel in return for the developer's agreement to incorporate some public amenity, such as a plaza or a park, into his project. (In some cases, the developer will instead give the municipality cash to enable it to purchase the desired amenity.) The value of the "zoning bonus" to the developer is the value of the increased space and rents enabled by relaxation of height and bulk limits. Recognizing this, municipalities will carefully calculate the bonus so that it equals or just slightly exceeds the cost to the developer of providing the amenity. See 2 Williams, American Planning Law § 49 (1974).

Transferable development rights (TDRs) have been widely used to ameliorate the effects of landmark preservation programs like the one in *Penn Central*. They have also been used in programs aimed at preserving ecologically or aesthetically important open spaces. Indeed, TDRs can be employed anytime a landowner is prohibited from developing its land to the bulk and height limits that generally apply in its district. *A*, who owns a regulated 18-story landmark in a district that is generally zoned to allow buildings thirty stories high, can be given a transferable development right for twelve stories; *A* can then sell this right to *B*, another landowner in the district, enabling *B* to build to forty-two stories—twelve stories over the generally applicable limit. (Alternatively, the city may buy the development rights from the affected landowner for cash, and itself reconvey the rights to some other landowner in the district, also for cash.) The TDR concept is considered in two essays by its leading academic exponent, Costonis, The Chicago Plan: Incentive Zoning and the Preservation of Urban Landmarks, 85 Harv.L.Rev. 574 (1972); Costonis, Development Rights Transfer: An Exploratory Essay, 83 Yale L.J. 75 (1973).

Can municipalities increase the amenities or cash they obtain from developers under incentive zoning programs by setting height and bulk limits lower than they otherwise would, so long as the limits are not set so low as to constitute a taking? Can municipalities acquire transferable development rights and, while holding them, impose more stringent limitations on height and bulk, thus increasing the value of the TDRs in their portfolio? In *Penn Central*, did the Supreme Court accept TDRs as the equivalent of cash for purposes of paying just compensation? What limits, if any, are there to a municipality's ability to finance its acquisition of amenities and cash by coining, and paying what is essentially play money?

7. Consider, in reflecting on *Euclid, Nectow, Belle Terre, Pennsylvania Coal* and *Penn Central*, and in reading the cases on aesthetic and exclusionary zoning that follow, whether the "takings" question is best considered, not in isolation, but rather in connection with a particular regulation's specific source in the police power. For example, government has generally been permitted to regulate unsafe or noxious uses even though the regulation cuts deeply into a private owner's use of his land. One reason for this result is that government's police power to protect "safety" and "health" is commonly thought to be greater than its power to protect less palpable "welfare" interests. But is it also relevant that, in these "safety" and "health" cases, the landowner's property interest will usually be less substantial than it is in "welfare" contexts? The owner of a brick factory in a residential neighborhood is not losing all that much when a zoning ordinance closes his operation down, for his neighbors probably could have shut him down anyway, under a nuisance theory. The fact that his neighbors had a private nuisance action against him for running a brickyard effectively means that he had no property

C. AESTHETICS

BRYAN v. CITY OF CHESTER, 212 Pa. 259, 61 A. 894 (1905). BROWN, J.: Under the police powers of a municipality it may prohibit the erection of insecure billboards within its limits, prevent the exhibition from secure ones of immoral or indecent advertisements or pictures, and protect the community from any actual nuisance resulting from the use of them. But this is not what the city of Chester attempted to do by its ordinance of December 1, 1903. There is a recital in the preamble of the ordinance that, in the sense of councils, showbills and advertising boards are unsightly, and very often are either a nuisance or create one; and thereupon those bodies ordained that in the future no additional boards shall be erected or constructed within the city limits, but permitting those already constructed and used to continue for the purpose of advertising. To say nothing of this inconsistent discrimination, the ordinance means that, though as a matter of fact a billboard may not be unsightly to the eyes of any other person than those of the members of councils, and may not be a nuisance nor create one, and the advertisements on it may neither shock nor offend public decency, an owner of private property cannot erect one on his land. This is a gross attempt at interference with the lawful use of private property, and the learned judge below properly declared the ordinance void, in concisely saying: "I know of no principle upon which it can be sustained. It is not a police regulation, nor for the preservation of health or the abatement or prevention of a nuisance, nor is it a fence or fire regulation." To this we do not feel called upon to add anything, contenting ourselves with quoting the following from Crawford v. City of Topeka, 51 Kan. 756, 33 Pac. 476. "All statutory restrictions of the use of property are imposed upon the theory that they are necessary for the safety, health, or comfort of the public; but a limitation without reason or necessity cannot be enforced. In what way can the erection of a safe structure for advertising purposes, near the front of a lot, endanger public safety any more than a like structure for some other lawful purpose? . . . Although the police power is a broad one, it is not without limitation, and a secure structure, which is not an infringement upon the public safety, and is not a nuisance, cannot be made one by legislative fiat, and then prohibited. It is doubtless within the power of the city to prohibit the erection of insecure billboards or other structures, require the owners to maintain them in a secure condition, and to provide for their removal at the expense of the owners in case they become dangerous. Perhaps regulations may be made with reference to the manner of construction, so as to insure safety; but the prohibition of the erection of structures upon the lot line, however safe they might be, would be an unwarranted invasion of private right."

STATE EX REL. STOYANOFF v. BERKELEY

Supreme Court of Missouri, 1970.
458 S.W.2d 305.

PRITCHARD, Commissioner.

Upon summary judgment the trial court issued a peremptory writ of mandamus to compel appellant to issue a residential building permit to respondents. The trial court's judgment is that the below-mentioned ordinances are violative of Section 10, Article I of the Constitution of Missouri, 1945, V.A.M.S., in that restrictions placed by the ordinances on the use of property deprive the owners of their property without due process of law. Relators' petition pleads that they applied to appellant Building Commissioner for a building permit to allow them to construct a single family residence in the City of Ladue, and that plans and specifications were submitted for the proposed residence, which was unusual in design, "but complied with all existing building and zoning regulations and ordinances of the City of Ladue, Missouri."

It is further pleaded that relators were refused a building permit for the construction of their proposed residence upon the ground that the permit was not approved by the Architectural Board of the City of Ladue. Ordinance 131, as amended by Ordinance 281 of that city, purports to set up an Architectural Board to approve plans and specifications for buildings and structures erected within the city and in a preamble to "conform to certain minimum architectural standards of appearance and conformity with surrounding structures, and that unsightly, grotesque and unsuitable structures, detrimental to the stability of value and the welfare of surrounding property, structures and residents, and to the general welfare and happiness of the community, be avoided, and that appropriate standards of beauty and conformity be fostered and encouraged." It is asserted in the petition that the ordinances are invalid, illegal and void, "are unconstitutional in that they are vague and provide no standard nor uniform rule by which to guide the architectural board," that the city acted in excess of statutory powers in enacting the ordinances, which "attempt to allow respondent to impose aesthetic standards for buildings in the City of Ladue, and are in excess of the powers granted the City of Ladue by said statute."

Relators filed a motion for summary judgment and affidavits were filed in opposition thereto. Richard D. Shelton, Mayor of the City of Ladue, deponed that the facts in appellant's answer were true and correct, as here pertinent: that the City of Ladue constitutes one of the finer suburban residential areas of Metropolitan St. Louis, the homes therein are considerably more expensive than in cities of comparable size, being homes on lots from three fourths of an acre to three or more acres each; that a zoning ordinance was enacted by the city regulating the height, number of stories, size of buildings, percentage of lot occupancy, yard sizes, and the location and use of buildings and land for trade, industry, residence and other purposes; that the zoning regulations were made in accordance with a comprehensive plan "designed to promote the health and general welfare of the residents of the City of Ladue," which in furtherance of said objectives duly enacted said Ordinances numbered 131 and 281. Appellant also asserted in his answer that these ordinances were a reasonable exercise of the city's governmental, legislative and police powers, as determined by its legislative body, and as stated in the above-quoted preamble to the ordinances. It is then pleaded that relators' description of their proposed residence as " 'unusual in design' is the understatement of the year. It is in fact a monstrosity of grotesque design, which would seriously impair the value of property in the neighborhood."

The affidavit of Harold C. Simon, a developer of residential subdivisions in St. Louis County, is that he is familiar with relators' lot upon which they seek to build a house, and with the surrounding houses in the neighborhood; that the houses therein existent are virtually all two-story houses of conventional architectural design, such as Colonial, French Provincial or English; and that the house which relators propose to construct is of ultra-modern design which would clash with and not be in conformity with any other house in the entire neighborhood. It is Mr. Simon's opinion that the design and appearance of relators' proposed residence would have a substantial adverse effect upon the market values of other residential property in the neighborhood, such average market value ranging from $60,000 to $85,000 each.

As a part of the affidavit of Russell H. Riley, consultant for the city planning and engineering firm of Harland Bartholomew & Associates, photographic exhibits of homes surrounding relators' lot were attached. To the south is the conventional frame residence of Mrs. T.R. Collins. To the west is the Colonial two-story frame house of the Lewis family. To the northeast is the large brick English Tudor home of Mrs. Elmer Hubbs. Immediately to the north are the large Colonial homes of Mr. Alex Cornwall and Mr. L. Peter Wetzel. In substance Mr. Riley went on to say that the City of Ladue is one of the finer residential suburbs in the St. Louis area with a minimum of commercial or industrial usage. The development of residences in the city has been primarily by private subdivisions, usually with one main lane or drive leading therein (such as Lorenzo Road Subdivision which runs north off of Ladue Road in which relators' lot is located). The homes are considerably more expensive than average homes found in a city of comparable size. The ordinance which has been adopted by the City of Ladue is typical of those which have been adopted by a number of suburban cities in St. Louis County and in similar cities throughout the United States, the need therefor being based upon the protection of existing property values by preventing the construction of houses that are in complete conflict with the general type of houses in a given area. The intrusion into this neighborhood of relators' unusual, grotesque and nonconforming structure would have a substantial adverse effect on market values of other homes in the immediate area. According to Mr. Riley the standards of Ordinance 131, as amended by Ordinance 281, are usually and customarily applied in city planning work and are: "(1) whether the proposed house meets the customary architectural requirements in appearance and design for a house of the particular type which is proposed (whether it be Colonial, English Tudor, French Provincial, or Modern), (2) whether the proposed house is in general conformity with the style and design of surrounding structures, and (3) whether the proposed house lends itself to the proper architectural development of the City; and that in applying said standards the Architectural Board and its Chairman are to determine whether the proposed house will have an adverse affect on the stability of values in the surrounding area."

Photographic exhibits of relators' proposed residence were also attached to Mr. Riley's affidavit. They show the residence to be of a pyramid shape, with a flat top, and with triangular shaped windows or doors at one or more corners.

Although appellant has briefed the point that it is a constitutional exercise of the police power for the Legislature to authorize cities to enact zoning ordinances, it is apparent that relators do not contest that issue. Rather, relators' position is that "the creation by the City of Ladue of an architectural board for the purpose of promoting and maintaining 'general conformity with the style and design of surrounding structures' is totally unauthorized by our Enabling Statute." It is further contended by relators that Ordinances 131 and 281 are invalid and unconstitutional as being an unreasonable and arbitrary exercise of the police power (as based entirely on aesthetic values); and that the same are invalid as an unlawful delegation of legislative powers (to the Architectural Board). . . .

. . . In Marrs v. City of Oxford (D.C.D.Kan.) 24 F.2d 541, 548, it was said, "The stabilizing of property values, and giving some assurance to the public that, if property is purchased in a residential district, its value as such will be preserved, is probably the most cogent reason back of zoning ordinances." The preamble to Ordinance 131, quoted above in part, demonstrates that its purpose is to conform to the dictates of § 89.040, with reference to preserving values of property by zoning procedure and restrictions on the use of property. This is an illustration of what was referred to in Deimeke v. State Highway Commission, Mo., 444 S.W.2d 480, 484, as a growing number of cases recognizing a change in the scope of the term "general welfare." In the Deimeke case on the same page it is said, "Property use which offends sensibilities and debases property values affects not only the adjoining property owners in that vicinity but the general public as well because when such property values are destroyed or seriously impaired, the tax base of the community is affected and the public suffers economically as a result."

Relators say further that Ordinances 131 and 281 are invalid and unconstitutional as being an unreasonable and arbitrary exercise of the police power. It is argued that a mere reading of these ordinances shows that they are based entirely on aesthetic factors in that the stated purpose of the Architectural Board is to maintain "conformity with surrounding structures" and to assure that structures "conform to certain minimum architectural standards of appearance." The argument ignores the further provisos in the ordinance: ". . . and that unsightly, grotesque and unsuitable structures, *detrimental to the stability of value and the welfare of surrounding property, structures, and residents,* and *to the general welfare and happiness of the community,* be avoided, and that appropriate standards of beauty and conformity be fostered and encouraged." (Italics added.) Relators' proposed residence does not descend to the "'patently offensive character of vehicle graveyards in close proximity to such highways'" referred to in the Deimeke case. Nevertheless, the aesthetic factor to be taken into account by the Architectural Board is not to be considered alone. Along with that inherent factor is the effect that the proposed residence would have upon the property values in the area. In this time of burgeoning urban areas, congested with people and structures, it is certainly in keeping with the ultimate ideal of general welfare that the Architectural Board, in its function, preserve and protect existing areas in which structures of a general conformity of architecture have been erected. The area under consideration is clearly, from the record, a fashionable one. In State ex rel. Civello v. City of New Orleans, 154 La. 271, 97 So. 440, 444, the court said, "If by the term 'aesthetic considerations' is meant a regard merely for outward appearances, for good taste in the matter of the beauty of the neighborhood itself, we do not observe any substantial reason for saying that such a consideration is not a matter of general welfare. The beauty of a fashionable residence neighborhood in a city is for the comfort and happiness of the residents, and it sustains in a general way the value of property in the neighborhood."

In the matter of enacting zoning ordinances and the procedures for determining whether any certain proposed structure or use is in compliance with or offends the basic ordinance, it is well settled that courts will not substitute their judgments for the city's legislative body, if the result is not oppressive, arbitrary or unreasonable and does not infringe upon a valid pre-existing nonconforming use. The denial by appellant of a building permit for relators' highly modernistic residence in this area where traditional Colonial, French Provincial and English Tudor styles of architecture are erected does not appear to be arbitrary and unreasonable when the basic purpose to be served is that of the general welfare of persons in the entire community. . . .

The judgment is reversed.

NOTES

1. What vision of the public health, safety, welfare and morals underlay the enactment of the billboard ordinance in Bryan v. City of Chester? The enactment of the architectural control ordinance in *Stoyanoff?*

The preservation or creation of such amenities as scenic highways and architecturally homogeneous neighborhoods has only gradually and partially obtained a secure foothold in the police power. Courts originally took a jaundiced view of aesthetic regulations, holding that the presence of an aesthetic objective would defeat an otherwise valid land use control measure. Most courts in the country have since arrived at the position that the presence of an aesthetic objective will not defeat an ordinance so long as the ordinance can also be justified in terms of some other, more acceptable element of the police power—health, safety or the protection of property values. A few states now hold that aesthetic objects alone are sufficient to sustain land use legislation. For a head count of the states, see Bufford, Beyond the Eye of the Beholder: A New Majority of Jurisdictions Authorize Aesthetic Regulation, 48 U.M.K.C.L.Rev. 125 (1980).

Some courts adopting the centrist position, that an aesthetic objective does not defeat an ordinance that also rests on some more traditional element of the police power, will sift through the ordinance to determine the presence of that traditional health or safety objective. The search occasionally leads to ludicrous results. For example, in St. Louis Gunning Advertising Co. v. City of St. Louis, 235 Mo. 99, 145, 137 S.W. 929, 942 (1911), the court reached far to uphold a billboard ordinance on health and safety grounds: "In cases of fire they [billboards] often cause their spread and constitute barriers against their extinction; and in cases of high wind, their temporary character, frail structure and broad surface, render them liable to be blown down . . . behind these obstructions the lowest form of prostitution and other acts of immorality are frequently carried on, almost under public gaze; they offer shelter and concealment for the criminal while lying in wait for his victim; and last, but not least, they obstruct the light, sunshine and air, which are so conducive to health and comfort."

Other courts adopting the centrist position do not require a concurrent health or safety objective, and will uphold an aesthetic regulation if it is at least likely to advance the public welfare by protecting property values within the community. Thus, the *Stoyanoff* ordinance would be upheld on the ground that to allow plaintiffs' "ultra modern" design in a neighborhood of traditional English Tudor, Colonial and French Provincial homes would depress property values in the neighborhood. Is a measure based on property values really independent of aesthetic judgments? What would have caused land values to drop other than the aggregate reaction of neighbors and prospective buyers to a visually offensive use? Is there any difference between this approach and the newer, less widely accepted position that validates aesthetic regulations apart from any showing that they preserve land values?

For a challenging critique of orthodox theory, see Costonis, Law and Aesthetics: A Critique and a Reformulation of the Dilemmas, 80 Mich.L.Rev. 355 (1982). For an excellent overview of developments in the area, see Rowlett, Aesthetic Regulation Under the Police Power: The New General Welfare and the Presumption of Constitutionality, 34 Vand.L.Rev. 603 (1981).

2. *Aesthetics and the First Amendment.* Aesthetic regulations sometimes run head-on into free speech interests protected under the First Amendment to the United States Constitution, as applied to the states under the Fourteenth Amendment. Indeed, the early reluctance to validate these regulations doubtless stemmed in part from the concern that to allow city councils to legislate what is beautiful, as well as what is safe and healthful, might improperly chill artistic and political expression.

Ironically, one of the first decisions to accept aesthetics as a legitimate, independent object of local regulation, and to reject the First Amendment claim, upheld an ordinance that was directly aimed at curbing political speech. People v. Stover, 12 N.Y.2d 462, 240 N.Y.S. 2d 734, 191 N.E.2d 272 (1963) (upholding enforcement of city ordinance, prohibiting front yard clotheslines, against defendants who had placed a clothesline, "filled with old clothes and rags," in their front yard as a form of protest against local taxes; recognizing that the clothesline was a form of nonverbal expression protected under the First Amendment, the court held that it was subject to reasonable regulation, presumably intended to reduce traffic hazards by providing clear visibility at street corners).

The United States Supreme Court has sketched several guidelines for regulation in the area. Although the Court's decisions generally sustain aesthetics as a basis for regulation, even against charges that such regulations violate the First Amendment, the guidelines are clouded, both by the absence of a clear majority, and by the proliferation of concurring and dissenting opinions.

In Young v. American Mini Theatres, Inc., 427 U.S. 50, 96 S.Ct. 2440, 49 L.Ed.2d 310 (1976), the Court, in a 5–4 decision, upheld a Detroit zoning ordinance that prohibited "adult" movie theatres, bookstores and peep shows from locating within 1000 feet of each other. Justice Stevens' plurality opinion started from the premise that society's interest in protecting erotic expression is less compelling than its interest in protecting political expression, and concluded that "[w]e are not persuaded that the Detroit zoning ordinances will have a significant deterrent effect on the exhibition of films protected by the First Amendment." 427 U.S. at 60, 96 S.Ct. at 2447. Justice Powell, writing separately on the point, viewed the case as "presenting an example of innovative land-use regulation, implicating First Amendment concerns only incidentally and to a limited extent"; 427 U.S. at 73, 96 S.Ct. at 2453. He applied a four-part test to uphold the ordinance: the ordinance must be (1) within the constitutional power of the government to enact; (2) it must further "an important or substantial governmental interest"; (3) the interest must be unrelated to the suppression of free expression; and (4) if the ordinance imposes restraints on First Amendment freedoms, they must be no greater than is essential for the furtherance of the interest. 427 U.S. at 79–80, 96 S.Ct. at 2456–2457.

Yet, the municipal power validated in *Young* was not intended to be "infinite or unchallengeable," and in Schad v. Borough of Mt. Ephraim, 452 U.S. 61, 101 S.Ct. 2176, 68 L.Ed.2d 671 (1981), the Court overturned appellant's conviction under a zoning ordinance that prohibited all live entertainment, including live nude dancing, in the Borough. Writing for the majority, Justice White asserted that "when a zoning law infringes upon a protected liberty, it must be narrowly drawn and must further a sufficiently substantial governmental interest." 452 U.S. at 69, 101 S.Ct. at 2183. Justice Blackmun, concurring, thought that "the presumption of validity that traditionally attends a local government's exercise of its zoning powers carries little, if any weight where the zoning regulation trenches on rights of expression protected under the First Amendment." 452 U.S. at 77, 101 S.Ct. at 2187. Chief Justice Burger, joined by Justice Rehnquist, dissented: "At issue here is the right of a small community to ban an activity incompatible with a quiet, residential atmosphere. The Borough of Mount Ephraim did nothing more than employ traditional police power to provide a setting of tranquility." 452 U.S. at 85, 101 S.Ct. at 2191.

In Metromedia, Inc. v. City of San Diego, 453 U.S. 490, 101 S.Ct. 2882, 69 L.Ed.2d 800 (1981), a 6–3 decision that generated five opinions, the Court overturned a San Diego ordinance that prohibited off-site billboard advertising, but permitted on-site commercial advertising. (Advertising is "on-site" when it touts goods or services available on the premises where the advertising is located.) Justice White's plurality opinion concluded that the ordinance was valid as applied to *commercial* advertising, but invalid as applied to *noncommercial* advertising, because the ordinance completely proscribed noncommercial billboard advertising while allowing some forms of commercial advertising, and because noncommercial speech is entitled to greater protection than commercial speech. The plurality opinion suggested, however, that a narrowing construction that would remove the prohibition respecting noncommercial signs could make the ordinance valid. On remand, the California Supreme Court held that it could not so construe the legislation and invalidated the entire ordinance. Metromedia, Inc. v. City of San Diego, 32 Cal.3d 180, 185 Cal.Rptr. 260, 649 P.2d 902 (1982).

Can *Young, Schad* and *Metromedia* be reconciled with Belle Terre v. Boraas, page 1088 above? To what extent does the First Amendment require every municipality to permit every form of speech within its boundaries? Is a municipality under an obligation to bear a "fair share" of all protected uses within a region? Compare the next principal case, Southern Burlington County N.A.A.C.P. v. Mt. Laurel, p. 1128.

See generally, Marcus, Zoning Obscenity: Or, the Moral Politics of Porn, 27 Buffalo L.Rev. 1 (1977).

3. *Architectural Controls*. The principal criticism levelled against architectural review ordinances is that they delegate excessive discretionary authority to administrative agencies, exposing landowners to arbitrary and standardless decisions. For example, the landowners in *Stoyanoff* argued that the ordinance represented an unconstitutional delegation of power to the Architectural Board; that the Board could not be given "the power to determine what is unsightly and grotesque"; and that the standards, "whether the proposed structure will conform to proper architectural standards in appearance and design, and will be in general conformity with the style and design of surrounding structures and conducive to the proper architectural development of the City" were inadequate. 458 S.W.2d at 311. Although the argument failed in *Stoyanoff*, it has succeeded elsewhere. See, for example, Pacesetter Homes, Inc. v. Village of Olympia Fields, 104 Ill.App.2d 218, 244 N.E.2d 369 (1968).

Courts will sometimes look outside the express terms of the applicable enabling legislation to find the necessary constraining standards. Architectural principles and the architecture profession provide a ready source of guidelines. See Reid v. Architectural Board of Review, 119 Ohio App. 67, 192 N.E.2d 74, 77 (1963) ("When borne in mind that the members of the Board are highly trained experts in the field of architecture, the instruction that they resolve these questions on 'proper architectural principles' is profoundly reasonable since such expression has reference to the basic knowledge on which their profession is founded"). Similarly, the judicial willingness to uphold architectural controls in designated historical districts probably stems from the belief that the period's architectural style will implicitly confine the Board's discretion. See, for example, City of New Orleans v. Impastato, 198 La. 206, 3 So.2d 559 (1941) (upholding architectural controls for New Orleans' historic French Quarter).

See generally, Bohlman & Dundas, Local Control of Architecture: Is it Legal?, 9 Real Estate L.J. 17 (1980); Anderson, Architectural Controls, 12 Syracuse L.Rev. 26 (1960).

4. *Historic Preservation*. The Supreme Court's decision in Penn Central Transportation Co. v. New York City, page 1100, above, gave the burgeoning preservationist movement a substantial boost. Al-

though the federal government had indicated a programmatic interest as early as the Antiquities Act of 1906, 16 U.S.C.A. §§ 431 *et seq.*, it was not until the 1960's that all levels of government became actively involved. By the time *Penn Central* was decided, all fifty states and more than 500 municipalities, including many of the nation's largest cities, had enacted laws aimed at preserving landmark buildings and historic districts. According to the former executive director of New York's Landmarks Commission, *Penn Central* spurred the enactment of rigorous landmark preservation ordinances in Washington, D.C. and in Louisville, Kentucky, and "mayors and city council members all over the nation are looking at their local laws and are realizing that now they have Supreme Court backing." Quoted in Cahan, Rescuing Our Architectural Heritage, 6 Barrister, Fall 1979 at 46.

Federal efforts at historic preservation combine a variety of techniques. For example, the 1966 Historic Preservation Act, 16 U.S.C.A. §§ 470 *et seq.* (1976), authorized grants in aid for preservationist purposes and, probably more important, authorized the creation of a National Register of Historic Places to list landmarks nominated by the states. Any federally-assisted project affecting a registered landmark must take the project's effects into account, and the responsible agency must give the Advisory Council on Historic Preservation the opportunity to comment on these effects. 16 U.S.C.A. § 470(a), (f) (1976). A building's designation as an historic landmark also provides the basis for federal income tax incentives to its restoration and disincentives to its demolition. See 26 U.S.C.A. § 46(a)(2)(F) (25% investment tax credit for rehabilitation of historic residential, commercial and industrial buildings; substantial tax penalty must be paid on demolition of any of these properties).

Local efforts have generally followed the regulatory patterns adopted in New York City and summarized in *Penn Central*. Historic district regulations will typically require that any new construction or demolition not be inconsistent with buildings already in the district. See, for example, the Massachusetts Historic Districts Act, Mass.Gen. Laws Ann. c. 40C (1973; Supp.1983). Because they have a substantial impact on landowners within a designated historic district, these ordinances usually give local residents some say in the designation decision, sometimes requiring a specified percentage of residents to agree to the designation.

Historic preservation law has been reviewed in several extensive symposia, among them, 36 Law & Contemp. Probs. 309 (1971); 8 Conn.L.Rev. 199 (1976); 12 Wake Forest L.Rev. 1 (1976); 1 Pace L.Rev. 569 (1981); and 11 N.C.Cent.L.J. 195 (1980).

5. Professor Carol Rose has traced three dominant themes in the evolution of historic preservation. "The first of these, especially characteristic of the nineteenth century, is the idea that historic preservation should seek to inspire the observer with a sense of patriotism. Thus, nineteenth-century preservation activities revolved

around structures associated with famous individuals or events; the movement to save Mount Vernon is perhaps the epitome of this approach. The second theme has a cultural, artistic, and architectural focus emerging at about the turn of the century with the entry of professional artists and architects into historic preservation. The protagonists of this view thought preservation activities should focus on the artistic merit of buildings or groups of buildings and on the integrity of their architectural style. In recent years a third strand has appeared that incorporates some elements of the earlier two. Its most notable characteristic is a concern for the environmental and psychological effects of historic preservation. Indeed, this approach to preservation coincided with the environmental movement, and like that movement centers on the relationship of human beings to their physical surroundings. It stresses the 'sense of place' that older structures lend to a community, giving individuals interest, orientation, and a sense of familiarity in their surroundings." Rose, Preservation and Community: New Directions in the Law of Historic Preservation, 33 Stan.L.Rev. 473, 479–480 (1981).

According to Professor Rose, the central questions in historic preservation law are, "What elements of the past are to be preserved, and why should their preservation take the form of maintaining buildings or groups of buildings?" 33 Stan.L.Rev. 478. These questions are important and deserve to be considered carefully, for the historical designation of a run-down area is typically the prelude to a dramatic social upheaval: the eviction of lower income tenants, restoration of buildings and sale or rental of the restored buildings to middle or upper income residents (a process sometimes called "gentrification").

6. *Environmental Protection*. The environmental protection movement that began in the 1960's produced several significant innovations in resource management techniques aimed at controlling air, water and land pollution. Earlier pollution control efforts had, like land use controls generally, relied primarily on private and public nuisance actions, on easement and covenant arrangements, and on zoning ordinances separating industrial and residential uses.

The federal government was the main source of innovation. The 1967 Air Quality Act, 42 U.S.C. §§ 7401 *et seq.* (1981), started from the premise that air pollution does not respect municipal, or even state boundaries and is not efficiently manageable under uniform standards. It charged the federal government to identify *air quality control regions*—areas that include most sources of contaminants in an urban area, as well as most persons and property affected by these contaminants—and *air quality criteria*—scientific evaluations of the harms threatened by any contaminant or combination of contaminants. The Act directed the states to use the federally-established air quality criteria as the basis for setting *air quality standards* prescribing the allowable concentration of contaminants in the air over any designated air quality control region. Many states, in turn, directed their local governments within air quality regions to convert air quality standards into *emission control standards* prescribing the extent to which each polluter in the region would have to curtail its emissions in order for the overall level prescribed by the air quality standard to be achieved. The Act has since been amended to strengthen the federal government's role in the prescription and enforcement of standards. See generally, Goldstein & Ford, The Management of Air Quality: Legal Structures and Official Behavior, 21 Buffalo L.Rev. 1 (1971).

The 1969 National Environmental Policy Act, 42 U.S.C.A. §§ 4321 *et seq.* (1976), takes a different tack, making federal agencies accountable for the environmental effects of their activities. NEPA directs all federal agencies to "utilize a systematic, interdisciplinary approach which will insure the integrated use of the natural and social sciences and environmental design arts in planning and in decision-making which may have an impact on man's environment," and to:

> include in every recommendation or report on proposals for legislation and other major Federal actions significantly affecting the quality of the human environment, a detailed statement by the responsible official on (i) the environmental impact of the proposed action, (ii) any adverse environmental effects which cannot be avoided should the proposal be implemented, (iii) alternatives to the proposed action, (iv) the relationship between local short-term uses of man's environment and the maintenance and enhancement of long-term productivity, and (v) any irreversible and irretrievable commitments of resources, which would be involved in the proposed action should it be implemented. 42 U.S.C. § 4332(A)(C) (1976).

More than half the states have taken a similar approach, requiring state agencies to file environmental impact reports. See F. Grad, 2 Environmental Law § 9.07 (1980); Hagman, NEPA's Progeny Inhabit the States—Were the Genes Defective? 7 Urb.L.Ann. 3 (1974). For a skeptical appraisal of NEPA's efficacy, see Sax, The (Unhappy) Truth about NEPA, 26 Okla.L.Rev. 239, 240 (1973) ("I know of no solid evidence to support the belief that requiring articulation, detailed findings, or reasoned opinions enhances the integrity or propriety of the administrative decisions. I think the emphasis on the redemptive quality of procedural reform is about nine parts myth and one part coconut oil").

Air quality control and federal, state and local accountability for environmental effects are just two examples of the new resource management techniques. Other legislation has sought to control activities involving water pollution, solid waste disposal, radiation, pesticides, power plant siting and automotive emissions. The techniques have ranged from direct regulation and accountability to tax incentives and the imposition of civil penalties designed to tax polluters at

D. EXCLUSIONARY EFFECTS

SOUTHERN BURLINGTON COUNTY N.A.A.C.P. v. TOWNSHIP OF MT. LAUREL

Supreme Court of New Jersey, 1975.
67 N.J. 151, 336 A.2d 713.

HALL, J.

This case attacks the system of land use regulation by defendant Township of Mount Laurel on the ground that low and moderate income families are thereby unlawfully excluded from the municipality. The trial court so found and declared the township zoning ordinance totally invalid. Its judgment went on, in line with the requests for affirmative relief, to order the municipality to make studies of the housing needs of low and moderate income persons presently or formerly residing in the community in substandard housing, as well as those in such income classifications presently employed in the township and living elsewhere or reasonably expected to be employed therein in the future, and to present a plan of affirmative public action designed "to enable and encourage the satisfaction of the indicated needs." Jurisdiction was retained for judicial consideration and approval of such a plan and for the entry of a final order requiring its implementation.

The township appealed to the Appellate Division and those plaintiffs, not present or former residents cross-appealed on the basis that the judgment should have directed that the prescribed plan take into account as well a fair share of the regional housing needs of low and moderate income families without limitation to those having past, present or prospective connection with the township. The appeals were certified on our own motion before argument in the Division.

The implications of the issue presented are indeed broad and far-reaching, extending much beyond these particular plaintiffs and the boundaries of this particular municipality.

There is not the slightest doubt that New Jersey has been, and continues to be, faced with a desperate need for housing, especially of decent living accommodations economically suitable for low and moderate income families. The situation was characterized as a "crisis" and fully explored and documented by Governor Cahill in two special messages to the Legislature—*A Blueprint for Housing in New Jersey* (1970) and *New Horizons in Housing* (1972).

Plaintiffs represent the minority group poor (black and Hispanic)[3] seeking such quarters. But they are not the only category of persons barred from so many municipalities by reason of restrictive land use regulations. We have reference to young and elderly couples, single persons and large, growing families not in the poverty class, but who still cannot afford the only kinds of housing realistically permitted in most places—relatively high-priced, single-family detached dwellings on sizeable lots and, in some municipalities, expensive apartments. We will, therefore, consider the case from the wider viewpoint that the effect of Mount Laurel's land use regulation has been to prevent various categories of persons from living in the township because of the limited extent of their income and resources. In this connection, we accept the representation of the municipality's counsel at oral argument that the regulatory scheme was not adopted with any desire or intent to exclude prospective residents on the obviously illegal bases of race, origin or believed social incompatibility.

As already intimated, the issue here is not confined to Mount Laurel. The same question arises with respect to any number of other municipalities of sizeable land area outside the central cities and older built-up suburbs of our North and South Jersey metropolitan areas (and surrounding some of the smaller cities outside those areas as well) which, like Mount Laurel, have substantially shed rural characteristics and have undergone great population increase since World War II, or are now in the process of doing so, but still are not completely developed and remain in the path of inevitable future residential, commercial and industrial demand and growth. Most such municipalities, with but relatively insignificant variation in details, present generally comparable physical situations, courses of municipal policies, practices, enactments and results and human, governmental and legal problems arising therefrom. It is in the context of communities now of this type or which become so in the future, rather than with central cities or older built-up suburbs or areas still rural and likely to continue to be for some time yet, that we deal with the question raised.

Extensive oral and documentary evidence was introduced at the trial, largely informational, dealing with the development of Mount Laurel, including the nature and effect of municipal regulation, the details of the region of which it is a part and the recent history there-

---

3. Plaintiffs fall into four categories: (1) present residents of the township residing in dilapidated or substandard housing; (2) former residents who were forced to move elsewhere because of the absence of suitable housing; (3) nonresidents living in central city substandard housing in the region who desire to secure decent housing and accompanying advantages within their means elsewhere; (4) three organizations representing the housing and other interests of racial minorities. The township originally challenged plaintiffs' standing to bring this action. The trial court properly held that the resident plaintiffs had adequate standing to ground the entire action and found it unnecessary to pass on that of the other plaintiffs. The issue has not been raised on appeal. We merely add that both categories of nonresident individuals likewise have standing. No opinion is expressed as to the standing of the organizations.

of, and some of the basics of housing, special reference being directed to that for low and moderate income families. The record has been supplemented by figures, maps, studies and literature furnished or referred to by counsel and the *amici,* so that the court has a clear picture of land use regulation and its effects in the developing municipalities of the state.

This evidence was not contradicted by the township, except in a few unimportant details. Its candid position is that, conceding its land use regulation was intended to result and has resulted in economic discrimination and exclusion of substantial segments of the area population, its policies and practices are in the best present and future fiscal interest of the municipality and its inhabitants and are legally permissible and justified. It further asserts that the trial court was without power to direct the affirmative relief it did.

I

The Facts

Mount Laurel is a flat, sprawling township, 22 square miles, or about 14,000 acres, in area, on the west central edge of Burlington County. It is roughly triangular in shape, with its base, approximately eight miles long, extending in a northeasterly-southwesterly direction roughly parallel with and a few miles east of the Delaware River. Part of its southerly side abuts Cherry Hill in Camden County. That section of the township is about seven miles from the boundary line of the city of Camden and not more than 10 miles from the Benjamin Franklin Bridge crossing the river to Philadelphia.

In 1950, the township had a population of 2817, only about 600 more people than it had in 1940. It was then, as it had been for decades, primarily a rural agricultural area with no sizeable settlements or commercial or industrial enterprises. The populace generally lived in individual houses scattered along country roads. There were several pockets of poverty, with deteriorating or dilapidated housing (apparently 300 or so units of which remain today in equally poor condition). After 1950, as in so many other municipalities similarly situated, residential development and some commerce and industry began to come in. By 1960 the population had almost doubled to 5249 and by 1970 had more than doubled again to 11,221. These new residents were, of course, "outsiders" from the nearby central cities and older suburbs or from more distant places drawn here by reason of employment in the region. The township is now definitely a part of the outer ring of the South Jersey metropolitan area, which area we define as those portions of Camden, Burlington, and Gloucester Counties within a semicircle having a radius of 20 miles or so from the heart of Camden city. And 65% of the township is still vacant land or in agricultural use.

The growth of the township has been spurred by the construction or improvement of main highways through or near it. The New Jersey Turnpike, and now route I-295, a freeway paralleling the turnpike, traverse the municipality near its base, with the main Camden-Philadelphia turnpike interchange at the corner nearest Camden. State route 73 runs at right angles to the turnpike at the interchange and route 38 slices through the northeasterly section. Routes 70 and U.S. 130 are not far away. This highway network gives the township a most strategic location from the standpoint of transport of goods and people by truck and private car. There is no other means of transportation.

The location and nature of development has been, as usual, controlled by the local zoning enactments. The general ordinance presently in force, which was declared invalid by the trial court, was adopted in 1964. We understand that earlier enactments provided, however, basically the same scheme but were less restrictive as to residential development. The growth pattern dictated by the ordinance is typical.

Under the present ordinance, 29.2% of all the land in the township, or 4,121 acres, is zoned for industry. This amounts to 2,800 more acres than were so zoned by the 1954 ordinance. The industrial districts comprise most of the land on both sides of the turnpike and routes I-295, 73 and 38. Only industry meeting specified performance standards is permitted. The effect is to limit the use substantially to light manufacturing, research, distribution of goods, offices and the like. Some nonindustrial uses, such as agriculture, farm dwellings, motels, a harness racetrack, and certain retail sales and service establishments, are permitted in this zone. At the time of trial no more than 100 acres, mostly in the southwesterly corner along route 73 adjacent to the turnpike and I-295 interchanges, were actually occupied by industrial uses. They had been constructed in recent years, mostly in several industrial parks, and involved tax ratables of about 16 million dollars. The rest of the land so zoned has remained undeveloped. If it were fully utilized, the testimony was that about 43,500 industrial jobs would be created, but it appeared clear that, as happens in the case of so many municipalities, much more land has been so zoned than the reasonable potential for industrial movement or expansion warrants. At the same time, however, the land cannot be used for residential development under the general ordinance.

The amount of land zoned for retail business use under the general ordinance is relatively small—169 acres, or 1.2% of the total. Some of it is near the turnpike interchange; most of the rest is allocated to a handful of neighborhood commercial districts. While the greater part of the land so zoned appears to be in use, there is no major shopping center or concentrated retail commercial area—"downtown"—in the township.

The balance of the land area, almost 10,000 acres, has been developed until recently in the conventional form of major subdivisions. The general ordinance provides for four residential zones, designated R–1, R–1D, R–2 and R–3. All permit only single-family, detached dwellings, one house per lot—the usual form of grid development. Attached townhouses, apartments (except on farms for agricultural workers) and mobile homes are not allowed anywhere in the township under the general ordinance. This dwelling development, resulting in the previously mentioned quadrupling of the population, has been largely confined to the R–1 and R–2 districts in two sections—the northeasterly and southwesterly corners adjacent to the turnpike and other major highways. The result has been quite intensive development of these sections, but at a low density. The dwellings are substantial; the average value in 1971 was $32,500 and is undoubtedly much higher today.

The general ordinance requirements, while not as restrictive as those in many similar municipalities, nonetheless realistically allow only homes within the financial reach of persons of at least middle income. The R–1 zone requires a minimum lot area of 9,375 square feet, a minimum lot width of 75 feet at the building line, and a minimum dwelling floor area of 1,100 square feet if a one-story building and 1,300 square feet if one and one-half stories or higher. Originally this zone comprised about 2,500 acres. Most of the subdivisions have been constructed within it so that only a few hundred acres remain (the testimony was at variance as to the exact amount). The R–2 zone, comprising a single district of 141 acres in the northeasterly corner, has been completely developed. While it only required a minimum floor area of 900 square feet for a one-story dwelling, the minimum lot size was 11,000 square feet; otherwise the requisites were the same as in the R–1 zone.

The general ordinance places the remainder of the township, outside of the industrial and commercial zones and the R–1D district (to be mentioned shortly), in the R–3 zone. This zone comprises over 7,000 acres—slightly more than half of the total municipal area—practically all of which is located in the central part of the township extending southeasterly to the apex of the triangle. The testimony was that about 4,600 acres of it then remained available for housing development. Ordinance requirements are substantially higher, however, in that the minimum lot size is increased to about one-half acre (20,000 square feet). (We understand that sewer and water utilities have not generally been installed, but, of course, they can be.) Lot width at the building line must be 100 feet. Minimum dwelling floor area is as in the R–1 zone. Presently this section is primarily in agricultural use; it contains as well most of the municipality's substandard housing . . . .

The record thoroughly substantiates the findings of the trial court that over the years Mount Laurel "has acted affirmatively to control development and to attract a selective type of growth" and that "through its zoning ordinances has exhibited economic discrimination in that the poor have been deprived of adequate housing and the opportunity to secure the construction of subsidized housing, and has used federal, state, county and local finances and resources solely for the betterment of middle and upper-income persons."

There cannot be the slightest doubt that the reason for this course of conduct has been to keep down local taxes on *property* (Mount Laurel is not a high tax municipality) and that the policy was carried out without regard for non-fiscal considerations with respect to *people*, either within or without its boundaries. This conclusion is demonstrated not only by what was done and what happened, as we have related, but also by innumerable direct statements of municipal officials at public meetings over the years which are found in the exhibits. The trial court referred to a number of them. No official testified to the contrary.

This policy of land use regulation for a fiscal end derives from New Jersey's tax structure, which has imposed on local real estate most of the cost of municipal and county government and of the primary and secondary education of the municipality's children. The latter expense is much the largest, so, basically, the fewer the school children, the lower the tax rate. Sizeable industrial and commercial ratables are eagerly sought and homes and the lots on which they are situate are required to be large enough, through minimum lot size and minimum floor areas, to have substantial value in order to produce greater tax revenues to meet school costs. Large families who cannot afford to buy large houses and must live in cheaper rental accommodations are definitely not wanted, so we find drastic bedroom restrictions for, or complete prohibition of, multi-family or other feasible housing for those of lesser income.

This pattern of land use regulation has been adopted for the same purpose in developing municipality after developing municipality. Almost every one acts solely in its own selfish and parochial interest and in effect builds a wall around itself to keep out those people or entities not adding favorably to the tax base, despite the location of the municipality or the demand for varied kinds of housing. There has been no effective intermunicipal or area planning or land use regulation. All of this is amply demonstrated by the evidence in this case as to Camden, Burlington and Gloucester Counties. One incongruous result is the picture of developing municipalities rendering it impossible for lower paid employees of industries they have eagerly sought and welcomed with open arms (and, in Mount Laurel's case even some of its own lower paid municipal employees) to live in the community where they work.

The other end of the spectrum should also be mentioned because it shows the source of some of the demand for cheaper housing than the developing municipalities have permitted. Core cites were originally the location of most commerce and industry. Many of those facilities furnished employment for the unskilled and semi-skilled. These employees lived relatively near their work, so sections of cities always have housed the majority of people of low and moderate income, generally in old and deteriorating housing. Despite the municipally confined tax structure, commercial and industrial ratables generally used to supply enough revenue to provide and maintain municipal services equal or superior to those furnished in most suburban and rural areas.

The situation has become exactly the opposite since the end of World War II. Much industry and retail business, and even the professions, have left the cities. Camden is a typical example. The testimonial and documentary evidence in this case as to what has happened to that city is depressing indeed. For various reasons, it lost thousands of jobs between 1950 and 1970, including more than half of its manufacturing jobs (a reduction from 43,267 to 20,671, while all jobs in the entire area labor market increased from 94,507 to 197,037). A large segment of retail business faded away with the erection of large suburban shopping centers. The economically better situated city residents helped fill up the miles of sprawling new housing developments, not fully served by public transit. In a society which came to depend more and more on expensive individual motor vehicle transportation for all purposes, low income employees very frequently could not afford to reach outlying places of suitable employment and they certainly could not afford the permissible housing near such locations. These people have great difficulty in obtaining work and have been forced to remain in housing which is overcrowded, and has become more and more substandard and less and less tax productive. There has been a consequent critical erosion of the city tax base and inability to provide the amount and quality of those governmental services—education, health, police, fire, housing and the like—so necessary to the very existence of safe and decent city life. This category of city dwellers desperately needs much better housing and living conditions than is available to them now, both in a rehabilitated city and in outlying municipalities. They make up, along with the other classes of persons earlier mentioned who also cannot afford the only generally permitted housing in the developing municipalities, the acknowledged great demand for low and moderate income housing.

II

The Legal Issue

The legal question before us, as earlier indicated, is whether a developing municipality like Mount Laurel may validly, by a system of land use regulation, make it physically and economically impossible to provide low and moderate income housing in the municipality for the various categories of persons who need and want it and thereby, as Mount Laurel has, exclude such people from living within its confines because of the limited extent of their income and resources. Necessarily implicated are the broader questions of the right of such municipalities to limit the kinds of available housing and of any obligation to make possible a variety and choice of types of living accommodations.

We conclude that every such municipality must, by its land use regulations, presumptively make realistically possible an appropriate variety and choice of housing. More specifically, presumptively it cannot foreclose the opportunity of the classes of people mentioned for low and moderate income housing and in its regulations must affirmatively afford that opportunity, at least to the extent of the municipality's fair share of the present and prospective regional need therefor. These obligations must be met unless the particular municipality can sustain the heavy burden of demonstrating peculiar circumstances which dictate that it should not be required so to do.

We reach this conclusion under state law and so do not find it necessary to consider federal constitutional grounds urged by plaintiffs. We begin with some fundamental principles as applied to the scene before us. . . .

Frequently the decisions in this state, including those just cited, have spoken only in terms of the interest of the enacting municipality, so that it has been thought, at least in some quarters, that such was the only welfare requiring consideration. It is, of course, true that many cases have dealt only with regulations having little, if any, outside impact where the local decision is ordinarily entitled to prevail. However, it is fundamental and not to be forgotten that the zoning power is a police power of the state and the local authority is acting only as a delegate of that power and is restricted in the same manner as is the state. So, when regulation does have a substantial external impact, the welfare of the state's citizens beyond the borders of the particular municipality cannot be disregarded and must be recognized and served.

This essential was distinctly pointed out in *Euclid*, where Mr. Justice Sutherland specifically referred to ". . . the possibility of cases where the general public interest would so far outweigh the interest of the municipality that the municipality would not be allowed to stand in the way." (272 U.S. at 390, 47 S.Ct. at 119, 71 L.Ed. at 311). Chief Justice Vanderbilt said essentially the same thing, in a different factual context, in the early leading case of Duffcon Concrete Products, Inc. v. Borough of Cresskill, 1 N.J. 509, 64 A.2d 347 (1949), when he spoke of the necessity of regional considerations in zoning and added this:

> . . . The effective development of a region should not and cannot be made to depend upon the adventitious location of municipal boundaries, often prescribed decades or even centuries ago, and based in many instances on considerations of geography, of commerce, or of politics that are no longer significant with respect to

zoning. The direction of growth of residential areas on the one hand and of industrial concentration on the other refuses to be governed by such artificial lines. Changes in methods of transportation as well as in living conditions have served only to accentuate the unreality in dealing with zoning problems on the basis of the territorial limits of a municipality. (1 N.J. at 513, 64 A.2d at 350).

In recent years this court has once again stressed this non-local approach to the meaning of "general welfare" in cases involving zoning as to facilities of broad public benefit as distinct from purely parochial interest. See Roman Catholic Diocese of Newark v. Ho-Ho-Kus Borough, 42 N.J. 556, 566, 202 A.2d 161 (1964), id., 47 N.J. 211, 220 A.2d 97 (1966). In this case we pointed out local action with respect to private educational projects largely benefitting those residing outside the borough must be exercised "with due concern for values which transcend municipal lines." (47 N.J. at 218, 220 A.2d at 101). Likewise in Kunzler v. Hoffman, 48 N.J. 277, 225 A.2d 321 (1966), a case unsuccessfully attacking a use variance granted a private hospital to serve the emotionally disturbed in a wide area of the state, we rejected the contention that local zoning authorities are limited to a consideration of only those benefits to the general welfare which would be received by residents of the municipality, pointing out that "general welfare" in the context there involved "comprehends the benefits not merely within municipal boundaries but also those to the regions of the State relevant to the public interest to be served." 48 N.J. at 288, 225 A.2d at 327.

This brings us to the relation of housing to the concept of general welfare just discussed and the result in terms of land use regulation which that relationship mandates. There cannot be the slightest doubt that shelter, along with food, are the most basic human needs. "The question of whether a citizenry has adequate and sufficient housing is certainly one of the prime considerations in assessing the general health and welfare of that body." New Jersey Mortgage Finance Agency v. McCrane, 56 N.J. 414, 420, 267 A.2d 24, 27 (1970). The same thought is implicit in the legislative findings of an extreme, long-time need in this state for decent low and moderate income housing, set forth in the numerous statutes providing for various agencies and methods at both state and local levels designed to aid in alleviation of the need. It is plain beyond dispute that proper provision for adequate housing of all categories of people is certainly an absolute essential in promotion of the general welfare required in all local land use regulation. Further the universal and constant need for such housing is so important and of such broad public interest that the general welfare which developing municipalities like Mount Laurel must consider extends beyond their boundaries and cannot be parochially confined to the claimed good of the particular municipality. It has to follow that, broadly speaking, the presumptive obligation arises for each such municipality affirmatively to plan and provide, by its land use regulations, the reasonable opportunity for an appropriate variety and choice of housing, including, of course, low and moderate cost housing, to meet the needs, desires and resources of all categories of people who may desire to live within its boundaries. Negatively, it may not adopt regulations or policies which thwart or preclude that opportunity. . . .

We have spoken of this obligation of such municipalities as "presumptive." The term has two aspects, procedural and substantive. Procedurally, we think the basic importance of appropriate housing for all dictates that, when it is shown that a developing municipality in its land use regulations has not made realistically possible a variety and choice of housing, including adequate provision to afford the opportunity for low and moderate income housing or has expressly prescribed requirements or restrictions which preclude or substantially hinder it, a facial showing of violation of substantive due process or equal protection under the state constitution has been made out and the burden, and it is a heavy one, shifts to the municipality to establish a valid basis for its action or non-action. The substantive aspect of "presumptive" relates to the specifics, on the one hand, of what municipal land use regulation provisions, or the absence thereof, will evidence invalidity and shift the burden of proof and, on the other hand, of what bases and considerations will carry the municipality's burden and sustain what it has done or failed to do. Both kinds of specifics may well vary between municipalities according to peculiar circumstances. . . .

Without further elaboration at this point, our opinion is that Mount Laurel's zoning ordinance is presumptively contrary to the general welfare and outside the intended scope of the zoning power in the particulars mentioned. A facial showing of invalidity is thus established, shifting to the municipality the burden of establishing valid superseding reasons for its action and non-action. We now examine the reasons it advances.

The township's principal reason in support of its zoning plan and ordinance housing provisions, advanced especially strongly at oral argument, is the fiscal one previously adverted to, *i.e.*, that by reason of New Jersey's tax structure which substantially finances municipal governmental and educational costs from taxes on local real property, every municipality may, by the exercise of the zoning power, allow only such uses and to such extent as will be beneficial to the local tax rate. In other words, the position is that any municipality may zone extensively to seek and encourage the "good" tax ratables of industry and commerce and limit the permissible types of housing to those having the fewest school children or to those providing sufficient value to attain or approach paying their own way taxwise.

We have previously held that a developing municipality may properly zone for and seek industrial ratables to create a better economic balance for the community *vis-a-vis* educational and governmental costs engendered by residential development, provided that such was ". . . done reasonably as part of and in furtherance of a legitimate comprehensive plan for the zoning of the entire municipality." Gruber v. Mayor and Township Committee of Raritan Township, 39 N.J. 1, 9–11, 186 A.2d 489, 493 (1962). We adhere to that view today. But we were not there concerned with, and did not pass upon, the validity of municipal exclusion by zoning of types of housing and kinds of people for the same local financial end. We have no hesitancy in now saying, and do so emphatically, that, considering the basic importance of the opportunity for appropriate housing for all classes of our citizenry, no municipality may exclude or limit categories of housing for that reason or purpose. While we fully recognize the increasingly heavy burden of local taxes for municipal governmental and school costs on homeowners, relief from the consequences of this tax system will have to be furnished by other branches of government. It cannot legitimately be accomplished by restricting types of housing through the zoning process in developing municipalities.

The propriety of zoning ordinance limitations on housing for ecological or environmental reasons seems also to be suggested by Mount Laurel in support of the one-half acre minimum lot size in that very considerable portion of the township still available for residential development. It is said that the area is without sewer or water utilities and that the soil is such that this plot size is required for safe individual lot sewage disposal and water supply. The short answer is that, this being flat land and readily amenable to such utility installations, the township could require them as improvements by developers or install them under the special assessment or other appropriate statutory procedure. The present environmental situation of the area is, therefore, no sufficient excuse in itself for limiting housing therein to single-family dwelling on large lots. This is not to say that land use regulations should not take due account of ecological or environmental factors or problems. Quite the contrary. Their importance, at last being recognized, should always be considered. Generally only a relatively small portion of a developing municipality will be involved, for, to have a valid effect, the danger and impact must be substantial and very real (the construction of every building or the improvement of every plot has some environmental impact)—not simply a makeweight to support exclusionary housing measures or preclude growth—and the regulation adopted must be only that reasonably necessary for public protection of a vital interest. Otherwise difficult additional problems relating to a "taking" of a property owner's land may arise.

By way of summary, what we have said comes down to this. As a developing municipality, Mount Laurel must, by its land use regulations, make realistically possible the opportunity for an appropriate variety and choice of housing for all categories of people who may desire to live there, of course including those of low and moderate income. It must permit multifamily housing, without bedroom or similar restrictions, as well as small dwellings on very small lots, low cost housing of other types and, in general, high density zoning, without artificial and unjustifiable minimum requirements as to lot size, building size and the like, to meet the full panoply of these needs. Certainly when a municipality zones for industry and commerce for local tax benefit purposes, it without question must zone to permit adequate housing within the means of the employees involved in such uses. (If planned unit developments are authorized, one would assume that each must include a reasonable amount of low and moderate income housing in its residential "mix," unless opportunity for such housing has already been realistically provided for elsewhere in the municipality.) The amount of land removed from residential use by allocation to industrial and commercial purposes must be reasonably related to the present and future potential for such purposes. In other words, such municipalities must zone primarily for the living welfare of people and not for the benefit of the local tax rate. [Imp pt]

We have earlier stated that a developing municipality's obligation to afford the opportunity for decent and adequate low and moderate income housing extends at least to ". . . the municipality's fair share of the present and prospective regional need therefor." Some comment on that conclusion is in order at this point. Frequently it might be sounder to have more of such housing, like some specialized land uses, in one municipality in a region than in another, because of greater availability of suitable land, location of employment, accessibility of public transportation or some other significant reason. But, under present New Jersey legislation, zoning must be on an individual municipal basis, rather than regionally. So long as that situation persists under the present tax structure, or in the absence of some kind of binding agreement among all the municipalities of a region, we feel that every municipality therein must bear its fair share of the regional burden. (In this respect our holding is broader than that of the trial court, which was limited to Mount Laurel-related low and moderate income housing needs.) [elaboration]

The composition of the applicable "region" will necessarily vary from situation to situation and probably no hard and fast rule will serve to furnish the answer in every case. Confinement to or within a certain county appears not to be realistic, but restriction within the boundaries of the state seem practical and advisable. (This is not to say that a developing municipality can ignore a demand for housing within its boundaries on the part of people who commute to work in another state.) Here we have already defined the region at present as "those portions of Camden, Burlington and Gloucester Counties within a semicircle having a radius of 20 miles or so from the heart of Camden City." The concept of "fair share" is coming into more general use and, through the expertise of the municipal planning adviser, the county planning boards and the state planning agency, a reasonable figure for Mount Laurel can be determined, which can then be translated to the allocation of sufficient land therefor on the zoning map. We may add that we think that, in arriving at such a determination, the type of information and estimates, which the trial judge directed the township to compile and furnish to him, concerning the housing needs of persons of low and moderate income now or formerly residing in the township in substandard dwellings and those presently employed or reasonably expected to be employed therein, will be pertinent. . . .

III

The Remedy

As outlined at the outset of this opinion, the trial court invalidated the zoning ordinance *in toto* and ordered the township to make certain studies and investigations and to present to the court a plan of affirmative public action designed "to enable and encourage the satisfaction of the indicated needs" for township related low and moderate income housing. Jurisdiction was retained for judicial consideration and approval of such a plan and for the entry of a final order requiring its implementation.

We are of the view that the trial court's judgment should be modified in certain respects. We see no reason why the entire zoning ordinance should be nullified. Therefore we declare it to be invalid only to the extent and in the particulars set forth in this opinion. The township is granted 90 days from the date hereof, or such additional time as the trial court may find it reasonable and necessary to allow, to adopt amendments to correct the deficiencies herein specified. It is the local function and responsibility, in the first instance at least, rather than the court's, to decide on the details of the same within the guidelines we have laid down. If plaintiffs desire to attack such amendments, they may do so by supplemental complaint filed in this cause within 30 days of the final adoption of the amendments.

We are not at all sure what the trial judge had in mind as ultimate action with reference to the approval of a plan for affirmative public action concerning the satisfaction of indicated housing needs and the entry of a final order requiring implementation thereof. Courts do not build housing nor do municipalities. That function is performed by private builders, various kinds of associations, or, for public housing, by special agencies created for that purpose at various levels of government. The municipal function is initially to provide the opportunity through appropriate land use regulations and we have spelled out what Mount Laurel must do in that regard. It is not appropriate at this time, particularly in view of the advanced view of zoning law as applied to housing laid down by this opinion, to deal with the matter of the further extent of judicial power in the field or to exercise any such power. The municipality should first have full opportunity to itself act without judicial supervision. We trust it will do so in the spirit we have suggested, both by appropriate zoning ordinance amendments and whatever additional action encouraging the fulfillment of its fair share of the regional need for low and moderate income housing may be indicated as necessary and advisable. (We have in mind that there is at least a moral obligation in a municipality to establish a local housing agency pursuant to state law to provide housing for its resident poor now living in dilapidated, unhealthy quarters.) The portion of the trial court's judgment ordering the preparation and submission of the aforesaid study, report and plan to it for further action is therefore vacated as at least premature. Should Mount Laurel not perform as we expect, further judicial action may be sought by supplemental pleading in this cause.

The judgment of the Law Division is modified as set forth herein. No costs.

[The opinions of MOUNTAIN and PASHMAN, JJ., concurring, are omitted.]

NOTES

1. *Mt. Laurel* raised many more questions than it answered. What is a "developing" municipality? What is its relevant "region," and how is the municipality's "fair share" of that region's needs to be computed? The New Jersey Supreme Court answered some of these questions in the years immediately after *Mt. Laurel*. It held in Pascack Association, Ltd. v. Mayor & Council of Township of Washington, 74 N.J. 470, 379 A.2d 6 (1977), that fully-developed residential communities had no *Mt. Laurel* obligations. And in Oakwood at Madison, Inc. v. Township of Madison, 72 N.J. 481, 371 A.2d 1192 (1977), the court ruled that "fair share" allocations need not be "precise" or based on "specific formulae," and that the relevant region consisted of the area from which, in view of available employment and transportation, the population of the township would be drawn, absent invalid exclusionary zoning. 371 A.2d 1192. But it was not until *Mt. Laurel* came before it again, eight years later, that the court attempted to prescribe more comprehensive and detailed guidelines for implementing the original mandate. Southern Burlington County N.A.A.C.P. v. Township of Mt. Laurel, 92 N.J. 158, 456 A.2d 390 (1983) (*Mt. Laurel II*).

Mt. Laurel's response to the supreme court's 1975 decision had been weak: it rezoned 20 acres—less than one-quarter of one per cent of the town's entire area—to allow construction of low-income units. Developers had failed to respond at all: not a single unit of low income housing was built in the community. Reviewing this quiescence in *Mt. Laurel II*, the New Jersey Supreme Court concluded that, after "all this time, ten years after the trial court's initial order invalidating its zoning ordinance, Mt. Laurel remains afflicted with a blatantly exclusionary ordinance. Papered over with studies, rationalized by hired experts, the ordinance at its core is true to nothing but Mount Laurel's determination to exclude the poor." 456 A.2d at 410.

In a 248-page opinion, Chief Justice Wilentz sought to "put some steel" into *Mt. Laurel I*. The new decision declared that "every municipality's land use regulations should provide a realistic opportunity for decent housing for at least some part of its resident poor who now occupy dilapidated housing," and that already-developed communities should no longer be immunized from the *Mt. Laurel* mandate. To facilitate the efficient and informed determination of regional need and fair share, the court held that "[a]ny future *Mount Laurel* litigation shall be assigned only to those judges selected by the Chief Justice with the approval of the Supreme Court. The initial group shall consist of three judges, the number to be increased or decreased hereafter by the Chief Justice with the Court's approval. The Chief Justice shall define the area of the State for which each of the three judges is responsible: any *Mount Laurel* case challenging the land use ordinance of a municipality included in that area shall be assigned to that judge."

The Court recognized, too, that the "municipal obligation to provide a realistic opportunity for the construction of its fair share of low and moderate income housing may require more than the elimination of unnecessary cost-producing requirements and restrictions. Affirmative governmental devices should be used to make that opportunity realistic, including lower-income density bonuses and mandatory set-asides. Furthermore, the municipality should cooperate with the developer's attempts to obtain federal subsidies." Also, "[m]obile homes may not be prohibited unless there is solid proof that sound planning in a particular municipality requires such prohibition." 456 A.2d at 419.

A few other state courts have taken roughly the approach followed in *Mt. Laurel I*. See, for example, Surrick v. Zoning Hearing Board of the Township of Upper Providence, 476 Pa. 182, 382 A.2d 105 (1977); Berenson v. Town of New Castle, 38 N.Y.2d 102, 378 N.Y.S.2d 672, 341 N.E.2d 236 (1975). See generally, After Mt. Laurel (J. Rose & R. Rothman, eds. 1977).

2. After *Mt. Laurel II*, what strategems might wealthy suburban residents be expected to employ in order to keep the poor from entering their communities? Could they vote to double or triple property taxes—to levels well beyond what lower income families can afford—and spend the increased tax revenues on golf, tennis and polo clubs for community use? Could they do just the opposite, reducing taxes to a point at which no public services—police, fire, or sanitation—are provided at all, so that each household must contract for these services with private firms? What if wealthy residents sought to preserve the amenities offered by large-lot zoning by buying up private restrictive covenants on all vacant parcels in the township, limiting the development of these parcels to a one-acre minimum lot size?

Is there anything in *Mt. Laurel I* or *Mt. Laurel II* to prohibit any of these tactics? Can you draft a *Mt. Laurel III* opinion that would effectively prohibit them?

3. As became evident by the time of *Mt. Laurel II*, simply invalidating an exclusionary zoning ordinance offers no guarantee that housing will be built at prices the excluded poor can afford to pay. Does this suggest that the New Jersey Supreme Court was mistaken in *Mt. Laurel I* to give standing to the plaintiffs before it—none of whom, apparently, was prepared to build the housing sought—and that it should instead have given standing only to landowners whose actual and immediate development plans had been thwarted by the challenged zoning ordinance? At the very least, this approach would have focused the court's attention on the connection between the housing needs of the excluded poor and the ability of the marketplace to respond to these needs. The inclusionary zoning approach suggested in *Mt. Laurel II* is considered at note 5, page 1284, below.

Does the history of the *Mt. Laurel I* litigation indicate any limits on the ability of courts to produce major social and economic change? Are legislatures likely to be any more effective? See Burton, California Legislature Prohibits Exclusionary Zoning, Mandates Fair Share: Inclusionary Housing Programs A Likely Response, 9 San Fern.V.L. Rev. 19 (1981).

The Township of Mt. Laurel is situated in southern New Jersey, about fifteen minutes by car from Philadelphia, Pennsylvania. Doubtless, the two municipalities lie within the same "region." What reason is there for Philadelphia suburbs to take on a "fair share" of the regional need, absent a mandate from *their* supreme court or legislature? Is the problem one that calls for interstate compacts as are sometimes employed in the management of air quality problems that cross state boundaries?

See generally, Ellickson, Suburban Growth Controls: An Economic and Legal Analysis, 86 Yale L.J. 385 (1977); Sager, Tight Little Islands: Exclusionary Zoning, Equal Protection and The Indigent, 21 Stan.L.Rev. 767 (1969).

4. All zoning is potentially exclusionary. Height, bulk, setback and minimum lot size requirements exclude denser land uses that will often be more profitable to the developer and more economical to prospective occupants. Although *Mt. Laurel I* was the first state high court decision to overturn an ordinance on strictly exclusionary grounds, earlier state court decisions had invalidated specific ordinance provisions for cutting too deeply into landowners' potential profits, or for excluding more economical uses, or both.

a. *Minimum Lot Size.* Minimum lot size requirements are widely accepted as a legitimate means for enhancing visual amenities, reducing congestion and lowering the costs of water supply and sewage treatment. Yet, if the minimum is too large it may be invalidated as confiscatory or exclusionary. Thus, in National Land & Investment

Co. v. Kohn, 419 Pa. 504, 215 A.2d 597 (1965), the Pennsylvania Supreme Court invalidated an Easttown ordinance that required a minimum area of four acres per building lot in residential districts in approximately 30% of the Township. One factor influencing the court's decision was that, when divided into one-acre lots as originally planned, the value of plaintiff's land was approximately $260,000; under the four-acre restriction, "the value of the land, under the most optimistic appraisal, fell to $175,000." The court was even more troubled by the question "whether the township can stand in the way of the natural forces which send our growing population into hitherto undeveloped areas in search of a comfortable place to live. We have concluded not. A zoning ordinance whose primary purpose is to prevent the entrance of newcomers in order to avoid future burdens, economic and otherwise, upon the administration of public services and facilities cannot be held valid." 419 Pa. at 532, 215 A.2d at 612. See generally, Note, Large Lot Zoning, 78 Yale L.J. 1418 (1969).

b. *Minimum Floor Area.* Ordinances imposing minimum floor space requirements in residential developments were early upheld as reasonably aimed at controlling density, preserving neighborhood amenities and promoting public health by assuring that families would not live in cramped housing. See, for example, Lionshead Lake, Inc. v. Wayne Township, 10 N.J. 165, 89 A.2d 693 (1952). Concerned, no doubt, by the requirements' exclusion of more modest and economical housing, courts have recently begun to invalidate floor space minima on the ground that they bear no rational relationship to legitimate police power objects. See, for example, Home Builders League, Inc. v. Township of Berlin, 81 N.J. 127, 405 A.2d 381 (1979). See generally, Haar, Zoning for Minimum Standards: The Wayne Township Case, 66 Harv.L.Rev. 1051 (1953); Nolan & Horack, How Small a House? Zoning for Minimum Space Requirements, 67 Harv. L.Rev. 967 (1954).

c. *Restrictions on Multiple Family Dwellings.* In Appeal of Girsh, 437 Pa. 237, 263 A.2d 395 (1970), the Pennsylvania Supreme Court invalidated a zoning ordinance that effectively prohibited apartment houses anywhere in the township. The court relied on its earlier decision in National Land & Investment Co. v. Kohn, above, to reject the Township's argument that "apartment uses would cause a significant population increase with a resulting strain on available municipal services and roads, and would clash with the existing residential neighborhood." 437 Pa. at 243, 263 A.2d at 398. The court conceded that the town "can protect its attractive character by requiring apartments to be built in accordance with (reasonable) setback, open space, height, and other light-and-air requirements, but it cannot refuse to make any provision for apartment living. The simple fact that someone is anxious to build apartments is strong indication that the location of this township is such that people are desirous of moving in, and we do not believe Nether Providence can close its doors to those people." 437 Pa. at 245, 263 A.2d at 399.

d. *Restrictions on Mobile Homes and Mobile Home Parks*. Although conditions have improved substantially since the 1930's and 1940's, when mobile homes were dinky trailers and trailer courts were cramped and ill-kept, even the most gracious suburban governments still seek to exclude individual mobile homes or to confine them to carefully segregated mobile home parks. Courts have generally invalidated efforts at complete exclusion and, more recently, have also stricken ordinances limiting mobile homes to designated mobile home parks. See, for example, Robinson Township v. Knoll, 410 Mich. 293, 313, 302 N.W.2d 146, 150 (1981) ("Today we consider the *per se* exclusion not of trailers, but of mobile homes—and more than the label has changed with time. The mobile home today can compare favorably with site-built housing in size, safety and attractiveness"). See generally, Moore, The Mobile Home and the Law, 6 Akron L.Rev. 1 (1973).

e. *Phased Development*. Municipalities frequently attempt to justify minimum lot size and floor area requirements, as well as restrictions on multiple family dwellings and mobile homes, on the ground that, however indirectly, these regulations effectively conserve public expenditures. If a regulatory measure is in fact directly connected to rational management of the municipal budget, courts will be inclined to uphold it. Thus, in Golden v. Planning Board of Town of Ramapo, 30 N.Y.2d 359, 334 N.Y.S.2d 138, 285 N.E.2d 291 (1972), the New York Court of Appeals upheld a local ordinance that conditioned subdivision approval on the availability to the subdivision of sewers, drainage facilities, public parks, schools, roads and firehouses. Noting that it would "not countenance" any "community efforts at immunization or exclusion," the court ruled that, "far from being exclusionary, the present amendments merely seek, by the implementation of sequential development and timed growth, to provide a balanced cohesive community dedicated to the efficient utilization of land. The restrictions conform to the community's considered land use policies as expressed in its comprehensive plan and represent a bona fide effort to maximize population density consistent with orderly growth." 30 N.Y.2d at 378, 334 N.Y.S.2d at 149, 285 N.E.2d 302.

5. Federal courts have been far less hospitable to exclusionary claims than state courts. In the early 1970's, housing activists had hoped that the United States Supreme Court would overturn exclusionary ordinances on the ground that, by discriminating against the poor in search of housing, they violated the Constitution's equal protection clause and interfered with consumers' freedom of travel. The Supreme Court soon dashed these hopes. In Lindsey v. Normet, 405 U.S. 56, 92 S.Ct. 862, 31 L.Ed.2d 36 (1972), the Court held that housing is not a fundamental right. In San Antonio School District v. Rodriguez, 411 U.S. 1, 93 S.Ct. 1278, 36 L.Ed.2d 16 (1973), it held that wealth is not necessarily a suspect classification. In Belle Terre v. Boraas, 416 U.S. 1, 94 S.Ct. 1536, 39 L.Ed.2d 797 (1974), the Court dismissed the argument that zoning regulations inhibit the right to

travel. And, in Warth v. Seldin, 422 U.S. 490, 95 S.Ct. 2197, 45 L.Ed. 2d 343 (1975), it ruled that plaintiffs—nonprofit organizations, local taxpayers, low-income minority residents living in the general area, and a local homebuilders' association—lacked standing to attack the local zoning ordinance.

Federal courts will, however, overturn zoning ordinances shown to exclude individuals on the basis of race. In Village of Arlington Heights v. Metropolitan Housing Corp., 429 U.S. 252, 97 S.Ct. 555, 50 L.Ed.2d 450 (1977), the Supreme Court rejected a claim that, because the Village's refusal to rezone plaintiff's property to permit the construction of federally-financed low income housing had a racially discriminatory impact, it violated the equal protection clause. In the Court's view, plaintiff had to show discriminatory *intent*, not just *impact*, to prevail on the constitutional claim. The Court remanded for a determination whether the Village's refusal to rezone violated the Fair Housing Act of 1968, 42 U.S.C.A. § 3604(a). The Seventh Circuit Court of Appeals ruled that it did: "under the circumstances of this case defendant has a statutory obligation to refrain from zoning policies that effectively foreclose the construction of any low-cost housing within its corporate boundaries," and "at least under some circumstances a violation of section 3604(a) can be established by a showing of discriminatory effect without a showing of discriminatory intent." Metropolitan Housing Development Corp. v. Village of Arlington Heights, 558 F.2d 1283, 1285, 1290 (1977), *cert. denied* 434 U.S. 1025, 98 S.Ct. 752, 54 L.Ed.2d 772 (1978). Several years later, the Court of Appeals affirmed a district court decision approving and entering a consent decree between the parties. 616 F.2d 1006 (1980).

II. PLANNING LAW AND ADMINISTRATION

R. LINOWES & D. ALLENSWORTH, THE POLITICS OF LAND USE: PLANNING, ZONING AND THE PRIVATE DEVELOPER 7, 12–18 (1973)

PLANNING THEORY

Planning theory holds that the various steps of the planning process should follow an orderly and logical pattern. Community goals and objectives should be known before plans are prepared. Extensive study of existing community characteristics, problems, and opportunities should precede planning for the future. Plans should be developed before land uses are decided upon.

Planning theory holds that certain designated governmental powers should be used to carry out plans. These powers include zoning and subdivision regulations and key land-use controls that stipulate such things as land uses permitted by law, layout patterns, public improvements to be provided in new subdivisions, minimum lot sizes, and maximum population densities. Other governmental powers that can be used to implement plans include the official map, which sets aside land for future public use; urban renewal, which provides for the reuse of land; and code enforcement, which covers building construction, occupancy, and maintenance matters. Other public powers, especially those concerning highways and sewers, influence community development, and, according to planning theory, these powers should be exercised in a way that is consistent with community planning.

A plan may specify the particular governmental powers that will be called upon for its implementation and may detail how land-use controls are to be used. Land-use controls like zoning and subdivision regulation are viewed in planning theory as "tools" of planning; the primary mission of these tools is to make the plan a reality.

Planning theory requires that land-use controls and other governmental powers that impact on community development be understood and operate within the context of community planning. The argument is that if community development is to proceed along rational lines, standards are needed, and planning provides the means for the consideration, adoption, and enforcement of these standards. The theory is that with planning and plans, community development will be consciously directed, the likely impact of decisions will be known in advance, mistakes will be avoided, future needs for public and private facilities will be anticipated and met as they arise, resources will be set aside prior to the time they are needed, and a more pleasing, satisfying, and livable environment will ensue. All agencies and parties involved in community development are, by planning theory, supposed to work within a common frame and to have their activities judged by common standards provided by community planning. . . .

The Planning Board

The planning board stands at the pinnacle of the planning bureaucracy. It heads the independent planning commission. The planning board normally will have administrative authority over a planning staff. Of some 18,000 local governments that might be expected to have planning, about 10,700, or nearly 60 percent, have planning boards. Almost 90 percent of the cities with 5,000 or more population have planning boards. Planning boards contain an average of seven to eight members, and larger cities (50,000 or more population) have somewhat bigger boards.

Planning boards are composed chiefly of citizen members, commonly appointed by local governing bodies or chief executives. Some boards have ex officio members, and these may include representatives of important local bureaucracies (such as public works). The planning board normally will have the power to adopt and revise master plans, and it will supervise the planning staff, which actually prepares the plans. The planning board has advisory power over basic zoning decisions (rezonings), although a special majority of the governing body (generally two-thirds or three-quarters) may be required to override planning boards' zoning recommendations. The planning board likely will have the final voice in the administration of subdivision regulations, may review site plans for proposed commercial or mixed commercial-residential developments, and may prepare and maintain the official map. The planning board may recommend amendments to the zoning ordinance text and may have advisory authority over local capital budget proposals.

The Planning Staff

The planning staff normally serves in a planning commission under the direction of the planning board. Some planning staffs operate directly under a chief executive, and some legislative bodies have their own internal planning staffs. The planning staff carries out duties as assigned, and it may constitute an independent political force in and of itself. The planning staff usually will be headed by a director, and staff responsibilities will be divided among different divisions or sections that report to the director.

Increasingly, planning staffs are becoming professional; they frequently include members with advanced degrees in planning and with membership in the American Institute of Planners (AIP), the organization of professional planners. Planning staffs may include persons trained in other fields—such as engineering, architecture, geography, or public administration—as well as in city planning.

The Chief Executive

The chief executive of the local government may have administrative authority over the planning staff, and he may appoint members of the planning board as well as the director of planning. The chief executive likely will attempt to serve key community interests in planning, and elected executives are particularly sensitive to the views of citizens associations. Although the chief executive usually does not make the basic decisions in planning, he coordinates the local agencies whose programs impact on the planning process, and, by virtue of his legal powers and his political resources, he may influence planning decisions made by the planning board, the planning staff, and the local governing body.

The Governing Body

The governing body plays an important part in the planning process—even when the planning function is administered by an independent planning commission. The governing body may appoint the planning board and may adopt plans. Governing boards, being elected bodies, are vulnerable especially to citizens association influence, particularly in smaller communities and when elected on a ward or district basis.

In most communities the governing body makes the final zoning decisions, including those concerning the text and map of the zoning ordinance. The text is the written provisions of the ordinance, and the map depicts the sections of the text that govern land use on each lot regulated by the ordinance. A change in the map is called a rezoning, and proposed rezonings typically take up most of the time a community governing body spends on planning matters. Other planning-related decisions may be made by the governing body. . . .

Citizens Associations

Citizens associations are organized on a neighborhood basis, and they commonly wield considerable power over planning and zoning decisions that affect particular neighborhoods. Citizens associations concentrate most attention on zoning decisions, and they usually seek rulings that preserve the status quo. Citizens groups support strong controls and restrictions on land development.

Developers

Developers and other real estate forces are key activists in the planning process. Included in this category are land developers, home builders, large landowners, and investors in private land and improvements. Real estate groups generally favor planning and zoning decisions that promote community growth and expansion. Developers are concerned with subdivision control decisions, and they work for public decisions that facilitate the development process. They frequently are organized into interest groups, known as builders associations, perhaps on a single jurisdiction (city, county), submetropolitan, or metropolitan-wide basis; realtors are organized separately into local boards of realtors.

State Roads Agencies

The most important highway agency in the federal system is the state roads department. State roads departments are responsible for the construction and maintenance of interstate and state highways; they receive assistance from the federal government for construction purposes. Cities, counties, and townships may have authority over local streets and highways.

State highway departments may exercise significant influence over community development, as highways tend to shape urban development patterns. State roads agencies do not have to adhere to community plans or zoning in making highway location decisions. As a result of the Federal-Aid Highway Act of 1962, all metropolitan areas now have a transportation planning process, in which state highway departments and local governments are to work cooperatively in planning highway projects. The transportation planning process may lead to a coordination of local planning and state highway programming.

Sewer and Water Districts

Sewer and water lines can influence development patterns. Decisions to extend sewer lines into undeveloped areas are particularly important in this respect. In the major metropolitan areas, the sewage disposal function is commonly assigned to special sewerage districts (the Metropolitan St. Louis Sewer District is an example). Water supply is frequently a function of special districts as well (there are over 2,000 urban water supply districts in the country). Special districts with sewer and water responsibilities may have independent authority to locate sewer and water lines, and this authority may or may not be subject to advisory recommendations of the local planning commission or to the power of general-purpose local government (municipalities, counties).

The General Business Community

General business interests participate in planning somewhat independently of the real estate community. In the larger metropolitan areas, developers are organized separately from the general business community; the former, as noted, work through builders associations (Minneapolis Home Builders Association, for example), while the general business community is organized into chambers of commerce or boards of trade.

In the planning process, the general business groups may support or oppose developers. The two do not necessarily have the same views on planning and zoning. General business groups, for example, may oppose rezonings that generate competition for existing businesses. The two are more likely to agree on broad planning principles and concepts than on specific rezoning proposals. . . .

Education, Codes, Transit, Housing, Renewal, and Airport Agencies

School districts, building and housing codes agencies, urban mass transit authorities, public housing districts and community development departments, urban renewal authorities, and airport agencies, all usually local government units, are concerned with decisions made in the planning process and may be affected by these decisions. These agencies have programs that impact on community development.

Local school operations are significantly affected by planning and zoning decisions, and school agencies may participate in these decisions. It is basic land-use decisions that determine the number of children in the public schools and the amount of available property taxes, a common source of school financing. School location decisions and other school agency determinations can affect community development patterns and may in turn be influenced by planning policy.

Building and housing code agency decisions on building and housing construction, maintenance, and occupancy can affect environmental quality, housing conditions, and the housing supply. Urban rail transit authority decisions on the location of new transit lines, for example, can alter community development patterns and affect planning and zoning.

Decisions by public housing authorities and community development departments can affect the housing quality and housing supply for low- and moderate-income families, and urban renewal authority decisions can importantly mold land-use and reuse patterns in inner city areas. Airport bureaucracy decisions can influence urban development.

The education function in the community usually is handled by a special school district (nearly 22,000 of the 23,390 public school systems of the nation are run by special school governments), urban rail transit almost universally by a special district government (the Southeastern Pennsylvania Transportation Authority, SEPTA, in Philadelphia, is an example), public housing mostly by special districts, urban renewal not infrequently by special districts (there are over 2,000 housing and renewal authorities in the country), and airports often by special districts (Port of New York Authority, for example). The rail transit, public housing, urban renewal, and airport functions, when under special districts, normally are administered by governments called authorities.

Local planning agencies and key officials of general-purpose governments may play only a limited role in the decision-making processes of special districts, and this may make coordinated community development and planning difficult. Regardless of how these local functions are administered (by special districts or by general-purpose governments), there is no assurance that they will be coordinated through a central planning process.

A. THE COMPREHENSIVE PLAN

UDELL v. HAAS

Court of Appeals of New York, 1968.
21 N.Y.2d 463, 288 N.Y.S.2d 888, 235 N.E.2d 897.

KEATING, Judge.

The issue on this appeal is whether a 1960 amendment to the Building Zone Ordinance (altering the Zoning Map) of the Village of Lake Success, which reclassified appellant's property from Business "A" and "B" to Residence "C", is valid. Appellant claims that the rezoning was discriminatory, confiscatory and *ultra vires*.

The background of the dispute is this: The Village of Lake Success is a small, suburban community in the extreme westerly portion of Nassau County. It has a rather irregular shape, but generally is bounded on the south by the Northern State Parkway and on the north and east by the Town of North Hempstead. To the west lies its giant neighbor, the City of New York.

The village is approximately two square miles in size. Running through it in a generally north-south direction is the main artery of the village, Lakeville Road. That street intersects with Northern Boulevard, a major east-west thoroughfare in this section of Long Island.

The village's northern boundary appears to be completely arbitrary. For the most part, it is to the south of Northern Boulevard. However, along Lakeville Road, the village reaches out in a northerly direction to touch Northern Boulevard. The area is not large and is neck-like in shape, consisting of several hundred feet on either side of Lakeville Road extending from Northern Boulevard some 750 feet to University Road on the west side of Lakeville Road and some 600 feet to Cumberland Avenue on the east. Cumberland Avenue and University Road form what may be described as the base of the neck.

Prior to the 1960 rezoning in question, almost the entire neck was zoned for business. For a distance of some 400 feet south of Northern Boulevard, the area was zoned Business "A" which permitted retailing and similar uses as well as laboratories and office and public buildings. The rest of the neck was zoned Business "B" where essentially the only nonresidential use allowed was neighborhood retailing.

Two parcels of land were initially the subject of this litigation. They are located in this neck and constitute a substantial portion of it. However, as a result of this litigation, only one parcel is now in question. It consists of approximately two and one-half acres, covering all of the area formerly zoned Business "A" on the *east* side of Lakeville Road, except for a 100 by 100-foot plot in the northwest corner of the parcel at the intersection of Northern Boulevard and Lakeville Road which is occupied by a gasoline station. Twenty-four feet of the southern end of the parcel extend into the former Business "B" zone. Appellant also owns land, adjacent to and east of this property in the Town of North Hempstead.

When appellant assembled this east parcel in 1951, the only use being made of this property was in the northerly portion facing Northern Boulevard. It was then being operated as a restaurant.

Also in 1951, plaintiff acquired two and one-half acres of vacant lots on the *west* side of Lakeville Road. This property covered almost the entire block from Lakeville Road to University Place, one block to the west of Lakeville Road, and from Northern Boulevard for a distance of approximately 500 feet to the south towards University Road, except for a few lots facing University Place to the west. Like the northwest corner of the east parcel, the northeast corner of this property is also occupied by a gas station, not owned by appellant.

The zoning amendment, ordinance No. 60, placed the entire neck, except for a 100-foot-wide strip adjacent to Northern Boulevard, in a Residence "C" category. Thus, the northeast and the northwest corners of the east and west parcels, respectively, that is the land fronting on Northern Boulevard, are not directly involved in this proceeding since the rezoning did not affect those portions of appellant's property. Permitted uses in the new classification include public and religious buildings and residences with minimum plot size set at 13,000 square feet and minimum frontage of 100 feet on Lakeville Road.

The trial court held the rezoning with respect to the so-called *west* parcel unconstitutional as being confiscatory, but sustained the ordinance insofar as it affected the *east* parcel (Udell v. McFadyen, 40 Misc.2d 265, 243 N.Y.S.2d 156). The decision with respect to the west parcel rested on three grounds. First, there was the size and shape of the plot; second, the topography of the land, which sloped down some 15 feet from Lakeville Road to University Place; and third, the existing neighboring uses. After a careful evaluation of the evidence, the trial court concluded that "residential zoning precludes use for any purpose to which it is reasonably adaptable" (40 Misc.2d 265,

271, 243 N.Y.S.2d 156, 162). It also held the rezoning to be discriminatory, of which more will be said later.

With respect to the east parcel, however, a contrary conclusion was reached as to the validity of the ordinance. In essence, the court held that since the appellant also owned contiguous lots fronting on Summer Avenue in the Town of North Hempstead, residential use was practical for the east parcel since the residences could face Summer Avenue. In addition, it found residential zoning would not be inconsistent with the character of the neighborhood and that a nursery school located on the south side of the east parcel was not incompatible with residential use. The problem raised by the commerce of Northern Boulevard could be remedied by appropriate fencing.

Both sides appeal this decision. During the pendency of the appeal, the village passed a second amendatory ordinance rezoning the *west* parcel into a new Business "C" category, which permitted "such scientific and/or research laboratory use, offices for executive, administrative, banking or professional purposes, libraries, schools, telephone exchanges and municipal building uses, as may be approved by the Village . . . upon recommendation of the Planning Board". Following this second change, the village withdrew its appeal.

On the landowner's appeal, the Appellate Division affirmed. Justice Hopkins, dissenting, stated in a brief opinion that he could see no justification for treating the two properties differently and that the "same considerations that prompted the declaration of the invalidity of the ordinance exist on the one side of Lakeville Road as on the other" (27 A.D.2d 750, 751, 279 N.Y.S.2d 701).

We hold that ordinance No. 60 is invalid with respect to the *east* parcel as well as the *west* parcel. We have concluded that the rezoning was discriminatory and that it was not done "in accordance with [the] comprehensive plan" of the Village of Lake Success (Village Law, § 177). In our view, sound zoning principles were not followed in this case, and the root cause of this failure was a misunderstanding of the nature of zoning, and, even more importantly, of its relationship to the statutory requirement that it be "in accordance with a comprehensive plan."

Zoning is not just an expansion of the common law of nuisance. It seeks to achieve much more than the removal of obnoxious gases and unsightly uses. Underlying the entire concept of zoning is the assumption that zoning can be a vital tool for maintaining a civilized form of existence only if we employ the insights and the learning of the philosopher, the city planner, the economist, the sociologist, the public health expert and all the other professions concerned with urban problems.

This fundamental conception of zoning has been present from its inception. The almost universal statutory requirement that zoning conform to a "well-considered plan" or "comprehensive plan" is a reflection of that view. (See Standard State Zoning Enabling Act, U.S.

Dept. of Commerce [1926].) The thought behind the requirement is that consideration must be given to the needs of the community as a whole. In exercising their zoning powers, the local authorities must act for the benefit of the community as a whole following a calm and deliberate consideration of the alternatives, and not because of the whims of either an articulate minority or even majority of the community. (De Sena v. Gulde, 24 A.D.2d 165, 265 N.Y.S.2d 239 [2d Dept., 1965].) Thus, the mandate of the Village Law (§ 177) is not a mere technicality which serves only as an obstacle course for public officials to overcome in carrying out their duties. Rather, the comprehensive plan is the essence of zoning. Without it, there can be no rational allocation of land use. It is the insurance that the public welfare is being served and that zoning does not become nothing more than just a Gallup poll.

Moreover, the "comprehensive plan" protects the landowner from arbitrary restrictions on the use of his property which can result from the pressures which outraged voters can bring to bear on public officials. "With the heavy presumption of constitutional validity that attaches to legislation purportedly under the police power, and the difficulty in judicially applying a 'reasonableness' standard, there is danger that zoning, considered as a self-contained activity rather than as a means to a broader end, may tyrannize individual property owners. Exercise of the legislative power to zone should be governed by rules and standards as clearly defined as possible, so that it cannot operate in an arbitrary and discriminatory fashion, and will actually be directed to the health, safety, welfare and morals of the community. The more clarity and specificity required in the articulation of the premises upon which a particular zoning regulation is based, the more effectively will courts be able to review the regulation, declaring it ultra vires if it is not in reality 'in accordance with a comprehensive plan.'" (Haar, "In Accordance With a Comprehensive Plan", 68 Harv.L.Rev. 1154, 1157–1158.)

As Professor Haar points out, zoning may easily degenerate into a talismanic word, like the "police power", to excuse all sorts of arbitrary infringements on the property rights of the landowner. To assure that this does not happen, our courts must require local zoning authorities to pay more than mock obeisance to the statutory mandate that zoning be "in accordance with a comprehensive plan". There must be some showing that the change does not conflict with the community's basic scheme for land use.

One of the key factors used by our courts in determining whether the statutory requirement has been met is whether forethought has been given to the community's land use problems.

Where a community, after a careful and deliberate review of "the present and reasonably foreseeable needs of the community", adopts a general developmental policy for the community as a whole and amends its zoning law in accordance with that plan, courts can have some confidence that the public interest is being served. Where, however, local officials adopt a zoning amendment to deal with various problems that have arisen, but give no consideration to alternatives which might minimize the adverse effects of a change on particular landowners, and then call in the experts to justify the steps already taken in contemplation of anticipated litigation, closer judicial scrutiny is required to determine whether the amendment conforms to the comprehensive plan.

The role of these experts must be more than that of giving rationalizations for actions previously decided upon or already carried out. In recent years, many experts on land use problems have expressed the pessimistic view that the task of bringing about a rational allocation of land use in an ever more urbanized America will prove impossible. But of one thing, we may all be certain. The difficulties involved in developing rational schemes of land use controls become insuperable when zoning or changes in zoning are followed rather than preceded by study and consideration.

By this statement, we do not mean to imply that the courts should examine the motives of local officials. What we do mean is that the courts must satisfy themselves that the rezoning meets the statutory requirement that zoning be "in accordance with [the] comprehensive plan" of the community.

Exactly what constitutes a "comprehensive plan" has never been made clear. Professor Haar in his article discusses most of the meanings which courts have given the term. In the conclusion of his article he notes (68 Harv.L.Rev. 1173): "As we have seen, the courts have taken a number of rather different approaches in testing zoning measures for consonance with the enabling act mandate of 'accordance with a comprehensive plan.' None of the meanings suggested—broad geographical coverage, 'policy' of the planning or zoning commission, the zoning ordinance itself, the rational basis underlying the ordinance—do extreme violence to the statutory wording. But all of them share a common defect: they emphasize the question whether the zoning ordinance is a comprehensive plan, not whether it is in accordance with a comprehensive plan. Thus construed, the enabling act demands little more than that zoning be 'reasonable,' and impartial in treatment, to satisfy the constitutional conditions for exercise of the state's police power."

No New York case has defined the term "comprehensive plan". Nor have our courts equated the term with any particular document. We have found the "comprehensive plan" by examining all relevant evidence. As the trial court noted, generally New York cases "have analyzed the ordinance . . . in terms of consistency and rationality" (40 Misc.2d 265, 267–268, 243 N.Y.S.2d 156, 159). While these elements are important, the "comprehensive plan" requires that the rezoning should not conflict with the fundamental land use policies and development plans of the community. These policies may be garnered from any available source, most especially the master plan of the community, if any has been adopted, the zoning law itself and the zoning map.

In the case at bar, the search for the village's "comprehensive plan" is relatively easy. It may be found both in the village's zoning ordinance and in its zoning map.

In 1925 the Village of Lake Success adopted its first zoning ordinance. At least since 1938, appellant's parcel has been placed in a business use district. Over the years, various amendments were passed, none of them, however, affecting appellant's property. If anything, the changes tended to reinforce the conclusion that the community had decided that the neck of land was most appropriately fitted for business use because of its proximity to Northern Boulevard. Thus, in the early 1950s the west side of University Place near Northern Boulevard was rezoned for business use.

When appellant acquired the parcel, it had been zoned for business use for some 12 or 13 years and so it remained for the next 8 or 9 years.

In 1958 the village undertook to set forth expressly the essential development goals of the community. It did so in the form of an amendment to the zoning ordinance and entitled the statement a "developmental policy". According to the statement, Lake Success was and was to remain a suburban community of low density, one-family residential development. Other uses were to be permitted only to the extent that they were related to residential use, e.g., schools, churches, and community institutions, or as they might contribute to the strengthening of the tax base of the community.

If one examines the zoning map of the village as it stood prior to June, 1960, this policy is carried out almost perfectly. Only a small portion of the community's land was zoned for business use. It is important to note that almost, if not, every piece of property in the nonresidential category was located on the periphery of the community, usually adjacent to lands in neighboring communities with similar nonresidential use. Consistent with this "developmental policy", a portion of the northeast section of the community had previously been rezoned for commercial use.

Thus, as matters stood on the morning of June 21, 1960, the village had a zoning plan with stated community goals and a zoning map which consistently carried out these policies.

On June 21, 1960 Fred Rudinger, an associate of the appellant, appeared at the village's offices with a preliminary sketch for the development of the vacant west parcel with a bowling alley and a supermarket or discount house. That same evening, the village planning board recommended a change in zoning from business to residential use.

The minutes of that meeting indicate that, following a discussion of the severe traffic problem which had developed on Lakeville Road, a proposed amendment to the zoning map was recommended to the village trustees. A month or so later, this proposal became, in slightly modified form, ordinance No. 60.

Next, the following comment appears in the minutes: "Mr. Klein informed the Board that *by coincidence*, this morning, an informal preliminary sketch was submitted to him by Mr. Fred Rudinger for the development of the area with a bowling alley and a supermarket or discount house. The Board gave no opinion on this informal sketch and no further action was considered necessary." (Emphasis supplied.)

The reference to Mr. Rudinger's visit as being "by coincidence" appears somewhat odd since no zoning amendments had been considered previously. It is significant that no consideration was given to other possible alternatives for alleviating the traffic problem.

Only after adopting this recommendation did the planning board vote to ask the board of trustees to retain a planning expert to review the village's master plan. On July 5, 1960 the trustees retained Mr. Hugh Pomeroy to make just such an investigation. Later that same day, the planning board and the trustees met in joint session, and it was agreed that a required public hearing should be held promptly. On July 27, 1960 ordinance No. 60 became law following the holding of a public hearing two days earlier.

This history of ordinance No. 60 must immediately raise doubts whether this race to the statute books was in accord with sound zoning principles or was a subversion of them, for the process by which a zoning revision is carried out is important in determining the validity of the particular action taken. The village argues that there was no longer any need for shopping facilities in the area. Assuming that to be so, this does not explain why consideration was only given to zoning the area as "Residence C". A fair respect for the community's need for taxables, as set forth in its "developmental policy", required that some thought be given to other possible land use controls.

A more substantial justification for the rezoning was the serious traffic conditions on Lakeville Road. However, at the trial, the village's own expert, Mr. Frederick P. Clark, who was retained by the village after Mr. Pomeroy's death, admitted that business use of the east parcel would create less of a traffic problem than business use of the west parcel would. The reason for this was that access to the east parcel could be restricted to Northern Boulevard, while access to the west parcel would probably have to be from Lakeville Road.

The point here is not only that the expert's argument does not support the village's position, but that his testimony also conflicted sharply with the community's "developmental policy" and his own earlier recommendations for modifications of that policy, which he had made in 1962 when he drafted a proposed "Comprehensive Zoning Plan" for the community.

In that report, Mr. Clark had recommended the rezoning of various perimeter areas in the community for commercial and light manufacturing use to take account of property developments outside the community and to strengthen the tax base. For example, he suggested that the entire area of the community south of the Northern State Parkway be rezoned for commercial or light manufacturing. On cross-examination, Mr. Clark admitted that the east parcel was in a perimeter area. The fair implication, therefore, is that commercial use of this property would conform with his recommendations for land use control.

More pertinent is Mr. Clark's testimony at the trial: "In my opinion the property on the east side, the Andre property, could be used either for residential purposes as presently zoned or for business. I do not find in my study of it a marked superiority of one over the other. I believe it could be used for either as an appropriate use."

He later modified this statement to include the proviso that there should be no access from Lakeville Road. This concession by Mr. Clark was no mistake. In light of the recommendations of his "Comprehensive Zoning Plan of 1962", he had to agree that commercial use was at least equally desirable. Otherwise, he would have discredited his own planning work for the community. Mr. Clark's testimony establishes that the zoning amendment was neither in 1960 nor afterwards in harmony with the community's over-all land use plan.

Aside from this testimony, examining the zoning map, one would find it difficult to locate a more fitting area to use for commercial purposes than this isolated neck near Northern Boulevard of which the subject parcel is part.

Viewing the village's plans on a temporal basis, there is a consistency predating ordinance No. 60 and post-dating the change. In 1958 a large area in the northeast section of the village had been zoned for nonresidential use. After 1960 other changes of a similar nature were recommended in conformity with a policy of expanding areas of noncommercial use on the periphery of the community. The only significant deviation was the ordinance No. 60.

It is not disputed that the village officials faced a traffic problem in the Northern Boulevard-Lakeville Road area. Nevertheless, we can come to no other conclusion than that the rezoning was not "accomplished in a proper, careful and reasonable manner" (Rodgers v. Village of Tarrytown, 302 N.Y. 115, 122, 96 N.E.2d 731, 733, supra). Ordinance No. 60 not only did not conform to the village's general "developmental policy", but it was also inconsistent with what had been the fundamental rationale of the village's zoning law and map. The amendment was not the result of a deliberate change in community policy and was enacted without sufficient forethought or planning. The particular conditions existing in the area did not support the radical change, which ordinance No. 60 embodied.

More than 60% of the value of appellant's property, or $260,000, was wiped out because, to use the words of the village's first expert, "in his discussions he had found *it is the feeling of the Village* that it does not want extensive business in that area". (Emphasis supplied.)

These vague desires of a segment of the public were not a proper reason to interfere with the appellant's right to use his property in a manner which for some 20 odd years was considered perfectly proper. If there is to be any justification for this interference with appellant's use of his property, it must be found in the needs and goals of the community as articulated in a rational statement of land use control policies known as the "comprehensive plan". We find that appellant has demonstrated that ordinance No. 60 did not conform to the established "comprehensive plan" of the village. Hence, ordinance No. 60 must be held to be *ultra vires* as not meeting the requirement of section 177 of the Village Law that zoning be "in accordance with a comprehensive plan".

Turning then to the other claims of the appellant, we have also concluded that his claim of discrimination is equally valid.

Discrimination in zoning is usually thought of in terms of the injustice done to the landowner. In reality, it is also a wrong done to the community's land use control scheme. It is the opposite side of the coin, one side of which is "spot zoning".

Nevertheless, a claim of discrimination is not just another way of saying that the change does not accord with the comprehensive plan. When the claim is one of discrimination, the focus of inquiry is narrower. The issue is the propriety of the treatment of the subject parcel as compared to neighboring properties.

Trial Term found the rezoning here to be discriminatory because the rezoning did not affect the retail service area to the south on Lakeville Road. The court pointed out that, while those properties would of course be entitled to an exemption for existing nonconforming uses, there was nothing to differentiate that parcel from the appellant's west parcel, and the failure to include the existing retail area evidenced a discriminatory pattern of treatment. It also found that the "ordinance as enacted also discriminated against the east parcel" for the same reason that it discriminated against the west parcel, but also because, unlike the west parcel, most of the east parcel was already being used as a restaurant, that is for a nonconforming commercial use. Nevertheless, there was a "sufficient difference" between the two parcels to warrant their being treated differently (40 Misc.2d 265, 272, 243 N.Y.S.2d 156, 163).

The difference was the fact that the east parcel could be used for residential purposes, where the west parcel could not be. A property owner need not prove confiscation to establish discrimination. In almost every respect, the properties are alike. Also, on the north, west and southwest of the east parcel, the adjacent properties are now zoned for business use.

While not decisive, there is also the added factor that there is at present a nonconforming commercial use on part of the property, which is likely to persist. The treatment accorded the east parcel must take account of economic realities.

There is an inconsistency in the argument of the Trial Justice that there was nothing in the "surrounding residential uses . . . nor any other circumstances" to distinguish the retail service area from both the west and east parcels, and, on the other hand, that the east and west parcels were somehow different (40 Misc.2d 265, 272, 243 N.Y.S.2d 156, 163).

In any event, reversal is clearly warranted by the subsequent history of this case. The village might have met the Trial Justice's objection, had it rezoned the Lakeville Road retail area to Residence "C". Instead, contingent upon the Appellate Division's sustaining the finding of invalidity, the village rezoned the west parcel into a new category, Business "C", which permits allegedly non-traffic-creating business use, i.e., laboratories and office and public buildings. Subsequently, the village withdrew its appeal. As Justice Hopkins correctly pointed out, the village thus accepted the finding of invalidity. That being so, it removes all doubt that the treatment of the east parcel is discriminatory.

Having recognized that the west parcel could not fairly be zoned for residential use, the village was bound to show that dissimilar treatment of the east parcel was still warranted. The village offers no acceptable reason to justify the distinction and, as noted above, the position of the village's expert was, if anything, that the east parcel could properly be zoned for nonresidential use, but the west parcel should be restricted to residential use. That crucial concession removed any basis for an argument that the needs of the village required a different treatment of the east parcel from that of the west parcel.

Appellant has amply demonstrated that ordinance No. 60 constitutes unjustifiable discrimination. If we also consider the fact that, aside from the lack of any showing of purpose in distinguishing the two parcels, the substantial loss which appellant will sustain if the zoning change is upheld, the invalidity of the ordinance becomes unquestionably clear.

The order of the Appellate Division should be reversed and the judgment of the Supreme Court should be modified by striking out the first decretal paragraph and by substituting in place thereof a decretal paragraph declaring ordinance No. 60 to be *ultra vires*, unconstitutional and void as to the property of plaintiff located on the easterly side of Lakeville Road and the westerly side of Summer Avenue, with costs.

FULD, C.J., and BURKE, SCILEPPI, BERGAN, BREITEL and JASEN, JJ., concur.

Order reversed, with costs in all courts, and case remitted to Supreme Court, Nassau County, for further proceedings in accordance with the opinion herein.

NOTES

1. State courts have traditionally been cavalier about enforcing the Standard State Zoning Enabling Act's requirement that zoning be "in accordance with a comprehensive plan." For example, in the leading case of Kozesnik v. Township of Montgomery, 24 N.J. 154, 131 A.2d 1 (1957), the New Jersey Supreme Court held that a municipality which had not adopted a separate comprehensive plan could treat its zoning ordinance as itself a comprehensive plan; amendments to the zoning ordinance were thus viewed as amendments to—and necessarily in conformity with—the comprehensive plan. The court's conclusion that the enabling act did not require a comprehensive plan "in some physical form outside the ordinance itself," stemmed in part from the fact that New Jersey had passed its zoning enabling act *before* it enacted its planning enabling act. 24 N.J. at 166, 131 A.2d at 7.

Udell reflects a contemporary judicial trend to take comprehensive plans more seriously. State legislatures are moving in the same direction, ordering local governments to engage in comprehensive planning and attaching sanctions to the requirement that local land use regulations be consistent with the local plan. See, for example, West's Fla.Stat.Ann. § 163.3167 (Supp.1983) (local government's failure to plan will forfeit planning function to the next higher level of government).

See generally, Mandelker, The Role of the Local Comprehensive Plan in Land Use Regulation, 74 Mich.L.Rev. 899 (1976).

2. As municipalities across the country begin to adopt discrete and detailed comprehensive plans, questions will unavoidably arise concerning the proper procedures to be followed in amending these plans. Should the procedures be more extensive and rigorous than those required for amending a zoning ordinance? Can a local government kill two birds with one stone by amending its zoning ordinance *and* its comprehensive plan for the same purpose, at the same time?

Consider South of Sunnyside Neighborhood League v. Board of Commissioners of Clackamas County, 280 Or. 3, 569 P.2d 1063 (1977). Petitioners there contended "that the Clackamas County Board of Commissioners acted improperly in approving a proposed amendment to the county's comprehensive plan," changing "the designation of a 65-acre parcel on the plan map from 'medium density planned residential' to 'planned commercial'". Rejecting the Board of Commissioners' action, the Oregon Supreme Court remanded to the Board for entry of new findings of fact: "when a comprehensive plan map is amended to change the permissible use of a single tract of land, without any change in the plan's underlying policies, the proponent of the change has the burden of proving that the change in the plan map is consistent with the goals and policies expressed in the plan as a whole and that the change does not violate the specific provisions of any applicable statewide planning goal." 280 Or. at 18, 569 P.2d at 1075.

3. One function of comprehensive planning is to force municipalities to think about local land use patterns and demographics over the longer term. Another function is to clarify goals and to systematize the land use control devices employed to reach those goals. And, as *Udell* indicates, the plan also serves an important political function, protecting the landowner from "arbitrary restrictions on the use of his property which can result from the pressure which outraged voters can bring to bear on public officials."

Do these political and planning functions suggest that comprehensive plans also serve, or can be made to serve, an important economic function, solidifying landowners' expectations respecting the range of restrictions that will be applied to their land while they hold it for development or resale? Should these expectations be treated as property rights, so that any subsequent change in the comprehensive plan will constitute an unlawful taking? Does this possible economic function explain *Udell's* observation that the "vague desires of a segment of the public were not a proper reason to interfere with appellant's right to use his property in a manner which for some twenty odd years was considered proper"?

The Village's action in *Udell tightened* the restrictions on a parcel's development and thus prompted a confrontation between the Village and the landowner, who wanted the previous, less restrictive ordinance to apply. Should the requirement of conformity with a comprehensive plan differ when the municipality *loosens* the restrictions on a parcel's development? Note that here the resulting confrontation will be between the municipality and the parcel's neighbors, and that, in the hands of neighbors, the requirement that rezoning be in accordance with a comprehensive plan offers a powerful tool for delay. The developer must cool her heels and assuage her suppliers and creditors while a court tries to determine what the municipality's comprehensive plan is and whether the challenged rezoning complies with it. The effort will undoubtedly be complicated and lengthened by the fact that a plan may have several competing objects—more housing for the poor; more open space and park uses—and that while the rezoning is consistent with some of these objects, it is inconsistent with others.

Can a developer use a comprehensive plan affirmatively, to argue that her parcel should be rezoned from its present use to one that is less restrictive? See City of Louisville v. Kavanaugh, 495 S.W.2d 502 (Ky.1973) (parcel owner had unsuccessfully sought rezoning from single family to multifamily residential, relying on the fact that City's comprehensive plan projected multifamily use for his parcel; court ordered City Board of Aldermen to rezone as requested).

4. *The Source of Municipal Power to Plan and to Zone.* Constitutionally, the power to plan and to zone resides in state, not local, government. The Standard Zoning Enabling Act was the vehicle through which most states first delegated the zoning power to their local units of government. The Act phrased the delegation of power narrowly and specifically—to "regulate and restrict the height, number of stories, and size of buildings and other structures, the percentage of lot that may be occupied, the size of yards, courts, and other open spaces, the density of population, and the location and use of buildings, structures and land for trade, industry, residence, or other purposes." U.S. Dept. of Commerce Standard State Zoning Enabling Act § 1 (rev.ed. 1926). And, on the premise that municipalities possess only those powers specifically delegated to them by the state, or those necessarily implied, courts early refused to enlarge the local power to include objects or methods not specified in the Act. The result, well into the middle of the century, was a legal straitjacket, constraining local governments from embarking on innovative land use control programs.

As increasing numbers of states abandon the Standard Act's rigid format in favor of more flexible enabling acts, and as courts become more generous in defining the powers delegated by the Standard Act, the straitjacket has been partially loosened and local governments have been given room to experiment with new objects and techniques. See, for example, Golden v. Town of Ramapo, p. 1145, above, in which the New York Court of Appeals construed the Standard Act to authorize the Town's innovative phased development program. Many municipalities have also gained increased freedom to plan and zone as a result of state constitutional and statutory provisions giving them broad home rule powers.

B. THE ZONING SYSTEM

1. THE ZONING ORDINANCE

U.S. NATIONAL COMMISSION ON URBAN PROBLEMS, BUILDING THE AMERICAN CITY

201–202, 205 (1968).

Despite increasingly important changes, the form of today's land use regulations, and often their substance as well, still commonly fall within the conventional patterns established in the 1920's. Of course, no one local regulation is typical of these patterns: Objectives, techniques, and administrative practices reflect the varying desires of thousands of local governments. A rudimentary zoning regulation in a rural village may do little more than exclude a few noxious uses from residential areas, while a regulation for a large city or a prosperous suburb may establish an array of districts and a complex administrative process. There are, however, some elements that are common to most of the current regulations that fall within the conventional pattern.

(1) The zoning ordinance

a. *Regulated subjects.* A zoning ordinance typically prescribes how each parcel of land in a community may be used. Most regulations cover at least these subjects—

Use: First, zoning ordinances designate permitted "uses" (activities). Many divide uses into three basic categories: Dwellings, businesses, and industry. These basic categories are usually divided into subcategories. It is common practice, for example, to distinguish between one-family detached houses and apartment buildings, between "light" and "heavy" industry. Over the years ordinances have tended to establish more and more use categories. Ordinances with more than 20 different use categories are now common, and many ordinances now make specific provision for hundreds of listed uses.

Population density: A limitation on population density is also part of today's accepted zoning pattern. Most ordinances establish this limitation by setting a minimum required size for each lot. Alternatively, they may limit the number of families per acre or set a minimum required lot area for each dwelling unit on a lot. Some, particularly in large cities, establish more refined density controls that try to take account of the likelihood that more people will live in larger apartment units than in smaller ones.

Building bulk: Zoning regulations also limit building bulk. Usually, they do this by requiring yards along lot boundaries, by limiting building height, and by limiting the proportion of lot area that may be covered by buildings. Refinements of these devices have become common, in recent years, as communities have recognized that rigid yard and height requirements often deter imaginative design. "Floor area ratio" and "usable open space" requirements are among the increasingly common refinements.

Offstreet parking: As an addition to the original pattern, most zoning ordinances now contain offstreet parking requirements. These are intended to assure that new development provides for at least some of its own parking needs rather than adding to the number of parked cars on already crowded streets.

Other subjects: Many other requirements also appear in zoning regulations. Minimum house size, landscaping, signs, appearance of buildings, offstreet loading, view protection, and grading are just a few of the other subjects sometimes regulated.

b. *The zoning map.* In recognition of differing conditions and planning policies in different parts of each community, zoning regulations establish "zones" or "districts." Within each of these districts a uniform set of regulations dealing with uses, bulk and the like apply. Thus, for example, stores may be permitted in one district but not in another. To show the location and boundaries of these districts, the ordinance includes a zoning map.

The number of districts and the nature of the differences between them vary greatly from town to town. Most ordinances contain at least one district in which single-family detached dwellings are the only permitted residential use. Often there are several such "single family" districts, distinguished from each other primarily by differences in the required minimum lot size; one district may require each lot to contain at least 2 acres, another at least 1 acre, and so on. Many ordinances also contain general residence districts, in which other types of dwellings are also permitted; these, too, are often differentiated by density requirements. Ordinances also commonly contain a variety of commercial districts bearing such names as neighborhood retail, central business, heavy commercial, and commercial recreation. They are commonly distinguished from one another by variations in permitted activity, bulk, and parking requirements. And industrial districts may differ from each other with respect to permitted activities, bulk regulations, and "performance" regulations limiting the amount of smoke, noise, or odor that industries may produce.

In addition to the basic districts—those based on the traditional triad of dwellings, business and industry—scores of other kinds of districts have been devised since the early days of zoning and are now commonly used to fit local conditions and policies. Agricultural districts, industrial-park districts, and special districts for public land are examples. Some of the newer districts allow a mixture of traditionally separated uses, such as residential-office and residential-commercial districts. Others are intended to meet unique conditions of a particular area, such as flood plain districts. . . .

(3) Evolution of the regulatory pattern

Although today's regulations still normally resemble those of the 1920's in some respects, many also show marked differences from the early pattern. Regulatory techniques have been substantially refined, and standards have been generally raised. Objectives have become more ambitious, particularly where the old negativism has given way to the view that regulations should be part of a process to guide development affirmatively toward desired public objectives. And both techniques and objectives have been adapted to changes in the process of city building itself, particularly to the increased scale and pace of change since World War II.

a. *Refinement of regulatory techniques.* One direction of change has been toward refinement of regulatory techniques. Among the many common examples of such refinement are these:

Specification of permitted uses: Instead of listing prohibited uses in each district, as the oldest ordinances did, regulations now normally list uses permitted in each district and prohibit all others. This plugs loopholes and establishes more clearly the intent of the regulations to guide development affirmatively in desired directions.

Noncumulative regulations: Old zoning ordinances set up a kind of use pyramid. Residences were "highest," businesses next, and industry was at the bottom. Each district permitted all the "higher" uses but excluded the "lower" ones. Thus, while industry was prohibited in residence zones, residences were permitted in industrial zones. Recent ordinances, however, attempting to assure that land is put to its planned use are much more likely to prohibit residences in industrialized zones as well as *vice versa.*

More districts: Another sign of increasing refinement of control is the ever-increasing number of districts. A small suburban community that may have had half a dozen districts 30 years ago may have several times that many today.

More subjects regulated: There is a tendency to regulate more characteristics of development. Landscaping and screening provisions, for example, are now common. Many community regulations reflect public concern about such diverse matters as the appearance of buildings, the economic compatibility of the uses permitted in business areas, or the unwelcome glare from lights in parking lots.

Performance standards: Finally, a number of regulations contain performance standards. Performance standards fashion regulations more precisely to public objectives than do traditional or conventional regulations. Industrial performance standards, for example, may establish odor limits instead of prohibiting all paint plants. Performance standards hold great promise wherever the regulatory purpose is clear, where a standard can be precisely determined, and where compliance with it can be objectively and easily measured. Nevertheless, standards of this type are not even potentially available to govern many of the most important land-use relationships; there are simply too many purposes to be weighed in each situation and too many that defy objective measurement.

2. FLEXIBILITY IN ZONING

a. The Constitutional Setting

i. Nonconforming Structures and Uses

BELLEVILLE v. PARRILLO'S, INC.

Supreme Court of New Jersey, 1980.
83 N.J. 309, 416 A.2d 388.

CLIFFORD, J.

We granted certification to review the Appellate Division's reversal of defendant's conviction for violating the zoning ordinance of the Town of Belleville. Specifically, defendant was found guilty of extending a nonconforming use [1] when it changed its operation from a restaurant to a discotheque without having first obtained approval of the local board of adjustment. The Appellate Division concluded that "within the meaning and intent of our applicable statute, N.J.S.A. 40:55D-68, defendant did not either extend or enlarge its use of the premises." Our examination of the record satisfies us that a prohibited change in use was established beyond a reasonable doubt, that being the appropriate standard of proof in these *quasi*-criminal proceedings. We therefore reverse and reinstate the judgment of conviction.

1. *N.J.S.A.* 40:55D-5 defines a nonconforming use as "a use or activity which was lawful prior to the adoption, revision or amendment of a zoning ordinance, but which fails to conform to the requirements of the zoning district in which it is located by reason of such adoption, revision or amendment."

I

The record demonstrates that sometime prior to 1955 Parrillo's operated as a restaurant and catering service on Harrison Street, Belleville. On January 1, 1955 the Town enacted a new zoning ordinance of which all provisions pertinent here are still in effect. The system created under that ordinance provided for zoning under which specific permitted uses for each zone were itemized. Uses not set forth for a particular zone were deemed prohibited. Parrillo's was situated in a "B" residence zone, which did not allow restaurants. However, because it had been in existence prior to the effective date of the zoning ordinance, defendant's establishment qualified as a preexisting nonconforming use and, under the terms of the ordinance, was allowed to remain in operation.

In 1978 defendant's owners made certain renovations in the premises. Upon their completion Parrillo's opened as a discotheque. We readily acknowledge that included among those for whom the term "discotheque" has not, at least until this case, found its way into their common parlance are some members of this Court; and on the assumption that there may be others whose experience has denied them an intimate familiarity with the term and the milieu to which it applies, we pause to extend the benefit of definition. *Webster's Third New International Dictionary* 63a (1976) informs us that a discotheque is a "small intimate nightclub for dancing to recorded music; *broadly:* a nightclub often featuring psychedelic and mixed-media attractions (as slides, movies, and special lighting effects)". "Disco" appears to be an accepted abbreviation. Defendant's operation is closer to the broad definition above than it is to a small or intimate cabaret.

Shortly after they had opened under the new format, Parrillo's owners applied for a discotheque license as required by the Town's ordinance regulating dancehalls. Although the application was denied, defendant continued business as usual. Thereupon the municipal construction code official filed the charges culminating in the conviction under review. The municipal court imposed a fine of $250.00.

On a trial *de novo* after defendant's appeal to the Superior Court, Law Division, the defendant was again found guilty. That court correctly framed the issue as whether "a change from a business primarily conducted as a restaurant with incidental dancing and serving of liquor [can] survive the proscription of the prohibiting ordinance when the character of the operation shifts to a form primarily conducted as a dance hall with the serving of liquor and incidental eating." That court determined that the evidence adduced could "lead to no other conclusion" than that there had been a prohibited extension of a nonconforming use, and likewise entered a judgment of conviction.

The Appellate Division reversed. The error in that result is rooted in the court's approach to the case, which was to review separately each component of the municipality's proof supporting the contention that defendant's operation was not permitted as a nonconforming use. From that perspective it reasoned that since each aspect of the "new" business had been conducted previously, there was no impermissible change from the nature of the "old" business. The analysis was thus quantitative rather than, as it should have been, qualitative. Put differently, the focus in cases such as this must be on the quality, character and intensity of the use, viewed in their totality and with regard to their overall effect on the neighborhood and the zoning plan.

That was precisely the frame of reference of Judge Joseph Walsh in the trial *de novo* in Superior Court, Law Division. Contrary to the suggestion of the Appellate Division, Judge Walsh made extensive and specific findings of fact. They are amply supported by the record and are as follows:

> The business was formerly advertised as a restaurant; it is now advertised as a "disco". It was formerly operated every day and now it is open but one day and three evenings. The primary use of the dance hall was incidental to dining; now it is the primary use. The music was formerly provided by live bands and now it is recorded and operated by a so-called "disc-jockey". An admission charge of $3.00 on the Wednesday opening and $5.00 on the Friday and Saturday openings is now mandatory as opposed to any prior entry charge. There is no charge for Sunday. Formerly there was but one bar; now there are several.
>
> During the course of the testimony it was admitted that the business is operated as a "disco". Normal lighting in the premises was altered to psychedelic lighting, colored and/or revolving, together with mirrored lighting. The premises were crowded and there were long lines waiting to enter. There are now fewer tables than the prior use required and on one occasion there were no tables. The music was extremely loud and the premises can accommodate 431 persons legally. There have been numerous complaints from residents adjacent to the area. During the course of the testimony "disco" dancing was described by the owners as dancing by "kids" who "don't hold each other close". The bulk of the prior business was food catering; now there is none. The foods primarily served at the present time are "hamburgers" and "cheeseburgers", although there are other selections available to people who might come in earlier than the "disco" starting time.

On the basis of these findings Judge Walsh concluded that there had been a prohibited change in the use of the premises. He found to be dispositive the straightforward proposition that "a 'disco' is a place wherein you dance and a restaurant a place wherein you eat. It is as simple as that"—an unvarnished exercise in reductionism, perhaps, but one fully justified in this case. He concluded that the defendant had "abandoned all the pretenses of the continued existence of a restaurant as it was before." We agree with that conclusion.

II

Historically, a nonconforming use has been looked upon as "a use of land, buildings or premises that lawfully existed prior to the enactment of a zoning ordinance and which is maintained after the effective date of such ordinance even though it does not comply with the use restrictions applicable to the area in which it is situated." 6 R. Powell, *The Law of Real Property*, ¶ 871 (Perm.ed. 1979). Under the Municipal Land Use Act, N.J.S.A. 40:55D–1 *et seq.*, such property is deemed to have acquired a vested right to continue in such form, irrespective of the restrictive zoning provisions:

> Any nonconforming use or structure existing at the time of the passage of an ordinance may be continued upon the lot or in the structure so occupied and any such structure may be restored or repaired in the event of partial destruction thereof. [N.J.S.A. 40:55D–68.]

This statutory guarantee against compulsory termination, however, is not without limit. Because nonconforming uses are inconsistent with the objectives of uniform zoning, the courts have required that consistent with the property rights of those affected and with substantial justice, they should be reduced to conformity as quickly as is compatible with justice. In that regard the courts have permitted municipalities to impose limitations upon nonconforming uses. Such restrictions typically relate to the change of use, the enlargement or extension, or the repair or replacement, of nonconforming structures, and limits on the duration of nonconforming uses through abandonment or discontinuance.

The method generally used to limit nonconforming uses is to prevent any increase or change in the nonconformity. Under that restrictive view our courts have held that an existing nonconforming use will be permitted to continue only if it is a continuance of substantially the same kind of use as that to which the premises were devoted at the time of the passage of the zoning ordinance. In that regard nonconforming uses may not be enlarged as of right except where the change is so negligible or insubstantial that it does not warrant judicial or administrative interference. Where there is doubt as to whether an enlargement or change is substantial rather than insubstantial, the courts have consistently declared that it is to be resolved against the enlargement or change.

In the instant case it is acknowledged by all parties that the former restaurant had constituted a proper preexisting nonconforming use. The issue then becomes whether the conversion from a restaurant to a discotheque represented a substantial change, and was thus improper. Fundamental to that inquiry is an appraisal of the basic character of the use, before and after the change. . . .

III

We have already expressed our agreement with the municipal court and with Judge Walsh, presiding at the trial *de novo*, that defendant's conversion of the premises from a restaurant to a discotheque resulted in a substantial, and therefore impermissible, change. The entire character of the business has been altered. What was once a restaurant is now a dancehall. Measured by the zoning ordinance the general welfare of the neighborhood has been demonstrably affected adversely by the conversion of defendant's business. Our strong public policy restricting nonconforming uses requires reversal of the judgment below.

We observe that a *quasi*-criminal proceeding is a poor vehicle for a determination of the underlying issue in cases such as this. Only a penalty may be imposed, and the more demanding burden of proving a zoning ordinance violation beyond a reasonable doubt may inhibit the attainment of the ultimate goal sought by the municipal authorities, namely, preservation of the zoning plan and containment of nonconforming uses. Counsel for the Town in this case readily conceded at oral argument before us that the municipality would have done better to seek injunctive relief rather than to file a complaint in the municipal court.

Finally, we point out that the Court views with disfavor the conduct of the attorney of record for defendant. He has disregarded all written communications from the Clerk of this Court as to counsel's intentions on this appeal. He did not file any responsive papers or brief on the petition for certification; he did not furnish a copy of his Appellate Division brief in lieu of an answering brief to the petitioner's brief; he did not respond to the Clerk's notification with respect to argument before the Supreme Court; and he has not otherwise explained his silence. There may be good and sufficient reasons for the stance he has taken, but in the absence of any explanation whatsoever counsel's ostensible incivility to an arm of this Court—and hence to this Court directly—is *prima facie* the sort of discourtesy contemplated by *DR* 7–106(C)(6). Public announcement of counsel's dereliction herein should serve as notice to the bar that such disrespectful conduct will not be countenanced in the future.

Reversed. The cause is remanded to the Superior Court, Law Division, for entry there of a judgment of conviction.

ii. Vested Rights

BOARD OF SUPERVISORS OF FAIRFAX COUNTY v. MEDICAL STRUCTURES, INC.

Supreme Court of Virginia, 1972.
213 Va. 355, 192 S.E.2d 799.

SNEAD, Chief Justice.

Medical Structures, Inc. (Medical Structures) filed a Petition for Declaratory Judgment against the Board of Supervisors of Fairfax County alleging that Medical Structures was the owner of a tract of land in Fairfax County and that the County Board of Zoning Appeals had issued a special use permit allowing it to construct a nursing home on the property. It was further alleged that, subsequent to the issuance of the special use permit and to the filing of a site plan as required by county ordinance, the Board of Supervisors had unlawfully amended the zoning requirements having the effect of prohibiting petitioner's nursing home. This was done, it was alleged, arbitrarily and capriciously in disregard of Medical Structures' vested rights.

After hearing the evidence *ore tenus* the trial court entered a decree on September 2, 1971, in favor of Medical Structures to the effect that under the circumstances of the case Medical Structures obtained a vested right in a special use permit which could not be divested by the subsequent enactment of an amended zoning ordinance. The zoning amendments were held null and void as to Medical Structures, and the court directed the county to approve the site plan and upon the filing of the required application to issue a building permit.

The Board of Supervisors assigned as error (1) the finding of the trial court that the granting of a special use permit created a vested right to a given land use which could not be divested by subsequent legislative action, and (2) the order directing approval of Medical Structures' site plan and the issuance of a building permit in disregard of the amended ordinance.

The evidence establishes that on April 23, 1963, a special use permit was granted to Henry Rolfs, Medical Structures' predecessor in title, permitting a 160-bed nursing home on his property located on Columbia Pike in an R–17 zoning district (residential 17,000 square feet). At that time nursing homes were allowed in all residential districts under special use permits. The use permit on the subject property was extended a number of times and did not finally expire until January 8, 1970.

On December 24, 1968, Medical Structures purchased the property from Rolfs for $250,000, reflecting the value of the use permit and filed a site plan on March 7, 1969, as a prerequisite to the issuance of a building permit. The site plan was resubmitted to the county with alterations on June 16, August 18, and November 12, 1969, which procedure was not unusual in Fairfax County.

On January 7, 1970, John F. Chilton, chief of the land planning department of Fairfax County, affixed his signature to the site plan approving it and the requisite bonding, siltation and easement agreements. However, after consultation with the county attorney on the same day, Chilton eradicated his signature and notified Medical Structures on January 8, 1970, that the passage of amendments to the zoning ordinance on October 8 and November 19, 1969, prevented approval of its site plan. Chilton advised Medical Structures by letter that if the ordinance had not been amended, he would have approved the site plan, entitling Medical Structures to the issuance of a building permit before the expiration of the use permit on January 8, 1970.

The actions of the Board of Supervisors on October 8 and November 19 amended the zoning ordinance to prohibit nursing homes of over 50 beds in any residential district of less density than RT–10 (residential townhouses), which prohibition included Medical Structures' R–17 property. The amendments provided, however, a "grandfather clause" for an existing nursing home with future expansion plans for more than 50 beds located 2000 feet from the subject property on Columbia Pike in a district of less density than RT–10 or R–17.

Medical Structures spent considerable sums of money in the development and preparation of site plans and bond deposits. The uncontradicted evidence shows that it spent $59,600 for engineering and architectural plans alone and a total for the entire project of $247,500 exclusive of the purchase price. There was no evidence that the proposed construction would be harmful to the public health, safety, morals or general welfare.

The question whether the issuance of a special use permit and the filing of a site plan create a vested property right in the permittee is one of first impression for this Court.

The Board of Supervisors argues that for rights to vest from reliance upon a special use permit or building permit, one must go beyond mere expense in preparation, and construction must have actually and substantially begun. In support of its position, the Board of Supervisors relies on McClung v. County of Henrico, 200 Va. 870, 108 S.E.2d 513 (1959).

On the other hand, Medical Structures argues that once a diligently pursued site plan is filed in reliance upon existing zoning or the issuance of a special use permit, fairness dictates that a vested right is acquired in the land use.

In recent years some localities have enacted ordinances requiring the filing of a site plan in order to obtain a building permit. Under current planning practice in many urban localities, the site plan has virtually replaced the building permit as the most vital document in the development process. Every site plan submitted under the Fairfax County Zoning Ordinance (Chapter 30, Code of Fairfax County) must contain, among other things, topographical maps, surveys, engineering studies and proof of notice to landowners in the vicinity. The filing of such a plan creates a monument to the developer's intention, and when the plan is approved, the building permit, except in rare situations, will be issued.

Here, Medical Structures purchased the property in reliance upon the use permit allowing a 160-bed nursing home. It incurred in good faith expenses amounting to $59,600 in the preparation of site and architectural plans as well as other considerable development costs. Certainly, a substantial change in its position resulted therefrom.

We hold that where, as here, a special use permit has been granted under a zoning classification, a bona fide site plan has thereafter been filed and diligently pursued, and substantial expense has been incurred in good faith before a change in zoning, the permittee then has a vested right to the land use described in the use permit and he cannot be deprived of such use by subsequent legislation.

We further hold that the trial court did not err in ordering the approval of Medical Structures' site plan and the issuance of a building permit.

McClung v. County of Henrico, *supra*, relied upon by the Board of Supervisors, is factually different from the case at bar and is not controlling. In that case, after McClung was issued a building permit, the zoning ordinance was amended to prohibit the intended use. Thereafter, his rights were held to have expired for failure to start construction within ninety days after the amendment as provided by the zoning ordinance.

The decree of the trial court will be

Affirmed.

NOTES

1. Is there a principled distinction between Euclid v. Ambler—in which a developer who had acquired land, intending to put it to a specified use, was given no relief against an ordinance prohibiting that use—and cases like *Belleville*, implicitly holding that a developer who acquires land, *and* puts it to his intended use, will be immunized from an ordinance prohibiting that use? Is the difference one of credibility—that, in the latter case, the developer in fact put the land to the use that he only talked about in *Euclid?* Or is the difference dictated by a concern for the economic waste that would result from requiring the developer to shut down a going enterprise? What are the distinction's likely effects on a landowner's timing of his development activities?

Cases like *Euclid*—and *Belle Terre, Penn Central* and *Mt. Laurel*—raise the conflict between private property and the public interest to its highest, most abstract level. Cases like *Belleville* and *Medical Structures* reduce that conflict to more concrete and localized terms. In localizing these conflicts, the cases also bring the combatants into sharp relief—the landowner who wishes to avoid an applicable zoning ordinance, and his neighbors who wish to enforce it. What tradeoffs do *Belleville* and *Medical Structures* suggest these combatants can make with each other? Is it the role of local government to do anything more than mediate between the combatants?

2. *Amortization.* Prohibitions against extending a prior use, as in *Belleville*, represent one of two principal methods that municipalities employ to curb nonconforming uses and structures. The other method, amortization, enables the owner of a rezoned parcel to phase out its nonconforming use or structure over a predetermined period. "The term 'amortization' is derived from the notion that the nonconforming user can amortize his investment during the period of permitted nonconformity. It is reasoned that this opportunity to continue for a limited time cushions the economic shock of the restriction, dulls the edge of popular disapproval, and improves the prospects of judicial approval." 1 R. Anderson, American Law of Zoning § 6.65 (1968). Statutory amortization periods can be as short as one or two years—typically for nonconforming uses—and as long as fifty or sixty years—typically for nonconforming structures.

Courts will generally hold an amortization period constitutional if it is sufficiently long to enable the landowner to recover all or most of her original investment. The constitutional rationale is usually couched in the terms of standard police power analysis: "The distinction between an ordinance restricting future uses and one requiring the termination of present uses within a reasonable period of time is merely one of degree, and constitutionality depends on the relative importance to be given to the public gain and to the private loss. Zoning as it affects every piece of property is to some extent retroactive in that it applies to property already owned at the time of the effective date of the ordinance. The elimination of existing uses within a reasonable time does not amount to a taking of property nor does it necessarily restrict the use of property so that it cannot be used for any reasonable purpose. Use of a reasonable amortization scheme provides an equitable means of reconciliation of the conflicting interests in satisfaction of due process requirements. As a method of eliminating existing nonconforming uses it allows the owner of the nonconforming use, by affording an opportunity to make new plans, at least partially to offset any loss he might suffer . . . . If the amortization period is reasonable the loss to the owner may be small when compared with the benefit to the public." City of Los Angeles v. Gage, 127 Cal.App.2d 442, 460, 274 P.2d 34, 44 (2d Dist.1954).

Judicial support for amortization techniques has not, however, been unanimous. See, for example, Hoffmann v. Kinealy, 389 S.W.2d

745, 753 (Mo.1965) ("To our knowledge, no one has, as yet, been so brash as to contend that such a pre-existing lawful nonconforming use properly might be terminated *immediately*. In fact, the contrary is implicit in the amortization technique itself which would validate a taking *presently* unconstitutional by the simple expedient of *postponing* such taking for a 'reasonable' time . . . it would be a strange and novel doctrine indeed which would approve a municipality taking private property for public use without compensation if the property was not too valuable and the taking was not too soon . . .."). Also, several of the leading high court decisions sustaining amortization provisions were rendered over substantial dissents. See, for example, Harbison v. City of Buffalo, 4 N.Y.2d 553, 176 N.Y.S.2d 598, 152 N.E.2d 42 (1958) (4–3 decision; two members of the majority concurring in result only).

3. Constitutional considerations aside, is it fair or efficient to apply a uniform amortization period to all uses or structures, without regard for how long they have already existed or for the economics of the industry in which they are employed? One proponent of an individualized approach to amortization periods has noted that its use would probably halve present amortization periods based on a building's useful life: "In deciding whether to construct or purchase a structure with a useful economic life of 40 to 50 years, an investor usually considers only the returns in the early years of the project, both because it is almost impossible to estimate returns for more than 25 years with any degree of accuracy . . . and because the interest factor tends to reduce the present value of any returns received in the distant future to a very small amount (*e.g.*, the present value of $100 received in 25 years, discounted at a 12% required rate of return, is $5.90). Given these two factors, a project is not likely to be approved unless the investment will be returned in the first 25 years, even though the structure is built with a 50-year service life. Structures are built with 50-year, rather than 25-year service lives, because the marginal cost of constructing a building to last the additional 25 years is minimal." Note, A Suggested Means of Determining the Proper Amortization Period for Nonconforming Structures, 27 Stan.L.Rev. 1325, 1342 n. 74 (1975). Would such an individualized approach be administratively feasible?

4. *Vested Rights*. Once construction of an improvement is completed in compliance with the applicable zoning ordinance, the improvement and its permitted uses are protected against any change in the zoning ordinance under the rules respecting prior nonconforming structures and uses. But what if the rezoning occurs before construction is finished? Until two or three decades ago, the question rarely arose, for site acquisition and development usually proceeded quickly. But, with the contemporary emergence of large-scale phased developments, and with the proliferation of land use controls and permit requirements, the time needed for a project's completion

has in many places grown from two or three months to two or three years or more.

Courts in many states have adopted the doctrine of vested rights to protect developers from changes in the zoning and other land use controls that obtained at the time they first acquired their site and began planning its development. The doctrine explicitly focuses on two factors: the extent to which the developer has obtained the required governmental approvals, up to and including the final building permit; and the extent to which the developer has irretrievably committed time and money in good faith reliance on these approvals.

Judicial treatment of these two factors varies widely. Some courts will not require the developer to have obtained any permits, while others will ignore even the issuance of a building permit; some courts will require that the good faith expenditures be on the actual construction of improvements, while others will credit expenditures made on planning alone. Compare American National Bank & Trust Co. v. City of Chicago, 19 Ill.App.3d 30, 311 N.E.2d 325 (1974) (land acquisition costs, site planning and architect contracts, together with "probability" that permit would issue, sufficient to vest development right) with County Council for Montgomery County v. District Land Corp., 274 Md. 691, 337 A.2d 712 (1975) (expenditure of more than $1,000,000 on site studies and planning and issuance of building permit insufficient to vest development rights). *Medical Structures* reflects the majority position that substantial planning expenditures made in reliance on a permit that approximates a building permit will suffice.

Is there a principled distinction between the rule that categorically permits prior nonconforming structures to continue, and the rule that a developer can continue building a nonconforming structure only if she has relied on a building permit or equivalent permit issued before the change in zoning? Is it fair or efficient to allow the developer who completes her building before rezoning to continue occupying it, while requiring her counterpart, whom the rezoning fortuitously catches in the middle of development, to scrap his investment?

See generally, Cunningham & Kremer, Vested Rights, Estoppel, and the Land Development Process, 29 Hastings L.J. 623 (1978).

5. If a local official mistakenly grants a building permit in violation of the applicable zoning ordinance, may the municipality, once having discovered the mistake, revoke the permit and require the developer to remove improvements built in reliance on it? As a general rule, the answer is that the municipality may revoke. See, for example, Pettitt v. City of Fresno, 34 Cal.App.3d 813, 823, 110 Cal.Rptr. 262, 268 (1973) ("To hold that the City can be estopped would not punish the City but it would assuredly injure the area residents, who in no way can be held responsible for the City's mistake"). Courts sometimes correct these situations by holding that the developer has acquired a vested right in the improvement erected under the illegal

permit. See Petrosky v. Zoning Hearing Board of Upper Chichester Township, 485 Pa. 501, 402 A.2d 1385 (1979).

The decisions in these cases have a "damned if you do, damned if you don't" aspect: to hold that the municipality is not estopped will penalize the developer who relied to his detriment on an authoritative governmental act. But, to hold that the municipality is estopped will penalize the neighbors who would prefer that improvements on the parcel conform to requirements otherwise uniformly imposed throughout the district. Would it be better in these cases to allow the municipality to revoke the permit and require the developer to remove the illegal improvement, but also to require that the municipality indemnify the developer for any losses suffered? Such an approach would make the developer whole and would give the municipality an incentive to be more careful in its issuance of permits. See Heeter, Zoning Estoppel: Application of the Principles of Equitable Estoppel and Vested Rights to Zoning Disputes, 1971 Urb.L.Ann. 63, 97–98. Does nuisance law's gravity-utility calculus offer a better approach to the problem—balancing the costs to the developer of compliance against the cost to neighbors of noncompliance?

b. Administrative Decisions: Variances and Special Exceptions

NORTH SHORE STEAK HOUSE, INC. v. BOARD OF APPEALS OF INCORPORATED VILLAGE OF THOMASTON

Court of Appeals of New York, 1972.
30 N.Y.2d 238, 331 N.Y.S.2d 645, 282 N.E.2d 606.

BURKE, Judge.

In this article 78 proceeding, appellant North Shore Steak House, Inc. (hereafter North Shore) seeks to review a decision of the Board of Appeals of the Village of Thomaston (hereafter the Board) denying North Shore's application for: (1) a special exception permit to extend its parking area, on its split zoned lot, 25 feet into a single-family residence district, and (2) a hardship variance permitting accessory parking on the residentially zoned property beyond the 25-foot strip.

North Shore is the lessee of a plot of land used for a restaurant on the northwest corner of Northern Boulevard and Summer Street, in the Village of Thomaston in Great Neck, Long Island. The lease term is from May 1, 1961 to February 28, 2003. The premises front 181 feet on Northern Boulevard, a heavily traveled State highway, and have a depth of 286 feet along Summer Street. The zoning map provides that the Business "B" District has a depth of 200 feet and, therefore, the lot is split zoned, the rear 86 feet being in Residence "B" District zoned for single-family homes. The plot has been in single and separate ownership since 1903 and is improved with a main building, used as a restaurant since 1940, and an old stable, in the back of the premises, approximately 5 feet from the rear line.

All available space within the 200 feet business district has been blacktopped for parking during the past nine years. North Shore has made two small extensions to the main building which did not increase the seating capacity but did result in the loss of several parking spaces. The restaurant has seats for 170 people at the tables and an additional 18 at the bar. At present, there are parking spaces for 75 to 85 cars.

In December, 1969, North Shore, joined by the owner-lessor, Herman Weinman, made an application for a special exception permit, pursuant to article X (§ 3) of the Zoning Ordinance, which states:

"Section 3. They *may* in appropriate cases, after public notice and hearing, and subject to appropriate conditions and safeguards, and in harmony with the general purpose and intent of this ordinance, in addition to the powers and duties set forth in the Village Law of the State of New York and such powers as are heretofore in this ordinance given to them:

"(e) Where a zone boundary line divides a lot in single ownership at the effective date of this ordinance affecting a use district, as the case may be, permit a use authorized on either portion of such lot to extend to the entire lot, but not more than twenty-five (25) feet beyond the boundary line of the greater restricted zone." (emphasis supplied).

In addition, the application sought a variance for the balance of the rear 86 feet beyond the 25-foot strip, except for a 50-foot by 100-foot plot on the northeast corner, to be improved with a new one-family house fronting on Summer Street.

In rejecting the application for a variance, the Board found, among others, that (1) the premises were not unique or different from other split zoned property in the village (2) that the hardship, if any, was self-created (3) that the evidence that the variance would have an adverse effect on the adjoining property was not rebutted and (4) that a ratio of one car to every three or four seats is all that should be reasonably required. Based on these findings, the Board also concluded, without any additional findings or conditions, that the special exception permit "would not be in harmony with the general purpose and intent of the zoning plan and scheme".

Special Term, in sustaining the Board's determination, did so, not on the merits, but on the basis that a prior application by the owner-lessor in 1957 was *res judicata* in the absence of "changed circumstances". The majority in the Appellate Division did not rely on this rationale but concluded that the record did not support the view that the residential portion of the property could not be used for that purpose. In addition, citing Matter of Lemir Realty Corp. v. Larkin, 11

N.Y.2d 20, 226 N.Y.S.2d 374, 181 N.E.2d 407, it held there was a reasonable basis for the denial of the special exception permit.

In his dissent, Justice Gulotta agreed with the majority with respect to the denial of the variance but determined that the denial of the special exception permit was arbitrary and capricious since the Board "erroneously applied the same test to the special exception application" as that required for a hardship variance.

On this record, it cannot be said that the hardship variance was improperly denied. It was sought for accessory parking on the northwest corner of the property (measuring approximately 61 feet by 81 feet) beyond the 25-foot special exception area and next to the 50-foot by 100-foot plot on the northeast corner on which the owner-lessor planned to erect a new, conforming one-family house fronting on Summer Street. North Shore's contention, no doubt true, that this plot is more valuable as accessory parking is insufficient to warrant a hardship variance since the property, located in a residential zone, may be reasonably employed for that use as evidenced by the proposed new house on the adjoining parcel.

The denial of the special exception permit, based on factual findings used to support denial of the variance, ignores the fundamental difference between a variance and a special exception permit. A variance is an authority to a property owner to use property in a manner forbidden by the ordinance while a special exception allows the property owner to put his property to a use expressly permitted by the ordinance. The inclusion of the permitted use in the ordinance is tantamount to a legislative finding that the permitted use is in harmony with the general zoning plan and will not adversely affect the neighborhood. Denial of the permit on the ground that the extension of the parking lot 25 feet into the residential zone is "not . . . in harmony with the general purpose and intent of the zoning plan" is, thus, patently inconsistent.

The burden of proof on an applicant for a special exception permit is much lighter than that required for a hardship variance. It does not require the applicant to show that it has been denied any reasonable use of the property but only that the use is contemplated by the ordinance subject only to "conditions" attached to its use to minimize its impact on the surrounding area. North Shore has met that burden. The president of North Shore testified that 22 parking spaces are needed for employees' cars. Despite the employment of parking attendants at all times, a severe shortage of parking space exists at peak dining periods on weekends. A 25-foot by 81-foot extension would accommodate approximately 25 to 30 more cars. Because of congestion in the parking lot, cars tend to back up on Summer Street waiting to get into the parking area. This problem is further aggravated by the fact that a median was installed on Northern Boulevard three years ago preventing traffic traveling eastward from turning left into the driveway on Northern Boulevard. Instead, the traffic must proceed to Summer Street and make a left turn, adding to the congestion there.

The Board's expert, Mr. Reuter, conceded that North Shore had a parking problem and the restaurant needs 100 parking spaces. He admitted that there was an adjacent water tower, 80 feet to 100 feet tall, but declined to estimate the impact of the tower on residential values. In addition, he admitted that Briggs Auto Leasing had been issued a permit to extend a large parking area beyond the 200-foot business district on a plot less than two blocks from the restaurant and that the Methodist Church fronting on Northern Boulevard in the vicinity had parking well beyond the 200-foot line without harm to anyone. He, nonetheless, concluded that granting the permit would adversely affect property values and generate more traffic on Northern Boulevard.

In view of the changes which have already taken place in the immediate area, there is no basis for the conclusion that the addition of parking spaces for 25 or 30 cars, to be used primarily on weekends, will adversely affect property values or greatly increase traffic in the area. On the contrary, the uncontroverted evidence is that granting of the permit will have a beneficial impact by relieving traffic on Summer Street during peak dining hours while preventing any spillback onto heavily traveled Northern Boulevard by cars traveling eastward and unable to enter the front entrance of the parking lot. Nor does there appear to be any reasonable basis for the conclusion that the additional cars will increase noise or gas fumes in the immediate area, since North Shore has agreed to provide a 10-foot screen of shrubs or trees at the rear of the extension to protect the neighboring residences. Absent any support in the record for the conclusions advanced by the Board justifying the denial, and in view of the "erroneous standard" used, namely that applicable to a hardship variance, the decision of the Board with respect to the special permit, must be deemed arbitrary and capricious.

The argument, relied on by Special Term, that a prior application was *res judicata* is not applicable. In 1957 the present owner made an application for a use variance as well as a special exception permit for accessory parking in the residential zone. The application was denied and the denial sustained by Special Term. The denial was apparently on the basis that the additional parking was available on the 200-foot business zone despite the owner's reluctance to disturb the lawn and trees then present. Since then substantial changes have occurred. The 200-foot business zone has been completely blacktopped for parking; Northern Boulevard, a State highway, has been widened, eliminating on-street parking, previously permitted, as well as adding a median strip making it impossible for eastbound traffic to enter the parking lot from the front entrance. Substantial changes have also occurred in neighboring parcels in which parking has been extended into the residential area from the business zone.

In sum, North Shore has advanced sufficient proof of compliance with the ordinance justifying issuance of the special permit by the Board. The testimony of North Shore is virtually uncontroverted. As a result it would appear there is no room for the exercise of discretion on the part of the Board and no purpose would be served by remanding the matter for further hearings.

Accordingly the order of the Appellate Division should be modified to the extent of reversing the denial of the special exception permit and directing the Board to issue the permit subject to any reasonable conditions it deems appropriate and the remainder of the order insofar as it denied the application for a use variance should be affirmed.

FULD, C.J., and SCILEPPI, BERGAN, BREITEL, JASEN and GIBSON, JJ., concur.

Ordered accordingly.

NOTES

1. What difference in standards does *North Shore* suggest local boards of adjustment and zoning appeals should observe in acting on applications for variances and applications for special exceptions? Should courts apply a different standard in reviewing these two types of administrative decisions? Should there be any difference between the standard that administrative agencies apply in determining whether to grant a variance and the standard that courts apply in determining whether a zoning ordinance is unconstitutional as applied to a particular parcel? Compare Nectow v. City of Cambridge, page 1085, above.

In rejecting North Shore's application, the Village Board of Appeals relied in part on the ground that the applicant's hardship, if any, "was self-created" because North Shore had acquired its parcel knowing of the applicable zoning restriction. This disqualification finds some scattered support in judicial decisions. See, for example, Abel v. Zoning Board of Appeals, 172 Conn. 286, 374 A.2d 227 (1977). Does the "self-created hardship" disqualification make sense? Say that your client, *B*, wishes to buy Blackacre from *A* in order to develop a mobile home park. At the time *A* acquired the parcel, it was zoned to allow mobile home parks, but the parcel has since been rezoned to prohibit them. Under the self-created hardship rule, *B* would be barred from obtaining a variance, but *A* would not, and you would probably advise *B* to condition her purchase of Blackacre on *A*'s obtaining the necessary variance. (The value of the variance to *B* would doubtless be reflected in the purchase price.) Does this suggest that the only effect of the self-created hardship rule is to shift the risk of not obtaining a variance from the buyer, who acquires after the rezoning, to the seller who acquired before the rezoning?

Who—seller or buyer—has better access to the information needed to pursue the administrative action?

2. *Variance.* Variances, authorized by the 1926 Standard State Zoning Enabling Act, represent the earliest administrative device for flexing the rigid framework of Euclidean zoning. The Act gave boards of adjustment the power to "authorize, upon appeal in specific cases, such variance from the terms of the ordinance as will not be contrary to the public interest, where, owing to special conditions, a literal enforcement of the provisions of the ordinance will result in unnecessary hardship, and so that the spirit of the ordinance shall be observed and substantial justice done." U.S. Dept. of Commerce, Standard State Zoning Enabling Act § 7(3) (rev.ed.1926).

Will consonance with the "public interest" depend on the type of variance sought? How should "unnecessary hardship" be measured? The New York Court of Appeals addressed both questions in Consolidated Edison Co. of New York v. Hoffman, 43 N.Y.2d 598, 403 N.Y.S. 2d 193, 374 N.E.2d 105 (1978), holding that a local zoning board of appeals had abused its discretion in denying plaintiff's application for a variance to enable it to comply with federal agency requirements by building a cooling tower for its nuclear power generating plant. Noting that plaintiff utility was seeking relief not only from area restrictions—to accommodate the height of its proposed tower—but also from use restrictions—to accommodate the effluent discharge from the tower—the court drew a line between the standards applicable to the two types of variance: "To be granted an area variance, the applicant must satisfy the less demanding standard of showing that strict compliance with the zoning law will cause 'practical difficulties.' On the other hand, since a prohibited use, if permitted, will result in a use of the land in a manner inconsistent with the basic character of the zone, a heavier burden is placed on the applicant and the enabling act has been construed to require a showing of 'unnecessary hardship.' However, even in the case of an area variance, a significant factor is the magnitude of the variance sought, since the greater the deviation the more likely it is that the impact on the community will be severe." 43 N.Y.2d at 606, 403 N.Y.S.2d at 196, 374 N.E.2d 108.

In determining whether "unnecessary hardship" had been shown, the court started from the "traditional approach" which "has been to require the applicant to show that the land cannot yield a reasonable return if used only for a purpose allowed in the zone, that the circumstances which cause the hardship are unique to the land and not to general neighborhood conditions, and that the requested use will not alter the essential character of the locality." The court added, however, that in considering variance applications from public utilities, such essentially local concerns, "though important, are not the sole criteria, since utilities such as Con Edison, a gas, electric and steam corporation, are required to 'provide such service, instrumentalities and facilities as shall be safe and adequate and in all respects just and reasonable.' Indeed, consideration of the needs of a broader public are reasonably within the contemplation of the enabling legislation, which authorizes a zoning board to grant a variance 'so that the spirit of the local law or ordinance shall be observed, public safety and welfare secured and substantial justice done.' Thus, in resolving the question of hardship, the effect on the utility's customers is a significant factor to be considered by local zoning boards." 43 N.Y.2d at 607, 608, 403 N.Y.S.2d at 197, 374 N.E.2d 109.

3. *Special Exceptions (sometimes called Conditional Uses)*. Like variances, special exceptions seek to make zoning more flexible. Yet, as indicated in *North Shore*, the two devices rest on different premises. Variances aim to protect landowners from economic hardship. Special exceptions, by contrast, "are designed to meet the problem which arises where certain uses, although generally compatible with the basic use classification of a particular zone, should not be permitted to be located as a matter of right in every area included within the zone because of hazards inherent in the use itself or special problems which its proposed location may present. By this device, certain uses (e.g., gasoline service stations, electric substations, hospitals, schools, churches, country clubs, and the like) which may be considered essentially desirable to the community, but which should not be authorized generally in a particular zone because of considerations such as current and anticipated traffic congestion, population density, noise, effect on adjoining land values, or other considerations involving public health, safety, or general welfare, may be permitted upon a proposed site depending upon the facts and circumstances of the particular case." Zylka v. City of Crystal, 283 Minn. 192, 195, 167 N.W.2d 45, 48–49 (1969).

4. Professor Jan Krasnowiecki begins his provocative article, Abolish Zoning, 31 Syracuse L.Rev. 719, 720 (1980), with the truism that the "fundamental idea of zoning is that development is best controlled by a set of 'self-administering' rules laid down by the legislative body of a municipality long in advance of actual development." He then asserts, "I do not believe that zoning in practice bears any resemblance to this idea. I doubt that any significant development is occurring pursuant to preexisting zoning. I believe that all intensive development, certainly all residential development involving densities of more than four units to the acre, is occurring, if at all, only through a zoning change, variance, or some other form of administrative relaxation that is *applied for and granted on the threshold of development.*"

From this, Krasnowiecki concludes that "zoning cannot work, especially in a developing community. Failure to perceive this fact has led the courts on a wild goose chase in pursuit of an ideal that is not capable of attainment and that is, in any event, unsound. This failure has led commentators and statutory drafters on the same chase and has significantly delayed finding any realistic solution to the problem."

If Krasnowiecki's perception is correct, should zoning be abolished? If so, what kind of system should replace it? Unconstrained, *ad hoc* decisionmaking by local legislatures and administrative agencies? *Ad hoc* decisions constrained only by the goals set forth in the community's comprehensive plan? Since the battles in most of these cases involve developers pitted against their neighbors, would it be preferable to leave decisions to neighborhood referenda?

5. The main problem with the statutory standards governing variances and special exceptions, and with the judicial decisions that construe them, is not that they are too vague or too precise, nor that they are too heavily biased toward developers or toward neighbors, but is simply that they are probably irrelevant to the vast, unreviewed bulk of administrative decisions rendered by local boards. Political and economic pressures doubtless play a far larger role in these decisions than does the rule of law. For some empirical insights, see Dukeminier & Stapleton, The Zoning Board of Adjustment: A Case Study in Misrule, 50 Ky.L.J. 273 (1962); Comment, Zoning: Variance Administration in Alameda County, 50 Calif.L.Rev. 101 (1962).

c. LEGISLATIVE DECISIONS

i. Rezoning

CITY OF PHARR v. TIPPITT

Supreme Court of Texas, 1981.
616 S.W.2d 173.

POPE, Justice.

E.A. Tippitt and fourteen other landowners filed suit against the City of Pharr, Mayfair Minerals, Inc., and Urban Housing Associates seeking a judgment declaring a zoning ordinance invalid. The district court upheld the ordinance, but the court of civil appeals nullified it. We reverse the court of civil appeals judgment and affirm that of the trial court.

Mayfair Minerals, Inc. is the owner of 10.1 acres of land which the City of Pharr rezoned from R–1, single-family residence use to R–3, multi-family residence use. Urban Housing Associates, the developer, made the application for change of the single-family classification so that it could build fifty family units consisting of duplexes and quadruplexes. The Planning and Zoning Commission rejected its staff's recommendation that the zoning request be approved; but the

City Council, by a four to one vote, enacted an ordinance which rezoned the property. After the district court upheld the validity of the zoning ordinance, Tippitt was the only person who appealed from that judgment. Tippitt's single point of error, which point was sustained by the court of civil appeals, was that the City acted arbitrarily because the amendatory ordinance was spot zoning that was not warranted by any change in conditions in the area.

The land in question is a rectangular 10.1-acre tract. It is on the west side of a larger 60-acre tract. The 60-acre tract and additional large expanses of land to the south and southeast are vacant farmlands. The lands were zoned in 1974 for single-family residences. The tract in question is about two blocks east of Highway 281, a major highway that runs from north to south toward Mexico. The land along the highway is rapidly developing as a commercial strip by reason of a proposed new bridge that will cross the Rio Grande River into Mexico. Sam Houston Street is a major traffic artery that runs from west to east. The tract in question is south of and separated from Sam Houston Street by a 2.6-acre tract of land known as the Aycock tract. Moving clockwise from the north around the 10.1-acre tract, the Aycock tract is zoned for single-family residences. Farther north of there, on the north side of Sam Houston, there are many city blocks of land that were zoned for multiple-family residences. That area, however, was built as single-family residences. The land on the east, southeast, south, and southwest are undeveloped farmlands, all zoned for single-family residences. Bordering the 10.1-acre tract on the west is Richmond Heights Subdivision, which has been developed as single-family residences on the north end, but is not yet developed toward the south. Three hundred feet to the northeast of the tract, but south of Sam Houston, there is an area that is zoned for multiple housing. Two hundred feet to the west of the 10.1-acre tract is a small area that is zoned for industrial use.

Zoning is an exercise of a municipality's legislative powers. Thompson v. City of Palestine, 510 S.W.2d 579 (Tex.1974). The validity of an amendment to the City of Pharr's comprehensive zoning ordinance presents a question of law, not fact. In making its determination, courts are governed by the rule stated in Hunt v. City of San Antonio, 462 S.W.2d 536, 539 (Tex.1971): "If reasonable minds may differ as to whether or not a particular zoning ordinance has a substantial relationship to the public health, safety, morals or general welfare, no clear abuse of discretion is shown and the ordinance must stand as a valid exercise of the city's police power." We wrote in City of Fort Worth v. Johnson, 388 S.W.2d 400, 402 (Tex.1964), that "a zoning ordinance, duly adopted pursuant to Arts. 1011a–1011k, is presumed to be valid and the burden is on the one seeking to prevent its enforcement, whether generally or as to particular property, to prove that the ordinance is arbitrary or unreasonable in that it bears no substantial relationship to the health, safety, morals or general welfare of the community."

The burden on the party attacking the municipal legislative action is a heavy one. As expressed in Weaver v. Ham, 149 Tex. 309, 232 S.W.2d 704 (1950):

> The City had the power to enact the basic zoning ordinance, and to amend it, if a public necessity demanded it. While the presumption would be that the enactment of the amendatory ordinance was valid, that presumption disappears when the facts show and it was determined by the court that the City acted arbitrarily, unreasonably, and abused its discretion; that the ordinance is discriminatory and violates the rights of petitioners under the basic ordinance, and does not bear any substantial relation to the public health, safety, morals or general welfare; that it "constitutes unjustifiable spot zoning"; and that the ordinance is void.

These general rules for review of zoning ordinances have often been stated, but there has been little discussion of the actual legal criteria or standards against which legislative action should be tested. It has been suggested that such a statement would help to restrain arbitrary, capricious and unreasonable actions by city legislative bodies; improve the quality of the legislation; assist in eliminating *ad hoc* decisions, and focus the evidence from interested parties upon the real issues. We call attention to some of the important criteria:

First: A comprehensive zoning ordinance is law that binds the municipal legislative body itself. The legislative body does not, on each rezoning hearing, redetermine as an original matter, the city's policy of comprehensive zoning. The law demands that the approved zoning plan should be respected and not altered for the special benefit of the landowner when the change will cause substantial detriment to the surrounding lands or serve no substantial public purpose. The duty to obey the existing law forbids municipal actions that disregard not only the pre-established zoning ordinance, but also long-range master plans and maps that have been adopted by ordinance.

The adoption of a comprehensive zoning ordinance does not, however, exhaust the city's powers to amend the ordinance as long as the action is not arbitrary, capricious and unreasonable.

Second: The nature and degree of an adverse impact upon neighboring lands is important. Lots that are rezoned in a way that is substantially inconsistent with the zoning of the surrounding area, whether more or less restrictive, are likely to be invalid. For example, a rezoning from a residential use to an industrial use may have a highly deleterious effect upon the surrounding residential lands.

Third: The suitability or unsuitability of the tract for use as presently zoned is a factor. The size, shape and location of a lot may render a tract unusable or even confiscatory as zoned. An example of this is found in City of Waxahachie v. Watkins, 154 Tex. 206, 275 S.W.2d 477 (1955), in which we approved the rezoning of a residential lot for local retail use, because the lot was surrounded by a de facto business area. This factor, like the others, must often be weighed in relation to the other standards, and instances can exist in which the use for which land is zoned may be rezoned upon proof of a real public need or substantially changed conditions in the neighborhood.

Fourth: The amendatory ordinance must bear a substantial relationship to the public health, safety, morals or general welfare or protect and preserve historical and cultural places and areas. The rezoning ordinance may be justified, however, if a substantial public need exists, and this is so even if the private owner of the tract will also benefit.

Mr. Tippitt's attack upon the amendatory ordinance in this case is that it is spot zoning. The term, "spot zoning," is used in Texas and most states to connote an unacceptable amendatory ordinance that singles out a small tract for treatment that differs from that accorded similar surrounding land without proof of changes in conditions. Mr. Tippitt's present complaint of spot zoning invokes mainly inquiries about the second and third criteria stated above. Spot zoning is regarded as a preferential treatment which defeats a pre-established comprehensive plan. It is piecemeal zoning, the antithesis of planned zoning.

Spot zoning has uniformly been denied when there is a substantial adverse impact upon the surrounding land. The size of a rezoned tract in relation to the affected neighboring lands has been said by some authorities to be the most significant consideration in rezoning.

Amendatory ordinances which have rezoned a single city lot when there have been no intervening changes or other saving characteristic, have almost always been voided in Texas.

Proof that a small tract is unsuitable for use as zoned or that there have been substantial changes in the neighborhood have justified some amendatory ordinances. Here, too, the size, shape and characteristics of the tract have been determinative factors in upholding the amendments. On the other hand, an amendatory ordinance covering a 4.1-acre tract was invalidated in Thompson v. City of Palestine, *supra*. See 1 R. Anderson, *supra* § 5.07 at 253–54, for a study of size as a factor in spot zoning cases.

Amendatory zoning ordinances should be judicially tested against the same criteria that govern the action of the municipal legislative body. In this case, the 10.1-acre tract was not, as urged by the developer who made the application, an interim or automatic R–1 zoning following annexation. The tract had been previously comprehensively zoned, along with vast areas reaching south and southeast to the city limits after study, notice, and hearing. The zoning ordinance had classified lands of the city into districts known as residential, single-family (R–1); residential, two-family (R–2); residential, multi-family (R–3); residential, mobile home parks (R–MH); residential, mobile home subdivision (R–MHS); residential, townhouse subdivision (R–TH); general commercial (C), and industrial (M).

The impact of the amendatory R-3 zoning upon the neighborhood, according to some witnesses who lived west of the rezoned tract, would depress the values of their R-1 district. According to other testimony, the new development would enhance values of the entire southeast section of Pharr, and the existing homes in Richmond Heights would be protected by the city's requirement for a conditional permit which would compel the city's prior analysis of the design before development. The new development would require the backyards of the existing residences in Richmond Heights to back upon the backyards of the buildings in the rezoned tract. Most of the traffic from the rezoned tract would be directed to the east and north away from Richmond Heights. The new housing district would have its own internal streets and off-street parking.

The number of potential structures would not be substantially increased. Zoning for single-family dwellings would permit as many as forty-four family units, whereas the rezoning for multiple-housing (R-3) would permit fifty family units. There was evidence that the impact upon the surrounding area would be slight and even beneficial.

We do not regard the ordinance as spot zoning. The ten-acre tract is located in an undeveloped farming area. Large expanses of rural lands are located to the east, south and southeast, the direction in which the town must grow. To hold that the undeveloped land cannot be used for anything other than single-family residences (R-1) would mean, for all practical purposes, that there can be no more multiple housing in Pharr within its present city limits, since there is almost no presently undeveloped area which is available for R-3 housing. The size of this tract is large enough for planning as a self-contained orderly development which can in advance provide for the direction and the flow of traffic and assure a careful development of necessary public utilities. The development will not cause that measure of disharmony that occurs when there is a rezoning ordinance that permits a use that affects lands or tracts that are already developed. This is not an instance of an unplanned or piecemeal zoning of an isolated lot or small tract.

There is also evidence that rezoning would benefit and promote the general welfare of the community. The City of Pharr has a great need for multiple housing, the population has markedly increased since 1974, and there are only three small areas in Pharr that are presently zoned for multiple housing (R-3) which are not fully developed. The mayor testified that the need for multi-family housing will continue to grow. The City of Pharr, from the data included in the minutes of the zoning hearing, has 703 acres zoned for residential purposes of all kinds. Only 49 acres are actually used for multiple housing (R-3), and nine acres are actually used for duplexes (R-2). To relieve the City of Pharr's housing and utility needs, the City had agreed with the Housing and Urban Development Department to provide more space for multiple housing (R-3) construction. A block grant to the City of $3,000,000 had been made which included sums to provide needed extensions of sewer and water lines and the construction of a water reservoir. From the record it does not appear that the one complaining of the rezoning ordinance discharged his burden to prove that the City of Pharr acted arbitrarily, capriciously or unreasonably.

The judgment of the court of civil appeals is reversed and the judgment of the district court upholding the ordinance rezoning the tract in question is affirmed.

McGEE, J., notes his dissent.

NOTES

1. How much freedom should municipalities have in rezoning individual parcels? What interests, variously weighed in zoning decisions generally, should courts consider in determining whether to uphold piecemeal rezonings: The community's health, safety, welfare and morals? The interests of the individual landowner and his immediate neighbors? The interests of individuals living outside the community? Would the *Tippitt* court have reached the same result if it had been reviewing the grant of a variance instead of a rezoning?

Tippitt reflects what is probably the majority view on piecemeal rezonings. Maryland and a few other states apply a more rigorous standard, allowing municipalities to rezone individual parcels only if they can demonstrate that the rezoning is necessary to correct a mistake in the original zoning ordinance or to accommodate substantially changed neighborhood conditions. Md.Code 1957, Art. 66B, § 4.05(a).

Should the test for legitimacy differ depending on whether it is a developer or a neighbor who sought the piecemeal rezoning? In *Tippitt*, the rezoning had been sought by a developer and opposed by his neighbors. In other cases, the rezoning will have been sought by the neighbors and opposed by the developer; for example, apartment house owners in an R-3 district may have obtained a rezoning of the developer's parcel from R-3 to R-1 on the ground that more multiple family dwellings in the area would produce intolerable increases in traffic, noise and the demand for public services and facilities.

2. A few states take the position that piecemeal rezonings should not be treated as legislative acts at all, but rather as judicial decisions, and should therefore be encumbered by all the trappings of the judicial process. The position has dramatic procedural implications—shifting the burden of proof from landowner to legislature, widening and intensifying the standard of review on appeal, and requiring such due process guarantees as adequate notice to all concerned parties, a fair and public hearing, the right to cross-examination and written fact findings.

Fasano v. Board of County Commissioners, 264 Or. 574, 507 P.2d 23 (1973), is generally regarded as the leading case for this position. The court there struck down a zoning amendment that would have changed a parcel's permitted use from single-family residential to mobile home park, observing that it "would be ignoring reality to rigidly view all zoning decisions by local governing bodies as legislative acts to be accorded a full presumption of validity and shielded from less than constitutional scrutiny by the theory of separation of powers. Local and small decision groups are simply not the equivalent in all respects of state and national legislatures." Specifically, the court ruled that:

> Ordinances laying down general policies without regard to a specific piece of property are usually an exercise of legislative authority, are subject to limited review, and may only be attacked upon constitutional grounds for an arbitrary abuse of authority. On the other hand, a determination whether the permissible use of a specific piece of property should be changed is usually an exercise of judicial authority and its propriety is subject to an altogether different test . . . .
>
> Because the action of the commission in this instance is an exercise of judicial authority, the burden of proof should be placed, as is usual in judicial proceedings, upon the one seeking change. The more drastic the change, the greater will be the burden of showing that it is in conformance with the comprehensive plan as implemented by the ordinance, that there is a public need for the kind of change in question, and that the need is best met by the proposal under consideration. As the degree of change increases, the burden of showing that the potential impact upon the area in question was carefully considered and weighed will also increase. If other areas have previously been designated for the particular type of development, it must be shown why it is necessary to introduce it into an area not previously contemplated and why the property owners there should bear the burden of the departure.

264 Or. at 580–81, 586, 507 P.2d at 26, 29. The Oregon Supreme Court has since clarified the principles for determining when legislative decisions are to be treated as judicial decisions. See, for example, Neuberger v. City of Portland, 288 Or. 155, 603 P.2d 771 (1979), rehearing denied 288 Or. 585, 607 P.2d 722 (1980).

After *Fasano*, should legislative standards or judicial standards govern lawyers' activities before local legislatures on behalf of their land use clients? Lawyers will commonly approach individual legislators to press their client's position on a pending land use matter; yet to approach a judge *ex parte* on a pending matter would almost always be improper. Rezoning requests are often orchestrated with press releases and advertisements; rules of professional responsibility forbid lawyers to wage lawsuits through the media. See American

Bar Association, Model Code of Professional Responsibility, EC 7–33; 7–35 (1981).

A handful of states and the American Law Institute have adopted the *Fasano* approach. See American Law Institute, A Model Land Development Code § 2–312 (1976). A few states have expressly rejected the approach. See, for example, State by Rochester Association v. City of Rochester, 268 N.W.2d 885, 888 (Minn.1978) ("[O]ur narrow scope of review reflects a policy decision that a legislative body can best determine which zoning classifications best serve the public welfare").

For an insightful and provocative analysis of piecemeal land use decisions generally, see C. Rose, Planning and Dealing: Piecemeal Land Controls as a Problem of Local Legitimacy, 71 Calif. L.Rev. 837, 846 (1983) ("piecemeal local land decisions should not be classed as either 'legislative' or 'judicial'; these rubrics are drawn from a separation-of-powers doctrine more appropriate to larger governmental units. Piecemeal changes are quintessentially local matters, and any jurisprudential test of the reasonableness of piecemeal changes must identify and build upon the factors that lend legitimacy and institutional competence to local decisionmaking.")

3. *"Contract" and "Conditional" Zoning.* Municipalities will sometimes condition a parcel's rezoning on its owner's agreement to mitigate a development's adverse effects on neighboring parcels by such steps as building and maintaining an attractive buffer or providing a specified amount of off-street parking. These undertakings usually take the form of covenants executed and recorded by the developer either before or after the rezoning, depending on local practice.

In zoning's early years, these arrangements were generally condemned on the ground that the state cannot bargain away its police power. Although some states still take this view, most today would probably hold that, within prescribed limits, conditional zoning is not only tolerable but desirable. The New York Court of Appeals decision in Church v. Town of Islip, 8 N.Y.2d 254, 203 N.Y.S.2d 866, 168 N.E.2d 680 (1960), marked the beginning of this modern trend, upholding a rezoning from residential to business use that had been conditioned on the parcel owner's execution of covenants respecting maximum density and the installation of a fence and shrubbery buffer. Noting that since the Town Board could have rezoned the parcel for business use without any restrictions, the court failed "to see how reasonable conditions invalidate the legislation." Further, the court observed "[a]ll legislation 'by contract' is invalid in the sense that a Legislature cannot bargain away or sell its powers. But we deal here with actualities, not phrases. To meet increasing needs of Suffolk County's own population explosion, and at the same time to make as gradual and as little of an annoyance as possible the change from residence to business on the main highways, the Town Board imposes conditions." 8 N.Y.2d at 259, 203 N.Y.S.2d at 869, 168 N.E.2d at 683.

Even in states that allow "conditional" zoning, a failure to structure the arrangement properly may lead to its invalidation as "contract" zoning. Compare Baylis v. City of Baltimore, 219 Md. 164, 148 A.2d 429 (1959) (City Council had no power to enact ordinance making rezoning "conditional upon the execution of an agreement, set out in the ordinance, between the owners and the City") with Pressman v. City of Baltimore, 222 Md. 330, 343, 160 A.2d 379, 386 (1960) (rezoning valid; distinguishing *Baylis* on ground that, although conditions were proposed by planning commission, "the legislative body has not itself sought to impose conditions and has certainly not stated that its own action is dependent upon compliance with any condition"). See also, State *ex rel.* Zupancic v. Schimenz, 46 Wis.2d 22, 30, 174 N.W. 2d 533, 538 (1970) ("We hold that when a city itself makes an agreement with a landowner to rezone the contract is invalid; this is contract zoning. However, when the agreement is made by others than the city to conform the property in a way or manner which makes it acceptable for the requested rezoning and the city is not committed to rezone, it is not contract zoning in the true sense and does not vitiate the zoning if it is otherwise valid").

The distinction between valid "conditional" zoning and invalid "contract" zoning creates a dilemma both for developers and municipalities. Neither will be willing to act—by recording the covenant or rezoning the parcel—unless and until it is certain that the other will be equally forthcoming. Yet, the most effective vehicle for creating that certainty—conditions in a mutually binding executory contract—is unavailable because of the contract zoning bar. Can a city rezone the developer's parcel and then rescind the rezoning if the developer does not record its covenant? Can the developer record its covenant and later rescind it if the municipality fails to rezone? How would you try to structure the arrangement to satisfy the interests of both sides?

Who should hold the benefit of these covenants? If only neighboring landowners hold the benefit, they and the parcel's developer can later agree to terminate the covenant, possibly against the city's wishes. Yet, if the municipality holds the benefit, does it have an enforceable interest? Can a city seeking to enforce one of these covenants successfully rebut the argument that the benefit is unenforceable because it is held in gross? That the burden of the covenant does not run because it does not touch or concern the land? See pages 744 to 780, above.

4. A study of 360 rezoning applications in Atlanta, Georgia during the period 1970–1974 revealed that "[o]pposition to a rezoning application by a neighborhood group or individuals has a significant influence on the ultimate decision of the zoning authority. An examination of applications over a period of five years in Atlanta indi-

cates that an unopposed application had a 70 percent chance of a favorable outcome, whereas an opposed application had only a 43 percent chance of a favorable outcome." Ordway & Weaver, Preparing for a Zoning Ambush, 7 Real Estate Rev. 40, 41 (1977).

The authors also measured the relative success of arguments employed by applicants and their opponents:

SUCCESSFUL ARGUMENTS USED BY APPLICANTS IN OPPOSED REZONING CASES

	Arguments Used by Applicants	Times Used (Sample Size: 360 cases)	Success Ratio (%)
(1)	Use will create new jobs, stimulate the economy, and bring people back to the city.	11	73
(2)	Proposed use will not significantly affect traffic.	31	63
(3)	Proposed use will be a marketing success, or use is desired by prospective user.	35	54
(4)	Unnecessary hardship or mistake in original zoning.	21	52
(5)	Has contacted neighbors and has neighborhood support.	21	48
(6)	Project will be an asset to the community.	21	48

SUCCESSFUL ARGUMENTS USED BY OPPONENTS IN REZONING CASES

	Arguments Used by Opponents	Times Used (Sample Size: 360 cases)	Success Ratio (%)
(1)	Proposed rezoning is adverse to neighborhood restoration efforts.	18	100
(2)	Spot zoning.	24	96
(3)	Applicant wants to make a profit off the neighborhood.	14	86
(4)	Proposed use will cause a breakdown of the "community."	14	86
(5)	Use not consistent or compatible with existing uses.	19	84
(6)	No market support for proposed use.	12	83
(7)	Proposed use is not consistent with master plan.	50	78

Arguments Used by Opponents	Times Used (Sample Size: 360 cases)	Success Ratio (%)
(8) Residential character of the neighborhood must be preserved.	119	73
(9) Proposed use is detrimental to the area.	59	73
(10) Proposed use will lower property values.	38	71
(11) Proposed use will trigger an exodus out of neighborhood.	41	70

Id. at 42–43. Does the apparent political weight of these positions correspond to their legal merit?

ii. Floating Zones and PUDs

CHENEY v. VILLAGE 2 AT NEW HOPE, INC.

Supreme Court of Pennsylvania, 1968.
429 Pa. 626, 241 A.2d 81.

ROBERTS, Justice.

Under traditional concepts of zoning the task of determining the type, density and placement of buildings which should exist within any given zoning district devolves upon the local legislative body. In order that this body might have to speak only infrequently on the issue of municipal planning and zoning, the local legislature usually enacts detailed requirements for the type, size and location of buildings within each given zoning district, and leaves the ministerial task of enforcing these regulations to an appointed zoning administrator, with another administrative body, the zoning board of adjustment, passing on individual deviations from the strict district requirements, deviations known commonly as variances and special exceptions. At the same time, the overall rules governing the dimensions, placement, etc. of primarily public additions to ground, e.g., streets, sewers, playgrounds, are formulated by the local legislature through the passage of subdivision regulations. These regulations are enforced and applied to individual lots by an administrative body usually known as the planning commission.

This general approach to zoning fares reasonably well so long as development takes place on a lot-by-lot basis, and so long as no one cares that the overall appearance of the municipality resembles the design achieved by using a cookie cutter on a sheet of dough. However, with the increasing popularity of large scale residential developments, particularly in suburban areas, it has become apparent to many local municipalities that land can be more efficiently used, and developments more aesthetically pleasing, if zoning regulations focus on density requirements rather than on specific rules for each individual lot. Under density zoning, the legislature determines what percentage of a particular district must be devoted to open space, for example, and what percentage used for dwelling units. The task of filling in the particular district with real houses and real open spaces then falls upon the planning commission usually working in conjunction with an individual large scale developer.

The ultimate goal of this so-called density or cluster concept of zoning is achieved when an entire self-contained little community is permitted to be built within a zoning district, with the rules of density controlling not only the relation of private dwellings to open space, but also the relation of homes to commercial establishments such as theaters, hotels, restaurants, and quasi-commercial uses such as schools and churches. The present controversy before this Court involves a frontal attack upon one of these zoning districts, known in the trade as a Planned Unit Development (hereinafter PUD).

Spurred by the desire of appellant developer to construct a Planned Unit Development in the Borough of New Hope, in December of 1964 Borough Council began considering the passage of a new zoning ordinance to establish a PUD district in New Hope. After extensive consultation with appellant, council referred the matter to the New Hope Planning Commission for further study. This body, approximately six months after the project idea was first proposed, formally recommended to council that a PUD district be created. Council consulted with members of the Bucks County Planning Commission on the text of the proposed ordinance, held public hearings, and finally on June 14, 1965 enacted ordinance 160 which created the PUD district, and ordinance 161 which amended the Borough zoning map, rezoning a large tract of land known as the Rauch farm from low density residential to PUD. Pursuant to the procedural requirements of ordinance 160, appellant presented plans for a Planned Unit Development on the Rauch tract to the Borough Planning Commission. These plans were approved on November 8, 1965, and accordingly four days later two building permits, known as zoning permits 68 and 69, were issued to appellant. . . . Subsequently, permit number 75 was issued. Appellees, all neighboring property owners opposing the issuance of these permits, appealed to the zoning board of adjustment. The board, after taking extensive testimony, upheld ordinances 160 and 161 and accordingly affirmed the issuance of the permits. Appellees then appealed to the Bucks County Court of Common Pleas. That tribunal took no additional testimony, but reversed the board, holding the ordinances invalid for failure to conform to a comprehensive plan and for vesting too much discretion in the New Hope Planning Commission. This Court granted certiorari under Supreme Court Rule 68½.

The procedural posture of this case is identical to that of National Land & Investment Co. v. Easttown Twp. Bd. of Adjustment, 419 Pa.

504, 523, 215 A.2d 597, 607 (1965). Our scope of review may thus be stated by reference to that decision: "The zoning enabling act being silent as to a right of appeal, we consider this case on broad certiorari, reviewing the testimony, the evidence, and the entire record. Because the court below took no additional testimony, we will look at the decision of the board of adjustment to determine if, in upholding . . . [ordinances 160 and 161], the board committed an abuse of discretion or an error of law." Applying this standard, we hold that no error of law or abuse of discretion was committed by the New Hope Board of Adjustment, and that therefore the Court of Common Pleas of Bucks County must be reversed.

I.

Approximately one year before the PUD seed was planted in New Hope, Borough Council had approved the New Hope Comprehensive Plan. This detailed land use projection clearly envisioned the Rauch tract as containing only single family dwellings of low density. The court below therefore concluded that the enactment of ordinance 160, and more specifically the placing of a PUD district on the Rauch tract by ordinance 161 was not "in accordance with a comprehensive plan," as required by the Act of February 1, 1966, P.L. (1965) § 3203, 53 P.S. § 48203. See also Eves v. Zoning Bd. of Adjustment, 401 Pa. 211, 164 A.2d 7 (1960).

The fallacy in the court's reasoning lies in its mistaken belief that a comprehensive plan, once established, is forever binding on the municipality and can never be amended. Cases subsequent to *Eves* have made it clear, however, that these plans may be changed by the passage of new zoning ordinances, provided the local legislature passes the new ordinance with some demonstration of sensitivity to the community as a whole, and the impact that the new ordinance will have on this community. As Mr. Chief Justice Bell so artfully stated in Furniss v. Lower Merion Twp., 412 Pa. 404, 406, 194 A.2d 926, 927 (1963): "It is a matter of common sense and reality that a comprehensive plan is not like the law of the Medes and the Persians; it must be subject to reasonable change from time to time as conditions in an area or a township or a large neighborhood change." This salutary rule that comprehensive plans may be later amended by the passage of new zoning ordinances has been approved not only in *Furniss*, but also in Donahue v. Zoning Bd. of Adjustment, 412 Pa. 332, 194 A.2d 610 (1963) and Key Realty Co. Zoning Case, 408 Pa. 98, 182 A.2d 187 (1962).

Given this rule of law allowing postplan zoning changes, and the presumption in favor of an ordinance's validity, we are not in a position, having reviewed the record in the present case, to say that the zoning board committed an abuse of discretion or an error of law when it concluded that ordinances 160 and 161 were properly passed. Presented as it was with evidence that the PUD district had been under consideration by council for over six months and had been specifically recommended by the borough planning commission, a body specially equipped to view proposed ordinances as they relate to the rest of the community, we hold that the board, within its sound discretion, could have concluded that council passed the ordinances with the proper overall considerations in mind. The PUD district established by ordinance 160 is not the type of use which by its very nature could have no place in the middle of a predominantly residential borough. It is not a steel mill, a fat rendering plant, or a desiccated egg factory. It is, in fact, nothing more than a miniature residential community.

Closely tied to the comprehensive plan issue is the argument raised by appellees that ordinances 160 and 161 constitute spot zoning outlawed by *Eves*, supra. Given the fact situation in *Eves*, however, as well as the post-*Eves* cases, we do not believe that there is any spot zoning here. In *Eves*, the municipality created a limited industrial district, F-1, which, by explicit legislative pronouncement, was not to be applied to any particular tract until the individual land owner requested that his own tract be so re-zoned. The obvious evil in this procedure did *not* lie in the fact that a limited industrial district might be placed in an area previously zoned, for example, residential. The evil was the *pre-ordained* uncertainty as to where the F-1 districts would crop up. The ordinance all but invited spot zoning where the legislature could respond to private entreaties from land owners and re-zone tracts F-1 without regard to the surrounding community. In *Eves*, it was almost impossible for the F-1 districts to conform to a comprehensive plan since tracts would be re-zoned on a strictly ad hoc basis.

Quite to the contrary, no such "floating zone" exists in the present case. On the very day that the PUD district was created by ordinance 160, it was brought to earth by ordinance 161; and, as discussed supra, this *was* done "in accordance with a comprehensive plan." Speaking of a similar procedure in Donahue v. Zoning Bd. of Adjustment, 412 Pa. 332, 194 A.2d 610 (1963), this Court faced squarely an attack based upon *Eves* and responded thusly:

"It was this case by case review [in *Eves*] which demonstrated the absence of a comprehensive plan and which sought to enable the Board of Supervisors [the local legislative body] to exercise powers they did not statutorily possess.

In the instant case, the new classification was established and the zoning map amended within a very short period of time [in the case at bar, on the same day]. Under the rules of statutory construction which are likewise applicable to ordinances, these ordinances should be read together as one enactment. So construed, Ordinances 151 [creating new zone] and 155 [amending zoning map] do not create the 'floating zone', anchored only upon case by case application by landowners, which we struck down in *Eves*.

While it is true that the change here was made upon request of a particular landowner, this does not necessarily create the evils held invalid in *Eves* where the defects were specifically created by the very terms of the ordinances. It is not unusual for a zoning change to be made on request of a landowner, and such change is not invalid if made in accordance with a comprehensive plan." 412 Pa. at 334–335, 194 A.2d at 611.

We think *Donahue* is completely controlling on the issue of alleged spot zoning and compels the conclusion that ordinances 160 and 161 do not fall on that ground.

II.

The court below next concluded that even if the two ordinances were properly *passed*, they must fall as vesting authority in the planning commission greater than that permitted under Pennsylvania's zoning enabling legislation. More specifically, it is now contended by appellees that complete project approval by the planning commission under ordinance 160 requires that commission to encroach upon legislative territory whenever it decides where, within a particular PUD district, specific types of building should be placed.

In order to appreciate fully the arguments of counsel on both sides it is necessary to explain in some detail exactly what is permitted within a PUD district, and who decides whether a particular land owner has complied with these requirements. Admittedly the range of permissible uses within the PUD district is greater than that normally found in a traditional zoning district. Within a New Hope PUD district there may be: single family attached or detached dwellings; apartments; accessory private garages; public or private parks and recreation areas including golf courses, swimming pools, ski slopes, etc. (so long as these facilities do not produce noise, glare, odor, air pollution, etc., detrimental to existing or prospective adjacent structures); a municipal building; a school; churches; art galleries; professional offices; certain types of signs; a theatre (but not a drive-in); motels and hotels; and a restaurant. The ordinance then sets certain overall density requirements. The PUD district may have a maximum of 80% of the land devoted to residential uses, a maximum of 20% for the permitted commercial uses and enclosed recreational facilities, and must have a minimum of 20% for open spaces. The residential density shall not exceed 10 units per acre, nor shall any such unit contain more than two bedrooms. All structures within the district must not exceed maximum height standards set out in the ordinance. Finally, although there are no traditional "set back" and "side yard" requirements, ordinance 160 does require that there be 24 feet between structures, and that no townhouse structure contain more than 12 dwelling units.

The procedure to be followed by the aspiring developer reduces itself to presenting a detailed plan for his planned unit development to the planning commission, obtaining that body's approval and then securing building permits. Of course, the planning commission may not approve any development that fails to meet the requirements set forth in the ordinance as outlined above. . . .

. . . [Q]uite logically, the job of approving a particular PUD should rest with a single municipal body. The question then is simply which one: Borough Council (a legislative body), the Planning Commission (an administrative body), or the Zoning Board of Adjustment (an administrative body)?

There is no doubt that it would be statutorily permissible for council itself to pass a PUD ordinance and simultaneous zoning map amendment so specific that no details would be left for any administrator. The ordinance could specify where each building should be placed, how large it should be, where the open spaces are located, etc. But what would be the practical effect of such an ordinance? One of the most attractive features of Planned Unit Development is its flexibility; the chance for the builder and the municipality to sit down together and tailor a development to meet the specific needs of the community and the requirements of the land on which it is to be built. But all this would be lost if the Legislature let the planning cement set before any developer could happen upon the scene to scratch his own initials in that cement. Professor Krasnowiecki has accurately summed up the effect on planned unit development of such legislative planning. The picture, to be sure, is not a happy one:

> "The traditional refuge of the courts, the requirement that all the standards be set forth in advance of application for development, does not offer a practical solution to the problem. The complexity of pre-established regulations that would automatically dispose of any proposal for planned unit development, when different housing types and perhaps accessory commercial areas are envisaged, would be quite considerable. Indeed as soon as various housing types are permitted, the regulations that would govern their design and distribution on every possible kind of site, their relationship to each other and their relationship to surrounding properties must be complex unless the developer's choice in terms of site, site plan, and design and distribution of housing is reduced close to zero. It is not likely . . . that local authorities would want to adopt such a set of regulations." Krasnowiecki, Planned Unit Development: A Challenge to Established Theory and Practice of Land Use Control, 114 U.Pa.L.Rev. 47, 71 (1965).

Left with Professor Krasnowiecki's "Hobson's choice" of no developer leeway at all, or a staggering set of legislative regulations sufficient to cover every idea the developer might have, it is not likely that Planned Unit Development could thrive, or even maintain life, if the local legislature assumed totally the role of planner.

The remaining two municipal bodies which could oversee the shaping of specific Planned Unit Developments are both administrative agencies, the Zoning Board of Adjustment and the Planning Commission. As this Court views both reality and zoning enabling act, the Zoning Board of Adjustment is not the proper body. The Act of February 1, 1966, P.L. (1965) § 3207, 53 P.S. § 48207(g) specifically sets forth the powers of a borough zoning board of adjustment. These powers are three in number, and only three. The board may (1) hear and decide appeals where there is an alleged error made by an administrator in the enforcement of the enabling act or any ordinance enacted pursuant thereto; (2) hear and decide special exceptions; and (3) authorize the grant of variances from the terms of existing ordinances. These powers in no way encompass the authority to review and approve the plan for an entire development when such plan is neither at variance with the existing ordinance nor is a special exception to it; nor does (1) above supply the necessary power since the board would not be reviewing an alleged administrative error.

Moreover, from a practical standpoint, a zoning board of adjustment is, of the three bodies here under discussion, the one least equipped to handle the problem of PUD approval. Zoning boards are accustomed to focusing on one lot at a time. They traditionally examine hardship cases and unique uses proposed by landowners. As Professor Krasnowiecki has noted: "To suggest that the board is intended, or competent, to handle large scale planning and design decisions is, I think, far fetched." Technical Bulletin 52, Urban Land Institute, p. 38 (1965). We agree.

Thus, the borough planning commission remains the only other body both qualified and statutorily permitted to approve PUD. Of course, we realize that a planning commission is not authorized to engage in actual re-zoning of land. But merely because the commission here has the power to approve more than one type of building for a particular lot within the PUD district does not mean that the commission is usurping the zoning function. Indeed, it is acting in strict *accordance* with the applicable zoning ordinance, for that ordinance, No. 160, *permits* more than one type of building for a particular lot. To be sure, if the commission approved a plan for a PUD district where 30% of the land were being used commercially, *then* we would have an example of illegal re-zoning by an administrator. But no one argues in the present case that appellant's plan does not conform to the requirements of ordinance 160.

Nor is this Court sympathetic to appellees' argument that ordinance 160 permits the planning commission to grant variances and special exceptions. We fail to see how a development such as appellant's that meets every single requirement of the applicable zoning ordinance can be said to be the product of a variance or a special exception. The very essence of variances and special exceptions lies in their *departure* from ordinance requirements, not in their compliance with them. We therefore conclude that the New Hope Planning Commission has the power to approve development plans submitted to it under ordinance 160. . . .

The appeals from the orders of the Court of Common Pleas of Bucks County in appeals No. 110 and No. 111 are quashed. The orders of the court in appeals No. 112 and No. 113 are vacated and the records remanded for further proceedings consistent with this opinion. The order of the court in appeal No. 114 is reversed.

BELL, C. J., took no part in the consideration or decision of this case.

NOTE

Large-scale developers will often prefer the freedom offered by "density" or "cluster" zoning to the uniformity imposed by traditional Euclidean zoning. By clustering homes in one or more areas, rather than spreading them over a grid, developers can economize on street, sidewalk and public utility installations. They can also reduce grading and other site preparation costs by leaving many of the parcel's natural features, such as hills and trees, untouched. Many homebuyers, too, prefer cluster developments, and are happy to trade the privacy of a small backyard for the pleasures of far larger, shared recreation areas such as parks, playgrounds, pools and tennis courts.

Although courts today generally accept the concept of cluster zoning, questions continue to surround the concept's implementation. Conflict often arises when the developer submits its final development plans for government approval. The developer will want the plans to consist only of rough guidelines, enabling it to alter the development to meet problems that arise in the course of construction. The city will want the final plans to indicate not only the height, bulk and location of improvements and common areas, but also their design.

What recourse do neighbors have when a development, as built, violates the terms of the final approved plan? In Frankland v. City of Lake Oswego, 267 Or. 452, 517 P.2d 1042 (1973), the court found that defendant developer's project did not conform to its final plan, and ruled that plaintiff neighbors would be entitled to recover damages for the diminution in value of their parcels resulting from "the difference between the apartment constructed and the apartment represented in the sketches which have been approved by the City." 267 Or. at 480, 517 P.2d at 1055. The court remanded to allow the parties to introduce evidence on the issue whether injunctive or monetary relief was more appropriate in the circumstances.

Does the evolution from Euclidean zoning to cluster zoning suggest that the next evolutional step will be for government to keep its hands entirely off large-scale cluster developments, trusting developers to follow plans that will keep homebuyers happiest? Or is the pendulum likely to swing in the opposite direction? Does the answer depend on whether developers are able to demonstrate either that owners of neighboring parcels will suffer no damage from their developments, or that those who will be damaged have been bought off? On whether developers can also demonstrate that their projects will provide a "fair share" of housing for low and middle income people in the region?

Krasnowiecki, Planned Unit Development: A Challenge to Established Theory and Practice of Land Use Control, 114 U.Pa.L.Rev. 47 (1965), was particularly influential in swaying the judiciary toward validating the PUD concept. See also, Mandelker, Reflections on the American System of Planning Controls: A Response to Professor Krasnowiecki, 114 U.Pa.L.Rev. 98 (1965).

d. COMMUNITY DECISIONS

EASTLAKE v. FOREST CITY ENTERPRISES, INC.

Supreme Court of the United States, 1976.
426 U.S. 668, 96 S.Ct. 2358, 49 L.Ed.2d 132.

Mr. Chief Justice BURGER delivered the opinion of the Court.

The question in this case is whether a city charter provision requiring proposed land use changes to be ratified by 55% of the votes cast violates the due process rights of a landowner who applies for a zoning change.

The city of Eastlake, Ohio, a suburb of Cleveland, has a comprehensive zoning plan codified in a municipal ordinance. Respondent, a real estate developer, acquired an eight-acre parcel of real estate in Eastlake zoned for "light industrial" uses at the time of purchase.

In May 1971, respondent applied to the City Planning Commission for a zoning change to permit construction of a multi-family high-rise apartment building. The Planning Commission recommended the proposed change to the City Council, which under Eastlake's procedures could either accept or reject the Planning Commission's recommendation. Meanwhile, by popular vote, the voters of Eastlake amended the city charter to require that any changes in land use agreed to by the Council be approved by a 55% vote in a referendum. The City Council approved the Planning Commission's recommendation for reclassification of respondent's property to permit the proposed project. Respondent then applied to the Planning Commission for "parking and yard" approval for the proposed building. The Commission rejected the application, on the ground that the City Council's rezoning action had not yet been submitted to the voters for ratification.

Respondent then filed an action in state court, seeking a judgment declaring the charter provision invalid as an unconstitutional delegation of legislative power to the people. While the case was pending, the City Council's action was submitted to a referendum, but the proposed zoning change was not approved by the requisite 55% margin. Following the election, the Court of Common Pleas and the Ohio Court of Appeals sustained the charter provision.

The Ohio Supreme Court reversed. Concluding that enactment of zoning and rezoning provisions is a legislative function, the court held that a popular referendum requirement, lacking standards to guide the decision of the voters, permitted the police power to be exercised in a standardless, hence arbitrary and capricious manner. Relying on this Court's decisions in Washington ex rel. Seattle Title Trust Co. v. Roberge, 278 U.S. 116, 49 S.Ct. 50, 73 L.Ed. 210 (1928), Thomas Cusack Co. v. Chicago, 242 U.S. 526, 37 S.Ct. 190, 61 L.Ed. 472 (1917), and Eubank v. Richmond, 226 U.S. 137, 33 S.Ct. 76, 57 L.Ed. 156 (1912), but distinguishing James v. Valtierra, 402 U.S. 137, 91 S.Ct. 1331, 28 L.Ed.2d 678 (1971), the court concluded that the referendum provision constituted an unlawful delegation of legislative power.

We reverse.

I

The conclusion that Eastlake's procedure violates federal constitutional guarantees rests upon the proposition that a zoning referendum involves a delegation of legislative power. A referendum cannot, however, be characterized as a delegation of power. Under our constitutional assumptions, all power derives from the people, who can delegate it to representative instruments which they create. In establishing legislative bodies, the people can reserve to themselves power to deal directly with matters which might otherwise be assigned to the legislature.

The reservation of such power is the basis for the town meeting, a tradition which continues to this day in some States as both a practical and symbolic part of our democratic processes. The referendum, similarly, is a means for direct political participation, allowing the people the final decision, amounting to a veto power, over enactments of representative bodies. The practice is designed to "give citizens a voice on questions of public policy." James v. Valtierra, *supra*, 402 U.S., at 141, 91 S.Ct., at 1333.

In framing a state constitution, the people of Ohio specifically reserved the power of referendum to the people of each municipality within the State.

> "The initiative and referendum powers are hereby reserved to the people of each municipality on all questions which such municipalities may now or hereafter be authorized by law to control by legislative action . . . ." Ohio Const., Art. II, § 1f.

To be subject to Ohio's referendum procedure, the question must be one within the scope of legislative power. The Ohio Supreme Court expressly found that the City Council's action in rezoning respondent's eight acres from light industrial to high-density residential use was legislative in nature. Distinguishing between administrative and legislative acts, the court separated the power to zone or rezone, by passage or amendment of a zoning ordinance, from the power to grant relief from unnecessary hardship. The former function was found to be legislative in nature.

II

The Ohio Supreme Court further concluded that the amendment to the city charter constituted a "delegation" of power violative of federal constitutional guarantees because the voters were given no standards to guide their decision. Under Eastlake's procedure, the Ohio Supreme Court reasoned, no mechanism existed, nor indeed could exist, to assure that the voters would act rationally in passing upon a proposed zoning change. This meant that "appropriate legislative action [would] be made dependent upon the potentially arbitrary and unreasonable whims of the voting public." 41 Ohio St.2d, at 195, 324 N.E.2d, at 746. The potential for arbitrariness in the process, the court concluded, violated due process.

Courts have frequently held in other contexts that a congressional delegation of power to a regulatory entity must be accompanied by discernible standards, so that the delegatee's action can be measured for its fidelity to the legislative will. Assuming, *arguendo*, their relevance to state governmental functions, these cases involved a delegation of power by the legislature to regulatory bodies, which are not directly responsible to the people; this doctrine is inapplicable where, as here, rather than dealing with a delegation of power, we deal with a power reserved by the people to themselves.

In basing its claim on federal due process requirements, respondent also invokes Euclid v. Ambler Realty Co., 272 U.S. 365 (1926), but it does not rely on the direct teaching of that case. Under *Euclid*, a property owner can challenge a zoning restriction if the measure is "clearly arbitrary and unreasonable, having no substantial relation to the public health, safety, morals, or general welfare." *Id.*, at 395, 47 S.Ct., at 121. If the substantive result of the referendum is arbitrary and capricious, bearing no relation to the police power, then the fact that the voters of Eastlake wish it so would not save the restriction. As this Court held in invalidating a charter amendment enacted by referendum:

> "The sovereignty of the people is itself subject to those constitutional limitations which have been duly adopted and remain unrepealed." Hunter v. Erickson, 393 U.S., at 392, 89 S.Ct., at 561.

But no challenge of the sort contemplated in Euclid v. Ambler Realty is before us. The Ohio Supreme Court did not hold, and respondent does not argue, that the present zoning classification under Eastlake's comprehensive ordinance violates the principles established in Euclid v. Ambler Realty. If respondent considers the referendum result itself to be unreasonable, the zoning restriction is open to challenge in state court, where the scope of the state remedy available to respondent would be determined as a matter of state law, as well as under Fourteenth Amendment standards. That being so, nothing more is required by the Constitution.

Nothing in our cases is inconsistent with this conclusion. Two decisions of this Court were relied on by the Ohio Supreme Court in invalidating Eastlake's procedure. The thread common to both decisions is the delegation of legislative power, originally given by the people to a legislative body, and in turn delegated by the legislature to a *narrow segment* of the community, not to the people at large. In Eubank v. Richmond, 226 U.S. 137 (1912), the Court invalidated a city ordinance which conferred the power to establish building setback lines upon the owners of two-thirds of the property abutting any street. Similarly, in Washington ex rel. Seattle Title Trust Co. v. Roberge, 278 U.S. 116 (1928), the Court struck down an ordinance which permitted the establishment of philanthropic homes for the aged in residential areas, but only upon the written consent of the owners of two-thirds of the property within 400 feet of the proposed facility.

Neither *Eubank* nor *Roberge* involved a referendum procedure such as we have in this case; the standardless delegation of power to a limited group of property owners condemned by the Court in *Eubank* and *Roberge* is not to be equated with decision-making by the people through the referendum process. The Court of Appeals for the Ninth Circuit put it this way:

> "A referendum, however, is far more than an expression of ambiguously founded neighborhood preference. It is the city itself legislating through its voters—an exercise by the voters of their traditional right through direct legislation to override the views of their elected representatives as to what serves the public interest." Southern Alameda Spanish Speaking Organization v. Union City, California, 424 F.2d 291, 294 (1970).

Our decision in James v. Valtierra, upholding California's mandatory referendum requirement, confirms this view. Mr. Justice Black, speaking for the Court in that case, said:

> "This procedure ensures that *all the people* of a community will have a voice in a decision which may lead to large expenditures of local governmental funds for increased public services . . . ." 402 U.S., at 143, 91 S.Ct., at 1334 (emphasis added).

Mr. Justice Black went on to say that a referendum procedure, such as the one at issue here, is a classic demonstration of "devotion to democracy . . . ." *Id.*, at 141. As a basic instrument of democratic government, the referendum process does not, in itself, violate the Due Process Clause of the Fourteenth Amendment when applied to a rezoning ordinance. Since the rezoning decision in this case was properly reserved to the People of Eastlake under the Ohio Constitution, the Ohio Supreme Court erred in holding invalid, on federal constitutional grounds, the charter amendment permitting the voters to decide whether the zoned use of respondent's property could be altered.

The judgment of the Ohio Supreme Court is reversed, and the case is remanded for further proceedings not inconsistent with this opinion.

Reversed and remanded.

Mr. Justice POWELL, dissenting.

There can be no doubt as to the propriety and legality of submitting generally applicable legislative questions, including zoning provisions, to a popular referendum. But here the only issue concerned the status of a single small parcel owned by a single "person." This procedure, affording no realistic opportunity for the affected person to be heard, even by the electorate, is fundamentally unfair. The "spot" referendum technique appears to open disquieting opportunities for local government bodies to bypass normal protective procedures for resolving issues affecting individual rights.

Mr. Justice STEVENS, with whom Mr. Justice BRENNAN joins, dissenting.

The city's reliance on the town meeting process of decisionmaking tends to obfuscate the two critical issues in this case. These issues are (1) whether the procedure which a city employs in deciding to grant or to deny a property owner's request for a change in the zoning of his property must comply with the Due Process Clause of the Fourteenth Amendment; and (2) if so, whether the procedure employed by the city of Eastlake is fundamentally fair?

I

We might rule in favor of the city on the theory that the referendum requirement did not deprive respondent of any interest in property and therefore the Due Process Clause is wholly inapplicable. After all, when respondent bought this parcel, it was zoned for light industrial use and it still retains that classification. The Court does not adopt any such rationale; nor, indeed, does the city even advance that argument. On the contrary, throughout this litigation everyone has assumed, without discussing the problem, that the Due Process Clause does apply. Both reason and authority support that assumption.

Subject to limitations imposed by the common law of nuisance and zoning restrictions, the owner of real property has the right to develop his land to his own economic advantage. As land continues to become more scarce, and as land use planning constantly becomes more sophisticated, the needs and the opportunities for unforeseen uses of specific parcels of real estate continually increase. For that reason, no matter how comprehensive a zoning plan may be, it regularly contains some mechanism for granting variances, amendments, or exemptions for specific uses of specific pieces of property. No responsibly prepared plan could wholly deny the need for presently unforeseeable future change.

A zoning code is unlike other legislation affecting the use of property. The deprivation caused by a zoning code is customarily qualified by recognizing the property owner's right to apply for an amendment or variance to accommodate his individual needs. The expectancy that particular changes consistent with the basic zoning plan will be allowed frequently and on their merits is a normal incident of property ownership, when the governing body offers the owner the opportunity to seek such a change—whether that opportunity is denominated a privilege or a right—it is affording protection to the owner's interest in making legitimate use of his property.

The fact that an individual owner (like any other petitioner or plaintiff) may not have a legal right to the relief he seeks does not mean that he has no right to fair procedure in the consideration of the merits of his application. The fact that codes regularly provide a procedure for granting individual exceptions or changes, the fact that such changes are granted in individual cases with great frequency, and the fact that the particular code in the record before us contemplates that changes consistent with the basic plan will be allowed, all support my opinion that the opportunity to apply for an amendment is an aspect of property ownership protected by the Due Process Clause of the Fourteenth Amendment.

This conclusion is supported by the few cases in this Court which have decided zoning questions, and by many well-reasoned state-court decisions. In both Eubank v. City of Richmond, 226 U.S. 137, 33 S.Ct. 76, 57 L.Ed. 156 and Washington ex rel. Seattle Title Trust Co. v. Roberge, 278 U.S. 116, 49 S.Ct. 50, 73 L.Ed. 210 the Court invalidated ordinances for procedural reasons. In *Eubank* the Court held that the method of imposing a building-line restriction on a property owner was defective. In *Roberge*, which is more analogous to this case, the Court invalidated the requirement that the owners of two-thirds of the property within 400 feet must give their approval to the plaintiff's proposed use of his property. Implicitly, both cases hold that the process of making decisions affecting the use of particular pieces of property must meet constitutional standards.

Although this Court has decided only a handful of zoning cases, literally thousands of zoning disputes have been resolved by state courts. Those courts have repeatedly identified the obvious difference between the adoption of a comprehensive citywide plan by legislative action and the decision of particular issues involving specific uses of specific parcels. In the former situation there is generally great deference to the judgment of the legislature; in the latter situation state courts have not hesitated to correct manifest injustice. . . .

II

When we examine a state procedure for the purpose of deciding whether it comports with the constitutional standard of due process, the fact that a State may give it a "legislative" label should not save an otherwise invalid procedure. We should, however, give some deference to the conclusion of the highest court of the State that the procedure represents an arbitrary and unreasonable way of handling a local problem. . . .

The essence of fair procedure is that the interested parties be given a reasonable opportunity to have their dispute resolved on the merits by reference to articulable rules. If a dispute involves only the conflicting rights of private litigants, it is elementary that the decision-maker must be impartial and qualified to understand and to apply the controlling rules.

I have no doubt about the validity of the initiative or the referendum as an appropriate method of deciding questions of community policy. I think it is equally clear that the popular vote is not an acceptable method of adjudicating the rights of individual litigants. The problem presented by this case is unique, because it may involve a three-sided controversy, in which there is at least potential conflict between the rights of the property owner and the rights of his neighbors, and also potential conflict with the public interest in preserving the city's basic zoning plan. If the latter aspect of the controversy were predominant, the referendum would be an acceptable procedure. On the other hand, when the record indicates without contradiction that there is no threat to the general public interest in preserving the city's plan—as it does in this case, since respondent's proposal was approved by both the Planning Commission and the City Council and there has been no allegation that the use of this eight-acre parcel for apartments rather than light industry would adversely affect the community or raise any policy issue of citywide concern—I think the case should be treated as one in which it is essential that the private property owner be given a fair opportunity to have his claim determined on its merits.

As Justice Stern points out in his concurring opinion, it would be absurd to use a referendum to decide whether a gasoline station could be operated on a particular corner in the city of Cleveland. The case before us is not that clear because we are told that there are only 20,000 people in the city of Eastlake. Conceivably, an eight-acre development could be sufficiently dramatic to arouse the legitimate interest of the entire community; it is also conceivable that most of the voters would be indifferent and uninformed about the wisdom of building apartments rather than a warehouse or factory on these eight acres. The record is silent on which of these alternatives is the more probable. Since the ordinance places a manifestly unreasonable obstacle in the path of every property owner seeking any zoning change, since it provides no standards or procedures for exempting particular parcels or claims from the referendum requirement, and since the record contains no justification for the use of the procedure in this case, I am persuaded that we should respect the state judiciary's appraisal of the fundamental fairness of this decisionmaking process in this case.

I therefore conclude that the Ohio Supreme Court correctly held that Art. VIII, § 3, of the Eastlake charter violates the Due Process Clause of the Fourteenth Amendment, and that its judgment should be affirmed.

STATE THEATRE CO. v. SMITH, 276 N.W.2d 259, 263–264, (S.D. 1979), HENDERSON, J.: SDCL 11–4–5 is not a typical "protest" statute. Normally enabling acts provide for the filing of protest petitions by a specified number of property owners within a prescribed distance of the land affected by the amendment under consideration. If sufficient protests are filed, a larger affirmative vote of the municipal legislative body than normally needed to enact an ordinance is required to adopt the protested amendment and render the protest ineffective. These provisions have been held constitutional when challenged as an unlawful delegation of legislative power.

SDCL 11–4–5 does allow protest by neighboring property owners but does not include a provision for subsequent municipal legislative action. The statute is, therefore, analogous to what are referred to as "consent" statutes. These statutes require that the consent of a certain number of affected neighbors be obtained before a zoning ordinance is amended. The legislative body has no power to overrule; the neighbors are given the ultimate power to block the amendment.

The validity of consents has long been debated; the absence of standards relating to the giving of consents has been a major ground for the invalidity of consent statutes. There appear to be two categories of consent statutes: those requiring consent to establish a restriction and those requiring consent to waive a restriction. The former are invalid and the latter valid.

The distinction between the two types of statutes is best illustrated by State v. City of Minneapolis, 255 Minn. 249, 97 N.W.2d 273 (1959) and O'Brien v. City of Saint Paul, 285 Minn. 378, 173 N.W.2d 462 (1969).

In State v. City of Minneapolis, supra, the relators' property was zoned commercial. The relators wanted to build an office building on their commercial property. Two-thirds of the relators' neighbors subsequently filed, under authority of a Minneapolis ordinance, consents to rezone relators' property to residential. The consent clause of the ordinance was struck down as an unlawful delegation of power to impose restrictions on real property.

The O'Brien v. City of Saint Paul, supra, case involved an application to change zoning from a Residential Class A to a Residential Class C. Class C permitted apartment buildings; Class A permitted single-family dwellings. A Minnesota statute required the consent of neighboring landowners before the amendment of zoning ordinances. The court held that this statute did not constitute an unconstitutional delegation of legislative authority to private persons. The adjoining property owners were not vested with the power to impose restrictions as was the case in State v. City of Minneapolis, supra. Instead, they had the right to waive restrictions which were already established by the city.

QUESTIONS

Is *Eastlake* a good decision? Are the procedural safeguards that surround legislative acts necessary when the electorate votes directly? Can a court overturn a land use referendum or initiative on the ground that it is not "in accordance with a comprehensive plan"? Would, and should, the United States Supreme Court have reached the same result if the Ohio Supreme Court had characterized the City Council's action in rezoning respondent's parcel as "quasi-judicial" rather than "legislative"? Compare Leonard v. City of Bothell, 87 Wn.2d 847, 854, 557 P.2d 1306 (1976) (rezoning of 141-acre lot was "quasi-judicial" action and, since referendum elections are limited to legislative acts by governmental body, was not subject to a referendum; "amendments to the zoning code or rezone decisions require an informed and intelligent choice by individuals who possess the expertise to consider the total economic, social, and physical characteristics of the community").

What limits, if any, are there to Justice Stevens' position that a developer's opportunity to apply for rezoning "is an aspect of property ownership protected by the Due Process Clause of the Fourteenth Amendment"? Note that the position turns the traditional argument, that land use regulations "take" private property, on its ear, for it makes the regulatory system, rather than common law rules, the source of property rights. Consider whether the majority completely answered Justice Stevens by saying that his argument "fails to take into account the mechanisms for relief potentially available to property owners whose desired land use changes are rejected by the voters. First, if hardship is occasioned by zoning restrictions, *administrative* relief is potentially available. Indeed, the very purpose of 'variances' allowed by zoning officials is to avoid 'practical difficulties and unnecessary hardship.'" 426 U.S. 668, 679 n.13, 96 S.Ct. 2358, 2365 n.13.

Would, and should, *Eastlake* have been decided differently if the zoning amendment had been initiated by neighbors and had tightened, rather than loosened, the restrictions on respondent's parcel? Do you agree with State Theatre Company v. Smith, that a distinction should be drawn between statutes requiring consent to establish a restriction and statutes requiring consent to waive a restriction? How, if at all, should consent mechanisms be structured to account for the varying intensities of preference held by neighbors close to and far from the affected parcel?

See generally, Glenn, State Law Limitations on the Use of Initiatives and Referenda in Connection with Zoning Amendments, 51 S.Cal.L.Rev. 265 (1978).

3. THE ZONING SYSTEM AT WORK: THE 2030 VALLEJO CASE

a. Factual and Legal Background

On April 2, 1963, Perry Liebman acquired a 106-foot by 137.5-foot lot at 2030 Vallejo Street, San Francisco, California. The parcel is situated in the city's Pacific Heights section, a north-facing slope about one mile long that leads down to San Francisco Bay and offers stunning views of the Bay, the Golden Gate Bridge and the hills of Marin County beyond. Pacific Heights was then, as it is now, primarily residential, developed with medium density housing—some detached, one- or two-family homes, row houses, and a few high rise apartments built in the 1920's. Several landmark quality mansions dot the area. The parcel that Liebman acquired is on the north, Bay side of Vallejo Street, ninety-nine feet west of Vallejo's intersection with Laguna, about halfway—four blocks—down the slope leading to the Bay. Most of the lots in the immediate vicinity of 2030 Vallejo were, at the time of Liebman's purchase, developed with detached residential structures two or three stories high.

Under the zoning ordinance in force at the time Liebman acquired 2030 Vallejo, the parcel was in an R–4 district, permitting multi-story, multi-family dwellings and noncommercial private clubs and lodges as well as all principal uses permitted in the more restrictive R–1–D through R–3 districts. [City Planning Code, Part II, San Francisco Municipal Code § 205.1 (May 2, 1960).] The district was surrounded by R–4 or higher residential use districts and by two C–2 districts (community retail business and service; dwelling).

San Francisco Zoning Map
May 2, 1960
(as amended through July 10, 1964)

Sheet 2

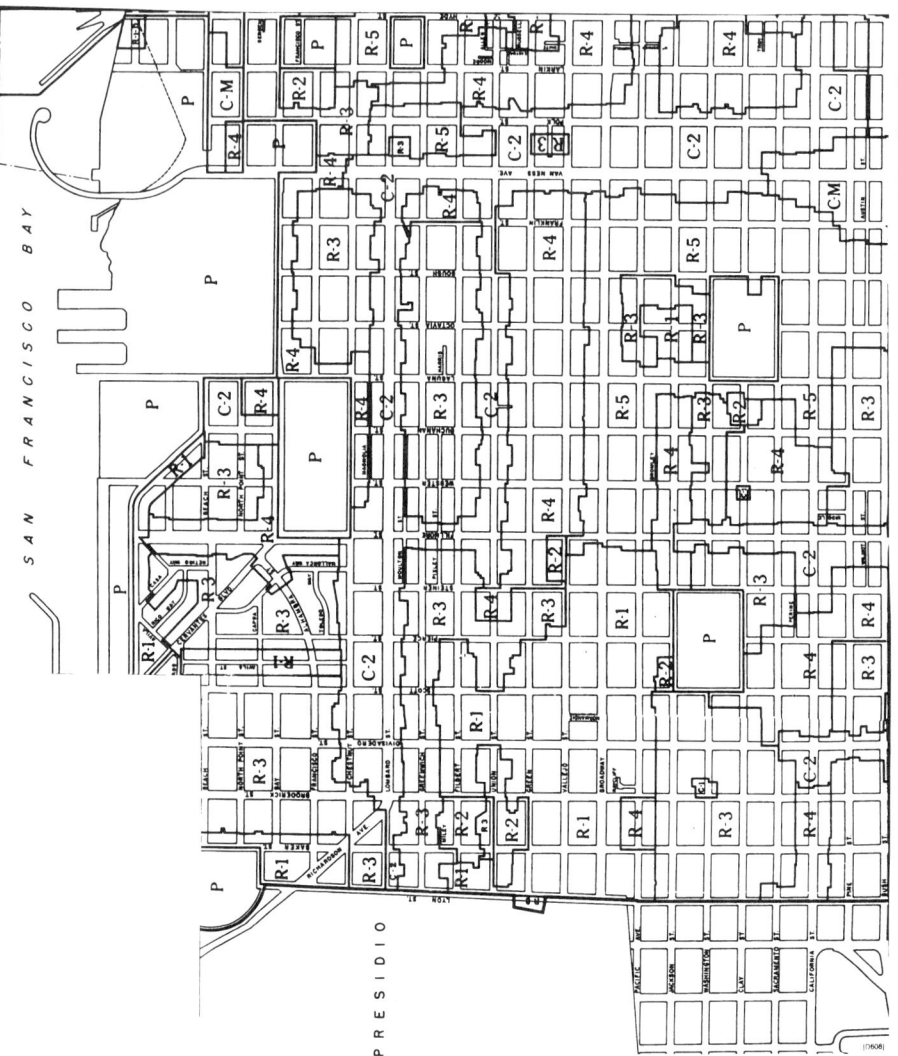

Courtesy of San Francisco Department of City Planning

Liebman's purpose in buying 2030 Vallejo was to build a multiple unit high-rise apartment building. According to plans prepared by Liebman's architects, Schram and White, early in 1964, the building would be eleven stories high, consist of 53 units, and would be set back approximately 15 feet in the front yard, 25 feet in the rear yard and 11 feet on each side. Five-foot balconies would ring each of the top ten floors, and 62 underground parking spaces would be provided for residents and their guests. As proposed, the building complied with almost all of the requirements prescribed for an R–4 district. Thus, the height permitted in the district was 105 feet; Liebman's building was to be exactly 105 feet high. Maximum permitted lot coverage was 75%; the lot coverage proposed was 54%. Side yards were not required; Liebman's plans called for two side yards, each 11 feet wide. The maximum number of dwelling units permitted was 74 (calculated as 1 per 200 square feet of lot area), but only 53 were proposed (1 per 275 square feet of lot area). Although 62 parking spaces were proposed, only 53 were required.

The one major requirement that Liebman's plans did not meet—and that became the focus of all the administrative and judicial proceedings that ensued—was the maximum permitted floor area ratio (FAR), the primary bulk control in an R–4 district. The maximum permitted FAR was 4.8:1 (4.8 square feet of floor space to every 1 square foot of lot space). Applying this ratio to the 14,575 square foot 2030 Vallejo parcel meant that the maximum allowable floor space was 69,960 square feet. Liebman's proposal called for 80,293 square feet of floor space—an excess of 10,333 square feet, or roughly 15%. Effectively, Liebman's proposed FAR was 5.51:1—a ratio that would have been well within the 10:1 FAR permitted in the R–5 districts just to the south of 2030 Vallejo. Liebman's proposed FAR would also have been permitted in an R–4 district if 2030 Vallejo had been a corner lot, for which the Code provided an allowance of an extra 25% in computing the size of the lot.

FAR PROVISIONS OF CITY PLANNING CODE

Section 120.1 Height and Bulk, Measurement

. . .

(c) The term "floor area ratio" as used herein shall mean the ratio of the aggregate gross floor area of a building, exclusive of parking or loading spaces, cellars and basement areas used only for storage or for services incidental to the operation or maintenance of the building, to the area of the lot upon which the building is located. For the purpose of this calculation the area of a corner lot may first be increased by one-fourth ($\frac{1}{4}$), and the area of an interior lot where the rear lot line abuts upon an alley or street may first be increased by adding ten (10) feet to the depth.

Section 120.2 Height and Bulk, Exceptions

. . . The height and bulk limitations of this Code relating to use districts shall not apply to the following features of a building:

(a) A chimney, church spire, flag pole, scenery loft, transmission tower, fire tower or hose tower;

(b) A cupola, water tank or other mechanical appurtenance, or a stairway bulkhead; if not used for dwelling purposes or for any commercial purpose not necessary to a permitted use of the building;

(c) Any structure necessary to a permitted manufacturing or industrial process if not used to provide additional floor space. . . .

Section 122 Floor Area Ratio

No building in any R-3, R-3.5, R-4, R-5, C or M district shall exceed the floor area ratio specified in the following table for the district in which the building is located.

TABLE 1

Maximum Permitted Floor Area Ratio

District	Floor Area Ratio
R-3, R-3.5 (except dwellings)	1.8 to 1
R-4 (all buildings)	4.8 to 1
R-5 (all buildings)	10.0 to 1
C-1, C-2 (all buildings)	3.6 to 1
C-3 (all buildings)	16.0 to 1
C-M (all buildings)	9.0 to 1
M-1, M-2 (all buildings)	5.0 to 1

Provided that in a C-2 district, on a lot which is nearer to an R-5 district than to any other R district, the Floor Area Ratio shall be 10 to 1. The distance to the nearest R district shall be measured from the mid-point of the front lot line, or from a point directly across the street therefrom, whichever gives the greater ratio.

Recognizing a need to clarify the Code's use of the term "floor area," the Department of City Planning issued an interpretive zoning bulletin on June 6, 1963.

ZONING BULLETIN 63.2

DEFINITION OF "FLOOR AREA" FOR COMPUTING FLOOR AREA RATIO

. . .

III. *Definition*: In order to provide for reasonable and accurate application of floor area ratio standards within the meaning and intent of the Planning Code, "floor area" is hereby defined as follows:

Floor area is the sum of the gross areas of the several floors of a building or buildings, measured from the exterior faces of exterior walls or from the center lines of party walls separating two buildings. Where columns are outside and separated from an exterior wall (curtain wall) which encloses the building space or are otherwise so arranged that the curtain wall is clearly separate from the structural members, the exterior face of the curtain wall shall be the line of measurement, and the area of the columns themselves at each floor shall also be counted.

A. In particular, "floor area" *includes:*

(1) basement and cellar space including tenants' storage areas and all other space except that used only for storage or services incidental to the operation or maintenance of the building.

(2) elevator shafts, stairwells, exit enclosures and smokeproof enclosures, at each floor.

(3) floor space in penthouses except as specifically excluded in this definition.

(4) attic space (whether or not a floor has been laid) capable of being made into habitable space.

(5) floor space in balconies or mezzanines in the interior of the building.

(6) floor space in open or roofed porches, arcades or exterior balconies if such porch, arcade or balcony is located above the ground floor or first floor of occupancy above basement or garage and is used as the primary access to the interior space it serves.

(7) floor space in accessory buildings, except for floor space used for accessory off-street parking or loading.

(8) any other floor space not specifically excluded.

B. "Floor area" *shall not include:*

(1) elevator or stair bulkheads, accessory water tanks, or cooling towers, other mechanical appurtenances and areas, or other features listed in Section 120.2 of the Planning Code and located at the top of the building.

(2) outside stairs to the first floor of occupancy at the face of the building which the stairs serve, or fire escapes.

(3) floor space used for accessory off-street parking.

(4) floor space used for accessory off-street loading.

(5) arcades, plazas, porches, breezeways, porticos, etc. (whether roofed or not), if at or near street level, accessible to the public and not substantially enclosed by exterior walls.

(6) balconies, porches, roof decks, terraces or courts except those used for primary access as defined in Item A (6), provided that:

(a) If more than 70% of the perimeter of such an area is enclosed, either by building walls (exclusive of a railing or parapet not more than 3 feet 8 inches high) or by such walls and interior lot lines, and the clear space is less than 15 feet in either dimension, the area shall not be excluded from "floor area" unless it is fully open to the sky (except for roof eaves, cornices or belt courses which project not more than two feet from the face of the building wall).

(b) If more than 70% of the perimeter of such an area is enclosed, either by building walls (exclusive of a railing or parapet not more than 3 feet 8 inches high), or by such walls and interior lot lines, and the clear space is 15 feet or more in both dimensions, (1) the area shall be excluded from "floor area" if it is fully open to the sky (except for roof eaves, cornices or belt courses which project no more than two feet from the face of the building wall), and (2) the area may have roofed areas along its perimeter which are also excluded from "floor area" if the minimum clear open space between any such roof and the opposite wall or roof (whichever is closer) is maintained at 15 feet (with the above exceptions) and the roofed area does not exceed 10 feet in depth; (3) in addition, when the clear open area exceeds 625 square feet, a canopy, gazebo, or similar roofed structure without walls may cover up to 10% of such open space without being counted as "floor area".

(c) If, however, 70% or less of the perimeter of such an area is enclosed, by building walls (exclusive of a railing or parapet not more than 3 feet 8 inches high) or by such walls and interior lot lines, and the open side or sides face on a yard, street or court whose dimensions satisfy the requirements of this Code and all other applicable codes for instances in which required windows face upon such yard, street or court, the area may be roofed to the extent permitted by such codes in instances in which required windows are involved.

IV. *Guiding Principles in the Application of Floor Area Ratio Provisions:* The Department of City Planning will be guided by the following principles in applying the City Planning Code provisions pertaining to the floor area ratio:

(1) Consistency of interpretation.

(2) Ease of comprehension and administration.

(3) Minimum bias in favor of one or another system of construction.

(4) Effect of interpretation on the purpose and intent of the City Planning Code.

While the Department endeavors to review preliminary plans that are submitted for advice on conformity to the Planning Code, the comments of the Department based on preliminary plans cannot guarantee an approval of final plans, especially as experience indicates that working drawings often involve an increase in floor area over that shown in the preliminary plans.

QUESTIONS

What legitimate land use and planning objectives are served by density restrictions like FAR? It is commonly thought that density restrictions assure the availability of needed light and air, space for community facilities, and individual feelings of openness and privacy. Density restrictions may also, through their implicit population limits, effectively control traffic and parking and aid in determining the appropriate size of public facilities like schools. There are density control alternatives to FAR. Population can be more directly controlled by restricting the number of persons who can live in a dwelling unit, or by limiting the number of families permitted to live in a building. Bulk limitations—coverage, height and cubage—will more directly affect amenities such as light and air. See generally, 1 N. Williams, American Planning Law, Chap. 34 (1974).

What legal and political steps would you have counseled the neighbors to take in objecting to Liebman's proposal? Would your suggestions and strategy depend on your client's specific objective—unobstructed light and air (neighbors immediately adjacent to the parcel); unobstructed view (neighbors behind the parcel); or aesthetics (neighbors within eye range of the parcel)? Which, if any, of these concerns are directly related to the purposes of FAR? Which might better have been pressed at the legislative stage, when the zoning ordinance was being enacted and height limitations and design review were being decided on? Since Liebman's proposal called for fewer than the permitted number of dwelling units and more than the required number of parking spaces, could the neighbors have effectively rested any of their arguments on density concerns respecting excessive population?

Representing Liebman, what steps would you have recommended to minimize the expense and risks that so frequently attend attempts to obtain a variance or other relief from code requirements? Would it have been wise to challenge Zoning Bulletin 63.2 on the ground that it interpreted Code § 120 too restrictively? To try to persuade the Zoning Administrator to change his interpretation? (Apparently, during July and the first part of August, 1964, Liebman persuaded the Zoning Division to change its interpretation of the Code to exclude side balconies from the computation of FAR. The change is reflected in the updated August 14, Zoning Bulletin 63.2, above.) Would Liebman have been wise to reduce his proposed floor area so that, at least, it would have been less than 10% in excess of the permitted FAR? Section 302(b) of the City Planning Code provided that in the case of variances of less than 10% "the determination of the Zoning Administrator may be made without holding a public hearing. In other cases, a public hearing shall be held." Anticipating objections from neighbors, what forces might Liebman have tried to marshall to his side? The local Chamber of Commerce? Real Estate Board? Building Trades Council? Pro-housing groups? What steps might Liebman have taken to reduce the neighbors' concerns?

Representing the neighbors or Liebman, how would you have shaped your overall strategy to accommodate, and benefit from, the following realities of land use decisionmaking in San Francisco, *circa* 1964:

Zoning Administrator. Clyde Fisher, the City's Zoning Administrator responsible for the initial decision on variance requests, was an experienced member of the Planning Department's professional staff who could be expected to rest his decisions primarily on planning principles and theory. In a rare testimonial, Norman Williams, himself an outstanding land use scholar, has called Fisher "one of the country's outstanding planning lawyers." 1 N. Williams, American Planning Law 692 n.17 (1974).

Board of Permit Appeals. The City's Board of Permit Appeals, responsible for reviewing the Zoning Administrator's decisions, could be expected to weigh political and economic considerations more heavily than would the Zoning Administrator. Appointed by the Mayor, and serving at his pleasure, the Board at this time consisted of two savings and loan executives, an insurance broker, a lawyer, and one other individual. Members were paid $15.00 for each meeting they attended. According to one massive study, in "California prior to 1967, as most everywhere in the country, boards of adjustment and appeal gave out zoning variances on a wholesale basis despite their illegality. The variance was *the* flexibility device." DiMento, *et al.*, Land Development and Environmental Control in the California Supreme Court: The Deferential, The Preservationist, and the Preservationist-Erratic Eras, 27 U.C.L.A. L.Rev. 859, 954 (1980).

Judiciary. The state courts were responsible for reviewing administrative actions taken by the Board of Permit Appeals. In exercising their power of judicial review, California courts during this period paid great deference to the administrative decision. Thus, the perceived illegality of Board variance practice "was possible because of lax judicial review. Courts refused to review the boards' reasons for granting a variance. Evidence to support issuance was presumed to be present, a doctrine accepted by the California Supreme Court . . . as late as 1962. As of 1965, no appellate court in California had ever reversed the issuance of a variance." DiMento, *et al., id.*

b. THE ADMINISTRATIVE PROCESS

On June 30, 1964 Liebman filed a building permit application with the San Francisco Department of Public Works. This, the first formal step in the land use approval process, had been preceded by several informal contacts and discussions between Liebman's representatives and Planning Department officials. Liebman's application was disapproved on July 20, 1964.

DISAPPROVAL OF BUILDING PERMIT APPLICATION

July 20, 1964

Mr. Perry Liebman
3106 Fillmore Street
San Francisco, Calif. 94123

Re: Building Permit Application No. 301813
Location: Vallejo St., N/L, 98' W of Laguna St.
Assessor's Block 555 Lots 10 & 13
In an R–4 (High Density Multiple Residential) zoning district

Dear Mr. Liebman:

This is to notify you that the above application for a permit has been disapproved by the Zoning Administrator on this date because this application is for an eleven story, fifty-three unit apartment building with an aggregate gross floor area of 89,080 sq. ft. on a lot where a maximum gross floor area of 69,960 sq. ft. can be permitted and with a rear yard of 22 ft. where a 25 ft. rear is required.

Section 120 of the City Planning Code defines "floor area ratio" as the ratio of the aggregate gross floor area of a building, exclusive of parking or loading spaces, cellars and basement areas used only for storage or for services incidental to the operation or maintenance of the building, to the area of the lot upon which the building is located. Section 124 of this code specifies a maximum permitted floor area ratio of 4.8 to 1 for this interior, 14,575 sq. ft. R–4 parcel. The proposed 89,080 sq. ft. building would have a floor area ratio of 6.1 to 1 rather than the maximum 4.8 to 1 permitted.

Section 134 of the City Planning Code requires a 25 ft. rear yard for buildings with four or more stories of residential occupancy. Section 126 of that Code permits balconies to extend three feet into a required rear yard as proposed on this building except that, "In the case of required yards, the aggregate length of all bay windows, balconies, fire escapes and chimneys that project into the required open area shall be no more than 2/3 the buildable width along a rear building wall." The proposed building has a balcony at each floor extending 3 ft. into the required 25 ft. rear yard for the full 84 ft. width of the building: this is 13 ft. 8 in. wider than the maximum width of 70 ft. 8 in. permitted as 2/3 of the width, in this case of 106 ft.

Because, as you know, from your many conferences with members of the Zoning Division Staff, this proposed building does not comply with the City Planning Code as to floor area and rear yard requirements outlined above, this application must be disapproved.

Please consult Mr. Johnson of the Zoning Division of the Department of City Planning (KL 8–3056) within 10 days of the date of this letter regarding any further explanation of this disapproval.

Very truly yours,

Clyde O. Fisher, Jr.
Zoning Administrator

Liebman appealed the Zoning Administrator's disapproval to the Board of Permit Appeals. On August 3, 1964, the Board refused to hear the appeal unless it came as an appeal from a variance decision. On August 6, 1964, Liebman filed an application for a FAR variance as authorized by section 302 of the City Planning Code.

SECTIONS 302, 303 OF SAN FRANCISCO PLANNING CODE

SEC. 302. **Variances.** The Zoning Administrator shall receive, investigate, hear and determine all applications for variances from the strict application of the provisions of this Code. He shall have the power to grant only such variances as may be in harmony with the general purpose and intent of this Code and in accordance with the general and specific rules contained herein, subject to such conditions and safeguards as he may impose. He shall have the authority to grant such variances only when the strict and literal interpretation and enforcement of the provisions of this Code would result in practical difficulties, unnecessary hardships or results inconsistent with the general purposes of this Code, and only to the extent necessary to overcome such practical difficulties and unnecessary hardships. The procedure shall be as follows:

(a) **Applications.** An application for such variance shall be filed with the Zoning Administrator by the owner, or an authorized agent of the owner of the property involved. Applications shall be upon forms prescribed therefor, and shall contain or be accompanied by all information required to assure the presentation of pertinent facts for the permanent record. Each such application shall include a verification by the owner or his authorized agent attesting to the truth and correctness of all facts, statements and information presented.

(b) **Hearings.** Upon the filing of a verified application, the Zoning Administrator shall set a reasonable time not to exceed thirty (30) days thereafter for considering the same and shall give notice thereof to the applicant and may give notice to any other interested person. If the variance requested is solely for a modification of any regulation of this Code which is expressed by a number or in terms of a ratio, fraction or percentage, and involves a deviation from the expressed requirement of less than ten (10) per cent of such number, ratio, fraction or percentage, the determination of the Zoning Administrator may be made without holding a public hearing. In all other cases, a public hearing shall be held.

(c) **Notice of Public Hearings.** The Zoning Administrator shall give notice of the time and place of every public hearing on a variance application and the purpose thereof by mailing a notice not less than ten (10) days prior to the date of such hearing to the owners of all property adjoining the property involved, and to the owners of all property abutting on the same street, or streets, and within three hundred (300) feet of the property involved, using for this purpose the names of the last known owners as shown on the records of the Assessor. The failure to send notice by mail to any property owner, where the address of such owner is not a matter of public record, shall not invalidate any proceedings in connection with any variance. The Zoning Administrator shall make a record of the pertinent evidence presented at such public hearings which shall be maintained as a part of the public records of the Department of City Planning.

(d) **Determination.** The Zoning Administrator shall grant the requested variance in whole or in part if, from the facts presented in connection with the application, or at the public hearing, or determined by investigation, it appears and the Zoning Administrator specifies in his findings the facts which establish: (1) that there are exceptional or extraordinary circumstances or conditions applying to the property involved, or to the intended use of the property, that do not apply generally to other property or uses in the same class of district; (2) that owing to such exceptional or extraordinary circumstances the literal enforcement of specified provisions of the Code would result in practical difficulty or unnecessary hardship; (3) that the variance is necessary for the preservation of a substantial property right of the petitioner possessed by other property in the same class of district; (4) that the granting of the variance will not be materially detrimental to the public welfare or materially injurious to the property or improvements in the vicinity; and (5) that the granting of such variance will be in harmony with the general purpose and intent of this Code and will not adversely affect the Master Plan.

(e) **Procedure.** The Zoning Administrator shall act upon every such application for variance within a reasonable time. Unless deferred at the request of the applicant, his decision shall be rendered within sixty (60) days from the date of conclusion of the hearing or, where no public hearing is involved, within a minimum period of sixty (60) days from the date of filing. Failure of the Zoning Administrator to act as herein provided shall entitle the applicant to cause the record to be placed before the Planning Commission for determination at its next following regular meeting. Upon making his decision, the Zoning Administrator shall forthwith transmit a copy thereof to the applicant and to the Director of Planning. No variance granted shall become effective until ten (10) days thereafter. If no appeal is filed, such granted variance shall thereafter govern the approval of any application for a permit or license affected thereby.

(f) **Conditions.** In granting any variance under the provisions of this section the Zoning Administrator shall specify the character and extent thereof, and shall also specify such reasonable conditions in connection therewith as are necessary to secure the objectives of this Code. Once any portion of the variance privilege is utilized all such specifications pertaining thereto shall become immediately operative, and must be complied with. Violation of any such condition shall constitute a violation of this Code.

SEC. 303. **Appeals.**

(a) **Right of Appeal.** The determination of the Zoning Administrator shall be final in all matters in his jurisdiction except that appeals therefrom may be taken by any person aggrieved or by any officer, board or commission of the City to the board, committee or agency empowered by the Charter of the City to receive and act upon such appeals. Filing notice of appeal as hereafter provided shall stay all proceedings in furtherance of the action appealed from.

(b) **Notice of Appeal.** Notice of appeal from any determination of the Zoning Administrator shall be filed with said board, committee or agency within ten (10) days from the date of such determination, in such form as may be required. An appeal from any order, requirement, decision, determination, or interpretation by the Zoning Administrator in the administration or enforcement of the provisions of this Code, shall set forth specifically wherein it is alleged that there was error in interpretation of the provisions thereof, or abuse of discretion on the part of the Zoning Administrator. Appeal from any ruling, decision, or determination by the Zoning Administrator denying or granting any variance shall set forth the particulars wherein the application for variance is alleged to have met or to have failed to meet, as the case may be, the five (5) conditions set forth in Section 302(d).

(c) **Procedure.** The procedure and requirements for the transmittal of the record, notice of hearing, and hearing in connection with any appeal shall be as specified in Chapter 19 of the Administrative Code.

(d) **Decision.** Upon the hearing of any such appeal, said board, committee or agency may approve, disapprove, or modify the ruling, decision or determination appealed from or, in lieu thereof, make such other additional determination as it shall deem proper in the premises, subject to the same limitations as are placed upon the Zoning Administrator by this Code or by the City Charter. If the decision of the said board, committee or agency differs from that of the Zoning Administrator, it shall, in its decision, specify wherein there was error in the interpretation of the provisions of this Code, or abuse of discretion on the part of the Administrator, and shall specify in its findings the facts relied upon in making such determination. In granting any variance, it shall specify the character and extent thereof and also such reasonable conditions in connection therewith as are necessary to secure the objectives of this Code. Thereafter, such decision shall govern the approval of any application for a permit or license affected thereby.

Because Liebman's new application expressly eliminated the excessive rear balcony extension, FAR became the only point of noncompliance. A public hearing on Liebman's variance application was held on September 2, 1964. Thirty-two opponents of record appeared, and sixteen letters of opposition were received by the Zoning Administrator. One of the more forceful and explicit letters came from a neighbor at 2068–70 Vallejo.

LETTER OPPOSING GRANT OF VARIANCE

Dear Mr. Fisher:

> Re: Application for Zoning Deviation
> Applicable to Property on Vallejo Street N/L, 99 ft. W. of Laguna Street — Assessors Block 555, Lots Numbers 10 and 13 — Notice VZ–64–61 —
> Dated 8/20/64

This will acknowledge your notice of a hearing on this matter which was held on September 2, 1964.

I was unable to attend because I was out of the city when this hearing was scheduled. Some of my neighbors were out of the city also, and I am advised by other property owners in this block they did not get any notice of this hearing. This hearing was set at a time when many of us were out of the city at the close of a summer vacation, which made it impossible to attend the hearing and register opposition.

Therefore, first I ask you to set this matter for a further hearing when summer vacations are over so I and other property owners can attend and present our views on this matter. This would be the equitable thing to do unless, of course, you reject this application and not allow any deviation from the present R–4 zoning applicable to this property.

I have spoken with a number of property owners in this block and have not found one of them who favors the deviations applied for by this property owner. I join with them and urge you to give proper consideration to all of us who are living in this block and neighborhood—and ask that you reject this application and not grant any deviation on the present zoning of the property.

All of us look forward to orderly and proper development of any property in the area. As a matter of fact, we welcome it. However, to grant this application for deviation requested would be entirely contrary to orderly and proper development. I cite below some of the reasons I am opposed to the granting of any deviation to present zoning.

1. The owner of this property knew the zoning of it when he bought it, and purchased it with full knowledge of the R-4 zoning restrictions and limitations. Therefore this is in no way a case of hardship brought about by something of which he was not fully aware, because it was a matter of public record.

Moreover, he can improve this property under present R-4 zoning limits and restrictions, and have a fine property that will be in keeping with the area and the general conditions of other properties existing in this block!

2. It is my understanding he has pleaded at the hearing on September 2, that test borings revealed subsoil conditions which will make the cost of his foundation work more expensive. It is well known in this neighborhood that soil conditions are such that foundation work is more expensive than in some other areas. If this owner had made inquiry on the subject from some of us who live within a few feet of his property, he could have known something about this, or public records could have been consulted to shed some light on this point.

3. This owner is requesting deviations apparently from R-4 which would indeed be the equivalent of changing the whole neighborhood and in particular do damage to owners who have invested heavily in this block and who *make their homes here.*

Owners, like myself who bought or built property in good faith, relying on R-4 zoning, would suffer great injustice and possible financial loss, if any deviations are granted this owner. We are entitled to have the zoning left as it is at present.

4. I have consulted with an architect who worked, like many others, long and dedicated hours in the present zoning of *our city.* He advises me that much study and consideration was given to all zoning, and after having viewed the property in question—it is his opinion it should remain R-4 as it is now zoned.

To grant any deviations on this property would be a sad commentary indeed on the talents, qualifications, and hard work of our many fine citizens who, in their wisdom, placed R-4 on this property.

For this reason alone, there is good reason to deny this application.

5. This block and neighborhood is already highly congested with the parking of automobiles in the neighborhood, both day and night—to the extent that extraordinary hazards exist in traffic safety and in fire fighting. There is a girls' school in the block next to this property, to the west.

This applicant proposes to put in one and a small fraction of garage space to each living unit he wants to build.

What is to provide parking space for relatives and visitors who come to visit with occupants of these living units? The streets of San Francisco in this area are already much overcrowded.

As an example, driveways of present owners must frequently be cleared by the police. Towing away parked vehicles blocked driveways, before owners and residents can get in or out of their garage.

Approximately a month ago, I wanted to get out of my garage at 8:00 a.m. It was completely blocked, and became necessary to call the S.F. Police who had to have the vehicle towed away, which took approximately $1\frac{1}{4}$ hours. The policeman who came to handle this situation showed me that he had cleared 6 driveways that morning at the request of owners in the area, since 6:00 a.m.

Why make such conditions worse by granting zoning deviations which could only create more congestion and make for less safe traffic conditions—and also result in more expensive use of our police department which could well devote itself to more serious matters?

6. This building will cut off much light from the East, in the mornings for us property owners who have lower buildings to the West of the property in question—and all of us are in low-rise buildings, well within the R–4 zoning restrictions.

To grant the deviations requested would deny us more light and possibly more air—which the present zoning gives us.

There are many other reasons which could be advanced to deny this application.

I urge you to deny it in its entirety.

If deviations are granted, I shall feel it my duty to join with others who may wish to take this matter into the courts, if necessary, to get proper relief. This is not necessary, and would be an unjust expense imposed on present property owners who have lived and made their home in this block for many years. It can be avoided by simply adhering to the present R–4 zoning now applicable.

I am the owner of property located at 2068–70 Vallejo Street, on the same side of the street as the property in question—and located approximately 74 feet west of the property under discussion.

Thank you.

The Zoning Administrator announced his decision in a letter to Liebman dated October 8, 1964.

DECISION OF ZONING ADMINISTRATOR DENYING APPLICATION FOR VARIANCE

Dear Sir:

This is to notify you and other interested parties that your application under the City Planning Code for a variance pertaining to the above property and described as follows:

> FLOOR AREA RATIO VARIANCE SOUGHT: Proposal is to construct an 11-story 53-unit apartment house with a floor area ratio of 5.51 sq. ft. of floor area to each sq. ft. of lot area where, in R–4, a ratio of 4.8 to one is the maximum otherwise permitted by the City Planning Code. The area of this property is 14,575 sq. ft., which, at a ratio of 4.8 to one, would permit 69,960 sq. ft. of floor area; the building as proposed would have 80,293 sq. ft. of floor area;

which application was considered by the Zoning Administrator at a public hearing on September 2, 1964 (the record of which remained open through September 16 for any further written evidence the parties might wish to submit), has been decided as follows:

Denied.

I. FINDINGS OF FACT AND BACKGROUND

A. Chronology of Zoning Division Review of this Matter . . .

B. Nature of the Proposed Building

1. The building proposed in this case has many of the attractive features ascribed to it by the applicant:

(a) It has 53 relatively spacious dwelling units, at a ratio of one unit per 275 square feet of lot area, compared with the 74 units that would be the maximum permissible number on this lot at the R–4 density limit of one unit per 200 square feet of lot area;

(b) The building is free-standing, with side yards of 11 feet where no side yards are required;

(c) Although the building has the minimum permitted rear yard of 25 feet, into which balconies extend 3 feet as permitted, the building covers approximately 54% of its site compared with the maximum permitted coverage of 75%;

(d) The 5-foot balconies extending around the building at its 10 upper floors provide approximately 21,000 square feet of usable outdoor area immediately accessible to the dwelling units; and,

(e) 62 parking spaces are provided where a minimum of 53 are required.

2. On the other hand:

(a) Buildings with the maximum number of units permitted by the one unit per 200 square feet of lot area density factor in R–4 are not often built because of their questionable rentability and the difficulty of providing required parking for that number of units;

(b) The actual number of people in the lesser number of large units proposed in this case might equal the likely number of people in a larger number of smaller units; and,

(c) It is not at all clear that a 62:53 parking ratio in such a building and location would prevent greater congestion on the streets than already exists, and 4 of the 62 spaces would be located in the porte cochere area and thus of limited usefulness for long-term parking.

C. The Testimony at the September 2 Hearing

1. The principal spokesmen for the applicant were his attorney and his soils engineer.

2. The attorney stated he still felt that 1,760 square feet of floor area represented by the smoke towers should be excluded from the 80,293 square foot figure.

3. The remainder of his presentation is well summarized by the outline of the applicant's claims listed on his application form under each of the 5 requirements that must be met for the granting of a variance, with the first two of these claims embodying the essence of his case and being as follows:

"A. Peculiar subsoil conditions require extraordinarily expensive foundation work, thus increasing cost of this building, or any other R–4 building.

"B. Prime quality residential neighborhoods in and adjacent to area in which building to be constructed demand exceptional quality of building design, exceptional degree of landscaping potential, maximal use of light and air, and minimal congestion of traffic and population."

4. A series of persons spoke in opposition to the application, but a summary of their statements is not necessary here in the light of the denial of this application.

II. CONCLUSIONS BASED UPON THE ABOVE FINDINGS

The Charter and Section 302 of the Planning Code specify five requirements that must all be met if a variance is to be granted, and the Charter and Code also specify that this variance decision must set forth the findings upon which these requirements are deemed to be, or not to be, met in each case. The five requirements, therefore, are listed below and, on the basis of the findings herein set forth, they are deemed to be, or not to be, met in this case as indicated.

Requirement 1. That there are exceptional or extraordinary circumstances or conditions applying to the property involved, or to the intended use of the property, that do not apply generally to other property or uses in the same class of district:

Requirement *not* met because:

(a) The applicant's claim to a variance by analogy to the planned unit development concept of the Planning Code overlooks the basic legal differences between that concept and the variance concept, the planned unit development concept being designed to provide a flexible planning approach to parcels of unusual size (generally 3 acres or more, compared with the $^1/_3$ acre in this case), and the variance concept providing a legal safety valve for unduly oppressive situations meeting 5 specific requirements that have little similarity to the standards specified by the Planning Code (Section 304 ff.) for planned unit developments.

(b) In variance cases, quality of building design may be a relevant factor, but it cannot be the principal basis for a variance.

(c) Concerning the subsoil conditions, although the applicant's expert testified that "this site is adverse for multi-unit developments in comparison with similar hillside building lots in this particular area," there was considerable conflict of evidence on this point at the hearing.

(d) It is questionable, in any event, whether subsoil conditions could justify the type and extent of variance here sought.

(e) It is also apparent that the subsoil conditions are not a principal reason for this variance application, in that the soils expert stated his proposal to the applicant for a soils investigation was dated May 7, 1964, several months after the problem of excessive floor area was first mentioned to the Zoning Division; moreover, applicant's attorney stated at the hearing that the plans for this building were well advanced when his client learned of Zoning Bulletin 63.2 in the fall of 1963.

Requirement 2. That owing to such exceptional or extraordinary circumstances the literal enforcement of specified provisions of the Code would result in practical difficulty or unnecessary hardship:

Requirement *not* met because:

(a) No hardship has been claimed other than as a result of circumstances that are not exceptional or extraordinary for purposes of Requirement 1 above.

(b) If it should be claimed that the "changed interpretations" of Zoning Bulletin 63.2 have caused unnecessary hardship, even if the last remaining interpretation question in this case—concerning the 1,760 square feet of smoke towers—were resolved in applicant's favor, the building would still have 78,500 square feet of floor area for FAR purposes, or 8,500 square feet over the maximum permitted on this lot.

(c) In any event, after thorough study of the question, it is believed that the area represented by smoke towers should be included in the computation of floor area for FAR purposes, and the fact that they were excluded in the case of the Hartford Building (the first case in which the question was of any moment) and that the Superior Court upheld their exclusion in that case does not prohibit the Zoning Division from adopting the sounder interpretation of including them that has been followed in every subsequent case, including that of the Wells Fargo-Dillingham Building (where the question was of considerable moment).

Requirement 3. That the variance is necessary for the preservation of a substantial property right of the petitioner, possessed by other property in the same class of district:

Requirement *not* met because:

(a) The great majority of lots in the R-4 vicinity of this lot have less than half their permitted FAR of 4.8, and of all R-4 lots within a 300-foot radius only two are developed in excess of 4.8 and were so developed years ago under the zoning standards of a by-gone era.

(b) No FAR variance of the proportions requested in this case has been applied for previously anywhere in the city.

(c) Besides the 80,293 square feet of floor area included in the FAR computation in this case, there is an additional 52,000 square feet of floor area not so included: 21,350 square feet on balconies, 27,500 square feet in parking area, and 3,150 square feet on the entry level—for a grand total of 132,000 square feet on a lot of 14,575 square feet, even further in excess of the surrounding pattern of R-4 development.

(d) In these circumstances, there is neither merit nor logic behind applicant's claims under this "parity" requirement, claims summarized as follows on his application form:

"A. Owner's right to build unit according to the generally high-grade residential construction and habitation standards within the district and neighboring prime residential districts.

"B. Right to maximize development of land notwithstanding adverse soil conditions."

Requirement 4. That the granting of the variance will not be materially detrimental to the public welfare or materially injurious to the property or improvements in the vicinity:

Requirement *not* met on the basis of the foregoing findings and conclusions.

Requirement 5. That the granting of such variance will be in harmony with the general purpose and intent of this Code and will not adversely affect the Master Plan:

Requirement *not* met on the basis of the foregoing findings and conclusions.

This decision will become effective if no appeal from this decision has been filed as provided in Section 303 of the City Planning Code on or before the last date for filing as noted above.

Very truly yours,

Clyde O. Fisher, Jr.
Zoning Administrator

Attachment: Mailing List to Parties of Record.

Liebman appealed the Zoning Administrator's decision to the Board of Appeals, which heard the matter on October 19, 1964 and, on November 2, 1964, rendered its decision overruling the Zoning Administrator and granting the requested variance. On November 20 the Zoning Administrator requested a rehearing.

REQUEST FOR REHEARING BY BOARD

November 20, 1964

Board of Permit Appeals
227 City Hall
San Francisco 94102

                          Re: Request for Rehearing of
                                   Vallejo Street, North Line
                                   98 Feet West of Laguna Street

Gentlemen:

A rehearing is respectfully requested of your decision dated November 10, 1964 in the above case, in which you overruled my denial of a variance under the Floor Area Ratio provisions of the City Planning Code for 10,333 square feet of floor area beyond that permitted on the subject lot.

The basis of this decision, as stated in the findings therein, is essentially (1) that the proposed apartment building is "attractive", and (2) that certain subsoil difficulties were discovered after the building had been designed with an excessive floor area.

A rehearing is requested for the reason that such a basis constitutes a radical departure from the concept of zoning variances, has no support in the law of zoning and is thus devoid of reference or citation to that law, and substitutes completely unspecified criteria for variances as a guide for property owners and public officials in place of the guides specified in the Charter, Planning Code and body of law that exists with regard to zoning variances.

I. THE "ATTRACTIVE BUILDING" CLAIM

The finding that this building has "attractive features" and would conform to higher development standards in certain instances than the minimum standards of the Planning Code overlooks the fact that (1) the Planning Code expressly states (Section 103) its standards "shall be held to be *minimum* requirements", and (2) that new high-rise apartment buildings rarely sink to these minimum standards in San Francisco today. It has never before been suggested that a variance to go below certain Planning Code minimums is justified just because certain other minimums are not quite reached.

Comparative data for several recently built high-rise apartment buildings within a mile or so of the subject lot are presented at the end of this letter. These buildings are those for which these data are readily available in the records of the Department of City Planning and are representative of the experience of the Department with high-rise buildings generally under the 1960 Planning Code.

These data show no building that sinks to more than one Planning Code minimum, if any, and the data is presented simply to show how the applicant for this floor area variance has totally failed to sustain his burden of proving "exceptional or extraordinary circumstances", the first requirement for a variance, on this novel basis.

Instead, this finding is simply a statement of the "planned unit development" argument made by the applicant in his hearing before the Zoning Administrator, but with that term itself no longer being used because the planned unit development concept has no legal applicability in variance cases, as pointed out in the decision of the Zoning Administrator.

Lastly, and of serious legal and practical consequences, even if "attractiveness" were to be a basis for a variance, this decision is devoid of any criteria for determining what Planning Code minimums are to be varied for this reason and to what quantitative extent.

II. THE SUBSOIL CONDITIONS CLAIM

The findings do not deny that the subsoil conditions claimed as the other basis for this variance were not discovered until several months after the Department of City Planning was informed that this building had already been designed with this excessive floor area, thus raising a question as to the full circumstances of this case. Nor, parenthetically, is there any denial that a representative of the applicant attempted to persuade the Zoning Administrator to act upon this variance application without a public hearing.

The evidence presented to show "unusual subsoil conditions" on the subject lot was itself questioned by an engineer familiar with such matters and resident in the area. More important, however, the applicant has the burden of proving "exceptional or extraordinary circumstances . . . that do not apply generally to other property or uses in the same class of district", and he submitted no evidence to distinguish the subject lot from other Pacific Heights properties or other R–4 districts generally.

Even if the subsoil conditions of this lot were shown to be different from those of other property in the same class of district, the question then arises as to whether every lot in San Francisco is to have zoning regulations geared just to its particular subsoil conditions and, if so, by what criteria are those regulations to be determined. The decision in this case is devoid of any such criteria.

III. THE FIVE REQUIREMENTS FOR A VARIANCE

The decision of the Board, in its findings in support of the conclusion that the *exceptional or extraordinary circumstances* requirement is met, goes no further than the two claims discussed above.

The findings in support of the second requirement for a variance, that these circumstances result in *unnecessary hardship*, a hardship going considerably beyond that relating to property generally as a result of the reciprocal benefits and burdens of a zoning ordinance, also go no further than the foregoing two claims.

The findings in support of the third requirement, *that the variance is necessary for the preservation of a substantial property right of the petitioner, possessed by other property in the same class of district*, start by stating "appellant like every property owner in the City has a right to build a building better in its overall merits than the Code requires through mechanical application of its several specific criteria". It is absolutely true that property owners have, and invariably do exercise, the right to build high-rise apartment buildings at more than minimum Planning Code standards—but it has never been suggested that this right gives rise to another and seemingly contradictory right to build at less than those minimums by variance.

The further finding here, that "without the variance appellant cannot economically proceed with this attractive building", is quite correct in that *this building* could not be built without a variance because of its excessive floor area, and thus this variance application has been filed. Despite the extensive financial analysis that goes into the planning of a building of this magnitude, no detailed economic data were submitted to support any claim that a building cannot also be built within the floor area limitations of the Planning Code in this case.

Moreover, applicant has the burden of proving under the "parity" concept of this third requirement for a variance that other property in the same class of district already has as much or more than he seeks by variance, and no such evidence was submitted. On the other hand, the public records of the Department of City Planning support the conclusion to the contrary in the decision of the Zoning Administrator, that "the great majority of lots in the R-4 vicinity of this lot have less than half their permitted FAR of 4.8, and of all R-4 lots within a 300-foot radius only two are developed in excess of 4.8 and were so developed years ago under the zoning standards of a by-gone era", and even a cursory field observation reveals, for example, there are no buildings over 3 or 4 stories in size in the R-4 district on either side of Vallejo Street in the subject block, along either side of Vallejo Street in the block to the west, in the entire Assessor's Block (Number 555) in which the subject lot is located, or in the Assessor's Block (Number 556) to the west, thus resulting in floor area ratios less than half that of the 11-story building proposed in this case.

The findings of the Board's decision relating to the *fourth and fifth requirements* for a variance raise no considerations beyond those listed under the first three requirements. These findings, however, do violence to the plain meaning of these requirements—such as the one that the variance harmonize with the general purpose and intent of the Planning Code—when a new and incomprehensible basis for the granting of variances is adopted, disregarding the specific variances criteria of the Charter and Planning Code, and substituting for them no criteria that provide a guide for property owners and public officials in the administration of the City Planning Code.

Many buildings are attractive, most buildings are designed well above Planning Code minimums, and many lots in San Francisco have subsoil peculiarities. There is no showing in this case why some or all of these factors justify a variance for 15% more floor area than the Planning Code permits on this lot, nor is there any indication how the 15% figure was arrived at, rather than a figure of 5%, or 50% extra, or no extra or even less than that.

No Planning Code can be fairly and equitably administered if the sole guide for a variance is to be that someone has applied for it.

For these reasons it is requested that a rehearing of this appeal be granted.

Very truly yours,

Clyde O. Fisher, Jr.
Zoning Administrator

COMPARATIVE DATA ON RECENTLY BUILT
HIGH-RISE APARTMENT BUILDINGS
November 20, 1964

Showing extent to which 4 new buildings, and a proposed building on Vallejo Street near Laguna, exceed the minimum standards of the City Planning Code

Building	Dwelling Units No.	Dwelling Units % of Max. Allowable	Coverage % of Max. Allowable	Parking Spaces No.	Parking Spaces Spaces Per Unit	Floor Area % of Max. Allowable
Royal Towers (Green St. S/L 137.5' E of Taylor)	77	43%	76%	112	1.45	100%
Pacific, N/W Corner Buchanan	65	56%	79%	65	1.00	84%
Green Hill Tower (Green St. N/L 65' E of Leavenworth)	53	75%	81%	63	1.19	95%
Franklin St. W/L 63' S of Clay	45	68%	95%	45	1.00	100%
Vallejo, N/L 98' W Laguna (proposed building)	53	72%	72%	62	1.15	115%

The Zoning Administrator's request was strongly supported by the newly-formed Broadway, Vallejo, Laguna Property Owners Association, consisting of 55 neighbors. The Association had on October 15, 1964 sent a letter to the Board of Permit Appeals expressing its opposition to the proposed variance. The Association also retained an attorney, J. Joseph Sullivan, who, writing to the Board on November 20, gave as one ground in support of the request for a rehearing that:

> Due to the lack of facilities of your Board, notices of the Appeal hearing of the Zoning Administrator's Variance denial decision which was to be held by your Board on October 19, 1964 were only obtained through a notice given, at the request of your office, through the Department of City Planning, mailed on October 15th, 1964 and received through the mails by interested parties only two or three days prior to your hearing. This did not allow time for preparation of evidence and personal appearance before your Board of those who had testified during the original Zoning Administrator's hearings.

On November 23, 1964 Liebman filed letters opposing the rehearing request, but the request was granted the same day. Following a rehearing on December 14, 1964, the Board rendered its decision on January 11, 1965.

BOARD OF PERMIT APPEALS DECISION ON REHEARING

BOARD OF PERMIT APPEALS

CITY AND COUNTY OF SAN FRANCISCO

Perry Liebman,
                Appellant,
      vs.
Clyde Fisher,
Zoning Administrator,
                Respondent.

No. V-3754
Notice of Decision

TO: __PERRY LIEBMAN__ Address: __3106 Fillmore Street, San Francisco, California__ Applicant, and __CLYDE FISHER__ Zoning Administrator of the City and County of San Francisco:

NOTICE IS HEREBY GIVEN that the appeal of __PERRY LIEBMAN__, the Appellant above named, from decision of __CLYDE FISHER__ Zoning Administrator of the City and County of San Francisco,

(_____) granting (X) denying the application of the Appellant
(_____) above named, or the application of _____
(_____) _____

for a variance relating to property located at __2030 Vallejo Street__ identified as Assessor's Block No. __555__ Lot No. __10 & 13__ and in __R-4__ District under the City Planning Code, which variance was described by the Zoning Administrator as follows:

"FLOOR AREA RATIO VARIANCE SOUGHT: Proposal is to construct an 11-story 53-unit apartment house with a floor area ratio of 5.5 sq. ft. of floor area to each sq. ft. of lot area where, in R-4, a ratio of 4.8 to one is the maximum otherwise permitted by the City Planning Code. The area of this property is 14,575 sq. ft., which, at a ratio of 4.8 to one, would permit 69,960 sq. ft. of floor area; the building as proposed would have 80,293 sq. ft. of floor area;"

came on regularly for hearing before the Board of Permit Appeals of the City and County of San Francisco on December 14, 1964, and the said decision of the Zoning Administrator was DISAPPROVED with such conditions as are necessary to secure the objectives of the Planning Code, on January 11, 1965, as follows:

The decision of the Zoning Administrator denying the variance is DISAPPROVED. The variance as requested by appellant from Section 122 (Floor Area Ratio) of the City Planning Code is hereby granted pursuant to Section 303(d) of said Code, in accordance with the plans submitted with Building Permit Application No. 301813, as amended by Variance Application VZ64–61.

The Board of Permit Appeals finds that there was error on the part of the Zoning Administrator, hereafter called "ZA", pertaining to the five conditions (called "Requirements" in Opinion of ZA), of Section 302(d) of the Planning Code as set forth below and for the facts and reasons herein specified with regard to each condition.

1. *That there are Exceptional or Extraordinary Circumstances or Conditions Applying to the Property Involved, or to the Intended use of the Property, that do not Apply Generally to other Property or uses in the same Class of District.*

FINDINGS

Condition met because:

A. An unusual subsoil condition exists on the lots involved. According to the testimony of appellant's soils engineer, a member of a nationally recognized soils engineering firm, the site probably contains a buried stream channel or draw, the type and depth of which are not typical of other building sites in hillside areas. He further testified that because of this exceptional condition: (1) This site is adverse for multi-unit development in comparison with similar hillside building lots in this particular area; (2) Foundation costs on the proposed building have been increased from $2\frac{1}{2}$ to 3 times the cost anticipated without the exceptional soils condition; and (3) Development of these lots for any multi-story structure similar to the proposed building in excess of 50 feet in height is difficult.

B. The Appellant proposes to build according to development standards which are more restrictive in terms of producing the results intended by the Planning Code than are the provisions of the Code themselves. ZA himself noted such standards in his Findings. Therefore, his intended use of the property is unique and constitutes an exceptional circumstance, when compared with the conventional development of property according to the standards found in the Code.

These high standards were designed to effect many attractive features in terms of the Code's purposes, including:

(1) 53 relatively spacious dwelling units, at a ratio of one unit per 275 square feet of lot area, compared with the 72 units that would be the maximum permissible number on this lot at the R–4 density limit of one unit per 200 square feet of lot area. (See Findings of ZA paragraph I B 1(a).)

(2) The building is free standing, with side yards of 11 feet where no side yards are required. (See Findings of ZA paragraph I B 1(b).) Such side yards provide open corridors of light and air on both sides of the building, a highly unusual feature for an interior lot building, and also a result most consistent with the overall goals of the Code.

(3) The building covers only approximately 54% of its site, compared with the maximum permitted coverage of 75%. (See Findings of ZA paragraph I B 1(c).)

(4) The building has five-foot balconies which extend around the building on all sides on its 10 upper floors. These balconies provide approximately 21,000 square feet of usable outdoor area immediately accessible to the dwelling units. (See Findings of ZA paragraph I B 1(d).) The balconies create additional light and air on the sides of the buildings.

(5) 62 parking spaces, where the Code requires only 53, an increase of 16% over Code Minimum parking. (See Findings of ZA paragraph I B 1(e).)

Specifications of Error or Abuse of Discretion.

ZA abused his discretion in failing to find that an unusual and adverse subsoil condition exists on the lots involved. The only competent evidence based upon a professional investigation of the soil which the record contains was supplied by appellant's soils engineer. A copy of his testimony is part of the record. Testimony conflicting with such evidence consisted solely of the opinion of a neighbor, also an engineer, who had made no study of the site, and whose qualifications failed to indicate any special familiarity with the soils topography of San Francisco's hilly terrain.

In the light of this abuse of discretion and the further fact that ZA conceded both that the proposed building contains the same attractive features as found by the Board, and that quality of building design is a relevant factor in variance cases, the Board concludes that ZA erred in so interpreting the Code as to conclude that this condition was not met by appellant.

2. *That owing to such exceptional or extraordinary circumstances the literal enforcement of specified provisions of the Code would result in practical difficulty or unnecessary hardship.*

FINDINGS

Condition *met* because:

The subsoil condition obviously constitutes a practical difficulty for development, if the Code be literally enforced, as noted by the Board under Condition 1. Also appellant's adoption of "superior to Code" building development standards for the proposed building, imposes practical difficulty and hardship for the appellant in developing the property far beyond that imposed by the literal Code provisions. This latter self-imposed development discipline, more rigid than the provisions of the Code requirements, will produce results in terms of the basic purposes of the Code which more than offset the variance, as also already noted under Condition 1. Thus, the Board concludes that the literal enforcement of the Code in the face of these two exceptional circumstances would create practical difficulties and unnecessary hardship for not only the appellant, but also for the surrounding neighborhood. The last conclusion is based on the fact that the features of the building upon which appellant bases his variance request produce solutions to the common neighborhood objections to moderate high-rise development, i.e., loss of view, light and air, overcrowded land, and traffic congestion.

Specifications of Error or Abuse of Discretion.

The Board concludes that ZA's findings that Condition 2 was not met by appellant is in error, because it was based on an erroneous interpretation by ZA of the Code in regard to the exceptional circumstances shown by appellant. The Board concludes that ZA's finding is further in error because it would result in a hypertechnical enforcement of a single provision of the Code pertaining to the height and bulk of a building to defeat a project which the Board finds fully governed by the remaining height and bulk limitations of the Code, and which will clearly promote the overall purposes of the entire Code, and completely offset the variance. The Board finds that such a practice in interpreting the Code would unquestionably discourage architects and builders from looking to imaginative development solutions according to the spirit of the Code.

3. *That the Variance is Necessary for the Preservation of a Substantial Right of the Petitioner, Possessed by Other Property in the Same Class of District.*

FINDINGS

Condition *met* because:

Appellant has a right to develop his property, notwithstanding adverse soil conditions. Because the Board finds that the variance in this case amounts to no more than an immaterial breach of the Code fully compensated by features of the building not demanded by the Code, and because the record shows that without the variance appellant cannot economically proceed with this attractive building, the Board finds that the variance is necessary to preserve that basic property right of appellant.

Specifications of Error or Abuse of Discretion.

ZA's failure to find that this condition was met by appellant constitutes an abuse of discretion on his part, because such failure is based upon the following erroneous conclusions:

(1) Conclusion (a) of ZA under Condition 3 is immaterial. In it, ZA himself recognizes the inconclusiveness of comparing development before and after the existing zoning legislation. Furthermore, in the light of the same evidence the Planning Code was adopted so as to zone R-4 the entire area referred to by ZA.

(2) Conclusion (b) of ZA under Condition 3 is immaterial and irrelevant, because no evidence was introduced in the record which would

enable the Board to compare other Floor Area Ratio variance requests with the application before it on this appeal.

(3) Conclusion (c) of ZA under Condition 3 is immaterial and irrelevant, since all the square foot areas noted by ZA are permitted by the Code.

(4) ZA's Conclusion (d) falls with his erroneous Conclusions (a)–(c) upon which it is based.

(5) ZA's comparison of the proposed building with 4 others described in his rehearing request likewise constitutes an abuse of discretion. Two of the buildings are not comparable because they are located in R–5 districts, while two others are owned by the occupants as distinct from the apartment building appellant proposes.

4. *That the Granting of the Variance will not be Materially Detrimental to the Public Welfare or Materially Injurious to the Property or Improvements in the Vicinity.*

FINDINGS

Condition *met* because

A. On the basis of its foregoing Findings, and its analysis of ZA's conclusions under Conclusions 1 through 3, the Board concludes that the granting of the variance will not be materially detrimental to the public welfare, and not materially injurious to the property or improvements in the vicinity.

B. The Board finds further that if constructed according to the plans submitted to the Board on this appeal, the proposed building will:

(1) Provide the vicinity with highest quality multi-unit development.

(2) Improve all the property in the vicinity through use of multi-unit standards allowing for maximum landscaping, light and air, parking, safety and privacy, as well as minimal traffic density and lot coverage.

(3) Improve lots which, because of adverse soil characteristics, require extraordinary development costs for any similar multi-unit building in excess of 50 feet.

Specifications of Error or Abuse of Discretion.

ZA has erred and abused his discretion in connection with Condition 4 in the same respects as pointed out by the Board in its consideration of ZA's errors and abuse of discretion under Conditions 1 through 3 above, because those same erroneous conclusions constitute the basis of ZA's conclusion under Condition 4.

5. *That the Granting of such Variance will be in Harmony with the General Purpose and Intent of the Planning Code and will not Adversely affect the Master Plan.*

FINDINGS

Condition *met* because:

The Board finds that the variance is fully compensated through the attractive features of the proposed building, which features result in a building thoroughly in harmony with the general purposes of the Code and Master Plan. Paraphrasing the general purposes of the Code as set forth in Section 101, the Board finds that the proposed building will:

A. Protect and enhance the character and stability of this prime residential area of this Pacific Heights District in which the proposed building is to be built.

B. Provide exceptional access to light, air and view, exceptionally low lot coverage and population density, exceptional privacy, ease of access and safety from fire.

C. Promote the purpose of the Code in obviating traffic interference on streets and thoroughfares.

D. Exemplify the spirit of the Code by affording light and air on all sides of this non-corner lot building, an exceptional result which, if followed by other builders, would lead to supplementing landscaping and use of light and air by adjacent R-4 developments.

Specifications of Error or Abuse of Discretion.

A. ZA has erred and abused his discretion in connection with Condition 5 in the same respects as pointed out by the Board in its consideration of ZA's errors and abuse of discretion under Conditions 1 through 4, because those same erroneous conclusions constitute the basis of ZA's conclusion under Condition 5.

B. ZA's treatment of appellant's case under this condition reflects an erroneous interpretation of the Planning Code. ZA has disregarded the spirit and fundamental purposes of the Planning Code as set forth in Section 101, in favor of a mechanical, literalistic construction of the Code. In effect, he has concluded that the Planning Code is so inflexible as to preclude a property owner in this City from imposing higher development standards upon himself than does the Code, if such higher standards can only be reached through an immaterial breach of a minor Code provision, fully offset by these high standards themselves. ZA pursues this conclusion even when the higher standards advanced by appellant in this case promote the very purposes of the Code established by Section 101: "To protect the character and stability of residential areas . . . ; . . . to promote the orderly development of such areas; . . . to provide adequate light, air, privacy and convenience of access, and to secure safety from fire . . . ; to prevent overcrowding of land and undue congestion of population; . . . to obviate the danger to public safety caused by undue interference with existing or prospective traffic movements . . . ."

ZA concedes that appellant's proposed building is clearly designed with these goals in mind. Nevertheless, in denying appellant a variance ZA has *"literally enforced"* one section of the Code, Section 122, while side stepping his obligation to enforce the *entire* Code including Section 101, and including Section 302. This latter section *expressly* permits "variances from strict application of the Code" when such variances are "in harmony *with the general purpose and intent of this Code*", and literal Code enforcement would result in "practical difficulties, unnecessary hardships or results inconsistent with the general purposes of this Code". As already observed, the Board has found that such results would follow in this case from literal Code enforcement.

ZA's request for rehearing reiterates his hypertechnical approach through his protest that the Board's first decision granting the variance substituted " . . . unspecified criteria as a guide for variances in place of the provision of the Charter and Planning Code." (Page 1 of Request for Rehearing.) The Board concludes, however, that the Code sets up no criteria for the granting of variances other than the five conditions examined in the foregoing opinion. (See Section 302 of the Planning Code.)

SYNOPSIS OF PROCEEDINGS. . . .

DATED: January 18, 1965.

BOARD OF PERMIT APPEALS OF THE CITY AND COUNTY OF SAN FRANCISCO

(SEAL)

President

Secretary

An article on the Board of Appeals decision appeared in the February 24, 1965, San Francisco Examiner under the headline, "Zoning Law—How It Was Bent". The article zeroed in on the report by Liebman's soils engineer, "that the site 'probably contains a buried stream, channel or draw, the type and depth of which are not typical of other building sites in the hillside areas.'" According to the article, "Planning Director James McCarthy inked this sarcastic commentary on a memo to Fisher: 'Adverse soil justifies more area. The stream is under this lot ONLY. The logic is so compelling!' The timing of the soils report bothered Fisher as much as its logic. For not until May 7, 1964 was the report proposed, about nine months after Schram and White told Fisher's assistant, Robert Passmore, they had designed the building with too much floor area because they liked their experimental cost-cutting structural design." San Francisco Examiner, p. 43 col. 1 (Feb. 24, 1965).

Photo: Brian Sutphin

View of 2030 Vallejo from corner of Vallejo and Buchanan (from left to right: 2090 Vallejo, 2080 Vallejo, 2072–2076 Vallejo, 2068–2070 Vallejo, 2058 Vallejo, 2030 Vallejo)

Photo: Brian Sutphin

Buildings at 1940–1998 Vallejo, between Laguna and Octavia (2030 Vallejo is at left, rear)

Photo: Brian Sutphin
View of 2030 Vallejo from corner of Vallejo and Laguna

Photo: Brian Sutphin

2010 Vallejo (2030 Vallejo is at left)

Photo: Brian Sutphin

View of 2030 Vallejo from corner of Green and Laguna, one block north of Vallejo

Photo: Brian Sutphin

2012–2014 Broadway (2030 Vallejo visible in background at right)

Photo: Brian Sutphin

View from back porch of 2012-2014 Broadway (San Francisco Bay visible in background)

QUESTIONS

What motives, interests and concerns probably lay behind the positions taken by the Zoning Administrator, the Board of Permit Appeals, the Broadway, Laguna, Vallejo Association, and Perry Liebman? What steps or strategies not pursued would you have counseled each to take in pursuing these objectives? Which of the two decisionmakers—Zoning Administrator or Board of Permit Appeals—was more likely to respond to political and economic pressures in the Pacific Heights area? In the City? Did either or both take a mediatory position, attempting to accommodate the interests of developer, neighbors and public to the City's land use plan? Did either or both take an advocacy position? Can you think of ways in which the Zoning Administrator could have effectively met the Board's concerns without sacrificing his own interests?

What arguments might the Association have made in order to prevail before the Zoning Administrator, and to buttress the Administrator's position on appeal to the Board of Permit Appeals? Should the Association have emphasized or de-emphasized the fact that the vast majority of its members lived in the existing high rise apartment buildings at 1940 Broadway, 1960 Broadway and 1940 Vallejo? Note that the location of these buildings relative to 2030 Vallejo suggests that these residents were probably concerned not so much with impeded light, air or view, as with an aesthetic affront. Would it have been more effective for these neighbors to try to line up behind the owner of 2012 Broadway, whose view was directly obstructed, and the owners immediately adjacent to 2030 Vallejo, whose light and air were directly obstructed? Note that depriving the few residents at 2012 Broadway of their view meant conferring the benefit of the same view on the many more residents at 2030 Vallejo. Does this imbalance in cost and benefit cut for or against the claim of the owner at 2012 Broadway? How would the owner at 2012 Broadway, and the neighbors, have calculated the amount they might offer to buy off Liebman's right to build above a specified height and to get him to agree to a restrictive covenant encumbering the land? How successful do you think the owners at 2012 Broadway and those immediately adjacent to 2030 Vallejo would have been in getting their neighbors at 1940 and 1960 Broadway, and at 1940 Vallejo, to chip in to a fund to buy off Liebman's development right?

Representing Liebman, what steps and strategies would you have pursued in attempting to win the Zoning Administrator over to your side? To win over the neighbors? Would it have been an effective strategy for Liebman to tell the neighbors that, if he could not obtain the requested FAR variance, he would submit new plans calling for a building that complied with R–4 requirements in all respects, but that covered the entire permitted 75% of the lot (rather than the 54% first proposed); that had no side yards (rather than two eleven-foot side yards, as first proposed); and that had 74 dwelling units (rather than the 53 units first proposed)?

Would Liebman have been wise to try to come to terms with the neighbors immediately adjacent to 2030 Vallejo, whose light and air were obstructed, and the neighbors on Broadway, whose view was directly obstructed, thus isolating the bulk of the Association's membership, all of whom were apparently concerned only with the proposed building's aesthetic effects?

Recall the study, at page 1194, above, identifying the relative success of arguments used by applicants and opponents in rezoning cases. Are these arguments likely to enjoy any greater or lesser success when advanced in variance, as opposed to rezoning, proceedings? Recall that, unlike legislators voting to rezone an area, administrative agencies must make fact findings and give reasons for their decisions.

c. JUDICIAL REVIEW OF THE ADMINISTRATIVE PROCESS

The Board's January 11 decision ended the administrative phase and prepared the stage for a change of characters and scene. The Zoning Administrator dropped out of the proceedings, and the Broadway, Laguna, Vallejo Association retained a prominent downtown law firm, Heller, Ehrman, White & McAuliffe, to represent it in the judicial proceedings. The lead attorney was Caspar Weinberger, then a partner in the firm, and later Secretary of Health, Education and Welfare in the Nixon Cabinet, and Secretary of Defense in the Reagan Cabinet. Working with him was M. Laurence Popofsky, then an associate, and later a partner in the firm. Liebman was represented by the San Francisco firm of Feldman, Waldman & Kline; active participants throughout the various proceedings were an associate, Richard B. Morris, who subsequently became Executive Secretary of the Bar Association of San Francisco and the State Bar of California, and Jesse Feldman, a partner in the firm.

On March 4, 1965, the Association petitioned the Superior Court in and for the City and County of San Francisco for a writ of mandate to compel the Board to reverse its decision. On May 25, 1965, approximately one and one-half months after hearing argument, Superior Court Judge Andrew Eyman rendered his decision denying the petition and upholding the Board's decision. Judge Eyman's decision rested on two central conclusions of law:

> 3. Respondent Board of Permit Appeals duly complied with all applicable provisions of the Charter, Planning Code and other municipal ordinances of the City and County of San Francisco governing said appeal of Respondent and Real Party in Interest Perry Liebman. The Notice of Decision of Respondent Board of Permit Appeals duly specified wherein there was error in the interpretation of the provisions of the Planning Code or abuse of discretion on the part of Respondent Clyde O. Fisher, Jr., Zoning Administrator, and specified in its findings the facts relied upon by Respondent Board of Permit Appeals in making its decision, all as required by Section 303(d) of said City Planning Code. The Board of Permit Appeals duly complied with the requirement of Section 117.3 of the Charter and Section 303(d) of the City Planning Code imposing on the Respondent Board of Permit Appeals the same limitations as are placed upon the Zoning Administrator. These limitations are set forth in Section 302(d) of the City Planning Code. They provide that the Zoning Administrator shall grant the variance if it appears that certain requirements specified in Section 302(d) are found. Respondent Board of Permit Appeals complied with these limitations by specifying in its Notice of Decision its findings of fact establishing the existence of each of the five conditions contained in said Section 302(d).
>
> 4. Respondent Board of Permit Appeals proceeded within its jurisdiction in granting said variance. Respondent Board of Permit Appeals did not proceed without or in excess of its jurisdiction.

The Association promptly filed an appeal.

On June 8, 1965, the Association filed a petition for writ of supersedeas with the appropriate appeals court, the District Court of Appeal for the First District, seeking to prohibit construction of the building while the appeal was pending. The Association argued that to allow Liebman to begin construction would effectively defeat the purpose of the appeal since, by the time the appeal was resolved, the building would be an accomplished fact. The Association also argued that the public would be endangered during the course of excavation. Liebman responded on June 18.

DECLARATION OF PERRY LIEBMAN

1 CIVIL NO. 22889

IN THE DISTRICT COURT OF APPEAL STATE OF CALIFORNIA FIRST APPELLATE DISTRICT DIVISION THREE

Broadway, Laguna, Vallejo Association, et al.,
    Petitioners and Appellants,
vs.
Board of Permit Appeals of The City And County of San Francisco and Perry Liebman, Real Party in Interest, et al.,
    Respondents.

DECLARATION OF PERRY LIEBMAN

I, PERRY LIEBMAN, hereby declare as follows:

I am one of the respondents in this matter, and I am also the owner of the building site situated at 2030 Vallejo Street, San Francisco, California. I am also the president of Liebman Construction Company. I have developed the plans for the proposed apartment building to be constructed at 2030 Vallejo Street, and my company will be the general contractor on the job of constructing that building. I make this declaration in connection with the above-entitled matter.

I have been advised by my architects, Schram & White, that should the present zoning variance be withdrawn by the Courts, the building could be modified to meet floor area ratio Planning Code requirements by eliminating the presently planned eleventh floor and two ground floor apartments, leaving a maximum of 1600 square feet of living space on the ground floor.

I have also been advised by T.Y. Lin, Kulka, Yang & Associates, consulting structural engineers for the building, that if such changes were made there would be no need or justification for changing the presently planned foundation. (A copy of the letter of T.Y. Lin, Kulka, Yang & Associates to me is attached hereto as Appendix A.)

As president of the construction firm for the building, I am intimately involved in all of the cost estimates and other related details of the planning for the construction of the subject building. Accordingly, I declare that if the commencement of construction of the apartment building is delayed for an additional ten to twelve month period from the present time, I will incur substantial damages by way of increased costs for the proposed building. The following is my best estimate of such damages following as a direct result from such delay:

1. Forfeiture of cash deposit I have made with The Prudential Life Insurance Company of America in connection with the construction loan commitment that the company has made for this project. (Such forfeiture is expressly provided for in the event that the building is not completed, and is not being leased to tenants, by December 9, 1965). If construction could begin in the near future, I am informed that an extension of this default date could be obtained. $32,000.00

2. Increased labor costs for carpenters, laborers, cement finishers and other members of the general contractors work force. The union contracts involved are pending re-negotiation, and the unions concerned have requested an increase of $1.80 per hour over the present scale of $5.00 per hour. I estimate a settled increase of $1.00 per hour. $50,000.00

3. Increased labor costs for plumbers, pipe fitters and similar types of skilled labor. These costs arise from escalation in provisions of the controlling union contracts and are predicated on computations of J. Gibbs Sons, the plumbing subcontractor presently considered for the plumbing work. $15,000.00

4. Increased labor costs for electricians. Again, this increase will be due to an escalation provision of the governing union contract, as computed by Dahl-Beck Electric Corp., the prospective electrical subcontractor. $3,000.00

5. Increased labor costs for a crew of 12 men for drywall work, again under existing escalation provisions of union contracts. $7,000.00

6. The plasterers' union contract is being re-negotiated. It is estimated that there will be an increase in their wages. $1,250.00

7. Increased labor costs for floor workers, and for installers of doors and windows, again due to escalation provisions of existing union contracts. $4,000.00

8. In addition to the foregoing losses, I estimate a loss of rent for the building. Based on my experience and general knowledge related to similar buildings, I expect 50% occupancy for the first year, and of this rental income approximately 50% would be charged to ex-

penses and loan interest. For this building at 50% occupancy I expect a gross rental of $10,000.00 per month. $60,000.00

Total damages $162,250.00

In specifying the foregoing damages, I have completely omitted any estimate or allowance for increased cost of materials, notwithstanding the steadily rising costs of materials we have recently experienced and expect to continue to experience.

I declare further that I have fully discussed the above-entitled matter with my attorneys. They have advised me that I have a meritorious position in this appeal.

Based on the foregoing counsel of my architects, engineers and attorneys, and the foregoing analysis of my expected losses due to delay in construction, I hereby declare that if permitted to commence construction of the proposed building:

(1) I will modify the building as recommended by my architect by removing the top floor and two ground level apartments even after construction, to meet floor area ratio requirements of the City Planning Code if I should lose the appeal; and

(2) I will not change the present planned foundation, nor hold up its construction, pending the outcome of the appeal, once commenced.

I declare under penalty of perjury that the foregoing is true and correct. Executed at San Francisco, California.

Dated: June 18, 1965.

Perry Liebman

On July 12, 1965, the court of appeal denied the Association's petition, thus allowing Liebman to proceed with construction. According to Liebman's later-filed reply brief in the court of appeal, construction was "well-along" by January, 1966.

On October 31, 1966, the court of appeal released its decision affirming the superior court's decision seventeen months earlier, 54 Cal.Rptr. 562. Declaring that "the crucial inquiry here is whether the facts as found by the Board are sufficient to support its decision," and reviewing the Board's factfinding in detail, the court of appeal concluded that "these evidentiary findings constitute substantial evidence and sufficiently support the five findings cast in the language of the ordinance [Planning Code Section 302(d)]."

On December 1, 1966, the Association petitioned for a hearing in the California Supreme Court and Liebman answered on December 16. The court granted the petition on January 4, 1967.

BROADWAY, LAGUNA, VALLEJO ASSOCIATION v. BOARD OF PERMIT APPEALS

Supreme Court of California, 1967.
66 Cal.2d 767, 59 Cal.Rptr. 146, 427 P.2d 810.

TOBRINER, Associate Justice.

We must decide whether the San Francisco Board of Permit Appeals exceeded the scope of its authority in granting a variance under the circumstances of this case. That variance rested upon the alleged attractiveness of the proposed building, coupled with the belated discovery of subsoil conditions requiring a more costly foundation than anticipated. We conclude that the approval of a variance on such a basis would undermine the foundation of a comprehensive zoning law.

The controversy before us arose in 1963, when a developer (the real party in interest) contacted the Zoning Division of the Department of City Planning concerning a proposal to construct an 11-story, 53-unit apartment building on R-4 property located at 2030 Vallejo Street in San Francisco. The zoning division advised the developer that the proposed structure would contravene the floor area ratio regulations, which comprise the primary bullk and density control mechanism of the City Planning Code. The developer nonetheless refused to modify his plans before applying for a building permit in June 1964; in July the zoning division disapproved the developer's application.

Confronted with this obstacle to the execution of his project unless he obtained a variance, the developer undertook a study of subsoil conditions on his Vallejo Street property. Although he commenced the study several months after informing the Department of City Planning that the proposed structure was already designed, the developer, and ultimately the Board of Permit Appeals, relied exclusively upon this study to support the assertion that "unusual subsoil conditions" required a variance from the floor area ratio regulations.

After completing his subsoil investigation, the developer applied for a floor area variance in August 1964. He urged that the "unusual conditions" disclosed by his study would cause unnecessary hardship if the planning code were strictly enforced. He argued further that a variance from the requirements of a "minor" code provision seemed appropriate since his building would possess "attractive features" above and beyond those required by other code provisions.

The variance requested by the developer, however, did *not* involve a relatively unimportant code provision. On the contrary, the consensus among zoning authorities is that, in terms of controlling population density and structural congestion, the technique of restricting the ratio of a building's rentable floor space to the size of the lot on which it is constructed possesses numerous advantages, both theoretical and practical, shared by no other method of controlling building bulk or density. The developer in the present case thus sought more than relief from a purely technical requirement of an insignificant ordinance; he requested instead a variance from a regulation which has become a cornerstone of contemporary building codes.

To protect such crucial provisions from circumvention, the City Planning Code prohibits the granting of a variance unless the appropriate persons, beginning with the zoning administrator, have first determined that five specified conditions have been met. Having concluded that the developer's application complied with *none* of those conditions, the zoning administrator denied the application in October 1964.

Recognizing the need to accord appropriate weight to the expert administrator's ruling, the draftsmen of the City Planning Code provided that his determination could be overcome only by relevant and specific findings by the Board of Permit Appeals. In reversing the zoning administrator's decision in January 1965, the board purported to comply with the planning code by setting forth its findings with respect to all five code conditions. Acting under the mistaken belief that the board's ultimate conclusion was thereby insulated from judicial review, the trial court deemed itself powerless to grant a writ of mandate to compel the board to set aside its variance order. The petitioner, an association of interested property owners, then instituted this appeal.

Although the San Francisco Board of Permit Appeals possesses broad discretionary power in passing upon permit and licensing matters, it plays a more narrowly confined role in the variance area. Before granting a variance despite the zoning administrator's denial, the board must specify which aspects of the administrator's ruling it deems erroneous and must set forth in its findings "the facts relied upon in making [its] determination." (City Planning Code, § 303(d).)

This requirement for specific findings differentiates the present case from Siller v. Board of Supervisors (1962) 58 Cal.2d 479, 25 Cal. Rptr. 73, 375 P.2d 41, relied upon in the amicus curiae brief filed in support of respondents. That brief cites *Siller* for the proposition that a zoning board's action in granting a variance must be sustained in the absence of a clear and convincing showing of arbitrariness or caprice. Neither in *Siller*, nor in any other decision of similar import . . . did the governing provisions require the administrative board to specify its subsidiary findings and its ultimate conclusions.

The presumption that an agency's rulings rest upon the necessary findings and that such findings are supported by substantial evidence . . . does not apply to agencies which must expressly state their findings and must set forth the relevant supportive facts. In variance cases, the San Francisco Board of Permit Appeals is such an agency.

In a mandate proceeding to review the granting of a variance by that board, the variance order may be sustained only if the board's findings suffice to establish compliance with all of the statutory criteria and are supported by substantial evidence in the record.

The basic difficulty with the board's findings in the instant case is not that they lack evidentiary support but rather that they lack legal relevance; even if they are assumed to be correct, those findings simply do not meet the requirements of the planning code.

Viewed in the light most favorable to the board and to the developer, the evidence disclosed by the record before us supports the following findings of fact: (1) After the developer had been told that the proposed building would violate the floor area ratio regulations he undertook a study of his property which revealed that unusual subsoil conditions at that location would increase foundation costs for any structure similar to the one he proposed; (2) such increased costs would render the foundation of the proposed building from two and one-half to three times as expensive as the developer had anticipated; (3) because of this unexpectedly high fixed cost, the reduction of rentable floor space in this or any similar building to a level consistent with the floor area ratio regulations would prevent the developer from realizing as high a rate of return as he had hoped to obtain from his investment; and (4) the proposed building, apart from its excessive floor area, would conform to limitations more exacting than those imposed by the planning code with respect to height, lot coverage, number of dwelling units, uncovered areas, and parking facilities. Accepting these findings as true, we have concluded that they fail as a matter of law to satisfy the statutory criteria.[5]

1. *Exceptional Circumstances*

The first criterion which a variance application must meet is that there be "exceptional or extraordinary circumstances or conditions applying to the property involved, or to the intended use of the property, that do not apply generally to other property or uses in the same class of district." (City Planning Code, § 302(d).) The board purported to find two such "exceptional circumstances" here: (a) the unusual subsoil condition "applying to the property involved"; and (b) the attractive architectural features "applying to . . . the intended use of the property." Neither of these circumstances, however, satisfies the code criterion.

a. *Unusual Subsoil Condition*

We turn first to the subsoil condition belatedly discovered by the developer. On the evidence before it, the board could make no finding, nor did it attempt to make one, linking the subsoil condition to the asserted need for a floor area variance. Unlike cases in which

---

5. Since we conclude that the first three criteria have not been met, we do not pause to consider whether the last two have been satisfied.

topographical conditions prove to be physically incompatible with attempted adherence to a zoning provision, the case before us presents no logical relationship between the condition identified and the variance requested.

Admittedly, the soil conditions beneath the developer's property restrict its income potential; but the mere fact that a floor area variance would enable the developer to increase the rate of return upon his invested capital can hardly transform the developer's subsoil problem into the sort of "exceptional circumstance" contemplated by the code. In a word, "profit motive is not an adequate ground for a variance." (Beirn v. Morris (1954) 14 N.J. 529, 534–535, 103 A.2d 361, 363)

We recognize that virtually *any* circumstance which would lead a commercial real estate developer to seek a variance may ultimately be translated into economic terms: The developer attempts to obtain relief from a particular zoning provision in order to augment the earning power or the market value of his property. We must be careful to distinguish, however, between those circumstances which prevent a builder from profitably developing a lot within the strictures of the planning code and those conditions which simply render a complying structure *less profitable than anticipated.* If conditions which merely reduce profit margin were deemed sufficiently "exceptional" to warrant relief from the zoning laws, then all but the least imaginative developers could obtain a variety of variances, and the "public interest in the enforcement of a comprehensive zoning plan" (County of San Diego v. McClurken (1951) 37 Cal.2d 683, 690, 234 P.2d 972, 977) would inevitably yield to the private interest in the maximization of profits.

Keeping in mind this fundamental difference between circumstances which prevent a variance applicant from economically developing his property and those which simply reduce his expected earnings, we note that in the present case the board determined only that the "unusual subsoil condition" would increase the cost of the proposed building or of any similar high-rise structure. The board did not determine, however, that the subsoil condition in question would similarly increase the cost of a differently designed building.

Moreover, even if we were to assume, as did the board, that the developer could properly insist upon constructing an apartment building similar to the one he originally proposed, we would still confront a fatally defective record: The board made no finding in this case that the developer could not earn a *reasonable return* upon his investment after modifying his building to the extent necessary to comply with the floor area regulations, nor would the evidence before the board have supported any such conclusion.

In this connection, we note that in July 1965 the petitioners sought a writ of supersedeas to halt construction of the building pending appeal. The court denied the writ after the developer filed under penalty of perjury a declaration stating that if he were permitted to proceed with construction he would thereafter modify the building "by removing the top floor and two ground level apartments even after construction, to meet floor area ratio requirements of the City Planning Code if [he] should lose the appeal." Thus the developer assured the court that he would make the required modifications if the variance were later held improper. Having implied that he could proceed economically with his project even after altering it to comply with the governing floor area regulations, the developer can hardly claim now that his apartment building will yield an unreasonably low profit unless he is permitted to spread his foundation costs over a rentable floor area beyond that permitted by the code. At most, the developer may urge a reduction in expected revenue; as we have explained, however, such a claim does not rise to the "exceptional" level demanded by the code.

b. *Attractive Architectural Features*

Nor do the various architectural limitations incorporated in the developer's proposed structure constitute "extraordinary . . . conditions applying to . . . the intended *use* of the property" (italics added) within the meaning of the first variance criterion.

First, the concept of "intended use of the property" does not encompass the contemplated *design* of a building to be constructed on that property but refers only to the *activity* which is to be conducted there.[7] Second, an "intended use" does not constitute an "exceptional circumstance" unless it does not "apply generally to other . . . uses in the same class of district." In this regard, the board found only that the developer proposed "to build according to development standards which are more restrictive . . . than are the provisions of the Code themselves." The board then drew the conclusion that "[t]herefore, [the developer's] intended use of the property is unique and constitutes an exceptional circumstance." That conclusion was of course a non sequitur. The board made no finding, nor could it have done so on the evidence before it, that *other* buildings in the same zone were not *likewise* built "according to development standards . . . more restrictive . . . than . . . the provisions of the Code themselves."

2. *Unnecessary Hardship*

Even if the circumstances identified by the board could qualify under the first criterion, however, the variance should still have been

---

7. A broader construction of "intended use" might bring the code provision into conflict with state law, since Government Code section 65906 authorizes variances "only when, because of special circumstances applicable to the property, including size, shape, topography, location or surroundings, the strict application of the zoning ordinance deprives such property of privileges enjoyed by other property in the vicinity and under identical zoning classification." (See Comment (1962) 50 Cal.L.Rev. 101, 104, 110 & fn. 61.)

denied since the developer did not show that, as a result of such circumstances, "literal enforcement of [the floor area ratio regulations] would result in practical difficulty or unnecessary hardship." (City Planning Code, § 302(d).) The board found: (a) that, since the building would benefit the community, enforcement of the code would work a hardship upon the surrounding neighborhood; (b) that the developer's adoption of "superior to code" building standards would impose a hardship upon him if the variance were denied; and (c) that "the subsoil condition obviously constitutes a practical difficulty for development."

a. *Benefit to the Community*

With regard to the community benefit, the board's finding was neither relevant as a matter of law nor supportable as a matter of fact. Although impact upon the surrounding neighborhood is an important factor in the variance formula, the planning code specifically provides for its consideration under the fourth and fifth criteria. In requiring a showing that literal enforcement would cause hardship, the second criterion looks only to burdens upon the variance applicant.

Even if it had been legally relevant, however, the board's determination that the community would suffer if the floor area regulations were literally enforced would find no support whatever in the evidence. Accepting as true the board's finding that the "attractive features" of the developer's building would benefit the neighborhood, it does not follow that the community would sacrifice such benefits if the code were strictly enforced. Nothing in the record suggests that if his variance application should be denied the developer would forego his project or eliminate any of its beneficial features; indeed, the developer has indicated the contrary under penalty of perjury. Although a denial of a variance would cut into the developer's profit margin, the community derives benefit not from his financial gain but from his conforming building.

b. *Superior Building Standards*

Turning to the board's inclusion of the developer's adoption of superior building standards as an element of hardship upon the developer, we need only note that such self-imposed burdens cannot legally justify the granting of a variance.

c. *Practical Difficulty*

All that remains of the board's findings with regard to hardship is its observation that "the subsoil condition obviously constitutes a practical difficulty for development." But the only such "difficulty" supportable on this record must stem from the developer's claim of increased foundation cost. In this connection, the board simply concluded that *any economic sacrifice flowing from enforcement of the* floor area regulations should be deemed "unnecessary" in this case because the proposed building would more than comply with all *other* requirements pertinent to bulk and dimension. In reaching this conclusion, the board asserted that the floor area regulations merely duplicate those governing such factors as height, lot coverage, number of units, and open space. Apart from its shallowness, the board's approach rests upon an impermissible assumption: that the draftsmen engaged in an idle act when they added the floor area ratio regulations as independent requirements of the planning code.

The board's characterization of any resulting difficulty or hardship as *automatically* "unnecessary" in this case must stand or fall with the broad notion that a variance applicant may earn immunity from one code provision merely by overcompliance with others. Since few buildings are designed at planning code minimums, variance applications based upon this open-ended theory would soon become commonplace. The board would then be empowered to decide which code provisions to enforce in any given case; that power does not properly repose in any administrative tribunal.

3. *Preservation of Parity*

Entirely apart from "exceptional circumstances" and "unnecessary hardship," the planning code requires that a variance be denied unless it is "necessary for the preservation of a substantial property right of the [applicant] possessed by other property in the same class of district." (City Planning Code, § 302(d).) The board's findings in this case completely fail to establish compliance with this "parity" requirement.

In this connection, the board simply said: "[Developer] has a right to develop his property, notwithstanding adverse soil conditions. Because the Board finds that the variance in this case amounts to no more than an immaterial breach of the Code fully compensated by features of the building not demanded by the Code, and because the record shows that without the variance [the developer] cannot economically proceed with this attractive building, the Board finds that the variance is necessary to preserve that basic property right of [the developer]."

These findings, whether or not accurate, simply do not relate to the matter at hand. Neither the "immateriality" of the developer's breach, nor the extent to which self-imposed building features might "compensate" for it, bears upon the parity issue; nor can we attach any significance to the truism that the developer cannot construct this particular building without the variance he seeks.

Under its findings with respect to "exceptional circumstances," however, the board offered one conclusion of conceivable relevance to our present inquiry: "This site is adverse for multi-unit development in comparison with similar hillside building lots in this particular area." If the "adversity" to which the board referred were such that enforcement of the floor area regulations would effectively deprive the developer of the ability to construct a reasonably profitable multi-unit structure in an area zoned for multi-unit construction, then the requisite disparity of treatment might be established. As we have seen, however, that is not the case. At most, the developer here has suggested that, unless code requirements are relaxed, multi-unit development will prove somewhat less profitable on his lot than on other lots in the same zone. The short answer to the developer's argument is that zoning variances were never meant to insure against financial disappointments.

Although a variance must be denied unless all five of the specified code conditions have been independently fulfilled, the board's findings in the present case fail to establish compliance with the first three of those conditions; the board's decision to grant a variance therefore exceeded its statutory authority.

The variance sought by the developer in this case would confer not parity but privilege; to sanction such special treatment would seriously undermine present efforts to combat urban blight and municipal congestion through comprehensive zoning codes. So selective an application of the provisions of the City Planning Code would destroy the uniformity of the zoning laws which is their essence.

The judgment is reversed and the cause is remanded to the trial court with directions to issue a writ of mandate requiring the board to vacate its order awarding a variance and to affirm the zoning administrator's original decision denying that variance, and with additional directions to the trial court to grant such further relief as is appropriate.

TRAYNOR, C.J., and PETERS, MOSK, BURKE and SULLIVAN, JJ., concur.

McCOMB, Justice.

I dissent. I would affirm the judgment of the superior court denying a writ of mandate, for the reasons expressed by Mr. Justice Ageé in the opinion prepared by him for the Court of Appeal in Broadway, Laguna, Vallejo Ass'n v. Board of Permit Appeals (Cal. App.) 54 Cal.Rptr. 562.

QUESTIONS

The supreme court's decision in *Broadway, Laguna* doubtless came as a surprise to Liebman and his lawyers. With the decision, the court "signaled the beginning of a new era of judicial review of land development and environmental control controversies . . . . Few perceived at the time that these cases ushered in a new era of California Supreme Court review of governmental land-use decisions. During this new era, if a government made an environmentally insensitive decision, it would lose." Aside from certain narrow exceptions, "neighbors and public interest groups *never* lost in the 1966–1977 period and developers and landowners *nearly always* lost." DiMento, *et al.*, Land Development and Environmental Control in the California Supreme Court: The Deferential, the Preservationist, and the Preservationist-Erratic Eras, 27 U.C.L.A.L.Rev. 859, 863, 879 (1980).

According to the DiMento study, "because *Broadway, Laguna* involved a *height* variance, regarded as less hostile to zoning than a *use* variance, only cautious attorneys took note. A leading California land-use lawyer opened a subsequent speech as follows: 'Because the . . . case could note the demise of the variance as *the* implement for flexibility . . . alternative solutions for flexibility must be found.' Less cautious attorneys took the court at its word and believed that the strict scrutiny was applied in *Broadway, Laguna* only because of the peculiar provisions in the San Francisco ordinance. The incautious were proved wrong by *Topanga* [Topanga Association for a Scenic Community v. County of Los Angeles, 11 Cal.3d 506, 113 Cal.Rptr. 836, 522 P.2d 12] in 1974. Strict scrutiny of variances was by then sweeping the country." *Id.* 955.

Representing Liebman, could you have made any arguments connecting the adverse subsoil condition to the need for an FAR variance? Would you have attempted to quantify the income lost as a result of the subsoil condition and compliance with the FAR requirement? If so, how would you go about doing the computation? In retrospect, does the supreme court's repeated reference to Liebman's Declaration of June 18, as evidence that the building could be operated at a profit even if FAR requirements were met, suggest that Liebman made a strategic error in filing the Declaration?

Did the Association—or the Court of Appeal—make a strategic error in not demanding more than a declaration as the basis for denying the writ of supersedeas? Recall the materials on improving trespassers and easements by estoppel, pages 60 and 676 above, and consider whether a wrongdoer who has unlawfully made a valuable improvement will always enjoy a strategic advantage over the rightdoer who puts off improving land until her rights in it have been established. Should the Association have insisted—or the court required—that Liebman at least file a bond securing the performance of his promise in the event he lost the appeal?

Norman Williams has called *Broadway, Laguna* "the leading case on FAR restrictions." 1 N. Williams, American Planning Law 696 (1974). Calling the supreme court's decision "the strongest legal blow yet struck at San Francisco's powerful Board of Permit Appeals", an article in the May 27, 1967, *San Francisco Chronicle* said that the decision against Liebman "will evidently cost him the top floor of his new 11-story $2 million structure." Do you think it did?

d. Postscript

It would be logical—but mistaken—to assume that following the supreme court's decision in *Broadway, Laguna*, Liebman removed the top floor and two ground floor apartments at 2030 Vallejo. As in private disputes, so in zoning matters, a final judicial decree frequently represents only a prelude to further negotiations. The principal difference is that negotiations following zoning decisions must accommodate the fact that the state is a party and that its interests, mission, personnel and processes are directly implicated. In a word, it is generally a far more complicated task to strike a bargain in these cases than in cases involving an equal number of private parties.

What happened, then, after the California Supreme Court rendered its decision? The Association returned to superior court seeking an order requiring Liebman to remove the top floor and two ground floor apartments from the building in accordance with Liebman's Declaration of June 21, 1965. Liebman replied on August 8, 1967, that a writ of mandate could not effectively issue against him since he was a private individual and not an officer of the court and, further, that his June 21 Declaration did not constitute a stipulation that the trial court was bound to enforce. In support of this second point, Liebman argued that his Declaration was the basis only for an *offer* to stipulate, an offer that had been rejected by the Association; further, there was nothing to show that the district court of appeal had relied on the Declaration in denying the writ of supersedeas. Liebman also claimed that the interests of third parties—his construction lender, permanent lender, and the tenants in the building—would be adversely affected by compliance with the order; that other, less onerous methods of correcting the FAR violation were available; and that he could lawfully submit a new application for a variance, so long as it was supported by additional factual evidence which was not presented to the Zoning Administrator or to the Board of Permit Appeals in conjunction with the prior application. And, as the clincher, Liebman called the court's attention "to the affidavit of Perry Liebman, herein, in which he sets forth the circumstances of his present legal insolvency. He is without sufficient funds to effect the removal of the top floor and two ground level apartments and he is without borrowing capacity to obtain the funds for that purpose."

Six days before filing his reply, Liebman had acquired an option to purchase the premises at 2010 Vallejo, a 4,169 square foot parcel adjacent to the 2030 property on the east. As this parcel, like 2030 Vallejo, was situated in an R–4 district, a 4.8 FAR applied, allowing a 20,012 square foot building on the parcel. At the time Liebman acquired the option to the premises, 2010 Vallejo consisted of a three-story, six-unit apartment house of approximately 9000 square feet—roughly 11,000 square feet less than the permitted maximum. Since the building at 2030 Vallejo exceeded the permissible maximum by 10,333 square feet, Liebman figured that by purchasing 2010 Vallejo and combining it with the 2030 parcel for purposes of the zoning ordinance, the new parcel would in the aggregate satisfy all FAR zoning requirements. Discussions with the Association, aimed at achieving this result, proceeded slowly but with apparent effect, for on December 22, 1967, Liebman and a partner acquired the 2010 Vallejo parcel and, in early January, 1968, Liebman and the Association agreed to cooperate in terminating the dispute. According to Laurence Popofsky of Heller, Ehrman, "We were satisfied that a San Francisco court would be reluctant to order destruction of the top floor of the building if any viable alternative could be proposed. Since the building was up, there was little to be gained in practical terms so far as the neighborhood was concerned; hence the proposed solution, duly recorded and binding for all time, seemed like a reasonable 'out.' As for the claimed insolvency, we assumed it would be cured by the lenders, as presumably it was."

AGREEMENT

This agreement is made with reference to the following facts:

Broadway, Laguna, Vallejo Association, Michele Weill, Glenn A. Stackhouse, Maude H. Lyons and L.P. Brassy ("Petitioners"), the Board of Permit Appeals of the City and County of San Francisco, its officers and commissioners, the Zoning Administrator of the City and County of San Francisco, and Perry Liebman are parties litigant in certain proceedings now pending in the Superior Court of the State of California in and for the City and County of San Francisco ("Action No. 552685").

Said proceedings are upon remand from the decision of the Supreme Court of the State of California in Broadway, etc., Assn. v. Board of Permit Appeals, 66 AC 798 (May 26, 1967). The Court therein determined that, under the facts presented in the record, the Board of Permit Appeals erred in awarding a variance from the floor area ratio regulations with regard to a then proposed structure upon Assessor's Block No. 555, Lots 10 and 13, more commonly known as 2030 Vallejo Street.

The construction of the proposed structure was completed during the process of appellate review pursuant to foundation and building permits granted by the Department of Public Works.

All parties now desire that a just and equitable method be found whereby said structure can be made to comply with said floor area ratio regulations.

A recorded option to purchase that certain property known as 2010 Vallejo Street, Lot No. 9, adjacent to the subject property, has been obtained on Liebman's behalf.

R. Spencer Steele, Zoning Administrator, and Robert Kenealey, Esq., Deputy City Attorney, have acknowledged that the acquisition of title to said property by Perry Liebman, the execution and filing in the office of the Recorder of the City and County of San Francisco of the Notice of Special Restrictions in the form appended hereto as Exhibit "A", and the combining of Lot 9 with Lots 10 and 13 in the manner indicated therein will eliminate any floor area ratio violation presently existing.

The parties do therefore agree as follows:

1. Perry Liebman has exercised said option. Upon the acquisition of 2010 Vallejo Street by Perry Liebman, the combination of 2010 Vallejo Street with 2030 Vallejo Street in the manner indicated in Exhibit "A", and the filing of a notice in the form of said Exhibit "A", all parties in the above proceedings on remand agree to stipulate in the form of stipulation attached hereto as Exhibit "B" and to cooperate in the termination of said proceedings in accordance with the terms of said Exhibit "B".

2. In consideration for Petitioners' agreement to join in said stipulation, Perry Liebman agrees to pay Petitioners' actual costs, disbursements and attorney's fees incurred in all court proceedings in Action No. 552685 up to a maximum of $5,000.00 upon the execution of said stipulation and the entry of the order referred to therein.

3. This agreement is understood to be a compromise with respect to the positions asserted by the parties hereto in Action No. 552685 and shall not estop or prevent any party hereto from seeking or initiating new enforcement proceedings in the future in the event the floor area of the structure at 2030 Vallejo is found to be in violation of zoning regulations by reason of the subsequent severance of 2030 Vallejo from 2010 Vallejo through the foreclosure of liens upon either parcel or through other action effecting such severance.

DATED: _____

    Heller, Ehrman, White & McAuliffe

    By _____
      M. Laurence Poposky,
      Attorneys for
      Petitioners

    Perry Liebman

The City Attorney and Zoning Administrator of the City and County of San Francisco hereby approve of this agreement and acknowledge that the representations attributed to them therein are true and correct.

Thomas O'Connor, City Attorney

By _____
  Robert A. Kenealey,
  Deputy City Attorney

R. Spencer Steele, Zoning Administrator

EXHIBIT A

Department of City Planning   Recorded at: Book _____
                                                  Page _____

NOTICE OF SPECIAL RESTRICTIONS UNDER THE CITY PLANNING CODE

I

The undersigned owners of that certain real property situate in the City and County of San Francisco, State of California generally described as 2030 Vallejo Street and 2010 Vallejo Street (Assessor's Block No. 555, Lots 9, 10 and 13) and more particularly described as follows:

Parcel one: COMMENCING at a point on the northerly line of Vallejo Street, distant thereon 147 feet westerly from the westerly line of Laguna Street; and running thence westerly along said line of Vallejo Street 58 feet; thence at a right angle northerly 137 feet 6 inches; thence at a right angle easterly 58 feet; thence at a right angle southerly 137 feet 6 inches to the point of commencement. BEING a part of Western Addition Block No. 243.

Parcel two: COMMENCING at a point on the northerly line of Vallejo Street, distant thereon 99 feet westerly from the westerly line of Laguna Street; running thence westerly along said line of Vallejo Street 48 feet; thence at a right angle northerly 137 feet 6 inches; thence at a right angle easterly 48 feet; thence at a right angle southerly 137 feet 6 inches to the point of commencement. BEING a part of Western Addition Block No. 243.

Parcel three: COMMENCING at a point on the northerly line of Vallejo Street, distant thereon 68 feet and 9 inches westerly from the westerly line of Laguna Street; thence westerly along said line of Vallejo Street 30 feet and 3 inches; thence at a right angle northerly 137 feet and 6 inches; thence at a right angle easterly 30 feet and 3 inches; thence at a right angle southerly 137 feet and 6 inches to the point of commencement. BEING a portion of Western Addition Block No. 243.

hereby give notice that there are special restrictions on the use of said property under Part II, Chapter II of the San Francisco Municipal Code (City Planning Code).

II

Said special restrictions are as follows:

To satisfy the floor-area ratio requirement of the City Planning Code, all property described above must be retained as one parcel of land. This shall be accomplished by recording in the Recorder's Office a single deed covering all of the above property and requesting the assessment of all such property as one parcel.

III

The use of said property contrary to these special restrictions shall constitute a violation of the City Planning Code, and no release, modification or elimination of these special restrictions shall be valid unless notice thereof is recorded on the Land Records by the Zoning Administrator of the City and County of San Francisco.

The owners of said property may apply for the removal of said restrictions if and when said restrictions are no longer necessary to satisfy the floor-area ratio requirement of the City Planning Code.

DATED January 9, 1968 at San Francisco, California.

/s/ _____
Perry Liebman

/s/ _____
Bernard Schnitzer

EXHIBIT B

FELDMAN, WALDMAN & KLINE
2700 Russ Building
235 Montgomery Street
San Francisco, California 94104
Telephone: 981–1300

Attorneys for Perry Liebman
Respondent and Real Party in Interest

IN THE SUPERIOR COURT OF THE STATE OF CALIFORNIA
IN AND FOR THE CITY AND COUNTY
OF SAN FRANCISCO

Broadway, Laguna, Vallejo Association, Michele Weill, Glenn A. Stackhouse, Maude H. Lyons, L.P. Brassy, Petitioners, vs. Board of Permit Appeals of the City and County of San Francisco; and Perry Liebman, Real Party in Interest, et al., Respondents.	NO. 552685 Stipulation to Issue Writ of Mandate and Terminate Proceedings

IT IS HEREBY STIPULATED AND AGREED by and between the parties that the Court in this proceeding on remand after the opinion of the Supreme Court of the State of California in the above matter filed May 26, 1967 issue a Writ of Mandate in the form appended hereto, said Writ of Mandate being in full compliance with that opinion and with the remittitur issued pursuant thereto, and that all proceedings in this action be terminated.

DATED: _____, 1967.

Respondents

By _____
Robert Kenealey,
Deputy City Attorney

Heller, Ehrman, White & McAuliffe

By _____
M. Laurence Popofsky,
Attorneys for Petitioners

Jesse Feldman, Attorney
for Respondent Perry
Liebman, Real Party in
Interest.

FELDMAN, WALDMAN & KLINE
2700 Russ Building
235 Montgomery Street
San Francisco, California 94104
Telephone: 981-1300

Attorneys for Perry Liebman
Respondent and Real Party in Interest

IN THE SUPERIOR COURT OF THE STATE OF CALIFORNIA
IN AND FOR THE CITY AND COUNTY OF SAN FRANCISCO

Broadway, Laguna, Vallejo Association, Michele Weill, Glenn A. Stackhouse, Maude H. Lyons, L.P. Brassy,
Petitioners,
vs.
Board of Permit Appeals of the City and County of San Francisco; and Perry Liebman, Real Party in Interest, et al.,
Respondents.

NO. 552685
WRIT OF MANDATE

IT IS HEREBY COMMANDED that respondent Board of Permit Appeals, its officers and commissioners, (1) vacate their order in Appeal V-3754 entered on January 11, 1967, disapproving the decision of the Zoning Administrator and granting respondent Perry Liebman the variance sought in Application VZ64.61 with respect to that certain property located at 2030 Vallejo Street, North Line 99 feet west of Laguna Street (Assessor's Block No. 555, Lots No. 10 and 13), and (2) enter a new order affirming the decision of respondent Clyde O. Fisher, Jr., Zoning Administrator of the City and County of San Francisco, in VZ64.61;

IT IS HEREBY FURTHER COMMANDED (1) that respondent Zoning Administrator of the City and County of San Francisco reinstate his original order in VZ64.61 denying the application of respondent Perry Liebman for a variance and (2) that respondent Department of Public Works of the City and County of San Francisco and Myron Tatarian, as Director of said Department, vacate all building permits based upon said variance and immediately thereupon grant and issue, without any fees or charges whatsoever to Perry Liebman, a new permit by reason of a new application which has been submitted by respondent Perry Liebman based upon the combination, heretofore accomplished by said respondent of property at 2010 Vallejo Street, (Assessor's Block No. 555, Lot No. 9), with said 2030 Vallejo Street property in such manner as to comply with said floor-area ratio requirements.

ATTEST my hand and the seal of this Court on _____, 1967.

MARTIN MONGAN, Clerk

By _____

ORDER

Let the within Writ issue.

Dated: _____

_____
Judge of the Superior Court

QUESTIONS

What would have happened if 2010 Vallejo had not been available for purchase? Is it reasonable to assume that land is *always* available for purchase, the only question being at what price? If the owner of 2010 Vallejo knew that Liebman was behind the offer to buy the parcel, how much more than "fair market value" might he have been able to obtain from Liebman for the land? (Recall that there was a small building on the other side of 2030 Vallejo that evidently would have served Liebman's purpose just as well.) Apart from strategic behavior, what effect did development of the 2030 Vallejo parcel probably have on the value of the 2010 Vallejo parcel? Clearly, by interfering with light, air and other amenities, it diminished the parcel's value for use as a six-unit residence. But, might it have increased the lot's value for purposes of high rise development?

From the viewpoint of the Zoning Administrator, would you have been satisfied that the ultimate result—combination of the 2030 and 2010 Vallejo parcels for purposes of computing FAR—achieved the density objectives established by the Code? From the viewpoint of the Board of Permit Appeals? The California Supreme Court? From the Association's viewpoint, would you have been happy with the ultimate outcome of the case? From Liebman's viewpoint? With the benefit of hindsight, what different steps would you have counseled the Association or Liebman to take from the outset?

C. SUBDIVISION REGULATION

Like zoning, subdivision regulation gives local government a powerful tool for ordering private land use and allocating the social costs of development. At a first glance, a typical subdivision ordinance might appear to have only a modest reach—requiring simply that for a parcel to be lawfully subdivided, and for lots in the subdivision to be sold, a map describing the subdivision must first be filed in the appropriate government office. The ordinance's true reach lies in the requirements it imposes for the map to be accepted for filing. Among the more moderate requirements are that the map contain an accurate legal description of the subdivision lots and a sensibly designed "infrastructure"—well-planned and engineered street, drainage, water and sewerage systems and sidewalks, street and traffic signs, traffic lights and fire hydrants. The ordinance may also require the developer to install and pay for the subdivision's complete infrastructure and to provide space and funds for parks, schools, fire stations and other facilities to serve the subdivision.

The history of subdivision regulation in this country reveals a gradual evolution from modest goals toward more ambitious objects. The first subdivision regulations were primarily concerned with improving land conveyancing procedures. The use of lengthy metes and bounds descriptions to identify a parcel each time it was transferred meant not only wasted time and effort, but also unavoidable errors and omissions in deed descriptions. To overcome these problems, early subdivision ordinances required that every subdivision be surveyed, legally described, and then drawn on a map, with each individual lot identified on the map by number or letter. Thus, instead of rehearsing an extensive description each time a parcel was sold, the parcel could be simply described by reference to the map—for example, "Lot 7, in Block 49 in Barton's Subdivision, according to the plat thereof recorded as document No. 173711, deed records of Cook County, Illinois."

These early ordinances also required the developer to plot out all internal roads serving the subdivision. It was but a small step from this descriptive function to a set of qualitative requirements—that the internal roads connect to streets outside the subdivision and that they be wide enough to accommodate fire trucks and other firefighting apparatus. A series of similarly small steps led to the requirements that the subdivision be proximate to fire and police stations and to water and sewage service, and then to the requirement that the subdivider itself install the infrastructure facilities needed to service the subdivision. (Municipalities had long assessed individual lot owners for the cost of installing the water and sewer mains that served their homes; making the subdivider pay was viewed as simply a more efficient method for collecting these charges.)

The Standard City Planning Enabling Act of 1928 brought these scattered efforts at subdivision description and regulation into the planning mainstream by authorizing regulations that "may provide for the proper arrangement of streets in relation to other existing or planned streets and to the master plan, for adequate and convenient open spaces for traffic, utilities, access of firefighting apparatus, recreation, light and air, and for the avoidance of congestion of population, including minimum width and area of lots. Such regulations may include provisions as to the extent to which streets and other ways shall be graded and improved and to which water and sewer and other utility mains, piping, or other facilities shall be installed as a condition precedent to the approval of the plat." U.S. Dept. of Commerce, A Standard City Planning Enabling Act § 14.

Today, a developer seeking subdivision approval will typically begin by talking with local officials to determine their feelings about the proposed project and the changes that may be required to make the project more acceptable to the community. Eventually, the developer will submit a preliminary map, identifying lots, roads, utilities and easements, for approval by the local planning commission or other designated agency. Copies of the proposed map will be distributed for comment to interested public agencies such as the public health department, parks and recreation department, the school board, the municipal engineer, and the fire and police departments. The planning commission will then review the comments from these interested agencies, as well as from its own planning staff, and, after negotiating with the developer over site design and subdivision exactions, will make its decision to approve or disapprove the preliminary map.

If the preliminary map is approved, the developer must then install the infrastructure facilities agreed upon in the plan or, alternatively, obtain a bond guaranteeing that the required infrastructure will be completed according to plan within a specified period. Once the developer has made, or bonded, all of the infrastructure improvements, and met all other conditions attached to the preliminary map, the commission will approve the final map, the developer will file the map with the appropriate governmental agency and, finally, will begin developing and selling parcels.

The next principal case, Board of Education v. Surety Developers, Inc., addresses the question of how subdivision regulations should be coordinated with other land use control regulations. Other questions abound. What are the limits to a municipality's power to impose conditions on developers? Should the answer turn on whether the conditions imposed call for dedication of land or for cash payments? These questions, and others, are considered in the notes following *Surety Developers*.

BOARD OF EDUCATION OF SCHOOL DIST. NO. 68 v. SURETY DEVELOPERS, INC.

Supreme Court of Illinois, 1976.
63 Ill.2d 193, 347 N.E.2d 149.

UNDERWOOD, Chief Justice:

The basic issue presented by this case concerns the authority of a county board to require a real estate developer to contribute land or money for school facilities as a condition to the issuance of special use permits necessary to development of a subdivision. The circuit court of Du Page County held that such authority did not exist, the appellate court reversed and we granted leave to appeal.

Defendant, Surety Developers, Inc., a building and land development corporation, acquired early in 1958 about 465 acres of unimproved farm land in an unincorporated area of Du Page County. At the time of purchase, defendant intended to divide the land into lots of one or more acres, to service the lots with individual septic tanks and wells, and to sell the vacant lots as so improved. Subsequent seepage tests, however, showed the land unsuitable for individual septic tanks.

The R-2 residential zoning of the area permitted defendant to develop an alternate plan involving dividing the land into lots of less than one acre, and building homes on the smaller lots. The zoning regulations, however, required that lots of this size be served by public water and sewage treatment facilities. No public facilities were available which could be economically extended to serve defendant's property. Consequently, in order to develop the land, defendant would have to build community water and sewer systems, permissible only if the County Board of Supervisors granted a special use permit.

Defendant filed applications for special use permits to build a permanent community sewage treatment plant, two temporary sewage treatment plants, two permanent well sites, and a permanent water tower. On July 31, 1958, the county zoning board of appeals held a public hearing to consider the special use applications. A majority of the approximately 150 persons in attendance opposed the request, citing, among other grounds, that the school could not absorb the projected increase in enrollment. During the 1958–59 school year, plaintiff school district had only a five-classroom school located more than a mile from the proposed development, with an enrollment of 97 students.

The zoning board of appeals, by letter to the County Board of Supervisors, recommended denial of the special use applications, indicating:

"The Board is unanimously of the opinion that the issuance of these Special Use Permits will allow a subdivision development that is entirely out of character with the uses of adjacent and adjoining property and which would tend to diminish their property values, add to the hazards on the public streets and highways and place a considerable burden on the country school which serves the area."

The zoning board of appeals' recommendation was to be first considered by the building and zoning committee, which would then make its recommendation to the full Board of Supervisors. Defendant began to discuss this problem with individual Board members, was granted a hearing before the committee, and attempted without success to negotiate with plaintiff. On August 19, 1958, after meeting with the committee, defendant, by letter to it, proposed the following plan in response to the committee's expressed concern regarding schools:

"Insofar as our development will create the need for additional class room facilities in the Goodrich School District, it is our intent to be cooperative with those needs. We therefore agree to the following:

1. We will furnish houses as temporary school facilities at a minimum rental to the School Board, if required, until permanent school facilities can be erected.

2. We will furnish the ground, build a permanent school facility and lease same to the Goodrich School District at a nominal rental of $1.00 per year for a period not to exceed five years, the School Board to purchase said facilities prior to the expiration of the rental term at 80% of the total costs of the facilities."

The county board thereafter granted three of the four requested special uses, denying only the requested operation of the temporary sewage treatment plants. Each special use permit contained as a condition the verbatim proposals in defendant's letter to the committee. The board also approved defendant's first subdivision plat, and within 13 months defendant secured approval of two more subdivision plats in the same area.

Defendant intended to build homes selling in the $14,000 to $17,000 range. It sought the approval of the Veterans Administration (V.A.), since, if that agency determined that the subdivision met its requirements for planning, construction and general acceptability, the V.A. would agree to guarantee private financing when homes were sold to veterans. While the V.A. was still considering the matter, several of plaintiff's representatives visited the agency's Chicago office to complain of the burden that defendant's development would place on the school system. On November 14, 1958, the V.A. wrote a letter to defendant suggesting that as a condition of V.A. approval of the subdivision plans, defendant take responsibility to insure the availability of schools. Defendant replied that it shared this concern and was presently meeting with plaintiff to draw up a formal agreement. Defendant also requested that the V.A. grant conditional approval with the understanding that no loans or sales to veterans would be closed until plaintiff and defendant had signed an agreement. On December 12, 1958, the V.A. issued the conditional approval.

On March 24, 1959, plaintiff and defendant signed an agreement that was, in substance, the same as the conditions of the special use permits, and defendant's original proposal. Plaintiff notified the V.A. of the agreement and the condition was deleted from the V.A.'s approval.

Defendant subsequently began to experience difficulties performing under the agreement. After a series of correspondence and conversations, plaintiff and defendant entered into a new agreement on February 15, 1960. Defendant agreed to donate to plaintiff an improved parcel of land for use as school grounds (stipulated value $35,000), to pay plaintiff $50,000 as an initial contribution toward the construction of the permanent school, and to pay an additional $200 for each home thereafter constructed and occupied in the subdivision. Plaintiff agreed to erect a school building on the site, to request the voters to approve a bond issue, and to cancel the March 24 agreement when defendant made the initial deposit.

All parts of the February 15 agreement were performed except the requirement that defendant pay $200 per home toward the cost of the new school facilities. In 1969, plaintiff brought an action in the circuit court of Du Page County to collect those amounts. At the time of trial, payments for 1030 homes were in issue. Defendant asserted there and maintains here that both contracts were unenforceable because compelled by the attachment to the special use permits of illegal conditions, and counterclaimed for the value of the land ($35,000), and the $50,000 contribution. The trial court agreed and entered judgments for defendant on the complaint and awarded defendant $85,000 on the counterclaim both of which, as earlier noted, were reversed by the appellate court.

The essence of defendant's position is that the conditions imposed on the special use permits were not voluntarily initiated or agreed to by defendant, were not authorized by statute, and bore no relationship to the special use requested by defendant. It urges that Rosen v. Village of Downers Grove (1960), 19 Ill.2d 448, 167 N.E.2d 230, and Duggan v. County of Cook (1975), 60 Ill.2d 107, 324 N.E.2d 406, sustain its position. Additionally, it urges that the conditions imposed deprived it of its property without compensation contrary to the holdings of Pioneer Trust and Savings Bank v. Village of Mount Prospect (1961), 22 Ill.2d 375, 176 N.E.2d 799, and People ex rel. Exchange National Bank of Chicago v. City of Lake Forest (1968), 40 Ill.2d 281, 239 N.E.2d 819.

The authority of a county board of supervisors to attach conditions to a special use permit derives from section 1 of "An Act in relation to county zoning" (Ill.Rev.Stat.1973, ch. 34, par. 3151; formerly par. 152i), as interpreted in Kotrich v. County of Du Page (1960), 19 Ill.2d 181, 166 N.E.2d 601. *Kotrich* involved the validity of the same special use ordinance now before us. It was there held that the special use technique is authorized by statute, and the court said, in relation to the ordinance, "It also empowers the board of supervisors to impose 'such . . . conditions as it considers necessary to protect the public health, safety and welfare.' A fair reading of the ordinance shows that it contemplates that the county board will weigh the desirability of the proposed use against its potential adverse impact." 19 Ill.2d 181, 187, 166 N.E.2d 601, 604.

Six weeks later the court announced its opinion in *Rosen*. The issue there was the validity of a village ordinance enacted under the Revised Cities and Villages Act, which authorized the creation of a plan commission, the adoption of an official plan and the commission's examination of proposed subdivision plats to insure their conformity with the requirements of the official plan. The village plan commission had approved two subdivision plats, subject to the condition that the landowners secure a certificate of compliance from local boards of education. In the case of one of the landowners, the board of education issued its certificate only after the landowner agreed, in effect, to pay the school districts $325 for each lot sold in the subdivision. This court there stated, citing Petterson v. City of Naperville (1956), 9 Ill.2d 233, 137 N.E.2d 371, that under the statute a "developer of a subdivision may be required to assume those costs which are specifically and uniquely attributable to his activity and which would otherwise be cast upon the public." (19 Ill.2d 448, 453, 167 N.E.2d 230, 233.) However, since the $325 per lot assessment had been determined by considering factors totally unrelated to the proposed subdivision and since the statute did not authorize the imposition of monetary charges as a condition to plat approval, this court held that the circuit court properly enjoined those practices. Whether a municipality could, under the statute, require the dedication of land for school grounds was not considered.

Pioneer, too, was concerned with the validity of a village ordinance. The specific portion there in issue required that a subdivider dedicate land for public use according to a stated formula. The court there restated the *Rosen* test in the following language:

"If the requirement is within the statutory grant of power to the municipality *and* if the burden cast upon the subdivision is specifically and uniquely attributable to his activity, then the requirement is permissible; if not, it is forbidden and amounts to a confiscation of private property in contravention of the constitutional prohibitions rather than reasonable regulation under the police power." (Emphasis supplied.) 22 Ill.2d 375, 380, 176 N.E.2d 799, 802.

The significance of this statement is that land dedication requirements in Illinois that were not specifically and uniquely attributable to the activity of the subdivider were now constitutionally infirm, as well as unauthorized by statute. The "specifically and uniquely attributable" test was reaffirmed as a constitutional requirement in People ex rel. Exchange National Bank of Chicago v. City of Lake Forest (1968), 40 Ill.2d 281, 286–87, 239 N.E.2d 819, and, while *Rosen* and *Pioneer* concerned village ordinances enacted under the authority of a municipal plat and subdivision statute, which has a county counterpart in section 25.09 of the statute relating to the powers of county boards (Ill.Rev.Stat.1973, ch. 34, par. 414), and the present case concerns the special use technique authorized by section 1 of the County Zoning Act (Ill.Rev.Stat.1973, ch. 34, par. 3151), which has a municipal counterpart in section 11–13–1.1 of the Illinois Municipal Code (Ill.Rev.Stat.1973, ch. 24, par. 11–13–1.1), defendant is correct in asserting that the elevation of the *Rosen* test to a constitutional basis in *Pioneer* applies to land dedication requirements regardless of the legislation involved.

As earlier indicated, *Rosen* and *Pioneer* both held invalid the contributions required of the developers in those cases. At no time, however, has this court held that land dedication requirements for school grounds are unauthorized by the Municipal Code or predecessor statutes. Nor has it held that land dedication requirements for school grounds are automatically in violation of the Constitution. Quite the contrary is true, for the implications of both *Rosen* and *Pioneer* are that land dedication requirements proportioned to the needs specifically and uniquely attributable to the developer's activities would be valid.

We note that the American Law Institute in its Model Land Development Code similarly recommends that a county be empowered to authorize the conditioning of a special development permit on the developer's dedication of land for schools, or fees in lieu of dedication, so long as the demands are "reasonably allocable to the development—measured in terms of the need for such facilities created by the development." A Model Land Development Code (Proposed Official Draft No. 1, 1974), sec. 2–103(3), Note, at 44–47. . . .

Defendant urges that the conditions imposed relating to schools bear no reasonable relationship to a special use permitting community sewer and water facilities. We do not agree that so restricted a view is required. Neither we nor the county board members need blind ourselves to the applicant's ultimate objective in seeking the permit or the ultimate result of its issuance. Once issued, defendant was free to develop a small-lot subdivision with an unmistakable impact upon the existing school system, and intended to do so. The extent of that impact is demonstrated by the fact that at the time this case was tried there were approximately 1400 children in the two elementary schools in defendant's subdivision, 98% of whom were from this development.

Plaintiff has suggested that our "specifically and uniquely attributable" test is more narrowly drawn than the Constitution demands, and urges that we reexamine this test in light of more recent holdings in other jurisdictions. We consider such reexamination unnecessary here, however, for in our opinion the conditions imposed in this case were designed to alleviate a school problem specifically and uniquely attributable to defendant's activity. *Pioneer* involved the addition of a 250-lot subdivision to an existing municipality. The court found that the school needs were the result of the total development of the community and not specifically and uniquely attributable to the new addition—yet the village plan commission attempted to require the developer to pay the entire cost of remedying a problem not entirely of his making. The dedication requirement was simply not limited to the portion of the school needs specifically and uniquely attributable to the developer's activity. By contrast, the subdivision before us was not an addition to an existing municipality but the commencement of a new one. This case arose precisely because defendant chose to purchase and develop land in a sparsely settled rural area, so far from public sewer and water facilities that it had to construct community facilities. Defendant dramatically changed the character of the surrounding area. By the time defendant submitted its third subdivision plat for approval in September, 1959, it was appearing before the Board of Trustees for the newly incorporated Village of Woodridge rather than the Du Page County Board of Supervisors. The conditions imposed by the county board on the special use permit required defendant to dedicate land for a school site and to contribute a modest percentage towards the cost of a school building which defendant would erect and sell to the school board at a reduced figure. As earlier noted, at the time of trial in 1972, nearly 98% of the students attending the schools subsequently built in defendant's development lived inside the development. While this factor is not by itself determinative, we find ample evidence that the need for more schools was almost entirely attributable to defendant's activity; the conditions imposed clearly were reasonable in light of defendant's contribution to the creation of the school problem.

We hold, therefore, that the conditions were authorized by statute, were a reasonable regulation under the police power, and in conformity with the tests enunciated in *Rosen* and *Pioneer*. . . .

What we have said, we think, substantially disposes of defendant's arguments that the contracts were the result of duress since those arguments were predicated on the alleged illegality of the conditions imposed upon the special use permits. Complaint is also made of the school district's intervention in defendant's negotiations with the Veterans Administration seeking financing guarantees for veterans who purchased defendant's homes. The Veterans Administration, however, also had a responsibility: to ascertain that defendant's subdivision and available facilities, including schools, were adequate and merited approval. We see nothing sinister in the fact that in doing so it listened to the view of, or consulted with, school district representatives.

The present action is, of course, founded on the second contract, which substantially differs from the original. This second contract, however, was negotiated at defendant's urging and presumably to its advantage; it was not required by the county board. Since we have held the first contract valid, the second is obviously so.

The judgment of the appellate court is affirmed and the cause remanded to the circuit court of Du Page County for further proceedings consistent with this opinion.

Affirmed and remanded.

SCHAEFER, Justice (dissenting):

By this decision the court has conferred upon county boards the power to impose requirements of cash payments as conditions for the granting of permits for special uses. No such authority has ever been granted by any statute, either to counties or municipalities, and all of the previous decisions of this court have denied that such an authority exists. . . .

When the *Rosen* case was decided in 1960, and when Pioneer Trust and Savings Bank v. Village of Mount Prospect, 22 Ill.2d 375, 176 N.E.2d 799, was decided in 1961, the statute which required plan commission approval of a plat of subdivision authorized the imposition of "reasonable requirements for public streets, alleys, ways for public service facilities, parks, playgrounds, school grounds, and other public grounds." (Ill.Rev.Stat.1959, ch. 24, pars. 53–2, 53–3; 19 Ill. 2d at 451, 167 N.E.2d at 233.) Shortly after *Pioneer* was decided, the statute was altered to provide:

> "Whenever the reasonable requirements provided by the ordinance including the official map shall indicate the necessity for providing for a school site, park site, or other public lands within any proposed subdivision for which approval has been requested, and no such provision has been made therefor, the municipal authority may require that lands be designated for such public purpose before approving such plat. Whenever a final plat of subdivision, or part thereof, has been approved by the corporate authorities as complying with the official map and there is designated therein a school site, park site or other public land, the corporate authorities having jurisdiction of such use, be it a school

board, park board or other authority, such authority shall acquire the land so designated by purchase or commence proceedings to acquire such land by condemnation within one year from the date of approval of such plat; and if it does not do so within such period of one year, the land so designated may then be used by the owners thereof in any other manner consistent with the ordinance including the official map and the zoning ordinance of the municipality." Laws of 1961, at 2762; Ill.Rev.Stat.1961, ch. 24, par. 11–12–8.

The General Assembly has never authorized the sale of special use permits, nor has it ever authorized county or municipal governing bodies to exact cash contributions from real estate developers as the price of approval of plats of subdivision. If such legislation should ever be adopted, it would give rise to serious constitutional questions which need not now be addressed. It is enough at this time and on this record to note that the county board exercised in this case an authority that was never conferred upon it by the General Assembly.

NOTES

1. How close a connection should be required between the burden that a subdivision imposes on a community and the land dedication or cash exaction that the community requires of the subdivider? As noted in *Surety Developers*, Illinois' "specifically and uniquely attributable" test is more stringent than the test applied elsewhere in the country. Should the test differ depending on whether the contribution is a condition of subdivision approval or, as in *Surety Developers*, is a condition of some other land use approval such as a special use permit? What difference, if any, is there between concessions required as a condition of subdivision approval and concessions required as a condition to rezoning, page 1193 above?

What limits are there to a municipality's power to extract concessions from developers? Do transferable development rights and incentive zoning programs, pages 1114 to 1115, above, suggest that government is far from exhausting its constitutional power to force developers to pay for the right to develop?

2. What limits *should* there be to the municipal power to extract concessions from developers? Does the answer turn on who pays for the concession? Although it is commonly thought that the cost of these contributions is passed by developers on to consumers in the form of higher housing prices, it is far more likely, at least in the typical housing market, that the developer passes most or all of the cost back to the landowner who sells to him. The reason is simply that, other things being equal, homebuyers will pay no more for a house in Community *A*, that extracts concessions, than they will for an identical house in neighboring Community *B*, that does not; as a result, for developers in Community *A* to price competitively, they must pay less for their land than developers in Community *B*. (How-

ever, other things will not necessarily be equal: buyers should be willing to pay more for a home in Community A to the extent that the subdivision exactions confer benefits on residents in that subdivision not generally available to residents in Community B.) See generally, Adelstein & Edelson, Subdivision Exactions and Congestion Externalities, 5 J. Legal Studies 147 (1976).

Can this tax on landowners be justified on the ground that it merely enables the municipality to recapture some of the value—reflected in the land's appreciation—that the municipality has effectively contributed to the land through collective measures such as police protection, cultural activities, and wise land use planning generally?

3. *Exaction of Fees.* Although courts in this country generally accept the principle that municipalities can condition subdivision approval on the developer's dedication of land to meet communal subdivision needs, many courts have categorically invalidated requirements that the developer pay the municipality cash to support off-site improvements such as schools, parks, and recreational, police and fire facilities. See, for example, Gordon v. Village of Wayne, 370 Mich. 329, 121 N.W.2d 823 (1963) (exactions not authorized by enabling act); Hillis Homes, Inc. v. Snohomish County, 97 Wn.2d 804, 650 P.2d 193 (1982) (exaction constituted unauthorized tax).

One reason sometimes given for this distinction between on-site dedication requirements and fees for off-site improvements is that the dedication of land within the subdivision will be far more certain to confer benefits on the subdivision's residents. Should the distinction make a difference? Say that, because applicable state law prohibits cash exactions, a municipality requires a developer to dedicate two acres for a park, even though both the municipality and the developer would much prefer a $10,000 cash payment. Can the municipality legally waive the dedication in return for the fee? Should it be able to? Who would have standing to complain? At the least, should courts distinguish between situations in which the cash exaction is entirely independent of land dedication requirements and those in which the exaction is imposed as an alternative to land dedication? For example, if a subdivision site is topographically unsuited to development of a park, can the municipality demand that a cash payment instead be applied toward development of a park somewhere close to the subdivision?

Is it preferable for municipalities to resolve their fiscal dilemmas through the exaction of subdivision fees rather than through large lot and other exclusionary zoning techniques like those attacked in *Mt. Laurel*, page 1128, above? At the least, should cities be given latitude to decide whether fee exactions—independently or in combination with other techniques—represent the wisest way to channel resources toward meeting the city's "fair share" of regional concerns?

4. The Utah Supreme Court has pioneered the use of cost-benefit analysis in determining the validity of municipal fee requirements.

In Lafferty v. Payson City, 642 P.2d 376 (Utah 1982), the court reviewed two sets of municipal fees levied on the construction of new homes. One, an "impact fee" of $1,000 per dwelling, was stated by the authorizing ordinance to be necessary "because of an emergency situation created by property development within the city limits; the City needed additional revenue to offset the costs of the necessary increases in municipal services. This fee was in addition to all other municipal fees." The second, a "connection fee," was charged for connecting residents to city services—"$1,000 for sewer; $450 for water (3/4-inch hookup); $250 for electricity (100 amp service)."

Ruling that the impact fee represented an illegal, discriminatory tax on new housing, the court distinguished earlier decisions sustaining fees to finance specific municipal services or capital expenditures "on the basis that a reasonable charge for a specific service is permissible whereas a general fee that amounts to a revenue measure is not." 642 P.2d at 378. The court then ruled that the city had failed to justify the connection fees, in terms of the seven factors that the court had earlier held, in Banberry Development Corp. v. South Jordan City, 631 P.2d 899 (Utah 1981), should be considered "in determining the relative burden already borne and yet to be borne by newly developed properties and other properties":

(1) the cost of existing capital facilities;

(2) the means by which those facilities have been financed;

(3) the extent to which the properties being charged the new fees have already contributed to the cost of the existing facilities;

(4) the extent to which they will contribute to the cost of existing capital facilities in the future;

(5) the extent to which they should be credited for providing common facilities that the municipality has provided without charge to other properties in its service area;

(6) extraordinary costs, if any, in serving the new property; and

(7) the time-price differential inherent in fair comparisons of amounts paid at different times.

The objective of this analysis "is to assure that municipal fees pertaining to newly developed properties do not require them to bear more than their equitable share of the capital costs (in comparison with other properties) in relation to benefits conferred. If properly applied, those seven factors should put the new homeowner on essentially the same basis as the average existing homeowner with respect to costs borne in the past and to be borne in the future, in comparison with benefits already received and yet to be received. The municipality has the burden of disclosing the basis of its calculations to whoever challenges the reasonableness of the fees, and its allocations need not achieve precise mathematical equality." 642 P.2d at 379.

5. *"Inclusionary Zoning."* Many suburban communities across the country have sought to increase the housing available to low and middle income families through "inclusionary" zoning ordinances requiring developers to price a specified percentage of new units for sale to families in these income groups. The Palo Alto, California program, for example, requires developers to provide one unit of below market rate (BMR) housing for every ten market rate units in a subdivision or multiple family dwelling. (As an alternative to providing BMR housing directly, developers may pay a prescribed in-lieu fee, to be spent by a local non-profit housing corporation on BMR housing elsewhere in the community.) Eligible "moderate-income" families are defined as those with income between 80% and 120% of the median income in the county. Recipients, originally chosen by lottery, were subsequently selected on the basis of a waiting list of eligible, interested families. A unit, once sold to a qualified family, can only be resold to another eligible family; a mandatory ceiling on the sales price prevents the seller from reaping the capitalized benefit of the subsidy. See Dept. of Planning and Community Environment, City of Palo Alto, Palo Alto's BMR Program (1980).

Inclusionary zoning got off to a shaky start in the courts. The country's first inclusionary zoning ordinance—in Fairfax County, Virginia—was struck down in Board of Supervisors of Fairfax County v. DeGroff Enterprise, Inc., 214 Va. 235, 198 S.E.2d 600 (1973), on the grounds that it exceeded the authority granted by the state enabling act and violated the state constitutional guarantee "that no property will be taken or damaged for public purposes without just compensation."

Can BMR programs pass muster under the test, generally applied to subdivision exactions, requiring that some rational connection be shown between the communal burden imposed by the new development and the benefit exacted? When will a new housing development *ever* exacerbate a housing shortage in the community? Would it be easier to sustain a program, like one adopted in San Francisco, California, requiring office building developers to provide either new housing or in-lieu fees in proportion to the square footage—and hence the likely number of new office workers—in their buildings? See California Builder, p. 8 (April, 1981).

For a careful analysis of the law, politics and economics of inclusionary zoning, see Ellickson, The Irony of "Inclusionary" Zoning, 54 S.Cal.L.Rev. 1167 (1981). See generally, H. Franklin, D. Falk & A. Levin, In-Zoning: A Guide for Policy-Makers on Inclusionary Land Use Programs (1974); King, Inclusionary Zoning: Unfair Response to the Need for Low Cost Housing, 4 West. New England L.Rev. 597 (1982).

6. How should the line be drawn between those developments that are subject to dedication and exaction requirements and those that are not? Plaintiffs in Associated Home Builders of Greater East

Bay, Inc. v. City of Walnut Creek, 4 Cal.3d 633, 94 Cal.Rptr. 630, 638, 484 P.2d 606, 614 (1971), argued that the California statute authorizing subdivision exactions "arbitrarily imposes its requirements only upon subdividers whereas those who do not subdivide are free from its exactions. The example is suggested of an apartment house built on land which is not subdivided. The future occupants may live the same distance from a public park and have the same right to use the recreational facilities as the residents of a nearby subdivision, yet the builder of the apartment house is not required to contribute to park facilities because he has constructed his apartment without subdividing."

Though recognizing that the "point has some arguable merit," the court rejected it on the ground that "the apartment is generally vertical, while the subdivision is horizontal. The Legislature could reasonably have assumed that an apartment house is thus ordinarily constructed upon land considerably smaller in dimension than most subdivisions and the erection of the apartments is, therefore, not decreasing the limited supply of open space to the same extent as the formation of a subdivision." Is it relevant that, if and when the apartment house is converted into condominiums, the conversion *will* be considered a subdivision and exactions *will* be allowed? See Norsco Enterprises v. City of Fremont, 54 Cal.App.3d 488, 126 Cal.Rptr. 659 (1st Dist.1976).

For purposes of authorizing exactions, why should any line at all be drawn between subdivision developments and non-subdivision developments or, for that matter, between developments that need some form of governmental consent—subdivision approval, rezoning, variance, or special exception—and those that fully comply with existing regulations? Many municipalities have employed "site plan reviews" as a vehicle for forcing concessions from developers whose proposed projects involve neither a subdivision of land nor any changes in existing zoning. Site plan review procedures have generally been upheld. See, for example, Goldberg v. Zoning Commission of Town of Simsbury, 173 Conn. 23, 376 A.2d 385 (1977).

7. *Official Maps.* As should by now be evident, the public land use planning process generates a profusion of maps—zoning maps, subdivision maps, and the maps annexed to the municipality's comprehensive plan. Yet another map—the "official map"—antedates all of these, and continues to be used across the country to locate existing and proposed streets, highways, drainage and sewage systems, parks and other public improvements within the municipality. The main purpose of official maps today is to require developers to conform their subdivisions to the planned municipal infrastructure and thus to avoid economic waste. Regulations issued in connection with official maps prohibit developers from building improvements on lands that have been identified for future streets or highways. Thus, once the municipality eventually installs the street or highway, it will not have

to destroy, and compensate for, an improvement that stands in its way.

Do official maps unconstitutionally take property without just compensation? Courts generally sustained early map acts that did not prohibit improvements on planned streets, but only warned developers that their improvements were at risk of later condemnation for construction of public roads. See, for example, Baumann v. Ross, 167 U.S. 548, 17 S.Ct. 966, 42 L.Ed. 270 (1897). The next generation of official map acts, which actually prohibited development on planned streets, encountered only slightly rougher going in the courts. What of an official map that widens street lines and leaves an abutting landowner with only 2 $\frac{1}{2}$ feet of land? See In re Sansom Street, 293 Pa. 483, 143 A. 134 (1928) (unconstitutional as a "taking" of property).

III. EMINENT DOMAIN

A. "PUBLIC USE" AND "PUBLIC PURPOSE"

POLETOWN NEIGHBORHOOD COUNCIL v. CITY OF DETROIT

Supreme Court of Michigan, 1981.
410 Mich. 616, 304 N.W.2d 455.

PER CURIAM.

This case arises out of a plan by the Detroit Economic Development Corporation to acquire, by condemnation if necessary, a large tract of land to be conveyed to General Motors Corporation as a site for construction of an assembly plant. The plaintiffs, a neighborhood association and several individual residents of the affected area, brought suit in Wayne Circuit Court to challenge the project on a number of grounds, not all of which have been argued to this Court. Defendants' motions for summary judgment were denied pending trial on a single question of fact: whether, under 1980 PA 87; M.C.L. § 213.51 *et seq.*; M.S.A. § 8.265(1) *et seq.*, the city abused its discretion in determining that condemnation of plaintiffs' property was necessary to complete the project.

The trial lasted 10 days and resulted in a judgment for defendants and an order on December 9, 1980, dismissing plaintiffs' complaint. The plaintiffs filed a claim of appeal with the Court of Appeals on December 12, 1980, and an application for bypass with this Court on December 15, 1980.

We granted a motion for immediate consideration and an application for leave to appeal prior to decision by the Court of Appeals to consider the following questions:

Does the use of eminent domain in this case constitute a taking of private property for private use and, therefore, contravene Const. 1963, Art. 10, § 2?

Did the court below err in ruling that cultural, social and historical institutions were not protected by the Michigan Environmental Protection Act?

We conclude that these questions must be answered in the negative and affirm the trial court's decision.

I

This case raises a question of paramount importance to the future welfare of this state and its residents: Can a municipality use the power of eminent domain granted to it by the Economic Development Corporations Act, to condemn property for transfer to a private corporation to build a plant to promote industry and commerce, thereby adding jobs and taxes to the economic base of the municipality and state?

Const.1963, Art. 10, § 2, states in pertinent part that "[p]rivate property shall not be taken for public use without just compensation therefor being first made or secured in a manner prescribed by law." Art. 10, § 2 has been interpreted as requiring that the power of eminent domain not be invoked except to further a public use or purpose. Plaintiffs-appellants urge us to distinguish between the terms "use" and "purpose", asserting they are not synonymous and have been distinguished in the law of eminent domain. We are persuaded the terms have been used interchangeably in Michigan statutes and decisions in an effort to describe the protean concept of public benefit. The term "public use" has not received a narrow or inelastic definition by this Court in prior cases. Indeed, this Court has stated that " '[a] public use changes with changing conditions of society' " and that " '[t]he right of the public to receive and enjoy the benefit of the use determines whether the use is public or private' ".[3]

The Economic Development Corporations Act is a part of the comprehensive legislation dealing with planning, housing and zoning whereby the State of Michigan is attempting to provide for the general health, safety, and welfare through alleviating unemployment, providing economic assistance to industry, assisting the rehabilitation of blighted areas, and fostering urban redevelopment.

Section 2 of the act provides:

"There exists in this state the continuing need for programs to alleviate and prevent conditions of unemployment, and that it is accordingly necessary to assist and retain local industries and commercial enterprises to strengthen and revitalize the economy of this state and its municipalities; that accordingly it is necessary to provide means and methods for the encouragement and assistance of industrial and commercial enterprises in locating, purchasing, constructing, reconstructing, modernizing, improving, maintaining, repairing, furnishing, equipping, and expanding in this state and in its municipalities; and that it is also necessary to encourage the location and expansion of commercial enterprises to more conveniently provide needed services and facilities of the commercial enterprises to municipalities and the residents thereof. *Therefore, the powers granted in this act constitute the per-*

---

3. Hays v. Kalamazoo, 316 Mich. 443, 453–454, 25 N.W.2d 787, 169 A.L.R. 1218 (1947), quoting from 37 Am.Jur., Municipal Corporations, § 120, pp. 734–735.

formance of essential public purposes and functions for this state and its municipalities." M.C.L. § 125.1602; M.S.A. § 5.3520(2). (Emphasis added.)

To further the objectives of this act, the legislature has authorized municipalities to acquire property by condemnation in order to provide industrial and commercial sites and the means of transfer from the municipality to private users.

Plaintiffs-appellants do not challenge the declaration of the legislature that programs to alleviate and prevent conditions of unemployment and to preserve and develop industry and commerce are essential public purposes. Nor do they challenge the proposition that legislation to accomplish this purpose falls within the Constitutional grant of general legislative power to the legislature in Const.1963, Art. 4, § 51, which reads as follows:

> "The public health and general welfare of the people of the state are hereby declared to be matters of primary public concern. The legislature shall pass suitable laws for the protection and promotion of the public health."

What plaintiffs-appellants do challenge is the constitutionality of using the power of eminent domain to condemn one person's property to convey it to another private person in order to bolster the economy. They argue that whatever incidental benefit may accrue to the public, assembling land to General Motors' specifications for conveyance to General Motors for its uncontrolled use in profit making is really a taking for private use and not a public use because General Motors is the primary beneficiary of the condemnation.

The defendants-appellees contend, on the other hand, that the controlling public purpose in taking this land is to create an industrial site which will be used to alleviate and prevent conditions of unemployment and fiscal distress. The fact that it will be conveyed to and ultimately used by a private manufacturer does not defeat this predominant public purpose.

There is no dispute about the law. All agree that condemnation for a public use or purpose is permitted. All agree that condemnation for a private use or purpose is forbidden. Similarly, condemnation for a private use cannot be authorized whatever its incidental public benefit and condemnation for a public purpose cannot be forbidden whatever the incidental private gain. The heart of this dispute is whether the proposed condemnation is for the primary benefit of the public or the private user.

The Legislature has determined that governmental action of the type contemplated here meets a public need and serves an essential public purpose. The Court's role after such a determination is made is limited.

> " 'The determination of what constitutes a public purpose is primarily a legislative function, subject to review by the courts

when abused, and the determination of the legislative body of that matter should not be reversed except in instances where such determination is palpably and manifestly arbitrary and incorrect.'" Gregory Marina, Inc. v. Detroit, 378 Mich. 364, 396, 144 N.W.2d 503 (1966).

The United States Supreme Court has held that when a legislature speaks, the public interest has been declared in terms "well-nigh conclusive." Berman v. Parker, 348 U.S. 26, 32, 75 S.Ct. 98, 102, 99 L.Ed. 27 (1954).

The Legislature has delegated the authority to determine whether a particular project constitutes a public purpose to the governing body of the municipality involved. The plaintiffs concede that this project is the type contemplated by the Legislature and that the procedures set forth in the Economic Development Corporations Act have been followed. This further limits our review.

In the court below, the plaintiffs-appellants challenged the necessity for the taking of the land for the proposed project. In this regard the city presented substantial evidence of the severe economic conditions facing the residents of the city and state, the need for new industrial development to revitalize local industries, the economic boost the proposed project would provide, and the lack of other adequate available sites to implement the project.

As Justice Cooley stated over a hundred years ago "the most important consideration in the case of eminent domain is the necessity of accomplishing some public good which is otherwise impracticable, and . . . the law does not so much regard the means as the need." People ex rel. Detroit & Howell R. Co. v. Salem Twp. Board, 20 Mich. 452, 480–481 (1870).

When there is such public need "[t]he abstract right [of an individual] to make use of his own property in his own way is compelled to yield to the general comfort and protection of community, and to a proper regard to relative rights in others." *Id.* Eminent domain is an inherent power of the sovereign of the same nature as, albeit more severe than, the power to regulate the use of land through zoning or the prohibition of public nuisances.

In the instant case the benefit to be received by the municipality invoking the power of eminent domain is a clear and significant one and is sufficient to satisfy this Court that such a project was an intended and a legitimate object of the Legislature when it allowed municipalities to exercise condemnation powers even though a private party will also, ultimately, receive a benefit as an incident thereto.

The power of eminent domain is to be used in this instance primarily to accomplish the essential public purposes of alleviating unemployment and revitalizing the economic base of the community. The benefit to a private interest is merely incidental.

Our determination that this project falls within the public purpose, as stated by the Legislature, does not mean that every condemnation proposed by an economic development corporation will meet with similar acceptance simply because it may provide some jobs or add to the industrial or commercial base. If the public benefit was not so clear and significant, we would hesitate to sanction approval of such a project. The power of eminent domain is restricted to furthering public uses and purposes and is not to be exercised without substantial proof that the public is primarily to be benefited. Where, as here, the condemnation power is exercised in a way that benefits specific and identifiable private interests, a court inspects with heightened scrutiny the claim that the public interest is the predominant interest being advanced. Such public benefit cannot be speculative or marginal but must be clear and significant if it is to be within the legitimate purpose as stated by the Legislature. We hold this project is warranted on the basis that its significance for the people of Detroit and the state has been demonstrated. . . .

The decision of the trial court is affirmed.

The clerk is directed to issue the Court's judgment order forthwith, in accordance with GCR 1963, 866.3(c).

No costs, a public question being involved.

FITZGERALD, Justice (dissenting).

This Court today decides that the power of eminent domain permits the taking of private property with the object of transferring it to another private party for the purpose of constructing and operating a factory, on the ground that the employment and other economic benefits of this privately operated industrial facility are such as to satisfy the "public use" requirement for the exercise of eminent domain power. Because I believe the proposed condemnation clearly exceeds the government's authority to take private property through the power of eminent domain, I dissent.

I

In the spring of 1980, General Motors Corporation informed the City of Detroit that it would close its Cadillac and Fisher Body plants located within the city in 1983. General Motors offered to build an assembly complex in the city, if a suitable site could be found. General Motors set four criteria for the approval of a site: an area of between 450 and 500 acres; a rectangular shape (³/₄ mile by 1 mile); access to a long-haul railroad line; and access to the freeway system. The city evaluated a number of potential sites and eventually made an in-depth study of nine sites. Eight of the sites were found not to be feasible, and the ninth, with which we are concerned, was recommended. It occupies approximately 465 acres in the cities of Detroit and Hamtramck. A plan was developed to acquire the site, labeled the Central Industrial Park, under the Economic Development Corporations Act, 1974 PA 338. As authorized by the statute, the project plan contemplated the use of condemnation to acquire at least some of the property within the site. . . .

II

The city attaches great importance to the explicit legislative findings in the Economic Development Corporations Act that unemployment is a serious problem and that it is necessary to encourage industry in order to revitalize the economy of this state, and to the legislative declaration that the use of eminent domain power pursuant to a project under the act, "shall be considered necessary for public purposes and for the benefit of the public". It is undeniable that such legislative pronouncements are entitled to great deference. However, determination whether a taking is for a public or a private use is ultimately a judicial question. Through the years, this Court has not hesitated to declare takings authorized by statute not to be for public use in private cases. This is as it must be, since if a legislative declaration on the question of public use were conclusive, citizens could be subjected to the most outrageous confiscation of property for the benefit of other private interests without redress. Thus, while mindful of the expression of the legislative view of the appropriateness of using the eminent domain power in the circumstances of this case, this Court has the responsibility to determine whether the authorization is lawful.

Our role was well stated by Justice Cooley in "A Treatise on Constitutional Limitations". Writing subsequent to the Court's decision in People ex rel. Detroit and Howell R. Co. v. Salem Township Board, 20 Mich. 452 (1870), he noted:

> "The question what is a public use is always one of law. Deference will be paid to the legislative judgment, as expressed in enactments providing for an appropriation of property, but it will not be conclusive." 2 Cooley, Constitutional Limitations (8th ed.), p. 1141.

III

Our approval of the use of eminent domain power in this case takes this state into a new realm of takings of private property; there is simply no precedent for this decision in previous Michigan cases. There were several early cases in which there was an attempt to transfer property from one private owner to another through the condemnation power pursuant to express statutory authority. In each case, the proposed taking was held impermissible.

The city places great reliance on a number of slum clearance cases here and elsewhere in which it has been held that the fact that the property taken is eventually transferred to private parties does not defeat a claim that the taking is for a public use. Despite the superficial similarity of these cases to the instant one based on the ultimate disposition of the property, these decisions do not justify the condemnation proposed by the city. The public purpose that has been found to support the slum clearance cases is the benefit to the public health and welfare that arises from the elimination of existing blight, even though the ultimate disposition of the property will benefit private interests. As we said in *In re Slum Clearance, supra*:

"It seems to us that the public purpose of slum clearance is in any event the one *controlling* purpose of the condemnation. The jury were not asked to decide any necessity to condemn the parcels involved for any purpose of resale, but only for slum clearance. . . .

". . . [T]he resale [abating part of the cost of clearance] is not a primary purpose and is incidental and ancillary to the primary and real purpose of clearance." 331 Mich. 720. (Emphasis original.)

However, in the present case the transfer of the property to General Motors after the condemnation cannot be considered incidental to the taking. It is only through the acquisition and use of the property by General Motors that the "public purpose" of promoting employment can be achieved. Thus, it is the economic benefits of the project that are incidental to the private use of the property.

The city also points to decisions that have found the objective of economic development to be a sufficient "public purpose" to support the expenditure of public funds in aid of industry. What constitutes a public purpose in a context of governmental taxing and spending power cannot be equated with the use of that term in connection with eminent domain powers. The potential risk of abuse in the use of eminent domain power is clear. Condemnation places the burden of aiding industry on the few, who are likely to have limited power to protect themselves from the excesses of legislative enthusiasm for the promotion of industry. The burden of taxation is distributed on the great majority of the population, leading to a more effective check on improvident use of public funds.

IV

The courts of other states have occasionally dealt with proposals to use condemnation to transfer property from one set of private owners to others, justified on the ground that the resulting economic benefits provide the requisite public use or public purpose. Some decisions have upheld the use of eminent domain powers on that basis; others have found the proposed taking to exceed the power of the government to take private property. While these cases are instructive, they are not controlling of the disposition of this case. Each is presented against the background of a particular state's constitutional and statutory framework. The peculiar facts of the development projects involved also make it difficult to compare them with the present case. In addition, each is decided in the context of that state's body of case law which may have given either a broad or a narrow interpretation to the term "public use."

Despite the limited value of decisions in other states, several points can be made. First, while it is difficult and perhaps futile to categorize individual states as utilizing a "broad" or "narrow" interpretation of "public use" for condemnation purposes, Michigan law seems most consistent with that of states that give a more limited construction to the term. While our decisions have sometimes used the phrase "public purpose" (a phrase often associated with a broad interpretation), the result of our decisions has been to limit the eminent domain power to situations in which direct governmental use is to be made of the land or in which the private recipient will use it to serve the public. The slum clearance cases are really the only significant departure from these principles, and, as noted above, those decisions have been sustained only because of the conclusion that the clearing of a blighted area is a public use. In this respect, the scope of "public use" in Michigan is quite similar to that in states that have rejected development projects on the theory that they would improve general economic conditions. Certainly, we have never sustained the use of eminent domain power solely because of the economic benefits of development as have cases that allowed condemnation in similar circumstances.

Second, it is worth noting that the Maryland and Minnesota cases cited above are distinguishable in that in each it was the governmental unit that selected the site in question for commercial or industrial development. By contrast, the project before us was initiated by General Motors Corporation's solicitation of the city for its aid in locating a factory site.

V

The majority relies on the principle that the concept of public use is an evolving one; however, I cannot believe that this evolution has eroded our historic protection against the taking of private property for private use to the degree sanctioned by this Court's decision today. The decision that the prospect of increased employment, tax revenue, and general economic stimulation makes a taking of private property for transfer to another private party sufficiently "public" to authorize the use of the power of eminent domain means that there is virtually no limit to the use of condemnation to aid private businesses. Any business enterprise produces benefits to society at large. Now that we have authorized local legislative bodies to decide that a different commercial or industrial use of property will produce greater public benefits than its present use, no homeowner's, merchant's or manufacturer's property, however productive or valuable to its owner, is immune from condemnation for the benefit of other private interests that will put it to a "higher" use. As one prominent commentator has written:

> "It often happens that the erection of a large factory will be of more benefit to the whole community in which it is planned to build it than any strictly public improvement which the inhabitants of the place could possibly undertake; but even if the plan was blocked by the refusal of the selfish owner of a small but necessary parcel of land to part with it at any price, the public mind would instinctively revolt at any attempt to take such land by eminent domain." 2A Nichols, Eminent Domain § 7.61[1] (rev. 3d ed.).

The condemnation contemplated in the present action goes beyond the scope of the power of eminent domain in that it takes private property for private use. I would reverse the judgment of the circuit court.

[The opinion of RYAN, J., dissenting, is omitted.]

NOTES

1. The history of eminent domain in the United States suggests that *Poletown*, far from being an aberration, belongs to a long tradition of government subsidy to private industry. In colonial times, eminent domain's two principal objects were the construction of roads—often to connect private lands to public highways—and the construction of mills for use by neighboring farmers. Both forms of condemnation flourished after the Revolution, particularly the Mill Acts which were eventually broadened to authorize the condemnation of dam sites for privately owned sawmills, paper mills and other private industrial uses. Private companies, chartered by the state to build railroads, bridges, canals, turnpikes, and later, power and telephone lines, were given authority to condemn the land they needed. Since these firms were public utilities or common carriers, required to serve the public on a nondiscriminatory basis, they were thought to qualify as a "public use." And, because these firms were typically subject to rate regulation, there was little concern that they would manipulate the economic benefits of condemnation to their own ends rather than to the advantage of their customers. See generally, M. Horwitz, The Transformation of American Law, 1780–1860, 63–66 (1977); Scheiber, Property Law, Expropriation, and Resource Allocation by Government: The United States, 1789–1910, 33 J.Econ.Hist. 232 (1973).

There is a modern trend to delegate the eminent domain power to institutions such as hospitals, universities and cemetery associations which, though not public utilities or common carriers, are thought to have some special claim on the public interest. Can these delegations be justified in the usual terms of public use and benefit? In any other terms?

2. Why could GM not have assembled the disputed parcel on its own? The standard answer—given to justify eminent domain generally—is that, absent eminent domain, individual landowners can hinder major public projects by refusing to sell their parcels or, more likely, by refusing to sell at other than an "extortionate" price. Meandering roads and incomplete sites would result.

Does this answer make any sense? Does it make sense in the specific context of *Poletown*? Is it relevant that, throughout the twentieth century, private developers assembling sites for office buildings, industrial parks and shopping centers have, by following careful strategy and playing good poker, managed to overcome holdout problems without the aid of eminent domain?

3. What difference is there between the "public use" or "public purpose" required to justify exercises of the eminent domain power, and the enhancement of public "health, safety and welfare," required to justify exercises of the police power? Should courts give the same, virtually total, deference to legislative judgments on public use or purpose that they give to legislative judgments about health, safety and welfare? Is it relevant that in the standard condemnation case it is a compensated landowner who is claiming invalidity, while in the standard zoning case it is an uncompensated owner who is making the claim?

4. *"Public Use" and "Public Purpose."* What difference is there between "public *use*," required by the Michigan constitution, and "public *purpose*," required by some other state constitutions? Justice Ryan, dissenting in *Poletown*, noted that while the Michigan constitution required "public use" to support the eminent domain power, it required "public purpose" to support exercises of the taxing power. 304 N.W.2d 472. For Ryan, the distinction made a difference. Recognizing a long tradition of judicial deference to legislative determination of public purpose in tax cases, Ryan observed that eminent domain cases "evince no like commitment to minimal judicial review. Instead, it has always been the case that this Court has accorded little or no weight to legislative determinations of 'public use.'" Further, Ryan thought the distinction to be fully justified: "The character of governmental interference with the individual in the case of taxation is wholly different from the case of eminent domain. The degree of compelled deprivation of property is manifestly less intrusive in the former case: it is one thing to disagree with the purposes for which one's tax money is spent; it is quite another to be compelled to give up one's land and be required, as in this case, to leave what may well be a lifelong home and community." 304 N.W.2d at 474.

The *Poletown* majority expressly acknowledged that "condemnation for a private use or purpose is forbidden." What room did the decision leave for making any such finding in a future case? In an economic system that purports to rely on the operation of private markets, when will lawful conduct ever lack a public purpose? After *Poletown*, would GM's activities in the new plant be considered "state action" for purposes of the applicable constitutional guarantees?

See generally, Ross, Transferring Land to Private Entities by the Power of Eminent Domain, 51 Geo.Wash.L.Rev. 355 (1983).

5. One student writer, after reviewing the long history of the public use requirement in American law, concluded that the "Supreme Court has repudiated the doctrine of public use. Most state courts have arrived at the same conclusion, although rarely with so much directness. Doubtless the doctrine will continue to be evoked nostalgically in dicta and may even be employed authoritatively in rare, atypical situations. Kinder hands, however, would accord it the permanent interment in the digests that is so long overdue." Comment, The Public Use Limitation on Eminent Domain: An Advance Requiem, 58 Yale L.J. 599, 614 (1949).

Recent state high court decisions suggest that the requiem may have been premature and that *Poletown* will by no means be the final word. For example, in Petition of City of Seattle, 96 Wn.2d 616, 638 P.2d 549 (1981), the Washington Supreme Court ruled that the City's proposed acquisition of a downtown area in order to develop and strengthen retailing activities was not a public use, even though the project might forestall urban decay, and even though the project would include a public square, park, museum and off-street parking areas. In City of Owensboro v. McCormick, 581 S.W.2d 3 (1979), the Kentucky Supreme Court struck down the state's Local Industrial Authority Act to the extent that it gave municipalities the power to condemn private property for reconveyance to private enterprise; "no 'public use' is involved where the land of A is condemned merely to enable B to build a factory or C to construct a shopping center." 581 S.W.2d 8. And, in Karesh v. City Council of City of Charleston, 271 S.C. 339, 247 S.E.2d 342 (1978), the South Carolina Supreme Court held that the city could not condemn land in order to lease it to a private firm for construction of a convention center and parking facility that would contain retail shops replacing existing retail stores in the area.

The *Seattle* and *Owensboro* opinions, like Justice Fitzgerald's dissenting opinion in *Poletown*, sought to distinguish the large body of case law upholding condemnation for purposes of slum clearance and urban renewal. In Justice Fitzgerald's words, the "public purpose that has been found to support the slum clearance cases is the benefit to the public health and welfare that arises from the elimination of existing blight, even though the ultimate disposition of the property will benefit private interests." Is it a difference of kind or degree that slum areas have no value, or even negative value, as compared to the positive value of residential areas such as Poletown? If the difference is one of degree, is it self-evident that the degree of improvement, from lower to higher use, will invariably be greater when a slum is turned into a subsidized housing project than when a residential area is converted to the site for an automobile factory?

6. *Private Condemnation.* Several state constitutions include provisions like the first sentence of Washington Const. Art. 1 § 16, "Private property shall not be taken for private use, except for private ways of necessity, and for drains, flumes or ditches on or across the lands of others for agricultural, domestic or sanitary purposes." Can these provisions, which effectively enable landlocked owners to condemn rights of way over their neighbors' parcels, be reconciled with the Fifth and Fourteenth Amendments to the United States Constitution, which contain no comparable authority for private condemnation? Can they be sustained on the ground that they are integral to the state law definition of "property" and are thus immune from federal constitutional review? See PruneYard Shopping Center v. Robins, page 70 above. Or do they violate the "core" common law property rights identified in Justice Marshall's concurring opinion in *PruneYard*?

How can "private necessity" be reconciled with eminent domain's orthodox "public use" predicate? Flora Logging Co. v. Boeing, 43 F.2d 145, 148 (D.Or.1930), offers the standard rationale: "The people of the state have, by their Constitution, legislative enactment, and decisions of their highest court, expressed their opinion that the public welfare of the state demands that right of way for the transportation of the raw products of the forest should not be made impossible by the owner of property refusing to consent to sell the right to cross his land."

Brown v. McAnally, 97 Wn.2d 360, 644 P.2d 1153 (1982), graphically illustrates the dilemma created by the distinction between "private necessity" and "public use." Plaintiff there owned a landlocked parcel which it wished to subdivide into residential lots. As a condition of approving the subdivision map, the county required that the subdivision be connected to existing public highways by a fifty-foot road to be built over neighboring parcels. Although the county refused to condemn and build the roadway itself—"it would not be beneficial to the County to allocate road funds to such a minor road"—it did agree to take title to the road once plaintiff had built it. The Washington Supreme Court struck down plaintiff's private condemnation of a fifty-foot easement on the ground that it "greatly exceeds" the rights contemplated by the state constitution and the implementing legislation: "Respondents were attempting to *privately* condemn property rights, under RCW 8.24, which they would ultimately put to a *public use*. By so doing they not only sought to circumvent the limited power of condemnation authorized by RCW 8.24, but to acquire rights greater than would otherwise be available to them, *i.e.*, rights legally afforded only to counties under RCW 8.08. Further, this tactic would also aid the County to evade the strict statutory proof required of counties seeking to exercise the right of eminent domain under RCW 8.08." 97 Wash.2d at 372, 644 P.2d at 1160–1161.

Is there any economic justification for private condemnation provisions? Although courts often assert that, absent these provisions, it will be "impossible" for a landlocked owner to use her parcel productively, it seems clear that the problem is not impossibility, but rather judicial displeasure at one landowner's attempt to "extort" her landlocked neighbor. Say that the value of Whiteacre, a landlocked parcel, is $5,000 without access to a public road and $150,000 with access, and that the value of neighboring parcel, Blackacre is $200,000 without any easement across it, and $192,000 encumbered by an easement connecting Whiteacre to the public road that adjoins Blackacre. Since the benefit to Whiteacre of enjoying the easement outweighs the cost to Blackacre of suffering it, economic efficiency dictates that the easement should exist. But does it follow that the easement would not be granted absent condemnation? Presumably, Whiteacre's owner will be willing to pay any amount up to $145,000 for the easement, and Blackacre's owner will be willing to accept any amount in excess of $8,000. The two will presumably strike a bargain at some price in between.

Should the availability of private condemnation turn on whether more than one parcel lies between Whiteacre and the public road, raising the prospect that transaction costs will defeat private negotiations? On whether Whiteacre is bordered by other parcels, owned by others, who might compete with Blackacre's owner in accepting bids for the right of way easement? For a thoughtful elaboration of the issue, see Berger, The Public Use Requirement in Eminent Domain, 57 Or.L.Rev. 203 (1978).

7. *Eminent Domain as a Redistributive Tool.* Can a state use the eminent domain power to redistribute land from a handful of major landowners to the masses of tenants living on their lands? The Hawaii Land Reform Act, Hawaii Rev.Stat. ch. 516 (1976), sought to do just that, authorizing the Hawaii Housing Authority to condemn the residential lands of the state's few large landholders, who traditionally rented out residential parcels under long term leases, and to resell the lands in fee to the tenants. In Midkiff v. Tom, 483 F.Supp. 62, 67–68 (D.Hawaii 1979), the district court upheld the Act against constitutional attack. ("In order to uphold the constitutionality of chapter 516, this Court believes all it need do is look at the broadest possible rationale for the statute—that of redistributing residential land and changing the pattern of residential ownership in Hawaii. I believe this purpose is within reach of the police power, and hence the takings authorized by the statute are for a public purpose . . . . [T]he Legislature had the right to conclude that Hawaii's system of landholding was injurious to the social and economic health of the community.")

The Ninth Circuit Court of Appeals reversed, holding that the act unlawfully authorized the taking of property for a private purpose. 702 F.2d 788, 798 (1983): "We see a naked attempt . . . to take the private property of A and transfer it to B solely for B's private use and benefit." The court distinguished Berman v. Parker, 348 U.S. 26, 75 S.Ct. 98, 99 L.Ed. 27 (1954), an urban renewal case, on the ground that the "transformation from slum to healthy thriving community represents a change in the use of the land," while the Hawaii act would not alter the use of property at all. Also, unlike *Berman*, the Hawaii act provides for no "intermediate step in which the government holds the property for the accomplishment of a public purpose. The lessee simply retains possession of residential property throughout the condemnation process until he receives fee simple title." 702 F.2d at 796–797.

8. *Condemnation of Private Business.* Can a city use the eminent domain power to condemn a local business—such as General Motors—that threatens to move its operations out of town? When the Oakland Raiders professional football team announced its plans to relocate in Los Angeles, the City of Oakland instituted a condemnation proceeding to acquire all property rights in the team. In City of Oakland v. Oakland Raiders, 32 Cal.3d 60, 183 Cal.Rptr. 673, 646 P.2d 835 (1982), the California Supreme Court rejected the team's claim that only real property, and not intangible business property, could be taken by eminent domain. The court also ruled that, as a matter of law, the proposed use could qualify as a "public use." The court remanded for a determination whether in fact the proposed use did constitute a public use under the terms of the applicable eminent domain statute.

Would it have been better to characterize the case as involving not eminent domain—in which land is condemned so that it can be put to a different, more socially valuable use—but rather nationalization—in which title to a business is transferred from private to public ownership without any change in the firm's business?

9. The constitutional phrase, "just compensation," has almost universally been interpreted to mean "fair market value"—a measure that will indemnify the condemnee in some, but not all, cases. For example, condemnees are not entitled to relocation expenses or to the value of their personal attachment to home and neighborhood. These uncompensated values were doubtless very high for Poletown residents, forced out of a neighborhood in which they had lived for years. According to Justice Ryan, Poletown was a "tightly-knit residential enclave of first- and second-generation Americans, for many of whom their home was their single most valuable and cherished asset and their stable ethnic neighborhood the unchanging symbol of the security and quality of their lives." 304 N.W.2d at 470.

> Is the question whether the public use or public purpose requirehas been met properly separable from the question whether the ee is likely to be fully compensated for his loss?

B. "JUST COMPENSATION"

COUNTY OF RAMSEY v. MILLER

Supreme Court of Minnesota, 1982.
316 N.W.2d 917.

YETKA, Justice.

Richard Miller appeals following a jury verdict on valuation in a condemnation proceeding in Ramsey County. We reverse and remand for a new trial.

Appellants owned approximately 79.9 acres of land in the City of New Brighton. The property is scenic wooded land along Rice Creek, with approximately 23 acres of high ground and the remaining 57 acres within the flood plain of Rice Creek. The surrounding area is a developed residential neighborhood. The City of New Brighton had constructed a bridge over Rice Creek through the center of the property and had installed public water and sewer facilities in preparation for development.

In 1975, Ramsey County began condemnation proceedings to acquire the subject property owned by appellants for a park and open space system. The district court found the proposed taking necessary and appointed commissioners who awarded damages of $415,000 in June 1976. Appellant owners appealed the award to Ramsey County District Court and, after a jury trial in June 1980, were awarded a judgment of $665,000. Appellants moved for additur or a new trial on the grounds, among others, that evidence supporting the development cost approach to determine market value was erroneously excluded and that other evidentiary rulings were erroneous. Respondent moved for remittitur. By order dated October 29, 1980, the court denied both motions, from which denial appellants appeal.

At trial on the issue of valuation, all witnesses agreed the highest and best use of the property was for residential development, but disagreed as to the number and types of residential units for which the property was suited. Opinions ranged from 20 units to 477 units. The applicable zoning would permit a maximum of 477 dwelling units under a planned residential development. Appellants were not permitted to introduce into evidence plats illustrating a proposed development plan. The parties introduced conflicting evidence on the support characteristics of the soil. The parties also introduced conflicting expert opinions on the likelihood of the granting by the Rice Creek Watershed District of the permit which would be required before a builder could put any fill in the flood plain.

Value witnesses expressed opinions of the value of the property as follows:

Witnesses for the county: $372,000; $280,000; and $415,000.

Witnesses for appellants: $2,027,250; $1,635,000; $2,330,000; and $1,700,000.

The county's witnesses were permitted to discuss comparable sales on which they based their opinions, but were prohibited from discussing specific prices of comparable sales except on cross-examination. Appellants' witnesses were permitted to describe in general the development cost approach by which they appraised the property, but were not permitted to discuss the numerical data or analyses underlying their opinions. Engineering testimony on the cost of development was also excluded.

Appellants' offer of proof not admitted into evidence establishes that in 1970 appellants submitted a proposed development plat to the city, on which the city deferred final action pending a study of the flood plain by the Army Corps of Engineers. Evidence was admitted that the Corps of Engineers' study, completed in November 1971, indicated that portions of the site would be under water in a 100-year flood. The court took judicial notice that on November 22, 1971, Ramsey County Commissioners passed a resolution authorizing acquisition of the property by negotiation or condemnation, but this evidence was not presented to the jury.

The issues on appeal are:

(1) Is specific numerical, analytical, and illustrative evidence supporting a development cost approach to valuation admissible?

(2) Was cross-examination of appellant landowner regarding the purchase price of the subject property prejudicial error to appellants?

(3) May a valuation witness be cross-examined regarding sales prices of comparable property not considered in his own valuation?

(4) Should appellants' proposed plat have been admitted as evidence of highest and best use?

(5) Must the court inform the jury of facts of which it took judicial notice?

(6) May the matter be remanded for consideration of whether the taking of the entire 80 acres was necessary?

Other errors alleged by appellants were not briefed to this court and, upon examination, are found to be without merit.

To determine the fair market value of property in a condemnation proceeding "[a]ny competent evidence may be considered, if it legitimately bears upon the market value." State v. Malecker, 265 Minn. 1, 5, 120 N.W.2d 36, 38 (1963) (footnote omitted). The measure of compensation is the amount which a purchaser willing, but not required, to buy the property would pay to an owner willing, but not required, to sell it, taking into consideration the highest and best use to which the property can be put. In appraising land for which the highest and best use indisputably is residential subdivision, an appraiser must consider the property in the same manner as would a prospective purchaser of the undeveloped land for that purpose.

As the trial court recognized, courts have traditionally used three methods of determining fair market value of real property: (1) market data approach based on comparable sales; (2) income-capitalization approach; and (3) reproduction cost, less depreciation. Of these, only comparable sales have been employed for unimproved property. Appellants claim, however, that comparable sales on which to base an opinion as to value are unavailable. The subject property is uniquely situated with creek frontage, trees, and natural scenic beauty in an area of heavy housing demand and convenient location. The county's witnesses described sales of comparable parcels on which they based opinions of the value of the subject property; on cross-examination, however, the properties to which the comparisons were made were shown to lack desirable features of the subject property. Appellants' witnesses testified that the comparable properties were so different that comparison was meaningless, and reached their own valuation opinions using the development cost approach instead.

The development cost approach is designed to reflect, through cash flow analysis, the current price a developer-purchaser would be warranted in paying for the land, given the cost of developing it and the probable proceeds from the sale of developed sites.[1] American Institute of Real Estate Appraisers, *The Appraisal of Real Estate*, 140 (7th ed. 1978).

Appellants' witnesses were permitted at trial to give their opinions as to the value of the property, as well as a general description of the development cost approach by which they appraised the property.

---

1. A typical "development cost" appraisal calculation would include these steps:

   1. Identify the economic bracket of the residents and check the range of sale prices of typical new homes in the area.
   2. By distribution, or comparison with lot sales in similar subdivisions, decide what figure represents a typical lot value in this category of development.
   3. Study and lay out a subdivision plan to develop typical lots.
   4. Project the total probable gross sale price for these lots.
   5. Estimate development costs to include:
      a. Engineering or other fees
      b. Cost of streets and utilities
      c. Advertising and cost of sales
   6. Estimate overhead and administrative costs to include:
      a. Taxes and inspection fees
      b. Financing fees and carrying costs
   7. Deduct these direct expenses for development from the figure derived in Step 4.
   8. Deduct an adequate profit allowance to provide incentive for the developer so that the calculated value of the raw land is exclusive of development profit. (Alternatively, profit may be provided for in the rate used for capitalization on the discounting process.)
   9. Deduct for time lag by discounting, at an appropriate risk rate, the annual net income flow over the time needed for completion and market absorption of the project.

American Institute of Real Estate Appraisers, *The Appraisal of Real Estate*, 148 (7th ed. 1978).

They were not, however, permitted to discuss the numerical data or analyses underlying their opinions. We believe the evidence supporting the development cost approach should have been admitted in this case. In holding that the prejudicial speculation of this type of testimony outweighed its probative value, the trial court noted that "there is an inherently speculative quality to the developmental approach to market value when the subject acreage is essentially raw, undeveloped land." In reaching this position, the trial court relied on State v. Malecker, 265 Minn. 1, 120 N.W.2d 36 (1963).

In *Malecker*, the owner of a large tract of rural property sought to calculate his damages resulting from the condemnation of a portion of his property by aggregating the individual diminutions in value for each of the 131 lots on an unregistered plat of the remainder. In affirming the lower court's exclusion of evidence under this "lot method" approach, this court offered four major objections to this form of evaluation:

1. The fair market value should reflect the "selling [of] the entire property as one big unit rather than selling the individual lots separately."

2. The cost of improving and preparing the land cannot be ignored because the landowner would otherwise receive a windfall.

3. The jury should not be concerned "with all of the uncertain costs of advertising, brokers' commissions, taxes, utilities, grading, and improvements which a protracted lot-by-lot sales campaign would inevitably require."

4. The land involved was raw, undeveloped land as opposed to unoccupied city property which implies that some potentiality of development must be shown.

Id. at 3–8, 120 N.W.2d at 38–40.

The "development cost approach" clearly satisfies the first two requirements of *Malecker*—the market value calculation assumes a single sale of the property to a developer and makes corresponding adjustments for the costs of preparing, improving, and selling the property. *See* footnote 1 above, steps 5 through 8.

The third requirement seeks to protect juries by declaring that evidence of the underlying facts and data of the development cost approach is "per se" speculative and thus inadmissible. However, as pointed out by Judge Parker's often quoted words:

> Artificial rules of evidence which exclude from the consideration of the jurors matters which men consider in their everyday affairs hinder rather than help them at arriving at a just result. In no branch of the law is it more important to remember this, than in cases involving the valuation of property, where "at best, evidence of value is largely a matter of opinion".

United States v. 25.406 Acres of Land, 172 F.2d 990, 995 (4th Cir. 1949).

The developmental cost approach is recognized as an accepted appraisal practice. Howard Shenehon, past international president of the Society of Real Estate Appraisers, testified that the development cost approach was a nationally recognized approach which had been accepted by lending institutions, assessors, developers, and builders. Peter Fisher, chairman of the Appraisal Review Committee of the American Institute of Real Estate Appraisers, described the development cost approach as "extremely reliable" and one which is relied upon by the Federal Home Loan Bank Board as well as by Midwest Federal Bank where he is employed. One of respondent's appraisal experts, James M. McKenzie, acknowledged that this was an "acceptable procedure when appraising development land."

The modern trend favors admissibility of all relevant evidence. Although Minn.R.Evid. 705 does allow an expert witness to give his opinion without first disclosing the facts or data upon which it is based, the rule clearly does not prohibit the introduction of such testimony. It seems a bit incongruous to prohibit an expert from testifying as to these matters on direct examination because they might confuse the jury while, at the same time, permitting such testimony on cross-examination when the clarification of the expert's position is clearly not always foremost in the questioner's mind. While the trial court may always exclude relevant evidence if its probative value is "substantially outweighed" by the danger of confusion of the issues, Minn.R.Evid. 403, we believe the careful use of preliminary jury instructions could do much to reduce any potential for confusion. The automatic exclusion of the underlying facts and data which support a "development cost approach" appraisal is contrary to the modern theme of the rules of evidence.

In *Malecker*, the court distinguished Board of County Comm'rs v. St. Paul & S.C.R.R., 28 Minn. 503, 11 N.W. 73 (1881), by noting that the lot method of appraisal was permissible in that case because city property was involved which was capable of being subdivided. The land involved in *Malecker*, however, was approximately 110 acres of rural property that had no utilities except electricity, no improvements, and roads that were only graded and graveled. The court thus suggested that some showing of a current potential for subdivision and sale was necessary.

Federal cases which have approved the development cost approach have also required some showing of minimal practicality. See, e.g., United States v. 47.3096 Acres, 583 F.2d 270 (6th Cir.1978) (valuation testimony based on hypothesized subdivision is excludible if development not shown to be reasonably probable); United States v. 100 Acres of Land, 468 F.2d 1261 (9th Cir.1972), *cert. denied*, 414 U.S. 864, 94 S.Ct. 37, 38 L.Ed.2d 84 (1973) (the subject property was generally unimproved, but it was part of a larger tract being developed and was the next area to be completed); United States v. 147.47 Acres, 352 F.Supp. 1055 (M.D.Pa.1972) (substantial physical work and actual sales of lots had taken place). This satisfies the requirement that "[e]lements affecting value that depend upon events or combinations of occurrences which, while within the realm of possibility, *are not fairly shown to be reasonably probable*, should be excluded from consideration . . .." Olson v. United States, 292 U.S. 246, 257, 54 S.Ct. 704, 709, 78 L.Ed. 1236 (1934) (emphasis added).

The factors which indicate if an event is reasonably probable are those that "fairly might be brought forward and reasonably be given substantial weight" in "fair negotiations between an owner willing to sell and a purchaser desiring to buy." *Id.* at 257, 54 S.Ct. at 709. With the use of computers, sophisticated buyers and sellers are able to consider accurately a myriad of variables in arriving at a current market value for undeveloped land. The factors involved in the development cost approach are clearly those that are "brought forward" and given "substantial weight" in "fair negotiations" between a willing seller and a willing buyer.

We take the position that, in light of current practices in the real estate area, the use of computer technology and the approach to a more liberal introduction of evidence as suggested by our new rules of evidence adopted in 1977, it was error to disallow the development cost approach in this case. We go several steps further. Since all relevant evidence relating to market value should be admissible, we hold that specific prices of comparable sales may be used on both direct testimony of witnesses, as well as on cross-examination, unless that evidence containing comparable sales is so remote in time as to be irrelevant. We see no reason to allow an expert to testify as to value and then permit the very bases for his testimony to come out only in cross-examination, if at all. Likewise, we believe that the assessed valuation of the property as shown in the county auditor's records should be admissible as bearing upon the fair market value of the property. Again, subject to the objection of the possible remoteness of time, the owner's acquisition costs and money expended for improvements should be admissible on both direct or cross-examination.

Finally, while the development cost approach will hereafter be permissible, specific numerical, analytical and illustrative evidence supporting the development cost approach appraisal will be allowed only if the party introducing such evidence can lay a proper foundation to show that (a) the land is ripe for development; (b) the owner can reasonably expect to secure the necessary zoning and other permits required for the development to take place; and (c) the development will not take place at too remote a time. To the extent that *Malecker* may be inconsistent, it is overruled.

In this particular case, therefore, appellants should have been permitted to introduce the planned development and proposed plat through expert witnesses. They would be required to prove that the landfill contemplated would be normally and reasonably permissible under either state statutes or watershed district regulations. The county board resolution should have been submitted to the jury because of the influence it might have had on the possibility that the permits needed for the landfill would have been issued.

We do not deem the final issue as to whether there was a necessity to acquire the entire 80 acres to have much merit. Appellants' own counsel did not seriously argue that point at the hearing held on initial petition for condemnation and has virtually conceded there was a public use involved.

The case is reversed and remanded for a new trial not inconsistent with this opinion.

KELLEY, J., took no part in the consideration or decision of this case.

NOTES

1. As stated in *Ramsey County*, the standard measure for just compensation is "the amount which a purchaser willing, but not required, to buy the property would pay to an owner willing, but not required, to sell it, taking into consideration the highest and best use to which the property can be put." Traditionally, the preferred technique for determining that amount has been the *market data* or *comparable sales* approach. *Ramsey County* reflects the modern trend to use other techniques where appropriate—the *income-capitalization* approach (primarily for rental properties) and the *reproduction cost less depreciation* approach (primarily for properties with unique improvements having no ready market).

One crucial variable under any of these measures is the parcel's "highest and best use." Determining highest and best use becomes particularly tricky when that use depends on governmental actions—rezoning, variances, special exceptions or subdivision map approvals—not yet taken. For example, do you think that *Ramsey County* provided adequate guidelines for discounting the parcel's theoretically best use—477 dwelling units—by the probability that, in order to appease neighbors and obtain development approvals, the developer would have to cut back on the number of units built? Is there any discrepancy between the eminent domain rule, allowing compensation to include the value of prospective land use approvals, and the "takings" rule, discussed at pages 1094–1116, above, denying compensation for losses suffered as a result of changes in land use legislation? Is it appropriate to compensate for the benefits that a local government has specially conferred in preparation for a parcel's development, such as the bridge, water and sewer facilities built by the City of New Brighton?

2. The willing seller-willing buyer measure will rarely leave the condemnee better off than if no condemnation had occurred. Typically it will leave him far worse off. Apart from the emotional jar of being required to move, a family whose home is taken by eminent domain will usually not be compensated for its relocation costs, including moving expenses, carrying charges and the possibly higher price and financing costs of a new home. Businesses do no better. A firm cannot recover either relocation expenditures or damages arising from destruction of its business, lost goodwill or the diminished value of equipment that, custom-built for the site condemned, will be less useful at some other site. (Although condemnors are not required to compensate for movable equipment, they must pay for fixtures and other improvements to the condemned parcel.) See D. Hagman, Urban Planning and Land Development Control Law 331–343 (1975).

One rationale for not compensating these losses is that they are too speculative. Do the rules of evidence in condemnation proceedings, discussed in *Ramsey County*, fully rebut this rationale? Another argument against compensation is that land is the sole constitutional object of compensation and these losses are unconnected to land. Does the *Oakland Raiders* case, page 1300, note 8, above, holding that intangible business property can be condemned, completely rebut this argument? Can the argument be reconciled with the constitutional position that nonconforming uses cannot be prohibited immediately upon the enactment of a zoning law but, rather, must be amortized over a reasonable period? See page 1176, above.

Is there any good reason for government to be so stingy in condemnation cases? Courts and legislatures have moved toward requiring more complete compensation. Some courts, for example, will partially compensate for relocation costs by treating them as an item that the seller would naturally include in setting her selling price. Similarly, at least two appraisal techniques—capitalized income and reproduction cost less depreciation—will often allow at least partial compensation for the diminished value of goodwill and equipment. State legislatures have begun to require compensation for specified relocation costs. See, for example, Mass.Gen.Laws Ann. ch. 79, § 6A (1978).

See generally, Aloi & Goldberg, A Reexamination of Value, Good Will and Business Losses in Eminent Domain, 53 Cornell L.Q. 604 (1968).

3. Recent empirical studies indicate that there will often be a substantial gap between the "just compensation" required by state and federal constitutions and the compensation that condemnees in fact receive. Apparently, the condemnation process itself tends to skew awards away from the just compensation ideal. For example, a study of condemnation proceedings in one Chicago urban renewal program found that, while high-valued parcels received more than

market value, low-valued parcels tended to receive less than market value. Munch, An Economic Analysis of Eminent Domain, 84 J.Pol. Econ. 473 (1976).

An earlier study of condemnation practices in Nassau County, New York, revealed that the process systematically understated the "fair market value" to be paid for both high and low value parcels. One reason lay in the way the county used its appraisals. Typically the county would order one appraisal; since condemnees rarely obtained their own appraisals, this appraisal became the benchmark for all subsequent negotiations. Because these appraisals were comparatively unsophisticated and were infrequently tested in court, the appraiser had every opportunity to bias his result downward in order to favor the county, his regular employer. On those occasions when the county did order a second appraisal, wide discrepancies appeared. "In barely half (51.3%) of the appraisal pairs was the second appraisal within 10% of the first. In 11.8% of the cases, the second appraisal varied from the first by fifty or more percentage points." Berger & Rohan, The Nassau County Study: An Empirical Look into the Practices of Condemnation, 67 Colum.L.Rev. 430, 440 (1967).

The settlement process also contributed to undercompensation in Nassau County. The first county official to contact the condemnee was a professional negotiator authorized to settle at a figure no higher than somewhere between 60% and 85% of the already understated first appraisal. If these negotiations failed, the matter was then turned over to a litigator on the county attorney's staff for further negotiation and, if these settlement efforts failed, for trial. Settlement agreements were reached for more than 85% of the parcels studied. According to the authors, "the condemnee who agreed to settle was shockingly underpaid. Only about one in six (15.7%) realized or bettered the County's low appraisal, a sum that an impartial observer might consider a *sine qua non* for 'just' compensation. Even regarding the next group of settlements—those between 90 and 99% of low appraisal—as within a tolerable range, nearly three claimants in five (56.9%) received under 90% of the County's low appraisal, and one in twelve (8.6%) received less than 50%!" Id. 442–443.

4. *Replacement Cost or Fair Market Value?* United States v. 564.54 Acres of Land, 441 U.S. 506, 99 S.Ct. 1854, 60 L.Ed.2d 435 (1979), raised the question whether the Fifth Amendment's just compensation clause requires the government to pay replacement cost rather than fair market value, which is often much lower. Condemnee, the Southeastern Pennsylvania Synod of the Lutheran Church of America, had rejected the government's $485,400 fair market value offer for three nonprofit summer camps it operated along the Delaware River, and demanded $5.8 million instead—the alleged cost of developing functionally equivalent substitute facilities. (The condemnee claimed that the larger award was necessary "because the new facilities would be subject to financially burdensome regulations

from which existing facilities were exempt under grandfather provisions.")

The district court ruled against the condemnee on the ground that replacement cost was payable only to government condemnees. The Third Circuit Court of Appeals reversed, observing that in condemnations of property belonging to states or their subdivisions, the Fifth Amendment requires an award of replacement cost "so that the functions carried out by or on behalf of members of the community may be continued." Since the Fifth Amendment refers expressly to private but not to public property, the court reasoned that the framers of the amendment could not have "intended to impose a greater obligation of indemnification on the national government toward the states and their subdivisions than toward private owners." 506 F.2d 796, 799–801.

The Supreme Court reversed. Acknowledging that in "giving content to the just compensation requirement of the Fifth Amendment, this Court has sought to put the owner of condemned property 'in as good a position pecuniarily as if his property had not been taken,'" the Court noted that the indemnity principle "has not been given its full and literal force. Because of serious practical difficulties in assessing the worth an individual places on particular property at a given time, we have recognized the need for a relatively objective working rule"—the concept of fair market value. Yet, the Court refused to accept fair market value as the sole measure of just compensation, for "there are situations where this standard is inappropriate . . . . Hence, we must determine whether application of the fair-market-value standard here would be impracticable or whether an award of market value would diverge so substantially from the indemnity principle as to violate the Fifth Amendment."

The Court found no such problem under the facts. First, "it is not at all unusual that property uniquely adapted to the owner's use has a market value on condemnation which falls far short of enabling the owner to preserve that use. Such a situation may often arise, for example where a family home has been built to the owner's tastes, but is old and deteriorated, or where property, like respondent's camps, is exempt from regulations applicable to new facilities." 441 U.S. at 514, 99 S.Ct. at 1858. Second, the rationale for awarding replacement cost on condemnation of lands belonging to the public entities—"the entity has an obligation to continue providing the facilities taken"—did not apply here. "Awarding replacement cost on the theory that respondent would continue to operate the camps for a public purpose would thus provide a windfall if substitute facilities were never acquired, or if acquired, were later sold or converted to another use." 441 U.S. at 515–516, 99 S.Ct. as 1859.

Do you agree with the Court's decision? What good reason is there to distinguish between the political forces that determine whether a governmental condemnee will replace its condemned facility, and the market forces that determine whether a private condemnee will devote its award to continuing its condemned facility or to pursuing some other activity?

5. *Governmental Actions Affecting Fair Market Value: De Facto Takings.* When, as a prelude to initiating an urban renewal project, the government declares an area to be blighted, owners in the area often allow their buildings to deteriorate in the years before the condemnation proceeding actually begins. Courts computing a parcel's fair market value will, as a general rule, exclude such decreases in value resulting directly from the government's announcement of its condemnation plans—commonly by computing value as of the date the condemnation plans were first announced, rather than as of the date when condemnation was begun.

What if the delay following the first government announcement is so protracted, and the consequent disincentive for the landowner to maintain her parcel so great, that the owner is effectively unable to earn a reasonable return from the parcel? Courts will in these circumstances sometimes hold that a compensable *de facto* taking of the parcel has occurred, so that if the government later abandons its condemnation plans, and no *de jure* taking occurs, the court will order compensation for the *de facto* taking. See, for example, Osborn v. City of Cedar Rapids, 324 N.W.2d 471 (Iowa 1982). (If, by contrast, a *de jure* taking does follow the *de facto* taking, the court will at that time compute the parcel's value as of the date the condemnation plans were first announced and award interest on that value from the date of the *de facto* taking.)

Many courts are reluctant to find a *de facto* taking in these circumstances, particularly if there is no subsequent *de jure* taking. Their main concern is probably that such a finding would dangerously expand the ground for inverse condemnation claims beyond the present, generally applicable, requirement that a physical invasion be shown. See page 1113, above. For example, in City of Buffalo v. J. W. Clement Co., 28 N.Y.2d 241, 321 N.Y.S.2d 345, 269 N.E.2d 895 (1971), the New York Court of Appeals ruled that no *de facto* taking had occurred at any time between 1954, when condemnation plans were first announced, and 1967 when condemnation proceedings were actually begun, even though in the interim the City repeatedly confirmed, and postponed, its condemnation plans, the whole area fell into disrepair, defendant Clement's parcel became unsalable and unrentable after 1963, and Clement acquired a new site for its plant and began directing all improvements and new machinery for its printing operations to that site. In the court's view, "to hold that there can be a *de facto* appropriation absent a physical invasion or direct legal restraint would, needless to say, be to do violence to a workable rule of law. It is our view that only the most obvious injustice compels such a result. The Appellate Division, discerning so substantial an interference with the use of the subject property, found the essential elements of ownership to have been destroyed and held that the city's action constituted a *de facto* taking. We firmly disagree with that determination." 28 N.Y.2d at 253–254, 321 N.Y.S.2d at 352, 269 N.E. 2d at 902.

Should the court have distinguished the case before it from cases in which there had been no subsequent *de jure* taking on the ground that here the city had authoritatively evidenced its intention to take Clement's land and damages were awardable in any event? Should *de facto* taking cases, in which government announces its condemnation plans but does not follow through with a *de jure* condemnation, be distinguished from inverse condemnation cases generally, in which there is not even a preliminary statement of intent to condemn? One possible ground for the distinction is the convenience of small numbers: in *de facto* taking cases, the government has identified the specific parcel or parcels affected, to the exclusion of the rest of the land in the community; asserted regulatory takings, by contrast, affect all or most of the land in the community to some degree.

1. PARTIAL TAKINGS

MERRILL TRUST CO. v. STATE

Supreme Court of Maine, 1980.
417 A.2d 435.

DUFRESNE, Active Retired Justice.

On October 20, 1970, the Department of Transportation of the State of Maine (hereinafter referred to as MDOT) on behalf of the State of Maine, pursuant to 23 M.R.S.A. § 153, acquired through eminent domain 9.19 acres of land owned by the plaintiff Merrill Trust Company, trustee under the will of Louis Oakes, together with certain easements in the nature of sloping and drainage rights over portions of the remaining property of the plaintiff. The expropriated land was part of a tract approximately 5,500 acres in size located in the unorganized township of Big Squaw, Piscataquis County. The purpose of the taking was to eliminate a curve in the Greenville to Rockwood highway, otherwise known as routes 6 and 15 and hereinafter referred to as the highway. The new section of highway, running north to south through the tract, recast the plaintiff's holdings into three parts, instead of two previously existing segments: a westerly portion of approximately 4,576 acres, an easterly portion of about 902 acres, and a 3.5 acre parcel isolated between the old highway and the new right of way.

Big Squaw Mountain and Mountain View Pond are located in the westerly portion of the tract. At the time of the taking, seven hundred and fifty acres around Big Squaw Mountain had been leased by the plaintiff to the Moosehead Winter Development Corporation and the improvements in that area consisted of a motel, base facilities for ski-lifts, a sanitation system and trails. Otherwise, the plaintiff's property was uninhabited woodland.

A series of three studies, made by various consulting firms relative to the long term land use development of the Squaw Mountain tract in the years 1966, 1968 and 1971, culminated in a classification of the area of the land acquired by MDOT in 1970 as developable land for recreational purposes.

The area taken by the State is comprised of three separate parcels which run severally along the old right of way, except for that portion which abuts the reference 3.5 acre islanded piece between the old and the new road. The largest acquisition, located on the east side of the highway and denominated "parcel 2–2" by the parties, represents an area of 8.03 acres, while the other two small strips of land, "parcel 2–1" and "parcel 2–3," measure .16 acre and 1 acre respectively.

The State appealed from the 1973 award of the Land Damage Board to the Superior Court pursuant to 23 M.R.S.A. § 157, where the case was heard, jury waived, in December 1978.

Each party presented an expert witness to testify to the fair market value of the land taken. The plaintiff's appraiser stated that the highest and best use was "recreational development," and concluded that its per acre value was $2,250.00, supporting, so he claimed, an award of $20,677.50 for the 9.19 acres which the State had condemned. Adding $1,125.00 per acre for severance damages in respect to the 3.5 acre plot isolated by the taking, he testified that the plaintiff was entitled to the total amount of $24,450.00 as just compensation for the State's action. On the other hand, the State's appraiser, who was an employee of MDOT, estimated that in his opinion the total damage award should be $700.00. Specifically, he testified that the highest and best use of the subject property was "woodland with recreational potential," and concluded that its value was $65.00 per acre for a total amount of $600.00. He allocated an additional $100.00 for the other interests (easements) acquired. He also determined that no severance damages were allowable either on account of the isolated 3.5 acre piece as such or in relation to the remaining property of the plaintiff, because, as he maintained, the plaintiff's total acreage ownership was worth some $1,500,000.00, whether viewed before or after the taking.

The presiding Justice rejected the appraisal approaches of both experts, but expressly stated that, in his attempt to reach a fairer evaluation of just compensation, he did take into consideration their testimony and the opinions they voiced. He concluded the plaintiff was entitled to a total award of damages in the amount of $12,000.00.

Specifically, the trial Justice found that the highest and best use of the property was "partially developed wooded land with potential for further recreational development." He first placed a fair market value of $275.00 per acre for parcels 2–1 and 2–3 on the west side of the highway, awarding $319.00 for the 1.16 acres of land taken and

$181.00 for easements and severance damage in connection therewith, for a total value of $500.00. From a value range of $275.00 to $2,000.00 per acre, he then estimated the worth of the 8.03 acres taken on the east side of the highway at the rate of $1,000.00 per acre, for a total damage of $8,030.00, to which he added the sum of $1,000.00 for easement and severance damages in relation to that taking. Finally, he found that the isolated piece between the old highway and the new section of road had suffered severance damages in the amount of $2,459.00.

The State timely appealed from the appropriate judgment entered upon the foregoing findings, and presently challenges the valuation formula utilized, and the damages awarded, by the Court below.

We deny the appeal and sustain the Superior Court.

I. *Fair Market Value—Parcels 2-1, 2-2 and 2-3.*

As its primary argument on appeal, the State earnestly contends that, in all instances of a partial taking, the exclusive method for valuing the portion condemned must be to estimate its worth as part of the whole. It is suggested that, under the holding of Timberlands, Inc. v. Maine State Highway Com'n, Me., 284 A.2d 894 (1971), the only valid valuation formula where severance damages are claimed is the difference between the value of the entire tract immediately before the taking and the value of the remainder immediately after the taking. This is contrary to the recognized traditional measure of damages for such partial takings which authorizes the use of an alternative concept, to wit, the value of the property actually taken together with the diminution in value of the part that remains (severance damage).

Nevertheless, pursuant to its stated argument, the State claims that the Superior Court erred in relying upon the suggested invalid appraisal of the plaintiff's expert witness, who grounded his professional opinion of market values upon a comparison to sales of one half acre lots. We reject this contention.

The defendant incorrectly interprets the holding of *Timberlands, supra*, wherein we wrote at 284 A.2d 898:

> The "before and after" formula, in partial taking cases, is the *ideal* formula where severance damages are claimed, since the parcel taken is generally of limited size or unusual shape, or both, and may have no independent use and little or no economic value, unless considered in its relationship to the remainder of the tract. (Emphasis supplied).
>
> . . . . Where the part taken has an independent economic use with a market value and may command a higher value as a separate entity, such value has been allowed.
>
> The owner of the land taken by the process of eminent domain has the right to this higher fair market value or at least to the

opportunity of proving it to the jury, as he is entitled to no less under the constitutional mandate than an exact equivalent for the injury.

The *before and after* test was devised for the benefit of the condemnee. The plaintiff is not restricted to the use of this formulation; rather, it is entitled to submit proof of its damages based upon the value of its holdings at their highest and best use. Had the condemnation not occurred, there is no showing that there would be any legal impediment to the plaintiff's subdivision of its 5500 acre tract. It logically follows that upon proper proof, the plaintiff is entitled to recover the higher value of the land taken, whether or not it asserts a claim for severance damages.

The defendant also argues that the values assigned to the various parcels by the Superior Court Justice were arbitrary, and without evidentiary support. The record reveals that, contrary to this assertion, the presiding Justice carefully followed the guidelines enunciated in *Timberlands*, reaching a highly rational conclusion in the face of such disparate appraisal testimony.

In estimating the value of the land acquired by the State, Walter Foster, the plaintiff's expert witness, relied upon six comparable sales which he adjusted for time, location, and development and promotional costs. The parcels had been sold in 1972 by Skylark Incorporated, a subsidiary of Scott paper, to various grantees and are located approximately one quarter mile south of the plaintiff's property. Each parcel measured 22,000 square feet and sold for $2,500.00, for a unit value of $5,000.00 per acre. Based upon this data, Mr. Foster concluded that the 9.19 acres condemned had an indicated value of $2,250.00 per acre. On the other hand, the State's expert witness, Henry Plimpton, estimated the "contributory value" of the subject property to be $65.00 per acre. He based this estimate in particular upon sales comparisons to two tracts of land: a 70 acre parcel which sold in 1966 for $2,900.00 or $41.00 per acre, and a 100 acre parcel, also sold in 1966, for $4,500.00 or $45.00 per acre. In ascertaining the extent of severance damages, however, Mr. Plimpton considered three sales of large tracts of land and concluded that the value of the entire 5500 acres was $1,500,000.00, both before and after the taking, an estimate which equates to a value of approximately $275.00 per acre.

The presiding Justice explained the basis for his finding on the record. Consistent with the *Timberlands* rationale, he determined that parcels 2–1 and 2–3 to the west had little independent economic value because of their "minimum depth," and affixed their value at $275.00 per acre by consideration of their relationship to the remainder of the tract. In valuing parcel 2–2, the presiding Justice looked to its size and shape. He found that part of the parcel had an independent economic use with a market value of $2,000.00 per acre, and that part thereof had no such independent value and was, therefore, worth $275.00 per acre. He then concluded that parcel 2-2 had an average value of $1,000.00 per acre. . . .

On the record before us the evidence, though in conflict, does support the finding of the Superior Court on the issue of the market values of parcels 2-1, 2-2 and 2-3.

II. *Severance Damages.*

The State challenges the sufficiency of the evidence to support the trial Justice's award of severance damages made in connection with each of the three parts of the plaintiff's remaining lands following the taking, contending that the Court's several findings of such damages was arbitrary and reversible error. We disagree.

Initially, may we repeat what we said in *Timberlands, supra*, 284 A.2d at 897, that "[w]hen only a part of a tract of land is taken in the exercise of the power of eminent domain, the general rule is that the just compensation which the Constitution guarantees to the owner includes not only the value of the part taken, but also the damages accruing to the residue."

In the instant case, the State's taking has segmented the plaintiff's lands three ways; some small portion (1.16 acres) was extracted from the land area to the west of the old right of way (with minimal severance damage impact as mentioned by the presiding Justice on the large area owned by the plaintiff on that side of the highway), while the plaintiff's property to the east of the old right of way was split in two separate parcels, the isolated piece and the rest of the property to the east of the new right of way.

Where only a portion of a landowner's property is taken and there remains to the condemnee a singular contiguous parcel suitable and adaptable to a unitary use, the general rule is to regard the entire remainder as a single entity for the purpose of assessing severance damages for the taking of a part. In instances, however, where a substantial portion of a contiguous remainder piece is suitable and adaptable to a higher and better economic use than the use to which the rest thereof can be put, a land owner may claim severance damages to that portion which may be put to the higher and better use and waive severance damages to the balance.

In this case, however, the partial taking left the owner with three completely separate parcels, the large area to the west of the old highway, the isolated piece between the old and the new right of way, and the remainder of the property to the east of the new section of highway. Under such circumstances, the severance damage rule, applicable to partial takings where there remains a single contiguous parcel suitable or adaptable to a unitary use, need not be the formula to measure the variation in values of such separate plots; and the approach used by the Court below in estimating the severance damages caused to the three different and discontinuous pieces of land of the plaintiff by reason of the taking as if they stood alone was proper.

In his decision, the presiding Justice said:

"Now I've applied two severance factors because the taking of parcel 2.2 severed part of the Plaintiff's land and the impact differs from the west side of the parcel to the east side of the parcel taken. My approach to the 3.5-acre parcel isolated between the new and the old highway is to find that the impact of the taking reduced the value of that acreage from the $1000 average that I found above to the $275 value that I applied originally on the west side of the highway."

In relation to the 3.5 acre piece, which suffered the greatest damage by being severed from the balance of the land east of the highway, he estimated that the plaintiff was entitled to an award of $2,459.00. This conclusion was well within the range of values testified to by the expert witnesses. (There was a mathematical error in computation, however, as the total should have been $2,537.50, some $78.50 short of the correct amount; this error favored the State.)

In connection with parcels 2–1 and 2–3 taken on the west side of the old highway, the single Justice allowed severance and easement damages of $181.00, and, on account of the taking of parcel 2–2, the sum of $1,000.00 as such severance and easement damages. There was evidence given by the State's expert respecting easement damages, but neither expert testified specifically in regard to severance damages in connection with the taking of parcels 2–1, 2–2 or 2–3. The State argues that, without specific expert evidence of severance damages focussing directly on each parcel, the Justice below committed reversible error in adjudicating the amount of such damages. Again, we disagree. . . .

The entry will be:

Appeal denied.

Judgment of the Superior Court entered June 22, 1979 affirmed.

NOTES

1. As indicated in *Merrill Trust*, *A*, whose land is partially condemned, will be compensated not only for the part taken, but also for damages to the part retained. Thus, if the state condemns a 25-foot strip of *A*'s land in order to expand an existing road into a superhighway, *A* will recover not only for the value of the strip, but also for consequential damage to the remainder of the parcel arising from the noise, fumes and lights produced by the increased traffic. Yet, *A*'s neighbor *B*, whose land on the other side of the highway has not been condemned, will not be entitled to consequential damages and thus will be entirely uncompensated even though he suffers identical damage from the increased traffic.

Is the different treatment of *A* and *B* fair? Is it efficient? One advantage of the rule is that it provides a bright line—physical appropriation—to distinguish the few situations in which compensation will be allowed from the innumerable claims of damage that will be pressed by landowners both adjacent to and distant from the public improvement. Note, too, that the alternative means for correcting the disparity between *A* and *B*—*reducing A*'s award to exclude consequential damages—will often be difficult. See Dennison v. State, 22 N.Y.2d 409, 293 N.Y.S.2d 68, 70, 239 N.E.2d 708, 710 (1968) ("As we view the case, it would have been practically impossible for the court to separate the noise element from the other elements which, it is conceded, were properly considered—the loss of privacy, seclusion and view").

Some courts have begun to correct the disparity between *A*, whose land has been partially condemned, and *B* whose land has not, by holding that if *B* can show that the injury to his land is both substantial and unique, he may obtain compensation on an inverse condemnation theory. For example, in Varjabedian v. City of Madera, 20 Cal.3d 285, 142 Cal.Rptr. 429, 572 P.2d 43 (1977), the California Supreme Court ruled that plaintiffs could claim inverse condemnation by reason of an adjacent, noisome municipal sewage plant even though they could show no physical invasion of their parcel.

Does this increased liberality in inverse condemnation awards against noninvasive governmental activities suggest that the next step will be to hold that purely regulatory activities—such as the enactment of zoning ordinances—can constitute inverse condemnation? See generally, Note, Condemnation Blight and the Abutting Landowner, 73 Mich.L.Rev. 583 (1975).

2. The two principal formulae for compensating partial takings are the *before and after* formula (the difference between the fair market value of the entire parcel before the taking and the value of the remainder after the taking) and the *value plus damages* formula (the fair market value of the portion taken plus damage to the remainder, as measured by the difference between the fair market value of the remainder before and after the taking). While many states have adopted one formula to the exclusion of the other, some, like Maine, allow the condemnee to elect between them. And, although the value plus damages formula has historically been preferred by courts, the before and after test, favored by the commentators, is increasing in popularity. See, for example, Connor, Valuation of Partial Takings in Condemnation: A Need for Legislative Review, 2 Pac.L.J. 116 (1971).

The practical difference between the two formulae stems from the general rule that if a partial condemnation confers any benefits on the remainder—improved highway access, for example, or increased business traffic—these benefits must be set off against the condemnee's damages. Under the before and after formula these benefits will be set off against the entire compensation. By contrast, under the value plus damages formula, the benefits will be set off only against damages to the remainder, and not against the value of the portion taken. As a result, whenever benefits exceed total damages, the condemnee will receive no compensation at all under the before and after formula while, under the value plus damages formula, she will always receive the value of the portion taken. See 1 L. Orgel, Valuation Under Eminent Domain §§ 47–65 (2d ed. 1953).

Are there better ways to account for the value of benefits conferred by a partial taking? Compare Uniform Eminent Domain Code § 1002 (1974):

(a) Except as provided in subsection (b), the measure of compensation for taking of property is its fair market value determined under Section 1004 as of the date of valuation.

(b) If there is a partial taking of property, the measure of compensation is the greater of (1) the value of the property taken as determined under subsection (a) or (2) the amount by which the fair market value of the entire property immediately before the taking exceeds the fair market value of the remainder immediately after the taking.

3. *Contiguity.* Traditionally, in order to recover severance damages for a partial taking, a condemnee was required to show unity of title, unity of use and physical contiguity between the parcel taken and parcel or parcels retained. Although common ownership is still required, courts have begun to relax the earlier insistence on technical unity of title. See, for example, Symms v. Nelson Sand & Gravel, 93 Idaho 574, 468 P.2d 306 (1970) (condemnee, with fee interest in parcel condemned, entitled to severance damages to adjacent parcel held under lease). And, although many states still require strict physical contiguity, others will loosen the requirement to enable recovery if the parcels are proximate and economically interdependent. See, for example, City of Los Angeles v. Wolfe, 6 Cal.3d 326, 99 Cal. Rptr. 21, 491 P.2d 813 (1971) (although "general rule in this state is that contiguity is 'ordinarily essential,'" held: condemnee's parking lot, separated from condemnee's business premises by 250 feet, was contiguous for purposes of severance damages to the business premises).

Unity of use, however, continues to be required everywhere: "Regardless of contiguity and unity of ownership, ordinarily lands will not be considered a single tract unless there is unity of use. It has been said that 'there must be such a connection, or relation of adaptation, convenience, and actual and permanent use between them, as to make the enjoyment of the parcel taken, reasonably and substantially necessary to the enjoyment of the parcel left, in the most advantageous and profitable manner in the business for which it is used.' The unifying use must be a present use! A mere intended use cannot be given effect. If the uses of two or more sections of land are different and inconsistent, no claim of unity can be maintained. But the mere possibility of adaptability to different uses will not render segments of land separate and independent." Barnes v. North Carolina State Highway Commission, 250 N.C. 378, 109 S.E.2d 219, 225 (1959).

Do contiguity rules encourage landowners, faced with imminent condemnation proceedings, to engage in strategic behavior—buying up contiguous parcels to take advantage of severance damages and selling contiguous parcels to avoid benefit setoffs? (In the first case, the landowner should be willing to pay his neighbor some amount, above the after-condemnation market value, approaching the severance damages expected for that parcel; in the second case, the landowner should be willing to accept some amount, below the after-condemnation market value, approaching the benefit setoff for that parcel.) Note that in both cases the amount bid for the parcel in question should approximate what the parcel would bring if the condemnation had not occurred. Do you see why?

4. *Will Severance Damages Include Losses Arising From Reduced Access to Public Roads?* The question typically arises when government condemns part of a parcel in order to convert a freely accessible public road into a limited access superhighway, forcing the occupant of the remainder to take a more circuitous route to gain access to the highway. Although the diminution in value is clear, and would doubtless be compensable under the general principles announced in *Merrill Trust*, courts hesitate to include diminished access as an element of severance damages.

Ironically, the reason for this reluctance lies in a rule of inverse condemnation law that government *must* compensate an owner whose land abuts a public road any time the government completely blocks access to that road, even though the obstruction involves no direct condemnation or physical invasion of any part of the abutting owner's land. The rule has two limiting principles. First, the abutting owner must, to prevail, demonstrate that her injury is unique and not common to the public at large. Second, she must demonstrate that she has been deprived of all reasonable access. See generally, Note, Inverse Condemnation and the Right of Access of Abutting Property Owners, 9 Ind.L.Rev. 859, 881 (1976). It is this second limiting principle that explains the judicial reluctance to award severance damages for reduced access in direct condemnation actions.

The Alaska Supreme Court explored the connection between these inverse condemnation and direct condemnation rules in Triangle, Inc. v. State, 632 P.2d 965 (Alaska 1981), reviewing an award for the state's condemnation of part of plaintiff's parcel in the course of widening the highway on which plaintiff's property abutted; one result of the widening was that plaintiff lost its direct access to the highway, and its customers were required to travel an extra one-half mile to get to and from its night club. The trial court ruled against plaintiff's claim for severance damages arising from loss of direct access to the highway. The Alaska Supreme Court affirmed, holding that inverse condemnation law's reasonable access rule controlled: "the remaining access was sufficiently reasonable to avoid any need for the payment of compensation." 632 P.2d at 969. Justice Connor dissented, arguing that direct condemnation law's severance damages rule should govern.

2. DIVIDED INTERESTS

CHARLOTTE v. CHARLOTTE PARK & RECREATION COMM'N

Supreme Court of North Carolina, 1971.
278 N.C. 26, 178 S.E.2d 601.

The City of Charlotte instituted this proceeding to condemn property owned by The Charlotte Park and Recreation Commission (the Commission), used by it as a park and known as the Rose Garden, the taking being for the purpose of construction of a highway known as the Northwest Expressway. The Commission moved that its title to the property and its sole right to receive the award for its taking be determined. The City moved that a hearing be had upon all issues raised by the pleadings, other than the issue of damages, and that the court determine the nature and extent of the Commission's interest in the land and the measure of damages to be paid by the City. The case was so heard in the Superior Court without a jury. The following is a summary of the facts found by the Superior Court, to which findings no exception has been taken:

1. All parties known to claim any interest in the property have been named as defendants and properly served with process.

2. The property was conveyed to the City of Charlotte by Piedmont Realty Company by deed dated July 13, 1904, which deed contained the following provision:

> "To Have and To Hold unto the said party of the second part, its successors and assigns, to be improved, maintained and used by it for the purpose of furnishing to white people a park for their pleasure and comfort, and upon condition that whenever the said property shall cease to be used as a park for white purposes (sic), then the same shall revert to the party of the first part, its successors and assigns."

3. Subsequently, title to the property vested in the Commission, subject to the above quoted provision in the deed from Piedmont Realty Company, and such title was held by the Commission at the time of the taking in this proceeding by the City.

4. At the time of the taking, there was no intent on the part of the Commission to abandon the use of the property for a public park or any probability of the discontinuance of the use of the property for park purposes.

Upon these facts the Superior Court concluded as matters of law (summarized):

1. The Commission is the only party having any interest in the property condemned and is entitled to the entire amount of any award to be made.

2. The City has acquired title to the property in fee simple absolute, free and clear of any restriction as to use, rights of reverter or any other encumbrance.

3. "Plaintiff having acquired title in fee simple absolute, the measure of damages to be followed in determining the issue of damages shall be the difference between the fair market value of the entire tract immediately prior to March 11, 1969, on which date the taking occurred, and the fair market value of the remaining property immediately after the taking."

4. No request for appointment of commissioners having been made, the cause is transferred to the Civil Issue Docket for trial as to the issue of just compensation.

The City appeals, assigning as error the third of the above conclusions of law, the signing of the order by the Superior Court and the refusal of the court to sign an order tendered by the City. The order so tendered by the City and rejected by the court would have directed the judge, at the trial of the issue of damages, to include in his charge the following:

> "In determining the issue of damages, the measure of damages shall be the difference between the fair market value of the entire tract *with its use limited to that of a public park* immediately prior to March 11, 1969, and the fair market value of the remaining property *with its use limited to that of a public park* immediately after the taking." (Emphasis added.) . . .

LAKE, Justice.

The deed from Piedmont Realty Company conveyed to the City of Charlotte a fee simple determinable estate, sometimes called a base or qualified fee, in the land here in question. The Superior Court found, without objection, that by virtue of certain acts of the Legislature this estate in the land was vested in the Commission at and prior to the time of the retaking of the land by the City in this condemnation proceeding.

The conveyance of the fee simple determinable estate left in the grantor, Piedmont Realty Company, a possibility of reverter, which is not an estate in the land but is a reversionary interest therein. Though the record before us does not so show, it is stated in the brief of the Commission that Abbott Realty Company, itself now defunct, was "a supposed transferee of Piedmont Realty Company." . . .

A fee simple determinable estate terminates automatically upon the occurrence of the event, which gives rise to the reverter, and no entry upon the land by the holder of the possibility of reverter is necessary to bring about the reversion of the fee simple absolute to him. Thus, had the Commission put the land to a use other than that specified in the deed from Piedmont Realty Company, which the record does not indicate, the Commission's right in the land would have terminated immediately. The taking of the land under the power of eminent domain does not, however, cause a reversion of the title to the grantor or its successor or transferee.

In this proceeding the City, in its declaration of taking, asserted that it thereby acquired a fee simple absolute in the land described as taken. Thus, the City in this proceeding has taken by condemnation both the fee simple determinable estate and the possibility of reverter. These were taken simultaneously. There was no interval following the taking of the fee simple determinable estate, for use for a purpose other than that stated in the deed from Piedmont Realty Company, in which the reverter could have occurred. The condemnation destroyed the possibility of reverter. The court below has found, without objection, that at the time of the taking by this proceeding there was no intent on the part of the Commission to abandon its use of the land as a park and that there was then no probability that such use by the Commission would be discontinued.

The right to compensation for a taking of property by the power of eminent domain is in those who owned compensable interests in the property immediately prior to the filing of the complaint and declaration of taking. In condemnation proceedings, where there are several separately owned interests in the condemned property, a proper method for determining compensation to be paid the holder of each interest is, first, to determine the value of the property taken, as a whole, and then apportion the award among the several claimants. The taker of the property, thus having its total liability determined, is not affected by or interested in the division of the award by the court.

Although there is authority to the contrary, the weight of authority supports the view that if, at the time of the taking of both the fee simple determinable estate and the possibility of reverter, the event which would otherwise have terminated the fee simple determinable estate is not a probability for the near future, the owner of the fee simple determinable estate is entitled to the full award of compensation for the taking, the possibility of reverter being considered of no value. In the present instance, those whom the City has designated as claimants of the possibility of reverter have either failed to file answer, or have filed answer disclaiming any interest in the award and asserting that they have transferred such interest as they might otherwise have to the Commission. Thus, there was no error in the conclusion of the Superior Court that the Commission is entitled to the full award to be made in this case.

It appears from the record that substantially all, but not all, of the tract of land affected by this taking has been condemned. The Commission asserts that the remainder is of no value as a park. "Where a portion of a tract of land is taken for highway purposes, the just compensation to which the landowner is entitled is the difference between the fair market value of the property *as a whole* immediately before and immediately after the appropriation of the portion thereof." Barnes v. North Carolina State Highway Commission, 250 N.C. 378, 109 S.E.2d 219. The market value of the property is to be determined on the basis of conditions existing at the time of the taking. It is not limited by the use then actually being made of the property, but is determined in the light of all uses to which the property was then adapted and for which it could have been used. All factors pertinent to a determination of what a buyer, willing to buy but not under compulsion to do so, would pay and what a seller, willing to sell but not under compulsion to do so, would take for the property must be considered.

The City contends that the application of this rule requires that the land be valued on the basis of its use as a public park only, since the Commission could not use it for any other purpose without terminating its estate therein. Although there is authority to that effect, in our opinion the better view, which is supported by the weight of authority, is that, in the absence of exceptional circumstances, if both the fee simple determinable estate and the possibility of reverter are condemned and if, at the time of the taking, the event which would otherwise terminate the fee simple determinable is not a probability for the near future, the award is made on the basis of the full market value of the land without restrictions as to its use. There is no injustice to the taker in this ruling for, having condemned both the fee simple determinable and the possibility of reverter, it has acquired a fee simple absolute. It is, therefore, required to pay only the value of the property which has been taken. If any injustice results, it falls upon the holder of the possibility of reverter. In the present case, according to the record before us, the holder or holders of that interest in the land have either filed no answer and made no claim to any portion of the award or have expressly disclaimed any interest therein and have requested that it be paid to the Commission.

A number of the cases cited by the City in support of its position are, in our opinion, distinguishable. In Boston Chamber of Commerce v. Boston, 217 U.S. 189, 30 S.Ct. 459, 54 L.Ed. 725, the city condemned land for use as a street. The land was subject to an easement of way, light and air in favor of an adjoining property owner. The Supreme Court of the United States held that the Fourteenth Amendment required the city to pay only the value of the land after taking this encumbrance into account. There, the encumbrance was not taken, or destroyed, by the condemnation proceeding since the purpose of the condemnation was to provide a public street and would, necessarily, preserve the easement of way, light and air. Not having taken or destroyed the right of the owner of the dominant estate, the city was properly held liable for the value of the servient estate only. In Rogers v. State Roads Commission, 227 Md. 560, 177

A.2d 850, and in State Highway Commission v. Callahan, 242 Or. 551, 410 P.2d 818, the taker was the grantor of the fee simple determinable and, therefore, was already the owner of the possibility of reverter. Not having taken this interest, that is, not having taken the fee simple absolute, it should not be required to pay for it, and the award was properly limited to the value of the fee simple determinable estate. Staninger v. Jacksonville Expressway Authority, 182 So. 2d 483 (Fla.Dist.Ct.App.), and State v. Reece, 374 S.W.2d 686 (Tex. Civ.App.), involved zoning restrictions and restrictions imposed by a covenant. These are distinguishable for the reason that the condemnation proceeding was not a taking or a destruction of the restriction. Furthermore, such restrictions are distinguishable from a possibility of reverter in that those restrictions forbid a use to be made of property, whereas the possibility of reverter does not forbid a use but transfers title to the property if it occurs. Where, as in the case before us, both the fee simple determinable and the possibility of reverter have been taken in the same condemnation proceeding, the full fee simple absolute has been taken and its full value should be paid by the taker to the party or parties rightfully entitled.

It follows that the measure of damages set forth in the third conclusion of law by the court below is the correct measure to be applied in this case and there was no error in the court's refusal to limit such damages to the value of the property as used for a public park.

No error.

NOTES

1. *Condemnation of Estates in Land and Future Interests.* It is clear that when government takes land that has been divided into present and future possessory interests, the present possessor will always receive some part or all of the condemnation award. The principal issue, considered in *Charlotte,* is whether and to what extent the future interest holder can share in the award.

As a general rule, the more certain it is that the future interest will become possessory, the more likely it is that its owner will be compensated. Most courts hold that reversioners or remaindermen are categorically entitled to compensation; their share of the award will differ, though, depending upon whether their interest is vested or contingent. Possibilities of reverter, rights of entry and executory interests, because they are uncertain ever to vest in possession, are generally not compensated; if, however, the defeasing event has occurred, and possession is in view, compensation may be paid if the statute of limitations has not run. And, there appears to be growing support for the rule, at least nominally followed in *Charlotte,* that these interests may be compensated if their vesting is "a probability for the near future."

Once having determined that a future interest is too distant and speculative to be compensated, should a court give the entire award to the present possessor as if he held an unencumbered fee simple absolute? Would it be preferable—and more consistent with the original parties' intent—for the entire award to be paid into court, impressed with a trust, and reinvested in some other asset subject to the terms and conditions of the original grant? California's Code of Civil Procedure § 1265.420 provides that when the property taken is subject to a life tenancy, the life tenant or any other person having an interest in the property, may petition the court to order:

(a) An apportionment and distribution of the award based on the value of the interest of life tenant and remaindermen.

(b) The compensation to be used to purchase comparable property to be held subject to the life tenancy.

(c) The compensation to be held in trust and invested and the income (and, to the extent the instrument that created the life tenancy permits, principal) to be distributed to the life tenant for the remainder of the tenancy.

(d) Such other arrangement as will be equitable under the circumstances.

Would, and should, *Charlotte* have been decided the other way if the holders of the possibility of reverter had pressed their claims in court? If they had pressed their claims and succeeded in proving that their interests would probably vest in the near future, how could they have proved the value of the reverter interest? Should the valuation account for the restriction that the parcel be used "as a park for white purposes"? Compare Charlotte Park and Recreation Commission v. Barringer, page 501 above, validating such racially restrictive conditions appearing in fees simple determinable. Is the rule in *Charlotte*, that compensation need not be paid to holders of remote possibilities of reverter and other future interests, good authority for the validity of title legislation abolishing these interests prospectively and retrospectively?

See generally, Courter & Maskery, The Effect of Condemnation Proceedings upon Possibilities of Reverter and Powers of Termination, 38 U.Det.L.J. 46 (1960); Browder, The Condemnation of Future Interests, 48 Va.L.Rev. 461 (1962).

2. *Condemnation of Easements, Covenants and Servitudes.* If *A* holds the benefit of an easement over *B*'s neighboring parcel, Blackacre, *A* will be entitled to compensation in the event Blackacre is condemned and the easement destroyed. (Of course if, in condemning and using Blackacre, the government does not interfere with the easement, *A* will receive no compensation.) Should the compensation rule differ when *A*'s easement was created by implication? By necessity? By prescription? By estoppel?

Covenants, unlike easements, are only irregularly compensated and the trend seems to be against compensation. The reason most commonly given for treating easements and covenants differently is the ancient bromide that easements are interests in land, and hence real property, while covenants are "mere" contracts, and hence not. In Board of Public Instruction v. Town of Bay Harbor Islands, 81 So. 2d 637 (Fla.1955), for example, the court refused to order compensation for the lost benefit of residential restrictive covenants on the ground that they "convey no interest in the land, are not true easements, and at best may be relied upon and enforced between the parties thereto and their successors with notice." 81 So.2d at 642. The court was particularly concerned that, in the event of "the construction of a public building in a large subdivision containing many separate ownerships, a determination of the varying degrees of damage, if any, which might be claimed by the individual lot owners would present obstacles of an unwarranted nature in the exercise of the sovereign power. It would afford little, if any, actual benefit to the landowner." 81 So.2d. at 643–644.

What contemporary justification is there for the rule against compensating covenants? Should the noncompensation rule be confined to the subdivision context described in *Bay Harbor*? Should a line be drawn between negative covenants and affirmative covenants? Between covenant benefits held in gross and those held appurtenant?

3. *Condemnation of Leasehold Estates.* As a general rule, landlords and tenants, like other holders of substantial future and present possessory interests in land, are entitled to share in any eminent domain award according to their respective interests—the landlord receiving the property's value in fee less the amount of the tenant's award, and the tenant receiving the difference, if any, between the parcel's fair rental value and the reserved rental for the remainder of the lease term. The two exceptions to this general rule are that the landlord will not be compensated if the reversion is so distant—for example, if it follows a 99-year term—that its value is speculative or not even *de minimis*, and the tenant will not be compensated if her term is so short that it is unlikely to have any market value.

In determining fair rental value, courts often employ an eclectic mix of techniques. For example, in State Dept. of Highways v. Schumacher, 180 Mont. 329, 590 P.2d 1110 (1979), the state condemned a large parcel, part of which was subject to a leasehold interest, for highway purposes. The lessor had operated a slaughterhouse on his portion of the land and the lessee had operated—believe it or not—a maggot ranch. In valuing the leasehold interest of the maggot ranch, the court started from the proposition that the "test of just compensation for property condemned is 'market value,' which is what a willing buyer would pay to a willing seller for the estate or interest being valued," and then went on to indicate the sorts of factors to be considered in determining market value: " 'the length of the lease, the rent to be paid, the cost or expense of operation of the business, the advantages or disadvantages of the operation of the business in that location and the fact that the lessee is relieved of such additional expense.'" 180 Mont. 334, 590 P.2d. 1114–1115. The court also noted that, as maggot production is a skill possessed "by very few people in the United States," it would be difficult to readily establish a fair market value through an overview of comparable sales . . . . In such cases . . . evidence of acceptable alternative means of valuing the lease, such as reproduction cost and revenue produced, is admissible." *Id.* Finally, the court took into account that $7\frac{1}{2}$ years of the 10-year lease term remained, as well as an option to renew for a second 10-year term. See generally, Horgan & Edgar, Leasehold Valuation Problem in Eminent Domain, 4 U.S.F.L. Rev. 1 (1969).

What are the effects of condemnation on the rights and liabilities of landlord and tenant *inter se*? Condemnation of the entire premises and of the entire leasehold term will terminate the landlord-tenant relationship. Partial condemnation, in which the condemnor takes only part of the premises or part of the term, leaves the landlord-tenant relationship intact. The tenant may recover from the condemnor for the value of the portion lost, but remains liable to the landlord for the rent and other leasehold obligations. See generally, 2 M. Friedman, Leases §§ 13.1, 13.2 (1974).

Representing a landlord, how would you draft a lease provision that would effectively give the landlord the entire condemnation award? Representing a tenant, how would you draft a lease provision relieving the tenant from lease obligations in the event of partial condemnation? In terms of negotiating strategy, what connections are there between the two provisions?

IV. REPRISE: WHY PROPERTY?

SAX, SOME THOUGHTS ON THE DECLINE OF PRIVATE PROPERTY

58 Washington Law Review 481–496 (1983).

A case could be made for the proposition that property rights have been in a state of more-or-less continuous decline for many decades, and that there is nothing to report on that front but more of the same. I do not agree. I believe that we have moved in recent years from a situation (characterized by conventional urban zoning) in which we generally encourage developmental rights, though recognizing they must from time to time be restrained, to one in which developmental activity has itself become suspect. As a result, we are in the midst of a major transformation in which property rights are being fundamentally redefined to the disadvantage of property owners.

Because this transition is, by and large, taking place without compensation, it has become commonplace for courts to describe what is occurring in conventional terms. The proliferation of recent historic preservation laws is routinely characterized, for example, as if it were nothing but a continuation of long-accepted zoning practices. In fact, I submit, such laws and many others—wetlands and coastal protection, open space zoning, growth control and the resurgent public trust doctrine—mark a transition the full effects of which have hardly begun to be recognized or felt.

As good an example as any is the recent decision of the United States Supreme Court in Penn Central Transportation Co. v. City of New York.[6] After dutifully reciting all the conventional cases in which regulation without compensation was sustained, the majority in effect concluded that the city's refusal to allow Penn Central to build a high-rise above Grand Central Station, which had been designated an architectural landmark, was indistinguishable from a half-century's land regulation and zoning cases. Justice Rehnquist, in dissent, insisted that something importantly different was happening in *Penn Central*. He was right, but he too failed to recognize the full significance of the majority's decision: Rejection of the very claim that there existed a private property right capable of being taken.

What made *Penn Central* an unconventional case? For one thing, the owner in that case was denied the opportunity to pursue an established business expectation, though the majority opinion denied

---

6. 438 U.S. 104 (1978).

it. Building on air rights had become a conventional economic activity, and one in which many owners had invested great sums of money.

Moreover, the case cannot be justified on the conventional "external harm" theory which is the source of most traditional property regulation. It cannot be said, for example, that the proposed use was a nuisance-like activity that would intrude on the uses others were making of their property. Unlike the case in which an owner wishes to build a factory or to maintain a quarry in a residential neighborhood, Penn Central only asked to be allowed to do what its neighbors had already done, to construct a high-rise building. Neither can it be said—beyond the limits of so-called noxious uses or nuisances—that there was even a conflict between the uses Penn Central wanted to make of its property and those that its neighbors wanted to make of theirs. Thus, *Penn Central* was not a case like Miller v. Schoene,[14] in which some choice had to be made between competing and incompatible uses, neither of which could be viewed as wrongful. This illustrates the distinctiveness of the *Penn Central* decision, because Miller v. Schoene has long been viewed as at the outer limit of permissible regulation.

Moreover, as Justice Rehnquist emphasized in his dissent, there was no plausible reciprocity of advantage in the case, a feature common to much traditional zoning. Indeed, *Penn Central* is precisely the opposite of a reciprocity case; one landowner was prevented from doing something that all his neighbors had been permitted to do. And he was prevented not because he had done something wrongful or intrusive, but because he had done something admirable—he had built an architecturally distinguished building.

The most accurate way of looking at *Penn Central* is to say that the owner was required to continue conferring a benefit on his neighbors. The owner's situation in *Penn Central* resembles the situation of a landowner who has, up to the present time, refrained from building on his lot, thereby providing his neighbors a scenic amenity. Now he wishes to stop providing that benefit, and to use his property as his neighbors have already used their adjoining tracts. Yet the law requires him to continue bestowing amenity value upon his neighbors even though they have no similar obligation. How can such a result be explained or justified? That is the question Justice Rehnquist raised, and the majority opinion in the case provides no satisfactory answer.

In the pages that follow I propose an explanation of why cases like *Penn Central* are being decided as they are. I argue that *Penn Central* and its companions do not turn on the compensation/no compensation issue, which has traditionally dominated legal thinking about property. Instead, they address the allocational function of

14. 276 U.S. 272 (1928) (no deprivation of property without due process of law by the state requiring destruction of ornamental cedar trees in order to avoid infecting apple orchards in the vicinity with cedar rust).

property. Put as bluntly as possible my thesis is this: We have endowed individuals and enterprises with property because we assume that the private ownership system will allocate and reallocate the property resource to socially desirable uses. Any such allocational system will, of course, fail from time to time. But when the system regularly fails to allocate property to "correct" uses, we begin to lose faith in the system itself. Just as older systems of property, like feudal tenures, declined as they became nonfunctional, so our own system is declining to the extent it is perceived as a functional failure. Since such failures are becoming increasingly common, the property rights that lead to such failures are increasingly ceasing to be recognized. Thus, the interesting question in the *Penn Central* case is not why the owner failed to receive compensation, but why private ownership of Grand Central Station did not lead to the correct allocation, that is, to maintaining the property as an unobstructed, architecturally distinctive railroad station.

In speaking of the "correct" allocation, I mean to suggest no omniscience either on my part or that of the New York Landmarks Preservation Commission. Rather, I intend only to observe that in cases like *Penn Central* and many other modern situations such as open space preservation or coastal protection, there is widespread agreement that nondevelopment is the correct result, and widespread recognition that conventional bargaining between the owner and potential users of the property is not bringing about that result. I also mean to contrast the outcome in such cases with an earlier belief that demolishing old structures so as to allow vigorous new development was the right result. It is this difference rather than the question whether the owner is being compensated or not that is generating disillusionment with private developmental rights.

Before turning to the reasons for the perceived allocational failure of traditional property, however, I want to comment briefly on the relationship between compensation and allocation. One might say that the ability of the public to avoid compensation significantly affects the allocation decision, for the simple reason that the public will want something (preservation of an historic structure, for example) much more if it is free than if it costs it millions of dollars. But the choice is not always that simple. For example, if a high-rise is not built above Grand Central Station, the public—whether or not it pays compensation to the owner—is foregoing the benefits that come from development. As the employer and welfare provider of last resort, it risks the loss of economic activity, of jobs and of housing, losses not significantly felt by any individual. The public does not casually eschew the benefits of economic development. For this reason, one must view laws constraining development, such as historic preservation ordinances, as allocational choices that are not "free" to the community even when no compensation is paid the owner. Such decisions reflect changing public values, and not simply public avidity for obtaining free benefits.

Why are values changing, and why does the property system not automatically adapt to them? One important explanation may lie in the difference between the different kinds of benefits flowing from property—"exclusive" and "nonexclusive" consumption benefits. In a case of exclusive consumption (a residence or a shopping center, for example), virtually all benefits flow exclusively to those who occupy and use the land. In such a case, where there are no significant externalities, one expects the direct users to be able to organize, calculate and bid for the opportunity to enjoy those benefits. In general, the community as a whole is content to have the property allocated to whomever among such competing exclusive use bidders is willing to make the highest bid. The conventional property system is organized to facilitate such allocations, and such allocations only.

If, however, the "competitors" include those who benefit from maintenance of an existing historic building, the consumption is nonexclusive. That is to say, the number of people who will potentially benefit is much greater: Benefits are not limited to actual occupants; the nature of the benefits will differ among various people in the group; they are likely to be quite small as to any individual; and there is no way of assuring that every beneficiary will contribute, for benefits will flow to all potential beneficiaries whether or not they have contributed (the so-called free-rider problem).

Moreover, it is often particularly difficult for any individual to calculate the value of nonexclusive benefits to him. Such benefits often have a substantial uncertainty or "option element" to them. One may be confident that he will benefit from the presence of the building in some way (just as he benefits from the existence of many as-yet-unread books in the public library), but it is much more difficult to put a price tag on that value than to put such a price tag on his apartment or on a hamburger he consumes.

For all these reasons—diffuseness, smallness of individual interest, imperfect knowledge, differential values to a large number of people, and difficulty of pricing—the likelihood that nonexclusive consumers will organize to bid, and to bid the "right" price for such benefits, is doubtful.

Of course these very uncertainties also suggest reasons to lack confidence in the intervention of government to allocate the land to a given nonexclusive consumptive use through a legal mandate. What I have said to this point seeks to demonstrate not that allocation through law, rather than through bidding, is necessarily right, but only that allocation through conventional bidding—whereby the maximization of profit to the owner is assumed to produce the correct allocation—is fraught with difficulties.

When nonexclusive consumption benefits are very small by comparison to exclusive consumption values, the traditional system of allocation functions well. But as nonexclusive benefits rise in importance, the capacity of traditional private property transactions to allocate satisfactorily diminishes, and in such circumstances one should not be surprised to see diminishing confidence in the property system as an engine of allocation.

Another element of nonexclusive consumption makes private allocation through the property system still more unreliable. This element is what has sometimes, in a different context, been called the bandwagon effect. This effect describes a situation in which the value of something to any given individual is itself dependent on whether it has value to others. To take a banal example, the value to me of some fashionable item, like designer blue jeans, is linked to the fact that others value it. The value of my consumption to me is determined by the praise, support, or envy that others yield me as a result of my consumption. This phenomenon has an important and serious implication for things like historic preservation or wilderness. Some of the value of such things doubtless lies in their capacity to stimulate feelings of national identity or cultural solidarity, and their value to any individual rises as they are embraced by the entire community as public values.

I may, for example, derive benefits from using the wilderness as a hiker, or some historic site as a visitor, but I may also derive some benefits from wilderness or historic preservation in some remote area I will never use or see, arising from the commitment of Americans to preserve wilderness as a community value. A commitment to wilderness (or to symbols of America's historic greatness) yields such value to any given individual only if the community as a whole treats it as important. And in such cases the evidence of such value is an act of commitment by the whole community, such as embracing the national policy of historic preservation, wilderness, the flag or any of a host of symbols of national character or identity.

In such a case, even if a number of individuals could organize to bid for preservation and could outbid other potential users, that bid would not necessarily measure the whole value of preservation. Preservation may be more valuable to me simply because there is a community-wide commitment to preservation. Thus, for example, French people value their historic chateaux not only for their beauty, but also because the nation has "adopted" them as symbols of national greatness. Such benefit valuation can only be expressed through the instrumentality of the political community, which in practice means through government. Thus, the participation of the government using a legal mandate may serve not only as a device to identify the bidding value for a nonexclusive use, but also as a device for expressing a kind of value in addition to the sum of all purely individual uses or benefits.

As nonexclusive consumption values rise in importance, and the capacity of the property system to make correct allocations thereby diminishes, it seems inevitable that we begin to ask ourselves why we allow those private property rights to exist which increasingly produce unwanted results. At least as to land, where property rights are assigned by the public in the first instance (and putting aside those things that are more or less entirely the product of an individual's own creative efforts, such as a symphony or a poem), the assignment of property rights presupposes that private ownership would routinely produce socially desirable use allocations.

We assigned property to private owners in the undeveloped West, for example, because we assumed that the uses they would make of the property—settlement, security of the frontier, development of railroads, farms and mines—would maximize net social benefits. Had we not believed that the allocations brought about by private ownership would produce such results, it hardly seems likely that such rights would have been created. The application of a new kind of water right for the arid West in place of traditional riparian rights pointedly illustrates this assumption. One may also test it against the current debate over the proposed sale of public lands remaining in federal ownership.

It is, I suggest, precisely because it is widely believed that the highest and best use of much of that land lies in its retention for nondevelopmental nonexclusive uses, such as public recreation, wilderness and wildlife habitat, that there is strong resistance against selling it into private ownership. If it is believed that private ownership likely will not, for the reasons I have suggested above, sufficiently allocate the land to such nonexclusive uses, it is only to be expected that private rights will not be established.

The difficulty with land already patented into private ownership, of course, is one of fairness to the owners in the face of changing values, and I shall have something to say about that later. What I wish to emphasize, however, is not the compensation issue, but the growing conviction that for substantial areas of land the content of private ownership rights that we have long relied on is misallocating the land, and that what was long viewed as exceptional (government intervention to allocate correctly) is becoming commonplace. This change cannot help but impose enormous pressure upon our conception of the role that private ownership in land should play.

We have already seen some remarkable transformations, of which the rise of historic preservation ordinances is but one example. The perceived dominating importance of nonexclusive uses of shoreline has already given rise in the last decade to a greatly revived public trust doctrine. In that instance, the path of a judicially led transformation was paved by a long—though largely moribund—tradition of government retention of public rights in submerged shoreland that were never transferred into private ownership. The tradition was often ignored in the mid-nineteenth century, especially in places like California, where vast acreages of submerged shoreline were passed into private ownership to encourage development.

At the time, the private ownership of these lands seemed absolute. As the need for nonexclusive uses of the lands rose in the last decade, and as the availability of such lands shrank, we witnessed some remarkable judicial pyrotechnics. For instance, recent California Supreme Court decisions have redefined the nature of the grants made by the legislature in the 1860's,[19] questioned longstanding property rights in water,[20] and explicitly reversed previous decisions holding that absolute private rights had been granted,[21] thereby reinstating the public right of nonexclusive use on the inventive theory of implicit reservations in grants made more than a century ago.

However shocking such results may be to conventional legal sensibilities, they reveal a trend that is equally obvious in a range of other areas. That trend is exemplified not only by *Penn Central* but also by contemporary decisions upholding open space, coastal and wetland zoning.

Nonexclusive consumption benefits have always existed. Why should they be less in harmony with the property system now than they were in the past? The reasons, I suggest, are two, both related to the developmental use of property. First, the more development proceeds, the more the stock of such benefits (coastal access, historic structures, wilderness) declines. Second, and even more important, values are changing, so that the quantum of benefits from developmental activity (both exclusive and nonexclusive consumption benefits) is perceived as being less than it formerly was, while simultaneously the perceived benefits flowing from nondevelopmental, nonexclusive consumption are sharply increasing.

The building of the railroads, the irrigation of the arid West, the electrification of rural areas, the growth of great cities, even the belching steel mills of Pittsburgh or Gary, idealized America on the march, putting the world on wheels, serving as the breadbasket and the arsenal of democracy. Such images were at least as powerful as the current imagery of the wilderness or of our historic heritage. The nonexclusive consumption benefits of a symbolic sort that flowed from these activities were in harmony with conventional exclusive consumption benefits that flowed to users and builders. The profits that came to landowners in allocating property to development automatically brought in their wake a sense of common purpose to a public enlivened by an idea of progress tied to development. The developmental rights of property owners were truly an engine pulling us where we wanted to go.

Plainly, that animating sense of progress has declined. The change might best be analogized to the mining of a valuable mineral.

19. City of Berkeley v. Superior Ct., 26 Cal.3d 515, 606 P.2d 362, 162 Cal.Rptr. 327, *cert. denied*, 449 U.S. 840 (1980).

20. National Audubon Soc'y v. Superior Ct., 33 Cal.3d 419, 658 P.2d 709, 189 Cal.Rptr. 346 (1983).

21. City of Berkeley v. Superior Ct., 26 Cal.3d at 532, 606 P.2d at 372, 162 Cal. Rptr. at 337.

At first, the richest lodes are mined, and the productive output is very great per acre of land disturbed. As time goes on, the miner must move on to less and less concentrated ores, more and more land must be disrupted, and more energy must be expended to get the same level of output. Over time the benefits of developmental activity diminish, while the costs increase. Our sense of progress diminishes.

One might also say generally of developmental activity that the most important needs are taken care of first. As time passes the sense of accomplishment associated with new uses diminishes. Constructing suburban shopping centers or producing instant cameras cannot be expected to generate the enthusiasm that went with building transcontinental railroads. Those few contemporary activities that do excite us—the space program or the development of the computer—are little involved with controversies over resource use.

Of course, the transformation I have been describing is neither uniform nor unidirectional. Some development is still perceived as essential, as in a recent case where a long-established Detroit community, "Poletown," was destroyed to make way for a new General Motors plant.[23] Such examples are likely to be particularly notable in periods of economic difficulty such as we have been experiencing in the last few years. And, of course, some developmental activity, such as maintaining the supply of energy resources, is needed to sustain existing uses. An economy devoted to sustenance, however, is more likely to generate interest in the techniques of continuity, durability and sustained yield than in large-scale development and expenditure of resources.

There is yet a third way of understanding the ongoing transformation in the content of property rights. Social coherence demands evidence and symbols of common purpose, self-worth and solidarity. As developmental activity ceases to provide those things and we are much less persuaded that "America is on the march," we turn to other things. We seem to be turning to symbols of stability, of links with our past. History is an obvious outlet for such values. So, though less obviously, is the interest in ecology, a science focused on the stability and continuity of natural systems. It may be that as growth and development seem to become less valuable guides for future well-being, those things that speak to sustenance, continuity, adaptation and evolutionary change rise sharply in value. All the sorts of laws to which I referred earlier appear in various ways to speak to these themes: historic preservation, to the continuity of the social order; wetland and coastline regulation, to the sustaining marvel of productivity in the shorelands and estuaries; growth control, to the maintenance of viable communities seen as threatened by explosive and disorienting growth.

23. Poletown Neighborhood Council v. City of Detroit, 410 Mich. 616, 304 N.W.2d 455 (1981). See also Barbian v. Panagis, 694 F.2d 476 (7th Cir.1982).

It is notable, in regard to the law of urban land use, that one sees increasing emphasis in judicial opinions on the value of community stability as a basis for restrictive laws, as compared with earlier nuisance-type justifications. In the much quoted *Belle Terre* case,[25] the Supreme Court upheld family-only zoning in language that at first seems faintly archaic. It spoke of "family values, youth values, and the blessing of quiet seclusion[,] . . . a sanctuary for people."[26] Reliance on such values seems not at all out of place when considered in terms of the transformation I have been describing.

One could point to many examples of this change that reflect a shifting emphasis even within the confines of the Standard State Zoning Enabling Act, the model for conventional state laws that provide authorization for local zoning. The most familiar language of that law, and the part most relied upon in the past, spoke to nuisance-type problems: "to lessen congestion . . .; to secure safety from fire, panic, and other dangers; to promote health . . .; to prevent the overcrowding of land; to avoid undue concentration of population; to facilitate the adequate provision of transportation, water, sewerage . . . and other public requirements." For many years, the standard cases drew upon that nuisance-like language. In the leading zoning case of Village of Euclid v. Ambler Realty Co.,[29] for example, the Supreme Court used the example of a pig in the parlor instead of the barnyard. At one time billboard control was said to be justified because thieves and rapists could hide behind the signboards. In those days, development itself was viewed as the benefit and goal, and any constraints on developmental activities were thought to be exceptional. Use-separation zoning was probably viewed mainly as a means to facilitate—rather than to constrain—maximum development of the community as a whole.

Today one finds the promotion of nonexclusive benefits cited as a goal in itself—a very significant change. Where once aesthetics were thought an insufficient justification for zoning, today the Supreme Court easily accepts aesthetic regulation of billboards, and Justice Rehnquist can say, as he did in his dissent in the *Metromedia* case, "the aesthetic justification alone is sufficient to sustain a total prohibition of billboards within a community."[32] Similarly, the Court has recently noted—with no discussion or difficulty—that open space zoning substantially advances legitimate governmental goals, recognizing, though not deciding, that such regulation may impose very substantial constraints on the totality of property that would be developed.[33] It accepted the California legislature's determination to

---

25. Village of Belle Terre v. Boraas, 416 U.S. 1 (1974).

26. *Id.* at 9.

29. 272 U.S. 365 (1926).

32. Metromedia, Inc. v. City of San Diego, 453 U.S. 490, 570 (1981) (Rehnquist, J., dissenting).

33. Agins v. City of Tiburon, 447 U.S. 255 (1980).

prevent the "unnecessary conversion of open space land to urban uses."[34]

Movement away from the nuisance justification for zoning in favor of concern about neighborhood character, seeing the community as a common, reflects a shift from primary concern with exclusive consumption (with its connotations of individualization and privatization) to nonexclusive consumption (with its connotations of community and shared values). Even where important individual rights are at stake, as in cases involving the first amendment, one finds the Supreme Court, both in the billboard case [35] and in the adult theatre zoning case,[36] evincing great sympathy for the importance of maintaining community stability and character. As one begins to see urban and suburban land use less through the lens of individuals who have bought isolated tracts that need protection against intrusions from outside, and more as situations in which one has acquired a package of common amenities—such as quality schools, quietude, low levels of crime and the like—the values of nonexclusive consumption and of commonly enjoyed benefits come to the fore.

To be sure, none of this is entirely new, and it could be argued that even the most traditional zoning of a half-century ago was always more community-oriented than its nuisance-type justification implied. It may be that we are only now seeing the final result of a situation in which belief in free-wheeling development and individualism on the one hand, and the interest in community and what I have called nonexclusive consumption benefits on the other, are finally reaching an unresolvable tension. With this change the importance of protection and preservation becomes greater, relatively speaking, than that of development. Historic preservation looms larger than an additional high-rise; the coastline as a public amenity becomes more significant than the coastline as a commodity to be divided up and given over to exclusive housing development.

As I noted earlier, one sees precisely the same sort of changes occurring in the management of the public lands. What were once viewed as tracts largely to be parcelled out to timber companies and grazing and mining interests are more and more perceived in terms of opportunities for public recreation, for wildlife protection and reserves, and for archeological and paleontological sites.

I might note that the transition I have been describing is by no means limited to land use. The change away from enchantment with the virtues of productivity is also revealed in such small things as a resurgent interest in the activities of artisans and in folklore, folk art and Native American culture and its artifacts. In art and architecture, there has been a decline of interest in the chrome and glass

---

34. *Id.* at 261 (quoting Cal.Gov't Code § 65,561(b) (West Supp.1979)).

35. Metromedia, Inc. v. City of San Diego, 453 U.S. 490 (1981).

36. Young v. American Mini Theatres, Inc., 427 U.S. 50 (1976).

modernity that symbolized the industrial era at its apex. It is no longer so obvious that traditional communities should be cavalierly displaced for a new dam. When an energy boom town imposes itself upon an older community, that transformation is no longer seen as pure progress; much more often it is seen as a tragedy, though often still as an inevitable one. The disenchantment with urban renewal's community-destroying aspects is just an older example of the sort of attitudes that today are giving rise to the historic preservation movement in many cities.

What all this suggests is a transition in which an ever greater proportion of our well-being is realized in the form of shared wealth, or things that are nonexclusively consumed, rather than in the form of privatized or exclusive-consumption wealth. It seems a paradox that such changes should be occurring simultaneously with the blossoming of the "me" generation and the highly privatized gratification that goes with it. Perhaps the simultaneous rise of community-based nonexclusive benefits is a compensating substitute for the loss of more traditional social values focused around one's work and the more tightly-knit family.

Even where some of the output of nonexclusive consumption is privatized, as with the goods of artisans, such values require collective effort to maintain traditional cultures and communities. As we are already seeing, more attention is paid to assuring the quality of community-wide amenities, and less to simply increasing the stock of private, exclusive-possession goods. This means that developmental rights will increasingly give way to protection of community-wide amenities.

I want finally to say something about the question that has traditionally most concerned lawyers: the problem of compensation. If owners are to lose developmental rights, should they not be compensated for that loss? At one level, there is an easy, descriptive answer. They are losing such rights and, as the various categories of cases to which I have been referring demonstrate, they are usually not being compensated. Obviously, a number of such owners are being sharply disappointed, by conventional standards, in their expectations. Legislatures are alert to the problem, and in many cases (such as historic preservation and inclusionary zoning) mitigating benefits are being provided, though they fall far short of full compensation. Among these are tax abatements, density bonuses, and transferable development rights. We are in a transitional state and legislatures are using these devices to ease the pains of transition.

It also has to be recognized that the unwillingness to compensate property owners reflects a desire to bring about some redistribution, though it is redistribution of a peculiar sort. In withdrawing developmental rights (as opposed to existing uses), the legislatures and the courts are in fact leaving in place some long-existing uses, such as open space, coastal access, recreational opportunities, and historic structures. What is changing is not the quantum of de facto nonexclusive benefits, but the quantum of rights to destroy those benefits. Public privileges, long enjoyed, are becoming public rights.

One justification for such redistribution is sometimes made explicit in the cases, as it was in the New York Court of Appeals decision in *Penn Central*. It is simply that so much of the value that inures to property owners is itself the product of public investment in what we call infrastructure (transportation, utilities, etc.), rather than the product of individual enterprise, that the equitable claim owners have is really not so great. This, too, is understandable in a society that is increasingly attuned to land as community rather than as an amalgam of isolated, individualized tracts. And it is, of course, a recognition by the courts of the old saw that property owners grow rich in their sleep.

Finally, it is worth noting—and this may explain why the Supreme Court in *Penn Central* rejected the claim of investment-backed expectations—that we are already so far along in diminishing developmental rights that owners are viewed, in important respects, as already on notice. Anyone today who holds, or wishes to buy, historical properties, wetlands or coastal lands, or who plans developments in developing suburbs (to take but the most obvious examples), knows or should know that his opportunities for old-fashioned development are far from clear. Even such conventional strategies as acquiring property with the expectation of obtaining a rezoning for denser development have now been put in question in a number of states as a result of the so-called *Fasano* doctrine.[42] Surely canny owners must be learning to hedge their bets; the whole structure of expectations is in the process of change. It would be fascinating to learn, for example, whether at the time the plans for the development atop Grand Central Station were first put forward the developers thought about the possibility of a denial based on historic preservation, and whether their plans incorporated a hedge for that possibility.

In any event, the path of noncompensation seems rather clearly set, and it is becoming clearer not only that there will be less development, but also that owners will play a less central role in determining where the development that is allowed will take place. Because more land will be devoted in part to nonexclusive (and thus largely non-profit-producing) consumption, the corollary observation is that what development is to be allowed will more often be determined publicly rather than privately. Because developmental opportunities will be

---

42. In Fasano v. Board of County Comm'rs, 264 Or. 574, 507 P.2d 23 (1973), the Oregon Supreme Court shifted the burden of proof by abandoning the traditional presumption of validity and requiring the county to justify zoning changes. 507 P.2d at 29. Justice Stevens, dissenting in Eastlake v. Forest City Enters., Inc., 426 U.S. 668 (1976), asserts that it is reasonable to expect zoning changes to be granted freely. *Id.* at 682 (Stevens, J., dissenting) ("The expectancy that particular changes consistent with the basic zoning plan will be allowed frequently and on their merits is a normal incident of property ownership.").

scarcer, those that continue to exist are likely to be extremely profitable. One already sees this phenomenon in operation in communities that have elaborate growth management plans, such as Montgomery County, Maryland, where some areas are designated for greenbelt and agriculture, others for low density, and still others for high density development. The same sort of thing can be seen in places like Adirondack Park in New York, on the federal public lands, and in the California Desert Conservation Area. Elaborate land use planning schemes have zoned all of these areas for a variety of nondevelopmental and developmental uses.

A major problem I see ahead is one of controlling the potential for what Professor Hagman called "windfalls" in those limited areas where development will be concentrated.[47] To move in this direction we are going to have to come to terms with the prospect that planning (a word Americans don't much like), rather than property, is going to be a principal engine of social benefit production in the future, and that public (nonexclusive) rather than privatized (exclusive) benefits are going to loom much larger in long-term resource planning. These changes will not be easily assimilated in American thought and the American legal system. But the die is cast, and I see no evidence to suggest that the emerging pattern I have here tried to describe will not continue in its current direction.

47. D. Hagman & D. Misczynski, Windfalls for Wipeouts: Land Value Capture and Compensation (1978).

*

ACKNOWLEDGEMENTS

I gratefully acknowledge the permission kindly granted to reproduce all or part of the following materials:

Abbott, S., Housing Policy, Housing Codes and Tenant Remedies: An Integration, 56 Boston University Law Review 1 (1976).

American Bar Association, Code of Professional Responsibility (1980). Excerpted from the ABA Model Code of Professional Responsibility, August, 1980 by American Bar Association. All rights reserved. Reprinted with permission.

American Bar Association, Residential Real Estate Transactions: The Lawyer's Proper Role—Services—Compensation (1978). Copyright © 1978, American Bar Association. Reprinted with permission.

American Law Institute, Restatement of Property (1936, 1940). Copyright 1936, 1940 by the American Law Institute. Reprinted with the permission of the American Law Institute.

American Law Institute, Restatement of Property (Second) (1977). Copyright 1977 by the American Law Institute. Reprinted with the permission of the American Law Institute.

American Law Institute, Restatement of Torts (Second) (1979). Copyright 1979 by the American Law Institute. Reprinted with the permission of the American Law Institute.

Anderson, R., American Law of Zoning (1968). Reprinted from Robert M. Anderson, American Law of Zoning, by special permission. Copyright © 1968 by the Lawyers Co-operative Publishing Company.

Bade, E., Cases and Materials on Real Property and Conveyancing (1954).

Bancroft-Whitney Co., Percentage Rental Lease, CAL FORMS (1975).

Bar Association of Erie County and Greater Buffalo Board of Realtors, Inc., Contract of Sale.

Berger, C. and Rohan, P., The Nassau County Study: An Empirical Look into the Practices of Condemnation, 67 Columbia Law Review 430 (1967). Copyright 1967, © by the Directors of the Columbia Law Review Association, Inc. All rights reserved. This article originally appeared at Volume 67 page 430. Reprinted by permission.

Blumberg, R., Robbins, B., and Baar, K., The Emergence of Second Generation Rent Controls, 8 Clearinghouse Review 240 (1974).

Brakel, S., and McIntyre, D., URLTA in Operation: An Introduction, 1980 American Bar Foundation Research Journal 559.

Brown, C., Boundary Control and Legal Principles (2d ed. 1969). Copyright © 1957, 1969 by John Wiley & Sons, Inc. Reprinted by permission of John Wiley & Sons, Inc.

Brown, R., The Law of Personal Property (3d ed. 1975). Reprinted with permission from The Law of Personal Property (§§ 1.6, 4.2, 6.2) by Ray Brown (W. Raushenbush 3d ed.) published by Callaghan & Co., 3201 Old Glenview Rd., Wilmette, IL 60091.

Casner, A.J., ed., American Law of Property (1952, 1954, 1977).

Clark, C., Real Covenants and Other Interests Which "Run with Land" (2d ed. 1947). Reprinted with permission from C.E. Clark's Real Covenants and Other Interests Which "Run with the Land," (pp. 73, 99, 1947), published by Callaghan & Co., 3201 Old Glenview Rd., Wilmette, IL 60091.

Comment, The Public Use Limitation on Eminent Domain: An Advance Requiem, 58 Yale Law Journal 599 (1949). Reprinted by permission of the Yale Law Journal Company and Fred B. Rothman & Company from The Yale Law Journal, Vol. 58, pp. 599, 614.

Cribbet, J., Principles of the Law of Property (2d ed. 1975).

Cunnyngham, W., Making Land Surveys and Preparing Descriptions to Meet Legal Requirements, 19 Missouri Law Review 234 (1954).

Developments in the Law—Zoning, 91 Harvard Law Review 1427 (1978). Copyright © 1978 by the Harvard Law Review Association.

DiMento, J., Dozier, M., Emmons, S., Hagman, D., Kim, C., Greenfield-Sanders, K., Waldau, P., Woollacott, J., Land Development and Environmental Control in the California Supreme Court: The Deferential, The Preservationist, and the Preservationist-Erratic Eras, 27 University of California at Los Angeles Law Review 859 (1980). Originally published in 27 UCLA L.Rev. 859. Copyright 1980, The Regents of the University of California. All Rights Reserved.

Flick, C., Abstract and Title Practice (2d ed. 1958).

Frieden, B., Housing Allowances: An Experiment that Worked, 59 The Public Interest 15 (1980). Reprinted with permission of the author from: THE PUBLIC INTEREST, No. 59. (Spring, 1980), pp. 15–22, 25–27, 32, 35. Copyright © 1980 by National Affairs, Inc.

Frieden, B., and Solomon, A., The Nation's Housing: 1975–1985 (1977).

Friedman, L., A History of American Law (1973).

Glendon, M., The Transformation of American Landlord-Tenant Law, 23 Boston College Law Review 503 (1982).

Greater Buffalo Board of Realtors, Inc., Exclusive Right to Sell Listing Contract.

Grey, T., The Disintegration of Property, XXII NOMOS (1980). Reprinted by permission of New York University Press from Property (NOMOS XXII) edited by J. Roland Pennock and John W. Chapman. Copyright © 1980 by New York University.

Heskin, A., The Warranty of Habitability Debate: A California Case Study, 66 California Law Review 37 (1978). Copyright © 1978, California Law Review, Inc., Reprinted by permission.

Hines, N.W., Real Property Joint Tenancies: Law, Fact and Fancy, 51 Iowa Law Review 582 (1966). Copyright 1966 University of Iowa (Iowa Law Review).

Johanson, S., Reversions, Remainders, and the Doctrine of Worthier Title, 45 Texas Law Review 1 (1966). Published originally in 45 Texas L.Rev. 1, 12–13 (1966). Copyright © 1966 by the Texas Law Review. Reprinted by permission.

Johnson, C., Purpose and Scope of Recording Statutes, 47 Iowa Law Review 231 (1962). Copyright 1962 University of Iowa (Iowa Law Review).

Krasnowiecki, J., Abolish Zoning, 31 Syracuse Law Review 719 (1980).

Leach, W.B., Perpetuities in a Nutshell, 51 Harvard Law Review 638 (1938). Copyright © 1938 by the Harvard Law Review Association.

Levi, J., Hablutzel, P., Rosenberg, L., and White, J., Modern Residential Landlord-Tenant Code (1969).

Linowes, R. and Allensworth, D., The Politics of Land Use: Planning, Zoning and the Private Developer. Copyright © 1973 Praeger Publishers, Inc. Excerpted and reprinted by permission of Praeger Publishers.

Love, J., Landlord's Liability for Defective Premises: Caveat Lessee, Negligence, or Strict Liability?, 1975 Wisconsin Law Review 19. Copyright 1975 University of Wisconsin.

Merryman, J., Improving the Lot of the Trespassing Improver, 11 Stanford Law Review 456 (1959). Copyright 1959 by the Board of Trustees of the Leland Stanford Junior University.

Meyers, C., The Covenant of Habitability and the American Law Institute, 27 Stanford Law Review 879 (1975). Copyright 1975 by the Board of Trustees of the Leland Stanford Junior University.

Michelman, F., Property, Utility and Fairness: Comments on the Ethical Foundations of "Just Compensation" Law, 80 Harvard

Law Review 1165 (1967). Copyright © 1967 by the Harvard Law Review Association.

Mueller, W., Residential Tenants and Their Leases: An Empirical Study, 69 Michigan Law Review 247 (1970).

National Conference of Commissioners on Uniform State Laws, Uniform Land Transactions Act (1975).

Note, Damages: The Illogical Differences in Measuring Breach of Contract Damages When the Contract Involves Land Rather than Goods, 26 Oklahoma Law Review 277 (1973). Reprinted with permission of Oklahoma Law Review © 1973.

Note, The Great *Green* Hope: The Implied Warranty of Habitability in Practice, 28 Stanford Law Review 729 (1976). Copyright 1976 by the Board of Trustees of the Leland Stanford Junior University.

Note, The Home Owners Warranty Program: An Initial Analysis, 28 Stanford Law Review 357 (1976). Copyright 1976 by the Board of Trustees of the Leland Stanford Junior University.

Note, A Suggested Means of Determining the Proper Amortization Period for Nonconforming Structures, 27 Stanford Law Review 1325 (1975). Copyright 1975 by the Board of Trustees of the Leland Stanford Junior University.

Note, The Tract and Grantor-Grantee Indices, 47 Iowa Law Review 481 (1962). Copyright 1962 University of Iowa (Iowa Law Review).

Ordway, N. and Weaver, W., Preparing for a Zoning Ambush, 7 Real Estate Review 40 (1977).

Paschal, Joel Francis, Mr. Justice Sutherland: A Man Against the State. Copyright 1951 by Princeton University Press; renewed © 1979 by Princeton University Press.

Poland, M., Comments to § 60–503, Vernon's Kansas Statutes Annotated (1967).

Powell, R., Powell on Real Property (1982). Copyright 1982 by Matthew Bender & Co., Inc. and reprinted with permission.

RAND Corporation, Second Annual Report of the Housing Assistance Supply Experiments (May, 1976).

Richburg, K., "Angry Tenants Hit City Council on Rent Increase," Washington Post, November 25, 1980. © The Washington Post.

Rose, C., Planning and Dealing: Piecemeal Land Controls as a Problem of Local Legitimacy, 71 California Law Review 837 (1983). Copyright © 1983, California Law Review, Inc. Reprinted by permission.

Rose, C., Preservation and Community: New Directions in the Law of Historic Preservation, 33 Stanford Law Review 473

(1981). Copyright 1981 by the Board of Trustees of the Leland Stanford Junior University.

Rudden, B. and Moseley, H., An Outline of the Law of Mortgages (1967).

Rundell, O., Judge Clark on the American Law Institute's Law of Real Covenants: A Comment, 53 Yale Law Journal 312 (1944). Reprinted by permission of The Yale Law Journal Company and Fred B. Rothman & Company from The Yale Law Journal, Vol. 53, pp. 322, 325.

San Francisco Examiner, "Zoning Law—How It Was Bent," San Francisco Examiner, February 24, 1965.

Sax, J., Some Thoughts on the Decline of Private Property, 58 Washington Law Review 481 (1983). Reprinted by permission of the author and the Washington Law Review Association.

Sax, J., The (Unhappy) Truth About NEPA, 26 Oklahoma Law Review 239 (1973). Reprinted with permission of Oklahoma Law Review © 1973.

Schoshinski, R., Remedies for the Indigent Tenant: Proposal for Change, 54 Georgetown Law Journal 519 (1966). Reprinted with the permission of the publisher, © 1966 The Georgetown Law Journal Association.

Simes, L. and Taylor, C., Improvement of Conveyancing by Legislation (1960).

Simes, L. and Taylor, C., Model Title Standards (1960).

Skilton, R., Developments in Mortgage Law and Practice, 17 Temple Law Quarterly 315 (1943).

Thompson, G., Commentaries on the Modern Law of Real Property (1959).

Tiffany, H., The Law of Landlord and Tenant (1910). Reprinted with permission from The Law of Landlord and Tenant (pp. 1338–1339, Vol. 2, 1910), by H. Tiffany, published by Callaghan & Co., 3201 Old Glenview Rd., Wilmette, IL 60091.

Title Guarantee Company, Title Insurance Policy, N.Y.B.T.U. Form 100E (1969).

Waggoner, L., Reformulating the Structure of Estates: A Proposal for Legislative Action, 85 Harvard Law Review 729 (1972). Copyright © 1972 by the Harvard Law Review.

Washington Star, "Compliance on Repairs is Often Delayed," July 20, 1965.

Weissenberger, G., The Landlord's Duty to Mitigate Damages on the Tenant's Abandonment: A Survey of Old Law and New Trends, 53 Temple Law Quarterly 1 (1980).

*

INDEX

References are to Pages

ABANDONMENT
Easement, 812.
Personal property, 59–60.

ABATEMENT
Rent, by tenant, 956.

ABSTRACTS OF TITLE
Generally, 363–372.

ACCESSION
Personal property, 68.

ACQUIESCENCE
Nonpossessory interests, 812.

ACTUAL EVICTION
Quiet enjoyment, 856.
Under shopping center lease, 1040–1041.

ACTUAL NOTICE
Under recording acts, 334–335.

ADVERSE POSSESSION
Against government, 35–36, 56–57.
Concurrent estates, 638–639.
Disabilities, 57.
Elements of,
  Actual, Open, Visible,
    Notorious and Exclusive, 37–43.
  Claim of right, 43–50.
  Continuity, 50–60.
  Hostile, 43–50.
  Tax payments, 49–50.
Personal property, 57–59.
Prescriptive easements, 698–707.
Rationale, 32–33.
Squatters, 34–36.
Statute of limitations, 56.
Subterranean use, 41.
Tacking, 55.
Theory of protection, 24–36.

AESTHETIC ZONING
Generally, 1116–1128.

AFFIRMATIVE COVENANTS
See Covenants.

AFFIRMATIVE EASEMENTS
See Easements.

AFFIRMATIVE WASTE
Action for, 559.

AIR RIGHTS
Takings of, 1112–1113.
Trespass, 21–22.

ALIENABILITY
Condominium ownership, 1053–1059.
Economics of, 7.
Estates in land, 567–606.
Future interests, 548–549.
Leases, 852–877.
Policy favoring, 474.
Rule against perpetuities, 567–587.
Rule against restraints on alienation, 587–598.
Statutory reform, 599–606.

ALTERNATIVE CONTINGENT REMAINDERS
Future interest, 560–561.

AMELIORATIVE WASTE
Action for, 560–561.

AMORTIZATION
Mortgage, 206–207, 420.
Zoning, 1176–1177.

ANCIENT LIGHTS
Easements, 706–707.

ANTIDEFICIENCY RULES
Mortgage foreclosure, 443–445.

APPURTENANT EASEMENT
See Easements.

ARCHITECTS
Liability for housing defects, 294–295.

ARCHITECTURAL CONTROLS
Zoning, 1124.

ASSIGNMENT
Of commercial lease, 1029–1030.
Of lease, generally, 852–877.

ASSUMPTION
Of mortgage, 427–428.

INDEX

References are to Pages

BASE FEE
Estate in land, 498.

BONA FIDE PURCHASER
Recording act requirement, 321–337.

BROKERS
See Real Estate Brokers.

BUYER OF REAL ESTATE
Duties to broker, 184.
Post-closing rights against seller, 279–309.
Rights against broker, 183–184.
Rights respecting quality of premises, 281–295.

CHANGED CONDITIONS
Nonpossessory interests, 812–813.

CIVIL LAW
See also Roman Law.
Ownership in, 474–475.

CLUSTER ZONING
Generally, 1196–1204.

COASE THEOREM
Disputes between neighbors, 86–89.

COMMON RECOVERY
Fee tail, 502–503.

COMMUNITY PROPERTY
Generally, 656–664.

COMPETITION
Covenants against, 762–763.

COMPREHENSIVE PLAN
Generally, 1152–1164.

CONCURRENT ESTATES
Adverse possession, 638–639.
Coparcenary, 606.
Cotenant rights and liabilities, 624–640.
Joint tenancy, 607–624.
Partition, 640–646.
Tenancy by the entireties, 649–655.
Tenancy in common, 607–616.

CONDEMNATION
See Eminent Domain.

CONDOMINIUMS
Generally, 1044–1073.
Conversion, from rental housing, 988–989.
Discrimination, 1059–1073.
History, 1045–1046.
Management and control, 1047–1053.
Regulation, 1046–1047.
Restraints on alienation, 1053–1059.

CONSTRUCTIVE EVICTION
Quiet enjoyment, 856.
Under shopping center lease, 1040–1041.

CONSTRUCTIVE NOTICE
Under recording acts, 334.

CONTINGENT REMAINDER
Destructibility, 547.
Future interest, 530.

CONTRACT
Lease as, 816–822, 937–940.
Zoning, 1193–1194.

CONTRACT CONDITIONS
See Contract of Sale.

CONTRACT OF SALE
Conditions,
    Generally, 196–212.
    Financing, 200–205, 209–210.
    Good Faith, 206–207.
    Marketable Title, 196–200, 207–208.
    Reasonableness, 206–207.
    Time of essence, 210–211.
    Zoning, 209.
Earnest money deposit, 224–225.
Real estate, form, 186–187.
Real estate, generally, 186–236.
Remedies, 212–226.
Risk of loss, 226–236.
Statute of Frauds, 189–195.

CONVEYANCE
Lease as, 816–822.

CONVEYANCING
See Land Transfer.

COOPERATIVES
    Generally, 1044–1073.
Discrimination, 1059–1073.
Restraints on alienation, 1053–1059.

COPARCENARY
Concurrent estates, 606.

COPYHOLD
Estate in land, 470–471.

COTENANCIES
See Concurrent Estates.

COVENANT AGAINST ENCUMBRANCES
Generally, 296.

COVENANT FOR FURTHER ASSURANCES
Generally, 296.

COVENANT OF HABITABILITY
    Generally, 941–959.
Compared to quiet enjoyment, 952.
Effects of, 958–959.
Waiver of, 957.

COVENANT OF QUIET ENJOYMENT
In land sales, 296.
In leases, 843–858.

COVENANT OF RIGHT TO CONVEY
Generally, 296.

COVENANT OF SEISIN
Generally, 296.

COVENANT OF WARRANTY
Generally, 296.

COVENANTS
See also Encumbrances.
Generally, 719–780.
Affirmative covenants, 671.
Against competition, 762–763.
By implication, 730–744.
Changed conditions, 812–813.
Common neighborhood plan, 739–744.
Covenants, conditions and restrictions, 719–721.
Creation, 719–744.
Easements compared, 729.
Eminent domain, 1326–1327.
Habitability of leased premises, 941–959.
History, 729–730.
Implied into easement, 799.
Interpretation, 787–799.
Liens, 763–764.
Merger, 811–812.
Negative covenants, 671.
Of title, 295–310.
Privity requirement, 746–755.
Quiet enjoyment,
    In land sales, 296.
    In leases, 843–858.
Remedies, 787.
Running of benefit, 765–780.
Running of burden, 744–765.
Termination, 799–815.
To deliver possession, 834–843.
Touch or concern requirement, 755–765.

COVENANTS, CONDITIONS AND RESTRICTIONS
Forms, 673–674, 719–721.

COVENANTS OF TITLE
Generally, 295–310.

CRIMES
Trespass, 22–23.

CURATIVE ACTS
Title to real property, 390–391.

CURTESY
Property rights of husband and wife, 648–649.

CY PRES
Rule against perpetuities, 585.

DAMAGES
Contract of sale, 223–224.
Contract of sale, liquidated, 224–225.

DAMAGES—Cont'd
Eminent domain, severance, 1312–1321.
Landlord remedy, 901–902.
Mitigation, by landlord, 902–905.
Nuisance, 125.
Waste, 561.

DE DONIS CONDITIONALIBUS
Estates in land, 472.
Fee tail, 502–503.

DEBTOR PROTECTION
On mortgage foreclosure, 444–445.

DEED OF TRUST
See also Land Finance.
Generally, 419–420.
Default, 430–445.
Obligations of trustor, 422–430.

DEEDS
Generally, 237–239.
Acceptance of, 278.
Construction of, 239–244.
Delivery of, 260–279.
Description of property, 244–260.
Elements of, 238.
Escrow, 278–279.
Formalities, 238–239.
    Curative acts, 390–391.
Forms, 237.
In lieu of foreclosure, 444.
Merger, 279–281.
Post-closing liabilities, 279–309.

DEFAULT
On mortgage or deed of trust, 430–445.

DEFEASIBLE FEES
Estates in land, 485–501.
Fee simple determinable, 498.
Fee simple subject to condition subsequent, 498–494.
Fee simple subject to executory limitation, 499.

DEFICIENCY JUDGMENTS
Mortgage foreclosure, 443–445.

DELIVERY
Acceptance of, 278.
Escrow, 278–279.
Of deed, 260–279.
Of lease, 822.

DEPRECIATION
Deduction under federal income tax, 450–466.

DESCRIPTION OF LAND
In deeds, 244–260.

DISABILITIES
See Adverse Possession.

INDEX

References are to Pages

DISCRIMINATION
In condominiums, 1059–1073.
In housing, 980–987, 989–990.
In zoning, 1146.

DISTRAINT
See Distress.

DISTRESS
Landlord and tenant, 890.

DOCTRINE OF WORTHIER TITLE
Future interests, 526–527.

DOWER
Property rights of husband and wife, 648–649.

DUE ON SALE CLAUSE
Generally, 428–429.

EARNEST MONEY DEPOSIT
Contract of sale, 224–225.

EASEMENTS
See also Encumbrances.
Generally, 673–718.
Abandonment, 812.
Affirmative easement, 670, 680.
Ancient lights, 706–707.
Apportionment, 796–797.
Appurtenant easement, 714–715, 718.
By custom, 705.
By implication, 684–698.
By necessity, 684–698.
By prescription, 698–707.
Covenants compared, 729.
Creation of, 673–684.
Dedication to public, 704–705.
Eminent domain, 1326–1327.
In gross, 715–718.
Interpretation, 787–799.
History, 729–730.
Licenses compared, 683–684.
Light and air, 706–707.
Location of, 797–798.
Merger, 811–812.
Misuse, 813–814.
Negative easement, 670–671, 680–681.
Public easement, 704–705.
Running of benefit, 709–718.
Running of burden, 707–709.
Solar easement, 681–682.
Spite fences, 706–707.
Statute of Frauds, 679–680.
Termination, 799–815.

ECONOMICS
Coase Theorem, 86–89.
Effects of uncertainty, 7–8.
Efficiency, 89.

ECONOMICS—Cont'd
Nuisance law, 122–123.
Right to exclude, 6–7.
Takings of property, 1107–1108.
Transaction costs, 7, 88.

EFFICIENCY
Rights of neighbors, 86–89.

EMINENT DOMAIN
Generally, 1287–1328.
By private parties, 1298–1299.
Estates in land, 1321–1326.
History, 1295.
Inverse condemnation, 1113–1114.
Just compensation, 1301–1312.
Landlord-tenant, 1327–1328.
Nonpossessory interests, 1326–1327.
Partial takings, 1312–1321.
Public purpose, 1287–1300.
Public use, 1287–1300.
Severance damages, 1312–1321.

ENCUMBRANCES
Affecting marketable title, 208.
Covenant against, 296.

ENVIRONMENTAL PROTECTION
Land use controls, 1128.

EQUITABLE CONVERSION
Recording acts, 316–317.
Risk of loss, 234–235.

EQUITABLE SERVITUDES
See Servitudes.

ESCROWS
Generally, 278–279.
Tenant remedy, 957.

ESTATES
See Estates in Land.

ESTATES IN LAND
Generally, 467–669.
Alienability, 567–606.
Classification, 476–521.
Constructional preferences, 499–500.
De Donis Conditionalibus, 472, 502–503.
Defeasible fees, 485–501.
Doctrine of Worthier Title, 526–527.
Executory interests, 529.
Fee simple, 476–501.
Fee simple absolute, 467, 479–484.
Fee simple determinable, 498.
Fee simple subject to condition subsequent, 498–499.
Fee simple subject to executory limitation, 499.
Fee tail, 501–512.
Freehold estates, 472–473.
Future interests, 521–567.
History, 467–474, 521–527.

INDEX

ESTATES IN LAND—Cont'd
In America, 473–474.
Incidents, 470.
Life estate, 467, 512–521.
Marketability, 567–606.
Possibility of reverter, 521, 528.
Quia Emptores, 471–472.
Racial restrictions, 500–501.
Remainder, 467, 521, 529–530.
Reversion, 467, 521, 528.
Right of entry, 528.
Rule Against Perpetuities, 567–587.
Rule Against Restraints on Alienation, 587–598.
Rule in Shelley's Case, 526.
Seisin, 473.
Services, 470.
Shifting interests, 522.
Springing interests, 522.
Tenures, 469–470.
Term of years, 467.
Trusts, 525.
Uses, 522–525.
Valuation, 527–528.
Vesting, 529–530.
Villeins, 471.
Waste, 549–568.

ESTOPPEL
By deed, 362–363.
Nonpossessory interests, 812.

EVICTION
See Actual Eviction; Constructive Eviction; Retaliatory Eviction; Summary Proceedings.

EXCLUSIONARY ZONING
Generally, 1128–1146.

EXCLUSIVE USE CLAUSE
In commercial lease, 1041.

EXECUTORY INTERESTS
Estates in land, 529.
Statute of Uses, 524.

FEDERAL INCOME TAXATION
Historic preservation, 1125.
Of real property transfers, 446–466.

FEE SIMPLE
"And his heirs . . ." requirement, 477–478.
Estate in land, 476–501.

FEE SIMPLE ABSOLUTE
Estate in land, 467, 479–484.

FEE SIMPLE DETERMINABLE
Estate in land, 498.

FEE SIMPLE ON SPECIAL LIMITATION
Estate in land, 498.

FEE SIMPLE SUBJECT TO CONDITION SUBSEQUENT
Estate in land, 498–499.

FEE SIMPLE SUBJECT TO EXECUTORY INTEREST
Estate in land, 499.

FEE SIMPLE SUBJECT TO EXECUTORY LIMITATION
Estate in land, 499.

FEE TAIL
Generally, 501–512.
Common recovery, 502–503.
De Donis Conditionalibus, 502–503.
Statutory reform, 503–504.

FENCING-IN STATUTES
Trespass, 21.

FEUDALISM
Estates in land, 468–473.

FINANCING
See also, Deed of Trust; Land Finance; Mortgage.
Condition in contract of sale, 200–205, 209–210.

FINDERS' CASES
See Found Objects.

FITNESS OF PREMISES
Architect liability, 294–295.
Broker liability, 294–295.
Implied covenant in leases, 941–959.
Incidence of housing defects, 291.
Lender liability, 294–295.
Liability of seller and others, 281–295.

FIXTURES
As real property, 69–70.

FLOATING ZONES
Zoning, 1196–1204.

FLOOR AREA RATIO
Zoning, 1215–1220.

FORCIBLE ENTRY AND DETAINER
Applied to squatters, 34–35.
Landlord and tenant, 889–890.

FORECLOSURE
Of mortgage or deed of trust, 430–446.
  Antideficiency rules, 443–445.
  One-action rule, 445.
  Statutory redemption, 445.

FORMS
Bond and mortgage, 409–410.
Broker's Listing Agreement, 171–172.
Contract of Sale, 186–187.

FORMS—Cont'd
Covenants, Conditions, and Restrictions, 673–674, 719–721.
Residential lease, 908–913.
Retail lease, 1011–1015.
Title insurance policy, 373–378.
Warranty deed, 237.

FOUND OBJECTS
Rights in, 23–24.

FOUR UNITIES
Joint tenancy, 620–623.

FREE SPEECH
In shopping centers, 70.
Zoning, 1122–1124.

FREEHOLD ESTATES
See Estates in Land.

FUTURE INTERESTS
Generally, 521–567.
Alienability, 548–549.
Classification, 528–549.
Doctrine of Worthier Title, 526–527.
Executory interest, 529.
History, 521–527.
Possibility of reverter, 521–528.
Remainder, 521, 529–530.
Reversion, 521, 528.
Right of entry, 528.
Rule Against Perpetuities, 567–587.
Rule in Shelley's Case, 526.
Shifting interests, 522.
Springing interests, 522.
Uses, 522–525.
Valuation, 527–528.
Vesting, 529–530.
Waste, 549–568.

GRADUATED PAYMENT MORTGAGE
Generally, 421.

GRANTOR–GRANTEE INDEX
Recording system, 343–356.

HABITABILITY
Implied warranty of, 941–959.

HEIRS
Generally, 478.

HISTORIC PRESERVATION
Generally, 1124–1126.

HISTORY
Condominium, 1045–1046.
Covenants and easements, 729–730.
Eminent domain, 1295.
Estates in land, 467–474, 521–527.
Future interests, 521–527.
Land finance, 407–408.
Land use controls, 1074–1076.

HISTORY—Cont'd
Landlord and tenant, 820–821.
Police power, 1091–1092.
Recording acts, 310–312.
Rights of husband and wife, 647–649.
Rule Against Perpetuities, 586–587.
Subdivision regulation, 1272–1274.
Zoning, 1091–1092.

HOMEOWNER'S ASSOCIATION
In condominiums, 1072–1073.

HOMEOWNERS' WARRANTY PROGRAM
Generally, 289–291.

HOUSING
Codes, 927–936.
Condominiums, 1044–1073.
Cooperatives, 1044–1073.
Discrimination, 980–987, 989–990.
Inclusionary zoning, 1284.
Multiple family zoning, 1144.
Residential leases, 908–1010.
Substandard, 908–1010.
  Market for, 917–926.

HOUSING DEFECTS
See Fitness of Premises.

HUSBAND AND WIFE
Community property, 656–664.
Concurrent estates, 646–669.
Curtesy, 648–649.
Dower, 648–649.
Joint tenancy, 614–616.
Married Women's Acts, 648–657.
Rights in property, 646–669.
  History, 647–649.
Tenancy by the entireties, 649–659.

IMPLIED COVENANTS
Generally, 730–744.
Common neighborhood plan, 739–744.
Delivery of possession, 834–843.
Habitability, 941–959.
Quiet enjoyment, 843–858.

IMPROVEMENTS
By trespasser, 60–70.
Fixtures, 69–70.

IN GROSS EASEMENT
See Easements.

INCENTIVE ZONING
Generally, 1114–1115.

INCIDENTS
Estates in land, 470.

INCLUSIONARY ZONING
Generally, 1284.

INDEFEASIBLY VESTED REMAINDER
Future interest, 529.

INQUIRY NOTICE
Under recording acts, 334–336.

INVERSE CONDEMNATION
Generally, 1113–1114.

INVESTMENT PROPERTY
Federal income taxation, 448–466.

JOINT TENANCY
Generally, 607–624.
Cotenants' rights and liabilities, 624–640.
"Four Unities," 620–623.
Husband and wife, 614–616.
Murder by cotenant, 623.
Rules of construction, 607–616.
Severance, 616–624.
Simultaneous deaths, 623.

JUDICIAL FORECLOSURE
Of mortgage, 443.

JUST COMPENSATION
Eminent domain, 1301–1312.

LACHES
Nonpossessory interests, 812.

LAND FINANCE
Generally, 407–445.
Default, 430–445.
Due on sale clauses, 428–429.
History, 407–408.
Innovations, 420–422.
Obligations of debtor, 422–430.
Waste, 429–430.

LAND TRANSFER
Generally, 152.
Contract of sale, 186–236.
Costs of, 154–156.
Deeds, 237–279.
Delivery, 260–279.
Escrow, 278–279.
Federal income taxation, 446–466.
Finance, 407–445.
Lawyers, 156–170.
Liability for fitness of premises, 281–295.
Post-closing liabilities, 279–309.
Real estate brokers, 171–183.
Recording acts, 153–154.
Recording system, 310–407.
Risk of loss, 226, 236.
Statute of Frauds, 153, 189–195.
Statute of Uses, 153.
Steps in sale and transfer, 152–309.
Title assurance, 310–407.
Title insurance, 363–387.

LAND USE CONTROLS
See also Eminent Domain; Planning; Subdivision Regulations; Zoning.
Generally, 1074–1341.
Environmental protection, 1126–1128.
History, 1074–1076.

LANDLORD
See also Landlord and Tenant.
Acceptance of surrender, 905–907.
As slumlord, 925–926.
Commercial, 1010–1043.
Duties under commercial lease, 1032–1043.
Duty to mitigate, 902–905.
Liability for negligence, 866–877.
Remedies, 878–908.
Residential, 908–1010.
Retaliatory eviction, 959–973.
Strict liability, 867.
Tort liability, 858–868.

LANDLORD AND TENANT
Generally, 816–1043.
Actual eviction, 856.
Alternatives to regulation, 990–1010.
Assignments, 852–877, 1029–1039.
Commercial lease,
  Generally, 1010–1043.
Constructive eviction, 856.
Contract aspects, 816–822.
Conveyance aspects, 816–822.
Covenant of quiet enjoyment, 843–858.
Damages, 901–902.
Delivery, 822.
Discrimination, 980–987, 989–990.
Distress, 890.
Eminent domain, 1327–1328.
Escrow, 957.
Forcible entry and detainer, 889–890.
History, 820–821.
Holdover tenant, 825–834.
Housing codes, 927–936.
Illegal leases, 937–940.
Implied habitability warranty, 941–959.
Landlord duties under commercial lease, 1032–1043.
Model Residential Landlord and Tenant Act, 915.
Negligence, 866–867.
Periodic tenancy, 824.
Radius clause, 1031–1032.
Receivership as remedy, 957.
Reletting, 902.
Remedies, 841–842, 878–908, 954–957.
Rent abatement, 956.
Rent control, 973–990.
Residential leases, 908–1010.
Retaliatory eviction, 959–973.
Right to possession, 834–843.
Security deposit, 907–908.
Statute of Frauds, 822.

LANDLORD AND TENANT—Cont'd
Statutory lien, 890.
Strict liability of landlord, 867.
Sublease, 852–877, 1029–1036.
Substandard housing, 908–1010.
   Market for, 917–926.
Summary proceedings, 887–888.
Surrender, 905–907.
Tenancies, types of, 823–825.
Tenancy at sufferance, 825.
Tenancy at will, 824–825.
Tenant self-help, 956.
Term of years tenancy, 823–824.
Tort liability, 858–868.
   Commercial landlord, 1042–1043.
   Slumlordism, 952–953.
Waste, 877–878.
Uniform Residential Landlord and Tenant Act, 915–916.
Use clause, 1030–1031.

LATERAL SUPPORT
Generally, 126–151.
Statutes, 148–149.
Remedies, 148.

LAWYERS
Land transfers, 156–170.
   Ethics, 163–170.
Liability for title opinion, 371–372.

LEASE
See also Landlord and Tenant.
As illegal contract, 937–940.
Assignment, 852–877.
Commercial, 1010–1043.
   Assignment of, 1029–1030.
   Exclusive use clause, 1041.
   Radius clause, 1031–1032.
   Sublease of, 1029–1030.
   Use clause, 1030–1031.
Delivery of, 822.
Duties of commercial tenant, 1016–1032.
Implied covenant of quiet enjoyment, 843–858.
Implied obligation respecting waste, 877–878.
Implied warranty of habitability, 941–959.
Residential, 908–1010.
   Form, 908–913.
Retail, 1010–1043
   Form, 1011–1015.
Statute of Frauds, 822.
Subleases, 852–877.
Tenant review of, 914–915.

LEASEHOLD
See Landlord and Tenant; Leases.

LENDERS
Liability for housing quality, 294–295.

LICENSES
Generally, 683–684.

LIENS
Generally, 763–764.
Landlord and tenant, 890.

LIFE ESTATE
Estate in land, 467, 512–521.
Pur autre vie, 520.
Trusts, 520–521.

LIGHT AND AIR
Easements, 706–707.
Nuisance, 101–102.

LISTING AGREEMENT
Form, 171–172.
Types of, 180.

MARKETABILITY
Estates in land, 567–606.
Policy favoring, 474.
Rule Against Perpetuities, 567–587.
Rule Against Restraints on Alienation, 587–598.
Statutory reform, 599–606.

MARKETABLE TITLE
Contract of sale, 196–200, 207–208.

MARKETABLE TITLE ACTS
Generally, 388–397.
Constitutionality of, 604.

MARRIED WOMEN'S ACTS
Rights of husband and wife, 648–657.

MEASURING LIVES
Rule Against Perpetuities, 584.

MERGER
Contingent remainders, 547.
In real property deeds, 279–281.
Termination of nonpossessory interests, 811–812.

MISUSE
Easements, 813–814.

MITIGATION
By landlord, 902–905.

MOBILE HOMES
Zoning, 1145.

MODEL RESIDENTIAL LANDLORD AND TENANT CODE
Generally, 915.

MORTGAGE
   See also Land Finance.
Generally, 409–422.
Default, 430–445.
Form, 409–410.

INDEX

MORTGAGE—Cont'd
Lien theory, 410–411.
New forms, 420–422.
Obligations of mortgagor, 422–430.
Power of sale, 419–420.
Title theory, 410–411.
Waste, 429–430.

MULTIPLE LISTING SERVICE
See Real Estate Brokers.

NEGATIVE COVENANTS
See Covenants.

NEGATIVE EASEMENTS
See Easements.

NEGLIGENCE
Landlord liability, 866–867.

NEIGHBORS
See also Covenants; Easements; Nuisance; Servitudes; Zoning.
Rights of, 86–151.

NONCONFORMING STRUCTURE
Zoning, 1168–1172, 1176–1177.

NONCONFORMING USE
Zoning, 1168–1172, 1176–1177.

NONJUDICIAL FORECLOSURE
Of mortgage, 443–444.

NONPOSSESSORY INTERESTS
See also Covenants; Easements; Servitudes.
Generally, 670–815.
Elements of, 672–673.
Types of, 670–672.

NOTICE STATUTE
Recording act, 319–320.

NUISANCE
Generally, 90–126.
Damages, 125.
Economics, 122–123.
Interference with light, air, or view, 101–102.
Public nuisance, 124.
Remedies, 105–126.
Restatement of Torts, 99–100, 122–123.
Self-help abatement, 125–126.
Trespass compared, 102–103.
Visual offenses, 100–101.
Zoning, relation to, 103–104.

OFFICIAL MAPS
Generally, 1285–1286.

ONE-ACTION RULE
Mortgage foreclosure, 445.

OPTIONS
Rule Against Perpetuities, 586.

PARTITION
Concurrent estates, 640–646.

PERIODIC TENANCY
Generally, 824.

PERMISSIVE WASTE
Action for, 559–560.

PERSONAL PROPERTY
Abandonment, 59–60.
Accession, 68.
Adverse possession, 57–59.
Fixtures, 69–70.
Found objects, 23–24.
Rule of capture, 149–151.
Wild animals, 149–151.

PLANNED UNIT DEVELOPMENTS
Zoning, 1196–1204.

PLANNING
Generally, 1147–1164.
Comprehensive plan, 1152–1164.
History, 1074–1076.

POLICE POWER
Generally, 1077–1146.
Aesthetic zoning, 1116–1128.
History, 1091–1092.
Takings of property, 1094–1116.

POSSESSION
See also Adverse Possession.
Rights arising from, 21.
Personal property, 23–24.
Tenant's right to, 834–843.

POSSIBILITY OF REVERTER
Future interest, 521, 528.

POWER OF TERMINATION
See Right of Entry.

PRESCRIPTIVE EASEMENTS
Generally, 698–707.
Interpretation, 798.
Requirements, 702–704.

PRIVITY
For burden of covenant to run, 746–755.

PUBLIC EASEMENT
By custom, 705.
By dedication, 704–705.
By prescription, 704.

PUBLIC NUISANCE
See Nuisance.

PUBLIC PURPOSE
Eminent domain, 1287–1300.

INDEX
References are to Pages

PUBLIC USE
Eminent domain, 1287–1300.

PURCHASER FOR VALUE
Under recording system, 337–343.

PURCHASER WITHOUT NOTICE
Recording act requirement, 321–337.

QUALIFIED FEE
Estate in land, 498.

QUIA EMPTORES
Estates in land, 471–472.
Future interests, 529.

QUIET ENJOYMENT
Compared to covenant of habitability, 952.
Covenant of, 296.
Tenant's right to, 843–858.

RACE STATUTE
Recording act, 319.

RACE–NOTICE STATUTE
Recording act, 320–321.

RACIAL RESTRICTIONS
Estates in land, 500–501.
Zoning, 1128–1146.

RADIUS CLAUSE
In commercial lease, 1031–1032.

REAL ESTATE BROKERS
Duties to buyer, 183–184.
Duties to seller, 181.
Land transfer, 171–185.
Liability for housing quality, 294–295.
Listing agreement, 171–172.
Multiple listing service, 182–183.
Rights against buyer, 184.
Rights against seller, 181–182.
Unauthorized practice of law, 185.

REAL ESTATE BUYER
See Buyer of Real Estate.

REAL ESTATE CONTRACT
See Contract of Sale.

REAL ESTATE SELLER
See Seller of Real Estate.

REAL OBLIGATION
See Servitudes.

RECEIVERSHIP
Tenant remedy, 957.

RECORDING ACTS
See Recording System.

RECORDING SYSTEM
Actual notice, 334–335.
Bona fide purchaser, 321–336.
Conditions for protection, 321–343.
Constructive notice, 334.
Estoppel by deed, 362–363.
History, 153–154, 310–312.
Indices, 343–356.
Inquiry notice, 334–336.
Purchaser for value, 337–343.
Purchaser without notice, 321–336.
Recording acts, 317–321.
Reform, 388–407.
Title search, 343–363.

REGULATION OF LAND USE
Generally, 1074–1341.

RELETTING
Landlord remedy, 902.

REMAINDER
Alternative contingent, 530.
Contingent, 530.
Estate in land, 467.
Future interest, 521, 529–530.
Indefeasibly vested, 529.

REMEDIES
Contract of sale, generally, 212–226.
  Damages, 223–224.
  Liquidated damages, 224–225.
  Rescission, 225–226.
  Specific performance, 222–223.
  Uniform Land Transactions Act, 226.
Covenants and servitudes, 787.
Landlord, 878–908, 954–957.
Lateral support, 148.
Nuisance, 105–126.
On mortgage default, 443–444.
Subjacent support, 148.
Tenant, 841–842.
Trespass, 22.
Waste, 561.

RENEGOTIABLE RATE MORTGAGE
Generally, 421.

RENT
Abatement, 956.
Control, 973–990.
Percentage lease, 1011–1015.

RENT CONTROL
Generally, 973–990.

REPAIR AND DEDUCT
Tenant remedy, 956.

RESCISSION
Contract of sale, 225–226.

RESIDENCE
Federal income taxation, 446–448.

INDEX

RESTRAINTS ON ALIENATION
In condominiums, 1053–1059.
Indirect restraints, 597–598.
Restraints on marriage, 598.

RESTRAINTS ON MARRIAGE
Generally, 598.

RETALIATORY EVICTION
Generally, 959–973.
Summary proceedings, 971–973.

REVERSE ANNUITY MORTGAGE
Generally, 422.

REVERSION
Estates in land, 467.
Future interest, 521, 528.

REZONING
Generally, 1186–1196.

RIGHT OF ENTRY
Future interest, 528.

RISK OF LOSS
Contract of sale, 226–236.
Equitable conversion, 234–235.
Insurance proceeds, 235.
Uniform Land Transactions Act, 236.
Uniform Vendors and Purchasers Risk Act, 236.

ROMAN LAW
Improving trespasser, 67.

RULE AGAINST PERPETUITIES
Generally, 567–587.
Cy pres, 585.
Equitable approximation, 585.
Equitable reformation, 585.
Fertile octogenarian rule, 582–583.
History, 586–587.
Measuring lives, 584.
Options, 586.
Reform, 585.
Slothful executor rule, 583.
Unborn widow rule, 583.
Vesting, 581, 583–584.
Wait-and-see, 585.

RULE AGAINST RESTRAINTS ON ALIENATION
Generally, 587–598.

RULE IN SHELLEY'S CASE
Future interests, 526.

RULE OF CAPTURE
Generally, 130–146, 149–151.
Personal property, 149–151.

SECURITY DEPOSIT
Landlord and tenant, 907–908.

SEISIN
Generally, 473.
Covenant of, 296.

SELF–HELP
Abating nuisance, 125–126.
Tenant, 956.

SELLER OF REAL ESTATE
Duties to broker, 181–182.
Liability for fitness of premises, 281–295.
Post-closing liability to buyer, 279–309.
Rights against broker, 181.

SERVICES
Estates in land, 470.

SERVITUDES
See also Encumbrances.
Changed conditions, 812–813.
Eminent domain, 1326–1327.
Equitable servitudes, 671, 780–784.
Implied into easement, 799.
Interpretation, 787–799.
Merger, 811–812.
Real obligation, 671, 786–787.
Remedies, 787.
Termination, 799–815.

SEVERANCE
Damages, eminent domain, 1312–1321.
Joint tenancy, 616–624.

SHARED APPRECIATION MORTGAGE
Generally, 421–422.

SHARED OWNERSHIP
See also Concurrent Estates; Condominiums; Cooperatives.
Husband and wife, 646–669.

SHIFTING INTERESTS
Estates in land, 522.

SHOPPING CENTERS
Generally, 1010–1043.
Free speech in, 70.

SLUMLORDISM
As tort, 952–953.

SOLAR EASEMENTS
Generally, 681–682.

SPECIAL EXCEPTIONS
Zoning, 1179–1186.

SPECIFIC PERFORMANCE
Contract of sale, 222–223.

SPITE FENCES
Generally, 706–707.

SPRINGING INTERESTS
Estates in land, 522.

INDEX

References are to Pages

SQUATTERS
See Adverse Possession.

STATUTE OF FRAUDS
Easements, 679–680.
Exceptions to, 36.
History, 153.
Leases, 822.
Real estate contract, 189–195.
Uniform Land Transactions Act, 194–195.

STATUTE OF LIMITATIONS
Adverse possession, 32–33, 56.
Title to real property, 391–392.

STATUTE OF USES
Generally, 523–524.
Conveyancing, 524–525.
Executory interests, 524.
Land transfer, 153.
Testamentary transfers, 525.

STATUTORY REDEMPTION
Mortgage foreclosure, 445.

STRICT LIABILITY
Of landlord, 867.

SUBDIVISION EXACTIONS
Generally, 1272–1286.

SUBDIVISION REGULATIONS
Generally, 1272–1286.
History, 1272–1274.

SUBJACENT SUPPORT
Generally, 126–151.
Remedies, 148.
Statutes, 148–149.

SUBLEASE
Of commercial lease, 1029–1030.
Of lease, generally, 852–877.

SUBSURFACE RIGHTS
See also Subjacent Support.
Adverse possession, 42.
Trespass, 21–22.

SUMMARY PROCEEDINGS
Landlord and tenant, 887–888.
Retaliatory eviction defense, 971–973.

SUPPORT
Lateral, 126–151.
Subjacent, 126–151.

SURRENDER
Landlord acceptance of, 905–907.

TACKING
See Adverse Possession.

TAKING OF PROPERTY
See also Eminent Domain.
Generally, 1094–1116.
Air rights, 1112–1113.
Economics, 1107–1108.
Inverse condemnation, 1113–1114.
Tests for, 1108–1111.

TAX SHELTER
Depreciation deduction, 450–466.

TAXATION
See Federal Income Taxation.

TENANCIES
See Concurrent Estates; Landlord and Tenant.

TENANCY AT SUFFERANCE
Generally, 825.

TENANCY AT WILL
Generally, 824–825.

TENANCY BY THE ENTIRETIES
Concurrent estate, 469–656.
Cotenants' rights and liabilities, 624–640.

TENANCY IN COMMON
Generally, 607–616.
Cotenants' rights and liabilities, 624–640.
Rules of construction, 607–616.

TENANT
See also Concurrent Estates; Landlord and Tenant.
Commercial, 1010–1043.
Copyhold, 470–471.
Duties under retail lease, 1016–1032.
Escrow remedy, 957.
Holdover tenant, 825–834.
Receivership remedy, 957.
Remedies, 841–842, 954–957.
Repair and deduct remedy, 956.
Residential, 908–1010.
Right to possession, 834–843.
Right to quiet enjoyment, 843–858.
Security deposit, 907–908.
Tenant in capite, 468.
Tenant in demesne, 468.
Villeins, 471, 821.

TENURES
Generally, 469–470.
Copyhold, 470–471.
Frankalmoign, 469.
Military, 469.
Socage, 469.

TERM OF YEARS
See also Landlord and Tenant.
Generally, 823–824.
Estate in land, 467.

INDEX

References are to Pages

TESTAMENTARY TRANSFERS
Statute of Uses, 525.
Trusts, 525.

TIME OF ESSENCE
In contract of sale, 210–211.

TIMESHARING
Generally, 1047.

TITLE
Covenants of title, 295–310.

TITLE ABSTRACTS
Generally, 363–372.

TITLE ASSURANCE
Abstracts of title, 363–372.
Covenants of title, 295–310.
Curative acts, 390–391.
Marketable title acts, 388–397.
Recording system, 310–407.
Reforms, 388–407.
Statute of limitations, 391–392.
Title insurance, 363–387.
Title opinions, 363–372.
Title registration, 397–407.
Title search, 343–363.

TITLE INSURANCE
Generally, 363–387.
Form, 373–378.

TITLE OPINIONS
Generally, 363–372.

TITLE REGISTRATION
Generally, 397–407.

TITLE SEARCH
Generally, 343–363.

TORRENS SYSTEM
Generally, 397–407.

TORT
Landlord liability, generally, 858–868.
Liability of commercial landlord, 1042–1043.
Slumlordism as, 952–953.

TOUCH OR CONCERN
For burden of covenant to run, 755–765.

TRANSACTION COSTS
Land transfer, 154–156.

TRANSFER OF PERSONAL PROPERTY
Abandonment, 59–60.
Accession, 68.
Adverse possession, 57–59.
Fixtures, 69–70.
Lost items, 23–24.

TRANSFERABILITY
See Alienability.

TRANSFERABLE DEVELOPMENT RIGHTS
Generally, 1114–1115.

TRANSFERS OF LAND
See Land Transfer.

TRESPASS
Air rights, 21–22.
Criminal liability, 22–23.
Economics of, 6–7.
Fencing-in rule, 21.
Improving trespasser, 60–70.
Limits on, 70–86.
Nuisance, compared, 102–103.
Remedies, 22.
Subsurface rights, 21–22.
Theory of protection, 8–24.

TRUSTS
Generally, 525.
Deed of trust, 419–420.
Life estates, 520–521.

UNAUTHORIZED PRACTICE OF LAW
Real estate broker, 185.

UNIFORM LAND TRANSACTIONS ACT
Contract of sale, remedies, 226.
Risk of loss, 236.
Statute of Frauds, 194–195.

UNIFORM RESIDENTIAL LANDLORD AND TENANT ACT
Generally, 915–916.

UNIFORM VENDORS AND PURCHASERS RISK ACT
Risk of loss, 236.

USE CLAUSE
In commercial lease, 1030–1031.

USES
Generally, 522–525.

VARIABLE RATE MORTGAGE
Generally, 421.

VARIANCES
Zoning, 1179–1186, 1213–1272.

VESTED RIGHTS DOCTRINE
Land use regulation, 1173–1175, 1177–1178.

VESTING
Future interests, 529–530.
In interest, 529.
Rights of developer, 1173–1175, 1177–1178.
Rule Against Perpetuities, 581, 583–584.

INDEX
References are to Pages

VIEW
Interference with, 101–102.

VILLEINS
Estates in land, 471.
Tenants, 821.

WARRANTY
Covenant of, 296.

WARRANTY OF FITNESS
Generally, 281–295.

WARRANTY OF HABITABILITY
In housing sales, 281–295.

WASTE
Action for, 549–568.
Affirmative waste, 559.
Ameliorative waste, 560–561.
Landlord and tenant, 877–878.
Mortgagor's obligation, 429–430.
Permissive waste, 559–560.
Remedies, 561.

WATER
Withdrawal of, 130–146.

WIFE AND HUSBAND
Community property, 656–664.
Concurrent estates, 646–669.
Curtesy, 648–649.
Dower, 648–649.
Joint tenancy, 614–616.
Married Women's Acts, 648–657.
Rights in property, 646–669.
  History, 647–649.
Tenancy by the entireties, 649–656.

WORDS OF LIMITATION
Generally, 478.

WORDS OF PURCHASE
Generally, 478.

ZONING
Generally, 1165–1272.
Aesthetic zoning, 1116–1128.
Affecting marketable title, 209.
Amortization, 1176–1177.
Architectural controls, 1124.
Community decisions, 1204.
Comprehensive plan, 1152–1164.
Conditional zoning, 1193–1194.
"Contract" zoning, 1193–1194.
Exclusionary zoning, 1128–1146.
Floating zones, 1196–1204.
Floor area ratio, 1215–1220.
Free speech, 1122–1124.
Historic preservation, 1124–1126.
History, 1091–1092.
Incentive zoning, 1114–1115.
Inclusionary zoning, 1284.
Inverse condemnation, 1113–1114.
Judicial review, 1251–1264.
Minimum lot size, 1143–1144.
Mobile homes, 1145.
Multiple family dwellings, 1144.
Nonconforming structures, 1168–1172, 1176–1177.
Nonconforming uses, 1168–1172, 1176–1177.
Nuisance, relation to, 103–104.
Ordinances, 1165–1168.
Phased development, 1145.
Planned Unit Developments, 1196–1204.
Planning, 1147–1164.
Police power, 1077–1146.
Rezoning, 1186–1196.
Source of municipal power, 1164.
Special exceptions, 1179–1186.
Takings of property, 1094–1116.
Transferable development rights, 1114–1115.
Variances, 1179–1186, 1213–1272.
Vested rights, 1173–1175, 1177–1178.